lonely planet

G reek Islands

Paul Hellander
Kate Armstrong, Michael Clark, Des Hannigan,
Victoria Kyriakopoulos, Miriam Raphael, Andrew Stone

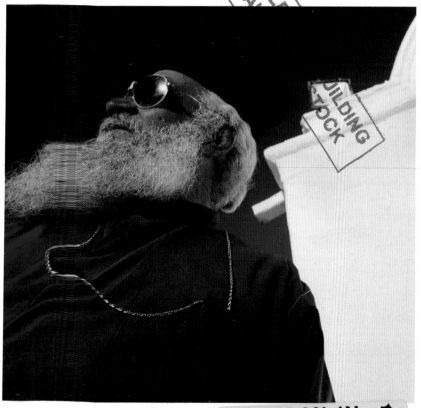

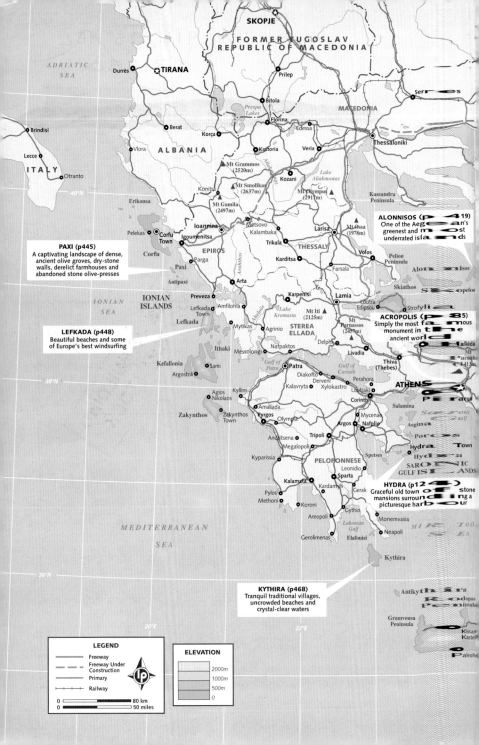

ADRIATIC
SEA

FORMER YUGOSLAV
REPUBLIC OF MACEDONIA

SKOPJE

Durrës
★ TIRANA
Prilep

Bitola

Florina

Berat
Korça
Edessa
Veria

Vlora
ALBANIA
Kastoria
Thessaloniki

MACEDONIA

Brindisi

Lecce
ITALY
Otranto

Erikousa

Mt Grammos
(2520m)
Konitsa
Mt Smolikas
(2637m)
Mt Olympus
(2911m)
Kozani
Lake
Aliakmonas

Kassandra
Peninsula

Mt Gamila
(2497m)

Ioannina
Metsovo
Kalambaka
Larisa
Mt Ossa
(1978m)

ALONNISOS (p419)
One of the Aegean's
greenest and most
underrated islands

Pelekas
Corfu
Town
Igoumenitsa
EPIROS
Trikala
THESSALY
Volos

PAXI (p445)
A captivating landscape of dense,
ancient olive groves, dry-stone
walls, derelict farmhouses and
abandoned stone olive-presses

Corfu
Parga
Karditsa
Farsala

Pelion
Peninsula
Alonnisos

Paxi
Skiathos
Skopelos

Antipaxi

IONIAN
SEA
IONIAN
ISLANDS
Preveza
Amfilohia
Arta
Karpenisi
Lamia
Loutra
Edipsou
Strofylia

ACROPOLIS (p85)
Simply the most famous
monument in the
ancient world

LEFKADA (p448)
Beautiful beaches and some
of Europe's best windsurfing

Lefkada
Town
Lefkada
Mytikas
Agrinio
STEREA
ELLADA
Mt Parnassos
(2457m)
Delphi
Livadia
Halkida
Mt
Parnitha
(1413m)

Ithaki
Nafpaktos
Thiva
(Thebes)

Kefallonia
Sami
Messolongi
Gulf of
Patra
Patra
ATHENS

Argostoli
Zakynthos
Zakynthos
Town
Diakofto
Derveni
Xylokastro
Kalavryta
Perahora
Loutraki
Corinth
Piraeus
Saronic
Gulf

Agios
Nikolaos
Kyllini
Amaliada
Pyrgos
Olympia
Argos
Mycenae
Nafplio
Salamina
Aegina
Poros

Andritsena
Megalopoli
Tripoli
Spetses
Hydra
Town
Hydra
SARONIC
GULF ISLANDS

Kyparissia
PELOPONNESE
Leonidio
Sparta

HYDRA (p124)
Graceful old town
mansions surrounding a
picturesque harbour

Kalamata
Kardamyli
Gerak
Gythio

Pylos
Methoni
Koroni
Areopoli
Monemvasia
Neapoli

MEDITERRANEAN
SEA
Gerolimenas
Elafonisi
Lakonian
Gulf

Kythira

KYTHIRA (p468)
Tranquil traditional villages,
uncrowded beaches and
crystal-clear waters

Antikythira
Kapodos
Peninsula

Gramvousa
Peninsula
Kissamos
Kasteli
Paleohora

LEGEND

Freeway
Freeway Under
Construction
Primary
Railway

0   80 km
0   50 miles

ELEVATION

2000m
1000m
500m
0

Saronic Gulf Islands

Sail the green waters surrounding the Saronic Gulf Islands (p115)

Uncover ancient rituals at the Temple of Aphaia (p120), Aegina

OTHER HIGHLIGHTS

- Beach-hop along the spectacular coastline of Spetses (p129).
- Party like a local among the bustling nightlife in Aegina Town, (p118), Aegina.
- Escape the throngs on pine-cloaked Angistiri (p121).

Wander the narrow, winding streets and lanes of Hydra Town (p126), Hydra

6

Cyclades

JOHN ELK III

Traverse Ancient Delos and encounter the magnificent Terrace of Lions (p161)

Wind your way around the magical island of Mykonos (p150)

CHERYL CONLON

OTHER HIGHLIGHTS

- Tour the golden-sand beaches of charming Koufonisia (p181).
- Experience quiet and peaceful Oia, Santorini and its beautiful sunset views (p199).
- Make friends with the locals while exploring the cliff-top villages of Folegandros (p203).

Stroll through picturesque white-washed Santorini (p191)

IZZET KER

Crete

Float down to the old harbour at Iraklio (p224)

JOHN ELK III

Soak up the rays on Crete's iconic Preveli beach (p244)

CHRIS CHRISTO

Step back in time and learn about the Minoan civilisation at Knossos (p233)

NEIL SETCHFIELD

Dodecanese

Reflect on the Monastery of St John the Theologian (p338), Patmos

PAUL DAVID HELLANDER

NOBORU KOMINE

Hike to the top of the amazing Acropolis of Lindos (p288), Rhodes

Roll down the ridge to the living museum that is Olymbos (p299), Karpathos

GEORGE TSAFOS

OTHER HIGHLIGHTS

- Weave through the labyrinthine interior of Rhodes Old Town (p282), Rhodes.
- Kick back on the unassuming island of Astypalea (p323).
- Walk along the cliffs, rocky inlets, valleys and bucolic meadows of Tilos (p309).

Northeastern Aegean

Meander over the medieval cobblestone streets in Chios (p363)

Laze away a summer's day on the beaches of Armenistis (p352), Ikaria

Gaze upon the tranquil pools at pretty-as-a-picture Skala Kalloni (p372), Lesvos

Evia & the Sporades

OTHER HIGHLIGHTS

- Clamber up the hillside to conquer the ruined fortress in captivating Skopelos Town, (p415), Skopelos.
- Take a dip in the Aegean's cleanest water, which encircles the isle of Alonnisos (p419).
- Journey to Karystos, Evia in summer to partake in the bacchanalian Wine & Cultural Festival (p408).

GEORGE TSAFOS

Experience local architecture in the traditional villages of Evia (p403)

Cruise down to the beautiful horseshoe-shaped Pefkos Bay (p429), Skyros

GEORGE TSAF

Ionians

Get in touch with the local icons at the
Church of Agios Spyridon (p438), Corfu

While away the afternoon at a waterfront
taverna in Loggos (p447), Paxi

Amble through ancient olive groves on Paxi (p445)

Curl up on the sand at Porto Katsiki (p452), Lefkada

Catch a breeze off the coast of Vasiliki
(p452), Lefkada

OTHER HIGHLIGHTS

- Head to Zakynthos to catch a glimpse of the
  endangered loggerhead turtle (p464).
- Stroll through the sprawling vineyards tucked
  beneath rugged mountains on
  Kefallonia (p454).
- Follow in the footsteps of Homer's Odyssey on
  the diminutive island of Ithaki (p459).

Take in the scene of sophisticated and
charming Corfu Town (p436), Corfu

Contents

Regional Map Contents

Northeastern Aegean Islands p346

Athens & the Mainland Ports p74

Ionian Islands p432

Evia & The Sporades p405

Saronic Gulf Islands p116

Dodecanese p276

Cyclades p134

Crete pp222-3

The Authors

PAUL HELLANDER
Coordinating Author, Athens & the Mainland Ports, Dodecanese

For Paul Greece is not merely a destination, it is a lifestyle and a 30-year love affair that sees no end. Fluent in the language after taking a hard-earned degree in Ancient, Byzantine and Modern Greek from his native UK, he has been in and out of his spiritual home, Greece, more times than he cares to remember. Imbued with a love of sun-bleached Aegean islands, Paul brings to this edition of *Greece* his vast experience of the Dodecanese islands and of Greece in general. Paul would happily retire to a small, stone island-cottage with a view. Until then he shall live on in Adelaide, South Australia.

Paul's Favourite Trip

I start in Athens (p73) with a leisurely lunch at Vizantino (p90) in Plaka. The following day I'll head to Piraeus (p97) and hop on a ferry to Ikaria (p347). I'll soon head south for spiritual inspiration on Patmos (p334) and eventually move on to laidback Lipsi (p339) for good food, good company and fine swimming. Next up is Leros (p331): I come here for the top-class food and nontouristy feel. From Leros I'll fly to Astypalea (p323), a stunning Cycladic-like island with brooding hills and fine beaches. Next stop is Kos (p315) for a touch of nightlife. Then I'll swing south to Tilos (p309) for some brisk walking and more fine food, topping off my trip with a few days in the old town of Rhodes (p280) with its Middle Age ambience and cosy comforts.

KATE ARMSTRONG
Ionian Islands

Kate grew up in Melbourne, the world's third largest Greek city, and by osmosis fell in love with all things Greek. At university she dabbled in classical art history, so Greece and the Cyclades were among her first backpacking pilgrimages to view her first (noncelluloid) *kouros*. She was excited, therefore, to return to the region to retrace Odysseus' steps in the Ionians. Her own 'epic' journeys over the last 15 years have been within Europe, South America and Africa and her itchy feet are currently grounded in Sydney where she works as a freelance writer. She is the author of travel articles and several books. This is her first Lonely Planet assignment.

LONELY PLANET AUTHORS

Why is our travel information the best in the world? It's simple: our authors are independent, dedicated travellers. They don't research using just the Internet or phone, and they don't take freebies in exchange for positive coverage. They travel widely, to all the popular spots and off the beaten track. They personally visit thousands of hotels, restaurants, cafés, bars, galleries, palaces, museums and more – and they take pride in getting all the details right, and telling it how it is. For more, see the authors section on www.lonelyplanet.com.

MICHAEL STAMATIOS CLARK
Evia & the Sporades

Born into a Greek-American community in Cambridge, Ohio, Michael's Greek roots go back to the village of Karavostamo on the eastern Aegean island of Ikaria, home of his maternal grandparents. He first worked his way to Greece as a deck hand aboard a Greek freighter, trading Greek lessons over strong coffee and backgammon. When not travelling to Greece, Michael teaches English to international students in Berkeley, California, listens to *rembetika* music after midnight and continues to search out the best sources of Greek olives, feta and retsina. For this edition, he updated the Evia & the Sporades chapters.

DES HANNIGAN
Saronic Gulf Islands, Cyclades

Des is a writer and photographer who has worked on travel guides for over 20 years. He first surfaced (literally) in Greece many years ago in Aegina harbour, having stepped off a boat into two feet of water. He's been floating around the country, whenever he can, ever since. Des lives on the edge of the Atlantic in sunny Cornwall, England. In a previous life he worked at sea, valuable experience for coping with the Greek ferry system, of which he is an enthusiastic admirer. It always gets him (eventually) to remote islands. Des worked on the previous editions of Lonely Planet's *Greece* and *Greek Islands* and has written guidebooks to Corfu and Rhodes for other publishers.

VICTORIA KYRIAKOPOULOS
The Culture, Food & Drink, Crete

Victoria is a freelance journalist based in Melbourne, Australia – when not living her 'other life' in Greece. She lived in Athens between 2000 and 2004, witnessing the city's angst-ridden pre-Olympic makeover. She was editor of Athens-based Greek diaspora magazine *Odyssey*, a contributor to the *Age*, *Sydney Morning Herald* and other Australian and international newspapers and magazines, as well as a researcher for several foreign TV programmes. Victoria wrote the 1st edition of Lonely Planet's *Athens Condensed* and *Best of Athens* and updated the 3rd edition of *Crete*. In Australia she has worked as a staff writer on the *Bulletin* and as a reporter for the Melbourne *Herald*.

MIRIAM RAPHAEL
Northeastern Aegean

Miriam has spent much of the last two years splashing around the Aegean for Lonely Planet. Always up for an adventure, she was only too happy to explore a side of Greece hidden from the tourist brochures. For this edition she trekked the Zagoria, ruin-hopped across Macedonia, embraced the Thessalonikan nightlife and ate her way though enough meze and grilled sardines to turn her into a merperson. When she's not playing *tavli* (backgammon) on a remote Aegean beach, Miriam is bodysurfing on a beach in Sydney, trying to decide where to go next.

ANDREW STONE
Kythira & Antikythira

Ever since his first trip to Greece as a teenager on an Inter-Railing holiday around Europe, Andrew has loved this friendly, ruggedly beautiful country. Having studied classical history, literature and politics as part of his degree, he eagerly accepted the offer from Lonely Planet to return to Greece. For *Greece*, Andrew explored Kythira, Antikythira and the Peloponnese, a region packed with historical, political and mythical significance for Western culture and a beautiful, diverse but unhyped chunk of Greece. Andrew has also written about other destinations around the Mediterranean for Lonely Planet.

Getting Started

The Greek islands are easy to hop around, with good public transport and a range of accommodation to suit every budget, from the backpacker to the five-star traveller. For some, planning involves no more than heading out and buying a ticket; for others, planning the trip is half the fun – and there is certainly no shortage of information to help them on their way.

WHEN TO GO

Spring and autumn are the best times to visit Greece. Most of the tourist infrastructure goes into hibernation in winter, particularly on the islands. Some of the smaller islands close completely, and islanders head off to alternative homes in Athens. Many hotels, along with cafés and restaurants, close their doors from the end of November until the beginning of April; bus and ferry services are either drastically reduced or plain cancelled.

See Climate (p484) for more information.

The cobwebs are dusted off in time for Easter, when the first tourists start to arrive. Conditions are perfect between Easter and mid-June, when the weather is pleasantly warm in most places; beaches and ancient sites are relatively uncrowded; public transport operates at close to full schedules; and accommodation is cheaper and easy to find.

From mid-June to the end of August is high season. It's party time on the islands and everything is in full swing. It's hot – in July and August the mercury can soar to 40°C in the shade just about anywhere; the beaches are crowded, the ancient sites are swarming with tour groups and in many places accommodation is booked solid. The season winds down in September, and conditions are ideal once more until the end of October.

By November, the endless blue skies of summer have disappeared. November to February are the wettest months. It can get surprisingly cold. Snow is common on the mainland and in the mountains of Evia and Crete; it occasionally snows in Athens. There are also plenty of sunny days, and some visitors prefer the tranquillity that reigns.

COSTS & MONEY

Greece is no longer a cheap country. Prices have rocketed since the adoption of the euro at the beginning of 2002. It is hard to believe that inflation is less than 3%, as claimed by the government, when prices for many services have risen by more than 50% in two years. Lonely Planet's researchers have recorded some quite dramatic price rises, particularly for accommodation options and restaurant meals.

A rock-bottom daily budget would be €45. This means hitching, staying in hostels or camping, and rarely eating in restaurants or taking ferries. Allow at least €90 per day if you want your own room and plan to eat out as well as see the sights. If you want comfy rooms and restaurants all the way, you will need €130 per day. These budgets are for individuals travelling in high season. Couples sharing a room can get by on less.

Your money will go further if you travel outside high season – there are fewer tourists around and you're able to negotiate better deals. Accommodation, which often eats up a large part of the daily budget, is a lot cheaper outside the high season, particularly on the islands. You will also be able to negotiate much better deals if you stay a few days. Families can achieve big savings by looking for rooms with kitchen facilities.

All prices quoted in this guidebook are for the high season (during July and August).

HOW MUCH?

Local telephone call per min €0.25

Minimum taxi fare €3

Litre of milk €1.50

Herald Tribune €2

Coffee €3-4

Soft drink (can) €1

Cinema ticket €7.50

TOP TENS

Best Beaches

When many people conjure up an image of the Greek islands, the first image to spring to mind is of a gorgeous, secluded beach. The Greek islands are justly famous for their beaches, so don't forget to pack your beach towel, hat and sunscreen. The following is a list of some of the Greek islands' finest beaches:

- Pori beach (p182), Koufonisia, Cyclades
- Ladiko beach (p287) and Glystra beach (p290), Rhodes, Dodecanese
- Ammoöpi beach (p297), Karpathos, Dodecanese
- Preveli beach (p244) and Elafonisi beach (p260), Crete
- Alyki beach (p399), Thasos, Northeastern Aegean

- Provatas beach (p210), Milos, Cyclades
- Psili Ammos (p361), Samos, Northeastern Aegean
- Banana beach (p413), Skiathos, Sporades
- Mylos beach (p452), Lefkada, Ionians
- Myrtos beach (p272), Kefallonia, Ionians

Must-See Movies

Predeparture planning is definitely best done in a comfy lounge chair with a bowl of popcorn in one hand and a remote in the other. Head down to your local video store to pick up these flicks, from the best-known Greek films to the very cheesiest. For more information on Greek cinema, see p51.

- *A Touch of Spice* (2003) directed by Tasos Boulmetis
- *My Big Fat Greek Wedding* (2002) directed by Joel Zwick
- *Nyfes* (2004) directed by Pandelis Voulgaris
- *Zorba the Greek* (1964) directed by Mihalis Cacoyannis
- *Never on Sunday* (1960) directed by Jules Dassin

- *Z* (1969) directed by Costa Gavras
- *Eleni* (1985) directed by Peter Yates
- *Eternity and a Day* (1998) directed by Theo Angelopoulos
- *For Your Eyes Only* (1981) directed by John Glen
- *Shirley Valentine* (1989) directed by Lewis Gilbert

Festivals & Events

Greeks love to celebrate, and there's almost always something, somewhere, that's worth the effort of having a celebration. The following list is our top 10 festivals and events in the Greek islands, but for a comprehensive list of all the main festivals and events throughout the year, go to p488.

- Skyros Carnival (p426), Sporades, February to March
- Easter (p488), everywhere, March to April
- Miaoulia Festival (p127), Hydra, Saronic Gulf Islands, June
- Summer on Lykavittos Hill (p87), Athens, June to August
- Hellenic Festival (p86), Theatre of Herodes Atticus, Athens, June to September

- Folegandros Festival (p205), Folegandros, Cyclades, July
- Santorini Jazz Festival (p199), Santorini, Cyclades, July
- Milos Festival (p208), Milos, Cyclades, July
- Panagia tou Harou (p341), Lipsi, Dodecanese, 24 August
- Samothraki World Music Festival (p391), Samothraki, Northeastern Aegean, August

DON'T LEAVE HOME WITHOUT...

Most travellers carry far too much gear, filling bags and backpacks with things that will never see the light of day. It's best to bring only the essentials: you can buy anything else you might need in Greece. The essentials:

▪ A sturdy pair of shoes for clambering around ancient sites and wandering through historic towns and villages, which tend to have lots of steps and cobbled streets.

▪ Good sunglasses – especially in summer.

▪ Your mobile phone. You can buy a local SIM card cheaply and keep in touch with family and friends.

▪ A few paperback novels to while away the hours riding ferries.

▪ A few photos of your family, your home and your region: they are great for answering the questions of curious locals.

▪ A handy digital camera. Greece is enviably overphotogenic. Send photos home via the Internet and make friends jealous.

TRAVEL LITERATURE

Travel writers can be a great source of inspiration for those planning to follow in their footsteps.

A Traveller's History of Athens (Richard Stoneman) A lively and compact look into Athens' complex and multifarious past.

Attic in Greece (Austen Kark) This tale revolves around the author's experiences in buying a house in the old town of Nafplio with his wife Nina. It's full of interesting insights gleaned through the author's time in Greece working for the BBC.

Falling for Icarus: A Journey Among the Cretans (Rory MacLean) A light yet fascinating tale of a man obsessed with building an aeroplane on Crete.

My Family and Other Animals (Lawrence Durrell) Durrell offers an hilarious account of his family's chaotic and wonderful life on Corfu.

Prospero's Cell (Lawrence Durrell) This classic collection of tales records brother Laurence's experience on Corfu in the 1920s. Worth reading for the fire engine story alone!

The Greek Book Centre reviews the latest Greek booksand has author profiles at www .ithacaonline.gr

The Colossus of Maroussi (Henry Miller) Few writers have matched the enthusiasm expressed in this classic tale. Miller's fervour never flags as he leaps from one adventure to the next. Some travellers get upset about being ripped off by a taxi driver on arrival; to Miller, it's another experience to be savoured.

The Greek Islands (Lawrence Durrell) This coffee-table collection of stunning photos is one of the most popular books of its kind.

The Mani (Patrick Leigh Fermor) Another ardent philhellene, Patrick Leigh Fermor is well known for his exploits in rallying the Cretan resistance in WWII. He now lives in Kardamyli in the Peloponnese.

INTERNET RESOURCES

Predictably enough, there has recently been a huge increase in the number of websites providing information about Greece and its islands.

Culture Guide (www.cultureguide.gr) Lots of information about contemporary culture and the arts.

Greek Ferries (www.greekferries.gr) One-stop site with access to all the latest international and domestic ferry information.

Greek National Tourist Organisation (www.gnto.gr) For concise tourist information.

Greek Search Engine (www.in.gr) The best starting point for those browsing the web.

Greek Travel Pages (www.gtp.gr) An excellent though basic online planner for travel and accommodation.

Lonely Planet (www.lonelyplanet.com) Has postcards from other travellers and the Thorn Tree bulletin board, where you can ask questions before you go or dispense advice when you get back.

Ministry of Culture (www.culture.gr) Information about ancient sites, art galleries and museums.

Itineraries
ISLAND HOPPING

ONE WEEK TO SPARE
One Week / Mykonos to Serifos

The first port of call from Athens is super chic **Mykonos** (p150). It's also the stepping-off point for the sacred island of **Delos** (p158), where the much-photographed Terrace of Lions from Naxos stand guard over the most important archaeological site in the Greek islands.

The next stop is **Naxos** (p169), famous for its wine, cheese and fresh produce. Explore the capital, **Hora** (p171), with its maze of alleys surrounding the ancient Venetian *kastro* (castle). The mountainous interior of the island is ideal for trekking, while **Agios Georgios beach** (p176) is perfect for windsurfing or sailing.

Onwards to **Santorini** (p191), surely the most spectacular of all the islands. The sheer cliffs of its volcanic caldera, created by one of the largest eruptions ever recorded, are a sight not to be missed.

If ferry schedules permit, try to stop at either **Folegandros** (p203) or **Serifos** (p214) on the journey back to Athens on the mainland. Both boast superb examples of Cycladic architecture, and the opportunity to relax away from the crowds.

This 400km tour is designed for people without much time who want to get a taste of what the islands have to offer. The island hop starts and finishes in Athens.

THE CYCLADES
Two Weeks / Syros to Serifos

From Athens head first to **Syros** (p144) and spend a couple of days exploring its graceful capital, **Ermoupolis** (p146), once the busiest and largest port in the Aegean. The next port of call is **Mykonos** (p150), from where you can make the short excursion across to the island of **Delos** (p158) and its impressive antiquities. You can recover on **Naxos** (p169), the greenest and most fertile of the Cyclades and a great place for walkers.

If time permits, take a detour for a couple of days to either **Koufonisia** (p181) or **Schinousa** (p180), Greece's island outback where the tone is decidedly low-key, otherwise head straight on to spectacular **Santorini** (p191). Its white cubic, clifftop houses defy gravity, while sunset from the village of Oia is perhaps the best in the Aegean Sea; divers can check out the activities of the new volcano that is developing underwater.

The journey back north starts with friendly **Folegandros** (p203), followed by **Milos** (p207), an underrated island that is often overlooked despite a wealth of attractions that range from its superior beaches to its unique Christian catacombs. The final port of call before returning to Athens is **Serifos** (p214), home to arguably the finest of all the Cycladic capitals.

The Cyclades are the quintessential Greek islands. Two weeks should be long enough to complete this 230km circuit from Athens, but a month is even better.

EVIA & THE SPORADES   Two Weeks / Rafina to Alonnisos

Start by catching a ferry from **Rafina** (p100) on the mainland to the port of
Marmari (p404) in southern Evia, and work up the island via **Eretria** (p404)
to its capital, **Halkida** (p404), where you can observe the extraordinary
tide patterns of the Evripous Channel that once so puzzled Aristotle. The
mountain village of **Steni** (p406), in central Evia, is a delightful stop en
route to the eastern port of **Kymi** (p406), the departure point for ferries
to remote **Skyros** (p424). This quaint island is best known for its strange
pre-Lenten goat carnival, and for its pretty Cycladic-style capital.

You'll need to double back to Halkida to continue to Skiathos, reached
from the mainland ports of **Agios Konstantinos** (p109) or **Volos** (p109).
Skiathos (p409) is one of Greece's premier resort areas, with dozens of
beaches to choose from as well as all manner of water sports. Head out
from **Skiathos Town** (p411) to explore the island's offerings.

Next stop is **Skopelos** (p414), where the pace is decidedly slower. **Skopelos Town** (p415) is a delightful place to explore and there are some
good walks. The final stop is **Alonnisos** (p419). It's no longer the Aegean's
best-kept secret, but it still boasts the cleanest water in the Aegean and
wonderful opportunities for walkers.

The Sporades can
be a challenge
for the island
hopper, thanks
to the absence of
easy connections
between Evia and
Skyros and the main
islands of the
Sporades further
north. This 360km
route takes you
through the islands.

IONIAN EXPERIENCE   Two Weeks / Corfu to Zakynthos

Start with a few days on **Corfu** (p433), exploring the sights of the old town and savouring the island's distinctive cuisine. Include a day trip over to the west-coast resort of **Paleokastritsa** (p443), lingering long enough to enjoy the sunset. Next up is tiny **Paxi** (p445), where visitors can explore a lost world of ancient, gnarled olive groves and derelict farmhouses. In the absence of ferry connections, you'll need to return to Corfu to move on to the next island south, **Lefkada** (p448).

The beaches of the west coast are the finest beaches in the Ionians, while **Vasiliki Bay** (p452), in the south, is renowned as a prime windsurfing spot. It's also the departure point for ferries to **Kefallonia** (p454), which arrive at the charming port of **Fiskardo** (p459), the only Kefallonian town not devastated by the great earthquake of 1953. Hop across from Fiskardo to **Ithaki** (p459) and spend a couple of days exploring the homeland of Homer's Odysseus, and then return to Kefallonia.

Call in at the stunning west-coast village of **Assos** (p458) and magic **Myrtos beach** (p459) on the journey south to Kefallonia's lively capital, **Argostoli** (p455), for connections to the final island in the group, **Zakynthos** (p462). Known to the Venetians as the 'Flower of the Orient', the island's capital, **Zakynthos Town** (p464), boasts some fine examples of Venetian and neoclassical architecture.

The Ionians are Greece's green islands, blessed with ample winter rains. Take this 500km trip outside of peak summer season (September to June) and have the islands to yourself.

THE EASTERN ISLAND RUN

Three Weeks / Rhodes to Alexandroupolis

You'll need to spend a few days on **Rhodes** (p277), exploring the old city and visiting the **Acropolis of Lindos** (p288), before setting sail for **Tilos** (p309). Laid-back Tilos is a great place for walkers and one of the few islands in the Dodecanese to have escaped the ravages of development.

The next stop is **Nisyros** (p312), where the eruptions of Mt Polyvotis have created a bizarre volcanic landscape. You'll need to call briefly at **Kos** (p315) to pick up a ferry onward to **Patmos** (p334), an island that St John found sufficiently inspiring to pen his *Book of Revelations*. Patmos has good connections to ultra laid-back **Ikaria** (p347), where you can laze on some of the Aegean's best beaches before continuing to **Chios** (p363) and the fabulous villages of the island's south.

The next stop is **Lesvos** (p372), birthplace of the poet Sappho, and which produces Greece's finest olive oil and ouzo. **Limnos** (p385) is little more than a transit point on the journey north to **Samothraki** (p390) and the superbly named **Sanctuary of the Great Gods** (p392).

The final leg is to the Thracian port of **Alexandroupolis** (p112), where travellers will find several good transport connections to Athens and Thessaloniki.

This 680km route takes travellers island hopping north from Rhodes through the islands of the Dodecanese and the Northeastern Aegean.

THE GRAND TOUR
One Month / Athens to Kythira

From **Athens** (p73), head first to spectacular **Santorini** (p191), whose capital **Fira** (p194) perches precariously atop the sheer walls of a volcanic caldera created by one of the greatest eruptions ever recorded. Next up is fertile **Naxos** (p169) famous for its crops and fine wines, followed by party island **Mykonos** (p150), favoured by backpackers and socialites alike. Be sure to take a day trip to visit the temples and sanctuaries of sacred **Delos** (p158) before moving on to laid-back **Ikaria** (p347) – where Icarus crash-landed after he flew too close to the sun.

Next up is **Samos** (p355), where the unspoiled villages of the interior offer lots of opportunities for walkers. **Kos** (p315) need be no more than a stopover en route to **Rhodes** (p277), the amazing fortress city built by the Knights of St John.

The journey west from Rhodes offers the possibilities of stops at either **Karpathos** (p294) or **Kasos** (p300) on the way to the Cretan port of **Sitia** (p268). Travel along Crete's northern coast to **Iraklio** (p224) and **Knossos** (p233), the ancient capital of Minoan Crete, before moving west to the pretty twin ports of **Rethymno** (p237) and **Hania** (p246) with their harbourside restaurants and buzzing bars. The exit point from Crete is the northwestern port of **Kissamos-Kastelli** (p260) to **Kythira** (p468). From Kythira, there's a choice of catching a ferry or flight back to Athens, or travelling back through the Peloponnese.

A month is long enough to have a really good look around the islands on this 1400km tour, and to experience the huge variety of attractions they have to offer.

TAILORED TRIPS

ANCIENT WONDERS

The ancient sites are one of the main reasons why travellers come to Greece and the islands have their fair share. You can take in all the big names and some of the lesser known ones while travelling through the islands.

You can explore the ancient sites in **Athens** (p73), head to the **Acropolis** (p85), or perhaps take a day trip to **Aegina** (p116) to see the **Temple of Aphaia** (p120). The sacred island of **Delos** (p158) is packed with ancient wonders and is guarded by the much photographed Terrace of Lions. To view the **Ireon** (p361), a massive temple to Hera that ranked as one of the wonders of the ancient world, head to Samos. The ancient **Asklipieion** (p321) is on Kos and is where the great Hippocrates once taught his approach to medicine. The island of **Rhodes** (p277) is home to the mighty fortress city built by the Knights of St John and is Europe's oldest inhabited medieval town. From Rhodes you can visit the spectacular **Acropolis of Lindos** (p288). Take in the Minoan palace of **Knossos** (p233) at Iraklio on Crete. If time permits, try to include the palaces at **Phaestos** (p236) and **Zakros** (p271) before heading on your way.

WALK ON THE WILD SIDE

The islands offer wonderful opportunities for walkers. The best time to go is in spring (especially April/May), when the weather is pleasantly warm and wildflowers transform the countryside into a riot of colour.

Batsi (p138), on Andros, is an ideal base for exploring the countryside along ancient cobbled paths. **Naxos** (p169), the largest of the Cyclades, has a mountainous interior, especially the **Tragaea** (p176) region, that is a favourite walking destination.

The coastal resorts of **Samos** (p355) may be a tour group fave, but the interior villages remain unspoiled. Travel through the Dodecanese to volcanic **Nisyros** (p312), where you can marvel at the landscape created by the eruptions from the crater **Polyvotis** (p314). Stop in **Tilos** (p309) for its picturesque **Potami Gorge** (p311), or **Symi** (p305) with its pretty port and neoclassical shipowner mansions carefully restored by Greeks and foreigners alike. Explore Europe's oldest inhabited medieval town, **Rhodes Old Town** (p280). Greece's most southerly island, **Crete** (p220) has many possibilities, starting with **Samaria Gorge** (p253), one of many excellent treks.

Snapshot

The years 2004 and 2005 have been challenging times for the inhabitants of the Greek islands. While Greeks at heart and concerned with the same issues as their mainland countrymen, Greek islanders share a diverse and scattered world with its own peculiarities and a mentality that is not unnaturally insular. While feeling equally proud at the national successes of Greece in the sporting and entertainment field, and showing equal disdain for politics as anywhere in Greece, islanders are united in their common lifestyle – living in microcosms of Greek society in a limited geographic space – yet are as different as they are similar.

The 2004 Summer Olympic Games were a huge shot in the arm for Greece's self-image. After weathering doubts that they would never pull it off, Greece surprised the world by staging one of the best presented and efficient Games of recent times. But at a cost. The budget blowout caused by increased security costs, lower than expected visitors and poor ticket returns means that Greece will be in the red for some years to come.

The Greek islands, while an integral part of the state, display some characteristics that sets them apart from the mainland. Their focus is more concerned with their own development and progress in areas that are often short of natural resources and hampered by tenuous transport links. Tourism has been and will always be the lifeline of their economy. In this each island often displays a rivalry with its neighbours as each seeks to share in what has been, in recent times, a fluctuating pot of tourist dollars. Many in the tourist and service industries across the Greek islands suffered badly during the 2004 summer. The anticipated windfall of hundreds of thousands of visitors to Greece and its islands before, during and after the Olympic Games never materialised, leaving many with hefty bills for renovations and investments. The tourist scene throughout the Aegean and Ionian seas in the summer of 2004 had never been thinner. Things were not much better by the beginning of the 2005 tourism scene, though by the end of the season the demand had picked up perceptibly and businesses across the archipelago were breathing more easily.

On larger islands life is less dependent on tourism and issues of concern range from the price of olives to the spiralling cost of real estate. On smaller islands transport is always a hot topic. Some places complain of poor ferry services, while others have been crying out for an airport for years.

The Greek islands by late-2005 are unquestionably undergoing change. While the islands are modernising rapidly and becoming more and more integrated into mainstream European Unionism, they are doing so at a slow cost. Creeping price increases are making life harder for islanders, where the cost of goods can be higher than on the mainland. The issue of sustainable tourism while keeping development within acceptable ecological boundaries, is becoming a more debated topic. At a more subliminal level, the sense that the islands are viewed as little more than insignificant outposts by government in Athens has imparted a perceptible underdog angst in the thinking of those who live there permanently.

There is nonetheless a resilience in the islanders' mindset, an adaptive attitude to change and a shared pan-insular spirituality that transcends day to day problems. The Greek island psyche is stronger than ever and more confident than it has been for a long time. The years to come will no doubt be testing for islanders, but they will inevitably succeed as the world they live in is unique and will never wither nor disappear.

History

The Greek Islands were the birthplace of two of Europe's earliest civilisations, the Cycladic and the Minoan.

Both can be traced to the introduction of Bronze Age smelting techniques in about 3000 BC by settlers from Phoenicia (on the coast of modern Lebanon). The Cyclades were the first to blossom. The Cycladic civilisation is divided into three periods: Early (3000–2000 BC), Middle (2000–1500 BC) and Late (1500–1100 BC). The most impressive legacy of this civilisation is the statuettes carved from Parian marble – the famous Cycladic figurines. The finest were produced in the Early Cycladic period. Like statuettes from Neolithic times, they depicted images of the Great Mother (the earth goddess). Other remains include bronze and obsidian tools and weapons, gold jewellery, and stone and clay vases and pots.

Greece Before History, by Priscilla Murray and Curtis Neil Runnels, is a good introduction to Greece's earliest days.

The people of the Cycladic civilisation were also accomplished sailors who developed prosperous maritime trade links. They exported their wares to Asia Minor (west of present-day Turkey), Europe and North Africa, as well as to Crete and continental Greece. The Cycladic civilisation lasted until about 1100 BC, but its later stages were increasingly dominated by the Minoan civilisation that evolved on nearby Crete.

The Minoans, named after the mythical King Minos, drew their inspiration from two great Middle Eastern civilisations: the Mesopotamian and the Egyptian. The civilisation reached its peak in the period between 2100 and 1500 BC, producing pottery and metalwork of remarkable beauty and a high degree of imagination and skill.

The famous palaces at Knossos, Phaestos, Malia and Zakros were built at this time. They were destroyed by a violent earthquake in about 1700 BC, but were rebuilt to a more complex, almost labyrinthine design with multiple storeys, sumptuous royal apartments, reception halls, storerooms, workshops, living quarters for staff and an advanced drainage system. The interiors were decorated with the celebrated Minoan frescoes, now on display in the archaeological museum at Iraklio (p226).

The Greek language has the longest written history of all languages in Europe and is second only to Chinese in the world. Greek can be traced back to the Linear B script of Minoan Crete.

After 1500 BC, the civilisation began to decline, both commercially and militarily, against Mycenaean competition from the mainland. The Minoan civilisation came to an abrupt end around 1100 BC during a period of major upheaval throughout the eastern Mediterranean that is normally referred to as the Age of Migrations, and which also swept away the Mycenaeans.

Some historians have suggested that the Minoans' demise was accelerated by the effects of the massive volcanic explosion on the Cycladic island of Santorini (Thira) in 1450 BC, an eruption vulcanologists believe was more cataclysmic than any on record. They theorise that the fallout of volcanic ash from the blast caused a succession of crop failures with resulting social upheaval.

For more on Linear B script, try www.ancient scripts.com/linearb.html.

The Mycenaeans' most impressive legacy is their magnificent gold jewellery and ornaments, the best of which can be seen in the National Archaeological Museum (p85) in Athens. The Mycenaeans wrote in what is called Linear B (an early form of Greek) and worshipped gods who were precursors of the later Greek gods.

TIMELINE	3000 BC	2000 BC
	Arrival of the Bronze Age in Greece triggers rise of Cycladic and Minoan civilisations	The Acropolis of Lindos in Rhodes is settled for the first time

DORIAN GREECE

By the time life had settled down, it was the Dorians who had emerged as the new power on the Greek mainland, replacing the old order with new city-states such as Sparta and Corinth. Thought to have arrived from northern Greece, the warlike Dorians brought a traumatic break with the past and the next 400 years are often referred to as Greece's 'dark age'. The Dorians worshipped male gods instead of fertility goddesses and adopted the Mycenaean gods of Poseidon, Zeus and Apollo, paving the way for the later Greek religious pantheon. They were also responsible for bringing the Iron Age to Greece, and for the development of a new style of pottery, decorated with striking geometrical designs.

Minotaur by Joseph Alexander MacGillivray is a comprehensive history of the at times controversial excavation and restoration work conducted by Sir Arthur Evans at Knossos.

The Dorians also spread their tentacles into the Greek Islands, founding the cities of Kamiros, Ialysos and Lindos on the island of Rhodes in about 1000 BC, while Ionians fleeing to the Cyclades from the Peloponnese established a religious sanctuary on Delos.

By the 8th century BC, when Homer's *Odyssey* and *Iliad* were first written down, the Greek city-states were powerful enough to start spreading their wings. Led by Athens and Corinth, which took over Corfu in 734 BC, the city-states created a Magna Graecia (Greater Greece) with southern Italy as an important component. Although the city-states spent much of their time fighting each other, they united behind Athens to repel the Persians twice, at Marathon (490 BC) and Salamis (480 BC).

THE GOLDEN AGE

The period that followed Salamis has become known as the classical (or golden) age. For Athens, it was a time of unparalleled growth and prosperity. In 477 BC it founded the Delian League, so called because the treasury was on Delos. Almost every state with a navy, including most of the Aegean islands, was forced to swear allegiance to Athens and to make an annual contribution of ships (and later money).

When Pericles became leader of Athens in 461 BC, he moved the treasury from Delos to the Acropolis and used its contents to build the Parthenon and the other monuments of the Acropolis (p85). The golden age ended with the Peloponnesian War (431–404 BC) in which the militaristic Spartans defeated the Athenians.

www.ancientgreece.com is a great web portal for all things ancient and Greek!

So embroiled were they in this war that they failed to notice the expansion of Macedonia to the north under King Philip II, who easily conquered the war-weary city-states.

Philip's ambitions were surpassed by those of his son Alexander the Great, who marched triumphantly into Asia Minor, Egypt, Persia and what are now parts of Afghanistan and India. After Alexander's untimely death in 323 BC at the age of 33, his generals divided his empire between themselves. The Dodecanese became part of the kingdom of Ptolemy I of Egypt, while the remainder of the Aegean islands became part of the League of Islands ruled by the Antagonids of Macedon.

ROMAN RULE & THE BYZANTINE EMPIRE

Roman incursions into Greece began in 205 BC. By 146 BC the mainland had become the Roman provinces of Greece and Macedonia. Crete fell in 67 BC, and the southern city of Gortyn became capital of the Roman

1000 BC	630 BC
The cult of the Great Gods is brought to Samothraki by mainland Thracians	Sappho was born in Eresos, Lesvos

province of Cyrenaica, which included a large chunk of North Africa. Rhodes held out until AD 70.

In AD 330 Emperor Constantine chose Byzantium as the new capital of the Roman Empire and renamed the city Constantinople. After the subdivision of the Roman Empire into Eastern and Western empires in AD 395, Greece became part of the Eastern Roman Empire, leading to the illustrious Byzantine age.

In the centuries that followed, Venetians, Franks, Normans, Persians, Arabs and, finally, Turks all took their turns to chip away at the Byzantine Empire. The Persians captured Rhodes in 620, but were replaced by the Saracens (Arabs) in 653. The Arabs also captured Crete in 824.

Other islands in the Aegean remained under Byzantine control until the sacking of Constantinople in 1204 by renegade Frankish crusaders in cahoots with Venice. The Venetians were rewarded with the Cyclades and they added Crete to their possessions in 1210.

THE CRUSADES

It is one of the ironies of history that the demise of the Byzantine Empire was accelerated not by invasions of infidels from the east, nor barbarians from the north, but by fellow Christians from the west – the Frankish crusaders.

The stated mission of the crusades was to liberate the Holy Land from the Muslims, but in reality they were driven as much by greed as by religious fervour. The first three crusades passed by without incident, but the leaders of the fourth crusade decided that Constantinople presented richer pickings than Jerusalem and struck a deal with Venice.

Constantinople was sacked in 1204 and much of the Byzantine Empire was partitioned into feudal states ruled by self-styled 'Latin' (mostly Frankish) princes. The Venetians, meanwhile, had also secured a foothold in Greece. Over the next few centuries they acquired all the key Greek ports, including the island of Crete, and became the wealthiest and most powerful traders in the Mediterranean.

Despite this sorry state of affairs, Byzantium was not yet dead. In 1259 the Byzantine emperor Michael VIII Palaeologos recaptured the Peloponnese and made the city of Mystras his headquarters. Many eminent Byzantine artists, architects, intellectuals and philosophers converged on the city for a final burst of Byzantine creativity. Michael VIII managed to reclaim Constantinople in 1261, but by this time Byzantium was a shadow of its former self.

THE OTTOMAN EMPIRE

The Byzantine Empire finally came to an end in 1453 when Constantinople fell to the Turks. Once more Greece became a battleground, this time fought over by the Turks and Venetians. Eventually, with the exception of Corfu, Greece became part of the Ottoman Empire.

Much has been made of the horrors of the Turkish occupation in Greece. However, in the early years at any rate, people probably marginally preferred Ottoman to Venetian or Frankish rule. The Venetians in particular treated their subjects little better than slaves. Ottoman power reached its zenith under Sultan Süleyman the Magnificent (r 1520–66), who expanded the empire to the gates of Vienna. His successor added

'It is one of the ironies of history that the demise of the Byzantine Empire was accelerated...by fellow Christians from the west'

300 BC

Hippocrates practices medicine on the island of Kos

AD 824

Arabs capture Crete

Cyprus to their dominions in 1570, but his death in 1574 marked the end of serious territorial expansion.

Although they captured Crete in 1669 after a 25-year campaign and briefly threatened Vienna once more in 1683, the ineffectual sultans of the late 16th and 17th centuries saw the empire go into steady decline. They suffered a series of reversals on the battlefield, and Venice succeeded in recapturing the Peloponnese (1685–87) in a campaign that saw them advance as far as Athens. The Parthenon was destroyed in the fighting by a shell that struck a store of Turkish gunpowder.

Chaos and rebellion spread across Greece. Pirates terrorised coastal dwellers and islanders, while gangs of *klephts* (anti-Ottoman fugitives and brigands) roamed the mountains. There was an upsurge of opposition to Turkish rule by freedom fighters – who fought each other when they weren't fighting the Turks.

The Unification of Greece 1770–1923, by Douglas Dakin, is the ultimate guide to Modern Greek history, tracing Greece's transition from Ottoman subject state to modern nation.

THE WAR OF INDEPENDENCE

The long-heralded War of Independence finally began on 25 March 1821, when Bishop Germanos of Patras hoisted the Greek flag at the monastery of Agias Lavras, near Patras in the Peloponnese. Fighting broke out almost simultaneously across most of Greece and the occupied islands, with the Greeks making big early gains. The fighting was savage, with atrocities committed on both sides. The islands weren't spared the horrors of war: in 1822, Turkish forces massacred 25,000 people on the island of Chios, while another 7000 died on Kasos in 1824.

Eventually, the Great Powers – Britain, France and Russia – intervened on the side of the Greeks, defeating the Turkish-Egyptian fleet at the Battle of Navarino in October 1827. Although fighting between Russian and Turkish forces continued until 1829, Greece was left free to organise its own affairs. Nafplio, in the Peloponnese, was declared the first capital.

It was there that the country's first president, Ioannis Kapodistrias, a Corfiot who had been the foreign minister for Tsar Alexander I, was assassinated in 1831. Amid anarchy, the European powers stepped in again and declared that Greece should become a monarchy. In January 1833, 17-year-old Prince Otto of Bavaria was installed as king of a nation (established by the London Convention of 1832) that consisted of the Peloponnese, Sterea Ellada (Central Greece), the Cyclades and the Sporades.

King Otho (as his name became) displeased the Greek people from the start, arriving with a bunch of upper-class Bavarian cronies to whom he gave the most prestigious official posts. He moved the capital to Athens in 1834.

Patience with his rule ran out in 1843, when demonstrations in the capital, led by the War of Independence leaders, called for a constitution. Otho mustered a National Assembly, which drafted a constitution calling for parliamentary government consisting of a lower house and a senate. Otho's cronies were whisked out of power and replaced by War of Independence freedom fighters, who bullied and bribed the populace into voting for them.

By the end of the 1850s, most of the stalwarts from the War of Independence had been replaced by a new breed of university graduates (Athens University had been founded in 1837). In 1862 they staged a

1453	1699
Turks capture Constantinople; most of Greece becomes part of the Ottoman Empire	Crete comes under Ottoman rule

bloodless revolution and deposed the king. But they weren't quite able to set their own agenda because, in 1863, Britain returned the Ionian islands (a British protectorate since 1815) to Greece. Amid the general euphoria that followed, the British were able to push forward young Prince William of Denmark, who became King George I.

His 50-year reign brought stability to the troubled country, beginning with a new constitution in 1864, which established the power of democratically elected representatives and pushed the king further towards a ceremonial role. An uprising in Crete against Turkish rule (1866–8) was suppressed by the sultan, but in 1881 Greece acquired Thessaly and part of Epiros as the result of another Russo–Turkish war.

In 1897 there was another uprising in Crete, and the hot-headed prime minister Theodoros Deligiannis responded by declaring war on Turkey and sending help to Crete. A Greek attempt to invade Turkey in the north proved disastrous – it was only through the intervention of the Great Powers that the Turkish army was prevented from taking Athens.

Crete was made a British protectorate in 1898, and the day-to-day government of the island was gradually handed over to the Greeks. In 1905 the president of the Cretan assembly, Eleftherios Venizelos, announced Crete's *enosis* (union) with Greece, although this was not recognised by international law until 1913. Venizelos went on to become prime minister of Greece in 1910 and was the country's leading politician until his republican sympathies brought about his downfall in 1935.

Although the Ottoman Empire was in its death throes at the beginning of the 20th century, it was still clinging onto Macedonia. It was a prize sought by the newly formed Balkan countries of Serbia and Bulgaria, as well as by Greece, leading to the Balkan wars. The first, in 1912, pitted all three against the Turks; the second, in 1913, pitted Serbia and Greece against Bulgaria. The outcome was the Treaty of Bucharest (August 1913), which greatly expanded Greek territory by adding the southern part of Macedonia, part of Thrace, another chunk of Epiros and the Northeastern Aegean Islands, as well as recognising the union with Crete.

In March 1913, King George was assassinated by a lunatic and his son Constantine became king.

'In March 1913, King George was assassinated by a lunatic and his son Constantine became king.'

WWI & SMYRNA

King Constantine, who was married to the sister of the German emperor, insisted that Greece remain neutral when WWI broke out in August 1914. As the war dragged on, the Allies (Britain, France and Russia) put increasing pressure on Greece to join forces with them against Germany and Turkey, and they made promises that they couldn't hope to fulfil, including offering land in Asia Minor. Venizelos, the prime minister of Greece, favoured the Allied cause, placing him at loggerheads with the king. Tensions between the two came to a head in 1916 and Venizelos set up a rebel government, first in Crete and then in Thessaloniki, while the pressure from the Allies eventually persuaded Constantine to leave Greece in June 1917. He was replaced by his more amenable second son, Alexander.

Greek troops served with distinction on the Allied side, but when the war ended in 1918 the promised land in Asia Minor was not forthcoming.

1827	1864
Ioannis Kapodistrias elected first president of independent Greece	Britain cedes the Ionian Islands to Greece

Venizelos took matters into his own hands and, with Allied acquiescence, landed troops in Smyrna (present-day Izmir) in May 1919 under the guise of protecting the half a million Greeks living in that city (just under half its population). With a firm foothold in Asia Minor, Venizelos now planned to push home his advantage against a war-depleted Ottoman Empire. He ordered his troops to attack in October 1920 (just weeks before he was voted out of office). By September 1921, the Greeks had advanced as far as Ankara.

The Turkish forces were commanded by Mustafa Kemal (later to become Atatürk), a young general who also belonged to the Young Turks, a group of army officers pressing for Western-style political reforms. Kemal first halted the Greek advance outside Ankara in September 1921 and then routed them with a massive offensive the following spring. The Greeks were driven out of Smyrna and many of the Greek inhabitants were massacred. Mustafa Kemal was now a national hero, the sultanate was abolished and Turkey became a republic.

The outcome of the failed Greek invasion and the revolution in Turkey was the Treaty of Lausanne of July 1923. This gave eastern Thrace and the islands of Imvros and Tenedos to Turkey, while the Italians kept the Dodecanese (which they had temporarily acquired in 1912 and would hold until 1947).

The treaty also called for a population exchange between Greece and Turkey to prevent any future disputes. Almost 1.5 million Greeks left Turkey and almost 400,000 Turks left Greece. The exchange put a tremendous strain on the Greek economy and caused great hardship for the individuals concerned. Many Greeks abandoned a privileged life in Asia Minor for one of extreme poverty in shantytowns in Greece.

King Constantine, restored to the throne in 1920, identified himself too closely with the war against Turkey and abdicated after the fall of Smyrna.

WWII & THE CIVIL WAR

Mediterraneo, directed by Gabriele Salvatores, is a classic Italian movie about a bunch of misfit soldiers sent to invade a magical Greek island where almost anything can happen.

In 1930 George II, Constantine's son, became king and appointed the dictator General Ioannis Metaxas as prime minister. Metaxas' grandiose ambition was to take the best from Greece's ancient and Byzantine past to create a Third Greek Civilisation, though what he actually created was more a Greek version of the Third Reich. His chief claim to fame was his celebrated *ohi* (no) to Mussolini's request to allow Italian troops to traverse Greece in 1940. Despite Allied help, Greece fell to Germany in 1941, after which carnage and mass starvation followed. Resistance movements sprang up, eventually polarising into royalist and communist factions.

A bloody civil war resulted, lasting until 1949 and leaving the country in chaos. More people were killed in the civil war than in WWII and 250,000 people were left homeless. The sense of despair that followed became the trigger for a mass exodus. Almost a million Greeks headed off in search of a better life elsewhere, primarily to Australia, Canada and the USA. Villages – whole islands even – were abandoned as people gambled on a new start in cities like Melbourne, Chicago and New York. While some have drifted back, the majority have stayed away.

1923	1947
Failed military campaign ends with population exchange between Greece and Turkey	The Dodecanese is declared part of Greece

THE COLONELS

Continuing political instability led to the colonels' coup d'état in 1967, led by Georgos Papadopolous and Stylianos Patakos. King Constantine (son of King Paul, who succeeded George II) staged an unsuccessful counter coup, then fled the country. The colonels' junta distinguished itself by inflicting appalling brutality, repression and political incompetence upon the people.

In 1974 they attempted to assassinate Cyprus' leader, Archbishop Makarios. When Makarios escaped, the junta replaced him with the extremist Nikos Samson, a convicted murderer. The Turks, who comprised 20% of the population, were alarmed at having Samson as leader. Consequently, mainland Turkey sent in troops and occupied North Cyprus, the continued occupation of which is one of the most contentious issues in Greek politics today. The junta, by now in a shambles, had little choice but to hand power back to civilians.

In November 1974 a plebiscite voted 69% against restoration of the monarchy and Greece became a republic. An election brought the right-wing New Democracy (ND) party into power. The ban on communist parties was then lifted, Andreas Papandreou formed the Panhellenic Socialist Union (PASOK).

ND won again in 1977, but the leader, Konstandinos Karamanlis' personal popularity began to decline. One of his biggest achievements was to engineer Greece's entry into the European Community (EC; now the European Union).

Democracy at Gunpoint, by Andreas Papandreou, former prime minister of Greece, is a compelling account of the coup d'état in Greece in 1967, which ushered in the infamous years of the Junta's colonels.

THE SOCIALIST 1980S

In 1981 Greece entered the EC (now the EU). Andreas Papandreou's PASOK won the next election, giving Greece its first socialist government. PASOK promised removal of US air bases and withdrawal from NATO, which Greece had joined in 1951.

Six years into government these promises remained unfulfilled, unemployment was high and reforms in education and welfare had been limited. Women's issues had fared better, however – the dowry system was abolished, abortion legalised, and civil marriage and divorce were implemented. The crunch for the government came in 1988 when Papandreou's affair with air stewardess Dimitra Liana (whom he subsequently married) was widely publicised and PASOK became embroiled in a financial scandal involving the Bank of Crete.

In July 1989, an unprecedented conservative and communist coalition took over to implement a *katharsis* (campaign of purification) to investigate the scandals. It ruled that Papandreou and four ministers should stand trial for embezzlement, telephone tapping and illegal grain sales. It then stepped down in October 1990, stating that the *katharsis* was complete.

1990–2000

An election in 1990 brought the ND back to power with Konstandinos Mitsotakis as prime minister. Intent on redressing the country's economic problems – high inflation and high government spending – the government imposed austerity measures, including a wage freeze for civil servants and steep increases in utility costs and basic services.

1981	2002
Greece becomes 10th member of the European Union	Greece drops the drachma and adopts the euro

By late 1992 corruption allegations were being made against the government and it was claimed that Cretan-born Mitsotakis had a secret collection of Minoan art. Allegations of government telephone tapping followed and by mid-1993 Mitsotakis supporters began to cut their losses, abandoning the ND for the new Political Spring party. The ND lost its parliamentary majority and an early election was held in October, which returned Andreas Papandreou's PASOK party with a handsome majority.

Papandreou's final spell at the helm was dominated by speculation about his health. He was finally forced to step down in early 1996, and his death on 26 June marked the end of an era in Greek politics.

Papandreou's departure produced a dramatic change of direction for PASOK, with the party abandoning his left-leaning politics and electing experienced economist and lawyer Costas Simitis as the new prime minister. Cashing in on his reputation as the Mr Clean of Greek politics, Simitis romped to a comfortable majority at a snap poll called in October 1996.

THE NEW MILLENNIUM

With the turn of the millennium the Simitis government focused on the push for further integration with Europe. This meant in general terms more tax reform and austerity measures. His success in the face of constant protest nonetheless earned him a mandate for another four years in April 2000. The goal of admission to the euro club was achieved at the beginning of 2001 and Greece adopted the euro as its currency in March 2002.

In April 2004 the Greek populace, perhaps tired of a long run of socialist policies, turned once more to the right and elected New Democracy leader Konstantinos Karamanlis as prime minister. This may have been a blessing in disguise for the socialists as they had been chiefly responsible for the preparations for the 2004 Olympic Games, which had for some time been dogged by delays and technical problems.

For the low-down on the Athens Olympic Games and the history of this famous Greek event visit www.athens2004.com.

Before the staging of the Olympic Games Greece's sporting prowess took an unexpected shot in the arm when against all odds they won the European football championships, giving Greeks the world over an enormous boost of self pride. As it happens the August Olympic Games were a resounding success and the Greeks put on a well organised (if poorly attended) spectacle. The fiscal cost to Greece is yet to be counted as the eventual cost of the Games far exceeded the original budget. Further national kudos was to be gleaned when Greece – again against the odds – won the Eurovision Song Contest with an English song sung by a Swedish-Greek diva called Elena Paparizou. Greeks the world over were again ecstatic.

Greece's relations with its neighbours – particularly Turkey – became warmer. Konstantinos Karamanlis made particular efforts to chip away at the frost with its neighbour Turkey, and they seem to have paid off with little to report on the brinkmanship front. A trend that all too often in the past had caused sabres to be rattled between the two military forces. On the Greek islands – particularly those of the Northeastern Aegean and the Dodecanese – the peace is likely to be shattered by the ear-piercing scream and roar of Turkish and Greek jets chasing each other in combat games.

Greece by mid-2005 was a developed and yet maturing EU nation with a rising standard of living coupled – perhaps ominously for many of its citizens – with a rising cost of living.

2004	2005
Athens hosts the 28th Modern Olympic Games	Greece wins the Eurovision Song Contest for the first time

The Culture

REGIONAL IDENTITY

With so many Greek islands sprawled across the furthest reaches of Greece, it is not surprising that Greek islanders maintain their own strong sense of identity. Even within the seven island groups, there are distinct differences in the various island histories, customs and traditions, influencing everything from their cuisine to music and dances. These distinctions mean that Greek islanders often identify with their island first (as Cretans, Ithacans or Kastellorizians, etc) and as Greeks second. Even though many have left the islands for the mainland, bigger islands or abroad, the connection to their ancestral island remains strong. Such diverse regional identities add to the complex psyche of the Greeks.

Greeks have long enjoyed a reputation as loyal friends and generous hosts. They pride themselves on their *filotimo* (dignity and sense of honour), and their *filoxenia* (hospitality, welcome, shelter), which you will find in even the poorest household.

Greeks are intensely patriotic and take pride in their country's rich cultural heritage. Yet they also display the insecurities of a relatively new nation as they struggle to catch up with the rapid social and economic changes of the past 30 years.

There is a residual mistrust of authority and little respect for the state; personal freedom and democratic rights are almost sacrosanct. Greeks remain highly individualistic, are dependent on family support networks and maintain a strong sense of community and neighbourhood. Yet until recently there was little sense of communal responsibility, especially in relation to the environment.

Patronage features prominently at all levels of Greek society. It's almost impossible to make any headway with local bureaucracy (or often get a job) without *meson,* the help of a friend or cousin working within the system.

Under occupation, Greeks maintained a sense of unity and common purpose through the church and religion remains a key part of Greek identity.

Anti-Americanism is an interesting undercurrent of the Greek psyche. Apart from general resistance to American hegemony, it originates from what many regard as undue US interference in Greek affairs during the civil war (p36), suspected CIA involvement in the colonels' coup in 1967 and US indifference over Cyprus.

The laid-back Greeks have a casual approach to timekeeping, with turning up to an appointment on time often referred to as 'being English'.

Most Greeks have a zest for life. They are forthright and argumentative and thrive on news, politics, gossip and debate.

Greece has the highest number of smokers in the EU.

Despite it virtually being the national pastime, Greece has the most expensive coffee in Europe.

LIFESTYLE

The lifestyle of the average Greek has changed beyond all recognition in the last 50 years. Grandparents who recall the devastated country that emerged from the civil war in 1949 can hardly believe the difference in the lives of their children or grandchildren, now part of the euro club.

There are still huge disparities in the standard of living across society and a stark rural-city divide, but Greeks generally enjoy a good quality of life.

Greeks are social animals and enjoy a rich communal life, regularly sharing meals and good times with their families or their *parea* (company). In the evenings, especially in summer, you will see people of all ages out on their *volta* (promenade), walking along seafront promenades or through town centres, often dressed up and refreshed from their siesta.

The cafés and bars of Greece's towns and cities are lively and sophisticated, and the fashion-conscious and consumerist Greeks have their share of yuppies in designer clothes, clutching the latest mobile phones and driving the latest-model cars.

Summer holidays are the highlight of the year, with the country virtually shutting during mid-August.

Island life is completely seasonal. On islands that survive largely on tourism, many islanders move to Athens for the winter. On the bigger islands, the beach resorts are deserted in winter for the towns and cities with schools and infrastructure. Winter can be very tough for the small permanent populations on isolated smaller islands, especially those without airports.

Every inhabited island has a ferry service of some sort, even if it is only a weekly supply boat.

Greeks have been feeling the financial pinch in recent times, with the cost of living rising sharply since the arrival of the euro – yet wages remain among the lowest in the EU. The general decline in tourism has severely impacted on island economies.

Greek society remains dominated by the family. Extended family plays an important role in daily life, with grandparents often looking after grandchildren while their parents are at work or out socialising. Many working Athenians send their children to their grandparents on the islands for the summer holidays.

It's uncommon for Greek children to move out of the family home before they are married unless they leave temporarily for university or work reasons. Many islands are losing their young people as they head to the mainland or bigger islands for work and educational opportunities.

Check out Greece's demographics at www.statistics.gr.

Greeks attach great importance to education, determined to provide their children the opportunities they lacked. The inadequacies of the public education system have spawned a big industry in private night schools, known as *frontistiria*. Greece also has the highest number of students in the EU studying at universities abroad.

POPULATION

Less than 15% of people live on the islands, the most populous of which are Crete, Evia and Corfu. Greece's population exceeded 11 million in 2004 and a third of the population (3.7 million) lives in the Greater Athens area.

THE GREEK DIASPORA

Greece was until recently a country of emigrants, with more than five million people of Greek descent living in 140 countries around the world. While about three million Greeks live in the US and Canada, the concentrated presence of about 300,000 Greeks in Melbourne, Australia, backs its claim as the third-largest population of Greek-speakers in the world (after Athens and Thessaloniki).

The biggest waves of migration were in the 15 years before the Balkan wars, after the 1922 Asia Minor purge and in the postwar years in the 1950s and '60s. Some islands were virtually deserted en masse, though strong sentimental connections remain.

Now a feature of many islands such as Kastellorizo, Ithaki and Kythira is the influx of diaspora Greeks who return annually for holidays, to buy or claim family properties and generally become involved in the political and cultural life of their ancestral islands.

Many older migrants are retiring in Greece, while there is a growing stream of young second- and third-generation Greeks repatriating permanently, lured partly by cultural curiosity and the seductive lifestyle.

More than two-thirds of the population live in cities – confirming that Greece is now largely an urban society.

Greece has a declining and ageing population. The main population growth has been the dramatic influx of migrants since 1991, with about one million migrants estimated to be living in Greece.

Albanians make up roughly half the legal migrants, followed by migrants from Eastern Europe, Pakistan, the former Soviet Union, India and North Africa.

MULTICULTURALISM

The influx of recent migrants has dramatically changed the ethnic mix in what was a largely homogeneous country. This is posing a major challenge for the state, which was not prepared for dealing with migrants or refugees, and also at a local community level. As migrants seek Greek residency and citizenship, they are challenging notions of Greek identity and nationality.

Albanians, the biggest migrant group, have become an economic necessity, doing jobs many Greeks no longer want to do. Many have settled on the larger islands where they work in the tourism industry in summer and construction and agriculture in the winter.

Many Greeks initially reacted with xenophobia and resented their presence, holding Albanians responsible for just about every crime committed, and there is still a long way to go before migrants are fully accepted into the community.

Indeed, a 2005 report by human rights watchdog Amnesty International criticised Greece's treatment of minorities and foreigners, particularly refugees, and accused authorities of failing to fight discrimination and comply with international asylum and detention standards.

Mixed marriages are becoming a phenomenon. Eastern European brides are common in rural areas, which Greek women desert for the cities.

Until recently, Greece's only recognised ethnic minority were the 300,000 ethnic Turks in western Thrace who were exempt from the population exchange of 1923.

Small numbers of Vlach and Sarakatsani shepherds live out a semi-nomadic existence in Epiros, while you will come across Roma (Gypsies) everywhere.

MEDIA

Greece has a disproportionate number of newspapers and TV stations – 30 national dailies (including 10 sports dailies) and seven national broadcasters. Openly partisan newspapers and largely sensationalist TV news coverage give the country's media owners an extremely influential role in shaping public opinion.

Ownership of key publications is spread around half a dozen major players. The most important of these is the Lambrakis Group, which publishes the serious paper *To Vima* and the populist *Ta Nea,* both of which consistently backed the Panhellenic Socialist Movement (PASOK) and continue to mount an opposition to the ruling New Democracy (ND) government, as do *Eleftherotypia* and *Ethnos.*

Kathimerini is traditionally the centre-right publication favoured by the establishment; *Eleftheros Typos* and *Apogevmatini* promote the ND line; and communist party views are represented by the daily *Rizospastis* and the weekly *Pontiki.* Controversial journalist Makis Triantafyllopoulos threw a spanner in the works by launching the top-selling Sunday paper *Proto Thema.*

The Cyclades, or Life Among the Insular Greeks, by James Theodore Bent, is still regarded as the greatest book about the people of the Greek islands.

Pulitzer prize–winning novel *Middlesex* by Greek-American writer Jeffrey Eugenides is an intriguing gender-bending tale of genetic mutation and the secrets of a refugee family from Asia Minor who fled to America.

The advent of private TV and radio in 1989 as well as changing lifestyles has brought a dramatic decline in newspaper readership, leading the papers to fight back with gimmicks, competitions, magazine inserts and free DVDs.

TV ownership is evenly spread among the same main players. Controversy over the media barons' conflicting business interests led to ultimately ineffective moves to strengthen media ownership rules. The contentious entangled relationship between media owners, journalists, big business and the government is what the Greeks have coined *diaplekomena*.

RELIGION

Religion is a key factor in Greek identity, with about 98% of the Greek population belonging to the Greek Orthodox Church. The remainder are Roman Catholic, Jewish or Muslim.

The Greek year is centred on the saint's days and festivals of the church calendar. While the younger generation aren't generally devout and don't attend church regularly, most observe the rituals and consider it part of their identity. You will notice taxi drivers, motorcyclists and people on public transport making the sign of the cross when they pass a church. There are hundreds of tiny churches dotted around the countryside built by individual families as thanksgiving for God's protection. The tiny roadside iconostases or chapels you see everywhere are similar dedications or shrines to people who died in road accidents.

Greece was one of the first places in Europe that Christianity emerged, with St Paul reputedly first preaching the gospel in AD 49 in the Macedonian town of Philippi. He later preached in Athens, Thessaloniki and Corinth.

Time, Religion & Social Experience in Rural Greece by Laurie Kain Hart is a fascinating account of village traditions, many of which are alive and well, buried beneath the tourist veneer.

The Greek Orthodox Church is closely related to the Russian Orthodox Church, together forming the third-largest branch of Christianity. Orthodox, meaning 'right belief', was founded in the 4th century by Constantine the Great, who was converted to Christianity by a vision of the Cross.

By the 8th century, differences of opinion and increasing rivalry were emerging between the pope in Rome and the patriarch of Constantinople. One dispute was over the wording of the Creed, which stated that the Holy Spirit proceeds 'from the Father', but Rome added 'and the Son'. Other bones of contention concerned the celibacy of the clergy (Orthodox priests could marry before being ordained) and fasting (the Orthodox Church also forbids wine and oil during Lent).

These differences became irreconcilable and in 1054 the pope and the patriarch excommunicated one another and went their separate ways. The brief visit to Athens by Pope John Paul II in May 2001 was the first by a pontiff for more than 1300 years and Greece's Orthodox church was represented at the highest levels at his funeral in 2005.

During Ottoman times religion was one of the most important criteria in defining a Greek, regardless of where they lived. The church was the principal upholder of Greek culture and traditions.

Greece doesn't have the same church–state separation as other Western countries, often causing friction in relations between the church and the government.

A small Roman Catholic population, which is largely of Genoese or Frankish origin, lives mostly in the Cyclades, especially on Syros, where they make up 40% of the population.

There are about 5000 Jews living in Greece today, with a small Jewish community in Rhodes (dating back to the Roman era).

> **PAYING YOUR RESPECTS**
>
> Dress appropriately if you wish to look around a church or monastery. Women should wear skirts that reach below the knees and have their arms and shoulders covered. Men should wear long trousers. Many monasteries have skirts and clothing on hand for tourists who rock up in shorts and strappy tops, but it's handy to have a sarong with you for such occasions.

WOMEN IN GREECE

Old attitudes towards the 'proper role' for women are changing fast as more Greek women become educated and enter the workforce, though 'mother' and 'sex object' are still the dominant role models in society. In provincial towns and villages Greek women still maintain traditional roles, while in the cities and large towns things are much more liberal.

While there are many benefits for mothers in the public sector, Greek women generally do it tough in the workplace. Women are significantly underrepresented in the workforce compared to their EU or international counterparts. There is no affirmative action and sexism prevails. Women generally earn less than their male counterparts and struggle to climb the corporate ladder.

There are women in many prominent positions in business and government, though more often than not they also happen to be the wives or daughters of prominent or wealthy men. Only 9% of seats in parliament are held by women.

On the domestic front, Greek women are famously house proud, trained from an early age to keep spotless homes and take pride in their culinary skills. It's rare for men to be involved in housework or cooking.

The male–female dynamic throws up some interesting paradoxes. Men give the impression that they rule the roost but, in reality, it's often the women who run the show, both at home and in business, while men sit around talking over endless coffees. This pattern is developed at home, where boys are waited on hand and foot while girls are involved in the domestic chores from an early age. However, this is also changing and young Athenian women are more likely to be found in a gym or beauty salon than in the kitchen.

From Tyrnavo's phallic festival and Easter tradition to the goat dancers of Skyros, *Festive Greece* by John L Tomkinson explores the fascinating (and sometimes wacky) folk and religious celebrations observed around Greece.

ARTS
Architecture

The influence of Ancient Greek architecture can be seen today in buildings from Washington, DC to Melbourne, Australia. Greek temples are a symbol of democracy and have been the inspiration for major architectural movements such as the Italian Renaissance and British Greek Revival.

The earliest known architectural sites of ancient Greece are the labyrinthine Minoan palace complexes in Crete, including the famous palace at Knossos (p233), and Akrotiri (p198) on Santorini.

The Mycenaeans later built citadels on a compact, orderly plan, fortified by strong walls.

The next great architectural advance came with the first monumental stone temples in the Archaic and classical periods, when temples became characterised by the famous orders of columns, particularly the Doric, Ionic and Corinthian. These orders were applied to the exteriors, which retained their traditional simple plan of porch and hall, but were now regularly surrounded by a colonnade or at least a columnar façade.

Doric columns feature cushion capitals, fluted shafts and no bases. The most famous Doric temple in Greece is the Parthenon (p85), but the Temple of Aphaia (p120) on Aegina and the small Doric temple of Isis (p160) on Delos, near Mykonos, are also fine examples.

The shaft of the Ionic column has a base in several tiers and has more flutes. Unlike the austere Doric style, its capital has an ornamented necking; it is less massive and generally more graceful. Two famous Ionic temples are the little temple of Athena Nike and the Erechtheion on the Acropolis (p85) in Athens.

Corinthian columns feature a single or double row of ornate leafy scrolls (usually acanthus). Introduced at the end of the classical period, the order was subsequently used by the Romans. A good example is the Temple of Olympian Zeus (p85) in Athens.

Theatre design was also a hallmark of the classical period. The Theatre of Dionysos (p85) was built into the slope of Athens' Acropolis in the 5th century BC, while theatres were also built at Dodoni, Megalopolis, Epidavros and Argos. They all feature excellent acoustics and most are still used for summer festivals. Less well-preserved theatres are found on several islands, including the marble theatre at Delos (p160), the ancient theatre at Eretria (p405) on Evia, the Hellenistic theatre of Samothraki (p392), and theatres in Thassos, Rhodes, Crete, Santorini and Milos.

In the Hellenistic period, the focus was on private houses and palaces, rather than temples and public buildings. Among the best existing examples are the houses at Delos (p158), built around peristyled (surrounded by columns) courtyards and featuring striking mosaics.

During the Byzantine period, the Parthenon in Athens was converted into a church and other churches were built throughout Greece. These usually featured a central dome supported by four arches on piers and flanked by vaults, with smaller domes at the four corners and three apses to the east. The external brickwork, which alternated with stone, was sometimes set in patterns. At Mt Athos and on Patmos (p334), where the first monasteries were built in the 10th century, the monastic buildings as well as the churches survive. At Meteora in central Greece, the monasteries were built high on precipitous rocks and for centuries were almost inaccessible.

Little architecture of the Ottoman period survives in Greece. The best examples are in the Thracian towns of Kavala, Xanthi and Didymotiho near the Turkish border. Ottoman architecture is also evident in the Cretan towns of Hania and Rethymno, and the old town of Rhodes.

After the War of Independence, Greece continued the neoclassical style that had been dominant in Western European architecture and sculpture from 1760 to 1820, thus providing a sense of continuity with its ancient past. This neoclassical style is apparent in Nafplio, initially the capital, and in Athens, notably in the trilogy of the National Library, Academy and University.

Architectural sensibilities unfortunately took a back seat for most of the 20th century, when political necessity and economic constraints shaped events. Many neoclassical buildings were destroyed in the untamed modernisation and expansion that took place in the 1950s, '60s and '70s, when most of the ugly mass of concrete apartment blocks that now characterise modern Athens (and most Greek towns) were built. This was largely attributed to the colonels' lifting height restrictions and the Karamanlis' introduction of *antiparochi,* a law which allowed people to demolish houses and hand over their land to builders in return for apartments in the new building. Most were hastily and cheaply constructed without architectural input.

The other scourge was the *afthaireta* (illegal buildings), which sprouted all over the country due to lax planning controls and corruption.

RA Tomlinson's *Greek Architecture* covers everything from the prehistoric settlements of Troy to the absorption of Hellenic Greece into the Roman Empire.

Until recently it was hard to think of any modern buildings of architectural note in Athens. The new metro stations are a brilliant exception, as are a few promising projects such as the new Acropolis Museum and the Olympic Stadium's stunning roof design (albeit the work of Spanish architect Santiago Calatrava).

Many neoclassical mansions are now heritage-protected and are being restored, while there have also been some innovative transformations of industrial spaces into cultural centres.

Theatre

Drama in Greece can be dated back to the contests staged at the Ancient Theatre of Dionysos in Athens during the 6th century BC for the annual Dionysia festival. During one of these competitions, Thespis left the ensemble and took centre stage for a solo performance. This is regarded as the first true dramatic performance – thus the term 'thespian'.

The so-called 'father of tragedy' was Aeschylus (c 525–456 BC), whose best-known work is the Oresteia trilogy. Sophocles (c 496–406 BC), regarded as the greatest tragedian, is thought to have written over 100 plays, of which only seven survive, including *Antigone, Electra* and his most famous play, *Oedipus Rex.*

Euripides (c 485–406 BC) was more popular than Aeschylus and Sophocles because his plots were considered more exciting. He wrote 80 plays, of which 19 are extant (although one, *Rhesus,* is disputed). His most famous works are *Medea, Andromache, Orestes* and *Bacchae.*

Aristophanes (c 427–387 BC) wrote often ribald comedies dealing with topical issues, ridiculing Athenians who resorted to litigation over trivialities in *The Wasps* and poking fun at their gullibility in *The Birds.*

You can see plays by ancient Greek playwrights at the Hellenic Festivals in Athens and Epidavros (p86), and festivals around the country.

The most distinguished modern Greek playwrights are Giorgos Skourtis, Pavlos Matessis and the father of post-war drama, Iakovos Kambanellis. Many of their plays have been translated and performed outside Greece.

Literature

The first, and greatest, ancient Greek writer was Homer, author of the *Iliad* and *Odyssey,* which tell the story of the Trojan War and the subsequent wanderings of Odysseus. Nothing is known of Homer's life; where or when he lived, or whether, as it is alleged, he was blind. The historian Herodotus thought Homer lived in the 9th century BC, and no scholar since has proved or disproved this.

Herodotus (5th century BC) was the author of the first historical work about Western civilisation. His highly subjective account of the Persian Wars, however, led some to regard him as the 'father of lies' as well as the 'father of history'. The historian Thucydides (5th century BC) was more objective in his approach, but took a high moral stance. He wrote an account of the Peloponnesian Wars, and also the famous *Melian Dialogue,* which chronicled talks between the Athenians and Melians prior to the Athenian siege of Melos (Milos).

Pindar (c 518–438 BC) is regarded as the pre-eminent lyric poet of ancient Greece. He was commissioned to recite his odes at the Olympic Games. The greatest writers of love poetry were Sappho (6th century BC) and Alcaeus (5th century BC), both of whom lived on Lesvos. Sappho's poetic descriptions of her affections for women gave rise to the term 'lesbian'.

Dionysios Solomos (1798–1857) and Andreas Kalvos (1796–1869), who were both born on Zakynthos, are regarded as the first modern

Sappho: A New Translation by Mary Bernard is the best translation of this great poet's work.

Collected Poems by George Seferis and *Selected Poems* by Odysseus Elytis are excellent English translations of these Greek poets.

Modern Greek Writing: An Anthology in English Translation profiles 50 of the most important Greek writers since 1821.

GREEK ISLAND TALES

The Greek Islands have inspired many novels and travel books by foreigners. Lawrence Durrell wrote *Prospero's Cell* about Corfu, *Reflections of a Marine Venus* about Rhodes, *The Dark Labyrinth* about Crete and *The Greek Islands*. His brother Gerald wrote *My Family and Other Animals* about their life on Corfu while Emma Tennant has a more contemporary take in *A House of Corfu*. Louis de Bernières novel *Captain Corelli's Mandolin* is based on Kefallonia, while John Fowles' bestselling novel *The Magus*, inspired by his time on Spetses, has become a literary classic.

Greek poets. Solomos' work was heavily nationalistic, and his *Hymn to Freedom* became the Greek national anthem. Other notable literary figures include Alexandros Papadiamantis (1851–1911) from Skyros and poet Kostis Palamas (1859–1943).

The best-known 20th-century poets are Georgos Seferis (1900–71), who won the 1963 Nobel Prize for literature, and Odysseas Elytis (1911–96), who won the same prize in 1979.

The most celebrated novelist of the early 20th century is Nikos Kazantzakis (1883–1957), whose unorthodox religious views created a stir. His novels, all of which have been translated into English, are full of drama and larger-than-life characters, such as the magnificent Alexis Zorbas of *Zorba the Greek* and the tortured Michalis of *Christ Recrucified,* which are two of his finest works.

Stratis Myrivilis (1892–1969), whose works include *Life in the Tomb, Vasilis Arvanitis* and *The Mermaid Madonna,* is one of the great prose writers of modern Greece.

Leading contemporary Greek writers include Thanassis Valtinos, Rhea Galanaki, Ziranna Ziteli, Nikos Dimou (best known for his controversial observations on Greek society and book *The Misery of Being Greek*), and Ersi Sotiropoulou, who wrote the acclaimed 1999 novel *Zigzagging Through the Bitter Orange Trees.*

Unfortunately not all contemporary work is translated into English. Panos Karnezis bypassed the translation issue by writing his novel *The Maze* and book of short stories, *Little Infamies,* in English.

Other writers attracting foreign publishers include Apostolos Doxiadis, whose novel *Uncle Petros and Goldbach's Conjecture* has been translated into several languages; Petros Markaris, who delves into Athens' underbelly in his crime noir novels *Late Night News* and *Deadline in Athens*; and prolific children's author and playwright (and criminologist) Eugene Trivizas, whose first book *The Three Little Wolves and the Big Bad Pig* has been translated into 15 languages.

Uncle Petros and Goldbach's Conjecture by Apostolos Doxiadis is an unlikely blend of family drama and mathematical theory. It tells the story of a mathematical genius' attempt to solve a problem that has defied the world's greatest minds.

Fine Arts
PAINTING

The lack of any comprehensive archaeological record of ancient Greek painting has left art historians largely to rely on the painted decoration of terracotta pots as evidence of the development of this art.

There are a few exceptions, such as the famous frescoes unearthed on Santorini and now housed in the National Archaeological Museum (p85) in Athens. These works were painted in fresco technique using yellow, blue, red and black pigments, with some details added after the plaster had dried. Stylistically, the frescoes are similar to the paintings of Minoan Crete.

Greek painting came into its own during the Byzantine period. Byzantine churches were usually decorated with frescoes on a dark blue background with a bust of Christ in the dome, the four Gospel writers in the pendentives supporting the dome and the Virgin and Child in the apse. They also featured scenes from the life of Christ (Annunciation, Nativity, Baptism, Entry into Jerusalem, Crucifixion and Transfiguration) and figures of the saints. In the later centuries, the scenes in churches and icons involved more detailed narratives, including cycles of the life of the Virgin and the miracles of Christ.

With the fall of Constantinople in 1453 many Byzantine artists fled to Crete, while many Cretan artists studied in Italy, where the Renaissance was in full bloom. The result was the 'Cretan school' of icon painting that combined technical brilliance and dramatic richness. In Iraklio alone there were over 200 painters working from the mid-16th to mid-17th centuries who were equally at ease in Venetian and Byzantine styles, and the technique spread through monasteries throughout Greece. The finest exponent of the Cretan school was Michael Damaskinos. Some fine examples of his work can be seen in Iraklio's church and museum of Agia Ekaterini.

The Cretan School was a formative influence for arguably Greece's most famous artist, El Greco (meaning 'The Greek' in Spanish; his real name was Dominikos Theotokopoulos). He was born and educated on Crete but found recognition as one of the great Renaissance painters in Spain.

Painting after the Byzantine period became more secular in nature, with 19th-century Greek painters specialising in portraits, nautical themes and representations of the War of Independence. Major 19th-century painters included Dionysios Tsokos, Andreas Kriezis, Theodoros Vryzakis, Nikiforos Lytras, Konstantinos Volanakis and Nicholas Gyzis.

From the first decades of the 20th century, artists such as Konstantinos Parthenis (one of the greatest modern Greek artists), Konstantinos Kaleas and, later, the expressionist George Bouzianis were able to use their heritage and at the same time assimilate various developments in modern art, a trend which continues among the new generation of artists.

Significant artists of the 'thirties generation' were cubist Nikos Hadjikyriakos-Ghikas, surrealist Nikos Engonopoulos, Yiannis Tsarouchis and Panayiotis Tetsis.

Other leading artists include Yannis Moralis, Giorgos Zongolopoulos (with his trademark umbrella sculptures), Dimitris Mytaras, Yannis Tsoclis, abstract artist Yannis Gaitis, Christos Caras and Alekos Fassianos.

Many internationally known artists are based abroad, including Pavlos, known for his distinctive use of paper; the kinetic artist Takis in Paris; and neon artist Stephen Antonakos, and sculptor and painter Chryssa in New York.

In the past 25 years, modern Greek painting has attracted serious sums at leading auction houses in London.

Athens has a burgeoning contemporary arts scene, hosting shows by local and international artists in galleries around Psyrri and Kolonaki. The National Art Gallery in Athens (p85) and the Rhodes Art Gallery have the most extensive collections of 20th-century art.

The World of the Ancient Greeks (2002) by archaeologists John Camp and Elizabeth Fisher is a broad and in-depth look at how the Greeks have left their imprint on politics, philosophy, theatre, art, medicine and architecture.

SCULPTURE

The sculptures of ancient Greece are works of extraordinary visual power and beauty that hold pride of place in the collections of the great museums of the world.

The prehistoric art of Greece has been discovered only recently, most notably the remarkable figurines produced in the Cyclades from the high-quality marble of Paros and Naxos in the middle of the 3rd millennium BC. Their primitive and powerful forms have inspired many artists since.

Displaying an obvious debt to Egyptian sculpture, the marble sculptures of the Archaic period are true precursors of the famed Greek sculpture of the classical period. They began to represent figures that were true to nature, rather than flat and stylised. For the first time in history a sculptured shape was made to reproduce the complex mechanism of the human body. Seeking to master the depiction of both the naked body and of drapery, sculptors of the period focused on *kouroi* (figures of naked youths), with their set symmetrical stance and enigmatic smiles. Many great *kouros* sculptures and draped female *kore* can be admired at the National Archaeological Museum (p85) in Athens.

Greek Art and Archaeology by John Griffiths Pedley is a super introduction to the development of Greek art and civilisation.

The sculptures of the classical period show an obsession with the human figure and with drapery. Unfortunately, little original work from this period survives. Most freestanding classical sculpture described by ancient writers was made of bronze and survives only as marble copies made by the Romans.

The quest to attain total naturalism continued on in the Hellenistic period; works of this period were animated, almost theatrical, in contrast to their serene Archaic and classical predecessors. These were revered by later artists such as Michelangelo, who was at the forefront of the rediscovery and appreciation of Greek works in the Renaissance. The end of the Hellenistic age signalled the decline of Greek sculpture's pre-eminent position in the art form. The torch was handed to the Romans, who proved worthy successors.

Two of the foremost modern sculptors, Dimitrios Filippotis and Yannoulis Halepas, were from Tinos, where marble sculpture tradition endures today. Contemporary Greek and international sculpture can be seen at the new National Glyptothèque (p85) in Athens.

POTTERY

The painted terracotta pots of ancient Greece have enabled us to appreciate in small measure the tradition of ancient pictorial art.

Practised from the Stone Age on, pottery is one of the most ancient arts. At first, vases were built with coils and wads of clay, but the art of throwing on the wheel was introduced in about 2000 BC and was then practised with great skill by Minoan and Mycenaean artists.

Minoan pottery is often characterised by a high centre of gravity and beak-like spouts, with flowing designs of spiral or marine and plant motifs. Painted decoration was applied as a white clay slip (a thin paste of clay and water) or was fired to a greyish black or dull red. The Archaeological Museum in Iraklio has a wealth of Minoan pots.

Mycenaean pottery shapes include a long-stemmed goblet and a globular vase with handles resembling a pair of stirrups. Decorative motifs are similar to those on Minoan pottery but are less fluid.

The 10th century BC saw the introduction of the Protogeometric style, with its substantial pots decorated with blackish-brown horizontal lines around the circumference, hatched triangles and compass-drawn concentric circles. This was followed by the new vase shape and more crowded decoration of the Geometric period. By the early 8th century BC figures were introduced, marking the introduction of the most fundamental element in the later tradition of classical art – the representation of gods, men and animals.

By the 7th century BC, Corinth was producing pottery with added white and purple-red clay slip. These pots often featured friezes of lions, goats and swans and a background fill of rosettes. In 6th-century Athens, artists used red clay with a high iron content. A thick colloidal slip made from this clay produced a glossy black surface that contrasted with the red and was enlivened with added white and purple-red. Attic pots, famed for their high quality, were exported throughout the Greek empire during this time.

Reproductions of all these styles are available at souvenir shops throughout the country. Some contemporary ceramicists are still making pots using ancient firing and painting techniques. Minoan-style pottery is made in Crete and the island of Sifnos (p211) continues its distinctive pottery tradition. You can also find traditional potters in the northern Athenian suburb of Marousi, once one of the big pottery centres of Greece.

Music
TRADITIONAL
Music has always been a feature of Greek life. Cycladic figurines holding musical instruments resembling harps and flutes date back to 2000 BC. Ancient Greek musical instruments included the lyre, lute, *piktis* (pipes), *kroupeza* (a percussion instrument), *kithara* (a stringed instrument), *aulos* (a wind instrument), *barbitos* (similar to a cello) and the *magadio* (similar to a harp).

The ubiquitous six- or eight-stringed bouzouki, the long-necked lutelike instrument associated with contemporary Greek music, is a relative newcomer to the scene. The *baglamas* is a tiny version used in *rembetika*.

The plucked strings of the bulbous *outi* (oud), the strident sound of the Cretan *lyra* (lyre) the staccato rap of the *toumberleki* (lap drum), the *mandolino* (mandolin) and the *gaïda* (bagpipe) bear witness to a rich range of musical instruments that share many characteristics with instruments all over the Middle East.

Every region in Greece has its own musical tradition. Regional folk music is divided into *nisiotika* (the lighter, more upbeat music of the islands), and the more grounded *dimotika* of the mainland – where the *klarino* (clarinet) is prominent and lyrics refer to hard times, war and rural life.

Crete's music has a presence in the world music scene as a genre in its own right, and is best exemplified by the legendary late Nikos Xylouris and *lyra* master Kostas Moundakis. Of all the regions, Crete has perhaps

---

RECOMMENDED LISTENING

Axion Esti (Mikis Theodorakis) The oratorio of Elytis' famous work or *Epitafios*.

Brazilero (Nikos Portokaloglou) Excellent movie soundtrack with contemporary Greek East–West sounds.

I Ekdikisi tis Gyftias (Nikos Papazoglou, Manolis Rasoulis & Nikos Xydakis) The classic 1970s album.

I Ellada Tou Markou Vamvakari (Markos Vamvakaris) Compilation from the original bouzouki master.

Mode Plagal II (Mode Plagal) For traditional Greek music with an ethnic jazz sound.

O Arhangelos Tis Kritis 1958–68 (Nikos Xylouris) Try this, or his first album *Nikos Xylouris*, for the voice of Crete's favourite son.

Nogo (Psarantonis) The eccentric Cretan's best instrumental work.

Rembetika (Stavros Xarhakos) Modern *rembetika* from the movie soundtrack.

Songs of the Mediterranean (Savina Yiannatou) With Primavera en Salonika.

Ta Authentika (Stelios Kazantzidis) A double-CD set of his popular songs.

Ta Tragoudia Tis Haroulas (Haris Alexiou) The album that made her the '80s queen of *laïka*; or try her recent two-CD anthology.

The Bodies and the Knives (Eleftheria Arvanitaki) Celebrated 1994 release with music by Armenian Ara Dinkjian.

To Hamogelo tis Tzokontas (Manos Hatzidakis) Timeless recording from the acclaimed composer, for a more Greek sound try *Skliros Aprilis tou 45*.

Tribute to Vasilis Tsitsanis (Yiorgos Dalaras) A contemporary interpretation of classic Tsitsanis, with Eleni Tsaligopoulou.

the healthiest music scene, with a popular following, regular performances and recordings by folk artists. The most prominent Cretan musician today is Xylouris' brother, Psarantonis.

Traditional music was shunned by the bourgeoisie during the period
after independence, when they looked to Europe – and classical music
and opera – rather than their eastern or 'peasant' roots.

In the 1920s urban blues music known as *rembetika* became popular,
entering the mainstream after WWII.

In the '50s and '60s a popular musical offshoot of *rembetika* – known
as *laïka* (urban folk music) took over and the clubs in Athens became
bigger, glitzier and more commercialised. The late Stelios Kazantzidis
was the big voice of this era.

During this period another style of music emerged led by two outstanding classically trained composers – Mikis Theodorakis and Manos
Hatzidakis. Known as *entehno* or 'artistic' music, it drew on folk music
and instruments but had more symphonic arrangements. Most significantly, they created popular hits with lyrics from the poetry of leading
poets such as Seferis, Elytis, Ritsos and Kavadias. Their music became
a form of political expression and social commentary during the junta
years, when it was banned. Theodorakis, who was jailed during this time,
is one of Greece's most prolific composers. Somewhat to his dismay, he
is best known for the classic 'Zorba' music.

All of the different Greek musical styles are still heard today and its
music is very much a part of the country's history and politics.

CLASSICAL

Since independence, Greece has followed mainstream developments in
classical music. Sopranos Elena Kelessidi and Irini Tsirakidou are the
latest to follow in the footsteps of the country's original opera superstar
Maria Callas. Greece's best-known conductor was Dimitris Mitropoulos,
who led the New York Philharmonic in the 1950s, while Loukas Kary-
tinos is Greece's leading conductor and artistic director of the National
Opera. Greece's most distinguished composers are Yiannis Markopoulos,
Stavros Xarhakos and the late Yannis Xenakis. Mezzo-soprano Agnes
Baltsa and acclaimed pianist Dimitris Sgouros are also internationally
known, while Greece's answer to Andrea Bocelli is popular tenor Mario
Frangoulis. Composer Vangelis Papathanasiou is best known for his film
scores, including *Chariots of Fire*.

Comparatively few Greek performers have made it big on the international scene – the 1970s icon Nana Mouskouri remains the best known,
along with the larger-than-life, kaftan-wearing Demis Roussos.

CONTEMPORARY

Contemporary Greek music veteran Georgos Dalaras has covered the
gamut of Greek music and collaborated with Latin and Balkan artists,
as well as Sting. Other distinguished Greek artists include Haris Alexiou, Dimitra Galani, Eleftheria Arvanitaki, Alkistis Protopsalti, Dionysis
Savopoulos, Yiannis Kotsiras, and singer-songwriters Nikos Papazoglou,
Sokratis Malamas, Nikos Portokaloglou, Alkinoös Ioannidis and Thanassis Papakonstantinou.

Acclaimed vocal artist Savina Yannatou, and ethnic jazz fusion artists
Kristi Stasinopoulou and Mode Plagal, are making a mark on the world
music scene, along with percussion ensemble Krotala.

The big pop and modern *laïka* performers are Anna Vissi, Notis Sfakia-
nakis, Despina Vandi, Yiannis Ploutarhos and Mihalis Hatziyiannis.

The comprehensive
www.rebetiko.gr has an
extensive discography
and database of more
than 2500 songs, while
Matt Barrett gives a
history and guide to the
main players in modern
Greek music at www
.greektravel.com/music
/index.html.

Contemporary Greek music also includes folk rock, heavy metal, rap and electronic dance music. Pop-rock band Raining Pleasure are breaking into Europe with English lyrics.

Popular Greek-Swedish singer Elena Paparizou shot to local stardom when she won the 2005 Eurovision song contest, while heart-throb pop icon Sakis Rouvas was last seen in LA seeking an international career.

During summer you can see many of Greece's leading acts in concerts around Greece. In winter they perform in the big clubs in Athens and Thessaloniki. The hugely popular nightclubs known as *bouzoukia* are glitzy, expensive, cabaret-style venues where the bouzouki reigns supreme. Musical taste can sometimes take a back seat at the lower-end clubs, referred to as *skyladika* or 'dog houses' – apparently because the crooning singers resemble a whining dog.

Dance

Music and dancing have been part of social life in Greece since the dawn of Hellenism. Some of today's folk dances derive from the ritual dances performed in ancient Greek temples. The *syrtos* is depicted on ancient vases and there are references to dances in Homer's works. Many folk dances are performed in a circular formation; in ancient times, dancers formed a circle in order to seal themselves off from evil influences or would dance around an altar, tree, figure or object. Dancing was part of military education.

Regional dance styles often reflect the climate or disposition of the participants. The islands, with their bright and cheery atmosphere, give rise to light, springy dances such as the *ballos* and the *syrtos,* while the graceful and most widely known *kalamatianos,* originally from Kalamata, reflects years of proud Peloponnese tradition. In Crete you have the graceful and slow *syrtos,* the fast and triumphant *maleviziotikos* and the dynamic *pentozali,* which has a slow and fast version, in which the leader impresses with high kicks and leaps.

The so-called 'Zorba dance', or *syrtaki,* is a stylised dance for two or three men or women with arms linked on each other's shoulders, though the modern variation is danced in a long circle with an ever-quickening beat.

The often spectacular solo male *zeïmbekiko,* with its whirling improvisations, has its roots in *rembetika,* while women have their own sensuous *tsifteteli,* a svelte, sinewy show of femininity evolved from the Middle Eastern belly dance.

Cinema & TV

Cinema in Greece took off after the end of the civil war and peaked in the 1950s and early '60s, when domestic audiences flocked to a flurry of comedies, melodramas and musicals being produced by the big Greek studios. Since those heydays, Greece's domestic film industry has long been in the doldrums, largely due to the demise of the studios with the advent of TV, and inadequate funding.

The problem was compounded by filmmakers taking on writer, director and producer roles, as well as the type of films being produced. The 'new Greek cinema' of the '70s and '80s was slow moving, loaded with symbolism and generally too avant-garde to have mass appeal.

The leader of this school is award-winning film director Theodoros Angelopoulos, winner of the 1998 Golden Palm award at the Cannes Film Festival for *Eternity and a Day.* He is considered one of the world's few remaining 'auteur' filmmakers.

Another internationally known Greek director is Paris-based Costa-Gavras, who won an Oscar in 1969 for *Z,* a story based on the 1967

Pantelis Voulgaris' acclaimed 2004 film *Brides* follows the fortunes of one of the 700 Greek mail-order brides who set off for America in the 1920s on the SS *Alexander,* bound for unknown husbands and lives.

The Greek Film Centre is responsible for support and development of film in Greece. Find out about Greek films, directors and what's in production at www.gfc.gr.

ON LOCATION

You've seen the movie but where in Greece was it shot?

Big Blue (1988) Memorable black-and-white opening scenes of unspoilt Amorgos.

Bourne Identity (2002) The final scenes were shot at the Sea Satin restaurant in Little Venice, Mykonos.

Captain Corelli's Mandolin (2001) Shot largely in the port of Sami, Kefallonia.

For Your Eyes Only (1981) James Bond explores Corfu's beaches, hotels and even the Turkish fort in Corfu Town.

Mediterraneo (1991) Italian soldiers are garrisoned on tiny, remote Kastellorizo in the Dodecanese.

Never on a Sunday (1960) Greece's big star Melina Mercouri received an Oscar nomination for her role as a prostitute in Piraeus.

Pascali's Island (1988) Ben Kingsley plays a Turkish spy on Symi during the dying days of Ottoman occupation.

Shirley Valentine (1989) The classic foreign woman's Greek island romance fantasy was in Mykonos.

Summer Lovers (1982) Darryl Hannah and Peter Gallagher got raunchy on Santorini, Mykonos and Crete.

Tomb Raider (2001-2) Lara Croft went diving off Santorini.

Zorba The Greek (1964) Where else but Crete? The famous beach dance scene was at Stavros, near Hania.

murder of communist deputy Grigoris Lambrakis in Thessaloniki by right-wing thugs. His most recent work was *Amen* (2003).

The 1990s saw a shift in cinematic style, with a new generation of directors achieving moderate commercial successes with lighter social satires and a more contemporary style and pace.

For the first time in many years, two Greek films gained cinematic releases outside Greece – Tassos Boulmetis' *Touch of Spice* (2003) and Pantelis Voulgaris' *Nyfes* (2004).

Greek TV serves up a constant diet of low-budget chat shows, Greek and foreign soaps, series, movies, sport and re-runs of Greek cinema classics, as well as local versions of international quiz shows, reality TV and talent shows.

Popular Greek series reflect local attitudes and preoccupations with sexual and gender roles; one example is younger women often being portrayed in relationships with older men, while comedies such as *Seven Deadly Mother-In-Laws* play on well-known stereotypes.

Tassos Boulmetis' 2003 film *A Touch of Spice (Politiki Kouzina)*, is a beautifully shot and bittersweet story about Greek refugees from Istanbul moving to Athens in the 1960s, told through a boy's passion for food. Filmed in Greece and Turkey, it stars the dashing George Corraface.

SPORT

Greece came under the international sports spotlight in an unprecedented way in 2004 with two unexpected triumphs – the successful staging of the Olympic Games in Athens and the Greek football team's astounding victory in the European Cup.

Despite the angst-ridden lead up to the Olympics, which was plagued by construction delays, budget blow-outs and terrorism fears, the Athens Olympics were an overwhelming success and the sports venues world-class. On the field, Greece won a record 16 Olympic medals, split evenly between men's and women's sports.

But it was Greece's football triumph a month before the Olympics that created the most euphoria and raised morale and national pride, which then carried through to the games and no doubt boosted attendances. Greek football is consequently riding high after many years in the doldrums. It remains the most popular spectator sport in Greece, and Greece is bidding to host the 2012 European Championships. Greece currently fields three teams in the European Champions League – Panathinaikos, Olympiakos and AEK.

Basketball is the other major sport in Greece, gaining popularity after the Greek national team became the European champions in 1987 – and was set for another boost after they became 2005 European champions.

Environment

THE LAND

Greece lies at the southern tip of the rugged Balkan Peninsula. Most of the mainland is mountainous and dominated by the Pindos Ranges. The country has land borders to the north with Albania, the Former Republic of Macedonia and Bulgaria; and to the east with Turkey.

The mainland, however, is but a small part of Greece. It also has some 1400 islands, of which 169 are inhabited. They contribute only a small percentage of the nation's total land mass of 131,900 sq km, but are responsible for extending Greek territorial waters over more than 400,000 sq km.

The majority of islands are spread across the shallow waters of the Aegean Sea between Greece and Turkey. These are divided into four main groups: the Cyclades, the Dodecanese, the islands of the Northeastern Aegean and the Sporades. The two largest Aegean islands, Crete and Evia, do not belong to any group.

The other island groups are the Saronic Gulf islands, which lie between Athens and the Peloponnese, and the Ionians, in the Ionian Sea between Greece and southern Italy, while Kythira stands alone below the southeastern tip of the Peloponnese.

Like the mainland, most of the terrain is extremely rugged. Crete has half a dozen peaks over 2000m, the highest of which is Mt Ida at 2456m. Evia, Karpathos, Kefallonia and Samothraki all boast peaks of more than 1500m.

Like the mainland, most of the ground is either too arid, too poor or too steep for intensive agriculture. There are several exceptions, like Naxos and Crete, both of which are famous for the quality of their produce, and verdant Samothraki.

Try Paul Sterry's *Complete Mediterranean Wildlife* for a general guide to the plants and animals of the region.

WILDLIFE
Animals

You're unlikely to encounter much in the way of wildlife on most of the islands. The exception is on larger islands like Crete and Evia, where squirrels, rabbits, hares, foxes and weasels are all fairly common. Reptiles are well represented too: snakes include several viper species, which are poisonous; you're more likely to see lizards though, all of which are harmless.

One of the pleasures of island-hopping in Greece is watching the dolphins as they follow the boats. Although there are many dolphins in the Aegean, the striped dolphin has recently been the victim of murbilivirus – a sickness that affects the immune system. Research into the virus is being carried out in the Netherlands.

Bird-watchers, however, have more chance of coming across something unusual in the Greek islands.

Not surprisingly, seabirds are a major feature. Assorted gulls, petrels, shearwaters and shags are common throughout the Aegean. The islands are also home to a rich variety of birds of prey, particularly the mountains of larger islands like Crete and Evia. They include the spectacular griffon vulture and several species of eagle as well as peregrine falcons, harriers and hawks. The website of the Hellenic Ornithological Society, www .ornithologiki.gr, has loads of information about what to see and where, as well as information about the society's outings and activities.

About 350 pairs (60% of the world's population) of the rare Eleonora's falcon nest on the island of Piperi, northeast of Alonissos in the Sporades.

You can get more information about dolphins from the Greek Society for the Protection & Study of Dolphins & Cetaceans at www .delphis.gr (in Greek only).

EARTHQUAKE ZONE

The earthquake that struck Athens on 7 September 1999, leaving 139 dead and 100,000 home-less, served as a savage reminder that Greece lies in one of the most seismically active regions in the world.

The quake was just one of more than 20,000 quakes recorded in Greece in the last 40 years or so. Fortunately, most of them are very minor in nature – detectable only by sensitive seismic monitoring equipment stationed throughout the country. The reason for all this activity is that the eastern Mediterranean lies at the meeting point of three continental plates: Eurasian, African and Arabian. The three push, shove and grind away at each other constantly, generating count-less, hardly recognisable earthquakes, as the land surface reacts to the intense activity beneath the earth's crust.

The system has two main fault lines. The most active is the North Aegean Fault, which starts as a volcano-dotted rift between Greece and Turkey, snakes under Greece and then runs north up the Ionian and Adriatic coasts. Less active but more dramatic is the North Anatolian Fault that runs across Turkey, which is renowned for major tremors like the 7.4 monster that struck western Turkey on 17 August 1999, leaving more than 40,000 dead. Seismologists maintain that activity along the two fault lines is not related.

More recently, on 14 August 2003 an earthquake measuring 6.4 hit the Ionian Island of Lefkada. While only causing minor damage, two unlucky British tourists, who had been walking below cliffs when it struck, were seriously injured.

The Eleonora's falcon can also be spotted on a number of other islands, including Naxos and Syros.

There are also a large number of migratory birds, most of which are merely passing by on their way from winter feeding sites in North Africa to summer nesting grounds in Eastern Europe.

The larger islands boast all the usual Mediterranean small birds – tits, wagtails, warblers, bee-eaters, larks, swallows, flycatchers, thrushes and chats – as well as some more distinctive species such as the hoopoe.

The Northeastern Aegean islands are extremely popular with bird-watchers, particularly Lesvos where birding has become big business. Other rewarding destinations for birders are the islands of Naxos, Sifnos and Syros in the Cyclades, and Kos and Tilos in the Dodecanese.

Birding in Lesvos by Richard Brooks is an excellent handbook for bird enthusiasts visiting this large northeast Aegean island.

ENDANGERED SPECIES

Europe's rarest mammal, the monk seal *(Monachus monachus)*, was once common in the Mediterranean, but is now on the brink of extinction in Europe – it survives in slightly larger numbers in the Hawaiian islands. There are only about 400 left in Europe, 250 of which live in Greece. There are 40 in the Ionian Sea and the rest are found in the Aegean. These crea-tures are susceptible to human disturbance and now live in isolated coastal caves. The majority of reported seal deaths are the result of accidental trapping, but the main threat to their survival is the destruction of habitat. Tourist boats are major culprits. For more information visit the Hellenic Society for the Study and Protection of the Monk Seal at www.mom.gr.

The waters around Zakynthos are home to the last large sea-turtle colony in Europe, that of the loggerhead turtle *(Caretta caretta)*. The loggerhead also nests in smaller numbers on the Peloponnese and Crete. The Sea Tur-tle Protection Society of Greece, Archelon, runs monitoring programmes and is always looking for volunteers. For details visit www.archelon.gr.

The golden jackal *(Canis aureus)* is a strong candidate for Greece's most misunderstood mammal. Although its diet is 50% vegetarian, in the past it has shouldered much of the blame for attacks on stock carried out by wild dogs. It was hunted to the brink of extinction until it was declared a protected species in 1990, and now survives only in central Greece and on the island of Samos. It's strictly nocturnal. The other 50% of its diet is made up of carrion, reptiles and small mammals.

The Cretan wild goat, the kri-kri, survives in the wild only in the Samaria Gorge area and on the tiny islet of Kri Kri, off Agios Nikolaos in Crete.

Plants

Greece is endowed with a variety of flora unrivalled in Europe. There are over 6000 plant species (some of which occur nowhere else) and more than 100 varieties of orchid, which flower from late February to early June. They continue to thrive on the islands because most of the land is too poor for intensive agriculture and has escaped the ravages of chemical fertilisers.

The Flowers of Greece & The Aegean, by William Taylor and Anthony Huxley, is the most comprehensive guide for the serious botanist.

The mountains of Crete boast some of the finest displays. Common species include anemones, white cyclamens, irises, lilies, poppies, gladioli, tulips and countless varieties of daisy. Look out for the blue-and-orange Cretan iris (*Iris cretica*), one of 120 wildflowers unique to Crete. Others are the pink Cretan ebony, the white-flowered symphyandra and the white-flowered *Cyclamen cretica*.

Other rare species found on the islands include the *Rhododendron luteum*, a yellow azalea, that grows only on Mytilini.

Spectacular plants include the coastal giant reed – you may get lost among high, dense groves on your way to a beach – as well as the giant fennel, which grows to 3m, and the tall yellow-horned poppy, both of which grow by the sea. The white-flowered sea squill grows on hills above the coast. The perfumed sea daffodil grows along southern coasts, particularly on Crete and Corfu. The conspicuous snake's-head fritillary (*Fritillaria graeca*) has pink flowers shaped like snakes' heads, and the markings on the petals resemble a chequerboard – the Latin word *fritillu* means dice box.

Another common species is the Cyprus plane (*Platanus orientalis insularis*), which thrives wherever there is ample water. It seems as if every village on the mainland has a plane tree shading its central square – and a Taverna Platanos.

Australian eucalypts were widely used in tree-planting programmes from the 1920s onwards, particularly on Crete.

RESPONSIBLE TRAVEL

Visitors should travel responsibly at all times. Follow these common-sense rules:

- Dispose of litter thoughtfully
- Do not discard items that could start a fire (cigarette butts, glass bottles etc) – forest fires are an annual torment
- Stick to footpaths wherever possible
- Close gates behind you
- Do not pick flowers or wilfully damage tree bark or roots – some of the species you see are protected
- Do not climb on walls or parts of buildings
- Respect landowners' property and do not trespass into private areas
- Take care when walking near cliffs – they can be dangerously slippery and quick to crumble
- Keep noise to a minimum and avoid disturbing wildlife
- Pay attention to signs and public warnings

THE EVIL OLIVE

It is a sad irony that the tree most revered by the Greeks is responsible for the country's worst ecological disaster. That tree is the olive. It was the money tree of the early Mediterranean civilisations, providing an abundance of oil that not only tasted great but could also be used for everything from lighting to lubrication. The ancient Greeks thought it was too good to be true and concluded it must be a gift from the gods.

In their eagerness to make the most of this gift, native forest was cleared on a massive scale to make way for the olive. Landowners were urged on by decrees such as those issued in the 6th century BC by the *arhon* (chief magistrate) of Athens, Solon, who banned the export of all agricultural produce other than olive oil and made cutting down an olive tree punishable by death.

Much of the land planted with olives was hill country unsuitable for agriculture. Without the surface roots of the native forest to bind it, the topsoil of the hills was rapidly washed away. The olive tree could do nothing to help; it has no surface root system, depending entirely on its impressive tap root.

Thus, the lush countryside so cherished by the ancient Greeks was transformed into the harsh, rocky landscape that greets the modern visitor.

NATIONAL PARKS

Visitors who expect Greek national parks to provide facilities on a par with those in countries such as Australia and the US will be disappointed. Although all have refuges and some have marked hiking trails, Greek national parks provide little else in the way of facilities. The only national park on the islands is Samaria Gorge (p253) on Crete. There are marine parks off the coast of Alonnisos (p419) in the Sporades, and at the Bay of Laganas (p466) on Zakynthos in the Ionians.

ENVIRONMENTAL ISSUES

Greece is belatedly becoming environmentally conscious; regrettably, it can be a case of closing the gate long after the horse has bolted. Deforestation and soil erosion are problems that date back thousands of years. Olive cultivation (see, above) and goats have been the main culprits, but firewood gathering, shipbuilding, housing and industry have all taken their toll.

Wildflowers of Greece, by George Sfikas, is one of an excellent series of field guides by this well-known Greek mountaineer and naturalist. His guides are readily available at bookshops throughout the country.

Forest fires are also a major problem, with an estimated 25,000 hectares destroyed every year. The 2000 summer season was one of the worst on record, particularly on the northeastern Aegean island of Samos.

Water shortages are a major problem on many islands, particularly smaller islands without a permanent water supply. These islands import their water by tanker, and visitors are urged to economise on water use wherever possible: small things, like turning the tap off while you brush your teeth, can make a big difference.

General environmental awareness remains at a depressingly low level, especially where litter is concerned. The problem is particularly bad in rural areas, where roadsides are strewn with soft-drink cans and plastic packaging hurled from passing cars. Environmental education has begun in schools, but it will be a long time before community attitudes change. Sadly, many tourists seem to follow the local lead instead of setting a good example.

Not surprisingly, Greece has been slow to embrace the organic movement. Less than 1% of available agricultural land is farmed organically – the lowest percentage in Europe.

For more details on contemporary environmental issues check out www.greece.gr/environment.

Greek Islands Outdoors

The Greek islands offer a plethora of possibilities for travellers who want to do more with their time than laze around on the beach waiting for the evening's partying to begin. Naturally enough, water sports of all descriptions are a speciality throughout the islands, but nowhere more so than in the Cyclades.

TREKKING

The Greek islands are a veritable paradise for trekkers, offering an extraordinary variety of landscapes ranging from remote coastal paths to dramatic mountain gorges.

Spring (April to May) is the best time. Walkers will find the countryside green and fresh from the winter rains, and carpeted with the spectacular array of wildflowers for which the islands are justly famous. Autumn (September to October) is another good time, but July and August, when the temperatures are constantly up around 40°C, are not much fun at all. Whatever time of year you opt to set out, you will need to come equipped with a good pair of walking boots to handle the rough, rocky terrain, a wide-brimmed hat and a high UV-factor sunscreen.

Some of the most popular treks, such as the Samaria Gorge (p253) on Crete, are detailed in this book, but there are possibilities just about everywhere. On small islands it's fun to discover pathways for yourself, and you are unlikely to get into danger as settlements or roads are never far away. You will encounter a variety of paths – *kalderimi* are cobbled or flagstone paths that link settlements and date back to Byzantine times – but sadly, many have been bulldozed to make way for roads.

If you're going to be venturing off the beaten track, a good map is essential. Unfortunately, most of the tourist maps sold around the islands are pitifully inadequate. The best maps are produced by Athens company Road Editions (see p491 for details).

The following is a brief description of the best trekking possibilities around the islands.

Captain Corelli's Mandolin (2001), directed by John Madden and starring Nicholas Cage and Penelope Cruz, is a biographical epic that looks at the life of an Italian soldier in German occupied Kefallonia in WWII.

Crete

The spectacular Samaria Gorge (p253) needs little introduction as it is one of Europe's most popular treks, as well as being one of the island's main tourist attractions, drawing thousands of walkers every year.

The gorge begins at Xyloskalo high on the southern slopes of the lofty Lefka Ori (White Mountains) and finishes at the coastal settlement of Agia Roumeli (p254). Its width varies from 150m to 3.5m (the famous Iron Gates) and its vertical walls reach 500m at their highest points. The gorge has an incredible number of wildflowers, which are at their best in April and May. It is also home to a large number of endangered species, including the Cretan wild goat, the kri-kri. You are unlikely to see too many of these shy animals, which show a marked aversion to trekkers.

Winter rains render the gorge impassable from mid-October until mid-April.

People who prefer to walk without the company of a cast of thousands will enjoy the coastal path that links the southwest coastal villages of Agia Roumeli and Hora Sfakion (p255). Another favourite is the two-hour

www.climbincrete .com is a detailed and comprehensive site on all you need to know on getting out and up onto Crete's rugged tracks and mountains. Also a good section on trekking.

stroll from Zakros to the remote Minoan palace site of Kato Zakros (p270) in eastern Crete. The walk passes through the mysterious sounding Valley of the Dead, so named because of the cave tombs dotted along the rugged cliffs that line the valley.

Cyclades

Naxos (p169) has long been a favourite destination for walkers, particularly the beautiful Tragaea region (p176) – a broad central plain of olive groves dotted with unspoiled villages and ancient Byzantine churches. The more energetic will enjoy the short but strenuous climb from the village of Filoti to the Cave of Zeus. Andros (p136) is another good choice, particularly the hills around the small west-coast resort of Batsi.

Rock climbing is now one of the hottest activities on the island of Kalymnos in the Dodecanese islands, yet it only started in 1997.

Dodecanese

Tranquil Tilos (p309) is one of the few islands in this group that has escaped the ravages of mass tourism. It's a terrific place for walkers, with dramatic cliff-top paths that lead to uncrowded beaches. For something completely different, there's nothing to rival the bizarre landscape of volcanic Nisyros (p312), where walkers can check the hissing craters that dot Mt Polyvotis for signs of activity.

Evia & the Sporades

Alonnisos (p419) enjoys a glowing reputation as the Aegean's cleanest and greenest island. In recent years it's been attracting growing numbers of walkers, who come to trek a network of established trails and swim at remote pristine beaches. Skopelos (p414) has a good set of trails and many organised walking tours are available, some of them ending conveniently at a restaurant or taverna.

Ionian Islands

Good things come in small packages, or so the saying goes. It's certainly the case on tiny Paxi (p445), the smallest of the main Ionian islands. Its landscape of ancient, gnarled olive groves and snaking dry-stone walls is a great choice for walkers who really want to escape the crowds.

On Ithaki (p459), the long-lost island homeland of Trojan War–hero Odysseus, mythology fans will enjoy seeking out the handful of sites associated with the Homeric legend.

THE ISLANDS BY BIKE

It's not the most obvious way to get around the Greek islands, but carting your own pedal-powered wheels from island to island is, when you get down to brass tacks, an ideal way to cart you and your baggage from place to place. First up, bicycles usually travel for free on the ferries so there is no extra outlay, nor do you have to pony up valuable cash to hire motorised wheels when you arrive. You can be last onto the ferry and first off – free to pedal off to the nearest beach or to look for accommodation. Islands do not have the frenzied traffic of the mainland and cycling is actually fun. While islands tend not to be so flat, a bike with a good set of gears will tackle most inclines with ease and then there is always the buzz of coming down the hill on the other side. While virtually any island will lend itself to some kind of two-wheeled activity the Dodecanese island of Kos (p315) is perhaps the best equipped and geographically most cyclist-friendly island. Bicycle hire outfits are everywhere and a bicycle is almost de riguéur for many visitors. Peletons of pedlars can be encountered all over the flat and winding lanes of the north coast of Kos and for once you feel that you belong. It is better to burn fat than oil, so pedal on and see the islands the natural way – on a bike.

Northeastern Aegean Islands

The Northeastern Aegean Islands are a long-time favourite with walkers. Samos (p355) is one of the most-visited islands in Greece, but most visitors stick to the resorts of the south coast – leaving the interior almost unscathed. The best walking area is around the delightful mountain villages of Manolates and Vourliotes (p362), set on the forested northern slopes of Mt Ambelos. Walkers who are still out and about at dusk may be lucky enough to spot one of the country's most-endangered species, the golden jackal (p54), which lives only on Samos and in parts of Central Greece. Lesvos (p372) is another good choice, especially for bird-watching.

Saronic Gulf Islands

Walking has always been the main form of transport on traffic-free Hydra (p124), where a well-maintained network of paths links the island's various beaches and monasteries.

DIVING & SNORKELLING

There are some excellent dive sites around the Greek islands, but diving is subject to strict regulations in order to protect the many antiquities in the depths of the Aegean.

Any kind of underwater activity using breathing apparatus is strictly forbidden unless under the supervision of a diving school. Diving is only permitted between sunrise and sunset, and only in specified locations. There are also strict controls on diving activities: underwater photography of archaeological finds is prohibited, as is spear fishing with diving equipment.

Don't be put off by all the red tape. Diving is rapidly growing in popularity, and there are diving schools on the islands of Corfu (p442), Crete (at Rethymno; p240), Evia (at Halkida; p404), Hydra (p127), Leros (at Xirokambos; p333), Milos (at Adamas; p208), Mykonos (p157), Paros (p167) and Antiparos (p168), Rhodes (p284), Santorini (at Kamari; p198) and Skiathos (p413). Most charge around €50 for a dive, and from €250 for courses; prices include all equipment.

Check out the **Internet Scuba Diving Club** (www.isdc.gr) for more information about diving. You'll also get useful information from the **Professional Association of Diving Instructors** (PADI; www.padi.com); its website has a list of all PADI-approved dive centres in Greece.

Snorkelling is enjoyable just about anywhere in the islands and has the advantage of being totally unencumbered by regulations. All the equipment you need – mask, fins and snorkel – are cheaply available everywhere.

Especially good places are Monastiri (p166) on Paros; Paleokastritsa (p443) on Corfu; Telendos Islet (near Kalymnos; p330); Ammoöpi (p297) in southern Karpathos; Xirokambos Bay (p333) on Leros; and anywhere off the coast of Kastellorizo (p302). Many dive schools also use their boats to take groups of snorkellers to prime spots.

Organised Tours

Trekking Hellas (☎ 210 323 4548; www.trekking.gr; Filellinon 7, Athens 105 57) offers four-day diving holidays on Paros that include dives off the islands of Iraklia, Schinousa, Koufonisia and Naxos. It also offers dives off Corfu and Lesvos.

WINDSURFING

Windsurfing is the most popular water sport in Greece. Many people reckon that Vasiliki Bay (p452), on the south coast of the Ionian island of Lefkada, is one of the best places in the world to learn the sport. Hrysi Akti (p167) on Paros is another favourite.

www.club-mistral.com is an excellent website on windsurfing holidays in Afiartis Bay, Karpathos in Greece's Dodecanese islands. Good information on accommodation and surfing conditions.

There are numerous other prime locations around the islands, including Afiartis Bay (p297) on Karpathos; Ormos Korthiou (p140) on Andros; Kalafatis beach (p157) on Mykonos; Agios Giorgios beach (p176) on Naxos; Milopotas beach (p188) on Ios; Prasonisi (p291) in southern Rhodes; around Tingaki (p321) on Kos; Kokkari (p362) on Samos; around Skala Sotira (p400) on Thasos; and Koukounaries beach (p413) on Skiathos.

You'll find sailboards for hire almost everywhere. Hire charges range from €10 to €25, depending on the gear and the location. If you are a novice, most places that rent equipment also give lessons; reckon on about €200 to €250 for a 10-hour beginners' course.

Sailboards can be imported freely from other EU countries, but importing boards from other destinations, such as Australia and the USA, is subject to some quaint regulations. Theoretically, importers need a Greek national residing in Greece to guarantee that the board will be taken out again. Contact the **Hellenic Windsurfing Association** (☎ 210 323 0330; www.ghiolman.com; Filellinon 7, Athens 105 57) for more information.

Greek Waters Pilot by Rod Heikell (1998) is the definitive sailing handbook to the Greek islands. If you plan to sail your way around the islands this complete guide will help you find your way without going astray.

YACHTING

Despite some disparaging remarks among backpackers, yachting is *the* way to see the Greek islands. Nothing beats the peace and serenity of sailing the open sea, and the freedom of being able to visit remote and uninhabited islands.

The free EOT booklet, *Sailing the Greek Seas,* although long overdue for an update, contains lots of information about weather conditions, weather bulletins, entry and exit regulations, entry and exit ports and guidebooks for yachties. You can pick up the booklet at GNTO/EOT offices either abroad or in Greece. The Internet is the place to look for the latest information – **Hellenic Yachting Server** (www.yachting.gr) has general information on sailing around the islands and lots of links.

The sailing season lasts from April until October, although the best time to go depends on where you are going. The most popular time is between July and September, which ties in with the high season for tourism in general. Unfortunately, it also happens to be the time of year when the *meltemi* (northeasterly wind) is at its strongest (see p484 for details). The *meltemi* is not an issue in the Ionian Sea, where the main summer wind is the *maïstros,* a light to moderate northwesterly that rises in the afternoon and usually dies away at sunset.

Organised Tours

Individuals can consider joining a yachting cruise, which usually have a maximum of around eight people. **Ghiolman Yachts & Travel** (☎ 210 323 3696; www.ghiolman.com; Filellinon 7, Athens 105 57) has a range of seven-day island cruises, including an Ionian cruise leaving Corfu every Saturday, a Dodecanese cruise leaving Rhodes every Thursday and a Cycladic cruise leaving Piraeus every Friday. Berths on board these boats are priced from €670, and include half-board and the services of an English-speaking guide. All three cruises operate weekly from early May to the end of September.

Trekking Hellas (☎ 2103 234 548; www.trekking.gr; Filellinon 7, Athens 105 57) also offers a range of yachting and sailing holidays around the Cyclades and the Ionians by caïque or by yacht.

Yacht Hire

You can hire a bare boat (a yacht without a crew) if two crew members have a sailing certificate. Prices start at about €1000 per week for a

---

ORGANISED TREKS

There are a number of companies running organised treks and one of the biggest is **Trekking Hellas** (☎ 2103 234 548; www.trekking.gr; Filellinon 7, Athens 105 57). Its programme includes a nine-day island-hopping trek through the Cyclades making stops at Tinos (p140), Mykonos (p150), Naxos (p169) and Santorini (p191), and an eight-day trek in western Crete that takes in the Samaria Gorge (p253). Both tours start and finish in Athens and cost about €160 per day, including transfers, full board and an English-speaking guide. Trekking Hellas also runs half-day weekend treks in the Lake Korision area of southern Corfu for €50, including transfers from Corfu Town.

You'll find more information about organised treks in Hania (p249) and Rethymno (p239).

28-footer that will sleep six and it will cost an extra €840 per week to hire a skipper.

Most of the big hire companies are based in and around Athens. They include the following:

Aegean Cruises (☎ 210 964 9967; www.aegean-cruises.gr; cnr Poseidonos & Davaki, Alimos 174 55)
Alpha Yachting (☎ 210 968 0486; www.alphayachting.com; Poseidonos 67, Glyfada 166 75)
Ghiolman Yachts & Travel (☎ 210 323 3696; www.ghiolman.com; Filellinon 7, Athens 105 57)
Hellenic Charters (☎ 210 960 7174; www.hellenic-charters.gr; Arsitotelous 19-21, Glyfada 166 74)
Vernicos Yachts (☎ 210 989 6000; www.vernicos.gr; Poseidonos 11, Alimos 174 55)

You'll find details about yacht-charter companies on the islands of Milos (at Adamas; p208), Paros (at Naousa; p166) and Syros (at Ermoupolis; p148) in the Cyclades.

62

Food & Drink

Greek cuisine is an integral part of Greek culture, steeped in tradition and ritual. Eating with family and friends is paramount to enjoying life, and people eat out regularly. Greeks are passionate about food, heading to the mountains for fresh meat or to tiny fishing villages to sample the day's catch.

Greek cookery is seasonal and varies according to each region's topography and history. Traditional island cuisine is influenced by often arid landscapes, the sea and the availability of local produce, often resulting in simple food made from fresh ingredients with intense flavours.

On many islands you will also find influences from the mainland and their various occupiers, as well as spices and flavours from historical trading partners or simply what grows wild such as fennel and capers. In Crete, you'll find the epitome of the healthy life-prolonging Mediterranean diet.

Many islands have indigenous grape varieties, producing unique wines such as those from the volcanic soil in Santorini or the famous sweet Muscat wine from Samos.

Greece's dining scene has become increasingly diverse and nowadays in most places you are not restricted to Greek cuisine. But exploring the local regional specialities is part of the joy of travelling around Greece, so avoid the bland 'tourist' establishments and seek out the real thing.

The Olive and the Caper by foodie and anthropologist Susanna Hoffman provides a lively exploration of Greek food culture, with interesting culinary sidebars on history, mythology, customs and regional specialities.

With as many anecdotes as recipes, Emma Tennant's Corfu Banquet: A Seasonal Memoir with Recipes is a delightfully evocative book.

STAPLES & SPECIALITIES

The essence of Greek cuisine lies in fresh, unadulterated seasonal produce, aromatic herbs and original flavours. Most restaurants will have a combination of *tis oras* (grills) and *mayirefta* (casseroles or oven-baked dishes), and a wide range of hot and cold appetisers and salads. *Mayirefta* are prepared early in the day and left to cool, which enhances the flavour, especially with dishes like *yemista* (stuffed vegetables) and *mousaka* (sliced eggplant and mincemeat arranged in layers and baked), which are often served lukewarm.

Bread

Psomi (bread) is a mandatory feature of every meal. The most common is *horiatiko*, white crusty country bread traditionally made in a wood oven, though now largely produced in industrial bakeries. You'll also find wholemeal bread and savoury breads made from olive oil and flavoured with olives, walnuts, cheese and herbs.

FETA

Feta is the national cheese of Greece, where it has been produced for about 6000 years. It's made from sheep's and/or goat's milk and most feta comes from mountainous areas, where flocks have to cover great distances to feed. This has a double advantage – the sheep feed on a greater variety of plants, transmitting their characteristics to the milk, and because they are constantly in motion their milk has less fat, as does the resulting cheese.

In 2002 the European Commission ruled that only feta produced in Greece can be called feta, giving it the same protected status as Parma ham and champagne. A legal challenge from the Dutch and Germans, who claimed feta was a generic term and the cheese was widely produced outside Greece, was rejected by the European Court of Justice. The ruling is to come into force in 2007.

Paximadia (rusks), a staple since ancient days, are made from barley or whole wheat and double-baked to produce a hard loaf that can keep for years. They are moistened with water and topped with tomato and olive oil in the Cretan *dakos*. The unusual *eptazymo* bread made from chickpeas is most commonly found in the Dodecanese and Crete.

Festive breads include the glazed mastic-flavoured *tsoureki* at Easter and *kouloures,* the elaborately decorated Cretan wedding bread.

Cheese

Greece probably produces as many different cheeses as there are villages, with the innumerable microclimates producing infinite variations in taste.

Most cheeses, including the national cheese feta, are made from goat and sheep's milk. Yellow cheeses such as *kaseri, kefalotyri* and *graviera* are also found all over Greece. Other cheeses include the ricotta-like *myzithra* (also hardened dry and grated in pasta dishes) and the soft *manouri* cheese from the north.

Cheeses used in *saganaki* (a tasty fried-cheese meze) include *kefalograviera* and *mastelo* from Chios.

As well as being the world's biggest olive-oil consumers, Greeks are also among the biggest cheese-eaters, with per capita consumption in excess of 2.6kg.

Fish & Seafood

In a land with miles of coastline, *psari* (fish) has long been a staple. Fish is cooked with minimum fuss – grilled whole and drizzled with *ladholemono* (a lemon and oil dressing). Good fishes for grilling are *tsipoura* (sea bream), *lavraki* (sea bass) and *fangri* (bream), while smaller fish like *barbounia* (red mullet) are delicious fried. Less common are *gopes* (bogue), *maridha* (whitebait), *gavros* (mild anchovy) and *sardeles* (sardines).

Kalamari (squid) is cut into rings and deep-fried, grilled whole, or stuffed with cheese, herbs or rice, while *soupies* (cuttlefish) is also common. You'll often see *ohtapodi* (octopus) hung out drying; it is great grilled, pickled or in a tomato stew with macaroni. Spaghetti with lobster is a decadent island speciality.

Cured fish such as *kolios* (mackerel) is a popular mezes, while isolated islands like Symi are renowned for their sun-dried preserved fish and seafood, on which its population once survived the winters. Salted cod served with *skordalia* (a pungent garlic and potato dip) is another tasty dish.

It is customary to go into the kitchen and choose the fish yourself. Fish is normally sold by the kilogram, so make sure they weigh it (uncooked) to avoid a shock when the bill arrives.

Don't kid yourself that there is enough fresh local fish to cater for the millions of tourists who descend on the islands each summer. Most places will state if the fish and seafood are frozen, though sometimes only on the Greek side of the menu (indicated by the abbreviated 'kat' or an asterisk). Smaller fish are often a safer bet – the odder the sizes, the greater chance they are local.

Gastronome Miles Lambert takes a journey through Greece via the country's tavernas in *Greek Salad: A Dionysian Travelogue*, an amusing portrayal of local characters and food culture.

Fruit & Vegetables

Vegetables are a key element of the Greek kitchen, where meat was traditionally saved for special occasions.

Green beans, broad beans and okra are all cooked in a tomato sauce with olive oil and are referred to as *ladera* – dishes cooked in olive oil. Artichokes and aubergines are also widely used (Santorini has its own white eggplant), while *yemista* are a summer favourite.

Extremely nutritious *horta* (wild greens) are best eaten warm and drizzled with olive oil and lemon juice. *Klimatofylla* (vine leaves) are wrapped around aromatic rice in dolmades.

Frouta (fruit), especially watermelon is often served at the end of a meal (gratis in many tavernas) instead of dessert. Citrus fruits are especially abundant, as are figs and grapes in season.

Legumes & Pulses

Many islanders rely on beans and pulses as the foundation of their winter diet. *Fava* (yellow split pea) is made into a tasty dip in the Cyclades, usually topped with onion and lemon juice. Chickpeas are made into soups and fritters, and roasted as a snack.

Yigandes, giant white beans, are cooked in a light tomato sauce seasoned with sweet dill, while *fakes* (lentils) make a hearty soup.

There are at least 100 edible *horta* (wild greens) on Crete, though even the most knowledgable would not recognise more than a dozen.

Meat & Poultry

Meat has become a prominent part of the Greek diet. Pork and lamb dominate, though kid (goat) is also popular. Local beef is relatively rare, but plenty is imported.

Grilled meats are a speciality, especially *païdakia* (lamb cutlets) and *brizoles* (pork chops). The popular *gyros,* from the word 'spin', is a slab of tightly stacked pork or chicken slices roasting on a vertical spit. In a restaurant you are more likely to find *souvlaki* – cubes of pork (or chicken or swordfish) on a skewer.

Many islands have their special meat dishes, such as veal *sofrito* in Corfu, *pancetta* (pork spare ribs) in Zakynthos or *tsigariasto* (braised lamb or goat) in Crete; while meat is commonly baked with potatoes, lemon and oregano, or cooked in stews or casseroles such as tomato-based *kokkinisto*.

Chicken is also widely used, with special dishes being reserved for the rooster *(kokoras)*.

You'll find excellent cured pork dishes, such as *apaki* in Crete, *louza* in the Cyclades or rare goat *pastourmas* in Ikaria and Karpathos. Every region also has its variation of the village *loukanika* (sausages).

Game is becoming increasingly rare, though you do find quail, hare and rabbit – the latter is made into *stifado,* a tomato and onion stew.

More than 75% of Greece's entire annual production of oil is good enough to be labelled extra virgin. Compare that to 50% for Italy and 30% for Spain.

Greeks being resourceful, almost every part of the animal is used – from *sikotakia* (fried chicken livers) and *kokoretsi* (spit-roasted offal wrapped in intestines) to rare delicacies such as *ameletita* ('unspeakables') – fried sheep's testicles. Greeks also swear by the hangover-preventing qualities of a steaming bowl of *patsa* (offal soup).

Olives & Olive Oil

Greece has hundreds of olive varieties. *Eleoladho* (olive oil) is the essential ingredient of Greek cuisine and the secret to making vegetables and legumes taste so good. Greeks consume more oil per capita than any other people: 30L annually. Many families take time off for the harvest to get their year's supply from their ancestral villages. There is a growing trend to produce organic oil. Greece exports much of its finest oil to Italy.

Pasta & Rice

Greeks are great eaters of *zymarika* (pasta). It is believed they acquired the taste from their former Venetian overlords, though others suggest the ancient Greeks invented the stuff.

Specialities include pastitsio, a sort of Greek lasagne, *hilopites,* a fettuccine-style pasta; *youvetsi,* a hearty dish of baked meat or poultry with tomato sauce and *kritharaki* (rice-shaped pasta).

Ryzi (rice) has been around since Alexander's expedition to India in the 3rd century, but became a staple during Ottoman rule. It is commonly used as stuffing in *yemista* and dolmades, or cooked in stock for pilaf.

Pies
Pites (pies) are among the most common fare in Greece, made with filo or a thicker pastry with a variety of fillings. *Tiropita* (cheese pie) and *spanakopita* (spinach pie) are the favourites, but variations include sausage, ham and cheese, mushrooms and peppers.

Soups & Salads
Soups are often a hearty meal in themselves, especially lentil and bean ones. *Avgolemono* (egg-and-lemon chicken soup) is delicious and light, while *kakavia* is a speciality originally cooked by fishermen with various fresh fish.

Horiatiki, translated as 'village salad', is the ubiquitous Greek salad, with tomatoes, cucumber, onions, feta and olives. Capers and small delicious tomatoes are a speciality in the Cyclades. In winter or spring you also get cabbage (with a little carrot) and lettuce salads.

Sweet Treats
Greeks don't normally eat dessert but sweets have a special place in the Greek diet. They are offered with coffee to guests and are taken as gifts when visiting someone's home.

Many islands have their own sweet specialities and it is worth perusing local bakeries and *zaharoplasteia* (patisseries).

Syros is known for its delicious *loukoumi* ('Grecian delight'; gummy squares usually flavoured with rosewater), while Andros and Mykonos are known for *amygdalota*, an almond confectionery. Two Zakythos specialities are sesame-seed and almond pastelli and nougatlike *mandolato*.

Honey, syrup and nuts are common ingredients. Dairy-based sweets such as *rizogalo* (rice pudding) and *galaktoboureko* (syrupy custard slice) are found at *galaktopoleia* (shop selling dairy products). Dodoni is an excellent local brand of ice cream.

Fruit preserves (spoon sweets), traditionally served as a welcome to guests, are also delicious on yoghurt or ice cream.

Yoghurt
Greek *yaourti* (yoghurt) is something to swoon about. Usually made from sheep's milk, it is thick, rich and flavourful. Have it for breakfast with honey, walnuts and fruit. Mass-produced brands of sheep and cow's milk yoghurt are widely available but look out for locally made yoghurt in villages and small towns.

CELEBRATIONS
Religious rituals and cultural celebrations invariably involve a feast and every morsel is laced with symbolism.

Apokries (Carnival; abstinence from meat) refers to the three weeks of indulgence before Lent, including the popular Tsiknopempti (Scorched Thursday), when you can smell the grills cooking meat everywhere.

The 40 days of Lent are the best time to eat vegetarian fare, with special dishes that have no meat or dairy products, or even oil if you go strictly by the book.

During Easter, red-dyed boiled eggs are an integral part of festivities. The resurrection mass on Saturday night is followed by a supper that

Feasting and Fasting in Crete by Diana Farr Louis is a portrait of the island and its culinary traditions, including 140 recipes and chapters on the island's wine, cheeses, herbs and religious feasts.

In *Prospero's Kitchen*, Diana Farr Louis and June Marinos present both rare and traditional recipes from the Ionian islands.

TRAVEL YOUR TASTE BUDS

Look out for the following specialities on your island travels:

ahinosalata – sea urchin eggs with lemon juice.

amygdalota – almond sweets from Andros and Mykonos.

astakomakaronada – decadent lobster spaghetti.

dakos – rusks topped with tomato, olive oil, *myzithra* cheese.

dolmades ke anthi – vine leaves and zucchini flowers stuffed with rice and herbs.

domatokeftedes – tasty tomato fritters from the Cyclades.

fava – yellow split-pea puree from Santorini.

hohlioi Bourbouristoi – Crete's famous snail dish.

horta – wild greens; nutritious and delicious.

loukoumi –Syros' renowned 'Turkish delight', also available throughout Greece.

marinated gavros – a delicious marinated small fish.

mastiha – Mastic-flavoured *ipovrihio* or 'submarine' sugar confectionary from Chios, served in a spoon dipped in a glass of water.

saganaki – a sharp, hard cheese fried until crispy on the outside and soft in the centre; you'll also see prawn or mussel *saganaki*.

Samos dessert wine – prized sweet wine from the local Muscat grape.

taramasalata – a thick pink or white puree of fish roe, potato, oil and lemon juice.

---

includes *mayiritsa*, an offal soup. Lamb is the centrepiece on Easter Sunday, when you will see lambs cooking on spits all over the countryside.

Another 40 days of fasting prior to Christmas is not as widely observed, and Christmas itself is a more low-key celebration. Pork is the traditional Christmas Day dish.

A golden-glazed cake called *vasilopita*, baked with a coin inside, is cut at midnight on New Year's Eve, giving the recipient good fortune for the ensuing year.

DRINKS

Retsina and ouzo may be Greece's most famous (or infamous) tipples, but there are plenty of other enticing options.

Wine

Krasi (wine) in Greece predates the written record. The wine god Dionysos was tramping the vintage even before the Bronze Age. By the time of Greek independence in 1829, however, there wasn't much of a wine industry. Farmers grew small vineyards and made wine for their own consumption. It wasn't until the 1960s that Greeks began producing wine commercially, largely the infamous retsina, the tart and distinctive wine flavoured with the resin of pine trees.

In the past 20 years, the industry has experienced a renaissance, making Greece an exciting source of modern wines.

While many wineries are producing Cabernets, Chardonnays and other foreign varieties, there is an encouraging trend to produce wine from unique Greek indigenous varieties. White wines to look out for include *moschofilero*, *roditis* and *savatiano*. Greek reds include *xinomavro*, *agiorgitiko* and *kotsifali*.

Island vineyards produce some distinctive indigenous wines, including *robola* in the Ionians (especially Kefallonia), *assyrtiko* and *athiri* in the Cyclades, particularly those grown in Santorini's volcanic soil.

As for retsina, nowadays it has a largely folkloric significance and is drunk by foreigners more than Greeks. You can find some decent

Boasting the largest collection of Greek recipes on the web is www .greek-recipe.com, which also includes a Greek culinary dictionary and cookbook reviews.

homemade retsina, but the most reliable is bottled and served chilled. You can also find more lightly resinated and sophisticated retsina produced by new-generation winemakers.

Spirits

Ouzo is made from distilled grapes and flavoured with aniseed, though similar *apostagmata* (spirits) are flavoured with mint, fennel and even hazelnut.

Ouzo is served in small bottles or *karafakia* (carafes) with a glass of water and bowl of ice cubes, and should be drunk diluted with the water (it turns a milky white). Ouzo is best drunk in summer with a prolonged meal of *mezedes,* cleansing the palate between flavours. Mixing it with cola is a foreign abomination. Some of the best ouzo is made in Mytilini.

Greece's fire water is *tsipouro,* a highly potent spirit produced from the fermented and distilled grape skins left over from winemaking. In Crete, a similar but smoother variation called *raki* or *tsikoudia* is drunk in copious quantities.

Greek brandies tend to be sweet and flowery on the nose, with some deliberately sweetened by Monemvasia or other sweet grapes. The dominant Greek brandy is Metaxa.

The Muscat of Samos is made into a unique and delicious sweet dessert wine.

Beer

The most common beers are locally brewed Amstel and Heineken or Greek brands Mythos, a Pilsner-type brew, and Alfa. In cities and tourist areas you can find a range of European beers and even Australia's Foster's.

Corfu's *tsitsibira* is a (non-alcoholic) local ginger beer that used to be drunk on all the Ionians.

Coffee & Tea

Greek coffee is struggling to maintain its place as the national drink, facing competition from the ubiquitous frappé, a home-grown frothy, iced instant coffee.

Greek coffee is traditionally brewed on hot sand in a special copper *briki* (pot) and served in a small cup. It should be sipped slowly, until you reach the mud-like grounds at the bottom (don't drink the sludge). It is best drunk *metrios* (medium, with one sugar), or you can have it *glykos* (sweet) or *sketos* (unsweetened).

Filter or espresso coffee is widely available and the latter also comes *freddo* (chilled).

While *tsai* (tea) is usually a sorry story in Greece (ask for a cuppa and you'll get hot water and a cheap teabag), the chamomile and mountain teas are excellent.

Water

Greece's diverse topography ensures a huge variety of underground springs. Almost every region has its own bottled spring water on the market.

Tap water meets European sanitation standards and is generally quite drinkable, especially in major cities. Many islands, however, have questionable, limited or no water supply, so it is best to stick to bottled water. Check with the locals.

The Illustrated Greek Wine Book by Nico Manessis is the definitive work for wine connoisseurs. It traces the history of Greek wine, profiles leading winemakers, wine regions and local varietals and reviews hundreds of wines.

For comprehensive details of the country's wine regions and producers, visit www.greekwine.gr.

A glass of water is traditionally served when you arrive at a restaurant or bar, and with coffee or sweets.

WHERE TO EAT & DRINK

The best way to choose a restaurant is to see where the Greeks are eating. Greeks are fussy eaters and are sticklers for fresh produce, preferring places with fresh-cut potatoes and avoiding frozen meat and seafood, and even farmed fish.

For quick meals it is best to stick to a taverna. Likewise if you are dining alone. Most tavernas are open for lunch and dinner, but restaurants may open for dinner only.

Dining options:

Bar restaurant A more recent arrival, these places become incredibly loud after 11pm, which is hardly conducive to dinner conversation.

Estiatorio Restaurant, where you once paid more for essentially the same dishes you got in a taverna, but with nicer setting and service. These days *estiatorio* refers to an upmarket restaurant serving more international-style cuisine.

For restaurant and cookbook reviews, profiles and informative articles on Greek and Mediterranean food, check out www .gourmed.gr.

Kafeneio One of the oldest institutions in Greece, *kafeneia* serve Greek coffee, spirits and little else, and are still largely the domain of men, especially in villages.

Mayireio These cookhouses offer big trays of the day's specials, including baked dishes and casseroles.

Mezedopoleio Serves lots of different *mezedes* (appetizers) that are shared and accompanied by the drink of your choice.

Ouzeri The traditional *ouzeri* served small plates of increasingly sophisticated meze with each round of ouzo. The Cretan equivalent is a *rakadiko*, while in the north you will find *tsipouradika*. Most now serve a range of *mezedes* with whatever you care to drink.

Psarotaverna A taverna specialising in fish.

Psistaria A taverna specialising in chargrilled or spit-roasted meat.

Taverna Traditional tavernas are casual and family-run (and child-friendly) places where the waiter will arrive with bread and cutlery in a basket, and a jug of water. Trendy, upmarket tavernas offer creative takes on Greek classics in fancier surrounds, with higher prices and good wine lists but not necessarily better value.

Quick Eats

The Glorious Foods of Greece by Award-winning Greek-American food writer Diane Kochilas is a superb regional exploration of Greek cuisine, its history and culture through a personal travelogue reflecting her passion.

Souvlaki is the favourite fast food of Greece, both the *gyros* and skewered versions wrapped in pitta bread, with tomato, onion and lashings of tzatziki. But western-style *fastfoudadika*, as fast-food joints are called, are making inroads. McDonalds has a relatively small presence (and introduced a McGreek version of *souvlaki*) but Greece has its own slavish imitator – Goody's. Plenty of places make *tost,* the Greek variation of toasted sandwiches, and cheese and spinach pies are widely available.

Street vendors on the islands sell *koulouria* (fresh sesame-covered bagel-like bread rings), nuts, fruit and, depending on the season, roasted chestnuts and corn.

VEGETARIANS & VEGANS

It's easy to go vegetarian in Greece. While no Greek would claim to be a vegetarian (at least none of our acquaintance), a combination of lean

---

BILL TIME

All restaurants add a per person 'cover' or service charge to the bill, normally a nominal amount to cover the bread etc. In fancier places this can be as steep as €5. Tax is included in the bill. It is customary to at least round up the bill or leave a small tip.

DOS & DON'TS

■ Do ask what the local speciality is in each region.

■ Do ask to look in the pots in the kitchen to select your meal.

■ Do select your own fish and get it weighed.

■ Don't insist on paying if you are invited out – it insults your host.

■ Don't refuse a coffee or drink – it's offered as a gesture of hospitality and goodwill.

---

times and the Orthodox faith's fasting traditions has produced many tasty meat-free dishes.

EATING WITH KIDS

Greeks love children and most tavernas are child-friendly, with no-one too fussed if children play between the tables. Children's menus are rare, even in tourist areas. For more information on travelling with children, see p484.

HABITS & CUSTOMS

Most Greeks think of breakfast as a cigarette and a cup of coffee so your best recourse is to take to the streets. Bakeries and pie shops are open early. English-style breakfasts are rare outside of tourist areas.

Though changes in working hours are affecting traditional meal patterns, lunch is still usually the big meal of the day and does not start until after 2pm.

Most Greeks wouldn't think of eating dinner before the sun went down, which coincides with shop trading hours, so restaurants don't fill up until after 10pm. Cafés do a roaring trade after the siesta, between 6pm and 8pm.

Dining is a drawn-out ritual, so if you are eating with locals pace yourself during the *mezedes* because there will be more to come. Greeks order way too much food, as they would rather throw it away than not have enough.

Greeks don't drink coffee after a meal and many tavernas still don't offer it – that is the domain of the café or *kafeneio*.

Foods of the Greek Islands by Aglaïa Kremezi explores the history, culture and cuisine of Greece's islands, with recipes collected on her travels and from New York's acclaimed Molyvos Greek restaurant.

COOKING COURSES

Several well-known cooking writers and chefs run cooking courses on the islands.

In Santorini, Rosemary Barron leads the **Tasting Places** (www.rosemary barronsgreece.com) course, while Aglaïa Kremezi and her friends open their kitchens and gardens on Kea for five-day hands-on **cooking workshops** (www.keartisanal.com).

Award-winning Greek-American food writer Diane Kochilas runs the **Glorious Greek Kitchen** (www.cuisineinternational.com) summer cooking course on her ancestral island Ikaria.

Also based in the islands, **Crete's Culinary Sanctuaries** (www.cookingincrete .com) combines cooking classes, farm tours, hiking and cultural excursions around the island.

In Flavours of Greece, Rosemary Barron explores the Greek kitchen through more than 250 different regional specialities, from meze to spit-roasted goat.

EAT YOUR WORDS

Get behind the cuisine scene by getting to know the language. For pronunciation guidelines see p513.

SMOKED OUT

Greeks are the biggest smokers in the EU: they smoke all the time, everywhere – even *during* a meal. In 2003 smoking was banned in public areas (bars and clubs are exempt) and all restaurants are required to have non-smoking areas – let us know if you find any!

Useful Phrases

I want to make a reservation for this evening.
Θέλω να κλείσω ένα τραπέζι για απόψε.   the·lo na kli·so e·na tra·pe·zi ya a·po·pse

A table for ... please.
Ένα τραπέζι για ... παρακαλώ.   e·na tra·pe·zi ya ..., pa·ra·ka·lo

I'd like the menu, please.
Το μενού, παρακαλώ.   to me·nu, pa·ra·ka·lo

Do you have a menu in English?
Έχετε το μενού στα αγγλικά;   e·hye·te to me·nu sta ang·li·ka?

I'd like ...
Θα ήθελα ...   tha i·the·la ...

Please bring the bill.
Το λογαριασμό, παρακαλώ.   to lo·ghar·ya·zmo, pa·ra·ka·lo

I'm a vegetarian.
Είμαι χορτοφάγος.   i·me hor·to·fa·ghos

I don't eat meat or dairy products.
Δε τρώω κρέας ή γαλακτοκομικά προϊόντα.   dhen tro·o kre·as i gha·la·kto·ko·mi·ka pro·i·on·da

Food Glossary

STAPLES

ψωμί	pso·mi	bread
βούτυρο	vu·ti·ro	butter
τυρί	ti·ri	cheese
αυγά	a·vgha	eggs
μέλι	me·li	honey
γάλα	gha·la	milk
ελαιόλαδο	e·le·o·la·dho	olive oil
ελιές	e·lyes	olives
πιπέρι	pi·pe·ri	pepper
αλάτι	a·la·ti	salt
ζάχαρη	za·ha·ri	sugar
ξύδι	ksi·dhi	vinegar

MEAT, FISH & SEAFOOD

μοσχάρι	moschari	beef
ροφός	ro·fos	blackfish
κοτόπουλο	ko·to·pu·lo	chicken
σουπιά	sou·pia	cuttlefish
κέφαλος	ke·fa·los	grey mullet
σφυρίδα	sfi·ri·da	grouper
ζαμπόν	zam·bon	ham
λαγός	la·ghos	hare
κατσικάκι	ka·tsi·ka·ki	kid (goat)
αρνί	ar·ni	lamb
αστακός	a·sta·kos	lobster
κολιός	ko·li·os	mackerel
μύδια	mi·di·a	mussels
χταπόδι	hta·po·dhi	octopus

χοιρινό	hyi·ri·*no*	pork
γαρίδες	gha·*ri*·dhes	prawns
κουνέλι	kou·*ne*·li	rabbit
μπαρμπούνια	bar·*bu*·nya	red mullet
σαρδέλες	sar·*dhe*·les	sardines
φαγρί/λιθρίνι/μελανούρι	fa·*ghri*/li·*thri*·ni/me·la·*nu*·ri	sea bream
καλαμάρι	ka·la·*ma*·ri	squid
ξιφίας	ksi·*fi*·as	swordfish
μοσχάρι	mo·*sha*·ri	veal
μαρίδες	ma·*ri*·dhes	whitebait

FRUIT & VEGETABLES

μήλο	*mi*·lo	apple
αγγινάρα	ang·gi·na·ra	artichoke
σπαράγγι	spa·*rang*·gi	asparagus
μελιτζάνες	me·li·*dza*·nes	aubergine (eggplant)
λάχανο	*la*·ha·no	cabbage
καρότο	ka·*ro*·to	carrot
κεράσι	ke·*ra*·si	cherry
σκόρδο	*skor*·dho	garlic
σταφύλια	sta·*fi*·li·a	grapes
(άγρια) χόρτα	(a·ghri·a) *hor*·ta	greens, seasonal wild
λεμόνι	le·*mo*·ni	lemon
κρεμμύδια	re·*mi*·dhi·a	onions
πορτοκάλι	por·to·*ka*·li	orange
ροδάκινο	ro·*dha*·ki·no	peach
αρακάς	a·ra·*kas*	peas
πιπεριές	pi·per·*yes*	peppers
πατάτες	pa·*ta*·tes	potatoes
σπανάκι	spa·*na*·ki	spinach
φράουλα	*fra*·u·la	strawberry
ντομάτα	do·*ma*·ta	tomato

DRINKS

μπύρα	*bi*·ra	beer
καφές	ka·*fes*	coffee
τσάι	*tsa*·i	tea
νερό	*ne*·ro	water
κρασί (κόκκινο/άσπρο)	kra·*si* (*ko*·ki·no/*a*·spro)	wine (red/white)

Athens & the Mainland Ports

Athens, the city of Athina the goddess of wisdom, inevitably evokes romantic associations. The sensation of seeing the Parthenon temple perched on the rocky hulk of the Acropolis for the first time is little short of magical – even for visitors who visit the capital repeatedly.

Often rushed through by travellers in search of their magical Greek island, Athens deserves much more than a brief dalliance. It is a city that never sleeps; it is a city of world-class museums, where antiquities still dot street corners or may lie buried and undiscovered under a layer of marble, cement and asphalt.

Its restaurants rival, if not surpass, those in other capitals and its nightlife is as sophisticated as that of New York, London or Rio di Janeiro, yet it is a safe as your own backyard. Accommodation ranges from homely pensions to world-class hotels. While the streets can seem like a Grand Prix on a busy day, you can swiftly move around on an underground metro system, or meander your way to one of Athens many beach suburbs on an air-conditioned tram. Nonpolluting trolley buses still thread their way through Athens.

Athens can exhilarate, exasperate and yet be exonerated in equal doses. As a city it is unique. It sits with one eye on the East and the other to the West. It's part of Europe yet has never forgotten its oriental roots. It is definitely worth a few days yet a month would hardly suffice. Athens is a city with a glorious past and a burgeoning future.

HIGHLIGHTS

▪ **Magic Moment**
That first glimpse of the Acropolis (p85)

▪ **Northern Delight**
Views over Thessaloniki from the city's historic Turkish Kastra (p101)

▪ **Dining**
A table (p90) with a view of the floodlit Acropolis

▪ **Showtime**
A performance at the Odeon of Herodes Atticus (p86)

▪ **Historical Experience**
Follow in the footsteps of Socrates at the Ancient Agora (p76)

▪ **Panorama**
The views from Lykavittos Hill (p86)

Acropolis ★ ★ Lykavittos Hill
Ancient Agora ★ ★
★ Odeon of
Herodes Atticus

▪ POPULATION: ATHENS 4.7 MILLION, ATTICA 3.7 MILLION | ▪ AREA: 3808 SQ KM

ATHENS ΑΘΗΝΑ

pop 3.7 million

HISTORY

The early history of Athens is so interwoven with mythology that it's hard to disentangle fact from fiction.

The Acropolis has been occupied since Neolithic times. It was an excellent vantage point and the steep slopes formed natural defences on three sides. By 1400 BC the Acropolis was a powerful Mycenaean city.

Its power peaked during the so-called golden age of Athens in the 5th century BC, following the defeat of the Persians at the Battle of Salamis. The city fell into decline after its defeat by Sparta in the long-running Peloponnesian War, but rallied again in Roman times when it became a seat of learning. The Roman emperors, particularly Hadrian, graced Athens with many grand buildings.

After the Roman Empire split into east and west, the power shifted to Byzantium (modern day Istanbul) and Athens fell into obscurity. By the end of Ottoman rule, Athens was little more than a dilapidated village (the area now known as Plaka).

Then, in 1834, the newly-crowned King Otho transferred his court from Nafplio in the Peloponnese and made Athens the capital of independent Greece. The city was rebuilt along neoclassical lines, featuring large squares and tree-lined boulevards with imposing public buildings. The city grew steadily and enjoyed a brief heyday as the 'Paris of the Mediterranean' in the late 19th and early 20th centuries.

This came to an abrupt end with the forced population exchange between Greece and Turkey, which followed the Treaty of Lausanne in 1923. The huge influx of refugees from Asia Minor virtually doubled the population overnight, forcing the hasty erection of the first of the many concrete apartment blocks that dominate the city today. The belated advent of Greece's industrial age in the 1950s brought another wave of migration, this time of rural folk looking for work.

The city's infrastructure, particularly road and transport, could not keep pace with such rapid and unplanned growth, and by the end of the '80s the city had developed a sorry reputation as one of the most traffic-clogged and polluted in Europe.

The 1990s appear to have been a turning point in the city's development. Jolted into action by the failed bid to stage the 1996 Olympics, authorities embarked on an ambitious programme to prepare the city for the 21st century. Two key elements have been an extension of the metro network and the construction of a new international airport.

These projects played an important role in the city's successful staging of the 2004 Olympics. The legacy of the games is that Athens today is a radically different city – a more attractive, cleaner, greener and efficient capital, though it is still a work in progress.

ORIENTATION

Although Athens is a huge, sprawling city, nearly everything of interest to short-term visitors lies within a small area bounded by Omonia Square (Plateia Omonias) to the north, Monastiraki Square (Plateia Monastirakiou) to the west, Syntagma Square (Plateia Syntagmatos) to the east and the Plaka district to the south. The city's two major landmarks, the Acropolis and Lykavittos Hill, can be seen from just about everywhere in this area.

Plaka, the old Ottoman quarter that was all that existed when Athens was declared the capital of independent Greece, nestles on the northeastern slope of the Acropolis. It may be touristy, but it's the most attractive and interesting part of Athens and the majority of visitors make it their base.

INFORMATION
Bookshops

Compendium Books (Map p88; ☎ 210 322 1248; Navarhou Nikodimou 5 & Nikis, Plaka) Specialises in books in English, and has a popular second-hand section.

Eleftheroudakis Plaka (Map p88; ☎ 210 322 9388; Nikis 20); Syntagma (Map p88; ☎ 210 331 4180; Panepistimiou 17) The seven-floor Panepistimiou store is the biggest bookshop in Athens, with a level dedicated to English books.

Reymondos (Map p88; ☎ 210 364 8188, Voukourestiou 18, Syntagma) Stocks books in English, and a wide range of foreign press and magazines.

Road Editions (Map p74; ☎ 210 361 3242; Ippokratous 39, Exarhia) A wide range of travel literature and all the Road Editions maps.

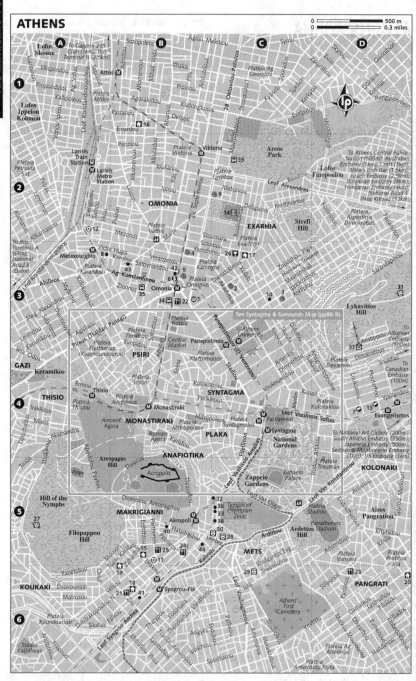

ATHENS

INFORMATION		
Athens Central Post Office	1	B3
Bits & Bytes Internet Café	2	C3
C@fe4U	3	C3
C@fe4U	4	B3
Cyberzone	5	B3
Eurochange	6	B3
German Embassy	7	D4
Laundry Self Service	8	A3
Museum Internet Café	9	C2
Road Editions	10	C3
Tourist Police	11	B5
Traffic Police	12	A2
UK Embassy	13	D4

SIGHTS & ACTIVITIES		
National Archaeological Museum	14	C2

SLEEPING		
Art Gallery Hotel	15	B5

Hostel Aphrodite	16	B1
Hotel Exarchion	17	C3
Marble House Pension	18	B6
Tony's Hotel	19	B6
Youth Hostel No 5	20	D6

EATING		
Gardenia Restaurant	21	B6
Marinopoulos	22	B3
Spondi	23	D6
To 24 Hours	24	B5
Veropoulos	25	B5

DRINKING		
AN Club	26	C3

ENTERTAINMENT		
Dora Stratou Theatre	27	A5
Granazi Bar	28	C5
Half Note Jazz Club	29	C6

Lamda Club	30	C5
Lykavittos Theatre	31	D3

TRANSPORT		
Avis	32	C5
Budget	33	C5
Bus No 049 to Piraeus	34	B3
Bus No 051 to Bus Terminal A	35	B3
Europcar	36	C5
Funicular Railway	37	D3
Hertz	38	C5
Mavromateon Bus Terminal (Lavrio & Rafina)	39	C2
Motorent	40	B5
Olympic Airlines	41	B6
Olympic Airlines	42	B3
OSE Office	43	B3
Sixt	44	B5

Emergency

Ambulance/First-Aid Advice (☎ 166) US citizens can ring ☎ 2107 212 951 for emergency medical aid.

Athens Central Police Station (☎ 210 770 5711/5717; Leof Alexandras 173, Ambelokipi)

ELPA Road Assistance (☎ 10400)

Fire Brigade (☎ 199)

Police Emergency (☎ 100)

SOS Doctors (☎ 1016 or 210 821 1888; ☻ 24hr) A pay service with English-speaking doctors.

Tourist Police (Map p74; ☎ 171 for emergency or 210 920 0724; 4th Fl, Veïkou 43-45, Koukaki; ☻ 8am-10pm) Provides 24-hour emergency help as well as general tourist information.

Traffic Police (Map p74; ☎ 210 528 4000; Deligianni 24-6, Omonia)

Internet Access

There are numerous Internet cafés around the city centre.

Most charge €1.50 to €4 per hour of computer time, whether you're connected to the Internet or not. C@fe4U has the cheapest rates.

Bits & Bytes Internet Café Exarhia (Map p74; ☎ 210 330 6590; Akadimias 78); Plaka (Map p88; Kapnikareas 19; per hr €3; ☻ 24 hr)

C@fe4U Exarhia (Map p74; ☎ 210 361 1981; Ippokratous 44; per hr €1; ☻ 24 hr); Omonia (Map p74; ☎ 210 520 1564; Tritis Septemvriou 24; per hr €2.50; ☻ 8am-11pm).

Cyberzone (Map p74; ☎ 210 520 3939; Satovriandou 7, Omonia; per hr €2.50, midnight-8am €1.50; ☻ 24 hr;)

Ivis Internet (Map p88; Mitropoleos 3, Syntagma; per hr €3; ☻ 24 hr)

Museum Internet Café (Map p74; ☎ 210 883 3418; 28 Oktovriou-Patision 46, Omonia; per hr €4.50; ☻ 9am-3am) Next to the National Archaeological Museum.

Internet Resources

www.cityofathens.gr City of Athens site with walks, events and other useful information.

www.cultureguide.gr Outlines the festivals and events happening in Athens and throughout Greece.

www.psirri.gr A guide to events in Psiri.

Laundry

Laundry Self Service (Map p74; Psaron 9, Omonia; per load €8.50; ☻ 8am-8pm Mon-Fri, 8am-2pm Sat & Sun) Near Plateia Karaïskaki.

Plaka Laundrette (Map p88; ☎ 210 321 3102; Angelou Geronta 10, Plaka; wash & dry 5kg €9; ☻ 8am-7pm Mon-Sat, 8am-1pm Sun)

Left Luggage

Some hotels store luggage, but most only pile them in a hall. Left-luggage facilities are at the airport and Pireaus train station (p100).

Pacific Luggage Storage (Map p88; ☎ 210 324 1007; Nikis 26; ☻ 8am-8pm Mon-Sat, 9am-2pm Sun) Charges €2 per day for up to four days, €7 per week.

Money

Bank opening hours are 8am to 2pm Monday to Thursday and 8am to 1.30pm on Friday. Banks at the airport are open 7am to 9pm.

Acropole Foreign Exchange (Map p88; ☎ 210 331 2765; Kydathineon 23, Plaka; ☻ 9am-midnight)

American Express (Map p88; ☎ 210 324 4979; Ermou 7, Syntagma; ☻ 8.30am-4pm Mon-Fri, 8.30am-1.30pm Sat)

Eurochange Omonia (Map p74; ☎ 210 324 3997; Agiou Konstantinou 34 & Marikas Kotopouli 1); Syntagma (Map p88; ☎ 210 322 0155; Karageorgi Servias 2; ☻ 9am-9pm) Exchanges Thomas Cook travellers cheques without commission.

National Bank of Greece (Map p88; cnr Karageorgi Servias & Stadiou, Syntagma; ☻ foreign exchange only: 3.30-6.30pm Mon-Thu, 3-6.30pm Fri, 9am-3pm Sat, 9am-1pm Sun) Has a 24-hour automatic exchange machine.

MORE FOR YOUR MONEY

The €12 admission charge to the Acropolis buys a collective ticket that gives entry to all the other significant ancient sites in Athens: the Ancient Agora, the Roman Agora, the Keramikos, the Temple of Olympian Zeus and the Theatre of Dionysos. The ticket is valid for 48 hours, otherwise individual site fees apply.

Post

Athens Central Post Office (Map p74; www.elta.gr; Eolou 100, Omonia; 7.30am-8pm Mon-Fri, 7.30am-2pm Sat) Unless specified otherwise, all poste restante is sent here.

Parcel Post Office (Map p74; Stadiou 4, Syntagma; 7.30am-2pm Mon-Fri) Parcels weighing over 2kg must be taken here, unwrapped, for inspection. The office is in the arcade.

Syntagma Post Office (Map p88; cnr Mitropoleos; 7.30am-8pm Mon-Fri, 7.30am-2pm Sat) If you're staying in Plaka, it's more convenient to get your mail sent here.

Telephone

Public phones all over Athens allow local, long distance and international calls. They only take phone cards, which are widely available at kiosks. Use call cards, which like Hronokarta, are available from kiosks for much cheaper rates.

Toilets

Public toilets are relatively scarce in Athens and keep inconsistent hours. The many fast-food outlets in central Athens are also handy for travellers. Cafés will let you use their facilities, but will usually expect you to buy something for the privilege.

Tourist Information

City of Athens Visitor Information Booths (195; www.cityofathens.gr) Manned over the summer at key locations.

EOT (Greek National Tourist Organisation; Map p74; 210 331 0392; www.gnto.gr; Amalias 26a, Syntagma; 9am-7pm Mon-Fri; 10am-4pm Sat-Sun) This helpful office has a handy free map of Athens, the week's ferry departure timetable and public transport information. You can also pick up a free copy of the glossy 'Athens & Attica' booklet.

EOT Airport Office (210 353 0445-7; Arrivals Hall; 9am-7pm Mon-Fri, 10am-4pm Sat & Sun) Has the same information and maps as its city office.

DANGERS & ANNOYANCES

Lonely Planet continues to hear from readers who have been taken in by one of the various bar scams that operate around central Athens. The scam runs something like this: friendly Greek approaches male traveller and discovers that the traveller knows little about Athens; friendly Greek then reveals that he, too, is from out of town. Why don't they go to this great bar that he's just discovered and have a beer? They order a drink and the friendly owner then offers another drink. Women appear, more drinks are provided and the visitor relaxes as he realises that the women are not prostitutes, just friendly Greeks. The crunch comes at the end of the night when the traveller is presented with a huge bill and the smiles disappear. The con men who cruise the streets playing the role of the friendly Greek can be very convincing: some people have been taken in more than once.

Other bars don't bother with the acting. They target intoxicated males with talk of sex and present them with outrageous bills.

SIGHTS
Ancient Agora

The **Agora** (Map p88; 210 321 0185; Adrianou; adult/concession €4/2; museum 8am-7.30pm Jun-Oct, 8am-5.30pm Nov-May) was the marketplace of and focal point of civic life. The main monuments are the **Temple of Hephaestus**, the 11th-century **Church of the Holy Apostles** and the **Stoa of Attalos**, which houses the museum.

Roman Agora

The Romans built an **Agora** (210 324 5220; cnr Pelopida Eolou & Markou Aureliou; adult/concession €2/1; 8am-7.30pm Jun-Oct, 8am-5.30pm Nov-May) east of the Ancient Agora. Visit the Tower of the Winds, built in the 1st century BC by Andronicus, a Syrian astronomer. This ingenious construction functioned as a sundial, weather vane, water clock and compass.

Changing of the Guard

Every Sunday at 11am a platoon of traditionally dressed *evzones* (guards) marches down Leof Vasilissis Sofias, accompanied by a band, to the Tomb of the Unknown Soldier in front of the **parliament building** (Map p88; Syntagma).

(Continued on page 85)

The Parthenon (p85), Athens

Odeon of Herodes Atticus (p87), Athens

Stoa of Attalos (p76), Athens

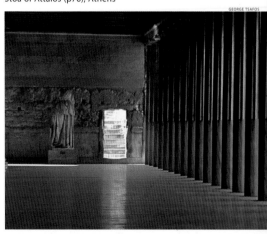

Temple of Hephaestus (p76), Athens

IZZET KERIBAR

View of Athens and Lykavittos Hill (p73)

JULIET C

Ancient artworks, Benaki Museum (p85), Athens

NEIL SE

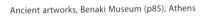

KIM WILDMAN

Fisherman, Hydra Town (p126), Hydra

CHRIS CHRISTO

Hillside ruins, Paleohora (p120), Aegina

Hydra Town harbour (p126), Hydra

MARK DAFFEY

Dried fish (p63)

CHRIS CHRISTO

ALAN BENSON

Balls of soft cheese (p63)

Grilled octopus (p63)

ALAN B

JON DAVISON

Volcanic cliffs, Santorini (p191)

Ancient ruins, Milos (p207)

CHRIS CHRISTO

Donkey transport, Fira (p193), Santorini

GLENN BEANLAND

PAUL DAVID HELLA

Harbour (p176), Halki

ALAN BENSON

Cobblestone street, Paros (p161)

Waterfront, Hora (p171), Naxos

DAMIEN SIM

Venetian fountain, Spili (p243), Crete

CHRIS CHRISTO

Street vendor, Rethymno (p237), Crete

NEIL SETCHFIELD

Olives and dolmades (p64)

NEIL SETCHFIELD

Waterfront at night, Rethymno (p237), Crete

JON DAVISON

84

Dishes at the covered food market (p252), Hania, Crete

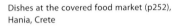

ALAN BENSON

GLENN BEANLAND

Venetian lighthouse (p248), Hania, Crete

Café culture, Rethymno (p237), Crete

NEIL SETCH

(Continued from page 76)

Keramikos

The city's cemetery from the 12th century BC to Roman times was the **Keramikos** (☎ 210 346 3552; Ermou 148; adult/concession €2/1; ☼ 8am-7.30pm Jun-Oct, 8am-5.30pm Nov-May). It was discovered in 1861 during the construction of Pireos, the street that leads to Piraeus. It is one of the most green and tranquil of Athens' ancient sites. The Keramikos is a five minute walk west of the Thision metro station.

Temple of Olympian Zeus

This is the largest **temple** (Map p74; ☎ 210 922 6330; adult/concession €2/1; ☼ 8am-7.30pm Jun-Oct, 8am-5.30pm Nov-May) in Greece and sits just east of the Acropolis. Construction was begun in the 6th century BC by Peisistratos, but was abandoned for lack of funds. Various other leaders had stabs at completing the temple, but it was left to Hadrian to complete the work in AD 131. It took over 700 years to build.

The temple is impressive for the sheer size of its 104 Corinthian columns (17m high with a base diameter of 1.7m), of which 15 remain – the fallen column was blown down in a gale in 1852. Hadrian put a colossal statue of Zeus in the cella and, in typically immodest fashion, placed an equally large one of himself next to it.

Museums & Galleries

One of the world's great museums, the **National Archaeological Museum** (Map p74; ☎ 210 821 7717; 28 Oktovriou-Patision 44; www.culture.gr; adult/concession €7/3; ☼ 1pm-7.15pm Mon, 8am-7.15pm Tue-Sun Jun-Oct, 8am-2.45pm Nov-May) houses important finds from Greece's archaeological sites. It was extensively re-furbished prior to the Olympic games and renovations are ongoing.

The crowd-pullers are the magnificent, exquisitely detailed gold artefacts from Mycenae and the spectacular Minoan frescoes from Santorini (Thira). The collection is arranged thematically and is beautifully presented with labels in English and Greek. Two new galleries with the Egyptian and Stathatos collections are expected to open in 2006.

The **Benaki Museum** (Map p88; ☎ 210 367 1000; www.benaki.gr; cnr Leof Vasilissis Sofias & Koumbari 1, Kolonaki; adult/concession €6/3, free admission Thu; ☼ 9am-5pm Mon, Wed, Fri & Sat, 9am-midnight Thu, 9am-3pm Sun) contains the collection of Antoine Benaki, accumulated during 35 years of avid collecting throughout Europe and Asia. The collection includes ancient sculpture, Bronze Age finds from Mycenae and Thessaly, two early works by El Greco and a stunning collection of Greek regional costumes.

The **Goulandris Museum of Cycladic & Ancient Greek Art** (Map p88; ☎ 210 722 8321; www.cycladic.gr; cnr Leof Vasilissis Sofias & Neofytou Douka, Kolonaki; adult/concession €5/2.50; ☼ 10am-4pm Mon, Wed-Fri, 10am-3pm Sat) houses a collection of Cycladic art second in importance only to that at the National Archaeological Museum. The museum was custom-built for the collection and the finds are beautifully displayed and labelled.

The emphasis in the **National Art Gallery** (Map p74; ☎ 210 723 5857; www.nationalgallery.gr; Leof Vasileos Konstantinou 50; adult/concession €6.50/3; ☼ 9am-3pm Wed-Sat, 6-9pm Mon & Wed, 10am-2pm Sun), opposite the Hilton Hotel, is on Greek painting and sculpture from the 19th and 20th centuries. There are also 16th-century works, a few works by European masters, including paintings by Picasso, Marquet and Utrillo, and Magritte's sculpture *The Therapist*. Greek sculpture of the 19th and 20th centuries is displayed in the sculpture garden and sculpture hall, reached from the lower floor. There are works by Giannolis Halepas (1851–1937), one of Greece's foremost sculptors.

The Acropolis

Most of the buildings that grace the **Acropolis** (Map p86; ☎ 210 321 0219; sites & museum adult/concession €12/6; ☼ 8am-7.30pm June-Oct, 8am-5.30pm Nov-May) were commissioned by Pericles during the golden age of Athens in the 5th century BC. The site had been cleared for him by the Persians, who destroyed an earlier temple complex on the eve of the Battle of Salamis.

The entrance to the Acropolis is through the **Beulé Gate**, a Roman arch that was added in the 3rd century AD. Beyond this is the **Propylaia**, which was the ancient entrance. It was damaged by Venetian bombardment in the 17th century, but has been restored. To the south of the Propylaia is the small **Temple of Athena Nike** (not accessible to visitors).

Standing over the Acropolis is a monument that epitomises the glory of ancient Greece: the **Parthenon**. It was completed in

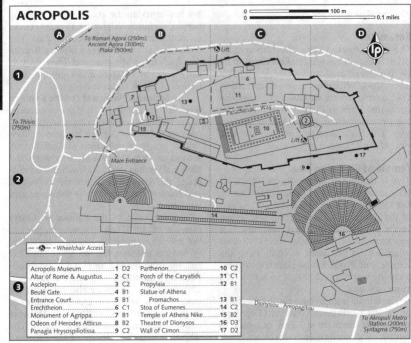

ACROPOLIS

0   100 m
0   0.1 miles

To Roman Agora (250m); Ancient Agora (300m); Plaka (500m)

Lift

To Thisio (750m)

Panathenaic Way

Main Entrance

Lift

Dionysiou Areopagitou

To Akropoli Metro Station (200m); Syntagma (750m)

— Wheelchair Access

Acropolis Museum	1 D2	Parthenon	10 C2
Altar of Rome & Augustus	2 C1	Porch of the Caryatids	11 C1
Asclepion	3 C2	Propylaia	12 B1
Beulé Gate	4 B1	Statue of Athena	
Entrance Court	5 B1	Promachos	13 B1
Erechtheion	6 C1	Stoa of Eumenes	14 C2
Monument of Agrippa	7 B1	Temple of Athena Nike	15 B2
Odeon of Herodes Atticus	8 B2	Theatre of Dionysos	16 D3
Panagia Hrysospiliotissa	9 C2	Wall of Cimon	17 D2

438 BC and is unsurpassed in grace and harmony. Its lines were ingeniously curved to counteract optical illusions. The base curves upwards slightly towards the ends, and the columns become narrower towards the top, with the overall effect of making it look straight.

Above the columns are the remains of a Doric frieze, which was partly destroyed by Venetian shelling in 1687. The best surviving pieces are the controversial Parthenon Marbles, which were carted off to Britain by Lord Thomas Elgin in 1801. The Parthenon, dedicated to Athena, contained an 11m-tall gold-and-ivory statue of the goddess completed in 438 BC by Phidias of Athens (only the statue's foundations survive today).

To the north is the **Erechtheion** with its popular Caryatids, the six maidens who support its southern portico. These are plaster casts. The originals (except for the one taken by Lord Elgin) are in the site's museum.

Lykavittos Hill

This striking rocky landmark (277m) in central Athens rises out of a sea of concrete

to offer the finest views in Athens. On clear days there are panoramic views of the city, the Attic basin, the surrounding mountains and the islands of Salamis and Aegina. A fairly steep path leads to the summit from the top of Loukianou. Alternatively, you can take the **funicular railway** (Map p74; ☎ 210 721 0701; return €4.50; ⏱ 9am-3am, half-hourly), referred to commonly as the *télépherique*, from the top of Ploutarhou. At the top is the chapel of Agios Georgios and a rather expensive café-cum-restaurant.

The open-air Lykavittos Theatre, located northeast of the summit, is used during the Summer on Lykavittos Hill festival programme (opposite).

FESTIVALS & EVENTS
Hellenic Festival

The annual **Hellenic Festival** is the city's most important cultural event, running from mid-June to late September. It features a line-up of international music, dance and theatre at the **Odeon of Herodes Atticus** (Map p88). The setting is quite stunning, backed by a floodlit Acropolis.

The festival has been going from strength to strength, and line-ups in recent years have included Marcel Marceau, the French National Opera Company of Paris and Ian Anderson's Jethro Tull, as well as a mix of opera, modern dance and theatre both ancient and modern.

Tickets can be bought at the **Hellenic Festival box office** (Map p88; ☎ 210 928 2900; www .hellenicfestival.gr; Panepistimiou 39, Syntagma (in arcade); 8.30am-4pm Mon-Fri, 9am-2pm Sat). Tickets go on sale three weeks before a performance. There are student discounts for most performances on production of an International Student Identity Card (ISIC; see p486).

Summer on Lykavittos Hill

The **Lykavittos Theatre** (Map p74; ☎ 210 722 7233) on the Hill of Lykavittos makes a spectacular setting for a series of performances by Greek and international stars from June to the end of August. The theatre provides a spectacular setting for an eclectic annual programme – choices for 2005 included ancient Greek theatre, the Soweto Gospel Choir and the Rocky Horror Picture Show.

SLEEPING
Budget
HOSTELS

Student & Travellers' Inn (Map p88; ☎ 210 324 4808; www.studenttravellersinn.com; Kydathineon 16; dm €12-15, s/d/tr €45/55/66;) This popular and well-run place in the heart of Plaka has a mixture of dorms and simple rooms for up to four people, with or without private bathroom and air-con. It has a cheery yellow-and-blue colour scheme and some rooms have fine old timber floors. Facilities include a pleasant shady courtyard with large-screen TV, Internet access and a travel service. Breakfast is from €3.50 and rooms are heated in winter.

Youth Hostel No 5 (Map p74; ☎ 210 751 9530; www .athens-yhostel.com; Damareos 75; dm €12) The dorms here are basic and dated, but it's a cheery place in quiet Pangrati. Owner Yiannis is a bit of a philosopher, and visitors are encouraged to add their jokes and words of wisdom to the noticeboards. Facilities include coin-operated hot showers (€0.50), communal kitchen, TV room and laundry. If it's full you can sleep on the covered rooftop (€10). Take trolleybus No 2 or 11 from Syntagma to the Filolaou stop on Frinis, or it's a long walk from Evangelismos metro station.

Hostel Aphrodite (Map p74; ☎ 210 881 0589; www .hostelaphrodite.com; Einardou 12; dm €12-16; d/tr €24/54;) This well-run hostel is the cheapest budget option and is convenient for the Larisis train station. It has very clean, good-sized four and eight-bed dorms, some with ensuite bathrooms, as well as double rooms with and without private bathrooms – many with balconies. Facilities include Internet access, laundry and a travel agency. Breakfast from €2.50.

HOTELS
Plaka & Syntagma

Hotel Adonis (Map p88; ☎ 210 324 9737; fax 210 323 1602; Kodrou 3; s/d incl breakfast €53/82;) This comfortable if bland pension on a quiet street represents one of the best deals around. The rooms are neat and come with TV. There are great views of the Acropolis from the 4th-floor rooms and from the rooftop bar.

Adams Hotel (Map p88; ☎ 210 322 5381; adams@ otenet.gr; Herofontos 6; s/d €60/70;) A decent budget option in Plaka, this place has simple old-fashioned rooms with TV as well as larger family rooms (€120 to €140).

John's Place (Map p88; ☎ 210 322 9719; Patroou 5; s/d/tr €35/55/75) This small, old-style, family-run place is situated just west of Syntagma. It missed out on an Olympic makeover but is clean and the timber staircase, old doors and high ceilings retain some charm. The furnishings are dated, each room has a hand basin, some have air-conditioning but the bathrooms are all shared.

Monastiraki

Hotel Tempi (Map p88; ☎ 210 321 3175; www.travel ling.gr/tempihotel; Eolou 29; s/d/tr €38/58/70;) This friendly, family-run place is spotless, and the rooms at the front have balconies overlooking pretty Plateia Agia Irini, with its flower market and church – not to mention the Acropolis views. The rooms have had a makeover, and include satellite TV, though the bathrooms are still basic. There is a communal kitchen with a refrigerator and facilities for preparing hot drinks and snacks. Credit cards are accepted.

Makrigianni & Koukaki

Marble House Pension (Map p74; ☎ 210 923 4058; www.marblehouse.gr; Zini 35a, Koukaki; s/d/tr €42/48/55;) This pension in a quiet cul-de-sac off Zini is one of Athens' better budget hotels,

SYNTAGMA & SURROUNDS

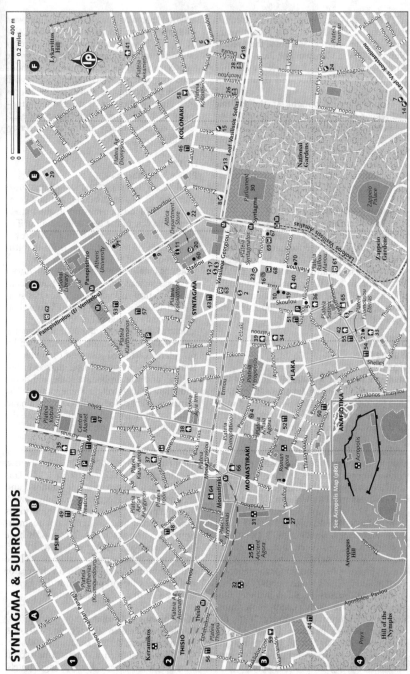

though it is a fair way from the tourist areas. Rooms have been updated, with new single beds and linen. All have a fridge and ceiling fans and some have air-con (€9 extra). Breakfast costs €5.

Hotel Tony (Map p74; ☎ 210 923 0561; www.hotel tony.gr; Zaharitsa 26; s/d/tr €45/55/75; ❋) This clean, well-maintained pension has been upgraded, with all but one of the rooms having ensuite bathrooms. All have fridges but air-con costs extra. Tony also has roomy well-equipped studio apartments nearby that are similarly priced, and excellent for families or longer stays.

Omonia & Surrounds
Hotel Exarchion (Map p74; ☎ 210 380 0731; www.ex archion.com; Themistokleous 55, Exarhia; s/d/tr €35/45/56-60; ❋) Right in the heart of bohemian Exarhia, this dated and rather bland 1960s high-rise hotel offers cheap and clean accommodation complete with washing facilities and an Internet café in the foyer. There's a rooftop café-bar from which you can watch the action below.

CAMPING
Athens Camping (☎ 210 581 4114; www.camping athens.com.gr; Leof Athinon 198; camp sites per adult/tent €6/4; ☯ year-round) This unattractive place, 7km west of the city centre on the road to Corinth, is the nearest camping ground to Athens. It has reasonable facilities but little else going for it.

Midrange
PLAKA & SYNTAGMA
Central Hotel (Map p88; ☎ 210 322 1553; www.central hotel.gr; Apollonos 21, Plaka; s/d/tr incl buffet breakfast from €99/121/165; ❋) This stylish hotel has been decorated in modern tones. It has comfortable rooms with all the mod cons and decent bathrooms. There is a lovely roof terrace with Acropolis views, which has a small Jacuzzi and sun lounges. Central is in a handy location between Syntagma and Plaka.

Niki Hotel (Map p88; ☎ 210 322 0913; www.nikihotel .gr; Nikis 27, Syntagma; s/d/q incl buffet breakfast €60/88/180; ❋) This small hotel bordering Plaka has undergone one of the more stylish makeovers in the area, with a contemporary design and furnishings. The rooms are well-appointed and there is a two-level suite for families with balconies offering Acropolis views.

MONASTIRAKI
Hotel Attalos (Map p88; ☎ 210 321 2801; www.attalos hotel.com; Athinas 29; s/d/tr €72/96/119; ❋) Though decor has never been its strong point, this nonetheless comfortable hotel was refurbished in 2004. Its best feature is the rooftop bar that offers wonderful views of the Acropolis by night, and the rooms at the back with Acropolis views from the balconies. All rooms have TV.

MAKRIGIANNI & KOUKAKI
Art Gallery Hotel (Map p74; ☎ 210 923 8376; www .artgalleryhotel.gr; Erehthiou 5; s/d €90/105; ❋) This

small, family-run place is full of personal touches and artwork. Some rooms are a little small but all have been refurbished, with new bathrooms. Original furniture from the '60s has been retained in the communal areas, maintaining its charm. There is a balcony with Acropolis views where you can have a generous breakfast (€7).

OMONIA & SURROUNDS

Fresh Hotel (Map p88; ☎ 210 524 8511; www.freshhotel .gr; Sofokleous 26 & Klisthenous, Omonia; d/ste incl buffet breakfast from €150/350; 🖳 🖃) This designer hotel led the trend for hip hotels in the gritty Omonia area. Once inside, the seediness gives way to chic rooms and suites with individual colour schemes, clever lighting and all the mod cons, while the fantastic rooftop with pool, bar and restaurant with Acropolis views couldn't be further from the world below.

Top End

There are some lovely luxury hotels in Athens but the upper end of the market is generally outrageously priced, though you can find the odd discount off season.

St George Lycabettus Hotel (Map p88; ☎ 210 729 0711/719; www.sglycabettus.gr; Kleomenous 2, Kolonaki; d from €145; 🖳 🖃 🅿) It's a bit of a hike up the hill to this boutique hotel at the foot of Lykavittos Hill, in chic Kolonaki. But you can look forward to cooling off in the rooftop pool and enjoying the spectacular view from the bar (and many of the rooms). The rooms are individually decorated and renovated. A luxury spa centre opened in 2005.

EATING

For most people, Plaka is the place to be. It's hard to beat the atmosphere of an afternoon coffee break in its cobbled streets or dining out beneath the floodlit Acropolis.

Budget

PLAKA

Taverna Vizantino (Map p88; ☎ 210 322 7368; Kydathineon 18; specials €4.80-8) This taverna is the best of the restaurants around Plateia Filomousou Eterias. Its menu is realistically priced and it's popular with locals year-round. The daily specials are good value, with dishes like stuffed tomatoes pastitsio and excellent fish soup (€6.80 with fish served on side).

Paradosiako (Map p88; ☎ 210 321 3121; Voulis 44a; specials €4-9) For great traditional fare at very fair prices you can't beat this inconspicuous, no-frills taverna on the edge of Plaka. There's a basic menu but it is best to choose from the daily specials, which include fresh and delicious seafood. Get there early before the Greeks arrive.

Taverna Damigos (Map p88; ☎ 210 322 5084; Kydathineon 41; mains €4.50-8; 🕒 11am-1am Sep-Jun) Opened by the Damigos family in 1865, this quaint place claims to be the oldest taverna in Plaka. The house speciality is *bakaliaros* (cod fried in batter), eaten with lashings of *skordalia* (garlic and potato dip), and washed down with plenty of house wine.

Platanos (Map p74; ☎ 210 321 8734; Diogenous 4; mayirefta €5-8; closed Sun) This age-old Plaka taverna is in a pleasant setting away from the main tourist drag, with tables outside in the courtyard under a giant plane tree. It is popular among locals and tourists for its reliable, delicious home-style fare, such as oven-baked potatoes with lemon and oregano.

SYNTAGMA

Ariston (Map p88; ☎ 210 322 7626; Voulis 10; pies €1-1.50; 🕒 10am-4pm Mon-Fri) Traditional *tiropites* (cheese pies) and their various permutations make the perfect snack or light meal. This place has been around since 1910, serving the best range of tasty, freshly baked pies with all manner of fillings.

MAKRIGIANNI & KOUKAKI

Gardenia Restaurant (Map p74; ☎ 210 922 5831; Zini 31; mains €3.50-6) The Gardenia is a typical old-fashioned neighbourhood place turning out solid taverna food at old-fashioned prices. Cheerful owners Nikos and Gogo reckon they have the best prices in Athens.

To 24 Hours (Map p74; ☎ 210 922 2749; Syngrou 44; mains €5-7.50; 🕒 24hr) This is something of an institution among Athenian night owls. The place never closes, except on Easter Sunday, and is busiest in the wee hours. The customers are as much of an attraction as the food: you'll be rubbing shoulders with cabbies, middle-aged couples dressed for the opera, and leather-clad gays from the area's many bars – all tucking into steaming bowls of the speciality, *patsas* (tripe soup). It also has a changing choice of other popular dishes.

KOLONAKI

Food Company (Map p74; ☎ 210 363 0373; Anagnostopoulou 47; mains €5-7) This casual café-style restaurant serves an interesting range of healthy salads, and hot and cold pasta and noodle dishes. The house wine is an excellent red from Nemea and the cheesecake is delicious.

Midrange
PLAKA & SYNTAGMA

Palia Taverna tou Psara (Map p88; ☎ 210 321 8734; Erehtheos 16, Plaka; mezedes €3.50-11.50, top fish per kg €47) Hidden away from the main hustle and bustle of Plaka, this fish tavern is a cut above the Plaka crowd. There is a choice of *mezedes* – the *melitzanokeftedes* (aubergine croquettes) are particularly good – but it is known as the best seafood tavern in Plaka. You'll need to get in early to secure a table on the terrace, which has views out over the city.

AKROPOLI & THISIO

Filistron (Map p88; ☎ 210 346 7554; Apostolou Pavlou 23, Thisio; mezedes €4.50-10; ⏰ closed Mon) You may be hard pressed finding a table for dinner at this excellent *mezedopoleio* which serves an interesting range of reasonably priced, tasty *mezedes* in a prized setting – a rooftop terrace looking out over the Acropolis. Try their baked potato with smoked cheese and pepper or the *mastelo*, a fried cheese from Chios in a tomato sauce.

To Steki tou Ilia (Map p88; ☎ 210 345 8052; Eptahalkou 5; chops portion €7.80; ⏰ 8pm-late) This *psistaria* specialising in tasty grilled lamb chops has achieved celebrity status. There are tables outside on the pedestrian mall opposite the church. For those who don't eat lamb, there are pork chops and steaks as well as dips, chips and salads.

MONASTIRAKI

Oineas (Map p88; ☎ 210 321 5614; Esopou 9, Psiri; 7; appetisers €5-9.50) This cheery place on a pedestrian street in Psiri stands out for the walls of kitsch Greek ads and retro paraphernalia. There are some creative dishes on the menu and excellent generous salads, best shared. Try the cheese pie made with *kataifi* (angelhair pastry).

Pak Indian Restaurant (Map p88; ☎ 210 321 9412; Menandrou 13; mains €8.50-13) This was one of the first and best-regarded of the Indian-Pakistani curry restaurants that sprouted around the backstreets of Omonia near the central Market. It is slicker than most and is popular with Greeks.

Top End

Athens has a great variety of upmarket, blow-the-budget dining options in Athens. Reservations are essential.

Spondi (Map p74; ☎ 210 752 0658; Pironos 5, Pangrati; mains €28-37; ⏰ 8pm-late) This excellent restaurant has been consistently voted Athens best and the accolades are deserved. Spondi offers Mediterranean *haute cuisine*, with heavy French influences, in a relaxed, classy setting. There is a lovely garden terrace draped in bougainvillea in summer. This is definitely a special-occasion place.

Self-Catering
MARKETS

You'll find the widest range of whatever's in season, and the best prices at the central markets on Athinas, halfway between Plateia Omonias and Plateia Monastirakiou. The **fruit and vegetable market** (Map p88) is on the western side of Athinas, and the **meat market** (Map p88) is opposite on the eastern side. The stretch of Athinas between the meat market and Plateia Monastirakiou is the place to shop for nuts and nibblies.

SUPERMARKETS

You can find the following supermarkets in central Athens:
Marinopoulos Konakki (Map p74; Kanari 9); Omonia (Map p74; Athinas 60)
Vasilopoulou (Map p88; Stadiou 19, Syntagma)
Veropoulos (Map p74; Parthenos 6, Koukaki)

DRINKING
Cafés

En Athinais (Map p88; ☎ 210 345 3018; Iraklidon 12, Thisio) There are great views from the tables outside this neoclassical building on the pedestrian walk.

Da Capo (Map p88; Tsakalof 1, Kolonaki) Reputed to have Athens' best coffee but is more a prime people-watching spot. It's self-serve if you can find a table.

Yellow Cafe (Map p88; ☎ 210 331 9029; Karageorgi Servias 9 & Voulis) This cheery café has a great range of sandwiches and juices as well as plenty of caffeinated options.

Of the local chains, **Flocafe** (Apostolou Pavlou, Thisio & other locations) has decent coffees, and great snacks and (unlike rival Starbucks) table service, while **Street Cafe** (Map p88; Koraï Arcade) has arguably the cheapest coffee in town. Both chains have several outlets.

Bars

Brettos (Map p88; ☎ 210 323 2110; Kydathineon 41, Plaka; ☺ 10am-midnight) This delightful Plaka bar has a wall of colourful bottles that is backlit at night. Huge barrels line one wall, and there are limited seats from which you can sample shots of Brettos' own ouzo, brandy and other spirits (€1.50 to €3) as well as wine from the family winery and distillery.

Mike's Irish Bar (☎ 210 777 6797; www.mikesirish bar.gr; Sinopis 6, Ambelokipi; ☺ 8pm-4am) A long-time favourite of the city's expat community, who come to play darts and sip pints of Guinness or Murphy's stout. There's live music nightly from 11.30pm.

Craft (☎ 210 646 2350; Leof Alexandras 205, Ambelokipi) At Greece's first (and only) boutique brewery, drinkers can sample the various house brews safe in the knowledge that there's plenty more bubbling away in the giant stainless-steel vats in the background. It is also a restaurant.

Gay & Lesbian Venues

The greatest concentration of gay bars is around Makrigianni, south of the Temple of Olympian Zeus. Most places open at 11pm, but you won't find much of a crowd until after midnight. Popular spots include the long-running **Granazi Bar** (Map p74; ☎ 210 924 4185; Lembesi 20, Makrigianni; admission €6 with free drink) and the **Lamda Club** (Map p74; ☎ 210 922 4202; Lembesi 15, Makrigianni; admission €6 with free drink).

ENTERTAINMENT

The best source of entertainment information is the weekly listings magazine *Athinorama*, but you'll need to be able to read some Greek to make much sense of it. It costs €1.50 and is available from *periptera* (kiosks) all over the city.

English-language listings appear daily in the *Kathimerini* supplement that accompanies the *International Herald Tribune*, while the *Athens News* carries a weekly entertainment guide.

Greek Folk Dancing

Dora Stratou Dance Company (Map p74; ☎ 210 921 4650; www.grdance.org; Dora Stratou Theatre, Filopappou Hill; adult/concession €15/10; ☺ performances 9.30pm Tue-Sat, 8.15pm Sun May-Sep) Every summer the Dora Stratou company performs its repertoire of folk dances at its open-air theatre on western side of Filopappou Hill. Formed

to preserve the country's folk culture, it has gained an international reputation for authenticity and professionalism. The theatre is signposted from the western end of Dionysiou Areopagitou. Take trolleybus 22 from Syntagma and get off at Agios Ioannis.

Live Music

Athens has a healthy rock music scene and is on most European touring schedules. In summer check Rockwave and other festival schedules, as you may be able to see your favourite band perform in open-air theatres around town.

Gagarin 205 Club (Liosion 205) Primarily a rock venue, with gigs on Fridays and Saturdays featuring leading rock and underground music bands. Tickets are available from **Ticket House** (Map p88; ☎ 210 360 8366; Panepistimiou 42).

AN Club (Map p74; ☎ 210 330 5056; Solomou 13-15, Exarhia) The small AN Club hosts lesser-known international bands, as well as some interesting local bands.

Half Note Jazz Club (Map p74; ☎ 210 921 3310; Trivonianou 17, Mets) Jazz fans should head to this club opposite the Athens First Cemetery. It hosts an array of international names.

Top-name international acts play at a variety of venues, including the spectacular **Lykavittos Theatre** (p87) on Lykavittos Hill and the **Panathinaïkos Football Stadium** (Leof Alexandras).

Nightclubs

Admission to most places ranges from €5, Monday to Thursday, to €10 Friday and Saturday. The price often includes one free drink. Subsequently, expect to pay about €3 for soft drinks, €5 for a beer and €8 for spirits. Clubs don't start to get busy until around midnight.

Lava Bore (Map p88; ☎ 210 324 5335; Filellinon 25; ☺ 10pm-5am) The Lava Bore stays open all year and caters largely to tourists. The formula stays the same: a mixture of mainstream rock and techno and (relatively) cheap drinks. It's more casual that most clubs. The admission fee includes one drink.

Venue (Map p88; ☎ 210 331 7801; Agias Eleousis & Kakourgiodikeio, Psiri) This popular club plays the latest dance music in Psiri during winter and in summer moves the partying to a massive venue at **Varkiza** (☎ 210 897 1763), which is 30km along the Athens-Sounion Rd.

Kalua (Map p88; ☎ 210 360 8304; Amerikis 6) This established downtown club plays mainstream music and the odd Greek disco hit and usually rocks till dawn. Don't even get there before midnight.

SHOPPING
Flea Market
This market is the first place to spring to people's minds when they think of shopping in Athens. It's the commercial area that stretches west of Plateia Monastirakiou and consists of shops selling goods running the whole gamut from high quality to trash. These shops are open daily during normal business hours.

However, when most people speak of the Athens flea market, they are referring to the Sunday **flea market** (Map p88; ☽ 7am-2pm Sun), which spills over into Plateia Monastirakiou and onto Ermou. A visit to Athens isn't complete without a visit to the Sunday market. All manner of things – from new to fourth-hand – are on sale.

There's everything to be found on sale from clocks to condoms, binoculars to *bouzouki* (stringed lutelike instrument), tyres to telephones, giant evil eyes to jelly babies, and wigs to welding kits.

Traditional Handicrafts
Hellenic Folk Art Gallery (Map p88; ☎ 210 325 0524; cnr Apollonos & Ypatias, Plaka; ☽ 9am-8pm Tue-Fri, 9am-3pm Mon & Sat) Run by the National Welfare Organisation, this is a good place for purchasing handicrafts. It has top-quality merchandise and your money goes to a good cause – the preservation and promotion of traditional Greek handicrafts. It has a wide range of knotted carpets, kilims, flokatis, needlepoint rugs and embroidered cushions, as well as a small selection of pottery, copper and woodwork.

Stavros Melissinos (Map p88; ☎ 210 321 9247; www.melissinos-art.com; Agias Theklas 2, Psiri; 10am-2pm & 4-7pm Mon-Sat, 10am-2pm Sun) Athens' famous septuagenarian sandal maker and poet Stavros Melissinos names the Beatles, Rudolph Nureyev, Sophia Loren and Jackie Onassis among his past customers. But fame and fortune have not gone to his head, he still makes the best-value sandals in Athens, a tradition continued by artist son Pantelis. Designs based on Ancient Greek styles in natural leather cost €15 to €23 a pair.

GETTING THERE & AWAY
Air
Athens is served by **Eleftherios Venizelos International Airport** (☎ 210 353 0000; www.aia.gr) at Spata, 27km east of the city. The airport, named after the country's leading 20th-century politician, opened in 2001. Built by a German consortium, the facilities are state of the art and immeasurably better than the former airport, Ellinikon. See Getting Around (p95) for public transport to/from the airport. For international flights to/from Athens see p497 .

DOMESTIC FLIGHTS
Most domestic flights are operated by **Olympic Airlines** (Map p74; ☎ 210 356 9111, 8011 144 444; www.olympicairlines.com; Leof Syngrou 96), which also has branch offices at **Syntagma** (Map p88; ☎ 210 926 4444; Filellinon 15) and **Omonia** (Map p74; ☎ 210 926 7218; Marikas Kotopouli 1). For flight information call ☎ 210 966 6666. The following tables give flight details from Athens to the islands and mainland ports in high season.

OLYMPIC AIRLINES FLIGHTS FROM ATHENS TO THE GREEK ISLANDS

Destination	Flights per week	Duration	Fare
Astypalea	5	1hr	€53
Chios	28	50min	€69
Corfu	14	1hr	€77
Crete (Hania)	35	50min	€84
Crete (Iraklio)	35	50min	€76
Crete (Sitia)	3	80min	€66
Ikaria	4	55min	€47
Kefallonia	14	65min	€75
Kos	21	55min	€93
Kythira	7	45min	€43
Leros	7	1hr	€54
Lesvos	28	50min	€78
Limnos	7	55min	€65
Milos	7	45min	€52
Mykonos	35	40min	€88
Naxos	8	45min	€56
Paros	8	40min	€56
Rhodes	35	1hr	€73
Samos	28	1hr	€79
Santorini	35	50min	€94
Skiathos	7	50min	€53
Skyros	2	35min	€35
Syros	7	35min	€64
Zakynthos	7	1hr	€74

OLYMPIC AIRLINES FLIGHTS FROM ATHENS TO OTHER MAINLAND PORTS

Destination	Flights per week	Duration	Fare
Alexandroupolis	28	65min	€75
Kavala	14	1hr	€75
Preveza	5	1hr	€62
Thessaloniki	49	55min	€90

Aegean Airlines (Map p88; reservations ☎ 801 112 00 00, 210 331 5502; www.aegeanair.com; Othonos 10, Syntagma) provides welcome competition on some of the most popular routes.

It has up to 12 flights per day to Thessaloniki, seven daily to Iraklio, six daily to Rhodes, at least four daily to Mykonos and Santorini, three daily to Hania and Lesvos, two daily to Alexandroupolis and Corfu, and one daily flight to Kavala.

Aegean Airlines has a convenient city centre sales office at).

Bus

There are two main intercity bus stations in Athens.

The first of these stations is **Terminal A** (☎ 210 512 4910; Kifisou 100) about 7km northwest of Plateia Omonias. It has regular departures to the Peloponnese, the Ionian Islands, and western and northern Greece. City bus No 051 (€0.45) runs between the terminal and the junction of Zinonos and Menandrou, near Omonia, every 15 minutes from 5am to midnight.

Terminal B (☎ 210 831 7181; Liosion 260) is about 5km north of Plateia Omonias off Liosion and has departures to central Greece and Evia. While the address is nominally Liosion 260 the terminal is actually one block further east on Agiou Dimitriou Oplon. Liosion 260 is where you will need to get off the No 024 bus that travels from outside the main gate of the National Gardens on Amalias.

From this stop you should turn right onto Gousiou and you'll then see Terminal B at the end of the street.

Buses for Rafina and Lavrio depart from the **SE Attiki Terminal** (Map p74; ☎ 210 821 0872; cnr Alexandras & Patision), which is commonly known as the Mavromateon Terminal. It is located 250m north of the National Archaeological Museum.

For international bus services see p499.

BUS DEPARTURES FROM ATHENS

Bus Terminal A

Destination	Duration	Fare	Frequency
Corfu*	11hr	€32.30	2 daily
Epidavros	2½hr	€9	2 daily
Igoumenitsa	8½hr	€32.60	4 daily
Kalavryta	3½hr	€12.30	1 daily
Lefkada	5½hr	€24.70	4 daily
Nafplio	2½hr	€9.70	hourly
Olympia	5½hr	€21.90	4 daily
Patra	3hr	€13.80	half-hourly
Zakynthos*	7hr	€24.40	8 daily

*prices inclusive of ferry transfers

Bus Terminal B

Destination	Time	Fare	Frequency
Agios Konstantinos	2hr	€11.50	hourly
Delphi	3hr	€11.80	6 daily
Halkida	1hr	€5.10	half-hourly
Karpenisi	5hr	€18.20	3 daily
Trikala	5½hr	€20.60	8 daily
Volos	5hr	€20	9 daily

Se Attiki Terminal (Mavromateon)

Destination	Duration	Fare	Frequency
Cape Sounion via coast road	1½hr	€4.20	hourly
Lavrio port	1¼hr	€3.60	half-hourly
Marathon	1¼hr	€2.60	hourly
Rafina port	1hr	€1.70	half-hourly

Car & Motorcycle

National Road 1 is the main route north. It starts at Nea Kifisia. Take Vasilissis Sofias from Syntagma or the Ymittos ring road via Kaisariani, linking up with the **Attiki Odos**, a toll motorway that links Elefsina with the airport and Central Attiki in the east. National Road 8, begins beyond Dafni and goes to the Peloponnese and northwestern Greece. Take Agiou Konstantinou from Omonia.

Leof Syngrou, near the Temple of Olympian Zeus, is lined with rental firms. Local companies offer better deals than multinationals. An average price for a small car is €46 per day.

Avis (Map p74; ☎ 210 322 4951; Leof Vasilissis Amalias 48)
Budget (Map p74; ☎ 210 921 4771; Leof Syngrou 8)
Europcar (Map p74; ☎ 210 924 8810; Leof Syngrou 36-38)
Hertz (Map p74; ☎ 210 922 0102; Leof Syngrou 12)
Sixt (Map p74; ☎ 210 922 0171; Leof Syngrou 23)

You can rent mopeds and motorcycles if you have the appropriate licence and the confidence to take on the traffic. **Motorent** (Map p74; ☎ 210 923 4939; www.motorent.gr; Rovertou Galli 1, Makrigianni) has a machines from 50cc to 250cc. High season prices for a 50cc scooter start at €18 per day or €110 per week.

Train

Intercity trains to central, northern Greece and the Peloponnese currently leave from **Larisis Train Station** (☎ 210 529 8837; cnr Deligianni & Filadelfias). All future intercity services are due to start operating from the new Central Station at Arharnon which, despite the name, will actually be a good 20km north of the city centre. The main access to the station will be by suburban train. The easiest way to get to the Larisis station is to catch the metro to the Larisa stop on Line 2, which is right outside Larisis station.

Under the new rail system, Larisis station will become a stop on the suburban line between Piraeus and Arharnon.

The **OSE** (☎ 1110; www.ose.gr; ☻ 24hr) has offices at **Omonia** (Map p74; ☎ 210 529 7516; Karolou 1; ☻ 8am-3pm Mon-Fri) and **Syntagma** (Map p88; ☎ 210 362 4402; Sina 6; ☻ 8am-3pm Mon-Sat), which handle advance bookings. See p499 for information on international train services.

GETTING AROUND
To/From the Airport
BUS

There are six special express bus services operating between the airport and the city, including a service between the airport and Piraeus. They leave from between gates 4 and 5 outside the arrivals area.

Service X92 runs between the airport and the northern suburb of Kifisia. Service X93 runs between the airport and the Terminal A (Kifisos) bus station. Service X94 runs between the airport and the Ethniki Amyna metro station. Service X95 operates between the airport and Plateia Syntagmatos and is the most convenient one for central Athens. This line operates 24 hours with services approximately every 20 minutes. The bus stop is outside the National Gardens on Amalias on the eastern side of Plateia Syntagmatos.

Service X96 operates between the airport and Plateia Karaïskaki in Piraeus. This line also operates 24 hours, with services approximately every 15 minutes. Service X97

runs between the airport and the Dafni metro station.

Tickets for all these services cost €2.90 and are valid for one trip only. The journey from the airport to central Athens takes between an hour and 1½ hours, depending on traffic conditions.

Additionally, KTEL Attikis runs express buses from the airport to the port of Rafina (€3) roughly every one hour and 40 minutes; and the port of Lavrio (€4, change at Markopoulo) roughly every two hours.

SUBURBAN RAIL & METRO

From the airport you can take the ultra-modern, Finnish-built suburban rail train (Proastiakos) to the Larisis train station, the Doukissis Plakentias metro station or to Nerantziotissa, on the Piraeus Kifisia ISAP Metro Line. Suburban trains from the airport run from 7.20am to 8.20pm, while trains to the airport from the Larisis train station run from 6.06am to 7.36pm. The trip takes 40 minutes and trains run every 30 minutes. The cost of the ticket between the airport and the Larisis train station is €6.

In parallel, the Metro network also runs to/from the airport by connecting with the metro network at Doukissis Plakentias. Take the metro if you wish to go directly to central Athens. The first metro leaves the airport at 6.30am and the last metro at 8.30pm. From Athens (Syntagma) the first metro leaves at 5.53am and the last one at 7.21pm. One-way tickets also cost €6.

TAXI

Taking a cab from or to the airport is a relatively easy business as long as the basic ground rules are understood and adhered to. Check that the meter is set to the correct tariff (day or night). You will be required to pay in addition to the fare a €3 surcharge on trips *from* the airport, a €2.50 toll for using the toll road connecting the airport to the city plus €0.30 for each piece of luggage over 10kg. Fares vary according to the time of day and level of traffic, but expect to pay about €20 from the airport to the city. In case of a dispute take the taxi driver's permit number and car registration number, and report the details to the tourist police. Drivers can and will be prosecuted for overcharging.

The trip from the airport to the city centre – via the much faster Ymyttos ring road and the Katehaki exit – should take between 40 and 55 minutes depending on traffic. Taxis to Piraeus will take longer and cost more as drivers may prefer to take the longer, but less congested southern loop route via Vari, Voula and Glyfada.

Around Athens

METRO

The slowly expanding **metro system** (www.ametro .gr) has transformed travel in central Athens. Journeys that once took an hour above ground can now be completed in much less time. The stations are an attraction in their own right, displaying finds from archaeological excavations. All have wheelchair access.

Ticket pricing still distinguishes between the old network (Line 1-ISAP) and the metro, and can be confusing. Travel on lines 2 and 3 costs €0.70, while Line 1 is split into three sections: Piraeus–Monastiraki, Monastiraki–Attiki and Attiki–Kifisia. Travel within one section costs €0.60 and a journey covering two or more sections costs €0.70.

Tickets must be validated at the machines at platform entrances. The penalty for travelling without a validated ticket is €29.

The trains run between 5am and midnight. They come every three minutes during peak periods, dropping to every 10 minutes at other times.

Line 1 (Green Line)

The old Kifisia–Piraeus line was the original metro system. Omonia and Attiki are transfer stations with connections to Line 2; Monastiraki is the transfer station for Line 3. Nerantziotissa is the transfer station for the suburban rail line.

Line 2 (Red Line)

Line 2 runs from Agios Antonios in the northwest to Agios Dimitrios in the southeast (check the boards so you don't confuse your saints). Attiki and Omonia are transfer stations for Line 1, while Syntagma is the transfer station for Line 3. Bear in mind that stations are being added as the line expands.

Line 3 (Blue Line)

Line 3 runs northeast from Monastiraki to Doukissis Plakentias, with the suburban airport train continuing from there. Syntagma is the transfer station for Line 2.

Bear in mind that stations are being slowly added as the line expands.

BUS & TROLLEYBUS

The blue-and-white local express and regular buses operate every 15 minutes from 5am until midnight.

Buses run 24 hours between the centre and Piraeus – every 20 minutes from 6am until midnight and then hourly. Trolleybuses also operate from 5am until midnight. The free map handed out by EOT shows most of the routes.

There is a €0.45 ticket valid on both buses and trolleybuses. Tickets must be purchased before you board, either at a transport kiosk or at most *periptera*, and validated on board. Plain-clothed inspectors make spot checks; the penalty for travelling without a validated ticket is €29.

TAXI

Taxis are yellow. To hail a taxi, stand on the pavement and shout your destination as they pass. If a taxi is going your way the driver may stop even if there are passengers inside. This does not mean the fare will be shared: each person will be charged the fare shown on the meter. If you get in one that does not have passengers, make sure the meter is on.

The flag fall is €0.85, with a €0.80 surcharge from ports and train and bus stations, and a €3 surcharge from the airport. After that, the day rate (tariff 1 on the meter) is €0.30 per km. The night tariff (tariff 2 on the meter) increases to €0.56 between midnight and 5am. Baggage is charged at the rate of €0.30 per item over 10kg. The minimum fare is €1.75.

TRAM

The **tram** (www.tramsa.gr) network that began operating in 2004 makes for a scenic journey along the coast to Faliro and Glyfada, but it is not the fastest means of transport.

Line 4 runs from Syntagma to the Faliro Peace and Friendship Stadium and Line 5 takes the same route to the coast then goes along the beach to Glyfada. The tram runs from 5am to 1am Monday to Thursday and is a 24-hour service from Friday night to Sunday. Services run every seven to eight minutes, reducing to every 40 minutes after midnight on Friday and Saturday. The trip from Syntagma to Faliro takes 43 to 47 minutes, while Syntagma to Glyfada takes 52 to 57 minutes. The central terminus is on Amalias, opposite the National Gardens. Purchase tickets at vending machines on the platforms (€0.60 adult, €0.30 student).

THE MAINLAND PORTS

This section is designed to provide all the information a traveller needs to get from the mainland to the islands. It begins with the ports that serve more than one island group: Piraeus, Rafina, Thessaloniki and Gythio. The remaining ports are grouped according to the island groups they serve.

PIRAEUS ΠΕΙΡΑΙΑΣ
pop 175,697

Apart from being a port for Athens, Piraeus is Greece's main port and one of the Mediterranean's major ports. It's the hub of the Aegean ferry network; centre for Greece's maritime export-import and transit trade; and base for its large merchant navy. Nowadays, Athens has expanded sufficiently to meld imperceptibly into Piraeus.

History

The histories of Athens and Piraeus are inextricably linked. Themistocles transferred his Athenian fleet from the exposed port of Phaleron (modern Faliro) to the security of Piraeus at the start of the 5th century BC. Piraeus was a flourishing commercial centre during the classical age but, by Roman times, it had been overtaken by Rhodes, Delos and Alexandria. During medieval and Turkish times Piraeus shrank to a tiny fishing village and by the time Greece became independent

it was home to fewer than 20 people. Its resurgence began in 1834 when Athens became the capital of independent Greece. By the start of the 20th century, Piraeus had superseded Syros as Greece's principal port.

Orientation

Piraeus is 10km southwest of Athens. The largest of its three harbours is the Great Harbour (Megas Limin), on the western side of the Piraeus peninsula, which is the departure point for all ferry, hydrofoil and catamaran services. Zea Marina (Limin Zeas) and the picturesque Mikrolimano (small harbour), on the eastern side, are for private yachts.

The metro and suburban train lines from Athens terminate at the northeastern corner of the Great Harbour on Akti Kalimassioti. The suburban train station is much handier for Cretan ferries while the metro station is convenient for other island ferries.

Information

Emporiki Bank (cnr Antistaseos & Makras Stoas) Has a 24-hour automatic exchange machine.

Internet Center (☎ 2104 111 261; Akti Poseidonos 24; ☽ 10am-11pm)

National Bank of Greece (cnr Antistaseos & Tsamadou) Near the Emporiki Bank

Post Office (cnr Tsamadou & Filonos; ☽ 7.30am-8pm Mon-Fri, 7.30am-2pm Sat)

Sleeping

There's no reason to stay at any of the shabby cheap hotels around the Great Harbour when Athens is so close. The cheap hotels are geared more towards accommodating sailors than tourists. Whatever happens, don't attempt to sleep out – Piraeus is the most dangerous place in Greece to do so.

WHICH PORT?

The following list details the ports serving each island group:

- Crete – Piraeus, Thessaloniki, Gythio, Kalamata
- Cyclades – Piraeus, Rafina, Thessaloniki, Lavrio
- Dodecanese – Piraeus, Thessaloniki, Alexandroupolis
- Evia & the Sporades – Rafina (Evia only), Agios Konstantinos, Volos
- Ionians – Patra, Igoumenitsa, Kyllini, Piraeus (Kythira only), Gythio (Kythira and Antikythira only), Neapoli (Kythira only)
- Northeastern Aegean – Piraeus, Thessaloniki, Kavala, Alexandroupolis
- Saronic Gulf Islands – Piraeus, Porto Heli, Ermione, Galatas

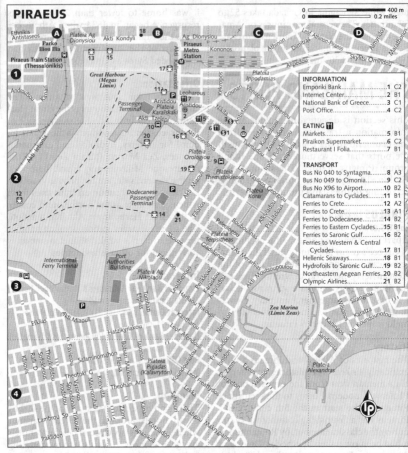

PIRAEUS

| 0 | 400 m |
| 0 | 0.2 miles |

INFORMATION
Emporiki Bank.....................1 C2
Internet Center....................2 B1
National Bank of Greece.....3 C1
Post Office...........................4 C2

EATING
Markets...............................5 B1
Piraikon Supermarket..........6 C2
Restaurant I Folia................7 B1

TRANSPORT
Bus No 040 to Syntagma.....8 A3
Bus No 049 to Omonia........9 C2
Bus No X96 to Airport........10 B2
Catamarans to Cyclades.....11 B1
Ferries to Crete..................12 A2
Ferries to Crete..................13 A1
Ferries to Dodecanese.......14 B2
Ferries to Eastern Cyclades..15 B1
Ferries to Saronic Gulf.......16 B2
Ferries to Western & Central
   Cyclades.........................17 B1
Hellenic Seaways...............18 B1
Hydrofoils to Saronic Gulf....19 B2
Northeastern Aegean Ferries..20 B2
Olympic Airlines.................21 B2

Eating

There are dozens of cafés, restaurants and
fast-food places along the waterfront at
Great Harbour.

Tiny **Restaurant I Folia** (☎ 210 421 0781; Akti
Poseidonos 30; mains €3-5), opposite the passenger
terminal, is perfect for a quick bite before
you board a ferry.

If you need to stock up on some supplies before your ferry trip, you should
head straight for the area just inland from
Poseidonos. You will also find fresh fruit
and vegetables for sale at the **markets** on
Demosthenous.

Located just opposite the markets is **Piraikon Supermarket** (☎ 210 411 7177; ⏰ 8am-8pm
Mon-Fri, 8am-4pm Sat).

Getting There & Away

AIR

Olympic Airlines (☎ 210 926 7560) has an office
at Akti Miaouli 27.

BUS

Buses Nos 040 and 049 operate 24 hours a
day and run between Piraeus and central
Athens. The buses run every 20 minutes
from 6am until midnight and then they
run hourly.

Bus No 040 operates between Akti Xave-
riou in Piraeus and Filellinon in Athens.
This is the only bus service that actually
passes closest to Zea Marina; the most
convenient stop is outside Hotel Savoy on
Iroön Polytehniou.

Bus No 049 runs between Plateia Themistokleous in Piraeus and Plateia Omonias in Syntagma, Athens. The fare is €0.45 on each service. E96 buses to the airport leave from the southwestern corner of Plateia Karaïskaki.There are no intercity buses to or from Piraeus.

FERRY

Piraeus is the busiest port in Greece with a bewildering array of departures and destinations, including daily services to all the island groups except the Ionians and Sporades.The following table lists all the destinations that can be reached by ferry. The information is for the high season – from mid-June to September.

For the latest departure information, pick up a weekly ferry schedule from EOT in Athens (p76). See the Getting There & Away sections for each island for specific details, and p503 for general information about ferry travel.

The departure points for ferry destinations are shown on the map of Piraeus. Note that there are two departure points for Crete.

Ferries for Iraklio depart from the western end of Akti Kondyli, but the ferries for other ports in Crete occasionally dock there as well.

The other departure point for Crete is on Akti Miaouli; it's a long way between the two, so check where to find your boat when you buy your ticket.

FERRIES FROM PIRAEUS

Crete

Destination	Duration	Fare	Frequency
Agios Nikolaos	12hr	€27.70	3 weekly
Hania	10hr	€23.50	2 daily
Iraklio	10hr	€30	2 daily
Kastelli-Kissamos	12hr	€20	2 weekly
Rethymno	10-12hr	€23.10	daily
Sitia	14½hr	€25.30	3 weekly

Cyclades

Destination	Time	Fare	Frequency
Anafi	11hr	€24.70	4 weekly
Folegandros	6-9hr	€18.40	4 weekly
Ios	7½hr	€23.30	4 daily
Kimolos	6hr	€16.60	2 weekly
Kythnos	2½hr	€11.30	daily
Milos	7hr	€17.90	2 daily
Mykonos	5½hr	€22.60	3 daily
Naxos	6hr	€21.70	6 daily
Paros	5hr	€22.40	6 daily
Santorini	9hr	€26.10	daily
Serifos	4½hr	€14.30	daily
Sifnos	5½hr	€16	daily
Syros	4hr	€19.40	3 daily
Tinos	4½hr	€20.80	daily

Dodecanese

Destination	Time	Fare	Frequency
Astypalea	12hr	€25.10	3 weekly
Halki	20hr	€33	4 weekly
Kalymnos	10-13hr	€31.30	daily
Karpathos	18½hr	€28	4 weekly
Kasos	17hr	€27.70	4 weekly
Kos	12-15hr	€33.50	2 daily
Leros	11hr	€28.40	daily
Lipsi	16hr	€27	weekly
Nisyros	13-15hr	€27.80	2 weekly
Patmos	9½hr	€27.20	daily
Rhodes	15-18hr	€39.80	2 daily
Symi	15-17hr	€32.60	2 weekly
Tilos	15hr	€27.80	2 weekly

Northeastern Aegean Islands

Destination	Time	Fare	Frequency
Chios	8hr	€21.20	daily
Fourni	10hr	€18	3 weekly
Ikaria	9hr	€20.20	daily
Lesvos	12hr	€26.20	daily
Limnos	13hr	€26	3 weekly
Samos	13hr	€24.70	2 daily

Saronic Gulf Islands

Destination	Time	Fare	Frequency
Aegina	1¼hr	€5	hourly
Hydra	3½hr	€8.40	2 daily
Poros	2½hr	€7.80	4 daily
Spetses	4½hr	€11.20	daily

HYDROFOIL & CATAMARAN

Hellenic Seaways (☎ 210 419 9000; cnr Akti Kondyli & Elotikou; www.hellenicseaways.gr) has hydrofoil and catamaran services from Piraeus to the Saronic Gulf Islands and the Cyclades.

The information in the hydrofoil and catamarans timetable following is for the high season, from mid-June to September.

For more information about these services, see the Transport chapter (p497) and the Getting There & Away sections for each island throughout this book.

HYDROFOILS & CATAMARANS FROM PIRAEUS

Cyclades

Destination	Time	Fare	Frequency
Kythnos	1¾hr	€22.10	5 weekly
Milos	4¼hr	€35.30	6 weekly
Mykonos	3½hr	€37.30	3 daily
Naxos	3¼hr	€37	2 daily
Paros	3-5hr	€37	3 daily
Ios	3¾hr	€41	1 daily
Santorini	5¼hr	€43.10	daily
Serifos	2¼hr	€27.90	daily
Sifnos	2¾hr	€31.50	daily
Syros	2½hr	€31.80	2 daily
Tinos	3¾hr	€34.20	daily

Peloponnese

Destination	Time	Fare	Frequency
Ermioni	2hr	€18.20	3 daily
Porto Heli	2hr	€21.60	4 daily

Saronic Gulf Islands

Destination	Time	Fare	Frequency
Aegina	35min	€8.60	hourly
Hydra	1¼hr	€17.30	6 daily
Poros	1hr	€15.40	4 daily
Spetses	2hr	€23.90	4 daily

METRO

The metro is the fastest and easiest way of getting from the Great Harbour to central Athens (see p96). The station is at the northern end of Akti Kalimassioti. Travellers should take extra care of valuables on the metro; the section between Piraeus and Monastiraki is notorious for pickpockets.

TRAIN

The Piraeus train station is the terminus of the new suburban rail network. Suburban trains run from here to the new Central Station at Arharnon (p95).

RAFINA ΡΑΦΗΝΑ

pop 11,909

Tucked into Attica's east coast, Rafina is Athens' main fishing port and second-most important port for passenger ferries. It is smaller than Piraeus and less confusing – and fares

are about 20% cheaper, but you have to spend an hour on the bus and €2 to get there.

The **port police** (☎ 22940 22300) occupies a kiosk near the quay, which is lined with fish restaurants and ticket agents. The main square, Plateia Plastira, is at the top of the ramp leading to the port.

Getting There & Away

BUS

There are frequent buses from the SE Attiki (Mavromateon) terminal in Athens to Rafina (€2, one hour) between 5.45am and 10.30pm. The first bus leaves Rafina at 5.50am and the last at 10.15pm.

CATAMARAN

Blue Star Ferries operates high-speed catamarans to the Cyclades. There is a daily 7.40am service to Tinos (€30.10, 1¾ hours), Mykonos (€34, two hours 10 minutes) and Paros (€34.60, three hours), and a 4pm service to Tinos and Mykonos.

FERRY

Blue Star Ferries run a daily service at 8.05am to Andros (€9.90, two hours), Tinos (€15, 3¾ hours) and Mykonos (€17, 4½ hours). It also has a 7.15pm daily ferry to Andros.

Hellas Ferries sails to Andros and Tinos in the mornings for the same price and adds Mykonos to the route in the afternoons.

There are also five ferries daily to the port of Marmari on the island of Evia (€5.10, one hour).

THESSALONIKI ΘΕΣΣΑΛΟΝΙΚΗ

pop 363,987

It may be Greece's second-largest city, but being second does not mean Thessaloniki (thess-ah-lo-nee-kih) lies in the shadow of, or tries to emulate, the capital. It is a sophisticated city with its own distinct character.

Thessaloniki sits at the top of the Thermaic Gulf. The oldest part of the city is the Turkish quarter, with streets circling the Byzantine fortress on the slopes of Mt Hortiatis.

Orientation

Thessaloniki is laid out on a grid stretching back from Leof Nikis, which runs from the port in the west to the White Tower (Lefkos Pyrgos) in the east. The two main squares, both abutting the waterfront, are Plateia Eleftherias, which doubles as a local bus terminal, and Plateia Aristotelous. The other main streets of Mitropoleos, Tsimiski, Ermou and Egnatia run parallel to Leof Nikis. Egnatia is the main thoroughfare, running east from Plateia Dimokratias. Kastra, the old Turkish quarter, is north of Plateia Dimokratias.

Information

BOOKSHOPS
Molho (☎ 2310 275 27; Tsimiski 10) Has a comprehensive stock of English-language books, magazines, newspapers and good maps of Greece by Road Editions and Emvelia Publications.

EMERGENCY
First-Aid Centre (☎ 2310 530 530; Navarhou Koundourioti 10)
Ippokration Hospital (☎ 2310 837 921; Papanastasiou 50) Two kilometres east of the city centre.
Tourist Police (☎ 2310 554 871; 5th floor, Dodekanisou 4; ⏰ 7.30am-11pm)

INTERNET ACCESS
IQ Station (☎ 2310 213 654; Agiou Dimitriou 59; per hr €2; ⏰ 24hr)
MultiPlayer (☎ 2310 968 289; Olymbou 124; per hr €2.20; ⏰ 9.30am-3amr)

LAUNDRY
Bianca Laundrette (Panagias Dexias 3; per 6kg load €6; ⏰ 8am-8.30pm Tue, Thu & Fri, 8am-3pm Mon, Wed & Sat;)

MONEY
National Bank of Greece (Tsimiski 11) Opens at the weekend for currency exchange.

POST
Main Post Office (Aristelous 26; ⏰ 7.30am-8pm Mon-Fri, 7.30am-2.15pm Sat, 9am-1.30pm Sun)
Port Post Office (Koundourioti 6; ⏰ 7.30am-2pm)

TOURIST INFORMATION
EOT (☎ 2310 500 310; Port Passenger Terminal; ⏰ 7.30am-3pm Mon-Fri, 8am-2pm Sat)

Sights
The **Archaeological Museum** (☎ 2310 830 538; Manoli Andronikou 6; admission €4; ⏰ 8.30am-3pm Tue-Sun, 10.30am-5pm Mon) houses finds from prehistoric Thessaloniki, including a well-preserved **Petralona hoard** – a collection of axes and chisels, and some filigree gold wreaths and jewellery from burial sites all over Macedonia.

The **Museum of Ancient Greek & Byzantine Instruments** (☎ 2310 555 263; Katouni 12-14; admission €4.40; ⏰ 9am-3pm & 5-10pm Tue-Sun) houses a superb collection of instruments from antiquity to the 19th century.

The imposing **Arch of Galerius**, at the eastern end of Egnatia, is the finest of the city's Roman monuments. It was erected in AD 303 to celebrate the emperor's victories over the Persians in 297. The nearby **Rotunda** was built as a mausoleum for Galerius, but never fulfilled this function; Constantine the Great transformed it into a church.

The 15th-century **white tower** (☎ 2310 267 832; Lefkos Pyrgos; adult €2; ⏰ 8am-7pm Tue-Sun & 12.30-7pm Mon) is both the city's symbol and most prominent landmark. During the 18th century the tower was used as a prison for insubordinate janissaries. In 1826 they were massacred there and it was known as the 'bloody tower'. After independence it was whitewashed as a gesture to expunge its Turkish function. You can climb to the top via a wide circular stairway – the views from the top are impressive and there is a small café.

The Turkish quarter of **Kastra**, with its narrow steep streets flanked by timber-framed houses and tiny, whitewashed dwellings with shutters, is all that is left of 19th-century Thessaloniki. The original ramparts of Kastra were built by Theodosius (379–475), but were rebuilt in the 14th century. From Kastra there are stunning views of modern Thessaloniki and the Thermaic Gulf.

Take bus No 22 or 23 from Plateia Eleftherias, or walk north along Agias Sofias, which becomes Vlatadon then Dimadou Vlatadou after Athinas, and turn right into Eptapyrgiou at the top.

Sleeping
Hotel Acropol (☎ 2310 536 170; fax 2310 528 492; Tandalidou 4; s/d €18/26) The Acropol is the best budget option. It's clean and quiet, and the rooms are basic but comfortable. There is a small courtyard for bicycle storage and luggage can also be stored for free.

Orestias Kastoria (☎ 2310 276 517; fax 2310 276 572; Agnostou Stratioti 14; s/d €40/50; ❄) The Orestias Kastoria occupies a beautifully renovated neoclassical building a little away from the main hotel strip. While the hotel is nominally D-class, the comfortable rooms are bright and airy, and come with TV and phone.

Hotel Alexandria (☎ 2310 536 185; fax 2310 536 154; Egnatia 18; s/d €45/50) This D-class hotel has been renovated in recent times and offers

THESSALONIKI

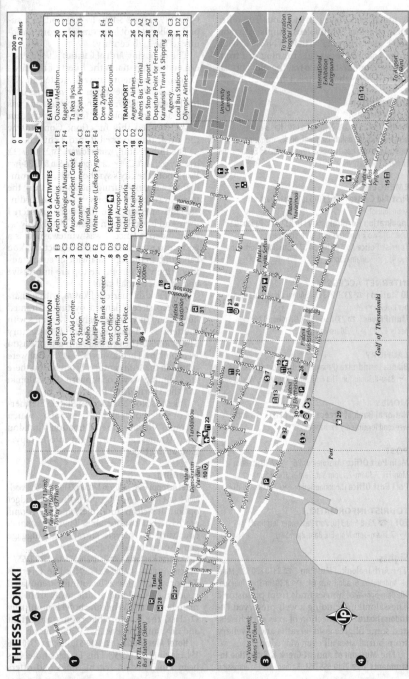

INFORMATION
Bianca Laundrette.....................	1 B3
EOT..	2 C3
First-Aid Centre.........................	3 C3
IQ Station.................................	4 D2
Molho......................................	5 C3
MultiPlayer...............................	6 E2
National Bank of Greece............	7 C3
Post Office................................	8 D3
Post Office................................	9 C3
Tourist Police............................	10 B2

SIGHTS & ACTIVITIES
Arch of Galerius........................	11 E3
Archaeological Museum..............	12 F4
Museum of Ancient Greek &	
Byzantine Instruments...........	13 C3
Rotunda...................................	14 E3
White Tower (Lefkos Pyrgos).....	15 E4

SLEEPING
Hotel Acropol...........................	16 C2
Hotel Alexandria.......................	17 D2
Orestias Kastoria.......................	18 D2
Tourist Hotel............................	19 C3

EATING
Ouzou Melathron.......................	20 C3
Ragoti......................................	21 E3
Ta Nea Ilysia.............................	22 C2
Ta Spata Psistaria......................	23 D3

DRINKING
Dore Zythos..............................	24 E4
Kourdisto Gourouni...................	25 D3

TRANSPORT
Aegean Airlines.........................	26 C3
Athens Bus Terminal.................	27 A2
Bus Stop for Airport..................	28 A2
Departure Point for Ferries........	29 C4
Karahatsis Travel & Shipping	
Agency.................................	30 C3
Local Bus Station......................	31 D2
Olympic Airlines........................	32 C3

clean, tidy rooms with bathroom and TV. There's a rather impressive modern lift to hoist your heavy backpacks to the rooms.

Tourist Hotel (☎ 2310 270 501; www.touristhotel .gr; Mitropoleos 21; s/d/tr €53/70/90; ✕) The C-class Tourist Hotel has a spacious lounge with comfortable armchairs and a TV. Rooms are good enough, though the reception area is a little spartan and small.

Eating

Ta Nea Ilysia (☎ 2310 536 996; Leondos Sofou 17; mains €3-6) This is a clean and cheery place equally popular with travellers and locals, conveniently near the west-end budget-hotel strip with moderately priced *mayirefta* (ready-cooked meals) including filling *mousakas* and a range of *ladera* (olive oil-based dishes).

Ta Spata Psistaria (☎ 2310 277 412; Aristotelous 28; mains €4.50-6) At this no-nonsense old-style restaurant, you choose from the dishes on display – a simple meal of beans, feta and half a litre of retsina is a good choice. Service is smart and businesslike.

Ragoti (☎ 2310 277 694; Venizelou 8; mains €5-8; ✕) It looks totally naff – fake baby's breath in vases on the table, black and white photos, and rows of beer mugs from around the world – but we can promise you Ragoti's is cult, an institution since 1928, and locals swear it's the best place in town for a meatball lunch.

Ouzou Melathron (☎ 2310 275 016; Karypi 21; mezedes €2.50-8) Regarded as the best *ouzeria* in town and definitely worth stopping by for a bite, if you don't mind waiting for a seat. Service is attentive, the food is presented with care and attention, and the atmosphere is very relaxed. Order a batch of *mezedes*, a small carafe of ouzo and unwind.

Drinking

Kourdisto Gourouni (☎ 2310 274 672; Agias Sofias 310) There's an old-world feel about this neat pub-cum-restaurant, with its wood-panelled baroque décor, prominent bar and beer taps serving seven types of draught ale. It's a good spot for a lazy lunch reading the newspaper, or an evening out with some good ales and even better company.

Dore Zythos (☎ 2310 279 010; Tsirogianni 7) Another classic place for revellers of all ages. Beers such as Fosters and Schneider Wheat, and a range of wines are on offer, as well as good Mediterranean food.

Getting There & Away

AIR

Thessaloniki's **airport** (☎ 2310 473 212) is 16km southeast of the city. **Olympic Airlines** (☎ 2310 368 666; Navarhou Koundourioti 1-3) and **Aegean Airlines** (☎ 2310 280 050; Venizelou 2) have offices in town.

Olympic Airlines has seven flights daily to Athens (€45 to €94, 55 minutes); daily flights to Limnos (€56, 50 minutes); six flights a week to Mytilini (€74, one hour 50 minutes); and between two and four flights weekly to Corfu (€74, 55 minutes), Iraklio (€97, 1½ hours), Mykonos (€92, one hour), Hania (€104, 2½ hours), Chios (€77, 2¾ hours), Skyros (€57, 40 minutes) and Samos (€88, one hour 20 minutes).

Aegean Airlines has similar flights to Athens (€76), and with lesser frequency to Iraklio (€90), Mytilini (€81), Rhodes (€108) and Santorini (€105).

There is no Olympic Airlines shuttle, but bus No 78 plies the airport route; it runs between the local bus station on Filippou and the airport – via the train station – every 30 minutes from 5am to 10pm. A taxi to the airport costs around €8.50.

See p497 for information on international flights to and from Thessaloniki.

BUS

Thessaloniki's main **KTEL Makedonias bus station** (☎ 2310 595 408; Monastiriou 319), situated 3km west of the city centre, has departures to Athens (€29.40, six hours, 13 daily), Alexandroupolis (€20.70, six hours, eight daily) and Kavala (€9.70, 1½ hours, hourly). Athens buses also depart from a small terminal located opposite the train station. Local bus No 1 travels between the bus station and the train station every 10 minutes.

FERRY

Minoan Lines operates three ferries weekly to Iraklio on Crete (€40, 23 hours), via Mykonos (€33, 13½ hours) and Santorini (€35.50, 19 hours). These boats also call twice weekly at Tinos (€32.50, 12½ hours) and Paros (€33, 15 hours), and once weekly at Skiathos (€15, 5¾ hours) and Syros (€30.50, 12¼ hours).

There are a further three boats (offering weekly services) just to Skiathos in July and August, as well as a Sunday ferry to Chios (€30, 18 hours) via Limnos (€20, eight hours) and Lesvos (€30, 13 hours); and a weekly boat that goes to Rhodes (€48, 21 hours) via Samos and Kos throughout the year.

Ferry tickets are available from **Karaharisis Travel & Shipping Agency** (☎ 2310 524 544; fax 2310 532 289; Navarhou Koundourioti 8).

HYDROFOIL & CATAMARAN

In summer hydrofoils and a catamaran travel more or less daily to the Sporades islands of Skiathos (€29, 3¼ hours), Skopelos (€28, four hours) and Alonnisos (€29, 4½ hours), via Nea Moudania (€15, one hour) in Halkidiki. Tickets for these can also be purchased from **Karaharisis Travel & Shipping Agency** (☎ 2310 524 544; fax 2310 532 289; Navarhou Koundourioti 8).

TRAIN

There are four regular trains daily to Athens (€14, 7½ hours), three daily to Alexandroupolis (€9.70, eight hours) and Larisa with connections to Volos (€6.80, 4½ hours).

There are seven express intercity services to Athens (€27.60, six hours) and two to Alexandroupolis (€16.20, 5½ hours).

GYTHIO ΓΥΘΕΙΟ
pop 4489

Gythio (*yee-thih-o*), once the port of ancient Sparta, is now an attractive fishing port at the head of the Lakonian Gulf. It is a convenient port of departure for the island of Kythira, and for Kissamos on Crete.

Orientation

Gythio is not too hard to figure out. Most things of importance to travellers are along the seafront on Akti Vasileos Pavlou. The bus station is at the northeastern end, next to a park known as the Perivolaki.

Vasileos Georgiou runs inland past the main square, Plateia Panagiotou Venetzanaki, and becomes the road to Sparta. The square at the southwestern end of Akti Vasileos Pavlou is Plateia Mavromihali, the hub of Marathonisi. The ferry quay is situated opposite this square.

Information

Café Mystery (☎ 27330 25177; cnr Kapsali & Grigoraki; per hr €4; 9am-1pm) Despite being almost opposite the telephone exchange, Internet connection is a problem.

EOT (☎ /fax 27330 24484; Vasileos Georgiou 20; 11am-3pm Mon-Fri) This is the information equivalent of Monty Python's famous 'cheese shop' sketch: it's remarkably information-free, even by EOT's lamentable standards.

Hassanakos Bookstore (☎ 27330 22064; Akti Vasileos Pavlou 39)

Post Office (cnr Ermou & Arheou Theatrou; 7.30am-2pm Mon-Fri)

Tourist Police (☎ 27330 22271; Akti Vasileos Pavlou)

Sights

Pine-shaded **Marathonisi Island** is linked to the mainland by a causeway at the southern edge of town. According to mythology, it was here that Paris (prince of Troy) and Helen (wife of Menelaus) consummated the affair that kicked off the Trojan Wars. The 18th-century Tzanetakis Grigorakis tower houses a small **Museum of Mani History** (☎ 27330 24484; €1.50; 9am-2pm) which relates Maniot history through the eyes of European travellers who visited the region between the 15th and 19th centuries. The architecturally minded will find an absorbing collection of plans of Maniot towers and castles upstairs.

Sleeping

Xenia Karlaftis Rooms to Rent (☎ 27330 22719 or 27330 22991; s/d/tr €25/35/40) The best budget option in town, ideally situated opposite Marathonisi. There's a communal kitchen area upstairs with a fridge and small stove for making tea and coffee. Manager Voula also has studios for rent 3km west of town.

Saga Pension (☎ 27330 23220; fax 27330 24370; 150m from port on Kranai; s/d €30/42;) The French-run Saga has comfortable rooms with TV and balconies overlooking Marathonisi Island on Kranai. There's also a restaurant.

Eating

Taverna Petakou (☎ 27330 22889; beside stadium on Xanthaki; mains €3-6) Another favourite with locals; there are no frills here. The day's menu is written down in an exercise book in Greek. It may include a hearty fish soup (€6) or a freshly cooked *mousakas* (€5).

Psarotaverna I Kozia (☎ 27330 24086; Akti Vasileos Pavlou 11; mains €6-10) Take your pick from the fish on display out front at this simple, cosy place between Rozakis Travel and the Hotel Kranai, and join the locals tucking into plates of grilled octopus (€7), calamari (€6) and other treats.

Saga Pension (☎ 27330 23220; 150m from port on Kranai; mains €6-9; daily lunch & dinner;) Good seafood at this French-run hotel, including a *bouillabaisse*-style hearty fish soup (€8) and spaghetti with shrimp (€7).

Getting There & Away

BUS

The **KTEL Lakonias bus station** (☎ 27330 22228; cnr Vasileos Georgiou & Evrikleos) has buses north to Athens (€17.40, 4¼ hours, five daily) via Sparta (€3.10, one hour).

FERRY

ANEN Lines (www.anen.gr) operates five ferries weekly to Kissamos on Crete (€21.40, 6½ hours), travelling via Kythira (€9.90, 2½ hours) and Antikythira (€15.80, 4½ hours), from July to early September. This drops to two services weekly in winter. **Rozakis Travel** (☎ 27330 22207; rosakigy@otenet.gr), on the waterfront near Plateia Mavromihali, sells tickets.

PORTS TO THE SARONIC GULF ISLANDS

There are connections to the Saronic Gulf Islands from several ports around the Argolis Peninsula of the eastern Peloponnese.

Porto Heli, at the southwestern tip of the peninsula, has at least four hydrofoils a day to Spetses (€5, 10 minutes) and Hydra (€11.30, 45 minutes), while nearby **Ermioni** has four a day to Hydra (€7, 20 minutes).

Galatas, on the east coast, is a stone's throw from Poros. Small boats (€0.50, five minutes) shuttle back and forth across the adjoining Poros Strait from 6am to 10pm.

All three ports can be reached by bus from **Nafplio**, the main town and transport hub of the Argolis. There are two buses daily from Nafplio to Galatas (€6.10, two hours), but travelling to Ermioni and Porto Heli involves changing at Kranidi (€6, two hours, three daily). There are hourly buses to Nafplio (€9, 2½ hours) from Terminal A in Athens.

PORTS TO THE CYCLADES

Lavrio ΛΑΥΡΙΟ

pop 8558

An unattractive industrial town on the east coast of Attica, 43km southeast of Athens, Lavrio, is the departure point for ferries to the islands of Kea and Kythnos, and for high-season catamaran services to the western Cyclades.

Getting There & Away

BUS

Buses run every 30 minutes to Lavrio departing from the Mavromateon terminal in Athens (€3.25, 1½ hours).

CATAMARAN

Hellenic Seaways operates from Lavrio between mid-June to September. There are departures daily except Wednesday to Kythnos (€14.50, 40 minutes), Syros (€25.50, 1¾ hours) and Mykonos (€30, 2¾ hours).

FERRY

Goutos Lines runs the F/B Myrina Express from Lavrio to Kea (€5.30, 1¼ hours) and Kythnos (€7.20, 3½ hours).

From mid-June, there are ferries to Kea every morning and evening Monday to Friday, and up to six daily at weekends. Six ferries weekly continue to Kythnos. In winter there are ferries to Kea every day except Monday, returning every day except Wednesday.

One service a week continues to Kythnos. EOT in Athens gives out a timetable for this route. The ticket office at Lavrio is opposite the quay.

PORTS TO THE IONIANS

Patra ΠΑΤΡΑ

pop 167,600

Named after King Patreas, who ruled the Peloponnese prefecture of Achaïa in about 1100 BC, Patra is Greece's third-largest city and the principal port for boats travelling to and from Italy and the Ionian Islands. Despite a history stretching back 3000 years, Patra is not wildly exciting. Few travellers stay around any longer than it takes to catch the next boat, bus or train.

The city was destroyed during the War of Independence and rebuilt on a modern grid plan of wide, arcaded streets, large squares and ornate neoclassical buildings.

Many of these old buildings, such as the Apollon Theatre, were being restored at the time of research in preparation for the city's role as Europe's City of Culture for 2006.

ORIENTATION

Patra's grid system means easy walking. The waterfront is known as Iroön Polytehniou at the northeastern end, Othonos Amalias in the middle and Akti Dimeon to the south.

Customs is at the Iroön Polytehniou end, and the main bus and train stations are on Othonos Amalias.

Most of the agencies selling ferry tickets are on Iroön Polytehniou and Othonos Amalias.

INFORMATION

Bookshops

Newsstand (☎ 2610 273 092; Agiou Andreou 77) Sells novels, as well as international newspapers and magazines.

Road Editions (☎ 2610 279 938; Agiou Andreou 50) Stocks Lonely Planet guides, maps and travel literature.

Emergency

First Aid Centre (☎ 2610 277 386; cnr Karolou & Agiou Dionysiou; 🕑 8am-8pm)

Port Police (☎ 2610 341 002)

Tourist Police (☎ 2610 695 191; 🕑 7am-9pm) Upstairs in the embarkation hall at the port.

Internet Access

Netp@rk (☎ 2610 279 699; Gerokostopoulou 37; 🕑 10-2am)

Plazanet Internet Café (☎ 2610 222 192; Gerokostopoulou 25; 🕑 10am-midnight)

Laundry

Skafi Laundrette (Zaïmi 49, wash & dry per load €7; 🕑 9am-3pm Mon-Sat, 5-8.30pm Tue, Thu & Fri)

Left Luggage

Train Station (🕑 6am-11pm) Charges €3.20 per item per day, or €1.60 if you have a train ticket.

Money

National Bank of Greece (Plateia Trion Symahon)

Post

Main Post Office (cnr Zaïmi & Mezonos; 🕑 7.30am-8pm Mon-Fri, 7.30am-2pm Sat, 9am-1.30pm Sun)

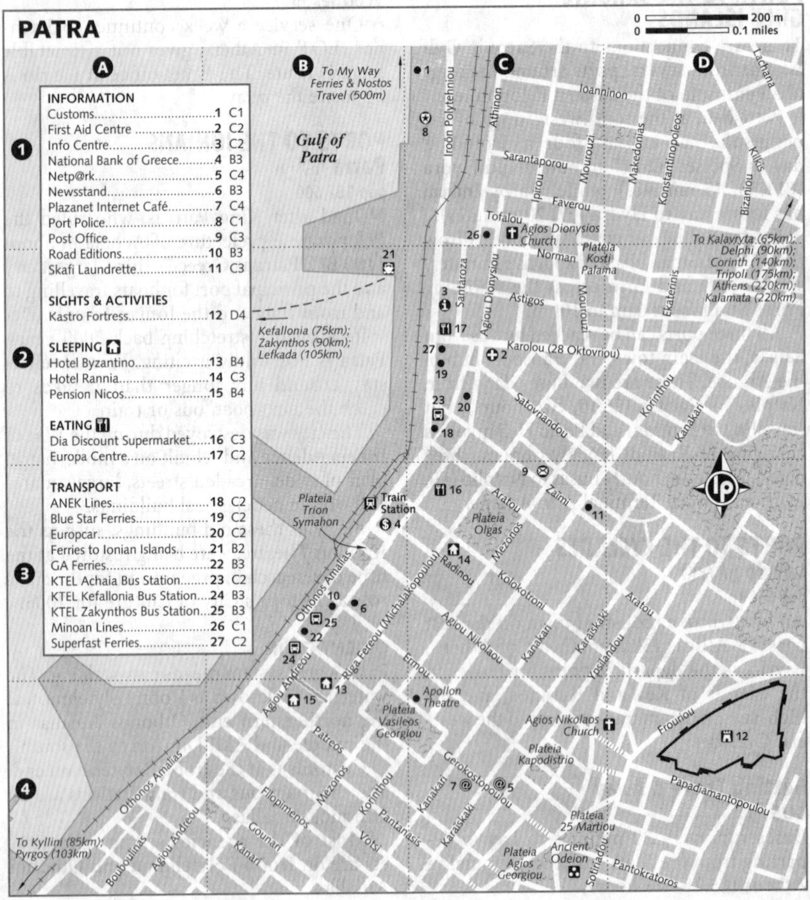
PATRA
0 200 m
0 0.1 miles
A B C D 1 2 3 4
INFORMATION
Customs 1 C1
First Aid Centre 2 C2
Info Centre 3 C2
National Bank of Greece 4 B3
Netp@rk 5 C4
Newsstand 6 B3
Plazanet Internet Café 7 C4
Port Police 8 C1
Post Office 9 C3
Road Editions 10 B3
Skafi Laundrette 11 C3
SIGHTS & ACTIVITIES
Kastro Fortress 12 D4
SLEEPING
Hotel Byzantino 13 B4
Hotel Rannia 14 C3
Pension Nicos 15 B4
EATING
Dia Discount Supermarket 16 C3
Europa Centre 17 C2
TRANSPORT
ANEK Lines 18 C2
Blue Star Ferries 19 C2
Europcar 20 C2
Ferries to Ionian Islands 21 B2
GA Ferries 22 B3
KTEL Achaia Bus Station 23 C2
KTEL Kefallonia Bus Station 24 B3
KTEL Zakynthos Bus Station 25 B3
Minoan Lines 26 C1
Superfast Ferries 27 C2
To My Way Ferries & Nostos Travel (500m)
Gulf of Patra
Kefallonia (75km); Zakynthos (90km); Lefkada (105km)
To Kalavryta (65km); Delphi (90km); Corinth (140km); Tripoli (175km); Athens (220km); Kalamata (220km)
To Kyllini (85km); Pyrgos (103km)
Iroon Polytehniou
Athinon
Ioanninon
Lachana
Sarantaporou
Ipirou
Mourouzi
Makedonias
Konstantinoupoleos
Kilkis
Bizaniou
Faverou
Tofalou
Agios Dionysios Church
Norman
Plateia Kosti Palama
Santaroza
Agiou Dionysiou
Astigos
Ekaterinis
Karolou (28 Oktovriou)
Satovriandou
Korinthou
Kanakari
Plateia Trion Symahon
Train Station
Aratou
Zaïmi
Plateia Olgas
Mezonos
Radinou
Riga Fereou (Michalakopoulou)
Kolokotroni
Othonos Amalias
Agiou Andreou
Agiou Nikolaou
Kanakari
Karaiskaki
Ypsilandou
Ermou
Apollon Theatre
Plateia Vasileos Georgiou
Agios Nikolaos Church
Frouriou
Plateia Kapodistrio
Patreos
Gerokostopoulou
Papadiamantopoulou
Mezonos
Korinthou
Filopimenos
Pantanasis
Plateia 25 Martiou
Ancient Odeion
Plateia Agios Georgiou
Sotiriadou
Pantokratoros
Gounari
Votsi
Kanari
Bouboulinas

Tourist Information

Info Centre (☎ 2610 461 740; infopatras@hol.gr; Othonos Amalias 6; ☺ 8am-10pm) Friendly and well organised, with maps, hotels and brochures about local points of interest. It also has an attractive display of local wine, olive oil and other produce.

SIGHTS

Kastro's wonderful old **fortress** (admission free; ☺ 8am-7pm Tue-Sun Apr-Oct, 8.30am-5pm Tue-Fri, 8.30am-3pm Sat-Sun Nov-Mar) stands on the site of the acropolis of ancient Patrai. The structure is of Frankish origin, remodelled many times over the centuries by the Byzantines, Venetians and Turks. It was in use as a defensive position until WWII and remains in good condition.

Set in an attractive park, it is reached by climbing the steps at the end of Agiou Nikolaou.

FESTIVALS & EVENTS

Patra is noted for the exuberance with which its citizens celebrate the city's annual carnival. The carnival programme begins in mid-January, and features a host of minor events leading up to a wild weekend of costume parades, colourful floats and celebrations at the end of February or early March. The event draws big crowds, so hotel reservations are essential if you want to stay overnight. Contact EOT (p76) for dates and details.

SLEEPING & EATING

Pension Nicos (☎ 2610 623 757; cnr Patreos & Agiou Andreou; s/d/tr €20/35/45) Nicos is easily the best budget choice. The sheets are clean, the water is hot and it's close to the waterfront.

Hotel Byzantino (☎ 2610 243 000; www.byzantino -hotel.gr; Riga Fereou 106; s/d €112/140; ❄ ▯) The Byzantino occupies a graceful old neoclassical building that has been tastefully restored. Every room is different, but all offer the same facilities: TV, fax, Internet access, minibar and safety box. Prices include breakfast.

Hotel Rannia (☎ 2610 220 114; fax 2610 220 537; Riga Fereou 53; s/d €30/45; ❄) The Rannia's shabby fittings cry out for renovation but it is clean and rooms have TV and phone. Other than this it has little to recommend it beyond price.

Europa Centre (☎ 2610 437 006; Othonos Amalias 10; mains €5.50-7; ☺ 7am-midnight) This convenient, cafeteria-style place is close to the international ferry dock. It has taverna dishes, spa-

ghetti and a good choice of vegetarian meals. It also serves a hearty breakfast (€7), and offers free luggage storage to customers.

Dia Discount Supermarket (Agiou Andreou 29) Ideally located for travellers planning to buy a few provisions and keep moving.

GETTING THERE & AWAY

Bus

The **KTEL Achaia bus station** (☎ 2610 623 888; Othonos Amalias) has buses to Athens (€13.90, three hours, half-hourly) via Corinth (€9.30, 1½ hours). It also has buses to Thessaloniki (€32.40, 9½ hours, three daily) and Kalamata (€16.40, four hours, two daily).

The **KTEL Kefallonia bus station** (☎ 2610 274 938; cnr Othonos Amalias & Gerokostopoulou) has five buses a day to Kyllini (€4.40, 1¼ hours), timed to meet ferries to Argostoli and Poros.

Buses to Zakynthos (€11.50 including ferry, 3½ hours, five daily) leave from the **KTEL Zakynthos bus station** (☎ 2610 220 219; Othonos Amalias 58). They also travel via Kyllini.

Ferry

There are daily ferries to Kefallonia (€11.50, 2½ hours) and Ithaki (€11.70, 3¾ hours). Fares to Corfu (7 hours) range from €24 with Blue Star Ferries up to €29 with ANEK.

See p501 for services to Italy. Ferry offices include the following:

ANEK Lines (☎ 2610 226 053; www.anek.gr; Othonos Amalias 25) Ancona and Trieste via Corfu and Igoumenitsa.
Blue Star Ferries (☎ 2610 634 000; www.bluestar ferries.com; Othonos Amalias 12) Ancona via Igoumenitsa.
GA Ferries (☎ 2610 276 059; Othonos Amalias & Gerokostopolou) Brindisi via Igoumenitsa.
Minoan Lines (☎ 2610 455 622; cnr Norman 1 & Athinon 2) Ancona via Igoumenitsa; Venice via Igoumenitsa and Corfu.
My Way Ferries (☎ 2610 420 639; www.maritimeway .com; Nostos Travel, Iroön Polytehniou 40) Brindisi via Kefallonia and Corfu.
Superfast Ferries (☎ 2610 622 500; Othonos Amalias 12) Ancona direct or via Igoumenitsa; Bari via Igoumenitsa.

Train

There are at least eight trains daily from Patra to Corinth; three are slow trains (€7, four hours) and five are Intercity (€10, 3½ hours). All trains between Patra and Corinth stop at Diakofto.

There are also two Intercity trains daily to Olympia (€8.65, two hours) via Pyrgos, as well as services to Kyparissia and Kalamata.

Igoumenitsa ΗΓΟΥΜΕΝΙΤΣΑ
pop 9104

Opposite the island of Corfu, Igoumenitsa (ih-goo-meh-*nit*-sah) is the main port of northwest Greece. Few travellers hang around any longer than it takes to buy a ticket. Ferries leave in the morning and evening, so there is little reason to stay overnight.

ORIENTATION
Ferries for Italy and Corfu leave from three separate quays situated close to each other on the waterfront at Ethnikis Andistasis. Ferries travelling to Ancona and Venice (in Italy) depart from the new port on the south side of town; those for Brindisi and Bari (in Italy) still utilise the old port situated in front of the main shipping offices; and ferries for Corfu (Kerkyra) and Paxi usually depart from just north of the new port. The bus station is on Kyprou, two blocks back from the waterfront.

SLEEPING & EATING
Hotel Aktaion (☎ /fax 26650 22707; Agion Apostolon 17; s/d €50/60) and **Jolly Hotel** (☎ 26650 23971; jollyigm@otenet.gr; Ethnikis Andistasis 44; s/d €55/65) are both comfortable C-class hotels on the waterfront with uninspiring, yet quiet rooms.

Alekos (☎ 26650 23708; Ethnikis Andistasis 84; mains €3.50-5.50) Popular with locals, Alekos is one of the better eating choices in town. There's a mixed batch of *mayirefta* and *tis oras* (to order), but the *mousakas* and veal with aubergines are worth trying.

O Salonikios (☎ 26650 26695; Pargas 5; breakfast €5) For breakfast and excellent Greek coffee try this little place tucked away in the backstreets near the Corfu ferry terminal.

GETTING THERE & AWAY
Bus
The **bus station** (☎ 26650 22309; Kyprou 29) has buses to Athens (€32.60, eight hours, five daily), Ioannina (€7, two hours, nine daily), Preveza (€7.60, 2½ hours, two daily) and Thessaloniki (€30.20, eight hours, one daily).

Ferry
There are ferries heading to Corfu Town hourly from 5am and 10pm (€6, 1¾ hours). Ferries also travel to Lefkimmi in southern Corfu (€6.20, one hour, six daily) and Paxi (€6.70, 1¾ hours, three weekly).

Most of the ferries to/from Italy also stop at Corfu.

Hydrofoil
There is a weekly hydrofoil service to/from Corfu (€12.40, 35 minutes) and Paxi (€13.40, one hour) in summer. Contact **Milano Travel** (☎ 26650 23565; milantvl@otenet.gr) for further details.

Kyllini ΚΥΛΛΗΝΗ
The tiny port of Kyllini (kih-*lee*-nih), which sits about 78km southwest of Patra, warrants a mention only as the jumping-off point for ferries to Kefallonia and Zakynthos. Most pass through Kyllini on buses from Patra that board the ferries that ply the Ionian.

GETTING THERE & AWAY
Bus
There are 10 buses daily to Kyllini (€4.40, 1¼ hours) from Patra, five from the KTEL Kefallonia bus station and five from the KTEL Zakynthos bus station.

Ferry
There are boats travelling to Zakynthos (€6, 1¼ hours, up to six daily), Poros (€7.20, 1½ hours, three daily) and Argostoli on Kefallonia (€11.50, 2½ hours, two daily).

PORTS TO KYTHIRA
Dangling from the tip of the southeastern tip of the Peloponnese, Kythira is the odd island out. It belongs in theory to the Ionian island group but in practice is administered from Athens. The best access is from the ports of Gythio and Neapoli.

Neapoli ΝΕΑΠΟΛΗ
pop 2727

Lying close to the tip of the eastern finger of the Peloponnese, Neapoli (neh-*ah*-po-lih) is a fairly uninspiring town, in spite of its location on a huge horseshoe bay. Most travellers come here only to catch a ferry to the island of Kythira, clearly visible across the bay.

SLEEPING & EATING
Hotel Aivali (☎ 27340 22287; Akti Voion 164; s/d €35/40; ✗) This small family hotel is ideally located right on the seafront close to the ferry dock for Kythira. All the rooms are equipped with TV and fridge. Like all the hotels in town, it's booked out during August.

Psarotaverna O Bananas (☎ 27340 22464; Akti Voion 158; mains €4-7.50) This excellent taverna is the perfect place to indulge your craving for seafood. Ask to take a look at the day's catch, or check out the daily specials, such as the seafood risotto (€7), or the fish baked with wine and herbs (€6).

GETTING THERE & AWAY
Bus
There are four buses daily from Neapoli to Sparta (€10.30, three hours), from where there are frequent buses to Athens.

Ferry
There are daily ferries travelling from Neapoli to Diakofto on Kythira (€6.40, one hour). Tickets are sold at **Voiai ANE** (☎ 27340 23980; fax 27340 23981), signposted on the seafront 100m west of the Hotel Aivali. The frequency varies from one a day in midwinter up to four a day in July/August.

PORTS TO THE SPORADES
Agios Konstantinos ΑΓΙΟΣ ΚΩΝΣΤΑΝΤΙΝΟΣ
pop 2674
The closest port serving the Sporades for travellers from Athens is Agios Konstantinos, 175km northwest of the capital.

SLEEPING & EATING
With judicious use of buses from Athens, you will not need to stay overnight.
Hotel Olga (☎ 2235 031 766; fax 2235 033 266; Eivoilou 6; s/d €25/35; ✖) The Olga is a good option if you get stuck. Like most of the town's hotels, it's right on the seafront.
Taverna O Stefanos (☎ 22350 32110; mains €3.50-7) Near the central square, Stefanos serves up tasty grills, generous salads and traditional oven-cooked dishes.

GETTING THERE & AWAY
Bus
There are hourly buses (from 6.15am) between Agios Konstantinos and Athens Terminal B bus station (€11.50, 2½ hours).

Ferry
Two **jet ferries** (☎ 22350 31874) make daily runs from Agios Konstantinos to Skiathos (€23.20, 2½ hours) and to Skopelos (€31.60, 3½ hours); to Alonnisos (€31.40, four hours) there are just two per week, usually on Friday and Sunday.

Hydrofoil
There are three hydrofoils daily to Skiathos (€23.20, 1½ hours) and Skopelos Town (€31.70, 2½ hours) and Alonnisos (€31.30, 2¾ hours). **Bilalis Travel Agency** (☎ 22350 31614), near the quay, sells tickets.

Volos ΒΟΛΟΣ
pop 84,425
A bustling city on the northern shores of the Pagasitic Gulf, Volos is the port for ferry and hydrofoil services to the Sporades.

According to mythology, Volos was ancient Iolkos, from where Jason and the Argonauts set sail on their quest for the Golden Fleece.

ORIENTATION
Volos is laid out on an easy grid system stretching inland parallel to the waterfront (called Argonafton), which is where most services for travellers are to be found. The main square, Plateia Riga Fereou, is at the northwestern end of Argonafton.

INFORMATION
National Bank of Greece (Argonafton)
Network (☎ 24210 30260; Iasonos 41; ✹ 24hr) Volos' largest Internet café.
Post Office (cnr Dimitriados & Agios Nikolaou)
Tourist Police (☎ 24210 76987; 28 Oktovriou 179)
Volos Information Centre and Hotels' Association of Magnesia (☎ 24210 20273; www.travel-pelion.gr; Gr Lambraki & Sekeri; ✹ 8am-10pm 1 Apr-30 Sep, 8am-8pm 1 Oct-31 Mar) Gives out town maps, bus and ferry schedules as well as information about hotels.

SLEEPING & EATING
Hotel Jason (☎ 24210 26075; fax 24210 26975; Pavlou Mela 1; s/d €30/40; ✖) You won't miss the ferry to the Sporades if you stay at this clean and roomy budget option just opposite the ferry quay.
Hotel Philippos (☎ 24210 37607; fax 24210 39550; info@philippos.gr; Solonos 9; s/d €45/65; ✖) The well-managed Philippos has bright, modern rooms with satellite TV, along with a spacious bar where breakfast and drinks are served.
O Haliabalias (☎ 24210 20234; Orpheos 8; mains €5-12) Tucked away on a pedestrian side street near Agios Nikolaos church, locals find their way here for variations on traditional ready-to-eat dishes like rabbit with tomatoes and carrots.

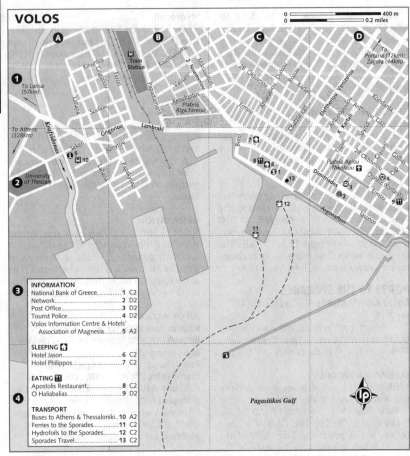

VOLOS

0 — 400 m
0 — 0.2 miles

Train Station

To Larisa (57km)

To Athens (328km)

University of Thessaly

To Portaria (12km); Zagora (44km)

Plateia Riga Fereou

Plateia Agiou Nikolaou

Pagasitikos Gulf

INFORMATION
National Bank of Greece..............1 C2
Network.......................................2 D2
Post Office..................................3 D2
Tourist Police.............................4 D2
Volos Information Centre & Hotels'
    Association of Magnesia...........5 A2

SLEEPING
Hotel Jason.................................6 C2
Hotel Philippos...........................7 C2

EATING
Apostolis Restaurant...................8 C2
O Haliabalias...............................9 D2

TRANSPORT
Buses to Athens & Thessaloniki..10 A2
Ferries to the Sporades..............11 C2
Hydrofoils to the Sporades........12 C2
Sporades Travel..........................13 C2

Apostolis Restaurant (☎ 24210 26973; Argonafton 15; mains €3-5) You can grab a quick lunch at this traditional waterfront eatery opposite the ferry quay. The folks will even pack it for takeaway if you're in a hurry to catch a ferry.

GETTING THERE & AWAY
Bus
There are 10 buses daily to Athens (€20, five hours) and seven to Thessaloniki (€13.40, three hours).

Ferry
There are two ferries daily to Skiathos (€12.40, 2½ hours), Glossa (Skopelos; €14.40, 3½ hours), Skopelos Town (€15.90, four hours)

and Alonnisos (€16.70, four hours). You can buy tickets from **Sporades Travel** (☎ /fax 24210 35846; Argonafton 33).

Hydrofoil
From the port of Volos there are four hydrofoils that travel daily to the island of Skiathos (€20.50, 1¼ hours) and Skopelos Town (€26.30, 2¼ hours); and three travelling to Glossa (Skopelos; €24, 1¾ hours) and Alonnisos (€27.80, 2½ hours). Tickets are available from **Sporades Travel** (☎ /fax 24210 35846; Argonafton 33).

Train
There is one intercity train daily to Athens (€19.50), and one to Thessaloniki (€14.40).

PORTS TO THE NORTHEASTERN AEGEAN

Kavala ΚΑΒΑΛΑ

pop 60,802

It's hard not to admire Kavala, one of Greece's most attractive cities. The town spills gently down the foothills of Mt Symvolon to a large harbour. The old quarter of Panagia nestles under a big Byzantine fortress.

Kavala is an important ferry hub with sea connections to the Northeast Aegean, the Dodecanese and Attica.

ORIENTATION

Kavala's focal point is Plateia Eleftherias. The two main streets, Eleftheriou Venizelou and Erythrou Stavrou, run west from here parallel with the waterfront Ethnikis Andistasis. The old quarter of Panagia occupies a promontory to the southeast of Plateia Eleftherias, reached by a steep signposted access road at the east side of the harbour.

INFORMATION

Cybernet (☎ 25102 30102; Erythrou Stavrou 64; per hr €2; ☺ 6am to 4am) Internet.

EOT (☎ 25102 22425; Plateia Eleftherias; ☺ 8am-2pm Mon-Fri) Staff can provide a map of the town and transport information.

National Bank of Greece (cnr Megalou Alexandrou & Dragoumi) Exchange machine and ATM.

Papadogiannis Bookshop (Omonias 46) Stocks a wide range of international newspapers and magazines.

Port Police (☎ 25102 23716; Omonias 119)

Post Office (cnr Hrysostomou Kavalas & Erythrou Stavrou)

Tourist Police (☎ 25102 22905; Omonias 119) In the same building as the regular police.

SIGHTS

If you've got time to spare, spend it exploring the streets of **Panagia**, the old Turkish quarter surrounding the massive Byzantine fortress on the promontory south of Plateia Eleftherias.

The pastel houses in the narrow, tangled streets of the Panagia quarter are less dilapidated than those of Thessaloniki's Kastra and the area is less commercialised than Athens' Plaka. The most conspicuous building is the **Imaret**, a huge structure with 18 domes, which overlooks the harbour from Poulidou.

The **archaeological museum** (☎ 25102 22335; Erythrou Stavrou 17; adult €2, free Sun & public holidays; ☺ 8am-3pm Tue-Sun) houses well-displayed finds from ancient Amphipolis, between Thessaloniki and Kavala.

SLEEPING & EATING

Giorgos Alvanos Rooms (☎ 25102 21781; Anthemiou 35; s/d €20/30) The best deal available for budget travellers and perhaps the cosiest environment in Kavala is the homely *domatia* housed in this beautiful 300-year-old house in Panagia.

Hotel Esperia (☎ 25102 29621; www.esperiakavala.gr; Erythrou Stavrou 44; s/d/tr €60/74/88; ▓) The B-class Esperia saves itself from complete mediocrity by dated but well-appointed rooms, and a good breakfast served on the terrace. The rooms have no soundproofing, but mercifully, sea views. Ask for a quieter room at the back of the hotel.

Hotel Nefeli (☎ 25102 27441; fax 25102 27440; Erythrou Stavrou 50; s/d €55/70; ▓) Renovated in 2002, this a good midrange choice where pleasant rooms are equipped with TV and large modern bathrooms.

There are lots of good places to eat in Panagia, particularly on Poulidou.

Taverna Kanados (☎ 25108 35172; Poulidou 27) and **Tembelhanio** (☎ 25102 32502; Poulidou 33b) both specialise in seafood. Although chicken rules the roost at **To Tavernaki tis Pareas** (☎ 25102 26535; Poulidou 25).

GETTING THERE & AWAY

Air

Olympic Airlines (☎ 25102 23622; Ethnikis Andistasis 8) and **Aegean Airlines** (☎ 25102 29000; Erythrou Stavrou 1) offer three flights a day to Athens from Hrysoupolis airport, 29km east of town. A taxi to the airport will cost around €20.

Bus

The **bus station** (☎ 25102 23593) has departures to Athens (€40, 9½ hours, three daily), Keramoti (€3.20, one hour, hourly) and Thessaloniki (€10.20, two hours, hourly).

Buses for Alexandroupolis (€10.95, two hours, seven daily) depart from outside the **bus stop** (Hrysostomou Kavalas 1), outside the 7-Eleven Snack Bar and opposite the KTEL office. Get departure times and tickets from inside the store.

Ferry

There are ferries to Skala Prinou on Thasos (per person/car €3.30/15, 1¼ hours, hourly).

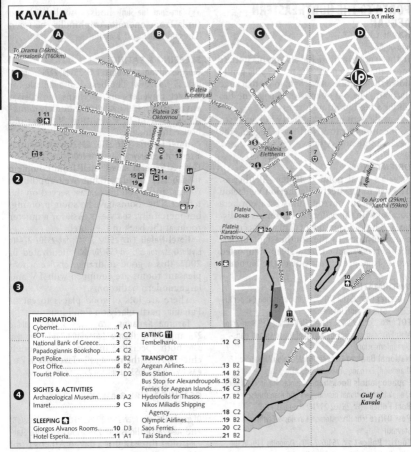

KAVALA

There is also an hourly service in summer from the small port of Keramoti, 46km east of Kavala, to Limenas (per person/car €1.50/10, 40 minutes).

In summer there are ferries to Samothraki (€13.50, four hours). Times and frequency vary month by month. Buy tickets and check the latest schedule at **Saos Ferries** (☎ 25108 35671) near the entrance to the Aegean Islands ferry departure point.

There are ferries to Limnos (€14.30, four to five hours) and Lesvos (€24.50, 10 hours). Some services also go through to Rafina (in Attica) and Piraeus via Chios and Samos. Tickets and the latest schedules are available from **Nikos Miliadis Shipping Agency** (☎ 25102 26147; fax 25108 38767; Karaoli-Dimitriou 36).

Hydrofoil
There are about nine hydrofoils daily to Limenas (€8, 40 minutes). Purchase tickets at the departure point at the port.

Both hydrofoil and ferry schedules are posted in the window of the port police near the hydrofoil departure point.

Alexandroupolis ΑΛΕΞΑΝΔΡΟΥΠΟΛΗ
pop 49,176
The capital of the prefecture of Evros, Alexandroupolis (ah-lex-an-*droo*-po-lih) is a modern town with a lively student atmosphere supplemented by a population of young soldiers. Most travellers come here in transit heading east to Turkey, or to catch ferries to Samothraki or to the Dodecanese

Islands. The maritime ambience of this town, and its year-round liveliness, make it a pleasant stopover. The town was named Alexandroupolis (Alexander's City) in honour of King Alexander and has been part of the Greek state since 1920. There are few sights, except for the still-operating, 19th-century lighthouse parked conspicuously on the main promenade, along which crowds flock on warm summer evenings, to stroll and relax in the many cafés and restaurants that stretch westwards from the port.

ORIENTATION
The town is laid out roughly on a grid system, with the main streets running east–west, parallel with the waterfront, where the lively evening *volta* (promenade) takes place. Karaoli Dimitriou is at the eastern end of the waterfront, with Megalou Alexandrou at the western end.

The two main squares are Plateia Eleftherias and Plateia Polytehniou, both just one block north of Karaoli Dimitriou.

The train station is on the waterfront just south of Plateia Eleftherias and east

of the port where boats leave for Samothraki and other ports south. The bus station is at Eleftheriou Venizelou 36, five blocks inland. The local bus station is on Plateia Eleftherias, just outside the train station.

INFORMATION
Bank of Piraeus (Leof Dimokratias) Has an ATM, as do other banks along the same street.
Eurobank (Leof Dimokratias) Has an ATM.
Fairy Tales Café (☎ 25510 33639; Nikiforou Foka 7; per hr €3; ◷ 9-3am) You can access the Internet here.
Kendro Typou (Leof Dimokratias) Foreign newspapers and magazines available here.
Municipal Tourist Information office (Camping Alexandroupolis; ☎ /fax 25510 28735; Leof Makris) Handles all official tourist information.
Port Police (☎ 25510 26468)
Post Office (cnr Nikiforou Foka & Megalou Alexandrou)
Tourist Police (☎ 25510 37424; Karaïskaki 6)

SIGHTS
The **Ethnological Museum of Thrace** (☎ 25510 36663; www.emthrace.com; 14th Maiou 63; adult €3; ◷ 10am-2pm & 6-9pm Tue-Sat) houses a superb collection of traditional artefacts and tools.

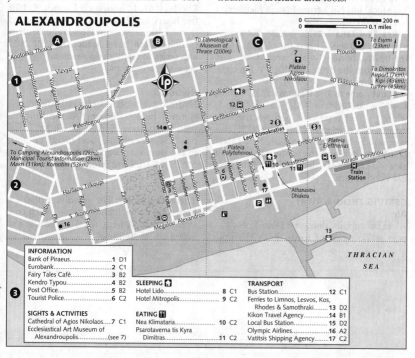

ALEXANDROUPOLIS

0   200 m
0   0.1 miles

To Ethnological Museum of Thrace (200m)

To Esymi (23km)

To Dimokritos Airport (7km); Kipi (43km); Turkey (45km)

To Camping Alexandroupolis (2km); Municipal Tourist Information (2km); Makri (11km); Komotini (53km)

THRACIAN SEA

INFORMATION		
Bank of Piraeus	1	D1
Eurobank	2	C1
Fairy Tales Café	3	B2
Kendro Typou	4	B2
Post Office	5	B2
Tourist Police	6	C2

SIGHTS & ACTIVITIES		
Cathedral of Agios Nikolaos	7	C1
Ecclesiastical Art Museum of Alexandroupolis	(see 7)	

SLEEPING		
Hotel Lido	8	C1
Hotel Mitropolis	9	C2

EATING		
Nea Klimataria	10	C2
Psarotaverna tis Kyra Dimitras	11	C2

TRANSPORT		
Bus Station	12	C1
Ferries to Limnos, Lesvos, Kos, Rhodes & Samothraki	13	D2
Kikon Travel Agency	14	B1
Local Bus Station	15	D2
Olympic Airlines	16	A2
Vatitsis Shipping Agency	17	C2

The excellent **Ecclesiastical Art Museum of Alexandroupolis** (☎ 25510 26359; Plateia Agiou Nikolaou; admission free; ⏰ 9am-2pm Tue-Fri, 10am-1pm Sat) is one of the best in the country. It has a priceless collection of icons and ecclesiastical ornaments brought to Greek Thrace by refugees from Asia Minor. The museum is in the grounds of the Cathedral of Agios Nikolaos.

SLEEPING & EATING

Hotel Mitropolis (☎ 25510 26443; Athanasiou Dhiakou; s/d €25/30) We love this cheap choice – it's close to the water, it's quiet and there's views! The rooms are bright and large, and the staff are accommodating. Head here first.

Hotel Lido (☎ 25510 28808; fax 25510 25156; Paleologou 15; s/d €35/45) The Hotel Lido is a quiet choice, with no-frills rooms (which are often full) and a distinct lack of atmosphere. The shared bathrooms are spartan but clean enough.

Camping Alexandroupolis (☎ /fax 25510 28735; Leof Makris; site per adult/tent €4.50/3.20) This spacious but rather characterless camping ground is on the beach 2km west of town. It's a clean, well-run site with good facilities. Take local bus No 7 from Plateia Eleftherias to reach the site.

Nea Klimataria (☎ 25510 26288; Plateia Polytehniou; mains €3.50-5) This is the place to head for hearty, home-cooked fare. Make your choice from the dishes on display. Draught wine is available.

Psarotaverna tis Kyra Dimitras (☎ 25510 34434; Karaoli Dimitriou 104; mains €4-8.50) This blue-and-white painted taverna is perhaps the oldest in Greece. In operation since 1875 and now watched over by the affable Kyra (Mrs) Dimitra, you'll find the freshest fish as well as a wide range of salads. Rice and mussels is a good choice.

GETTING THERE & AWAY

Air
Alexandroupolis' domestic Dimokritos airport is 7km east of town. Both Olympic Airlines and Aegean Airlines offer four flights a day to Athens (€75, 55 minutes). Olympic Airlines also has three flights a week to Siteia in Crete (€78, 1¾ hours). **Olympic Airlines** (☎ 25510 26361; Ellis 6 & Koletti) is in town, while **Aegean Airlines** (☎ 25510 89150) is at the airport.

A **taxi** (☎ 25510 28358) to the airport costs about €7.

Bus
The **bus station** (☎ 25510 26479; Eleftheriou Venizelou) has buses to Athens (€45.20, 12 hours, one daily) and Thessaloniki (€20.70, six hours, six daily) via Xanthi and Kavala.

Ferry
There are up to three boats daily to Samothraki (€8.30, two hours) in summer, which drops back to one daily in winter. Contact **Vatitsis Shipping Agency** (☎ 25510 26721; a_vati@otenet.gr; Kyprou 5) for timetables and tickets. Some services continue to Limnos, Agios Efstratios and eventually Lavrio in Attiki.

There is also a weekly G&A ferry to Rhodes (€41, 18 hours) via Limnos (€14.10, five hours) and Lesvos (€19.60, 11½ hours). It currently leaves on Monday at 8.30am. Contact **Kikon Travel Agency** (☎ 25510 25455; www.samothraki.com; Eleftheriou Venizelou 68) for tickets and reservations.

Hydrofoil
Hydrofoil services operate only during the summer months, linking Alexandroupolis with Samothraki (€16.50, one hour), Limnos (€30, three hours) and mainland ports to the west. Contact **Vatitsis Shipping Agency** (☎ 25510 26721; Kyprou 5) for schedules.

Train
There are trains to Thessaloniki (€10, seven hours, six daily), including one which continues on to Athens (€24, 14 hours) and intermediate stations.

Saronic Gulf Islands
Τα Νησιά του Σαρωνικού Κόλπου

SARONIC GULF ISLANDS

The islands of the Saronic Gulf straggle south from Athens, colourful stepping stones to Greece's wider Mediterranean world. The name Saronic derives from the mythical King Saron of Argos, who drowned while pursuing a deer that had swum into the gulf. The occasional king may still cruise the area today, but the deer are long gone.

The closest island to Athens is Salamina, too often dismissed as a mere suburb of the sprawling capital, yet it has a surprisingly green and peaceful hinterland. The first truly distinctive island is Aegina, a half-hour week-ender hop from Piraeus and with all the lively brashness that such proximity brings. Near-neighbour Angistri changes down to walking pace.

Further south is easygoing, popular Poros within shouting distance of the Peloponnese. Next comes Hydra, whose port is the exemplar of what island ports should be, an amphitheatre of white- and pastel-hued houses rising from a semi-circular harbour. Deepest south of all is Spetses, with one foot in the Argolic Gulf. It is an island of pine woods, that are still extensive despite their devastation by fires in recent years.

All of the Saronics have beaches, though none are dreamlike; Angistri and Spetses have the best of the bunch. The islands do not boast a feast of architectural glories either, although Aegina's Temple of Aphaia is a premier site.

If you are not fixated on beaches or bygones, the Saronics offer an authentic Greek island experience, and their proximity to Athens is a bonus.

HIGHLIGHTS

- **Wining & Dining**
  Dig into traditional dishes in tavernas in Poros (p124) and Spetses (p132)

- **Adrenaline Rush**
  Dive in the waters around Hydra (p127)

- **Ancient Wonder**
  Reconstruct in your mind the full glory of the Temple of Aphaia on Aegina (p120)

- **Living in Style**
  Live like an old 'admiral-pirate' in a mansion hotel in Hydra Town (p127)

- **Novel Outing**
  Browse through John Fowle's novel *The Magus* among Spetses' pine trees (p129)

Temple of Aphaia ★

Poros ★

Hydra Town ★

Spetses ★

- POPULATION: 48,471
- AREA: 318 SQ KM

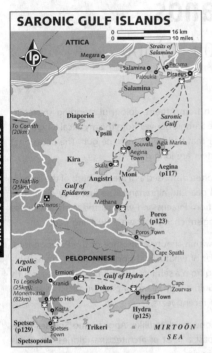

SARONIC GULF ISLANDS

GETTING THERE & AWAY
Ferry
Schedules for conventional ferries may change radically from 2006 onwards as more fast vessels join the fleet. You should always check details close to the date of your planned trip.

FERRIES FROM PIRAEUS' GREAT HARBOUR

Destination	Duration	Fare	Frequency
Aegina	1hr 10min	€5.60	hourly
Angistri	2hr	€8.10	2 daily
Hydra	3½hr	€9.30	daily
Poros	2½hr	€8.60	5 daily
Spetses	4½hr	€12.50	daily

Hydrofoil & Catamaran
Hellenic Seaways (☎ 21041 99000; www.hellenicsea ways.gr) operates a busy schedule to the islands and the nearby Peloponnesian ports with its Flying Dolphin hydrofoils and Flying Cat catamarans; see the destination sections for full details. **Euroseas** (☎ 21041 32105/6) is a relative newcomer to the fast fleet and runs a useful daily service from Piraeus, to

Hydra, Poros and Spetses. **Saronic Dolphins** (☎ 21042 24777) operates less frequently on the same routes as Hellenic Seaways, but offers discounts for advance bookings. All services depart from the Great Harbour at Piraeus.

Organised Tours
CHAT (☎ 210 322 3137; Xenofontos 9, Syntagma; www. chatours.gr), **GO Tours** (☎ 210 921 9555; Athanasiou 20), **Hop In Sightseeing** (☎ 210 428 5500), and **Key Tours** (☎ 210 923 3166/266; www.keytours.com; Kaliroïs 4, Makrigianni) all offer cruises from Piraeus to the islands of Aegina, Poros and Hydra.

The cruises leave Piraeus at 9am, returning at 7pm. You'll spend about an hour at each island – long enough for a sigh, souvenir, *souvlaki* and snapshot. They cost €85, including buffet lunch, but there are bargain tickets if you book through your hotel.

AEGINA ΑΙΓΙΝΑ

pop 13,552
Aegina (*eh*-ghi-nah) is a cheerful shakedown cruise for first-time Greek islandhoppers. A little down-at-heel, a little dusty and a little too accessible, this endearing island is nevertheless a worthwhile stopover.

Aegina was named after the daughter of the river god, Asopus. In the usual thuggish interlude she was abducted by Zeus and taken to the island for further research. The resulting offspring, Aeacus, was the grandfather of Achilles of Trojan War fame.

The island was a power player in the Hellenic world because of its strategic position at the mouth of the Saronic Gulf. By the 7th century BC, Aegina was the leading maritime power in the region and had amassed wealth through trade with Egypt and Phoenicia. The island's fleet made a major contribution to the Greek victory over the Persian fleet at the Battle of Salamis in 480 BC.

Athens grew uneasy about Aegina's maritime prowess and attacked and defeated the islanders in 459 BC. Aegina never regained its status although it enjoyed brief glory from 1827 to 1829, when it was declared the temporary capital of partly liberated Greece. Today the island boasts a more down-to-earth role as Greece's main producer of pistachio nuts. Bear in mind those ghosts of greater days, however; not least at Aegina's splendid Temple of Aphaia.

Getting There & Away

FERRY

In summer there are several ferries a day from Aegina Town to Piraeus (€5.90, one hour 10 minutes). Schedules should always be checked in advance. There are at least four boats daily to Poros (€5.10, 50 minutes) via Methana (€3.90, 40 minutes), two daily to Hydra (€6.50, two hours) and one to Spetses (€10.10, three hours).

The ferry companies have ticket booths at the entrance to the main quay, where there are lists of daily sailings. There are also services to Piraeus from Agia Marina (€4.90, one hour) and Souvala (€5, 1¼ hours). The Angistri Express goes to Angistri's main port of Skala (€2.30, 15 minutes, three daily).

HYDROFOIL & CATAMARAN

Hellenic Seaways (☎ 22970 24456; www.hellenic seaways.gr) operates almost hourly from 7am to 8pm between Aegina Town and the Great Harbour at Piraeus (€9, 35 minutes), but there are no services south to Poros, Hydra or Spetses. Tickets are sold at the quay in Aegina Town. **Vasilopoulos Hydrofoils** (☎ 22970 29027) also operates several trips daily.

Getting Around

There are frequent buses running from Aegina Town to Agia Marina (€1.70, 30 minutes), via Paleohora and the Temple of Aphaia. Other buses go to Perdika (€1, 15 minutes) and Souvala (€1.20, 20 minutes).

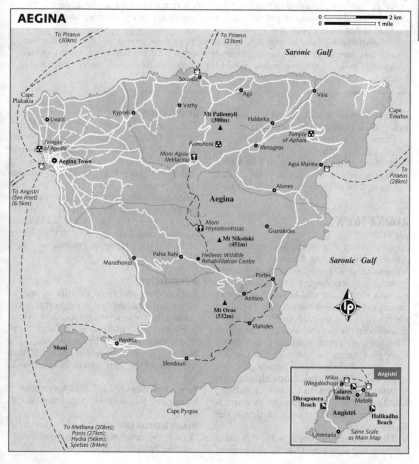

AEGINA

To Piraeus (30km)
To Piraeus (23km)

Saronic Gulf

Souvala
Cape Plakakia
Agli
Vaia
Cape Tourlos
Vathy
Kypseli
Mt Paliomyli (300m)
Haldeika
Livadi
Temple of Apollo
Paleohora
Temple of Aphaia
Moni Agiou Nektariou
Mesagros
Aegina Town
Agia Marina
To Angistri (See Inset) (6.5km)
To Piraeus (28km)
Alones

Aegina

Moni Hrysoleontissas
Gianakides
Mt Nikolaki (451m)
Pahia Rahi
Hellenic Wildlife Rehabilitation Centre
Marathonas
Portes
Saronic Gulf
Anitseo
Mt Oros (532m)
Vlahides
Perdika
Moni
Sfendouri
Cape Pyrgos

To Methana (20km); Poros (27km); Hydra (56km); Spetses (84km)

0 ___ 2 km
0 ___ 1 mile

Angistri
Milos (Megalohori)
Lalares Beach
Skala
Metohi
Dhragonera Beach
Angistri
Halikadha Beach
Limenaria
Same Scale as Main Map

A SALAMINA SAGA

Billed as the 'Greatest Battle of the Ancient World', the seaborne clash between Greeks and Persians in 480 BC (see p32) in the narrow strait between the Greek mainland and the island of Salamina seems hard to envisage today. The Battle of Salamis was a masterful recovery of fortunes for the Greeks under their gifted leader Themistokeles, whose understanding of wind patterns in the labyrinthine channels of the Greek islands ensured that 371 Greek ships routed a Persian fleet of 1207. Thus Salamina, one of the least tourist-favoured islands in Greece, rests on its historic laurels, while its modern image is that of a mere suburb of Athens and Piraeus amid the murky waters of the northern Saronic Gulf.

If you have a spare day, however, it's worth making the trip to Salamina, by public transport, or by bike if you can get hold of one. You can travel there and back to Salamina by ferry from Piraeus, but the following trip gives a vivid insight into how Athens triumphs over its urban gridlock. Catch the metro from Monastiraki to Piraeus, then take a Perama bus from outside the station's main entrance (€0.45, 40 minutes). It's a pleasantly chaotic trip through narrow roads jammed with traffic and overshadowed by buildings. Frequent signs of the cross made by fellow passengers reflect the remarkable number of churches passed rather than travel terror. Car ferries run all night from Peramato to Paloukia, Salamina's port; but catch the smaller passenger ferry (€0.70, 15 minutes) across this historic strait for a mind's-eye view of ghostly triremes and the chaos of that ancient sea battle.

If you're biking, head off into Salamina's surprisingly green interior and quiet coastal areas with their handful of small beaches. Otherwise catch a short bus ride to the island's modest capital of Koulouri, or to the equally modest resort of Selinia, from where you can catch a ferry directly back to Piraeus.

Departure times are displayed outside the ticket office on Plateia Ethnegersias.

There are numerous places in Aegina where you can hire cars and motorcycles. Advertised prices start from around €40 a day for a car and €15 per day for a 50cc machine, though deals are possible in quiet times.

AEGINA TOWN

pop 7410

Aegina Town can rock like downtown Athens, but its long harbour front and wide skies give it a sense of having some breathing space. Aegina Town lies on the island's west coast and is the capital and main port. The town has a tough, engaging charm to it and its racket ebbs and flows throughout the day and well into the night. The harbour front road is a speedway. Canopied cafés, packed with voluble locals, cram the inland promenade. Narrow lanes full of colourful shops slice across interlocking streets and a few crumbling neoclassical buildings survive as attractive accents from the town's heyday as the Greek capital.

The harbour is lined with colourful caïques, and with smart yachts in summer.

Orientation

The larger, outer quay, with its little church of St Nikolaos, is where the bigger ferries dock. The smaller, inner quay is where hydrofoils come in. A left turn from the end of the quays leads to Plateia Ethnegersias, where the bus terminal and post office are located, and then on to the Temple of Apollo and the north coast. A right turn at the end of the quays leads along the busy main harbour front to the Church of Panagytsa and on to Perdika and Agia Marina.

Information

Aegina does not have an official tourist office, but you can find some useful information at www.aeginagreece.com. Alpha Bank and Bank of Piraeus are located opposite the end of the hydrofoil quay. The National Bank of Greece is about 300m to the right of the ferry quays. All the banks have ATMs.

Kalezis Bookshop (☎ 22970 25956) Midway along the waterfront; has a selection of foreign newspapers and books.

Nesant Internet Café (☎ 22970 24053; Afeas 13; per 10 min €1; ☺ 10am-2am) Located several blocks inland from Xenon Pavlou Guest House.

Port police (☎ 22970 22328) At the entrance to the ferry quay.
Post office (Plateia Ethnegersias; ☯ 7.30am-2pm Mon-Fri)
Tourist police (Leonardou Lada; ☎ 22970 27777) Opposite the ferry quay.

Sights
Forlorn, yet defiant, the single surviving Doric column of the **Temple of Apollo** (☎ 22970 22637; adult/concession €2/1; ☯ 8.30am-3pm Tue-Sun) on the hill of Coloni, serves as Aegina Town's significant icon. The column is all that's left of the 5th-century BC temple, which once stood on the Hill of Kolona. The hill was the site of the ancient acropolis. Just below is the **Sanctuary Museum** (admission €3; ☯ 8.30am-3pm Tue-Sun), which displays artefacts from the temple.

Sleeping
Aegina has a fair selection of hotels and rooms, but you should consider booking ahead, especially at weekends.
Hotel Plaza (☎ 22970 25600; s/d €30/40) The Plaza is 100m north of Plateia Ethnegersias (keep left from the end of the ferry quays). It has been around for a while, but its enthusiastic young owner, who took over in recent years, is working hard to improve the already decent rooms.
Xenon Pavlou Guest House (☎ 22970 22795; Aiginitou 21; s/d/tr €35/55/65) Rooms and service are unfussy at this small family-run guesthouse tucked away beside the Church of Panagytsa about 500m along the main harbour front from the ferry quays.
Hotel Brown (☎ 22970 22271; brownhotel@aig .forthnet.gr; s/d/tr €60/75/100; ☒ P) The name of this fine hotel relates to its owner, George Brown, a local who has an English grandfather. Rooms are comfortable and stylish and the bungalows are nicely sequestered in a shaded garden. There's a generous buffet breakfast. The hotel is right at the far end of the main harbour front, about 80m beyond the Church of Panagytsa.
Eginitiko Arhontiko (☎ 22970 24968; www.aegin itikoarhontiko.gr; cnr Thomaïdou & Agios Nikolaou; s/d/tr €50/60/70, ste €120) This 19th-century sandstone *arhontiko* (mansion once belonging to an *arhon*, a leading town citizen) has rare character that makes up for some of its rather old-fashioned fittings. An upper salon has a beautiful painted ceiling. Turn

right from the ferry quays and after 150m go left and inland to reach a small square near the restored Markelos Tower, once the seat of the erstwhile Greek government of 1827–29. The hotel is on the left.

Eating
The inland side of the harbour front is lined with cafés and restaurants – ideal for relaxing among Aegina's café society, but not particularly good value.
Mezedopoleio To Steki (☎ 22970 23910; Pan Irioti 45; seafood mezedes €3.50-6) For great seafood, with attitude, head for this cramped, sunless, but somehow vivid place. It's right behind the fish market midway along the harbour front. As with its immediate neighbour I Agora, it's always packed with people tucking into hell-fired octopus (€4), grilled sardines (€4) or other *mezedes* (appetisers).
Babis (☎ 22970 23594; mains €4.50-12) A few metres beyond Hotel Brown, the spick-and-span Babis has an outside terrace that overlooks a tiny beach. It dishes up tasty staples, without fuss. The waiters run the gauntlet of the main road to deliver; so, respect.
Lidinos (The Garden; ☎ 69765 92666; Ahilleos 4; meals €3.50-7; ☯ 11am-late) Determinedly British in thought and deed, The Garden offers full English breakfast (€8), sandwiches and even Athens-made 'Cornish pasties'. There's a varied selection of wine, spirits and beers. It's down the street just beyond the Church of Panagytsa.
Kritikos Supermarket (☎ 22970 27772; Pan Irioti 53) It's self-caterers' country at this supermarket in the street behind the fish market. There's also a big modern branch outside town on the Agia Marina road.

Delicious local pistachio nuts are on sale everywhere, priced from €5 for 500g.

Entertainment
There are numerous bars on the waterfront and in the maze of streets behind.
Yes! Café (☎ 22970 28306; Dimokratias; ☯ 9am-3am) A flash landscape of sofas and modish lounge kit at this harbour front café is matched by easy-listening music by day and edgier spins at night. It all goes nicely with a decent selection of coffee, drinks and snacks.
Avli (☎ 22970 26438; Pan Irioti 17; ☯ 9am-3am) Established favourite of the post-bopping

SARONIC GULF ISLANDS

age group, Avli mixes '60s and Latin music and decks Greek sounds when Athenians hit town.

Lidinos (The Garden; ☎ 69765 92666; Ahilleos 4) Great wines, spirits and bottled beers, plus John Smith's and Guinness on draught, all smooth the late-night chat at the British-owned Lidinos.

Aegina has two outdoor cinemas, the Olympia and the more attractive **Akrogiali** (☎ 22970 53675; admission €7; ☺ mid-Jun–Aug) just outside town along the Perdika road and in a pretty garden setting.

AROUND AEGINA
Temple of Aphaia

The impressive **Temple of Aphaia** (☎ 22970 32398; adult/concession/under 18 €4/2/free; ☺ 8am-7.30pm), a local deity of pre-Hellenic times, is the major ancient site of the Saronic Gulf Islands. It was built in 480 BC, when Aegina was at its political height.

The temple's pediments were decorated with splendid Trojan War sculptures, most of which were spirited away in the 19th century. They fell into the hands of Ludwig I (father of King Otho) and now decorate Munich's Glyptothek. The temple is still impressive, despite the absence of the sculptures. It stands on a pine-covered hill with views over the Saronic Gulf as far as Cape Sounion.

Aphaia is 10km east of Aegina Town. Buses to Agia Marina stop at the site (€1.40, 20 minutes). A taxi from Aegina Town costs about €10.

Paleohora Παλαιοχώρα

The ruins of the settlement of Paleohora lie on a hillside 6.5km east of Aegina Town. Paleohora was the island's capital from the 9th century to 1826. It evolved as a refuge because of the vulnerability of coastal settlements to pirate attacks. The town served its purpose well until the implacable pirate, Barbarossa, arrived in 1537, laid waste Paleohora and enslaved the inhabitants.

The ruins of domestic buildings are extensive but often vestigial. What makes the site so compelling are the numerous small chapels, most fairly intact, that are dotted around the hillside. Remnants of frescoes can be seen in some and the Orthodox faithful still revere them, as should we all.

A modern iconic building lies beside the road to Agia Marina in the valley below

Paleohora. This is **Moni Agiou Nektariou**, an important place of pilgrimage. The monastery contains the relics of a hermit monk, Anastasios Kefalas, who died in 1920 and was said to work miraculous cures during his lifetime. Kefalas was canonised in 1961 – the first Orthodox saint of the 20th century. The enormous church that has been built to honour him is a sumptuous extravaganza, but a compelling one.

Buses from Aegina Town to Agia Marina stop at the turn-off to Paleohora (€1, 10 minutes).

Hellenic Wildlife Rehabilitation Centre

If you want harsh evidence of the damage caused by hunting to thousands of Greece's wild birds and animals, pay a visit to the **Hellenic Wildlife Rehabilitation Centre** (Elliniko Kentro Perithalifis Agrion Zoon; ☎ 22970 28367, 69772 31983; www.ekpaz.gr in Greek; ☺ 10am-7pm).

The centre is about 10km southeast of Aegina Town and 1km east of Pahia Rahi on the road to Mt Oros. Admission is free, but donations are appreciated. Volunteers are welcome and accommodation is supplied. There is no public transport – most visitors hire motorbikes or bicycles to get here; a taxi costs about €6.

Perdika Πέρδικα

If Aegina Town bounces you too much, you should head for the more relaxing fishing village of Perdika, about 9km south of town, at the southern tip of the west coast. Its long seafront terrace is crammed with tavernas and bars and is the hop-off point for the lovely little island of Moni, a few minutes away.

Buses run every couple of hours to Perdika from Aegina Town (€1, 15 minutes). Always check where the bus is leaving from on its return to Aegina Town. During festivals and busy times of year it does not turn around at the harbour, but leaves from the bus stop on the outskirts of town. A taxi is €9 one way.

Perdika's harbour inlet is very shallow and swimming is not much fun. Instead, catch one of the regular caïques (€2) from the harbour to Moni Islet, once targeted as the site for an exclusive casino, but now a nature reserve and with a magic little beach and summertime café. Peacocks and deer wander about peacefully and there are deep blue waters for more adventurous swimming over the rocky saddle behind the tree-lined beach. Make sure to catch the last boat back – or you sleep with the peacocks.

There are a couple of hotels and a few rooms in Perdika. **Villa Rodanthos** (☎ 22970 61400; www.villarodanthos.gr; s/d €45/65) is a charming, friendly option with rooms and apartments complete with kitchens. Rodanthos has a wonderful roof patio and a basement lounge and bar. It's about 100m along the right-hand branch road from the bus terminus.

There's a swathe of tavernas along the harbour-front terrace. **To Proraion** (☎ 22970 61577; mains €4-8) stands out, not just for its colourful flowers, but for excellent Greek food, including such tasty specialities as onion pie, as well as flavoursome fish and meat dishes.

Music bars jostle with the tavernas along the terrace, but keep going to the far end where you'll find **The Cross Eyed Seagull** (☎ 69488 43310; mains €3-7), which has the best and most laid-back views. It offers such Tex-Mex delights as buffalo wings and jalapeño peppers as well as burgers, sandwiches and toasties. It's a good late-night escape as well.

Beaches
Beaches are not Aegina's strong point. The east-coast town of **Agia Marina** is the island's main package resort. It has a shallow-water beach that is ideal for youngsters; but it's backed by a fairly chic-less main drag.

There are a couple of sandy patches by the roadside between Aegina Town and Perdika.

ANGISTRI ΑΓΚΙΣΤΡΙ

pop 700

Pine-cloaked Angistri is another escape from the fast-paced Aegina Town. It lies a mile or two off the west coast of the main island. Ease up when you get there.

The island's port, **Skala**, is a resort village these days, crammed with small hotels and apartment blocks, tavernas and cafés. Its beach, the best on the island, succumbs to lounger-life and a tide of tanning oil in July and August, but life, in general, still ticks away gently.

Orientation
A right turn coming off the ferry quay leads westwards to the small harbour beach and then along a paved walkway to a church on a low headland. Beyond here lies the long, but narrow, main beach. A kilometre further west takes you to **Mylos** (Megalochori), an attractive, small settlement with rooms and tavernas, but no beach. Turning left from the ferry quay takes you south in about half an hour to the pebbly and clothing optional **Halikadha Beach**.

Above Skala and now absorbed by it is the old settlement of **Metohi**.

The well-organised **Skala Tours** (☎ 22970 91356; pannek@aig.forthnet.gr) has an office in the main street, just inland from the main beach, and can help with accommodation and other services. There is a branch of Emboriki Bank just up from Skala Tours. It has an ATM, but it may dry up over busy holiday weekends. Where the main street meets the beach-front road is the **Aquarius Café Bar** (☎ 22970 91022), with a pleasant terrace and a well-run Internet facility (€1.50 per half hour).

Sleeping & Eating
There are dozens of sleeping places in Skala and its surroundings. In high season and on summer weekends it's best to book ahead; otherwise ask around or check through Skala Tours.

The welcoming **Alkyon** (☎ 22970 91378; s/d/tr €30/50/60; ☿ mid-Apr–Oct) is a 10-minute stroll east of the ferry quay. Its seafront rooms and apartments have a terrific outlook. Other rooms back onto the road. The Alkyon has a popular **taverna** (☎ 22970 91378; mains €4-8; ☿ mid-Apr–Oct) offering such delights as tuna salad, spaghetti with shrimps, and pork and chicken dishes in spicy sauces.

There are tavernas that offer reasonable Greek standards at similar prices in Skala and at the beaches.

Getting There & Away
Two ferries a day run from Piraeus via Aegina (€8.10, two hours) and four fast ferries run during July and August (€12.40, one hour).

The blue and yellow Angistri Express runs about three times daily from midway along Aegina Town's harbour front to Angistri's main port of Skala (€2.30,

SARONIC GULF ISLANDS

15 minutes) and then on to neighbouring Mylos (€2.40, 20 minutes).

An expensive last resort is the **water taxi service** (☎ 22970 91387/69722 29720; tickets €30) to Aegina.

Getting Around

About four buses a day run during the summer months from Skala and Mylos to the little village of Limenaria on the southeast coast. It's worth renting a moped (€15) or sturdy mountain bike (€8) to explore the island's coastline road. You can also follow tracks from Metohi overland through cool pine forest to reach the west coast beach of Dhragonera. Take a compass with you; the tracks divide often and route-finding can be frustrating.

POROS ΠΟΡΟΣ

pop 4500

Cheerful Poros lies curled up against the Peloponnese with only a few hundred metres of water between. It is too often dismissed as being 'package tour' country, but it's a rewarding holiday island like any other and is refreshingly unpretentious.

Poros is made up of two islands, Kalavria and Sferia. They are connected by a narrow isthmus, cut by a canal for small boats and spanned by a road bridge. Most people live on tiny Sferia, which is occupied mainly by the town of Poros. Sferia projects from the southern coast of Kalavria, a large, well-forested island that has most of the bigger, seasonal hotels.

Getting There & Away

FERRY

There are at least five ferries daily in summer and about four daily in winter, to Piraeus (€8.60, 2½ hours), via Methana (€2.90, 30 minutes) and Aegina (€5.10, one hour), two daily to Hydra (€4.20, one hour), and one to Spetses (€6.70, two hours). **Family Tours** (☎ 22980 25900; www.familytours.gr) handles tickets.

Small boats shuttle constantly between Poros and Galatas (€0.50, five minutes) on the mainland. They leave from the quay opposite Plateia Iroön in Poros Town. Car ferries to Galatas leave from the dock on the road to Kalavria.

HYDROFOIL & CATAMARAN

Hellenic Seaways (www.hellenicseaways.gr) has about eight services daily to Piraeus (€16.10, one hour). Most continue to Hydra (€7.90, 30 minutes), and on to Spetses (€12.60, one hour). **Marinos Tours** (☎ 22980 23423; Plateia Iroön) sell tickets.

Saronic Dolphins also operate to these destinations. **Hellenic Sun Travel** (☎ 22980 25901; www.hellenicsuntravel.com), opposite the ferry dock, is the local agent.

Getting Around

The Poros bus operates almost constantly on a route that starts near the main ferry dock on Plateia Iroön in Poros Town. It crosses to Kalavria and goes east along the south coast as far as Moni Zoödohou Pigis (€0.90, 10 minutes), then turns around and heads west as far as Neorion Beach (€0.90, 15 minutes).

Some of the caïques operating between Poros and Galatas switch to ferrying tourists to beaches during summer. Operators stand on the waterfront and call out destinations.

There are several places on the road to Kalavria offering bikes for hire, both motorised and pedal-powered. **Moto Stelios** (☎ 22980 23026) has bikes for €5 per day, and mopeds and scooters priced from €15.

POROS TOWN

pop 4102

Bustling Poros Town with its sunny, white houses and red-tiled roofs seems more like a lakeside resort in the mountains than an island port. Huge ferries glide by, seeming almost within touching distance, and smaller vessels scurry to and fro between the island and the mainland town of Galatas. Above the harbour front, narrow lanes and passageways link small squares and churches around the focal points of a handsome blue-domed clock tower and a cathedral. The town is a useful base from which to explore the ancient sites of the adjacent Peloponnese.

Orientation

The main ferry dock is at the western point of the town's long waterfront.

A right turn from the ferry dock lands you on the tapering square of Plateia Iroön. The square and adjoining waterfront are lined with cafés and tourist shops. The island bus

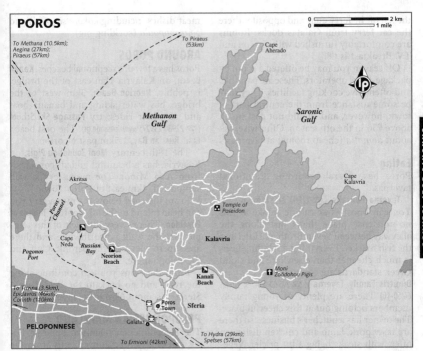

POROS

0 ————— 2 km
0 ————— 1 mile

To Methana (10.5km);
Aegina (27km);
Piraeus (57km)

To Piraeus
(53km)

Cape
Aherado

Methanon
Gulf

Saronic
Gulf

Akritsa

Cape
Kalavria

Poros
Channel

Temple of
Poseidon

Cape
Neda   Russian
Bay

Kalavria

Pogonos
Port

Neorion
Beach

Moni
Zoödohou Pigis

To Trizina (3.5km);
Epidavros (46km);
Corinth (110km)

Kanali
Beach

Poros
Town   Sferia

PELOPONNESE

Galatas

To Hydra (29km);
Spetses (57km)

To Ermioni (42km)

leaves from next to the kiosk at the eastern end of Plateia Iroön. Steps lead up from the inner corner of the square to the attractive lanes and squares of the upper town and to the clock tower and cathedral. A short distance south of Plateia Iroön is Plateia Karamis, set back from the waterfront road.

A left turn from the dock leads along the extended waterfront and on to the Kalavria road.

Information

Poros does not have a tourist office, but you can find some useful information at www.poros.gr.

Alpha Bank (Plateia Iroön) ATM.

Bank Emporiki (Plateia Iroön) ATM.

Coconuts Internet Café (☎ 22980 25407; Plateia Karamis; per 15 min €1.50; ☼ 9am-2am Feb-Nov)

National Bank of Greece (Papadopoulou) About 100m from the dock; has ATM.

Post office (Plateia Karamis; ☼ 7.30am-2pm Mon-Fri)

Suzi's Laundrette Service (Papadopoulou; ☼ 8am-2pm & 6-9pm Mon-Sat May-Oct, 9am-2pm Mon-Sat Nov-Apr) Next to the National Bank of Greece; €10 to wash and dry a 5kg load.

Tourist police (☎ 22980 22462/22256; Dimosthenous 10) Behind the Poros high school.

Sleeping

Seven Brothers Hotel (☎ 22980 23412; 7brothers@hol .gr; Plateia Iroön; s/d/tr €50/60/70; ✖) An excellent option at the heart of the waterfront, this modern hotel has fresh, comfy rooms that have been recently refurbished and are equipped with fridge, and tea and coffee makers.

Villa Tryfon (☎ 22980 22215/25854; off Plateia Agios Georgiou; s/d €35/50; ✖) Great views from the front rooms and a cheerful welcome are on offer here. All rooms have bathroom and kitchen facilities. To get here, turn left from the ferry dock and after 80m turn right up broad steps next to the Family Tours office. Turn left at the top of the steps in front of the public library and after 150m you'll see the place signposted up the steps to the right.

Hotel Dionysos (☎ 22980 23511/22530; dionysos@ saronics.com; Papadopoulou 78; s/d €50/65; ✖) The pleasantly dated Dionysos is a restored mansion located several hundred metres to the left of the ferry quay and opposite where the car ferry from Galatas docks. Rooms are comfortably furnished with air-con and TV. Breakfast is €8.

Off season you may be offered a room by package-hotel operators. These are passable, and often have cooking facilities. They may be some distance from the central part of town, however, and should not cost much above €30 in the off-season. Otherwise, ask about *domatia* (cheap rooms) at tavernas.

Eating

Poros has several rewarding traditional tavernas.

Taverna Pantelis (☎ 22980 22581; mains €2-5) You can boost your calorie intake at this no-nonsense place that's just along the alleyway between Seven Brothers Hotel and the fish market. Everything, including beer, is much cheaper than elsewhere and stolid Greek standards are conjured up.

Dimitris Family Taverna (☎ 22980 23709; mains €4.50-10) There are plenty of young family members helping out at this cheerful place. The owner has a butcher's business, so there are tasty pork, lamb and chicken dishes on offer, with steaks being a bit pricier. Vegetarians can still mix 'n' match such treats as butter beans in sauce and fried green peppers. Head up right from Taverna Platanos, then go left.

Taverna Karavolos (☎ 22980 26158; mains €4.50-7.40; ☺ 7pm-late) Karavolos means 'big snail' in Greek and is the nickname of the taverna's impressive owner. Snails are also a speciality of the house and are served in a thick tomato sauce (€4.50). *Mezedes* are inventive and there's a daily selection of main courses such as pork stuffed with garlic (€6). The home-produced wine is very persuasive. Karavolos is down past Platanos and left towards the waterfront.

O Kipos (The Garden; ☎ 22980 26139; Plateia Agios Georgiou; mains €4-16) A leafy balcony enhances the decent food at this taverna near Agios Georgios Cathedral. Foil-baked lamb with garlic, herbs and cheese costs €7, while a tasty mixed seafood platter is €12. Pastas and pizzas are €3.50 to €10.

Taverna Platanos (☎ 22980 24249; Plateia Agios Georgiou; mains €4.50-10) The Platanos is just beyond the cathedral, tucked away beneath an old plane tree in the dappled shade of a small square. It offers full-on spit-roast meat dishes including *kokoretsi* (offal) and *gouronopoula* (suckling pig).

AROUND POROS

Poros has a few unexceptional beaches. **Kanali Beach**, on Kalavria 1km east of the bridge, is pebbly. **Neorion Beach,** 3km west of the bridge, has water skiing and banana boat and air chair rides; try **Passage Ski School** (☎ 22980 23927; www.passage.gr). The best beach is at **Russian Bay**, 1.5km past Neorion.

The 18th-century **Moni Zoödohou Pigis**, on Kalavria, has a beautiful gilded iconostasis from Asia Minor. The monastery is well signposted, 4km east of Poros Town.

From the road below the monastery you can head inland to the 6th-century **Temple of Poseidon**. There's very little left of this temple, but the walk is worthwhile and there are superb views of the Saronic Gulf and the Peloponnese.

From the ruins you can continue along the road and go back to the bridge onto Sferia. It's about 6km in total.

PELOPONNESIAN MAINLAND

The Peloponnesian mainland opposite Poros can be explored conveniently from the island.

The ruins of ancient **Troizen**, legendary birthplace of Theseus, lie in the hills near the modern village of Trizina, 7.5km west of Galatas. There are buses to Trizina (€1.10, 15 minutes) from Galatas, leaving a walk of about 1.5km to the site.

The inspiring ancient theatre of Epidavros can be reached from Galatas.

Getting There & Around

Small boats run constantly between Galatas and Poros (€0.70, five minutes). A couple of buses daily depart Galatas for Nafplio (€6.80, two hours) and can drop you off at the ancient site of Epidavros.

HYDRA ΥΔΡΑ

pop 2719

Hydra (*ee*-drah) is the diva of the Saronic Gulf islands – and knows it. The good looks of Hydra Town, and the catwalk of its harbourside, still attract a resident troupe of artists, writers and *fashionistas* among the throng of cruise ship passengers, charter-

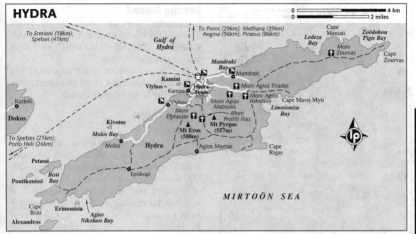

HYDRA

To Ermioni (18km);
Spetses (41km)

Gulf of
Hydra

To Poros (29km); Methana (39km);
Aegina (56km); Piraeus (86km)

Cape
Maniati

Ledeza
Bay

Zoödohou
Pigis Bay

Moni
Zourvas

Cape
Zourvas

Mandraki
Bay

Mandraki

Kamini

Vlyhos

Kamini

Hydra
Town

Moni Agios Triadas

Kastelli

Vlyhos

Moni
Efpraxias

Moni Agias
Matronis

Moni Agios
Nikolaos

Cape Mavri Myti

Limnioniza
Bay

Dokos

Kivotos

Moni
Profiti Ilias

Molos Bay

Mt Eros
(588m)

Mt Pyrgos
(557m)

To Spetses (21km);
Porto Heli (26km)

Molos

Hydra

Agios Mamas

Cape
Rigas

Petassi

Episkopi

Pontikonissi

Bisti
Bay

MIRTOÖN SEA

Cape
Bisti

Alexandros

Erimonisia

Agios
Nikolaos Bay

SARONIC GULF ISLANDS

yacht crews and regular tourists. The lingering whiff of moneyed celebrity means that you may pay for the privilege of visiting, but the deal is still worthwhile.

A rare bonus in modern Greece is the absence, even from Hydra Town, of scooters and rabid motorbikes. The island has no motorised transport, except for sanitation and construction vehicles. Donkeys and mules (hundreds of them) are the only means of transport. They load the air of the port with more diverting and more environmentally-friendly odours too.

History
The Turks had great difficulty in keeping a grip on many of the Greek islands and Hydra experienced only the light hand of a stretched Ottoman governance. Consequently the island prospered because enterprising Greeks from the Peloponnese settled here to escape Turkish mainland repression and taxes. The population was further boosted by an influx of Albanians. Agriculture was difficult, so these new settlers began building boats and took to the thin line between maritime commerce and piracy. By the 19th century, Hydra had become a substantial maritime power. From considerable profits, wealthy shipping merchants built most of the town's grand old mansions.

Hydra made a major contribution to the Greek War of Independence by supplying 130 ships for a blockade of the Turks. It also supplied leaders such as Georgios

Koundouriotis, who was president of the emerging Greek nation's national assembly from 1822 to 1827, and Admiral Andreas Miaoulis, who commanded the Greek fleet. Streets and squares all over Greece are named after these two.

Getting There & Away
FERRY
There is a daily ferry to Piraeus (€9.80, 3½ hours), sailing via Poros (€4.10, one hour), Methana (€6.10, 1½ hours), Aegina (€6.50, two hours) and Spetses (€6, one hour).

You can buy tickets from **Idreoniki Travel** (☎ 22980 54007; www.hydreoniki.gr), opposite the ferry dock.

HYDROFOIL & CATAMARAN
Hellenic Seaways (☎ 21041 99000; www.hellenic seaways.gr) has about eight services daily to Piraeus (€18.10, 1½ hours). Direct services take 1½ hours, but most go via Poros (€7.90, 30 minutes). There are also frequent services to Spetses (€9, 30 minutes), some of which call at Ermioni, adding 20 minutes to the trip. Many of the services to Spetses continue on to Porto Heli (€10.60, 50 minutes). Buy tickets from Idreoniki Travel.

Euroseas (☎ 22980 52184; www.euroseas.com) runs two boats a day to Piraeus (€17, two hours), Poros (€7.60, one hour) and Spetses (€8.50, 30 minutes). Tickets are bought from **Saitis Tours** (☎ 22980 52184) on the waterfront.

Saronic Dolphins also calls a couple of times daily. Saitis Tours sells tickets.

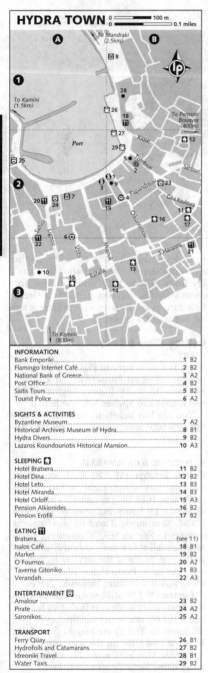

HYDRA TOWN

Getting Around

In summer, there are caïques from Hydra Town to the island's beaches. There are also **water taxis** (☎ 22980 53690), which will take you anywhere you like.

The donkey owners clustered around the port charge around €10 to transport your bags to the hotel of your choice.

HYDRA TOWN

pop 2526

Red-tiled houses with white- and pastel-coloured walls rise in stacked terraces above Hydra harbour. The waterfront throngs with life; from elbowing crowds to the cavorting of donkeys and mules and the carnival of smart yachts making less than smart landings amid a flurry of poorly aimed mooring lines. Behind the harbour front, narrow, stepped streets and alleyways draw you in to still corners and cool squares, with always a tempting rise towards the rock-studded slopes behind. Along the main streets that lead inland are plenty of shops, galleries and tavernas.

Information

There is no tourist office, but **Saitis Tours** (☎ 22980 52184; saitours@otenet.gr), on the waterfront near Tombazi, puts out a useful free guide called *Holidays in Hydra*. It has an ATM during opening hours. You can find information about the island at www .compulink.gr/hydranet.

The **post office** (7.30am-2pm Mon-Fri) is on a small side street between the Bank Emporiki and the National Bank of Greece, both of which have ATMs. The **Tourist Police** (☎ 22980 52205; Votsi; mid-May–end Sep) can be found sharing an office with the regular police.

You can check email at the **Flamingo Internet Café** (☎ 22980 53485; Tombazi; per 15 min €3; 11am-midnight).

Sights & Activities

The star attraction is the grand **Lazaros Koundouriotis Historical Mansion** (☎ 22980 52421; nhmuseum@tee.gr; adult/concession €4/2; 9am-4pm Tue-Sun), former home of one of the major players in the Greek independence struggle. It's a fine example of late-18th-century traditional architecture. The main reception rooms of the 2nd floor have been restored to their full splendour, furnished with all the finery of the period.

The **Historical Archives Museum of Hydra** (☎ 22980 52355; museumhy@otenet.gr; adult/child €3/1.50; ☺ 9am-4.30pm & 7.30-9.30pm Jul-Oct, 9am-4.30pm Nov-Jun) is close to the ferry dock on the eastern side of the harbour. It houses a collection of portraits and naval oddments, with an emphasis on the island's role in the War of Independence.

The **Byzantine Museum** (☎ 22980 54071; admission €2; ☺ 10am-5pm Tue-Sun Apr-Oct), upstairs at the Monastery of the Assumption of the Virgin Mary, houses a collection of icons and assorted religious paraphernalia. The entrance is through the archway beneath the clock tower on the waterfront. The monastery courtyard, cathedral and associated buildings offer a peaceful sanctuary.

Hydra Divers (☎ 22980 53900, 69447 08390; www .divingteam.gr) offers dives at a range of locations around the nearby Peloponnese coast. It has introductory dives for €60, and packages for experienced divers such as four dives for €125 using your own equipment. The company also runs daily boat trips to beautiful Bisti Bay (€10), on the southwestern side of the island, where people can hire snorkelling gear or try their hand at kayaking in the sheltered waters.

Festivals & Events
Hydriots celebrate their contribution to the War of Independence struggle by staging a mock battle in Hydra harbour during the **Miaoulia Festival**, held in honour of Admiral Miaoulis, in late June. It's accompanied by much carousing, feasting and fireworks. **Easter** is also celebrated in a colourful way.

Sleeping
Accommodation in Hydra is of a high standard, and you pay accordingly. These prices are for the high season, which in Hydra means weekends as well as July and August. Most owners will meet you at the harbour if pre-arranged and will organise luggage transfer.

BUDGET
Hotel Dina (☎ 22980 52248; Stavrou Tsipi; s/d €45/60) Cheap accommodation, for Hydra, is found at this small, old-fashioned place with its dated but reasonable rooms, several with views. It's tucked away up a steep, narrow alleyway off Sahtouri and is a Greek-speaking household.

THE AUTHOR'S CHOICE

Hotel Miranda (☎ 22980 55230/53953; www .mirandahotel.gr; Miaouli; s/d/tr incl breakfast €80/110/165; ☺ mid-Mar–mid-Nov; ☒) Built in 1810 as the mansion of a wealthy Hydriot sea captain, the Miranda was converted to a hotel in 1962. It retains many fine features of its traditional décor, including wooden-beamed and coved ceilings, the latter retaining their original motifs that were painted by Italian artists hired by many of Hydra's wealthy households. There is an overall mood of quiet, gracious living and the service is equally gracious and unassuming. Breakfast is enjoyed on a delightful patio. From the harbour front head inland on Miaouli and on beyond the square.

Pension Erofili (☎ /fax 22980 54049; www.pension erofili.gr; Tombazi; s/d/tr €45/55/65; ☒) Young, efficient owners add a sparkle to these very decent rooms that have TV and fridge. It also has a large family room with private kitchen. Head straight up Tombazi.

Pension Alkionides (☎ /fax 22980 54055; www .alkionideshydra.com; off Oikonomou; s/d/tr €55/60/75; ☒) The Alkionides is in a peaceful cul-de-sac and has a pretty courtyard. Rooms are smart, though some are quite small. They have tea and coffee making facilities. From the waterfront, head up Oikonomou.

MIDRANGE
Pension Bouayia (☎ 22980 52869; s/d/tr incl breakfast €60/80/100; ☒) Close proximity to Hydra's rock-studded slopes adds to the serenity of this pleasant place. It's built across terraces that are drenched in bougainvillea and geraniums. From the waterfront, head up Tombazi, turn left onto Sahtouri and keep going, bearing left at the football pitch.

Hotel Leto (☎ 22980 53385; www.letohydra.gr; off Miaouli; s incl breakfast €68-125, d €91-162, tr €147-214; ☒) One of Hydra's classiest hotels, Leto has handsome interiors and fine rooms and is one of the few establishments in the Cyclades to have a fully-equipped room for disabled use. The price ranges depend on such variables as size, balconies and floor location. Buffet breakfast is included and there's a fitness studio, sauna and bar. From the harbour front head inland on Miaouli and turn left at the square.

TOP END

Hotel Orloff (☎ 22980 52564; www.orloff.gr; Rafalia; s/d incl breakfast €165/185; ✖) A Russian admiral of the 18th century gave his name to this historic and beautiful stone mansion that exudes taste and style from its cool, vine-covered courtyard to its elegant rooms and furnishings. The buffet breakfast is served in the courtyard in summer. From the harbour front head inland on Miaouli and then turn right onto Rafalia after the square.

Hotel Bratsera (☎ 22980 53971; bratsera@yahoo .com; Tombazi; d incl breakfast €145-205, 4-bed ste incl breakfast €294-315; ✖ ⚲) The spacious Hotel Bratsera occupies the site of a former sponge factory. Merging the best of the new with decorative antiques and period details makes this another of Hydra's finest hotels. The hotel also boasts the town's only swimming pool. It's for guests only, but you can hop in if you eat at Bratsera's restaurant (below).

Eating

Hydra has dozens of tavernas and restaurants. Some of the cafés along the mid-waterfront push their luck with their high prices/low service; but near the ferry arrival, **Isalos Café** (☎ 02980 58845) offers decent snacks and beverages at reasonable cost.

Taverna Gitoniko (Manolis & Christina; ☎ 22980 53615; Spilios Haramis; mains €3.82-10.70) The Gitoniko taverna is better known by the names of its owners, an accolade that reflects the delightful family spirit of the place. Classic Greek favourites are well-prepared and there's a pleasant roof garden. Try the fresh green beans in oil with fava and tomato sauce, or beetroot salad – a flavoursome bowl of baby beets and boiled greens served with garlic mashed potato. Things gets busy at weekends and throughout August.

Verandah (☎ 22980 52259; Sahini; mains €7.50-12.50) *Haute* views over the harbour complement the cuisine at this fine place where you can enjoy it all between mouthfuls of spaghetti marinara, or pork fillet with gorgonzola cheese.

Bratsera (☎ 22980 52794; Tombazi; mains €8.50-15.20; ☒ 1-3.30pm & 8-11pm Apr-Oct) There's fine Mediterranean cuisine on offer at this restaurant that is attached to the hotel of the same name. There's a poolside terrace to

enhance the landscape. Starters, such as the spinach tart, have subtle tastes and mains include treats like veal fillet with thyme sauce.

There's a supermarket, fruit shop and fish market just inland, mid-harbour side. O Fournos is a mouthwatering bakery next to the Pirate club.

Entertainment

Hydra's waterfront fires up at night, when daytime cafés become hot music bars. Most bars are at the far end of the harbour where places like **Pirate** (☎ 22980 52711) and **Saronikos** (☎ 22980 52589) keep going until dawn. Most play lounge sounds by day and Pirate plays rock, while Saronikos goes Greek at night. A few blocks inland from the waterfront the cooler **Amalour** (☎ 69774 61357; Tombazi) does a lively line in cocktails and juices.

AROUND HYDRA

Hydra's stony, arid interior, now with some regenerating pine woods, is muscular and peaceful. Heading up Miaouli and onward offers a strenuous but worthwhile 2km walk up to **Moni Profiti Ilias**. Monks still live in the monastery, which offers some grand views down to the town. It's a further short walk from the monastery to the convent of **Moni Efpraxias**. Other paths and tracks lead over and down to the south coast, while you can stroll up to the top of Mount Eros, the highest point in the Saronic islands.

Hydra's shortcoming – or blessing – is its lack of appealing beaches to draw the crowds. There are a few strands all the same. **Kamini**, about a 1.5km walk along the coastal path from the port, has rocks and a very small pebble beach. **Vlyhos**, a 1.5km walk further on from Kamini, is an attractive village offering a slightly larger pebble beach, two tavernas and a ruined 19th-century stone bridge.

Bisti Bay on the southwestern side of the island has a decent pebble beach and its facilities are managed by Hydra Divers (p127), which operates a boat service from the port.

A path leads east from the port to the reasonable pebble beach at **Mandraki**.

Water taxis from the port to various beaches cost about €10.

SPETSES ΣΠΕΤΣΕΣ

pop 4,000

Of all the Saronics, Spetses feels as if it is off the beaten track. The novelist John Fowles used the island as the setting of his compelling book *The Magus* (1965). His portrayal – especially of heat and pine-scented seduction – probably sent many a reader hotfooting it on their first Greek island idyll.

Spetses' history replicates Hydra's. The island grew wealthy through shipbuilding, ran the British blockade during the Napoleonic Wars and refitted its ships to join the Greek fleet during the War of Independence.

The island's famed forests of Aleppo pine, legacy of the far-sighted and wealthy philanthropist Sotirios Anargyrios, were devastated by fires in 1990 and 2000. Much woodland survives however and the burnt areas slowly recover. Anargyrios was born on Spetses in 1848 and emigrated to the USA, returning in 1914 as a very rich man.

He bought two-thirds of the then largely barren island and planted the pines that stand today. He also financed the Spetses' road network and commissioned many of the town's grand buildings. He was a big fan of the British public (ie private) school system, and established Anargyrios & Korgialenios College, a boarding school for boys from all over Greece. John Fowles taught English at the college in 1950–51; the rest is literary history.

Getting There & Away

FERRY

From June to September there should be at least one ferry a day. The rest of the year one ferry runs on Friday, Saturday, Sunday and Monday. The ferry goes to Piraeus (€13.50, four hours), via Hydra (€4.90, one hour), Poros (€6.70, two hours) and Aegina (€10.10, three hours). You'll find departure times on the waterfront outside **Alasia Travel** (☎ 22980 74098; www.spetses-online/alasia.gr), which sells tickets. It's wise to check the situation regarding both summer and winter schedules for these ferries.

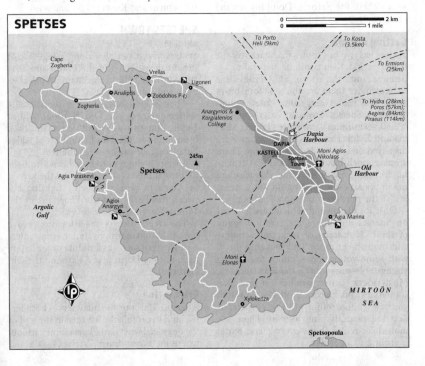

SPETSES

0 ——— 2 km
0 ——— 1 mile

To Porto Heli (9km)
To Kosta (3.5km)
To Ermioni (25km)

Cape Zogheria
Vrellas
Ligoneri
Analipsis
Zoödohos Pigi
Zogheria
Anargyrios & Korgialenios College

To Hydra (28km); Poros (57km); Aegina (84km); Piraeus (114km)

Dapia Harbour
DAPIA
245m
KASTELLI
Moni Agios Nikolaos
Spetses Town
Spetses
Old Harbour

Agia Paraskevi
Agioi Anargyri
Argolic Gulf
Agia Marina

Moni Elonas
MIRTOÖN SEA

Xylokeriza

Spetsopoula

SARONIC GULF ISLANDS

There are water taxis to Kosta (€15, 15 minutes), on the Peloponnese mainland. A larger ferry runs to Kosta about four times daily (€0.80, 10 minutes). There are three buses daily from Kosta to Nafplio (€5.90, 2¼ hours).

HYDROFOIL & CATAMARAN

Hellenic Seaways (☎ 21041 99000; www.hellenic seaways.gr) runs the red Flying Cats and Flying Dolphins. There are at least six services a day to Piraeus (€23.90, 2 hours 10 minutes). Most services travel via Hydra (€9, 30 minutes) and Poros (€12.60, 70 minutes). There are also daily connections to Ermioni (€6.60, one hour) and Porto Heli (€4.70, 20 minutes). Tickets are available from **Bardakos Tours** (☎ 22980 73141; Dapia Harbour), located opposite the water taxis.

Euroseas (www.euroseas.com) runs two boats a day to Piraeus (€22.50, two hours 10 minutes), via Hydra (€8.60, 30 minutes) and Poros (€12.10, one hour). Tickets are bought from **Mimoza Travel** (☎ 22980 75170; mimoza -kent@aig.forthnet.gr), which is on the waterfront just past Plateia Limenarhiou. Mimoza also sells tickets for Saronic Dolphins on the same route.

Getting Around

Spetses has two bus routes that start over the Easter period, then continue, depending on demand, until the end of May. From June to September there are three or four buses daily. The routes are; from Plateia Agiou Mama in Spetses Town to Agio Anargyri (€2.50, 40 minutes), travelling via Agia Marina and Xylokeriza. All departure times are displayed on a board by the bus stop. There are also hourly buses to Ligoneri (€1) departing from in front of the Hotel Possidonion, the impressive old building on the seafront just to the northwest of Dapia Harbour.

Only locally-owned vehicles are allowed on Spetses and there are not too many of these. Hundreds of racketing scooters and motorbikes more than make up for it, with some youngsters – and a few ageing youngsters – pursuing Grand Prix fantasies. Most riders (entire families on one bike sometimes) buzz around briskly, so watch yourself while strolling at blind corners, or doff the earmuffs and join in. There are motorbike-rental shops everywhere; rental is around €15 per day.

For quieter pedal power there are sturdy bikes (€7 per day) at **Mountain Bikes** (☎ 22980 74505) 100m beyond Plateia Agiou Mama along the lane to the right of the kiosk (they also make stylish furniture by way of fascinating contrast). Bikes (€5 per day) to suit all ages, as well as baby seats, are also on hire from the **Bike Center** (☎ 22980 74143), behind the fish market.

Spetses' horse-drawn carriages are an expensive way of getting around (€20 to Old Harbour and back). Prices are displayed on a board on Plateia Limenarhiou by the port.

BOAT

Water taxis (☎ 22980 72072; Dapia Harbour) go anywhere you want from opposite the Bardakos Tours office just up from the end of the ferry quay. Fares are displayed on a board. Sample one-way fares include €22 to Agia Marina and €45 to Agioi Anargyri, or €60 for a round trip of the island. Fares are per trip, not per person.

In summer, there are caïques from the harbour to Agioi Anargyri (€6 return), Zogheria (€4 return) and Kosta (€1.50 one way).

SPETSES TOWN

pop 3846

Spetses Town rambles along a big slice of the northeast coast of the island and rises steeply from behind the main Dapia Harbour and waterfront area.

There's evidence of an early Helladic settlement near the Old Harbour and at Dapia. Roman and Byzantine remains have been found in the area behind Moni Agios Nikolaos, halfway between the two.

Spetses is thought to have been uninhabited for almost 600 years before the arrival of Albanian refugees fleeing fighting between the Turks and the Venetians in the 16th century.

The Dapia district has a few impressive *arhontika* (old mansions) but the most interesting part of town, as antidote to the happy racket of the Dapia area, is around the Old Harbour.

Orientation

At Dapia Harbour the quay serves both ferries and hydrofoils. A left turn at the end of the quay leads east past Plateia Limenarhiou, where the horse-drawn carriages wait, and

along the waterfront road of Sotiriou Anargyriou, past the town beach and Plateia
Agiou Mama. Beyond here the seafront
road continues to the Old Harbour.

From the inner, left-hand corner of
Plateia Limenarhiou a narrow lane leads
to Plateia Orologiou, which is enclosed by
cafés, tavernas and shops and is overlooked
by its namesake clock tower.

Above Dapia Harbour is a café-crammed
terrace from where the road drops down
right and then bends sharply left along the
waterfront to become the road to Ligoneri.

Information

There is no tourist office on Spetses. Alpha
Bank at Dapia Harbour has an ATM and
there are ATMs just up to the right on the
harbour terrace.

1800 Net Café (☎ 22980 29498 near Hotel Posidonion;
per ½/1hr €2/3; ☼ 9am-midnight). Sessions are card-
timed; keep an eye on the lower right-hand screen for
time run out.

Mimoza Travel (☎ 22980 75170; mimoza-kent@aig
.forthnet.gr) On the waterfront just past Plateia Limenarhiou; can help with accommodation and other services.

Port police (☎ 22980 72245) Behind the inner harbour
terrace on the way to the Lascarina Bouboulina Museum.

Post office (☼ 7.30am-2pm Mon-Fri) On the street
running behind the hotels on Sotiriou Anargyriou.

Tourist police (☎ 22980 73100; ☼ mid-May–Sep)
Behind the inner harbour terrace on the way to the
Lascarina Bouboulina Museum.

Sights

The Spetses **museum** (☎ 22980 72994; adult/
concession €3/2; ☼ 8.30am-2pm Tue-Sun) is housed
in the old mansion of Hadzigiannis Mexis,
a shipowner who became the island's first
governor. While most of the collection is
devoted to folkloric items and portraits of
the island's founding fathers, there is also
a fine collection of ships' figureheads. To
reach the museum go from the top left-
hand corner of Plateia Orologiou, turn left
and then follow signposts for about five
minutes. When you reach a huge anchor,
you've landed.

The mansion of Spetses' famous daughter, the 19th-century seagoing Amazon
Lascarina Bouboulina, has been converted
into a **museum** (☎ 22980 72416; www.bouboulina
-spetses.gr; adult/child/concession €5/1/3; ☼ 9am-9pm
Tue-Sun Jun–mid-Sep, 10.30am-4.30pm mid-Sep–May).
You can only take a guided tour. These

run every 45 minutes from June to mid-
September, but less frequently the rest of
the year. Billboards around town advertise
the starting times of tours. To reach the
museum turn up right 20m beyond Hotel
Roumani.

The **Old Harbour**, which is about a 1.5km
stroll from Dapia, is an engaging place to
wander round. It is crammed with all types
of vessels, from working fishing boats to
minor-league private cruisers and yachts,
all interspersed with half-built caïques and
others being repaired. A pleasant jumble
of houses rises behind the long harbour
front.

Sleeping

BUDGET

Spetses has several pleasant sleeping options. Most places offer discounts outside
August.

Villa Marina (☎ 22980 72646; off Plateia Agiou
Mama; s/d €45/64; ❄) A charming place with
kind and friendly owners. It's just up to the
right of Plateia Agiou Mama, beyond the
row of restaurants. Pleasant rooms look out
onto a delightful little garden full of flowers,
while others front a big balcony with views
to the sea. All rooms have refrigerators and
there is a well-equipped communal kitchen
downstairs.

Hotel Kamelia (☎ 22980 72415; s/d/tr €35/45/50;
❄) Another welcoming place, the Kamelia
is tucked away inland from Plateia Agiou
Mama. Head along the lane that leads to the
right of the kiosk in the Plateia for 100m,
then bear right before a little bridge. In another 100m or so go right along a narrow
lane to a quiet square where Kamelia lies
drenched in bougainvillea.

MIDRANGE & TOP END

Hotel Roumani (☎ 22980 72344; www.hotelroumani
.gr; Dapia Harbour; s/d €65/75; ❄) This place has
been refurbished in recent years and has an
attractive and fresh décor. It's on the terrace
above Dapia Harbour, right at the heart of
things, and it stays open all year.

Nisiá (☎ 22980 75000; www.nissia.gr; d/tr incl
breakfast €230/275; ❄ 🐾) Hefty prices earn
you luxury at this peaceful complex with
its apartment-style rooms clustered around
a large swimming pool. It's about 300m
northwest of Dapia Harbour. The hotel has
a restaurant (mains €18 to €25).

SARONIC GULF ISLANDS

Eating

The cafés overlooking the harbour charge choke-on-your-coffee prices. For better food and better deals, veer off quickly.

O Roussos (☎ 22980 72212; Plateia Agiou Mama; mains €5-13) Hard to beat for decent traditional food at reasonable prices in an unpretentious setting.

Cockatoo (☎ 22980 74085; mains €1.50-10; ☿ noon-midnight) At the back of Plateia Limenarhiou, this is the place for budget food. You can get a *souvlaki* for €1.50 or a whole chicken for €10, to eat in or take away. Greek salads are €3.80.

Taverna O Lazaros (☎ 22980 72600; mains €5-6.50; ☿ 7pm-midnight) A steady hike of about 600m up from Dapia earns rewards at this popular taverna where the homemade *taramasalata* (thick puree of fish roe, potato, oil and lemon juice; €2.35) is the real thing. Other treats include young goat in lemon sauce (€6.80) and chicken in tomato sauce with spices. Vegetarians can weave their own choice and the retsina is very persuasive.

Orloff (☎ 22980 75255; mezedes €5-14, mains €8-14) If character is what you want, you won't find a better place than this, 600m from Plateia Agiou Mama on the coast road to the Old Harbour. The early-19th-century port-authority building has been converted into a stylish restaurant specialising in *mezedes*.

Self-caterers will find everything they need at **Kritikos Supermarket** (☎ 22980 74361; Kentriki Agora), next to the fish market on the waterfront. The entrance is up a covered passageway.

Entertainment

Bar Spetsa (☎ 22980 74131; ☿ 8pm-late) In every town, on every island, there's a bar that doesn't need to shout about itself and Bar Spetsa is one of them. It's the place for good company, great conversation and enduring music from the '60s and '70s. The bar is 50m beyond Plateia Agiou Mama, on the road to the right of the kiosk.

Balconi Wine Bar (☎ 22980 72594; Sotiriou Anargyriou; ☿ 10.30am-3am May-Oct, 7pm-3am Nov-Apr) Sip cocktails, wine and impressively sourced whisky (expensively, but in style) at this smart bar, next to the seafront Stelios Hotel, to a background of mainly classical music by day and jazz riffs in the evening. Mop up with fine cheeses and salami, or hand-cut smoked salmon.

AROUND SPETSES

Spetses' coastline is speckled with numerous coves with small, pine-shaded beaches. A 24km surfaced road skirts the entire coastline, so a scooter is the ideal way to explore.

The beach at **Ligoneri**, west of town, has the attraction of being easily accessible by bus. **Agia Paraskevi** and **Agioi Anargyri**, on the southwest coast, have good, albeit crowded, beaches; both have water sports of every description. **Agia Marina**, to the south of the old harbour, is a small resort with a beach that gets crowded.

The interior of the island is crisscrossed with woodland tracks, where a compass is useful.

Cyclades
Κυκλάδες

The Cyclades (kih-*klah*-dez) seem to be the Greek islands we long for – sun-blasted outposts of rock and dappled earth, anchored in crystal clear seas and speckled with white buildings. Add golden beaches, olive groves, pine forests, herb-strewn mountain slopes and terraced valleys, and the Cyclades become irresistible. The relaxed world of the taverna, easy living in the sun and a culture that is a fascinating mix of East and West tops up the appeal even more.

The reality is much harsher, at least for native islanders, who often struggle for a living. They raise livestock and grow food on reluctant soil, or chase a diminishing supply of fish from seas that are regularly rough and dangerous. Their winters are often grey, bleak and unforgiving.

Yet, the Cyclades are still irresistible, to many Greeks as well as to visitors, not least because of the fascinating variety that underpins all their other attractions. The islands range from big fertile Naxos, with its craggy mountains and landlocked valleys, to the tiny outliers of Donousa, Iraklia and Sikinos, where the sea dominates on every side.

The beaches of Mykonos, Santorini and los are awash with sun-lounger society and raucous diversion; their main towns seethe with commercialism. All of this has its appeal, but other islands, such as Andros, Amorgos and Sifnos, have kept tourism to a more sedate scale.

The Cyclades are so named because they form a circle *(kyklos)* around the island of Delos, one of the world's most haunting ancient sites. Closing that circle is still one of the most rewarding experiences for the dedicated traveller.

CYCLADES

HIGHLIGHTS

- **Authentic Greece**
  The old villages of Amorgos (p184) and Anafi (p201)

- **Spectacular Sunsets**
  View the best over Santorini's submerged volcano (p191)

- **Ancient & Sublime**
  The archaeological feast of Delos (p160)

- **Uncrowded Beaches**
  On the islands of the Little Cyclades (p178), lost in the Big Blue

- **Adrenaline Rush**
  Kiteboarding in Paros (p167)

- **Night Fever**
  All-night action on Mykonos (p156) and los (p190)

★ Mykonos
Delos

Paros ★

Little Cyclades ★ Amorgos

los ★

Santorini (Thira) ★
Anafi ★

■ POPULATION: 109,814	■ AREA: 2,429 SQ KM

HISTORY

The Cyclades have been inhabited since at least 7000 BC, awesome proof of their antiquity. Around 3000 BC the Cycladic civilisation, a culture sustained by its sea-farers, first achieved cohesion. During the Early Cycladic period (3000–2000 BC) there were settlements on the islands of Keros, Syros, Naxos, Milos, Sifnos and Amorgos, while other islands were probably colonised, if only seasonally. During this period the tiny, compelling Cycladic marble figurines were sculpted.

In the Middle Cycladic period (2000–1500 BC) many of the islands were occupied by the Minoans – at Akrotiri, on Santorini, a Minoan town has been excavated. At the beginning of the Late Cycladic period (1500–1100 BC), the Cyclades passed to the Mycenaeans. The Dorians followed in the 8th century BC, bringing Archaic culture with them.

By the middle of the 5th century BC the islands were members of a fully fledged Athenian empire. In the Hellenistic era (323–146 BC) they were controlled by Egypt's Ptolemic dynasties and then by the Macedonians. In 146 BC the islands became a Roman province and lucrative trade links were established with many parts of the Mediterranean.

After the division of the Roman Empire into western and eastern entities in AD 395, the Cyclades were ruled from Byzantium

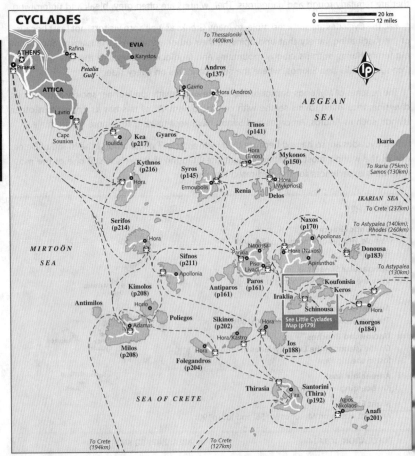

(Constantinople); but following the fall of Byzantium in 1204, the Franks ceded the Cyclades to Venice, which parcelled the islands out to opportunistic aristocrats. The most powerful aristocrats was Marco Sanudo (self-styled Duke of Naxos), who acquired Naxos, Paros, Ios, Santorini, Anafi, Sifnos, Milos, Amorgos and Folegandros, introducing a Venetian gloss that survives to this day in island architecture.

The Cyclades came under Turkish rule in 1537. Neglected by the Ottomans, they became backwaters prone to pirate raids, hence the labyrinthine, hilltop character of their towns – the mazes of narrow lanes were designed to disorientate invaders. Nevertheless, the impact of piracy led to the massive depopulation of the Cyclades; in 1563 only five of the islands were still inhabited.

The Cyclades' participation in the Greek War of Independence was minimal, but they became havens for people fleeing from islands where insurrections against the Turks had led to massacres. During WWII the islands were occupied by the Italians.

The fortunes of the Cycladics have been revived by the tourism boom that began in the 1970s. Until then, many islanders lived in deep poverty; many more gave up the economic battle and headed for the mainland, or to America and Australia, in search of work.

GETTING THERE & AWAY
Air
Olympic Airlines (www.olympicairlines.com) links Athens with Naxos, Syros, Santorini, Mykonos, Paros and Milos. From Mykonos there are flights to/from Thessaloniki, Santorini and Rhodes (see individual island sections for details).

Aegean Airlines (www.aegeanair.com) flies to Mykonos and Santorini from Athens and Thessaloniki.

Fast Boat & Catamaran
Large high-speed boats and catamarans are on the increase on Cyclades' routes, mainly during the late spring to early autumn period. The travel time is usually half that of regular ferries. Seats fill fast in July and August, especially on weekends, so it's worth

booking your ticket a day or so in advance. With increasing numbers of faster ferries joining the fleet and foreign operators, including British ferry companies, becoming involved, services to the islands may see some interesting developments in the next few years.

Ferry
Ferry routes separate the Cyclades into western, northern, central and eastern subgroups.

Most ferries services operating within the Cyclades connect one of these subgroups with the ports of Piraeus, Lavrio or Rafina on the mainland. The central Cyclades (Paros, Naxos, Ios and Santorini) are the most-visited and have the best ferry links with the mainland, usually to Piraeus.

The northern Cyclades (Andros, Tinos, Syros and Mykonos) have excellent connections with the mainland. The departure point for Andros is Rafina, but it's possible to reach it from Piraeus by catching a ferry to Syros, Tinos or Mykonos and connecting from there.

Lavrio is the mainland port for ferries serving Kea, from where connections south to the other western Cyclades are not good. Kythnos has a reasonable number of connections to Piraeus and good connections south to other islands. Milos, Serifos and Sifnos have welcomed greatly improved ferry connections with Piraeus in recent years. Folegandros and Sikinos have less frequent connections with the mainland.

The eastern Cyclades (Anafi, Amorgos, Iraklia, Schinousa, Koufonisia and Donousa) are the least-visited and have the fewest ferry links with the mainland. Amorgos, Iraklia, Schinousa and Koufonisia are best visited from Naxos; Anafi from Santorini.

Whilst planning your island-hopping it pays to bear this pattern of ferry routes in mind; however, Paros is the ferry hub of the Cyclades, and connections between different groups are usually possible via this port.

See table for an overview of high-season ferry services to the Cyclades from the mainland and Crete. The information relates to slower, traditional ferries.

FERRY CONNECTIONS TO THE CYCLADES

Origin	Destination	Dur	Fare	Freq
Agios Nikolaos (Crete)	Milos	7hr	€19	2 weekly
Iraklio (Crete)	Mykonos	9hr	€23	3 weekly
	Naxos	7½hr	€19.50	weekly
	Paros	7-8hr	€22	2 weekly
	Santorini	3¾hr	€14.70	3 weekly
	Syros	10hr	€23.40	weekly
	Tinos	10¼hr	€25	2 weekly
Lavrio	Kea	1¼hr	€5.90	2 daily
	Kythnos	3½hr	€7.70	6 weekly
	Syros	3½hr	€14.20	2 weekly
Piraeus	Amorgos	10hr	€18.60	10 weekly
	Anafi	11hr	€24.70	3 weekly
	Donousa	7hr	€17.80	3 weekly
Piraeus	Folegandros	6-9hr	€18.40	4 weekly
	Ios	7hr	€19.50	4 daily
	Iraklia	6¾hr	€17.40	3 weekly
	Kimolos	6hr	€17.30	2 weekly
	Koufonisia	8hr	€17.20	5 weekly
	Kythnos	2½hr	€11.20	2 daily
	Milos	5-7hr	€17.90	2 daily
	Mykonos	6hr	€22.60	3 daily
	Naxos	6hr	€18.20	6 daily
	Paros	5hr	€18.80	6 daily
	Santorini	9hr	€21.50	4 daily
	Serifos	4½hr	€14.90	daily
	Sifnos	5hr	€16	daily
	Sikinos	10hr	€20.30	7 weekly
	Syros	4hr	€16.20	3 daily
	Tinos	5hr	€14.10	2 daily
Rafina	Andros	2hr	€9.20	2 daily
	Mykonos	4½hr	€15.90	2 daily
	Tinos	3½hr	€18.20	2 daily
Sitia (Crete)	Milos	9hr	€19	3 weekly
Thessaloniki	Mykonos	15hr	€35	3 weekly
	Naxos	15hr	€34.50	weekly
	Paros	15-16hr	€35	2 weekly
	Santorini	19hr	€38.40	3 weekly
	Syros	12hr	€31.20	weekly
	Tinos	13hr	€35	2 weekly

GETTING AROUND

For information on travel within the Cyclades, see the individual island entries.

The Cyclades are more exposed to the northwesterly *meltemi* than other island groups. This is a fierce wind; it may be warm, but it can blast, and it often plays havoc with ferry schedules (especially for smaller vessels that ply the Little Cyclades routes and small hydrofoils). Keep this in mind if you're on a tight schedule.

ANDROS ΑΝΔΡΟΣ

pop 9999

Andros is an escapist's dream. It is the most northerly of the Cyclades and the second largest after Naxos; it is not overwhelmed by tourism, and has lonely mountains and terraced valleys to wander through. Andros boasts neoclassical mansions and Venetian tower-houses that contrast with the rough unpainted stonework of farm buildings and patterned dovecotes. Slate walls and cobbled footpaths wriggle across the rugged landscape. The island's natural beauty is enhanced even more by a strong archaeological and cultural heritage.

Andros is also one of the most fertile of the Cyclades; it produces citrus fruit and olives, and supports large swathes of pine, plane and cypress trees. The island has several beaches, many of them isolated. There are three main settlements: the unpretentious port of Gavrio, the cheerful resort of Batsi and the handsome main town, Hora, known also as Andros.

Getting There & Away

FERRY

At least three ferries daily leave Andros' main port of Gavrio for Rafina (€9.20, two hours). Daily ferries run to Tinos (€6.70, 1½ hours) and Mykonos (€8.90, 2½ hours); conveniently allowing daily connections to Syros and Paros in the high season. Services run direct to Syros, from May to October, three times a week (€7.40, two hours). Three ferries a week run to Paros (€12.10, four hours), and there's a weekly service to Naxos (€13.50, five hours) and Kea (€7.10, 8½ hours).

Getting Around

Around nine buses daily (fewer on weekends) link Gavrio and Hora (€3, 55 minutes) via Batsi (€1.50, 15 minutes); schedules are posted at the bus stop in Gavrio and Hora and outside Andros Travel in Batsi; otherwise, call ☎ 22820 22316 for information.

A **taxi** (☎ 22820 71171 in Gavrio, ☎ 22820 41081 in Batsi, ☎ 22820 22171 in Hora) from Gavrio to Batsi costs €5 and to Hora €22. Car hire is about €35 in August, about €25 in the off season.

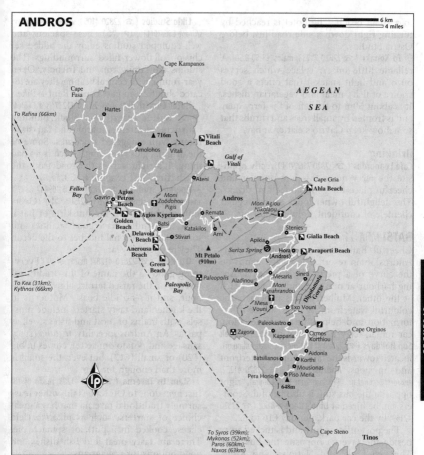

ANDROS

0   6 km
0   4 miles

AEGEAN SEA

CYCLADES

GAVRIO ΓΑΥΡΙΟ

Gavrio, on the west coast, is the main port of Andros. Apart from the flurry of ferry arrivals it is very low key, but there are pleasant beaches nearby.

Orientation & Information

The ferry quay is situated midway along the waterfront and the bus stop is right next to it. Turn left from the quay and walk along the front for 150m to get to the post office. You will find a bank with ATM midwaterfront.

Greek Sun Holidays (☎ 22820 41252; greeksun@
travelling.gr) Helpful; has an office at Gavrio, right opposite the ferry quay.

Port police (☎ 22820 71213) On the waterfront.

Sleeping & Eating

There are few sleeping places in Gavrio. A couple of options in the harbour area are essentially a last resort, but things improve just out of town.

Ostria Studios (☎ 22820 71551; www.ostria-studios
.gr; s/d/apt €55/60/67) These decent apartments in a big spacious complex of rising terraces are a good choice, especially for reduced prices off season. It is about 300m along the Batsi road.

Andros Holiday Hotel (☎ 22820 71384; www
.androsholiday.com; s incl breakfast €75-85, d incl breakfast
€85-95; ⊗ Easter–mid-Oct; Ⓟ 🐶 🏊) This resort-style hotel on the Batsi road overlooks the sea. It has a slightly well-worn ambience that is quite appealing. There's direct access

to a small beach. The hotel is reached by turning right down a side road just before Ostria Studios.

To Konaki (☎ 22820 71733; mains €3.50-8.50) A reliable little *ouzeri* (place which serves ouzo and light snacks) that offers a good choice of fish , meat and vegetarian dishes. It is about 50m to the left of the ferry quay and is fronted by small trees and shrubs that somehow keep Gavrio's clatter at bay.

Drinking

Café Leanordos (☎ 22820 71669) Directly opposite the ferry quay, this is a popular and cheerful place for good coffee and drinks. The delightful owner looks after a regular clientele of confident, voluble Andriots.

BATSI ΜΠΑΤΣΙ

Cheerful Batsi, 8km south of Gavrio, is Andros' main resort. The village stands on the curve of a pretty bay and has a fishing harbour at one end and a sandy beach at the other. Mulberry trees punctuate the colourful waterfront. A great source of information and help with accommodation, car rental, ferry tickets and more, is **Greek Sun Holidays** (☎ 22820 41198; greeksun@travelling.gr), located towards the far end of the waterfront and up steps. **Andros Travel** (☎ 22820 41252; androstr@otenet.gr; 9am-2pm & 6-9.30pm), right opposite the bus stop is also helpful. Scooters can be hired at **Dino's Rent-a-Bike** (☎ 22820 42169) by the car park, per day €16 to €22.

The post office is tiny and is tucked away beside the taverna opposite the bus stop. The taxi rank, and National and Alpha banks (with ATMs), are all midwaterfront.

Tours

Greek Sun Holidays & Andros Travel (☎ 22820 41 252) Organises island tours (€22) from May to October that take in Paleopolis and the village of Korthi on the Bay of Korthiou; Menites, with its elaborate fountain; Apikia with its old mansions, and the 8th-century Moni Agiou Nikolaou complete with beautiful murals. There are also small-group, guided half- and full-day walks (€18 to €28) following old paths through beautiful countryside.

Poseidon (☎ 22820 41696) This local boat runs there-and-back trips to nearby beaches (€10). Details can also be had from the Koala taverna.

Sleeping & Eating

For July and August it's wise to book accommodation well ahead.

Likio Studios (☎ 22820 41050; www.likiostudios.gr; s/d/apt €56/70/110;   ) These spacious and well-equipped studios enjoy the added seclusion of flower-filled surroundings. The studios are family run and friendly. Open year-round, with central heating, they are located about 250m past Dino's Rent-a-Bike.

Hotel Chryssi Akti (☎ 22820 41237; s/d €48/66;   ) A resort-style block building with acres of internal marble and fair-sized rooms with staggered balconies. Some of the original gloss is fading, which is no bad thing. It's right across the road from the beach. Breakfast is about €4.50.

Anemos Studios (☎ 22820 42305, 69447 83998; anemosst@syr.forthnet.gr; s/d €42/50;   ) Overlooking the sea, on the outskirts of Batsi, these fine studios have good facilities and some nice traditional touches to the décor. They're open all year.

Oti Kalo (☎ 22820 41287; mains €4-9) 'Everything good' is the name of this traditional taverna on the raised terrace above the harbour, and it's no idle boast. Mother is in the kitchen and tasty starters include mussels, with mains of meat and fish as well as pastas. An Andros speciality, *frutalia* (spicy sausage and potato omelette), comes in big (€20) or small (€17), but even the small is more than enough for two.

Stamatis Taverna (☎ 22820 41283; mains €4-18) Just next door to Oti Kalo is this other reassuringly traditional taverna that has a great choice of starters, such as *pikatiko* (feta cheese cooked in a pot), or spinach pie. There are tasty meat and fish dishes and good options for vegetarians.

Koala (☎ 22820 41696; mains €4.70-10) Midway along the line of waterfront tavernas is this cheerful place noted for its very big breakfasts (€7), its tasty pastas and pizzas (€4.70 to €10) and its local dishes.

Drinking & Entertainment

There are several lively music bars all clustered together at the inner corner of the waterfront where the road bends to the right. They include Nameless, Aqua and Kimbo, all of which play mainstream disco with modern Greek music when the local crowd is in.

Shopping

Gavrio has the usual swathe of gift shops.

Melita (☎ 22820 42005) For a special gift try this neat little pottery shop tucked between

CYCLADES

the Oti Kalo and Stamatis tavernas, for Andros-made ceramics.

HORA (ANDROS) ΧΩΡΑ (ΑΝΔΡΟΣ)
pop 1508

Hora, the delightful capital of Andros, lies on the east coast 35km east of Gavrio, where it unfolds its charms along a narrow rocky peninsula between two bays. It's an absorbing little town that reflects Venetian origins in numerous elegant neoclassical mansions underscored with Byzantine and Ottoman accents. Hora's cultural pedigree is even more distinguished by its Museum of Modern Art and the impressive Archaeological Museum.

Orientation & Information

If you arrive by car, turn right at the T-junction on Plateia Ieroy Loxoy, then left and then right again. Bear down right a few metres to a car park.

The bus station is on Plateia Goulandri, situated at the entrance to town. From the bus stop, cross the square to its bottom left-hand corner, head down a narrow lane past the taxi rank to reach a T-junction. The post office is up to the left.

Otherwise, turn right onto the, notionally, pedestrianised main street. The National Bank of Greece, and the Alpha Bank, both with ATMs, are halfway down the main street near a big church that has palm trees gracing its forecourt. Opposite the church, steps lead down to the old harbour area of Plakoura, and to Nimborio Beach.

Further down the main street is the pretty central square, Plateia Kaïri, with tree-shaded tavernas and cafés watched over by the Archaeological Museum. Steps descend from the square, north to Plakoura and Nimborio Beach and south to Paraporti Beach. The street passes beneath a short arcade and then continues along the promontory, bends left, then right and ends at Plateia Riva, a big, airy square with crumbling balustrades and a giant bronze statue.

Sights & Activities

Hora has two outstanding museums; both were donated to the state by Vasilis and Elise Goulandris, of the wealthy ship-owning Andriot family. The **Andros Archaeological Museum** (☎ 22820 23664; Plateia Kaïri; adult/child/

student €3/2/free; ✆ 8.30am-3pm Tue-Sun) contains impressive finds from the settlements of Zagora and Paleopolis (9th–8th century BC) on Andros' east coast, as well as items of the Roman, Byzantine and Early Christian periods. They include a spellbinding marble copy of the 4th-century bronze **Hermes of Andros** by Praxiteles.

The **Museum of Modern Art** (☎ 22820 22650; adult/student €6/3 Jun-Sep, €3/1.50 Oct-May; ✆ 10am-2pm & 6-8pm Wed-Mon, 10am-2pm Sun Jul-Sep, 10am-2pm Sat-Mon Oct-Jun) has earned Andros a reputation in the international art world. The main gallery features the work of prominent Greek artists but each year, from July to September, the gallery stages an exhibition of one of the world's great artists. To date there have been exhibitions featuring the work of Picasso, Matisse, Braque, Toulouse-Lautrec and Miro. To reach the gallery head down the steps from Plateia Kaïri towards the old harbour.

A huge **bronze statue** of a sailor stands in Plateia Riva, looking more Russian triumphalist than Andriot in its scale and style. It celebrates Hora's great seagoing traditions. The ruins of a **Venetian fortress** stand on an island that is linked to the tip of the headland by the worn remnants of a steeply arched bridge.

A great option is to hire a self-drive boat and head out to some of the west and north coast's glorious beaches, most of which are difficult to reach by road. **Riva Boats** (☎ 22820 24412, 69744 60330; Hora) have superb 4.5m Norwegian-built open boats with 20hp outboards. They are very seaworthy and come complete with life raft, anchor and even a mobile phone. You do not need a licence to drive these boats. They can carry four adults comfortably. Hire per boat for a minimum of one day is about €90.

Scooters and motorbikes can also be hired from Riva down at Nimborio Beach, and through Karaoulanis Rooms for €12 to €15. Riva also sells fishing tackle and boat fittings.

Sleeping & Eating

Karaoulanis Rooms (☎ 22820 24412, 69744 60330; www.androsrooms.gr; d/apt €50/100) There's a friendly and kind welcome at this tall harbourside house, where rooms and apartments have been recently refurbished to the highest standards. To get there, head down the steps opposite the big church halfway down the main street, and keep going to the harbour. Check here also for scooter and boat hire.

Alcioni Inn (☎ 22820 24522, 69734 03934; alcioni@hellastourism.gr; Nimborio; s/d €60/100) These self-catering rooms are very smart and comfortable. They are in the midst of the main waterfront, just across the road from the beach, but have a nicely secluded and relaxing atmosphere.

Niki (☎ /fax 22820 29155; s/d €55/75) There's great individuality at this handsome old house that's right on the main street and handy for just about everything. The owner has done a marvellous job in restoring the building and has retained beautiful timber ceilings and galleries. Downstairs is a large veranda where you can relax, get breakfast for about €8, or coffee.

Nonna's (☎ 22820 23577; Plakoura; mains €3-9) A small, down-to-earth meze place on the old harbour, next to Karaoulanis Rooms, Nonna's main dishes are mainly fish, fresh from the family's own boat. Monkfish and red mullet are two marvellous dishes that are often available. Vegetarians also have a great choice, from salads to zucchini pie.

Palinorio (☎ 22820 22881; Nimborio; mains €8-15; ☽ 11am-2am) Among the line of waterfront tavernas at Nimborio Beach, this is the one for a great choice of delicious traditional dishes, as well as good service and value.

DESIGNER DOVECOTES

There's nothing fancier than the pigeon fanciers' dovecotes of Andros and Tinos.

Peppering the wide open spaces of the islands are hundreds of these remarkable buildings, isolated within the landscape and reflecting distinctive architecture of great charm and skill. The breeding of pigeons has long been an island trade; the birds supplied meat for the winter months, droppings for field manure, and feathers for bedding.

It's said that the Venetians first introduced dovecotes to the Cyclades. They are like tiny palaces, 'embroidered' with symbols of trees, wagon wheels, triangles, chevrons, and sun symbols; all worked in slate and stone and then whitewashed, creating a rich interplay of light and shade. Most remaining dovecotes date from the 18th and 19th centuries.

Shellfish dishes are more expensive, but are prepared with skill.

Ernis (☎ 22820 22233; Plateia Kaïri) By the square, this is a pleasant little café and pastry shop.

Mickey's Cafe-Bar (☎ 22820 23508; ☽ 10am-4pm & 9pm-2.30am) Just up the street from Ernis, this hosts a buzzing music scene for young locals, day and night.

AROUND ANDROS

Between Gavrio and Paleopolis Bay are several pleasant beaches, including **Agios Kyprianos**, where there's a little church with a taverna close by, **Delavoia**, one half of which is naturist, **Anerousa** and **Green Beach**.

Paleopolis, 9km south of Batsi on the coast road, is the site of Ancient Andros, where the Hermes of Andros was found. The small, but intriguing, **Archaeological Museum of Paleopilis** (☎ 22829 41985; admission free; ☽ 8.30am-3pm Tue-Sun) was opened in 2005 and displays and interprets finds from the area.

The blue-green bay and resort at **Ormos Korthiou**, 20km south of Hora, has a lot of faded charm. You'll find several standard hotels and *domatia* (cheap rooms), as well as a handful of reasonably priced restaurants.

TINOS ΤΗΝΟΣ

pop 8574

On Tinos, religious pilgrims are brought to their knees by their devotion to the sacred icon of the Megalochari, the Holy Virgin, which takes pride of place in the splendid Church of Panagia Evangelistria in the main town of Hora. Religion took a firm grip on Tinos in centuries past and has not let go in recent times. The main religious focus may be Greek Orthodox, but Turkish rule was lax on Tinos and a legacy of the resilient Venetian influence is the survival of a substantial Roman Catholic community. Tinos is a beautiful island of rock-studded mountains and terraced hill slopes, dotted with over forty villages that look like marble outcrops up against the dark hills. Ornate dovecotes vie with handsome church belfries throughout the island and there is a rich artistic tradition here, not least in the sculptors' village of Pyrgos. All of this is reward enough for any kind of pilgrim.

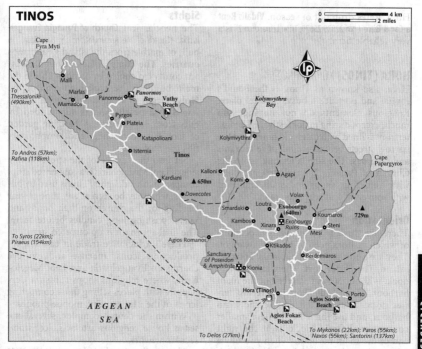

TINOS

0 ————— 4 km
0 ————— 2 miles

Cape
Fyra Myti

Malli

To
Thessaloniki
(490km)

Marlas
Mamados   Panormos   Panormos
                        Bay   Vathy
                              Beach

Pyrgos
Plateia

Katapolioani

To Andros (57km);
Rafina (118km)

Isternia

Kolymvythra   Kolymvythra
               Bay

Tinos

Cape
Papargyros

Kardiani   Kalloni
▲ 650m   Komi   Agapi

Dovecotes   Volax

To Syros (22km);
Piraeus (154km)

Smardaki   Loutra   Exobourgo
                      ▲(640m)   Koumaros   729m ▲
Kambos   Exobourgo
            Xinara   Ruins   Steni
Agios Romanos   Mesi

Sanctuary   Ktikados
of Poseidon
& Amphitrite Kionia   Berdemiaros

Hora (Tinos)   Porto

AEGEAN
SEA   Agios Sostis
                     Beach
          Agios Fokas
          Beach

To Delos (27km)   To Mykonos (22km); Paros (55km);
                     Naxos (55km); Santorini (137km)

CYCLADES

Getting There & Away

EXCURSION BOAT

The excursion boat *Tinos Sky* runs trips to Delos and Mykonos (about €20 to €25) from the middle port at 9am Tuesday to Sunday. You have two hours on Delos, four on Mykonos and return to Tilos at about 6pm. Trips run mid-June to mid-September.

FAST BOAT & CATAMARAN

There are at least three services daily to Mykonos (€7.50, 15 minutes) and Rafina (€28.20, 1¾ hours), plus daily services to Paros (€17, 1¼ hours), five weekly to Piraeus (€35.80, three hours) and one daily to Syros (€7.50, two hours).

FERRY

At least six ferries daily go to Mykonos (€3.75, 30 minutes), and four daily to Rafina (€14.10, 3½ hours) and Andros (€6.70, 1½ hours). There are at least two daily to Syros (€3.60, 50 minutes) and Piraeus (€18.20, six hours).

Four weekly ferries go to Ikaria via Mykonos (€17.60, 3½ hours).

Two ferries weekly go to Thessaloniki (€35, 12 hours), and there are daily services to Paros (€8.50, 2½ hours), and Santorini (€16.40, five hours).

Two weekly services run to Naxos (€11, 4¼ hours) and Iraklio on Crete (€25, 10¼ hours).

There are two weekly ferries to Amorgos (€17.20, 2¼ hours) and one weekly ferry to Skiathos (€23, 7¼ hours).

Getting Around

There are frequent buses, June to September, from Hora (Tinos) to Porto and Kionia (€1, 10 minutes) and several daily to Panormos (€3, one hour) via Kambos (€1, 15 minutes) and Pyrgos (€2.80, 50 minutes). At the time of writing buses left from the station on the waterfront, opposite the Blue Star Ferry Office, where there's a timetable in the window. There are plans to move the bus station near the Outer Port, in front of Windmills Travel on Kionion 2.

Motorcycles (per day €15) and cars (minimum per day €35) can be hired from a number of outfits along the waterfront at

Hora. Rates drop out of season. **Vidalis Rent a Car & Bike** (☎ 22830 25670; Trion Leararchon 2) is a very reliable firm.

HORA (TINOS) ΧΩΡΑ (ΤΗΝΟΣ)

Hora, also known as Tinos, is the island's capital and port. It's a busy, cheerful place. Religious elements do not impinge too much, except during major festivals. The waterfront is lined with cafés and hotels and the narrow streets behind are full of restaurants and tavernas. The streets leading up to the Church of Panagia Evangelistria are lined with numerous shops and stalls crammed with souvenirs and religious ware.

Orientation

There are three ferry quays, the locations of which visitors need to be very aware of. They are know as 'ports' by locals. Looking inland, The Outer Port, where large ferries dock, is about 300m to the left of the main harbour. The Middle Port, where fast ferries dock, is at the left end of the main harbour, and the Inner Port, where smaller conventional ferries dock, is at the right end of the main harbour. When you buy a ferry ticket it's essential to check which port your ferry is leaving from. Allow at least 20 minutes to walk from the centre of town to the Outer Port.

The uphill street of Leof Megaloharis, straight ahead from the middle of the main waterfront, is the route pilgrims take to the church. The narrower Evangelistria, to its right, also leads to the Church of Panagia Evangelistria.

Information

The post office is at the southeastern end of the waterfront, just past the bus station and the National Bank of Greece (with ATM) is 50m left of Hotel Posidonion.

Malliaris Travel (☎ 22830 24241; fax 22830 24243; malliaris@thn.forthnet.gr; Paralia) On the waterfront near Hotel Posidonion; handles ferry tickets.

Port police (☎ 22830 22348; Kionion) Just up from Windmills Travel.

Symposion (☎ 22830 24368; Evangelistria 13) A pleasant café-bistro that has Internet access (per half-hour €3).

Windmills Travel & Tourism (☎ 22830 23398; www.windmillstravel.com; Kionion 2) Halfway between the new ferry quay and the central waterfront, this is very helpful and can arrange accommodation, car hire and much more.

Sights

The neoclassical **Church of Panagia Evangelistria** (Church of the Annunciation; 🕑 8am-8pm) is built of marble from the island's Panormos quarries. The complex lies within a pleasant courtyard cooled by arcades. Inside the main building the acclaimed icon of the Holy Virgin is draped with gold, silver, jewels and pearls, and is surrounded by gifts from supplicants. A hanging garden of fabulous chandeliers and lampholders fills the roof space.

Set into the surface of the street on one side of Leof Megaloharis is a rubberised strip, complete with sidelights. This is used by pilgrims, who may be seen at any time of year heading for the church on their hands and knees, pushing long candles before them. The final approach is up carpeted steps.

There's a lucrative trade in candles, reproduction icons, incense and evil-eye charms on Evangelistria and Leof Megaloharis, where religious shops rub shoulders happily with places selling those competing icons of the 21st century, mobile phones.

Within the church complex, several **museums** house religious artefacts, icons and secular artworks.

The small **archaeological museum** (☎ 22830 22670; Leof Megaloharis; admission €2; 🕑 8am-3pm Tue-Sun) on the right-hand side of the street as you descend from the church, has a small collection that includes impressive clay *pithoi* (storage jars), grave reliefs and sculptures.

Sleeping

Avoid Hora on 25 March (Annunciation), 15 August (Feast of the Assumption) and 15 November (Advent), unless you want to join the roofless masses who sleep on the streets at these times.

BUDGET

Camping Tinos (☎ 22830 22344; www.camping.gr/tinos; sites per adult/tent €6/3, bungalows with/without bathroom €25/18) This is a fine site with good facilities. It's south of the town, near Agios Fokas, about a five-minute walk from the ferry quay, and is clearly signposted from the waterfront. A minibus meets ferries.

MIDRANGE & TOP END

Oceanis (☎ 22830 22452; oceanis@mail.gr; Akti G Drosou; s/d €30/50; ❄) Immaculate and modern, yet is run with confident, old-fashioned style.

CYCLADES

THE AUTHOR'S CHOICE

Metaxy Mas (☎ 22830 25945; Plateia Palladas; mains €7.50-16) You can tell a great restaurant as soon as you walk in, and Metaxy Mas is such a place. There's a merging of modern with traditional in the décor, and the service has that magic combination of courtesy and warmth. The food is modern Mediterranean. Try starters such as *yigantes me spanaki* (giant beans with spinach), or the truly succulent cheese pie. Mains treats include veal casserole or cuttlefish with spinach, and for vegetarians there's aubergines roasted with cheese or mushrooms in egg and lemon sauce. Desserts are dreamlike and the wine list has some of the best mainland wines while the house wine, at €6 to €8 a kilo, is still worth every sip.

Rooms are not huge, but you won't beat them for smartness. They even have some genuine, if small, single rooms. There's a lift to all floors. Breakfast is €6.

Boreades (☎ 22830 23845; s €40-50, d €45-65, apt €140) A fairly ordinary location belies the style and comfort of this interesting place that manages to convey an almost country-house ambience with its interior plan and creative décor. Breakfast in the sunny lounge is €7.

Hotel Posidonion (☎ 22830 23121; fax 22830 25808; Paralia 4; s/d €55/70) Located midwaterfront, Posidonian is a long-established, unfussy hotel. Communal lounges overlooking the harbour are an endearing feature. Much refurbishment has taken place in recent years and most rooms are well-appointed and comfortable.

Eating

Waterfront places serve standard fare, but away from the front there are some worthwhile places and one particularly outstanding restaurant (see boxed text, above).

Pallada Taverna (☎ 22830 23516; Plateia Palladas; mains €4-9) A popular place, Pallada offers Greek dishes such as tasty veal, pork and lamb specialities. It has persuasive retsina and other local wines from the barrel. Follow the waterfront road left from the Middle Port round a busy corner and where things open out, go sharp right onto Plateia Palladas.

To Koutouki tis Elenis (☎ 22830 24857; G. Gagou 5; mains €6-12) Tucked away off the bottom of Evagelistrias, is this cosy little place, jostling for space with other tavernas and cafés. It offers several tasty dishes including rabbit *stifado* (cooked in a tomato purée) and a worthwhile fish soup.

Drinking & Entertainment

Koursaros (☎ 22830 23963; 8am-3am) A relaxed centre of non-religious music on Tinos, this bar, at the outer end of the line of cafés across from the Middle Port, plays an engaging mix of rock, funk and jazz.

In the pleasantly seedy back street behind the Pallada Taverna you'll find Tinos' little clubland with fairly raw venues such as Volto and Sibylla whacking out clubby standards and Greek floorburners.

AROUND TINOS

To make the most of Tinos and its numerous villages, beaches and dramatic countryside, you need to get out of Hora's religious-commercial grip and go exploring.

At **Porto**, 6km east of Hora, there's a lovely, uncrowded beach facing Mykonos, while about 1km further on from Porto is the even lovelier **Pahia Ammos Beach**.

Kionia, 3km northwest of Hora, has several small beaches. Near the largest beach are the scant remains of the 4th-century-BC site of the **Sanctuary of Poseidon & Amphitrite**.

About 12km north of Hora on the north coast is **Kolymvythra Bay**, where there are two fine sandy beaches, the smaller with sun loungers, umbrellas and a seasonal café, the larger backed by reed beds.

On the north coast, 28km northwest of Hora, is the seaside village of **Panormos** from where the distinctive green marble, quarried in nearby **Marlas**, was once exported. The waterfront at Panormos is lined with tavernas.

Pyrgos, on the way to Panormos, is a heartwarming little village where even the cemetery is a feast of carved marble. Look for the tiny marble inlays in the street surfaces of the village, depicting anchors, ships, shells and other symbols. During the late 19th century and early 20th century Pyrgos was the centre of a remarkable tradition of sculpture and fine vernacular architecture.

Just across the road from the car park at the entrance to the village is the **Museum**

House of Yannoulis Halepas (adult/child €5/2.50; 10.30am-2.30pm & 5-8pm Apr–mid-Oct) a compelling place, where the sculptor's humble rooms and workshop, with their striated plaster walls and slate floors, have been preserved. An adjoining gallery has splendid examples of the work of local sculptors. Outstanding are *Girl on a Rock* by Georgios Vamvakis, *Hamlet*, by Loukas Doukas and a copy of the superb *Fisherman* by Dimitrios Filippolis.

About 6km directly north of Hora is the tiny village of **Volax**, a scribble of white houses at the heart of an amphitheatre of low hills studded with thousands of dark-coloured boulders. Behind the doorways, Volax really is old Greece. There's a small **folklore museum** (ask at the nearest house for the key), an attractive Catholic chapel and a small outdoor theatre. There are a couple of tavernas at the entrance to Volax.

The ruins of the Venetian fortress of **Exobourgo** lie 2km south of Volax, on top of a mighty 640m rock outcrop. Head south from Volax past the Koumaras turn-off on the road to Steni, then go right up a side road that ends at a church. From here it's a steep but reasonable 15-minute walk to the summit where the view will take away whatever breath you have left.

SYROS ΣΥΡΟΣ

pop 16,766

Syros is the big boss of the Cyclades: the ferry hub of the northern islands, the legal and administrative centre of the entire group and home to Ermoupolis, the most handsome of all Cycladic towns. If you break the lightest of laws anywhere in the Cyclades, you'll be whisked off to court in Syros. It's probably best to make your visit to Syros voluntary instead. The rewards for travellers are substantial and include exposure to authentic Greek culture and society, great eating and sleeping options and a handful of small but pleasant beaches. Because Syros' core economy does not depend on tourism, there is none of the overt commercialism of more tourist-bound islands. Local shipbuilding has declined, but Syros still has textile manufacturing, dairy farms and a thriving horticultural industry.

History

Excavations of an Early Cycladic fortified settlement and burial ground, at Kastri in the island's northeast, date from the Neolithic period, 2800–2300 BC.

In the Middle Ages, Syros was the only Greek island with an entirely Roman Catholic population, a result of conversion by the Catholic Franks who took over the island in 1207. This ensured that during Turkish rule, Syros enjoyed effective neutrality, and the protection of the French. During the War of Independence thousands of refugees from islands ravaged by the Turks fled to Syros. They brought with them an infusion of Greek Orthodoxy and fresh commercial incentives. Through their energies they built a new settlement (now called Vrodado), and made the port town of Ermoupolis the commercial, naval and cultural centre of Greece during the 19th century.

Getting There & Away

AIR

Olympic Airlines (22810 88018; fax 22810 83536; www.olympicairlines.com; Akti Papagou, Ermoupolis) operates at least one flight daily, except Thursday and Saturday, to Athens (€64, 35 minutes). The Olympic Airlines office is at the airport, but you can buy tickets at tourist agencies.

FAST BOAT & CATAMARAN

Services depart daily for Piraeus (€33, 2½ hours), Rafina (€27, 1¾ hours), Paros (€13.30, 45 minutes), Naxos (€13.80, 1½ hours), Mykonos (€12, 30 minutes) and Tinos (€7.50, two hours).

FERRY

There are at least four ferries departing daily from Syros to Piraeus (€21, four hours), two to Tinos every day except Tuesday (€5, 50 minutes), and four to Mykonos (€7, 1¼ hours).

There are two daily to Paros (€7.50, 1¾ hours) and Naxos (€10, three hours). There are daily connections to Andros via Tinos (€9, 2¾ hours) and two direct connections weekly (1¾ hours, €7.40).

At least four ferries weekly go to Amorgos (€14, 4½ hours), Ios (€14, 2¾ hours), Ikaria (€10.70, 2½ hours), Milos (€14.70, six hours), Samos (€17.10, 4½ hours) and

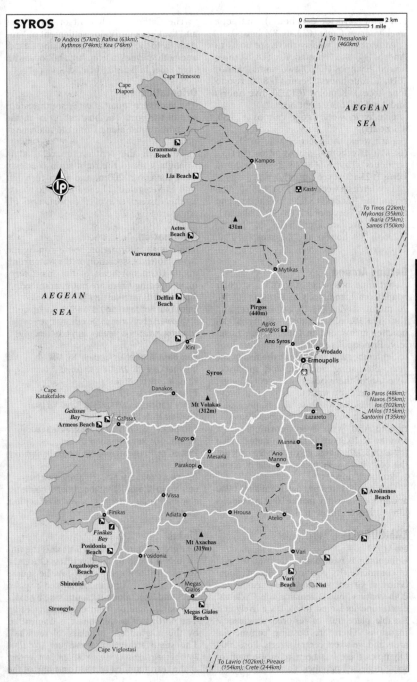

SYROS

0 — 2 km
0 — 1 mile

To Andros (57km); Rafina (63km); Kythnos (74km); Kea (76km)

To Thessaloniki (460km)

Cape Trimeson

Cape Diapori

A E G E A N
S E A

Grammata Beach

Lia Beach

Kampos

Kastri

Aetos Beach

431m

Varvarousa

Mytikas

A E G E A N
S E A

Delfini Beach

Pirgos (440m)

Agios Georgios

Kini

Ano Syros

Vrodado
Ermoupolis

Syros

Cape Katakefalos

Danakos

Galissas Bay
Armeos Beach

Galissas

Mt Volakas (312m)

Lazareto

To Tinos (22km); Mykonos (35km); Ikaria (75km); Samos (150km)

To Paros (48km); Naxos (55km); Ios (102km); Milos (115km); Santorini (135km)

Pagos

Mesaria

Manna

Parakopi

Ano Manno

Vissa

Finikas

Adiata

Hrousa

Atelio

Azolimnos Beach

Finikas Bay
Posidonia Beach

Angathopes Beach

Shinonisi

Posidonia

Mt Axachas (319m)

Vari

Vari Beach

Nisi

Strongylo

Megas Gialos

Megas Gialos Beach

Cape Viglostasi

To Lavrio (102km); Pireaus (154km); Crete (244km)

CYCLADES

Santorini (€18.10, 5¼ hours); and one weekly serves Crete (€23.40, 8½ hours).

At least twice weekly there are boats to Andros (€7.40, 1¾ hours), Kea (€8.70, three hours), Kythnos (€7.60, two hours), Sifnos (€10,80, four hours), Serifos (€8.80, two to four hours), Kimolos (€12.20, five hours) and Anafi (€16.30, eight hours).

Five ferries weekly go to Patmos (€23.50, 4½ hours).

Each week, three ferries head to Sikinos (€10.10, five hours), Folegandros (€11.30, six hours), Lavrio (€14.20, 3½ hours) and Leros (€25.10, seven hours).

Two ferries a week go to Kos (€28.40, nine hours) and Rhodes (€33.20, 15½ hours), and one goes to Thessaloniki (€31.20, 12 hours).

There are weekly ferries to Iraklio (€23.40, 7½ hours) and Nisyros (€20.30, 11 hours).

Getting Around

About nine buses per day run a circular route from Ermoupolis to Galissas (€1.10, 20 minutes) Vari (€1.10, 30 minutes) and Kini (€1.30, 35 minutes) calling at all beaches mentioned in this section. Buses leave Ermoupolis every half hour from June to September and every hour the rest of the year, alternating clockwise and anticlockwise. All of these buses will eventually get you to where you want to go, but it's always worth checking which service is quickest.

There is a bus from Ermoupolis bus station to Ano Syros every morning except Sunday at 10.30am (€1, 15 minutes). **Taxis** (☎ 22810 86222) charge €5 to Ano Syros from the port; it's a very pleasant walk of about 1.5km back down.

Cars can be hired per day from about €40 and mopeds per day from €10 at numerous hire outlets on the waterfront.

ERMOUPOLIS ΕΡΜΟΥΠΟΛΗ

pop 11,799

Ermoupolis is named after Hermes, the god of commerce. Its position as the maritime centre of Greece was lost to Piraeus in the 20th century, but it remains the Cyclades' capital and its largest town. It's a lively and likeable place, full of restored neoclassical mansions. There are bustling commercial areas and well-kept central streets. Post-2004 Olympics there has been refurbishment of some neglected pavements and stairways.

The Catholic settlement of Ano Syros and the Greek Orthodox settlement of Vrodado lie to the left and right, looking inland, and both spill down from high hilltops, with even taller hills rising behind.

Orientation

The main ferry quay is at the southwestern end of the port. The bus station is on the waterfront, just along from the main ferry quay.

To reach the central square, Plateia Miaouli, walk to the right from the ferry quay for about 200m, and then turn left into El Venizelou. There are public toilets at the eastern end of the port, and off Antiparou.

Information

There is an information booth run by the Syros Hotels' Association on the waterfront, about 100m northeast of the main ferry quay; opening times are not guaranteed.

Alpha Bank (El Venizelou) Has ATM.

Enjoy Your Holidays (☎ 22810 87070; Akti Papagou 4) Opposite the bus station on the waterfront; very helpful with accommodation information, ferry tickets and other details.

Euro Bank (Akti Ethnikis Antistasis) Has ATM.

Internet Café (☎ 22810 85330; ground fl, Town Hall, Plateia Miaouli; per 20 min €2)

Piraeus Bank (Akti P Ralli) Has ATM.

Police station (☎ 22810 82610; Plateia Vardaka) Beside the Apollon Theatre.

Port police (☎ 22810 82690/88888; Plateia Lakis Kyriarchias) On the eastern side of the port.

Post office (Protopapadaki) Offers Western Union money transfer.

Teamwork Holidays (☎ 28810 83400; www.teamwork.gr; Akti Papagou 18) Just across from the main ferry quay; just as helpful and offers same services as Enjoy Your Holidays.

Sights

The great square of **Plateia Miaouli** is the finest urban space in the Cyclades. Once the sea reached this spot, but today the square is located well inland and is flanked by palm trees and lined along its south side by cafés and bars, some of them engagingly seedy. The north side of the square is dominated by the magnificent neoclassical **town hall**. The small **archaeological museum** (☎ 22810 88487; Benaki; admission free; 🕑 8.30am-3pm Tue-Sun) at the rear, founded in 1834 and one of the oldest in Greece, houses a tiny collection of ceramic and marble vases, grave stelae and some very fine Cycladic figurines.

The interesting **Industrial Museum of Ermoupolis** (☎ 22810 84764; Papandreos; adult/concession €2.50/1.50; ☒ 10am-2pm Wed-Mon, 6-9pm Thu-Sun Jun-Sep; 10am-2pm Mon, Thu & Fri, 10am-2pm & 6-9pm Wed, Sat & Sun Oct-May) is about 1km from the centre of town. It was opened in 2004 as a celebration of Syros' industrial and ship-building traditions, and occupies old factory buildings. There are over 300 items to keep you absorbed.

The Vrodado district and Ermoupolis merge fairly seamlessly, but **Ano Syros** – a medieval settlement with narrow alleyways and whitewashed houses – has great

individuality. It's a fascinating place to wander around and has views of neighbouring islands. Be wise and catch the bus up to Ano Syros. From the bus terminus, head into the steeply rising alleyways and bear up right through peaceful enclaves to reach the finest of the Catholic churches, the 13th-century **Agios Georgios** cathedral, with its star-fretted barrel roof and baroque capitals. Follow your nose down from the church, past stunning viewpoints to reach the main street where you'll find a little **museum** (☒ 10am-1pm Mon-Sat Jul-Aug) celebrating the life of Markos Vamvakaris, the famous *rembetika* (Greek blues) singer, who was born in Ano Syros. It's next to a lovely

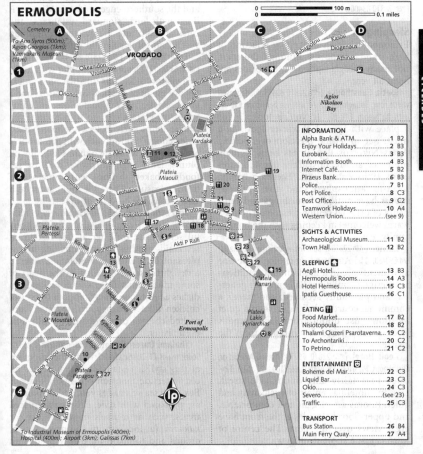

ERMOUPOLIS

INFORMATION
Alpha Bank & ATM.....................1 B2
Enjoy Your Holidays..................2 B3
Eurobank.................................3 B3
Information Booth......................4 B3
Internet Café...........................5 B2
Piraeus Bank............................6 B3
Police....................................7 B1
Port Police..............................8 C3
Post Office..............................9 C2
Teamwork Holidays.................10 A4
Western Union.....................(see 9)

SIGHTS & ACTIVITIES
Archaeological Museum............11 B2
Town Hall...............................12 B2

SLEEPING
Aegli Hotel.............................13 B3
Hermopulis Rooms...................14 A3
Hotel Hermes.........................15 C3
Ipatia Guesthouse...................16 C1

EATING
Food Market...........................17 B2
Nisiotopoula..........................18 B2
Thalami Ouzeri Psarotaverna...19 C2
To Archontariki.......................20 C2
To Petrino.............................21 C2

ENTERTAINMENT
Boheme del Mar......................22 C3
Liquid Bar..............................23 C3
Okio.....................................24 C3
Severo...............................(see 23)
Traffic..................................25 C3

TRANSPORT
Bus Station............................26 B4
Main Ferry Quay.....................27 A4

little balcony with terrific views and a handsome **bust of Vamvakaris** overseeing it all.

Just down some steps at the midpoint of the main street are, possibly, the best-kept public toilets in Greece.

Activities

Cyclades Sailing (☎ 22810 82501; csail@otenet.gr) can organise yachting charters, as can **Nomikos Sailing** (☎ 22810 88527); call direct or book through **Teamwork Holidays** (☎ 28810 83400).

Tours

You can book a day coach trip (adult/child €20/5) round the island on Tuesday, Thursday and Saturday through **Teamwork Holidays** (☎ 28810 83400).

Sleeping

Ermoupolis has an interesting selection of high-standard rooms, although there are not many budget options. Most places are open all year.

Ipatia Guesthouse (☎ 22810 83575; ipatiaguest@ yahoo.com; Babagiotou 3; s/d without bathroom €30/40, with bathroom €40/60) If you're looking for a place with special character Ipatia is a must. Set in a fine position overlooking Agios Nikolaos Bay, it has been lovingly preserved and retains all the finest features of its 19th-century past. There's a comfy, lived-in atmosphere and the spacious rooms have antique furnishings and remnants of original ceiling frescoes. There's a warm welcome, in keeping with the house's family feel.

Ethrion (☎ 22810 89066; www.ethrion.gr; Kosma 24; s/d €50/60; 🌐) A rewarding choice, these fine apartments are in a modern, but traditionally designed building. Balconies are generous and pleasantly secluded, and there's a communal courtyard. Ethrion is in a quiet location, just uphill from Hermoupolis Rooms, yet is just a few minutes from the centre.

Aegli Hotel (☎ 22810 79279; hotegli@otenet.gr; Klisthenous 14; s/d incl breakfast €83/100; 🌐 🖳) Located in a fairly anonymous side street, this fine hotel has an air of exclusivity and quiet. Rooms are elegant and comfortable, and upper-floor balconies at the front have great views over the port. The centre of town is just a short stroll away.

Hotel Hermes (☎ 22810 83011; fax 22810 87412; Plateia Kanari; s/d incl buffet breakfast €52/88) There's a great deal of old-fashioned charm in the air at this long-established, well-appointed hotel that dominates the eastern side of the waterfront. Rooms are smart, with bright interiors. The buffet breakfast is fine. The Hermes also has a good restaurant offering grills and pasta (mains €6 to €12).

Hermoupolis Rooms (☎ 22810 87475; Naxou; d €45) A reasonably priced option tucked away in narrow Naxou, a short climb up from the waterfront. The small, self-contained rooms open onto tiny, bougainvillea-cloaked balconies.

Eating

The waterfront, especially along Akti P Ralli and the southern edge of Plateia Miaouli, is lined with fairly standard restaurants and cafés, but dip into the quieter corners and you'll find some splendid eateries.

To Arhontariki (☎ 22810 81744; Emm Roidi 8; mains €3.50-12) Deservedly popular with locals and visitors alike, this fine place has an extensive menu of classical Greek dishes and a good selection of regional wines, including Santorini vintages, to go with them. Even simple items such as leek pie or *saganaki* (fried cheese) and spinach with mushrooms are delicious, while such mains as veal with plums, lamb with artichoke and, for sea foodies, baked shrimps with tomato, add to the pleasure. There's a roof garden and Greek music is on offer at times.

To Petrino (☎ 22810 87427; Stefanou 9; mains €5.50-9) Tasty traditional dishes and cheerful service are on offer at this restaurant set amid swathes of bougainvillea in the pleasant little enclave of Stefanou. There's a delightful sense of being in the heart of some mountain village, which makes such dishes as Kotopoula ala Spetsiota (pieces of chicken fillet with peppers, tomatoes and melted cheese) or squid stuffed with feta, even tastier.

Thalami Ouzeri Psarotaverna (☎ 22810 85331; Souri; mains €6-20) Seafood is by the kilogram at this stylish restaurant that occupies an old waterside mansion on Agios Nikolaos Bay. The sea serenades you, and fish dishes are prepared with style. Reasonably priced treats, such as mussels in wine sauce, or *kakavia* (a local soup comprising fish, onions and tomatoes) are only part of an excellent menu. To get there, go east along Souri (which runs off the eastern side of Plateia Miaouli) to its end.

Nisiotopoula (☎ 22810 81214; Antiparou 20; mains €3.30-6) For terrific budget eating, this unfancy, busy taverna offers a good range of Greek staples that include delicious soups, pies, and omelettes as well as chicken and pork dishes.

The best place to buy fresh produce is the small, but well-stocked morning **food market** (Hiou).

Entertainment

The best music bars are clustered along the waterfront on Akti P Ralli. They play mostly lounge music by day and a mix of house, funk and modern Greek music by night. They draw a great local crowd and rock into the early hours.

Boheme del Mar (☎ 22810 83354) Heads up the young scene.

Liquid Bar (☎ 22810 82284) Near Boheme del Mar and also lively.

Severo (☎ 22810 88243) Next door, this has a great racy atmosphere and good DJs.

A couple of busy little bars:

Traffic (☎ 22810 86197)

Okio (☎ 22810 84133)

GALISSAS ΓΑΛΗΣΣΑΣ

A short bus ride west of Ermoupolis takes you into another world. The west-coast resort of Galissas is a small resort with one of the best beaches on Syros, several cheerful bars and restaurants and some great places to stay. The main bus stop is at an intersection behind the beach.

Sleeping

Oasis (☎ 22810 42357; s/d/studios €20/35/45) The welcome at this lovely little farm is charming. Rooms and recently built studios are bright and airy. It's about 400m back from the village. Either head down the track opposite Karmelina's Rooms, or follow signs from the main bus stop intersection in the village.

Karmelina's Rooms (☎ 22810 42320; s/d €20/30) There are only a few rooms here and they are very small, but they overlook a little Eden of a garden and there's a communal kitchen. No English is spoken, but smiles and kindness say it all. Stay on the bus beyond the main village stop for about 500m until a bus

shelter appears at the junction with the main road, this is right beside Karmelina's.

Hotel Benois (☎ 22810 42833; www.benois.gr; s/d incl breakfast €50/70; 🞄) A long-established family-run hotel with a comfy atmosphere combining courtesy with old-fashioned service, backed-up by pleasant, spick-and-span rooms. It's close to the beach at the northern entrance to the village.

Two Hearts Camping (☎ 22810 42052; www .twohearts-camping.com; sites per adult/tent €6/4) Set in a pistachio orchard about 400m from the village and beach, this camping ground has reasonable facilities; from the main bus stop, cross the intersection and follow the signs. A minibus meets ferries in high season.

Eating & Drinking

Savvas (☎ 22810 42998; mains €5.50-9) Great cooking and a long-established family tradition make this one of the best tavernas around. Try the chicken fillet stuffed with bacon, cheese and mushrooms. It's just a few metres from the bus stop.

Socrates (☎ 22810 43284; mains €4-8) A delightful garden terrace at this well-run place sets off tasty dishes such as *giovetsi* (choice pieces of lamb in a tomato sauce, baked with pasta). Turn right at the junction by the bus stop and it's about 100m on the left.

Giasou Yianni (☎ 22810 42065; mains €5-7.30) A down-to-earth locals' favourite, with great Greek food, tucked away off the approach road to the beach.

Also recommended is the Green Dollars Bar on the beach road, for daytime snacks and music while you drink. Rock and reggae are favourites from 10am to 4am.

AROUND SYROS

The beaches south of Galissas all have *domatia* and some have hotels. Some beaches are narrow roadside strips of dullish sand, but they're not too busy. They include **Finikas**, **Posidonia** and **Angathopes**. Back on the main road and on the south coast proper, **Megas Gialos** has a couple of roadside beaches.

The pleasant **Vari Bay**, further east, has a decent sandy beach with some development, including a couple of hotels and a beachfront taverna. **Kini**, out on its own on the west coast, north of Galissas, has a good long beach and is developing into a popular resort with standard modern hotels, studios, cafés and tavernas.

MYKONOS ΜΥΚΟΝΟΣ

pop 9306

Mykonos carries its glamorous and faintly louche reputation with some style, but expensively so. Under the gloss it's a charming and hugely entertaining place, where high camp and celebrity posturing are balanced by the cubist charms of a traditional Cycladic town, and by local people who have had 40 years to get a grip on tourism and have not lost their Greek identity in doing so.

Be prepared for the oiled-up lounger lifestyle of the island's packed main beaches, the jostling street scenes and the relentless, and sometimes forlorn, partying. Yet there's still a handful of off-track beaches worth fighting for. Plus the stylish bars, restaurants and shops have great appeal, and you can still find a quieter pulse amid the labyrinthine old town. Add to all this the nearby sacred island of Delos, and Mykonos really does live up to expectations as an intriguing destination.

Mykonos is packed in July and August, and earlier in the season crowds of youngsters arrive in swarms on school and college trips that are not necessarily educational.

Getting There & Away

AIR

Olympic Airlines (☎ 22890 22490 in Hora, ☎ 22890 22327 at airport; www.olympicairlines.com; Fabrika Sq, Hora; ☉ 8am-3.30pm Mon-Fri) runs five flights daily to Athens (€94, 40 minutes) and Rhodes (€90, two hours, daily except Sunday). The office is by the southern bus station in Hora.

Aegean Airlines (☎ 22890 28720 airport; www.aegeanair.com) has daily flights to Athens (€94, 45 minutes) and Thessaloniki (€87, 50 minutes).

Sky express (☎ 28102 235000; www.skyexpress.gr) has about four flights a week to Iraklio, Crete (€125, one hour 30 minutes) via Santorini (€70, 35 minutes) and one flight a week direct to Iraklio (45 minutes). It also runs four flights a week to Rhodes (€125, two hours) via Santorini. You can book tickets through Mykonos Accommodation Centre (see p152).

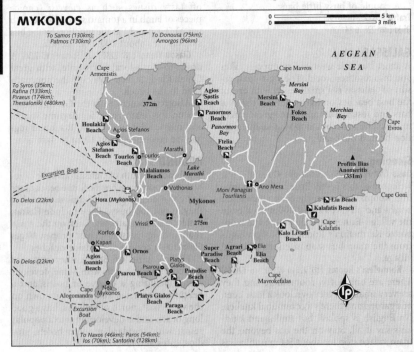

MYKONOS

0 ——— 5 km
0 ——— 3 miles

AEGEAN SEA

To Samos (130km);
Patmos (130km)

To Donousa (75km);
Amorgos (96km)

Cape Armenistis

To Syros (35km);
Rafina (133km);
Piraeus (174km);
Thessaloniki (480km)

372m

Agios Sostis Beach

Cape Mavros

Mersini Bay

Mersini Beach

Merchias Bay

Houlakia Beach

Agios Stefanos

Panormos Beach

Panormos Bay

Fokos Beach

Cape Evros

Agios Stefanos Beach

Tourlos Beach

Tourlos

Marathi

Ftelia Beach

Malaliamos Beach

Lake Marathi

Excursion Boat

Vothonas

Moni Panagias Tourlianis

Ano Mera

Profitis Ilias Anomeritis (351m)

To Delos (22km)

Hora (Mykonos)

Mykonos

Lia Beach

Cape Goni

Kalafatis Beach

Vrissi

275m

Cape Kalafatis

Korfos

Kalo Livadi Beach

Kapari

Ornos

Super Paradise Beach

Agrari Beach

Elia

To Delos (22km)

Agios Ioannis Beach

Platys Gialos

Psarou

Elia Beach

Psarou Beach

Paradise Beach

Cape Mavrokefalas

Cape Alogomandra

Nea Mykonos

Platys Gialos Beach

Paraga Beach

Excursion Boat

To Naxos (46km); Paros (54km);
Ios (70km); Santorini (128km)

FAST BOAT & CATAMARAN

There are at least three daily services connecting Mykonos with Tinos (€7.40, 15 minutes). Four daily services go to Rafina (€31.80, two hours) and three go to Piraeus (€39, three hours) and Syros (€11.40, 30 minutes). There are three daily services to Paros (€13.10, one hour), which connect with services to Naxos (€19, 1½ hours), Santorini (€27.50, three to four hours) and Ios (€23, 2¾ hours). One service daily continues to Iraklio on Crete (€46, 5 hours).

FERRY

Mykonos has two ferry quays: the Town Quay at Tourlos, where some conventional ferries and smaller fast ferries dock, and the New Quay, which is 2.5km north of town and where the bigger fast ferries, and some conventional ferries dock. You should always check when buying outgoing tickets which quay your ferry leaves from. There are bus connections to the New Quay; a taxi is €4.

Mykonos has daily services to Rafina (€15.90, 4½ hours) via Tinos (€3.70, 30 minutes) and Andros (€8.90, 2½ hours); and to Piraeus (€23.60, six hours) via Tinos and Syros (€6.80, 1½ hours).

There are three ferries a week to Santorini (€14.70, six hours).

There is one ferry a week to Thessaloniki (€35, 12 hours) and Crete (€23, nine hours).

There are three ferries a week to Samos (€17, 4½ hours) and Ikaria (€12.20, 2¼ hours).

Getting Around
TO/FROM THE AIRPORT

Buses do not serve Mykonos' airport, which is 3km southeast of the town centre. Make sure you arrange an airport transfer with your accommodation (expect to pay around €6) or take a **taxi** (☎ 22890 22400, airport ☎ 22890 23700); there's a fixed fare of €5.

BUS

Hora (Mykonos) has two bus stations. The **northern bus station** (☎ 22890 23360; Polikandrioti) has frequent departures to Agios Stefanos via Tourlos (€1.10), Ano Mera, (€1), Elia (€1.20), Kalo Livadi Beach (€1.30) and Kalafatis Beach (€1.50). Trip durations range from 20 minutes to 40 minutes. The **southern**

bus station (☎ 22890 23360; Fabrika Sq) serves Agios Ioannis Beach (€0.90), Ornos, (€1), Platys Gialos (€1.10) Paraga (€1.20) and Paradise Beach (€1.30). Trips range from 15 minutes to 40 minutes.

CAÏQUE

Caïque services leave Hora (Mykonos) for Super Paradise Beach, Agrari and Elia Beaches (June to September only) and from Platys Gialos to Paradise (€4), Super Paradise (€5), Agrari (€4.50) and Elia (€5) beaches.

CAR & MOTORCYCLE

Most car and motorcycle rental firms are around the southern bus station in Hora. Expect to pay per day for cars, depending on model, about €46 to €90 in high season, €36 to €68 in low season. For scooters it's about €17 to €35 in high season, €12 to €23 in low season. A very reliable hire agency is the Mykonos Accommodation Centre (p152).

TAXI

Taxis gather at Hora's Taxi Sq and by the bus stations. The minimum fare is €2, but there's a charge of €0.30 for each item of luggage. Fares to beaches: Paradise €6.50, Ornos €3.80, Platys Gialos €5 and Elia €9.50.

HORA (MYKONOS) ΧΩΡΑ (ΜΥΚΟΝΟΣ)
pop 6467

Mykonos, or Hora, the island's port and capital, is a warren of narrow alleyways that wriggle between white-walled buildings, their stone surfaces webbed with white paint. In the heart of the Little Venice area, tiny flower-bedecked churches jostle with trendy boutiques and there's a deluge of bougainvillea round every corner. Without question, you will soon pass the same junction twice. It's entertaining at first, but can become frustrating as throngs of equally lost people and pushy aficionados add to the stress. For quick-fix navigation, familiarise yourself with main junctions and the three main streets of Matogianni, Enoplon Dinameon and Mitropoleos that form a horseshoe behind the waterfront. The streets are thronged with chic fashion salons, cool galleries, jangling jewellers, languid and loud music bars, brightly painted houses and torrents of crimson flowers – plus a catwalk cast of thousands.

Orientation

The town waterfront is about 400m to the south of the ferry quay, beyond the tiny, rather dull, town beach. A busy square, Plateia Manto Mavrogenous (usually called Taxi Sq), is 150m beyond the beach and on the edge of Hora. East of Taxi Sq, the inner waterfront leads towards the Little Venice neighbourhood and the town's famous hilltop row of rather flyblown windmills. Due south of Taxi Sq, the busy streets of Matogianni, Zouganelli and Mavrogenous lead into the heart of Hora.

The northern bus station is 250m south of the ferry quay, at the junction of Agiou Stefanou and Polikandrioti. The southern bus station is on Plateia Remezzo, on the southern edge of town. The Old Jetty, from where boats leave for Delos, is at the western end of the waterfront.

Information

Mykonos has no official tourist office. When you get off at the town ferry quay, you will see a low building with numbered offices. No 1 is the **Hoteliers Association of Mykonos** (☎ 22890 24540; www.mykonosgreece.com; Town Quay; ☻ 8am-midnight). The Association will book a room on the spot, but do not accept telephone bookings prior to your arrival. No 2 is the **Association of Rooms, Studios & Apartments** (☎ 22890 26860; ☻ 9am-10pm).

BOOKSHOPS

International Press (☎ 22890 23316; Kambani 5) Has international newspapers and a good range of magazines and books; it's a block in from the waterfront, just along from Taxi Sq.

EMERGENCY

First Aid Clinic (☎ 22890 22274; Agiou Ioannou)
Hospital (☎ 22890 23994) Located about 1km along the road to Ano Mera.
Police (☎ 22890 22716; Plateia Laka) Next door to the post office.
Port police (☎ 22890 22218; Akti Kambani) On the waterfront, near the Delos boat quay.
Post office (☎ 22890 22238; Laka) In the southern part of town.
Tourist police (☎ 22890 22482) At the airport.

INTERNET ACCESS

Angelo's Internet Café (☎ 22890 24106; Xenias; per hr €3.50) On the road between the southern bus station and the windmills.

Earth Internet Café (☎ 22890 22791; Zani Pitaraki 4; per 15 min €1)

MONEY

Several banks by the ferry quay have ATMs.
National Bank of Greece (Taxi Sq) Has an ATM.

TRAVEL AGENCIES

Delia Travel (☎ 22890 22322; travel@delia.gr; Paralia) Halfway along the inner waterfront, this is also the French Consul and sells tickets for Delos trips.
Mykonos Accommodation Centre (☎ 22890 23408; www.mykonos-accommodation.com; 1st fl, Enoplon Dinameon 10) Well-organised and very helpful for a range of requirements. Can also arrange midrange, top end and gay-friendly accommodation.
Sea & Sky (☎ 22890 22853; Kambani) Efficient information and ferry tickets.
Windmills Travel (☎ 22890 23877; www.windmills -travel.com; Fabrica Sq) By the southern bus station, this is another helpful office.

Sights

MUSEUMS

There are five museums. The **archaeological museum** (☎ 22890 22325; admission adult/concession €3/1.50 ☻ 9am-3.30pm Wed-Sat & Mon, 10am-3pm Sun) is near the Town Quay. It houses pottery from Delos and some grave stelae and jewellery from the island of Renia (Delos' necropolis). Chief exhibits include a statue of Hercules in Parian marble.

The **Aegean Maritime Museum** (☎ 22890 22700; Tria Pigadia; admission adult/concession €3/1.5; ☻ 10.30am-1pm & 6.30-9pm Apr-Oct) has a fascinating collection of nautical paraphernalia from all over the Aegean, including models of ancient vessels and the old lighthouse of Mykonos.

Next door, **Lena's House** (☎ 22890 22390; Tria Pigadia; admission free; ☻ 6.30-9.30pm Mon-Sat 7-9pm Sun Apr-Oct) is a charming sanctuary amid the conspicuous modernity of Hora. It is a late-19th-century, middle-class Mykonian house (with furnishings intact) and takes its name from its last owner, Lena Skrivanou. Donations are appreciated.

The **folklore museum** (☎ 22890 22591; Paraportianis; admission free; ☻ 4.30-8.30pm Mon-Sat Apr-Oct), housed in an 18th-century sea captain's house, features a large collection of memorabilia and furnishings. The museum is near the Delos quay.

The **agricultural museum** (☎ 22890 22748; Agiou Ioannou; admission free; ☻ 4-6pm Jun-Sep), near

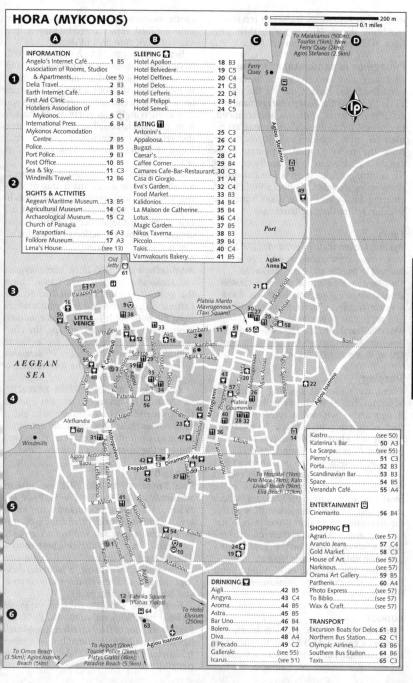

HORA (MYKONOS)

0 ————— 200 m
0 ————— 0.1 miles

INFORMATION
Angelo's Internet Café............1 B5
Association of Rooms, Studios
& Apartments....................(see 5)
Delia Travel...............................2 B3
Earth Internet Café....................3 B4
First Aid Clinic..........................4 B6
Hoteliers Association of
Mykonos..............................5 C1
International Press......................6 B4
Mykonos Accomodation
Centre..................................7 B5
Police......................................8 B5
Port Police...............................9 B3
Post Office..............................10 B5
Sea & Sky...............................11 C3
Windmills Travel.....................12 B6

SIGHTS & ACTIVITIES
Aegean Maritime Museum....13 B5
Agricultural Museum..............14 C4
Archaeological Museum.........15 C2
Church of Panagia
Paraportiani........................16 A3
Folklore Museum....................17 A3
Lena's House......................(see 13)

SLEEPING
Hotel Apollon........................18 B3
Hotel Belvedere.....................19 C5
Hotel Delfines........................20 C4
Hotel Delos............................21 C3
Hotel Lefteris.........................22 D4
Hotel Philippi........................23 B4
Hotel Semeli.........................24 C5

EATING
Antonini's..............................25 C3
Appaloosa..............................26 C4
Bugazi...................................27 C3
Caesar's.................................28 C4
Caffee Corner.........................29 B4
Camares Cafe-Bar-Restaurant..30 C3
Casa di Giorgio......................31 A4
Eva's Garden..........................32 C4
Food Market...........................33 B3
Kalidonios..............................34 B4
La Maison de Catherine.........35 B4
Lotus.....................................36 C4
Magic Garden........................37 B5
Nikos Taverna........................38 B3
Piccolo..................................39 B4
Takis.....................................40 C4
Vamvakouris Bakery..............41 B5

Kastro.................................(see 50)
Katerina's Bar.........................50 A3
La Scarpa.............................(see 55)
Pierro's..................................51 C3
Porta.....................................52 B3
Scandinavian Bar....................53 B3
Space....................................54 B5
Verandah Café........................55 A4

ENTERTAINMENT
Cinemanto.............................56 B4

SHOPPING
Agrari.................................(see 57)
Arancio Jeans.........................57 C4
Gold Market...........................58 C3
House of Art........................(see 57)
Narkisous............................(see 57)
Orama Art Gallery..................59 B5
Parthenis...............................60 A4
Photo Express.....................(see 57)
To Biblio............................(see 57)
Wax & Craft.......................(see 57)

TRANSPORT
Excursion Boats for Delos.61 B3
Northern Bus Station...........62 C1
Olympic Airlines...................63 B6
Southern Bus Station..........64 B6
Taxis.....................................65 C3

DRINKING
Aigli.......................................42 B5
Angyra...................................43 C4
Aroma....................................44 B5
Astra......................................45 B5
Bar Uno..................................46 B4
Bolero....................................47 B4
Diva.......................................48 A4
El Pecado...............................49 C2
Galleraki.............................(see 55)
Icarus.................................(see 51)

AEGEAN
SEA

CYCLADES

To Malaliamos (500m);
Tourlos (1km); New
Ferry Quay (2km);
Agios Stefanos (2.5km)

Ferry
Quay

Port

Agias
Anna

LITTLE
VENICE

Old
Jetty

Paraportianis

Plateia Manto
Mavrogenous
(Taxi Square)

Kambani

Agias Kiriakis

Plateia
Goumenio

Litous

Alefkandra

Windmills

Agiou Antoniou

Baou

Enoplon

Fabrika Square
(Platias Yialos)

To Hotel
Elysium
(250m)

To Hospital (1km);
Ano Mera (7km); Kalo
Livadi Beach (9km);
Elia Beach (10km)

To Ornos Beach
(3.5km); Agios Ioannis
Beach (5km)

To Airport (2km);
Tourist Police (2km);
Platys Gialos (4km);
Paradise Beach (5.5km)

the road to Ano Mera, features a renovated windmill, the miller's house, a threshing floor, wine-press and other artefacts.

CHURCH OF PANAGIA PARAPORTIANI

Mykonos' most famous church, located beyond the Delos Ferry Quay on the way to Little Venice, is the **Panagia Paraportiani**. It is actually five small churches amalgamated, in classical Byzantine style, into one asymmetrical entity, looking as if it has grown from the rocky ground. Opening times can be variable but it is usually open in the mornings. Admission is free but donations are appreciated. Visitors should avoid entering during services, unless for genuine worship rather than sightseeing.

Tours

Mykonos Accommodation Centre (☎ 22890 23408; www.mykonos-accommodation.com; 1st fl, Enoplon Dinameon 10) Organises guided tours to Delos (see p160). The centre also offers a big range of tours to other islands such as Naxos, Paros, Santorini and Tinos, as well as Mykonos bus tours and boat cruises, wine and culture tours, and exclusive gay boat cruises.

Windmills Travel (☎ 22890 23877; www.windmills -travel.com) The booking agent for snorkelling (30 minutes €25) and island cruises (€35, four weekly).

Sleeping

There are scores of sleeping options in Mykonos, but between July and September if you arrive without a reservation and find reasonably priced accommodation, grab it – 'budget' in Mykonos is relative to high prices generally. Otherwise check out the local accommodation organisations (see p152). If you choose *domatia* from owners meeting ferries – they rev up into one of the most raucous scrums in the Cyclades – check their exact location and ask if they charge for transport (some do). If you plan to stay in Hora and want somewhere quiet, think carefully about *domatia* on the main streets – bar noise until dawn is *de rigueur*.

During late July and early August some hotels will only accept minimum stays of three nights.

BUDGET

Hotel Philippi (☎ 22890 22294; chriko@otenet.gr; Kalogera 25; s €60-70, d €75-90) In the heart of Hora, this charming place has a wonderful garden ambience that smacks of more

exotic locations. Bright, clean rooms open onto a railed veranda overlooking a lush oasis of trees, flowers and shrubs.

Hotel Apollon (☎ 22890 22223; fax 22890 24237; Paralia; d without shower €45, s/d with shower €50/65) Located in the middle of the main waterfront, this delightful slice of traditional Mykonos has a time-lock entrance foyer that takes you into a satisfyingly non-glitzy world. Rooms here are old-fashioned and well-kept, and the friendly owner has a no-nonsense laugh that puts trendy Mykonos in its place.

Hotel Delfines (☎ 22890 22292; Mavrogenous; s/d/ tr €60/80/100) Right on the main drag of Mavrogenous, this long-established place was in at the dawn of tourism in Mykonos. Don't expect state-of-the-art décor or lavish, spacious rooms; but the welcome is kindly.

MIDRANGE

Hotel Lefteris (☎ 22890 27117; lefterishot@yahoo .com; Apollonos 9; s/d €79/99) Tucked away above the main streets, just up from Taxi Sq, the Lefteris is a great choice if you want a refuge from the hubbub. It's also an international meeting place for all age groups, the conversation is always good and the welcome is kind and friendly. Its rooms are straightforward and comfy and the roof terrace is a great place to relax.

Hotel Delos (☎ 22890 22517; fax 22890 22312; s/d €70/80; ☒ Apr–mid-Nov) In a quiet spot at the town end of Hora's little beach, life at Hotel Delos really is peaceful and detached. Rooms are refreshingly bright and large and those at the front have a clear sea view.

TOP END

Hotel Belvedere (☎ 22890 25122; www.belvedere hotel.com; Rohari; s & d €230-415, tr €276-457; Ⓟ ☒ ☒) Wispy Mykonos style enhances the modernist landscape and furnishings of this swish hotel, where sea and town views are panoramic in all but the cheapest rooms. There's even a sushi bar as well as a mainstream restaurant. Throw in Jacuzzis, massage therapy, a fitness studio and a cinema, and who needs a backpack?

Hotel Semeli (☎ 22890 27466; semeliht@otenet .gr; Rohari; s/d €270/305, studios €360-480; Ⓟ ☒ ☒) Right next door to the Belvedere, the Semeli has the same luxuriousness, but in a more traditional Cycladic style and with soothing pastel décor.

Hotel Elysium (☎ 22890 23952; www.elysium hotel.com; s/d/tr €170-238/190-258/304; ☒ Apr-Oct; P ☒ ☒ ☐) A top quality gay hotel located high above the town, in the School of Fine Arts area, but within short distance of the centre. There are many special features: suites and deluxe rooms have personal computers and there's a spa facility for a separate charge.

More top-end accommodation is available around the beaches (see p157) and Ano Mera.

Eating

High prices don't necessarily reflect high quality in many Mykonos eateries. There are, however, excellent, good-value restaurants of all kinds.

BUDGET

Antonini's (☎ 22890 22319; Taxi Sq; dishes €3.50-14) You won't go wrong at this local hang-out with its standard, but reliable, Greek food and gossipy view of the world passing by the terrace.

Camares Cafe-Bar-Restaurant (☎ 22890 28570; Akti Kambani; dishes €4-15) This place is on the waterfront just round from Taxi Sq. It offers decent helpings of meat dishes, salads and seafood and the surroundings and style suggest that Mykonos might be an everyday Greek harbour town after all.

Piccolo (☎ 22890 22208; Drakopoulou 18; snacks €3.70-7.50) An impeccable little food place where you can get a great selection of sandwich fillings, from Myconian prosciutto of Manouri cheese, tomato and oregano, to smoked eel or salmon. The home-made cakes are also delicious.

Vamvakouris Bakery (☎ 22890 27207; Aghios Efthymios) The engaging medieval ambience of this bakery makes it a tourist attraction in its own right; but you still won't beat the wood-fired bread or the tasty walnut cake for taste.

There's a cluster of cheap fast-food outlets and creperies around town:

Bugazi (☎ 22890 24066; snacks €3-6) Off the edge of Taxi Sq.

Jimmy's (22890 28754; Ipirou) This long-established place is at the busy junction of Enoplon Dinameon and Ipirou. It dishes out *gyros* (Greek version of doner kebab) for €2, and other gut-busting mouthfuls for €5 to €7.

Caffee Corner (☎ 22890 23287; Drakopoulou) Near Piccolo; has a terrific selection of great coffees and teas.

THE AUTHOR'S CHOICE

Kalidonios (☎ 22890 27606; Dilou 1/Garasimou; mains €6.60-19.95) The chef-owner and staff at this enjoyable restaurant put heart and soul into their work and the result on the plates is outstanding. Try the delicious *kolokithokeftedhes* (fried courgette balls) or *imam baildi* (baked aubergines stuffed with chopped onion, garlic, parsley, tomatoes and feta) - it's worth getting your tongue round the name, and then the food. Mains include delicious pastitsio and pastas, while a fillet of bream at €16.95 is worth every melting bite. Desserts are delicious. House wines and a more expensive, but worthy, wine list complement the food while the surroundings are relaxing and the service enthusiastic and friendly.

There are also several supermarkets and fruit stalls, particularly around the southern bus station area, and there's a food market on the waterfront where Mykonos' famous pelicans hang out. There's an excellent **fruit and veg shop** (Kalogera 21) in the heart of town.

MIDRANGE

Magic Garden (☎ 22890 26217; Tourlianis; dishes €7-15) You are drawn into a genuine garden environment beyond the welcoming entrance bar at this long-standing and well-run restaurant. The food's interesting too, with treats such as shrimps in ouzo, and baked lamb with yogurt, garlic and nutmeg.

Eva's Garden (☎ 22890 22160; Platia Goumenio; dishes €8-21) Authentic Greek cooking makes for tasty dishes here, from the dolmades and *spanakopita* (spinach pie) to generous meat treats.

Casa di Giorgio (☎ 69325 61998; Mitropoleos 1; mains €7-21) This place has a big, pleasant terrace and offers delicious pizzas and pastas, as well as good meat and seafood dishes.

TOP END

La Maison de Catherine (☎ 22890 22169; cnr Gerasimou & Nikou; meals €14-28) This Mykonos' institution offers traditional Greek cuisine that has more than a great touch of subtle, international flair. The service and surroundings are equally classy; this top establishment matches efficiency behind the scenes with a relaxing ambience out front.

CYCLADES

Appaloosa (☎ 22890 27086; Mavrogenous 1, Plateia Goumenio; mains €7.50-19) Get ready for a big night at this friendly, popular place with its cosmopolitan buzz. There's a strong Mexican influence in the delicious starters and mains, and there are salads, grills and pasta dishes too. Expect a terrific line in tequila and cocktails, all backed by cool music.

Lotus (☎ 22890 22881; Matogianni 47; dishes €7-12) A local favourite with great character and style; you can also enjoy drinks here to the soothing strains of classical greats such as Puccini.

Drinking

Rosy sunsets, windmill views, glowing candles and water lapping at your feet are a major draw of the waterside bars in the Little Venice quarter (Venetia). The music leans towards smooth soul and easy-listening, but at quieter times bar staff play more esoteric and satisfying sounds. A good spot is the friendly **Galleraki** (☎ 22890 27188; Little Venice) where they turn out superb cocktails. Nearby is the view-happy **Verandah Café** (☎ 22890 27400; Little Venice) while **La Scarpa** (☎ 22890 23294; Little Venice) lets you leans back from the sea on its cosy cushions. Further north **Katerina's Bar** (☎ 22890 23084; Agion Anargiron) has a cool balcony and eases you into the action with DJs and dancing.

Deeper into town the relentlessly stylish **Aroma** (☎ 22890 27148; Enoplon Dinameon) is the place for a critic's eye-view, from a strategic corner, of the evening cat walk. It's open for breakfast and coffee as well.

Further down Enoplon Dinameon is **Astra** (☎ 22890 24767), where the décor is modernist Mykonos at its best, and where some of Athens' top DJs feed the ambience with rock, funk, house and drum 'n' base. Just across from Astra, cocktail-cool **Aigli** (☎ 22890 27265) has another useful terrace for people-watching. Matogianni has a couple of music bars, including **Angyra** (☎ 22890 24273) which sticks with easy listening and mainstream.

Bar Uno (☎ 22890 26144; Matogianni 42) is a lively corner place that rocks happily to just about every playlist. **Bolero** (☎ 22890 24877; Malamatenias), in a quiet alleyway off Kalogera, has a more restrained diet of jazz, funk and Latin. **Scandinavian Bar** (☎ 22890 22669; Ioanni Voinovich 9), just in from the east end of the waterfront, is more down-to-earth, although its cocktail nomenclature is a bit weary.

For dance club action **Space** (☎ 22890 24100; Laka) is the place. The night builds superbly through a mix of techno, house and progressive, and the bar-top dancing really fires up the late-night action. **El Pecado** (☎ 22890 24100; Polikandrioti) is run by the same team but features lounge and dance for a more relaxing scene. Entry is around €10 to both clubs.

GAY BARS

Mykonos has long been feted as a gay travel destination, combining camp style with sun-seducing indulgence. A healthy, and mutual, tolerance of tendencies has made gay life less overt here, but the island still maintains many gaycentric clubs and hang-outs.

Kastro (☎ 22890 23072; Agion Anargiron) In Little Venice, this is a good place to start the night with cocktails as the sun sets.

Diva (☎ 22890 27271; Little Venice) Just round the corner is this relaxing spot, where there's a mixed crowd with a loyal lesbian core.

Porta (☎ 22890 27807; Ioanni Voinovich) Around 11pm things get a bit livelier at this popular, cruisey bar that gets close-quarters crowded late in the evening.

Pierro's (☎ 22890 22177; Agia Kyriaki) The night rounds off – usually with sensation – at this dance club playing heavy-beat house, which also has superbly extroverted drag action. It's just in from Taxi Sq.

Entertainment

Cinemanto (☎ 22890 27190; admission €7; ☼ summer) Screenings are at 9pm and 11pm in the garden setting of this open-air cinema that runs new films every few days. There's a bar and you get a tasty *souvlaki* (cubes of meat on skewers) for €2.

Shopping

You could spend all your money covering just a few metres of Hora's packed shopping streets. The entire gang vies for attention, including Dolce & Gabbana, Naf Naf, Diesel and Body Shop; but for something special try **Parthenis** (☎ 22890 23089; Alefkandra Sq) featuring the stylish designs – in black and white only – of Athens designer and longtime Mykonos resident Dimitris Parthenis.

There are lots of art and craft galleries, but the **Orama Art Gallery** (☎ 22890 26339; Fournakia, off Enoplon Dinameon), shows the highly original work of Louis Orosko and Dorlies Schapitz.

Every now and then Hora produces a fascinating clutch of everyday, yet highly individualistic shops, such as those found halfway down Florou Zouganeli. Try **Arancio Jeans** (☎ 22890 28321; Florou Zouganeli 25) for great gear, **Wax & Craft** (☎ 22890 28903; Florou Zouganeli 23) for handmade candles and natural cosmetics, **Narkisous** (☎ 22890 23743; Florou Zouganeli) for flowers, **Agrari** (☎ 22890 23598; Florou Zouganeli 21) for wines and honey and **To Biblio** (☎ 22890 27737; Florou Zouganeli 19) for books. There's also the **House of Art** (☎ 69443 86143; Florou Zouganeli 14-16) gallery and even a useful **Photo Express** (☎ 22890 26350; Florou Zouganeli 17) thrown in for good measure.

Jewellery shops are a Mykonos' fixture but a good bet is **Gold Market** (☎ 22890 22770; Agias Annas) right at the entrance to town.

AROUND MYKONOS
Beaches

Mykonos' beaches are a key element in the island's indulgent lifestyle. They are in good supply and most have golden sand and are in great locations. They are not huge enough to escape the crowds, and they are extremely popular and busy from June onwards. Do not expect seclusion, although there is often a sense of *exclusion* as various cliques commandeer the sun loungers; segregation zones for style and sheer snobbery dominate at some locations.

The best beaches really do get packed and you need to be a party person for the likes of Paradise and Super P. It can all get very claustrophobic, but it's heaven for the gregarious.

Most beaches have a varied clientele, and attitudes to toplessness and nudity also vary; but there are some fairly distinct orientations.

The nearest beaches to Hora (Mykonos), and the island's least glamorous, are **Malaliamos**, the tiny and crowded **Tourlos**, 2km to the north, and **Agios Stefanos**, 2km beyond. About 3.5km south of Hora is the packed and noisy **Ornos**, from where you can hop onto boats for other beaches. Just west is **Agios Ioannis**. The sizeable package-holiday resort of **Platys Gialos** is 4km from Hora on the southwest coast. All of the above beaches are family-orientated.

Platys Gialos is the caïque jump-off point for the glitzier beaches to the east, such as Paradise and Super P.

About 1km south of Platys Gialos is the pleasant **Paraga Beach**, which has a small gay section. About 2km east of here is the famous **Paradise**, which is not a recognised gay beach, but has a lively younger scene. **Super Paradise** (aka **Plintri** or **Super P**) has a fully gay section. Mixed and gay-friendly **Elia** is the last caïque stop and a few minutes walk from here is the small and pleasant **Agrari**. Nudity is commonplace on all these beaches. Caïques from Platys Gialos to the beaches cost from €3 to €5 one way.

North-coast beaches can be exposed to the Meltemi wind, but **Panormos** and **Agios Sostis** are fairly sheltered; Panormas is now high on the popular list; Agios Sostis less so because of poor road access. Both have a mix of gay and non-gay devotees.

For out-of-the-way beaching you need to head for the likes of **Lia** on the southeast coast, or the smaller **Fokos** and **Mersini** on the east coast; but you'll need tough wheels and undercarriage to get there.

ACTIVITIES

Very well organised and with lots of experience **Dive Adventures** (☎ 22890 26539; www.diveadventures.gr; Paradise Beach) offers a full range of diving courses with multilingual instructors. Two introductory dives cost €100, snorkelling costs €30.

On a great location at the delightful Kalafatis Beach **Planet Windsailing** (☎ 22890 72345; www.pezi-huber.com; Kalafatis Beach) offers one-hour or one-day windsurfing for €20 or €50 respectively, or a three-hour beginner's course for €75. You can also hire a canoe (per hour/day €10/30).

Also at Kalafatis, the friendly **Kalafati Dive Center** (☎ 22890 71677; www.mykonos-diving.com; Kalafatis Beach) has the full range of diving courses. One beach-dive with tank and weight is €18, or with all equipment it's €30; a boat dive with tank and weight will cost you €35, or with all equipment €50. A Discover Scuba Diving session is €45.

SLEEPING

Mykonos' beaches have two camping grounds, which have budget bungalows and whose minibuses meet the ferries. There are many top-end places around the coast; in between there doesn't seem to be much choice.

Budget

Mykonos Camping (☎ 22890 24578; www.mycamp
.gr; sites per adult/tent €10/4; bungalows per person €25)
This is a decent budget option by the pleas-
ant Paraga Beach (a 10-minute walk from
Platys Gialos) and has reasonable facilities
and bungalows that sleep two.

Midrange & Top End

Villa Katerina (☎ 22890 23414; fax 22890 22503; 2-6
person studios €111-234; P ⬛) Classic Cycladian
style and a blue-and-white colour scheme
enhance the quiet charms of this pleasant
place. It's 300m uphill from Agios Ioannis'
popular family beach.

Princess of Mykonos (☎ 22890 23806; fax 22890
23031; s/d/tr incl breakfast €200/225/260; P ⬛ ⬛) It
costs about 25% more for sea views at this
swish hotel that merges traditional island
style with Art-Deco touches. You're never
short of an interesting conversation piece
here. The hotel is above the fairly oversub-
scribed Agios Stefanos beach.

Ornos Beach Hotel (☎ 22890 23216; fax 22890
22483; s&d €120-140; P ⬛ ⬛) Overlooking
the busy beach, the traditional-style Ornos
is right in the middle of the action and is
handy for beach-hopping caïques.

EATING

Tasos Trattoria (☎ 22890 23002; Paraga Beach; mains
€7.50-19) A popular traditional taverna in the
heart of Paraga Beach, which does terrific
fish dishes, as well as chicken, pork and
veal.

Ano Mera Ανω Μέρα

The village of Ano Mera, 7km east of
Hora, is the island's only inland settlement.
Founded in the 16th century by Cretan settlers who had island-hopped from Folegandros it's a breezy, down-to-earth place with
a big central square flanked on three sides
by tavernas. If driving from Hora, keep on
past the village then go up right to a big
car park adjoining the main square. There
is an ATM booth between the car park and
the square.

You can visit the 6th-century **Moni Panagias Tourlianis** (☎ 22890 71249). It has a fine
marble bell tower and 16th-century icons
painted by members of the Cretan School,
but pride of place goes to a beautiful
wooden iconostasis carved in Florence in
the late 1700s.

Ano Mera Hotel (☎ 22890 71215; fax 22890 71230;
s/d €70/74; ☾ Jun-Sep; ⬛ ⬛) This big hotel has
decent rooms arranged round a big central
square. The swimming pool is just across
the road. To find it follow the road to Agrari
Beach from the village for about 400m.

The popular **Vangelis** (☎ 22890 71577; dishes
€4-12), which offers tasty spit roasts and fish
dishes including *kakavia* (fish soup), is in
Ano Mera's central square.

DELOS ΔΗΛΟΣ

The Cyclades fulfill their collective name
(*kyklos*) by encircling the sacred island of
Delos (☎ 22890 22259; sites & museum €3.50; ☾ 9am-
3pm Tue-Sun); but Mykonos clutches the island jealously to its heart. Delos, without a
permanent population other than a myriad
of ghosts, is an enchanting contrast to the
relentless liveliness of modern Mykonos,
although in high summer you share it all
with fellow visitors. The island is one of
the most important archaeological sites in
Greece, and certainly the most important in
the Cyclades. It lies a few kilometres off the
west coast of Mykonos.

History

Delos won early acclaim as the mythical
birthplace of the twins Apollo and Artemis
and was first inhabited in the 3rd millennium BC. In the 8th century BC, a festival
in honour of Apollo was established; the
oldest temples and shrines on the island
(many donated by Naxians) date from this
era. The dominant Athenians coveted Delos
as an island from where they could control
the Aegean. They had full control by the
5th century BC.

In 478 BC Athens established an alliance known as the Delian League that
kept its treasury on Delos. A cynical decree
ensured that no one could be born or die
on Delos, thus strengthening Athens control over the island by expelling the native
population.

Delos reached the height of its power in
Hellenistic times, becoming one of the three
most important religious centres in Greece
and a flourishing centre of commerce. Many
of its inhabitants were wealthy merchants,
mariners and bankers from as far away as
Egypt and Syria. They built temples to their

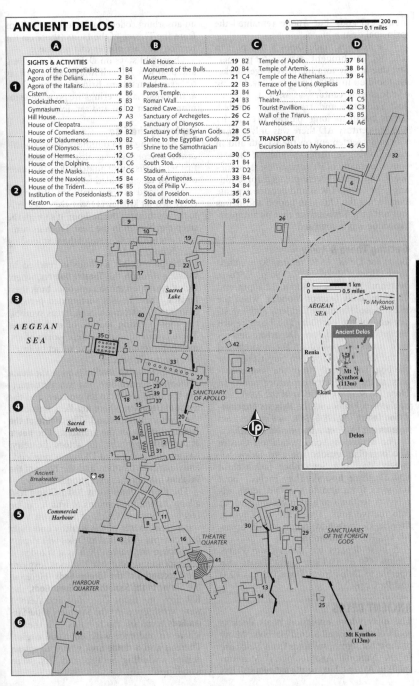

ANCIENT DELOS

CYCLADES

homeland gods, but Apollo remained the principal deity.

The Romans made Delos a free port in 167 BC. This brought even greater prosperity, due largely to a lucrative slave market that sold up to 10,000 people a day. During the following century, as ancient religions lost relevance and trade routes shifted, Delos began its long, painful decline. By the 3rd century AD there was only a small Christian settlement on the island, and in the following centuries the ancient site was looted of many of its antiquities; its stonework and fittings were pillaged for buildings elsewhere. The island became a pirate lair during the Ottoman period and it was not until the Renaissance that its antiquarian value was recognised.

Getting There & Away

Boats for Delos (€6.50 return, 30 minutes) leave Hora (Mykonos) at 9am, 9.50am, 10.15am, 11.10am, 11.40pm, 12.20pm and 12.50pm, daily (except Monday, when the site is closed) from the Old Jetty at the western end of the harbour. The boats return between 11am and 3pm. Departure and return times are posted on the noticeboard at the Old Jetty. You can buy tickets for the boat trip directly from the boat operators at the Old Jetty departure point. In Hora (Mykonos), **Delia Travel** (☎ 22890 22322; travel@delia.gr; Paralia) and the **Mykonos Accommodation Centre** (☎ 22890 23408; www.mykonos-accommodation.com; 1st fl, Enoplon Dinameon 10) sell tickets.

The Mykonos Accommodation Centre also organises guided tours to Delos between May and September (adult/child €30/23, three hours). They include boat transfers from and to the Old Jetty, admission to the site and museum and an informative tour. Tours are in English, French, German and Italian and in Spanish and Russian on request.

A boat departs for Delos from Platys Gialos (€9) at 10.15am daily. Boats also operate to Delos from Tinos (€20 to €25) and Paros (€40).

ANCIENT DELOS

The quay where excursion boats dock is south of the tranquil Sacred Harbour. Many of the most significant finds from Delos are in the National Archaeological Museum (p85) in Athens, but the **site museum** still has an absorbing collection, including the lions from the Terrace of the Lions (those on the terrace itself are plaster-cast replicas).

Overnight stays on Delos are forbidden, and boat schedules allow a maximum of six or seven hours there. Bring water and food, as the cafeteria's offerings are poor value for money. Wear a hat and sensible shoes.

Exploring the Site

The following is an outline of some significant archaeological remains on the site. For further details, buy a guidebook at the ticket office, or take a guided tour.

The island is very flat, but the rock-encrusted **Mt Kythnos** (113m) rises elegantly to the southeast of the harbour. It's worth the steep climb, even in the heat. From its summit there are terrific views of the surrounding islands on clear days.

The path to Mt Kythnos is reached by walking through the **Theatre Quarter**, where Delos' wealthiest inhabitants once built their houses. These houses surrounded *peristyle* courtyards, with mosaics (a status symbol) the most striking feature of each house. These colourful mosaics were works of art, mostly representational and offset by intricate geometric borders.

The most lavish dwellings were the **House of Dionysos**, named after the mosaic depicting the wine god riding a panther, and the **House of Cleopatra**, where headless statues of the owners were found. The **House of the Trident** was one of the grandest. The **House of the Masks**, probably an actors' hostelry, has another mosaic of Dionysos resplendently astride a panther, and the **House of the Dolphins** has another exceptional mosaic.

The **theatre** dates from 300 BC and had a large **cistern**, the remains of which can be seen. It supplied much of the town with water. The houses of the wealthy had their own cisterns – essential as Delos was almost as parched and barren then as it is today.

Descending from Mt Kythnos, explore the **Sanctuaries of the Foreign Gods**. Here, at the **Shrine to the Samothracian Great Gods**, the Kabeiroi (the twins Dardanos and Aeton) were worshipped. At the **Sanctuary of the Syrian Gods** there are the remains of a theatre where an audience watched ritual orgies. There is also a **shrine** area where Egyptian deities, including Serapis and Isis, were worshipped.

The **Sanctuary of Apollo**, to the northeast of the harbour, contains temples dedicated to the main man, and is the site of the much-photographed **Terrace of the Lions**. These proud beasts, carved from marble, were offerings from the people of Naxos, presented to Delos in the 7th century BC to guard the sacred area. To the northeast is the **Sacred Lake** (dry since it was drained in 1925 to prevent malarial mosquitoes breeding) where, according to legend, Leto gave birth to Apollo and Artemis.

PAROS ΠΑΡΟΣ

pop 12,853

Paros welcomes you with open arms to its broad bay and main port, Parikia, beyond which the island rises through undulating slopes to Mt Profitis Ilias (770m). White marble made Paros famous and prosperous from the Early Cycladic period onwards – most famously the *Venus de Milo* was carved from Parian marble, as was Napoleon's tomb.

Paros is the main ferry hub of the Cyclades and for onward travel to other island chains in the Aegean. The busy port town of Parikia bursts into frantic activity around the ferry quay whenever vessels arrive. The other major settlement, Naoussa, on the north coast, is a delightful resort with a colourful fishing harbour. At the island's heart is the peaceful mountain village of Lefkes.

The smaller island of Antiparos, 1km southwest of Paros, is easily reached by car ferry or excursion boat.

Getting There & Away

AIR

Olympic Airlines (☎ 22840 91257 at airport, ☎ 22840 21900 in Parikia; fax 22840 22778; www.olympicairlines.com; Plateia Mavrogenous; ⏲ 8am-2.30pm Mon-Fri) has daily flights to Athens (€55.35, 35 minutes).

FAST BOAT & CATAMARAN

There are three services daily to Piraeus (€39.10, 2½ hours) and one a day to Rafina (€32.80, 2½ hours), at least two daily to Naxos (€10.20, 30 minutes), Tinos (€16.90, 1¼ hours), Syros (€13, 45 minutes),

CYCLADES

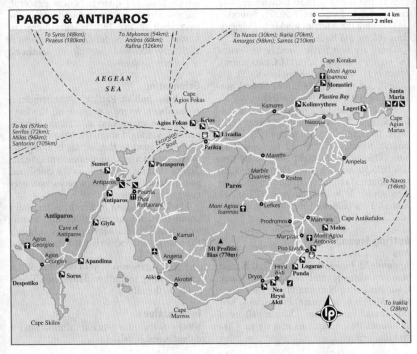

PAROS & ANTIPAROS

0 — 4 km
0 — 2 miles

To Syros (48km);
Piraeus (180km)

To Mykonos (54km);
Andros (60km);
Rafina (126km)

To Naxos (30km); Ikaria (70km);
Amorgos (98km); Samos (210km)

*AEGEAN
SEA*

Cape Korakas

Moni Agiou
Ioannou

Monastiri

Cape
Agios Fokas

Plastira Bay

Kamares

Kolimvythres

Santa
Maria

To Ios (57km);
Serifos (72km);
Milos (96km);
Santorini (105km)

Lageri

Cape
Agias
Marias

Naoussa

Agios Fokas

Krios

Excursion
Boat

Livadia

Parikia

Marathi

Ampelas

Sunset

Parasporos

*Marble
Quarries*

Kostos

To Naxos
(14km)

Antiparos

Paros

Pounta
*Thea
Restaurant*

Antiparos

Moni Agiou
Ioannou

Lefkes

Antiparos

Glyfa

Cave of
Antiparos

Kamari

Prodromos

Marmara

Cape Antikefalos

Molos

Agios
Georgios

Angeria

Mt Profitis
Ilias (770m)

Marpissa

Moni Agiou
Antonios

Agios
Georgios

Apandima

Piso Livadi

Soros

Aliki

Akrotiri

Dryos

Hrysi
Akti

Logaras

Punda

Despotiko

Nea
Hrysi
Akti

To Iraklia
(28km)

Cape
Mavros

Cape Skilos

LP

Mykonos (€13.10, one hour), Ios (€17.70, 1½ hours), Santorini (€23.76, 2¼ hours) and Amorgos (€17.70, 1½ to two hours). There is also one service daily to Iraklio on Crete (€43.90, four hours).

FERRY

There are price differences of about one to three euros between ferry companies whose vessels operate on the same ferry route. The more expensive price is given here.

There are around six boats daily to Piraeus (€23.40, five hours) and Naxos (€6.10, one hour), three daily to Ios (€10.60, 2½ hours) and Santorini (€14.20, three to four hours). There are daily services to Mykonos (€8, 1¾ hours), Syros (€7.30, 1½ hours), Tinos (€8.70, 2½ hours) and Amorgos (€11, three to 4½ hours).

Six weekly go to Koufonisia (€12.60, 4½ hours); three weekly go to Sikinos (€7.20, three to four hours), and Anafi (€13.30, six hours).

Five weekly go to Andros (€12.10, 4½ hours).

Four weekly go to Astypalea (€20.20, six hours) and Ikaria (€13,30 four hours) and two a week to Samos (€16.50, 7½ hours).

There are three ferries weekly to Folegandros (€7.40, 3½ hours).

There are two ferries weekly to Serifos (€7.60, three hours), Sifnos (€4, two hours), Milos (€11, 4½ hours), Kimolos (€9.30, 4½ hours), Schinousa (€8.40, four hours) and Donousa (€9, two to four hours).

There is one boat weekly to Thessaloniki (€35, 15 to 16 hours), Crete (€22, seven to eight hours), Skiathos (€27.50, 10 hours), Rhodes (€26.90, 12 to 15 hours), Kos (€16.90, six to eight hours), Kalymnos (€25.50, seven hours), Patmos (€15.35, four hours), Leros (€17, five hours), Kastellorizo (€30, 20 hours), Nisyros (€22.40, 11 hours), Tilos (€24.40, 10½ hours) and Symi (€27.20, 14 hours).

Getting Around

BUS

Around 12 buses daily link Parikia and Naoussa directly and seven buses daily from Parikia to Naoussa via Dryos, Hrysi Akti, Marpissa, Marmara, Prodromos, Kostos, Marathi and Lefkes. There are 10 buses to Pounta (for Antiparos) and six to Aliki (via the airport).

CAR, MOTORCYCLE & BICYCLE

There are rental outlets along the waterfront in Parikia and all around the island. One of the best in Parikia is **European Car Rental** (☎ 22840 21771; www.paroscars.de; D Vasileou) opposite the marina. Minimum rental per day in August for a car is about €30, for a motorbike €15.

TAXI

Taxis (☎ 22840 21500) gather to the right of the roundabout in Parikia. Fixed fares: airport €9, Naoussa €8, Pounta €7, Lefkes €8, and Piso Livadi €12. There are extra charges for luggage.

TAXI BOAT

Taxi boats leave from the quay for beaches around Parikia. Tickets ranging from €6 to €10 are available on board.

PARIKIA ΠΑΡΟΙΚΙΑ
pop 4522

Paros' capital and port is Parikia. It's a bright, cheerful town with an often frantic waterfront that contrasts dramatically with its Cycladic old quarter, where peaceful, narrow streets wriggle around the built-over shell of the 13th-century Venetian *kastro* (castle). The fortification crowns a slight rise above the waterfront, southeast of the ferry quay.

Orientation

The busy hub of Parikia is the windmill roundabout, where you come off the ferry quay. The main square, Plateia Mavrogenous, is straight ahead from the windmill. The busy road to the left leads along the northern waterfront to the beach at Livadia. The road to the right follows the café-lined southwestern waterfront, a pedestrian precinct in high season.

Market St (Agora in Greek) is the main commercial thoroughfare running southwest from Plateia Mavrogenous through the narrow and pedestrianised streets of the old town.

The bus station is 50m to the right of the quay (looking inland), and the post office is 350m to the left.

Information

Kiosks on the quay give out information on *domatia* and hotels.

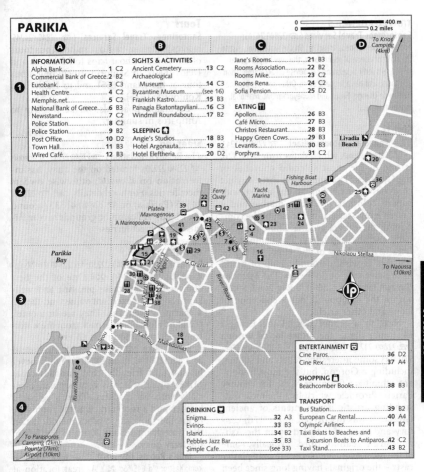

PARIKIA

INFORMATION
Alpha Bank.........................1 C2
Commercial Bank of Greece..2 B2
Eurobank...........................3 C3
Health Centre....................4 C2
Memphis.net......................5 C2
National Bank of Greece......6 B3
Newsstand.........................7 C2
Police Station.....................8 C2
Police Station.....................9 B2
Post Office.......................10 D2
Town Hall........................11 B3
Wired Café.......................12 B3

SIGHTS & ACTIVITIES
Ancient Cemetery..............13 C2
Archaeological
  Museum.........................14 C3
Byzantine Museum.........(see 16)
Frankish Kastro.................15 B3
Panagia Ekatontapyliani.....16 C3
Windmill Roundabout........17 B2

SLEEPING
Angie's Studios.................18 B3
Hotel Argonauta................19 B2
Hotel Eleftheria................20 D2

Jane's Rooms....................21 B3
Rooms Association.............22 B2
Rooms Mike.....................23 C2
Rooms Rena.....................24 C2
Sofia Pension...................25 D2

EATING
Apollon...........................26 B3
Café Micro........................27 B3
Christos Restaurant...........28 B3
Happy Green Cows............29 B3
Levantis..........................30 B3
Porphyra.........................31 C2

ENTERTAINMENT
Cine Paros.......................36 D2
Cine Rex.........................37 A4

SHOPPING
Beachcomber Books...........38 B3

TRANSPORT
Bus Station......................39 B2
European Car Rental..........40 A4
Olympic Airlines................41 B2
Taxi Boats to Beaches and
  Excursion Boats to Antiparos..42 C2
Taxi Stand.......................43 B2

DRINKING
Enigma...........................32 A3
Evinos............................33 B3
Island............................34 B2
Pebbles Jazz Bar...............35 B3
Simple Cafe..................(see 33)

0 —— 400 m
0 —— 0.2 miles

To Krios
Camping
(4km)

Livadia
Beach

To Naoussa
(10km)

To Parasporos
Camping (2km);
Pounta (7km);
Airport (10km)

CYCLADES

BOOKSHOPS

Newsstand (Ekatontapylianis) Great selection of newspapers, magazines and books in all languages.

EMERGENCY

Police (☎ 22840 23333; Plateia Mavrogenous)
Port police (☎ 22840 21240) Back from the northern waterfront, near the post office.

INTERNET ACCESS

Memphis.net (☎ 22840 23768; per 15 min €1; 9am-midnight Jun-Aug, 10am-10pm Sep-Apr) This place has an impressive range of services, including hook-ups for notebook computers and digital picture transfer.

Wired Café (☎ 22840 22003; Market St; 10.30am-2.30pm & 6-11pm Mon-Sat, 6-11pm Sun; per 30 min €2)

Head here for Internet access in a relaxed atmosphere. Also has connections for laptop computers and digital picture transfer.

MEDICAL SERVICES

Health Centre (☎ 22840 22500; Prombona)

MONEY

All the following banks have ATMS.
Alpha Bank (Ekatontapylianis)
Commercial Bank of Greece (Plateia Mavrogenous)
Eurobank (Ekatontapylianis)
National Bank of Greece (Plateia Mavrogenous)

POST

Post office (☎ 22840 21236) Located 450m to the left of the ferry quay.

TRAVEL AGENCIES

Santorineos Travel Services (☎ 22840 24245; bookings@santorineos-travel.gr) On the waterfront, just to the right of windmill roundabout, the very helpful Santorineos sells ferry tickets and can advise on accommodation and tours, and has a luggage store. Other services include bureau de change, FedEx and Moneygram (international money transfers).

Sights

The **Panagia Ekatontapyliani** (☎ 22840 21243; 7.30am-9.30pm), which dates from AD 326, is one of the most splendid churches in the Cyclades. The building is three distinct churches: Agios Nikolaos, the largest, with superb columns of Parian marble and a carved iconostasis, is in the east of the compound; the others are the Church of Our Lady and the Baptistery. The name translates as Our Lady of the Hundred Gates, but this is wishful rounding up of a still impressive tally of doorways. The **Byzantine Museum** (admission €1.50; 9.30am-2pm & 6-9pm), within the compound, has a collection of icons and other artefacts.

Next to a school behind the Panagia Ekatontapyliani, the **Archaeological Museum** (☎ 22840 21231; admission €2; 8.30am-3pm Tue-Sun) has some interesting reliefs and statues, including a Gorgon, but the most important exhibit is a fragment of the 4th-century Parian Chronicle, which lists the most outstanding artistic achievements of ancient Greece. It was discovered in the 17th century and most of it ended up in the Ashmolean Museum, Oxford. Typically, some of the most exquisite pieces are only plaster casts – the originals having long since been 'displaced' to museums in New York and Germany.

North along the waterfront there is a fenced **ancient cemetery** dating from the 7th century BC; it was excavated in 1983. Roman graves, burial pots and sarcophagi are floodlit at night.

The **Frankish Kastro** was built on the remains of a temple to Athena built by Marco Sanudo, Venetian Duke of Naxos, in AD 1260. Not much of the kastro remains, save for a large wall that is a jigsaw of unpainted column bases and dressed blocks, where pigeons now roost in the cracks. To find the kastro, head southwest along Market St and take the first right-hand turn.

Tours

Santorineos Travel Services (☎ 22840 24245; bookings@santorineos-travel.gr) can book bus tours of Paros (€22), boat trips to Mykonos and Delos (€40), to Santorini (including a bus tour of the island €55) and to Iraklia and Koufonisia (€35).

Excursion boats also make the trip to Antiparos in summer.

Sleeping

The **Rooms Association** (☎ 22840 22722, after hours ☎ 22840 22220), located on the quay, has information on *domatia*; otherwise owners meet ferries. For hotel details, call ☎ 22840 24555 (Parikia) or ☎ 22840 41333 (around the island). All camping grounds have minibuses that meet ferries.

BUDGET

Rooms Rena (☎ 22840 22220; fax 22840 21427; Epitropakis; s/d/tr €25/40/50;) One of the best choices in town, these pleasant and well-kept rooms are excellent value, and there's a charming welcome. They are in a quiet, but handy location just back from the waterfront. Air conditioning is €5 extra.

Rooms Mike (☎ 22840 22856; roommike@otenet.gr; s/d/tr €25/35/45, studios €30/40/50) You'll never be short of friendly chat and advice at Mike's place, which is very popular, especially with backpackers. There's a shared kitchen and a roof terrace. Some rooms are in another building, a block inland. It's on the waterfront, about 200m to the left of the ferry quay.

Jane's Rooms (☎ 22840 21338; www.janesrooms.com; Kastro; s/d €45/65;) A great location at the heart of the atmospheric Kastro area enhances these pleasant rooms that have fridges, sea views and balconies, and a communal roof terrace. Inquire for details about apartments (singles €40, doubles €50, triples €70) that are also available on the north side of the bay at Krios, 1.5km out of town.

Hotel Eleftheria (☎ 22840 22047; Livadia; s/d €40/50;) This cheerful and welcoming hotel is near Livadia Beach and has bright, clean rooms and a rooftop terrace; breakfast is available. Head left from the ferry quay for 800m and it's about 100m inland.

Parasporos Camping (☎ 22840 22268; sites per adult/tent €7/4) A popular and well-equipped site 2km south of Parikia, Parasporos is 300m from the beach.

Krios Camping (☎ 22840 21705; www.greek-tourism
.gr/krios-camping; sites per adult/tent €7/4; 🚌) This
appealing site, on the north shore of Parikia
Bay, is about 2.5km from the port. It has a
restaurant (dishes from €3.50 to €7) and a
minimarket. It runs a taxi boat across the
bay to Parikia every 10 minutes for €2 per
person (return). The boat pulls in just to the
left of the ferry quay, facing inland.

MIDRANGE

Sofia Pension (☎ 22840 22085; www.sofiapension
-paros.com; d/tr €85/95; P 🚌) This lovely place
is about 350m from the port on a quiet
street. Rooms are spacious and immaculate,
and many have sea views. The property is
set within landscaped gardens and patios
that are full of colour and are lovingly cared
for. The owners are charming and helpful. Head left from the ferry quay for about
600m, then head inland for about 150m.

Hotel Argonauta (☎ 22840 21440; www.argonauta
.gr; Plateia Mavrogenous; s/d €60/70; 🚌) You cannot beat this long-established family-run
hotel for its central location overlooking
Plateia Mavrogenous, or for its welcoming atmosphere. There are charming traditional touches to furnishings, the rooms
are spotless and comfy and have double-
glazing.

Angie's Studios (☎ 22840 23909/6977; www.angies
-studios.gr; Makedonias; d €60; 🕐 Apr-Oct; P 🚌)
Another friendly place, these handsome
studios are a short stroll from the centre
of town. They're big and extremely well-
kept and each has its own kitchen. There's a
patio surrounded by a garden area glowing
with bougainvillea and flowers, and there
are generous discounts in the off season.

Eating

Levantis (☎ 22840 23613; Kastro; dishes €9-13.50)
Stylish and with attentive service, Levantis
is in the heart of Kastro and has a courtyard garden setting and attractive grey-and-
orange décor. There are subtle international
touches to the cuisine. Starters include such
delights as aubergine rolls filled with *myzithra* (sheep's-milk cheese) and sun-dried
tomatoes. Salads are imaginative and mains
include such treats as rigaloni with spinach, wild mushrooms and roasted cherry
tomatoes, honey-spiced lamb, and grilled
calamari with spicy sausage and fennel. Desserts include white chocolate and

amaretto mousse with sour cherries. The
wine list is excellent, as is the house wine.

Happy Green Cows (☎ 22840 24691; dishes €10-15;
🕐 7pm-midnight) This intriguing little place (the
name was inspired by a dream) has witty,
kitsch décor and cheerful service. Food is
ethnic with a creative flair and there's a delicious line in *mezedes* (appetisers). Dishes are
named cheekily: try 'Tina' – chicken with
vegetables in a creamy curry sauce (€12), or
'Grandma's Secret' – smooth zucchini croquettes, crispy potatoes and yogurt sauce
(€12). You can drink into the early hours,
after the kitchen closes. To get there head
down G Gravari and look out for a narrow
alleyway on the left.

Porphyra (☎ 22840 22693; dishes €5-12.50) Set
back from the busy eastern waterfront, Porphyra does a great line in creative seafood:
shellfish and traditionally prepared fresh
fish, calamari and prawns.

Café Micro (☎ 22840 24674; Market St) A friendly
gathering spot for locals and visitors, this
bright place in the heart of the old town
does good breakfasts for €4 and offers coffee and snacks, fresh fruit and vegetarian
juices. There's drinks and music at night.

Also recommended:

Apollon (☎ 22840 21875; Market St; mains €8-22)
Upmarket; exudes attention to detail, right down to the
linen tablecloths and photo gallery of famous guests.

Christos Restaurant (☎ 22840 24666; mains €4.50-8)
On the seafront; for sturdy Greek dishes and home-made
pasta.

Argonauta Taverna (☎ 22840 23303; mains 4.50-9)
Attached to the hotel of the same name and offering reliable Greek standards.

Drinking

Island (☎ 22840 25046) Just west of the Windmill Roundabout, Island is a great local bar
with footstomping Greek music and late-
night dancing.

Pebbles Jazz Bar (☎ 22840 22283) Perched
above the seafront, on the edge of Kastro
is this cool place that plays classical music
by day and jazz in the evenings, with occasional live performers.

Enigma (☎ 22840 24664; D Vasileou) A stylish
place that goes hard into the wee hours, when
there's a touch more Greek to the sounds.

There are more bars are along the southwestern waterfront, including some busy
rooftop places like **Evinos** (☎ 22840 23026;
Kastro) and Simple Cafe.

Shopping

Beachcomber Books (☎ 22840 28282, 69736 20525; Market St) A veritable Aladdin's Cave of just about everything other than electrical goods. Second-hand books lead the field, but there are all sorts of bits and pieces. A cheerful experience all round.

NAOUSSA ΝΑΟΥΣΑ

pop 2316

Sunny Naoussa, on the north coast of Paros, has transformed itself from a quiet fishing village into a popular tourist resort, and has done so without losing its charm, or its harbourside atmosphere. There are good beaches nearby and the resort is fast becoming a food fanciers' destination with top tavernas and a couple of excellent restaurants. Behind the waterfront is a maze of narrow whitewashed streets, peppered with fish and flower motifs and with a mix of smart boutiques and souvenir shops.

Orientation & Information

The bus from Parikia terminates at the main square just in from the waterfront, where a dried-up river bed road leads inland. The main street of Naoussa lies to the left of the river bed. If arriving by car be warned: harbourside parking is banned from June to September. Signs are not clear, but the €35 fines are.

Naousa Information (☎ 22840 52158; ☼ 10am-midnight Jul-Aug, 11am-1pm & 6-10pm mid-Jun–Jul) can find you accommodation and is based in a booth by the main square, where the bus terminates.

The post office is a tedious uphill walk from the central square. An Alpha Bank (with ATM) is by the bus station.

Sights

Naoussa's **Byzantine museum** (admission €1.70; ☼ 11am-1.30pm & 7-9pm Tue, Thu, Sat & Sun) is housed in the blue-domed church, about 200m uphill from the central square on the main road to Parikia. A small **folklore museum** (☎ 22840 52284; admission €1.70; ☼ 9am-1pm & 6-9pm), which focuses on regional costumes, can be reached by heading inland from the main square to another blue-domed church. Turn right behind the church.

The best beaches in the area are **Kolimvythres**, which has interesting rock formations; and **Monastiri**, which has some good

snorkelling and a clubbing venue. Low-key **Lageri** is also worth seeking out. **Santa Maria**, on the other side of the eastern headland, is good for windsurfing. They can all be reached by road, but caïques go from Naoussa to each of them during July and August.

Activities

Kokou Riding Centre (☎ 22840 51818) has morning (€45), evening (€30) and one-hour (€25) horse rides, and can arrange pick up from Naoussa's main square for a small charge.

Tours

Naousa Paros Sailing Center (☎ 22840 52646; sailing@par.forthnet.gr) offers sailing tours to Naxos, Delos or Iraklia. A full day per person is €90, and departs at 10am. Half-day tours and yacht charters are also available.

Sleeping

There are two camping grounds, both with minibuses which meet ferries.

Naousa Camping (☎ 22840 51595; sites per adult/tent €6/4) This pleasant camping ground is at Kolimvythres. It has a small taverna and lovely bays nearby.

Surfing Beach (☎ 22840 52491; fax 22840 51937; info@surfbeach.gr; sites per adult/tent €7.40/3.55) A fairly large site, but with reasonable facilities and a good location at Santa Maria. The site has a windsurfing and a water-skiing school.

Hotel Stella (☎ 22840 51317; www.hotelstella.gr; s/d €45/65) Deep in the heart of the old town and within a leafy, colourful garden, this friendly hotel has excellent rooms and good facilities. It's best reached by heading up the main street, turning left at the National Bank, going beneath an archway, then turning right and up past a small church.

Hotel Galini (☎ 22840 51210; fax 22840 51949; s/d €45/55) Opposite the blue-domed local church (Byzantine museum), on the main road into town from Parikia, this charming and friendly little hotel has unfussy rooms that are being steadily updated.

Pension Anna (☎ 22840 51328, 69739 01135; s/d €40/60) Anna's has immaculate, comfortable rooms in a charming building surrounded by colourful shrubs and flowers. Turn right as you come into town from Parikia, just before the main square.

Hotel Madaky (☎ 22840 51475; fax 22840 52968; s/d €45/55; ☒) You pay €10 extra for air-conditioning at this very pleasant family-run hotel where rooms are spacious and comfortable. It's a quiet place, set back to the right of the main square facing inland.

Eating

Christos (☎ 22840 51442; dishes €12-23; ☺ 7pm-1am Apr-Oct) There's style and quality in abundance at this outstanding restaurant where you eat in a beautiful courtyard sheltered by leafy vines overhead and with paintings on the walls. The food matches the attentive service and is modern Mediterranean with exquisite touches, all backed by a superb wine list. To get there, head up the main street, and it's on the left after about 50m.

Perivolaria (☎ 22840 51598; dishes €6.50-18) Another of Naoussa's better eateries, Perivolaria has a delightful garden area where you can enjoy first-class Greek and international cuisine, including delicious pizzas and pastas. It is reached along the river road from the main square.

Moshonas (☎ 22840 51623; dishes €3.50-9) Seafood is by the kilogram at this long established and popular *ouzeri*. It's right on the edge of the harbour where the restaurant's own fishing caïques tie up and deliver the freshest catch straight to the kitchen.

Entertainment

In July and August, **Naousa Paros** (☎ 22840 52971; paros-dance@ach.gr; admission €8), a nationally known folk-dancing group based in Naoussa, perform every Sunday; book at Naoussa Information.

AROUND PAROS

Lefkes Λεύκες

Lefkes, 9km southeast of Parikia, is the island's highest and loveliest village, and was its capital during the Middle Ages. It boasts the **Agias Trias Cathedral**, an impressive building whose entrance is shaded by olive trees. But the village's real charm is the serenity of its pristine alleyways and buildings. Lefkes clings to a natural amphitheatre amid hills whose summits are dotted with old windmills. Siesta is taken seriously here, so tread lightly in the afternoon heat.

From the central square, a signpost points to a well-preserved Byzantine path, which leads in 3km to the village of **Prodromos**. At the edge of the village, keep left at a junction (signposted) with a wider track.

Sections of the route retain their original paving.

Down on the coast is the developing resort and harbour of **Piso Livadi**, where there is a pleasant beach and an ATM. **Candaca Travel** (☎ 22840 41449, 69464 62104; candaca@otenet .gr) at Piso Livadi can arrange accommodation and car rental, and also has Internet access.

Beaches

There is a fair scattering of beaches round the island's coastline, including a good one at **Krios**, accessible by taxi boat (return €4) from Parikia. Paros' top beach, **Hrysi Akti** (Golden Beach), on the southeast coast, is hardly spectacular, but it has good sand, several tavernas and is popular with windsurfers.

There is a decent enough beach at **Aliki** on the south coast.

SIGHTS & ACTIVITIES

The waters around Paros are ideal for adventure watersports, including diving and windsurfing. The straits between Paros and Antiparos are especially suited to windsurfing and the spectacular new sport of kiteboarding – effectively windsurfing in midair.

Located near Aliki and billed as a 'traditional historic museum', the fascinating **Scorpio's Museum** (☎ 22840 91129; ☺ 10am-2pm May-Sep) has remarkable models of fish, boats, lighthouses and much more, all the work of local man Benetos Skiadias. The museum is signposted just opposite the airport.

Down the coast at Pounda, **Eurodivers Club** (☎ 22840 92071; www.eurodivers.gr; Pounda) offers an impressive range of diving courses and dives for all levels and interests. A PADI open-water certification course costs €410.

Paros Kite Pro Centre (☎ 22840 92071; www .paroskite-procenter.com), well-run by the same team as Eurodivers Club, offers a range of courses, including an introductory kiteboarding session (one hour €30). More intensive courses start at €180.

At Hrysi Akti, **Fanatic Fun Centre** (☎ 69383 07617; www.fanatic-paros.com) has equipment for various watersports, including catamaran sailing, water-skiing and windsurfing. Board hire per hour costs from €15, and one-week courses are €140.

SLEEPING & EATING

Piso Livadi has a number of modern rooms and apartments, a few decent tavernas and there's a camping ground on the outskirts of town.

Anna's Studios (☎ 22840 41320; www.annasinn.com; Piso Livadi; s/d/studios €45/50/57; ⊠) Located at Piso Livadi these waterfront rooms and studios are immaculate. The studios are a little way out of the harbour area.

Young Inn (☎ 69764 15232; www.young-inn.com; Aliki; dm €12, s/d €30/50) Right down at the south of the island this cheerful place is orientated around young and international guests. There's always plenty going on and scooter rental can be arranged. There are discounts for groups.

Halaris Taverna (☎ 22840 43257; mains €4-12) There are a number of tavernas and cafés on the waterfront at Piso Livadi, but Halaris is a great choice. Starters range from zucchini croquettes to home-made cheese and spinach pies. The seafood mains are particularly good.

ENTERTAINMENT

The all-day clubbing venue **Punda Beach Club** (☎ 22840 41717; www.pundabeach.gr), at Viva Punda, is a huge complex with a swimming pool, bars, restaurants, gym, live-music shows and a relentlessly crowded beach scene.

ANTIPAROS ΑΝΤΙΠΑΡΟΣ

pop 1037
You feel the pace of life slow down delightfully as soon as you step ashore on Antiparos. The island is proud of its distinctiveness and of its independence from its larger neighbour; forget this at your peril in front of local people. The main village and port (also called Antiparos) is a bright and friendly place. There's a touristy gloss round the waterfront and main streets, but the village runs deep inland to quiet squares and alleyways that give way suddenly into open fields. Off the waterfront, streets are pedestrianised.

Getting There & Away

In summer, frequent excursion boats depart for Antiparos from Parikia.

There is also a half-hourly car ferry that runs from Pounta on the west coast of Paros to Antiparos (one way €0.60, per car €6.60; 10 minutes); the first ferry departs for Antiparos at around 7.15am and the last boat returning leaves Antiparos at 12.30am.

Getting Around

The only bus service on Antiparos runs, in summer, to the cave in the centre of the island (€1). The bus continues to Soros and Agios Georgios.

Orientation & Information

To reach the village centre from the Pounta ferry quay, head right along the waterfront and turn left into the main street, Market St, by Anarghyros restaurant. If you've come by excursion boat, walk straight ahead from the arrival quay.

Halfway up the main street are an Emporiki Bank and National Bank of Greece, both with ATMs. The post office is also here. The central square is reached by turning left at the top of the main street and then right, behind Smiles Cafe.

There are several travel agencies, including **Antiparos Travel Agency** (☎ 22840 61300; fax 22840 61465; ⊠ Jun–mid-Oct) by the waterfront, which can help you with your accommodation needs. **Blue Island Divers** (☎ 22840 61493; www.blueisland-divers.gr) can also arrange accommodation and car hire.

To reach the kastro, another Marco Sanudo creation, go under the stone arch that leads north off the central square.

Sights

Despite previous looting of stalactites and stalagmites, the **Cave of Antiparos** (admission €3.50; ⊠ 10.15am-3pm summer) is still awe-inspiring. It is 8km south of the port. Follow the coast road south until you reach a signed turn-off into the hills.

There are buses from the port (one way €1, hourly).

Activities

On the main pedestrian thoroughfare, with a gear and clothes shop attached, **Blue Island Divers** (☎ 22840 61493; www.blueisland-divers.gr) is friendly and helpful, and has a wide range of dive options. The owners have a great knowledge of the Antiparos scene. Accommodation and car rental can also be arranged. A four-day PADI open-water course is €340 and an advanced course is €260. A snorkelling day trip per adult/child is €20/10. Trips to suit your wishes are happily arranged.

Tours
MS Thiella (☎ 22840 61028) runs tours around the island daily, stopping at several beaches. The price is €35 and covers refreshments and lunch; you can book at Antiparos Travel Agency.

Sleeping
Camping Antiparos (☎ 22840 61221; sites per adult/tent €4.50/2.20) This camping ground is planted with bamboo and is on a pleasant beach 1.5km north of the quay; signs point the way.

Anarghyros (☎ 22840 61204; mak@par.forthnet .gr; s/d €30/45; ✖) This well-run, well-kept hotel is excellent value. It's right on the waterfront but double glazing cuts out any external noise. There's a decent restaurant (dishes from €4.50 to €8) attached.

Hotel Mantalena (☎ 22840 61206; mantalena hotel@par.forthnet.gr; d €60; ✖) Another good accommodation choice, the Mantalena is family-run and is located a short distance beyond the Anarghyros. It's set back from the main drag and has a fairly peaceful

---

THE AUTHOR'S CHOICE

Thea (☎ 22840 91220, 69457 51015; dishes €9-12) A taste of old Greece and Asia Minor hangs in the air of this great restaurant. It's an experience in every way, from its lovely waterside location near the Antiparos ferry quay on the Paros side of the straits, to the 465 different vintages that are kept in a wine room–cum-bar – which even has a glass floor with bottles nestling beneath your feet. The wine list must be one of the best in Greece. The food is prepared with love and care, and with the finest ingredients; even the olive oil is carefully sourced. For appetisers try roasted *Chaloumi* with Florina peppers, capers, olives and parsley, or *Ampelosarmades*, with rice, pine nuts, raisins and yogurt sauce, made using an old recipe from Constantinople. Mains include Capadocian lamb with apricots, or Kidonato beef with quinces, rice and plums, and there is much more. Background music is from a selection of 4500 CDs of world music. What more could you ask for...?

---

atmosphere. There's a pleasant terrace and rooms are comfortable.

Eating & Drinking
The main street of Antiparos has many cafés and tavernas serving Greek staples and fish dishes.

Maki's (☎ 22840 61616; dishes €4-10) One of the best, where the seafood is generally excellent, and includes such treats as prawn *souvlaki* with calamari.

Yam Bar Restaurant and Cocktail Bar (☎ 69782 30103; dishes €6-9; ☹ 8pm-4am mid-Jun–mid-Sep) Signposted left off the top end of Market St, this is a relaxing spot, with views of the sea. You can enjoy delicious cold plates of chicken, pasta and other treats while listening to a general mix of music, including Latin and house and occasional jazz.

Soul Sugar is along to the right from the top of the main street. It plays funk, disco and house into the small hours, and serves great cocktails.

NAXOS ΝΑΞΟΣ

pop 18,188
Myth and beauty have blessed Naxos with racy romanticism. It was on Naxos that Theseus is said to have abandoned Ariadne after she helped him escape the Cretan labyrinth. In keeping with even mythic soap opera, she didn't pine long, and was soon entwined with Dionysos, the god of wine and ecstasy and the island's favourite deity. Naxian wine has long been considered a fine antidote for a broken heart; but the very air of Naxos is intoxicating enough and you should take your time at this delightful island and its superb beaches, lively port, mountainous interior and enchanting villages, such as Halki and Apiranthos.

Naxos is more fertile than most of the other islands and produces olives, grapes, figs, citrus fruit, corn and potatoes. Mt Zeus (1004m; also known as Mt Zas or Zefs) is the Cyclades' highest peak and is the central focus of the island's mountainous interior.

Naxos is believed to have been inhabited continuously since the Neolithic period and was a cultural centre of classical Greece; its abundant marble facilitated fine sculpture and architecture. It was a flourishing centre of Byzantium, and Venetian and Frankish influences have also left a powerful mark.

The island is a wonderful place to explore on foot, as many old paths between villages, churches and other sights still survive. There are a number of walking guides and maps, including the useful *Central Naxos – A Guide with Map* (€8), available from local bookshops.

Getting There & Away

AIR
There is at least one flight daily and two on Sunday to Athens (€56, 45 minutes). Olympic Airlines is represented by **Naxos Tours** (☎ 22850 22095; naxostours@naxos-island.com), on the waterfront, which also sells ferry tickets.

FAST BOAT & CATAMARAN
There are at least two catamarans travelling daily to Paros (€13.90, 30 minutes), Mykonos (€15.20, 1½ hours) and Piraeus (€39.10, 3¼ hours). There are also daily services to Ios (€16.60, 50 minutes), Santorini (€22.60, 1½ hours) and Iraklio on Crete (€38.80, 3¼ hours), and four weekly to Syros (€13.80, 1½ hours).

FERRY
There are price differences of about €1 to €3 between ferry companies whose vessels operate on the same ferry route. The more expensive price is given here.

Naxos has around six ferry connections daily with Piraeus (€23.10, five hours),

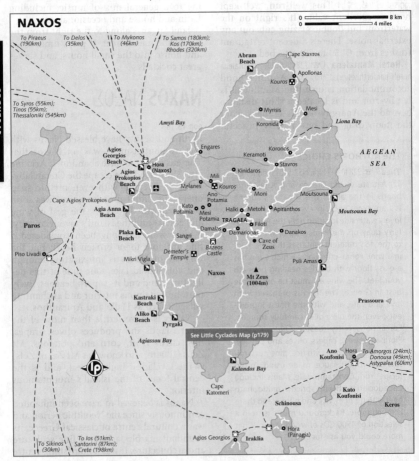

NAXOS

0 ___ 8 km
0 ___ 4 miles

To Piraeus (190km); To Delos (35km); To Mykonos (46km); To Samos (180km); Kos (170km); Rhodes (320km)

To Syros (55km); Tinos (55km); Thessaloniki (545km)

Abram Beach
Cape Stavros
Apollonas
Kouros
Myrisis
Mesi
Liona Bay
Amyti Bay
Koronida
Engares
Koronos
AEGEAN SEA
Agios Georgios Beach
Keramoti
Stavros
Hora (Naxos)
Kinidaros
Agios Prokopios Beach
Mili
Kouros
Melanes
Ano Potamia
Moni
Cape Agios Prokopios
Moutsouna
Agia Anna Beach
Kato Potamia
Halki
Metohi
Apiranthos
Moutsouna Bay
Paros
Mesi Potamia
TRAGAEA
Filoti
Plaka Beach
Damalas
Damarionas
Danakos
Piso Livadi
Sangri
Bazeos Castle
Cave of Zeus
Demeter's Temple
Mikri Vigla
Naxos
Psili Amas
Mt Zeus (1004m)
Kastraki Beach
Prassoura
Aliko Beach
Pyrgaki
Agiassou Bay

See Little Cyclades Map (p179)

Ano Koufonisi
Hora
To Amorgos (24km); Donousa (45km); Astypalea (60km)
Kalandos Bay
Kato Koufonisi
Cape Katomeri
Schinousa
Keros
To Sikinos (30km); To Ios (51km); Santorini (87km); Crete (198km)
Agios Georgios
Iraklia
Hora (Panagia)

Paros (€6.60, one hour), Ios (€8.60, 1¼ hours) and Santorini (€13.70, three hours), as well as four daily with Mykonos (€9.20, three hours).

There is one daily boat to Tinos (€11, 4¼ hours), Syros (€9.25, three hours), Iraklia (€5.50, 1¼ to 5¼ hours), Schinousa (€6, 1¾ to five hours), Koufonisia (€7, 2½ to 4¼ hours), Amorgos (€9.50, two to 5¾ hours), Donousa (€6.50, one to four hours), Samos (€16.30, 3½ hours) and Ikaria (€12.20, 1½ hours).

There are five ferries weekly to Anafi (€10.60, seven hours).

There are two boats weekly to Astypalea (€20.10, 5½ hours), Rhodes (€22.80, 14 hours), Sikinos (€8.10, three hours) and Folegandros (€8.80, three hours).

One goes weekly to Thessaloniki (€34.50, 15 hours), Kos (€16, 8¼ hours), Iraklio (€19.50, seven hours) and Andros (€13.50, five hours).

Getting Around

TO/FROM THE AIRPORT
The airport is 3km south of Hora. There is no shuttle bus, but buses to Agios Prokopios Beach and Agia Anna pass close by. A taxi costs €12.

BUS
Frequent buses run to Agia Anna (€1.20) from Hora. Five buses daily serve Filoti (€1.60) via Halki (€1.20), four serve Apiranthos (€2.30) via Filoti and Halki, at least three serve Apollonas (€4), Pyrgaki (€2) and Melanes (€1.20). There are less frequent departures to other villages.

Buses leave from the end of the wharf in Hora; timetables are posted outside the bus information office which is located in front of the bus station and the Naxos Tourist Information Centre in Hora.

CAR, MOTORCYCLE & BICYCLE
You can hire cars per day from about €40 and motorcycles from about €15, as well as 21-speed all-terrain bicycles, from the waterfront outlets in Hora. **Fun Car** (☎ 22850 26084; Plateia Protodikiou) is a good bet. Bicycle hire starts at €8. You'll need all the gears – the roads are steep and winding and, although surfaces are being improved, recent winter storms have caused damage on lesser-used mountain roads.

HORA (NAXOS) ΧΩΡΑ (ΝΑΞΟΣ)
pop 6533
The bustling and engaging Hora, on the west coast of Naxos, is the island's port and capital. It's a large town, divided into two historic neighbourhoods – Bourgos, where the Greeks resided, and the hilltop Kastro, where the Venetian Catholics lived.

Orientation
The ferry quay is at the northern end of the waterfront, with the bus terminal at its inland end. The waterfront, Protopapadaki, is lined with cafés and restaurants. Behind the waterfront, narrow alleyways scramble beneath archways up to the Kastro.

A left turn from the end of the ferry quay will lead you to a causeway over to Palatia Islet and the unfinished Temple of Apollo, Naxos' most famous landmark, known as the Portara. There is not much else to see here other than the two columns and their crowning lintel surrounded by fallen masonry.

There are a few swimming spots along the waterfront promenade below the temple. Southwest of the town is the pleasant, but busy, beach of Agios Georgios.

Information
Booths on the quay have information about hotels and *domatia*, but a good bet is to head for the privately owned Naxos Tourist Information Centre.

BOOKSHOPS
Zoom (☎ 22850 23675; Protopapadaki) A large, well-stocked newsagent and bookshop that has most international newspapers and one of the biggest selection of books, in various languages, in the entire Cyclades.

EMERGENCY
Police (☎ 22850 22100) Southeast of Plateia Protodikiou.
Port police (☎ 22850 22300) Just south of the quay.

INTERNET ACCESS
Rental Center (☎ 22850 23395; per hr €3; Plateia Protodikiou)
Zas Travel (☎ 22850 23330; fax 22850 23419; Protopapadaki; per hr €4)

MEDICAL SERVICES
Medical Centre (☎ 22850 23550; Prantouna)

CYCLADES

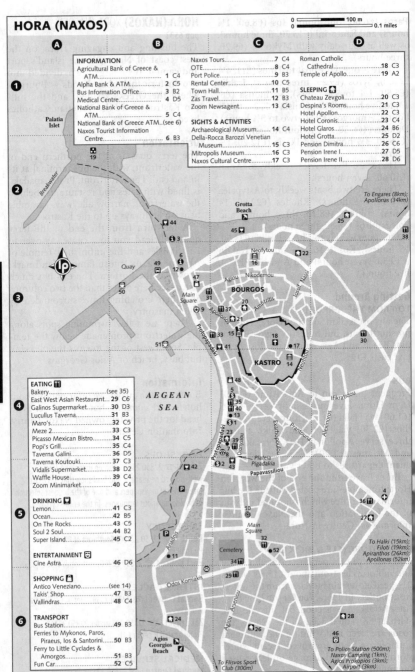

HORA (NAXOS)

MONEY

All the following banks have ATMs. There's also an ATM outside the Naxos Tourist Information Centre.

Agricultural Bank of Greece (Protopapadaki)
Alpha Bank (cnr Protopapadaki & Papavassiliou)
National Bank of Greece (Protopapadaki)

POST

Post office (Odos Komiakis) Past the OTE, across Papavasiliou, left at forked road.

TELEPHONE

OTE (telecommunications office; Protopapadaki) Has several phone kiosks outside.

TOURIST INFORMATION

Naxos Tourist Information Centre (NTIC; ☎ 22850 25201, emergency ☎ 22850 24525; apollon-hotel@ naxos-island.com) Opposite the quay, this is an excellent source of in-depth advice on accommodation, excursions and rental cars; luggage storage is available (€1.50). The NTIC does not sell ferry tickets.

TRAVEL AGENCIES

Both the following sell ferry tickets and organise accommodation, tours and rental cars.

Naxos Tours (☎ 22850 22095; naxostours@naxos -island.com; Plateia Pigadakia)
Zas Travel (☎ 22850 23330; fax 22850 23419; Proto-papadaki)

Sights

To see the Bourgos area, head inland and up to the right from the main square into the winding backstreets. The most alluring part of Hora, however, is the residential **Kastro**, with its narrow alleyways, timber-lined archways and whitewashed houses. Marco Sanudo made the town the capital of his duchy in 1207, and several Venetian mansions survive, many with well-kept gardens and the insignia of their original residents. Take a stroll around the Kastro during siesta to experience its hushed, medieval atmosphere.

A short distance behind the northern end of the waterfront is a remarkable area of Naxian history and religious culture. Here, several churches and chapels, including the 18th-century **Metropolis**, are obvious symbols of Orthodoxy. Below ground however is a more venerable Naxos, and within the **Mitropolis Museum** (☎ 22850 24151; admission free;

8.30am-3pm) are fragments of a Mycenaean city of the 13th to 11th centuries BC that was abandoned because of the threat of flooding by the sea. It's a haunting place and is well-laid out, with glass walk-over panels revealing ancient foundations, and larger areas of excavated buildings.

The **archaeological museum** (☎ 22850 22725; admission €3; 8.30am-3pm Tue-Sun) is in the Kastro, housed in the former Jesuit school where the novelist Nikos Kazantzakis was briefly a pupil. The contents include Hellenistic and Roman terracotta figurines. There are also, more interestingly, some early Cycladic figurines.

Close by the **Della Rocca-Barozzi Venetian Museum** (☎ 22850 22387; guided tours adult/student €5/3; 10am-3pm & 7-10pm), a handsome old tower house of the 13th century, is within the Kastro ramparts, by the northwest gate. A visit takes you into the fascinating world of the historic Kastro and its Frankish and Venetian past. There are changing art exhibitions in the vaults. Tours are multilingual. The museum also runs **tours** (adults/students €15/10) of the Kastro at 11am from Tuesday to Sunday; tours last just over two hours. Special **evening cultural events** are held at the museum several times a week and comprise traditional music and dance concerts, classical and contemporary music recitals, dance, drama and Greek shadow theatre.

The Roman Catholic **cathedral** (6.30-8.30pm), also in the Kastro, is worth visiting. The **Naxos Cultural Centre** (☎ 22850 22470; Kastro) nearby has exhibitions over summer. Phone for details as exhibition opening times and entrance fees vary greatly.

Activities

Flisvos Sport Club (☎ 22850 24308; www.flisvos -sportclub.com; Agios Georgios) offers a range of windsurfing options, starting with a beginner's course of six hours for €150, or a four-hour Hobie Cat sailing course for €95. The club also organises walking trips and rents mountain bikes for €7.50 a day; and arranges mountain-bike tours.

Naxos Horse Riding (☎ 69488 09142) organises daily evening horse rides (5pm to 8pm), both inland and on beaches (per person €40). You can book a ride up until 6pm the day before and can arrange pick-up and return, to and from the stables. Beginners and advanced riders are catered for and there is pony riding for very young children. Bookings can also be made at the **Naxos Silver Gallery** (☎ 22850 24130) in Plateia Pigadakia.

Tours

Naxos Tourist Information Centre (☎ 22850 25201, emergency ☎ 22850 24525; apollon-hotel@naxos-island. com) Offers day tours of the island by bus (€18) or caïque (including barbecue €38). One-day walking tours (two people €44) are offered three times weekly.

Flisvos Sport Club (☎ 22850 24308; www.flisvos -sportclub.com; Agios Georgios) You can book a half-day guided mountain-bike tour for €20.

Excursion Boats There are frequent excursions to Mykonos (€35), Delos (€35) and Santorini (€50); book through travel agents.

Sleeping

BUDGET

Naxos has a rapacious mob of *domatia* hawkers meeting ferries. If you're not interested be firm but polite, and keep moving; Hora has plenty of good accommodation options.

Pension Irene I (☎ 22850 23169; irenepension@ hotmail.com; s/d €25/35) Located a little bit out of the town centre, but peaceful and well run and in pleasant leafy surroundings, this popular place has comfortable rooms and there are cooking facilities. Head down Prantouna from the seafront for about 400m and it's the first lane on the right before the Medical Centre.

Pension Irene II (☎ 22850 23169; irenepension@ hotmail.com; s/d €30/50; ⚲) Run by the same people as Irene I and is an excellent option. Rooms are bright and comfortable with pleasant balconies, and the swimming pool is a surprising and irresistible bonus. Take the road on the southeast corner of the main square, walk for about 200m and then go left for about 50m.

Pension Dimitra (☎ /fax 22850 24922; Agios Georg ios; s/d/tr €45/53/70) Although some way from the centre and in an anonymous street, this is a charming, very Greek place, with clean and comfy rooms. Only Greek is spoken, but communication is by smiles and kindness anyway. Agios Georgios Beach is just 100m away.

Despina's Rooms (☎ 22850 22356; fax 22850 22179; Kastro; s/d €40/45) Tucked away on the edge of the Kastro, this cheerful family home has a selection of rooms, some with great sea views. Rooms on the roof terrace are popular despite their small size. There's a communal kitchen.

There are several camping grounds near Hora. All have good facilities. Minibuses meet the ferries. The sites are all handy to good beaches and there's an approximate price per person of €7.

Naxos Camping (☎ 22850 23500; ⚲) About 1km south of Agios Georgios Beach.

Camping Maragas (☎ 22850 24552) At Agia Anna Beach.

Plaka Camping (☎ 22850 42700; fax 22850 42701) At Plaka Beach, 6km from town.

MIDRANGE

Hotel Grotta (☎ 22850 22215; www.hotelgrotta.gr; Grotta; s/d incl breakfast €50/70; P ⚲) Overlooking Grotta Beach and in an area of archaeological importance, this delightful modern hotel has comfortable and immaculate rooms and great sea views from the front; all enhanced by friendly service.

Hotel Apollon (☎ 22850 22468, 69766 18384; www .naxostownhotels.com; Fontana; s/d incl breakfast €65/85; P ⚲ 🖳) The stylish and welcoming Apollon has thoughtful touches that capture a sense of Naxian good living, and spacious, well-equipped rooms. The hotel is in a quiet area a few minutes from the waterfront.

Hotel Glaros (☎ 22850 23101; fax 22850 24877; www.hotelglaros.com; Agios Georgios; s incl breakfast €55-60, d incl breakfast €70-75; ⚲ 🖳) Friendly, well-run Hotel Glaros has bright décor that reflects the colours of sea and sky. An added bonus is that Agios Georgios beach is only a few steps away. The owners also have attractive apartments nearby (€60 to €85).

Chateau Zevgoli (☎ 22850 26123; www.naxos townhotels.com; Kastro Bourgo; s/d €70/80; ⚲) There's a great sense of being in the heart of old Naxos at Zevgoli, with its charming garden setting within the Kastro. The experience is enhanced by the traditional Naxian style of rooms and furnishings.

Hotel Coronis (☎ 22850 22297/8; fax 22850 23984; Protpapadaki; s/d/tr €60/78/95; ⚲) Refurbishment in the past few years has made this standard resort-style hotel into a decent option. Rooms are bright and clean, and most look over the harbour. There is a lift to all floors.

Eating

Naxian specialities include *kefalotiri* (hard cheese), honey, *kitron* (a liqueur made from the leaves of the citron tree – see p176), *raki* (Greek fire water), ouzo and fine white wine.

Meze 2 (☎ 22850 26401; Paralia; mains €2.50-9) This is what a great old-style *mezedopoleio-ouzeri* (restaurant specialising in appetisers, light snacks and ouzo) is all about. The emphasis is on fish, and even the local fishermen eat here. Superb seafood is prepared and served by family members in an atmosphere that is never less than sociable and genuinely local. You can even drop in and order special fish dishes the day before.

Lucullus Taverna (☎ 22850 22569; Agiou Nikodemou; dishes €7.50-14) Lucullus has been operating for over 100 years and still offers great local food, such as *lemonato* (veal in a fresh lemon and white-wine sauce) with vegetables and garlic (€8.50), or a fisherman's pasta of shrimps, tomatoes, dill and garlic. The walls are hung with all sorts of fascinating artefacts.

Picasso Mexican Bistro (☎ 22850 25408; dishes €4.75-12.50; ⊗ 7pm-till late) To sample great Tex-Mex, head for this popular place. Tables fill quickly with aficionados of tacos, nachos, burritos and fajitas. It also does great salads as well as hefty Buffalo Steaks. There's a beach version, Picasso on the Beach at Plaka Beach, open mid-June to September.

Maro's (☎ 22850 25113; mains €3-8) Located a bit out of the centre, but worth the stroll, this grill house has a traditional Greek approach to food. Plenty of home-grown ingredients go into classic local dishes. Maro's popularity with locals says everything. To get there, take the road on the southeast corner of the main square for about 30m.

East West Asian Restaurant (☎ 22850 24641; off Agiou Arseniou; dishes €5.60-13) There's always a friendly welcome at this fine restaurant where you can enjoy Thai, Chinese or Indian favourites, such as southern shrimp masala (€13) or its beef version (€9). Dishes include excellent vegetarian options.

Waffle House (☎ 22850 23007; Plateia Pigadakia; waffles €3-6.50) The lively Pigadakia has a great selection of ice creams as well as waffles and also does breakfasts (€5 to €10).

Also recommended are the following places; all charging about €4 to €9 for a main dish.

Taverna Koutouki (Kastro) Famous for its outside tables in a narrow alleyway on the way up to Kastro.

Popi's Grill (Protopapadaki) The best place for *souvlaki*.

Taverna Galini (Prantouna)

Near the Zoom newsagent and bookshop is the town's best bakery. Next door is the Zoom Minimarket. The cheapest supermarkets are Galinos and Vidalis, both a little way out of town.

Drinking
BARS
Lemon (☎ 22850 24734; Protopapadaki) With its relaxing décor Lemon is one of the best waterfront places from which to watch the world go by.

On The Rocks (Plateia Pigadakia) Has plenty of character to go with its marvellous cocktails. You can enjoy Havana cigars with Cuban-style daiquiris that go well with sounds that vary between funk, house, electronic and live performances.

Jam (Plateia Pigadakia) Also recommended is this spot just across the way from On The Rocks. It's a long-established music bar that plays rock and assorted sounds.

Soul 2 Sol on the way to the Portara, is open for morning coffee as well as being a music bar playing a good mix of contemporary sounds until late.

Entertainment
CINEMAS
Cine Astra (☎ 22850 25381; Andreas Papandreou; adult/child €7/5) About a five-minute walk from the main square. It shows newly released mainstream films and has a bar. Sessions are 9pm and 11pm.

NIGHTCLUBS
Ocean (☎ 22850 26766; Seafront; ⊗ 11.30pm-3am May–mid-Sep, 11.30pm-late Fri & Sat rest of year) For clubbing, head to this place. It's a big space and features house and some modern Greek music and runs special nights with guest DJs. Entrance is between €5 and €8.

Super Island (Grotta; ⊗ 11.30pm-3am May–mid-Sep, 11.30pm-late Fri & Sat rest of year) Right on the waterfront, at Grotta Beach, this is even bigger and features similar sounds, but with more modern Greek. Entrance is about €8.

SUNSET CONCERTS
Della Rocca-Barozzi Venetian Museum (☎ 22850 22387; Kastro) Evening concerts, featuring traditional instruments, are held several times a week in the museum grounds, accompanied. Events start about 8pm and entry is €14 to €20 depending on seat position.

CYCLADES

Shopping

Takis' Shop (☎ 22850 23045; Plateia Mandalaraki) For one of the finest wine selections in the Cyclades head straight for Takis, just one block behind the waterfront. Takis Giannoulis knows all about Greek wines and among his splendid stock are such fine names as Lazaridis from Northern Greece, Tslepos from the Peloponnese and Nanousakis from Crete, all masterful vintages. You can also find Vallindras *kitron* liqueur (see right) and ouzo here. Adjoining is Takis' jewellery shop, where fine individual pieces often reflect ancient designs and the imagery of the sea.

Antico Veneziano (☎ 22850 26206; Kastro) An upmarket antique store and gallery in a restored home in the Kastro, this makes for a fascinating visit.

In the streets heading up to the Kastro there are several shops selling fine embroidery and hand-made silver jewellery.

AROUND NAXOS

Beaches

Agios Georgios is Naxos' town beach and starts right on the southern edge of the waterfront. It gets crowded, but is safe for youngsters as the water is very shallow.

The next beach south of Agios Georgios is **Agios Prokopios** in a sheltered bay. This is followed by **Agia Anna**, a stretch of shining white sand, quite narrow but long enough to feel uncrowded. Development is increasing here, but not too heavily.

Cruises run to different destinations daily from Agia Anna. They head either to Iraklia and Koufonisia, Schinousa and Koufonisia, or Antiparos; book at travel agents (see p173).

Sandy beaches continue down as far as **Pyrgaki** and include **Plaka, Aliko, Kastraki.**

One of the best of these southern beaches is **Mikri Vigla**, whose name translates as 'little lookout', a watching place for pirates, and reference to the rocky headland, all golden granite slabs and boulders, between superb beaches. The settlement here is a little scattered and is punctuated by half-finished buildings in places, but there's a sense of escapism and open space.

There are *domatia* and tavernas near most beaches. A great option is **Oasis Studios** (☎ 22850 75494; www.oasisnaxos.gr; s/d €60/75; P 🛞 🖳 🕱) at Mikri Vigla. It is close to the

beach and has lovely big rooms with kitchens. The owner and staff are friendly and helpful, and there's a sociable outside terrace with a swimming pool and bar. Much local information is available and they can help you arrange horse riding, windsurfing and kitesurfing on the nearby beaches.

The perfect beach location, backed by great food, makes **Taverna sto Liofago** (☎ 22850 75214, 69371 37737; dishes €3.50-7) a great favourite. It has been doing business for decades and offers a variety of tasty traditional dishes. The *keftedhaki* (meat balls) are a speciality.

Tragaea Τραγαία

The lovely Tragaea region is a vast plain of olive groves and unspoilt villages, harbouring numerous little Byzantine churches. **Filoti**, on the slopes of Mt Zeus, is the region's largest village. It has an ATM booth, accessed with card, just down from the main bus stop. On the outskirts of the village (coming from Hora), an asphalt road leads off right into the heart of the Tragaea. This road brings you to the isolated hamlets of **Damarionas** and **Damalas**.

From Filoti, you can also reach the **Cave of Zas (Zeus)**, a large natural cavern at the foot of a cliff on the slopes of Mt Zeus. About 800m south of Filoti there's a junction signposted Aria Spring and Zas Cave. If travelling by bus ask to be dropped off here. The side road ends in 1.2km. From the road-end parking, follow a walled path past the **Aria Spring**, a fountain and picnic area, and continue uphill to reach the cave.

HALKI ΧΑΛΚΕΙΟ

The delightful village of **Halki** lies at the heart of the Tragaea, about 20 minutes from Naxos town. It is one of the island's unmissable experiences, not least for its handsome villas and tower houses, legacy of a rich history as the one-time centre of Naxian commerce.

The main road skirts Halki. There is some roadside parking but you may find more at the schoolyard at the north end of the village. Lanes lead off the main road to the little square at the heart of the village.

Since the late 19th century Halki has had strong connections with the production of **kitron**, a delicious liqueur. The citron (*Citrus medica*) was introduced to the

Mediterranean area in about 300 BC and thrived on Naxos for centuries. The fruit is barely edible in its raw state, but its rind tastes delicious when preserved in syrup as a *ghlika kutaliu*, a popular dessert in Greece. *Kitroraki*, a *raki*, can be distilled from grape skins and citron leaves and by the late-19th century the preserved fruit and a sweet version of *kitroraki*, known as *kitron*, were being exported in large amounts from Naxos. In the 1960s most citron trees were uprooted to make way for more useful, profitable crops.

Kitron production has enjoyed a happy renaissance in recent years and the **Vallindras Distillery** (☎ 22850 31220; Halki; ☺ 10am–11pm summer, 10am–6pm winter) in Halki's main square still distils *kitron* the old-fashioned way. There are free tours of the old distillery's atmospheric rooms that still contain ancient jars and copper stills. *Kitron* tastings round off the trip and a selection of the distillery's products are on sale. You can book a tour by phone or just turn up.

Halki is also home to the ceramics gallery-shop **L'Olivier** (☎ 22850 32829; www.fish-olive-creations.com; Halki), which is full of the enthralling work of Katharina Bolesch and Alex Reichardt. Katharina Bolesch's stoneware pottery, the designs of which are inspired by the ancient and sacred themes of the olive and the fish, has earned her an international reputation. Katharina's partner Alex Reichardt decorates many of her pieces. He also makes beautiful pendants and jewellery based on the fish motif, and fashions truly luminous lamps using Naxian marble. L'Olivier is opening another nearby gallery and workshop in 2006. (Poor quality imitations of Katharina Bolesch's work are sold elsewhere on Naxos, so be warned.) L'Olivier also sells fine artefacts in olive wood, and olive products such as oil and soap.

Halki adds to its reputation for originality with the fascinating shop **Era** (☎ 22859 31009; eraproducts@mail.gr), where delicious marmalade, jam and spoon sweets are made and sold. There are no *domatia* in Halki, but Filoti has serviceable rooms at much lower rates than you'll find anywhere else in the Cyclades. Ask at the tavernas by the main bus stop.

In a perfect location in the heart of Halki's central square, **Yianni's Taverna** (☎ 22850 31214; dishes €5.50-7.50) is well known for its good local meat dishes and delicious fresh salads with *myzithra*.

The **Citron Café** (☎ 22850 31602) is next to the Vallindras Distillery and is a charming place that has retained the traditional style of old Halki.

Panagia Drosiani

The **Panagia Drosiani** (☺ 10am–7pm May–mid-Oct) just below **Moni**, 2.5km north of Halki, is one of the oldest and most revered churches in Greece. It has a warren of cave-like chapels and several of the frescoes date back to the 7th century. Donations are appreciated.

Sangri Σαγκρί

The handsome tower-like building of **Bazeos Castle** (☎ 22850 31402; ☺ 10am–5pm & 6-9pm) stands prominently in the landscape about 2km east of the village of Sangri, and was built in its original form as the Monastery of Timios Stavros (True Cross) during the 17th century. The monks abandoned the site in the early 19th century and it was later bought by the Bazeos family, whose modern descendants have refurbished the building and its fascinating late-medieval rooms with great skill and imagination. The castle now functions as a cultural centre and stages art exhibitions and the annual **Naxos Festival** during July and August, when concerts, plays and literary readings are held. Price of admission to these varies.

About 1.5km south of Sangri is the impressive **Temple to Demeter** (Dimitra's Temple; ☎ 22850 22725; ☺ 8.30am-3pm Tue-Sun). The ruins and reconstructions are not large, but they are historically fascinating and the hilltop location is impressive. There is a site **museum** with some fine reconstructions of temple features. Signs point the way from Sangri.

Apiranthos Απείρανθος

Apiranthos is an atmospheric alpine village of unadorned stone houses, marble-paved streets and alleyways that scramble up the slopes of Fanari Mountain. There is an enduring sense of a much older Greece here that is not contrived, and all the more tangible because of it. This is the kind of place in which to read Kazantzakis novels.

Apiranthos was once an emery-mining centre. Its inhabitants are descendants of refugees who fled Crete to escape Turkish repression; they have retained a strong individuality and an impressive richness in their dialect. The village was always noted for its spirited politics and its populism. Its most famous son is Manolis Glezos, the resistance fighter who during WWII replaced the Nazi flag with the Greek one atop the Acropolis. He later became the parliamentary representative for the Cyclades. Apiranthos is also known for producing accomplished academics. The village has an impressive trio of museums.

On the main road, to the right of the start of the village's main street, is the **museum of natural history** (admission €3; ⊗ 8.30am-2pm Tue-Sun). The **geology museum** (admission €3; ⊗ 8.30am-2pm Tue-Sun) and the **archaeology museum** (admission free; ⊗ 8.30am-2pm Tue-Sun) are part way along the main street. The latter has a marvellous collection of small Cycladian artefacts. The museums are sometimes open from 7pm to 10pm in summer, but it should be noted that all the opening times stated here are 'flexible', in keeping with the admirable local spirit of independence.

Just before the main square, which is dominated by a huge plane tree, is **Stoy Lefteris** (☎ 22850 61333; dishes €8-15) where you can eat in a peaceful terrace garden overlooking the valley. There are good meat dishes, a selection of delicious home-made sweets and baklava, and a range of local products on sale in the streetfront shop.

There is parking at the entrance to Aparanthos, on the main Hora–Apollonas road.

Moutsouna Μουτσούνα

The road from Apiranthos to Moutsouna descends in an exhilarating series of S-bends through spectacular mountain scenery. Formerly a busy port, shipping out the emery mined in the region, Moutsouna is a quiet place now, although there is some development. Seven kilometres south of the village is the fine beach of **Psili Amas**.

There are a few pensions and tavernas, mainly at Moutsouna but some are scattered along the coast road. A good option is **Ostria Studios** (☎ 22850 68235; d €70-80) which is in a garden setting.

Apollonas Απόλλωνας

Apollonas, on the north coast, was once a tranquil fishing village, but is now a popular resort. It has a pleasant beach.

Coachloads of day-trippers come to see the gargantuan 7th-century BC **kouros**, which lies in an ancient quarry a short walk from the village. It is signposted to the left as you approach Apollonas on the main inland road from Hora. This 10.5m statue may have been abandoned unfinished because it cracked. Apollonas has several *domatia* and tavernas.

The inland route from Hora to Apollonas winds through spectacular mountains – a worthwhile trip. With your own transport you can return to Hora via the west-coast road, passing through wild and sparsely populated country with awe-inspiring sea views. Several tracks branch down to secluded beaches, such as **Abram**.

LITTLE CYCLADES
ΜΙΚΡΕΣ ΚΥΚΛΑΔΕΣ

For the dedicated island lover the chain of small islands between Naxos and Amorgos is paradise. Variously called the Little Cyclades, Minor Islands, Back Islands and Lesser Islands, only four – Donousa, Koufonisia (comprising Ano Koufonisia and Kato Koufonisia), Iraklia and Schinousa – have permanent populations. All were densely populated in antiquity, as shown by the large number of ancient graves found here. During the Middle Ages, the islands were inhabited by wild goats and by even wilder pirates. Post-independence, intrepid souls from Naxos and Amorgos re-colonised, but until the advent of modern tourism, the only visitors were Greeks rediscovering their roots. Now, the islands welcome growing numbers of independent-minded tourists. Most are looking for fine beaches and a relaxed lifestyle without overt commercialism, although Koufonisia especially is edging towards becoming a conventional, though still low-key, resort.

DON'T BE SHORT CHANGED

Only Koufonisia has an ATM and, although money can usually be changed at the general store or post agency on the other islands, rates are fierce – it's best to bring cash with you.

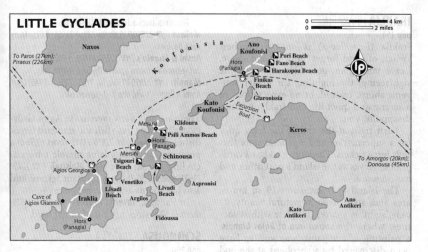

LITTLE CYCLADES

0 ——— 4 km
0 ——— 2 miles

Naxos

To Paros (27km);
Piraeus (226km)

Koufonisia

Ano
Koufonisi

Hora
(Panagia)

Pori Beach
Fano Beach
Harakopou Beach

Finikas
Beach

Glaronissia

Kato
Koufonisi

Excursion
Boat

Keros

Mesana
Klidoura

Hora
(Panagia)

Psili Ammos Beach

Mersini
Tsigouri
Beach

Schinousa

Agios Georgios

Aspronisi

To Amorgos (20km);
Donousa (45km)

Venetiko

Livadi
Beach
Argilos

Livadi
Beach

Cave of
Agios Giannis

Iraklia

Hora
(Panagia)

Fidoussa

Kato
Antikeri

Ano
Antikeri

Donousa is the northernmost of the group and farthest from Naxos. The others are clustered near the southeast coast of Naxos. Each has a public telephone and post agency.

Getting There & Away

Links with the Little Cyclades are regular but can be quite severely curtailed when sea conditions are poor, so make sure you have plenty of time before committing yourself – these islands are not meant for last-minute flying visits or even for overnight stops.

For anyone planning to explore the Little Cyclades, the sturdy little ferry **Express Skopelitis** (☎ 22850 71256/519; Katapola, Amorgos) provides a lifeline service (daily from mid-June to September, Monday to Saturday for the rest of the year) between Naxos and Amorgos via all of the islands. The *Sko-pelitis* is impressively punctual, but again, adverse weather conditions can affect its schedule. Sailings may be cancelled if wind speeds rise above Force 5 on the Beaufort scale. Most seating is second-deck and upper-deck level. When it's windy, work out which side is protected from the wind and sea and stay there, or you may get very wet. Regardless of sea conditions, locals head straight below for the comfy, air-conditioned cabin and coffee bar where they engulf themselves in cigarette smoke.

In high season the *Skopelitis* starts its weekly schedule from Katapola (Amorgos), at 6am on a Monday morning and calls at Aegiali (Amorgos; €4, 50 minutes), Donousa (€4.80, one hour 20 minutes), Koufonisia (€6, 3½ hours), Schinousa (€7, four hours), Iraklia (€7.40, 4½ hours) and Naxos (€9.50, six hours). It then leaves Naxos at 1pm and reverses the circuit, reaching Katapola at 4.45pm, from where it returns to Naxos direct. This is the schedule on Monday, Wednesday, Friday, Saturday and Sunday (excluding Donousa on Sunday, and Aegiali on Monday, Wednesday and Sunday evenings). On Tuesday and Thursday the *Skopelitis* does just one complete circuit, leaving Naxos at 3pm and docking overnight at Katapola.

There is also one weekly ferry from Donousa to Syros (€9.10, 3½ hours) and three weekly ferries to Paros (€12.80, two to four hours).

A useful weekly link from Donousa to Astypalea and the Dodecanese is the rather lumbering *MV Dimitroula* (you hear it before you see it). It calls at Donousa on its outward trip from Piraeus to Rhodes via Paros and Naxos on Tuesday, and calls in again on its return trip on Friday.

Three weekly ferries go from Schinousa to Paros (€7.50, four hours).

Three times a week the fast boat *Blue Star Naxos* travels from Piraeus to Koufonisia and twice a week to Iraklia and Schinousa via Naxos, continuing on to Amorgos. A few other large ferries stop at the islands during high season, often in the dead of night.

IRAKLIA HPAKΛEIA

pop 151

Iraklia (i-*ra*-klee-a) is one of the best switch-off-and-forget options anywhere. Leave your glam gear behind, forget the sightseeing, the nightlife, the dreary souvenir shops. Instead, bring expectations of a serene and quiet life and Iraklia will not disappoint you.

Turn right at the end of the ferry quay for a supermarket and a general store that sells ferry tickets. The store also has a cardphone, serves as the island's post office and has *domatia*.

The island only measures 19 sq km in area and, apart from its natural beauty, its only 'sight' is a cave, complete with stalactites, where the **sacred icon of Agios Giannis**, a painting of the saint, was said to have been discovered by a shepherd at the end of the 19th century. The icon is now in the church at the village of **Panagia**, where a **festival** is held each year on the last weekend in August.

The port and main village is **Agios Georgios**. It's very quiet and has an attractive cove-like harbour, complete with a pleasant little beach.

A surfaced road leads off to the left from the end of the ferry quay, going about 500m, to **Livadi** – the island's best beach. About 1km further on is the village of **Hora**, (also known as Panagia). The **Cave of Agios Gioannis** is situated 1.25km from Agios Georgios.

Sleeping & Eating

All *domatia* and tavernas are in Agios Georgios, although a few open on the beach at Livadi in high season. *Domatia* owners meet the boats, but the shortage of rooms makes it a sellers' market – take whatever you can get and don't bother looking for bargains. In high season it's definitely advisable to book.

Anna's Place (☎ 22850 71145; s/d €35/67) Anna's, near the road to Livadi, is the top place on the island. Rooms are very pleasant with kitchen and fridge, and most have good views.

Alexandra (☎ 22850 71482; fax 22850 71545; d €45) At the top of the hill above Agios Georgios, this is on the way to Livadi beach. It's a modern place and rooms have pleasant patios. The beach is about 500m away.

Rooms include the following:

Melissa (☎ 22850 71539; fax 22850 71561; d €25) Fairly basic doubles.

Anthi & Angelo's (☎ 22850 71486; d €40) Standard, but reasonable rooms open in the high season only.

Manolis (☎ 22850 71569; fax 22850 71561; d €45) Like Anthi & Angelo's and also high-season only.

There are only a few tavernas in Agios Georgios, all serving fresh fish and standard Greek dishes. **Perigiali** (☎ 22850 71118; dishes €3.50-6) a popular place, has a large marble table encircling an old pine tree. **Maistrali** (☎ 22850 71807; dishes €3.50-7) has a pleasant terrace and also has rooms and Internet access.

In Panagia, **Taverna to Steki** (☎ 22850 71579; dishes €3.50-6) does tasty traditional food.

SCHINOUSA ΣΧΙΝΟΥΣΑ

pop 206

Schinousa (skih-*noo*-sah) is a slow-paced, likeable island with a couple of fine beaches and a thoroughly lived-in **Hora (Panagia)** located on the breezy crest of the island with sweeping views of the sea. Hora's narrow main street visibly flinches as vehicles rumble through.

Ferries dock at the fishing harbour of **Mersini**. Hora is a hot 1km uphill, so try to get a lift with one of the locals. *Domatia* owners always meet ferries.

There's a public telephone in the main square and a couple of general stores sell stamps. Tickets are sold at the port a few minutes before boats arrive. There is a travel agency at Grispos Tsigouri Beach Villas in Tsigouri, which has ferry information and tickets.

On the way down to Tsigouri beach is a little **folk museum** that features a reconstructed bread oven. Opening hours go with the flow of island life.

Dirt tracks lead from Hora to several beaches around the coast. The nearest are **Tsigouri** and **Livadi**, both uncrowded outside August. Haul a little further to great beaches at **Almiros** and **Aligaria**. Take food and water, because, with the exception of Tsigouri, there are no shops or tavernas at the beaches.

Sleeping

There are a few rooms down at Mersini, but if you want to see the rest of the island you're much better off staying in Hora.

> **THERE BE PIRATES**
>
> Pirates push people about, and in the Cyclades of old, the story is that they pushed coastal communities to build new towns inland, out of sight of the sea and high up, if possible.
>
> The maze-like alleyways of Mykonos Town and of a score of other Cycladic villages are said to have evolved as a way of confusing raiders. There's probably some truth in all of this, although throughout history communities have often sought the high ground for one reason or another.
>
> The Greek islands have certainly had their fair share of villains afloat. In Greek hagiography it is usually Turkish or North African pirates who get the blame; yet even the Rhodes-based Knights of St John were lightly disguised freebooters as they sailed along the thin line between crime and enterprise.
>
> Records show that the Little Cyclades suffered from home-grown maritime gangsters too. In 1797 a boat carrying people from Naxos and Schinousa was boarded by men from the Mani in the Peloponnese (always a troublesome breed) who robbed the passengers and stripped them of their clothes. In 1822, local ruffians went on a rampage through the Little Cyclades. Armed ships from Amorgos eventually caught up with them near Thira (Santorini) and killed most of them.
>
> And those were the 'Good old Days'…

Iliovasilema (☎ 22850 71948; iliovasilema@schinousa.gr; Hora; s/d €35/50) Ideally located on the western outskirts of the village, looking south over the island, this bright, clean place has good-sized rooms and most of the balconies have fine views.

Anna Domatia (☎ 22850 71161; Hora; s/d €20/35) Just behind the main street on the westside of the village, these unfussy rooms are clean and comfortable and there's a friendly welcome.

Grispos Tsigouri Beach Villas (☎ 22850 71930; fax 22850 71176; www.grisposvillas.com; Hora; s/d/tr incl buffet breakfast €65/80/95; 🐾) Rooms are a good size at this complex on the edge of Tsigouri beach, and there's a spacious feel to the surroundings. It's about 250m down the dusty beach track from Hora.

Eating

There are a couple of very standard tavernas and one excellent restaurant.

Margarita (☎ 22850 74278; dishes €5-9) This would be a popular place anywhere in Greece. It's midway along the village street, down an alleyway, and is run by friendly young owners with a real interest in what they are doing. The terrace has dreamy views of the sea. The food is modern Greek and includes pricier seafood options, all creatively prepared and backed by a good wine list. A great choice is the mixed plate of delicious treats.

Loza (☎ 22850 71864; dishes €4.50-7) In Hora, this is the café on the main street with the very big umbrella shading its terrace. It does breakfasts for €7.50 as well as salads and pizzas, but it's also a bakery producing delicious pastries, including baklava and walnut pie.

Grispos (dishes €3-6) At Tsigouri beach, this has a restaurant attached to its villa complex and offers good island standards.

KOUFONISIA ΚΟΥΦΟΝΗΣΙΑ
pop 366

Koufonisia has more of a tourist gloss than its neighbours and is the most visited island in the Little Cyclades group; yet it retains its small-island charm, while its sizeable fishing fleet imparts a strong down-to-earth element to life. Koufonisia is really two islands, Ano Koufonisi and Kato Koufonisi, but it's Ano that's permanently inhabited.

The beaches are all golden sand, lapped by crystal-clear water. Like most low-lying islands, Kato seems to be lit more intensely by the sun and the reflecting sea. Locals are hospitable and friendly, and food and accommodation options are more plentiful and sophisticated than on any of the neighbouring islands.

A caïque ride away, **Kato Koufonisi**, has some beautiful beaches and a lovely church. Archaeological digs on **Keros**, the rocky mountain of an island that looms over Koufonisia to the south, have uncovered over 100 Early Cycladic figurines, including the famous harpist and flautist now on display in Athens' Archaeological Museum.

Orientation & Information

Koufonisia's only settlement spreads out behind the ferry quay and around an attractive harbour filled with moored fishing boats. The large town beach, which is flat and used by traffic, gives a great sense of space to the waterfront. The older part of town, the *hora* (main town), is on the low hill behind the quay.

From the quay head right and, where the sand begins, take the first road to the left. Continue to the junction, then turn left onto the village's pedestrianised main street.

There are supermarkets along the road leading in from the beach and there's an inconspicuous ticket agency (look for the dolphins painted right above the door) halfway along the main street. The post office is on the first road leading sharply off left as you come from the ferry quay.

Koufonisia Tours (☎ 22850 71671; www.koufonis siatours.gr) organises accommodation on the island.

The flat, hard sand of the town beach draws a few swimmers. Cars drive across it to reach the south-coast road and everyone uses it as a football pitch.

Sights

BEACHES

Koufonisia has a number of very good beaches amid its coastal landscape of low sand dunes punctuated by rocky coves and caves.

A walk along the south coast road is the best way to reach the island's beaches. The road runs for a couple of kilometres from the eastern end of the town beach to **Finikas**, **Harakopou** and **Fano** beaches. All these beaches tend to become swamped with grilling bodies in July and August and nudity increases as you go. A small bus runs to and from Finikas, mainly to coincide with ferry arrivals.

Beyond Fano the low-lying coast offers several potential swimming places and the path continues to the great bay at **Pori**, where there are acres of dunes, dappled with shrubs and maritime flora, and a long crescent of sand that slides effortlessly into the ultimate Greek-island dream sea. Pori can also be reached by an inland road that heads east from the junction with the pedestrianised main street of the *hora*.

Tours

Koufonisia Tours (☎ 22850 71671; www.koufonis siatours.gr), based at Villa Ostria, organises caïque trips to Keros, Kato Koufonisi and to other islands of the Little Cyclades. Bike hire is also available.

Sleeping

Wild camping is not permitted on Koufonisia. There is an excellent selection of *domatia* and hotels.

Koufonisia Camping (☎ 22850 71683; sites per person €6) This site is by the tree-lined beach at Harakopou. Facilities are fairly basic and not always salubrious, but closeness to the beach is a bonus.

Akrogiali (☎ 22850 71685, 69424 48263; s/d €45/60) Get ready for a good-natured welcome, mainly in Greek, at this cheerful family-run place right on the waterfront beyond the town beach. Rooms are bright and clean and they have tea- and coffee-making facilities. Adjacent houses also have rooms.

Lefteris Rooms (☎ 22850 71458; d/tr €40/45) Lefteris is behind the town beach, above the restaurant of the same name. The rooms are colourful and pleasant, with those at the back more peaceful.

Ermis (☎ 22850 71693; fax 22850 74214; s/d €50/60) Fine spacious rooms with stylish fittings and big generous balconies overlooking the sea make this quiet and attractive place a good choice. Not all rooms have sea views. It's on the road running parallel to the waterfront and adjoins the post office.

Villa Ostria (☎ 22850 71671; www.koufonissiatours .gr; s/d incl breakfast €60/70) This excellent hotel is up on the hill, above the beach, and manages to create a pleasant exclusive feel, not least because of its charming garden area. Rooms are smart and comfortable and have fridges. The hotel is reached by going up the road at the eastern end of the beach, then taking the first left.

Eating

Capetan Nikolas (☎ 22850 71690; dishes €4.50-7) A famous institution, this terrific place looks out over the little harbour on the west side of the village. It's family-run and bursting with life and good nature. The food is delicious, with lip-smacking grilled fish, such as sea-bream, a speciality. You browse for your selection in the kitchen and fish is by the kilogram.

Lefteris (☎ 2285071458; dishes €3.50-5.50) Down-to-earth and with a strong family team running things, Lefteris has one of the biggest outside terraces in the world, a great leafy space overlooking the town beach. It's below the rooms of the same name and does reasonably priced Greek standards. It's open for breakfast and lunch as well.

Out of town, there are seasonal tavernas at some of the beaches, but they are often subject to the vagaries of the season.

Drinking

Koufonisia caters for a fairly sophisticated music bar set and has a number of venues.

Scholeio (☎ 22850 71837; ⏱ 6pm-3am) At the west-end of the village's main street, this is an intimate little bar and creperie which does great cocktails and plays jazz, blues and rock among other choice sounds.

Sorokos (☎ 2285071704; ⏱ 4pm-3am) Down at the end of the eastern waterfront, beyond the town beach and in a terrific location overlooking the water. It has a nice Bohemian style, great drinks and snacks and good sounds, ranging from early-hours lounge music to hotter notes in the night.

DONOUSA ΔΟΝΟΥΣΑ
pop 110

Forget tomorrow's schedule; stop the world and get off at Donousa, the least accessible of the Little Cyclades. It's not on the route of many ferries to more popular islands so you'll have some castaway time on your hands.

Agios Stavros is Donousa's main settlement and the island's port. It has a pleasant little **beach**, which also serves as a drive-through for infrequent vehicles and foot traffic. Behind the beach there are lush vegetable gardens and vineyards. **Kendros**, situated 1.25km to the east of Agios Stavros, along a rather ugly bulldozed track, is a sandy and secluded beach with a seasonal taverna. **Livadi**, a dusty 1km trek further east, sees even fewer visitors. Both Kendros and Livadi are popular with nudists. Bulldozed tracks have marred Donousa in places, but there are still delightful paths and tracks that lead into the hills to utterly timeless little hamlets such as **Mersini**. At a number of points across the island there are taps supplying drinkable water.

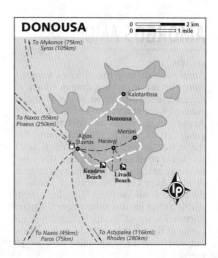

There is one public telephone, up a steep hill above the waterfront; look for the skeletal satellite dish. You can get telecards at the souvenir shop just up from the quay-end of the beach.

There is no cash withdrawl facility here, but there is a ticket agency, **Roussos Travel** (☎ 22850 51648) on the waterfront.

Sleeping & Eating

Although Donousa is out of the way for most travellers it's wise to think ahead and book rooms in advance during the high season. Most rooms on the island are fairly basic but are well kept, clean and in good locations.

Spiros Skopelitis Rooms (☎ 22850 51586; s/d €35/40) Just behind the town beach, these pleasant little bungalows have kitchens and are in a garden setting that has a nice desert-island feel.

Prasino Studios (☎ 22850 51579; d €35-41, apt €65) Overlooking the beach is this pleasant complex with a mix of rooms.

To Iliovasilema (☎ 22850 51570; d/studios €35/45) Overlooking the beach, this place has reasonable rooms, some with kitchens. It also has a popular restaurant with a fine terrace and a good selection of food (dishes €5.50 to €18).

Aposperitis (dishes €3.50-6) Next to Spiros Skopelitis, this serves standard dishes.

The hub of village life is Kafeneio To Kyma by the quay, where things liven up late into the night.

AMORGOS ΑΜΟΡΓΟΣ

pop 1869

Amorgos (ah-mor-*ghoss*) rises savagely from the sea in a long dragon's back of rugged mountains whose summits always seem to wear tiny scarves of violet cloud. Approaching ferries are dwarfed by the great curtain wall of the mountains, but the effect is exhilarating. The island's southeast coast is unrelentingly steep and boasts an extraordinary monastery embedded in a huge cliff. The northwest coast of the island is no less forbidding, but relents a little at the narrow inlet where the main port and town of Katapola lies. Amorgos is one of the most beautiful Greek islands, but you need to work quite hard to get there.

Amorgos's other port town, Aegiali, lies at the island's northern end and is more of a resort, with a fine beach. The enchanting Hora (also known as Amorgos), nestles high up in the mountains above Katapola.

Getting There & Away

The ferry *Express Skopelitis* has services to Naxos and other islands in the Little Cyclades (see p179).

Most ferries stop at both Katapola and Aegiali, but be sure to check if this is the case with your ferry. There are several boats weekly to Paros (€11, three hours) and Piraeus (€25, 10 hours). There are also services from Katapola to Astypalea (€11, 2½ hours, three weekly) and Syros (€14, 4½ to 9½ hours, three weekly).

FAST BOAT & CATAMARAN

Three boats a day run from Katapola to Ios (€18, 2¾ hours), Tinos (€26, 2¾ hours) and Andros (€27.50, 3½ to 6¼ hours). Several services will also stop at Aegiali.

Getting Around

Regular buses go from Katapola to Hora (€1, 15 minutes), Moni Hozoviotissis (€1, 15 minutes), Agia Anna Beach (€1.20, 20 minutes) and less frequent services go to Aegiali (€1.80, 30 minutes); however there are fewer services on weekends. There are

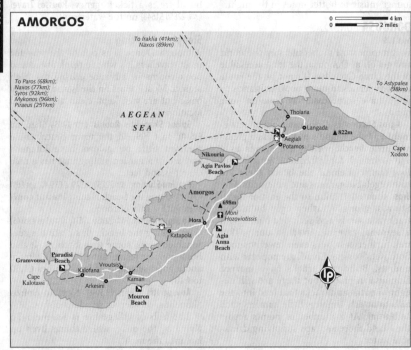

AMORGOS

0 — 4 km
0 — 2 miles

To Iraklia (41km);
Naxos (89km)

To Paros (68km);
Naxos (77km);
Syros (92km);
Mykonos (96km);
Piraeus (251km)

**AEGEAN
SEA**

To Astypalea
(98km)

Tholaria

Langada ▲822m

Aegiali
Potamos

Cape
Xodoto

Nikouria

Agia Pavlos
Beach

Amorgos

▲698m

Moni
Hozoviotissis

Hora

Katapola

Agia
Anna
Beach

Gramvousa

Paradisi
Beach

Vroutsis

Kalofana

Kamari

Cape
Kalotassi

Arkesini

Mouron
Beach

CYCLADES

also buses from Aegiali to the picturesque village of Langada. Schedules are posted on bus windscreens.

Cars and motorcycles are available for rent from the travel agencies **N Synodinos** (☎ 22850 71201; synodinos@nax.forthnet.gr; Katapola; ◷ year-round) and **Aegialis Tours** (☎ 22850 73107; fax 22850 73394; www.amorgos-aegialis.com; Aegialis).

KATAPOLA ΚΑΤΑΠΟΛΑ

Katapola, the principal port, is a pleasant place that straggles along the curving shore-line of a dramatic bay in the most verdant part of the island. Remains from the ancient Cretan city of **Minoa**, as well as a **Mycenaean cemetery**, lie above the port and can be reached by a steep uphill walk. Amorgos has also yielded many Cycladic finds; the largest figurine in the National Archaeo-logical Museum in Athens was found in the vicinity of Katapola.

Orientation & Information

Boats dock either in front of Katapola's central square or to the right (facing in-land). The bus station is to the left along the main waterfront, on the western shore of the bay.

A bank (with ATM) is midwaterfront and there's an ATM next to N Synodinos. There is a post office on the square.

Hotel Minoa (☎ 22850 71480; per hr €2.50) Internet access is available.

N Synodinos (☎ 22850 71201; synodinos@nax.forthnet .gr) This very helpful travel agency offers ferry tickets, money exchange and car rental (per day in high season €50). It is open year-round.

Police (☎ 22850 71210) In Hora.

Port police (☎ 22850 71259) On the central square.

Sleeping & Eating

Domatia owners usually meet ferries and are among the most restrained and polite in the Cyclades.

Eleni's Rooms (☎ 22850 71628; roomseleni@hack -box.net; s/d/apt €45/53/95) Located in a great position at the far end of the village, to the right from the ferry quay arrival point, these bright and airy rooms rise through several levels. You can even hop down in seconds for a morning swim.

Pension Sofia (☎ 22850 71494; s/d/apt €35/48/65) Tucked away behind the waterfront amid gardens and little meadows, Sofia's is reached by heading inland from the main

square, past a butcher's shop, then turning left beneath an archway and continuing for about 200m. Rooms are fresh and colourful and the welcome is charming.

Pension Galini (☎ 22850 71711; s/d/apt €35/48/90) Right next door to Sofia's, and has similar rooms.

Diosmarini (☎ 22850 71636; diosmarini@yahoo .com; d/tr/apt €48/60/95) On the northern shores of the bay and about 1km from the ferry quay, Disomarini is a delightful option with lovely big rooms in a handsome and mod-ern Cycladic-style building. There are airy views from most balconies.

Katapola Community Camping (☎ 22850 71802; sites per adult/tent €5/5) This shady site is set back from the northern end of the bay. Turn left from the quay (as you face inland) and continue past the turn-off for Hora. Turn right at the next paved road and walk about 100m.

Vitsentzos (☎ 22850 71518; dishes €4.50-6) On the northern side of the bay, Vitsentzos is a deservedly popular taverna with a terrace on the waterfront and a spotless interior of exposed stonework and varnished wooden floor. Food is traditional with modern touches. Seafood is by the kilogram.

Mouragio (☎ 22850 71011; dishes €3.80-7) You cannot miss Mouragio, if only because it always seems so busy. It's on the main water-front near the ferry quay, and really is hugely popular. The entire family turns out terrific fish and shellfish dishes without fuss and with good humour. Try the fish soup (€7) for a start.

Drinking

Moon Bar (☎ 22850 71598) You get a world out-look and a view of the bay at this relaxing place on the northern waterfront.

Le Grand Bleu (☎ 22850 71633) Just along from Psaropoula is this popular bar named after the film *The Big Blue*, which was partly filmed in Amorgos. It plays rock, reggae and modern Greek music.

HORA ΧΩΡΑ

The enchanting Hora spreads like a drift of snow across its rocky ridge. It stands 400m above sea level and is capped by a 13th-century *kastro* atop a prominent rock pinnacle. Old windmills stand like sentinels on surrounding cliffs. Yet in spite of its traditional style, the village has several sophisticated shops, bars

CYCLADES

and cafés that enhance its appeal without eroding its timelessness.

The bus stop is on a small square at the edge of town. The post office is on the main square, reached by a pedestrian laneway from the bus stop.

Hora's **Archaeology Museum** (☀9am-1pm & 6-8.30pm Tue-Sun) is on the main pedestrian thoroughfare, near Café Bar Zygos.

Sleeping & Eating

Hora has a handful of pleasant pensions.

Pension Ilias (☎ 22850 71277; s/d/tr €40/50/75) Just down from the bus stop is this unpretentious place with decent rooms.

View To Big Blue (☎ 22850 71814/69322 48867; s/d €40/50) At the top end of the village, just before the upper car park and radio tower, is this brand new establishment, opened in 2005. Rooms are very bright and comfy and the views from the front balconies are superb.

Café Bar Zygós (☎ 22850 71350; ☀8am-3am; snacks €2.50-10) This café lies at the heart of Hora's main street and is framed by vivid flowers. It's a charming place inside and out, and has a rooftop terrace. They offer breakfast, sandwiches and baguettes, salads and cold plates as well as coffee, delicious cakes, candied fruit and ice cream, all to accompanying Greek music by day, and '80s and '90s rock at night.

Keep heading up the winding main street to reach **Tsagaradiko** (☎ 69448 72275; dishes €3-7) a great little *mezedes* place with tables on a lovely little square.

MONI HOZOVIOTISSIS
ΜΟΝΗ ΧΟΖΟΒΙΩΤΙΣΣΗΣ

A visit to the 11th-century **Moni Hozoviotissis** (☀8am-1pm & 5-7pm) is unforgettable, as much for the spectacular scenery as for the monastery itself. The dazzling white building clings precariously to a cliff-face above the east coast. A few monks still live there and tours are sporadic, but worthwhile (and free).

The monastery contains a miraculous icon found in the sea below the cliff, which arrived (allegedly unaided) from Asia Minor, Cyprus or Jerusalem – depending on which legend you're told. Modest dress is absolutely required (long trousers for men, a long skirt or dress and covered shoulders for women).

A great round-trip is to catch the bus from Katapola to Hora, stroll the length of Hora's main street and on to an upper car park below a radio tower. Go down to the right of the car park viewpoint, through a gate and then follow a zigzag track with exhilarating views to reach the road. Turn left here to reach a junction, the left branch of which leads in 500m to the monastery. You can then catch the bus back to Katopola from the junction, or walk down to Agia Anna beach, which is 1.5km downhill, and catch the bus from the car park there, after a dip.

AEGIALI ΑΙΓΙΑΛΗ

Aegiali is Amorgos' other port and has more of a resort style, not least because of the fine sweep of sand that lines the inner edge of the bay on which it stands. Above the main village lie steep slopes and impressive crags.

Nautilus Travel Agent (☎ 22850 73032), which is a few metres up to the right of the bus stop and opposite Aegiali's Tours, sells ferry tickets and provides general tourist information.

Tours

Aegiali's Tours (☎ 22850 73107; fax 22850 73394; www.amorgos-aegialis.com), opposite the Nautilus Travel Agency, organises a daily bus outing (€20) around the island that departs at 9.30am and returns at 4.30pm, with stops at Agia Pavlos, Moni Hozoviotissis, Hora and Mouron.

Sleeping

As in Katapola, *domatia* owners meet the ferries.

Aegiali Camping (☎ 22850 73333; sites per adult/tent €6/4) This is a pleasant and shaded site on the road behind Lakki Village; go left from the port and follow the signs.

Lakki Village (☎ 22850 73253; info@lakkivillage.gr; s/d/tr incl breakfast €55/65/75, 2-/3-/4-person apt incl breakfast €82/92/109; ✱) Right behind the middle of the beach, Lakki has good rooms and apartments within a fairly extensive complex. There's a pleasant garden area between the beach and the buildings, which serves as the terrace of the attached taverna.

Grispos Hotel (☎ 22850 73412; fax 22850 73557; 2-/4-person studios €70/94; ℗ ✱) Reached by an uphill climb, from near the end of the harbour waterfront, these rooms are well worth the effort. Located in a well maintained, modern building with very friendly owners, they are big, bright and well equipped.

Eating

To Limani (☎ 22850 73269; dishes €3-7) Excellent traditional fare is prepared with home-grown produce at Limani. It's behind the church and just up from the waterfront. There's a lovely roof garden, to which food is whisked up in a little lift. The downstairs walls exhibit works by local artists. Seafood is by the kilogram.

To Koralli (☎ 22850 73217; dishes €3-6.50) A great location with extensive views enhances the excellent food at this cheerful restaurant, which offers delicious fish and *mezedes* platters. It's reached by a flight of steps at the eastern end of the waterfront.

Restaurant Lakki (☎ 22850 73253; dishes €3.50-8) The popular beachside restaurant of Lakki Village uses home-grown ingredients in its traditional dishes. The big shaded garden is relaxing.

AROUND AMORGOS

On the east coast, south of Moni Hozoviotissis, is **Agia Anna Beach**, the nearest beach to both Katapola and Hora. Don't get excited; the car park is bigger than any of the little pebbly beaches strung out along the rocky shoreline, and all the beaches fill up quickly. There's a small *cantina* next to the car park on the cliff-top, selling food and drinks.

Langada and **Tholaria** are the most picturesque of the villages inland from Aegiali.

IOS ΙΟΣ

pop 1838
Branded – unfairly at times – as the party capital of the Cyclades, Ios offers much more than hedonism and hangovers. It has a couple of the best beaches in the islands and traditional Greek life goes on sturdily beyond the wall-to-wall bars and nightclubs, and despite the often relentless routine of heavy drinking. Commercial interests play up the party image and it's all fuelled by a sometimes shrill insistence that everyone is having a fantastic time, whether

they like it or not. But all of this packaged fun is concentrated in corners and Ios rises above the image. All the same, you do need to have staying power for the action in the centre of Hora.

Getting There & Away

FAST BOAT & CATAMARAN

There are daily catamarans to Santorini (€12.50, 40 minutes), Naxos (€16.60, one hour), Paros (€17.70, 1½ hours) and Iraklio and Rethymno on Crete (€34.40, 2½ hours). Services travel once a week to Amorgos (€18, two hours) and Mykonos (€28, 2¾ hours).

FERRY

There are at least four daily connections with Piraeus (€21, seven hours), Paros (€9.60, 2½ hours) and Naxos (€8.60, 1¼ hours). There are daily boats to Santorini (€6.50, 1¼ hours), five weekly to Sikinos (€4.10, 30 minutes), Folegandros (€5.60, 1½ hours) and Anafi (€7.90, three hours) and four weekly to Syros (€14, 2¾ hours).

There are two boats weekly to Kimolos (€14, 2½ hours), Sifnos (€11.20, five hours), Serifos (€11.40, six hours) Kythnos (€15.50, 8½ hours), and three weekly to Milos (€14, 3½ hours).

Getting Around

In summer, crowded buses run between Ormos, Hora (€1) and Milopotas Beach (€1) about every 15 minutes. Private excursion buses go to Manganari Beach (€6, 10.30am and 12.30am) and Agia Theodoti Beach (€1, in July and August).

Caïques travelling from Ormos to Manganari per person cost €9 for a return trip (departing 11am daily). Ormos and Hora both have car and motorcycle rental that can be booked through the Plakiotis Travel Agency (p188) and Acteon Travel (p188).

HORA, ORMOS & MILOPOTAS
ΧΩΡΑ, ΟΡΜΟΣ & ΜΥΛΟΠΟΤΑΣ

Ios has three population centres, all very close together on the west coast: the port, Ormos, the capital, Hora (also known as the 'village'), 2km inland, by road, from the port, and Milopotas, the beach 1km downhill from Hora. Gialos Beach stretches west of the port.

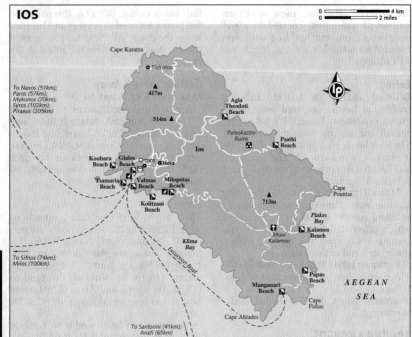

Orientation

The bus terminal in Ormos is straight ahead from the ferry quay on Plateia Emirou. If you don't mind the heat it's possible to walk from the port to Hora by turning left from Plateia Emirou, then right up a stepped path after about 100m. It's about 1.2km.

In Hora, the big cathedral opposite the bus stop, on the other side of the dusty car park and play area, is the main landmark. Plateia Valeta is the central square. There are public toilets up the hill behind the main square.

The road straight ahead from the bus stop leads to Milopotas Beach.

Information

There's an ATM right by the information kiosks at the ferry quay. In Hora, the National Bank of Greece, behind the church, and the Commercial Bank, nearby, both have ATMs.

The post office in Hora is a block behind the Town Hall side of the main road.

Acteon Travel (☎ 22860 91343; acteon@otenet.gr)

On the square near the quay, and in Hora and Milopotas. This also has Internet access (per hour €5).

Ali Baba's (☎ 22860 91558; Hora; per hr €5) Has Internet access.

Hospital (☎ 22860 91227) On the way to Gialos, 250m northwest of the quay; there are several doctors in Hora.

Plakiotis Travel Agency (☎ 22860 91221; plaktr2@otenet.gr) On the Ormos waterfront and with an office in Hora, opposite the bus stop, this is very helpful.

Port police (☎ 22860 91264) At the southern end of the waterfront, just before Ios Camping.

Sights

Hora (population 1632) is a lovely Cycladic village with a myriad of laneways and simple houses. It's most charming during daylight hours when the bars are shut and it recaptures the atmosphere of other island towns.

The **archaeological museum** (admission free; ☽ 8.30am-3pm Tue-Sun) is in the town hall by the bus stop.

Activities

Banana rides (€10), canoe rental (per hour €8) and mountain-bike rental (per day €10) all available at **Yialos Watersports** (☎ 22860 92463,

69449 26625; ralfburgstahler@hotmail.com; Gialos Beach).
Hire windsurfing equipment (per hour €15,
per half-day €30, lessons free), or take a
tube ride (€12 to €15).

Mylopotas Water Sports Center (☎ 22860
91622; www.ios-sports.gr; Milopotas Beach) has snorkelling and windsurfing gear, pedal boats
and canoes for hire. Windsurfing rental
(per hour/day €18/50), waterskiing (per
10/15 minutes €20/30) and tube rides (€15
to €20) are available. There's also a speed
boat taxi.

Windsurfing (per hour €15, per day €35,
two-hour beginners' course €30) is on offer
at **Meltemi Water Sports** (☎ 22860 91680, 69321
153912; www.meltemiwatersports.com; Milopotas) at the
beach opposite the Far Out Camping. There
is also self-drive motor boats (per day €80)
and laser sailboats (per hour €25), plus
canoes and pedalos for hire. Tube rides cost
from €15 to €25. Meltemi runs a similar
scene at Manganari Beach and has a water
taxi from Milopotas to other beaches.

Sleeping
ORMOS
There are many advantages to staying in
Ormos. The port has several good sleeping
options, plenty of reasonable eating places,
a couple of handy beaches and regular bus
connections to Hora.

Ios Camping (☎ 22860 92035; fax 22860 92101; sites
per person €7; ☒) Tucked away on the westside of Ormos, this site has good facilities
including a restaurant in high season. Head
right all the way round the waterfront.

Hotel Poseidon (☎ 22860 91091; www.poseidon
hotelios.gr; s/d/tr €63/75/95; ☒ ☒) One of the
best options on Ios, the Poseidon has terrific views over Ormos from its front balconies and there's a lovely swimming pool.
Rooms are spacious and well equipped.
Head along the waterfront from the ferry
quay and you'll find a flight of steps leading
up to the hotel.

GIALOS BEACH
I Corali (☎ 22860 91272; www.iosgreece/corali.htm; s/d incl
breakfast €50/60; ℗ ☒) These sparkling rooms
are attached to the restaurant of the same
name and are right on Gialos Beach. There's
a colourful garden at the rear and the delightful owners create a happy atmosphere.

Hotel Helena (☎ 22860 91276; www.hotelhelena
.gr; s/d €48/60) Set a short way back from the

midpoint of the beach is this friendly, well-
run place. It has a cool patio and bright,
clean rooms.

HORA
Francesco's (☎ 22860 91223; www.francescos.net; dm
€11, s €30-35, d €40-45) The famous and well-
run Francesco's, with good clean dormito-
ries and rooms, is near the centre of things
and is a lively meeting place for the international younger set. The party spirit rules
supreme. It has a busy bar and terrace with
great views of the bay. To get there head
up the main street from the cathedral and
follow signs to the left.

Markos Village (☎ 22860 91059; www.markovlg
.otenet; dm/s/d €19/35/45; ☒ ☐ ☒) Friendly
Markos is another popular backpacking
place and has pleasant rooms. There's an
upbeat yet easygoing ambience round the
pool and bar. There's free Internet use. To
get there, head uphill from the bus stop,
turn up right and then left.

MILOPOTAS
Milopotas has some very good small hotels.

Hotel Nissos Ios (☎ 22860 91610; www.nissosios
hotel.gr; Milopotas Beach; s/d/tr €45/65/78; ☒) The
best hotels keep up to date and the Nisos
Ios does so with enthusiasm. All rooms
are bright and fresh, colourful wall murals
add a cheerful touch, the atmosphere is
good-natured, and the beach is just across
the road. A recent addition is an outdoor
Jacuzzi.

Paradise Rooms (☎ 22860 91621; parios11@otenet
.gr; Milopotas Beach; s/d €50/60; ☒) These sparkling
rooms, about halfway along the beachfront,
are family run, and the beautiful garden is
looked after with love and skill. Breakfast
costs from €3 to €4.

Paradise Apartments (☎ 22860 91621; Milopotas
Beach; apt €90-135; ☒ ☒) Run by a member
of the same family, these apartments are
located a short distance away from Paradise
Rooms, in a secluded setting and with a
lovely pool and big patio. At both places
guests can get a 50% reduction at Mylopotas Water Sports Center.

Far Out Camping (☎ 22860 91468; www.farout
club.com; Milopotas Beach; sites per adult/tent €7/1.50,
small/large bungalows €9/15, std €75; ☐ ☒) If you
want plenty of action, backed by wall-to-
wall facilities, this is the place. There's everything from bungy jumping to five-a-side

football, and Meltemi Water Sports is just across the road. There's a bar, restaurant and four swimming pools. The 'bungalows' range from small tent-sized affairs to neat little 'roundhouses' with double and single beds.

Purple Pig Stars Camping & Bungalows (☎ 22860 91302; www.purplepigstars.com; Milopotas Beach; sites per person €8, dm €20, d €40; 🔊) This smaller site at the start of the beach has a more detached atmosphere and a more relaxing pace. It's shaded pleasantly by trees.

Eating
ORMOS

Susana (☎ 22860 51108; dishes €2.50-7) Popular with locals, this standard taverna offers efficient service and straightforward food. It's set back from the street in a wide square, by Acteon Travel, and does pastas and pizzas for €4 to €7.

GIALOS BEACH

To Corali (☎ 22860 91272; dishes €5-9) You won't find tastier wood-fired pizzas than at this popular place, right by the beach and in front of the hotel of the same name. There are even tables on the beach. They do pastas and salads as well and it's a great spot for coffee, drinks and ice cream.

HORA

Pithari Taverna (☎ 22860 91379; dishes €3.50-8) A friendly, unfussy taverna in the pleasant little square beside the cathedral, above the car park and play area, Pithari is an excellent option for good Greek food. Its tables, set out in front of the church, make you think that Hora really is a traditional Greek village after all.

Lord Byron (☎ 22860 92125; dishes €7-14) A long-established Ios favourite, the Lord Byron has moved to new premises near the main square. The ambience is relaxing and intimate and the food is still a great fusion of Greek and Italian. Dishes range from shrimp cooked in savoury tomato sauce with feta cheese and ouzo, to penne with wild mushroom and cream sauce; and it all comes in generous helpings.

Ali Baba's (☎ 22860 91558; dishes €6-10) Another great Ios favourite, this is the place for tasty Asian and international dishes, including *pad thai* and Dinosaur Ribs of awesome proportions. The service is very upbeat and

there's entertainment. To get there from the main square, go past Porky's, take the first right, then at a junction, keep straight ahead for a few metres, and then turn left.

Old Byron (☎ 22860 92125; dishes €3-15; 🕖 7pm-late) The Lord Byron's previous location lives on as a wine bar and eatery offering cold plates, with Greek and contemporary music for background. It is reached by taking the right fork just up the main street from the cathedral.

Porky's (☎ 22860 91143) Just off the main square, this is a long-time favourite that does toasties, salads, crepes and hamburgers.

There are also numerous *gyros* stands where you can get a cheap bite.

MILOPOTAS

Drakos Taverna (☎ 22860 91281; dishes €2.20-9) Seafood is by the kilogram at this popular taverna that overlooks the sea at the southern end of the beach. You get the feeling that the fish may well hop straight from the water into the kitchen, and then onto your plate.

Harmony (☎ 22860 91613; dishes €3-12) Just along the northern arm of Milopotas beach, this place really has got the franchise on relaxation, with its hammocks, deckchairs and great music. Children are well looked after here. There's live music too and the full-moon parties should not be missed. Tex-Mex food is the main attraction. Ask about professional massages.

Entertainment

Ios' nightlife is relentless in its promise of full-on fun, even for those being sick down the front of the free T-shirts handed out to anyone who sinks seven shots in a row. At night Hora's tiny central square is transformed into a noisy, open-air party and by midnight it's so crowded you won't be able to fall down, even if you need to. Be young and carefree – but, women especially, should also be careful.

Sweet Irish Dream (☎ 22860 91141) For a taste of mainstream and table-top dancing, visit this place, where the Guinness on-tap has probably travelled further than you have. It's on the right-hand side of the road as you enter Hora.

Ios Club (☎ 22860 91410) High above the rest with a terrific terrace and sweeping views. Head here for a cocktail and watch the sun set to classical, Latin and jazz music. It also does Greek food with international influences (dishes €3.50 to €9). To find it, walk right along the pathway by Sweet Irish Dream.

Ali Baba's (☎ 22860 91558) Adds to its many attractions with a good mix of entertainment that includes the latest Hollywood films most nights at 7pm, mainstream music, bands playing cover versions and live gigs.

Orange Bar (☎ 22860 91814) About 150m beyond the main square, this is an easy-paced music bar playing rock, reggae and pop.

Di Porto (☎ 22860 91685; Gialos Beach) Near To Corali, at sea level, this place is good for Greek music.

NIGHTCLUBS

Superfly (☎ 22860 92259; Hora Central Sq) Playing funky house tunes.

Disco 69 (☎ 22860 91064; Hora Central Sq) Has hardcore drinking to a background of disco and current hits.

Slammer Bar (☎ 22860 92119; Hora Central Sq) Hammers out house, rock and Latin.

Other popular late night bars and clubs on the square:

Red Bull (☎ 22860 91019)
Flames Bar (☎ 22860 92448)
Blue Note (☎ 22860 92271)

There are a couple of big dance clubs on the Milopotas road, but they don't open until July. **Mojo Club** (☎ 69727 59318; admission €15) does floor-burning progressive, drum 'n' bass and trance.

Scorpion's is another late-night dance-to-trance and hip-hop venue with laser shows.

AROUND IOS

Apart from the nightlife, the beaches are what lure travellers to Ios. Vying with Milopotas as one of the best is **Manganari**, a long swathe of fine white sand on the south coast, reached by bus or by excursion boat in summer (see p187).

From Ormos, it's a 10-minute walk past the little church of Agia Irini for **Valmas Beach**. **Kolitzani Beach**, south of Hora, down the steps by Scorpion's, is also nice. **Koubara**, a 1.3km walk northwest of Ormos, is the official clothes-optional beach. **Tsamaria**, nearby, is nice and sheltered when it's windy elsewhere.

Agia Theodoti, **Psathi** and **Kalamos Beaches**, all on the northeast coast, are more remote.

Moni Kalamou, on the way to Manganari and Kalamos, stages a huge **religious festival** in late August and a **festival of music and dance** on 7 September.

SANTORINI (THIRA)
ΣΑΝΤΟΡΙΝΗ (ΘΗΡΑ)

pop 13,402

Brace yourself for fabulous Santorini, regarded by many as the most spectacular of all the Greek islands. Known officially as Thira, the island is visited annually by vast numbers of holidaymakers who gaze in wonder at the submerged caldera, epicentre of what was probably the biggest volcanic eruption in recorded history. Santorini is unique and should not be missed, but you need to be ready for relentless crowds and commercialism. The caldera is truly awesome and, if you want to experience the full dramatic impact, it's worth arriving by a slower ferry with open decks, rather than by catamaran or hydrofoil. The main port is Athinios. Buses (and taxis) meet all ferries and then cart passengers to Fira, the capital, which fringes the edge of towering cliffs like a snowy cornice.

History

Minor eruptions have been the norm in Greece's earthquake record; but Santorini has bucked the trend with attitude throughout history. Eruptions here were genuinely earth shattering, and so wrenching that they changed the shape of the island several times.

Dorians, Venetians and Turks occupied Santorini, as they did all other Cycladic islands, but its most influential early inhabitants were the Minoans. They came from Crete some time between 2000 and 1600 BC, and the settlement at Akrotiri dates from the apogee of their great civilisation.

The island was circular then and was called Strongili (Round One). About 1650 BC, a colossal volcanic eruption caused the centre of Strongili to sink, leaving a caldera with high cliffs – now one of the world's most dramatic sights. Some archaeologists have speculated that this catastrophe destroyed not only Akrotiri but the structure, and eventually the essence, of the Minoan civilisation. Another theory that has fired the already overheated imaginations of some writers, artists and mystics since ancient times, claims that the island was part of the mythical lost continent of Atlantis.

Getting There & Away

AIR

Olympic Airlines (☎ 22860 22493; www.olympicairlines .com; Fira; ⏰ 8.30am-3.30pm Mon-Sat), on the road to Kamari, operates five flights daily to Athens (€94, 45 minutes). At the time of writing flights to other islands were not confirmed.

Aegean Airlines (Airport ☎ 22860 28500; www .aegeanair.com) has three flights daily to Athens (€88, 45 minutes) and daily flights to Thessaloniki (€110, 45 minutes).

From Easter to September, **Sky express** (☎ 28102 235000; www.skyexpress.gr) has at least four flights a week to Iraklio, Crete (€65, 30 minutes), four flights a week to Mykonos (€70, 35 minutes) and daily flights to Rhodes (€90, one hour). Book online or enquire at travel agents.

FAST BOAT & CATAMARAN

Daily services go to Ios (€12.80, 30 minutes), Naxos (€23.60, 1½ hours), Paros (€25.30, 2¼ hours), Mykonos (€28, three to four hours), Iraklio on Crete (€30.20 1¾ hours) and Piraeus (€45, 5¼ hours).

FERRY

Santorini is the southernmost island of the Cyclades, and as a major tourist destination it has good connections with Piraeus and Thessaloniki on the mainland, as well as with Crete. Santorini also has useful services to Anafi, Folegandros and Sikinos.

There are at least four boats daily to Naxos (€13.70, three hours), Paros (€14.90, three to four hours), Ios (€6.50, 1¼ hours), Piraeus (€27.80, nine hours) and two boats a week to Tinos (€14, five hours), Kythnos (€19.50, eight hours) and Folegandros (€8.10, 1½ to 2½ hours). Change at Naxos for Amorgos.

Seven boats weekly go to Anafi (€6.50, one hour), Sifnos, (€13.10, six hours), Thessaloniki (€38.90, 18 to 19½ hours), Sikinos (€7.50, 2½ hours), Iraklio on Crete (€14.70, 3¾ hours) and Skiathos (€32.90, 13½ hours).

SANTORINI (THIRA)

0 — 4 km
0 — 2 miles

To Sifnos (105km); Serifos (120km); Milos (131km)

To Ios (41km); Naxos (87km); Paros (105km); Mykonos (128km); Syros (135km); Piraeus (240km); Thessaloniki (627km)

Paradise Beach
Baxedes
Sigalas Winery
Pori Beach
Oia
Cape Riva
Ammoudi
Finikia
Armeni Beach
Potamos Beach
Potamos
Santorini (Thira)
Agrilla
Manolas
Imerovigli
Vourvoulos
Gialos Beach
Thirasia
Firostefani
Fira
Karterados Beach
Cape Trypiti
Fira Skala
Monolithos
Monolithos Beach
Nea Kameni
Karterados
Hot Springs
Palia Kameni
Messaria
Aspronisi
Vothonas
Athinios
Exo Gonia
Mesa Gonia
Pyrgos
Megalohori
Mt Profitis Ilias (567m)
Kamari
Moni Profiti Ilia
Kamari Beach
Ancient Thira
Cape Mesa Vouno
Cape Akrotiri
Akrotiri
Ancient Akrotiri
Emporio
Perissa
567m
Black Beach
White Beach
Red Beach
Perivolos Beach
Agios Georgios Beach
Vlihada Beach
Cape Evo Mytis

AEGEAN SEA

To Crete (128km)
To Anafi (56km)

SANTORINI'S UNSETTLING PAST

Santorini's violent volcanic nature is visible everywhere – in black-sand beaches, raw lava-layered cliffs plunging into the sea, earthquake-damaged dwellings and in the soil's fertility, which supports coiled-up grape vines. The volcano may be dormant, but it's not dead. Minor tremors – that may just wake you fleetingly at night – are fairly common.

Always unstable, Santorini was part of a series of volcanoes over a million years ago. The volcanoes became dormant and around 3000 BC the first human settlers arrived to take advantage of the fertile soil. From evidence found at Akrotiri, it appears that they led very idyllic lives and fashioned a highly sophisticated culture.

But the peace and harmony didn't last, and around 1650 BC a chain of earthquakes and eruptions culminated in one of the largest explosions in the history of the planet. Thirty cubic kilometres of magma spewed forth and a column of ash 36km high jetted into the atmosphere. The centre of the island collapsed, producing a caldera that the sea quickly filled. The eruption also generated huge tsunamis that travelled with dangerous force all the way to Crete and Israel; nearby Anafi was engulfed by one such gigantic wave. It's widely held that the catastrophe was responsible for the demise of Crete's Minoan culture, one of the most powerful civilisations in the Aegean at that time.

After the Big One, Santorini settled down for a time and was even recolonised. In 236 BC volcanic activity separated Thirasia from the main island. Further changes continued intermittently. In 197 BC the islet now known as Palia Kameni appeared in the caldera, and in AD 726 there was a major eruption that catapulted pumice all the way to Asia Minor. The south coast of Santorini collapsed in 1570, taking the ancient port of Eleusis with it. An eruption in 1707 created Nea Kameni Islet next to Palia Kameni.

A major earthquake measuring 7.8 on the Richter scale savaged the island in 1956, killing scores of people and destroying most of the houses in Fira and Oia. The renaissance is remarkable; the resilience and insouciance of locals even more so. For lovers of impermanence, precariousness and drama, Santorini is incomparable.

There are two weekly ferries running to Mykonos (€15.20, six hours), Milos (€14.50, four hours), Kimolos (€13.70, 3½ hours), Syros (€18.60, 5¼ hours) and Serifos (€15.70, seven hours).

Getting Around
TO/FROM THE AIRPORT
There are frequent bus connections in summer between Fira's bus station and the airport. Enthusiastic hotel and *domatia* staff meet flights, and some also return guests to the airport.

BOAT
From the seafront at Ancient Akrotiri, you can catch a caïque to Red Beach, White Beach and Black Beach for around €6. Caïques also run regularly from Perissa to Red Beach.

BUS
In summer, buses leave Fira hourly for Akrotiri (€1.40) and every half-hour for Oia (€0.10), Monolithos (€1), Kamari (€1)

and Perissa (€1.60). There are less frequent buses to Exo Gonia (€1), Perivolos (€1.60) and Vlihada (€1.70).

Buses leave Fira, Kamari and Perissa for the port of Athinios (€1.40, 30 minutes) 1½ hours before most ferry departures. Buses for Fira meet all ferries, even late at night

CABLE CAR & DONKEY
Cable cars (every 20 minutes, 7am to 10pm daily) shunt cruise-ship and excursion-boat passengers up to Fira from the small port below, known as Fira Skala. One way tickets per adult cost €3.50 or for a child €1.50, luggage is €1.50. You can make a more leisurely upward trip by donkey (€3).

CAR, MOTORCYCLE & BICYCLE
Fira has many firms that rent cars, motorcycles and bicycles. Car is the best way to explore the island as the buses are intolerably overcrowded in summer and you'll usually be lucky to get on one at all. Be very patient and cautious when driving – the narrow roads, especially in Fira, can be a nightmare.

CYCLADES

TAXI

For **taxis** (☎ 22860 23951/2555) there's a stand in the main square. A taxi from Athinios to Fira costs €8 (set fare).

FIRA ΦΗΡΑ
pop 2113

Crowds of fellow visitors and the often brash commercialism of Fira have not diminished the town's dramatic aura. Views from the edge of the caldera over the layered, multi-coloured cliffs are breathtaking and at night the caldera's edge is a frozen cascade of lights that eclipses the displays of the jewellery shops in the streets behind.

Orientation

The central square is Plateia Theotokopoulou. The main road, 25 Martiou, runs north-south, intersecting the square and is lined with travel agencies. The **bus station** (25 Martiou) is 50m south of Plateia Theotokopoulou. West of 25 Martiou, towards the edge of the caldera, the streets are pedestrian alleyways; Erythrou Stavrou, one block west of 25 Martiou, is the main commercial thoroughfare.

Another block west, Ypapantis, known also as Gold St because of its many jewellers, runs along the crest of the caldera and provides some staggering panoramic views. Head north on Nomikou for the cable-car station. If you keep walking along the caldera – the way steepens, but it's well worth it – you'll come, eventually, to the cliff-top villages of Firostefani and Imerovigli. Keep going and you'll reach Oia, but it's a long, hot 8km.

Information

Fira doesn't have an EOT (Greek National Tourist Organisation) or tourist police. It's best to seek out the smaller travel agents in the town, where you'll receive more helpful service.

There are toilets near the taxi rank.

EMERGENCY

Hospital (☎ 22860 22237) On the road to Kamari and Akrotiri.

Police station (☎ 22860 22649; Karterados) About 2km from Fira.

Port police (☎ 22860 22239; 25 Martiou) North of the square.

INTERNET ACCESS

PC World (☎ 22860 25551; Central Sq; per 30 min €2.10; 🕙 10am-2am May-Oct, 10am-10pm rest of year) A good range of services.

LAUNDRY

Laundrette (Danezi) Next to Pelican Hotel; it charges €10 for washing and drying an average load. Locked luggage storage (€1.50) is also available.

MONEY

There are numerous ATMs scattered around town.

Alpha Bank (Plateia Theotokopoulou) Represents American Express and has an ATM.

National Bank of Greece (Dekigala) Between the bus station and Plateia Theotokopoulou, on the caldera side of the road. Has an ATM.

POST

Post office (Dekigala)

TRAVEL AGENCIES

Dakoutros Travel (☎ 22860 22201; Dekigala) Sells ferry tickets and tours.

Pelican Tours & Travel (☎ 22860 22220; fax 22860 22570; Plateia Theotokopoulou) A useful agency that books accommodation and ferry tickets.

Sights & Activities
MUSEUMS

A single ticket costing €9 is valid for the Museum of Prehistoric Thera, the Archaeological Museum and the sites at Akrotiri and Ancient Thira.

Near the bus station, the **Museum of Prehistoric Thera** (☎ 22860 23217; Mitropoleos; admission €3; 🕙 8.30am-3pm Tue-Sun) houses extraordinary finds that were excavated from Akrotiri (where, to date, only 5% of the area has been excavated). Most impressive is the glowing gold ibex figurine, measuring around 10cm in length and dating from the 17th century BC. Many of Akrotiri's thrilling wall paintings are on display.

The **Archaeological Museum** (☎ 22860 22217; M Nomikou; adult/student €3/free; 🕙 8.30am-3pm Tue-Sun), near the cable-car station, houses finds from Akrotiri and Ancient Thira, some Cycladic figurines, and Hellenistic and Roman sculptures.

Megaron Gyzi Museum (☎ 22860 22244; Agiou Ioannou; adult/concession €3/1.50; 🕙 10.30am-1pm & 5-8pm Mon-Sat, 10.30am-4.30pm Sun May-Oct) Behind the Catholic cathedral, this has local

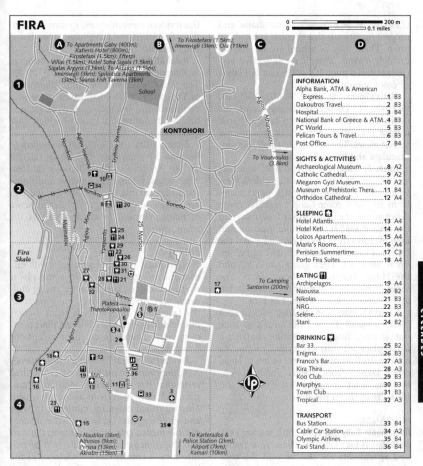

FIRA

0 — 200 m
0 — 0.1 miles

To Apartments Gaby (400m);
Kafieris Hotel (800m);
Firostefani (1.5km); Efterpi
Villas (1.5km); Hotel Sofia Sigala (1.5km);
Sigalas Argyris (1.5km); To Aktaion (1.5km);
Imerovigli (3km); Spiliotica Apartments
(3km); Skaros Fish Taverna (3km)

To Firostefani (1.5km);
Imerovigli (3km); Oia (11km)

School

KONTOHORI

To Vourvoulos
(3.8km)

Koneou

Fira
Skala

Danezi

Plateia
Theotokopoulou

To Camping
Santorini (200m)

To Karterados &
Police Station (2km);
Airport (7km);
Kamari (10km)

To Nautilos (3km);
Athinios (9km);
Perissa (13km);
Akrotiri (15km)

INFORMATION
Alpha Bank, ATM & American
  Express..............................1 B3
Dakoutros Travel.....................2 B3
Hospital...............................3 B4
National Bank of Greece & ATM..4 B3
PC World...............................5 B3
Pelican Tours & Travel...............6 B3
Post Office.............................7 B4

SIGHTS & ACTIVITIES
Archaeological Museum............8 A2
Catholic Cathedral...................9 A2
Megaron Gyzi Museum..............10 A2
Museum of Prehistoric Thera.....11 B4
Orthodox Cathedral.................12 A4

SLEEPING
Hotel Atlantis.........................13 A4
Hotel Keti..............................14 A4
Loizos Apartments....................15 A4
Maria's Rooms.........................16 A4
Pension Summertime.................17 C3
Porto Fira Suites......................18 A4

EATING
Archipelagos..........................19 A4
Naoussa................................20 B2
Nikolas.................................21 B3
NRG.....................................22 B3
Selene..................................23 A4
Stani....................................24 B2

DRINKING
Bar 33...................................25 B2
Enigma..................................26 B3
Franco's Bar............................27 A3
Kira Thira...............................28 A3
Koo Club................................29 B3
Murphys................................30 B3
Town Club..............................31 B3
Tropical.................................32 A3

TRANSPORT
Bus Station.............................33 B4
Cable Car Station......................34 A2
Olympic Airlines.......................35 B4
Taxi Stand..............................36 B4

CYCLADES

memorabilia, including fascinating photographs of Fira before and immediately after the 1956 earthquake.

Tours

Tour agencies operate various trips, including a bus-and-boat tour (€35), that lasts from four to eight hours depending on the itinerary, taking in Akrotiri, Thirasia, the volcanic island of Nea Kameni, Palia Kameni's hot springs and Oia; book at travel agencies.

The **Bella Aurora**, an exact copy of an 18th-century schooner, scoots around the caldera every afternoon on a sunset buffet dinner tour (€35), stopping for sight-seeing at Nea Kameni and for ouzo at Thirasia. Most travel agencies sell tickets.

Sleeping
BUDGET

Throughout Fira there are scores of sleeping options, but few budget places and prices soar in high season. *Domatia* touts at the port reach impressive heights of hysteria in their bids for attention. Some claim their rooms are in town, when they're actually a long way out; be tough and ask to see a map showing the exact location. If you're looking for a caldera view, expect to pay at least double the prices elsewhere. Many hotels in Fira, especially on the caldera rim, cannot be reached by vehicle. If you have heavy luggage, this is worth remembering.

Camping Santorini (☎ 22860 22944; fax 22860 25065; www.santorinicamping.gr; sites per adult/tent

€7.20/3.60; (**P** **☼**) There's some shade and modest facilities at this site that is handy to town. There may be school groups staying in high season. There's a self-service restaurant and a pool. It's 400m east of Plateia Theotokopoulou.

Maria's Rooms (☎ 22860 25143, 69732 54461; Agiou Mina; d €60; **☼**) These entertaining rooms, just down from Hotel Keti, open onto a shared terrace that offers unbeatable caldera and sunset views. The rooms are small, but immaculate and blissfully peaceful.

Loizos Apartments (☎ 22860 24046; www.loizos .gr; s/d €55/65; **☼**) Who needs a caldera view when this friendly place has great views from its front rooms and breakfast room down across the island towards Kamari and the distant sea? It's in a quiet location and only minutes from the caldera edge and the centre of town. Rooms are bright and clean. Breakfast is €4. Keep going south beyond the Hotel Atlantis for about 100m. The same owners have similar accommodation at Messaria, 2.5km southeast of Fira.

Pension Summertime (☎ 22860 24313; fax 22860 25438; s/d €40/50) There's not much to look out at from this little pension, but it's a smart place with attractive small rooms. It's a mere stroll from the centre of town. Head down Danezi from Plateia Theotokopoulou, turn left, then right in a few metres, and it's halfway down the street.

MIDRANGE

Apartments Gaby (☎ 22860 22057; Nomikou; s €45, d €60-90, 3-/4-bed r €108/130) These fine rooms and apartments are just beyond the convention centre on the caldera-edge path. They have a wonderful local feeling that transcends Fira's surface gloss. The rooms on the series of roof terraces guarantee fantastic sunset views.

Hotel Keti (☎ 22860 22324; www.hotelketi.gr; Agiou Mina; d €70; **☼**) One of the smaller view-to-die-for places, Keti is tucked away at the quieter southern end of town on the edge of the caldera and features attractive traditional rooms dug into the cliffs.

TOP END

Porto Fira Suites (☎ 22860 22849; www.portofira.gr; Agiou Mina; 2-4–person ste incl breakfast €280-414; **☼** **☼**) One of Fira's top-rated hotels, this caldera-edge place is an old Venetian mansion that merges traditional style with all the modern conveniences. Rooms are stylishly furnished and have huge stone-based beds and Jacuzzis.

Hotel Atlantis (☎ 22860 22232; www.atlantishotel .gr; Mitropoleos; s/d incl breakfast €174/245; **P** **☼** **☼**) The Atlantis dominates the southern end of Ypapantis and is a handsome place with cool, relaxing lounges and terraces, and bright airy bedrooms, most of which have great views.

Efterpi Villas (☎ 22860 22541; www.efterpi.gr; Firostefani; 2-3–person studios €160-190, apt €215-280; **☼** **☼**) Another of those famous caldera-edge hotels, Efterpi has pleasant traditional rooms carved into the cliffside. Furnishings are simple and there's a wonderful sense of being removed from the crush of the main town.

Eating

Fira has many tourist-trap eateries with dismal and overpriced food. In some places singles, and even families with young children, may find themselves unwelcome in the face of a pushy attitude from owners desperate to keep tables full and their turnover brisk. There are excellent exceptions however.

Nikolas (☎ 22860 24550; Erythrou Stavrou; dishes €5-7) At the heart of Fira, this long-established restaurant has tasty traditional Greek cuisine, including such treats as beef stew with onions, grilled calamari, cuttlefish in wine and white eggplant (in season). The absence of table menus gets you chatting to the staff and the choice changes regularly. The culture here is emphatically traditional in the best of ways; straightforward and courteous, and expecting the same in return.

Naousa (☎ 22860 24869; Erythrou Stavrou; dishes €3-17) Serves excellent, reasonably priced Greek classics, with new specials daily, in a pleasant upstairs venue. The lamb in lemon sauce is delicious; seafood dishes likewise.

Stani (☎ 22860 23078; Erythrou Stavrou; dishes €4.50-12) Just up from Bar 33, Stani's has a remarkable range of Greek standards served in a roof-top setting.

Archipelagos (☎ 22860 23673; Ypapantis; dishes €16-27) Caldera-hugging on several levels, this popular restaurant offers classic Mediterranean cuisine. The surroundings are gourmet as well. Those finest of fish, John Dory, monkfish and hake, are prepared with panache, and there's mussels, and octopus, plus, for high fliers, good meat dishes and duck.

Selene (☎ 22860 22249; Agiou Mina; dishes €19.50-22) Pay a visit between wedding receptions for some cracking cuisine at this top Fira restaurant. Or gaze down on the cool terrace from the walkway above if you're not into zucchini with smoked eel and white cheese, or fava balls stuffed with capers and tomatoes, followed by a rich choice of meat and such fish dishes as delectable sea bass. Romance blossoms unabated, even between the wedding receptions.

Nautilos (☎ 22860 27052; Ayia Irini; dishes €5-10) It's worth the trip to this smart restaurant, 3km south of Fira on the main road, for good modern Greek cuisine, while a real bonus is the chance of hearing live Greek music. Nautilos also has very luxurious apartments (€170) complete with a swish pool.

NRG (Erythrou Stavrou; dishes €2-5.70) Next to Koo Club, this is among the best town-centre cafés for Indian curry (€4.50), tortillas, crepes, ice cream, coffee and cool ambience.

There are several *gyros* stands up from the main square.

FIROSTEFANI & IMEROVIGLI

To Aktaion (☎ 22860 22336; dishes €8-16) On the edge of the square in Firostefani, this above-the-ordinary taverna has been going for years and serves up tasty Greek specialities such as excellent *mousaka* (sliced eggplant and mincemeat arranged in layers and baked) to go with the spectacular views.

Skaros Fish Tavern (☎ 22860 23616; dishes €3-12) A classic *mezedopoleio* (restaurant specialising in *mezedes*) further along the caldera's edge in Imerovigli, Skaros offers diners a great range of *mezedes* (appetisers) and fish dishes.

Drinking

Kira Thira (☎ 22860 22770; Erythrou Stavrou) The oldest bar in Fira has entrances on the streets to either side. Locals always use one entrance. Guess which one and you'll feel even more at home in this candle-lit bar with its smooth jazz, ethnic sounds and occasional live music.

Tropical (☎ 22860 23089; Marinatou) You feel the vibe yards away from the door of Tropical, which has a winning mix of rock, soul and

CYCLADES

SANTORINI WINES

Santorini's two lauded wines are its crisp, clear dry whites, and the amber-coloured, unfortified dessert wine *vinsanto,* both produced from the ancient indigenous cultivar *assyrtiko*. Most vineyards hold tastings and tours, and there are also two fascinating wine museums. There are several wineries that hold tastings in summer:

Antoniou (☎ 22860 23557; Megalohori; 🕙 10am-7pm)

Boutaris (☎ 22860 81011; www.boutari.gr; Megalohori; 🕙 10am-7pm)

Canava Roussos (☎ 22860 31349; 🕙 10am-10pm) On the way to Kamari.

Hatzidakis (☎ 22860 32552; hatzidakiswinery@san.forthnet.gr) Call before you visit this small organic winery based in the village of Pyrgos near Moni Profiti Ilia.

Santo Wines (☎ 22860 22596; santowines@san.forthnet.gr; 🕙 9am-sunset) Near Pyrgos.

Sigalas (☎ 22860 71644; 🕙 11am-1pm & 6-8pm) Off the beach road near Oia.

Antoniou winery was designed early by a winemaker with his eye on the export market. Built into the cliffs directly above Athinios port, the *canava* (wine cellar) is a masterpiece of free-form ingenuity: wine was once piped down to waiting boats. Wine is no longer made at this site, but it's a fascinating place to visit.

The winegrowers cooperative, **Santo Wines** (☎ 22860 22596, santowines@san.forthnet.gr; 🕙 9am-sunset) in Megalohori has a showcase selection of regional produce taken from all over Greece.

The atmospheric **Volcan Wine Museum** (Lava; ☎ 22860 31322; www.waterblue.gr; admission €1.70; 🕙 noon-8pm), housed in a traditional *canava* on the way to Kamari, has some interesting displays, including a 17th-century wooden wine press. Admission to the museum includes three tastings. On Sunday nights there's a traditional Greek night with a buffet, local dancers, and the added spice of belly dancing.

There's also the Art Space gallery-winery outside Kamari, see p199.

occasional jazz, plus friendly efficient staff and unbeatable balcony views. There's an international crowd on most nights and a stylish local crew.

Franco's Bar (☎ 22860 24428; Marinatou) Things move at a cooler pace at this ultimate sunset venue simply because of its sheer elegance and impeccable musical taste – it's always classical here. Think poise and composure. The ambience suits it, while management and staff have the old-fashioned courtesy and style of true class.

Entertainment

After midnight Erythrou Stavrou is the clubbing caldera of Fira.

Koo Club (☎ 22860 22025; Erythrou Stavrou) This five-bar joint fills its spacey levels with mainstream and Greek hits, plus a touch of hip hop.

Murphy's (☎ 22860 22248; Erythrou Stavrou) A hot-spot bar that soothes with afternoon lounge sounds, then really rocks from late evening. They're flashing their heels, and more, along the bar top by the early hours.

Town Club (☎ 22860 22820; Erythrou Stavrou) A charmingly kitsch confection which plays a mix of modern Greek and mainstream.

Enigma (☎ 22860 22466; Erythrou Stavrou) All white walls and tense chrome, this place is gently flayed with voluminous muslin drapes; cool, edgy and favouring house and mainstream hits.

Bar 33 (☎ 22860 23065; Erythrou Stavrou) A lively bouzouki place.

Shopping

Shopoholics will swoon over Fira's swathe of fashion shops in which you can get everything and anything from Armani and Versace to Timberland and Reef. It will cost you though.

Fira's jewellery and gold shops are legion. The merchandise gleams and sparkles, which is more than can be said of the merchants.

Grapes thrive in Santorini's volcanic soil, and the island's wines are famous all over Greece and beyond. Local wines are widely available in Fira and elsewhere.

Sigalas Argyris (La Cava; ☎ 22860 22802) In Firostefani, this has a good selection of wines and local delicacies such as caper leaves and thyme honey.

AROUND SANTORINI

Ancient Akrotiri Αρχαίο Ακρωτήρι

Excavations at **Akrotiri** (☎ 22860 81366; adult/student €5/3; ☺ 8.30am-3pm Tue-Sun), the Minoan outpost that was buried during the catastrophic eruption of 1650 BC, began in 1967 and have uncovered an ancient city beneath the volcanic ash. Buildings, some three storeys high, date to the late 16th century BC. Outstanding finds are the stunning frescoes and ceramics, many of which are now on display at the Museum of Prehistoric Thera in Fira (see p194).

The site at Akrotiri was always visually disappointing, its overall context having been compromised by the construction of a 'bio-climatic' roof aimed at protecting the ruins from the damaging effects of the weather. Tragedy still haunts Akrotiri, however, and at the time of writing the site was closed indefinitely, pending an official investigation, after one visitor was killed and several others injured when a section of the roof collapsed during summer 2005. Visitors are advised to check the situation carefully on their arrival on Santorini and to make their own decisions.

On the way to Akrotiri, pause at the enchanting traditional settlement of **Megalohori** for some fine wineries (see boxed text, p197).

Kamari Καμάρι

pop 1351

Kamari is 10km from Fira and is Santorini's best-developed resort. It has a long beach of black sand, with the rugged limestone cliffs of Cape Mesa Vouno framing its southern end. The beachfront road is pedestrianised and is thick with eateries and bars. There's an enviable mood of easy living here.

Lisos Tours (☎ 22860 33765; lisostours@san.forth net.gr) has an office on the main road into Kamari, and another just inland from the centre of the beach, and is especially helpful and knowledgeable about Santorini generally. They sell ferry tickets and can arrange accommodation and car rental. All kinds of tours can be sorted through Lisos, including fixed-wing flights over the caldera, horse riding and kayaking. There's Internet access and a bureau de change.

Just inland from the beach, **Volcano Diving Centre** (☎ 22860 33177; www.scubagreece.com) offers caldera dives from €55 to €80 with all equipment supplied. It also has courses for beginners (from €65) and snorkelling trips (€30).

Cinema Kamari (☎ 22860 31974; www.cinekamari .gr; admission €7), on the main road coming into Kamari, is a great open-air theatre set in a thicket of trees, showing recent releases at 9pm and 11.15pm daily. In July it hosts the three-day **Santorini Jazz Festival** (☎ 22860 33452; www.jazzfestival.gr), featuring lively perform-ances by Greek and foreign musicians.

Just outside Kamari, do not miss **Art Space** (☎ 22860 32774; Exo Gonia), at Argiro's Canava, one of the oldest wineries on the island. The atmospheric old wine caverns are hung with superb artworks while sculptures transform lost corners and niches. The collection is curated by the owner and features some of Greece's finest modern artists. Wine mak-ing is still in the owner's blood, so a tasting of his *vinsanto* greatly enhances the whole experience.

SLEEPING
Kamari has plenty of *domatia* and hotels.

Aegean View Hotel (☎ 22860 32790; www.aegean view-santorini.com; studios/apt €130/150; P ⊠ ▣ ⊕) You definitely do not need caldera views at this outstanding place that lies over sev-eral levels below sculpted cliffs. It has ter-rific views out over Kamarito, the sea and to distant Anafi. The spacious studios and apartments are superbly laid out and have first-class facilities, including small kitchen areas. Head up the steep road that leads to Ancient Thira and the hotel is easily located on the right, beneath steep cliffs.

Hotel Selini (☎ /fax 22860 32625; s/d incl breakfast €35/45) This is a reliable, family-run, mid-range hotel. Rooms are a good size and the hotel is centrally placed, just a few blocks in from Kamari beach.

Anna's Rooms (☎ 22860 22765; s/d €25/35) Straightforward furnishings without frills, these rooms above the Lisos Tours office in Kamari are an ideal budget option. It's a bit of a hike to the beach but the location is quiet.

EATING
Kamari has many eateries along its water-front and inland streets. Many are fairly standard but there are some choice places.

Eanos (☎ 22860 31161; dishes €4.20-14.60) Right on the beach, towards the south end of the

waterfront, this is a long-established tav-erna that does excellent Greek food, includ-ing terrific *mousaka*. Food is cooked on a wood-burning stove and pasta is also on offer.

Amalthia (☎ 22860 32780; dishes €3.50-12) A couple of blocks inland at the southern end of town, Amalthia has a marvellous garden area and terrace, and friendly serv-ice. It offers well-prepared Greek dishes; the lamb is particularly good, as is the pasta and pizza.

Taverna the Fat Man (☎ 22860 32932; dishes €3.20-9) This place is right at the back of town on the road into Kamari. It's worth visit-ing for traditional Greek cuisine, including the meat and fish, but also the vegetarian dishes. Arthuro's chicken in tasty 'Zorba Sauce' is a speciality.

Ancient Thira Αρχαία Θήρα
First settled by the Dorians in the 9th cen-tury BC, **Ancient Thira** (admission €2; ⏰ 8.30am-2.30pm) consists of Hellenistic, Roman and Byzantine ruins. The ruins include temples, houses with mosaics, an agora, a theatre and a gymnasium. There are splendid views from the site.

If you're driving, take the road from Kamari. It takes about 45 minutes to walk to the site, along the path from Perissa, on rocky, difficult ground.

Oia Οία
pop 763
The village of Oia (*ee*-ah), known locally as Pano Meria, was devastated by the 1956 earthquake, although for the visitor there's little overt evidence as good restoration work has taken place. It's a delightful place, once home to wealthy sea captains. Though much quieter than tourist-frenzied Fira, its streets still have their share of trendy bou-tiques and expensive jewellery shops. Built on a steep slope of the caldera, many of its dwellings nestle in niches hewn into the volcanic rock. Oia is famous as a sunset view 'must' and its narrow passageways get crowded in the evenings.

ORIENTATION & INFORMATION
From the bus, turn around, head left and uphill to reach the rather empty-looking central square and the main street, Nikolaou Nomikou, which skirts the caldera.

CYCLADES

Alpha Bank Branches on Main St, near blue-domed church, and outside Karvounis Tours. With ATM.

Atlantis Books (☎ 22860 72346; www.atlantisbooks .org; Nikolaou Nomikou) A highly original and very enthusiastic little bookshop run with flair and stocking a fascinating range of titles. Cultural events, for a small number of people, are often staged.

Karvounis Tours (☎ 22860 71290; www.idogreece .com; Nikolaou Nomikou) For information, booking hotels, renting cars and bikes, and making international calls.

SIGHTS & ACTIVITIES

The **maritime museum** (☎ 22860 71156; adult/ student €3/1.50; ⏰ 10am-2pm & 5-8pm Wed-Sun) is housed in an old mansion and has entertaining displays on Santorini's maritime history. Exhibits here include a very arched figurehead. It is located along a narrow lane that leads off right from Nikolaou Nomikou about 100m south of the Museum Hotel.

Ammoudi, a tiny port with good tavernas and colourful fishing boats, lies 300 steps below Oia. In summer, boats and tours go from Ammoudi to Thirasia daily; check travel agents for departure times.

SLEEPING

Oia Youth Hostel (☎ /fax 22860 71465; dm incl breakfast €15; ⏰ May–mid-Oct) Oia's hostel is exceptional for its cleanliness, comfort and facilities. It has a small bar and a lovely rooftop terrace with great views. To find it, head on from the bus terminus for about 100m.

Hotel Museum (☎ 22860 71515; santorini@museum hotel.net; Nikolaou Nomikou; studios/apt €118/140; ⛶ 🏊) Once a consular mansion this lovely building later became a museum and then a hotel of great style. The swimming pool is a work of art, and décor and furnishings are delightful.

Katikies (☎ 22860 71401; katikies@otenet.gr; Nikolaou Nomikou; d €285; studios €395-660; ⛶ 🖥 🏊) One of Santorini's most beautiful hotels, Katikies is at the east end of the village, just below the main street. It revels in luxury and its cliff-edge pool is spectacular. Rooms here are traditional and super swish.

Chelidonia (☎ 22860 71287; www.chelidonia.com; Nikolaou Nomikou; studios €129, apt €155-189) These excellent traditional cave apartments have pleasant wooden furnishings and great views from the verandas. The office is right on the main street.

EATING & DRINKING

1800 (☎ 22860 71485; Nikolaou Nomikou; dishes €13-29; ⏰ 6.30-11.30pm) Enthusiasm for slow food and the finest Mediterranean cuisine make this one-time sea-captain's mansion an institution. Nice touches, with magical use of herbs and subtle sauces, produce such joys as fillet of sea bream with cherry tomatoes, olives and baked fennel (€26). Or enjoy vanilla-scented pear, brie, prosciutto and walnut with vinaigrette. The stylish dining room and terrace-patio add to the pleasure.

Edwin Polski Lokal (☎ 22860 71971; snacks €1.70-2, dishes €4.28-12.50) Away from the main froth of visitors, but just down from the caldera edge is this cheerful little place with its rarely empty terrace. Tasty salads, plates and home-cooked *gyros* are on offer.

Skala (☎ 22860 71362; Nikolaou Nomikou; dishes €6-14) A caldera-view terrace enhances the good Greek cuisine of Skala. This includes lamb and meat dishes, salads and imaginative starters that make good use of traditional produce, while mixing in international influences.

GETTING THERE & AWAY

The last of the regular buses to and from Fira (see p193 for details) leaves Oia at 11.20pm in summer. After that, three to four people can bargain for a shared taxi for about €10.

Oia has no petrol station, the nearest being about 10km along the road to Fira.

Other Beaches

Santorini's black-sand beaches become so hot at times that a sun lounger or mat is essential. The best beaches are on the east coast.

One of the main beaches is **Perissa**, which is very long and can get busy. **Perivolos** and **Agios Georgios**, further south, are more relaxed. **Red Beach**, near Ancient Akrotiri, is breathtaking – high red cliffs and hand-size pebbles submerged under clear water. **Vlihada**, also on the south coast, is even nicer. On the north coast near Oia, **Paradise** and **Pori** are both worth a stop.

SLEEPING & EATING

The main concentration of rooms can be found in and around Perissa.

Hostel Anna (☎ 22860 82182; annayh@otenet.gr; dm €8-10, d €15; ⏰ Feb-Oct; 🖥 🏊) At the entrance to Perissa, Anna's is a friendly, relaxed hostel and is a great place to meet fellow travellers. A minibus picks up guests from the ferry port. To find the hostel contact office at the port, look for the sign on the Blue Star Ferry Office.

Stelio's Place (☎ 22860 81860; www.steliosplace .com; s/d/tr €50/60/75; P ⊠ ⊠) Just in from the beach at Perissa and down a quiet cul-de-sac is Stelio's, a bright and well-run complex. Airport and port transfers are by arrangement.

Most beaches have a range of tavernas and cafés.

THIRASIA & VOLCANIC ISLETS
ΘΗΡΑΣΙΑ & ΗΦΑΙΣΤΕΙΑΚΕΣ ΝΗΣΙΔΕΣ

Unspoilt Thirasia was separated from Santorini by an eruption in 236 BC. The cliff-top *hora*, **Manolas**, has tavernas and *domatia*. It's an attractive place, noticeably more relaxed and reflective than Fira could ever be.

The *Nisos Thira* leaves Athinios port for Thirasia on Monday and Friday, and on Wednesday mornings, but does not return to Santorini. Tickets are available only at the port. Take care of youngsters when on the upper deck near the rails (which have some child-size gaps, especially on the port side). There are also morning and afternoon boats to Thirasia from Oia's port of Ammoudi.

The islets of **Palia Kameni** and **Nea Kameni** are still volcanically active and can be visited on half-day excursions from Fira Skala and Athinios. Two-hour trips to Nea Kameni are also possible. A day's excursion taking in Nea Kameni, the **hot springs** at Palia Kameni, Thirasia and Oia is about €28.

ANAFI ΑΝΑΦΗ

pop 273

Anafi is the perfect antidote to Santorini's souped-up tourism. It may seem hopelessly out of reach at times but ferry connections have improved, so persevere. the rewards are a slow-paced, traditional lifestyle, islanders with time to smile, and a refreshing lack of commercialism. But pencil in a potential extra day or two, in case weather curtails ferry services.

The island's small port is **Agios Nikolaos**. From here, the main village, **Hora**, is a 10-minute bus ride up a winding road, or a steep 1km hike up a less winding walkway. Hora's main pedestrian thoroughfare leads uphill from the first bus stop and has most of the *domatia*, restaurants and minimarkets.

There is a post office, that opens occasionally, next to Panorama rooms at the entrance to Hora.

Jeyzed Travel (☎ 22860 61253; jeyzed@san.forth net.gr), halfway along Hora's main street, sells ferry tickets, exchanges money, can help with accommodation and rents motor bikes. It also has Internet access.

There are several lovely beaches near Agios Nikolaos. Palm-lined **Klissidi**, a 10-minute walk east of the port, is the closest and most popular.

Anafi's main sight is the monastery of **Moni Kalamiotissas**, a 6km walk from Hora in the extreme east of the island, near the meagre remains of a **sanctuary to Apollo**. At 470m, **Monastery Rock** is the highest rock formation in the Mediterranean Sea, outstripping even Gibraltar. There is also a ruined **Venetian kastro** at Kastelli, east of Klissidi.

Sleeping & Eating

Camping is tolerated at Klisidi Beach, but the only facilities are at nearby tavernas. *Domatia* owners prefer long stays, so if you're only staying one night you should take whatever you can get. In high season, contact Jeyzed Travel in advance to be sure of a room; places at Klissidi fill fast.

Villa Apollon (☎ 22860 61348; fax 22860 61287; vapollon@panafonet.gr; d/studios €120/150) At Klissidi

ANAFI

0 ——— 4 km
0 ——— 2 miles

AEGEAN SEA

Hora   Kastelli   Monestery Rock (470m)

Agios Nikolaos

Klissidi Beach   Moni Kalamiotissas

To Santorini (56km);
Ios (65km);
Paros (130km);
Naxos (140km);
Pireaus (270km)

Beach, these pleasant rooms are a good size and have an authentic traditional style.

Rooms to Let Artemis (☎ 22860 61235; d €45) These are just above the sea at Klissidi, and there's a restaurant attached.

Rooms in Hora are all very similar. Many have good views across Anafi's rolling hills to the sea and to the great summit of Monastery Rock. The recommended options below are easily found on the main street, and all charge about €30 or €35 for a single or double.

Panorama (☎ 22860 61292)
Paradise (☎ 22860 61243)
Anafi Rooms (☎ 22860 61271)

There are also several tavernas in Hora all of which are in the main street and easily found. The cheerful cook at **Astrakhan** (☎ 22860 61249; mains €4.50-7) serves up good Greek standards here, as if everyone is family. You stand the chance of some fine fish dishes at **Liotrivi** (☎ 22860 61209; mains €4-6), with the catch supplied from the family's boat.

Klissidi has a few tavernas, with similar prices.

Getting There & Away
There are five ferries weekly to Ios (€7.70, three hours), Naxos (€10.60, four hours) and Paros (€13.30, six hours). Seven ferries weekly go to Santorini (€6.50, one hour), four go to Folegandros (€9.40, five hours) and Sikinos (€8.20, four hours). Three go to Piraeus (€24.70, 11 hours), and two go to Syros (€16.30, eight hours).

Getting Around
A small bus takes passengers from the port up to the *hora*. Caïques serve various beaches and nearby islands.

SIKINOS ΣΙΚΙΝΟΣ

pop 238
Off-the-beaten-track, Sikinos (*see-kee-noss*) is another welcome island refuge after the heat and hubbub of Santorini. The island is blessed with pleasant beaches and a swooping landscape of terraced hills and mountains that plunge dramatically down to the sea. The port of **Alopronia**, and the villages of **Hora** and **Kastro** that comprise

SIKINOS

the hilltop capital, are the island's only settlements. Hora/Kastro is accessible by a 3.4km winding, uphill road leading up from the port. Here you'll find a post office and there's also a futuristic ATM booth, all shiny glass with card-slot access, in the central square of Kastro. Ferry tickets can be purchased in advance at **Koundouris Travel** (☎ 22860 51168) in Kastro and also down at the port before scheduled departures. There is no petrol station on the island.

Sights
The settlement of **Kastro** is a charming place with winding alleyways, brilliant white in the sun, and lovely old houses. At its heart is the main square and the **church of Pantanassa**. On its northern side, the land falls steeply to the sea. The fortified **Moni Zoödohou Pigis** stands on a hill above the town.

Sikinos' main excursion is a one-hour scenic trek (or five-minute drive along an ugly, bulldozed road) southwest to **Episkopi**. The remains here are believed to be those of a 3rd-century-AD Roman mausoleum that was transformed into a church in the 7th century, and then became **Moni Episkopis** (admission free; ⏱ 6.30-8.30pm) 10 centuries later. From here you can climb to a little **church** and **ancient ruins** perched on a precipice to the south, from where the views are spectacular.

Caïques run to good beaches at **Agios Georgios, Malta** – with ancient ruins on the hill above – and **Karra**. **Katergo**, a swimming place with interesting rocks, and **Agios Nikolaos Beach**, are both within easy walking distance of Alopronia.

Sleeping & Eating

In Hora/Kastro, there are a few basic *domatia* that charge about €30 for a double; ask at tavernas and the local shop. Alopronia has most of the accommodation.

Lucas Rooms (☎ 22860 51076; fax 22860 51075; Alopronia; s/d/studios €35/45/60) These very pleasant rooms are in a quiet location on the hillside, 500m uphill from the port. They are bright and clean and have airy views from their balconies. Studios are similar in quality, but are down at the beach.

Porto Sikinos (☎ 22860 51220; portosikinos@hit360 .com; Alopronia; d incl breakfast €69.60) This attractive hotel is about 100m from the quay. Rooms rise in a series of terraces and have great balcony views. There's also a bar and restaurant.

To Steki tou Garbi (dishes €3-6; Kastro) A good grill house just round the corner from Koundouris Travel. There are also decent tavernas at Agio Georgios.

Lucas (☎ 22860 51076; dishes €3.50-6; Alopronia) Down at the port, this is the favourite taverna, offering Greek standards without frills.

There's a supermarket next to Lucas.

Getting There & Away

Seven ferries weekly go to Piraeus (€20.30, 10 hours) and six weekly go to Santorini (€7.50, 2½ hours). There are five weekly to Ios (€4.10, 30 minutes), two to Naxos (€8.10, three hours) and Syros (€10.10, six hours), six to Paros (€7.20 four hours), four to Folegandros (€5, 45 minutes), Kimolos (€7.50, 2½ hours) and Anafi (€8.20, four hours), three weekly to Milos (€11.30, three hours), two weekly to Sifnos (€8.90, five hours), Serifos (€10.80, five hours) and Kythnos (€14.20, seven hours).

Getting Around

The local bus meets all ferry arrivals and runs between Alopronia and Hora/Kastro every half hour in August, less frequently at other times of the year (€0.90, 20 minutes). A timetable is sometimes posted near the minimarket. It's wise to be in good time.

FOLEGANDROS
ΦΟΛΕΓΑΝΔΡΟΣ

pop 667

Folegandros (fo-*leh*-gan-dross) has a winning combination of dramatic landscapes, a persuasive sense of timelessness and the friendliest of local people. The modern world has not overwhelmed Folegandros, perhaps because conspicuous tourism has not been able to get a foothold.

The island is a rocky ridge, barely 12km in length and just under 4km at its widest point. Much of the land is over 200m in height, the highest point being Agios Eleftherios at 414m. Beaches are small and do not invite too much development. Throughout a long history of human settlement the island's ruggedness led to its use as a place of exile for political prisoners, from Romans times right up to the Greek state during the 20th century, and as late as the military dictatorship of 1967–74. Now, it simply captivates visitors.

There are several good beaches; but be prepared for strenuous walking to reach some of them.

The capital is the concealed cliff-top Hora, one of the most appealing villages in the Cyclades. Boats dock at the cheerful little harbour of Karavostasis, on the east coast. The only other settlement is Ano Meria, 4km northwest of Hora.

Getting There & Away

There are four services weekly to Piraeus (€19.20, six to nine hours), Santorini (€7.60, 1½ to 2½ hours), Ios (€6, 1½ hours), Paros (€7.40, four hours), Naxos (€9, three hours) and Sikinos (€5, 45 minutes).

Three weekly services go to Syros (€11.30 five hours), Milos (€6.70, 2½ hours), Sifnos (€7.50, four hours) and Serifos (€9.60, five hours).

Two weekly ferries go to Kimolos (€5.10, 1½ hours) and Anafi (€9.50, five hours).

Once weekly there's a ferry to Kythnos (€13.50, six hours).

Getting Around

The local bus meets all ferry arrivals and takes passengers to Hora (€1). From Hora there are buses to the port one hour before

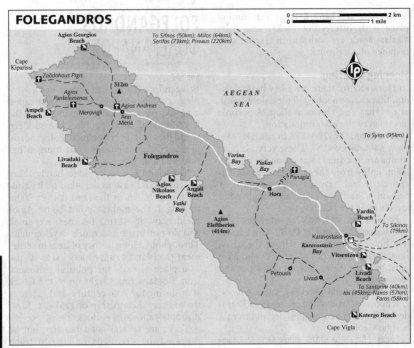

FOLEGANDROS

all ferry departures, even for the late night services. Buses from Hora run hourly to Ano Meria (€0.30), stopping at the road leading to Angali Beach. The bus stop for Ano Meria is located on the western edge of town, next to the Sottovento Tourism Office.

There is a **taxi service** (☎ 22860 41048, 69446 93957) on Folegandros, and you can hire cars for about €35 to €40 per day and motorbikes from €15 to €20 per day from a number of outlets.

KARAVOSTASIS ΚΑΡΑΒΟΣΤΑΣΙΣ
pop 55
Folegandros' port is a sunny little place serviced by a sprinkling of *domatia* and tavernas, and with a pleasant little pebble beach called **Hochlida**. Within a kilometre north and south of Karavostasis lie a series of other beaches, all pleasant and all easily reached by short walks. In season boats leave Karavostasis for beaches further afield.

Karavostasis is a terrific place to watch the world of boats go by.

Sleeping & Eating
Camping Livadi (☎ 22860 41204; sites per adult/tent €5/3) This site is at Livadi Beach, 1.2km from Karavostasis. It has a kitchen, minimarket, bar, restaurant and laundry. To get there turn left on the cement road skirting Karavostasis Beach.

Aeolos Beach Hotel (☎ 22860 41205; s/d/studios €40/60/85) Right behind Karavostasis beach in a quiet area, this friendly hotel has a pretty garden and clean straightforward rooms.

Vrahos (☎ 22860 41450; www.hotel-vrahos.gr; s/d incl breakfast €75/98) This fine hotel is in traditional Cycladic style, with ever-rising terraces. Room balconies have great views of the bay. There's an outdoor bar and breakfast area with views of the surrounding islands. It's at the far end of the beach beyond the Aeolos Beach Hotel.

Restaurant Kati Allo (☎ 22860 41272; dishes €4.50-6.30) Seafood is by the kilogram at this reliable eatery, where food, including salads, is prepared fresh on ordering. It has a pleasant terrace and is right behind the Karavostasis beach.

There are a couple of good beach-side bars. Evangelos is right on Karavostasis beach and is the place for relaxed drinks, snacks and great conversation.

HORA ΧΩΡΑ

pop 316

The delightful Hora, complete with a dozen pretty little churches and a medieval *kastro* filled with whitewashed houses draped in bougainvillea, draws you in with unassuming charm to its meandering main street that drifts happily from leafy square to leafy square. On its north side Hora stands on the edge of a very formidable cliff.

Orientation

The port–Hora bus turnaround is in the square, called Pounta. From here follow a road to the left into Dounavi Sq, from where an archway on the right, the Paraporti, leads to the densely-packed *kastro*, where the walls have been incorporated into dwellings. Dounavi Sq leads on to Kontarini Sq, then to Piatsa Sq and, finally, to Maraki Sq. Keep on through Maraki Sq to reach many of the music bars and the bus stop for Ano Meria and most beaches.

Information

There's no bank, but there is an ATM on the far side of Dounavi Sq, next to the community offices. The post office is on the port road, 200m downhill from the bus turnaround.

Travel agencies can exchange travellers cheques.

Maraki Travel (☎ 22860 41273; fax 22860 41149; Dounavi Sq; ☻ 10.30am-noon & 5-9pm) Hs a monopoly on the sale of ferry tickets. Also has a ticket booth at the port.

Police (☎ 22860 41249) Straight on from Maraki Sq.

Sottovento Tourism Office (☎ 22860 41444; sottovento@folegandrosisland.com) At the west end of town; doubles as the Italian Consulate and is very helpful on all tourism matters, including accommodation, international and domestic flights and boat trips.

Sights

It is an enduring pleasure just lingering among the well-preserved churches, flower-draped houses and cheerful squares of Hora. The medieval **kastro**, a tangle of narrow streets spanned by low archways, dates from when Marco Sanudo ruled the island back in the 13th century. The houses'

wooden balconies blaze with bougainvillea and hibiscus.

The extended village, outside the *kastro*, is just as attractive. From Pounta Sq and the bus turnaround, a steep path leads up to the large church of the Virgin, **Panagia** (☻ 6-8pm), which sits perched on a dramatic cliff-top above the town.

Tours

Sottovento Tourism Office (☎ 22860 41444; sottovento@folegandrosisland.com) runs boat trips around the island (adult/child including lunch €25/15). Departures are 10am Monday, Wednesday and Friday in summer. If you have snorkelling gear, take it along.

Festivals & Events

The annual **Folegandros Festival**, staged in late July, features a series of concerts, exhibitions and special meals, at venues around the island.

Sleeping

In July and August most *domatia* and hotels will be full, so book well in advance, or try the Sottovento Tourism Office.

Hotel Polikandia (☎ 22860 41322; polikandia@hotmail.com; s/d/tr €60/80/90; ☒) Just before the port–Hora bus turnaround, this is a pleasant and airy place with good-sized rooms arranged round a delightful reception and flower-filled garden area.

Anemomylos Apartments (☎ 22860 41309; www.AnemomilosApartments.com; d €115-200; ☒) Exhilarating views from seaward rooms are among the delights of these superb apartments. Rooms are cool and stylish and fine antiques add to the ambience. Anemomylos is just up from the bus turnaround. One unit is equipped for disabled use.

Folegandros Apartments (☎ 22860 41239; www.folegandros-apartments.com; studio apt from €90-160 ☒ ☒) These very fine apartments have tasteful furnishings and bright décor throughout and are arranged round a pool. They're just uphill from the bus turnaround.

Kallisti (☎ 22860 41555; www.kallisti.net.gr; s/d/tr €85/90/110; ☒ ☒ ☒) The very smart Kallisti merges sparkling modern facilities with charming Cycladic style – beds have the traditional stone bas, rather than wooden, as per Cycladic custom. The hotel is on an airy hillside at the western edge of Hora, but is just a short walk from the centre.

Eating

Pounta (☎ 22860 41063; dishes €4.50-8) A charming taverna on Pounta Sq within a walled garden full of flowers. Service is friendly and the food is excellent; from tasty breakfasts to evening meals of rabbit stew, lamb and vegetarian dishes. It's all served on delightful crockery made by one of the owners, Lisbet Giouri; you can buy examples of her work.

Piatsa Restaurant (☎ 22860 41274; dishes €2.50-7.50) Piatsa is on Hora's second square and offers excellent Greek cuisine such as *matsata* (hand-made pasta), usually with cockerel or rabbit – an island speciality.

Chic (☎ 22860 41515; dishes €4-8.50) Chic adjoins Piatsa, with similar classical Greek cuisine as well as tasty vegetarian dishes, including spinach pie with cheese, raisins and pine nuts.

Other recommended places:

To Mikro (☎ 22860 41550) Charming place near the middle square; for coffee, crepes and tasty cakes.

Nikos Fish Taverna (☎ 22860 41179; dishes 4.50-11) Just in front of To Mikro.

Pizza Pazza (☎ 22860 41549; dishes €4-10) Above the Greco Cafe-Bar.

Melissa (☎ 22860 41067; Kontarini; dishes €1.70-6) Serves good home-cooked food under an umbrella of pepper trees.

Nicolas (☎ 22860 41226; Dounavi; dishes €2.50-6) Dispenses entertaining chat with a range of dishes, including grills and pastas.

Entertainment

Folegandros has its own 'West End' – a clutch of great music bars at the western edge of Hora.

Greco Café-Bar (☎ 22860 41456) Next door to the Sottovento Tourism Office, and featuring vivid and appealing wall murals, the friendly ambience here is enhanced by a great mix of sounds from a stock of over 1000 CDs.

Avli Club (☎ 22860 41100) Near Greco's, early evening lounge music gives way to rock, disco, Latin and Greek here, as things liven up into the night.

Apanemo (☎ 22860 41562) Further along the road, is this pleasant bar that has a lovely garden.

Kellari (☎ 22860 41515) In Pounta Sq, this is a cosy little wine bar that plays Greek music and has a good selection of Greek wines.

Anikto (☎ 22860 41463) A good place for a late-night drink to the tones of Latin and jazz. It's on the road that leads west towards the Ano Meria bus stop.

Further on still from Apanemo is a long-established and fine little bar, Laoumi, that plays ethnic, funk, soul, South American and Caribbean sounds, with style.

AROUND FOLEGANDROS

Ano Meria Άνω Μεριά
pop 291

The settlement of Ano Meria is a scattered community of small farms and dwellings that stretches for several kilometres. This is traditional island life where tourism makes no intrusive mark and life happily wanders off sideways.

The **folklore museum** (admission €1.50; ☿ 5-8pm) is on the eastern outskirts of the village. Ask the bus driver to drop you off nearby.

There are several good traditional tavernas in Ano Meria, including **I Synantisi** (☎ 22860 41208; dishes €4-8) and **Mimi's** (☎ 22860 41377; dishes €3.50-7), which specialise in the local hand-made pasta dish *matsada*.

Beaches

For **Livadi Beach**, 1.2km southeast of Karavostasis, follow the signs for Camping Livadi. Further round the coast on the southeastern tip of the island is **Katergo Beach**, best reached by boat from Karavostasis.

The sandy and pebbled **Angali** beach on the coast opposite to Hora, is a popular spot, but you should remember that while it's a 1km downhill walk from where the bus drops you off, it's a steep and sweaty hike back up. There are several *domatia* here and two reasonable tavernas.

About 750m over the hill by footpath, west of Angali is the nudist beach of **Agios Nikolaos**. **Livadaki** beach is over 2km further west again, but is best reached by another 1.5km trek from the bus stop near the church of Agios Andreas at Ano Meria. Boats connect these west coast beaches in high season. **Agios Georgios** is north of Ano Meria and requires another demanding walk. Have tough footwear, sun protection and, because most beaches have no shops or tavernas, make sure you take food and water.

In July and August, weather permitting, excursion boats make separate trips from Karavostasis to Kartergo, Angali and Agios Nikolaos and from Angali to Livadaki beach.

MILOS ΜΗΛΟΣ

pop 4771

The most westerly of the Cyclades, Milos (*mee*-loss), is a big, good-natured island. It has dramatic coastal landscapes with colourful and crazy rock formations that reflect its volcanic origin. Milos also has hot springs, marvellous beaches and some absorbing ancient sites. A boat trip around the island allows you to visit most of Milos' beaches (many inaccessible by road), coves and geologically interesting places.

Filakopi, an ancient Minoan city in the island's northeast, was one of the earliest settlements in the Cyclades. During the Peloponnesian Wars, Milos was the only Cycladic island not to join the Athenian alliance. It paid dearly in 416 BC, when avenging Athenians massacred the adult males and enslaved the women and children.

The island's most celebrated export, the beautiful *Venus de Milo* (a 4th-century BC statue of Aphrodite, found in an olive grove in 1820) is far away in the Louvre (allegedly having lost its arms on the way to Paris in the 19th century).

Getting There & Away

AIR

There is a daily flight to/from Athens (€52 one way, 40 minutes). The **Olympic Airlines office** (☎ 22870 22380; fax 22870 21884; www.olympic airlines.com) is in Adamas, just past the main square, on the road to Plaka.

FAST BOAT & CATAMARAN

One weekly service goes to Santorini (€27, 1¾ hours), and one daily to Sifnos (€11.50, 1¾ hours) and Serifos (€12.50, 1¼ hours). At least one daily goes to Piraeus (€35, 3¾ hours). Three weekly go to Kythnos (€20, 2½ hours).

FERRY

The *Nisos Kimolos* departs five times daily from Pollonia for Kimolos at 9am, 11am, 2.15pm, 6.30pm and 10.40pm (per person €1.65, plus €1.30 for a motorbike and €7 for a car; 20 minutes).

From the main port of Adamas there are two ferries daily to Piraeus (€19, five to seven hours); one daily to Sifnos (€6, 1¼ hours), Serifos (€7, two hours) and Kythnos

(€10, 3½ hours); and six weekly to Kimolos (€4, one hour).

Three times weekly a ferry sails to the Cretan port of Sitia (€19, nine hours) and then on to Karpathos (€36.50, 12 hours) and Rhodes (€53.50, 13 hours).

There are three weekly ferries to Folegandros (€7, 2½ hours) and Sikinos (€8, three hours), and two weekly to Paros (€11, 4½ hours).

There is one weekly ferry to Santorini (€13, four hours), Ios (€14, 5½ hours) and Syros (€14.70, six hours).

Getting Around

There are no buses to the airport, so you'll need to take a **taxi** (☎ 22870 22219) for €6, plus €0.30 per piece of luggage, from Adamas. A taxi to Plaka is €5.

Buses leave Adamas for Plaka and Trypiti (both €1) every hour or so. Buses run to Pollonia (€1, four daily), Paleohori (€1.20, three daily), Provatas (€1.20, three daily) and Arhivadolimni (Milos) Camping, east of Adamas (three daily). Cars, motorcycles and mopeds can be hired along the waterfront.

ADAMAS ΑΔΑΜΑΣ

pop 1391

Although Plaka is the capital, the pleasant, if low-key port of Adamas has most of the accommodation and a waterfront which transforms into a lively evening scene.

Orientation

To get to the town centre from the quay, turn right at the waterfront. The central square, with the bus stop, taxi rank and outdoor cafés, is at the end of this stretch of waterfront, where the road curves inland. Just past the square is a road to the right that skirts the town beach.

Information

ATMs can be found outside Vichos Tours and in the main square. The post office can be along the main road, 50m from the main square, on the right.

Municipal Tourist Office (☎ 22870 22445; www .milos-island.gr; 8am-midnight mid-Jun–mid-Sep) Opposite the quay; one of the most helpful in the Cyclades.

Police (☎ 22870 21378) On the main square, next to the bus stop.

Port police (☎ 22870 22100) On the waterfront.

CYCLADES

MILOS & KIMOLOS

Vichos Tours (☎ 22870 22286; vichostours@in.gr) Right on the waterfront, sells air and ferry tickets, finds accommodation, rents cars and handles organised tours.

Sights & Activities

The **mining museum** (☎ 22870 22481; admission free; ⊙ 9.15am-1.45pm & 6.45-9.15pm) has some interesting geological exhibits and traces the island's long mining history. To get there, take the first right after the central square and continue along the waterfront for about 500m.

Dive courses are offered by **Milos Diving Center** (☎ 22870 41296; www.milosdiving.gr), based at Pollonia. This outfit is a member of the International Association for Handicapped Divers.

Tours

Milos Round 1 & 2 (☎ 22870 23411; tours €20; ⊙ May-Sep) Has tour boats departing daily at 9am, stopping at beaches around the island and pausing at Kimolos for lunch. Return is at 6pm. Buy tickets on the waterfront.

Andromeda Yachts (☎ 22870 23680; ⊙ May-Sep) Has sailing trips (per person €50) to the island's nicest beaches and coves; includes a seafood lunch, ouzo and sweets. Sailing tours (€240) take place in the southwest Cyclades. Book through travel agencies or Andromeda on the waterfront.

Festivals & Events

The **Milos Festival**, a well-orchestrated event, is held in early July and features traditional dancing, cooking and jazz.

Sleeping

In summer, lists of *domatia* are given out at the tourist office on the quay, but decent accommodation is thin on the ground – make sure you call ahead.

Arhivadolimni (Milos) Camping (☎ 22870 31410; fax 22870 31412; www.miloscamping.gr; Arhiva-dolimni; sites per adult/tent €6/4, bungalows €70) This camping ground has excellent facilities, including a restaurant, bar and bike rental. It's 4.5km east of Adamas; to get there, follow the signs along the waterfront from the central square or take the bus (see p207).

Hotel Delfini (☎ 22870 22001; fax 22870 22294; d incl breakfast €60; 🆒) This is a charming place with charming owners, run with old-fashioned courtesy. Rooms are comfy, clean and with good facilities. It's along to the left of the ferry quay, and is tucked in behind the Lagada Beach Hotel.

Portiani Hotel (☎ 22870 22940; www.portiani milos.com; s/d incl buffet breakfast €75/120; 🅿 🆒) The port's main waterfront hotel is right next to the square, but the fine rooms have a pleasant air of seclusion, and are worth the price, if you want all mod cons, including a lift. The upper balconies have great views. The buffet breakfast features delicious local products.

Villa Helios (☎ 22870 22258; fax 22870 23974; heaton.theologitis@utanet.at; apt €80-85; 🈀 mid-May–mid-Oct; 🆒) In an unbeatable location, high above the port, are these stylish, beautifully furnished, apartments for two or four people. New apartments were added in 2005.

Lagada Beach Hotel (☎ 22870 23411; fax 22870 23416; s incl breakfast €48-80, d incl breakfast €60-100, apt €120; 🅿 🆒 🈁)To the left of the ferry quay and dominating the fairly scrappy Lagada Beach is this big complex of resort-style rooms. They are functional and well-equipped and the newer rooms are quite swish.

Eating

I Milos (☎ 22870 22210; dishes €2.50-8) At the far end of the line of waterfront cafés and tavernas in the main square is this likeable place. It offers breakfast (€4.10 to €6.20) and is great for coffee. Lunch dishes include pizzas and pastas. The sweet of tooth should try the *lukumadhes* (fried balls of dough flavoured with cinnamon and served with syrup).

Flisvos (☎ 22870 22275; dishes €4.50-7) Fish is by the kilogram at this excellent waterfront taverna, to the right of the ferry quay. It serves good charcoal-grilled Greek specialities without fuss. Salads are crisp and fresh and the cheese and mushroom pies are delicious.

Aragosta (☎ 22870 22292; dishes €14-27) Top place, top food, top prices; but worth the experience; This stylish place is just up the first stairway above the waterfront. If you're in the mood for breast of duck with figs in a black cherry sauce (€16), or a layered seafood lasagne (€14), this is for you. Desserts are scrumptious; go for the chocolate and lime mousse. Aragosta is also one of the best local lounge-music café-bars around.

There's a terrific bakery and a cake shop with mouth-watering fare just round from the main square on the left-hand side of the road.

Entertainment

Halfway up the first staircase along from the ferry quay, near Aragosta, are a couple of popular music bars including Ilori and Vipera Lebetina, playing disco, pop and Greek music during July and August.

Akri (☎ 22870 22064) Further uphill, opposite Villa Helios, this is in a beautiful location with a fine terrace overlooking the port. Music favours freestyle, funk, and Latin. Upstairs is an elegant gallery selling superb glass jewellery, paintings, pottery and sculpture, many by island artists.

PLAKA & TRYPITI ΠΛΑΚΑ & ΤΡΥΠΗΤΗ

Plaka, 5km uphill from Adamas, is a typical Cycladic town with white houses and labyrinthine lanes. It merges with the settlement of Trypiti to the south and rises above a sprawl of converging settlements, yet has a distinctive and engaging character.

Plaka is built on the site of Ancient Milos, which was destroyed by the Athenians and rebuilt by the Romans.

Both Plaka and Trypiti have *domatia*; ask at tavernas.

Sights & Activities

The **archaeology museum** (☎ 22870 21629; admission €3; 🈀 8.30am-3pm Tue-Sun) is in Plaka, just downhill from the bus turnaround. It's in a handsome old building and contains some riveting exhibits, including a plaster cast of *Venus de Milo* that was made by Louvre craftsmen – as a sort of Venus de Mea Culpa perhaps. Best of all is a perky little herd of tiny bull figurines from the Late-Cycladic period.

The **Milos Folk & Arts Museum** (☎ 22870 21292; ☽ 10am-2pm & 6-9pm Tue-Sat, 10am-2pm Sun & Mon) has fascinating exhibits, including traditional costumes, woven goods and embroidery. Old photographs and domestic artefacts add colour to island culture. It's signposted from the bus turnaround in Plaka.

At the bus turnaround, go right for the path to the **Frankish Kastro** built on the ancient acropolis and offering panoramic views of most of the island. The 13th-century church, **Thalassitras**, is inside the walls.

There are some Roman ruins near Trypiti, including Greece's only Christian **catacombs** (☎ 22870 21625; admission free; ☽ 8am-7pm Tue-Sun). Stay on the bus towards Trypiti and get off at a T-junction by a big signpost indicating the way. Follow the road down for about 500m to where a track (signed) goes off to the right. This leads to the rather forlorn, but somehow thrilling spot where a farmer found the Venus de Milo in 1820; you can't miss the huge sign. A short way further along the track is the well-preserved **ancient theatre**, which hosts the **Milos Festival** every July. Back on the surfaced road, head downhill to reach the 1st-century catacombs. A stepped path leads down from the road past a small cave, then on down to the well-lit main chamber with its side galleries that contained the tombs. Take plenty of drinking water.

Eating

Arhontoula (☎ 22870 21384; dishes €3.60-9) All the family are busy at this cheerful and popular restaurant. It's just along the main street from the bus turnaround in Plaka and does great *mezedes*, main dishes of meat and fish, and fresh salads.

Utopia Café (☎ 22870 23678) One of best views in the Cyclades can be enjoyed from the cool terrace of Utopia. Head down the narrow alley opposite Arhontoula and prepare to have your breath taken away.

Methysmeni Politia (☎ 22870 23100; dishes €4.50-12) Halfway down the road to the catacombs, and a welcome break on your way back up, is this reliable and popular taverna. It offers a good selection of Greek dishes, and pastas.

AROUND MILOS

The village of **Klima**, below Trypiti and the catacombs, was the port of ancient Milos. Whitewashed buildings, with coloured doors and balconies, have boat houses on the ground floor and living quarters above.

Plathiena is a lovely sandy beach below Plaka, to the north. On the way to Plathiena you can visit the fishing villages of **Areti** and **Fourkovouni**. **Mandrakia** is a fishing hamlet northeast of Plaka. The beaches of **Provatas** and **Paleohori**, on the south coast, are long and sandy, and Paleohori has hot springs. **Pollonia**, on the north coast, is a fishing village-cum-resort with a beach and *domatia*. The boat to Kimolos departs here.

KIMOLOS ΚΙΜΩΛΟΣ

pop 769

This small island lies just northeast of Milos. It receives a steady trickle of visitors, especially day-trippers arriving from Pollonia, on the northeastern tip of Milos. There are *domatia*, tavernas, bars and pleasant beaches. *Domatia* owners meet ferries. Expect to pay single/double rates of about €35/50.

The boat docks at the port of **Psathi**, from where it's 3km to the pretty capital of **Horio**. The taverna **To Kyma** (☎ 22870 51001; dishes €3.50-7) is fine for Greek standards.

There's no petrol station on Kimolos so, if bringing a car or moped from Milos, make sure you've got enough fuel.

Beaches can be reached by caïque from Psathi. At the centre of the island is the 364m-high cliff on which sits the fortress of **Paleokastro**.

Getting There & Away

Boats go daily to and from Pollonia on Milos, departing from Kimolos at 8am, 10am, 1.15pm, 5.30pm and 10pm (see p207 for more details on boats to Kimolos).

There are daily boats to Sifnos (€4.40, 1½ hours) and Serifos (€5.90, 3¾ hours). There are six weekly boats to Piraeus (€17.50, eight hours) and Kythnos (€9.10, three hours).

There are three ferries weekly to Adamas (€4.65, one hour) and Syros (€11, five hours) and two weekly to Folegandros (€6, 1½ hours) and Sikinos (€6, 2½ hours).

Two weekly ferries go to Paros (€8.70, 4½ hours) and Santorini (€13.20 3½ hours).

CYCLADES

SIFNOS ΣΙΦΝΟΣ

pop 2900

Beautiful Sifnos (*see*-fnoss) hides its assets from passing ferries behind a curtain of high barren hills. Beyond all this, however, is a fascinating and abundant landscape of terraced olive groves and almond trees, with oleanders in the valleys and juniper and aromatic herbs covering the hillsides. There are numerous dovecotes, whitewashed houses and chapels. Sifnos is a sizeable island and has a number of substantial settlements. Plenty of old paths link the villages and walking on Sifnos is particularly satisfying. The Anavasi map series *Topo 25/10.25 Aegean Cyclades/Sifnos* is useful for footpath details.

During the Archaic period the island was very wealthy because of its gold and silver resources, but by the 5th century BC the mines were exhausted and Sifnos' fortunes were reversed. The island has a long tradition of pottery making, basket weaving and cooking.

SIFNOS

0 _____ 4 km
0 _____ 2 miles

To Serifos (24km);
Kythnos (63km);
Paros (74km);
Piraeus (146km)

AEGEAN SEA

Cape Heronisos

Heronisos

Agios Dimos

476m

Kamares Bay

Kamares

Sifnos

Ano Petali

Artemonas

Kastro

Apollonia

Seralia

Kato Petali

Katavati

Exambelas

680m

Moni Profiti Ilia

To Milos (50km);
Santorini (105km)

Moni Hrysopigis

Faros

Fasolou Beach

Hrysopigis Beach

Vathi

Platys Gialos

Vathi Bay

201m

Platys Gialos Bay

Cape Kondou

Kitriani

Getting There & Away

FAST BOAT & CATAMARAN

There is a daily catamaran to Piraeus (€32.90, 2¾ hours), four weekly to Kythnos (€11.20, 1¼ hours) and one daily to both Serifos (€10.90, 20 minutes) and Milos (€11.70, 45 minutes).

FERRY

There are daily ferries to Milos (€5.90 two hours), Piraeus (€16.70, five hours) via Serifos (€5.40, one hour) and Kythnos (€7.50, 2½ hours). There are three ferries weekly to Kimolos (€5.40, 1½ hours), Folegandros (€7.50, four hours), Sikinos (€8.90, five hours) and Santorini (€11.20, six hours), and two weekly to Paros (€4, two hours) and Syros (€7.80, 5½ hours).

Getting Around

Frequent buses link Apollonia with the following: Kamares (€1), with some services continuing on to Artemonas (€1), Kastro (€1), Vathi (€1.50), Faros (€1.20) and Platys Gialos (€1.50).

Meropi Taverna (☎ 22840 31672) runs a taxiboat service to anywhere on the island. **Taxis** (☎ 22840 31347) hover around the port and Apollonia's main square. Representative fares from Kamares are, to Apollonia (€5.50), to Platys Gialos (€10), and to Vathi (€11). Cars can be hired from **Stavros Hotel** (☎ 22840 31641) in Kamares, and from **Apollo Rent a Car** (☎ 22840 32237) in Apollonia, for €35 to €40.

KAMARES ΚΑΜΑΡΕΣ

The port of Kamares (kah-*mah*-rehs) has a resort atmosphere, not least because of its large beach. There are lots of waterfront cafés and tavernas and a very good mix of shops, from food stores to craft shops. The bus stop is by the tamarisk trees just past the inland end of the ferry quay.

Information

There are toilets near the tourist office, plus an ATM booth that is accessed by card insert, and has the best air-conditioning in the Cyclades.

Municipal tourist office (☎ 22840 31977/31975; ☿ 10.30am-2.30pm & 5-11pm Easter-Oct, 10am-11pm Sun-Tue & Thu, 11am-5pm Wed, 10am-10pm Fri & Sat Sep-Easter) Opposite the bus stop is this very helpful office. Opening times may vary depending on boat arrivals and

CYCLADES

the office does open for late boats. It can find accommodation, for a refundable €3, anywhere on the island, has a luggage storage (per item €0.50) and sells a useful clutch of information sheets about the island, walking trips, bus schedules and ferry times.

Yamas Café Bar Internet (☎ 22840 31202; per hr €5) Halfway along the waterfront. and up some steps. It also serves light snacks and breakfasts.

Sleeping & Eating

Domatia owners rarely meet boats, and in high season it's best to book ahead.

Camping Makis (☎ 22840 32366; www.makis camping.gr; sites per adult/tent €6/3, r from €40; P 🖳) There's a relaxed, friendly atmosphere at this pleasant site just behind the beach and 600m north of the port. It has an outdoor café, a barbecue area, mini-market, laundry and shaded sites. There's Internet access for €6 per hour.

Hotel Afroditi (☎ 22840 31704; www.hotel -afroditi.gr; s/d incl breakfast €55/70; P 🞨) A gem of a place, with charming family owners, Afroditi is right behind the beach, beyond Hotel Boulis. Rooms are very pleasant; there are sea views to the front and mountain views to the rear.

Simeon (☎ 22840 31652; fax 22840 31035; s/d/apt €40/45/90) Simeon's highly-placed upper front rooms are the ones to go for; they're small, but the balconies have exhilarating views down across the port and along the beach to soaring mountains beyond. It's high above the waterfront, up steepish steps. You can't miss the sign.

Stavros Hotel (☎ 22840 31641/33383; www.sifnos travel.com; s/d/tr €50/60/65; 🞨) It's right on the midwaterfront and has had a sparkling refurbishment in recent years. Rooms are comfy and bright and are a reasonable size. Attached to the hotel is an information office that can arrange car hire and has a book exchange.

Hotel Kamari (☎ 22840 33383; www.sifnostravel .com; s/d/tr €40/50/55) Owned by the same family as Stravros, this place has similar prices and standards. It's 400m up the road to Apollonia.

Argyris (☎ 22840 32352; mains €3.80-7.80) On the other side of the bay to the main waterfront is this popular restaurant. It has a terrific waterside location and offers several delicious treats, such as starters of mushrooms and feta, and mains of lamb in wine. The house wine is more than satisfactory.

There are several reasonably priced waterfront eateries serving good Greek staples for about €4 to €8; they include the cheerful family run Posidonia; a good choice where you can get a full breakfast for €5.80.

APOLLONIA ΑΠΟΛΛΩΝΙΑ

The engaging capital of Sifnos is situated on the edge of a plateau 5km uphill from the port.

The stop for buses to and from Kamares is on Apollonia's busy central square, where the post office is located. Because of congestion, all other buses pick up passengers about 50m further on, at a T-junction. There is a big car park at the entrance to Apollonia. Initial impressions of the village are of frantic traffic, but step off the main road onto the pedestrian thoroughfare behind the museum and Apollonia is transformed.

There is an Alpha Bank (with ATM) and the Piraeus Bank and National Bank of Greece, both with ATMs are just round the corner on the road to Artemonas; the police are another 50m beyond. **The Bookshop** (☎ 22840 33523), just down from the bus stop, has newspapers and a good selection of books in various languages.

The interesting little **Museum of Popular Art** (☎ 22840 33730; admission €1; ☯ 10am-2pm & 7.30-11.30pm Tue-Sun), on the central square and just opposite the post office, contains a splendid confusion of old costumes, pots, textiles and photographs that could keep you going for hours.

Sleeping & Eating

Mrs Dina Rooms (☎ 22840 31125, 69455 13318; s/d €30/45) These pleasant rooms are great value and include views towards the village of Kastro, bright flowers everywhere and a kindly welcome. They are located a couple of hundred metres along the road south towards Vathi and Platys Gialos.

Gerontios Rooms (☎ 22840 32316; s/d/tr €40/45/53) Another fine choice, these flower-bedecked rooms are set high above the village centre and have wide views to the village of Kastro. Again you could not wish for a more cheerful and kindly welcome. You get there from the centre of Apollonia by heading north towards Ano Petali.

Hotel Sifnos (☎ 22840 31624; s/d/tr €50/70/80) Right at the heart of the pretty main street is this family-run hotel with adjoining taverna. It has well-kept rooms and the taverna offers tasty Greek dishes (€5 to €8.20).

Apostoli to Koutouki (☎ 22840 31186; dishes €5-9) Fish is by the kilogram at this long-established place on the main pedestrianised street. It also serves meat and chicken specialities.

AROUND SIFNOS
Sights & Activities
Not to be missed is the walled cliff-top village of **Kastro**, 3km from Apollonia. The former capital, it is a magical place of buttressed alleyways and whitewashed houses. It has a small **archaeological museum** (☎ 22840 31022; admission free; ☽ 8.30am-3pm Tue-Sun).

A pleasant path circumnavigates the village. Midway round the northern side, above the glittering sea, is the charming little art workshop of **Maximos** (☎ 22840 33692) whose speciality is hand-made jewellery in original gold and silver motifs. Prices for these works of art start at about €6 and are far below the usual charged for work of this quality. There is also accommodation here (see below).

The attractive resort of **Platys Gialos**, 10km south of Apollonia, has a great sandy beach, entirely backed by tavernas, *domatia* and shops. The bus terminates at the beach's southwestern end. **Vathi**, on the west coast, is a lovely sandy bay with several tavernas. **Faros** is a cosy little fishing hamlet with a couple of nice beaches nearby, such as the little beach of **Fasolou**, up the steps and over the headland from the bus stop.

Sleeping & Eating
KASTRO
There are several *domatia* here, ask at shops and cafés.

Windmill Room (☎ 22840 33045; ☽ Apr-Sep; d €40) For something different, just before the entrance to Kastro, there's this place, built into a little cliff and with a charming owner who lives in the house above. There's a 25% reduction for more than one night.

Maximos (☎ 22840 33692; €45) There's another quirky little room at Maximos (see above): a tiny two-person 'terrace' with unbeatable sea views.

To Astro (☎ 22840 31476; mains €4-7) The first taverna you come to in Kastro and it certainly

lives up to its name (meaning 'the Star'). It's one of those Greek tavernas that you dream about. Lovingly run by the owner-cook it offers delicious island dishes including octopus with olives, lamb in traditional Sifniot style and many other delights.

PLATYS GIALOS
Although there are plenty of sleeping places here, most cater for package tourists.

Camping Platys Gialos (☎ 22840 71286; sites per adult/tent €5/4) Those with tents can try this reasonable site in an olive grove, about 700m from the beach.

Platys Gialos Hotel (☎ 22840 71324; fax 22840 71325; s/d €140/160; P ✖) In an enviable position overlooking the far end of the beach, this peaceful hotel has lovely terraces and a garden area. Rooms have imaginative, old fashioned fittings. It has a loyal clientele, so it's wise to book well in advance.

Angeliki Rooms (☎ 22840 71288; d/tr €47/55) This has pleasant rooms just back from the bus terminus, and right on the beach.

To Koutouki (☎ 22840 71330; dishes €5-9) Run by the family that has the same-name place in Apollonia. Fish is by the kilogram and is prepared with style. To Koutouki is on Platys Gialos beach.

VATHI
There are several sleeping options here, for ordinary mortals and for the mega rich alike.

Areti Studios (☎ 22840 71191; d/apt €50/80) is a great choice. It place occupies a handsome garden, rooms are fresh and bright and the welcome is friendly. If you are driving, the approach is down a rough, and at times very narrow, track that goes off left just before the main road ends. Grit your teeth.

Elies Resort (☎ 22840 34000; www.eliesresorts .com; d €330, apt €450-900; P ✖ ⬚ ⬚) One of Greece's classiest stopovers, this opened in 2004 to coincide with the Athens Olympics. The huge complex, with gorgeous pool and gourmet restaurant, is subtly merged into the hillside above Vathi Bay and spills down to a beach. Rooms here are sumptuous; apartments are virtually houses, with the most expensive having their own terrace pool. Enjoy...

Vathi has a good choice of beachfront tavernas offering Greek standards.

SERIFOS ΣΕΡΙΦΟΣ

pop 1414

Serifos (*seh-ri-fohs*) is eye-catching from the start, not least because of its fabulous *hora*, a scribble of white houses crowning a high and rocky peak, 2km to the north of Livadi. It serves as a dramatic backdrop to the port. The island is barren and rocky, but has a few pockets of greenery that are the result of tomato and vine cultivation. There are some pleasant paths linking various villages; the Anavasi map series *Topo 25/10.26 Aegean Cyclades/Serifos* is useful.

Getting There & Away

Three times weekly a catamaran runs to Sifnos (€10.80, 25 minutes), Milos (€13.10, 1¼ hours) and Piraeus (€29.20, 2¼ hours).

There is a daily ferry to Piraeus (€14.90, 4½ hours), Sifnos (€5.40, one hour), Milos (€6.50, two hours) and Kimolos (€7.40, 2½ hours).

Four times weekly the Piraeus ferry stops at Kythnos (€6.90, 1½ hours), and twice weekly boats go to Paros (€7.60, three hours), Syros (€8.80, two to four hours) and Folegandros (€9.60, five hours).

There are weekly boats to Santorini (€15.20, seven hours), Ios (€11.40, six hours) and Sikinos (€10.80, five hours).

Getting Around

There are frequent buses between Livadi and Hora (€1, 15 minutes); a timetable is posted at the bus stop by the yacht quay. Vehicles can be hired from Krinas Travel in Livadi.

LIVADI ΛΙΒΑΔΙ

pop 537

This unassuming and pleasant port is at the end of an elongated bay. In spite of growing popularity there's still a reassuring feeling that the modern world has not entirely taken over. Just over the headland that rises from the ferry quay lies the fine, tamarisk-fringed beach at **Livadakia**. A walk further south over the next headland, **Karavi Beach** is the unofficial clothes-optional beach.

Information

There is an Alpha Bank (with ATM), on the waterfront and an ATM under the Bakery sign opposite the yacht quay. In previous

years there was an official tourist information office that was open mid-July to August on the waterfront, but opening has been uncertain in recent years.

The post office is midway along the road that runs inland from opposite the bus stop and then bends sharply right.

Krinas Travel (☎ 22810 51488; www.serifos-travel .com) Just where the ferry quay joins the waterfront road, this helpful agency sells ferry tickets and organises car (per day €50) and scooter (per day €16) hire.

Malabar Café (☎ 22810 52333; per 30 min €2) There's a single Internet station here, in the complex behind the middle of the waterfront. Internet access is accompanied by loud music and robust pool playing over your left shoulder.

Port police (☎ 22810 51470) Up steps from the quay.

Sleeping & Eating

Coralli Camping (☎ 22810 51500; fax 22810 51073; www .coralli.gr; adult/tent €6/5, bungalows s/d €45/55; P) This well-equipped site, shaded by tall eucalypts, is just a step away from sandy Livadakia Beach. Bungalows have mountain or sea view. There's also a restaurant and minimarket, and a minibus meets all ferries.

Hotel Areti (☎ 22810 51479; fax 22810 51547; s/d/tr €50/65/75) One of the best bets on Serifos. It has been refurbished recently and has bright clean rooms with well-thought out fittings. Areti is high above the ferry quay and is best reached up the steps that lead from the landward end of the quay over to Livadakia beach, or up a dirt road leading off left from halfway along the ferry quay.

Alexandros-Vassilia (☎ 22810 51119; fax 22810 51903; s/d €50/66) is a family-run complex of rooms fronted by a taverna and is right on the beach front of Livadakia. Rooms and studios are a good size and are clean and well equipped, with studios having cooking facilities. Good-sized balconies and plenty of tumbling greenery enhances the surroundings. The taverna does sturdy Greek staples for €4.50 to €9.

Eliza (☎ 22810 51763; fax 22810 51763; apt €65-85; 🏖) Set back about 80m from the waterfront on the road to Hora, these big reasonable rooms, with cooking facilities enjoy the benefit of a colourful, leafy garden.

Yacht Club Serifos (☎ 22810 51888) There's a terrific ambience at this waterfront café-bar that does breakfast for €4.50 to €11 and snacks and sandwiches for €2.80 to €5.50. Music ranges from lounge by day, to mainstream, rock, disco and funk late into the night. Enquire at the Yacht Club about diving trips and courses.

Also recommended for reliable Greek standards; both on the waterfront:
Stamatis (☎ 22810 51309; mains €3.50-7)
Taverna Takis (☎ 22810 51159; mains €5-11.50)

Entertainment

Metalleio (☎ 22810 51755) Most stylish of all, this is tucked away along the parallel inland road to the waterfront. It has one of the best playlists around and features an eclectic array of sounds from around the world, including jazz, funk, Afro, Asian groove, Latin, tribal and hip hop. Live acts such as Mode Plagal are featured, all in a very hip lounge bar landscape. It opens about 9pm and keeps going until the early hours.

There are a couple of fairly loud music bars such as the Malabar Café (opposite) and, in the same complex, the Captain Hook Club. The Yacht Club Serifos is still one of the coolest venues.

HORA ΧΩΡΑ

The Hora of Serifos spills like a snow drift from the summit of a rocky hill above Livadi and is one of the most striking of Cycladic capitals. Ancient steps lead up from Livadi, though they are fragmented by the snaking road that links the two. You can walk up, but in the heat of summer, going up by bus may be the wiser decision. Just up from the bus terminus, steps climb into the wonderful maze of Hora proper, and lead to the charming main square, watched over by the imposing neoclassical town hall. From the square, narrow alleys and more steps lead ever upwards to the remnants of the ruined 15th-century **Venetian Kastro**; an eagle's nest if ever there was one.

Back downhill, there's a **post office** just up from the bus turnaround.

Hora has a small **archaeological museum** (☎ 22810 51138; admission free; 🕑 8.30am-3pm Tue-Sun) displaying fragments of mainly Hellenic and Roman sculpture excavated from the *kastro*. Exhibits are sparse, and the museum tiny, but it is a pleasure to visit. Panels in Greek and English spell out fascinating details, including the legend of Perseus. There's a **folk museum** (☎ 22810 51181; 🕑 6-9pm Mon-Fri, 9am-noon & 6-9pm Sat & Sun Jul-Aug) a long way down the steps to Livadi, on the lower edge of Hora. Entrance is free, but donations are welcomed.

There is a pleasant walk on a fine cobbled pathway that starts just above the archeological museum and leads up the mountain to the little church of **Aghios Georgios**. The views are superb.

Sleeping & Eating

There are only a few small rooms in Hora. Ask at the local shops.

Stou Stratou (☎ 22810 52566; plates €5.50-14) In the main square are the tables of this bar-café where the tradition of the *mezedopoleio* is alive and well. There's tasty *mezedes* (€3.50 to €4.50) and choices from a vegetarian plate to a mixed plate of Cretan smoked pork, ham, cheese, salami, stuffed vine leaves, feta, potato, tomatoes and egg, that will keep two people more than happy. Also available are breakfasts, ice creams, delicious sweets, cocktails and a range of drinks. There's an added pleasure in the stylish menu – more of a booklet – that features the work of famous artists as well as excerpts from a number of writers, including George Seferis, Baudelaire, Racine and Joni Mitchell.

I Platia (☎ 22810 51261; dishes €4.50-10) Just by the bus turnaround, this is an ideal place for a great night out. It has a fine bar area and an outside terrace. Delicious *mezedes* and local dishes are a speciality and it does an excellent choice of breakfasts. There's music in the bar, and occasional live sessions of Greek traditional music, including *rembetika*.

CYCLADES

AROUND SERIFOS

About an hour's walk north of Livadi (or a shorter drive) along a track (negotiable by motorbike) is **Psili Ammos Beach**. A path from Hora heads north for about 4km to the pretty village of **Kendarhos** (also called Kallitsos), from where you can continue by road for another 3km to the 17th-century fortified **Moni Taxiarhon**, which has impressive 18th-century frescoes. The walk from the town to the monastery takes about two hours. You will need to take food and water as there are no facilities in Kendarhos.

KYTHNOS ΚΥΘΝΟΣ

pop 1700

Few foreigners discover the muted charms of Kythnos (*kee*-thnos); but once you escape from the port, the island reveals those charms, not least in its pleasantly relaxed way of life. Kythnos is more of a weekend destination for mainlanders, but also attracts a regular flotilla of expensive private cruisers. Their glossy arrival makes for

much evening entertainment on the quay; a bigger vessel shoulders in amongst its smaller rivals, only to be quickly dwarfed by the next even bigger arrival.

The main settlements are the port of Merihas and the capital Hora (or Kythnos). There's an Emboriki bank (with an ATM) on the road above the waterfront, and an ATM on the waterfront just past the flight of steps as you come from the ferry quay. **Antonios Larentzakis Travel Agency** (☎ 22810 32104/32291) sells ferry tickets, can arrange accommodation and rents cars and motorbikes. It's up the flight of steps near Ostria Taverna. Hora has the island's post office and **police** (☎ 22810 31201). The **port police** (☎ 22810 32290) are on the waterfront in Merihas.

Getting There & Away

FAST BOAT & CATAMARAN

There are three services weekly to Piraeus (€23, 1½ hours), Sifnos (€11.20, 1¼ hours), Milos (€20, 2½ hours) and Serifos (€13, 45 minutes).

A once weekly catamaran goes to Mykonos (€19, 1¾ hours) and to Tinos (€19, 2¼ hours).

FERRY

There are at least two boats to Piraeus daily (€11.30, 2½ hours). Most services coming from Piraeus continue to Serifos (€6.50, 1½ hours), Sifnos (€7.10, 2½ hours), Kimolos (€9.10, three hours) and Milos (€9.50, 3½ hours).

There are six weekly ferries to Lavrio (€7.30, 3½ hours), three weekly to Syros (€8.70, two hours) and two weekly to Kea (€5.40, 1¼ hours), Folegandros (€12.90, six hours), Sikinos (€14.20, seven hours) and Santorini (€17.70, eight hours).

A ferry runs once weekly to Andros (€10, five hours).

Getting Around

There are regular buses from Merihas to Dryopida (€1), continuing to Kanala (€1.90) or Hora (€1.10). Less regular services run to Loutra (€1.90). The buses supposedly meet the ferries, but usually they leave from the turn-off to Hora in Merihas.

Taxis (☎ 69447 43791) are a better bet, except at siesta time. It's €10 to Hora and €6 to Dryopida. There are, however, only a few taxis on the island.

KYTHNOS

0 — 4 km
0 — 2 miles

To Syros (74km);
Tinos (81km);
Mykonos (98km)

Cape Kefalos

AEGEAN SEA

To Lavrio (48km)

▲ 297m

Loutra

Kythnos

▲ 308m

Fikiado Beach   Apokrousi Beach   Hora

Episkopi Beach

To Piraeus (96km)

Merihas

Dryopida

Cape Tzoulis

Flambouria Beach

▲ 302m

To Kimolos (41km);
Serifos (52km);
Sifnos (63km);
Milos (85km);
Santorini (155km)

Kanala

Dimitrios Beach

Cape Berou

MERIHAS ΜΕΡΙΧΑΣ
pop 289

Merihas (*meh*-ree-hass) does not have a lot going for it other than a bit of waterfront life and a slightly grubby beach. But it's a reasonable base and has most of the island's accommodation. There are better beaches within walking distance north of the quay (turn left facing inland) at **Episkopi** and **Apokrousi**.

Sleeping & Eating

Domatia owners usually meet boats and there are a number of signs along the waterfront advertising rooms; alternatively enquire at Larentzakis Travel Agency (opposite). A lot of places block-book during the season and there is an element of reluctance towards one-night stopovers. You should definitely book ahead for July and August.

Kythnos Hotel (☎ 22810 32247; d/tr €55/70) It's essential to book ahead here in high season and at weekends. It's the town's main hotel and has good rooms and a fine location above the harbour.

Ostria (☎ 22810 32263; dishes €4.50-12) On the waterfront near the quay, Ostria has reasonable Greek fare. Seafood is by the kilo.

Taverna to Kandouni (☎ 22810 32220; dishes €4-12) Near the port police on the waterfront, Kandouni specialises in grilled meats; it also has rooms to let for about €60 for a double.

AROUND KYTHNOS

The capital, **Hora** (also known as Kythnos) is a pleasant enough place, but struggles to match the charm of many Cycladic capitals. From Hora there's a pleasant 6km walk south to **Dryopida**, a picturesque town of red-tiled roofs and winding streets set within a gentle landscape of terraced fields. You can either walk the 6km back by road to Merihas or catch a bus or taxi.

There are good **beaches** at **Flambouria** about 2.5km south of Merihas, and near **Kanala** on the southeast coast.

KEA ΚΕΑ (ΤΖΙΑ)

pop 2417

Kea does not seem to offer travellers much up front, but this is an island that wears its many charms quietly and its distant prospect of bare hills is belied by lovely green valleys filled with orchards, olive groves,

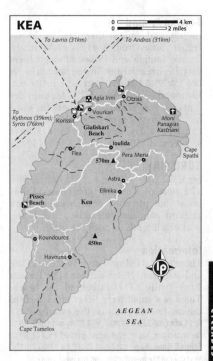

almond and oak trees. The main settlements on the island are the port of Korissia, and the delightful capital, Ioulida, about 5km inland. There are several fine beaches and some excellent signposted footpaths. Local people use the name Tzia for their island.

The most northerly island of the Cyclades, Kea is more often associated with mainland Attica and has few ferry links to the other islands. It's a popular daytrip, weekend and summer escape for Athenians. Boats here are usually packed on Fridays and you should avoid the Sunday night ferry to Lavrio, unless you enjoy controlled rioting. If you do plan a Sunday departure make sure you get your ticket before Friday.

Getting There & Away

Services connect Kea with Lavrio (€5.90, 1¼ hours) on the mainland at least twice daily. Three weekly ferries go to Kythnos (€5.80, 1¼ hours) and on to Syros (€8.20, four hours). One weekly boat goes to Andros (€7.80, six hours).

Getting Around

In July and August there are, in theory, regular buses from Korissia to Vourkari, Otzias, Ioulida and Pisses although there may be irregularities in the schedules. A **taxi** (☎ 22880 21021/228) may be a better bet, to Ioulida (€5) especially. Motorcycle-rental and car-rental is well above the usual high-season prices on other islands. Expect to pay, per day, anything from €25 for a scooter and €50 for a car.

KORISSIA ΚΟΡΗΣΣΙΑ

pop 555

The port of Korissia (koh-ree-*see*-ah) is bland, but there are enough eateries and cafés to pass the time. The north-facing port beach tends to catch the wind.

Information

There is an ATM next door to the Art Café and also near Hotel Karthea. The Piraeus Bank (with ATM) is behind the beach. There is a small ferry ticket office next to the car-rental agency on the waterfront.
Art Café (☎ 22880 21181; ⏰ 8.30am-midnight), On the waterfront; has Internet access (per half-hour €3.50).
Stegali Bookshop (☎ 22880 21435; fax 22880 21012) Next door to the tourist office, this is a great source of information; the selection of books is very good too. There is an ATM next to Stegali Bookshop.
Tourist information office (☎ 22880 21500) The official tourist office, opposite the ferry quay, has lists of *domatia* in Greek, but not much more.

Sleeping & Eating

Domatia owners don't meet ferries. It's wise to book in high season and at weekends.
Hotel Brillante Zoi (☎ 22880 22685; www.hotel brillante.gr; s/d incl breakfast €90/105, apt incl breakfast €135-150) This very fine hotel has rooms with individual décor and handsome furnishings. It has a charming garden setting and is midway along the beach road, about 300m from the ferry quay. The hotel is only robbed of sea views by the presence of Hotel Tzia opposite.
Hotel Tzia (☎ 22880 21305; fax 22880 21140; s/d/tr €50/55/60; 🅿) A rather dull building owned by the municipality of Kea; but it has decent, clean rooms and an enviable location right on the beach.
Hotel Karthea (☎ 22880 21204; fax 22880 21417; s/d/tr €50/65/78) Utterly functional in both style and service, the Karthea is convenient

enough for the port and it's rooms are clean and comfortable. Those at the rear overlook a quiet garden area. There's no lift to the several floors. In 1974, the deposed colonels of the Greek Junta were said to have been imprisoned in the newly opened hotel for a short time. Enough said.

There are several tavernas along the waterfront, all dishing up fairly standard fare for about €3.50 to €7, with **Akri** (☎ 22880 21196) being one of the best. The **Art Café** (☎ 22880 21181) has a pleasant ambience and is great for people watching.

Kea has more supermarkets than most, all catering for the weekender influx as well as for local needs.

IOULIDA ΙΟΥΛΙΔΑ

pop 700

Ioulida (ee-oo-*lee*-tha) is a delightful scramble of narrow alleyways and rising lanes that lies along the rim of a natural amphitheatre amongst the hills. It was once a substantial settlement of ancient Greece, but few relics remain and even the **Venetian kastro** has been incorporated into private houses. The houses have red-tiled roofs like those of Dryopida on Kythnos.

The bus turnaround is on a square just at the edge of town. From the turnaround, an archway leads into the village. At a T-junction, a left turn leads, not too rewardingly, to what's left of the *kastro*. Turning right and uphill takes you into the more interesting heart of Ioulida proper. The post office is part-way up on the right.

Sights

Ioulida's **archaeological museum** (☎ 22880 22079; admission free; ⏰ 8.30am-3pm Tue-Sun) is just before the post office on the main thoroughfare. It houses some intriguing artefacts, mostly from Agia Irini (see opposite).

The famed **Kea Lion**, chiselled from slate in the 6th century BC, lies on the hillside beyond the last of the houses. Head uphill from the museum, and pass a junction with a board giving directions and times to Karthea, Otzias, Ellinika – and the Kea Lion, only a few hundred metres further on. Walk past the cemetery and the Lion, with its Mona Lisa smile, is just round the hillside. The smile may reflect the mythical tale of the Lion chasing rampaging nymphs from the island, because they were killing local women.

Sleeping & Eating

There are a few *domatia* in Ioulida, and several decent tavernas. Ask about rooms at tavernas.

Recommended eateries, both with good Greek dishes at about €4.50 to €10, with lamb and fresh fish costing more:

Estiatorio I Piatsa (☎ 22880 22195) Just inside the archway.

Kalofagadon (☎ 22880 22118) On the main square.

There's an excellent bakery, just past the post office.

AROUND KEA

The beach road from Korissia leads past **Gialiskari Beach** for 2.5km to where the waterfront quay at tiny **Vourkari** is lined with yachts and cafés. **Vourkariana Art Gallery** (☎ 22880 21458) is set back midwaterfront among the cafés and restaurants; it stages changing exhibitions of world-class art works over the summer.

Just across the bay from Vourkari are the truncated remains of the Minoan site of **Agia Irini**.

The road continues for another 3km to a fine sandy beach at **Otzias**. A dirt road continues beyond here for another 5km to the 18th-century **Moni Panagias Kastriani** (☎ 22880 24348), which has terrific views.

Pisses is the island's best beach and is 8km southwest of Ioulida. It is long and sandy, and backed by a verdant valley of orchards and olive groves, with rugged hills rising above.

Crete
Κρήτη

Crete is Greece's largest, most diverse and arguably most beautiful and fascinating island.

Crete's turbulent history is evident across the island, from the ruins of Minoan palaces and the fortresses built by successive invaders, to the cave that is the legendary birthplace of Zeus. The Venetian ports of Hania and Rethymno are two of Greece's most evocative cities.

Crete is defined by the diversity of its landscape. Spectacular mountain ranges are dotted with caves and sliced by dramatic gorges. The rugged interior is interspersed with vast plateaus and fertile plains. The east boasts Europe's only palm tree–forest beach and the south some of the most stunning beaches and isolated coves.

Cretans are proud and hospitable people who maintain their culture and customs, particularly their strong musical tradition and *mantinades,* the famous rhyming couplets. Throughout the island you will come across traditional mountain villages and agricultural settlements. The young might drive four-wheel-drives but you will still pass shepherds tending their flocks and come across men in traditional dress.

An abundance of fresh produce and the distinct Cretan cuisine – renowned for its life-prolonging qualities – makes Crete a foodie's dream.

Crete has has the dubious honour of hosting nearly a quarter of Greece's tourists. Much of the north coast has been commandeered by hotels and resorts, while cheap package tourism has spoilt many southern coastal villages that were once backpacker favourites.

HIGHLIGHTS

- **Alfresco Dining**
  Romantic dinners in Hania's Old Town (p246)

- **Minoan Magnificence**
  The Palace at Knossos (p233)

- **History Explored**
  The treasures in Iraklio's archaeological museum (p226)

- **Sparkling Seas**
  Scuba diving in Rethymno (p237)

- **Longest Trek**
  The Samaria Gorge (p253)

- **Stunning Beaches**
  Preveli and the southern Rethymno beaches (p244)

- **Chill-Out Spot**
  Kato Zakros (p270) in far-eastern Crete

- **POPULATION: 540,045**
- **AREA: 8335 SQ KM**

HISTORY

Although Crete has been inhabited since Neolithic times (7000–3000 BC), for most people its history begins with the Minoan civilisation. The glories of Crete's Minoan past remained hidden until British archaeologist Sir Arthur Evans made his dramatic discoveries at Knossos in the early 1900s. The term 'Minoan' was coined by Evans and derived from the King Minos of Greek mythology. Nobody knows what the Minoans called themselves.

Among the ruins unearthed by Evans were the famous Knossos frescoes. Artistically, the frescoes are superlative; the figures that grace them have a naturalism lacking in contemporary Cycladic figurines, ancient Egyptian artwork (which they resemble in certain respects), and the Archaic sculpture that came later. Compared with candle smoke–blackened Byzantine frescoes, the Minoan frescoes, with their fresh, bright colours, look as if they were painted yesterday (see the boxed text, below).

Early in the 3rd millennium BC an advanced people migrated to Crete and brought with them the art of metallurgy. Many elements of Neolithic culture lived on in the Early Minoan period (3000–2100 BC), but the Middle Minoan period (2100–1500 BC) saw the emergence of a society of unprecedented artistic, engineering and cultural achievement. It was during this time that the famous palace complexes were built at Knossos, Phaestos, Malia and Zakros.

Also during this time, the Minoans began producing their exquisite Kamares pottery (see Iraklio's archaeological museum, p226) and silverware, and became a maritime power trading with Egypt and Asia Minor.

Around 1700 BC the complexes were destroyed by an earthquake. Undeterred, the Minoans built bigger and better palaces on the sites of the originals, as well as new settlements in other parts of the island.

Around 1500 BC, when the Minoan civilisation was at its peak, the palaces were destroyed again, signalling the start of the Late Minoan period (1500–1100 BC). This destruction was probably caused by Mycenaean invasions, although the massive volcanic eruption on the island of Santorini (Thira) may also have been responsible. Knossos was the only palace to be salvaged. It was finally destroyed by fire around 1400 BC.

The Minoan civilisation was a hard act to follow. The war-orientated Dorians, who arrived in 1100 BC, were pedestrian by comparison. The 5th century BC found Crete, like the rest of Greece, divided into city-states. The glorious classical age of mainland Greece had little impact on Crete, and the Persians bypassed the island. It was

---

THE MYSTERIOUS MINOANS

Of the many finds at Knossos and other Minoan sites, it is the celebrated frescoes that have captured the imagination of experts and amateurs alike, shedding light on a civilisation hitherto a mystery. The message they communicate is of a society that was powerful, wealthy, joyful and optimistic.

Gracing the frescoes are graceful white-skinned women with elaborately coiffured glossy black locks, dressed in stylish gowns that reveal perfectly shaped breasts. The bronze-skinned men are tall, with tiny waists, narrow hips, broad shoulders and muscular thighs and biceps; the children are slim and lithe. The Minoans seemed to know how to enjoy themselves. They played board games, boxed and wrestled, played leap-frog over bulls and over one another, and performed bold acrobatic feats.

As well as being literate, they were religious, as frescoes and models of people partaking in rituals testify. The Minoans' beliefs, like many other aspects of their society, remain an enigma, but there is sufficient evidence to confirm that they worshipped a nature goddess, often depicted with serpents and lions. Male deities were distinctly secondary.

The frescoes suggest women enjoyed a respected position in society, leading religious rituals and participating in games, sports and hunting. Minoan society may have had its dark side, however. There is evidence of human sacrifice being practised on at least one occasion, although probably in response to an extreme external threat.

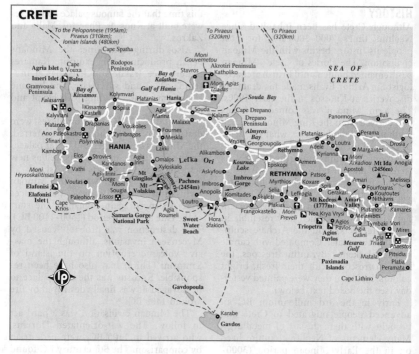

also ignored by Alexander the Great, so was never part of the Macedonian Empire.

By 67 BC, Crete had fallen to the Romans. The town of Gortyna in the south became the capital of Cyrenaica, a province that included large chunks of North Africa. Crete, along with the rest of Greece, became part of the Byzantine Empire in AD 395. In 1210 Crete was occupied by the Venetians, whose legacy is one of mighty fortresses, ornate public buildings and monuments, and handsome dwellings.

Despite the massive Venetian fortifications, which sprang up all over the island, by 1669 the whole of the mainland was under Turkish rule. The first uprising against the Turks was led by Ioannis Daskalogiannis in 1770. This set the precedent for many more insurrections, and in 1898 the Great Powers (Great Britain, France and Russia) intervened and made the island a British protectorate. It was not until the signing of the Treaty of Bucharest in 1913 that Crete officially became part of Greece, although the island's parliament had declared a de facto union in 1905.

Crete saw heavy fighting during WWII. Germany wanted the island as an air base, and on 20 May 1941 German parachutists landed on Crete. It was the start of 10 days of fierce fighting that became known as the Battle of Crete. For two days the battle hung in the balance until Germany won a bridgehead for its air force at Maleme, near Hania. The Allied forces of Britain, Australia, New Zealand and Greece then fought a valiant rearguard action which enabled the British Navy to evacuate 18,000 of the 32,000 Allied troops on the island. The German occupation of Crete lasted until the end of WWII.

During the war a large and active resistance movement was subject to heavy reprisals from the Germans. Many of Crete's mountain villages were bombed and their occupants shot. Among the bravest members of the local resistance were the so called 'runners' who relayed messages on foot over the mountains. One of these runners, George Psyhoundakis, wrote a book, *The Cretan Runner*, based on his experiences during the war.

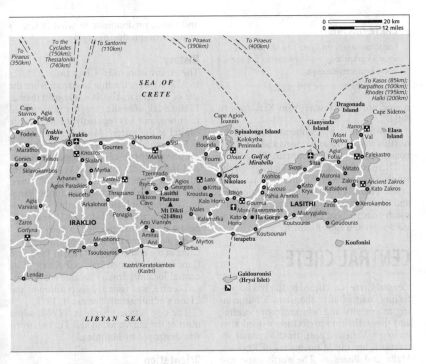

GETTING THERE & AWAY

This section provides an overview of air and boat options to and from Crete. For more comprehensive information, see the relevant sections under specific town entries.

Air

Crete has two international airports. The main and biggest one is at Iraklio and there is a smaller one at Hania. Sitia's small domestic airport was expanded and was due to start operating international charters in 2006. All three have flights to Athens and Thessaloniki; Iraklio also has flights to Rhodes.

Ferry

Crete has ports at Iraklio, Souda (for Hania), Rethymno, Agios Nikolaos, Sitia and Kissamos.

The following table lists the main connection to/from Crete by ferry, though these stop at different islands en route. Sailing times vary on some routes because of the type of craft used. These are high-season schedules; services are reduced by about half during low season.

MAIN FERRY CONNECTIONS TO CRETE

Origin	Destination	Duration	Fare	Frequency
Gythio	Kissamos	7hr	€22.10	5 weekly
Kalamata	Kissamos	10hr	€23.40	weekly
Kythira	Kissamos	4hr	€16.40	5 weekly
Piraeus	Agios Nikolaos	12hr	€30	3 weekly
	Souda (Hania)	5¾-9hr	€21.90	daily
	Souda (Hania)*	4½hr	€46.30	daily
	Iraklio	6-10hr	€29	daily
	Kissamos	19hr	€22	5 weekly
	Rethymno	10hr	€28.70	daily
	Sitia	14½hr	€30.50	3 weekly
Rhodes	Agios Nikolaos	12hr	€26.40	3 weekly
	Sitia	11hr	€26	3 weekly
Santorini	Iraklio	3¾hr	€16	4 weekly
Santorini	Iraklio*	1¾hr	€31	daily
Thessaloniki	Iraklio	23hr	€46.50	4 weekly

*high speed services

GETTING AROUND

A national highway skirts the north coast from Hania in the west to Agios Nikolaos in the east, and is being extended west to Kissamos and east to Sitia. Buses link the major northern towns from Kissamos to Sitia.

Less-frequent buses operate between the north-coast towns and resorts and the south coast, via the inland mountain villages.

There is nothing like the highway on the south coast; parts of this area have no roads at all. There is no road between Paleohora and Hora Sfakion, the steepest part of the south coast; a boat connects the two towns via Sougia and Agia Roumeli.

CENTRAL CRETE

Central Crete is occupied by the Iraklio prefecture, named after the island's burgeoning major city and administrative capital, and the Rethymno prefecture, named after its lovely Venetian port. Iraklio's major attractions are the Minoan sites of Knossos, Malia and Phaestos. The north coast east of Iraklio has been heavily exploited and, consequently, spoiled by package tourism, particularly around Hersonisos and Malia.

Rethymno has resorts spanning the coast to the east and one significant resort to the south, but much of the southern coast is still relatively unspoilt.

IRAKLIO ΗΡΑΚΛΕΙΟ
pop 130,914

Crete's capital Iraklio (ee-*rah*-klee-oh), also called Heraklion, is a bustling modern city and the fifth largest in Greece. Hectic, densely populated Iraklio lacks the architectural charm of Hania and Rethymno but is nonetheless a dynamic city. It has a lively city centre, chic boutiques, quality restaurants and buzzing cafés. Continuing redevelopment of the waterfront and new roads are helping to make the city more attractive. The port sees a constant procession of ferries, while charter jets bring thousands of visitors to Crete each year via Iraklio. Nearby the Minoan ruins of Knossos are the major drawcard, while further inland bucolic vistas of hillsides, full of olive trees

and vines, predominate in what is Crete's prime wine-producing region.

History

The Arabs who ruled Crete from AD 824 to AD 961 were the first to govern from the site of modern Iraklio. It was known then as El Khandak, after the moat that surrounded the town, and was reputedly the slave-trade capital of the eastern Mediterranean.

El Khandak became Khandakos after Byzantine troops finally dislodged the Arabs, and then Candia under the Venetians who ruled the island for more than 400 years. While the Turks quickly overran the Venetian defences at Hania and Rethymno, Candia's fortifications withstood a 21-year siege before finally surrendering in 1669.

Hania became the capital of independent Crete at the end of Turkish rule in 1898, and Candia was renamed Iraklio. Because of its central location, Iraklio became a commercial centre, and resumed its position as the island's administrative centre in 1971.

The city suffered badly in WWII, when most of the old Venetian and Turkish town was destroyed by bombing.

Orientation

Iraklio's two main squares are Plateia Eleftherias, near the museum, and Plateia Venizelou, recognisable by its famous landmark Morosini Fountain (better known as the Lion Fountain), inland from the old harbour. The city's major intersection (25 Avgoustou/1821 and Dikeosynis/Kalokerinou) is just south of Venizelou square.

The pedestrianised Dedalou, Koraï and Perdikari streets are the heart of the city's café and dining scene.

Iraklio has three intercity bus stations. The ferry port is 500m east of the old harbour. Iraklio's airport is 3km east of the city centre.

Information
BOOKSHOPS
Newsstand (☎ 28102 20135; Plateia Venizelou) Wide range of foreign press and magazines, and a selection of guidebooks, maps and books on Crete.

Road Editions (☎ 28103 44610; Handakos 29) A specialist travel bookshop with the best selection of maps.

EMERGENCY
Tourist Police (☎ 28102 83190; Dikeosynis 10; ⏰ 7am-10pm)

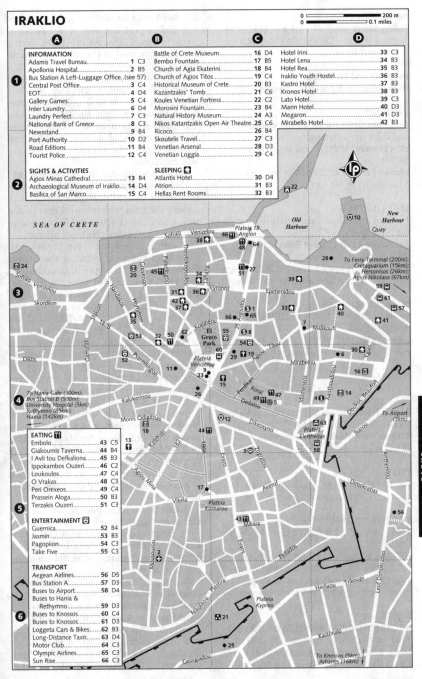

IRAKLIO

0 — 200 m
0 — 0.1 miles

INFORMATION
Adamis Travel Bureau.....................**1** C3
Apollonia Hospital.........................**2** B5
Bus Station A Left-Luggage Office..(see **57**)
Central Post Office........................**3** C4
EOT..**4** D4
Gallery Games..............................**5** C4
Inter Laundry...............................**6** D4
Laundry Perfect.............................**7** C3
National Bank of Greece..................**8** C3
Newsstand...................................**9** B4
Port Authority..............................**10** D2
Road Editions...............................**11** B4
Tourist Police...............................**12** C4

SIGHTS & ACTIVITIES
Agios Minas Cathedral....................**13** B4
Archaeological Museum of Iraklio....**14** D4
Basilica of San Marco.....................**15** C4
Battle of Crete Museum..................**16** D4
Bembo Fountain............................**17** B5
Church of Agia Ekaterini.................**18** B4
Church of Agios Titos.....................**19** C4
Historical Museum of Crete.............**20** B3
Kazantzakis' Tomb.........................**21** C6
Koules Venetian Fortress.................**22** C2
Morosini Fountain.........................**23** B4
Natural History Museum..................**24** A3
Nikos Katantzakis Open Air Theatre..**25** C6
Ricoco.......................................**26** B4
Skoutelis Travel............................**27** C3
Venetian Arsenal..........................**28** D3
Venetian Loggia............................**29** C4

SLEEPING
Atlantis Hotel..............................**30** D4
Atrion.......................................**31** B3
Hellas Rent Rooms........................**32** B3
Hotel Irini..................................**33** C3
Hotel Lena..................................**34** B3
Hotel Rea...................................**35** B3
Iraklio Youth Hostel......................**36** B3
Kastro Hotel................................**37** B3
Kronos Hotel...............................**38** B3
Lato Hotel..................................**39** C3
Marin Hotel................................**40** D3
Megaron....................................**41** D3
Mirabello Hotel...........................**42** B3

EATING
Embolo......................................**43** C5
Giakoumis Taverna........................**44** B4
I Avli tou Defkaliona......................**45** B3
Ippokambos Ouzeri........................**46** C2
Loukoulos...................................**47** C4
O Vrakas....................................**48** C3
Peri Orexeos................................**49** C4
Prassein Aloga..............................**50** B3
Terzakis Ouzeri.............................**51** C3

ENTERTAINMENT
Guernica....................................**52** B4
Jasmin.......................................**53** B3
Pagopiion...................................**54** C3
Take Five...................................**55** C3

TRANSPORT
Aegean Airlines............................**56** D5
Bus Station A...............................**57** D3
Buses to Airport...........................**58** D4
Buses to Hania & Rethymno............**59** D3
Buses to Knossos..........................**60** C4
Buses to Knossos..........................**61** D3
Loggeta Cars & Bikes.....................**62** B3
Long-Distance Taxis.......................**63** D4
Motor Club.................................**64** C3
Olympic Airlines...........................**65** C3
Sun Rise....................................**66** C3

SEA OF CRETE

Old Harbour

New Harbour
Quay

To Ferry Terminal (200m);
Cretaquarium (15km);
Hersonisos (26km);
Agios Nikolaos (67km)

To Hania Gate (300m);
Bus Station B (500m);
University Hospital (5km);
Rethymno (85km);
Hania (142km)

To Airport (3km)

To Knossos (5km);
Arhanes (16km)

CRETE

INTERNET ACCESS

Gallery Games (☎ 28102 82804; www.gallerygames
.net; Koraï 14; per hr €1.50; ☷ 24hr) High-speed access;
printers and PC games.

INTERNET RESOURCES

www.heraklion-city.gr Useful information.

LAUNDRY

Most laundries charge €6 for wash and dry,
and offer dry cleaning.
Inter Laundry (☎ 28103 43660; Mirabelou 25;
☷ 9am-9pm)
Laundry Perfect (☎ 28102 20969; Idomeneos
& Malikouti 32; ☷ 9am-9pm)

LEFT LUGGAGE

Iraklio Youth Hostel also offers left-luggage
facilities (per day €2).
Bus Station A Left-Luggage Office (☎ 28102
46538; per day €1; ☷ 6.30am-8pm)
Iraklio Airport Luggage Service (☎ 28103 97349; per
day €2.50-5; ☷ 24hr) Near the local bus stop at the airport.

MEDICAL SERVICES

Apollonia Hospital (☎ 28102 29713; Mousourou)
Inside the old walls.
University Hospital (☎ 28103 92111) At Voutes, 5km
south of Iraklio, it's the city's best-equipped medical facility.

MONEY

Most of the city's banks and ATMs are on
25 Avgoustou.
Adamis Travel Bureau (☎ 28103 46202; 25 Avgoustou 23) Represents American Express.
National Bank of Greece (25 Avgoustou 35) Has a
24-hour exchange machine.

POST

Central Post Office (☎ 28102 34468; Plateia Daskalo-
gianni; ☷ 7.30am-8pm Mon-Fri, 7.30am-2pm Sat)

TOURIST INFORMATION

There is a KTEL tourist office inside Bus
Station A.
EOT (Greek National Tourism Organisation; ☎ 28102
46299; Xanthoudidou 1; ☷ 9am-9pm Jul-Oct, 8.30am-
2.30pm Nov-Jun) Has maps, brochures and transport information; located opposite the archaeological museum.

Sights

ARCHAEOLOGICAL MUSEUM OF IRAKLIO

This outstanding **museum** (☎ 28102 24630;
Xanthoudidou 2; admission €6, incl Knossos €10; ☷ 1-
7.30pm Mon, 8am-7.30pm Tue-Sun Jun-Oct, noon-3pm

Mon, 8am-3pm Tue-Sun late Oct-May) is second in
size and importance only to the National
Archaeological Museum in Athens. Even a
superficial perusal of the contents requires
half a day.

The exhibits, arranged in chronological
order, include pottery, jewellery, figurines
and sarcophagi, as well as some famous
frescoes, mostly from Knossos and Agia
Triada. All testify to the remarkable imagination and advanced skills of the Minoans.
Unfortunately, the exhibits are not very
well explained.

Room 1 is devoted to the Neolithic and
Early Minoan periods. Room 2 has a collection from the Middle Minoan period.
Among the most fascinating exhibits are the
tiny, glazed colour reliefs of Minoan houses
from Knossos, called the 'town mosaic'.

Room 3 covers the same period with
finds from Phaestos, including the famous
Phaestos Disk. The symbols inscribed on
this 16cm diameter disc have not been de-
ciphered. The famous **Kamares pottery vases**,
named after the sacred cave of Kamares
where the pottery was first discovered, are
also on display. Case 40 contains fragments
of 'eggshell ware', so called because of its
fragility. The four large vases in case 43
were part of a royal banquet set. They are
of exceptional quality and are some of the
finest examples of Kamares pottery.

Exhibits in Room 4 are from the Middle
Minoan period. Most striking is the 20cm
black stone **Bull's Head**, which was a libation
vessel. The bull has a fine head of curls,
from which sprout horns of gold. The eyes
of painted crystal are extremely lifelike.
Also in this room are relics from a shrine
at Knossos, including two fine **snake goddess**
figurines.

Room 5 contains pottery, bronze figurines and seals, as well as vases imported
from Egypt and some Linear A and B tablets – the latter have been translated as
household or business accounts from the
palace at Knossos.

Room 6 is devoted to finds from Minoan
cemeteries. Especially intriguing are two
small clay models of groups of figures that
were found in a *tholos* (tomb shaped like
a beehive). One depicts four male dancers
in a circle, their arms around each other's
shoulders. The dancers may have been
participating in a funeral ritual. The other

model depicts two groups of three figures in a room flanked by two columns. Each group features two large seated figures being offered libations by a smaller figure. It is not known whether the large figures represent gods or departed mortals. On a more grisly level, there is a display of the bones of a horse sacrificed as part of Minoan worship.

The finds in Room 7 include the beautiful, fine-gold bee pendant found at Malia, which depicts two bees dropping honey into a comb. There are also three celebrated vases from Agia Triada. The **Harvester Vase**, of which only the top part remains, depicts a light-hearted scene of young farm workers returning from olive picking. The **Boxer Vase** shows Minoans indulging in two of their favourite pastimes – wrestling and bull-grappling. The **Chieftain Cup** depicts a more cryptic scene: a chief holding a staff, and three men carrying animal skins.

Room 8 holds the finds from the palace at Zakros. Don't miss the gorgeous crystal vase that was found in over 300 pieces and was painstakingly put back together again. Another exhibit is a beautiful elongated libation vessel decorated with shells and other marine life.

Room 10 covers the Postpalatial period (1580–1200 BC) when the Minoan civilisation was in decline and being overtaken by the warlike Mycenaeans. Nevertheless, there are still some fine exhibits, including a child (headless) on a swing in case 143.

Room 13 is devoted to Minoan sarcophagi. However, the most famous and spectacular of these, the **sarcophagus from Agia Triada**, is upstairs in Room 14 (the Hall of Frescoes). This stone coffin, painted with floral and abstract designs and ritual scenes, is one of the best examples of Minoan art.

The most famous of the Minoan frescoes are displayed in Room 14. Knossos-sourced frescoes include the **Procession Fresco**, the **Griffin Fresco** (from the Throne Room), the **Dolphin Fresco** (from the Queen's Room) and the amazing **Bull-Leaping Fresco**, which depicts a seemingly double-jointed acrobat somersaulting on the back of a charging bull. Other frescoes here include the lovely **Frescoes of the Lilies** from Amnisos and fragments of frescoes from Agia Triada.

There are more frescoes in Rooms 15 and 16. Room 16 has a large wooden model of Knossos.

The museum was expected to undergo some disruption during construction of a new office and storage wing, which began in 2005 and will eventually free up four exhibition rooms for the collection. The museum will close temporarily at some point while the main building is refurbished and exhibitions are rearranged.

HISTORICAL MUSEUM OF CRETE

A fascinating collection from Crete's more recent past is displayed at the **historical museum** (☎ 28102 83219; Sofokli Venizelou; admission €3; ⏰ 9am-4pm Mon-Fri, 9am-2pm Sat summer, 9am-3pm Mon-Sat winter). The 1st floor covers the period from Byzantine to Turkish rule, displaying plans, charts, photographs, ceramics and maps. This floor also has the only El Greco painting in Crete – *View of Mt Sinai and the Monastery of St Catherine* (1570). Other rooms contain frescoes, coins, jewellery, liturgical ornaments, vestments and medieval pottery.

The 2nd floor has a reconstruction of the **library of author Nikos Kazantzakis** (see p229), with letters, manuscripts and books. Some dramatic photographs of a ruined Iraklio are displayed in the **Battle of Crete** section and there is an outstanding **folklore collection** on the 3rd floor.

OTHER ATTRACTIONS

Iraklio burst out of its **city walls** long ago, but these massive fortifications, with seven bastions and four gates, are still very conspicuous, dwarfing the concrete structures of the 20th century. Venetians built the defences between 1462 and 1562. You can follow the walls around the heart of the city for views of Iraklio's neighbourhoods, although it is not a particularly scenic city.

The 16th-century **Koules Venetian fortress** (Iraklio Harbour; admission €2; ⏰ 8.30am-3pm Tue-Sun), at the end of the Old Harbour's jetty, was called Rocca al Mare under the Venetians. It stopped the Turks for 22 years and then became a Turkish prison for Cretan rebels. The exterior is most impressive with reliefs of the Lion of St Mark. The interior has 26 overly restored rooms and good views from the top. The ground-level rooms are used as art galleries, while music and theatrical events are held in the upper level.

The vaulted arcades of the **Venetian Arsenal** are opposite the fortress.

CRETE

Several other notable vestiges from Venetian times survive in the city. Most famous is **Morosini Fountain** (Lion Fountain) on Plateia Venizelou, which spurts water from four lions into eight ornate marble troughs. Built in 1628, the fountain was commissioned by Francesco Morosini while he was governor of Crete. A marble statue of Poseidon with his trident used to stand at the centre, but was destroyed during the Turkish occupation. Opposite is the three-aisled 13th-century **Basilica of San Marco**. It has been reconstructed many times and is now a public **art gallery** (☎ 28103 99228; admission free; ⊙ 9am-9pm Mon-Fri). A little north is the attractively reconstructed 17th-century **Venetian Loggia**. It was a Venetian version of a gentleman's club; the male aristocracy came here to drink and gossip. It is now the Town Hall.

The delightful **Bembo Fountain**, at the southern end of 1866, was built by the Venetians in the 16th century. The ornate hexagonal edifice next to the fountain was a pump house added by the Turks, and now functions as a pleasant *kafeneio* (coffee house).

The **Church of Agia Ekaterini** (☎ 28102 88825; Monis Odigitrias; adult/concession €2/1; ⊙ 9am-6pm Mon-Sat, 10am-6pm Sun), next to Agios Minas Cathedral, is now a museum housing an impressive collection of icons. Most notable are the six icons painted by Mihail Damaskinos, the mentor of El Greco.

The **Church of Agios Titos** (Agiou Titou) was constructed after the liberation of Crete in AD 961 and was converted to a Catholic church and then a mosque. It has been rebuilt twice after being destroyed by the big fire in 1554 and then the 1856 earthquake, and has been an Orthodox church since 1925.

You can pay homage to Crete's most acclaimed contemporary writer, Nikos Kazantzakis (1883–1957; see opposite), by visiting his **tomb** at the Martinengo Bastion (the largest and best-preserved bastion) in the southern part of town. The epitaph on his grave, 'I hope for nothing, I fear nothing, I am free', is taken from one of his works.

The **Battle of Crete Museum** (☎ 28103 46554; cnr Doukos Beaufort & Hatzidaki; admission free; ⊙ 8am-3pm) chronicles this historic battle through photographs, letters, uniforms and weapons.

The excellent **Natural History Museum** (☎ 28103 24711; www.nhmc.uoc.gr; Paraliaki Leoforos; adult/child €4.50/free; ⊙ 9am-3pm) was due to move to the former electricity company building on the harbour front in 2005. Apart from the broader evolution of humankind, it explores Crete's flora and fauna, ecosystem and habitats, and its caves, coastline and mountains, as well as Minoan civilisation.

Activities

The **Mountaineering and Skiing Club of Iraklio** (EOS; ☎ 28102 27609; www.interkriti.org/orivatikos/orivat.html; Dikeosynis 53; ☎ 8.30pm-10.30pm) arranges mountain climbing, cross-country walking and skiing excursions across the island most weekends.

For a dive in Crete's clear warm waters try **Diver's Club** (☎ 28108 11755; www.diversclub-crete.gr; Agia Pelagia), about 25km west of Iraklio.

LINEAR B SCRIPT

The methodical decipherment of the Linear B script by English architect and part-time linguist Michael Ventris was the first tangible evidence that the Greek language had a recorded history longer than any scholar had previously believed. The decipherment demonstrated that these mysterious scribblings was an archaic form of Greek 500 years older than the Ionic Greek used by Homer.

Linear B was written on clay tablets that lay undisturbed for centuries until they were unearthed at Knossos. Further clay tablets were unearthed later on the mainland at Mycenae, Tiryns and Pylos on the Peloponnese and at Thebes (Thiva) in Boeotia in Central Greece.

The clay tablets, found to be mainly inventories and records of commercial transactions, consist of about 90 different signs, and date from the 14th to the 13th centuries BC. Little of the social and political life of these times can be deduced from the tablets, though there is enough to give a glimpse of a fairly complex and well-organised commercial structure.

The language is undeniably Greek, thus giving the modern-day Greek language the second-longest recorded written history, after Chinese. The language Linear A, an earlier script believed to be of either Anatolian or Semitic origin, remains to this day undeciphered.

NIKOS KAZANTZAKIS – CRETE'S PRODIGAL SON

Crete's most famous contemporary literary son is Nikos Kazantzakis. Born in 1883 in Iraklio, the then Turkish-dominated capital, Kazantzakis spent his early childhood in the ferment of revolution and change that was creeping upon his homeland. In 1897 the revolution that finally broke out against Turkish rule forced him to leave Crete for studies in Naxos, Athens and later Paris. It wasn't until he was 31, in 1914, that he finally turned his hand to writing by translating philosophical books into Greek. For a number of years he travelled throughout Europe – Switzerland, Germany, Austria, Russia and Britain – thus laying the groundwork for a series of travelogues in his later literary career.

Kazantzakis was a complex writer and his early work was heavily influenced by the prevailing philosophical ideas of the time. The nihilistic philosophies of Nietzsche influenced his writings. Throughout his work he is tormented by a tangible metaphysical and existentialist anguish. His relationship with religion was always troubled. He was a nonbeliever, yet he always toyed with the idea that perhaps God did exist. His self-professed greatest work is *Odyssey*, a modern-day epic loosely based on the trials and travels of the ancient hero Odysseus (Ulysses). The weighty and complex opus of 33,333 iambic verses never fully realised Kazantzakis' aspirations to be held in the same league as Homer, Virgil or the Renaissance Italian, Tasso.

Ironically it was only much later in his career when Kazantzakis belatedly turned to novel writing that his star finally shone. It was through works such as *Christ Recrucified* (1948), *Kapetan Mihalis* (1950; now known as *Freedom and Death*) and *The Life and Manners of Alexis Zorbas* (1946) that he became internationally known. This last work gave rise to the image of the ultimate, modern Greek male 'Zorba the Greek', immortalised by Anthony Quinn in the movie of the same name.

Kazantzakis died while travelling in Germany on 26 October 1957. Despite resistance from the Orthodox Church, he was given a religious funeral and buried in the southern Martinenga Bastion of the old walls of Iraklio.

Iraklio for Children

If the kids are museumed out and the heat is getting to them, the indoor playground **Ricoco** (☎ 28102 22333; per child €5; ☿ 10am-10pm Mon-Sat, 5pm-10pm Sun) could be a godsend. It's upstairs in the arcade off Plateia Venizelou, near the Morosini Fountain. The **Natural History Museum** (opposite) is another safe bet.

Tours

Iraklio's myriad travel agents run coach tours the length and breadth of Crete. Try the helpful **Skoutelis Travel** (☎ 28102 80808; www.skoutelis.gr; 25 Avgoustou 24), which also arranges airline and ferry bookings, accommodation and car hire, and has useful ferry information online.

Festivals & Events

Iraklio's **Summer Arts Festival** takes place at the **Nikos Kazantzakis Open Air Theatre** (☎ 28102 42977; Jesus Bastion; box office ☿ 9am-2.30pm & 6.30-9.30pm), near the moat of the Venetian walls, the nearby Manos Hatzidakis theatre and at the Koules fortress. Check www.heraklion -city.gr for the programme.

Sleeping

Iraklio's accommodation is weighted towards the needs of business travellers. Many hotels were upgraded in the lead-up to the 2004 Olympics. There are few *domatia* (cheap rooms) but not enough cheap hotels to cope with the number of budget travellers in high season.

BUDGET

Mirabello Hotel (☎ 28102 85052; www.mirabello -hotel.gr; Theotokopoulou 20; s/d without bathroom €37/40, d with bathroom €65; ☯) One of the most pleasant budget hotels in Iraklio, the relaxed Mirabello is on a quiet street in the centre of town. The rooms are immaculate, although a little cramped, with TV and phones. Some rooms share single-sex bathrooms.

Hotel Lena (☎ 28102 23280; www.lena-hotel.gr; Lahana 10; s/d without bathroom €30/40, d/tr with bathroom €50/70; ☯) Renovated extensively in 2003, Hotel Lena has 16 comfortable, airy rooms with phone, TV and double-glazed windows, but the bathrooms are still rather basic.

CRETE

Hellas Rent Rooms (☎ 28102 88851; fax 28102 84442; Handakos 24; dm/d/tr without bathroom €10/30/40) Many travellers enjoy the lively atmosphere at this de facto youth hostel, which has a rooftop garden bar. Shared bathrooms are basic but clean, and most rooms have balconies. Breakfast is available on the terrace from €2.50.

Hotel Rea (☎ 28102 23638; www.hotelrea.gr; Kalimeraki 1; s/d without bathroom €25/30, d with bathroom €35) Popular with a wide range of backpackers, Rea has an easy, friendly atmosphere. Rooms all have fans and sinks, although some bathrooms are shared. There's a small, basic communal kitchen.

Iraklio Youth Hostel (☎ 28102 86281; heraklioyou thhostel@yahoo.com; Vyronos 5; dm/d/tr without bathroom €10/25/35) This Greek Youth Hostel Organisation establishment is rather scruffy and run-down, but it's the cheapest option for single travellers. The dorms are as basic as you can get.

MIDRANGE

Atrion (☎ 28102 46000; www.atrion.gr; Hronaki 9; s/d incl breakfast €95/110; ⊠) Fully refurbished in 2003, this is now one of the city's more pleasant hotels. Rooms are tastefully decked out in neutral tones, with TV, fridge, hairdryers and data ports. The top rooms have sea views and small balconies.

Kastro Hotel (☎ 28102 84185; www.kastro-hotel .gr; Theotokopoulou 22; s incl breakfast from €50, d incl breakfast €80-135; ⊠ ⛶) A refurbished, modern, cheery B-class hotel in the back streets, the Kastro is an excellent choice. The large rooms have fridges, TV, hairdryers, phones and ISDN Internet connectivity.

Kronos Hotel (☎ 28102 82240; www.kronoshotel .gr; Sofokli Venizelou 2; s/d incl breakfast €44/55; ⊠ ⛶) This well-maintained older waterfront hotel has comfortable rooms with double-glazed windows and balconies, phone and TV, and most have a fridge. It is one of the better-value C-class hotels in town. Ask for one of the rooms with sea views.

Hotel Irini (☎ 28102 26561; www.hotelirini.com; Idomeneos 4; s/d incl breakfast €66/93; ⊠) Close to the old harbour, Irini is a mid-sized establishment with 59 large, airy rooms with TV, radio and telephone, and plants and flowers on the balconies.

Marin Hotel (☎ 28103 00018; www.marin_hotel .gr; Doukos Beaufort 12; s incl breakfast €60, d incl breakfast €80-90; ⊠ ⛶) This refurbished hotel reopened in 2005. The seafront rooms have great views of the harbour and fortress and some have big balconies. All rooms are well-appointed, though nondescript and on the small side.

TOP END

Lato Hotel (☎ 28102 28103; www.lato.gr; Epimenidou 15; s/d €100/127; ⊠ ⛶) This refurbished boutique hotel overlooking the old and new harbours is one of Iraklio's prime hotels. It has a smart contemporary design and furnishings. Most rooms have spectacular views, especially the spacious suites, and there is a great rooftop restaurant.

Atlantis Hotel (☎ 28102 29103; www.grandhotel .gr; Ygias 2; s/d €115/165; ⊠ ⛶ ⛻) The Atlantis' makeover has maintained its status as one of the city's best hotels. The rooms are comfortable, stylish and well equipped, and there is a health studio, sauna and small pool.

Megaron (☎ 28103 05300; www.gdmmegaron.gr; Doukos Beaufort 9; s/d €225/255, ste from €325; ⊠ ⛻) This once-derelict historic building on the harbour has been stunningly transformed with top design and fittings throughout. There are comfortable beds, Jacuzzis in the VIP suites, plasma-screen TVs and a fax in every room. The rooftop restaurant and bar have fine harbour views and the glass-sided pool is unique.

Eating

Iraklio has some excellent restaurants to suit all tastes and pockets. Many restaurants are closed on Sunday.

BUDGET

Giakoumis Taverna (☎ 28102 80277; Theodosaki 5-8; mayirefta €5-7; ⊗ closed Sun) Theodosaki is lined with tavernas catering to the market on 1866 and this is one of the best. There's a full menu of Cretan specialities and turnover is heavy, which means that the dishes are freshly cooked.

O Vrakas (☎ 69778 93973; Plateia 18 Anglon; mezedes €4.50-8) This small street-side *ouzeri* (place which serves ouzo and light snacks) grills fresh fish alfresco in front of diners. It's cheap and unassuming and the menu is limited, but still very popular with locals. Grilled octopus with ouzo is a good choice.

Ippokambos Ouzeri (☎ 28102 80240; Sofokli Venizelou 3; seafood mezedes €4.20-7) Many locals come to this taverna at the edge of the tourist-driven waterfront dining strip. Take a peek inside at the fresh trays and pots of *mayirefta* (ready-cooked meals) such as baked cuttle-fish, and dine at one of the sidewalk tables or on the promenade across the road.

MIDRANGE

Terzakis Ouzeri (☎ 28102 21444; Marineli 17; mezedes €2.50-6.80) On a small square opposite the Agios Dimitrios church, this excellent *ouzeri* has a good range of *mezedes* (appetisers), *mayirefta* and grills. Try the sea urchin salad or, if you are really game to try a local speciality, ask if they have *ameletita* ('unmentionables'), which are fried sheep testicles.

Peri Orexeos (☎ 28102 22679; Koraï 10; mains €6-8) Right on the busy Koraï pedestrian strip, this restaurant offers excellent modern Greek food with creative takes like *kataïfi* (angel-hair pastry) with creamy chicken, huge salads, and solid Cretan cuisine. There's also a wicked chocolate dessert.

I Avli tou Defkaliona (☎ 28102 44215; Kalokerinou 8; meat dishes €4.20-13; ☽ dinner) This traditional taverna with wicker chairs, checked table-cloths and plastic grapevines is known for its delicious food. After the tourists leave at around 11pm, the locals pile in, the owner often takes out his accordion and the festivities commence.

Embolo (☎ 28102 84244; Miliara 7; mains €3.20-6.50) Run by former musician Giannis Stavrakakis from Anogia, Embolo dishes up fine Cretan food – excellent grills, *pites* (pies) and large salads. Live music is normally played on Thursday, Friday and Saturday.

Also recommended is Paraskies, opposite I Avli tou Defkaliona.

TOP END

Prassein Aloga (☎ 28102 83429; cnr Handakos & Kydonias 21; mains €9.50-15) This little rustic-style café/restaurant and its associated delicatessen (situated opposite) have excellent innovative Mediterranean food from an ever-changing menu. It has dishes based on ancient Greek cuisine, such as pork medallions with dried fruit on wild rice.

Loukoulos (☎ 28102 24435; Koraï 5; mains €10-19) Loukoulos is one of the poshest restaurants in town, offering Mediterranean specialities served on fine china, accompanied by soft classical music. There's an elegant interior or you can dine in the garden terrace.

Entertainment

Pagopiion (☎ 28103 46028; Plateia Agiou Titou; ☽ 10am-late) This former ice factory is the most original café/bar/restaurant on the island. The restaurant serves innovative but pricey dishes and salads and it becomes a lively bar after 11pm.

Guernica (☎ 28102 82988; Apokoronou Kritis 2; ☽ 10am-late) A great combination of traditional décor and contemporary music makes this one of Iraklio's hippest bar/cafés. The rambling old building has a delightful terrace garden for the summer and a cosy fireplace in winter.

Take Five (☎ 28102 26564; Akroleondos 7; ☽ 10am-late) An old favourite on the edge of El Greco Park, this place doesn't really get going until after sundown when the outside tables fill up with a diverse crowd. It's a gay-friendly place. The music and ambience are low-key, but the coffees aren't cheap.

Jasmin (☎ 28102 88880; Handakos 45; ☽ noon-late) This friendly bar/café, with its pleasant back terrace, specialises in serving up herbal teas and hot chocolates, but is also a bar in the evenings, playing rock and world music.

Getting There & Away

AIR

Aegean Airlines (www.aegeanair.com) City (☎ 28103 44324; fax 28103 44330; Leof Dimokratias 11); Airport office (☎ 28103 30475)

Olympic Airlines (www.olympicairlines.com) City (☎ 28102 44824; 25 Avgoustou 27; ☽ 8am-3.30pm Mon-Fri); Airport office (☎ 28103 37203)

Domestic

Olympic Airlines has flights at least five flights daily to Athens (from €76) from Iraklio's Nikos Kazantzakis airport. It also has daily flights to Thessaloniki (€98) and Rhodes (€78).

Aegean Airlines flies to Athens (from €76, five daily) and Thessaloniki (€110, two daily).

International

Iraklio has lots of charter flights from all over Europe, with flights to London available from €80 to €150. Skoutelis Travel (p229) is a good place to ask. **GB Airways** (www.gbairways.com) began weekly scheduled flights from Gatwick in May 2005.

CRETE

BOAT

Minoan Lines (☎ 21041 45700, 28102 29624; www .minoan.gr) operates ferries each way between Iraklio and Piraeus (seven hours). The ferries depart from both Piraeus and Iraklio at 10pm. Fares start at €29 for deck class and €54 for cabins. The Minoan Lines' high-speed boats, the F/B *Festos Palace* and F/B *Knossos Palace,* are much more modern and comfortable than their ANEK rivals.

In summer, Minoan runs extra six-hour services (deck class €29) on weekends and some weekdays, departing Iraklio and Piraeus at 11am and arriving at 5pm. This is the most convenient way to get to/from Iraklio.

Minoan runs four ferries weekly to Thessaloniki (€46.50, 21 hours) via Santorini (€16, four hours), stopping at different islands each time, including Mykonos (€25, nine hours), Paros (€24.50, seven hours), Tinos (€26.50, 10¼ hours), Naxos (€21.50, seven hours), Syros (€23.50, eight hours) and Skiathos (€39, 17¾ hours).

Hellenic Seaways (www.hellenicseaways.gr) has a daily high-speed service to Santorini (€31, 1¾ hours), Ios (€36.70, 2½ hours) Paros €47.80, 3¼ hours), Naxos (€41.70, 4¼ hours) and Mykonos (€48.70, 4¾ hours).

ANEK Lines (☎ 28102 44912; www.anek.gr) has daily ferries between Iraklio and Piraeus (€29, eight hours) at 9pm.

LANE Lines leaves Iraklio for Sitia, Karpathos (€17.40, seven hours), Rhodes (€26.40, 10 hours), and continues to Kasos, Halki, Kalymnos, Kos, Samos, Chios, Mytilene and Alexandroupolis (though this marathon is not recommended).

Iraklio Port Authority (☎ 28102 44912) at the port has ferry schedule information.

BUS

Iraklio has three intercity bus stations. **Bus Station A** (☎ 28102 46534; www.bus-service-crete-ktel .com), which serves eastern Crete (including Knossos), is on the waterfront near the quay, though there are plans to relocate it. A bus station servicing Hania and Rethymno is opposite Station A. Station B, just beyond Hania Gate, west of the city centre, serves Phaestos, Agia Galini and Matala.

There are buses every half-hour (hourly in winter) to Rethymno (€6.50, 1½ hours) and Hania (€11.50, 2½ hours), See the following tables for other destinations. Services reduce on weekends.

Buses from Bus Station A

Destination	Duration	Fare	Frequency
Agia Pelagia	45min	€2.60	3 daily
Agios Nikolaos	1½hr	€5.30	19 daily
Hersonisos/Malia	45min	€2.30/3	half-hourly
Ierapetra	2½hr	€8.10	7 daily
Knossos	20min	€1	6 hourly
Lasithi Plateau	2hr	€4.70	2 daily
Sitia	3¼hr	€11.20	6 daily

Buses from Bus Station B

Destination	Duration	Fare	Frequency
Agia Galini	2hr	€6	8 daily
Anogia	1hr	€2.90	5 daily
Matala	2½hr	€5.80	5 daily
Phaestos	1½hr	€4.80	4 daily

Getting Around

Bus No 1 goes to and from the airport every 15 minutes between 6am and 1am. It leaves from near the Astoria Capsis Hotel on Plateia Eleftherias. A taxi to the airport costs around €8 to €10.

Long-Distance Taxis (☎ 28102 10102/68/24) from Plateia Eleftherias can take you to all parts of Crete. Sample fares include Agios Nikolaos (€43), Rethymno (€54) and Hania (€92).

The airport has the full range of multinational car-rental companies, but you'll likely get the best deal from local car- and motorcycle-hire outlets, which are largely located on 25 Avgoustou.

Loggeta Cars & Bikes (☎ 28102 89462; Plateia Kallergon 6) Next to El Greco Park.
Motor Club (☎ 28102 22408; Plateia 18 Anglon)
Sun Rise (☎ 28102 21609; 25 Avgoustou 46)

AROUND IRAKLIO
CretAquarium

This massive new **aquarium** (☎ 28103 37801; www.hcmr.gr) is part of the Thalassocosmos marine science complex established by the Hellenic Centre for Maritime research at the former American base at Gournes, 15km east of Iraklio. It is the largest aquarium in the Eastern Mediterranean region and is one of the most hi-tech in the world, with interactive multimedia features. There are 23 tanks, holding 1.6 million litres of sea water, and with 50 viewing points to see the 4000 sea organisms in residence.

Arhanes

The village of Arhanes, 16km south of Irak-lio, once boasted one of the island's great Minoan palaces. Today only scraps of the palace (signposted from the main road) remain, but Arhanes is a vibrant village with meticulously restored old houses and pleasant squares with excellent tavernas. It's considered a model of EU-funded rural town revival.

The **Archaeological Museum of Arhanes** (☎ 28107 52712; admission free; ◷ 8.30am-3pm Wed-Mon) has several interesting finds from regional archaeological excavations. The exhibits include *larnakes* (coffins) and musical instruments from Fourni and an ornamental dagger from the Anemospilia temple.

South of Arhanes, in the otherwise unremarkable village of **Houdetsi**, the much-lauded musician Ross Daly has established a **museum of musical instruments** (☎ 28107 41027; www.labyrinthmusic.gr; admission €3; ◷ 10am-8pm Mar-Oct) displaying his extensive collection of mostly stringed instruments. The restored stone manor is the base for the Labyrinth Musical Workshop which each summer hosts leading international musicians and holds concerts in the lovely grounds.

There are buses hourly from Iraklio to Arhanes (€1.40, 30 minutes).

KNOSSOS ΚΝΩΣΣΟΣ

Knossos (k-nos-*os*), 5km from Iraklio, was the capital of Minoan Crete and the **site** (☎ 28102 31940; admission €6, incl Archaeological Museum of Iraklio €10; ◷ 8am-7pm Jun-Oct, 8am-3pm Nov-May) is the island's major tourist attraction.

The ruins of Knossos, home of the mythical Minotaur kept by King Minos, were uncovered in the early 1900s by the British archaeologist Sir Arthur Evans. Heinrich Schliemann, who had uncovered the ancient cities of Troy and Mycenae, had had his eye on the spot but was unable to strike a deal with the landowner.

Evans was so taken by his discovery that he spent 35 years and £250,000 of his own money excavating and reconstructing parts of the palace. Some archaeologists have disparaged Evans' controversial reconstruction, believing he sacrificed accuracy to his overly vivid imagination. However, most nonexperts agree that Sir Arthur did a good job and the reconstructions allow you to visualise what a Minoan palace looked like.

You will need to spend about two to three hours at Knossos to explore it thoroughly. The café at the site is expensive – you'd do better to bring a picnic along.

History

The first palace at Knossos was built around 1900 BC. In 1700 BC it was destroyed by an earthquake and rebuilt to a grander and more sophisticated design. It is this palace that Evans reconstructed. It was partially destroyed again sometime between 1500 and 1450 BC. It was inhabited for another 50 years before it was devastated once and for all by fire.

The city of Knossos consisted of an immense palace, residences of officials and priests, the homes of ordinary people, and burial grounds. The palace comprised royal domestic quarters, public reception rooms, shrines, workshops, treasuries and storerooms, all built around a central court. Like all Minoan palaces, it also doubled as a city hall, accommodating all the bureaucracy.

Until 1997 it was possible to enter the royal apartments, but the area was cordoned off before it disappeared altogether under the continual pounding of tourists' feet. Extensive repairs are under way but it is unlikely to open to the public again.

Exploring the Site

Thanks to Evans' reconstruction, the most significant parts of the complex are instantly recognisable (if not instantly found). On your wanders you will come across many of Evans' reconstructed columns, most painted deep brown-red with gold-trimmed black capitals. Like all Minoan columns, they taper at the bottom.

It is not only the vibrant frescoes and mighty columns which impress at Knossos; keep your eyes open for the little details which are evidence of a highly sophisticated society. Things to look out for include the drainage system, the placement of light wells, and the relationship of rooms to passages, porches, light wells and verandas, which kept rooms cool in summer and warm in winter.

The usual entrance to the palace complex is across the **Western Court** and along the **Corridor of the Procession Fresco**. The fresco depicted a long line of people carrying gifts to present to the king; unfortunately only

CRETE

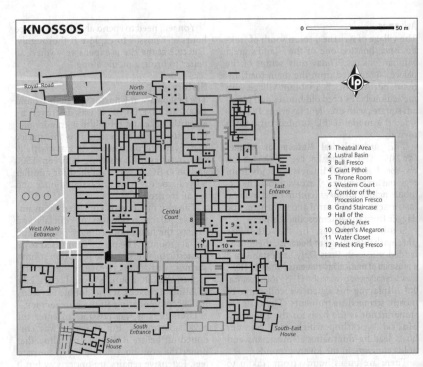

KNOSSOS

0 —————— 50 m

Royal Road

North Entrance

East Entrance

West (Main) Entrance

Central Court

South Entrance

South House

South-East House

1 Theatral Area
2 Lustral Basin
3 Bull Fresco
4 Giant Pithoi
5 Throne Room
6 Western Court
7 Corridor of the Procession Fresco
8 Grand Staircase
9 Hall of the Double Axes
10 Queen's Megaron
11 Water Closet
12 Priest King Fresco

fragments remain. A copy of one of these fragments, called the **Priest King Fresco**, can be seen to the south of the Central Court.

If you leave the Corridor of the Procession Fresco and walk straight ahead to enter the site from the northern end, you will come to the **Theatral Area**, a series of steps that could have been a theatre or the place where people gathered to welcome important visitors arriving by the Royal Road.

The **Royal Road** leads off to the west. The road, Europe's first (Knossos has lots of firsts), was flanked by workshops and the houses of ordinary people. The **Lustral Basin** is also in this area. Evans speculated that this was where the Minoans performed a ritual cleansing before religious ceremonies.

Entering the **Central Court** from the north, you pass the relief **Bull Fresco** which depicts a charging bull. Relief frescoes were made by moulding wet plaster, and then painting it while still wet.

Also in the northern section of the palace are the **Giant Pithoi**, large ceramic jars used for storing olive oil, wine and grain. Evans found over 100 *pithoi* at Knossos, some 2m

high. The ropes used to move them inspired the raised patterns decorating the jars.

Once you have reached the Central Court, which in Minoan times was surrounded by the high walls of the palace, you can begin exploring the most important rooms of the complex.

From the northern end of the west side of the Central Court, steps lead down to the **Throne Room**. This room is fenced off but you can still get a pretty good view of it. The centrepiece, the simple, beautifully proportioned throne, is flanked by the **Griffin Fresco**. (Griffins were mythical beasts regarded as sacred by the Minoans.) The room is thought to have been a shrine, and the throne the seat of a high priestess, rather than a king. The Minoans did not worship their deities in great temples but in small shrines, and each palace had several.

On the 1st floor of the west side of the palace is the section Evans called the **Piano Nobile**, for he believed the reception and state rooms were here. A room at the northern end of this floor displays copies of some of the frescoes found at Knossos.

Returning to the Central Court, the impressive **Grand Staircase** leads from the middle of the eastern side of the palace to the royal apartments, which Evans called the **Domestic Quarter**. This section of the site is now cordoned off and is off limits to visitors. Within the royal apartments is the **Hall of the Double Axes**. This was the king's megaron, a spacious double room in which the ruler both slept and carried out certain court duties. The room had a light well at one end and a balcony at the other to ensure air circulation. The room takes its name from the double axe marks on its light well, the sacred symbol of the Minoans.

A passage leads from the Hall of the Double Axes to the **Queen's Megaron**. Above the door is a copy of the **Dolphin Fresco**, one of the most exquisite Minoan artworks, and a blue floral design decorates the portal. Next to this room is the queen's bathroom, complete with terracotta bathtub and **water closet**, touted as the first ever to work on the flush principle; water was poured down by hand.

Getting There & Away

Regular buses run from Iraklio (see p232) from the bus station and from outside the Lion Fountain.

MALIA ΜΑΛΙΑ

The Minoan site of **Malia** (☎ 28970 31597; admission €4; ⓨ 8.30am-3pm Tue-Sun), 3km east of the resort of Malia, is the only cultural diversion on the northern stretch of coast east of Iraklio, which otherwise has surrendered lock, stock and barrel to the package-tourist industry. Malia is smaller than Knossos and

---

WINE COUNTRY

Just south of Iraklio and Knossos is one of Crete's largest wine-producing regions. The state-of-the-art **Boutari Winery** (☎ 28107 31617; www.boutari.gr; Skalani; tour & tasting €4.50; ⓨ 10am-6pm), about 8km from Iraklio, is set on a hill in the middle of the Fantaxometoho estate and has a stunning tasting room and showroom overlooking the vineyard. Tours include a quirky futuristic video on Crete in an impressive cellar cinema where you watch the hi-tech show with headphones and a glass of wine.

Phaestos and consisted of a palace complex and a town built on a flat, fertile plain, not on a hill.

Entrance to the ruins is from the **West Court**. At the extreme southern end of this court there are eight circular pits which archaeologists think were used to store grain. To the east of the pits is the main entrance to the palace, which leads to the southern end of the **Central Court**. At the southwest corner of this court you will find the **Kernos Stone**, a disc with 34 holes around its edge. Archaeologists still don't know what it was used for.

The **Central Staircase** is at the north end of the west side of the palace. The **Loggia**, just north of the staircase, is where religious ceremonies took place.

There are buses to Malia from Iraklio every 30 minutes (€2.70, one hour).

Buses travelling along the north coast can drop you at the site.

ZAROS ΖΑΡΟΣ

pop 2215

About 46km south of Iraklio, Zaros is a refreshingly unspoilt village that's known for its spring water and bottling plant. Various excavations in the region indicate that the Minoans and the Romans settled here, lured by the abundant supply of fresh water.

If you have your own wheels, the Byzantine monasteries and traditional villages tucked away in the hills are worth exploring. **Moni Agiou Nikolaou**, which is at the mouth of the verdant **Rouvas Gorge**, contains some 14th-century paintings. A few kilometres later, the **Moni Agiou Andoniou Vrondisiou** is noteworthy for its 15th-century Venetian fountain and early 14th-century frescoes.

Just outside the village, the lovely shady park at **Votomos** has a small lake and a taverna, café and children's playground, which makes a great picnic stop. From the lake, there is a walking path to Moni Agiou Nikolaou monastery (900m) and Rouvas Gorge (2.5km).

At the lake, **I Limni** (☎ 28940 31338; trout per kg €22; ⓨ 9am-late) has fresh grilled trout and excellent Cretan specialities.

In the village, the charming **Studios Keramos** (☎ /fax 28940 31352; s/d incl breakfast €25/35; ⌘) is decorated with Cretan crafts, weaving and family heirlooms. Many of the rooms have antique beds and furniture. Owner Katerina

CRETE

is up early cooking up a copious traditional Cretan breakfast – don't miss it.

There are two afternoon buses daily to Zaros from Iraklio (€3.40, one hour).

GORTYNA ΓΟΡΤΥΝΑ

Conveniently, Crete's three other major archaeological sites lie close to each other forming a rough triangle some 50km south of Iraklio. It's best to visit them all together.

Lying 46km southwest of Iraklio, and 15km from Phaestos, on the plain of Mesara, is **Gortyna** (☎ 28920 31144; admission €4; ☺ 8am-7pm, to 5pm winter), pronounced *gor*-tih-nah. It's a vast and wonderfully intriguing site with bits and pieces from various ages strewn all over the place. The site was a settlement from Minoan to Christian times. In Roman times, Gortyna was the capital of the province of Cyrenaica.

The most significant find at the site was the massive stone tablets inscribed with the **Laws of Gortyna**, dating from the 5th century BC and dealing with just about every imaginable offence. The tablets are on display at the site.

The 6th-century **Basilica** is dedicated to Agios Titos, a protégé of St Paul and the first bishop of Crete.

Other ruins at Gortyna include the 2nd-century-AD **Praetorium**, which was the residence of the governor of the province, a **Nymphaeum**, and the **Temple of Pythian Apollo**. The ruins are on both sides of the main Iraklio–Phaestos road.

PHAESTOS ΦΑΙΣΤΟΣ

The Minoan site of **Phaestos** (☎ 28920 42315; admission €4/2, incl Agia Triada €6; ☺ 8am-7.30pm Jun-Oct, 8am-5pm Nov-Apr), 63km from Iraklio, was the second most important palace city of Minoan Crete. Of all the Minoan sites, Phaestos (fes-*tos*) has the most awe-inspiring location, with all-embracing views of the Mesara Plain and Mt Ida. The layout of the palace is identical to Knossos, with rooms arranged around a central court.

In contrast to Knossos, the palace at Phaestos has very few frescoes. It seems the palace walls were mostly covered with a layer of white gypsum. There has been no reconstruction. Like the other palatial-period complexes, there was an old palace here that was destroyed at the end of the Middle Minoan period. Unlike the other

sites, parts of this old palace have been excavated and its ruins are partially superimposed upon the new palace.

The entrance to the new palace is by the 15m-wide **Grand Staircase**. The stairs lead to the west side of the **Central Court**. The best-preserved parts of the palace complex are the reception rooms and private apartments to the north of the Central Court; excavations continue here. This section was entered by an imposing portal with half columns at either side, the lower parts of which are still *in situ*. Unlike the Minoan freestanding columns, these do not taper at the base. The celebrated Phaestos disc was found in a building to the north of the palace. The disc is now in Iraklio's archaeological museum (p226).

Getting There & Away

Nine buses a day head to Phaestos from Iraklio (€4.80, 1½ hours), also stopping at Gortyna. There are also buses from Agia Galini (€1.70 minutes, seven daily) and Matala (€1.50, 30 minutes, five daily).

AGIA TRIADA ΑΓΙΑ ΤΡΙΑΔΑ

Pronounced ah-*yee*-ah trih-*ah*-dha, the small Minoan site of **Agia Triada** (☎ 28920 91564; admission €3, incl Phaestos €6; ☺ 10am-4.30pm summer, 8.30am-3pm winter), 3km west of Phaestos, was smaller than the other royal palaces but built to a similar design. This, and the opulence of the objects found at the site, indicate that it was a royal residence, possibly a summer palace of Phaestos' rulers. To the north of the palace is a small town where remains of a stoa (long, colonnaded building) have been unearthed.

Finds from the palace, now in Iraklio's archaeological museum, include a sarcophagus, two superlative frescoes and three vases: the Harvester Vase, Boxer Vase and Chieftain Cup.

The road to Agia Triada takes off to the right, about 500m from Phaestos on the road to Matala. There is no public transport to the site, although it is possible to catch a local cab from Phaestos, or even walk.

MATALA ΜΑΤΑΛΑ

pop 100

Matala (*ma*-ta-la), on the coast 11km southwest of Phaestos, was once one of Crete's best-known hippie hang-outs. When you see the dozens of eerie **caves** speckling the rock slab on the edge of the beach, you'll see why '60s hippies found it, like, groovy man, and turned them into a modern troglodyte city. The caves were originally Roman tombs cut out of the sandstone rock in the 1st century AD and have been used as dwellings for many centuries.

Matala expanded to the point where much of its original appeal was lost and these days it is a struggling resort, though it still has its loyal returnees every summer. The beautiful sandy **beach** below the caves is one of Crete's best and the resort is a convenient base to visit Phaestos and Agia Triada. The caves are normally fenced off at night and a fee charged but there was no guard – and free entry – at the time of research.

Orientation & Information
The bus stop is on the central square, one block back from the waterfront, and there is parking before the town and beach. There are ATMs in the village. There is no tourist office.

Monza Travel (☎ 28920 45757) You can change money here.

Zafiria Internet (☎ 28920 45498; per hr €4; ☼ 10am-late) For checking email.

Sleeping & Eating
The street running inland from Hotel Zafiria is lined with budget accommodation. Eating in Matala is hardly an experience in *haute cuisine*.

Pension Andonios (☎ 28920 45123; fax 28920 45690; d/tr €25/30) Run by the genial Antonis, this comfortable pension has attractively furnished rooms set around a lovely courtyard, many with kitchenette, and the top rooms have balconies.

Fantastic Rooms to Rent (☎ 28920 45362; fax 28920 45292; s/d/tr €20/25/25, d & tr with kitchen €30; ⬚) Has been here since the hippie heydays, and has added a newer block at the back. The rooms are plain but comfortable, many with kitchenette, phone, kettle and fridge.

Hotel Zafiria (☎ 28920 45366; fax 28920 45725; d incl breakfast €40; ⓟ ⬚ ⬚) The sprawling Hotel Zafiria takes up a whole block on Matala's main street. There is a spacious lobby bar and the comfortable rooms have balconies, sea views and telephones. A new pool has been added beneath the cliffs.

Matala Community Camping (☎ /fax 28920 45720; sites per person/tent €4.10/3.20) is a reasonable, shaded, although rather uneven, site just back from the beach.

Gianni's Taverna (☎ 28920 45719; mains €5-7) Towards the end of the main street, Gianni's Taverna is a no-frills place with good-value grills, including a mixed grill with salad and potatoes (€7).

You could also try Waves on the beach and Corali, opposite the fountain, for good-value *mayirefta*.

Getting There & Away
There are buses between Iraklio and Matala (€5.80, 2½ hours, five daily), and between Matala and Phaestos (€1.50, 30 minutes, five daily).

VORI ΒΩΡΟΙ
pop 755

In the village of Vori, 4km east of Tymbaki past Phaestos, you will find the outstanding private **Museum of Cretan Ethnology** (☎ 28920 91112; admission €3; ☼ 10am-6pm Apr-Oct, by appointment in winter ☎ 28920 91110). The modern museum provides a fascinating insight into traditional Cretan culture, with exhibits following themes such as rural life, war, customs, architecture, music, and the herbs, flora and fauna that form the basis of the Cretan diet. There some are some beautiful weavings, furniture, woodcarvings and musical instruments. It's well signposted from the main road.

RETHYMNO ΡΕΘΥΜΝΟ
pop 27,868

Rethymno (*reth*-im-no) is Crete's third-largest town and one of the most picturesque, with a charming harbour and massive Venetian fortress. The delightful Venetian-Ottoman quarter is a maze of narrow streets, graceful wood-balconied houses and ornate Venetian monuments, with minarets adding a touch of the Orient. The city has a campus of the University of Crete, bringing a student population that keeps the town alive outside the tourist season. An added attraction is a beach right in town.

The approaches to the town couldn't be less inviting. The modern town has sprawled out along the coast, dotted with big package hotels along the stretch on the sandy beach to the east.

CRETE

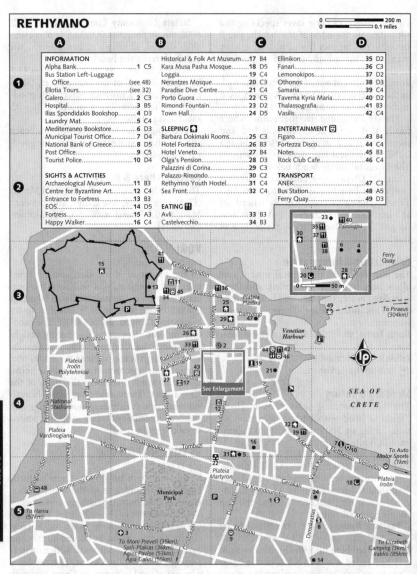

RETHYMNO

0 _____ 200 m
0 _____ 0.1 miles

INFORMATION
Alpha Bank............................1 C5
Bus Station Left-Luggage
    Office..............................(see 48)
Ellotia Tours........................(see 32)
Galero..................................2 C3
Hospital................................3 B5
Ilias Spondidakis Bookshop....4 D3
Laundry Mat.........................5 C4
Mediterraneo Bookstore.......6 D3
Municipal Tourist Office........7 D4
National Bank of Greece........8 D5
Post Office...........................9 C5
Tourist Police.....................10 D4

SIGHTS & ACTIVITIES
Archaeological Museum.......11 B3
Centre for Byzantine Art.....12 C4
Entrance to Fortress............13 B3
EOS.....................................14 D5
Fortress..............................15 A3
Happy Walker.....................16 C4

Historical & Folk Art Museum....17 B4
Kara Musa Pasha Mosque........18 D5
Loggia..................................19 C4
Nerantzes Mosque................20 C3
Paradise Dive Centre.............21 C4
Porto Guora.........................22 C5
Rimondi Fountain.................23 D2
Town Hall............................24 D5

SLEEPING
Barbara Dokimaki Rooms.....25 C3
Hotel Fortezza....................26 B3
Hotel Veneto.......................27 B4
Olga's Pension.....................28 D3
Palazzini di Corina...............29 C3
Palazzo Rimondo.................30 C2
Rethymno Youth Hostel.......31 C4
Sea Front.............................32 C4

EATING
Avli.....................................33 B3
Castelvecchio......................34 B3

Ellinikon.............................35 D2
Fanari..................................36 C3
Lemonokipos.......................37 D2
Othonos..............................38 D3
Samaria...............................39 C4
Taverna Kyria Maria.............40 D2
Thalassografia.....................41 B3
Vasilis..................................42 C4

ENTERTAINMENT
Figaro.................................43 B4
Fortezza Disco.....................44 C4
Notes..................................45 B3
Rock Club Cafe....................46 C4

TRANSPORT
ANEK..................................47 C3
Bus Station.........................48 A5
Ferry Quay..........................49 D3

History

The site of Rethymno has been occupied since Late Minoan times. In the 3rd and 4th centuries BC, the town was called Rithymna, an autonomous state of sufficient stature to issue its own coinage. A scarcity of references to the city in Roman and Byzantine times suggest it was of minor importance.

The town thrived under the Venetians, who ruled from 1210 until 1645, when the Turks took over. Turkish forces ruled until 1897, when it was taken by Russia as part of the Great Powers' occupation of Crete.

Rethymno became an artistic and intellectual centre after the arrival of a large number of refugees from Constantinople in 1923.

Orientation

Rethymno is a fairly compact town with most of the major sights and places to stay and eat near the old Venetian harbour. The beach is on the eastern side, around from the Venetian harbour.

If you arrive by bus, you will be dropped at the rather inconveniently located terminal at the western end of Igoumenou Gavriil, about 600m west of the Porto Guora (although this was due to relocate). If you arrive by ferry, the old quarter is at the end of the quay.

Information

BOOKSHOPS

Ilias Spondidakis bookshop (☎ 28310 54307; Souliou 43) Stocks novels in English, books about Greece, tapes of Greek music and has a small second-hand section.

Mediterraneo Bookstore (☎ 28310 23417; Mavrokordatou 2) Stocks English books, travel guides and foreign press.

EMERGENCY

Tourist police (☎ 28310 28156; ☽ 7am-10pm) In the same building as the municipal tourist office.

INTERNET ACCESS

Galero (☎ 28310 54345; Plateia Rimini; per hr €3; ☽ 6am-late)

LAUNDRY

Laundry Mat (☎ 28310 29722; Tombazi 45; wash & dry €8.50) Self-service laundry, next door to the youth hostel.

LEFT LUGGAGE

Bus Station Left-Luggage Office (☎ 28310 22659; cnr Kefalogiannidon & Igoumenou Gavriil) The bus station stores luggage for €1.50 per day.

MEDICAL SERVICES

Hospital (☎ 28210 27491; Triandalydou 17; ☽ 24hr)

MONEY

Alpha Bank (Pavlou Koundouriotou 29) Has a 24-hour automatic exchange machine and ATM.

National Bank of Greece (Dimokratias) On the far side of the square opposite the town hall.

POST

Post office (☎ 28310 22302; Moatsou 21; ☽ 7am-7pm)

TOURIST INFORMATION

Municipal tourist office (☎ 28310 29148; Eleftheriou Venizelou; ☽ 9am-9pm Mon-Fri Jun-Sep) Very convenient and helpful.

TRAVEL AGENCIES

Ellotia Tours (☎ 28310 24533; elotia@ret.forthnet.gr; Arkadiou 161; ☽ 9am-9pm Mar-Nov)

Sights

Rethymno's 16th-century **fortress** (fortezza; ☎ 28310 28101; adult/concession €3/2.50; ☽ 8am-8pm Jun-Oct) is the site of the city's ancient acropolis. Within its massive walls a great number of buildings once stood, of which only a church and a mosque survive intact. The ramparts offer good views, while the site has lots of ruins to explore.

The **Archaeological Museum** (☎ 28310 54668; admission €3; ☽ 8.30am-3pm Tue-Sun), near the entrance to the fortress, was once a prison. The exhibits are well labelled in English and contain Neolithic tools, Minoan pottery excavated from nearby tombs, Mycenaean figurines and a 1st-century-AD relief of Aphrodite, as well as an important coin collection.

Rethymno's **Historical & Folk Art Museum** (☎ 28310 23398; Vernardou 28-30; admission €3; ☽ 9.30am-2.30pm Mon-Sat) gives an excellent overview of the area's rural lifestyle, with its collection of old clothes, baskets, weavings and farm tools.

Pride of place among the many vestiges of Venetian rule in the old quarter goes to the **Rimondi Fountain** with its spouting lion heads and Corinthian capitals and the 16th-century **Loggia**, now a museum shop.

At the southern end of Ethnikis Antistaseos is the well-preserved **Porto Guora** (Great Gate), a remnant of the defensive wall.

The **Centre for Byzantine Art** (☎ 28210 50120; Ethnikis Antistaseos) is a great example of a restored Venetian/Turkish mansion and has a terrace café with great views of the old town. Other Turkish legacies in the old quarter include the **Kara Musa Pasha Mosque**, which has a vaulted fountain, and the **Nerantzes Mosque**, which was converted from a Franciscan church in 1657.

Activities

The **Happy Walker** (☎ /fax 28310 52920; www.happywalker.com; Tombazi 56) runs various walks in the region, including complete walking holidays.

Rethymno's chapter of the **EOS** (Greek Alpine Club; ☎ 28310 57766; http://eos.rethymnon.com; Dimokratias 12) can give advice on mountain climbing in the region.

The **Paradise Dive Centre** (☎ 28310 26317; pdcr@otenet.gr; Eleftheriou Venizelou 57) runs diving activities and PADI courses for all grades of divers.

Several companies at the harbour offer boat excursions to nearby caves, Panormo village and Marathi beach.

Festivals & Events

Rethymno's main cultural event is the annual **Renaissance Festival** (☎ 28310 51199; www .cultureguide.gr; ☒ Jul-Sep), primarily held in the Erofili Theatre at the fortress. Most years there's a **Wine Festival** in mid-July in the municipal park. There are lively carnival celebrations in February.

Sleeping

BUDGET

Sea Front (☎ 28310 51981; www.rethymnoatcrete.com; Arkadiou 159; s/d €30/35; ☒) This delightful pension has six fresh and cheerful studio apartments with sea views and ceiling fans. They can be noisy at night, however.

Olga's Pension (☎ 28310 28665; Souliou 57; s/d/tr €25/35/45; ☒) Friendly Olga's is tucked away on colourful Souliou. A quirky network of terraces, all bursting with flowers and greenery, connects a wide range of basic but colourful rooms, some with sea views. Most have a fridge, TV, fan, air-con and basic bathrooms.

Barbara Dokimaki Rooms (☎ 28310 24581; irodok@yahoo.com; Damvergi 14; s €30, d €40-60, tr €65; ☒) This well-located complex of rooms in a Venetian building with a newer 2nd-floor addition is set around a pleasant courtyard. The rooms are simple rooms with timber floors and some period features. They have TV and air-con and dated but functional bathrooms.

Rethymno Youth Hostel (☎ 28310 22848; www .yhrethymno.com; Tombazi 41; dm without bathroom €8) The hostel is friendly and well run with free hot showers. Breakfast is available (€2) and there's a bar in the evening. There is no curfew and the place is open all year.

Elizabeth Camping (☎ 28310 28694; sites per person/tent €6.55/4.38) Located near Mysiria beach, 3km east of Rethymno, this is the nearest camping ground. There's a taverna, snack bar and mini-market, plus a communal fridge, free beach umbrellas and sun lounges, and a weekly beach BBQ. An Iraklio-bound bus can drop you here.

MIDRANGE & TOP END

Hotel Fortezza (☎ 28310 55551; www.fortezza.gr; Melissinou 16; s/d incl breakfast €57/69; ℗ ☒ ☒) Housed in a refurbished old building in the heart of the old town, the tasteful rooms have TVs, telephones and air-con. After a day of roaming through Rethymno, it's pleasant to relax by the swimming pool.

Hotel Veneto (☎ 28310 56634; www.veneto.gr; Epimenidou 4; studio/ste incl breakfast €112/127; ☒) The oldest part of the hotel dates from the 14th century and many traditional features have been preserved without sacrificing modern comforts. There's a stunning pebble mosaic in the foyer and the eye-catching rooms of polished wood floors and ceilings have iron beds, satellite TV and kitchenettes. Rates drop significantly out of high season.

Palazzo Rimondi (☎ 28310 51289; rimondi@otenet .gr; Xanthoulidou 21 & Trikoupi 16; ste €164-213; ☒) This charming Venetian mansion in the heart of the old city has its exquisite individually decorated studios with kitchenettes. There's a small splash pool in the courtyard where breakfast is served.

Palazzini di Corina (☎ 28310 21205; www .corina.gr; Damvergi 9; d incl breakfast €120, ste €160-220; ☒ ☒) This regal Venetian mansion right near the harbour is one of the classiest boutique hotels in town. It has been beautifully restored, with exposed stone walls, timber vaulted ceiling, iron beds and lovely internal mosaic courtyard, and is superbly decorated with antique furniture.

Eating

The waterfront and Venetian harbour are lined with similar tourist restaurants fronted by fast-talking touts. Rethymno does have some fine restaurants – the best are inland from the harbour.

BUDGET

Taverna Kyria Maria (☎ 28310 29078; Moshovitou 20; Cretan specials €2.40-6.50). For authentic atmosphere, head inland to this traditional taverna. It has outdoor seating under a leafy trellis, and meals end with a complimentary dessert and shot of raki.

Samaria (☎ 28310 24681; Eleftheriou Venizelou; mayirefta €4.50-5.50) One of the few waterfront tavernas where you'll see local families eating. There's a large range of *mayirefta* in trays inside, the soups and grills are excellent and the fruit and raki are complimentary.

THE AUTHOR'S CHOICE

The moment you walk into the enclosed garden of this stunningly restored Venetian villa you know you are in for a sensory and culinary treat. The ambience and artful displays at **Avli** (☎ 28310 26213; www.avli.com; cnr Xanthoudidou 22 & Radamanthyos; mains €11-18) set the scene for superb contemporary Cretan and Mediterranean cuisine. Local produce and aromatic herbs feature heavily in dishes such as wild goat with thyme and honey, or the lamb with wild greens. Avli is one of Greece's best restaurants and has one of the country's top wine lists – the wine bar in the adjacent old stables boasts more than 200 Greek wines. If you want to complete the romantic experience there are four classy suites with Jacuzzis upstairs.

MIDRANGE

Thalassografia (☎ 28310 52569; Kefalogiannidon 33; mezedes €4.20-8.90) This excellent *mezedopoleio* (restaurant specialising in *mezedes*) is the place to watch the sunset and try some fine Cretan *mezedes*, as well as a few pastas and more hearty meals. It's a casual place with a breathtaking setting, taking in views over the sea and the imposing fortress.

Fanari (☎ 28310 54849; Kefalogiannidon 15; mezedes €2.50-6) West of the Venetian harbour, this welcoming waterfront taverna serves good *mezedes*, fresh fish and Cretan cuisine. The *Bekri mezes* (pork with wine and peppers) is excellent or try the local speciality, *apaki* (smoked pork). The home-made wine is decent, too.

Castelvecchio (☎ 28310 50886; Himaras 29; mains €7-13) The affable Valantis will make you really feel at home in the garden terrace of this family taverna located on the edge of the *fortezza*. Try the *klefyiko* (slow oven-baked lamb) or the variation on *mousaka* (sliced eggplant and minced meat arranged in layers and baked), with yogurt.

Lemonokipos (☎ 28310 57087; Ethnikis Antistaseos 100; mains €5.80-8) Dine among the lemon trees in the lovely courtyard of this well-respected taverna in the old quarter. It's good typical Cretan fare, with a good range of vegetarian dishes and lots of tasty appetisers.

Vasilis (☎ 28310 22967; Nearhou 10) The enticing display of fish in the showcase is no mere show. Hemmed in amongst the harbour-side fish tavernas, local foodies consider this atmospheric old-style taverna the best. The top fish are €41 per kilogram.

Also recommended:
Othonos (☎ 28310 55500; Petihaki 27) For Cretan food.
Ellinikon (☎ 28310 52526; Petihaki 11) For *mezedes*.

Entertainment

Rock Club Cafe (☎ 28310 31047; Petihaki 8; 🕙 9pm-dawn) Has been one of Rethymno's trendiest hang-outs for a while and still kicks on. A crowd of young professionals and tourists fills the club nightly.

Fortezza Disco (Nearhou 20; 🕙 11pm-dawn) Of the lively clubs around the Venetian port, this is the town's showpiece disco. It's big and flashy with three bars, a laser show and a well-groomed international crowd that starts drifting in around midnight.

Notes (☎ 28310 29785; Himaras 17; 🕙 10pm-late) A classic little bar with a polished-wood bar, run by a musician who has an excellent selection of Greek music and encourages art.

Figaro (☎ 28310 29431; Vernardou 21; ☎ noon-late) Housed in an ingeniously restored old building, Figaro is an atmospheric 'art and music' all-day bar that attracts a subdued crowd for drinks, snacks and its excellent mix of music.

Getting There & Away

BOAT

ANEK (☎ 28310 29221; www.anek.gr; Arkadiou 250) operates a daily ferry between Rethymno and Piraeus (€28.70, nine hours), leaving both Rethymno and Piraeus at 8pm.

BUS

From the **bus station** (☎ 28310 22212; Igoumenou Gavriil) there are hourly summer services to both Hania (€6, one hour) and Iraklio (€6.50, 1½ hours). There are also six buses a day to Plakias (€3.50, one hour), five to Agia Galini (€4.80, 1½ hours), three to Moni Arkadiou (€2.10, 40 minutes), one to Omalos (€11.30, two hours) and two to Preveli (€3.50). There are three daily buses to Hora Sfakion (€5.80, two hours) via Vryses. Services are greatly reduced in the low season.

Getting Around

Auto Motor Sports (☎ 28310 24858; www.auto motosport.com.gr; Sofokli Venizelou 48) rents cars and has 300 motorbikes, from mopeds and 50cc bikes to a Harley 1200cc.

CRETE

AROUND RETHYMNO

Moni Arkadiou Μονή Αρκαδίου

Surrounded by attractive hill country, the 16th-century **Moni Arkadiou** (Arkadi; ☎ 28310 83136; admission €2; ☺ 9am-7pm Apr-Oct) is 23km southeast of Rethymno. The most impressive of the buildings is the Venetian baroque church. Its striking façade has eight slender Corinthian columns and an ornate triple-belled tower.

In November 1866 the Turks sent massive forces to quell insurrections which were gathering momentum throughout the island. Hundreds of men, women and children who had fled their villages used the monastery as a safe haven. When 2000 Turkish soldiers attacked the building, rather than surrender, the Cretans set light to a store of gunpowder. The explosion killed everyone, Turks included, except one small girl, who lived to a ripe old age in a village nearby. Busts of the woman, and the abbot who lit the gun powder, stand outside the monastery.

There are three daily buses from Rethymno to the monastery (€3.30, 30 minutes).

Margarites Μαργαρίτες

pop 331

Known for its tradition of pottery, this town, 27km from Rethymno, is invaded by tour buses in the morning. There are more than 20 ceramic studios and the pottery is of mixed quality and taste. Amongst the garish pieces that line the main street, there are good-quality, authentic local designs at a few places. The traditional potters use local clay collected from the foot of Mt Psiloritis, which is of such fine quality it needs only one firing and no glazing – the outside smoothed with a pebble. You will see many pieces bearing the flower motif of the area.

The most traditional place is the workshop of septuagenarian potter **Manolis Syragopoulos** (☎ 28340 92363) who is the only one still using manual wheels and a wood-fired kiln to make pottery the way his great grandfather did. It's about 1km outside the town on your left.

Other stand-out places include Konstantinos Gallios' excellent studio **Ceramic Art** (☎ 28340 92304) and the slick **Kerameion** (☎ 28340 92135) on the main street, which has many pieces based on Minoan designs.

There are wonderful views over the valley from the taverna terraces on the main square.

From Margarites, you can visit **Ancient Eleftherna** with its extraordinary Roman cisterns. There are two buses daily from Rethymno (€2.70, 30 minutes).

ANOGIA ΑΝΩΓΕΙΑ

pop 2454

If ever there was a village that embodies quintessential Crete, it is Anogia, a bucolic village perched on the flanks of **Mt Psiloritis** 37km southwest of Iraklio. Anogia is well known for its rebellious spirit and its determination to hang on to its undiluted Cretan character. Its famous **weddings** involve the entire village. It's also known for its stirring music and has spawned a disproportionate number of Crete's best-known musicians.

Anogia is a macho town where the *kafeneia* (coffee shops) on the main square are frequented by moustachioed men, the older ones often wearing traditional dress. The women stay behind the scenes or flog traditional crafts that hang all over the shops in town.

During WWII Anogia was a centre of resistance to the Germans, who massacred all the men in the village in retaliation for their role in sheltering Allied troops and aiding in the kidnap of General Kreipe. Today, Anogia is the centre of a prosperous sheep-husbandry industry and a burgeoning tourist trade, bolstered as much by curious Greeks as by foreign travellers seeking a Crete away from the hype of the coastal resorts.

The town is spread out on a hillside with the textile shops in the lower half and most accommodation and businesses in the upper half. There's an Agricultural Bank with an ATM, and post office in the upper village. You can check mail at **Infocost** (☎ 28340 31808; per hr €3; ☺ 5pm-late) in the upper village.

In the upper village, the friendly **Hotel Aristea** (☎ 28340 31459; d incl breakfast €40) has good views from the simple but well-outfitted rooms with TV, private bathrooms and balconies, and there's an excellent set of new studios next door.

The oldest restaurant in town, **Ta Skalomata** (☎ 28340 31316; grills €3.50-6.80) provides a wide variety of grills and Cretan dishes at very reasonable prices. Zucchini with cheese and aubergine (€3.20) is very tasty, as is their home-baked bread. The restaurant is on the eastern side of the upper village and enjoys great views.

There are five buses daily from Iraklio (€2.90, one hour), and two buses daily Monday to Friday from Rethymno (€3.90, 1¼ hours).

SPILI ΣΠΗΛΙ
pop 642

Spili (spee-lee) is a pretty mountain village with cobbled streets, rustic houses and plane trees. Its centrepiece is a unique Venetian fountain, which spurts water from 19 lion heads. Bring along your own water containers and fill up with the best water on the island. Tourist buses regularly stop in the town during the day, but in the evening Spili belongs to the locals. It is a great base for exploring the region or at least a good spot for lunch.

The bus stop is just south of the square. There are two ATMs and the post office on the main street and you can check mail at Café Babis near the fountain.

Signposted from the main road, **Heracles Rooms** (☎ /fax 28320 22411; s/d €24/30) has clean and nicely furnished rooms with great mountain views and insect screens on the door.

Costas Inn (☎ 28320 22040; fax 28320 22043; d/tr incl breakfast €35/45) is the only pension encountered which offers bathrobes, all part of the homy atmosphere at these well-kept, pleasant rooms. They also have satellite TV, radio, ceiling fans, fridge, use of a washing machine and, for those on longer stays, the pool at a nearby estate. Breakfast is downstairs at **Taverna Costas** (Cretan specials €2.50-5), which has good home cooking and organic wine and raki.

Maria and Costas (☎ 28320 22436; mains €4-6) is easily recognisable from the gourds hanging in the vine- and wisteria-covered courtyard on the main road. The restaurant does decent charcoal-grilled meats.

PLAKIAS ΠΛΑΚΙΑΣ
pop 177

The south coast town of Plakias, 37km from Rethymno, was once a tranquil fishing village before it became a tourist resort. It's a spread-out town that maintains a relaxed outlook and is popular with backpackers and independent travellers. Off-season it attracts many families and an older crowd.

Plakias offers a good range of independent accommodation, some pretty decent eating options, good regional walks, a large sandy beach and enough nightlife to keep you entertained.

Orientation & Information

It's easy to find your way around Plakias, whose main street skirts the beach and another runs parallel to it one block back. The bus stop is at the middle of the waterfront.

Plakias has two ATMs. The post office is on the street off Monza Travel.

Monza Travel Agency (☎ 28320 31882) Near the bus stop, offers currency exchange and can help with accommodation, car hire and excursions.

Ostraco Bar (☎ 28320 31710; per hr €4.50; ☼ 9am-late) You can check email at this place on the main street.

Youth Hostel Plakias (☎ 28320 32118; per hr €4.50) Also for checking email.

Sleeping

Pension Thetis (☎ 28320 31430; fax 28320 31987; studio €40-50; ☒) Thetis is a very pleasant, family-oriented set of studios. Upgraded in 2004, the rooms have fridge, cooking facilities, coffee maker and TV. Relax in the cool and shady garden where there is a small play park for kids.

Castello (☎ /fax 28320 31112; info@castello-plakias .com; studio €30-33; P ☒) It is the relaxed owner Christos and his leafy and shady garden that makes this place a happy haven. All rooms are cool, clean and fridge-equipped and have cooking facilities. There are also big two-bedroom apartments (€45 to €50) ideal for families.

Pension Afrodite (☎ 28320 31266; kasel@hol.gr; s/d €30/40; ☒) This upmarket pension is in a lovely garden and the cheery, spotless rooms have more mod cons than some hotels, including a kettle, safe and hairdryer. The breakfast is excellent but you can get a lower rate without it.

Neos Alianthos Garden (☎ 28320 31280; www .alianthos.gr; d incl breakfast €59; ☒ ☒) This small hotel is at the entrance to town, next to the road overlooking the sea. It's comfortably furnished in traditional Cretan style and has two pools.

Hotel Livykon (☎ 28320 31216; fax 28320 31420; s/d €20/25; ☒) This fairly ordinary hotel on the seafront has basic, small and relatively cheap

CRETE

rooms. The room rate does at least include air-conditioning and there is a fridge.

Youth Hostel Plakias (☎ 28320 32118; www.yhplakias.com; dm without bathroom €7.50; 🖳) For independent travellers this is *the* place to stay in Plakias. Manager Chris from the UK has created a very friendly place with spotless dorms, green lawns, volleyball court and Internet access. Many guests stay for months. It's a 10-minute signposted walk from the bus stop.

Eating

Taverna Sofia (☎ 28320 31333; mains €4.50-7) In business since 1969, Sofia's is a solid choice, with daily specials. Choose from the clay pots in the window. Try the lamb in yogurt or lamb fricassee. The same family runs the other Sofia on the waterfront near the bus stop.

Taverna Christos (☎ 28320 31472; mains €4.10-9.50) An established waterfront taverna, Christos has a romantic tamarisk-shaded terrace overlooking the sea. It has a good choice of the main Cretan dishes and fresh fish.

Next door, Gio Ma is proving a tough competitor, sharing the prime spot on the waterfront.

O Tasomanolis (☎ 28320 31129) This traditional fish taverna on the western end of the beach is run by a keen fisherman. You can sample his catch on a pleasant terrace overlooking the beach, grilled and accompanied with wild greens and wine. Top fish are €45. He also takes boat trips to Preveli. Some other options:

Kri Kri (☎ 28320 32223; pizzas €5-11) For wood-fired pizza try this spot, near the bus stop.

Nikos Souvlaki (☎ 28320 31921) A popular and cheap *souvlaki* place.

Getting There & Away

In summer there are six buses a day to Rethymno (€3.50, one hour). It's possible to get to Agia Galini from Plakias by catching a Rethymno bus to the Koxare junction (referred to as Bale on timetables) and waiting for a bus to Agia Galini. Plakias has good bus connections in summer, but virtually none in winter. The bus stop has a timetable.

Getting Around

Cars Alianthos (☎ 28320 31851; www.alianthos.com) is a reliable car-hire outlet.

Easy Ride (☎ 28320 20052; www.easyride.reth.gr), close to the post office, rents out mountain bikes, bicycles, scooters and motorcycles.

AROUND PLAKIAS

Moni Preveli Μονή Πρέβελη

Standing in splendid isolation above the Libyan Sea, 14km east of Plakias and 35km from Rethymno, is the well-maintained **Moni Preveli** (☎ 28320 31246; admission €2; ⏰ 8am-7pm mid-Mar–May, 8am-1.30pm & 3.30-7.30pm Jun-Oct). Like most of Crete's monasteries, it played a significant role in the islanders' rebellion against Turkish rule. It became a centre of resistance during 1866, causing the Turks to set fire to it and destroy surrounding crops. After the Battle of Crete in 1941, many Allied soldiers were sheltered here by Abbot Agathangelos before their evacuation to Egypt. In retaliation the Germans plundered the monastery. The monastery's **museum** contains a candelabra presented by grateful British soldiers after the war.

From June through August there are two buses daily from Rethymno to Moni Preveli (€3.50).

Preveli Beach

At the mouth of the Kourtaliotis Gorge, Preveli or Palm Beach (Paralia Finikodasous) is one of Crete's most photographed and popular beaches. The river Megalopotamos meets the back end of the beach before it conveniently loops around and empties into the Libyan Sea. The palm-lined banks of the river have freshwater pools ideal for a swim and there are also pedal boats for hire. The beach is fringed with oleander bushes and palm trees.

A steep path leads down to the beach from a large car park below Moni Preveli, or you can get to within several hundred metres of the beach by following a signposted 5km-long rough dirt road from a stone bridge to the left just off the Moni Preveli main road. You can also get to Preveli Beach from Plakias by boat from June through August or by taxi boat from Agia Galini.

AGIOS PAVLOS & TRIOPETRA
ΑΓΙΟΣ ΠΑΥΛΟΣ & ΤΡΙΟΠΕΤΡΑ

It's not surprising that the fabulous remote sandy beaches of Agios Pavlos and Triopetra have been chosen by yoga retreats.

These unspoilt and peaceful beaches, about 53km from Rethymno, surrounded by sand dunes and rugged cliffs are arguably one of the most beautiful stretches of unspoilt coastline in Crete.

Agios Pavlos is little more than a few rooms and tavernas around a small cove with a sandy beach, but the best beaches are on the subsequent sandy coves, which are about a 10-minute walk over the cliffs. The sand dunes reach all the way to the top, which can get nasty on very windy days.

The coves stretch all the way to the three giant rocks, known as Triopetra, that stick out of the sea. The long stretch of beach beyond can be reached from Agios Pavlos (about 300m is drivable dirt road) or via a 12km-long windy asphalt road from the village of Akoumia, on the Rethymno–Agia Galini road.

Agios Pavlos Hotel & Taverna (☎ 28320 71104; www.agiospavloshotel.gr; d €30) is a family-run place with simple rooms in the main building. It has small balconies overlooking the sea, as well as rooms under the shady terrace below the taverna (*mayirefta* €3.50 to €6), which has good Cretan food. The café-bar next door is the place for breakfast and drinks, and has Internet facilities.

Yirogiali Taverna & Rooms (☎ 28320 71122; d/tr/q €25/30/35; Triopetra; 🗙), right on the big beach, is run by two brothers, with their mother cooking in the kitchen. The rooms are a recent addition, with marble floors and bathrooms, attractive timber furniture, fridge, TV and balconies.

There is no public transport to these beaches.

AGIA GALINI ΑΓΙΑ ΓΑΛΗΝΗ
pop 1260

Agia Galini (a-ya ga-*lee*-nee) is another erstwhile picturesque fishing village where package tourism and overdevelopment has spoilt much of its original charm. Hemmed in against the sea by large sandstone cliffs and phalanxes of hotels and *domatia*, Agia Galini can be rather claustrophobic – an ambience that is made worse by the ugly cement blocks in the harbour.

It is probably the most touristy southern beach resort. While it still gets lively during peak season, it has become a more sedate resort attracting a middle-aged crowd and families. Still, it does boast 340 days of sunshine a year, and some places remain open out of season, which is probably the best time to go.

It's a convenient base to visit Phaestos and Agia Triada, and although the town beach is crowded there are boats to better beaches. It has a friendly and lively atmosphere at night but, unless you are after nightlife, you might ultimately be better off elsewhere.

Orientation & Information
The bus station is at the top of Eleftheriou Venizelou, which is a continuation of the approach road. The central square, overlooking the harbour, is downhill from the bus station. You'll walk past the post office on the way. There are four ATMs and travel agencies with currency exchange, while the OTE is on the square.

Cosmos Internet (☎ 28320 91262; per hr €5; 🕙 9am-late) Go online here.

Laundry (🕙 10am-2pm & 5-10pm) Just off the square.

Sleeping
Adonis (☎ 28320 91333; hoteladonis@hotmail.com; r €45-90; 🗙 🖭) This pleasant hotel is spread over several buildings but the rooms, studios and apartments all have use of the large pool. Rooms are light and clean and most have been refurbished. Some have balconies with sea views.

Stohos Rooms & Taverna (☎ 28320 91433; d incl breakfast €40-50; 🗙) On the main beach, with apartments upstairs with kitchenettes and big balconies, and huge studios downstairs which are ideal for families or groups. Friendly Fanourios presides over the excellent taverna downstairs. Try the *klefyiko* or other clay-oven dishes, or the grills (€5.50 to €7.50).

Erofili Hotel (☎ 28320 91319; hotelerofili@hotmail .com; d incl breakfast €30-40; 🗙) Run by the laid-back Miro and his turtle mascot, this pleasant 10-room hotel has loads of character and a traditional feel. There are plain rooms and some with air-con, fridge and TV. All have great sea views and the lower rooms have a garden terrace. It's signposted to the right off the main road. Miro also takes sailing trips (€20).

Hotel Rea (☎ /fax 28320 91390; hoter-rea@gmx .net; s/d €20/25; 🗙) On the main road near the port, this budget hotel is dated, but has clean, reasonably sized twin and double rooms with pine furniture.

CRETE

Agia Galini Camping (☎ 28320 91386; sites per person/tent €5/3) Next to the beach, 2.5km east of the town, this camping ground is signposted off the Iraklio–Agia Galini road. It's well shaded and has a restaurant and mini-market.

Eating

Faros (☎ 28320 91346) Inland from the harbour, this no-frills place is one of the oldest fish tavernas in town, dishing up reasonably priced fresh fish (per kilogram €30) as well as a range of grills and *mayirefta*.

Madame Hortense (☎ 28320 91215; specials €6-13) The most atmospheric and elaborate restaurant/bar in town is on the top floor of the three-level Zorbas complex on the harbour. Cuisine is Greek Mediterranean, with a touch of the East.

La Strada (☎ 28320 91053; pizzas €5-7.50, pastas €4-6) On the first street left of the bus station, this place has excellent pizzas, pastas and risottos.

Also recommended are Kostas, the fish taverna at the eastern end of the beach, and Bozos on the harbour for traditional Cretan food.

Getting There & Away
BUS

In peak season there are nine buses each day to Iraklio (€5.50, two hours), five to Rethymno (€4.80, 1½ hours), nine to Phaestos (€1.50, 40 minutes) and five to Matala (€2.50, 45 minutes).

TAXI BOAT

In summer there are daily boats from the harbour to the beaches of Agios Giorgios, Agiofarango and Preveli (Palm Beach), but they are expensive (€15 to €20).

WESTERN CRETE

The westernmost part of Crete comprises the prefecture of Hania, named after the charming old Venetian city that is the region's capital – and one of the island's better attractions. The region's most famous attraction, however, is the spectacular and memorable Samaria Gorge. The area's south-coast towns of Paleohora and Sougia are laid-back resorts worthy of a visit.

HANIA XANIA
pop 53,373

Hania (hahn-*yah*; also spelt Chania) is unreservedly Crete's most evocative city. Its beautiful Venetian quarter is a web of atmospheric streets that tumble onto a magnificent harbour. Restored Venetian townhouses have been converted into chic restaurants and boutique hotels, while ruins house stunning restaurants. The prominent former mosque and other remnants of the city's Turkish rulers add to Hania's exotic charm. Hania has a lively tradition of artisanship and boasts some of the island's finest restaurants. The Old Town is one of the best places in Crete to spend a few days.

The Hania county gets its fair share of package tourists, but most of them stick to the beach developments that stretch out to the west. Hania is a main transit point for trekkers heading for the Samaria Gorge.

History

Hania is the site of the Minoan settlement of Kydonia, which was centred on the hill to the east of the harbour. Little excavation work has been done, but the finding of clay tablets with Linear B script (see the boxed text, p228) has led archaeologists to believe that Kydonia was both a palace site and an important town.

Kydonia met the same fiery fate as most other Minoan settlements in 1450 BC, but soon re-emerged as a force. It was a flourishing city-state during Hellenistic times and continued to prosper under Roman and Byzantine rule.

The city became Venetian at the beginning of the 13th century, and the name was changed to La Canea. The Venetians spent a lot of time constructing massive fortifications to protect the city from marauding pirates and invading Turks. This did not prove very effective against the latter, who took Hania in 1645 after a two-month siege.

The Great Powers made Hania the island capital in 1898 and it remained so until 1971, when the administration was transferred to Iraklio.

Hania was heavily bombed during WWII, but enough of the Old Town survives for it to be regarded as Crete's most beautiful city.

Orientation

Hania's bus station is on Kydonias, two blocks southwest of Plateia 1866, one of the main squares. From Plateia 1866, the Old Harbour is a short walk north up Halidon.

Most accommodation is to the left as you face the harbour. The headland separates the Venetian port from the crowded town beach in the modern quarter, called Nea Hora. Accommodation can also be found in the back streets behind the mosque.

Koum Kapi is a rejuvenated precinct in the old Turkish quarter further east, lined with waterfront cafés, bars and restaurants.

Boats to Hania dock at Souda, about 7km southeast of town.

Information

BOOKSHOPS

Mediterraneo Bookstore (☎ 28210 86904; Akti Koundourioti 57) An extensive range of English language novels and books on Crete, as well international press.

Newsstand (☎ 28210 95888; Skalidi 8) A wide range of international press and magazines, books, Crete guides and maps.

Pelekanakis (☎ 28210 92512; Halidon 98) Has maps, guidebooks and books in 11 languages.

EMERGENCY

Tourist police (☎ 28210 73333; Kydonias 29; ⏲ 8am-2.30pm) At the Town Hall; also occasionally at the mosque in Old Harbour.

INTERNET ACCESS

Manos Internet (☎ 28210 94156; Zambeliou 24; per hr €3; ⏲ 9am-late)

Vranas Studios Internet (☎ 28210 58618; Agion Deka 10; per hr €3; ⏲ 9am-11pm)

INTERNET RESOURCES

www.chania.gr The Municipality of Hania's website has information on the city and cultural events.

www.chania-guide.gr Has good information on Hania city and prefecture.

LAUNDRY

Laundry Fidias (☎ 28210 52494; Kallinikou; wash & dry €6)

Old Town Laundromat (☎ 28210 59414; Karaoli & Dimitriou 38; wash & dry €7; ⏲ 9am-2pm & 6-9pm Mon-Sat) Also does dry cleaning.

LEFT LUGGAGE

KTEL bus station (☎ 28210 93052; Kydonias 73-77; per day €1.50)

MEDICAL SERVICES

Hania Hospital (☎ 28210 22000; Mournies) Located south of town.

MONEY

Most banks are concentrated around the new city, while there are a few stand-alone ATMs in the Old Town on Halidon. There are numerous places to change money outside banking hours.

Alpha Bank (cnr Halidon & Skalidi) Has 24-hour automatic exchange machine.

Citibank (Halidon) Has ATM.

Emboriki (Halidon) Has ATM.

National Bank of Greece (cnr Tzanakaki & Giannari) Has 24-hour exchange machine.

POST

Post Office (☎ 28210 28445; Tzanakaki 3; ⏲ 7.30am-8pm Mon-Fri, 7.30am-2pm Sat)

TOURIST INFORMATION

Municipal Tourist Information Office (☎ 28210 36155; tourism@chania.gr; Kydonias 29; ⏲ 8am-2.30pm) Located under the Town Hall, it provides helpful practical information and maps.

TRAVEL AGENCIES

Diktynna Travel (☎ 28210 41458; www.diktynna -travel.gr; Sfakion 36)

Tellus Travel (☎ 28210 91500; Halidon 108; www .tellustravel.gr; ⏲ 8am-11pm) Rents out cars, changes money, arranges air and boat tickets and sells excursions.

Sights

MUSEUMS

Hania's **Archaeological Museum** (☎ 28210 90334; Halidon 30; admission €2, incl Byzantine Collection €3; ⏲ 8.30am-3pm Tue-Sun) is housed in the 16th-century Venetian Church of San Francisco. The Turkish fountain in the grounds is a relic from the building's days as a mosque. The museum houses a well-displayed collection of finds from western Crete dating from the Neolithic to the Roman era. Exhibits include statues, vases, jewellery, three splendid floor mosaics and some impressive painted sarcophagi from the Late-Minoan cemetery of Armeni.

The **Naval Museum** (☎ 28210 91875; Akti Koundourioti; admission €2.50; ⏲ 9am-4pm) has an interesting collection of model ships dating from the Bronze Age, naval instruments, paintings, photographs and memorabilia from the Battle of Crete. The museum is

HANIA

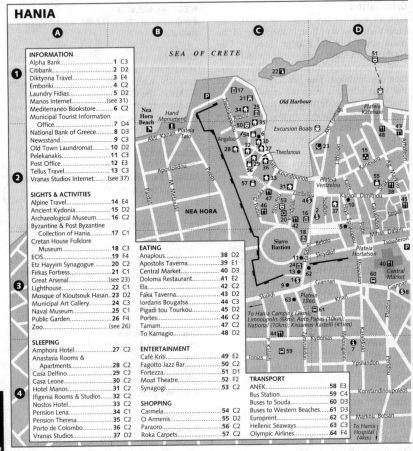

INFORMATION

Alpha Bank	1 C3
Citibank	2 D2
Diktynna Travel	3 E4
Emboriki	4 C2
Laundry Fidias	5 D2
Manos Internet	(see 31)
Mediterraneo Bookstore	6 C2
Municipal Tourist Information Office	7 D4
National Bank of Greece	8 D3
Newsstand	9 C3
Old Town Laundromat	10 D2
Pelekanakis	11 C3
Post Office	12 E3
Tellus Travel	13 C3
Vranas Studios Internet	(see 37)

SIGHTS & ACTIVITIES

Alpine Travel	14 E4
Ancient Kydonia	15 D2
Archaeological Museum	16 C2
Byzantine & Post Byzantine Collection of Hania	17 C1
Cretan House Folklore Museum	18 C3
EOS	19 F4
Etz Hayyim Synagogue	20 C2
Firkas Fortress	21 C1
Great Arsenal	(see 23)
Lighthouse	22 C1
Mosque of Kioutsouk Hasan	23 D2
Municipal Art Gallery	24 C3
Naval Museum	25 C1
Public Garden	26 F4
Zoo	(see 26)

SLEEPING

Amphora Hotel	27 C2
Anastasia Rooms & Apartments	28 C2
Casa Delfino	29 C2
Casa Leone	30 C2
Hotel Manos	31 C2
Ifigenia Rooms & Studios	32 C2
Nostos Hotel	33 C2
Pension Lena	34 C1
Pension Theresa	35 C2
Porto de Colombo	36 C2
Vranas Studios	37 D2

EATING

Anaplous	38 D2
Apostolis Taverna	39 E1
Central Market	40 D3
Doloma Restaurant	41 E2
Ela	42 C2
Faka Taverna	43 D2
Iordanis Bougatsa	44 C3
Pigadi tou Tourkou	45 D2
Portes	46 C2
Tamam	47 C2
To Karnagio	48 D2

ENTERTAINMENT

Café Kriti	49 E2
Fagotto Jazz Bar	50 C2
Fortezza	51 D1
Moat Theatre	52 F2
Synagogi	53 C2

SHOPPING

Carmela	54 C2
O Armenis	55 D2
Paraoro	56 C2
Roka Carpets	57 C2

TRANSPORT

ANEK	58 E3
Bus Station	59 C4
Buses to Souda	60 D3
Buses to Western Beaches	61 D3
Europrent	62 C3
Hellenic Seaways	63 C3
Olympic Airlines	64 F4

---

housed in the Firkas Fortress on the headland, once the old Turkish prison.

The **Byzantine and Post Byzantine Collection of Hania** (☎ 28210 96046; Theotokopoulou; admission €2, incl Archaeological Museum €3; ◷ 8.30am-3pm Tue-Sun) is in the impressively restored Church of San Salvatore, on the western side of the fortress. It has a small but fascinating collection of artefacts, icons, jewellery and coins, including a fine mosaic floor and a prized icon of St George slaying the dragon.

Hania's quaint and jam-packed **Cretan House Folklore Museum** (☎ 28210 90816; Halidon 46; admission €2; ◷ 9.30am-3pm & 6-9pm) contains a selection of crafts and implements including weavings with traditional designs.

OTHER ATTRACTIONS

The massive fortifications built by the Venetians to protect their city remain impressive. The best-preserved section is the western wall, running from the **Firkas Fortress** to the **Siavo Bastion**. You can walk up to the top of the bastion for some good views of the Old Town.

The Venetian **lighthouse** at the entrance to the harbour was getting some tender loving care in 2005. You can walk 1.5km around the sea wall to get there.

You can escape the crowds of the Venetian quarter by taking a stroll around the Turkish **Splantzia quarter** – a delightful tangle of narrow streets and little squares. You can see excavation works at the site of **Ancient**

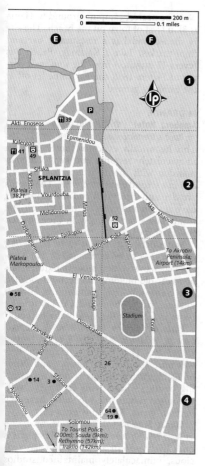

Hania's magnificent covered **food market** is worth a visit even if you don't want to shop. The excellent cheap eateries within the market offer a unique dining experience. Hania's three-level **Municipal Art Gallery** (☎ 28210 92294; www.pinakothiki-chania.gr; Halidon 98; ☉ 10am-1pm & 7-10pm Mon-Fri, 10am-1pm Sat) hosts exhibitions of modern Greek art.

Activities

Alpine Travel (☎ 28210 50939; www.alpine.gr; Boniali 11-19) organises a range of trekking programmes.

EOS (☎ 28210 44647; www.eoshanion.gr; Tzanakaki 90), the Hania branch of the Greek Mountaineering Association, has information about serious climbing in the Lefka Ori, Greece's mountain refuges, the E4 trail, and Crete in general. It runs regular weekend excursions.

Trekking Plan (☎ 28210 60861; www.cycling.gr), 8km west of town in Agia Marina next to the Santa Marina Hotel, offers treks to the Agia Irini Gorge and the Imbros Gorge, and climbs of Mt Gingilos. It also organises mountain-bike tours, canyoning, rappelling, rock-climbing and kayaking trips.

Hania for Children

If your five-year-old has lost interest in Venetian architecture, head to the **public garden** between Tzanakaki and Dimokratias, where there's a playground, a small **zoo** with a resident *kri-kri* (Cretan goat) and a children's resource centre with a small selection of books in English. Just outside town the giant water park **Limnoupolis** (☎ 28210 33246; Varypetro; day pass adult/concession €16/11; afternoon pass €11/8; ☉ 10am-8pm) has enough slides and rides to keep kids amused for the day and cafés and pool bars for adults. Buses leave regularly from the KTEL bus station (€1.60).

Tours

Historian **Tony Fennymore** (☎ 28210 87139, 69725 37055; www.fennyscrete.ws; 2-hr walking tour €12; ☉ Apr-Jul & Sep-Oct) puts Hania's history, culture and architecture in context during his informative walking tour of the Old Town. The tours start from the 'Hand' monument on Plateia Talo at the northern end of Theotokopoulou. His witty and indispensable walking guide *Fenny's Hania* (€7.50) is available at Roka Carpets (p252).

Boat excursions from the harbour take you to the nearby islands of Agii Theodorou

Kydonia, to the east of the old harbour at the junction of Kanevaro and Kandaloneou.

On the eastern side of Hania's inner harbour you will see the prominent **Mosque of Kioutsouk Hasan** (also commonly known as the Mosque of Janissaries), which has been restored and houses regular art exhibitions.

The **Great Arsenal** has been stunningly restored and is now home to the Centre for Mediterranean Architecture, which hosts regular events and exhibitions.

Identified as one of the world's top 100 endangered Jewish monuments, the **Etz Hayyim Synagogue** (Parodos Kondylaki; ☎ 28210 86286; www.etz-hayyim-hania.org; ☉ 9am-12.30pm & 6-8pm) was restored in 1999.

CRETE

and Lazaretto and the Gulf of Hania. The **M/S Irini** (☎ 28210 52001; cruises €15; sunset cruises €8, children under 7 free) runs daily cruises on a lovely 1930s cruiser, including free snorkelling gear, and sunset cruises with complimentary fruit and raki.

Sleeping
BUDGET

Pension Theresa (☎ /fax 28210 92798; Angelou 2; s €35, d €40-50; ☒) This creaky old house with a steep spiral staircase and antique furniture is the most atmospheric pension in Hania. It attracts many artists and writers. Some rooms have a view, but there's always the stunning vista from the rooftop terrace where you can use the communal kitchen. The rooms are spotless and all have TV, air-con and lofts with an extra bed, making it ideal for small families, though some are on the tight side.

Pension Lena (☎ 28210 86860; lenachania@hotmail .com; Ritsou 5; s/d €25/50; ☒) Lena's is a friendly, cosy pension in an old Turkish building where you can help yourself to a room if the owner, Lena, is not there. It has an old-world feel and a scattering of antiques. Originally from Hamburg, Lena makes all guests feel welcome.

Hotel Manos (☎ 28210 94156; www.manoshotel .gr; Zambeliou 24; s/d without view €30/40, s/d with view €40/50; ☒ ▣) This is one of the oldest small waterfront hotels in Hania and it's certainly showing its age. But despite the dated and basic décor it is clean and spacious, with fridge and air-con. The front rooms have a small balcony and harbour views.

Anastasia Rooms & Apartments (☎ 28210 88001; anastasia_ap@acn.gr; Theotokopoulou 21; r €38, studio €50-65; ☒) These stylish, spotless and well-equipped studios have new beds and furnishings. They are all two-level with lounge/sofa bed. The bathrooms are basic and the upstairs rooms have balconies.

Ifigenia Rooms & Studios (☎ 28210 94357; www .ifigeniastudios.gr; Gamba & Parodos Agelou; studio €30-70; ☒) This network of five refurbished houses around the Venetian port offers a range of options. All rooms have air-con and some deluxe apartments have kitchenettes, Jacuzzis and views. Some bathrooms are very basic and the faux old-world décor in some rooms is a little contrived.

Hania Camping (☎ 28210 31138; camhania@otenet .gr; Agii Apostoli; caravan/sites per person/tent €7/5/3.50;

☒) The nearest camping ground to Hania is 3km west of town on the beach. The site is shaded and has a restaurant, bar and mini-market. Take a Kalamaki Beach bus (every 15 minutes) from the southeast corner of Plateia 1866 and ask to be let off at the camping ground.

MIDRANGE

Amphora Hotel (☎ 28210 93224; www.amphora .gr; Parodos Theotokopoulou 20; d €80-110, ste 130; ☒) This historically evocative hotel is in an immaculately restored and kept Venetian mansion with rooms around a courtyard and in a second connected wing. The rooms are elegantly decorated and the top rooms have air-con and views of the harbour. The front rooms can be noisy in the summer. Breakfast is €10.

Nostos Hotel (☎ 28210 94740; fax 28210 94743; Zambeliou 42-46; s/d incl breakfast €40/80; ☒) Mixing Venetian style and modern fixtures, this 600-year-old building has been remodelled into classy split-level rooms/units, all with kitchen, fridge, phone and TV. Try to get a room in front for the view of the harbour.

Porto de Colombo (☎ 28210 70945; colompo@ otenet.gr; Theofanous & Moschon; d/ste incl breakfast €70/88; ☒) The Venetian mansion that was once the French embassy and office of Eleftherios Venizelos is now a charming boutique hotel with 10 lovely, well-appointed rooms; the top suites have fine harbour views. Air-con is extra €5.

Vranas Studios (☎ 28210 58618; www.vranas .gr; Agion Deka 10; studio €40-55; ☒) This place is on a lively pedestrian street and has spacious, immaculately maintained studios with kitchenettes. All rooms have polished wooden floors, balconies, TVs and telephones. Air-con is also available.

TOP END

Casa Delfino (☎ 28210 93098; www.casadelfino.com; Theofanous 7; d/apt incl buffet breakfast €185-298; ☒) This elegant 17th-century mansion is the most luxurious hotel in the Old Town. There are 22 individually decorated and well-appointed suites, including a palatial, split-level apartment with a Jacuzzi that sleeps up to four people. Breakfast is in the splendid pebble-mosaic courtyard.

Casa Leone (☎ 28210 76762; www.casa-leone.com; Parodos Theotokopoulou 18; s & d incl breakfast €80-130; ☒) This Venetian residence has been converted into a classy and romantic boutique hotel. The rooms are spacious and well appointed, with balconies overlooking the harbour. There are honeymoon suites, the usual mod cons and extras like hairdryers.

Eating

Hania has some of the finest restaurants in Crete. Unfortunately, most of the prime-position waterfront tavernas are generally mediocre, often overpriced and fronted by annoying touts. Head for the back streets, where some of the best tavernas are housed in roofless Venetian ruins.

BUDGET

The two tavernas in the food market are good places to seek out cheap traditional cuisine. Their prices are almost identical and the quality is excellent.

Iordanis Bougatsa (☎ 28210 90026; Kydonias 96; 150g bougatsa slice €2.10) Continuing the business started by his great-grandfather in 1924, Iordanis churns out endless trays of his famous delicious creamy *bougatsa* (filo pastry filled with *myzithra* cheese sprinkled with a little icing sugar). It's opposite the bus station.

Doloma Restaurant (☎ 28210 51196; Kalergon 8; mayirefta €3.50-5.80; Mon-Sat) This unpretentious restaurant is half-hidden amid the vines and foliage that surround the outdoor terrace. The traditional cooking is faultless. Pick from the trays of about 14 types of *mayirefta* cooked daily.

MIDRANGE

To Karnagio (☎ 28210 53366; Plateia Katehaki 8; Cretan specials €5-10.50) This place is on every Haniot's list of favourite restaurants. Its outdoor tables near the harbour make it appealing to tourists but it has not sacrificed one whit of authenticity. There is a good range of seafood (try the grilled cuttlefish) and classic Cretan dishes, plus a fine wine list.

Tamam (☎ 28210 58639; Zambeliou 49; mains €5.50-9) Housed in old Turkish baths, Tamam presents a superb selection of vegetarian specialities – try the spicy avocado dip on potato (€6) – and inspired dishes such as the Tas kebab veal with spices and yogurt or the Beyendi chicken with creamy aubergine purée.

Anaplous (☎ 28210 41320; Sifaka & Melhisedek; starters €2.30-6.20; dinner) This atmospheric restaurant is housed in the ruins of a 14th-century Venetian building. The owners are passionate about presenting authentic Cretan cuisine using fresh seasonal produce. The signature dessert with yogurt and nuts is a work of art. There is quality live acoustic music by a young local duo.

Portes (☎ 28210 76261; Portou 48; mains €6-8.50) Affable Susanna from Limerick cooks up Cretan treats with a difference at this superb restaurant in the Old Town. After testing her mettle at Tamam for many years, she has opened her own place with a broad menu. Try her divine marinated *gavros* (little fish) or stuffed fish baked in paper.

Apostolis Taverna (☎ 28210 43470; Akti Enoseos 6; fish per kg up to €45) In the quieter eastern harbour, this is a well-respected place for fresh fish and Cretan dishes. A seafood platter for two, including salad, is €26. Service is friendly and efficient, and there's a good wine list and a view over the harbour.

Faka Taverna (☎ 28210 42341; Plateia Katehaki; appetisers €2-5.50) This is another of those quiet, unassuming places that doesn't dish up bland tourist fare. The cuisine is solid and genuine. Good local choices include Cretan rice or artichokes and broad beans. There's a children's menu and small playpen.

Pigadi tou Tourkou (☎ 28210 54547; Sarpaki 1-3; mains €9.50-14.50; dinner) Features from this former steam bath, including the well it is named after (Well of the Turk), are incorporated into the cosy design of this popular restaurant, which has tantalising dishes inspired by Crete, Morocco and the Middle East. The service can, however, be indifferent and inconsistent and the prices have crept up.

Ela (☎ 28210 74128; Kondylaki 47; mains €6.50-12; noon-1am) This 14th-century building was a soap factory, then a school, distillery and cheese-processing plant. Now Ela serves up a decent array of Cretan specialities, while musicians create a lively ambience. The tacky board outside tells you it's in every guidebook but the accolades are not undeserved.

Entertainment

The harbour's lively waterfront bars and clubs are mostly patronised by tourists. Party animals head to the clubs in Platanias and Agia Marina, 11km west of Hania, but there are some lively bars in the Old Town.

CRETE

Synagogi (☎ 28210 96797; Skoufou 15) Housed in a roofless Venetian building that was once a synagogue, this is a popular lounge bar at night, frequented by trendy locals.

Fortezza (☎ 28210 46546) This café, bar and restaurant, installed in the old Venetian ramparts across the harbour, is the best place in town for a sunset drink. A free barge takes you across the water, from the bottom of Sarpidona to the sea wall wrapping around the harbour.

Fagotto Jazz Bar (☎ 28210 71877; Angelou 16; ☺ 7pm-2am Jul-May) A Hania institution housed in a restored Venetian building, Fagotto offers the smooth sounds of jazz and light rock and blues. Jazz paraphernalia includes a saxophone beer tap.

Café Kriti (☎ 28210 58661; Kalergon 22; ☺ 8pm-late) Also known as Lyrakia, this rough-and-ready joint, with a decorative scheme that relies on saws, pots, ancient sewing machines and animal heads, is the place to hear live Cretan music.

Shopping

Hania offers the best combination of souvenir hunting and shopping for crafts on the island, with many local artisans at work in their stores. The best shops are along Zambeliou and Theotokopoulou. Skrydlof is 'leather lane', and the Central market is worth a look.

Carmela (☎ 28210 90487; Angelou 7) Carmela produces unique ceramics using ancient techniques and has a tempting range of original jewellery designs with stones collected on her travels, as well as unusual pieces handcrafted by young Greek artisans.

Paraoro (☎ 28210 88990; Theotokopoulou 16) Artist Stamatis Fasoularis makes his distinctive series of decorative metal boats, which all have a functional use, including candles, light fittings and a steamship oil burner. There's also jewellery and crafts from local and Athens-based artists.

Roka Carpets (☎ 28210 74736; Zambeliou 61) You can watch the charming Mihalis Manousakis weave his wondrous rugs on a 400-year-old loom, using methods that have remained essentially unchanged since Minoan times. This is one of the few places in Crete where you can buy genuine, hand-woven goods.

O Armenis (☎ 28210 54434; Sifaka 29) Owner Apostolos Pahtikos has been making traditional Cretan knives since he was 13 and has passed on the trade to his son. You can watch them work as they match the blades to carefully carved handles. A kitchen knife costs €15. The workshop is at Sifaka 14.

Getting There & Away

AIR

Olympic Airlines (☎ 28210 58005; www.olympic airlines.com; Tzanakaki 88) operates five daily flights to/from Athens (€84). There are also four flights a week to/from Thessaloniki (€115).

Aegean Airlines (☎ 28210 63366; www.aegeanair .com) has four daily flights to Athens (€79) and two to Thessaloniki.

BOAT

Hania's main port is at Souda, about 7km southeast of town. There are frequent buses to Hania (€0.90), as well as taxis (€8).

ANEK (☎ 28210 27500; www.anek.gr; Plateia Sofokli Venizelou) has a daily boat at 9pm from Piraeus to Hania (€21.90, nine hours) and at 8pm from Hania to Piraeus. In July and August there is also a morning ferry at 9am from Piraeus (€21.90).

Hellenic Seaways (☎ 28210 75444; www.hellenic seaways.gr; Plateia 1866 14) has a high-speed catamaran service that take only 4½ hours (€46.30), although the seating is airplane style. It leaves Piraeus at 3.45pm and Hania at 9pm.

Port Police (☎ 28210 89240) can provide ferry information.

BUS

Buses depart from Hania's **bus station** (☎ 28210 93052; Kydonias 73-77) for the following destinations:

Destination	Duration	Fare	Frequency
Elafonisi	2¼hr	€8	daily
Falasarna	1½hr	€6	3 daily
Hora Sfakion	1hr 40min	€5.80	3 daily
Iraklio	2¾hr	€11.50	21 daily
Kissamos-Kastelli	1hr	€3.70	14 daily
Moni Agias Triadas	30min	€1.80	2 daily
Omalos			
(for Samaria Gorge)	1hr	€5.20	4 daily
Paleohora	1hr 50min	€5.80	4 daily
Rethymno	1hr	€6	21 daily
Sougia	1hr 50min	€5.40	daily
Stavros	30min	€1.60	6 daily

Getting Around

There are five buses a day running to the airport (€1.20). A taxi to the airport will cost about €15.

Local blue buses (☎ 28210 27044) meet the ferries at the port of Souda, just near the dock. In Hania, the bus to Souda (€0.90) leaves from outside the food market, and buses for the western beaches leave from the main bus station on Plateia 1866.

Most motorcycle-hire outlets are on Halidon, but the companies at Agia Marina are competitive and bring cars to Hania.

Auto Papas (☎ 28210 68124; Agia Marina) About 10km west of Hania.

Europrent (☎ 28210 40810, 28210 27810; Halidon 87)

National (☎ 28210 38185; Agia Marina) About 10km out of town.

AKROTIRI PENINSULA
ΧΕΡΣΟΝΗΣΟΣ ΑΚΡΩΤΗΡΙ

The Akrotiri (ahk-ro-*tee*-rih) Peninsula, to the east of Hania, has a few places of fairly minor interest, as well as being the site of Hania's airport, port and a military base. There is an immaculate **military cemetery** at Souda, where about 1500 British, Australian and New Zealand soldiers who lost their lives in the Battle of Crete are buried. The buses to Souda port from outside the Hania food market can drop you at the cemetery.

Almost at the northern tip of the peninsula is the lovely sandy beach of **Stavros**, famous as the dramatic backdrop for the final dancing scene in the classic film *Zorba the Greek*. It can get crowded but is your best bet on a windy day.

There are two working monasteries on the Akrotiri Peninsula. The impressive 17th-century **Moni Agias Triadas** (☎ 28210 63310; admission €1.50; ☒ 8am-7pm) was founded by the Venetian monks Jeremiah and Laurentio Giancarolo, converts to the Orthodox faith. A small store sells the monastery's fine wine, oil and raki.

The 16th-century **Moni Gouvernetou** (☎ 28210 63319; museum admission €1.50; ☒ 8am-2pm & 4-8pm) is 4km north of Moni Agias Triada. The church inside the monastery has an ornate sculptured Venetian façade.

There are two buses Monday to Saturday at 6.30am and 1pm to Moni Agias Triadas from Hania's bus station (€1.80, 40 minutes). There are six buses daily to Stavros beach (€1.60).

HANIA TO XYLOSKALO
ΧΑΝΙΑ ΠΡΟΣ ΞΥΛΟΣΚΑΛΟ

The road from Hania to the beginning of the Samaria Gorge is one of the most spectacular routes on Crete. It heads through orange groves to the village of **Fournes** where a left fork leads to **Meskla**. The main road continues to the village of **Lakki**, 24km from Hania. This unspoilt village in the Lefka Ori Mountains affords stunning views wherever you look. The village was a centre of resistance during the uprising against the Turks, and during WWII.

From Lakki, the road continues to **Omalos** and Xyloskalo, start of the Samaria Gorge. A number of visitors choose to stay at Omalos in order to make the earliest start possible on the Samaria Gorge.

The big stone-built **Hotel Exari** (☎ 28210 67180; fax 28210 67124; s/d €20/25) has pleasant, well-furnished rooms with TV, bathtub and balconies. The owner Yiorgos will give walkers lifts to the start of the Samaria Gorge and can deliver luggage to Sougia for groups. There is an attached taverna. Rooms at the friendly **Hotel Gingilos** (☎ 28210 67181; s/d/tr €20/25/30) are rather sparse, but are large (the triples are huge), very clean and have tasteful timber furniture and TV. There is a communal balcony and a taverna downstairs.

Hotel Neos Omalos (☎ 28210 67269; www.neos-omalos.gr; s/d €20/30) is the poshest hotel, with comfortable, modern, nicely decorated rooms that include phone, baths with shower curtains, and satellite TV.

The EOS (Greek Mountaineering Club) maintains the **Kallergi Hut** (☎ 28210 33199; dm without bathroom members/nonmembers €8/12), located in the hills between Omalos and the Samaria Gorge. It boasts 43 beds, electricity, hot water, and makes a good base for exploring Mt Gingilos and surrounding peaks.

SAMARIA GORGE
ΦΑΡΑΓΓΙ ΤΗΣ ΣΑΜΑΡΙΑΣ

Despite the crowds who tramp through the **Samaria Gorge** (☎ 28250 67179; admission €5; ☒ 6am-3pm 1 May–mid-Oct), a trek through this stupendous gorge is still an experience to remember.

At 18km, the Samaria (sah-mah-rih-*ah*) Gorge is supposedly the longest in Europe. It begins just below the Omalos Plateau, carved out by the river that flows between the peaks of Avlimaniko (1858m) and Volakias (2147m). Its width varies from 150m to 3m and its vertical walls reach 500m at their highest points. The gorge has an incredible number of wild flowers, which are at their best in April and May.

It is also home to a large number of endangered species, including the Cretan wild goat, the *kri-kri,* which survives in the wild only here and on the islet of Kri-Kri, off the coast of Agios Nikolaos. The gorge was made a national park in 1962 to save the *kri-kri* from extinction. You are unlikely to see too many of these shy animals, which show a marked aversion to trekkers.

An early start (before 8am) helps to avoid the worst of the crowds, but even the early bus from Hania to the top of the gorge can be packed. There's no spending the night in the gorge so you are going to have to complete the hike in the time allocated.

The trek from **Xyloskalo**, the name of the steep stone pathway with wooden rails that gives access to the gorge, to **Agia Roumeli** takes from between 4½ hours for the sprinters to six hours for the strollers. Early in the season it's sometimes necessary to wade through the stream. Later, as the flow drops, it's possible to use rocks as stepping stones.

The gorge is wide and open for the first 6km, until you reach the abandoned settlement of **Samaria**. The inhabitants were relocated when the gorge became a national park. Just south of the village is a small church dedicated to **Saint Maria of Egypt**, after whom the gorge is named.

The gorge then narrows and becomes more dramatic until, at the 11km mark, the walls are only 3.5m apart – the famous **Iron Gates** (Sidiroportes). Here a rickety wooden pathway leads trekkers the 20m or so over the water and through to the other side.

The gorge ends at the 12.5km mark just north of the almost abandoned village of **Old Agia Roumeli**. From here it's a further uninteresting 2km hike to the welcoming seaside resort of Agia Roumeli, where most hikers end up taking a refreshing dip in the sea.

What to Bring

Rugged footwear is *absolutely essential* for walking on the uneven ground covered by sharp stones. Don't attempt the walk

in unsuitable footwear – you will regret it. Even soft sports shoes are unsuitable. You'll also need a hat and sunscreen. There's no need to take water. While it's inadvisable to drink water from the main stream, there are plenty of cool springs along the way. There is nowhere to buy food until you reach either entrance to the gorge, so bring some energy food to snack on.

Getting There & Away

There are excursions to the Samaria Gorge from every sizable town and resort on Crete. Most travel agents have two excursions: 'Samaria Gorge Long Way' and 'Samaria Gorge Easy Way'. The first comprises the regular trek from Omalos; the second starts at Agia Roumeli and takes you as far as the Iron Gates.

Obviously it's cheaper to trek the Samaria Gorge under your own steam. Hania is the most convenient base. There are buses to Xyloskalo (Omalos; €5.20, 1½ hours) at 6.15am, 7.30am, and 8.30am. There's also a direct bus to Xyloskalo from Paleohora (€5.50, 1½ hours) at 6.15am.

AGIA ROUMELI ΑΓΙΑ ΡΟΥΜΕΛΗ
pop 121

These days most travellers just pass through Agia Roumeli waiting to catch the boat to Hora Sfakion, but it's pleasant enough for a stopover, although the surrounding mountains can make it very hot and stifling. The beach gets exceptionally hot and thus impossible to sit on for long unless you hire a beach umbrella and sun lounge.

If you've just trekked through the gorge and you're in no hurry to leave, there are quite a few places to stay and decent places to eat.

Farangi Restaurant (☎ 28250 91225; specials €4-6) has excellent Cretan specials and there are some tidy rooms (singles/doubles/triples €18/30/35; 🔀) above the restaurant, where you can crash for the night.

Hotel-Restaurant Kri-Kri (☎ 28250 91089; fax 28250 91489; s/d/tr €25/30/40; 🔀) is one of the larger hotels in town, with clean, simple rooms with a fridge and small balcony. There is a very good restaurant downstairs.

There are two boats daily from Agia Roumeli to Hora Sfakion (€5.40, one hour) via Loutro (€3.50, 45 minutes). They connect with the bus back to Hania. There's also a boat from Agia Roumeli to Paleohora (€7.20, 1.5 hours) at 5.15pm, calling in at Sougia (€3.70, 45 minutes). The boat ticket office is near the beach.

AROUND AGIA ROUMELI

The small but rapidly expanding fishing village of **Loutro** (Λουτρό) lies between Agia Roumeli and Hora Sfakion. The town is little more than a crescent of white-and-blue *domatia* around a tiny beach. It's a pleasant, lazy resort that is never overwhelmed with visitors, although it can get busy in July and August. Loutro is the only natural harbour on the south coast of Crete and is only accessible by boat or on foot. The absence of cars and bikes makes it quiet and peaceful.

Given the captive market, the tavernas that line the waterfront in Loutro are all surprisingly good. **The Blue House** (☎ 28250 91127; bluehouseloutro@chania-cci.gr; d €40) has spacious, well-appointed rooms with big verandas overlooking the port and a taverna serving excellent *mayirefta* (€4 to €5), including delicious garlicky spinach and a great *bureki* (small pastry pie) baked with zucchini, potato and goat's cheese.

An extremely steep path leads up from Loutro to the village of **Anopolis** (Ανώπολη) but it's far easier the take the ferry from Hora Sfakion.

HORA SFAKION ΧΩΡΑ ΣΦΑΚΙΩΝ

pop 351

Hora Sfakion (*ho*-rah sfah-*kee*-on) is a small coastal port where hordes of walkers from the Samaria Gorge spill off the boat and onto the bus. Most people pause only long enough to catch the next bus out, but it is pleasant enough in its own right with its fair share of sleeping and eating options. It's also a convenient spot for heading westwards to other resorts or taking a ferry to Gavdos.

Hora Sfakion played a prominent role during WWII when thousands of Allied troops were evacuated by sea from the town after the Battle of Crete.

The ferry quay is at the eastern side of the harbour. Buses leave from the square up the hill on the eastern side. There is one ATM. The post office is on the square. There is no tourist office or tourist police. The car park charges €3.

Accommodation in the village is of a reasonable quality and value. Up the steps at the western end of the port, **Rooms Stavris** (☎ 28250 91220; stavris@sfakia-crete.com; s/d €21/24; 🔀) has clean rooms – some with and kitchenettes and fridges. **Hotel Samaria** (☎ 28250 91261; fax 28250 91161; s/d €20/30; 🔀) is a decent waterfront hotel with clean, pleasantly furnished rooms with balconies, while next door **Livikon** (☎ 28250 91211; s/d/tr/q €25/35/45/55; 🔀) has similar prices but bigger colourful rooms that are ideal for families or larger groups.

Both restaurants have a good selection of *mayirefta* (€4 to €6) and vegetarian dishes on display, as well as the usual grills.

Getting There & Away

BOAT

Boat tickets are sold in the **booth** (☎ 28250 91221) in the car park. From June through August there is one daily boat from Hora Sfakion to Paleohora (€9, three hours) via Loutro, Agia Roumeli and Sougia. The boat leaves at 1pm. There are also an additional three boats a day to Agia Roumeli (€5.40, one hour) via Loutro (€2.20, 20 minutes). From 1 June there are boats (€10.20, 1½ hours) to Gavdos island (see p259) on Friday, Saturday and Sunday leaving at 10.30am and returning at 5pm.

BUS

There are four buses a day from Hora Sfakion to Hania (€5.80, two hours) – the last one leaves at 7.15pm after the last boat from Agia Roumeli. In summer there are three daily buses to Rethymno via Vryses (€5.80, 1 hour). There are two buses daily to Frangokastello (€1.50, 25 minutes).

AROUND HORA SFAKION

The road from Vryses to Hora Sfakion cuts through the heart of the Sfakia region in the eastern Lefka Ori. The inhabitants of this region have long had a reputation for fearlessness and independence – characteristics they retain to this day.

One of Crete's most celebrated heroes, Ioannis Daskalogiannis, was from Sfakia. In 1770, Daskalogiannis led the first Cretan insurrection against Ottoman rule. When help promised by Russia failed to materialise, he gave himself up to the Turks to save his followers. The Turks skinned him alive in Iraklio.

The Turks never succeeded in controlling the Sfakiots, and this rugged mountainous region was the scene of fierce fighting. The story of their resistance lives on in the form of folk tales and *rizitika* (local folk songs).

The village of **Imbros**, 23km from Vryses, is at the head of the beautiful 8km **Imbros Gorge** (admission €2), which is far less visited than the Samaria Gorge. To get there, take any bus bound for Hora Sfakion from the north coast and get off at Imbros. Walk out of the village towards Hora Sfakion and a path to the left leads down to the gorge. The gorge path ends at the village of **Komitades**, from where it is an easy walk by road to Hora Sfakion. The Happy Walker (p239) organises treks through this gorge.

FRANGOKASTELLO ΦΡΑΓΚΟΚΑΣΤΕΛΛΟ

pop 153

Frangokastello is a magnificent 14th-century fortress on the coast 15km east of Hora Sfakion. It was built by the Venetians as a defence against pirates and rebel Sfakiots, who resented the Venetian occupation as much as they did the Turkish.

It was here in 1770 that Ioannis Daskalogiannis surrendered to the Turks. On 17 May 1828 many Cretan rebels were killed here by the Turks. Legend has it that at dawn each anniversary their ghosts, the *'drosoulites'*, can be seen marching along the beach.

The wide, white-sand beach beneath the fortress slopes gradually into shallow warm water, making it ideal for kids. Most accommodation is set back from the shore, leaving the area's natural beauty largely untouched. Frangokastello is popular with day-trippers. Frangokastello is a peaceful retreat.

On the beach east of the castle, **Flisvos** (☎ 28250 92069; fax 28250 92042; r €35; 🕿) has pleasant rooms with a fridge and balcony and nice touches like mosquito screens on the windows. There is a decent taverna downstairs.

Two daily buses from Hora Sfakion stop at Frangokastello (€1.50).

SOUGIA ΣΟΥΓΙΑ

pop 109

Sougia (*soo*-yah), 67km from Hania, is a tiny laid-back beach resort with a wide curve of sand-and-pebble beach and a tree-lined coastal road. Sougia's tranquillity has been preserved only because it lies at the foot of a narrow, twisting road that would deter most tour buses and locals strongly resist an umbrella/lounge takeover of the beach.

Information

Sougia doesn't have a post office. There is an ATM next to Pension Galini.

Internet Lotos (☎ 28230 51191; per hr €3; 🕑 7am-late) Check email here.

Roxana's snack store (☎ 28230 51668; 🕑 5am-late) Sells bus tickets.

www.sougia.info Check out this website for information.

Sleeping

Aretousa Rooms to Rent (☎ 28230 51178; fax 28230 51178; s/d €25/35; 🕿) Inland, on the road to Hania you'll find this place, which has lovely rooms with wood-panelled ceilings and balconies

Pension Galini (☎ /fax 28230 51488; s/d/tr €35/40/43) Next door to Aretousa, Galini has equally beautiful rooms.

Some other options:

Santa Irene Hotel (☎ 28230 51342; www.sougia .info/hotels/santairene; s/d €40/50; 🕿 💻) On the seafront; has smart, well-furnished standard hotel rooms and apartments.

Arhontiko (☎ 28230 51200; r €40-50; 🕿) Has spacious, tasteful new studios and apartments.

Oceanis (☎ 28230 51176; d/tr €35/40; 🕿) Has plain but roomy accommodation overlooking the beach with basic coffee and tea facilities.

There's no camping ground, but the eastern end of the beach is popular with freelance campers.

Eating

Polyfimos (☎ 28230 51343; mains €5.20-7.80; 🕑 dinner) Tucked off the Hania road behind the police station, ex-hippy Yianni makes his own oil, wine and raki and makes *dolmades* (vine leaves stuffed with rice, and sometimes meat) from the vines that cover the shady courtyard. The food is excellent and service from the affable Savvas delightful.

Taverna Rembetiko (☎ 28230 51510; mayirefta €3.50-6) Serves various Cretan specialities such as *bureki* and stuffed zucchini flowers.

Kyma (☎ 28230 51670; mixed fish €18) On the beach, this has a good selection of *mayirefta* and fresh fish.

Getting There & Away

There's a daily bus travelling from Hania to Sougia (€5.35, 2½ hours) at 1.45pm. Buses going from Sougia to Hania leave at 7am and 6pm.

Sougia is also on the Paleohora–Hora Sfakion boat route. Boats leave at 10am for Agia Roumeli (€3.70, one hour), Loutro (€6.70, 1½ hours) and Hora Sfakion (€6.70, two hours). For Paleohora (€4.30, one hour) to the west there is a departure at 5.15pm. There is also a boat on Tuesday at 9am for the island of Gavdos (€9, three hours).

PALEOHORA ΠΑΛΑΙΟΧΩΡΑ

pop 2213

Paleohora (pal-ee-o-hor-a) was discovered by hippies back in the '60s and from then on its days as a tranquil fishing village were numbered. Despite the mid-sized hotels and package tourists, the place is still appealing and retains a certain laid-back feel. The number of backpackers is dwindling and it has become more of a family destination, though it gets livelier in the peak of summer. It is also the only beach resort on Crete that does not go into total hibernation in winter.

The little town lies on a narrow peninsula with a long, curving tamarisk-shaded sandy beach exposed to the wind on one side and a sheltered pebbly beach on the other. On summer evenings the main street and beach road is closed to traffic and the tavernas move onto the road.

Orientation & Information

Paleohora's main street, Eleftheriou Venizelou, runs north–south. There are three ATMs, an OTE and laundry on the main drag. The post office is at the northern end of Pahia Ammos beach. Boats leave from the old harbour at the southern end of the beach.

Erato Internet (☎ 28230 8301; Eleftheriou Venizelou; per hr €3)

Municipal tourist office (☎ 28230 41507; Eleftheriou Venizelou; ☽ 10am-1pm & 6-9pm Wed-Mon May-Oct) Closed at time of research; due to open along the beach.

Notos Internet (☎ 28230 42110; notos@grecian.net; Eleftheriou Venizelou; per hr €2; ☽ 8am-10pm)

Sights & Activities

It's worth clambering up the ruins of the 13th-century **Venetian castle** for the splendid view of the sea and mountains. The castle was built so the Venetians could keep an eye

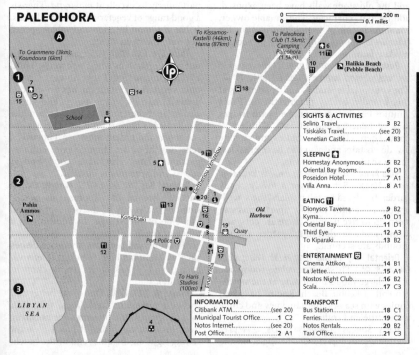

PALEOHORA

SIGHTS & ACTIVITIES	
Selino Travel	3 B2
Tsiskakis Travel	(see 20)
Venetian Castle	4 B3

SLEEPING
Homestay Anonymous	5 B2
Oriental Bay Rooms	6 D1
Poseidon Hotel	7 A1
Villa Anna	8 A1

EATING
Dionysos Taverna	9 B2
Kyma	10 D1
Oriental Bay	11 D1
Third Eye	12 A3
To Kiparaki	13 B2

ENTERTAINMENT
Cinema Attikon	14 B1
La Jettee	15 A1
Nostos Night Club	16 B2
Scala	17 C3

INFORMATION	
Citibank ATM	(see 20)
Municipal Tourist Office	1 C2
Notos Internet	(see 20)
Post Office	2 A1

TRANSPORT	
Bus Station	18 C1
Ferries	19 C2
Notos Rentals	20 B2
Taxi Office	21 C3

CRETE

on the southwestern coast from this commanding position on the hill-top. There's not much left of the fortress, however, as it was destroyed by the Venetians, the Turks, the pirate Barbarossa in the 16th century, and later the Germans during WWII.

From Paleohora, a six-hour walk along a scenic **coastal path** leads to Sougia, passing the ancient site of Lissos.

Tours

Travel agents around town offer dolphin-watching trips (€16):

Tsiskakis Travel (☎ 28230 42110; www.notoscar.com; Eleftheriou Venizelou)

Selino Travel (☎ 28230 42272; selino2@otenet.gr) Also sells boat tickets.

Sleeping

Homestay Anonymous (☎ 28230 41509; www.anon ymoushomestay.com; s/d/tr €22/25/28) This excellent small pension has been refurbished to provide private bathrooms and shared cooking facilities in the courtyard garden, but retains its simple charm and good value. The rooms are clean and tastefully furnished and the old stone walls have been exposed, adding to its character. The amiable owner, Manolis, is full of useful information for travellers. Rooms can connect to accommodate families.

Poseidon Hotel (☎ 28230 41374; www.interkriti .net/hotel/paleohora/poseidon; s/d/apt €25/30/40; ✷ ▯) The comfortable studios and apartments at this friendly, breezy place right on Pahia Ammos beach come equipped with fridges and kitchenettes and all have a little balcony. There's Internet facilities and satellite TV downstairs and you can have breakfast in the shady café downstairs.

Villa Anna (☎ 28103 46428; anna@her.forthnet.gr; apt €50-70; ✷) Set amongst a lovely shady garden bordered by tall poplars, these well-appointed, family-friendly apartments can sleep up to five people. There are cots, and swings and a sandpit in the garden and the grounds are secured.

Oriental Bay Rooms (☎ 28230 41076; s/d/tr €30/35/38; ✷) These immaculate rooms are in the large modern building at the northern end of Pebble Beach. Rooms have balconies with sea or mountain view and come with kettle and fridge.

Haris Studios (☎ 28230 42438; www.paleo choraholidays.com; d/apt €30/42; ✷) Right on the

dramatic rocky seafront around from the port, these friendly well-fitted studios are open all winter. The top rooms are nicer and have great views. The bathrooms are basic but functional. Scottish Flora cooks up a feast for guests once a week, often the day's catch from keen fisherman partner Haris.

Camping Paleohora (☎ 28230 41120; sites per person/tent €3/2.50) This large camping ground is 1.5km northeast of the town, about 50m from Pebble Beach. There is a taverna but no mini-market and facilities are a bit primitive.

Camping Grammeno (☎ /fax 28230 42125) This promising new camp site started operating at Grammeno Beach, about 3km west along the road to Koundoura, in 2005.

Eating

Dining in Paleohora is generally of a good standard and reasonably priced, with plenty of choices.

Dionysos Taverna (☎ 28230 41243; mains €4-6) One of the oldest tavernas in town, the popular Dionysos is known for top-grade food, particularly its excellent *mayirefta*. There is a good range of vegetarian dishes and grills. It has a roomy interior and tables spread out onto the main street.

Third Eye (☎ 28230 41234; mains €4-4.50) It's not just vegetarians who flock to the Third Eye, just inland from Pahia Ammos. Crete's only vegetarian restaurant has an eclectic menu of curries, salads, pastas and Greek and Asian dishes, much of it made from the family farm's organic produce. There is live *rembetika* and Indian music on Thursdays, reflecting the owner Ethymis' extra-culinary passions. They also have good budget rooms and apartments upstairs.

Oriental Bay (☎ 28230 41322; mayirefta €3.50-5) Part of Oriental Bay Rooms, this beachside taverna is one of the best options on this side of the village. In addition to a range of cheap vegetarian choices, such as green beans and potatoes, there are dishes such as 'rooster's kiss' (chicken fillet with bacon) and 'drunk cutlet' (pork chop in red wine).

Kyma (☎ 28230 41110) One of the better and cheapest places for fresh, local fish. Run by a fisherman, the offerings are normally from his own catch and it has a pleasant setting right on the quiet end of the beach, with a few tables outside under the trees. Top fish are €39 per kilogram.

Grammeno (☎ 28230 41505) For traditional Cretan food it is worth the trip to this exceptional taverna, on the road to Koundoura, about 2km west of Paleohora.

To Kiparaki (☎ 28230 42281) Also recommended is the Asian-style food at this Dutch-run place.

Entertainment

Cinema Attikon (tickets €5) Most visitors to Paleohora spend at least one evening here. Screenings at this well-signposted outdoor cinema start at 10pm.

Nostos Night Club (btwn Eleftheriou Venizelou & the Old Harbour) Has an outdoor terrace bar and a small indoor club playing Greek and Western music.

La Jettee, behind the Elman hotel, is right on the beach and has a nice garden, while Skala, by the port, is an old-time classic bar.

For late-night clubbing, Paleohora Club next to Camping Paleohora used to be popular for all-night, full-moon parties but is now a less-appealing indoor club. Most people head in the other direction to Castaway on the way to Koundoura, which has a pool bar.

Getting There & Away

BOAT

In summer there is a daily ferry from Paleohora to Hora Sfakion (€9, three hours), via Sougia (€4.40, 50 minutes), Agia Roumeli (€7.20, 1½ hours) and Loutro (€9, 2½ hours). The ferry leaves Paleohora at 9.30am, and returns from Hora Sfakion at 1pm. There are also three boats a week in summer to Gavdos (€10.20, 2½ hours), which leave Paleohora at 8.30am and return at 1pm. Tickets can be bought at **Selino Travel** (☎ 28230 42272; selino2@otenet.gr).

BUS

In summer there are four buses a day from the small **bus station** (☎ 28230 41914) to Hania (€5.80, two hours). There is also one daily service to Omalos (€5.50, 1½ hours) – for the Samaria Gorge – that departs at 6am.

Getting Around

Notos Rentals (☎ 28230 42110; notosgr@yahoo.gr; Eleftheriou Venizelou) rents out cars, motorcycles and bicycles.

From mid-April M/B *Elafonisos* ferries people to the west-coast beach of Elafonisi (€5, one hour). The service increases from three times a week to daily in mid-May through September. It departs at 10am and returns at 4pm.

The **taxi office** (☎ 28230 41128) is near the port. Sample fares: Kissamos (€35), Hania (€50; airport €55) and Elafonisi (€50).

GAVDOS ΓΑΥΔΟΣ

pop 98

Gavdos, in the Libyan Sea 65km from Paleohora, is the most southerly place in Europe and is the island for those craving total isolation and peace. The island has three tiny villages and lovely, unspoilt beaches, some of which are accessible only by foot or boat. Gavdos attracts a loyal following of campers, nudists and free spirits seeking natural beaches, long walks and laid-back holidays. There are no hotels but several of the locals rent rooms, and there are tavernas.

Until the late 1960s Gavdos had little water, electricity or phone lines. While water is now plentiful, there can still be the odd electricity shortages and blackouts.

While a day trip to Gavdos is possible, you won't appreciate the island's real appeal unless you take the time to chill out and get into the spirit of the place. Make sure you bring a torch (flashlight) for getting around at night as you only have the stars to guide you.

Sarakiniko Studios (☎ 28230 42182; www.gavdostudios.gr; s/d/tr studio incl breakfast €20/30/40, small apt incl breakfast €60-75), located above Sarakiniko beach, is perhaps the best place to stay on the island. You can be picked up at the port or it is a 20-minute walk north of the port. You can camp (per person €5) nearby, under the trees, and have access to the bathroom facilities.

In summer there are boats from Paleohora on Monday, Tuesday and Thursday (€10.20, 2½ hours). The Tuesday morning boat is faster and leaves Gavdos at 3pm, which makes it feasible to do it as a day trip (though you risk getting stranded in bad weather). In June and July there are boats from Hora Sfakion to Gavdos on Friday, Saturday and Sunday (€16.30, 1½ hours) and a weekly boat from Sougia (€10.20, two hours) on Tuesday. The only ferry that takes cars is on Monday night at 7pm from

Hora Sfakion (2½ hours) and returns on Tuesday at 7am. In August there is an extra boat from Hora Sfakion on Thursday.

ELAFONISI ΕΛΑΦΟΝΗΣΙ

As one of the loveliest sand beaches in Crete it's easy to understand why people enthuse so much about Elafonisi, at the southern extremity of Crete's west coast. The beach is long and wide and is separated from Elafonisi Islet by about 50m of knee-deep turquoise water on its northern side. The islet is marked by low dunes and a string of semi-secluded coves that attract a sprinkling of naturists. Unfortunately it is invaded by busloads of daytrippers.

There is one boat daily from Paleohora to Elafonisi at 10am (€4.50, one hour) from mid-June through September, as well as daily buses from Hania (€8, 2½ hours) and Kissamos (€5.20, 1¾ hours). The buses leave Hania at 8.30am and Kissamos at 9am, and both depart from Elafonisi at 4pm.

KISSAMOS ΚΙΣΣΑΜΟΣ
pop 3821
The north-coast town of Kissamos is near the port that serves the ferry from the Peloponnese or Kythira, and access from Hania is now faster on the new highway. Kissamos is a rural working town that neither expects nor attracts much tourism, though many small family hotels have sprouted in recent years. While it is not immediately appealing, it is worth more than a passing glance. The huge Kissamos Bay has some fine pebble and sand beaches and the almost bucolic feel to the region is a welcome antidote to the bustling Crete further east. There's a string of waterfront tavernas and bars lining the seafront promenade but the place only ever gets busy in August. Kissamos is good base for walking, touring and unwinding. Cruises to the Gramvousa Peninsula (opposite) leave from Kissamos port.

In antiquity, Kissamos was the main town of the province of the same name. When the Venetians came along and built a castle here, it became known as Kastelli. The name persisted until 1966 when authorities decided that too many people were confusing it with Crete's other Kastelli, near Iraklio. The official name reverted to Kissamos, though it is still often called Kastelli or Kissamos-Kastelli. Parts of the castle wall survive to the west of Tzanakaki square. The town's museum was due to reopen in 2006.

Orientation & Information
The port is 3km west of town. From June through August a bus meets the boats; otherwise a taxi costs around €4. The bus station is on the main square, Plateia Tzanakaki, and the main commercial street, Skalidi, runs east from Plateia Tzanakaki.

Kissamos has no tourist office, but has a reasonably informative website www.kissamos.net. The post office is on the main through road while there are a number of banks with ATMs along Skalidi.

Activities
Strata Walking Tours (☎ 28220 24336; www.stratatours.com) offers a range of walking tours for small groups, from leisurely day trips to full-on 15-day round trips reaching as far as the south coast.

Sleeping
Bikakis Family (☎ 28220 22105; www.familybikakis.gr; Iroön Polemiston 1941; s/d €20/25, studio €30; ❄) This would have to be the best budget option in Kissamos town. The rooms and studios sparkle and most have garden and sea views. Owner Giannis not only makes guests feel very welcome, he is also an expert on herbal teas and local knowledge.

Argo Rooms for Rent (☎ /fax 28220 23563; Plateia Teloniou; s/d €25/30) The C-class Argo has a great location on the seafront, with many of the well-appointed rooms directly overlooking the beach promenade. It's about 300m from Plateia Tzanakaki.

Thalassa (☎ 28220 31231; www.thalassa-apts.gr; Paralia Drapanias; studios €40-50; ❄ 🖳) The isolated Thalassa is an ideal spot to retreat to with a stack of books. The immaculate studios are airy and well-fitted out with irons, hairdryers and ISDN computer ports. There's a barbecue on the lawn and a small playground and it's just across from the beach, 100m east of Camping Mithymna.

Camping Mithymna (☎ 28220 31444; fax 28220 31000; sites per person/tent €5/3) An excellent shaded site 6km east of town, abutting the best stretch of beach on Kissamos Bay. There's a taverna, bar and shop and there are also rooms for rent nearby. Take a bus to the village of Drapanias and walk 1km through olive groves to the site.

Eating

Papadakis Taverna (☎ 28220 22340; mains €5-7)
One of the oldest tavernas in town, this place is well patronised by local diners. The taverna has a very relaxing setting overlooking the beach and serves well-prepared fish dishes such as oven-baked fish (€6), or fish soup.

Kellari Taverna (☎ 28220 23883; Cretan specials €4-6) This well-regarded taverna on the eastern end of the beach strip has an extensive range of home-cooked Cretan dishes, grills and fresh fish. It is owned by the same family that runs Strata Walking Tours.

O Stimadoris (☎ 28220 22057; mains €4-7) This well-respected fish taverna is about 2km west of town, just before the small fishing harbour. The owners are fishermen and therefore the fish is always fresh. Try an unusual salad made of seaweed in vinegar – *salata tou yialou*. The small tavern is like a mini-museum while the room with sea views regularly hosts weddings.

Restaurant Kastell (☎ 28220 22144; mains €4-6) Also recommended for home-style cooking is this place, opposite the bus station on the square.

Getting There & Away

BOAT

ANEN Ferries operates the *F/B Myrtidiotissa* on a route that takes in Antikythira (€9.40, two hours), Kythira (€16.40, four hours), Gythio (€22.10, five hours) and Kalamata (€23.40, seven hours). It does serve Piraeus eventually but it's far quicker to leave from Hania. It leaves Kissamos five times a week. You can buy tickets from **Horeftakis Tours** (☎ 28220 23250) and the **ANEN Office** (☎ 28220 22009; Skalidi).

BUS

From Kissamos' **bus station** (☎ 28220 22035), there are 15 buses a day to Hania (€3.70, 40 minutes), where you can change for Rethymno and Iraklio; three buses a day for Falasarna (€2.60, 20 minutes); one bus a day to Paleohora (€5.80, 1¼ hours) and two to Elafonisi (€5.20, 1¼ hours).

Getting Around

Hermes (☎ 28220 23678; www.hermesrentacar.net; Skalidi) rents cars, while you can pick up a bike or mountain bike at **Moto Fun** (☎ 28220 23440; www.motofun.info; Plateia Tzanakaki).

AROUND KISSAMOS

Falasarna Φαλάσαρνα

pop 21

Falasarna, 16km west of Kissamos, was a Cretan city-state in the 4th century BC but there's not much of the ancient city left to see. It attracts a mixed bunch of travellers due to its long, wide stretch of sandy beach, which is considered one of the best in Crete. It is split up into several coves by rocky spits and is known for its stunning sunsets and the pink hues reflecting from the fine coral in the sand. There is no village, just a scattering of widely spaced rooms and tavernas among the greenhouses that somewhat mar the approach to the beach.

One of the first places you will come across, signposted to the left along a gravel track, is **Rooms for Rent Panorama** (☎ 28220 41336; panorama@chania-cci.gr; d/tr €48/50; ☒), with spotless and comfortable studios and a well-run and friendly restaurant downstairs with a great view of the beach.

From June through August there are three buses daily from Kissamos to Falasarna (€2.60) as well as three buses from Hania (€6).

Gramvousa Peninsula

Χερσόνησος Γραμβούσας

North of Falasarna is the wild and remote Gramvousa Peninsula. There is a wide track, which eventually degenerates into a path, along the east-coast side to the stunning sandy beach of **Balos**, on the west side of the peninsula's narrow tip. The idyllic beach is overlooked by the two islets of **Agria** (wild) and **Imeri** (tame). To reach the track, take a west-bound bus from Kissamos and ask to be let off at the turn-off for the village of **Kalyviani** (5km from Kissamos). Walk the 2km to Kalyviani, then take the path that begins at the far end of the main street. The shadeless walk is around 3km – wear a hat and take plenty of water. If you have wheels (preferably a jeep) you can get to a point from where it is another 40-minute walk.

You don't have to inflict this punishment upon yourself to see this beautiful and rugged part of the island. There are daily **cruises** (☎ 28220 24344; www.gramvousa-balos .com.gr) to Gramvousa. In summer there are daily cruises around the peninsula to Imeri Gramvousa, which is crowned with a **Venetian castle** from which there are stunning

CRETE

views of the peninsula. It's a steep 20-minute walk to the top and there is a small beach below which gets crowded if the boats are full. Best to wait, as the cruise then stops at Balos, where you can swim in its turquoise lagoon-like waters. Tickets per adult/concession cost €20/10 and can be bought on the day at Kissamos port. Departures are at 10am, 10.15am and 12.15pm and return at 5.45pm and 7.30pm. The trip can be rough if it is windy.

EASTERN CRETE

Lasithi, Crete's easternmost prefecture, may receive far fewer visitors than the rest of the island, but the exclusive resorts around Elounda and Agios Nikolaos are the stronghold of Crete's high-end tourism. Agios Nikolaos is the region's contribution to the party scene. The Lasithi Plateau, the fertile region tucked in the Mt Dikti ranges, provides excellent cycling opportunities through quiet rural villages to the Dikteon Cave, where legend has it that Zeus was born. The east's other main attractions are the famous palm forest and beach at Vaï and the remote Minoan palace of Zakros.

LASITHI PLATEAU ΟΡΟΠΕΔΙΟ ΛΑΣΙΘΙΟΥ

The Lasithi Plateau, 900m above sea level, is a vast expanse of pear and apple orchards, almond trees and fields of crops. It would have been a stunning sight when it was dotted by some 20,000 metal windmills with white canvas sails. They were built in the 17th century to irrigate the rich farmland. There are less than 5000 still standing today and few of the original windmills are in service, most having been replaced by less-attractive mechanical pumps.

The plateau's rich soil has been cultivated since Minoan times. The inaccessibility of the region made it a hotbed of insurrection during Venetian and Turkish rule. Following an uprising in the 13th century, the Venetians drove out the inhabitants of Lasithi and destroyed their orchards. The plateau lay abandoned for 200 years. Food shortages led the Venetians to cultivate the area and build the irrigation trenches and wells that still service the region.

There are 20 villages dotted around the periphery of the plateau, the largest of which is **Tzermiado** (population 747), with a couple of ATMs and a post office. The town sees a fair amount of tourism from the tour buses going to the Dikteon Cave.

Hotel Kourites (☎ 28440 22194; s/d incl breakfast €25/40) is a fairly basic hotel on the left as you enter the village from the east side. It has simple rooms with small balconies. There are additional rooms and apartments available in nearby buildings and you have free use of the bicycles. The **Restaurant Kourites** (specials €4.50-7.30) serves filling and wholesome fare and there are many dishes made in the wood oven – try the suckling pig.

A better option to stay overnight might be the relaxing village of **Agios Georgios** (pronounced *agh*-ios ye-*or*-gios; population 554), where **Hotel Maria** (☎ 28440 31774; s/d €20/25) on the north side of the village has spacious stucco rooms decorated with weavings (although beds are very narrow). Maria also does the cooking at **Taverna Rea** (☎ 28440 31209; specials €5-6) on the main street, which rustles up excellent grilled local meats (her husband is the butcher) and other staple Cretan fare based on fresh seasonal local produce. They also rent studios upstairs from the taverna.

The other main village is **Psyhro** (population 212) which is the closest village to the Dikteon Cave. Its main street has a few tavernas, and plenty of souvenir shops selling 'authentic' rugs and mats of non-Cretan origin. It is prettier and less dusty than Tzermiado and makes for a better rest stop. Buses to Psyhro drop you at the end of the town where it's about a kilometre walk uphill to the cave.

The **Zeus Hotel** (☎ 28440 31284; s/d €30/40) is a rather featureless D-class hotel on the west side of the village near the start of the Dikteon Cave road. **Stavros** (☎ 28440 31453; mains €5-8) has a neat folksy interior and serves a good range of traditional Cretan dishes, such as goat with lemon. Most of the meat and produce is from the family farm.

Petros Taverna (☎ 28440 31600; grills €6), opposite the entrance to the cave, is run by former cave guardian Petros Zarvakis. It has great views from the balcony. He also organises regular hikes up to Mt Dikti, camping out under the stars.

DIKTEON CAVE ΔΙΚΤΑΙΟΝ ΑΝΤΡΟΝ
Lasithi's major sight is the **Dikteon Cave**
(adult/child €4/2; ☺ 10am-6.30pm Jun-Oct, 10am-4pm
Nov-May), just outside the village of Psyhro.
Here, according to legend, Rhea hid the
newborn Zeus from Cronos, his offspring-
gobbling father.

The cave, also known as the Psyhro Cave,
covers 2200 sq metres and features both
stalactites and stalagmites. It was excavated
in 1900 by the British archaeologist David
Hogarth, who found numerous votives
indicating it was a place of cult worship.
These finds are housed in the archaeological museum in Iraklio (p226).

It is a steep 15-minute (800m) walk up
to the cave entrance. You can take the
fairly rough but shaded track on the right
with great views over the plateau or the
unshaded paved trail on the left of the car
park next to the Chalavro taverna. You can
also let a donkey do the hard work (€10 or
€15 return).

Getting There & Away
Public transportation around the Lasithi
Plateau is tricky. From Iraklio there is a bus
daily to Lasithi (€4.70, two hours). From
Agios Nikolaos there are two buses weekly
to the Lasithi villages. Buses go through
Tzermiado and Agios Georgios before ter-
minating at Psyhro at the foot of the road
leading to the Dikteon Cave.

AGIOS NIKOLAOS ΑΓΙΟΣ ΝΙΚΟΛΑΟΣ
pop 10,080
Lasithi's capital, Agios Nikolaos (*ah*-yee-
os nih-*ko*-laos), is an undeniably attractive
former fishing village set around a pleasant
harbour and a small, picturesque lake connected to the sea.

In the early 1960s it became a chic hide-
away for the likes of Jules Dassin and Walt
Disney, but by the end of the decade package tourists were arriving in force and it
became an overdeveloped tourist town. It's
had its ups and downs ever since.

'Agios' remains popular, drawing people
from nearby resorts at night when the ambience turns more vibrant and cosmopolitan. While there is superficially little to
attract the independent traveller, there is
reasonable accommodation, prices are not
too horrendous and there is enough activity
to cater for all tastes.

Orientation
The bus station is on the southern side of
town about 100m from the town's centre at
Plateia Venizelou. The de facto town centre
is around the Voulismeni Lake, 150m from
Plateia Venizelou.

Information
Most banks, ATMs, travel agencies and
shops are on Koundourou and the parallel
pedestrianised 28 Oktovriou.
Anna Karteri Bookshop (☎ 28410 22272;
Koundourou 5) Well stocked with maps, and books in
English and other languages.
General Hospital (☎ 28410 66000; Knosou 3) On the
west side of town.
Laundry To Teleio (Paleologou 13; wash & dry €6)
Municipal Tourist Office (☎ 28410 22357; www
.agiosnikolaos.gr; ☺ 8am-9pm Apr-Nov) Right by the
bridge; changes money and assists with accommodation.
National Bank of Greece (Nikolaou Plastira) Has a
24-hour exchange machine.
OTE (☎ 28410 95330; Sfakianaki 10; ☺ 8am-2pm)
Polyhoros Internet Cafe (☎ 28410 24876; 28
Oktovriou 13; per hr €4; ☺ 9am-2am)
Post Office (☎ 28410 23744; 28 Oktovriou 9;
☺ 7.30am-2pm Mon-Fri)
Tourist Police (☎ 28410 91408; Erythrou Stavrou 47;
☺ 7.30am-2.30pm Mon-Fri)

Sights
The **Archaeological Museum** (☎ 28410 22943; Paleologou Konstantinou 74; admission €3; ☺ 8.30am-3pm
Tue-Sun) has an extensive and well-displayed
collection from eastern Crete. The exhibits
are arranged in chronological order beginning with Neolithic finds from Mt Tragista-
los, north of Kato Zakros, and early Minoan
finds from Agia Fotia. The highlight is *The
Goddess of Myrtos*, a clay jug from 2500 BC
found near Myrtos.

The **folk museum** (☎ 28410 25093; Paleologou
Konstantinou 4; admission €3; ☺ 10-4pm Sun-Fri), next
to the municipal tourist office, has a well-
displayed collection of traditional handicrafts and costumes.

The town beaches of **Ammos** and **Kytroplatia
Beach** are smallish and can get crowded. The
sandy beach at **Almyros** about 1km south of
town is the best of the lot and tends to be less
crowded than the others. There's little shade
but you can rent umbrellas. **Ammoudara Beach**,
1.5km further south along the road to Ierapetra, is a little better and supports a fairly
busy restaurant and accommodation scene.

CRETE

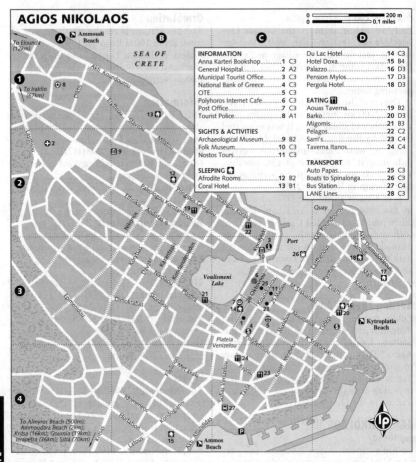

AGIOS NIKOLAOS

Tours

Travel agencies offer bus tours to Crete's top attractions and the boats along the harbour advertise their various boat trips. **Nostos Tours** (☎ 28410 22819; nostos@agn.forthnet.gr; Koundourou 30; ☼ 8am-9pm) has boat trips to Spinalonga (€15) that include a swim stop on the Kolokytha Peninsula, as well as guided tours of Phaestos, Zaros and Matala (€32), the Samaria Gorge (€37), and the Lasithi Plateau and Knossos (€35).

Sleeping
BUDGET & MIDRANGE

Pension Mylos (☎ 28410 23783; Sarolidi 24; d €34; ☒) From the fake flowers on the bed to the family photos and icons on the walls, this quaint

pension is an extension of the friendly elderly owner's home. The front rooms have sensational views (try for room 2) and all have a fridge and TV. The sprightly Georgia swears by the hard mattresses.

Du Lac Hotel (☎ 28410 22711; www.dulachotel.gr; 28 Oktovriou 17; s/d/tr €35/50/70; ☒) This refurbished hotel on the lake has standard rooms and spacious fully fitted out studios, both have stylish contemporary furnishings and nice bathrooms. There are lovely views over the lake.

Pergola Hotel (☎ 28410 28152; fax 28410 25568; Sarolidi 20; s/d with view €25/30; ☒) This family-run hotel has a homy feel. Rooms are comfortable and all have fridges, although TV, air-con and breakfast are extra. There is a pleasant veranda under a pergola to relax or have breakfast. Front rooms have balconies and sea views.

Hotel Doxa (☎ 28410 24214; www.doxa-hotel.com.gr; Idomeneos 7; s/d incl breakfast €40/55; ⚄) The plant-filled lobby sets a homely tone for this hotel, which has an attractive terrace for breakfast or drinks. Pleasant and clean rooms are equipped with fridges, hairdryers and satellite TVs and some have views.

Afrodite Rooms (☎ 28410 28058; Korytsas 27; d/tr €20/30) Also recommended is this budget place.

TOP END

Palazzo (☎ 28410 25086; www.palazzo-apartments; apt €90-110; ⚄ 🖳) Opposite Kytroplatia Beach, these classy apartments sleeping up to four people are the closest thing to a boutique hotel in town. It has 10 charming individually decorated apartments with mosaic-tiled floors and marble bathrooms and the front rooms have lovely balconies with views. There's free email downstairs.

Coral Hotel (☎ 28410 28363; www.hermes-hotels.gr; Akti Koundourou 68; d incl breakfast €94; ⚄ 🖳) Renovated in 2002, this handy and well-run B-class hotel on the northern waterfront is about as upmarket as places get in town. Rooms have satellite TV and fridges, and there is a pleasant roof garden and pool if you can't face the beach.

Eating

The lakeside restaurants, while visually tempting, tend to serve bland and often overpriced tourist 'Greek' food. Head further afield for the genuine article.

Barko (☎ 28410 24610; Akti Pagalou 8; mezedes €2.60-8) Now in flashier premises on Kytroplatia Beach, this excellent *oinomayirio* (wine cook house) has superb Cretan-style mezes dishes (try the dolmades and zucchini flowers). Its new location has given tourists easier access to the fine cuisine locals have enjoyed for some years.

Aouas Taverna (☎ 28410 23231; Paleologou Konstantinou 44; mezedes €2-8) This is a family-run place where dishes include specialities such as herb pies and picked bulbs. The interior is plain but the enclosed garden is refreshing and the *mezedes* are wonderful.

Taverna Itanos (☎ 28410 25340; Kyprou 1; mayirefta €5-9) This vast, friendly taverna with beamed ceilings and stucco walls has a few

tables outside on the pavement. The food is traditional Cretan, with trays of excellent *mayirefta* out the back. Try the lamb in filo with potato, feta, tomato and peas.

Migomis (☎ 28410 24353; Nikolaou Plastira 20; mains €8.50-18) Overlooking Voulismeni Lake from up high, Migomis is one of the better and pricier lakeside eating places. The cuisine is Greek international and the views and ambience are stunning. The fancy menu includes ostrich, and has Asian influences.

Pelagos (☎ 28410 25737; Katehaki 10; seafood dishes €6.60-17) For fresh fish and seafood, this place, in a beautifully restored house with a lovely garden, is considered one of the best restaurants in Agios Nikolaos.

Sarri's (☎ 28410 28059; Kyprou 15; mains €6-7.50) Tucked away in the back streets, Sarri's is a good spot for breakfast, lunch or dinner on the shady garden terrace. Check the daily specials board.

Getting There & Away

BOAT

LANE Lines (☎ 28410 89150; www.lane.gr) has ferries three times a week to Piraeus (€30, 14 hours), via Milos (€20) and Santorini (€20). There is also a service from Piraeus via Milos to Agios Nikolaos, Sitia, Kasos, Karpathos, Halki and Rhodes.

BUS

Buses leave from Agios Nikolaos' **bus station** (☎ 28410 22234; Sofoklis Venizelou) for Elounda (€1.10, 16 daily), Ierapetra (€2.80, eight daily), Iraklio (€5.30, half-hourly), Kritsa (€1.10, 10 daily) Lasithi Plateau (€3.50, two daily) and Sitia (€5.90, seven daily).

Getting Around

Auto Papas (☎ 28410 22344; www.autopapas.gr; 28 Oktovriou 30) rents cars and scooters (50cc scooter per day €5).

ELOUNDA ΕΛΟΥΝΤΑ

pop 1655

There are magnificent mountain and sea views along the 11km road north from Agios Nikolaos to Elounda (el-*oon*-da). A cluster of luxury resorts occupy the lovely coves along the coast. The first elite hotel was built here in the mid-1960s, quickly establishing Elounda as the playground for Greece's glitterati and high flyers – soon after, the world's rich and famous followed

suit. Elounda boasts some of the most exclusive resorts in Greece.

Past the resorts, the once-quiet fishing village of Elounda now bristles with
package tourists, though it's quieter than
neighbouring Agios Nikolaos. Busloads of
day-trippers rock up on their way to Spinalonga Island. The pleasant but unremarkable sandy town beach, to the north of the
port, can get very crowded. Elounda has
limited appeal unless you are lucky enough
to be staying in one of the posh resorts.

Information
The **Municipal Tourist Office** (☎ 28410 42464;
Y 8am-11pm Jun-Oct), on the main square,
helps with accommodation and information, and changes money.

Sleeping
While there are some nice places around,
Elounda is not particularly good value in
peak season and many hotels are booked
out by tour operators.

Corali Studios (☎ /fax 28410 41712; studio €55-70;
X) On the northern side, about 800m from
the clock tower the self-catering Corali is
set in lush lawns with a shaded patio.

Portobello Apartments (2-/4-bed apt €55-60; X)
Next door to Corali and under the same
management, these are spacious.

Hotel Aristea (☎ 28410 41300; fax 28410 41302;
s/d/tr incl breakfast €30/45/55; X) In the town
centre is this uninspiring but decent and
clean option. Most rooms at least have a sea
view, double-glazed windows, TV, fridge
and hairdryers.

Elounda Beach (☎ 28410 41412; www.elounda
beach.gr; r from €250; X R) Places like this
is what Elounda is really about. Elounda
beach ranks among the world's great luxury resorts. From 'simple' affairs with fresh
flowers, bathrobes and twice-daily maid
service, you can upgrade all the way to the
royal suites with a private indoor swimming pool, personal fitness trainer, butler
and cook (for a mere €15,000 per night).
See what we mean?

Eating
There's a big range of overpriced, bland
places to eat, bristling with eager touts.

Nikos (☎ 28410 41439; mains €4-7) A no-frills
place that is cheap and honest enough,
though service can be bit erratic.

Ferryman (☎ 28410 41230; local fish platter for 2
€44) On the pretty waterfront, the Ferryman
claims its moment of fame from being featured in the TV series *Who Pays the Ferryman*. The waterfront tables are lovely at
night, the service is excellent and, while it is
pricey, the consensus is that it's worth it.

Megaro (☎ 28419 42220) On the corner of
the square, this is also recommended. The
owner fishes from his own boat.

Getting There & Away
The price of a ferry across to Spinalonga
has skyrocketed to €10 (concession €5),
with all the boats at Elounda Harbour now
part of a cooperative that eliminated any
competition.

There are 16 buses daily from Agios
Nikolaos to Elounda (€1.10, 20 minutes).

SPINALONGA ISLAND
ΝΗΣΟΣ ΣΠΙΝΑΛΟΓΚΑΣ
Spinalonga Island lies just north of the
Kolokytha Peninsula. The island's massive
fortress (admission €2; Y 9am-6pm) was built by
the Venetians in 1579 to protect Elounda
Bay and the Gulf of Mirabello. It withstood
Turkish sieges for longer than any other
Cretan stronghold, finally surrendering in
1715, some 30 years after the rest of Crete.
The Turks used the island as a base for
smuggling. Following the reunion of Crete
with Greece, Spinalonga Island became a
leper colony. The last leper died here in
1953 and the island has been uninhabited
ever since. It is still known among locals as
'the island of the living dead'. The island is
a fascinating place to explore. It has an aura
that is both macabre and poignant.

Regular excursion boats visit Spinalonga
from Agios Nikolaos (€15) with tour guides
and swim stops (see p264), while ferries take
you across from the port in Elounda (€10).
You could also take a cheaper boat from
Plaka (5km further north). The boats from
Agios Nikolaos pass Bird Island and Kri-Kri
Island, one of the last habitats of the *kri-kri*,
Crete's wild goat. Both these uninhabited
islands are designated wildlife sanctuaries.

KRITSA ΚΡΙΤΣΑ
pop 1614
The village of Kritsa (krit-*sah*), perched
600m up the mountainside 11km from Agios Nikolaos, is a pretty mountain village

renowned for its strong tradition of needle-work and weaving. The village appears to have morphed into a tourist attraction, with busloads of tourists swarming through the streets all summer and villagers eager to exploit these invasions to the full. It creates a colourful atmosphere but not much of the stuff on sale is handmade these days and the rug designs are not necessarily authen-tic. It's still possible to find the traditional geometric designs of Crete and the odd finely crocheted blankets and tablecloths, but they are becoming a rarity.

On the way to Kritsa, it is worth stopping at the tiny, triple-aisled **Church of Panagia Kera** (☎ 28410 51525; admission €2.30; ☿ 8.30am-3pm Mon-Fri, 8.30am-2pm Sat). The frescoes that cover its interior walls are considered the most outstanding examples of Byzantine art in Crete. It's on the right, 1km before the vil-lage, on the Agios Nikolaos road.

In late August, Kritsa stages a traditional **Cretan wedding** replete with songs, dancing and traditional food (admission about €9).

The taverna/*kafeneio* **Platanos** (☎ 28410 51230; mains €4.50-6) retains a traditional feel and has a lovely setting under a giant plane tree and vine canopy. There's a standard menu of grills and *mayirefta* and it's well regarded by locals.

There are hourly buses from Agios Niko-laos to Kritsa (€1, 15 minutes).

ANCIENT LATO ΑΡΧΑΙΑ ΛΑΤΩ

The ancient city of **Lato** (admission €3; ☿ 8.30am-3pm Tue-Sun), 4km north of Kritsa, is one of Crete's few non-Minoan ancient sites. Lato (lah-*to*) was founded in the 7th century BC by the Dorians and at its height was one of the most powerful cities in Crete. It sprawls over the slopes of two acropolises in a lonely mountain setting, commanding stunning views down to the Gulf of Mirabello.

The city's name derived from the god-dess Leto whose union with Zeus produced Artemis and Apollo, both of whom were worshipped here.

In the centre of the site is a deep well, which is cordoned off. As you face the Gulf of Mirabello, to the left of the well are some steps which are the remains of a **theatre**. Above the theatre was the **prytaneion**, where the city's governing body met. The circle of stones behind the well was a threshing floor. The columns next to it are

the remains of a stoa which stood in the agora. There are remains of a pebble mosaic nearby. A path to the right leads up to the **Temple of Apollo**.

There are no buses to Lato. The road to the site is signposted to the right on the approach to Kritsa. If you don't have your own transport, it's a pleasant 4km walk through olive groves along this road.

GOURNIA ΓΟΥΡΝΙΑ

The important Minoan site of **Gournia** (☎ 28410 24943; admission €3; ☿ 8.30am-3pm Tue-Sun), pronounced goor-*nyah*, lies just off the coast road, 19km southeast of Agios Nikolaos. The ruins, which date from 1550 to 1450 BC, consist of a town overlooked by a small palace. The palace was far less ostentatious than the ones at Knossos and Phaestos, because it was the residence of an overlord rather than a king. The town is a network of streets and stairways flanked by houses with walls up to 2m in height. Trade, domestic and agricultural imple-ments found on the site indicate Gournia was a thriving little community.

Near the site is **Gournia Moon Camping** (☎ / fax 28420 93243; sites per person/tent €5.30/5; ⊗), the closest camping ground to Agios Nikolaos. The shaded and well-organised site has a taverna, swimming pool, snack bar and mini-market.

Gournia is on the Sitia and Ierapetra bus routes from Agios Nikolaos and buses can drop you at the site.

MOHLOS ΜΟΧΛΟΣ
pop 91

Mohlos (*moh*-los) is a pretty fishing vil-lage bedecked in hibiscus, bougainvillea and bitter laurel and reached by a 6km winding road from the main Sitia–Agios Nikolaos highway. In antiquity, it was joined to the homonymous island that now sits 200m offshore and was once a thriving Early Minoan community dating from the period 3000 to 2000 BC. Excavations still continue sporadically on Mohlos Island and at Mohlos village.

Mohlos is a chill-out place with decent accommodation, plenty of good walks and many interesting villages to explore nearby. There is reasonable swimming at the small pebble-and-grey-sand beach. Beware of strong currents further out in the small strait between the island and the village. Fishermen can take you across to the islet.

There is no bank, or post office in Mohlos and very few tourist facilities at all, other than a couple of gift shops and two minimarkets.

Yiannis Petrakis and his Belgian botanist wife Ann Lebrun run nature walks and guided jeep and bike tours (☎ /fax 28430 94725).

On the east side of the little harbour **Hotel Sofia** (☎ /fax 28430 94554; d/tr €30/35, apt €32-50; ❄) has basic, clean and comfortable rooms above the taverna with TV and fridge, as well as spacious, fully equipped two- to four-person apartments 200m east of the harbour. Good for families and longer stays, many have balconies with great views. Try the excellent home cooking at the taverna.

The pleasant **Spyros Rooms** (☎ /fax 28430 94204; d/tr €35/40; ❄) has clean and modern rooms, with fridges and air-con, just behind the village. See Spyros at the Kavouria restaurant. Signposted on the village's western side near a supermarket, the self-contained **Kyma** (☎ 28430 94177; solk@in.gr; studio €30) studios are spotless and good value.

To Bogazi (☎ 28430 94200; mezedes €1.50-6.50) on the harbour opposite the island and with a sea view on two sides, serves over 30 inventive *mezedes*, including many vegetarian-friendly dishes. For a main course, try the cuttlefish with fennel.

Also recommended is **Ta Kochilia** (☎ 28430 94432) for superb views, fresh fish and simple, good food.

There is no public transport to Mohlos. Buses between Sitia and Agios Nikolaos will drop you off at the Mohlos turn-off. From there you'll need to hitch or walk the 6km to Mohlos village.

SITIA ΣΗΤΕΙΑ
pop 8238

Sitia (si-*tee*-ah) is quieter than the prefecture capital Agios Nikolaos, though it can get quite busy in summer with a mainly domestic crowd. While the town is traveller-friendly, it exists for the locals, who live from agriculture and commerce rather than tourism. It makes a good jumping-off point for the Dodecanese islands. A sandy beach skirts a wide bay to the east of town. The main town is terraced up a hillside, overlooking the port. It has a pleasing mixture

of new and fading Venetian architecture, while its attractive harbour-side promenade lined with tavernas and cafés makes for a pleasant evening stroll. Even at the height of the season the town has a relatively laid-back feel compared with the commercialism further west.

Orientation & Information

The town's main square is Plateia Iroon Polytehniou – recognisable by its palm trees and statue of a dying soldier. There are lots of ATMs and places to change money in town. The bus station is at the eastern end of Karamanli, which runs behind the bay. Ferries dock about 500m north of Plateia Agnostou.

Akasti Travel (☎ 28430 29444; www.akasti.gr; Kornarou & Metakaki 4) Good source of information.

Itanos Hotel (per hr €4; ❄ 9.30am-2.30pm) Check email here.

National Bank of Greece (Plateia El Venizelou) Has a 24-hour exchange machine.

Post office (Dimokritou; ❄ 7.30am-3pm) To get here, follow El Venizelou inland and take the first left.

Tourist office (☎ 28430 28300; Karamanli; ❄ 9.30am-2.30pm & 5-8.30pm Mon-Fri, 9.30am-2.30pm Sat) On the promenade; has town maps.

Tourist police (☎ 28430 24200; Therisou 31)

Sights

Sitia's **archaeological museum** (☎ 28430 23917; Pisokefalou; admission €3; ❄ 8.30am-3pm Tue-Sun) houses a well-displayed collection of local finds spanning from Neolithic to Roman times, with emphasis on the Minoan. Among its prized exhibits is the *Palekastro Kouros* – a figure pieced together from fragments made of hippopotamus tusks and adorned with gold, believed to be the image of a Minoan god, as well as finds from the palace at Zakros. The museum is on the left side of the road to Ierapetra.

Towering over the town is the fort or **kazarma** (from 'casa di arma') which was a garrison under the Venetians. It is now used as an open-air theatre.

The **folklore museum** (☎ 28430 22861; Kapetan Sifinos 28; admission €2; ❄ 10am-2pm Mon-Fri) displays a fine collection of local weavings.

Sleeping

Hotel Arhontiko (☎ 28430 28172; Kondylaki 16; d/studio without bathroom €28/31) This small D-class guesthouse, uphill from the port, is in a beautifully maintained Neoclassical building and has a real old-world feel. It's spotless, with shared bathrooms and a lovely shady garden in the front.

Apostolis (☎ 28430 28172; Kazantzaki 27; d/tr €35/45) These upmarket *domatia* up from the waterfront have ceiling fans, and relatively modern bathrooms with handy touches such as shower curtains, and many have double beds. There's a communal balcony and fridge.

El Greco Hotel (☎ 28430 23133; elgreco@sit.forthnet.gr; Arkadiou 13; s/d €30/40; 🔆) For a modicum more comfort, El Greco has more character than the town's other C-class places. The rooms are very clean and presentable, and all have a fridge and phone. The hotel is well-signposted.

Itanos Hotel (☎ 28430 22900; www.itanoshotel.com; Karamanli 4; s/d incl breakfast €35/60; 🔆 🖥) The B-class Itanos has a conspicuous location on the waterfront, as well as a popular terrace restaurant. The comfortable rooms come equipped with satellite TV, balconies, fridge and sound-proofing.

Eating

Balcony (☎ 28430 25084; Foundalidou 19; mains €8.90-12.60) The finest dining in Sitia is on the 1st floor of this charmingly decorated old building. The Balcony has an exceptional and creative menu of fusion cuisine, with interesting dishes such as rooster in wine with noodles, or veal and rigatoni with four cheeses.

Gato Negro (☎ 28430 25873; Galanaki 3; mains €6.20-9.80) At the northern end of the harbour next to the pier, this popular restaurant uses produce from the owner's farm to create excellent Cretan dishes. Sample the rabbit in red sauce, or *kalitsounia* (filled pastries) with wild greens and finish off the night with the excellent raki.

Taverna O Mihos (☎ 28430 22416; Kornarou 117; mixed grill for 2 €17) This taverna in a traditional stone house one block back from the waterfront has excellent charcoal-grilled meats and Cretan cooking. There are also tables on a terrace nearby on the beach.

Symposio (☎ 28430 25856; Karamanli 12; grills €5-7) Symposio utilises all-Cretan natural products such as organic olive oil from Moni Toplou. The food is top class, with the rabbit in rosemary and wine sauce highly recommended.

Also recommended are the area's renowned *rakadika* (Cretan *ouzeri*). Try **Rakadiko Choulis** (☎ 28430 28298) on the waterfront for mezes and local raki.

Getting There & Away

AIR

Sitia's **airport** (☎ 28430 24666) opened an expanded international-size runway in 2003, and international flights were expected to begin operating in 2006. The airport (signposted) is 1km out of town. There is no airport bus; a taxi costs about €5.

Olympic Airlines (☎ 28430 22270; www.olympicairlines.com; 4 Septemvriou 3) has three weekly flights to Athens (€66, one hour), three flights a week to Thessaloniki (€125, three hours) via Alexandroupolis (€79, 1½ hours) and three flights a week to Preveza (€79, 1¾ hours).

BOAT

LANE Lines (☎ 28430 25555; www.lane.gr) link Sitia with Piraeus (€30.50, 14½ hours), Kasos (€16, four hours), Karpathos (€18, six hours), Halki (€23, 5½ hours) and Rhodes (€26, 10 hours) three times weekly. Departure times change annually, so check locally for latest information.

BUS

There are seven buses a day to Ierapetra (€4.60, 1½ hours), seven buses a day to Iraklio (€11.20, 3½ hours) via Agios Nikolaos (€5.90, 1½ hours), five to Vai (€2.50, one hour), and two to Kato Zakros via Palekastro and Zakros (€3.50, one hour). The buses to Vai and Kato Zakros run only between May and October.

AROUND SITIA

Moni Toplou Μονή Τοπλού

The imposing **Moni Toplou** (☎ 28430 61226; admission €2.50; 🕐 9am-1pm & 2-6pm Apr-Oct), 18km east of Sitia on the back road to Vaï, looks more like a fortress than a monastery. It was often treated as such, being ravaged by both the Knights of St John and the Turks. Its star attraction is an 18th-century icon by Ioannis Kornaros, with 61 small beautiful scenes inspired by an Orthodox prayer.

An excellent **museum** tells the history of the monastery and has a fine collection of icons, engravings and books, as well as weapons and military souvenirs from the resistance. The well-stocked shop sells ecclesiastical souvenirs and books on Crete, plus the monastery's award-winning organic olive oil and wine.

The monastery is a 3km walk from the Sitia–Palekastro road. Buses can drop you off at the junction.

Vaï Βάï

The beach at Vaï, on Crete's east coast 24km from Sitia, is famous for its palm forest. There are many stories about the origin of these palms, including the theory that they sprouted from date pits spread by Roman legionaries relaxing on their way back from conquering Egypt. While these palms are closely related to the date, they are a separate species unique to Crete.

In July and August you'll need to arrive early to appreciate the setting, because the place gets packed. It's possible to escape the worst of the ballyhoo – jet skis and all – by clambering over a rocky outcrop (to the right, facing the sea) to a small secluded beach. Alternatively, you can go over the hill in the other direction to a quiet beach frequented by nudists.

There is a taverna and café at Vaï but no accommodation. About 3km north is the ancient Minoan site of **Itanos**. Below the site are several good swimming spots.

There are buses to Vaï from Sitia (€2.50, one hour, five daily).

PALEKASTRO ΠΑΛΑΙΚΑΣΤΡΟ

pop 1084

Palekastro (pah-*leh*-kas-tro) is a small farming town in the midst of a rocky, barren landscape, but within easy striking distance of the lovely Kouremenos Beach, Vaï Beach and Moni Toplou. About 1km from town is the small archaeological site of Ancient Palekastro, where archaeologists believe a major Minoan Palace is buried. Excavations continue on the site, which uncovered the *Palekastro kouros* now residing in the Archaeological Museum in Sitia (p268).

The **tourist office** (☎ 28430 61546; ☒ 9am-10pm May-Oct), changes money and is also a good source of information on rooms and transport. There's an ATM next door. The bus stop is in the centre of town.

In town, **Hotel Hellas** (☎ 28430 61240; hellas _h@otenet.gr; s/d €20-40; ☒) has simple rooms

with air-con, TV, telephone, updated bathrooms and double-glazed windows, while downstairs at the taverna, Marika cooks up reputedly the best lunch in town, with hearty home-style cooking.

The closest beaches to Palekastro are **Kouremenos**, a nearly deserted pebble beach with excellent windsurfing and **Hiona Beach**, which has some fine fish tavernas.

Opposite Kouremenos Beach, **Casa di Mare** (☎ 28430 25304; casadimare@hotmail.com; studio €40-60; ☒ ☒) has six spacious, comfortable studios with stone floors and rustic-style decor that sleep up to four. There's a small pool among the olive groves.

Further along, **Glaros Apartments** (☎ 28430 61282; Kouremenos; d/q studio €50/65; ☒) has light and spacious self-contained studios surrounded by lawns and a lovely garden behind the restaurant.

There are five buses a day from Sitia that stop at Palekastro on the way to Vaï. The are also two buses daily from Sitia to Palekastro (€1.80, 45 minutes) that continue to Kato Zakros (€2.80).

ZAKROS & KATO ZAKROS ΖΑΚΡΟΣ & ΚΑΤΩ ΖΑΚΡΟΣ

pop 793

The village of Zakros (*zah*-kros), 37km southeast of Sitia, is the nearest permanent settlement to the Minoan site of Zakros, a further 7km away.

Kato Zakros (*kah*-to *zah*-kros) is a beautiful little seaside settlement located next to the archaeological site. Little more than a long stretch of pebbly beach shaded by pine trees with a string of welcoming tavernas, it is just about the most tranquil place to stay on Crete's southeastern coast.

The settlement is unlikely ever to expand thanks to restrictions imposed by the Culture Ministry's Archaeology and Antiquities department. There is an enjoyable and not-too-challenging 8km walk from Zakros to Kato Zakros through a gorge, known as the **Valley of the Dead** because of the cave tombs dotted along the cliffs. The gorge emerges close to the Minoan site.

Sleeping

The *domatia* in Kato Zakros fill up fast in the high season, so it is best to book. If there are no rooms available you can camp at the southern end of the beach.

Stella's Apartments (☎ /fax 28430 23739; studio €60-70) These charming stone-built studios are in a verdant, pine-tinged setting 800m along the old road to Zakros. Decorated with wooden furniture made by the owner, they have barbecues and hammocks and are perfect for longer stays. The engaging owners can take guests on free treks and walks.

Four good places are all under the same **management** (☎ 28430 26893; akrogiali@sit.forthnet .gr). The first two enjoy superb sea views from the communal balcony:

Athena Rooms (d €35; 🖳) The better-quality choice; the rooms are very pleasant with heavy stone walls.

Rooms Coral (☎ 28430 27064; d €35; 🖳) Next door to Athena, this has excellent, small but spotless rooms equipped with Internet connections.

Poseidon Rooms (d without/with bathroom €20/35) Budget.

Katerina Apartments (apt €50) New; opposite Stella's and sleeps up to four.

Eating

Taverna Akrogiali (☎ 28430 26893; mains €4.50-9) At the end of the beach, this taverna is a popular place with relaxed seaside dining and excellent food and service from the inimitable owner Nikos Perakis.

Restaurant Nikos Platanakis (☎ 28430 26887; specials €4.50-7) This well-regarded restaurant has a wide range of Greek staples such as rabbit stew, and rarities including pheasant and partridge when in season. Nikos' grilled meat and fish are also excellent.

Getting There & Away

There are buses to Zakros from Sitia via Palekastro (one hour, €2.80, two daily). From June to August, the buses continue to Kato Zakros.

ANCIENT ZAKROS

The smallest of Crete's four palatial complexes, **Ancient Zakros** (☎ 28430 26897; admission €3; ⏰ 8am-7pm) was a major port in Minoan times, maintaining trade links with Egypt, Syria, Anatolia and Cyprus. The palace comprised royal apartments, storerooms and workshops flanking a central courtyard.

The town occupied a low plain close to the shore. Water levels have risen over the years so that some parts of the palace complex are submerged. The ruins are not well preserved, but a visit to the site is worthwhile for its wild and remote setting.

XEROKAMBOS ΞΕΡΟΚΑΜΠΟΣ

pop 34

Xerokambos (kse-*ro*-kam-bos) is a quiet, unassuming agricultural settlement on the far southeastern flank of Crete. Its isolation has so far meant that tourism is pretty much low-key and most certainly of the unpackaged kind. There are a couple of splendid beaches, a few scattered tavernas and a smattering of studio accommodation that is ideal for people wanting peace and quiet.

The smallish, but cosy **Ambelos Beach Studios** (☎ /fax 28430 26759; studio €40) have kitchenettes and fridges. There is a barbecue and outdoor wood oven for guests, and a tree-shaded courtyard.

Villa Petrino (☎ 28430 26702; www.xerokampos .com; d €35; 🖳) has large fully equipped apartments, which are suitable for families, overlooking the garden. The top rooms have beach views.

The only beachside taverna in Xerokambos is **Akrogiali Taverna** (☎ 28430 26777; mayirefta €3.50-4.50), 50m from Ambelos Beach near the Ambelos Beach Studios. The food ranges from grills and fish to their special home-cooked *mayirefta*.

There are no buses to Xerokambos. To get there by car from Zakros take the Kato Zakros road, on the outskirts of Zakros. Turn left at the signpost for Livyko View Restaurant. This 8km dirt road is drivable in a conventional vehicle. Otherwise there is a good paved road from Ziros.

IERAPETRA ΙΕΡΑΠΕΤΡΑ

pop 11,678

Ierapetra (yeh-*rah*-pet-rah) is Europe's most southerly major town. It was a major port of call for the Romans in their conquest of Egypt. Ierapetra's main business continues to be agriculture and the greenhouses that mar the landscape along the coast, rather than tourism. Despite its wealth it is a largely unremarkable place. There are tavernas and cafés along the harbour, a small Venetian fort on the harbour and the odd remnant of a Turkish quarter.

Orientation & Information

The bus station is on the eastern side of town, one street back from the beachfront.

There is no tourist office, but travel agents can help with tourist information. There are ATMs around the main square.

CRETE

www.ierapetra.net Excellent website.
Post office (☎ 28420 22271; Vitsentzou Kornarou 7)
Net Internet Cafe (☎ 28420 25900; Koundourou 16; per hr €3.60; ☺ 9am-late) Check email here.

Sights & Activities

Ierapetra's one-room **archaeological museum** (☎ 28420 28721; Adrianou 2; admission €2; ☺ 8.30am-3pm Tue-Sun) is perfect for those with a short concentration span. It does have a good collection of headless classical statuary and a superb statue of the goddess of Demeter that dates from the 2nd century AD. Also notable is a *larnax*, or clay coffin, dating from around 1300 BC and decorated with 12 painted panels. The 1899 building was a school during Ottoman times.

South along the waterfront from the central square is the rather fragile 'Kales' **medieval fortress** (admission free; ☺ 8.30am-3pm Tue-Sun), which was built in the early years of Venetian rule and strengthened by Francesco Morosini in 1626.

Some 13.5km north of Ierapetra is the **Ha Gorge**, perhaps the most challenging gorge to traverse in all of Europe – it has reputedly been fully traversed by just 11 people.

The main **town beach** is near the harbour, while a second **beach** stretches east from the bottom of Patriarhou Metaxaki. Both have coarse, grey sand, but the main beach offers better shade.

Sleeping

Cretan Villa Hotel (☎ /fax 28420 28522; www.cretan-villa.com; Lakerda 16; s/d €30/35; ⊠) This well-maintained 18th-century house is the most atmospheric place in town. The traditionally furnished rooms have a fridge and TV, and there is a peaceful courtyard.

Astron Hotel (☎ 28420 25114; htastron@otenet.gr; Kothri 56; d incl breakfast €68-75; ⊠) The top hotel in town is the B-class Astron at the beach end of Patriarhou Metaxaki. The comfortable rooms are furnished with satellite TV and telephone; some have sea views.

Ersi (☎ 28420 23208; Plateia Eleftherias 19; s/d €20/30; ⊠) Refurbished in 2004, this central hotel is 30m from the beach. The neat rooms have a fridge, TV and sea views.

Koutsounari Camping (☎ 28420 61213; www.camping-koutsounari.epimlas.gr; sites per person/tent €4.90/3.50) About 7km east at Koutsounari, it has a restaurant, snack bar and minimarket. Ierapetra–Sitia buses pass the site.

Eating

Portego (☎ 28420 27733; Foniadaki 8; wood oven specials €2.50-8.50) This delightful restaurant serves excellent Cretan and Greek cuisine and specials cooked in the wood-fired oven (so is the bread). Try the lamb in a clay pot with yogurt. It is housed in the historic 1900s house with lovely courtyard for summer and there is a cool bar and *kafeneio*.

Odeion (Lasthenous 18; mezedes €3-4) This converted music school is believed to have been used as a torture chamber during the German occupation. These days its serves excellent *mezedes* in the basement to a generally younger crowd, while the 1st floor is a music bar. There is a pleasant garden in summer.

Napoleon (☎ 28420 22410; Stratigou Samouil 26; mains €5-6.50) This is one of the oldest and most respected establishments on the waterfront on the south side of town. There is fresh fish and Greek and Cretan specialities.

Getting There & Away

There are seven buses a day from Ierapetra's **bus station** (☎ 28420 28237; Lasthenous) to Iraklio (€8.10, 2½ hours), via Agios Nikolaos (€2.80, one hour) and Gournia; seven to Sitia (€4.60, 1½ hours) via Koutsounari (for camp sites); and six to Myrtos (€1.50, 30 minutes).

GAÏDOURONISI (HRYSI)

Just off the coast of Ierapetra, Gaïdouronisi (Donkey Island) – also known as Hrysi (Golden Island) – has good, sandy beaches, three tavernas and a stand of Lebanon cedars, the only one in Europe. It can get crowded when the tour boats are in, but you can always find a quiet spot of your own.

From June through August excursion boats (€20) leave for the islet every morning and return in the afternoon.

MYRTOS ΜΥΡΤΟΣ
pop 440

Myrtos (*myr*-tos), on the coast 17km west of Ierapetra, is popular with older Dutch and English travellers who like the authentic village ambience. It has no big hotels, and there's a reasonable patch of beach and some decently priced places to stay and eat.

To get to the waterfront from the bus stop, head south and take the road to the right for 150m. There is no post office or bank. Internet is available at **Prima Tours** (☎ 28420 51035; www.sunbudget.net; per hr €3.50).

One of the best places to stay is **Big Blue** (☎ 28420 51094; www.forthnet.gr/big-blue; d/studio/apt €35/60/75; ❄), on the western edge of town. It is handy for the beach and you have a choice of more expensive, large airy studios with sea views, or cheaper, cosy ground-floor rooms. They all have cooking facilities.

The cosy, traditional-style **Cretan Rooms** (☎ 28420 51427; d €35) have balconies, fridges and shared kitchens and are popular with independent travellers. Owner Maria Dask-alaki keeps them neat and clean.

The reliable eating option is **Myrtos Taverna** (☎ 28420 51227; mayirefta €5-8) on the main road, attached to the Myrtos hotel, which is popular with both locals and tourists for its wide range of *mezedes* as well as for its vegetarian dishes and *mayirefta*. Also recommended is **Taverna Akti** (☎ 28420 51584; Greek specials €3.60-6.80) at the eastern end of the waterfront, for pleasant seafront dining and better than average food.

There are six buses daily from Ierapetra to Myrtos (€1.50, 30 minutes), while the Ano Viannos–Ierapetra bus also passes through Myrtos twice a week.

Dodecanese
Δωδεκάνησα

Strung out along the coast of western Turkey, like jewels upon an impossibly aquamarine sea, the Dodecanese both entrance and attract passers by – many of whom return year after year to sample some of the most culturally and geographically diverse islands in the Aegean.

These 18 islands (including satellites) are an entity unto themselves. Under Italian rule until 1947, they maintain an air of slight separateness and, not unnaturally, still attract large numbers of curious Italian visitors. The islands are a beguiling mix of sea, mountain and meadow and, because they are all close to one another, can easily be 'hopped'. They need that extra effort to get to but the rewards far outweigh the investment.

The spiritually inclined will make a beeline for Patmos. The developed resorts of Rhodes and Kos have beaches and bars galore, while Lipsi and Tilos have seductive beaches, minus the crowds. The far-flung islands of Agathonisi, Arki, Kasos and Kastellorizo await Greek-island aficionados in pursuit of traditional island life, while everyone gapes at the extraordinary volcanic landscape that geological turbulence has created on Nisyros. The islands' chequered history has also endowed them with a wealth of diverse archaeological remains.

HIGHLIGHTS

- **Wining**
  Rhodes' wine country (p292) on the slopes of Mt Attavyros

- **Dining**
  Romantic restaurants in Rhodes' Old Town (p286)

- **Getting Away from It All**
  Kasos (p300) – slow, laid back life unfussed by mainstream tourism

- **Sporting Event**
  Fast and furious windsurfing at Afiartis Bay (p297) on Karpathos

- **Historical Experience**
  Lindos (p288), the most famous of the ancient cities of the Dodecanese

- **Green Haven**
  Fertile, volcanic Nisyros (p312)

- **Adrenaline Rush**
  Rock climbing near Armeos (p329) on Kalymnos

- **Chill-out Spot**
  Patmos (p334), an island of tranquillity, spirituality and beautiful beaches

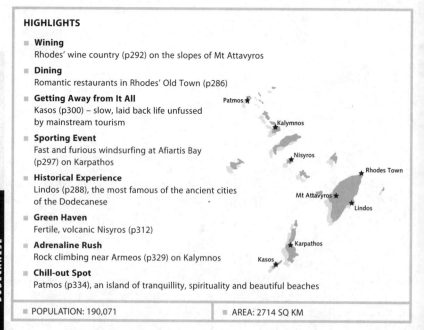

- POPULATION: 190,071
- AREA: 2714 SQ KM

DODECANESE

HISTORY

The Dodecanese islands have been inhabited since pre-Minoan times and by the Archaic period Rhodes and Kos had emerged as the dominant islands within the group. Distance from Athens gave the Dodecanese considerable autonomy and they were, for the most part, free to prosper unencumbered by subjugation to imperial Athens. Following Alexander the Great's death, Ptolemy I of Egypt ruled the Dodecanese.

The Dodecanese islanders were the first Greeks to become Christians. This was through the tireless efforts of St Paul, who made two journeys to the archipelago, and through St John, who was banished to Patmos, where he had his revelation.

The early Byzantine era saw the islands prosper, but by the 7th century AD they were plundered by a string of invaders. By the early 14th century it was the turn of the crusaders – the Knights of St John of Jerusalem, or Knights Hospitallers – who eventually became rulers of almost all the Dodecanese, building mighty fortifications, but not mighty enough to keep out the Turks in 1522.

The Turks were ousted by the Italians in 1912 during a tussle over possession of Libya. The Italians, inspired by Mussolini's vision of a vast Mediterranean empire, made Italian the official language and prohibited the practice of Orthodoxy. The Italians constructed grandiose public buildings in the Fascist style, which was the antithesis of archetypal Greek architecture. More beneficially, they excavated and restored many archaeological monuments.

After the Italian surrender of 1943, the islands became a battleground for British and German forces, with much suffering inflicted upon the population. The Dodecanese were formally returned to Greece in 1947.

GETTING THERE & AWAY

Air

Astypalea, Karpathos, Kos, Leros and Rhodes all have direct flights to Athens. In addition, Rhodes has flights to Iraklio, Kasos (via Karpathos), Thessaloniki, and in summer to Mykonos and Santorini (Thira) in the Cyclades, as well as to Kos, Leros and Astypalea.

Ferry & Hydrofoil

DOMESTIC

Ferry schedules to the Dodecanese are fairly complex, but they do follow a predictable and rarely varying pattern. Departure times in both directions tend to be geared to an early morning arrival at both Piraeus and Rhodes. This means that island hopping southwards can often involve some antisocial hours.

The table below, 'Ferry Connections to the Dodecanese', gives an overall view of ferry connections to the Dodecanese from the mainland and Crete in the high season. The services from Alexandroupolis are subject to seasonal demand, so always check the schedule before committing yourself to the trip.

Aegean Flying Dolphins operates daily hydrofoil services from the Northeastern Aegean island of Samos to the northern Dodecanese, and occasional services from Ikaria.

INTERNATIONAL

There are ferries and hydrofoils to the Turkish ports of Marmaris and Bodrum from Rhodes and Kos, respectively, and day trips to Turkey from Kastellorizo and Symi.

FERRY CONNECTIONS TO THE DODECANESE

Origin	Destination	Dur	Fare	Freq
Alexandroupolis	Kos	26hr	€44	weekly
	Rhodes	30hr	€44	weekly
Piraeus	Astypalea	10-12hr	€32	3 weekly
	Halki	22hr	€33	2 weekly
	Kalymnos	10-13hr	€26	daily
	Karpathos	18½hr	€33	4 weekly
	Kasos	17hr	€31	4 weekly
	Kos	12-15hr	€38	2 daily
	Leros	11hr	€26	daily
	Nisyros	13-15hr	€27	2 weekly
	Patmos	8-9½hr	€31	daily
	Rhodes	15-18hr	€38	2 daily
	Symi	15-17hr	€31	2 weekly
	Tilos	15hr	€30	2 weekly
Sitia	Halki	5½hr	€17	3 weekly
	Karpathos	4hr	€18	3 weekly
	Kasos	2½hr	€8	3 weekly
	Rhodes	10hr	€19	3 weekly
Thessaloniki	Kos	18hr	€39	weekly
	Rhodes	21hr	€45	weekly

DODECANESE

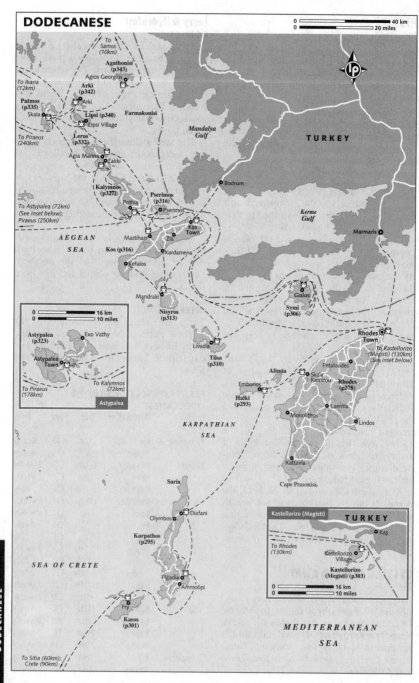

DODECANESE

RHODES ΡΟΔΟΣ

You'll either like Rhodes, or you'll love it. It's big, brash and bold, and is the largest island in the Dodecanese, with a population of over 98,000, Rhodes (*ro*-dos in Greek) is the top package-tour destination of the group. Enjoying 300 days of sunshine a year, and an east coast of virtually uninterrupted sandy beaches, it fulfils the two prerequisites of the sun-starved British, Scandinavians and Germans who flock here.

But beaches and sunshine are not its only attributes. Rhodes is a beautiful island with unspoilt villages nestling in the foothills of its mountains. The landscape varies from arid and rocky around the coast to lush and forested in the interior.

The World Heritage–listed Old Town of Rhodes is the largest inhabited medieval town in Europe, and its fortifications are the finest surviving example of the defensive architecture of that time. In the back streets of its labyrinthine interior you'll find a magical world of hidden alleyways and echoes of private lives lived out an aeon away from the modern tourist strip. Rhodes has attitude and spirit – in large doses.

History

The Minoans and Mycenaeans were among the first to have outposts on the islands, but it was not until the Dorians arrived in 1100 BC that Rhodes began to exert power and influence. The Dorians settled in the cities of Kamiros, Ialysos and Lindos and made each of them prosperous and autonomous states.

Rhodes continued to prosper until Roman times. It was allied to Athens in the Battle of Marathon (490 BC), in which the Persians were defeated, but had shifted to the Persian side by the time of the Battle of Salamis (480 BC). After the unexpected Athenian victory at Salamis, Rhodes hastily became an ally of Athens again, joining the Delian League in 477 BC. Following the disastrous Sicilian Expedition (416–412 BC), Rhodes revolted against Athens and formed an alliance with Sparta, which it aided in the Peloponnesian Wars.

In 408 BC, the cities of Kamiros, Ialysos and Lindos consolidated their powers for mutual protection and expansion by co-founding the city of Rhodes. Rhodes became

Athens' ally again, and together they defeated Sparta at the Battle of Knidos, in 394 BC. Rhodes then joined forces with Persia in a battle against Alexander the Great, but when Alexander proved invincible, quickly allied itself with him.

In 305 BC, Antigonus, one of Ptolemy's rivals, sent his son, the formidable Demetrius Poliorketes (the Besieger of Cities), to conquer Rhodes. The city managed to repel Demetrius after a long siege. To celebrate this victory, the 32m-high bronze statue of Helios Apollo (Colossus of Rhodes), one of the Seven Wonders of the Ancient World, was built (see the Colossus of Rhodes, p284).

After the defeat of Demetrius, Rhodes knew no bounds. It built the biggest navy in the Aegean and its port became a principal Mediterranean trading centre. The arts also flourished. When Greece became the battleground upon which Roman generals fought for leadership of the empire, Rhodes allied itself with Julius Caesar. After Caesar's assassination in 44 BC, Cassius besieged Rhodes, destroying its ships and stripping the city of its artworks, which were then taken to Rome. This marked the beginning of Rhodes' decline, and in AD 70 Rhodes became part of the Roman Empire.

When the Roman Empire split, Rhodes joined the Byzantine province of the Dodecanese. It was given independence when the crusaders seized Constantinople. Later the Genoese gained control. The Knights of St John arrived in Rhodes in 1309 and ruled for 213 years until they were ousted by the Ottomans, who were in turn kicked out by the Italians nearly four centuries later. In 1947, after 35 years of Italian occupation, Rhodes became part of Greece along with the other Dodecanese islands.

Getting There & Away

AIR

Olympic Airlines has at least five flights daily travelling to Athens (€75), two daily to Karpathos (€28), one daily to Kastellorizo (€25), two daily to Kasos (€34), four weekly to Thessaloniki (€117) one daily to Iraklio (€87), two weekly to Samos (€36) and three weekly to Astypalea (€30). Direct enquiries to **Olympic Airlines** (Map p281; ☎ 22410 24571; www.olympicairlines.com; Ierou Lohou 9).

Aegean Airlines (Map p281; ☎ 22410 24400; www.aegeanair.com; Ethelondon Dodekanision 20) offers flights to Athens, Thessaloniki and Iraklio at similar rates, plus direct connections to Larnaca (€106, one hour) and Rome (€153, two hours).

CAÏQUE

There is a daily caïque between Skala Kamirou, on Rhodes' west coast, and Halki (€12, 1½ hours). From Skala Kamirou services depart at 2.30pm, and from Halki at 6am.

CATAMARAN

The *Dodekanisos Express* starts its daily run up the Dodecanese at around 8.30am each day from Kolona harbour, stopping at Kos, Kalymnos and Leros daily, with stops at other times in Symi, Lipsi and Patmos.

There is usually a seasonal weekly service to Kastellorizo as well. Its sister vessel the *Dodekanisos Pride* runs a similar schedule starting at a similar time from Patmos.

Tickets can be bought at **Skevos Travel** (Map p281; ☎ 22410 22461; skeyos@rho.forthnet.gr; Amerikis 11) or **Dodekanisos Naftiliaki** (☎ 22410 70590; www.12ne.gr; Afstralias 3).

The Tilos-owned *Sea Star* links Rhodes with Tilos daily. Its schedules tend to fluctuate wildly, but there are one or two sailings daily and a weekly link to Nisyros. Check with **Triton Holidays** (Map p281; ☎ 22410 21690; www.tritondmc.gr; Plastira 9, Mandraki) for schedules and tickets.

There are two daily catamarans from Rhodes' Commercial Harbour to Marmaris

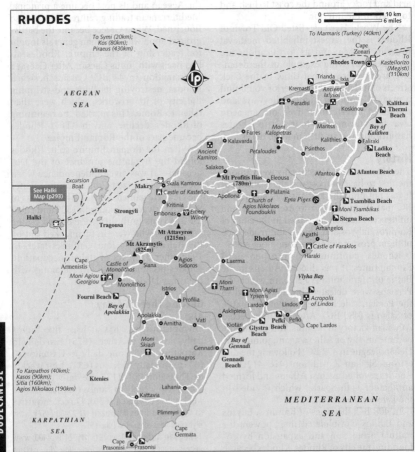

(50 minutes) from June to September at 8am and 4pm, respectively, dropping back to maybe only three or four services a week in winter. Tickets cost €30 one way plus the €15 Turkish arrival tax.

EXCURSION BOAT

There are excursion boats to Symi (€22 return) every day in summer, leaving Mandraki Harbour at 9am and returning at 6pm. You can buy tickets at most travel agencies, but it is better to buy them at the harbour, where you can check out the boats personally. Look for shade and the size and condition of the boat, as these vary greatly. You can buy an open return if you want to stay on Symi.

FERRY
Domestic

Rhodes is the main port of the Dodecanese and offers a complex array of departures. The following table lists scheduled domestic ferries from Rhodes to other islands in the Dodecanese and Piraeus in high season. The EOT office (p282) in Rhodes Town can provide you with current schedules.

Destination	Duration	Fare	Frequency
Astypalea	8-10hr	€21	2 weekly
Halki	1½-2hr	€8.50	daily
Kalymnos	4½hr	€12	6 weekly
Karpathos	5½hr	€18	3 weekly
Kasos	6½hr	€22	3 weekly
Kastellorizo	4-5hr	€17	4 weekly
Kos	3½hr	€18	daily
Leros	5½hr	€20	daily
Nisyros	4½hr	€12	2 weekly
Patmos	8½hr	€23	daily
Piraeus	15-18hr	€38	1-2 daily
Sitia	10hr	€25	3 weekly
Symi	1½hr	€7-13	1-2 daily
Tilos	2½hr	€18.50	4 weekly

International

There is a weekly passenger and car ferry service between Marmaris in Turkey and Rhodes (1¼ hours) on Friday at 4pm. The cost of ferrying a car to the Turkish mainland is €180 one way, while passengers pay €55, including taxes. Return rates usually work out cheaper. This service is run by the Turkish shipping line Aegean Shipping. Contact **Triton Holidays** (Map p281; ☎ 22410 21690;

www.tritondmc.gr; Plastira 9, Mandraki) upon arrival to arrange a crossing.

HYDROFOIL

Aegean Hydrofoils (Plateia Neoriou 6) on the quay operates the following services from Rhodes in the high season:

Destination	Duration	Fare	Frequency
Astypalea	5½hr	€37	weekly
Kalymnos	3½hr	€31	weekly
Kos	2hr	€25	2 daily
Leros	3½hr	€34	3 weekly
Patmos	3½hr	€39	3 weekly
Symi	50min	€13	2 weekly

Tickets are available from **Triton Holidays** (Map p281; ☎ 22410 21690; www.tritondmc.gr; Plastira 9, Mandraki). There is an additional daily hydrofoil, the *Aigili*, run and owned by Symi island, with a daily service (€11) to and from Gialos on Symi. Tickets are available from Triton Holidays or from the makeshift kiosk at the quay.

Getting Around
TO/FROM THE AIRPORT

The airport is 16km southwest of Rhodes Town, near Paradisi. There are 21 buses daily between the airport and Rhodes Town's west side bus station (€1.50, 25 minutes). The first leaves Rhodes Town at 5am and the last at 11pm; from the airport, the first leaves at 5.55am and the last at 11.45pm. Buses from the airport leave from the main road outside the airport perimeter.

BICYCLE

Bicycle Centre (Map p281; ☎ 22410 28315; Griva 39; per day €5) has a range of bicycles for hire.

BOAT

There are excursion boats to Lindos (return €15) every day in summer, leaving Mandraki Harbour at 9am and returning at 6pm.

CAR & MOTORCYCLE

There are numerous car and motorcycle rental outlets in Rhodes' New Town. Shop around and bargain because the competition is fierce. A reliable agency is **Drive Rent a Car** (☎ 22410 68243; www.driverentacar.gr; Australias 2). Call ahead for an aiport pickup,

DODECANESE

if required. Book through **Triton Holidays** (Map p281; ☎ 22410 21690; www.tritondmc.gr; Plastira 9, Mandraki) for even cheaper rates.

PUBLIC TRANSPORT

Rhodes Town has two bus stations, which service one half of the island each. From the **east side bus station** (Map p281; Plateia Rimini) there are 18 buses daily to Faliraki (€1.70), 14 to Lindos (€4.60), three to Kolymbia (€2.30), nine to Gennadi (€4.24) via Lardos, and four to Psinthos (€1.78).

From the **west side bus station** (Map p281), next to the New Market, there are buses every half-hour to Kalithea Thermi (€1.70, 15 minutes), 10 to Koskinou (€1.70, 20 minutes), five to Salakos (€3.50, one hour), two to Ancient Kamiros (€4.10, 55 minutes), one to Monolithos (€6, one hour 20 minutes) via Skala Kamirou, and one to Embonas (€5, one hour 10 minutes). The main tourist office gives out schedules.

Local buses around the city charge a flat €1.

TAXI

Rhodes Town's main **taxi rank** (Map p281) is east of Plateia Rimini. There are two zones on the island for taxi meters: Zone One is Rhodes Town and Zone Two (slightly higher) is everywhere else. Rates are a little higher between midnight and 6am.

Taxis tend not to use meters, but prefer to use set fare rates. All drivers carry a booklet setting out the current approved set fares. Request to see it if in doubt. Sample fares: airport €14, Filerimos €15, Petaloudes €23, ancient Kamiros €30, Lindos €34 and Monolithos €65. Taxi company contact phone numbers include ☎ 22410 64712, ☎ 22410 64734 and ☎ 22410 64778.

RHODES TOWN

pop 56,128

The heart of Rhodes Town is the Old Town, enclosed within massive walls. Avoid the worst of the tourist crowds by beginning your exploration early in the morning. At any time, away from the main thoroughfares and squares, you will find deserted serpentine alleyways. Much of the New Town to the north is dominated by package tourism, but it does have a few places of interest to visitors and the advantage of being right next to the town's best beaches.

Orientation

The Old Town is nominally divided into three sectors: the Kollakio, or Knights' Quarter, the Hora, and the Jewish Quarter. The Kollakio contains most of the medieval historical sights of the Old Town, while the Hora, often referred to as the Turkish Quarter, is primarily Rhodes Town's commercial sector and shows off most of the shops and restaurants. The Old Town is accessible by nine *pyles* (main gates) and two rampart-access portals. The whole town is a mesh of Byzantine, Turkish and Latin architecture, featuring quiet, twisting alleyways that are punctuated by lively squares.

The commercial centre of the New Town lies north of the Old Town and is easily explored on foot. Most commercial activity is centred on two blocks surrounding Plateia Kyprou. The hotel district is centred on a large sector bordered by 28 Oktovriou and G Papanikolaou.

The commercial harbour (Kolona) is east of the Old Town. Excursion boats, small ferries, hydrofoils and private yachts use Mandraki Harbour, further north.

Information

EMERGENCY

Emergency first aid & ambulance (☎ 22410 25555, 22410 22222)

INTERNET ACCESS

Mango Cafe Bar (Map p283; ☎ 22410 24877; www .mango.gr; Plateia Dorieos 3; per hr €5; ☼ 9.30am-midnight) In the Old Town.

Rock Style Internet Café (Map p281; ☎ 22410 57502; info@rockstyle.gr; Dimokratias 7; per hr €4; ☼ 7am-1am) Just south of the Old Town.

INTERNET RESOURCES

www.rhodesguide.com A comprehensive guide to what's on in Rhodes.

www.rodos.gr A good cultural and historical background to Rhodes.

LAUNDRY

Express Laundry (Map p281; Kosti Palama 5) Service washes for €4.

LEFT LUGGAGE

Planet Holidays (Map p281; ☎ 22410 35722; Gallias 6; per 2-hr period €3, up to 2 days €4) Prices can be negotiated for longer periods.

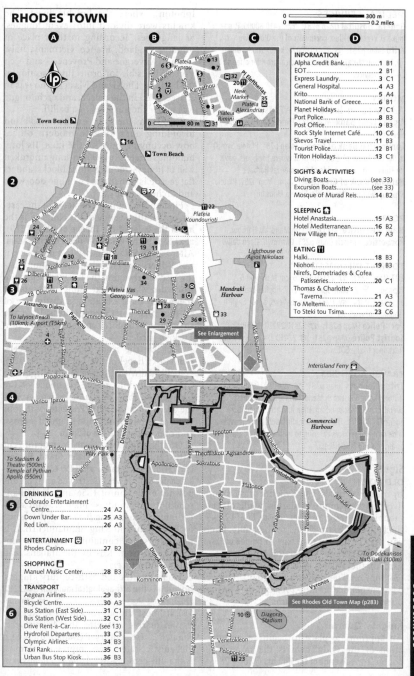

RHODES TOWN

0 — 300 m
0 — 0.2 miles

INFORMATION
Alpha Credit Bank...................**1** B1
EOT.....................................**2** B1
Express Laundry.....................**3** C1
General Hospital....................**4** A3
Krito....................................**5** A4
National Bank of Greece..........**6** B1
Planet Holidays.....................**7** C1
Port Police............................**8** B3
Post Office............................**9** B3
Rock Style Internet Café.........**10** C6
Skevos Travel........................**11** B3
Tourist Police.......................**12** B1
Triton Holidays....................**13** C1

SIGHTS & ACTIVITIES
Diving Boats....................(see 33)
Excursion Boats................(see 33)
Mosque of Murad Reis........**14** B2

SLEEPING
Hotel Anastasia.....................**15** A3
Hotel Mediterranean.............**16** B2
New Village Inn....................**17** A3

EATING
Halki...................................**18** B3
Niohori................................**19** B3
Nirefs, Demetriades & Cofea
Patisseries........................**20** C1
Thomas & Charlotte's
Taverna............................**21** A3
To Meltemi...........................**22** C2
To Steki tou Tsima.................**23** C6

DRINKING
Colorado Entertainment
Centre..............................**24** A2
Down Under Bar....................**25** A3
Red Lion..............................**26** A3

ENTERTAINMENT
Rhodes Casino......................**27** B2

SHOPPING
Manuel Music Center.............**28** B3

TRANSPORT
Aegean Airlines....................**29** B3
Bicycle Centre......................**30** A3
Bus Station (East Side)..........**31** C1
Bus Station (West Side).........**32** C1
Drive Rent-a-Car...............(see 13)
Hydrofoil Departures.............**33** C3
Olympic Airlines...................**34** B3
Taxi Rank............................**35** C1
Urban Bus Stop Kiosk............**36** B3

Town Beach

Town Beach

Plateia
Koundourioti

Lighthouse of
Agios Nikolaos

Mandraki
Harbour

See Enlargement

Interisland Ferry

To Ialysos Beach
(10km); Airport (15km)

Alexandrou Diakou

To Stadium &
Theatre (500m);
Temple of Pythian
Apollo (550m)

Children's
Play Park

Commercial
Harbour

To Dodekanisos
Naftiliaki (100m)

See Rhodes Old Town Map (p283)

Diagoras
Stadium

DODECANESE

Enlargement:
Plateia
Kyprou
New
Market
Plateia
Alexandrias
Plateia
Rimini

MEDICAL SERVICES

General Hospital (Map p281; ☎ 22410 80000; Papalouka El Venizelou) Just northwest of the Old Town.
Krito (Map p281; ☎ 22410 30020; krito@rho.forthnet.gr; Ioannou Metaxa 3) Private medical provider offering a 24-hour service.

MONEY

All the banks listed have ATMs.
Alpha Credit Bank (Map p281; Plateia Kyprou) In the New Town.
Commercial Bank of Greece (Map p281; Plateia Symis) In the Old Town, plus an ATM near where the boats leave for Turkey on the east side of Commercial Harbour.
National Bank of Greece New Town (Map p281; Plateia Kyprou) Old Town (Map p283; Plateia Mousiou)

POST

Main post office (Map p281) On Mandraki Harbour.
Post office branch (Map p283; Old Town) Open daily.

TOURIST INFORMATION

EOT (Map p281; ☎ 22410 35226; cnr Makariou & Papagou; ✆ 7.30am-3pm Mon-Fri) Supplies brochures and maps of the city. Has the *Rodos News*, a free English-language newspaper.
Port Police (Map p281; ☎ 22410 22220; Mandraki)
Tourist Police (Map p281; ☎ 22410 27423; ✆ 24hr) Next door to the EOT.

TRAVEL AGENCIES

Triton Holidays (Map p281; ☎ 22410 21690; www.tritondmc.gr; Plastira 9, Mandraki) Perhaps the best overall travel, tourist information and accommodation agency in Rhodes. The exceptionally helpful staff provide a wide range of services catering to individual needs, as well as air, sea and land tickets.

Sights

OLD TOWN

In medieval times, the Knights of St John lived in the Knights' Quarter, while other inhabitants lived in the Hora. The 12m-thick city walls are closed to the public but you may be able to take part in **guided walks** (☎ 22410 23359; tours €6), starting at the courtyard of the Palace of the Grand Masters (2.45pm on Tuesday and Saturday). These were suspended in mid-2005 but may be in operation again in the future.

Knights' Quarter

An appropriate place to begin an exploration of the Old Town is the imposing cobblestone **Avenue of the Knights** (Map p283;

Ippoton), where the knights lived. The knights were divided into seven 'tongues' or languages, according to their place of origin – England, France, Germany, Italy, Aragon, Auvergne and Provence – and each were responsible for protecting a section of the bastion. The Grand Master, who was in charge, lived in the palace, and each tongue was under the auspices of a bailiff.

To this day the street exudes a noble and forbidding aura, despite modern offices now occupying most of the inns. Its lofty buildings stretch in a 600m-long unbroken wall of honey-coloured stone blocks, and its flat façade is punctuated by huge doorways and arched windows.

First on the right, if you begin at the eastern end of the Avenue of the Knights, is the **Inn of the Order of the Tongue of Italy** (1519); next to it is the **Palace of Villiers de l'Isle Adam**. After Sultan Süleyman had taken the city, it was Villiers de l'Isle who had the humiliating task of arranging the knights' departure from the island. Next along is the **Inn of France**, the most ornate and distinctive of all the inns. On the opposite side of the street is a wrought-iron gate in front of a Turkish garden.

Back on the right side is the **Chapelle Française** (Chapel of the Tongue of France), embellished with a statue of the Virgin and Child. Next door is the residence of the Chaplain of the Tongue of France. Across the alleyway is the **Inn of Provence**, with four coats of arms forming the shape of a cross, and opposite is the **Inn of Spain**.

On the right is the truly magnificent 14th-century **Palace of the Grand Masters** (☎ 22410 23359; Ippoton; admission €6; ✆ 8.30am-7.30pm Tue-Sun). It was destroyed in the gunpowder explosion of 1856 and the Italians rebuilt it in a grandiose manner, with a lavish interior, intending it as a holiday home for Mussolini and King Emmanuel III. It is now a museum, containing sculpture, mosaics taken from Kos by the Italians, and antique furniture.

Housed in the old 15th-century knights' hospital is the **archaeological museum** (☎ 22410 27657; Plateia Mousiou; admission €3; ✆ 8am-4pm Tue-Sun). Its most famous exhibit is the exquisite Parian marble statuette, the *Aphrodite of Rhodes*, a 1st-century-BC adaptation of a Hellenistic statue. Less impressive to most is the 4th-century-BC *Afroditi Thalassia* in

RHODES OLD TOWN

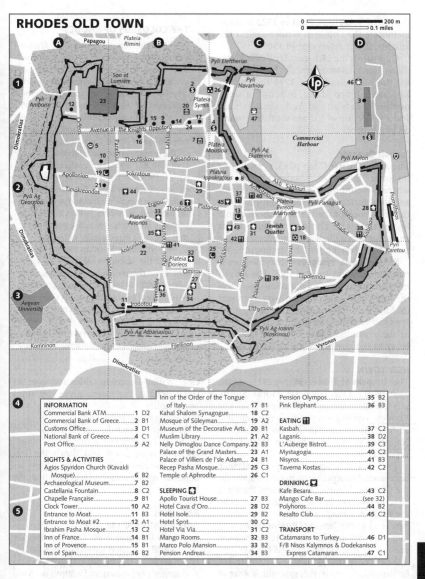

the next room. The **Museum of the Decorative Arts** (☎ 22410 72674; Plateia Argyrokastrou; admission €2; ☷ 8.30am-3pm Tue-Sun), further north, houses a collection of artefacts from around the Dodecanese.

On Plateia Symis, there are the remains of a 3rd-century-BC **Temple of Aphrodite**, one of the few ancient ruins in the Old Town.

Hora

Bearing many legacies of its Ottoman past is the **Hora** (Map p283). During Turkish times, churches were converted to mosques, and many more Muslim houses of worship were built from scratch, although most are now dilapidated. The most important is the pink-domed **Mosque of Süleyman**, at the top of Sokratous. Built in 1522 to commemorate the Ottoman victory against the knights, it was renovated in 1808.

Opposite is the 18th-century **Muslim library** (Plateia Arionos; Sokratous; admission free; ☯ 9.30am-4pm Mon-Sat). Founded in 1794 by Turkish Rhodian Ahmed Hasuf, it houses a small number of Persian and Arabic manuscripts and a collection of Korans written by hand on parchment.

Jewish Quarter

The **Jewish Quarter** (Map p283) is an almost forgotten sector of Rhodes Old Town, where life continues at an unhurried pace and local residents live seemingly oblivious to the hubbub of the Hora, no more than a few blocks away. This area of quiet streets and sometimes dilapidated houses was once home to a thriving Jewish community.

Kahal Shalom synagogue (www.rhodesjewish museum.org; Dosiadou), built in 1577, has a commemorative plaque to the many members of Hora's Jewish population who were sent to Auschwitz during the Nazi occupation. Jews still worship here and it is usually open in the morning. Close by is **Plateia Evreon Martyron** (Square of the Jewish Martyrs).

NEW TOWN

The **Acropolis of Rhodes** (Map p281), southwest of the Old Town on Monte Smith, was the site of the ancient Hellenistic city of Rhodes. The hill is named after the English admiral Sir Sydney Smith, who watched for Napoleon's fleet from here in 1802. It has superb views.

The restored 2nd-century-AD **stadium** once staged competitions in preparation for the Olympic Games. The adjacent **theatre** is a reconstruction of one used for lectures by the Rhodes School of Rhetoric. Steps above here lead to the **Temple of Pythian Apollo**, with four re-erected columns. This unenclosed site can be reached on city bus No 5.

North of Mandraki, at the eastern end of G Papanikolaou, is the graceful **Mosque of Murad Reis** (Map p281). In its grounds are a Turkish cemetery and the Villa Cleobolus, where Lawrence Durrell lived in the 1940s, writing *Reflections on a Marine Venus*.

If you fancy a flutter, the impressive **Rhodes Casino** (Map p281; ☎ 22410 97500; www .casinorodos.gr; G. Papanikolaou 4) is a combination of casino, hotel, convention centre and

THE COLOSSUS OF RHODES

Whether the famous *Colossus of Rhodes* ever actually existed can never be proven, since there are no remains and no tangible evidence other than the reports of ancient travellers. The statue was apparently commissioned by Demetrius Poliorketes in 305 BC, after he finally capitulated to Rhodian defiance following his long and ultimately failed siege of Rhodes in that same year.

The bronze statue was built over 12 years (294–282 BC) and when completed stood 32m high. What is not clear is where this gargantuan statue stood. Popular medieval belief has it astride the harbour at Mandraki (as depicted on today's T-shirts and tourist trinkets), but it is highly unlikely that this is the case, as it is technically unfeasible.

An earthquake in either 225 or 226 BC toppled the statue, most likely on land, where the remains lay undisturbed for 880 years. In AD 654 invading Saracens had the remains broken up and sold for scrap to a Jewish merchant in Edessa (in modern-day Turkey). The story goes that after being shipped to Syria, it took almost 1000 camels to convey it to its final destination.

café. With 34 gaming tables and over 300 slot machines the casino gives you ample opportunity to double – or half – your holiday savings in no time.

The town **beach** begins north of Mandraki and continues around the island's northernmost point and down the west side of the New Town. The best spots will depend on the prevailing winds, but tend to be on the east side.

Activities

GREEK DANCING LESSONS

The **Nelly Dimoglou Dance Company** (Map p283; ☎ 22410 20157; deyappet@otenet.gr; Andronikou 7; admission per person €8, per group €11) gives lessons and stages performances (9.30pm on Monday, Wednesday and Friday) in folk dance theatre.

SCUBA DIVING

Three diving schools operate out of Mandraki: **Waterhoppers Diving Centre** (☎ /fax 22410 38146, ☎ 69329 63173; water-hoppers@rodos.com; Perikleous 29), **Diving Centres** (☎ 22410 61115; fax

22410 66 584; Lissavonas 33) and **Scuba Diving Trident School** (☎ /fax 22410 29160; S Zervou 2). All offer a range of courses, including a 'One Day Try Dive', for €40 to €50. You can get information from their boats at Mandraki harbour (Map p281). Kalithea Thermi is the only site around Rhodes where diving is permitted.

Sleeping
BUDGET

The Old Town has a reasonable selection of budget accommodation.

Hotel Isole (Map p283; ☎ 22410 20682; fax 22410 33684; www.hotelisole.com; s/d incl breakfast €30/45; 🔀) Sequestered away in the back streets, but helpfully signposted, is this cosy pension consisting of seven homely rooms in blue and white. There's a welcoming lobby lounge with a small bar. Between them hosts Louisa and Guido Barone speak five languages to their guests.

Mango Rooms (Map p283; ☎ 22410 24877; www.mango.gr; Plateia Dorieos 3; s/d €30/47) This place has clean, nicely furnished rooms with bathroom, TV, ceiling fan, safety box and refrigerator. It's open all year and has heating in winter.

Pink Elephant (Map p283; ☎ 22410 22469; www.pinkelephantpension.com; Timakida 9; s/d €34/40) The fan-equipped and very presentable rooms here have large bathrooms, though there are some cheaper rooms with shared bathrooms. Owners Mari and Sylvia make guests feel at home away from home. One night stays are fine.

Hotel Spot (Map p283; ☎ 22410 34737; www.spothotelrhodes.com; Perikleous 21; s/d incl breakfast €35/60; 🔀 ▣) The Spot has exceptionally clean, pleasant and tastefully decorated rooms, each with a fridge. English speaking owner Lee is an impeccable host. There is also a small book exchange and left-luggage facilities.

Pension Olympos (Map p283; ☎ /fax 22410 33567; www.pensionolympos.com; Agiou Fanouriou 56; s/d €35/45; 🔀) This pension has pleasant rooms with fridge and TV, and an attractive little courtyard. Dream away on its wrought-iron country-style beds with soft mattresses.

Most of the New Town's hotels are modern and characterless, but there are a couple of exceptions.

New Village Inn (Map p281; ☎ 22410 34937; www.newvillageinn.gr; Konstantopedos 10; s/d €24/35) This cosy inn has tastefully furnished rooms with

refrigerator and fan, and a traditional stone-walled courtyard festooned with plants.

Hotel Anastasia (Map p281; ☎ 22410 28007; www.anastasia-hotel.com; 28 Oktovriou 46; s/d incl breakfast €35/41) This old-style, renovated hotel, in a former Italian mansion, is a quiet getaway. The high-ceilinged rooms with tiled floors are spotless. The lush garden sports a tortoise and cat family. Italian is spoken.

MIDRANGE

Apollo Tourist House (Map p283; ☎ 22410 32003; www.apollo-touristhouse.com; Omirou 28c; s/d €35/70) Fully reconstructed in 2004, this is a small, quality pension comprising six rooms, the best of which boasts a four-post bed. Rooms all have good views and there is a cosy courtyard for breakfasts or the occasional barbecue.

Pension Andreas (Map p283; ☎ 22410 34156; fax 22410 74285; www.hotelandreas.com; Omirou 28d; s/d €60/70 🔀) In one of the quietest parts of the Old Town this exceptionally friendly small boutique hotel, with ever-helpful staff, has 11 tastefully decorated and individually named rooms. There is a very social breakfast bar with terrific views across the Old Town. Open all year.

Hotel Cava d'Oro (Map p283; ☎ 22410 36980; fax 22410 77332; www.cavadoro.com; Kistiniou 15; s/d €60/90; Ⓟ 🔀) A handy choice for visitors with luggage as the taxi can come to the door. Constructed from an 800-year-old building the rooms have solid walls and attractive furnishings including wrought iron beds.

TOP END

Discounted New Town hotel deals can be booked via Triton Holidays (see p282).

Hotel Via Via (Map p283; ☎ /fax 22410 77027; www.hotel-via-via.com; Lisipou 2; d €75-90 🔀) This pristine boutique hotel, in a discreet quarter of the Old Town, has tastefully furnished and individually named rooms and is open all year. There's a gorgeous sun roof where breakfast is served by welcoming Belgian owner Bea.

Marco Polo Mansion (Map p283; ☎ 22410 25562; www.marcopolomansion.web.com; Agiou Fanouriou 40-42; s/d €90/170) Featured in glossy European magazines, this old-fashioned Anatolian inn is decorated in rich Ottoman-era colours. A cool and shady lodging, right in the heart of the Old Town, it is run by the effervescent Effie Dede.

Hotel Mediterranean (Map p281; ☎ 22410 24661; fax 22410 22828; www.mediterranean.gr; Kos 35; s/d €70/110; P ✖ ▣) This luxurious beach-side hotel is one of the best-located up-market establishments in the New Town, and worth investigating. Fronting the more sheltered east beach, it offers all the creature comforts you would expect from a top hotel, yet offers that personal discreet touch often missing elsewhere. Excellent in-house restaurant.

Eating
BUDGET
Old Town
Avoid the restaurant touts and tack along Sokratous and around Plateia Ippokratous. Hit the backstreets to find less touristy places to eat.

Taverna Kostas (Map p283; ☎ 22410 26217; Pythagora 62; mains €5-7) Popular Kostas is good value and has stood the test of time with its great grills and fish dishes. It can't be beaten on quality and quantity.

Mystagogia (Map p283; ☎ 22410 32981; Themistokleous 5; mezedes €4-10) Mystagogia draws its charm as much from the open fireplace for winter meals as from its carefully cooked dishes. Owner Filippos serves up top class home-made *mezedes* – the platter is recommended – and always plays quality background music.

Laganis (Map p283; ☎ 22410 35571; Alhadef 16; mains €4-7) In the backstreets of the Old Town, this restaurant close to the Karetou Gate is a low-key, family-style taverna. It's simple, unpretentious and doesn't rely on the clientele of the less discerning restaurants along the main strip. Try the excellent fish *souvlaki* or mussels Laganis (filled with cheese and oven baked).

New Town
The New Town has some surprisingly good places to eat, as long as you are prepared to look.

Halki (Map p281; ☎ 22410 33198; Kathopouli 30; mezedes €2.50-5; ☽ dinner) Halki is a down-to-earth and thoroughly idiosyncratic eatery. Choose from an enticing display of *mezedes*, and down them with excellent draught wine.

Niohori (Map p281; ☎ 22410 35116; I Kazouli 29; mains €3-6) In an area dominated by fast and mediocre food choices it's refreshing to find at least one genuine option left. Blink, however, and you've missed it. Hidden away in the back streets Niohori serves up grills from its own butcher shop, as well as an array of filling and low-cost *mayirefta* (ready-cooked meals).

Thomas & Charlotte's Taverna (Map p281; ☎ 22410 73557; Georgiou Leondos 8; mains €5-9) This taverna serves a wide selection of standard Greek dishes. Try the tasty *klefyiko*, a slow-cooked mixture of meat and vegetables served wrapped in greaseproof paper.

Feverish touting reaches its acme at people-watching patisseries such as Nirefs, Demetriades and Cofea, which border the New Market. Nevertheless, they're convivial meeting places.

MIDRANGE & TOP END
Old Town
Nisyros (Map p283; ☎ 22410 31741; Agiou Fanouriou 45-47; mains €6.50-11) A beautiful and tastefully decorated restaurant with impeccable service and a wide range of Greek dishes. Dining is in a leafy, secluded courtyard.

L'Auberge Bistrot (Map p283; ☎ 22410 34292; www.bistrotrhodes.com; Praxitelous 1; mains €11-17) This French bistro can take some finding (it's best approached from Koskinou gate), which may explain its high-quality food and repeat clientele. The resident French chef creates excellent bouillabaisse, as well as other 'French international' dishes from a small but select menu. Excellent, reasonably priced wines.

Kasbah (Map p283; ☎ 22410 78633; Platonos 4-8; mains €11-15; ☽ dinner, closed Mon) If you crave something other than Greek food, Kasbah serves excellent Moroccan dishes. Couscous dishes predominate, with one especially for vegetarians. Ambience is Middle Eastern, and piped world music entertains you as you dine.

New Town
To Steki tou Tsima (Map p281; ☎ 22410 74390; Peloponisou 22; mezedes €5-7) To Steki is an unpretentious and totally untouristy fish restaurant on the south side of Old Town. Sample from an imaginative, and occasionally unusual, array of fish (such as *yermanos*) and shellfish-based *mezedes* – try *fouskes*.

To Meltemi (Map p281; ☎ 22410 30480; cnr Plateia Kountourioti & Rodou; mains €6-13) Virtually the New Town's only beachside taverna, To

Meltemi sits proudly adjacent to the waterfront just north of Mandraki Harbour. To a nautical theme, with faded photos and piped old-school music, dishes are served up attentively and include oven-baked feta and an original 'Meltemi salad'.

Entertainment

OLD TOWN

Kafe Besara (Map p283; ☎ 22410 30363; Sofokleous 11-12) This Aussie-owned place is one of the Old Town's liveliest bars, and a great place to hang out.

Mango Cafe Bar (Map p283; ☎ 22410 24877; Dorieos 3) This bar claims to have the cheapest drinks in the Old Town, as well as Internet access (see p280), and is the preferred haunt of local expats, scuba divers and die-hard travellers.

Resalto Club (Map p283; ☎ 22410 20520; Plateia Damagitou; ⏰ 11pm-late) This Greek music centre features live music on weekends. The repertoire ranges from *entehno* (artistic compositional) to *laïko tragoudi* (popular) to *rembetika* (blues).

Sound & Light Show (Map p283; ☎ 22410 21922; www.hellenicfestival.gr; admission €6) This impressive show takes place from Monday to Saturday next to the walls of the Old Town, off Plateia Rimini and near the Amboise Gate. English-language sessions are staggered but in general begin at either 9.15pm or 11.15pm. Other languages offered are French, German and Swedish.

A largish complex known as Polyhoros (Map p283) is home to a number of stylish night clubs and bars in the middle of the Old Town.

NEW TOWN

There is a plethora of discos and bars in New Town. The two main areas are Top Street (Alexandrou Diakou) and the Street of Bars (Orfanidou), where a cacophony of Western music blares from every establishment.

Down Under Bar (Map p281; ☎ 22410 32982; Orfanidou 37) For a wild night of dancing on the bar, make for this Aussie-influenced watering hole.

Red Lion (Map p281; Orfanidou 9) For something more subdued, this bar has the relaxed atmosphere of a British pub. Ron and Vasilis will gladly answer questions about Rhodes for the price of a drink.

Colorado Entertainment Centre (Map p281; ☎ 22410 75120; www.coloradoclub.gr; cnr Akti Miaouli & Orfanidou 57) The Colorado consists of six venues in one – Studio Fame, Heaven Club R&B, Colorado Live, Förfesten, Swedco Café and IN 4 U Music Bar – and is more fun than you can shake your rear end at.

Shopping

Look out for gold and silver jewellery, leather goods and ceramics in the Old Town are. Shoes are also a good buy, with styles not always found back home.

Manuel Music Center (Map p281; ☎ 22410 28266; 25 Martiou 10-13) All the latest CDs and more are on sale here, including good-quality Greek music – ie not 'Zorba the Greek does Syrtaki' tourist music.

Getting Around

Local buses leave from the **urban bus stop** (Map p281) on Mandraki. Bus No 2 goes to Analipsi, No 3 to Rodini, No 4 to Agios Dimitrios and No 5 to Monte Smith. You can buy tickets at the kiosk on Mandraki.

EASTERN RHODES

Rhodes' best beaches are on the east coast. There are frequent buses to Lindos, but some beaches are a bit of a trek from the road. It's possible to find uncrowded stretches of coast even in the high season.

Kalithea Thermi, 10km from Rhodes Town, is a derelict Italian-built spa. Within the complex are crumbling colonnades, domed ceilings and mosaic floors. Buses from Rhodes Town stop opposite the turn-off to the spa. The beach is used by Rhodes' diving schools (see p284). To the right there's a small sandy beach (with a snack bar); take the track that veers right from the turn-off to the spa. Kalithea is slowly being restored.

Ladiko Beach, touted locally as 'Anthony Quinn Beach', is in fact two back-to-back coves with a pebbly beach on the north side and volcanic rock platforms on the south. The swimming is good and development is relatively low-key.

At Kolymbia, further down the coast, a right turn leads in over 4km of pine-fringed road to the **Epta Piges** (Seven Springs), a beautiful cool, shady valley where a lake fed by springs can be reached either along a path or through a tunnel. This is a popular tourist attraction in its own right. There are no buses around here, so take a Lindos bus and get off at the turn-off.

Back on the coast, **Kolymbia** and **Tsambika** are good but crowded beaches. A steep road (signposted) leads inland 1.5km to **Moni Tsambikas**, from where there are terrific views. The monastery is a place of pilgrimage for childless women. On 18 September, the monastery's festival day, women climb up to it on their knees and then pray to conceive.

Arhangelos, 4km further on and inland, is a large agricultural village with a tradition of carpet weaving and making goatskin boots by hand. Just before Arhangelos there is a turn-off to **Stegna Beach**, and just after to the lovely sandy cove of **Agathi**; both are reasonably quiet. The 15th century **Castle of Faraklos**, above Agathi, was a prison for recalcitrant knights and the island's last stronghold to fall to the Turks. The fishing port of **Haraki**, just south of the castle, has a pebbled beach. There are more beaches between here and Vlyha Bay, 2km from Lindos.

Lindos Λίνδος
pop 1091

Perhaps the most famous tourist sight after the Old Town in Rhodes is the sparkling white village of Lindos, 47km from Rhodes, crowned by its ancient Acropolis. Buses and boats make a beeline daily to this still pretty village. Be advised: your enjoyment will be shared by thousands of others, so time your visit carefully. Go late or early, or better still stay for a night or two and savour the quieter evening ambience, when rooftop moonlight dining is *de rigueur*.

The village is a showpiece of dazzling white **17th-century houses**, many boasting courtyards with black-and-white *hohlakia* (pebble mosaic) floors. Once the dwellings of wealthy admirals, many have been bought and restored by foreign celebrities. The main thoroughfares are lined with tourist shops and cafés, so you need to explore the labyrinthine alleyways to fully appreciate the place.

Lindos is the most famous of the ancient cities of the Dodecanese, and was an important Doric settlement because of its excellent vantage point and good harbour. It was first established around 2000 BC and is

overlaid with a conglomeration of Byzantine, Frankish and Turkish remains.

After the founding of the city of Rhodes, Lindos declined in commercial importance, but remained an important place of worship. The ubiquitous St Paul landed here en route to Rome. The Byzantine fortress was strengthened by the knights, and also used by the Turks.

The 15th-century Church of Agios Ioannis, in the Acropolis, is festooned with 18th-century frescoes.

ORIENTATION & INFORMATION
The town is pedestrianised. All vehicular traffic terminates on the central square of Plateia Eleftherias, from where the main drag, Acropolis, begins. The donkey terminus is a little way along here. Turn right at the donkey terminus to reach the post office, after 50m.

By the terminus is the Commercial Bank of Greece, with an ATM. The National Bank of Greece, located on the street opposite the Church of Agia Panagia, also has an ATM.

There are two Internet cafés in Lindos, one near the post office the other in the lower village. Access per hour costs €3.50.

Lindos Lending Library (Acropolis) Privately owned and well stocked with English books. It also has a laundrette (per load €7.50).
Lindos Sun Tours (☎ 22440 31333; Acropolis) Has room-letting services and also rents cars and motorcycles.
Municipal Tourist Office (☎ 22440 31900; Plateia Eleftherias; ☺ 7.30am-9pm) Helpful, although staff are overworked.
Pallas Travel (☎ 22440 31494; Acropolis) Has room-letting services.

SIGHTS
The Acropolis of Lindos
Spectacularly perched atop a 116m-high rock is the **Acropolis** (☎ 22440 31258; admission €6; ☺ 8.30am-2.40pm Tue-Sun Sep-May, 8.30am-6pm Jun-Aug). It's about a 10-minute climb to the well-signposted entrance gate. Once inside, a flight of steps leads to a large square. On the left (facing the next flight of steps) is a *trireme* (warship), hewn out of the rock by the sculptor Pythocretes; a statue of Hagesandros, priest of Poseidon, originally stood on the deck of the ship. At the top of the steps ahead, you enter the Acropolis via a vaulted corridor. At the other end, turn sharp left through an enclosed room to

reach a row of storerooms on the right. The stairway on the right leads to the remains of a 20-columned **Hellenistic stoa** (200 BC). The Byzantine **Church of Agios Ioannis** is to the right of this stairway. The wide stairway behind the stoa leads to a 5th-century-BC propylaeum, beyond which is the 4th-century **Temple to Athena**, the site's most important ancient ruin. Athena was worshipped on Lindos as early as the 10th century BC, and this temple has replaced earlier ones on the site. From its far side there are splendid views of Lindos village and its beach.

Donkey rides to the Acropolis cost €5 one way – be aware that although it might not be strictly enforced here, places like the UK stipulate that anyone over 8 stone (112lbs/50.8kg) should not ride a donkey.

SLEEPING

Accommodation can be expensive, hard to find or already reserved, as much is prebooked. The first two places here are near each other on the north side of the village. Follow the donkeys heading to the Acropolis for about 150m to find them.

Lindos Pension (☎ 22440 31369; s/d €25/40) This is a good budget option. Rooms are small and plain, but clean and pleasant, and arranged around a courtyard.

Pension Electra (☎ 22440 31266; s/d €25/40; ☒) Electra has a roof terrace with superb views and a beautiful shady garden. Rooms all have fridges.

Filoxenia Guesthouse (☎ 22440 31266; www .lindos-filoxenia.com; d/ste incl breakfast €80/110; ☒) Consisting of five double rooms and three suites, these exceptionally tastefully decorated rooms make for a comfortable midrange choice.

EATING

Kalypso (☎ 22440 31669; mains €7-7.50) Set in one of Lindos' historic buildings, Kalypso is one of the better dining choices. Try either sausages in mustard, pork *stamnato* (in a pot) with oregano, wine and spices, or rabbit stew in red wine with pearl onions.

Mavrikos (☎ 22440 31232; mains €7-10) Lindos' longest established and most respected restaurant is right by the bus and taxi terminal. The extensive menu contains all the classic Greek dishes, but it is the quality that makes this place stand heads above other 'tourist' eating venues.

THE AUTHOR'S CHOICE

Lindian Village (Lindos; ☎ 22440 35900; fax 22440 47360; www.lindianvillage.gr; s €263, ste €650; ☒ ☐ ☒) An air of eclectic serenity permeates this relaxing and luxurious getaway just south of Lindos village. Comprising an established complex of well-appointed conventional hotel-style rooms, and a more recent 'village' of superior studios and apartments spread out over several acres, Lindian Village is the ultimate accommodation choice on Rhodes. The luxurious apartments each have private swimming pools and spa baths with secluded grass and patios, while the humbler upstairs studios simply boast spas and capacious verandas. Five restaurants pamper to a variety of tastes, while the fitness centre has every service and amenity ever invented, included a Turkish hammam. Two pools compete for bathers with the resort's own private beach. If you've got it, this is the place to spend it. Enjoy – you only live once!

WESTERN RHODES

Western Rhodes is greener and more forested than the east coast, but it's more exposed to winds so the sea tends to be rough, and the beaches are mostly of pebbles or stones. Nevertheless, tourist development is slowly making headway, especially in the suburb resorts of Ixia, Trianda and Kremasti. Paradisi, despite being next to the airport, has retained some of the feel of a traditional village.

Ancient Ialysos Αρχαία Ιαλυσός

Like Lindos, Ialysos, 10km from Rhodes, is a hotchpotch of Doric, Byzantine and medieval remains. The Doric city was built on Filerimos Hill, an excellent vantage point, and attracted successive invaders over the years. The only ancient remains are the foundations of a 3rd-century-BC temple and a restored 4th-century-BC fountain. Also at the site are the **Monastery of Our Lady** and the **Chapel of Agios Georgios**.

The ruined **fortress** (adult €4; ☉ 8am-5pm Tue-Sun) was used by Süleyman the Magnificent during his siege of Rhodes Town. No buses go to ancient Ialysos. The airport bus stops at Trianda, on the coast, and Ialysos is 5km inland from here.

Ancient Kamiros Αρχαία Κάμειρος

The extensive **ruins** (adult €4; ☉ 8am-5pm Tue-Sun) of the Doric city of Kamiros stand on a hillside above the west coast, 34km from Rhodes Town. The ancient city, known for its figs, oil and wine, reached the height of its powers in the 6th century BC. By the 4th century BC it had been superseded by Rhodes. Most of the city was destroyed by earthquakes in 226 and 142 BC, but the layout is still easily discernible.

From the entrance, walk straight ahead and down the steps. The semicircular rostrum on the right is where officials made speeches to the public. Opposite are the remains of a **Doric temple**, with one column still standing. The area next to it, with a row of intact columns, was probably where the public watched priests performing rites in the temple. Ascend the wide stairway to the ancient city's main street. Opposite the top of the stairs is one of the best preserved of the **Hellenistic houses** that once lined the street. Walk along the street, ascend three flights of steps and continue ahead to the ruins of the 3rd-century **great stoa**, which had a 206m portico supported by two rows of Doric columns. It was built on top of a huge 6th-century cistern that supplied the houses with rainwater through an advanced drainage system. Behind the stoa, at the city's highest point, stood the **Temple to Athena**, with terrific views inland.

Buses from Rhodes Town to Kamiros stop on the coast road, 1km from the site.

Ancient Kamiros to Monolithos
Αρχαία Κάμειρος προς Μονόλιθο

Skala Kamirou, 13.5km south of ancient Kamiros, is a fairly unremarkable place sporting a few market gardens, a scattering of tavernas and a petrol station. More importantly, it serves as the access port for travellers heading to and from the island of Halki (p292). The road south from here to Monolithos has some of the island's most impressive scenery. From Skala Kamirou, the road winds uphill with great views across to Halki. This is just a taste of what's to come at the ruined 16th-century **Castle of Kastellos**, reached by taking a rough turn-off from the main road, 2km beyond Skala Kamirou. There is a left fork to the wine-making area of Embonas (p292) 8km further on. The main road continues for another

9km to **Siana**, a picturesque village below Mt Akramytis (825m), famed for its honey and *souma* – a brew made from seasonal fruit, similar to Cretan *raki* (Greek fire water).

The village of Monolithos, 5km beyond Siana, has the spectacularly sited 15th-century **Castle of Monolithos** perched on a sheer 240m-high rock and reached via a dirt track. To enter, climb through the hole in the wall. Continuing along this track, bear right at the fork for **Moni Agiou Georgiou**, or left for the very pleasant shingled **Fourni Beach**.

Most people come this way en route to Halki via the afternoon caïque, or on a round-island tour. For lunch while waiting for the ferry you won't go far wrong at **O Loukas** (☎ 22460 31271; fish dishes €12-14), the closest taverna to the ferry jetty. The menu is limited but is good value. The daily lunch specials – including beer or wine – are €13.

SOUTHERN RHODES
South of Lindos, Rhodes becomes progressively less developed. Although **Pefki**, 2km south of Lindos, does attract package tourists, it's still possible to escape them, away from the main beach.

Lardos is a pleasant village 6km west of Lindos and 2km inland from Lardos Beach. From the far side of Lardos a right turn leads in 4km to **Moni Agias Ypsenis** (Monastery of Our Lady) through hilly, green countryside.

Heading south from Lardos, don't miss the almost hidden **Glystra Beach**, 4km south along the coast road. This diminutive bay is one of the best swimming spots along the whole eastern coastline.

The well-watered village of **Laerma** is 12km northwest of Lardos. From here it's another 5km to the beautifully sited 9th-century **Moni Tharri**, the island's first monastery, which has been re-established as a monastic community. It contains some fine 13th-century frescoes and is worth a visit.

Asklipieio, 8km north of Gennadi, is an unspoilt village with the ruins of yet another castle and the 11th-century **Church of Kimisis Theotokou**, which has fine Byzantine wall paintings.

Gennadi Γεννάδι
pop 655
Gennadi (ye-*nah*-dhi), 13km south of Lardos, is an attractive, largely untouched agricultural, seaside village masquerading as a

holiday centre. For independent travellers it is probably the best base for a protracted stay in the south. The village itself, a patchwork of narrow streets and whitewashed houses, is set several hundred metres back from the beach.

There's a few sleeping and eating choices. **Effie's Dreams Apartments** (☎ 2244 043 410; www .effiesdreams.com; d/tr €40/50; 🐱 🖳) offers both. It is right by an enormous 800-year-old mulberry tree and has modern, spotlessly clean studios with lovely rural and sea vistas from the communal balcony. The friendly Greek-Australian owners will meet you if you call ahead. Below the apartments, **Effie's Dream Cafe Bar** (☎ 22440 43410; snacks €2.50-4) serves drinks and tasty snacks such as country-style sausage with onions and peppers.

I Kouzina tis Mamas (☎ 22440 43547; pasta €4-5) in the main street specialises in pizza and pasta, as well as a wide range of Greek grills.

Gennadi to Prasonisi

Γεννάδι προς Πρασονήσι

From Gennadi an almost uninterrupted beach of pebbles, shingle and sand dunes extends down to **Plimmyri**, 11km south. It's easy to find deserted stretches.

From Plimmyri the main road continues to **Kattavia**, Rhodes' most southerly village. The 11km dirt road north to Messanagros winds through terrific scenery. From Kattavia a 10km road leads south to remote **Cape Prasonisi**, the island's southernmost point, once joined to Rhodes by a narrow sandy isthmus but now split by encroaching seas. It's a popular spot for windsurfing.

A good place to sleep is at **Lahania**, signposted 2km off the main highway, in **Studios Alonia** (☎ 22440 46027; studios €32), where each fan-cooled studio has a kitchenette and fridge. These are owned by the proprietors of **Taverna Platanos** (☎ 22440 46027; mains €3-5), a relaxed little taverna that makes for a popular Sunday outing. You dine on the tiny village square, amid running water, in the company of ducks.

Down on Prasonisi, **Faros Taverna** (☎ 22440 91030; mains €4-7) is one of two tavernas on the beach. The food is uncomplicated and features grills and fish, while the comfortable rooms (doubles €32) attract a mainly windsurfing crowd.

South of Monolithos

Rhodes' southwest coast doesn't see as many visitors as other parts of the island. It is lonely and exposed. Forest fires in recent years have devastated many of the west-facing hillsides and there is a general end-of-the-world feeling about the whole region.

The beaches south of Monolithos are prone to strong winds. From the important crossroads village of **Apolakkia**, 10km south of Monolithos, a road crosses the island to Gennadi, passing through the unspoilt villages of **Arnitha** and **Vati** with an optional detour to **Istrios** and **Profilia** where you can dine in rustic comfort at **To Limeri tou Listi** (☎ 22440 61578; mains €6-8) on dishes such as rooster in red-wine sauce or other solid country fare.

A turn-off to the left, 7km south of Apolakkia, leads to the 18th-century **Moni Skiadi**. It's a serene place with terrific views down to the coast, and there is free basic accommodation for visitors.

THE INTERIOR

The east–west roads that cross the island have great scenery and very little traffic. If you have transport they're well worth exploring. It's also good cycling territory if you have a suitably geared bicycle.

Petaloudes Πεταλούδες

Known as the Valley of the Butterflies, **Petaloudes** (adult €1-3; ⏱ 8.30am-sunset 1 May-30 Sep) is one of the more popular 'sights' on the package-tour itinerary. It is reached along a 6km turn-off from the west coast road, 2.5km south of Paradisi.

The so-called 'butterflies' are in fact strikingly coloured moths (Callimorpha quadripunctarea) that are lured to this gorge of rustic footbridges, streams and pools by the scent of the resin exuded by the styrax trees. Regardless of what you may see other people doing, do not make any noises to disturb the butterflies; their numbers are declining rapidly, largely due to noise disturbance. Better still, don't visit; leave them alone. If you must, there are buses to Petaloudes from Rhodes Town.

Around Petaloudes

From Petaloudes a winding cross-island road leads to the 18th-century **Moni Kalopetras**, built by Alexander Ypsilandis, the

DODECANESE

grandfather of the Greek freedom fighter. This same road leads north across the central mountain spine of roads through a rather dry landscape full of olive trees to the pretty village of **Psinthos**, which makes for a very pleasant lunch break.

From Psinthos you can choose to loop back to Rhodes Town (22km), via a fast but undistinguished direct route passing through **Kalythies**, or head further south and pick up the very pretty cross-island route from **Kolymbia** to **Salakos**.

In Psinthos you'll find the well-regarded **Pigi Fasouli Estiatorio** (☎ 22410 50071; mains €5-7), where you dine under cool plane trees next to running water – all to the sound of incessant cicadas. Good dishes on offer are goat and chickpeas, pork and lima beans and *pitaroudia* (small pies). Look for signs from the main square in Psinthos to find it.

Wine Country

From Salakos you may detour to **Embonas** on the slopes of Mt Attavyros (1215m), the island's highest mountain. Embonas is the wine capital of Rhodes and produces some of the island's best tipples. The red Cava Emery, or Zacosta and white Villare are good choices. You can taste and buy them at **Emery Winery** (☎ 22410 41208; www.emery.gr; admission free; ◷ 9.30am-3.30pm) in Embonas.

Embonas is no great shakes itself, despite being touted by the tourism authorities as a 'traditional village'. However, **Bakis** (☎ 22460 41247; mains €4-6.50) on the main square is a good spot to try some home-produced grills. The *païdakia* (spare-rib chops), or the *kondosouvli* (Cypriot-style spit-roast kebabs) are particularly succulent.

You may nonetheless wish to detour around Mt Attavyros to **Agios Isidoros**, 14km south of Embonas, a prettier and still unspoilt wine-producing village that you can visit en route to Siana.

HALKI ΧΑΛΚΗ

pop 313

Halki is an unquestionably pretty little island just 10km off the west coast of Rhodes. Nonetheless, it's an island with a difficult past and a curious present. Once home to a buoyant sponge-fishing economy, a fishing fleet and a large supporting population,

the island was all but abandoned when the sponge industry took a nose dive and the depredations of two wars forced many Halkiots to emigrate to the USA (particularly Florida). Now it's enjoying a quiet, though somewhat sanitised, revival. A steady flow of villa-rental holidaymakers are trickling in, looking for that ideal island in the sun, but without the tackiness and excess that sometimes mars its larger neighbour Rhodes. Halki is ideal for a quiet holiday, for book lovers, writers, poets, the spiritually inclined and incurable romantics.

Getting There & Away

CAÏQUE & BUS

Halki has a daily link at 6am to Skala Kamirou (€12, 1½ hours) on Rhodes. A bus to Rhodes Town connects at Skala Kamirou, except on Sunday, and it can be somewhat delayed on Saturday.

FERRY

LANE Lines serves Halki three times weekly in either direction, with services to Rhodes (€6.80, two hours), Pigadia on Karpathos (€9.50, three hours), Sitia on Crete (€17, 7½ hours) and Piraeus (€33, 22 hours). There is an occasional summer link to Santorini (€20, 15 hours). Ticket are available from Chalki Tours and Zifos Travel in Emborios (see opposite).

Getting Around

There are no buses and just one overpriced **taxi** (☎ 69444 34429; Emborios), that charges €4 to Pondamos Beach from Emborios, €6.50 to Ftenagia Beach and €33 return to the Monastery of Agiou Ioanni. There are no rental cars or motorcycles, but there are water taxis to the main beaches and excursions to the island of Alimnia (€30). Additionally, day excursions are run on Sundays in summer to Tilos (€20) by the two Skala Kamirou caïques.

EMBORIOS ΕΜΠΟΡΕΙΟΣ

pop 52

The picturesque port village of Emborios resembles Gialos on Symi, but on a smaller scale. The port is draped around a horseshoe bay, and surrounded by former sea captains' mansions – some renovated, others still in a state of disrepair – which rise up in a colourful architectural display.

Cars are all but banned from the harbour, so the Emborios waterside enjoys a tranquil, motor-free setting.

Orientation & Information

Boats arrive at the middle of the small village harbour. All commercial services and most accommodation options are within 200m of the disembarkation point. There is no official tourist office on Halki but the free quarterly English-and-Greek newspaper, *The Halki Visitor*, available on the island, is a good source of information.

There's an ATM on the harbour front.

Chalki Tours (☎ 22460 45281; fax 22460 45219) For assistance on accommodation, travel, excursions and money exchange.

Diafora (☎ 22460 45061; per 30 min €10) Internet access; at the Pondamos Beach and Kania crossroads.

Doctor (☎ 22460 45206; ☒ 9am-noon & 6-8pm Mon-Fri) Can be contacted on call.

Post office (☒ 9am-1.30pm Mon-Fri) On the harbour.

www.chalki.gr A useful reference point.

www.halkivisitor.com Another useful site.

Zifos Travel (☎ 22460 45028; zifos-travel@rho.forthnet .gr) For assistance on accommodation, travel, excursions and money exchange.

Sights

Halki's main visual feature are the old **captains' mansions** that festoon the harbour. Many have been, or are being, restored to their former glory, others are in a complete state of disrepair. Either way they give Halki that picturesque look that visitors so appreciate.

The impressive stone **clock tower** at the southern side of the harbour is a gift from the Halkiots of Florida. While the clock tower may look good, don't rely on it for the time; each of the four faces is stuck on a different hour of the day.

The **Church of Agios Nikolaos** has the tallest belfry in the Dodecanese and boasts a particularly well-made and impressive *hohlaki* (pebbled) courtyard on the east side. There is a small upstairs **museum** (adult €2; ☒ 6-7pm Mon & Fri, 11am-noon Sun) with ecclesiastical exhibits.

Sleeping

Most villa and studio accommodation is block-booked by foreign tour companies. What little private accommodation there is can be in high demand, so bookings are essential. There is no hotel as yet on the island though the old sponge factory on the harbour is slowly being renovated into a hotel.

Captain's House (☎ /fax 22460 45201; captains house@ath.forthnet.gr; d €40) This beautiful 19th-century mansion, with period furniture and a tranquil tree-shaded garden, is the most pleasant place to stay. It is owned by a retired Greek sea captain, Alex, and his British wife Christine. Bookings are absolutely essential.

Mouthouria (☎ 22460 45071; francesm@otenet.gr; house €75) Rent a whole renovated captain's house that can accommodate up to six people. It's spacious, fully equipped, has superb south side harbour views and is ideal for longer stays. The access stairs may be a bit steep if you are hauling heavy luggage.

Villa Praxithea (☎ 69724 27272; fax 22410 70175; www.villapraxithea.com; apt €140-210) If you fancy the idea of fishing from your balcony, check out these two fully-furnished and privately rented apartments. They accommodate from between six and eight people and, fishing aside, they are right on the water's edge, handy for swimming off a private landing.

Eating

Mavri Thalassa (☎ 22460 45021; mains €4-6) This restaurant at the end of the harbour is well regarded by locals and does particularly good fish dishes. The whole grilled calamari, when available fresh, is delicate and soft, and the local, minuscule Halki shrimps just melt in your mouth.

Maria's Taverna (☎ 22460 45300; mains €4-7) Offers good and reliable home-cooked fare, with Halki lamb stew being the house speciality. It also enjoys a good location under the trees, although this can cause a slight problem with falling leaves when the wind is blowing.

Avra (☎ 6945148196; mains €4-7) Avra is a Georgian-run taverna with fast, efficient service and an inventive and tempting menu. There are excellent chicken dishes and Halki shrimps are again a good bet. Bookings are recommended. Just drop by earlier and let the owner know you are coming later.

AROUND HALKI

Podamos Beach is the closest and the best beach. It is 1km from Emborios in the direction of Horio. The narrowish beach is sandy and the water is rather shallow – not the best for snorkelling. For food you can try the somewhat pricey **Podamos Beach Taverna** (☎ 22460 45295; mains €5-7; ☼ lunch). **Ftenagia Beach**, past the headland and 500m to the south of Emborios, doesn't have much sand, but there is excellent rock swimming and the snorkelling is far better. The **Ftenagia Beach Taverna** (☎ 69459 98333; mains €5-7; ☼ lunch & dinner) is a cosy waterside eatery with friendly service and top-class dishes on offer.

Horio, a 30-minute walk along Tarpon Springs Blvd from Emborios, was once a thriving community of 3000 people, but it's now derelict, bar a small church and a few renovated structures, and is essentially uninhabited. A path leads from Horio's churchyard to a **Knights of St John castle**, with spectacular views.

Moni Agiou Ioanni is a two-hour, unshaded 8km walk, along a broad concrete road from Horio. The church and courtyard, protected by the shade of an enormous cypress tree, is a quiet, tranquil place, but it comes alive each year on 28–29 August during the feast of the church's patron, St John.

KARPATHOS ΚΑΡΠΑΘΟΣ

pop 6084

If ever there was a Greek island that combined the right mix of size, attractiveness, remoteness, water activities and general good feel, it might just be the elongated island of Karpathos (*kar*-pah-thos), midway between Crete and Rhodes. Karpathos has rugged mountains, numerous beaches – among the best in the Aegean – and unspoilt villages. So far, it has not succumbed to the worst excesses of mass tourism.

The island is traversed by a north–south mountain range. For hundreds of years the north and south parts of the island were isolated from one another and so they developed independently. It is even thought that the northerners and southerners have different ethnic origins. The northern village of Olymbos is of fascination to ethnologists for the age-old customs of its inhabitants.

Karpathos has a relatively uneventful history. Unlike almost all other Dodecanese islands, it was never under the auspices of the Knights of St John. It is a wealthy island, receiving more money from emigrants living abroad (mostly in the USA) than any other Greek island.

Getting There & Away
AIR
In summer there are 10 flights weekly to and from Athens (€68 to €79), up to three daily to Rhodes (€28, 25 minutes) and seven weekly to Kasos (€22, 10 minutes). **Olympic Airlines** (☎ 22450 22150; www.olympicairlines.com) is on the central square in Pigadia. The airport is 13km southwest of Pigadia.

FERRY
LANE Lines of Crete provides three services weekly to Rhodes (€18.50, four hours) via Halki (€11.50, three hours), as well as to Piraeus (€33, 18½ hours) via Milos (€36, 13 hours). Kasos (€7.50, 1½ hours) is also served by the same three-weekly services; all services stop at both Diafani and Pigadia.

Note that these ferries also serve the ports of Sitia (€18, 4¼ hours) and Agios Nikolaos (€20, seven hours) in Crete. Tickets can be bought from **Possi Travel** (☎ 22450 22235; possitvl@hotmail.com; Apodimon Karpathion) in Pigadia.

Getting Around
TO/FROM THE AIRPORT
There is no airport bus. Travellers must take a taxi (€12) or seek independent transport.

BUS
Pigadia is the transport hub of the island; a schedule is posted at the **bus terminus** (☎ 22450 22338; 28 Oktovriou). Buses serve most

KARPATHOS

0 ——— 6 km
0 ——— 4 miles

of the settlements in southern Karpathos, including the west coast beaches; fares are between €1.50 and €2. There is no bus between Pigadia and Olymbos or Diafani in the north, but a bus meets the excursion boats from Pigadia at Diafani and transports people to Olymbos.

CAR, MOTORCYCLE & BICYCLE

Drive Rent-a-Car (☎ 22450 23873; drivekarpathos@yahoo.gr; M Mattheou), on the east side of Pigadia, rents cars and motorcycles. **Possi Travel** (☎ 22450 22148; possitvl@hotmail.com; Apodimon Karpathion) also arranges car and motorcycle hire.

The precipitous, and at times hairy, 19.5km stretch of road from Spoa to Olymbos is unsurfaced, but you can drive it, with care; do not tackle this road by motorcycle or scooter. If you rent a vehicle and plan to drive to Olymbos, make it a small jeep and fill up your tank before you leave.

EXCURSION BOAT

In summer there is a daily excursion boat from Pigadia to Diafani (return including the bus to Olymbos €20, one-way not including the bus to Olymbos €8). There are also frequent boats to the beaches of Kyra Panagia and Apella (€10). Tickets can be bought at the quay.

From Diafani, excursion boats go to nearby beaches and occasionally to the uninhabited islet of Saria, where there are some Byzantine remains

TAXI

Pigadia's **taxi rank** (☎ 22450 22705; Dimokratias) is near the bus station. A price list is displayed. Sample one-way taxi fares from Pigadia are as follows: Ammoöpi (€6), Arkasa (€15), Pyles (€14), Kyra Panagia (€17), airport (€12).

PIGADIA ΠΗΓΑΔΙΑ
pop 1692

After being spoilt with the picturesque harbours of Symi, Chalki and Kastellorizo, Pigadia (pi-*gha*-dhi-ya), Karpathos' capital and main port, does not immediately grab your attention. It's a modern town and is attractive enough in its own way, but without any eminent buildings or sites. Much of the cement-based architecture was erected during a boom in the 1960s and '70s. Upon

DODECANESE

further investigation, however, Pigadia is a pleasant and busy town. It is built on the edge of **Vrondi Bay**, a 4km-long sandy beach where you can rent water-sports equipment. A 2km walk southwest along the beach are the remains of the early Christian **Basilica of Agia Fotini**.

Orientation & Information

The ferry quay is at the northern end of the wide harbour. It's a short walk to the centre of Pigadia, which is punctuated by the main street, Apodimon Karpathion. This in turn leads west to the central square of Plateia 5 Oktovriou.

Caffe Galileo Internet 2000 (☎ 22450 23606; Apodimon Karpathion; per hr €4; ☼ 9am-2pm & 6pm-1am) Offers Internet access.

National Bank of Greece (Apodimon Karpathion) Has an ATM.

Police (☎ 22450 22224) Near the hospital at the western end of town.

Possi Travel (☎ 22450 22148; possitvl@hotmail.com; Apodimon Karpathion) The main travel agency for ferry and air tickets.

Post office (Ethnikis Andistasis) Also near the hospital.

Pot Pourri (☎ 22450 29073; Apodimon Karpathion; per hr €3; ☼ 7am-1am) Also offers Internet access.

Tourist Information Office (☎ 22450 23835; ☼ Jul-Aug) In a kiosk in the middle of the seafront.

www.inkarpathos.com Mainly local information – mixed Greek and English.

www.karpathos.com General travel and island information in English.

Sleeping

There's plenty of accommodation in Pigadia; a few enterprising owners meet the boats.

Elias Rooms (☎ 22450 22446; www.eliasrooms .com; s/d r €20/25, s/d apts €25/35; ☐) Cozy Elias Rooms is located in a quiet part of town with great views and a lot of convenience. Owner Ilias Hatzigeorgiou is a mine of local information.

Avra Hotel (☎ 22450 22388; fax 22450 23486; 28 Oktovriou 50; s/d €20/25) This E-class hotel has small but comfortable rooms with ceiling fan, fridge and a small common kitchen.

Hotel Karpathos (☎ 22450 22347; fax 22450 22248; s/d €30/35; ☼) This C-class hotel has well-lit, airy rooms with TV and fridge, though the hotel itself looks a shade old and jaded.

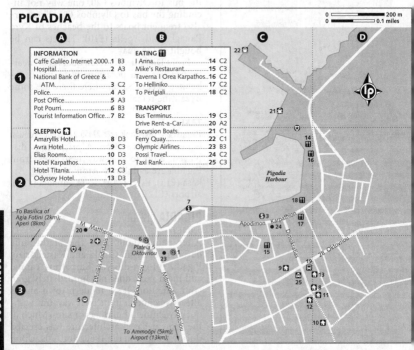

PIGADIA

0 ———— 200 m
0 ———— 0.1 miles

INFORMATION	
Caffe Galileo Internet 2000..1	B3
Hospital.............................2	A3
National Bank of Greece & ATM................................3	C2
Police................................4	A3
Post Office.........................5	A3
Pot Pourri..........................6	B3
Tourist Information Office...7	B2

SLEEPING	
Amaryllis Hotel....................8	D3
Avra Hotel..........................9	C3
Elias Rooms.......................10	D3
Hotel Karpathos.................11	D3
Hotel Titania.....................12	C3
Odyssey Hotel....................13	D3

EATING	
I Anna.............................14	C2
Mike's Restaurant.............15	C3
Taverna I Orea Karpathos..16	C2
To Helliniko.....................17	C2
To Perigiali......................18	C2

TRANSPORT	
Bus Terminus....................19	C3
Drive Rent-a-Car...............20	A2
Excursion Boats.................21	C1
Ferry Quay.......................22	C1
Olympic Airlines................23	B3
Possi Travel......................24	C2
Taxi Rank........................25	C3

Pigadia Harbour

To Basilica of Agia Fotini (2km); Aperi (8km);

Matthaiou

Plateia 5 Oktovriou

Apodimon Karpathion

To Αμμοόπι (5km); Airport (13km);

DODECANESE

Hotel Titania (☎ 22450 22144; www.titania karpathos.gr; s/d €35/50; ❄) This C-class hotel, opposite Hotel Karpathos, has spacious, pleasant rooms equipped with fridge, phone and TV, and is open all year.

Amarylis Hotel (☎ /fax 22450 22375; www.amarylis .gr; s/d €35/50; ❄) In a quiet part of Pigadia is this C-class hotel, offering a mixture of airy and exceptionally clean studios and apartments. All have kitchenettes and TVs, and at least half of them enjoy sea views.

Odyssey Hotel (☎ 22450 23762; www.odyssey -karpathos.gr; studios €50/65 ❄) Helen Stamatiadis, one of the friendliest and most charming hosts in town, runs this small complex of fully equipped studios, catering for between four to six people. Great for a longer stay or a discreet getaway.

Eating

There are a lot of places to choose from in Pigadia. Some are a bit too touristy, with their easy-to-pick picture menus, others are just that little more genuine. Among these are the following (make sure you try *makarounes* – pasta cooked with cheese and fried onions):

Mike's Restaurant (☎ 22450 22727; grills €5-8) One of the longer-standing and more popular eateries, Mike's serves up consistently good, solid fare at reasonable prices. Among the specials are chicken spaghetti and stuffed zucchini flowers.

Taverna I Orea Karpathos (☎ 22450 22501; mains €4-6) Near the quay, I Orea Karpathos serves a wide range of consistently well-prepared traditional Karpathian dishes, and reputedly the best *makarounes* in Pigadia.

To Helliniko (☎ 22450 23932; Apodimon Karpathion; daily specials €5-11) Boasting a pleasant outdoor terrace and a tasteful interior, the Helliniko is locally popular and open all year. Check the daily specials board for the best deal. The Karpathian goat *stifado* (cooked in a tomato purée) is particularly commendable.

I Anna (☎ 22450 22820; Apodimon Karpathion; fish per kg €35) Ignore the fading picture menus and tacky restaurant sign. Here you will be rewarded with Pigadia's freshest fish, caught daily off the owner's own boats. Other suggested dishes are fisherman's macaroni with octopus, shrimps and mussels, or the Karpathian sardines in oil.

To Perigiali (☎ 22450 22334; Apodimon Karpathion; mains €3-8) Lurking unobtrusively among its more boisterous neighbours, this little *ouzeri* (place which serves light snacks and ouzo)-taverna is also a cut above the rest. Fish *mezedes* feature predominantly, though you might try the rich Karpathian salad with capers, or steamed snails.

SOUTHERN KARPATHOS

Ammoöpi Αμμοοπή

If you are seeking sun and sand, and some of the best and clearest water for snorkelling in the whole of the Aegean, head for Ammoöpi (amm-oh-oh-*pee*), 5km south of Pigadia. Ammoöpi is a scattered beach resort without any real centre or easily identifiable landmarks.

In addition to snorkelling, die-hard windsurfers in the know head for the broad **Afiartis Bay**, a further 8km south of Ammoöpi, to enjoy some world-class conditions. The bay supports windsurfing centres and caters for advanced surfers at the northern end and beginners in the sheltered Makrygialos Bay lagoon at the southern end. While most surfers come on package tours from Germany, casual 'blow-ins' are more than welcome. One particularly good outfit is **Pro Center** (☎ 22450 91062; www.windsurfen -karpathos.com; Afiarti).

SLEEPING & EATING

All sleeping and eating recommendations are at the northern (more accessible) end of Ammoöpi. There is a pretty wide choice of accommodation and dining options, though much gets prebooked by tour operators. The places to eat are rather scattered.

Hotel Sophia (☎ /fax 22450 81078; www.sophia hotel.gr; d/tr €40/47; ❄) For starter, this is a quiet and comfortable midrange hotel at the northern end of the settlement.

Blue Sea Hotel (☎ /fax 22450 81036; huguette@rho .forthnet.gr; d €45) Just in front of Hotel Sophia, this has 27 comfortable double rooms, each with fridge and ceiling fan.

Vardes (☎ 22450 81111; www.hotelvardes.com; studios €56; ❄) For a really laid-back and relaxing choice try Vardes, a small block of tasteful, spacious and airy studios, set back against the hillside among a lush olive grove and a few banana palms. All have large, breezy rooms, shaded balcony, phone and TV.

Taverna Ilios (☎ 22450 81148; mains €5-7) Just back from the main beach, offers Greek and international cuisine with large portions.

Ammoöpi Taverna (☎ 22450 81138; mains €4-7) At the far northern end, and right on the beach; the food here is uniformly good – look for the daily specials (the clove-laced *mousaka*, sliced eggplant and mincemeat arranged in layers and baked, excels). There is a fairly genuine 'Greek music night' every Friday.

Menetes Μενετές
pop 450
Menetes (me-ne-*tes*) is perched precariously on top of a sheer cliff overlooking the rolling landscape leading to Pigadia, 8km distant. It's a picturesque, unspoilt village with pastel-coloured neoclassical houses lining its main street. Behind the main street are narrow, stepped alleyways that wind between more modest whitewashed dwellings. The village has a small but well-presented **museum** (admission free) on the right as you come in from Pigadia. Opening hours are upon request – the owner of Taverna Manolis will open it up for you.

There is only one place to stay and that's on the north side of Menetes; **Mike Rigas Domatia** (☎ 22450 81269; d/tr €18/22) is signposted on the outside as Rigas Kato Nero. These eight rooms bask in a traditional flower-bedecked Karpathian house, caressed by a fruit and vegetable-filled garden and accompanied by a menagerie of languid dogs and cats.

Stop by **Taverna Manolis** (☎ 22450 81103; mains €5-7) for generous helpings of grilled meat, or take a break at **Dionysos Fiesta** (☎ 22450 81269; mains €4-6), specialising in local dishes, including omelette made with artichokes and Karpathian sausages.

Top culinary marks though, go to **Pelagia Taverna** (☎ 22450 81135; mains €4-6), on the road down to (or up from) Ammoöpi, where free-range goat and lamb are on offer. Opt for the rich Karpathian salad, the local manouri cheese and excellent *fava* (chickpeas).

Arkasa & Finiki Αρκάσα & Φοινίκι
Arkasa (ar-*ka*-sa), 9km further on, and on the west coast, straddles a ravine. It is changing from a traditional village into a low-key resort. Turn right at the T-intersection to reach the village square.

A turn-off left, just before the ravine, leads 500m to the remains of the 5th-century **Basilica of Agia Sophia**, where two chapels stand amid mosaic fragments and

columns. **Agios Nikolaos Beach** is just south across the headland from here.

The serene fishing village of Finiki (fi-ni-ki) lies 2km north of Arkasa. The best swimming is at **Agios Georgios Beach** between Arkasa and Finiki.

One of the more attractive places to sleep is **Glaros Studios** (☎ 22450 61015, fax 22450 61016; Agios Nikolaos; studios €52-55), right on Agios Nikolaos Beach. Done out in Karpathiot style, these studios have raised sofa-like beds and large terraces with sun beds; they enjoy a cool sea breeze. There's a relaxed restaurant adjoining, which rustles up good *mayirefta* and grills.

Further along, to the left of the road to Finiki, **Eleni Studios** (☎ /fax 22450 61248; Arkasa; apt €50; 🐾) has fully-equipped and very neat apartments. For sea swimming though you're better of looking further afield.

Possibly the most relaxing place to eat is **Under The Trees** (☎ 69779 84791; Agios Georgios; mains €5-7.50). Abutting the only really decent bathing beach in the neighbourhood this simple seaside taverna puts effort into producing good quality, uncomplicated dishes based on a limited but reliable menu selection.

Some 9km north of Finiki, just before the road winds uphill to Lefkos, are the secluded **Pine Tree Studios** (☎ 69773 69948; Adia; d €35). These comfortable studios with views over to Kasos make for a quiet rural retreat and include an excellent restaurant. They also come equipped with fridge and kitchenette.

Lefkos Λευκός
pop 120
Lefkos (lef-*kos*), 13km north of Finiki and 2km from the coast road, is a burgeoning resort centred around a series of attractive, sandy coves. In summer Lefkos can get crowded, but at other times it still has a rugged, off-the-beaten-track feel about it.

Local boat owners sometimes take visitors to the islet of **Sokastro** where there is a ruined castle. Another diversion from the beaches is the remains of a **Roman cistern**, reached by walking inland and looking for the brown-and-yellow signpost to the catacombs.

Accommodation can often be block-booked but try calling the following places before you arrive. The three separate blocks of **Aegean View Studios** (☎ /fax 22450 71462; studios €45), run by a Greek-Australian, are a good bet. All are very close to the beach, airy and

have modern kitchenettes. High up are **Sunset Studios** (☎ 22450 71171; fax 22450 71407; www
.sunset-hotel.gr; studios €38-45), where the rooms
all have sea views and are immaculate.

For eating, head to the little harbour
where, of the handful of tavernas, **Dramundana**
(☎ 22450 71167; mains €5-7), is an unfussy, homely
place with a look-and-pick approach to dish
selection. They have good fish cakes and
fragrant chicken. Out on the approach road,
Small Paradise Taverna (☎ 22450 71184; mayirefta €3-
7) offers diners a vine-shaded terrace and a
range of uncomplicated, but home-cooked
mayirefta; goat in red wine sauce is one of
the owner's recommendations.

GETTING THERE & AROUND

There are two buses weekly to Lefkos and a
taxi from Pigadia costs €22. Hitching can be
slow as there is not much traffic.

Lefkos Rent A Car (☎ /fax 22450 71057) is a reliable outlet with competitive prices. The
owner will deliver vehicles, free of charge,
to anywhere in southern Karpathos.

NORTHERN KARPATHOS

Diafani Διαφάνι
pop 250

Diafani is Karpathos' small northern port,
where scheduled ferries stop six times
weekly and an excursion boat arrives daily
from Pigadia. It's a pretty low-key destination and is the only port of entry for travellers planning to visit Olymbos.

There's no post office, but there is a freestanding Commercial Bank ATM. There is
the usual scattering of cardphones and mobile phone networks are all fully covered.

Balaskas Hotel (☎ /fax ☎ 22450 51320; www
.balaskashotel.gr; d €30; ✖) is a pleasant hotel-
style option where all rooms have a fridge,
TV and phone. For a touch more comfort
Studios Niotis (☎ 22450 51529; studios €35-45, apt €50;
✖) are a very sensible choice. Strung along
a hillside on the south side of the port, there
is a choice of standard rooms, studios or a
couple of Karpathian-style apartments.

There are a number of places to dine along
the waterfront. **Chrysi Akti Taverna** (☎ 22450
51215; mains €4-6) is an ever-popular place
with stock fish and *mayirefta* dishes, and
where the service comes with a smile, while
I Gorgona (☎ 22450 51509; mains €3-6) is a casual,
Italian-style joint with good coffee, snacks
and pasta.

Olymbos Ολυμπος
pop 330

Clinging to the ridge of barren Mt Profitis
Ilias (716m), and 4km from Diafani, Olymbos is a living museum where, to this day,
the inhabitants speak in a vernacular that
contains some Doric words. Women wear
bright, embroidered skirts, waistcoats,
headscarves and goatskin boots, and still
bake their bread in outdoor communal
ovens. The interiors of the houses are
decorated with embroidered cloth, their
façades feature brightly painted, ornate
plaster reliefs and some of them retain
the wooden locks of a kind described by
Homer.

Olymbos, alas, is no longer a pristine
backwater caught in a time warp. Tourism
has taken hold in a big way and is now
a major money spinner. The 'traditional'
village is finding it ever harder to remain
genuine and is in danger of becoming a
kind of kitsch eco-Disney for day-trippers
from Pigadia. Olymbos is still fascinating,
but sadly rather overrated for what it ultimately has to offer.

There are a few unpretentious places to
stay. **Mike's Rooms** (☎ 22450 51304; d €25) are the
first you will come across, just beyond the
bus stop before you enter the village proper.
There's a restaurant downstairs. Within
the village, **Hotel Aphrodite** (☎ 22450 51307; fili
ppasfiliipakkis@yahoo.gr; d €35) is very close to the
central square, and has simply furnished,
airy rooms and impressive west-facing sea
views.

Makarounes (home-made pasta served
with fresh onions and melted local cheese)
are served up in Olymbos in most restaurants. The best place to eat would have to
be the delightfully sited **Taverna O Mylos**
(☎ 22450 51333; mains €3-7) on the north side
of the village. Built around a restored and
working windmill, the truly excellent food
is cooked in a wood oven and features organic meat and vegetable produce, including goat in red-wine sauce, artichokes and
filling *pites*.

At the south side of the village, on the
main street, **Olymbos Taverna** (☎ 22450 51252;
mains €3-4) is a good place for *makarounes*,
and there's a daily changing menu of *mayirefta* which includes artichokes in oil, or
mizithropitta (a pie made from a sweet cottage cheese).

KASOS ΚΑΣΟΣ

pop 980

You can't get much further away from mainland civilisation than Kasos – a craggy speck of land 11km south of Karpathos. This is really the end of the island line. It's the last Dodecanese island before Crete and, looking directly south, it is the last Greek island before Egypt. It is neither particularly easy to get to, nor to get away from, especially if the weather is inclement. Kasos is a rocky little island with prickly pears, sparse olive and fig trees, dry-stone walls, sheep and goats. Come here if you want to see how Greece once was; it's unpretentious, unassuming, undemanding and remote. Mist and clouds can blanket its craggy peaks yet there is a vibrancy to the island's social life and the Kasiots who, despite the odds, have clung on tenaciously to one of the last outposts of Aegean island culture.

History

Despite being diminutive and remote, Kasos has an eventful history. During Turkish rule the island flourished, and by 1820 it had 11,000 inhabitants and a large mercantile fleet. Mohammad Ali, the Turkish governor of Egypt, regarded this fleet as an impediment to his plan to establish a base on Crete from which to attack the Peloponnese and quell the uprising. On 7 June 1824, Ali's men landed on Kasos and killed around 7000 inhabitants. This massacre is commemorated annually on the anniversary of the slaughter, and Kasiots return from around the world to participate. During the late 19th century, many Kasiots emigrated to Egypt and around 5000 of them helped build the Suez Canal. Last century many emigrated to the USA.

Getting There & Away

AIR

There are up to eight flights weekly to Rhodes (€34, 1¼ hours) and Karpathos (€22, 10 minutes). **Olympic Airlines** (☎ 22450 41555; www.olympicairlines.com; Kritis) is in Fry. The airport is 800m west along the coast road from Fry (not 8km as signposted from near Bouka harbour).

EXCURSION BOAT

On Monday, Wednesday and Friday in summer, the **Athina excursion boat** (☎ 22450 41047) travels from Fry to the uninhabited Armathia Islet (return €8), where there are sandy beaches.

FERRY

LANE Lines of Crete includes Kasos on its long run to/from Rhodes and Piraeus via Karpathos, Crete and Milos. Sample fares: Piraeus (€31, 17 hours), Rhodes (€20, 6½ hours) and Sitia (€10, 2½ hours). There are usually four departures weekly in each direction.

Getting Around

The local bus serves all the villages of the island with a dozen or so scheduled runs; tickets are all €0.50. There are two **taxis** (☎ 22450 41158, 22450 41278) on the island, but they can be hard to find. Scooters can be rented from **Frangiskos Moto Rentals** (☎ 22450 41746) for €15 per day.

FRY ΦΡΥ

pop 270

Fry (pronounced *free*) is the island's capital and port. A pleasant, ramshackle kind of place, with little tourism, it can be thoroughly explored in under an hour. Its narrow whitewashed streets are usually busy with locals in animated discussion. The town's focal point is the very picturesque old fishing harbour of Bouka. The suburb of Emborio is located 1km east of Fry.

Orientation & Information

Fry's large harbour complex abuts the settlement 500m from its main square, Plateia Iroön Kasou. Turn left from the harbour to get to Emborio. Fry's main street is Kritis. Kasos does not have an EOT or tourist police.

The Commercial Bank's stand-alone ATM is on the south side of Fry, next to the port entrance. The post office is near this ATM. There's a Co-Operative Bank of the Dodecanese branch, with ATM, in Fry. **ACS Internet** (☎ 22450 42751; zwankie@otenet.gr; €4 per hr; ☷ 10am-2pm & 5pm-12am) Offers Internet access.

Kasos Maritime & Travel Agency (☎ 22450 41495; www.kassos-island.gr; Plateia Iroön Kasou) Emmanuel Manousos here is very helpful and will also exchange money.

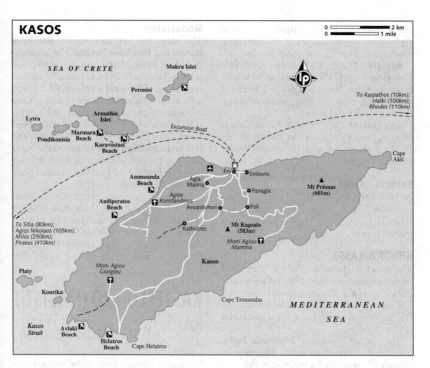

Kassian Travel (☎ 22450 42716; fax 22450 41801; hpetros@otenet.gr) Issues air and sea tickets. The office is just beyond the police station.

Police (☎ 22450 41222) Just beyond the post office.

Port police (☎ 22450 41288) Behind the Church of Agios Spyridon.

Sleeping

There is very little accommodation in Kasos but, with the exception of the days on either side of 7 June (Holocaust Memorial Day) – a room can normally be found quite easily. It is, however, recommended you book ahead in the high season.

Captain's House (☎ 22450 42716; fax 22450 41801; hpetros@otenet.gr; Fry; s/d €25/40) Comprising five airy and traditionally decorated apartments, this option is possibly the best accommodation choice on the island. Run by Kassian Travel.

Anagennisis Hotel (☎ 22450 41495; www.kassos -island.gr; Plateia Iroön Kasou; s/d €37/49; ✷) The only official hotel on the island overlooks Fry's main square. While the rooms are a little on the small side they have been renovated and the balcony doors have double insulation.

Blue Sky (☎ 22450 41047; Fry; studios €60) For a little extra outlay you can be self-contained in these comfortable studios, some 400m inland. All rooms have kitchenettes and fridge. Contact Kasos Maritime & Travel Agency.

Borianoula (☎ 22450 41495; www.kassos-island.gr; Emborio; studios €60) A little way out of Fry, in Emborio, are these four reasonable-sized, tastefully renovated apartments. See Kasos Maritime & Travel Agency for the keys.

Eating & Drinking

Fry is not over-endowed in the eating stakes, but there are at least one or two decent places to dine.

O Mylos (☎ 22450 41825; Plateia Iroön Kasou; mains €3.50-4.50) This, the most reliable eatery, is open year-round and overlooks the west side of the port; it's a popular gathering spot for locals. The food is wholesome, with fish, meat and casserole dishes on the menu as well as the odd *mayirefta*.

Restaurant Mihail Karagiannis (☎ 22450 41390; Fry; mains €4-5) Basic, generally busy and also open year-round, this dependable eating place, opposite Kasos Maritime & Travel Agency, is rough and ready but fine for a solid, no-frills grills and other fast fare.

Apangio (☎ 22450 41880; Bouka; mezedes €3-5) Enjoying a very atmospheric Bouka harbour location, the Apangio is a pleasant *ouzeri*-cum-café, serving select *mezedes*, drinks, snacks and coffee.

Cafe Zantana (☎ 22450 41880; Bouka) Kasiots congregate at this trendy café that overlooks Bouka harbour. Mihalis, the owner, makes excellent cappuccinos and cocktails.

Entertainment

Perigiali Bar (☎ 22450 41767; Bouka) This diminutive bar, between Bouka and Plateia Iroön Kasou, is Kasos' nightclub. The music played is predominantly Greek.

AROUND KASOS

The beach at **Emborio**, while a little short on atmosphere thanks to the rather scruffy backdrop of abandoned houses, is nonetheless sandy, and the water is clean and clear. It's the best close-by place for a quick and refreshing dip.

The rather mediocre **Ammounda Beach**, beyond the airport near the blue-domed church of Agios Konstandinos, is the next nearest to Fry. There are slightly better beaches further along this stretch of coast, one of them being the fine-pebble **Andiperatos Beach** at the end of the road system. Neither Ammounda or Andiperatos has shade.

The island's best beach is the isolated pebbled cove of **Helatros**, near Moni Agiou Georgiou, 11km southwest from Fry along a paved road. The beach has no facilities, very little shade and you'll need your own transport to reach it. **Avlaki** is another decent beach here, reached along a path from the monastery.

Agia Marina, 1km southwest of Fry, is a pretty village with a gleaming white-and-blue church. On 17 July the Festival of Agia Marina is celebrated here. From Agia Marina the road continues to verdant **Arvanitohori**, with wonderful fig and pomegranate trees.

Poli, 3km southeast of Fry, is the former capital, built on the ancient acropolis. **Panagia**, between Fry and Poli, now has fewer than 50 inhabitants; its once-grand sea captains' and many ship owners' mansions are either standing derelict or under repair.

Monasteries

The island has two monasteries: **Moni Agiou Mamma** and **Moni Agiou Georgiou**. The uninhabited Moni Agiou Mamma, on the south coast, is a 1½-hour walk from Fry or a 20-minute scooter ride. The road winds uphill through a dramatic, eroded landscape of rock-strewn mountains, crumbling terraces and soaring cliffs. Occasionally clouds and mist swirl over the road as it crests the ridge high above Poli and dips dramatically down to the monastery at the end of the paved road. A lively *panygyri* (annual religious feast) takes place here on 2 September every year.

Similarly, there are no monks at Moni Agiou Georgiou, but there is a resident caretaker for most of the year. Free accommodation may be available for visitors, but don't bank on it. The *panygyri* at Agiou Georgiou takes place in the week after Easter.

KASTELLORIZO (MEGISTI)
ΚΑΣΤΕΛΛΟΡΙΖΟ (ΜΕΓΙΣΤΗ)

pop 430

It takes a certain amount of decisiveness and a sense of adventure to come to tiny, rocky Kastellorizo (kah-stel-*o*-rih-zo). A mere speck on the map, its nearest Greek neighbour is Rhodes, 118km east, yet it is only 2.5km from the southern coast of Turkey and its closest neighbouring town, Kaş. Kastellorizo is named after the 'red castle' that once dominated the main port, but is also known as 'Megisti' (the largest), for it is the biggest of a group of 14 islets that surround this isolated Hellenic outpost.

Tourism is low-key, yet there are more Australian-Greek Kastellorizians here in summer than there are locals. There are no stunning beaches, but there are rocky inlets from where you can swim and snorkel, and swimming from the quay at the northside of the harbour is very pleasant. The island featured in the Oscar-winning Italian film *Mediterraneo* (1991), which was based on a book by an army sergeant.

History

Kastellorizo has a tragic history. Once a thriving trade port serving Dorians, Romans, crusaders, Egyptians, Turks and Venetians,

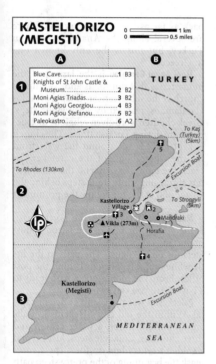

KASTELLORIZO (MEGISTI)

Blue Cave.............................1	B3
Knights of St John Castle & Museum...........................2	B2
Moni Agias Triadas.................3	B2
Moni Agiou Georgiou..............4	B3
Moni Agiou Stefanou.............5	B2
Paleokastro.........................6	A2

Kastellorizo came under Ottoman control in 1552. The island was permitted to preserve its language, religion and traditions, and its cargo fleet became the largest in the Dodecanese, allowing the islanders to achieve a high degree of culture and high levels of education.

Kastellorizo lost all strategic and economic importance after the 1923 Greece–Turkey population exchange. In 1928 it was ceded to the Italians, who severely oppressed the islanders. Many islanders chose to emigrate to Australia, where a disproportionate number still live.

During WWII, Kastellorizo suffered bombardment, and English commanders ordered the few remaining inhabitants to abandon the island. Most fled to Cyprus, Palestine and Egypt. When they returned they found their houses in ruins and re-emigrated. The island has never fully recovered from its population loss. In recent years, returnees have been slowly restoring buildings and the island is now enjoying a tenuous, but pleasant period of resurgence and resettlement.

Getting There & Away
AIR
In July and August there are daily flights to and from Rhodes (€25, 40 minutes), dropping to three weekly at all other times. You can buy tickets from **Dizi Tours & Travel** (☎ 22460 49241; dizivas@otenet.gr) or **Papoutsis Travel** (☎ 22460 70630; www.papoutsistravel .gr) located in Kastellorizo Village. You can either take a taxi (€5) to get from the airport to the port, or the local community bus (€1.50).

CATAMARAN & FERRY
Kastellorizo is the least well-connected island in the whole of the Dodecanese archipelago. Ferry links are subject to seasonal changes and the only direct domestic destination is Rhodes (€17, four hours). Call in at **Papoutsis Travel** (☎ 22460 70630; www.papoutsis travel.gr) for the latest details and tickets.

The *Dodekanisos Express* catamaran runs once a week to and from Kastellorizo from Rhodes (€33, 2½ hours), but the scheduled day changes yearly. Contact **Dodekanisos Naftiliaki** (☎ 22410 70590; info@12ne.gr) in Rhodes for the current schedules.

Getting Around
EXCURSION BOAT
Excursion boats go to the islets of **Ro**, **Strongyli** and the spectacular **Blue Cave** (Parasta), famous for its brilliant blue water, produced by refracted sunlight. Visitors are transferred from a larger caïque to a small motorised dingy in order to enter the very low cave entrance – claustrophobics be warned. Bring your bathing gear as the boatman usually allows visitors a quick dip in the cave itself.

The trip to the cave costs €8, and the longer trip to Ro, Strongyli and round Kastellorizo costs €15. All leave at around 8.30am daily.

Excursion Boat to Turkey
Islanders go on frequent shopping trips to Kaş in Turkey, and day trips (€15) are also offered to tourists. Look for the signs along the waterfront.

Currently, travellers cannot legally enter or exit Greece via Kastellorizo, though there is no problem with day trips. Passports in this case are retained by Turkish police until you board the boat for the return trip.

DODECANESE

KASTELLORIZO VILLAGE
pop 275
Besides Mandraki, its satellite neighbourhood over the hill and to the east, Kastellorizo Village is the only settlement on the island. Built around a U-shaped bay, the village's waterfront is skirted by imposing, spruced-up, three-storey mansions with wooden balconies and red-tiled roofs. It is undoubtedly pretty nowadays, but the alluring façade of today's waterfront contrasts starkly with backstreets of abandoned houses overgrown with ivy, crumbling stairways and winding stony pathways. Newer, brightly painted houses are emerging like gaudy mushrooms from among the ruins, while some of the older, ruined houses are slowly being restored to their former glory.

Orientation & Information
The quay is at the southern side of the bay. The central square, Plateia Ethelondon Kastellorizou, abuts the waterfront almost halfway round the bay, next to the yachting jetty. The settlements of Horafia and Mandraki are reached by ascending the wide steps at the east side of the bay.

There are a couple of cardphones and all Greek mobile service providers can be picked up on the island, as well as several Turkish mobile networks.

The National Bank of Greece, on the eastern waterfront, has an ATM. The post office is on the bay's western side.

Dizi Tours & Travel (☎ 22460 49241; dizivas@otenet.gr)
Kaz Bar (☎ 22460 49067; per hr €4) Internet access is provided at this waterfront eatery.
Papoutsis Travel (☎ 22460 70630; www.papoutsis travel.gr)
Police station (☎ 22460 49333) On the bay's western side.
Port police (☎ 22460 49333) At the eastern tip of the bay.

Sights
The **Knights of St John Castle** stands above the quay. A rickety metal staircase leads to the top from where there are splendid views of Turkey. Lower down the castle grounds, a well-displayed collection is held at the **museum** (☎ 22460 49283; admission free; ⏲ 7am-2.30pm Tue-Sun). Beyond the museum, steps lead down to a coastal pathway, from where more steps go up the cliff to a **Lycian tomb** with a Doric façade, which dates

back as far as the 4th century BC. There are several along the Anatolian coast in Turkey, but this is the only known one in Greece.

Moni Agiou Georgiou is the largest of the monasteries that dot the island. Within its church is the subterranean Chapel of Agios Haralambos, reached by steep stone steps. Greek children were given religious instruction here during Turkish times. The church is kept locked; ask around the waterfront for the whereabouts of the caretaker. To reach the monastery, ascend the conspicuous zigzagging white stone steps behind the village and at the top follow the prominent path.

Moni Agiou Stefanou, on the north coast, is the setting for one of the island's most important celebrations, the feast of Agios Stefanos on 1 August. The path to the little white monastery begins behind the post office. From the monastery, a path leads to a bay where you can swim.

Paleokastro was the island's ancient capital. Within the old city's Hellenistic walls are an ancient tower, a water cistern and three churches. Concrete steps, just beyond a soldier's sentry box on the airport road, mask the beginning of the pretty steep path to Paleokastro.

Sleeping
Accommodation in Kastellorizo Village runs the gamut from simple and small to traditional and spacious. The trouble is there's not too much of it. Book ahead in peak times to be sure of a bed.

Villa Kaserma (☎ 22460 49370; fax 22460 49365; d/tr €30/35; 🏊) Set back high on the western side of the harbour, this red-and-white coloured pension has oldish, fridge-equipped rooms with perhaps the best views of Kastellorizo harbour.

Pension Asimina (☎ 22460 49361; s/d €35/45; 🏊) Equipped with optional ceiling fans as well as fridge and TV, most of these very tidy double and triple rooms have private bathrooms. They are behind the fish market and to the right.

Pension I Orea Palameria (☎ 22460 49282; fax 22460 49071; d/tr €40/60) This converted building on the small square at the northwest corner of the waterfront has spotless rooms with kitchen and dining areas. Inquire about them at To Mikro Parisi.

Hotel Aegean (☎ 22460 49066; s/d €40/50) Housed in a brightly painted restored building, the most recent addition to the scene offers a cool and welcoming marble lobby and largish double rooms with TV and fridge. Located two blocks back from the southern waterfront, behind the fish market, the hotel may be a bit hard to find.

Pension Mediterraneo (☎ 22460 49007; www .mediterraneanpension.org; s & d €60) At the far western tip of the harbour are these smallish but otherwise comfortable rooms that offer a somewhat quieter accommodation choice and are very handy for a quick dip in the harbour.

Kastellorizo Hotel Appartments (☎ 22460 49044; fax 22460 49044; www.kastellorizohotel.gr; s/d €74/100; ❄ ⚑) The best accommodation is right here. All of these spacious and airy rooms have satellite TV, phone and fridge. The pint-sized pool is mainly for sitting in, but you can jump into the decidedly more capacious harbour from directly in front of the hotel.

Eating

Eating in Kastellorizo is generally a pleasant experience as the predominantly Greek and Italian clientele tends to be discerning. Most places are strung out along the waterfront.

To Mikro Parisi (☎ 22460 49282; mains €4.50-6) To Mikro Parisi has been going strong since 1974 and still serves generous helpings of grilled fish and meat. Fish soup is the house speciality, but the rich *stifado* is equally good.

Sydney Restaurant (☎ 22460 49302; mayirefta €3.50-4) Dishing up hearty home-cooked dishes and grilled fish, the Sydney, a little further around from To Mikro Parisi, is a popular low-key eatery with its tables teetering precariously on the harbour's edge.

Tis Ypomonis (☎ 22460 49224; mains €4-6; ❄ dinner) Sigposted in English as 'Serenity' this corner grill does a nightly roaring trade in *souvlaki* (cubes of meat on skewers), sausage and steaks, all cooked on a charcoal barbecue grill. Dine inside or on the busy street corner.

Akrothalassi (☎ 22460 49052; mains €3-5) Popular with visiting Greeks this relaxed taverna on the southwest side of the harbour serves up succulent grills and fish, as well as the

odd daily *mayirefta* such as green beans in *skordalia* (garlic and potato dip).

Kaz Bar (☎ 22460 49067; mezedes €2.50-4; ❄ 15 Jun-30 Sep) For a slightly different take on *mezedes,* visit owner Colin Pavlidis' barcum-restaurant on the middle waterfront. Pizzas, chicken wings and spring rolls, as well as original salads, feature on the menu and there's a good selection of Greek wines.

Entertainment

There are several easy-going cafés on the waterfront and Kaz Bar is a good place to kick off. Next door, Meltemi has tempting waterside chairs and cold beers while the gaudily painted Mythos Bar is another popular watering hole on the east side of the harbour.

SYMI ΣΥΜΗ

pop 2606

Symi is a rocky, dry island, 24km north of Rhodes. It lies within the geographical embrace of Turkey, 10km from the Turkish peninsula of Datça. The island has a scenic rocky interior, with pine and cypress woods. It has a deeply indented coast with precipitous cliffs and numerous small bays with pebbled beaches, and is enormously popular with day-trippers from Rhodes. Symi has good accommodation and eating choices and enjoys excellent transport links to the outside world. However, the island suffers from a severe water shortage and the day-tripper crowds can get a bit overwhelming at times. The main settlement and port is Gialos.

History

Symi has a long tradition of both sponge diving and shipbuilding. During Ottoman times it was granted the right to fish for sponges in Turkish waters. In return, Symi supplied the sultan with first-class boat builders and top-quality sponges scooped straight off the ocean floor.

These factors, and a lucrative shipbuilding industry, brought prosperity to the island. Gracious mansions were built and culture and education flourished. By the beginning of the 20th century the population was 22,500 and the island was launching some 500 ships a year. But the Italian occupation, the

DODECANESE

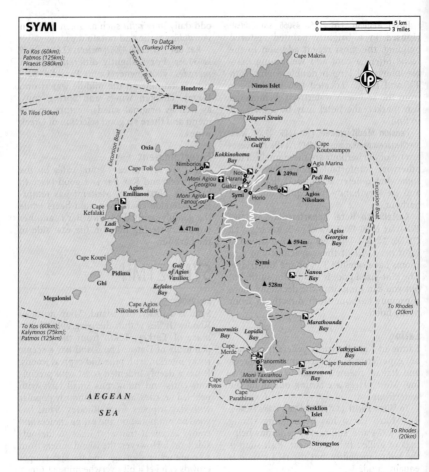

SYMI

0 — 5 km
0 — 3 miles

To Kos (60km);
Patmos (125km);
Piraeus (380km)

To Datça
(Turkey) (12km)

Cape Makria

Hondros

Nimos Islet

Platy

Diapori Straits

To Tilos (30km)

Nimborios
Gulf

Cape
Koutsoumpos

Oxia

Kokkinohoma
Bay

Cape Toli

Nimborios

Agia Marina

Cape
Emilianos

Moni Agiou
Georgiou

Nos
Harani
Gialos

▲ 249m

Pedi Bay

Cape
Kefalaki

Moni Agiou
Fanouriou

Symi

Pedi

Horio

Agios
Nikolaos

Ladi
Bay

▲ 471m

Cape Koupi

Agios
Georgios
Bay

▲ 594m

Pidima

Ghi

Gulf
of Agios
Vasilios

Symi

Megalonisi

Kefalos
Bay

Nanou
Bay

▲ 528m

Cape Agios
Nikolaos Kefalis

To Rhodes
(20km)

To Kos (60km);
Kalymnos (75km);
Patmos (125km)

Panormitis
Bay

Lopidia
Bay

Marathounda
Bay

Cape
Merde

Panormitis

Vathygialos
Bay
Cape Faneromeni

Cape
Potos

Moni Taxiarhou
Mihail Panormiti

Faneromeni
Bay

Cape Parathiras

AEGEAN

SEA

Sesklion
Islet

To Rhodes
(20km)

Strongylos

introduction of the steamship and Kalymnos'
rise as the Aegean's principal sponge producer
put an end to Symi's prosperity.

The treaty surrendering the Dodecanese islands to the Allies was signed in Symi's Hotel
(now Pension) Catherinettes on 8 May 1945.

Getting There & Away
EXCURSION BOAT
There are daily excursion boats running between Symi and Rhodes. The Symi-based
Symi I and *Symi II* (☎ 22460 71444; anes1@otenet
.gr; return €12) are the cheapest; tickets can be
bought on board.

Symi Tours (☎ 22460 71307; fax 22460 72292) has
excursion trips from Gialos to Datça in
Turkey (including Turkish port taxes €35).

FERRY, CATAMARAN & HYDROFOIL
Symi has only two long-haul ferries a week
heading north to other Dodecanese islands
and Piraeus. **ANES** (☎ 22460 71444) transports
cars between Symi and Rhodes (one-way
€5, one hour 10 minutes).

The *Dodekanisos Express* and *Dodekanisos
Pride* catamarans service the island at least
four times a week with connections to
Rhodes (€14, 50 minutes) and islands further north. One service calls in at Panormitis on the north side of the island.

Symi is connected by hydrofoil to Kos
(€17, one hour), Kalymnos (€21.30, 1½
hours) and Rhodes (€11, 50 minutes). The
Symi-owned *Aigli* hydrofoil also connects
Symi with Rhodes.

Getting Around
BUS & TAXI
The bus stop and taxi rank are on the south side of the harbour in Gialos. The green minibus makes frequent runs between Gialos and Pedi Beach (via Horio). The flat fare is €0.70. Taxis depart from a rank 100m west of the bus stop.

EXCURSION BOAT
Several excursion boats do trips to Moni Taxiarhou Mihail Panormiti and Sesklion Islet, where there's a shady beach. Check the boards for the best-value tickets. There are also boats to Agios Emilianos beach, on the far west side of Symi.

TAXI BOAT
The small boats *Katerina I* and *Katerina II* do trips (€8 to €13) to many of the island's beaches.

GIALOS ΓΙΑΛΟΣ
pop 2200
Gialos, Symi's port, is by all accounts a visual treat. Neoclassical mansions in a harmonious medley of colours are heaped up the hills flanking its harbour. Behind their strikingly beautiful façades, however, many of the buildings are derelict. It is a slightly claustrophobic place and can get unbearably hot in summer. Pervading its allure is a tangible neocolonial air, with a somewhat introverted and cliquish British-expat presence. Visitors tend to like Symi or leave it.

Orientation & Information
The town is divided into two parts: Gialos, the harbour, and Horio above it, crowned by the *kastro* (castle). Arriving ferries, hydrofoils and catamarans dock just to the left of the quay's clock tower; excursion boats dock a little further along. The centre of activity in Gialos is the promenade at the centre of the harbour. Kali Strata, a broad stairway, leads from here to hill-top Horio.

There is no official tourist office in Symi Town. The *Symi Visitor* is a free English-and-Greek-language newspaper distributed by portside newspaper vendors and restaurants.

The post office is by the ferry quay.

Kalodoukas Holidays (☎ 22460 71077; fax 22460 71491; kalodouka@rhoforthnet.gr) At the beginning of Kali Strata; sells a guide to walking the island.

Police (☎ 22460 71111) By the ferry quay.
Port police (☎ 22460 71205) By the ferry quay.
Roloï bar (☎ 22460 71595; per hr €4; 🕑 9am-3am) Access the Internet here, a block back from the waterfront.
Symi Tours (☎ 22460 71307; fax 22460 72292) Does excursion trips, including to Datça in Turkey.
www.symivisitor.com A useful source of island information and gossip.

Sights
Horio consists of narrow, labyrinthine streets crossed by crumbling archways. As you approach the **Knights of St John Kastro** dominating Horio, the once-grand 19th-century neoclassical mansions give way to the modest stone dwellings of the 18th century. The castle incorporates blocks from the ancient acropolis, and the **Church of Megali Panagia** is within its walls.

On the way to the *kastro*, Hellenistic, Byzantine and Roman exhibits, as well as some folkloric material, are kept in the **Archaeological and Folklore Museum** (admission €1.50; 🕑 10am-2pm Tue-Sun) in the Lieni suburb of Horio. In the port of Gialos the **Naval Museum** (admission €1.50; 🕑 10am-2pm Tue-Sun) has some noteworthy wooden models of ships and other naval memorabilia.

Activities
Symi Tours (☎ 22460 71307; fax 22460 72292) has multilingual guides who lead **guided walks** around the island. The publication *Walking on Symi* by Francis Noble (€7) is on sale at Kalodoukas Holidays.

Shutterbugs may care to take a **personal photography course** (☎ 69364 21715; www.symi dream.com); seek out Neil in his atelier in Horio for more details.

Sleeping
Most accommodation is in studios or a few private *domatia* (cheap rooms). There are a couple of good hotels as well.

Hotel Kokona (☎ 22460 71549; fax 22460 72620; Gialos; s/d €35/45) On the street to the left of the large church, this small and basic hotel has comfortable rooms.

Pension Catherinettes (☎ /fax 22460 72698; marina-epe@rho.forthnet.gr; Gialos; d €32-50) The historic Catherinettes (see History, p305) is on the north side of the harbour. The pink-stuccoed pension has wrought-iron balconies and some of the rooms have magnificently painted high ceilings.

DODECANESE

Hotel Fiona (☎ 22460 72755; www.symivisitor .com; Horio; s/d €45/55) This hotel in Horio has lovely rooms, with wood-panelled ceilings and great views, and is a shade cooler than accommodation in Gialos as it catches welcome breezes. To reach it, turn left at the top of the stairs and walk for 50m.

Hotel Nireus (☎ 22460 72400; www.nireus-hotel .gr; Gialos; s/d €47/80; 🏶) One of the two regular hotels in Gialos, the prominently sited Nireus, by the clock tower, has traditional rooms and suites with fridge, TV and phone.

Opera House Hotel (☎ 22460 72034; operasym@ otenet.gr; Gialos; studios €85-100; 🏶) Named after Australia's Sydney Opera House, these spacious studios in a peaceful garden are well signposted 150m back from the harbour and are fully self-contained.

Eating

There's a wide variety of places to eat in Gialos and Horio, with equally wide variances in quality. Choose carefully.

GIALOS

Taverna Neraïda (☎ 22460 71841; mains €4-5) Serving unpretentious and solid Greek dishes, Neraïda is an excellent, low-priced option, a block from the waterfront. Fish *souvlaki* features on the menu, as does a range of vegetarian dishes. Walk into the kitchen and select from the dishes on display.

Estiatorio Mythos (☎ 22460 71488; mezedes €4-10) This is a neat little harbourside taverna serving imaginative food. At lunch time Mythos serves mainly pasta dishes, while *mezedes* feature in the evening. For palate pleasing consider calamari stuffed with pesto, or fish fillet parcels in a saffron cream sauce.

Tholos (☎ 22460 72033; mains €5-9) Out on the headland just before Nos beach, this little low-key taverna is a good choice to escape the crowds in Gialos and dine on good-quality fare, including grills, *mezedes* and the ubiquitous fish dishes.

Mylopetra (☎ 22460 72333; mains €7-15) Considered to be the best restaurant on Symi, Mylopetra takes care with its ingredients and serves up Mediterranean-Greek creations, including home-made bread and pastas.

HORIO

Giorgos (☎ 22460 71984; mains €6-9) There is an always-changing and enticing *mayirefta* menu here, with such mouth-watering dishes as chicken stuffed with rice, herbs and pine nuts, lamb in vine leaves, or stuffed onions. Check prices before ordering as they are not always listed.

Restaurant Syllogos (☎ 22460 72148; mains €5-7) Similar in style to Giorgos, Syllogos also offers imaginative fare such as chicken with prunes, pork with leek, fish with rosemary and tomato, plus vegetarian options such as artichokes in egg and lemon sauce, or *spanakopita* (spinach pie).

Entertainment

There are several lively bars in the streets behind the south side of the harbour.

Vapori Bar (☎ 22460 72082) Drop by here during the day to read the free papers and then in the evenings for schmoozing, drinks and cruising.

Roloï Bar (☎ 22460 71595) A busy, happening little watering hole one block inland from the south side of the port, this is open most of the day and a large part of the night.

In Horio the **Jean and Tonic Bar** (☎ 22460 71819) is the self-styled 'late place', kicking in at 9pm and closing at dawn.

AROUND SYMI

Pedi is a little fishing village and busy mini-holiday resort in a fertile valley 2km downhill from Horio. It has some sandy stretches on its narrow beach and there are *domatia*, hotels and tavernas. Walking tracks down both sides of the bay lead to **Agia Marina** beach on the north side and **Agios Nikolaos** beach on the south side. Both are sandy, gently shelving beaches, suitable for children.

Nos Beach is the closest beach to Gialos. It's a 500m walk north of the campanile at Panormitis Bay. There is a taverna, bar and sun beds (per person €3).

Nimborios is a long, pebbled beach 3km west of Gialos. It has some natural shade as well as sun beds and umbrellas. You can walk there from Gialos along a scenic path – take the road by the east side of the central square and continue straight ahead; the way is fairly obvious, just bear left after the church and follow the stone trail. You can stay at **Niriides Apartments** (☎ 22460 71784; fax 22460 71892; www.niriideshotel.com; apts €60-80) in one of eight capacious units on the hillside, in a very quiet location.

Taxi boats are the only convenient way to get to **Agios Georgios Bay** and the more developed beach at **Nanou Bay**, which has sun beds, umbrellas and a taverna.

The remoter **Marathounda Bay** beach can be reached by road, while **Agios Emilianos** beach, on the far west side of Symi, is best reached by excursion boat.

Moni Taxiarhou Mihail Panormiti
Μονή Ταξιάρχου Μιχαήλ Πανορμίτη

An often winding but good sealed road leads you across the island, through scented pine forests, before dipping in spectacular zigzag fashion to the expansive, but protected Panormitis Bay. This is the site of Symi's principal attraction – the large **Moni Taxiarhou Mihail Panormiti** (Monastery of Archangel Michael of Panormitis). The large monastery complex, with its ornate Italianate campanile, occupies most of the foreshore of the bay and is open to visitors all day (admission free).

A monastery was first built here in the 5th or 6th century, but the present building dates from the 18th century. The *katholikon* (principal church of a monastic complex) contains an intricately carved wooden iconostasis, frescoes, and an icon of St Michael that supposedly appeared miraculously where the monastery now stands. St Michael is the patron saint of Symi, and protector of sailors.

The monastery is also a magnet for hoards of day-trippers who commonly arrive at around 10.30am on excursion boats; it is a good idea to visit early or after they have left.

The monastery complex comprises a **Byzantine museum** and **folkloric museum** (admission for both €1.50), a bakery with excellent bread and apple pies, and a basic restaurant-café to the north side.

Accommodation is available at the **guest house** (☎ 22460 72414; s/d €18/30) where bookings in July and August are mandatory.

TILOS ΤΗΛΟΣ

pop 533

Tilos is one of the few islands left in the Dodecanese that retains something of its traditional character, and where tourism has not widely impacted on the slow and carefree lifestyle of the islanders. Most visitors tend to be gentrified walkers from the UK, Italians in search of tranquillity, expat Tiliots from the USA or Australia, and a mixed bag of lost yachties.

Tilos lies 30km west of Rhodes. Among its highlights are good, uncrowded beaches, two abandoned villages and a well-kept monastery at the end of a spectacularly scenic road. It's a terrific island for walkers, with vistas of high cliffs, rocky inlets, valleys of cypress, walnut and almond trees, and bucolic meadows. The island's rich agricultural potential is little utilised nowadays since, rather than work the land for a pittance, young Tiliots have long preferred to leave for the mainland or emigrate overseas.

History

Mastodon bones – midget elephants that became extinct around 4600 BC – were found in a cave on the island in 1974. The cave, **Harkadio** (closed), is signposted from the Livadia–Megalo Horio road and is brilliantly illuminated at night. Erinna, one of the least known of ancient Greece's female poets, lived on Tilos in the 4th century BC.

Elephants and poetry aside, Tilos' history shares the same catalogue of invasions and occupations as the rest of the archipelago.

Getting There & Away
CATAMARAN

The Tilos-owned **Sea Star** (☎ 22460 44000) connects Tilos daily with Rhodes (€18.50) and once a week with Nisyros (€10). The time table changes annually, but there are up to two connections a day with Rhodes. Departures from Rhodes are usually timed to dovetail with incoming charter flights.

EXCURSION BOAT

There are a number of excursions advertised around Livadia. One is an all-inclusive beach barbecue excursion for €25 (food and wine included) and another is a multibeach island tour for the same price. Look for posters around Livadia for details.

FERRY

Tilos is poorly served by mainline ferries. Currently only G&A Ferries provide two services a week to Rhodes and two corresponding return links to islands to the north. Sample fares are Rhodes (€12, 3½ hours),

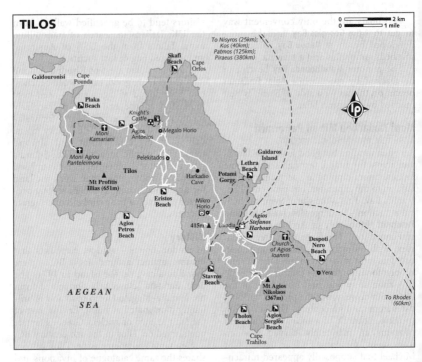

TILOS

0 ━━━━━━ 2 km
0 ━━━━━━ 1 mile

To Nisyros (25km);
Kos (40km);
Patmos (125km);
Piraeus (380km)

Gaïdouronisi

Cape
Pounda

Skafi
Beach   Cape
Orfos

Plaka
Beach

Knight's
Castle

Moni
Kamariani

Agios
Antonios   Megalo Horio

Moni Agiou
Panteleimona   Pelekitados

Gaïdaros
Island

Lethra
Beach

Tilos

Mt Profitis
Illias (651m)

Harkadio
Cave

Potami
Gorge

Eristos
Beach

Mikro
Horio

Agios
Petros
Beach

415m ▲   Livadia

Agios
Stefanos
Harbour

Church
of Agios
Ioannis

Despoti
Nero
Beach

Yera

Stavros
Beach

A E G E A N

S E A

Mt Agios
Nikolaos
(367m)

To Rhodes
(60km)

Tholos
Beach

Agios
Sergios
Beach

Cape
Trahilos

Kos (€10, three hours) and Piraeus (€30, 15 hours). Tickets are sold at **Stefanakis Travel** (☎ 22460 44310; stefanakis@rho.forthnet.gr) in Livadia.

Getting Around

Tilos' public transport consists of a bus that ploughs up and down the island's main road on a fairly regular basis. The timetable is posted at the bus stop in Livadia. The fares are €1 to Megalo Horio and €1.20 to Eristos Beach. On Sunday there is a special excursion bus to Moni Agiou Panteleimona (€4 return), which leaves Livadia at 11am and gives you one hour at the monastery. Tilos currently has only two **taxis** (☎ 69449 81727 or 69452 00436).

LIVADIA ΛΙΒΑΔΕΙΑ
pop 470

Livadia is the main village and port, though not the capital: that honour belongs to Megalo Horio, situated 8km northwest of the port. Livadia is a sleepy, pleasant enough place, though it can be a bit more hot and humid than other parts of the island. In

the village you will find most services and shops, as well as the bulk of the island's accommodation.

Orientation & Information

All arrivals are at Livadia. The small port is 300m southeast of the village centre. Tilos has no official tourist bureau. The Bank of the Dodecanese has a branch and an ATM in Livadia. The post office is on the central square.

Kosmos (☎ 22460 44074; www.tilos-kosmos.com; per hr €6; ☼ 9.30am-1pm & 7-11.30pm) This gift shop has Internet access. Its website is a useful source of information on Tilos. A local map of Tilos is available here for €2.50. There is also a book exchange and new books for sale.

Police (☎ 22460 44222) In the white Italianate building at the quay.

Port police (☎ 22460 44350) On the harbour.

Sea Star (☎ 22460 44000; fax 22460 44044; sea-star@ otenet.gr) Sells tickets for the Sea Star Catamaran.

Stefanakis Travel (☎ 22460 44310; stefanakis@rho .forthnet.gr) Between the port and the village, sells ferry tickets.

Tilos Travel (☎ 22460 44294; www.tilostravel.co.uk)

At the port; has helpful staff. Credit card withdrawals and money exchange are available, as well as car, motorbike and bike hire.

Sights & Activities
WALKS
There are a number of popular walks that can easily be made from Livadia. The most popular is to **Lethra Beach**, an undeveloped pebble and sand cove with limited shade, 3km north of Livadia. The trail starts at the far north side of the port and is fairly easy. Return via the very picturesque, oleander-strewn and goat-inhabited **Potami Gorge**, which will bring you to the main island highway.

A second walk is a longer return track to the small abandoned settlement of **Yera** and its accompanying beach at **Despoti Nero**. From Livadia follow the road south, around Agios Stefanos Bay and past the Church of Agios Ioannis, on the east side of the bay, and keep walking. Allow half a day for this hike.

Iain and Lyn Fulton of **Tilos Trails** (☎ 69460 54593; fulton@otenet.gr) are licensed guides and run a number of walks (per person €20) around the island, graded from easy to challenging.

Sleeping
Accommodation on the island is generally of a high standard, though much of it gets block-booked by low-key foreign tour operators.

Paraskevi Rooms (☎ 22460 44280; d €30) One of a couple of basic places on the waterfront in Livadia, this place has clean, simply furnished rooms with well-equipped kitchens.

Kosmos Studios (☎ 22460 44164; www.tilos-kosmos.com; d €42) These four well-presented, newish units are at the western end of the bay, 80m inland from the beach. They are fan-equipped and offer a free supermarket delivery service with Giannis and Maria's Supermarket.

Apollo Studios (☎ 22460 44379; www.apollostudios .com; d €57) Comprising seven double rooms with kitchenette and fan, these are small-ish but spotless, with sparkling tiled floors. They are in a very central location.

Eleni Beach Hotel (☎ 22460 44062; elenihtl@otenet .gr; s/d incl breakfast €50/60) This airy hotel, 400m south along the beach road, has beautiful,

tastefully furnished double rooms with refrigerator and telephone.

Irini Hotel (☎ 22460 44193; www.tilosholidays .gr; s/d incl breakfast €45/60; ☒) Catering mainly to the packaged travellers, the neat Irini also welcomes independents. The hotel is set back a little from the waterfront, in a citrus garden, and the rooms are very well appointed.

Ilidi Rock (☎ 22460 44193; www.tilosholidays.gr; apts €50; ☒) Run by the same management as the Irini Hotel, these very comfortable, self-contained apartments are above and to the right of the port and have access to a small, but private, pebbly beach.

Eating
Joanna's Cafe Bar (☎ 22460 44145; pizzas €6.50-10) This café-bar is a popular breakfast, brunch and evening hang-out, serving excellent coffee (try the Tilos coffee – a proper caffeine punch), yogurt and muesli, pizza, Italian wines and delicious home-made cakes.

Sofia's Taverna (☎ 22460 44340; mayirefta €3-6) This family-run taverna, 100m along the beach road, serves wholesome, home-cooked food as well as a good selection of starters.

Restaurant Irina (☎ 22460 44206; mayirefta €4-5) With its relaxing waterside location, Irina does great home-made food, including excellent *mousaka* and *paputsaki* (stuffed baby eggplant), and a rich, beefy *stifado*.

Taverna Blue Sky (☎ 22460 44259; mezedes €2-4) Blue Sky, on the harbour, is good for grilled fish and vegetarian *mezedes*. Now run by Italians this is reflected in the food, with pasta featuring prominently on the menu.

Calypso (☎ 22460 44382; mains €3.50-7) For a slightly unusual twist, the daily changing menu at Calypso showcases dishes such as shark with basmati rice or organic salads, combining elements from Greek, French and Vietnamese cuisines.

Entertainment
Mikro Horio Music Bar (☽ midnight-5am Jul & Aug) Serious ravers head for the abandoned village of Mikro Horio, 3km from Livadia, where this place belts out music most of the night. A minibus ferries revellers to and from the port.

There are a few summer bars on Livadia's waterfront, such as Ino and Bozi.

MEGALO HORIO ΜΕΓΑΛΟ ΧΩΡΙΟ
pop 50

Megalo Horio, the island's capital, is a serene whitewashed village. Its alleyways are fun to explore, and the village makes a great alternative base if you are looking for a taste of rural life in Tilos. There are *domatia*, a restaurant and at least one atmospheric bar to keep visitors bedded, fed and suitably watered. From here you can visit the **Knight's Castle**, a taxing 40-minute upwards walk along a track starting at the north end of the village. Along the way you will pass the **ancient settlement** of Tilos, which in its time stood precariously on rocky ledges overlooking Megalo Horio. The remains of stone houses can be clearly seen here.

The little **museum** (admission free) on the main street houses mastodon bones from Harkadio Cave. It's locked, but if you ask at the town hall on the 1st floor someone will show you around.

When it comes to sleeping you have two choices. **Elefantakia Studios** (☎ 22460 44242; d €30) on the main street is fairly uncomplicated. All rooms have little kitchenettes and fridges. Next door and up a notch are the secluded studios of **Miliou Rooms & Apartments** (☎ 22460 44204; d €35), sequestered in a tree-shaded garden which boasts a couple of banana palms.

To Kastro (☎ 22460 44232; mains €4.56) on the village's south side overlooking the Eristos plain below is the best place to eat. The fare features charcoal-grilled meats that including organic goat and locally raised pork, as well as fresh fish and a range of daily *mayirefta*.

After-dinner happenings take place at **Anemona** (☎ 22460 44090), which is perched at the northeastern side of the village near the start of the castle track, and is well illuminated at night. Greek music predominates.

AROUND MEGALO HORIO

Just before Megalo Horio, a turn-off to the left leads 2.5km to the pleasant, tamarisk-shaded **Eristos Beach**, a mixture of gritty sand and shingle. A signposted turn-off to the right from the junction leads to the quiet settlement of **Agios Antonios**, where the small Elpida Restaurant is the only reliable source of food and drink. The undeveloped **Plaka Beach**, 3km further west, is backed by shady trees and is clean and uncluttered.

The 18th-century **Moni Agiou Panteleimona** is 5km beyond here, along a scenic road. It is uninhabited but well maintained, with fine frescoes. The island's minibus driver takes groups of visitors here on Sunday. A well-attended and lively three-day annual **festival** takes place at the monastery, beginning on 25 July.

You can **camp** unofficially on Eristos Beach, but facilities are pretty basic. The best place to stay is at the expansive plant-festooned grounds and studios of **Eristos Beach Hotel** (☎ /fax 22460 44024; d €32) abutting the northern end of the beach. Here you'll find excellent, airy studios for up to four people with fridge and kitchenette. There is also an on-site restaurant. An alternative eating option is **Tropicana Taverna** (☎ 22460 44020; mains €3-4.40) on the Eristos road, where the owner serves up locally produced meat and vegetables and scrumptious *revithokeftedes* (chickpea rissoles).

NISYROS ΝΙΣΥΡΟΣ

pop 948

Nisyros (*nee-sih-ros*) is one of those quirky Greek islands that is not on the usual island-hopping circuit. It has no stunning sandy beaches and supports a rather low-key tourist infrastructure that favours individuals, yachties and lost souls. Nisyros is an almost round island and has something that no other Greek island has – its own volcano. The landscape is rocky, lush and green, all at the same time, yet it has no natural water.

The lunar landscape of the island's interior is offset by craggy peaks and rolling hillsides leading down to brown pebbly beaches that see relatively few visitors. The island's settlements are the main port of Mandraki, the fishing village of Pali and the crater-top villages of Emborios and Nikea.

Getting There & Away

Nisyros is linked by regular ferries to Rhodes (€10, three to five hours), Kos (€7, 1¾ hours) and Piraeus (€27, 17 hours). The small local ferries *Agios Konstantinos* and *Nisyros* link Mandraki with Kardamena on Kos (€7, two hours) departing Mandraki daily at 7am.

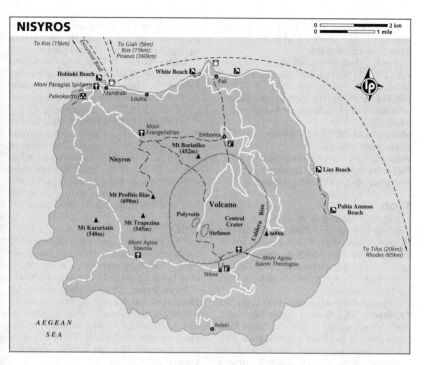

NISYROS

0 ————— 2 km
0 ————— 1 mile

To Kos (15km)
To Giali (5km)
Kos (15km);
Piraeus (360km)

Hohlaki Beach
White Beach
Moni Panagias Spilianis
Pali
Paleokastro
Mandraki
Loutra

Moni
Evangelistrias
Embonos

Mt Boriatiko
(452m)

Nisyros
Lies Beach

Mt Profitis Ilias
(698m)

Volcano
Pahia Ammos
Beach

Polyvotis   Central
Crater   Caldera Rim

Mt Kararatis   Mt Trapezina   Stefanos
(540m)   (545m)   600m

Moni Agiou
Stavrou
To Tilos (20km);
Rhodes (65km)

Moni Agiou
Ioanni Theologou

Nikea

AEGEAN
SEA
Avlaki

Sea Star (☎ 22460 44000) operates a catamaran service to Tilos and Rhodes once a week and there is a hydrofoil service to Kos and Rhodes once a week. In summer there are daily excursion boats from Kardamena, Kefalos and Kos Town on Kos (€13 to €18).

Getting Around
BUS
Bus companies run up to 10 excursion buses every day between 9.30am and 3pm to the volcano (€7 return) with around 40 minutes allowed to visit the volcano. These are in addition to the three daily buses that travel to Nikea (€1.70) via Pali. You'll find the bus stop is located at the quay.

EXCURSION BOAT
In July and August there are excursion boats (return €8) to the pumice-stone islet of Giali where there is a good sandy beach.

MOTORCYCLE
There are three rental outlets on Mandraki's main street. **Manos Rentals** (☎ 22420 31029) right on the quay is the most handy.

TAXI
There are two taxis on Nisyros: **Babis Taxi** (☎ 69456 39723) and **Irene's Taxi** (☎ 69733 71281). Sample fares from Mandraki: to the volcano (return €20), to Nikea (€11) and to Pali (€5).

MANDRAKI ΜΑΝΔΡΑΚΙ
pop 661
Mandraki is the sleepy port and capital of Nisyros. It has just the right amount of somnolence to make it great for a spot of aimless wandering. Its two-storey houses have brightly painted wooden balconies. Some are whitewashed but many are painted in bright colours, predominantly ochre and turquoise. The web of streets huddled below the monastery and the central square are especially captivating, and you can easily get lost for a while in their narrow confines.

Orientation & Information
The port is 500m northeast of the centre of Mandraki. Take the road right from the port and you will hit the centre. A shoreline

DODECANESE

road and an inner street both lead eventually to the tree-shaded Plateia Ilikiomeni, Mandraki's focal point.

The Co-Operative Bank of the Dodecanese has an ATM at the harbour and a branch in Mandraki.

Enetikon Travel (☎ 22420 31180; agiosnis@otenet.gr) 100m from the quay towards Mandraki. Provides tourist information.

Nisyrian Travel (☎ 22420 31411) On the quay. Provides tourist information.

Police (☎ 22420 31201) Opposite the quay.

Port police (☎ 22420 31222) Opposite the quay.

Post office (☎ 22420 31249) Opposite the quay.

Sights

Mandraki's main tourist attraction is the cliff-top 14th-century **Moni Panagias Spilianis** (Virgin of the Cave; ☎ 22420 31125; admission by donation; ☉ 10.30am-3pm), which is crammed with ecclesiastical paraphernalia. Turn right at the end of the main street to reach the steps up to the monastery.

The impressive Mycenaean-era acropolis, **Paleokastro** (Old Kastro), above Mandraki, has well-preserved Cyclopean walls built from massive blocks of volcanic rock. Follow the route signposted 'kastro', near the monastery steps. This eventually becomes a path. At the road, turn right and the kastro is on the left.

Hohlaki is a black-stone beach and can usually be relied upon for swimming unless the wind is up, when the water can get rough. It's on the western side of Moni Panagias Spilianis and is reached by a paved path.

Sleeping

Mandraki has a fairly limited amount of accommodation and owners do not usually meet incoming ferries. Book ahead to be assured of a bed.

Iliovasilema Rooms (☎ 22420 31159; d €25) Occupying one of the few central Mandraki spots, these fairly basic, but well-sited, rooms do cop a fair bit of noise from the waterfront tourist traffic.

Three Brothers Hotel (☎ 22420 31344; fax 22420 31640; iiibrother@kos.forthnet.gr; s/d €36/36; ✪) Closest to the port is this choice, overlooking the harbour and offering neat rooms with TV and fridge.

Hotel Porfyris (☎ 22420 31376; fax 22420 31176; diethnes@otenet.gr; s/d €35/40; ✪) Set at the back end of Mandraki, this hotel, with its early '90's

décor, is a cool oasis and, as well as a large reception area, has reasonable sized rooms equipped with fridge, TV and phone.

Haritos Hotel (☎ 22420 31322; www.haritos hotel.gr; d/tr €40/50; ✪ ✪) One of the better choices, the Haritos is located 200m along the Pali road. The rooms are well appointed and have fridge, TV and telephone.

Ta Liotridia (☎ 22420 31580; ste €150; ✪) For the absolute classiest and most romantic place to sleep in Mandraki, book one of the two suites above these two converted oil presses. Done out in classic Nisyriot style, with raised beds, solid furnishings, TV and a little cooker, the suites are not cheap but they're worth it for the sea views alone.

Eating

Ask for the island speciality, chickpea and onion patties (pitties), and wash them down with a refreshing soumada, a nonalcoholic local beverage made from almond extract.

Tony's Tavern (☎ 22420 31460; mains €3.50-5) Ex-Melbournian butcher Tony, on the waterfront, does great breakfasts and excellent meat and fish dishes, as well as a wide range of vegetarian choices. Try the gyros (Greek version of doner kebab) – probably the best on Nisyros.

Taverna Nisyros (☎ 22420 31460; grills €4-5) This taverna, just off the main street, is a cheap and cheerful little place and serves up good charcoal grills and souvlakia.

Kleanthes Taverna (☎ 22420 31484; mezedes €3.50-5) Good for a relaxed evening meal of mezedes and ouzo. Further east along the waterfront from Tony's, Kleanthes is a favourite among locals and visitors alike.

Restaurant Irini (☎ 22420 31365; Plateia Ilikiomeni; mayirefta €3-5) Irini's, on the leafy and shady central square, is recommended for its low-priced, no-nonsense and very good quality home-cooking.

Taverna Panorama (☎ 22420 31185; grills €3-5) Just off Plateia Ilikiomeni, heading to the Hotel Porfyris, is another commendable option. Try suckling pig or goat, or even the Cypriot-style herb-laced seftelies (sausages).

AROUND NISYROS
The Volcano Το Ηφαίστειο

Nisyros is on a volcanic line that passes through the islands of Aegina, Paros, Milos, Santorini, Nisyros, Giali and Kos. The island originally culminated in a mountain of 850m, but the centre collapsed 30,000 to 40,000 years ago after three violent eruptions. Their legacy are the white-and-orange pumice stones that can still be seen on the northern, eastern and southern flanks of the island, and the large lava flow that covers the whole southwest, around Nikea village. The first eruption partially blew off the top of the ancestral cone, but the majority of the sinking of the central part of the island came about as a result of the removal of magma from within the reservoir underground.

Another violent eruption occurred in 1422 on the western side of the caldera depression (called Lakki), but this, like all others since, emitted steam, gases and mud, but no lava. The islanders call the volcano Polyvotis because, during the Great War between the gods and the Titans, the Titan Polyvotis annoyed Poseidon so much that the god tore off a chunk of Kos and threw it at him. This rock pinned Polyvotis under it and became the island of Nisyros. The hapless Polyvotis from that day forth has been groaning and sighing while trying to escape – hence the volcano's name.

There are five craters in the **caldera** (admission €1.50; 9am-8pm). A not-so-obvious and unsignposted path descends into the largest one, **Stefanos**, where you can examine the multicoloured fumaroles, listen to their hissing and smell their sulphurous vapours. The surface is soft and hot, making sturdy footwear essential. Be careful you don't step into a fumarole, the steam can cause severe burns. Another unsignposted but more obvious track leads you in six to seven minutes to **Polyvotis**, which is smaller and wilder-looking, but does not allow you access to the caldera itself.

The easiest way to visit the volcano is by tourist bus, but you will share your experience with hoards of day-trippers. Better still, scooter in from Mandraki or walk down from Nikia. Get there before 11am and you may have the volcano entirely to yourself.

Emborios & Nikea Εμπορειός & Νίκαια
Emborios and Nikea perch on the volcano's rim. From each, there are stunning views down into the caldera. Only a handful of inhabitants linger on in Emborios. You may encounter a few elderly women sitting on their doorsteps crocheting, and their husbands at the *kafeneio* (coffee house). But generally, the winding, stepped streets are empty, the silence broken only by the occasional braying of a donkey or the grunting of pigs. There's one place to eat, the seasonal **To Balkoni tou Emboriou** (22420 31607; mains €3-5) where you can enjoy the view of the crater over lunch.

In contrast to Emborios, picturesque Nikea, with 35 inhabitants, buzzes with life. It has dazzling white houses with vibrant gardens and a central square with a lovely pebble mosaic. The bus terminates on Plateia Nikolaou Hartofyli. Nikea's main street links the two squares. The simple **Community Hostel** (22420 31203; Plateia Nikolaou Hartofyli; d €25) is your only choice of a place to stay.

The steep path down to the volcano begins from Plateia Nikolaou Hartofyli. It takes about 40 minutes to walk it one way. Near the beginning you can detour to the sign-posted **Moni Agiou Ioanni Theologou** where there is an annual feast on 25–26 September.

Pali Πάλοι
Pali is a small yachtie port with limited accommodation, yet a number of places to eat. The island's best beaches start here and continue on at **Lies**, 5.5km around the coast. **Pahia Ammos** beach is a further 1km from Lies along a coastal track.

If you decide to stay, then head for one of the comfy, self-contained studios at **Mammis' Apartments** (22420 31453; fax 22420 31181; www.mammis.com; d €50), on the last bend before you enter Pali.

Perhaps the best of the bunch of Pali's eating options is the **Captain's House** (22420 31016; grills €5-6), where you have a choice of home cooking or fish and meat grills, and where you can sit at lunch and watch the fishermen unravel their nets next to your table. It also rents motorbikes.

KOS ΚΩΣ

pop 17,890
Kos grows on you. It's a big island with a well-established package-tourism industry, a large selection of good beaches, some pretty mountain villages and lots of space for the visitor to spread out and find their own idyllic spot. While it doesn't have the prettiness of its smaller neighbours, it has a

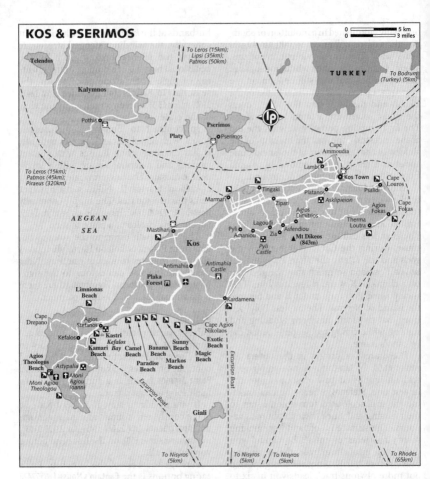

KOS & PSERIMOS

nice balance of attractions: good food and wine, scenery, sporting activities, antiquities and fine friendly people. It's also the third-largest island of the Dodecanese and one of its most fertile and well watered. It is second only to Rhodes in its wealth of archaeological remains and level of tourist development. A long, narrow island with a mountainous spine, it lies only a few kilometres from the Turkish town of Bodrum.

History

Kos' fertile land attracted settlers from the earliest days. So many people lived here by Mycenaean times that it sent 30 ships to the Trojan War. During the 7th and 6th centuries BC, Kos prospered as an ally of

the powerful Rhodian cities of Ialysos, Kamiros and Lindos. In 477 BC, after suffering an earthquake and subjugation to the Persians, it joined the Delian League and again flourished.

Hippocrates (460–377 BC), the father of medicine, was born and lived on the island. After Hippocrates' death, the Sanctuary of Asclepius and a medical school were built, which perpetuated his teachings and made Kos famous throughout the Greek world.

Ptolemy II of Egypt was born on Kos, thus securing it the protection of Egypt, under which it became a prosperous trading centre. In 130 BC Kos came under Roman domination, and in the 1st century AD it was administered by Rhodes, with which it came to share the same vicissitudes, right up to the tourist deluge of the present day.

Getting There & Away

AIR

There are three flights daily to Athens (€93, 55 minutes) and three flights a week each to Rhodes (€41, 20 minutes), Leros (€31, 15 minutes) and Astypalea (€46, one hour). **Olympic Airlines** (☎ 22420 28330; www.olympicairlines .com; Vasileos Pavlou 22) is in Kos Town. The **airport** (☎ 22420 51229) is 24km from Kos Town near the village of Antimahia.

FERRY

Domestic

Kos is well connected with all the islands in the Dodecanese and to Piraeus, with additional connections to the Cyclades. In summer there is a weekly ferry service from Kos Town to Samos and Thessaloniki. Services are offered by three ferry companies: **Blue Star Ferries** (☎ 22420 28914), **G&A Ferries** (☎ 22420 28545) and the **F/B Nisos Kalymnos** (☎ 22420 29900).

Sample fares: Rhodes (€17.50, 3½ hours), Piraeus (€38, 12 to 15 hours), Patmos (€14, four hours). Local ferries run to Pothia on Kalymnos from both Mastihari (€3.50, one hour, four daily) and Kos Town (€5, 1½ hours, two daily).

International

There are daily excursions boats in summer travelling from Kos Town to Bodrum in Turkey (one hour, €34 return). Boats leave at 8.30am and return at 4.30pm. Cars can be shipped across to Bodrum on a 4pm Turkish ferry for a rather steep €100 one way; contact Exas Travel for schedules.

HYDROFOIL & CATAMARAN

Kos is served by Aegean Hydrofoils and the *Dodekanisos Express* and *Dodekanisos Pride* catamarans. In the high season there are daily services to and from Rhodes (€27, two hours), with good connections to all the major islands in the group, as well as Samos (€25, four hours), Ikaria (€26, 3½ hours) and Fourni (€25, 3½ hours) in the Northeastern Aegean.

Information and tickets are available from the many travel agents in Kos Town, though **Exas Travel** (☎ 22420 28545) or **Hermes Shipping Agency** (☎ 22420 26607) are two of the better agencies.

Getting Around

TO/FROM THE AIRPORT

An Olympic Airlines bus (€3) leaves the airline's office two hours before the main Olympic flights. The airport is 26km southwest of Kos Town. Kefalos buses stop at the big roundabout near the airport entrance. A taxi to/from the airport from Kos Town will cost around €20.

BUS

The **bus station** (☎ 22420 22292; Kleopatras 7) is just west of the Olympic Airlines office. Buses regularly serve all parts of the island as well as the all-important beaches on the south side of Kos. A bus to the beaches will cost around €3.

CAR, MOTORCYCLE & BICYCLE

There are numerous car, motorcycle and moped rental outlets. You'll be tripping over bicycles to rent; prices range from €5 for an old bone-shaker to €10 for a top-notch mountain bike.

EXCURSION BOAT

From Kos Town there are many boat excursions around the island and to other islands. Examples of return fares: Kalymnos €10; Pserimos, Kalymnos and Platy €20; and Nisyros €20. There is also a daily excursion boat from Kardamena to Nisyros (€14 return) and from Mastihari to Pserimos and Kalymnos. In Kos Town these boats line the southern arm of Akti Koundourioti.

TAXIS

Taxis congregate at a stand on the south side of the port.

TOURIST TRAIN

You can take a guided tour of Kos in the city's (vehicular) Tourist Train (€3, 20 minutes), which runs 10am to 2pm and 6pm to 10pm starting from the Municipality Building. Or take a train to the Asklipieion and back (return €3), departing on the hour, 9am to 6pm Tuesday to Sunday, from the Municipal Tourist Office .

KOS TOWN

pop 14,750

Kos Town, on the northeast coast, is the island's capital and main port. The New Town, although modern, is picturesque and lush, with an abundance of palms, pines, oleander and hibiscus. The Castle of the Knights dominates the port, and Hellenistic and Roman ruins are strewn everywhere. It's a pleasant enough place and can easily be covered on foot in half a day. The Old Town was destroyed by an earthquake in 1933 and only part of it exists intact today.

Orientation

The ferry quay is north of the castle. The central square of Plateia Eleftherias is south of the harbourside street, Akti Koundourioti, along Vasileos Pavlou. Kos' Old Town is a smallish area bounded by Akti Koundourioti, Kolokotroni, Eleftheriou Venizelou and

Vasileos Pavlou; though its souvenir shops, jewellers and boutiques denude it of any old-world charm.

Southeast of the castle, the waterfront is called Akti Miaouli. It continues as Vasileos Georgiou and then Georgiou Papandreou, which leads to the beaches of Psalidi, Agios Fokas and Therma Loutra.

Information

BOOKSHOPS

Newsstand (☎ 22420 30110; Riga Fereou 2) Sells foreign-language newspapers and publications.

EMERGENCY

Police (☎ 22420 22222) Shares the Municipality Building with tourist police.

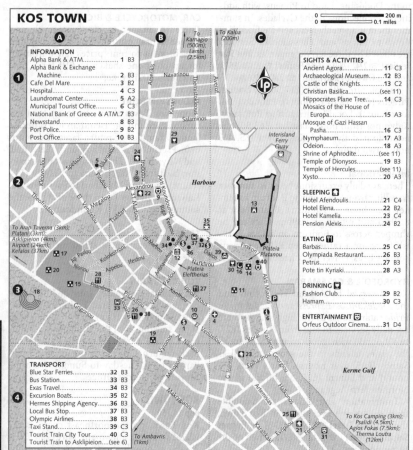

KOS TOWN

0 —————— 200 m
0 —————— 0.1 miles

INFORMATION	
Alpha Bank & ATM	1 B3
Alpha Bank & Exchange Machine	2 B3
Cafe Del Mare	3 B2
Hospital	4 C3
Laundromat Center	5 A2
Municipal Tourist Office	6 C3
National Bank of Greece & ATM	7 B3
Newsstand	8 B3
Port Police	9 B2
Post Office	10 B3

SIGHTS & ACTIVITIES	
Ancient Agora	11 C3
Archaeological Museum	12 B3
Castle of the Knights	13 C2
Christian Basilica	(see 11)
Hippocrates Plane Tree	14 C3
Mosaics of the House of Europa	15 A3
Mosque of Gazi Hassan Pasha	16 C3
Nymphaeum	17 A3
Odeion	18 A3
Shrine of Aphrodite	(see 11)
Temple of Dionysos	19 B3
Temple of Hercules	(see 11)
Xysto	20 A3

SLEEPING	
Hotel Afendoulis	21 C4
Hotel Elena	22 B2
Hotel Kamelia	23 C4
Pension Alexis	24 B2

EATING	
Barbas	25 C4
Olympiada Restaurant	26 B3
Petrus	27 B3
Pote tin Kyriaki	28 A3

DRINKING	
Fashion Club	29 B2
Hamam	30 C3

ENTERTAINMENT	
Orfeus Outdoor Cinema	31 D4

TRANSPORT	
Blue Star Ferries	32 B3
Bus Station	33 B3
Exas Travel	34 B3
Excursion Boats	35 B2
Hermes Shipping Agency	36 B3
Local Bus Stop	37 B3
Olympic Airlines	38 B3
Taxi Stand	39 C3
Tourist Train City Tour	40 C3
Tourist Train to Asklipieion	(see 6)

To Kamagio (500m); Lambi (2.5km)

To Kalua (200m)

Navarinou

Interisland Ferry Quay

Harbour

Alexandrou

To Arap Taverna (3km); Platani (3km); Asklipieion (4km); Airport (24km); Kefalos (37km)

Plateia Platanou

Plateia Eleftherias

To Ambavris (1km)

Kerme Gulf

To Kos Camping (3km); Psalidi (4.5km); Agios Fokas (7.5km); Therma Loutra (12km)

DODECANESE

Port police (cnr Akti Koundourioti & Megalou Alexandrou)
Tourist police (☎ 22420 22444)

INTERNET ACCESS
Cafe Del Mare (☎ 22420 24244; www.cybercafé.gr;
Megalou Alexandrou 4; per hr €4.50; ☽ 9am-1am) Has
Internet access.

INTERNET RESOURCES
www.kos-familyhotels.gr Alternative accommodation
site with more options.
www.koshotels.gr Comprehensive guide to Kos'
accomodation.

LAUNDRY
Laundromat Center (Alikarnassou 124; wash & dry €8)

MEDICAL SERVICES
Hospital (☎ 22420 22300; Ippokratous 32) In the centre
of town.

MONEY
Alpha Bank (Akti Koundourioti) Has a 24-hour automatic
exchange machine. Like most banks it also has an ATM, as
does the branch on El Venizelou.
National Bank of Greece (Riga Fereou) With ATM.

POST
Post office (El Venizelou)

TOURIST INFORMATION
Municipal Tourist Office (☎ 22420 24460; www
.kosinfo.gr; Vasileos Georgiou 1; ☽ 8am-2.30pm &
3-10pm Mon-Fri, 9am-2pm Sat May-Oct) Has general
information on Kos Town.

TRAVEL AGENCIES
Exas Travel (☎ 22420 28545) Hydrofoil and catamaran
tickets.

Sights
ARCHAEOLOGICAL MUSEUM
There's a fine 3rd-century-AD mosaic in
the vestibule of the **archaeological museum**
(☎ 22420 28326; Plateia Eleftherias; admission adult/stu-
dent €3/2; ☽ 8am-2.30pm Tue-Sun). The most renowned statue is that of Hippocrates.

ARCHAEOLOGICAL SITES
The **ancient agora** (admission free) is an open site
south of the castle. A massive 3rd-century-
BC stoa, with some reconstructed columns,
stands on its western side. On the north side
are the ruins of a **Shrine of Aphrodite**, **Temple of
Hercules** and a 5th-century **Christian basilica**.

North of the agora is the lovely cobblestone Plateia Platanou, where you can pay
your respects to the **Hippocrates Plane Tree**,
under which Hippocrates is said to have
taught his pupils. Plane trees don't usually
live for more than 200 years, though in all
fairness this is certainly one of Europe's
oldest. This once-magnificent tree is held
up with scaffolding, and looks to be in its
death throes. Beneath it is an old sarcophagus converted by the Turks into a fountain. Opposite the tree is the well-preserved
18th-century **Mosque of Gazi Hassan Pasha**, its
ground-floor loggia now converted into
souvenir shops.

From Plateia Platanou a bridge leads
across Finikon (called the Ave of Palms)
to the **Castle of the Knights** (☎ 22420 27927; Leof
Finikon; admission €4; ☽ 8am-2.30pm Tue-Sun). Along
with the castles of Rhodes Town and Bodrum, this impregnable fortress was the
knights' most stalwart defence against the
encroaching Ottomans. The castle, which
had massive outer walls and an inner keep,
was built in the 14th century. Damaged
by an earthquake in 1495, it was restored
by the Grand Masters d'Aubuisson and
d'Amboise (each a master of a 'tongue' of
knights – see p282 for more on this) in
the 16th century. The keep was originally
separated from the town by a moat (now
Finikon).

On the west of the town, facing Grigoriou,
turn right to reach the **western excavation site**.
Two wooden shelters at the back of the site
protect the 3rd-century mosaics of the **House
of Europa**. The best-preserved mosaic depicts
Europa's abduction by Zeus in the guise of
a bull. In front of here is an exposed section
of the **Decumanus Maximus** (the Roman city's
main thoroughfare) which runs parallel to the
modern road, then turns right towards the
nymphaeum, which consisted of once-lavish
latrines, and the **xysto**, a large Hellenistic
gymnasium with restored columns. On the
opposite side of Grigoriou is the restored
3rd-century **odeion**. The **Temple of Dionysos**
consist of a few scant ruins and is located a
short distance from the main site.

Sleeping
Pension Alexis (☎ 22420 28798; fax 22420 25797; Irodotou 9; s/d €25/30 ☒) This convivial travellers'
pension has long been a budget favourite
with visitors to the island. It has very clean

rooms, a communal kitchen and a large relaxing veranda and garden.

Hotel Afendoulis (☎ 22420 25321; fax 22420 25797; afendoulishotel@kos.forthnet.gr; Evripilou 1; s/d €35/50; 🖳 🐱) The ebullient, English-speaking Alexis Zikas runs this very relaxed, traveller-friendly establishment. The rooms are tastefully decorated and all have phones. Breakfast is optional, but is offered until late in case you are a late riser.

Hotel Kamelia (☎ 22420 28983; fax 22420 27391; kamelia_hotel@hotmail.com; Artemisias; s/d €25/45) On a quiet tree-lined street, the Kamelia is a pleasant C-class hotel with simple but comfortable rooms.

Hotel Elena (☎ 22420 22740; Megalou Alexandrou 7; d/tr €24/31) This D-class hotel is a reasonable budget option, though it looks a little tired and old at first glance.

Kos Camping (☎ 22420 23275; Psalidi; sites per adult/tent €6.50/4) This site, 3km along the eastern waterfront, is Kos' only camping ground. It's a well-kept, shaded site with a taverna, snack bar, kitchen and laundry.

Eating

The restaurants lining the central waterfront are generally expensive and poor value; avoid them and head for the backstreets or even further afield.

Barbas (☎ 2240 027856; Evripilou 6; mains €3-5) Right opposite Hotel Afendoulis is this busy little *psistaria* (restaurant serving grilled food) with streetside tables and fetching décor. The grills are the speciality and the chicken *souvlaki* or fillet is to die for: it's succulent and melts in your mouth. The chef also serves up a range of equally delicious *mayirefta*.

Olympiada Restaurant (☎ 22420 23031; Kleopatras 2; mains €3.50-4) For reliable, predictable and unfussy food, the unpretentious Olympiada behind the Olympic Airlines office delivers the goods, among which are a variety of stuffed dishes – tomatoes, aubergines, zucchini and vine leaves to name but a few.

Pote tin Kyriaki (☎ 22420 27872; Pisandrou 9; mezedes €3.50-5; 🕑 dinner, closed Sun) You can't get more untouristy than this quirky, *ouzeri*-style restaurant, with its idiosyncratic owner and menus written by hand in school exercise books. The food is topnotch too. Try the various styles of *pites* (pies) and *mezedes*.

Karnagio (☎ 22420 27900; Ethelondon Polemiston & Filinou; specials €7.50-16.50) If you see the owner in a wetsuit don't be surprised. He catches the fish for the restaurant, so it's fresh. Apart from fish, the specials are inventive, including paella, stuffed squid, pot-baked prawns and filling fish soup.

Arap Taverna (Memis; ☎ 22420 28442; Platani; mains €4-7) It's worth the slight detour to reach this Turkish-influenced restaurant on the main square in Platani, 3km southwest from Kos town. Go for the yogurt-flavoured dishes like *yiaourtoglou* (fried aubergines and courgette slices in yogurt), or *kavourma* (pork cubes with hot green chillies in a tomato sauce).

Ambavris (☎ 22420 25696; mains €4-8) For sheer ambience as well as top-quality food walk 15 minutes south out of town to this relaxed and totally non-touristy taverna. You would not know about this place if you hadn't read about it. Unassuming, quality dishes are all served up with a smile and good attitude.

Petrus (☎ 22420 49480; Ippokratous 3; mains €16-24) Petrus is a classy bistro-wine bar featuring a European-Greek menu with French and Swiss overtones. There's a tempting selection of cold salads, grills and specials. Memorable is the delectable stuffed chicken with ham and parmesan cheese, or the roast partridge with fresh vegetables combined tastefully with olive oil, oregano and pepper. An extensive wine list offers a choice of between 30 and 40 top-class wines.

Entertainment

Kos Town has two streets of bars, Diakon and Nafklirou, that positively pulsate in the high season.

Hamam (Akti Koundourioti 1) Most bars belt out techno, but this plays Greek music.

Fashion Club (☎ 22420 22592; Kanari 2) One of Kos Town's more popular and longer-standing clubs, with three bars to wet your whistle in.

Kalua (☎ 22420 24938; Akti Zouroudi 3) Further round the north side of the harbour, Kalua serves up a mixed menu of music, including R&B. It's an outdoor venue and also has a swimming pool.

Orfeus (☎ 22420 25036; Fenaretis 3; adult €6; 🕑 summer only) This outdoor cinema screens a wide range of movies.

HIPPOCRATES – THE FIRST GP

Hippocrates is often called the father of medicine, yet little is known for certain about his life. He is believed to have lived between 460 and 377 BC, but 'facts' about his birth and medical practices owe more to mythology than to hard evidence. The earliest known biography of him is *Life of Hippocrates* by Soranus, a Roman physician, published about AD 100, more than 400 years after Hippocrates' death.

Hippocrates' fame probably resulted from about 80 anonymously written medical works that became part of the collection of the Library of Alexandria after about 200 BC. These writings became linked with Hippocrates and are known by scholars as the *Hippocratic corpus*. However, it cannot be proved that Hippocrates actually wrote any of them.

Hippocrates' medicinal methods challenged the practices of many physicians, who hitherto had used magic and witchcraft to treat disease. They taught that diseases had natural causes and could therefore be studied, and possibly cured, according to the workings of nature. With Hippocratic medicine, a well-trained physician could cure illness with knowledge gained from medical writings or from experience. Modern medicine is based on this assumption.

AROUND KOS TOWN
Asklipieion Ασκληπιείον

The island's most important ancient site is the **Asklipieion** (☎ 22420 28763; Platani; admission adult/student €4/3; ⏰ 8.30am-6pm Tue-Sun), built on a pine-covered hill 3km southwest of Kos Town. From the top there is a wonderful view of Kos Town and Turkey. The Asklipieion consisted of a religious sanctuary to Asclepius (the god of healing), a healing centre and a school of medicine, where the training followed the teachings of Hippocrates.

Hippocrates was the first known doctor to have a rational approach to diagnosing and treating illnesses. Until AD 554, when an earthquake destroyed the Asklipieion, people came from far and wide to be treated here, as well as for medical training.

The ruins occupy three levels. The **propylaea** (approach to the main gate), Roman-era public **baths** and remains of guest rooms are on the first level. On the next level is a 4th-century-BC **altar of Kyparissios Apollo**. West of this is the **first Temple of Asclepius**, built in the 4th century BC. To the east is the 1st-century-BC **Temple to Apollo**; seven of its columns have been re-erected. On the third level are the remains of the once-magnificent 2nd-century-BC **Temple of Asclepius**.

Frequent buses and the Tourist Train go to the site, but it is pleasant to cycle or walk there.

AROUND KOS

Kos' main road runs southwest from Kos Town, with turn-offs for the mountain villages and the resorts of Tingaki and Marmari.

Between the main road and the coast is a quiet road, ideal for cycling, winds through flat agricultural land as far as Marmari.

The nearest decent beach to Kos Town is the crowded **Lambi Beach**, 4km to the northwest. Further round the coast, **Tingaki**, 10km from Kos Town, has an excellent, long pale-sand beach. **Marmari Beach**, 4km west of Tingaki, is slightly less crowded. Windsurfing is popular at all three beaches. In summer, there are boats from Marmari to the island of Pserimos.

Vasileos Georgiou (later G Papandreou) in Kos Town leads to the three crowded beaches of **Psalidi**, 3km from Kos Town, **Agios Fokas** (7km), and **Therma Loutra** (11km). The latter has hot mineral springs that warm the sea.

Mastihari Μαστιχάρι

Mastihari (mas-ti-*ha*-ri), north of Antimahia and 30km from Kos Town, is an important village in its own right. It's a resort destination, but also an arrival/departure point for ferries to Pothia on Kalymnos. It is better equipped to cater for independent travellers, with a good selection of *domatia* all within a hop, skip and jump of an excellent, though sometimes windy, beach. Mastihari is just that little bit more 'Greek' than Marmari and Tingaki. From here there are also excursion boats to Kalymnos and the island of Pserimos, where there's a decent beach and a couple of tavernas.

There are plenty of accommodation choices in Mastihari and many cater to independent travellers. Among these options

DODECANESE

is the pleasant **Rooms to Rent Anna** (☎ 22420 59041; d €25-35), 200m inland along the main road and on the left. **To Kyma** (☎ 22420 59045; kyma@kosweb.com; s/d €30/35) is a pleasant, small, family-run hotel with smallish but presentable rooms that enjoy a good sea breeze. There is a clean and homely communal kitchen for guests' use. Overlooking the west beach, **Rooms Panorama** (☎ /fax 22420 59145; studios €30; ❄) are tidy, fully-equipped studios, most of which have a kitchenette.

Right on the central square, the busy **Kali Kardia Restaurant** (☎ 22420 59289; fish €7-11) is commendable – the fish is particularly good – as is laid-back **O Makis** (☎ 22420 59061; mains €4-7), which serves as a taverna and grill house, with lots of good salads also on offer.

Mountain Villages

Several attractive villages are scattered on the northern slopes of the green and wooded alpine-like Dikeos mountain range. At **Zipari**, 10km from the capital, a road to the southeast leads to **Asfendiou**. Along the way, 3km past Zipari, you will pass **Taverna Panorama** (☎ 22420 69367; mezedes €3-5; ☺ evenings), which enjoys a great night-time view with barely a tourist in sight, as most head for Zia. Enjoy good *mezedes* and excellent service in the company of a mainly Greek clientele.

From Asfendiou, a turn-off to the left leads to the pristine hamlet of **Agios Dimitrios**. The road straight ahead leads to the village of **Zia**, which is touristy but worth a visit for the surrounding countryside, honey, herbs and spices, and some great sunsets.

For eating choices in Zia the almost out-of-sight **Kefalovrysi** (☎ 22420 69605; mains €5-8), a six-minute walk from the square to the upper end of the village, takes top marks for its well priced, high-quality cuisine. Among the more original choices are tomato balls, *salamoura* (pork cubes with onions) and Florina peppers stuffed with cheese. Also in Zia, **Taverna Olympia** (☎ 22420 69121; mains €4.50-7) is a less obvious choice – as it doesn't have the views – but it earns its good reputation based on solid, reliable local cuisine and repeat clientele.

Lagoudi is a small, unspoilt village to the northwest of Zia. From here you can continue to **Amaniou** (just before modern Pyli) where there is a left turn to the ruins of

the medieval village of **Pyli**, overlooked by an interesting ruined **castle**. The village of Pyli has a pleasant eating venue in **Palia Pygi** (☎ 22420 41510; mains €5-7), a little taverna overlooking a lion-headed fountain just off the central square. It serves up fragrant grills and filling *mayirefta*.

Kamari & Kefalos Bay Καμάρι & Κέφαλος

From Antimahia the main road continues southwest to the huge Kefalos Bay, fringed by a 12km stretch of sand, which is divided into roughly seven 'name' beaches, forming the soft sandy, underbelly of Kos. Each is signposted from the main road. The most popular is **Paradise Beach**, while the most undeveloped is **Exotic Beach**; **Banana Beach** (also known as Langada Beach) is a good compromise.

Agios Stefanos Beach at the far western end is dominated by a vast Club Med complex. The beach, reached along a short turn-off from the main road, is still worth a visit to see the island of **Agios Stefanos** (named after its church), which is within swimming distance, and the ruins of two 5th-century basilicas to the left of the beach as you face the sea.

Kefalos, 43km southwest of Kos Town, is a sprawling village perched high above **Kamari Beach**. It's a pleasant place with few concessions to tourism. The central square, where the bus terminates, is at the top of the 2km road from the coast. There is a post office and bank with an ATM here.

Daily excursion boats leave from Kamari for Nisyros (€16). There are a couple of sleeping and eating places worth seeking out; walk about 150m west from the seafront bus stop to find them. **Anthoula Studios** (☎ 22420 71904; studios €39) is a spotless set of airy and roomy studios surrounded by a flourishing vegetable garden. Also nearby, **Rooms to Let Katerina** (☎ 22420 71397; studios €38) are a similar choice, although they are a bit smaller. For eating **Stamatia** (☎ 22420 71245; mains €3-7) has been in business since 1935 and stands apart from the general mediocrity, with a good range of well-prepared classic fish and meat dishes.

The southern peninsula has the island's most wild and rugged scenery. **Agios Theologos Beach** is on the east coast, 7km from Kefalos at the end of a winding sealed road. You can't miss **Restaurant Agios Theologos**

(☎ 69745 03556; fish €9-11), which enjoys the best sunsets in Kos, as well as serving up good fish dishes such as white snapper, plus home-made goats' cheese and scrumptious home-baked bread.

ASTYPALEA ΑΣΤΥΠΑΛΑΙΑ

pop 1238

Astypalea (ah-stih-*pah*-lia), the most westerly island of the archipelago, is a butterfly-shaped hideaway that is more often than not missed by even seasoned travellers to the region. It is the kind of place you go to 'get away' and often end up staying. Treeless in the main, with bare, gently contoured hills, green valleys and sheltered coves, activity is centred upon an appealing hill-top *hora* (main town), a lively port, and a couple of small and unassuming beach resorts – all with an instant appeal.

Astypalea is also an island in search of a sense of belonging. Geographically and architecturally it is more akin to the Cyclades, but administratively it is a Dodecanese island. Sited more or less equidistant between its nearest Cycladic neighbour, Amorgos to the northwest, and its fellow Dodecanese island, Kos to the east, Astypalea effectively has a foot in both camps. The island undergoes a short, sharp summer season from mid-July to mid-August, when accommodation, unless prebooked, is almost impossible to find. The best time to visit is June or September.

Getting There & Away

AIR

There are five flights weekly from Astypalea to Athens (€53, 50 minutes) plus three flights weekly to Leros (€41, 20 minutes), Kos (€46, one hour) and Rhodes (€46, 1½ hours). **Astypalea Tours** (☎ 22430 61571), in Astypalea Town, is the agent for Olympic Airlines.

FERRY

Astypalea has up to five services a week in summer to Piraeus (€32, 10 to 12 hours) via Naxos (€22, 3¾ hours) and Paros (€26, 4¾ hours) and two a week to Rhodes (€18, seven to nine hours) via Kalymnos and Kos.

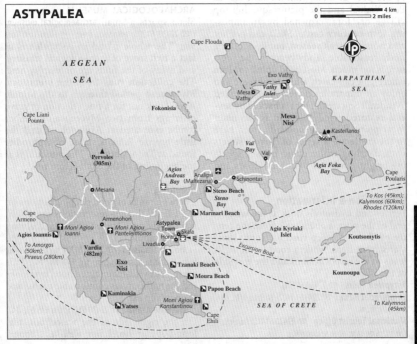

ASTYPALEA

The local ferry *F/B Nisos Kalymnos* calls in three times a week, linking the island with Kalymnos. Ferry tickets are available from **Paradisos Ferries Agency** (☎ 22430 61224; fax 22430 61450; www.astypalea-paradissos.com) or from **Astypalea Tours** (☎ 22430 61571).

Getting Around
BUS
From Skala a bus travels three times daily to Hora and Livadia (€1) and from Hora and Skala to Analipsi (Maltezana) (€1.50) via Marmari Beach. There are three taxis on the island. Hire cars or scooters from **Vergoulis** (☎ 22430 61351) in Skala.

EXCURSION BOAT
From June to August there is a daily excursion boat the *Seabird* (☎ 69744 36338) to the more remote western beaches of Agios Ioannis, Kaminakia and Vatses, or to the islets of Koutsomytis or Kounoupa. Tickets (€10) can be bought on the boat.

SKALA & HORA ΣΚΑΛΑ & ΧΩΡΑ
The main settlement of Astypalea consists of the port of Skala (known officially as Pera Yialos) and the picturesque hill-top village of Hora, crowned by an imposing 15th-century castle. Skala can get hot and noisy in peak season, but does offer a fairly reasonable sandy beach if the pressure is too much. Most head uphill to Hora where you can catch a hill-top breeze and enjoy an unparalleled view. The so-called Windmill Square in Hora is backed by several restored windmills and is the main focal point. Leading upwards from here to the castle are a series of narrow streets with dazzling-white cubic houses sporting brightly painted balconies, doors and banisters.

Orientation & Information
Ferries and hydrofoils dock at the western end of the port, a 300m walk from the centre of Skala. A steep road to Hora (1km) starts from here, while a road to the right leads to the airport (8km) and the east side of the island.
Astypalea Tours (☎ 22430 61571)
Commercial Bank (☎ 22430 61402) With an ATM, on the waterfront.
Municipal Tourist Office (☎ 22430 61412) Adjoins the quayside café; open seasonally.

Police (☎ 22430 61207) In a prominent Italianate building on the waterfront.
Port police (☎ 22430 61208) Co-located with the police.
Post office (☎ 22430 61223) At the top of the Skala–Hora road.
www.astypalaia.com Gives a good rundown on the island's facilities and sights.

Sights
CASTLE
Astypalea was occupied by the Venetian Quirini family, one of whom, Giovanni, built the imposing **castle** (admission free; ☾ dawn to dusk) starting in 1413. In the Middle Ages the population lived within its walls in order to escape the depredations of piracy that was rife in the Aegean Sea, but gradually the settlement outgrew them. The last inhabitants left in 1953, following a devastating earthquake, as a result of which the stone houses collapsed. Above the tunnel-like entrance is the **Church of Our Lady of the Castle** and within the walls is the **Church of Agios Giorgios**. The castle is currently being restored.

ARCHAEOLOGICAL MUSEUM
Skala sports a small **archaeological museum** (☎ 22430 61206; admission free; ☾ 11am-1pm Tue-Sun). The whole island of Astypalea is in fact a rich trove of archaeological treasure, and many of the finds are on display here. The collection runs from the prehistoric Mycenaean period through to the Middle Ages. Look out for a fine selection of grave offerings from two Mycenaean chamber tombs excavated at Armenohori, and the little bronze Roman statue of Aphrodite found at Trito Marmari. The museum is at the beginning of the Skala–Hora road.

Sleeping
There's a range of good sleeping options on the island, though reservations are essential in July and August as demand always exceeds supply.
Hotel Paradissos (☎ 22430 61224; fax 22430 61450; www.astypalea-paradisos.com; s/d €30/40; ✷) This ageing but well-maintained hotel overlooking the harbour has comfortable rooms and is open all year.
Hotel Australia (☎ 22430 61275; d/tr €45/50; ✷) On the right side of the waterfront, this long-popular hotel has well-kept rooms

with fridge and phone, and a friendly Greek-Australian owner. There's an excellent in-house restaurant too.

Avra Studios (☎ 22430 61363; d €50; ✖) For location you can't beat these five fully self-contained and spacious studios right on Skala beach. From the two front studios, with their own shaded patios, you are liter-ally 5m from the beach.

Akti Rooms (☎ 22430 61114; www.aktirooms.gr; d/tr €65/70; ✖) On the east side of the harbour, this block of rooms enjoys some superb harbour views from its balconies. All rooms have a fridge, phone and TV. Restaurant Akti, a popular restaurant and café, is here.

Eating

Restaurant eating tends to be good on Astypalea, though the choice of places is fairly limited.

To Akrogiali (☎ 22430 61863; mains €3-8.50) Dine on the beach, literally, or on a pleas-ant slate-paved patio punctuated by a huge tamarisk tree. The smell of freshly cooked food from the busy kitchen complements the friendly service and good-quality meals at this excellent taverna.

Restaurant Akti (☎ 22430 61114; mains €4-8.50) For the best harbourside dining seats in Astypalea, try this place. Perched high up, overlooking the harbour entrance, the few available tables are enormously popular and so is the food, which includes fisherman's pasta or *poungia* (local cheese foldovers).

Maïstrali (☎ 22430 61691; mains €4-8) Tucked away in the little street behind the harbour is this yachtie-popular eatery that has a pre-dictably fish-based menu, but occasional *mayirefta* such as succulent lemon goat. Service is brisk and friendly and dining is alfresco on the shaded, stepped veranda.

Barbarosa (☎ 22430 61577; mains €4-12; ✖ dinner) The best place to tempt your taste buds is here in Hora. Many of the meals are wok-cooked and ginger features prominently in some dishes, such as lamb with fennel and avocado. The stuffed pork with cheese and plum is another taste-bud tickler worth investigating.

LIVADIA ΛΙΒΑΔΕΙΑ

The little resort of Livadia lies in the heart of a fertile valley 2km from Hora. Its wide pebble-and-fine-gravel beach is one of the best on the island, but can get fairly

crowded in summer. There are at least a couple of recommendable sleeping options. First up are the smallish, but well-equipped **Venetos Studios** (☎ 22430 61490; fax 22430 61423; studios €50-60; ✖), set around a shady orange-tree grove. On the seafront itself are the neat studios of **Manganas** (☎ 22430 61468; fax 22430 59818; astyroom@otenet.gr; studios €50-60; ✖) some 20m from the beach and each with kitchenettes and fridges.

There are a handful of places to eat at Li-vadia. **Astropelos** (☎ 22430 61473; mains €4-6) serves up a small, but imaginative range of menu items, including the always popular pasta with lobster. **Trapezakia Exo** (☎ 22430 61083; snacks €3.50-4.50) is a neat little snack bar-restaurant at the western end of the beach strip. Snack on sandwiches or enjoy the cut-tlefish speciality.

EAST OF SKALA

To the east of Skala is the easterly wing of the 'butterfly' – the waist being marked by a narrow isthmus that barely joins the two halves of the island. **Marmari**, 2km northeast of Skala, has three bays with pebble-and-sand beaches and is home to Astypalea's **Camping Astypalea** (☎ 22430 61900; sites per adult/tent €5/3). Though it only operates from June to September, this shaded ground is right next to the beach and has a mini-market. **Steno Beach**, 2km further along, is one of the better but least frequented beaches on the island. It's sandy, has shade and is well protected. This is the point where the island is just 105m wide.

Analipsi (also known as Maltezana) is 7km beyond Marmari in a fertile valley on the isthmus. A former Maltese pirates' lair, it's a scattered, pleasantly laid-back settle-ment with a long sand and pebble beach, shaded by tamarisk trees. The water is clean and shallow. There are the remains of the **Tallaras Roman baths** with mosaics on the settlement's outskirts.

Accommodation is concentrated in Mal-tezana. **Maltezana Rooms** (☎ 22430 61446; fax 22430 61370; d €30) is a pretty reasonable op-tion, just east of the quay set back 50m from the beach. **Villa Varvara** (☎ /fax 22430 61448; studios €45/54; ✖) has 12 blue-and-white painted studios overlooking a veg-etable garden and is just 100m from the beach; all have TVs and fridges. The most expensive accommodation here, and on the island overall, is **Hotel Maltezana Beach** (☎ 22430 61558; fax 22430 61669; www.maltezana beach.gr; s/d €65/90; P ✖), on the middle section of the foreshore. The cubed, white studios are all tastefully decorated and rooms have TV, fridge and hairdryer.

Eating choices in Maltezana include **To Steki tou Manoli** (☎ 22430 61111; mains €3.50-5), which dishes up locally caught fish at a very reasonable price as well as a local take on bouillabaisse. There's also **Astakos** (☎ 22430 61865; mains €3-5) just over the headland at Schinontas. Try *strapatsada* (a wild-greens mélange mixed with egg yolk), or *bourloto* (a spicy cheese mix baked in the oven).

KALYMNOS ΚΑΛΥΜΝΟΣ

pop 16,441

Kalymnos (*kah*-lim-nos), only 2.5km south of Leros, is a mountainous and arid island, speckled with fertile valleys. Kalymnos is renowned as the 'sponge-fishing island', but with the demise of that industry it is now exploiting its tourist potential. It faces a tough job. The general diffidence of islanders towards tourists doesn't help, and while there is plenty on offer to entice travellers – good food, accommodation and rugged scenery – the pull of neighbouring Kos on the package-tourism industry is just too strong. New adventure enterprises in rock climbing are drawing growing numbers of visitors, however, and if you do make it across to Kalymnos via the local ferry you will find an island that is still generally in touch with its traditions.

Getting There & Away

AIR

Most people fly to Kos and transfer to the Mastihari–Pothia local ferry. Kalymnos' airport is scheduled to open in June 2006, however the angle of the runway means planes will only be able to land on days when the winds are favourable.

Olympic Airlines is represented by **Kapellas Travel** (☎ 22430 29265; fax 22430 51800; kapellas@klm.forthnet.gr) in Pothia.

FERRY

Kalymnos is linked to Rhodes (€16, five hours) and Piraeus (€26, 10 to 13 hours) and islands in between, including a useful

link to Astypalea (€10, three hours). Services are provided by **G&A Ferries** (☎ 22430 23700) and the **F/B Nisos Kalymnos** (☎ 22430 29612). In high season there is usually at least one ferry a day.

Car and passenger ferries leave between three and four times daily between 7am and 8pm from Pothia to Mastihari on Kos (€3, 50 minutes) and twice daily from Pothia to Kos Town (€5, 1½ hours). There are also services between Astypalea and Leros and Lipsi.

HYDROFOIL & CATAMARAN

Daily hydrofoils link Kalymnos with most islands in the north and south Dodecanese group, such as Rhodes (€35, 3½ hours) and Patmos (€20, 1½ hours), and Samos (€24, 3½ hours) in the Northeastern Aegean. Tickets can be bought from **Magos Travel** (☎ 22430 28777; magos@klm.forthnet .gr) in Pothia.

The *Dodekanisos Express* and *Dodekanisos Pride* catamarans call in four times daily during summer on their runs up and down the Dodecanese chain. Fares are similar to those of the hydrofoil. Tickets are issued by **G&A Ferries** (☎ 22430 23700).

There is a daily caïque (€7) from Myrties to Xirokambos on Leros at 1pm. and half-hourly services to Telendos.

Getting Around

BUS

In summer there is a bus departing from opposite the cathedral, on the hour, from Pothia to Masouri (€1) via Myrties, to Emborios (€1.50) and to Vathys (€1.50), four times daily. Buy tickets from Pilatos Minimarket in Pothia.

EXCURSION BOAT

From Myrties there is a daily excursion boat to Emborios (€7), leaving at 10am and returning at 4pm. Day trips to the **Kefalas Cave** (€19), impressive for its stalactites and stalagmites, run from both Pothia and Myrties.

TAXI

Shared taxis cost a little more than buses and run from the Pothia **taxi stand** (☎ 22430 50300; Plateia Kyprou) to Masouri. They can also be flagged down en route. A regular taxi to Myrties costs €5 and to Vathys €10.

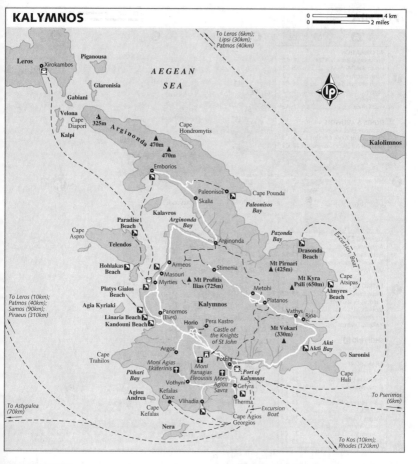

POTHIA ΠΟΘΙΑ

pop 10,500

Pothia (*poth*-ya), the port and capital of Kalymnos, is a fairly large town by Dodecanese standards. It is built amphitheatrically around the slopes of the surrounding valley, and its visually arresting melange of colourful mansions and houses draped over the hills makes for an particularly photogenic sight when you first arrive. While Pothia can be a tad brash and very busy, and its narrow vehicle-plagued streets a challenge to all pedestrians, it is nonetheless the focus of the island's life, and you will be passing through the main town at some point in your stay, even if you choose not to linger for very long.

Orientation & Information

Pothia's quay is located at the southern side of the port. Most activity, however, is centred on the main square, Plateia Eleftherias, abutting the lively waterfront. The main commercial centre is on Venizelou (more commonly known as Emboriki to the locals), along which are most of the shops.

The National, Commercial and Ionian Banks, all with ATMs, are close to the waterfront. The post office is a 10-minute walk northwest of Plateia Eleftherias.

Kapellas Travel (☎ 22430 29265; fax 22430 51800; kapellas@klm.forthnet.gr)

Magos Travel (☎ 22430 28777; magos@klm.forthnet.gr) Hydrofoil and catamaran tickets.

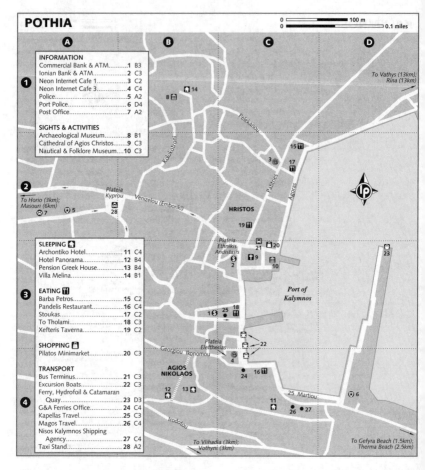

POTHIA

0   100 m
0   0.1 miles

INFORMATION
Commercial Bank & ATM............1 B3
Ionian Bank & ATM.....................2 C3
Neon Internet Cafe 1..................3 C2
Neon Internet Cafe 3..................4 C4
Police..5 A2
Port Police..................................6 D4
Post Office..................................7 A2

SIGHTS & ACTIVITIES
Archaeological Museum..............8 B1
Cathedral of Agios Christos........9 C3
Nautical & Folklore Museum....10 C3

SLEEPING 🏠
Archontiko Hotel........................11 C4
Hotel Panorama.........................12 B4
Pension Greek House..................13 B4
Villa Melina................................14 B1

EATING 🍴
Barba Petros...............................15 C2
Pandelis Restaurant...................16 C4
Stoukas......................................17 C2
To Tholami.................................18 C3
Xefteris Taverna.........................19 C2

SHOPPING 🛍
Pilatos Minimarket....................20 C3

TRANSPORT
Bus Terminus.............................21 C3
Excursion Boats..........................22 C3
Ferry, Hydrofoil & Catamaran
Quay.......................................23 D3
G&A Ferries Office.....................24 C4
Kapellas Travel...........................25 C3
Magos Travel..............................26 C4
Nisos Kalymnos Shipping
Agency....................................27 C4
Taxi Stand..................................28 A2

To Vathys (13km);
Rina (13km)

To Horio (3km);
Masouri (6km)

Plateia
Kyprou

Venizelou (Emboriki)

HRISTOS

Plateia
Ethnikis
Andistasis

Port of
Kalymnos

Plateia
Eleftherias

Georgiou Ikonomou

AGIOS
NIKOLAOS

Irodotou

To Vlihadia (3km);
Vothyni (3km)

25 Martiou

To Gefyra Beach (1.5km);
Therma Beach (2.5km)

Neon Internet Cafe 1 (☎ 22430 48318; per hr €5;
🕑 9.30am-midnight)
Neon Internet Cafe 2 (☎ 22430 28343; per hr €5;
Plateia Elefherias; 🕑 7.30am-midnight)
Police (☎ 22430 29301; Patriarhou Maximimou) Before
the post office.
Port police (☎ 22430 29304) On the port's eastern side.

Sights
North of Plateia Kyprou, housed in a neoclassical mansion that once belonged to a
wealthy sponge merchant, is the **Archaeological Museum** (☎ 22430 23113; admission adult/student
€2/1; 🕑 8.30am-2pm Tue-Sun). In one room there
are some Neolithic and Bronze-Age objects.
Other rooms are reconstructed as they were
when the Vouvalis family lived here.

In the centre of the waterfront is the
Nautical & Folklore Museum (☎ 22430 51361;
admission adult/student €2/1; 🕑 8am-1.30pm Mon-Fri,
10am-12.30pm Sat & Sun). Its collection is of traditional regional dress, plus a section on the
history of sponge diving.

Sleeping
While there is a fair selection of sleeping
options in Pothia, most travellers head out
of the town to the resorts. One good reason
to take a room in Pothia is to be on hand
to catch the notoriously early morning ferry
heading south.

Pension Greek House (☎ 22430 23752; s/d/studios
€20/30/35) This pension, inland from the port,
is a pleasant budget option with four cosy

wood-panelled rooms with kitchen facilities. More expensive and better-equipped studios are also available.

Hotel Panorama (☎ 22430 23138; smiksis2003@ yahoo.gr; s/d incl breakfast €25/45; ✦) This small hotel is situated high up and enjoys one of the best views in Pothia. The Panorama is clean and breezy and it has a pleasant breakfast area. Rooms have TV and fridge.

Archontiko Hotel (☎ /fax 22430 24149; s/d €35/45; ✦) At the southern end of the quay is this cool and pleasant hotel in a renovated century-old mansion. All the rooms have fridges, TV and phone.

Villa Melina (☎ 22430 22682; fax 22430 23920; antoniosantonoglu@yahoo.de; s/d €40/50; ✦ ✦) Pothia's most enticing accomodation is equally suitable for romantic couples seeking a hideaway, or travellers in search of old-world peace and quiet. This stately villa harks from another age, featuring palm trees, a lush garden and a swimming pool.

Eating

Xefteris Taverna (☎ 22430 28642; mains €3-5.50) This century-old and pretty basic taverna serves delicious, inexpensive food. The meal-sized dolmades and the *stifado* are recommended.

To Tholami (☎ 22430 51900; mains €3.50-5) This well-established eatery, tucked away on the seafront, is popular with locals and visitors alike. Recommended dishes are octopus patties and grilled tuna steaks.

Stoukas (☎ 22430 24546; mains €6-8) Of the handful of waterside *ouzeria* this one is about the closest you can get to the sea. Dishes are solid and well-cooked, and the service is friendly. The Kalymnian salad *mermizeli* features here, as does a rich prawn *saganaki* in tomato sauce, worth sampling.

Barba Petros (☎ 22430 29678; fish €6-11) Close to Stoukas on the eastern waterfront, this is another of the better and more reliable choices in town; the crab salad is a delicious and filling starter. Fish and grills are well prepared.

Pandelis Restaurant (☎ 22430 51508; mains €4.50-6) The specialities at this homely eatery are goat in red-wine sauce and the home-made dolmades, but all the food here is well worth the testing and tasting.

AROUND POTHIA

Running northwards from the port is a busy, densely populated valley with a series of almost contiguous settlements. The ruined **Castle of the Knights of St John** (or Kastro Hrysoherias) looms to the left of the Pothia–Horio road. There is a small **church** inside the battlements.

On the east side of the valley **Pera Kastro** was a pirate-proof village inhabited until the 18th century. Within the crumbling walls are the ruins of stone houses and six tiny, well-kept churches. Steps lead up to Pera Kastro from **Horio**; it's a strenuous climb but the splendid views make it worthwhile.

A tree-lined road continues from Horio to **Panormos** (also called Elies), a pretty village 5km from Pothia. Its pre-war name of Elies (olives) derived from its abundant olive groves, which were destroyed in WWII. An enterprising postwar mayor planted many trees and flowers to create beautiful panoramas wherever one looked – hence its present name, meaning 'panorama'. The sandy beaches of **Kandouni**, **Linaria** and **Platys Gialos** are all within walking distance of Panormos.

MYRTIES, MASOURI & ARMEOS
ΜΥΡΤΙΕΣ, ΜΑΣΟΥΡΙ & ΑΡΜΕΟΣ

From Panormos the road continues to the west coast, with stunning views of Telendos Islet, until it winds down into **Myrties** (myr-*tyez*), **Masouri** (mah-*soo*-ri) and **Armeos** (ar-*me*-os). These contiguous and busy resort centres host the lion's share of Kalymnos' modest package-holiday industry. The three centres are essentially one long street, packed head to tail with restaurants, bars, souvenir shops and minimarkets. Towards land, apartments and studios fill the hillside, while on the sea side an extinct volcano plug separates the dark sand beach into two distinct sections – Myrties beach, with Melitsahas harbour, and the marginally better Masouri and Armeos beaches.

There are exchange bureaus, car and motorcycle rental outlets and one Internet café.

In recent years Kalymnos has become something of a mecca for **rock climbers**. Some spectacular limestone walls backing the resorts now attract legions of climbers looking for some seriously challenging extreme sport. There are about 21 documented climbs awaiting the adventurous. The **Municipal Athletics Organisation** (☎/fax 22430 51601; www.kalymnos-isl.gr) is a good place to start for the full low-down on the activity that pulls in visitors from as early as March onwards.

Most accommodation in Masouri and Myrties is block-booked by tour groups, but there are a couple of places that deal with walk-ins. On the Myrties side of the resort strip are the 12 smallish, but comfy **Fotini Studios** (☎ 22430 47016; mmagoulias@yahoo .gr; d €32), each with a fridge and cooking ring. Every room has a view over the small harbour of Melitsahas. Towards Masouri, and occupying an excellent beachside location, **Acroyali** (☎ 22430 47521; acroyali@klm.forth net.gr; d/t €35/45; 🏠) is a set of impressive and spacious self-contained studios, just a few short metres from the beach. Each studio has a wide private balcony.

There's no shortage of places to eat. A top choice is **I Drosia** (☎ 22430 48745; seafood mezedes €5-12) overlooking Melitsahas harbour. Among the excellent *mezedes* on offer are *kalognomones* (local mussels), *ahini* (sea urchins) and a real treat – whole squid stuffed with creamy feta cheese.

In Masouri, **Kelly's** (☎ 22430 48390; mains €3-6) serves up breakfast, lunch and dinner with staples like *mousaka* and *stifado* and a smattering of French-influenced dishes. **Babis Bar** (☎ 22430 47864) in Myrties is a mix of food café, Internet joint, bar and general hangout, favoured by expats and travellers alike. It's a good spot for breakfast with all the trimmings.

From Myrties there's a daily caïque to Xirokambos on Leros (€7), and Emborios (€7) in the north of Kalymnos, as well as half-hourly boats to Telendos (below).

TELENDOS ISLET ΝΗΣΟΣ ΤΕΛΕΝΔΟΣ

The lovely, tranquil and (almost) traffic-free islet of Telendos, with a little quayside hamlet, was part of Kalymnos until separated by an earthquake in AD 554. Nowadays it's a great escape from the busy resort strip opposite.

If you turn right from Telendos' quay, you will pass the ruins of the early Christian **basilica** of Agios Vasilios. Further on, there are several pebble-and-sand beaches. To reach the far superior, 100m-long and fine-pebbled **Hohlakas Beach**, turn left from

the quay and then right at the sign to the beach. Follow the paved path up and over the hill for 10 minutes. **Paradise Beach** on the northern side of Telendos is a nudist haven. Walk for five minutes past On the Rocks Café and Rooms.

Telendos has quite a few rooms and one hotel to stay in. All have pleasant, clean rooms with bathroom. Opposite the quay is **George's** (☎ 22430 47502; d €25), while adjoining the café of the same name is **On the Rocks Cafe Rooms** (☎ 22430 48260; www.otr.telendos.com; studios €40; 🏠) offering four studios equipped with every convenience imaginable, including fridge, satellite TV, double glazing and mosquito nets. Guests can also access the Internet and will be picked up for free at Melitsahas harbour on Kalymnos.

Telendos' only hotel as such is **Hotel Porto Potha** (☎ 22430 47321; portopotha@klm.forthnet.gr; s/d €25/30; 🏊), 100m beyond On the Rocks Cafe. Rooms are airy and bright and there's a large lobby where guests come to relax and watch TV over a drink.

The best place to eat is **On the Rocks Cafe** (☎ 22430 48260; mains €5-8) where Greek-Australian owner, Georgos, serves well-prepared meat and fish dishes as well as vegetarian *mousaka*, and baked or grilled tuna and swordfish. It becomes a lively music bar at night – with over 300 cocktails to choose from – and on Friday and Monday evenings there are 'Greek Nights'.

In a little lane behind the waterfront, **Barba Stathis** (☎ 22430 47953; mains €5-6) does a great spin on octopus in red sauce and cooks up top-class stuffed peppers and tomatoes.

Caïques for Telendos depart every half-hour from the Myrties quay between 8am and 1am (one way €1.50).

EMBORIOS ΕΜΠΟΡΕΙΟΣ

The scenic west coast road winds a further 11.5km from Masouri to Emborios, where there's a pleasant, shaded sand-and-pebble beach, as well as a minimarket and **Artistico Café** (☎ 22430 40115) for evening entertainment that sometimes features live guitar renditions.

One of the better places to stay is **Harry's Apartments** (☎ 22430 40062; d/tr €27/33), made all the more attractive by its lush flower garden and adjoining **Paradise Restaurant** (☎ 22430 40062; mains €3.50-6.50) run by the charming

Evdokia. She rustles up a good line in vegetarian dishes such as *revithokeftedes* (chickpea rissoles) and *pites* with fillings such as aubergine, vegetables and onion. Stuffed courgette flowers is another one of her specialities.

VATHYS & RINA ΒΑΘΥΣ & ΡΙΝΑ

Vathys, 13km northeast of Pothia, is one of the most beautiful and peaceful parts of the island. Vathys means 'deep' in Greek and refers to the slender fjord that cuts through high cliffs into the fertile valley, where narrow roads wind between citrus orchards. There is no beach at Vathys' harbour, Rina, but you can swim off the jetty at the south side of the harbour. **Water taxis** (☎ 22430 31316) take tourists to quiet coves nearby.

Vathys has two places to stay, both at the little harbour of Rina. **Hotel Galini** (☎ 22430 31241; fax 22430 31100; d incl full breakfast €30) is marginally better on the basis of convenience. Higher up on the hill, however, and messier to get to with heavy luggage, is **Pension Manolis** (☎ 22430 31300; s/d €21/25), with neat basic rooms and private bathrooms enjoying the best views. The pension has a communal kitchen and is surrounded by an attractive garden.

A few harbourside tavernas ring the port. Of these **Restaurant Galini** (☎ 22430 31241; mains €4-5) is part of Hotel Galini and is a friendly place to eat. Roast local pork and grilled octopus are two of its recommended dishes. In a stone-clad building opposite is the cosy and intimate **Taverna tou Limaniou** (The Harbour's Taverna; ☎ 22430 31206; mains €4.50-5.50). Ask for the pork and chicken special, or the garlic prawn *saganaki*.

LEROS ΛΕΡΟΣ

pop 8207

Travellers looking for an island that is unmistakably Greek and still relatively untouched by mass commercial tourism will find it on Leros. This medium-sized island in the northern Dodecanese offers an attractive mix of sun, sea, rest and recreation, a stunning medieval castle and some excellent dining opportunities. It has a comfortable 'lived-in' feel and enjoys a life of its own outside the frenzy of mass tourism encountered on some of the more commercialised islands in the group.

Leros also offers gentle hilly countryside, dotted with small fields and huge, impressive, almost landlocked bays, which look more like lakes than open sea. The immense natural harbour at Lakki was the principal naval base of the Italians in the eastern Mediterranean, and is now a curious living architectural museum of Fascist Italian Art-Deco buildings.

Getting There & Away

AIR

There is a flight daily to Athens (€54, one hour) as well as three flights a week to Rhodes (from €41, two hours 10 minutes) via Kos (from €38, 15 minutes). There are also three flights a week to Astypalea (from €39, 10 minutes). **Olympic Airlines** (☎ 22470 22844; www.olympicairlines.com) is in Platanos, before the turn-off for Pandeli. The **airport** (☎ 22470 22777) is near Partheni in the north. There is no airport bus.

EXCURSION BOAT

The caïque *Katerina* leaves Xirokambos at 7.30am daily for Myrties on Kalymnos (one way €7). In summer the Lipsi-based caïques make trips between Agia Marina and Lipsi, while the Patmos-based *Patmos Star* links Leros with Lipsi and Patmos three times a week.

FERRY

Leros is on the main north–south route for ferries between Rhodes and Piraeus. There are daily departures from Lakki to Piraeus (€26, 11 hours), Kos (€8.50, 3¼ hours) and Rhodes (€19.50, 7¼ hours), as well as two weekly to Samos (€11, 3½ hours). Buy tickets at **Leros Travel** (☎ 22470 24000 in Lakki, ☎ 22470 23000 in Agia Marina).

HYDROFOIL & CATAMARAN

In summer hydrofoils and catamaran call in every day at Agia Marina, linking the island with Patmos (€13, 45 minutes), Lipsi (€10.60, 20 minutes), Samos (€22, two hours), Kos (€16.50, one hour) and Rhodes (€38, 3¼ hours).

Getting Around

The hub for Leros' buses is Platanos. There are four buses daily to Partheni via Alinda and six buses to Xirokambos via Lakki (€1 flat fare).

LEROS

0 — 2 km
0 — 1 mile

To Lipsi (10km);
Patmos (25km);
Samos (50km)

Trypiti

**Arhangelos
Islet**

Faradonisia

Cape
Tesmari

Strongyli

Chapel of
Agia Kioura

**Partheni
Bay**

Cape
Asfoungaros

**Blefoutis
Bay**

**Blefoutis
Beach**

Cape
Markelos

Mt Markelos
(264m) ▲

Temple of
Artemis

Partheni

Leros

▲ Mt Klidi
(320m)

Cape
Panosimi

**Agios
Nikolaos
Bay**

Cape
Katakrotiri

Alinda

**Alinda
Bay**

Cape Kastro

Kokkali

Agia
Marina

**Castle of
Pandeli**

Agios Isidoros

Krithoni

Cape Aspro

Gourna Bay

Gourna

Platanos
▲
204m

Pandeli

Drymonas

Cape
Ikonisma

Vromolithos

**Pandeli
Bay**

Agia Kyriaki

To Lipsi (15km);
Patmos (25km);
Piraeus (300km)

Mt Patelia
(248m) ▲

Lakki

To Kalymnos (20km);
Kos (35km)

Cape
Katsouni

**Lakki
Bay**

Lepida

▲
233m

Cape
Angistro

▲
255m

Paleokastro

Xirokambos

▲
288m

Piganousa

A E G E A N

S E A

Cape
Xirokambos

**Xirokambos
Bay**

Cape
Diapori

Gabiani

Velona

Kalpi

To Kalymnos (20km)

To Kalymnos (15km)

Car, motorcycle and bicycle rental outlets tend to be centered on the Alinda tourist strip. There are plenty of taxis.

LAKKI ΛΑΚΚΙ
pop 2366

Arriving at Lakki (lah-*kee*) by boat is akin to stepping into a long-abandoned Federico Fellini film set. The grandiose buildings and wide tree-lined boulevards dotted around the Dodecanese are best (or worst) shown here, for Lakki was built as a Fascist showpiece during the Italian occupation. Very few people linger in Lakki, though it has decent accommodation and restaurants, and there are some nice and secluded swimming opportunities on the road past the port. The port has Internet access and the town has banks and ATMs.

XIROKAMBOS ΞΗΡΟΚΑΜΠΟΣ

Xirokambos Bay, on the south of the island, is a low-key resort with a gravel-and-sand beach and some good spots for snorkelling. Just before the camping ground, on the opposite side, a signposted path leads up to the ruined fortress of **Paleokastro**.

Xirokambos is home to Leros' only camp site. **Camping Leros** (☎ 22470 23372; adult/tent €6.50/4.50) has tent sites that are interwoven into a shady olive grove. Look for it on the right 3km from Lakki. There is a small restaurant and bar on site and you'll also find **Panos Diving Club** (☎ 22470 23372; www.lerosdiving .com) here, offering a series of wreck dives and training courses.

For a spot of self-contained comfort, **Villa Alexandros** (☎ 22470 22202; d €48; 🞩) is a very presentable option. The self-contained studios each have a kitchenette and fridge, fly screens on the windows and look out onto a pleasant flower garden. You'll find it 150m back from the beach.

For eating, a good bet is **To Aloni** (☎ 22470 26048; mains €3.50-7). Abutting the beach this is a well-shaded and modern fish taverna. Fish dominates the menu but there is also an extensive array of *mezedes* dishes on offer.

PLATANOS & AGIA MARINA
ΠΛΑΤΑΝΟΣ & ΑΓΙΑ ΜΑΡΙΝΑ
pop 3500

Platanos (*plah*-ta-nos), the capital of Leros, is 3km north of Lakki. It's a bustling and picturesque village spilling over a narrow hill and pouring down to **Pandeli** to the south, and the port of **Agia Marina** (ay-*i*-a ma-*ri*-na) to the north. The bustling port has a more authentic ambience than the neighbouring **Alinda** resort a little further to the north, though there is no swimming to speak of. Platanos is the commercial centre of the island and is also the starting point for the path up to the **Castle of Pandeli** (☎ 22470 23211; admission castle €2, castle & museum €3; 🕒 8am-1pm & 5-8.30pm), from where there are stunning views in all directions around Leros; the museum is also worth a look.

Orientation & Information

The focal point of Platanos is the lively central square, Plateia N Roussou. From this square Harami leads to Agia Marina. The bus station and taxi rank are both about 50m along the Platanos–Lakki road.

The National Bank of Greece is on the central square. There are two ATMs at Agia Marina including a handy one at the port itself. Thepost office is on the right side of Harami, while the Tourist Information Kiosk is on Agia Marina quay.

Enallaktiko Café (☎ 22470 25746; per hr €4; 🕒 10am-midnight) Internet access; in Agia Marina.

Laskarina Tours (☎ 22470 24550; fax 22470 24551) In Platanos; very helpful and also organises trips around the island.

Police (☎ 22470 22222) In Agia Marina.

Sleeping & Eating

Tassos II Appartments (☎ /fax 22470 23769; Agia Marina; d €45; 🞩) These fully equipped studios with kitchen, ironing facilities, satellite TV, coffee maker, money safe and hairdryer, are excellent value. They are on the left along the main road leading to Alinda.

Crithoni Paradise Hotel (☎ 22470 25120; leros paradise@hotmail.com; s/d €90/125; 🅿 🞩 🞩) Complete with palm trees, bars, restaurant and relaxing lounges for afternoon cocktails, this A-class hotel is the best on the island.

Ouzeri-Taverna Neromylos (☎ 22470 24894; Agia Marina; mains €4-5.50) The most atmospheric of the tavernas at Agia Marina, this one is next to a former watermill. Night-time dining is best when lights illuminate the watermill.

Entertainment

Agia Marina is the heart of the island's nightlife, with several late-night music bars. Possibly the most lively hang-out is

DODECANESE

Enallaktiko Cafe where you can shoot pool, play video games or sip an ouzo on ice and chill out at sunset.

PANDELI & VROMOLITHOS
ΠΑΝΤΕΛΙ & ΒΡΩΜΟΛΙΘΟΣ

Head south from Platanos and you'll soon hit **Pandeli**, a little fishing village-cum-resort with a sand-and-shingle beach. Keep on going around the headland via the footpath and you'll stumble on **Vromolithos** where you'll find an even better, narrow shingly beach with some tree shade in the middle section. A scattering of sleeping and eating choices serve both settlements.

At a pinch Pandeli wins in the sleeping stakes as there's a bit more concentrated daytime activity and nightlife to pull in the punters. Easy to spot for its striking blue-and-white columned façade, **Rooms to Rent Kavos** (☎ 22470 23247; d €35) is a sensible choice. Rooms are largish, sport balconies and have fans and a fridge. Grab a front room if you want a harbour view. Up on the hill is the always popular **Pension Rodon** (☎ 22470 22075; d €30). Open year-round it is a reliable and welcoming choice with comfortable rooms.

At Pandeli, **Psaropoula** (☎ 22470 25200; mains €5-8) is right on the beach and is as good as any of the several tavernas plying their trade here. Psaropoula has a wide-ranging menu featuring fish; the prawn *souvlaki* with bacon is recommended.

KRITHONI & ALINDA ΚΡΙΘΩΝΙ & ΑΛΙΝΤΑ

Krithoni and Alinda are contiguous resorts on the wide Alinda Bay, running about 3km northwest from Agia Marina. Most of the action is concentrated at the Alinda end, where the only real danger is from the parades of kamikaze motorcyclists who roar indiscriminately up and down the narrow beachside road. The beach is pebbled and the water is very clean. Further to the north around the bay are some quieter coves and beaches.

On Krithoni's waterfront there is a poignant, well-kept **war cemetery**. After the Italian surrender in WWII, Leros saw fierce fighting between German and British forces; the cemetery contains the graves of 179 British, two Canadian and two South African soldiers.

Not surprisingly for the island's main resort area there are plenty of sleeping choices.

THE AUTHOR'S CHOICE

Dimitris o Karaflas (☎ 22470 25626; mezedes €3-7) You sometimes have to look high and wide to find something different in the culinary stakes in Greece. On Leros look no further than this truly outstanding *mezedopoleio* (restaurant specialising in *mezedes*). High up, overlooking Krithoni and Vromolithos, this popular eating locale would win on its views alone. While the basic fresh ingredients are the same as in most restaurants in Greece, it's the original way owner Dimitris 'the bald' combines them in a wide-ranging menu of *mezedes* (appetisers) that makes the difference. Delicious options include a cheese mix called *batiris*, or *pita kaisarias* a savoury pie featuring *pastourmas* (spicy smoked beef). Then there are main courses which include the bud-tickling chicken in retsina and pork in red sauce. Don't miss out on a real Lerian treat.

Hotel Gianna (☎ /fax 22470 24135; s/d €35/45) is just behind the war cemetery and far enough away from the 'strip' to be quiet. All rooms are pleasantly furnished. For some comfortable self-catering **Tassos Studios I** (☎ 22470 22769; fax 22470 23769; studios €42; 🖳) has beautiful, fully-equipped mini-apartments close to Krithoni beach, run by the same owners as Tassos II in Agia Marina.

Hotel Alinda (☎ 22470 23266; fax 22470 23383; s/d €30/40; 🖳) is an older style, but spick and span hotel, with 41 small but comfortable rooms offering good value for money. The highly regarded in-house restaurant does a good line in home-made *mayirefta*.

Finikas Taverna (☎ 22470 22695; mezedes €2.50-4.20) is a waterfront taverna in Alinda offering 15 types of salad and 20 different *mezedes*. When available, the delicious fish soup is worth opting for, as is the swordfish steak.

PATMOS ΠΑΤΜΟΣ

pop 3044

Patmos could well be the ideal Greek island destination, with a beguiling mix of qualities. It appeals in equal doses to the culturally inclined, the religiously motivated, gastronomes, sun worshippers, shoppers, yachties, bookaholics and travellers simply seeking to unwind. Patmos is a place of pilgrimage for both Orthodox and Western Christians, for it was here that St John wrote his divinely inspired revelation (the Apocalypse). Patmos is, without doubt, the best place to come and experience Orthodox Easter. Blessed with fine beaches and excellent food the island is instantly palatable, enticing the visitor to linger and to almost certainly return another time.

History

In AD 95, St John the Divine was banished to Patmos from Ephesus by the pagan Roman Emperor Domitian. While residing in a cave on the island, St John wrote the Book of Revelations. In 1088 the Blessed Christodoulos, an abbot who came from Asia Minor to Patmos, obtained permission from the Byzantine Emperor Alexis I Komninos to build a monastery to commemorate St John. Pirate raids necessitated powerful fortifications, so the monastery looks like a mighty castle.

Under the Duke of Naxos, Patmos became a semi-autonomous monastic state, and achieved such wealth and influence that it was able to resist Turkish oppression. In the early 18th century a school of theology and philosophy was founded by Makarios and it flourished until the 19th century.

Gradually the island's wealth became polarised into secular and monastic entities.

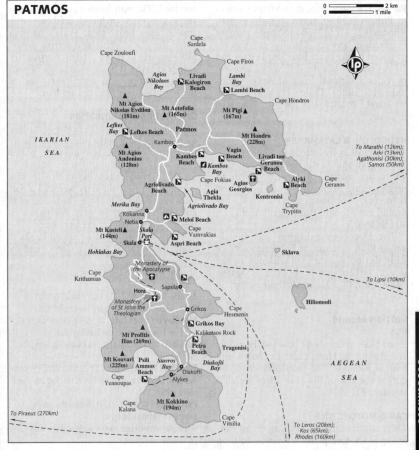

PATMOS

The secular wealth was acquired through shipbuilding, an industry that diminished with the arrival of the steam ship.

Getting There & Away

EXCURSION BOAT

The local **Patmos Star** (☎ 69776 01633) leaves Patmos daily for Lipsi and Leros at 10am (return €8) and returns from Lipsi at 3.30pm.

The Patmos-based **Delfini** (☎ 22470 31995) goes to Marathi every day in the high season and Monday and Thursday at other times (return €15). Twice a week it also calls in at Arki. From Marathi a local caïque will take you across to Arki (1¼ hours).

FERRY

Patmos is connected with two ferry services to Piraeus (€30.50, seven to eight hours), Rhodes (€27, six to 7½ hours) and a number of islands in between. Mainline services are provided by the faster Blue Star Ferries and G&A Ferries, while the *F/B Nisos Kalymnos* provides additional links to Arki, Agathonisi and Samos. Tickets are sold by **Apollon Travel** (☎ 22470 31324; apollontravel@stratas.gr) in Skala.

HYDROFOIL & CATAMARAN

There are daily hydrofoils to Rhodes (€22, 2½ hours) and destinations in between. There are additional services north to neighbouring Samos (€14, one hour) and Ikaria (€17, one hour). Twice a week a hydrofoil runs to and from Agathonisi (€13, 40 minutes).

The *Dodekanisos Express* and *Dodekanisos Pride* catamarans link Patmos twice daily during summer with islands to the south. Tickets can be bought at **Apollon Travel** (☎ 22470 31324; apollontravel@stratas.gr) in Skala.

Getting Around

BUS

From Skala there are 11 buses daily in July and August to Hora, eight to Grikos and four to Kambos. The frequency drops off during the rest of the year. Fares are all a standard €1.

CAR & MOTORCYCLE

There are motorcycle and car rental outlets in Skala. Competition is fierce, so shop around. **Australis Motor Rentals** (☎ 22470 32723) rents scooters for around €10 per day.

EXCURSION BOAT

Boats go to Psili Ammos beach from Skala, departing about 10.30am and returning about 4pm.

TAXI

Taxis (☎ 22470 31225) congregate at Skala's taxi rank. Sample fares include Meloï Beach €3, Lambi €6, Grikos €4 and Hora €4.

SKALA ΣΚΑΛΑ

Patmos' port town is Skala (*ska*-la), a bright and glitzy place, draped around a curving bay and only visible from arriving ships once the protective headland has been rounded. The port bustles and large cruise ships are often anchored offshore while smaller ones heave to at Skala's harbour. Once the cruise ships and ferries depart, Skala reverts to being a fairly normal, livable port town. It has a wide range of good accommodation and restaurants, and all the island's major facilities are here.

Orientation & Information

All transport arrives at the centre of the long quay, smack bang in the middle of Skala. To the right the road leads to the yacht port at Netia and on to the north of the island. To the left the road leads to the south side of the island. From near the ferry terminal a road leads inland and up to Hora. The bus terminal and taxi rank are at the quay. All main services are within 100m of the ferry quay.

There are two ATM-equipped banks in Skala: the National Bank of Greece and the Commercial Bank.

Apollon Travel (☎ 22470 31324; apollontravel@stratas.gr)

Astoria Travel (☎ 22470 31205; fax 22470 31975) On the waterfront near the quay, has helpful staff.

Blue Bay Internet Café (☎ 22470 31165; per hr €5; ☒ 9am-2pm; 4-8pm) At the Blue Bay Hotel.

Hospital (☎ 22470 31211) Two kilometres along the road to Hora.

Municipal Tourist Office (☎ 22470 31666; ☒ summer only) Shares the same building as the post office and police station.

Port police (☎ 22470 31231) Behind the quay's passenger-transit building.

www.patmos-island.com A useful website with information on Patmos.

Sleeping

BUDGET

Hotel and studio owners usually meet all arrivals at the port, but it's best to call ahead and arrange a pick up, as mainline ferries often arrive at unsocial hours.

Pension Maria Pascalidis (☎ 22470 32152; s/d €15/20) One of the better budget options is this place, on the road leading to Hora. The simple but quite presentable rooms are set amid a leafy citrus-tree garden.

Yvonne's Studios (☎ 22470 33066; s/d €30/40) These very pleasant self-contained studios are in the street behind the waterfront in quiet Hohlakas Bay. Call into Yvonne's shop in Skala and ask for Theologos.

Domatia Katina (☎ /fax 22470 31327; s/d €35/45) These four tidy rooms are out on the northern edge of Skala and each have good views, a kitchenette and a four-post bed. The ever-hospitable Katina will pick you up from the port if you call ahead.

Pension Avgerinos (☎ /fax 22470 32118; d €44) In a slightly quieter, elevated part of Netia, affording good views over the bay, this homely choice is run by a welcoming Greek-Australian couple. All rooms are cosy and comfortable.

MIDRANGE

Captain's House (☎ 22470 31793; s/d incl breakfast €55/75; 🖭 🔀) Each comfortable room here has a TV, fridge and phone. The front rooms have the best views but do get the noise from the often boisterous nightlife nearby.

Doriza Bay Hotel (☎ 22470 32702; fax 22470 33141; www.portoscoutari.com; d/maisonettes €40/65; 🔀) High above the south side of Hohlakas Bay is this new (in 2005) complex. Choose a spacious two-storey maisonette with internal spiral staircase, or a very comfortable double room.

Hotel Blue Bay (☎ 22470 31165; www.bluebay.50g .com; s/d incl breakfast €72/109; 🖳 🔀) This Australian-Greek–owned waterfront hotel has very clean, pleasantly furnished rooms and is at the quieter far southern end of Skala, just round the last bend.

Eating

Grigoris Taverna (☎ 22470 31515; mains €3-5) Grigoris, on the corner of the Hora road, is always very popular, and his dolmades are recommended along with his range of grills and *mayirefta*.

> ### THE EVIL WIZARD OF PATMOS
>
> At the northern end of Skala harbour on Patmos floats a prominent buoy, a few swimming strokes offshore, widely believed to mark the petrified remains of Patmos' own sorcerer, the evil wizard Yennoupas. Lying just beneath the surface of the water, this stack of rock is a potential shipping hazard, which not even drilling or dynamiting has been able to remove. Legend has it that while St John was on Patmos writing up his gospel, a local wizard-cum-sorcerer by the name of Kynops ('dog-faced' in Greek) used to retrieve effigies of the dead from the seabed as a form of gruesome local entertainment. Kynops (known today by the derivative name Yennoupas) challenged John to a duel of miracles. John's response was to petrify Kynops while he was still searching for effigies underwater. The rock has since refused to be dislodged and it is believed that fish caught near here taste foul. A volcanic cave on the now inaccessible Cape Yennoupas is believed to have been Kynops/Yennoupas' lair when he was still fit to practise his own macabre form of Patmian sorcery.

Pandelis Taverna (☎ 22470 31230; mains €3-6) One of the more picturesque is this busy little taverna that has been in business for over 50 years. The service is efficient and the street dining is atmospheric. The best bets are the daily *mayirefta*.

Hiliomodi Ouzeri (☎ 22470 34080; mezedes platter €9) For the freshest fish on the island head to this *ouzeri* for its excellent seafood and very reasonably priced seafood-based *mezedes*. Open all year, the Hiliomodi is patronised as much by locals as by visitors.

Vegghera (☎ 22470 32988; mains €8-14) Yachties and high-society diners tend to head for this swish French and Mediterranean cuisine restaurant. It's right opposite the yacht marina in Netia. Top-notch food and service – while the ambience is a little more formal than elsewhere.

Entertainment

Skala's musical nightlife revolves around a scattering of bars and the odd club or two. These include the following.

Consolato Music Club (☎ 22470 31794; 🕙 9pm-late) A popular place that is open all year.

Aman (☎ 22470 32323) Predisposes people to sitting outside on its tree-shaded patio and listening to music to the feel of a cold beer or cocktail.

HORA

Huddled around the monasteries of St John are the immaculate whitewashed houses of Hora. These houses are a legacy of the island's great wealth in the 17th and 18th centuries. Some of them have been bought and renovated by wealthy Greeks and foreigners.

The immense **Monastery of St John the Theologian** (☎ 22470 31398; admission free; ☼ 8am-1.30pm daily, 4-6pm Tue, Thu & Sun), with its buttressed grey walls, crowns the island of Patmos. A 4km vehicular road winds up from Skala, but many people prefer to walk up the Byzantine path which starts from a signposted spot along the Skala–Hora road.

Some 200m along, a dirt path to the left leads through pine trees to the **Monastery of the Apocalypse** (☎ 22470 31234; admission free, treasury €3; ☼ 8am-1.30pm daily, 4-6pm Tue, Thu & Sun), built around the cave where St John received his divine revelation. In the cave you can see the rock that the saint used as a pillow, and the triple fissure in the roof, from which the voice of God issued and which is said to symbolise the Holy Trinity.

The finest frescoes of this monastery are those in the outer narthex. The priceless contents in the monastery's **treasury** include icons, ecclesiastical ornaments, embroideries and pendants made of precious stones.

For atmospheric dining and people-watching, **Vangelis Taverna** (☎ 22470 31967; mains €4.50-6) on the lively central square is your best bet. Good menu choices include *bekri mezedes* and the similar *spetsofaï* – rich and spicy cubed-meat concoctions. **Loza** (☎ 22470 32405) on the northwest corner of Hora is the best spot for a sunset drink and snack with stunning views over Skala.

NORTH OF SKALA

The pleasant, tree-shaded **Meloï Beach** is just 2km northeast of Skala. Here you'll find **Stefanos Camping** (☎ 22470 31821; sites €6.50), the island's only camp site, with bamboo-shaded sites, a minimarket, café-bar and motorcycle rental facilities. Between Skala and Meloï, and set back alone abutting a verdant vegetable garden, are **Stefanos Studios** (☎ 22470 31415; studios €25-35 ☒). Tastefully furnished in pine they are airy, spacious and have full kitchenette facilities. The vegetables in the garden can be picked and eaten for free. **To Meloï** (☎ 22470 31888; grills €3-5), at pretty Meloï Beach, is a well-regarded and inexpensive fish taverna with a predictable menu mix of *mayirefta*, fish and grills.

Heading north, just out of Skala on the hill enjoying stunning views, is the plush **Porto Scoutari Hotel** (☎ 22470 33123; fax 22470 33175; www.portoscoutari.com; d/tr incl breakfast €70-130; ☐ ☒ ☒). This is the classiest and most romantic place to sleep on Patmos. Each self-contained and individually named studio is impeccably decorated, and comes with a large personal porch. There's even an on-site church, should you wish to get married and honeymoon in the same location.

A turn-off right from the main road leads to the relatively quiet and shaded **Agriolivado Beach**. Further along you'll quickly reach the inland village of **Kambos**, from where the road descends to the shaded and shingle **Kambos Beach**, where there's a bit of a Greek hangout scene happening in midsummer. Eating choices include **To Agnanti** (☎ 22470 32733; mezedes €3-5), a neat little *ouzeri* with a range of reasonably priced *mezedes*. At the northern end of the beach is the cool **George's Place** (☎ 22470 31881; snacks €3-5) where you can play backgammon to laid-back

THE AUTHOR'S CHOICE

Benetos (☎ 22470 33089; Sapsila; mains €7-14; ☼ dinner) This is perhaps the most enticing place to dine on Patmos and is almost hidden away from casual view. It is a working boutique farmhouse and specialises in Mediterranean fusion dishes with an occasional Japanese kick. Dine on 'food with light' on a sheltered stone patio with a bamboo roof. Among the suggested dishes are the chef's fragrant sashimi, courgette flowers stuffed with mushrooms and cheese, or delicate Norwegian salmon in a mayonnaise and wasabe cream sauce. The service is professional and attentive and the clientele comprise mainly diners who enjoy paying for just that extra bit of pampering and quality.

music, graze on a light lunchtime snack, and drink.

The main road soon forks left to **Lambi**, 9km from Skala, where there is an impressive beach of multicoloured pebbles. High up above the beach on the approach road, the locally revered **Psistaria Leonidas** (☎ 22470 31490; mains €3.50-6) rustles up a wide range of home-made *mayirefta*, various fish of the day plates and highly recommended *saganaki* dishes.

Under the protected lee of the north arm of the island are several more beaches, including the shaded **Livadi tou Geranou Beach** with a small church-crowned island opposite, replete with the mini chapel of **Agios Georgios**. If you're wanting lunch here, try the excellent **Livadi Geranou Taverna** (☎ 22470 32046; mains €3-5) overlooking the sea pulls in a fair share of the local beach drifters. The food is home-style, honest and relatively inexpensive.

SOUTH OF SKALA

Sapsila is a quiet little corner 3km south of Skala, ideal for book lovers who want space, peace and quiet, and a couple of under-used beaches to read on.

The best chill-out spot for a week or more with a stack of novels are the immaculate, self-contained **Mathios Studios** (☎ /fax 22470 32583; www.mathiosapartments.gr; d/tr studios €40/50 🌐). These eight fully-equipped and tastefully decorated studios are set in a quiet, leafy garden 200m from Sapsila Beach. Owner Giakoumina makes all guests feel very welcome.

Grikos, 1km further along over the hill, is a relaxed low-key resort with a narrow sandy beach and shallow, clean water. Eating is best undertaken at a couple of places on the southwest side of Grikos Bay. **Flisvos Restaurant** (☎ 22470 31764; mains €3-5) is a well-shaded, modern taverna dishing up standard grills and *mayirefta* with particularly good baked *revithia* (chickpeas), while 100m further along is **Ktima Petra** (☎ 22470 33207; mains €4-7) emphasising organic and home-grown produce. The stuffed and baked goat just melts in your mouth and the organic cheese and vegetables simply ooze flavour. There's also a good wine list representative of Greece's best vines.

Diakofti, the last settlement in the south, is reached by a round-about sealed road, or a rougher and shorter coastal track passing the startling **Kalikatsos Rock**, abutting pebbly **Petra Beach**. The long, sandy, tree-shaded **Psili Ammos** beach can be reached by excursion boat or walking track; here you'll find a popular, seasonal beach taverna.

LIPSI ΛΕΙΨΟΙ

pop 698

Lipsi (lip-*see*), 12km east of Patmos and 11km north of Leros, is the kind of place that is easily missed by passing travellers. And, once discovered, travellers feel disinclined to share their find with others. It's a friendly place with the right balance of remoteness and 'civilisation'. There is comfortable accommodation, a satisfying choice of quality restaurants and a good selection of underpopulated beaches. Lipsi gained national and international fame in the summer of 2002 when the now-convicted leader of the November 17 terrorist group was found to be living a double life among the islanders. Apart from two or three days a year in August, when pilgrims and revellers descend upon Lipsi for its major festival, you can have most of it to yourself.

Getting There & Away

FERRY

Lipsi is not particularly well served by ferries. The F/B *Nisos Kalymnos* calls eight times a week in summer, linking Lipsi with Samos, Agathonisi, Leros and Kalymnos. The small *Patmos Star* arrives from Patmos three days a week at around 11am and continues on to Leros. On the way back it departs for Patmos at 3.30pm (return €11, one hour). The local caïque *Popie* runs to Leros (€5, 1½ hours) on Tuesday, Wednesday and Thursday (weather permitting) throughout the year.

HYDROFOIL & CATAMARAN

In summer hydrofoils call at Lipsi up to four times daily on their routes north and south between Samos and Kos, with further links to Patmos and Ikaria. The *Dodekanisos Express* and *Dodekanisos Pride* catamarans call in up to six times a week in summer. Sample fares are Rhodes (€42, 4½ hours) and Patmos (€9.50, 30 minutes).

DODECANESE

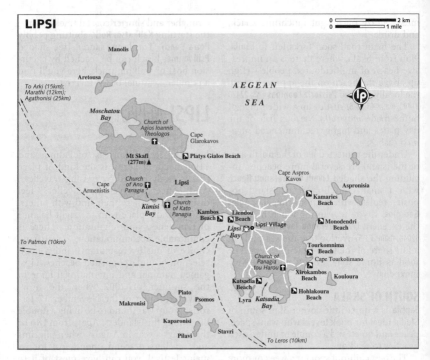

LIPSI

0 ⊏⊐⊐⊐⊐⊐⊐ 2 km
0 ⊏⊐⊐⊐⊐⊐ 1 mile

Manolis

Aretousa

To Arki (15km);
Marathi (12km);
Agathonisi (25km)

A E G E A N

S E A

Moschatou
Bay

Church of
Agios Ioannis
Theologos

Cape
Glarokavos

Mt Skafi
(277m) ▲

Platys Gialos Beach

Cape Aspros
Kavos

Aspronisia

Church
of Ano
Panagia

Lipsi

Kamaries
Beach

Cape
Armenistis

Church
of Kato
Panagia

Kambos
Beach

Liendou
Beach

Monodendri
Beach

Kimisi
Bay

Lipsi
Bay

Lipsi Village

To Patmos (10km)

Tourkomnima
Beach

Church of
Panagia
tou Harou

Cape Tourkolimano

Xirokambos
Beach

Kouloura

Piato

Psomos

Katsadia
Beach

Makronisi

Lyra

Katsadia
Bay

Hohlakoura
Beach

Kaparonisi

Pilavi

Stavri

To Leros (10km)

Getting Around

Lipsi has a minibus going every hour to the beaches of Platys Gialos (€1), and Katsadia and Hohlakoura (both €1) between 10am and 5.30pm. Two **taxis** (☎ 69424 09677 or 69424 09679) also operate on the island. There are one or two motorcycle rental outlets.

LIPSI VILLAGE

pop 600
Orientation & Information

All boats dock at Lipsi Port, where there are two quays. The ferries, hydrofoils and catamaran all dock at the larger, outer jetty, while excursion boats dock at a smaller jetty nearer the centre of Lipsi village. It's a 500m walk from the outer jetty to the village centre.

The post office is on the central square, and there is a freestanding Commercial Bank ATM at the port.

Laid Back Holidays (☎ 22470 41141; www.lipsiweb .gr) In Lipsi village; happy to help out with any queries.
Police (☎ 22470 41222) Near the ATM at the port.
Port police (☎ 22470 41133) Also close by the port ATM.

Tourist Office (☎ 22470 41185; ⊗ 9am-2.30pm) This small office is in the main upper village square; offers a few maps, timetables and accommodation advice.

Sights & Activities

Of macabre political interest is the **pink villa**, once occupied by the leader of the ultra-secretive November 17 terrorist group, who lived for a number of years under a pseudonym among the unsuspecting islanders. The solitary-standing villa is visible high on the bluff to the north side of the small boat harbour. While it's not open to visitors, the outer gate of the compound can be reached via a cement track on the north side of the bluff.

Lipsi's **museum** (admission free; ⊗ 11am-1pm) is hardly earth shattering, but contains a small collection of odd items such as pebbles and bottles of holy water from various locations around the world. It's on the main village square, opposite the large church.

Black Beauty and *Margarita* do 'Five Island' **boat trips** to Lipsi's offshore islands for €10; these are a popular diversion for a sail, picnic and swim. Both excursion boats can be found at Lipsi's small quay and depart at around 10am each day.

Festivals & Events
The annual religious festival of **Panagia tou Harou** takes places around 24 August when the island fills up with visitors from all over the Dodecanese. After a religious festival and procession through the island's narrow roads with an icon of the Virgin Mary, all-night revelry takes place in the lower village square with live music, food and wine.

Sleeping
O Glaros (☎ 22470 41360; d €30) Set back on the hill, about 100m from the village's small boat harbour, are these smallish but airy and comfortable rooms with a wide communal balcony and a well-equipped shared kitchen.

Studios Kalymnos (☎ 22470 41141; www.studios -kalymnos.lipsi-island.gr; d €36) One of the more appealing, and certainly the most friendly places to stay, is at these neat and airy studios, 800m from the quay on the east side of the village. Studios Kalymnos is set in a cool garden with a barbecue for guests, and has soothing chill-out music.

Hotel Calypso (☎ /fax 22470 41420; d/tr €45/50; ☒) You'll find this D-class hotel opposite the excursion boat quay. The rooms are reasonably comfortable and the location is pretty central for harbour nightlife.

Rooms Galini (☎ 22470 41212; d €45) Galini is high up, overlooking the harbour about half way along. Rooms here are pleasant, well-lit and sport a refrigerator, cooking ring and balcony.

Rizos Studios (☎ 69762 44125; fax 22470 44225; d/tr €44/50) These exceptionally well-located studios, enjoying a view over Liendou Bay, are tastefully decorated with hand-painted walls and decorations. They are equipped with every kitchen utensil imaginable. Sheffield-born host Anna welcomes guests with a flashing smile.

Eating
The harbour has the lion's share of eating places, but there are a couple of cafés in and around the quieter upper square.

Rock (☎ 22470 41180; mezedes €2.50-4) This coffee bar and *ouzeri* offers some unusual *mezedes* such as sea urchins, while the succulent grilled octopus is a standard

meze – best taken at sunset over a small glass of ouzo with ice.

Yiannis Restaurant (☎ 22470 45395; grills €5-6) The long-standing and ever-popular *psistaria* near the main ferry quay features grills in the main, though you will find the odd *mayirefta* and one or two mezedes-style dishes for vegetarians.

Kalipso Restaurant (☎ 22470 41060; grills €4-5) Adjoining the hotel of the same name, Kalipso serves up wholesome, low-priced food, mixing a few *mayirefta* dishes with the stock fish and meat grills.

Tholari (☎ 22470 41 060; mains €4-7.50) Run by a Tasmanian-Greek family, this low-key diner in the middle of the harbour rustles up popular dishes like prawn *saganaki* or a rich rabbit stew.

Pefko (☎ 22470 41404; mains €4-7) If the blue-and-yellow paint job décor doesn't grab you then the excellent menu dishes will. Try the *ambelourgou* (lamb in yogurt wrapped in vine leaves), or the Pefkos special – oven-baked beef with aubergines.

Karnagio (☎ 22470 41422; mains €8-13) One of the more innovative eating options is at this rather imposing restaurant at the far and not-so-attractive side of the harbour. The food makes up for the location. While fish and pasta dominate, the culinary permutations transcend the banal.

AROUND THE ISLAND
Lipsi has quite a few beaches and all are within walking distance of Lipsi Village. Some are shaded, some are not; some are sandy, others gravelly and at least one is for nudists. Getting to them makes for pleasant walks through countryside dotted with smallholdings, olive groves and cypress trees. The minibus services the main ones.

Liendou Beach is the most accessible and naturally the most popular beach. The water is very shallow and calm; this is the best beach for children. It's 500m from Lipsi village, just north of the ferry port over a small headland.

Next along is sandy **Kambos Beach**, a 1km walk along the same road that leads to Platys Gialos. Take the dirt road off to the left. There is some shade available.

Beyond Kambos Beach the road takes you, after a further 2.5km, to **Platys Gialos**, a lovely but narrow sandy beach. Water here is turquoise-coloured, shallow and ideal for children. Nearby is the decent **Kostas Restaurant** (☎ 69449 63303; grills €4-5; 8am-6pm Jul-Aug, later on Wed & Sat) which dishes up excellent fish and grill dishes as well as the odd suckling pig.

South, 2km from Lipsi Village, is the sand-and-pebble **Katsadia Beach**, shaded with tamarisk trees and easily reached on foot, or by the hourly minibus.

There is one distinguished place to eat, the **Dilaila Cafe Restaurant** (☎ 22470 41041; mains €5-8) which is right on the beach. The shady restaurant-cum-bar is caressed by an eclectic range of musical selections during the day and evening. Make sure to ask for 'mad feta' a spicy, baked feta cheese melange. Accommodation can be found at the airy and tastefully furnished **Katsadia Studios** (☎ 22470 41317; d €50) which overlooks the beach.

The pebble **Hohlakoura Beach**, to the east of Katsadia, offers neither shade nor facilities. Further north, **Monodendri** is the island's unofficial nudist beach. It stands on a rocky peninsula, and there are no facilities. It is a 3km walk to get there, though it is reachable by motorcycle.

ARKI & MARATHI
ΑΡΚΟΙ & ΜΑΡΑΘΙ

Studded like earrings off the eastern side of Patmos these two almost-forgotten satellite islands attract relatively few visitors and, in the main, those that come tend to be yachties or off-beat Greek media personalities. There are no cars and few permanent residents, so they make ideal hideaways for a few solitary days.

Getting There & Away

The F/B *Nisos Kalymnos* calls in up to four times a week as it shuttles between Patmos and Samos on its vital milk run. In summer the Lipsi-based excursion boats visit Arki and Marathi, and a number of Patmos-based caïques do frequent day trips (return €15).

ARKI ΑΡΚΟΙ
pop 50

Tiny Arki, 5km north of Lipsi, is hilly, with shrubs but few trees. Its only settlement, the little west coast port, is also called Arki.

Islanders make a living from fishing and tourism.

There is no post office or police on the island, but there is one cardphone. Away from its little settlement, the island seems almost mystical in its peace and stillness.

The **Church of Metamorfosis** stands on a hill behind the settlement. From its terrace are superb views of Arki and its surrounding islets. The cement road between Taverna Trypas and Taverna Nikolaos leads to the path up to the church. The church is locked but ask a local if it's possible to look inside.

Several secluded **sandy coves** can be reached along a path skirting the right side of the bay. To reach the path, walk around the last house at the far right of the bay, go through a little wooden gate in the stone wall, right near the sea, and continue ahead.

Tiganakia Bay on the southeast coast has a good sandy beach. To walk there from Arki village, take the cement road that skirts the north side of the bay. Tiganakia Bay is reached by a network of goat tracks and lies at the far side of the headland. You will recognise it by the incredibly bright turquoise water and the offshore islets.

Arki has three tavernas, two of which run a few basic but comfortable rooms; bookings are necessary in August. First up, **O Trypas Taverna & Rooms** (☎ 22470 32230; www.arki.gr; d €30; mains €4-6) is to the right of the quay, as you face inland and has 17 rooms available.

Suggested dishes at the taverna are *fasolia mavromatika* (black-eyed beans) and *pastos tou Trypa* (a type of salted-fish dish). Nearby **Taverna Nikolaos Rooms** (☎ 22470 32477; d €24; mains €4-6) is the second option. The food is marginally better here; try the potatoes au gratin.

MARATHI ΜΑΡΑΘΙ

Marathi is the largest of Arki's satellite islets. Before WWII it had a dozen or so inhabitants, but now has only one family. The old settlement, with an immaculate little church, stands on a hill above the harbour. The island has a superb sandy beach. There are two tavernas on the island, both of which rent rooms and are owned by the island's only permanent inhabitants, who speak English. **Taverna Mihalis** (☎ 22470 31580; d €30; mains €4-6) is the more laid-back and cheaper of the two places to eat and sleep at, while **Taverna Pandelis** (☎ 22470 32609; d €40; mains €4-6) at the top end of the beach is a tad more upmarket and not as traveller-oriented as the former.

AGATHONISI ΑΓΑΘΟΝΗΣΙ

pop 158

Agathonisi is a sun-bleached, often ignored speck of strategic rock a couple of hours east of Patmos. The island attracts yachties, serious island-hoppers and the curious, as well as latter-day Robinson Crusoes all seeking what Agathonisi has to offer – plain peace and quiet. If you ignore the occasional low-level roar of Turkish jets playing war games, the most exciting event of the day is the departure or arrival of the daily ferry or hydrofoil. There are only three settlements of any stature on the island: the port of Agios Giorgios, and the villages of Megalo Horio and Mikro Horio, which are less than 1km apart.

Getting There & Away

Agathonisi is linked to Samos (€4, one hour) and Patmos (€6, two hours) about four times a week by the F/B *Nisos Kalymnos*. A hydrofoil also links the island with Samos and destinations further south on the other three days. Ferry agent **Savvas Kamitsis** (☎ 22470 29003) sells tickets at the harbour prior to departures.

Getting Around

There is no public transport, and it is a steep 1.5km uphill walk from Agios Giorgios to the main settlement of Megalo Horio; somewhat less to Mikro Horio. From Megalo Horio the island's eastern beach coves are all within a 2km to 3km walk.

AGIOS GIORGIOS ΑΓΙΟΣ ΓΕΩΡΓΙΟΣ

The village of Agios Giorgios (*agh*-ios ye-*or*-yi-os) is a languid settlement at the end of a protected fjord-like bay. It has a 100m-long curved, pebbled beach, where you can comfortably swim, but **Spilia Beach**, 900m southwest around the headland, is quieter; a track around the far side of the bay will take you there. A further 1km walk will bring you to **Gaïdouravlakos**, a small bay and beach where water from one of the island's few springs meets the sea.

Orientation & Information

Boats dock at Agios Giorgios, from where roads ascend right to Megalo Horio and left to Mikro Horio. There is no tourist information, post office or bank.

The police are in a prominently marked white building at the beginning of the Megalo Horio road.

Sleeping & Eating

Pension Maria Kamitsi (☎ 22470 29003; fax 22470 29004; d €32) In the middle of the waterfront, the 13 comfortable rooms of Maria Kamitsi

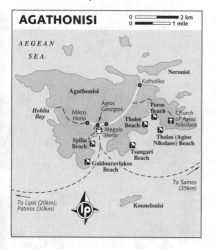

AGATHONISI

0 ——— 2 km
0 ——— 1 mile

AEGEAN
SEA

Neronisi

Katholiko

Agathonisi

Hohlia Bay | Mikro Horio | Agios Georgios | Poros Beach | Church of Agios Nikolaos

Tholos Beach

Megalo Horio

Spilia Beach | Tholos (Agios Nikolaos) Beach

Tsangari Beach

Gaïdouravlakos Beach

To Samos (35km)

To Lipsi (20km); Patmos (30km)

Kounelonisi

are the easiest to find and more likely to have vacancies in the high season. There is a communal fridge for every three rooms.

Domatia Giannis (☎ 22470 29062; d/tr €38/46 🔀) Above and just behind the Glaros Restaurant are these five airy rooms – the best accommodation on the island. Most have harbour views, are well constructed and enjoy modern furnishings.

Glaros Restaurant (☎ 22470 29062; mains €4.50-6.50) Of the few harbourside eateries, Glaros is probably the best place to dine. Owners Voula and Giannis are very engaging and make *markakia* (feta cheese fingers in vine leaves with a special sauce) among other standard *mayirefta*, grills and fish dishes, all made out of predominantly organic produce.

George's Taverna (☎ 22470 29101; fish €6-11) Closer to the ferry quay is the taverna of the affable George and his German staff. Food is predictably reasonable, though limited to meat and fish grills and the occasional goat in lemon sauce. Service can be a bit slow.

AROUND AGATHONISI

Megalo Horio is the only village of any size on the island. Somnolent and unhurried for most of the time, it comes to life each year with religious festivals on 26 July (Agiou Panteleimonos), 6 August (Sotiros) and 22 August (Panagias), when, after church services, the village celebrates with abundant food, music and dancing.

There are a series of accessible beaches to the east of Megalo Horio: pebbled **Tsangari Beach**, pebbled **Tholos Beach**, sandy **Poros Beach** and pebbled **Tholos (Agios Nikolaos Beaches)**, close to the eponymous church. All are within easy walking distance.

Further out at the end of the line is the small fishing harbour of **Katholiko** with the uninhabited and inaccessible islet of **Neronisi** just offshore.

If you prefer an even quieter stay than at the port, **Studios Ageliki** (☎ 22470 29085; s/d €25/30) in Megalo Horio will serve you very well. The four basic, but quite comfortable studios all have stunning views over a small vineyard and down to the port, and come equipped with kitchenette, fridge and bathroom. Eating in the village is unfortunately limited to the reliable **Restaurant I Irini** (☎ 22470 29054; mains €5-6) on the central square, or the **Kafeneio Ta 13 Adelfia** (mains €3-4) on the south side of the central square, serving up budget snacks and meals.

Northeastern Aegean Islands

Τα Νησιά του Βορειοανατολικού Αιγαίου

Strewn across the northeastern corner of the Aegean Sea, these far-flung islands are one of Greece's best-kept secrets. Their refreshingly green interiors are marked by rolling hills, jagged mountains, thick forests and gushing streams. Along their indented shores you'll find everything from pebbly coves to magnificent stretches of sand.

Hikers and fresh-air enthusiasts can choose from a wide range of trails that offer stunning coastal views and the chance to explore ancient sites.

Part of their appeal derives from the individual character of each island. Sure, they lack the white-washed churches of the Cyclades, and the party atmosphere of the Dodecanese, but these islands more than make up for it with largely unspoilt scenery, welcoming locals, delicious fresh produce and village life that is relatively undisturbed by the tourist dollar.

If you're determined to find your own place in the sun try the Fourni Islands situated near Ikaria, or Psara and Inousses, close to Chios, or Agios Efstratios near Limnos; these are some of the most seldom visited islands in the group, ensuring blissful days of sea and solitude.

Most of the islands lie closer to Turkey than to the Greek mainland, but rest assured, you're still very much in Greece. The Turkish influence is barely visible, even though the islands were part of the Ottoman Empire until 1912. Far more noticeable is the military presence, particularly on Limnos and Samos, where army and airforce bases take up large parts of the islands.

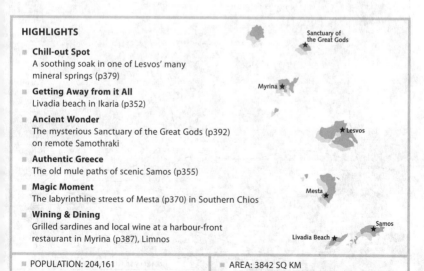

HIGHLIGHTS

- **Chill-out Spot**
  A soothing soak in one of Lesvos' many mineral springs (p379)

- **Getting Away from it All**
  Livadia beach in Ikaria (p352)

- **Ancient Wonder**
  The mysterious Sanctuary of the Great Gods (p392) on remote Samothraki

- **Authentic Greece**
  The old mule paths of scenic Samos (p355)

- **Magic Moment**
  The labyrinthine streets of Mesta (p370) in Southern Chios

- **Wining & Dining**
  Grilled sardines and local wine at a harbour-front restaurant in Myrnia (p387), Limnos

- POPULATION: 204,161
- AREA: 3842 SQ KM

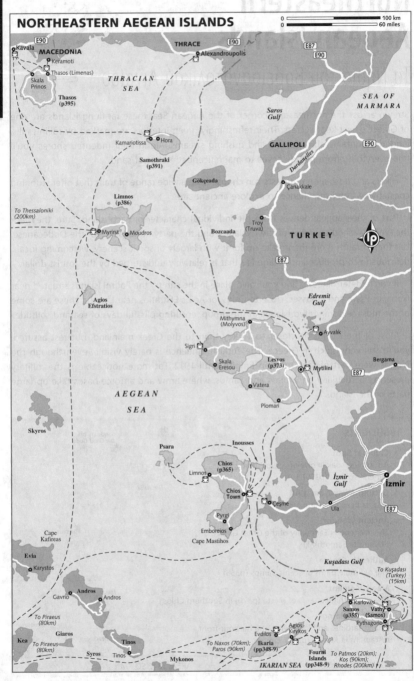

NORTHEASTERN AEGEAN ISLANDS

0 ——————— 100 km
0 ——————— 60 miles

GETTING THERE & AWAY
Air
Samos, Chios, Lesvos and Limnos have air links with Athens and Thessaloniki; Ikaria has flights just to Athens. Lesvos is connected to both Limnos and Chios by local flights.

Ferry
Ferry schedules make it difficult to plan an itinerary that takes in all the islands, especially in the off season. Samothraki and Thasos are particularly difficult to reach as there is no connection between these two islands. Ferry connections are much easier in the southernmost islands.

The table provided – Ferry Connections to the Northeastern Aegean Islands – gives an overview of the scheduled domestic ferries to this island group, when travelling from mainland ports during the high season. Further details and information on inter-island links can be found under individual island entries.

In summer there are daily ferry departures from Samos to Kuşadası (for Ephesus) in Turkey and from Chios to Çeşme. Ferries from Lesvos to Ayvalık run four times weekly.

FERRY CONNECTIONS TO THE NORTHEASTERN AEGEAN ISLANDS

Origin	Destination	Dur	Fare	Freq
Alexandrou-	Chios	12½hr	€24.50	weekly
polis	Lesvos (Mytilini)	9hr	€20.70	weekly
	Limnos	5hr	€17.90	2 weekly
	Samos	16hr	€29.80	weekly
	Samothraki	2hr	€8.30	daily
Kavala	Chios	16hr	€24.50	weekly
	Lesvos (Mytilini)	10hr	€24.70	2 weekly
	Limnos	5hr	€15.30	4 weekly
	Thasos			
	(Skala Prinos)	1¼hr	€3.30	hourly
Keramoti	Thasos	40min	€2	hourly
Piraeus	Chios	8hr	€22.50	daily
	Ikaria	9hr	€19	daily
	Lesvos (Mytilini)	12hr	€27.90	daily
	Limnos	13hr	€25.50	3 weekly
	Samos	13hr	€26	2 daily
Rafina	Limnos	13hr	€21.20	4 weekly
	Sigri	9hr	€18.20	4 weekly
Thessaloniki	Chios	18hr	€34.20	weekly
	Lesvos	13hr	€30.20	2 weekly
	Limnos	7hr	€22.10	2 weekly

Hydrofoil
In summer there are regular hydrofoil links between Kavala and Thasos, and some hydrofoils travelling between Alexandroupolis and Samothraki. Hydrofoils also operate out of Samos west towards Ikaria, south towards the Dodecanese, and north towards Chios and Lesvos.

IKARIA & THE FOURNI ISLANDS
ΙΚΑΡΙΑ & ΟΙ ΦΟΥΡΝΟΙ

area 255 sq km

Rugged Ikaria (ih-kah-*ree*-ah) is arguably the most striking of the north Aegean islands. With its sheer cliffs, deep ravines and forest-covered mountains, topped with ephemeral swirling mist, it has a wonderfully mythical feel. After a day spent in the olive and lemon groves, walking through the vineyards or in the cool of the pine forests, it seems fitting that Ikaria is said to be the birthplace of Dionysos, the Greek god of wine, fruitfulness and vegetation.

According to legend, the Ikarians were the first people to make wine, and while it was once considered the best in Greece (so good it even got a mention in Homer), a devastating phylloxera outbreak in the mid-1960s decimated the vines. Production is now low-key, but you will be able to try the deliciously light, cloudy red in any of the local tavernas.

Ikaria's radioactive springs are no myth; their therapeutic powers have drawn visitors for many centuries. Most of these springs can still be visited for cures or relaxation.

Long neglected by mainland Greece, Ikaria was once used as a dumping ground for dissidents. Ikarians call their island 'The Red Rock' because when the Greek government made it illegal to be a communist in 1946, some 15,000 were exiled here. Walls are still graffitied with red sickles and plastered with posters for leftist causes.

The lack of attention has had the happy effect of giving the island a special charm. Tourism is developing at a snail's pace and no one seems terribly interested in making money. Ikaria is a world away from its neighbours Samos and Mykonos, and

IKARIA & THE FOURNI ISLANDS

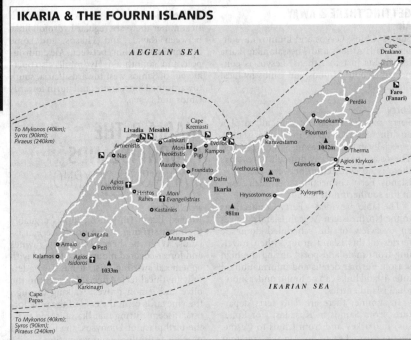

it also has what they lack: idyllic coves and unspoilt beaches, particularly Livadia and Mesahti near Armenistis. The island's capital is the port of Agios Kirykos on the south coast. Evdilos on the north coast is its second harbour, and a good base to enjoy the beaches and the lush, heavily indented northern coastline.

Getting There & Away

AIR

In summer there are four flights weekly to Athens (€47, 55 minutes), usually departing at 5.30pm. **Olympic Airlines** (☎ 22750 22214; www .olympicairlines.com) has an office in Agios Kiry-kos, and tickets can also be bought from **Blue Nice Agency** (☎ 22750 31990; fax 27750 31752) in Evdilos. There is no bus to the airport and a taxi will cost around €10 from Agios Kirykos.

CAÏQUE

A caïque leaves Agios Kirykos at 1pm on Monday, Wednesday and Friday for Fourni, the largest island in the miniature Fourni archipelago. The caïque calls at

Fourni (the main settlement) and usually at Hrysomilia or Thymena, where there are *domatia* (cheap rooms) and tavernas. Tickets cost €4 one way. There are also day excursion boats to Fourni from Agios Kirykos and from Evdilos which cost around €15.

FERRY

Nearly all ferries that call at Ikaria's ports of Evdilos and Agios Kirykos are on the Piraeus–Samos route; generally there are departures daily from Agios Kirykos and three to four weekly from Evdilos, travelling in both directions. There are five ferries a week to Mykonos (€13, 2½ hours) and Samos (€7.40, five hours) and four to Syros (€14, 2½ hours). Tickets are available at **Icariada Holidays** (☎ 22750 22277; icariada@hol.gr) and **GA Ferries agency** (☎ 22750 22426) in Agios Kirykos, or from **Blue Nice Agency** (☎ 22750 31990; fax 27750 31752) in Evdilos.

Chios-based **Miniotis Lines** (☎ 22710 24670; www.miniotis.gr; Neorion 23) also runs a couple of small boats twice weekly to Chios (€20, 8½ hours) from Agios Kirykos, via Fourni and Samos.

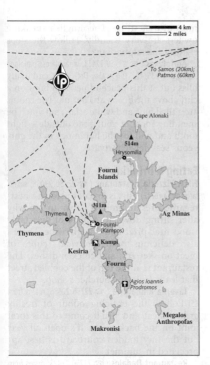

HYDROFOIL

Agios Kirykos handles the majority of Ikaria's hydrofoil services. There are year-round hydrofoils from Piraeus (€37.20, four hours) that go three times daily in winter and daily from June to October, stopping either at Agios Kirykos or Evdilos and continuing on to Samos, and vice versa. In summer there are two connections weekly to the Fourni Islands (€9.40, 20 minutes), four to Pythagorio on Samos (€16.60, 1¼ hours), two to Patmos (€15.70, 1¼ hours) and Kos (€29, 2¾ hours), and weekly services to Chios (€20, 7½ hours). There's also one boat a week each to Paros (€24, two hours) and Naxos (€21, 1½ hours). Check with **Dolihi Tours Travel Agency** (☎ 22750 23230; fax 22750 22346) or **Icariada Holidays** (☎ 22750 23322; icariada@hol.gr) in Agios Kirykos for the latest information.

Getting Around
BUS

Ikaria's bus services are almost as mythical as Icarus, but they do occasionally run. In summer a bus is supposed to leave Evdilos

for Agios Kirykos at 8am daily and return to Evdilos at around noon. However, it's best not to count on these buses as they exist to serve the schools during term time.

Buses to the villages of Hristos Rahes (near Moni Evangelistrias), Xylosyrtis and Hrysostomos from Agios Kirykos are even more elusive and depend mainly on the whims of the local drivers. It is usually preferable to share a taxi with locals or other travellers for long-distance runs, including to the airport. A taxi from Agios Kirykos to Evdilos will cost around €20.

CAR & MOTORCYCLE

This is an island where you really need your own transport. Cars can be rented from **Dolihi Tours Travel Agency** (☎ 22750 23230; fax 22750 22346) in Agios Kirykos, **Nas Travel** (☎ 22750 71396; fax 22750 71397) in Evdilos and Armenistis, and **Aventura Car & Bike Rental** (☎ 22750 31140; aventura@otenet.gr) in Evdilos and Armenistis. Expect to pay from €35 per day for a car and €15 per day for a bike.

TAXI BOAT

In summer there are daily taxi boats from Agios Kirykos to Therma and to the sandy beach at Faro (also known as Fanari) on the northern tip of the island. A return trip costs around €12.

AGIOS KIRYKOS ΑΓΙΟΣ ΚΗΡΥΚΟΣ
pop 1879

Agios Kirykos is Ikaria's capital and main port, but it's far from a bustling metropolis. The most exciting action in town is the arrival and departure of ferries. Other than watching boats come and go, there are radioactive springs, a few decent restaurants, embryonic nightlife and a little nest of old streets to explore. The pebbled beach at Xylosyrtis, 4km to the southwest, is the best of a bunch of stony beaches near town.

Orientation

Excursion boats and hydrofoils tie up in the town centre near Dolihi Tours Travel Agency. Ferries berth about 150m south of the centre at the ferry quay. To reach the central square turn right and walk along the main road. As you walk away from the quay, turn left on the central square; the bus stop is just west of the square.

Information

Alpha Bank, next to Dolihi Tours; and the National Bank of Greece, on the central square, both have ATMs. The police all share a building up the steps above Dolihi Tours. The post office is on the left of the central square.

Dolihi Tours Travel Agency (☎ 22750 23230; fax 22750 22346) At the bottom of the steps that lead to Agios Kirykos' police building. The staff can also arrange accommodation.

Icariada Holidays (☎ 22750 23322; icariada@hol.gr) Helpful staff sell ferry and plane tickets. They can also arrange accommodation in the Fourni Islands. Opposite the water.

Police (☎ 22750 22222)
Port police (☎ 22750 22207)
Tourist police (☎ 22750 22222)

Sights & Activities

Opposite the police building and up the steps from Dolihi Tours, are the **radioactive springs** (admission €5; ☯ 7am-2.30pm & 5-9pm Jun-Oct) which have recently been renovated. A dip supposedly cures a multitude of afflictions, including arthritis and infertility. A pleasant walk 2km northeast of Agios Kirykos, at Therma, are more **hot springs** (☎ 69771 47014; admission €5; ☯ 7am-2.30pm & 5-9pm Jun-Oct). This thriving spa resort has many visitors in summer.

Housing many local finds is Agios Kirykos' small **archaeological museum** (☎ 22750 31300; admission free; ☯ 10am-3pm Tue & Wed, Fri-Sun Jul & Aug). Pride of place is given to a large, well-preserved stele (500 BC) depicting in low relief a mother (seated) with her husband and four children. The museum is signposted and is near the hospital.

Sleeping

Hotel Kastro (☎ 22750 23480; www.island-ikaria.com /hotels/kastro.asp; d incl breakfast €60; ☒ ☒) Agios Kirykos' best-appointed hotel has a spectacular rooftop pool and bar. You will probably spend all your time taking in the lovely views from the terraces, but the rooms are nicely furnished with balconies and all mod cons. The hotel is up the steps from Dolihi Tours; at the top of the steps turn left and continue for about 20m.

Hotel Akti (☎ 22750 23905; fax 22750 22694; s/d €20/40; ☒) Recently remodelled, Hotel Akti sits on the rocks overlooking the sea and port. It's a great choice with small, but attractive, rooms with fridge, TV and

mosquito netting. The English-speaking owners are very friendly. Follow the steps right of the Alpha Bank.

Agriolykos (☎ 22750 22433; vmanolaros@panafone .tgr; s/d/tr €35/42/51; ☯ May-Oct) You can truly bliss out at this peaceful pension built on a cliff above the beach at Therma. The rooms are a tiled blue and white affair, but you'll be spending most of your time outside – fight tooth and nail for the hammock in the gorgeous sea-view courtyard.

Eating & Drinking

Filoti Pizzeria Restaurant (☎ 22750 23088; small/ large pizza €6/12) This is one of the town's best-regarded restaurants. It's easy to see why after sitting down to a plate of delectable wood-fired pizza and draught wine. There's also delicious pasta, *souvlaki* (cubes of meat on skewers) and chicken dishes. The restaurant is at the top of the cobbled street that leads from the butcher's shop.

Taverna Klimataria (☎ 22750 22686; mains from €5) Follow the enticing odour of freshly grilled meat and you'll come to this local joint on the backstreets. It's open all year but the tiny hidden courtyard is best appreciated in summer.

Restaurant Dedalos (☎ 22750 22473; mains from €5) On the main square, this restaurant offers delicious fresh fish dishes, including a good fish soup. You won't be disappointed with the house wine.

Café Aperihou (☎ 22750 24073) Perched on the rocks above the port, this is a natural meeting place for an ouzo, or an early morning pre-ferry coffee, in the window seats or on the balcony. The café is known for its occasional wild parties.

AGIOS KIRYKOS TO THE NORTH COAST

The island's main north–south asphalt road begins west of Agios Kirykos and links the capital with the north coast. As it climbs up to the island's mountainous spine there are dramatic mountain, coastal and sea vistas. The road winds through several villages, some with traditional stone houses topped with rough-hewn slate roofs. It then descends to Evdilos, 41km by road from Agios Kirykos.

Take the journey for the views but if you are travelling by bus from Agios Kirykos you will probably have to stay overnight in Evdilos, or even Armenistis. Alternatively,

IKARIAN PANIGYRIA

Locals break loose during *panigyria*, night-long festivals held on saints' days throughout the summer. Drinking and carousing in a village can be a wonderful way to get to know the islanders, but it will cost you more than you might expect – since these festivals serve as important fundraisers for the local community, the food and wine can be pricey. Make sure you get into the spirit of things though – don't just order a salad!

Festivals held in villages in the western end of the island take place on the following dates:

Kampos 5 May
Agios Isidoros 14 May
Armenistis 40 days after Orthodox Easter
Pezi 14 May
Hristos Rahes & Dafne 6 August
Langada 15 August
Agios Kirykos & Ikarian Independence Day 17 July
Evdilos 14-17 August
Agios Sofia 17 September

get a taxi back to Agios Kirykos for around €25. Hitching is usually OK, but there's not much traffic.

EVDILOS ΕΥΔΗΛΟΣ

pop 461

Evdilos, the island's second port, is a drowsy fishing village which perks up late in the evening. To see some lovely old houses and a cute little church, walk up Kalliopis Katsouli, the cobbled street leading uphill from the waterfront square.

You may prefer to head further west to the island's best beaches; there's also a reasonable beach to the east of Evdilos. To get to the eastern beach, walk 100m up the hill from the square and take the path down past the last house on the left.

Information

There is an ATM at both the eastern and western ends of the waterfront. At the western end, you'll also find the ticket agencies for **NEL** (☎ 22750 31572) and **Hellas Ferries** (☎ 22750 31990). **Aventura** (☎ 22750 31140), in a side street leading from the centre of the waterfront, rents cars and bikes, sells tickets and gives out general information.

Courses

Hellenic Culture Centre (☎ 22750 61140, 22750 61139; www.hcc.gr; ☒ May-Oct) This centre in the village of Arethousa, 7km from Evdilos, offers courses in Greek language, culture and literature. All levels of language proficiency are catered for; many professional translators undertake the three-month intensive course.

Sleeping

Hotel Atheras (☎ 22750 31434; www.atheras-kerame.gr; s/d/tr €49/59/69; ☒ ☒) The white-on-white decor makes a stunning contrast to the blue Aegean. Breezy, friendly and modern, there's also a pool bar for a lazy after-beach drink and most rooms have balconies. It's in the backstreets, about 200m from the port.

Karame Studios (☎ 22750 31434; www.atheras-kerame.gr; d studio/apt €59/69; ☒ ☒) If you want to be closer to Karame beach, these studios are 1km before Evdilos. There's the choice of simple studios and apartments for four people, with a separate kitchen. The spacious decks are great for relaxing in the sun, and there's a restaurant onsite, built into a windmill.

Hotel Evdoxia (☎ 22750 31502; www.evdoxia.gr; d €60; ☒) At the top of the hill is this small B-class hotel, worth considering if you don't mind the climb from the centre of town. There is a minimarket with basic provisions, a laundry service, money exchange and restaurant that serves good home-cooked food. They will pick you up free from the port.

Eating

To Koralli (☎ 22750 31924; Plateia Evdilou; mains from €5) This breezy eatery is a nice place for an outside meal. The modest menu does not try to set records in culinary innovation, but it does a good goat stew, and some tasty seafood dishes. There's a wide range of wine on offer.

To Steki (☎ 22750 31723; Plateia Evdilou; mains from €4) This little place on the harbour is open whatever the season, for cheese pies, large bowls of spaghetti and *soufiko* (an Ikarian speciality, like a Greek ratatouille).

Tsakonitis (☎ 22750 31684; Plateia Evdilou) Locals recommend this *ouzeri* (place which serves ouzo and light snacks), in a stone building on the waterfront, for its excellent and cheap rice pudding and home-made yogurt.

WEST OF EVDILOS
Kampos Κάμπος
pop 94

Kampos, 3km west of Evdilos, is a tiny village that was once mighty Oinoe (derived from the Greek word for wine), the island's capital. Little remains of Kampos' former glory, but its sandy beach is lovely and easily accessible. It also offers the possibility of relaxing country walks with stunning coastal views.

INFORMATION
Charismatic local Vasilis Dionysos (who speaks English) is a fount of information on Ikarian history and walking in the mountains. You will often find him in his well-stocked village store – it's on the right as you come from Evdilos. The village's post box is outside this shop and inside there is a metered telephone. There is a cardphone nearby.

SIGHTS & ACTIVITIES
As you enter Kampos from Evdilos, the ruins of a **Byzantine Palace** can be seen up on the right. In the centre of the village there is a small **museum** (☎ 22750 31300; admission free), which houses Neolithic tools, geometric vases, fragments of classical sculpture, figurines and ivory trinkets. Vasilis Dionysos at the village store has the key and will open it upon request.

THE AUTHOR'S CHOICE

Rooms Dionysos (☎ 22750 31300; dionisos@ hol.gr; d €35) Brothers Vasilis and Yiannis Kambouris, and Yiannis' Australian wife Demetra, run this wonderful family pension, replete with excellent Greek cooking, music and hospitality. The terrace offers splendid views and is a convivial meeting place for their happy guests, many of whom return year after year. Vasilis' generous breakfasts are (in)famous, so you might want to walk them off with a stroll through the surrounding countryside. Otherwise, head down to the nearby Kampos Beach to work on your tan. From Evdilos, take the dirt road to the right from near the cardphone and follow it round to the blue-and-white building on your left; you can't miss the bright blue trees! Alternatively, make your presence known at the village store.

Next to the museum is the 12th-century **Agia Irini**, the island's oldest church. It is built on the site of a 4th-century basilica. The columns standing in the grounds are from this original church. Agia Irini's frescoes are currently covered with whitewash because of insufficient funds to pay for its removal. Vasilis Dionysos also has the keys to the church.

The village is a good base for mountain walking. A one-day circular walk along dirt roads can be made, taking in the village of **Dafni**, the remains of the 10th-century Byzantine **Castle of Koskinas** and the villages of **Frandato** and **Maratho**. Take the trek up to the little Byzantine **Chapel of Theoskepasti**, jammed in beneath an overhanging lump of granite. Inside you will be shown the skulls of a couple of macabre internees. To get to the chapel and neighbouring **Moni Theoktistis**, where there are beautiful 300-year-old frescoes, look for the Frandato sign at the village of Pigi. A lovely woman named Evangelia runs a *kafeneio* (coffee house) at the monastery.

SLEEPING & EATING
Balcony (☎ 22750 31604; d/tr €35/50) It's a bit of a hike up a steep flight of steps to this collection of six apartments, but the views make it worthwhile. The studios are decorated with wrought-iron furniture, and have a kitchen and loft-sleeping area with twin mattresses; great for families. French doors lead out to a private sitting area with views down the coast.

Pashalia (☎ 22750 31346; mains from €4.50) This lovely family-run *ouzeria* is a great place to sit back, chat with the locals, and watch the day go by. For €1.50 you get an ouzo and a plate of home-made *mezedes* (appetisers) which might include wild mushrooms, freshly picked mountain asparagus and some delightful cheese courtesy of Katerina, the best-loved goat in Ikaria.

Armenistis Αρμενιστής
pop 130

Armenistis, 15km west of Evdilos, is the island's largest resort. It has two beautiful long beaches of pale golden sand, separated by a narrow headland composed of a harbour and a web of hilly streets. **Livadia Beach**, just to the east of Armenistis, is the perfect place to spend a lazy Ikaria day. Surfers will be happy to hear this beach gets constant waves during the summer season. As there are strong currents and the occasional drowning, there's a lifeguard service.

Tourism is the only business here, leaving the town somewhat lonely and stranded in the off season. **Dolihi Tours** (☎ 22750 71480; fax 22750 71340), on the road that skirts the sea, organises walking tours and jeep safaris on the island. **Aventura** (☎ 22750 71117), by the *zaharoplasteio* (patisserie) before the bridge, rents cars and sells tickets.

Just east of Armenistis a road leads inland to **Moni Evangelistrias**, **Agios Dimitrios** and the delightful hill village of **Hristos Rahes**. Hristos Rahes used to be famous for its 3am shopping, but not anymore; these days this rather eccentric little place is the centre for numerous trekking opportunities (see the boxed text, p354).

From Armenistis a road continues 3.5km west to the small and secluded pebbled beach of **Nas**, at the mouth of a stream. This is Ikaria's unofficial nudist beach. Behind the beach are some scant remains of a **Temple of Artemis**. Nas is a ramshackle settlement, popular with upmarket bohemians, and there's quite a few *domatia* and tavernas from which to watch the sunset (and the naked Germans!).

SLEEPING
Budget
Atsachas Rooms (☎ /fax 22750 71226; www.atsachas .gr; d €50) With a superb location at the eastern end of Armenistis beach, right on the water, you won't miss a swimming pool. Rooms are clean and nicely furnished, some have very well-equipped kitchens and most have sea-view balconies with a refreshing breeze. The café spills down to the divine garden below – definitely worth a stop for a cool drink or a bite to eat.

Rooms Fotinos (☎ 22750 71235; www.island-ikaria .com/hotels/PensionFotinos.asp; d €35; ❄) At the approach to the village, before the road forks, you will see this family-run pension on the left. Located in a spiffy white building, with light, airy rooms and a lovely flower-filled garden, the owners are extraordinarily accommodating, and there are the compulsory good views from the café.

Gallini (☎ 22750 71293; www.galinipension.gr; d €45; ❄ May-Oct) These 12 rooms hover above Armenistis. They are small but beautifully

furnished in traditional style and there's a lovely, landscaped terrace overlooking the sea. Kids will love the aviary.

Hotel Raches (☎ 22750 41269; s/d €30/35) Upstairs from Taverna Katoi these simple *domatia* make a good choice if you want to stay in Hristos Rahes. There are lovely valley views from the balconies, and a comfy communal area.

Midrange
Villa Dimitri (☎ /fax 22750 71310; www.villa-dimitri .de; 2-person studios & apt with private patios €50-65; ❄ March-Oct; ❄) The most exquisite accommodation on the island is this Cycladic-inspired pension belonging to Dimitris Ioannidopoulos. The studios, 800m west of Armenistis, spill down a cliff that overlooks the sea amid a riotous profusion of flowers and plants. Three renovated apartments now have a separate living room. Bookings are essential and should be for a minimum of one week.

Astra (☎ 22750 71255; €65-70) This friendly pension is up a steep driveway, just before Nas. The studios, with kitchenette, are brand new and fit up to four people. Of course the sea views from the spacious terrace are nothing short of outstanding. The complimentary hamper and bottle of wine also goes down a treat.

Hotel Daidalos (☎ 22750 71390; www.island -ikaria/hotels/hotelDaidalos.asp; s/d incl breakfast €58/72; ❄ ❄) On the western side of Armenistis Beach, this is a great place to enjoy the Aegean good life. The interior is cool and inviting, the rooms are tastefully furnished and the sea-water swimming pool surrounded by cedar trees is best of all.

EATING
Wherever you eat, see if you can try some of the locally made light but potent Fokianos wine.

Kelari (☎ 22750 71227; Gialiskari; mains from €6) Whether grilled or fried, the seafood here is the best in town, probably because it comes straight off the boats which pull up right outside this waterfront restaurant. The owner recommends the red snapper, but we say take whatever's fresh, it's all excellent. Opposite the supermarket, take the lower road and follow it around.

Pashalia Taverna (☎ 22750 71302; Armenistis; mains from €6; ❄ Jun-Nov) After a hard day at the beach you may be ready for rib-sticking fare such as *katsikaki* (kid goat) or filling pasta and veal in a clay pot. It's also a reliable breakfast spot for a coffee and a sea view. The taverna is the first place along the Armenistis harbour road.

Taverna Nas (☎ 22750 71486; Nas; mains from €6) This is the ultimate place for a romantic sunset meal, with stunning views over Nas and the sea beyond. The food doesn't compete, but with a piece of fresh fish and some Ikarian wine, it's a great place to spend the evening.

Taverna Katoi (☎ 22750 41269; Hristos Rahes; mains from €5) For a taste of true Ikaria, you really need to come and have a meal at this wonderfully charming taverna, tucked away in Hristos Rahes. It's a very quirky place, with every spare inch of space given over to a lifetime's hoarding of interesting bits and bobs. If the décor is making you lose concentration on the local roast pig and home-brewed wine, sit out on the leafy garden terrace.

FOURNI ISLANDS ΟΙ ΦΟΥΡΝΟΙ
pop 1469

If you are after the very quiet life, head to the mountainous Fourni Islands, a miniature archipelago lying between Ikaria and Samos. There are two inhabited islands: Fourni and Thymena, although Fourni is the only place where you will find accommodation. There's a good number of beaches dotted around the coast, and lots of rocky bays and inlets; once pirates' retreats, now contemplative hideaways. Kampi has two small sandy coves, but for something more remote head to Agios Ioannis Prodromos at the south of the island where there are several beaches below the monastery. The islands offer little else besides eating, sleeping, swimming and taking copious photos of sunsets, but that is their greatest attraction.

The largest community is in the capital of the group, **Fourni** (also called Kampos), which is the island's port. Fourni has one other village, tiny Hrysomilia, 10km north of the port; the island's only road connects the two.

Fourni has a **doctor** (☎ 22750 51202), and both local **police** (☎ 22750 51222) and **port police** (☎ 22750 51207).

For accommodation bookings, it is best to go through **Dolihi Tours Travel Agency**

(☎ 22750 23230; fax 22750 22346) in Agios Kirykos. Otherwise try **Nectaria's Studios** (☎ 22750 51365; d/tr €35/45) for comfortable, ultraclean *domatia* only 50m from the beach.

Most of the islanders make a living from fishing, sending their catch to the Athens fish market, so it's a great place for a fresh seafood meal at reasonable prices – definitely try the speciality: grilled Aegean lobster.

Getting There & Away
FERRY

Fourni lies on the ferry route between Piraeus and Samos. As well as daily boats to Ikaria (€3.20, 40 minutes), there are four ferries weekly to Samos (€6.75, two hours), and three weekly to Piraeus (€19.50, 10 hours) via Paros (€10, 3¼ hours) and Naxos (€8.70, four hours). These ferries stop at Mykonos (€9.20, 4½ hours) and Syros (€13.50, 5½ hours) twice a week. Tickets are available from the office on the corner of the waterfront and the main shopping street.

THE ROUND OF RAHES

Exploring the inland hill villages, collectively known as Rahes, offers a unique taste of local life and should not be missed. The community has published a walking map with excellent notes called *The Round of Rahes on Foot*; it's available at most tourist shops and supermarkets for €3.

The recommended loop can be done in one day (six hours), or, if you have less time or energy, split into easier, 45-minute walks. The paths are generally well-marked (once you get started!) and take you from Livadia Beach up through the villages, ending at Agion Polikorpos. Highlights include drinking in the splendid views, visiting the lovely churches and monasteries on the route, and glimpsing an oddity of the area, the strange 'anti-pirate' architecture – houses which have a sloping, one-sided roof, no windows or chimneys, just a low door that's obscured by a high wall in front.

Experienced walkers who are after something tougher might consider walking the Halaris Canyon to Nas, or crossing the island to Manganitis via Rahes.

If you are after more information, check out http://groups.yahoo.com/group /hikingikaria.

HYDROFOIL

Hydrofoils call at Fourni on the route from Ikaria to Samos and the Dodecanese (see p349 for details of services).

Getting Around

There are two caïques a week to Hrysomilia and three to Thymena. The boats operate year round and leave at 7.30am.

SAMOS ΣΑΜΟΣ

pop 32,814 / 477 sq km

Only 3km from Kuşadası, Turkey, Samos is a popular transit point for travellers heading to and from the Turkish mainland, but those who rush off without stopping are missing one of Greece's most splendid islands. Nature lovers and enthusiastic walkers flock to Samos for treks into the hinterland that reveal dense mountain greenery, populated by hordes of birds. Spring brings pink flamingos, wild flowers and the orchids that Samos grows for export. In summer the air grows heavy with the scent of flowers as the many jasmine bushes bloom. During the hottest days, cool mountain villages make an ideal escape from Samos' baking beaches and archaeological sites.

Unfortunately, Samos is incredibly popular with package tourists, who fill every available hotel room in July and August.

Samos has a glorious history as the legendary birthplace of Hera, wife and sister of God-of-all-Gods, Zeus, and is home to the Sanctuary of Hera, built by the tyrant Polycrates in the 6th century BC. The well-known mathematician Pythagoras was born in Samos around the same time. The island has been ruled at various times by the Romans, Venetians and Genoese, and also took part in a major uprising against the Turks in the early 19th century.

Samos has three ports: Vathy (Samos) and Karlovasi on the north coast, and Pythagorio on the south coast.

Getting There & Away

AIR

Olympic Airlines (www.olympicairlines.com) Vathy (☎ 22730 27237; cnr Kanari & Smyrnis); Pythagorio (☎ 22730 61213; Lykourgou Logotheti) has at least four flights daily from Samos to Athens (€73, 40 minutes) and two flights weekly to Thessaloniki (€149, one hour). The airport is 4km west of Pythagorio.

EXCURSION BOAT

In summer there are excursion boats four times weekly between Pythagorio and Patmos (return €35) leaving at 8am; a local bus will take you to the monasteries of St John. Daily excursion boats also go to the little island of Samiopoula (including lunch €25). There is also a boat tour of Samos once or twice a week, leaving from Pythagorio's harbour; it costs €40 and does not include lunch.

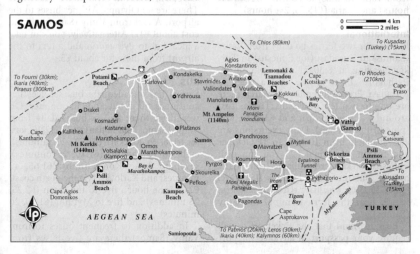

FERRY
Domestic
Samos is the transport hub of the North-eastern Aegean, with ferries to the Dodecan-ese and Cyclades as well as to the other Northeastern Aegean islands. Schedules are subject to seasonal changes, so consult any of the ticket offices for the latest versions. **ITSA Travel** (☎ 22730 23605; www.itsatravel .com; Themistokleous Sofouli) is the closest agency to the ferry terminal in Vathy. Your luggage can also be stored for free whether you buy a ticket or not. Ferries depart from both Vathy (Samos) and Pythagorio.

To Piraeus there are at least two ferries daily (€26, 13 hours). Two ferries daily go to Ikaria (€8.80, three hours) and five boats a week go to Fourni (€7, two hours); four weekly to Chios (€11.70, four hours); and one weekly to Lesvos (€16, 11 hours), Limnos (€25.50, 11 hours) and Alexandrou-polis (€29.80, 16 hours). At least five ferries a week go to Naxos (€20.10, seven hours) and Paros (€16.50, eight hours), with con-nections to Mykonos (€18.70, six hours), Ios and Santorini. There are about three ferries a week to Patmos (€6.90, 2½ hours), two each to Leros (€5.50, 3½ hours) and Kalymnos (€10, four hours), and one each to Kos (€11.50, 5½ hours) and Rhodes (€27, nine hours).

The *Aeolis Express* operates from Vathy (Samos) to Piraeus (€51, seven hours, six weekly). There are also two services weekly from Vathy (Samos) to Fourni (€12.50, 1¾ hours) and Ikaria (€15.75, 2¼ hours).

International
In summer two ferries go daily from Vathy (Samos) to Kuşadası (for Ephesus) in Tur-key, leaving at 8.30am and 5pm. From Pythagorio there is one boat a week to Kuşadası. From November to March there are one to two ferries weekly. Tickets cost around €47 open return and €37 one way (plus €10 port taxes). Daily excursions are also available from 10 May to 31 October and for an additional €25 you can visit Ephesus. Tickets are available from many outlets, but the main agent is **ITSA Travel** (☎ 22730 23605; www.itsatravel.com; Themistokleous Sofouli), near the ferry terminal in Vathy (Samos).

Bear in mind that the ticket office will require your passport in advance for port formalities. Turkish visas, where required, are issued upon arrival in Turkey. The fee depends upon nationality. Check with the Turkish diplomatic mission in your home country for the requirements. Visas are not required for daily excursions.

HYDROFOIL
In summer hydrofoils link Pythagorio four times daily with Patmos (€13.50, 1 hour), Leros (€14, two hours), Kos (€23, 3½ hours) and Kalymnos (€19, 2½ hours). Also from Pythagorio there are hydrofoils four times per week to Fourni (€12.75, 50 minutes) and Ikaria (€14.50, 1½ hours), daily to Lipsi (€13, 1½ hours) and once a week to Agath-onisi (€9, 35 minutes) as well as Mykonos three times a week (€17.70, six hours).

Also from Vathy (Samos) there are three hydrofoils a week to Patmos (€18.50, one hour), Kos (€25.50), Leros (€22.50) and Kalymnos (€25) as well as a daily boat to Naxos (€37.20, three hours) and Paros (€29.90, four hours). Schedules are subject to frequent changes, so contact the **tour-ist office** (☎ 22730 61389) or the **port police** (☎ 22730 61225), both in Pythagorio, for up-to-date information. Tickets are available from **By Ship Travel** (Pythagorio ☎ 22730 62285; fax 22730 61914; Vathy ☎ 22730 22116, Chem Sofouli 4) or **ITSA Travel** (☎ 22730 23605; www.itsatravel.com; Themistokleous Sofouli) in Vathy (Samos).

Getting Around
TO/FROM THE AIRPORT
There are no Olympic Airlines buses to the airport. A taxi from Vathy (Samos) should cost about €12. Alternatively, you can take a local bus to Pythagorio and a taxi to the airport from there for about €5.

BUS
Samos has an adequate bus service that continues till about 8pm in summer. On weekdays, there are six buses daily from Vathy (Samos) **bus station** (☎ 22730 27262; Ioan-nou Lekati) to Kokkari (€1.72, 20 minutes), eight to Pythagorio (€1.10, 25 minutes), seven to Agios Konstantinos (€1.65, 40 minutes) and Karlovasi (via the north coast; €2.75, one hour), five to the Ireon (€2.25, 25 minutes) and five to Mytilini (€1.10, 20 minutes).

In addition to frequent buses to/from Vathy (Samos) there are five buses from

Pythagorio to the Ireon (€1.25, 15 minutes) and four from Pythagorio to Mytilinii (€1.15, 20 minutes). Pay for your tickets on the bus. Services are greatly reduced on Saturday and none run on Sunday.

CAR & MOTORCYCLE

Samos has many car-rental outlets to choose from, including **Hertz** (☎ 22730 61730; Lykourgou Logotheti 77) and **Europcar** (☎ 22730 61522; Lykourgou Logotheti 65).

There are also many motorcycle-rental outlets on Lykourgou Logotheti. Many of the larger hotels can arrange motorcycle or car rental for you.

TAXI

The **taxi rank** (☎ 22730 28404) is in front of the National Bank of Greece in Vathy (Samos). In Pythagorio the **taxi rank** (☎ 22730 61450) is on the corner of the waterfront and Lykourgou Logotheti.

VATHY (SAMOS) ΒΑΘΥ (ΣΑΜΟΣ)

pop 2025

The island's capital is the large and bustling Vathy, also called Samos, on the northeast coast. The waterfront road is a string of bars, cafés and restaurants ranging from the tacky to the trendy. A harbourside walk is agreeable enough but the best part of town is Ano Vathy to the south, where 19th-century, red-tiled houses perch on a hillside and you can take it easy on a string of small beaches north of the Pythagoras Hotel. The best option is Gagou Beach situated about 1km north of the town centre.

Orientation

From the ferry terminal (facing inland) turn right to reach the central square of Plateia Pythagorou on the waterfront. It's recognisable by its four palm trees and statue of a lion. A little further along and a block inland are the shady municipal gardens. The waterfront road is called Themistokleous Sofouli. The bus station (KTEL) is on Ioannou Lekati.

Information

The Commercial Bank, on the east side of the square, and the National Bank of Greece, on the waterfront, just south of Plateia Pythagorou, have ATMs.

Diavlos NetCafé (☎ 22730 22469; Themistoklous Sofouli 160; per hr €4; ☯ 8.30am-11.30pm) Access is fast; it closes in the afternoon from November to April.

Hospital (☎ 22730 27407) On the waterfront, north of the ferry quay.

Municipal tourist office (☎ 22730 28530) Just north of Plateia Pythagorou in a little side street, it only operates during the summer season. The staff may assist in finding accommodation.

Police (☎ 22730 27980; Themistokleous Sofouli 129) On the south side of the waterfront.

Port police (☎ 22730 27890) Just north of the quay, one block back from the waterfront.

Post office (Smyrnis) Four blocks from the waterfront.

Tourist police (☎ 22730 27980; Themistokleous Sofouli 129) On the south side of the waterfront.

Sights

Apart from the charming old quarter of **Ano Vathy**, which is a peaceful place to stroll, and the **municipal gardens**, which are a pleasant place to sit, the main attraction is the **archaeological museum** (☎ 22730 27469; adult/student €3/2; ☯ 8.30am-3pm Tue-Sun), one of the finest in the islands. Many of the exhibits in this well laid-out museum are a legacy of Polycrates' time. They include a gargantuan (5.5m) *kouros* (male statue of the Archaic period) found in the Ireon (Sanctuary of Hera). In true Polycrates fashion, it was the largest standing *kouros* ever produced. The collection includes many statues, mostly from the Ireon, bronze sculptures, stelae and pottery.

Sleeping

Vathy does not have a camping ground. Be wary of touts who may approach you as you disembark and tell you that places listed in this guide are closed – it's usually not true.

Pythagoras Hotel (☎ 22730 28422; www.pythagoras hotel.com; Kallistratou 12; dm/s/d €15/20/35; Ⓟ ▢) This quiet hotel is an ideal place to unwind for a couple of days, with clean, simply furnished rooms, many of which have terrific sea views. Travellers meet and compare notes on the relaxing waterfront terrace, and there's good home-cooking (definitely try the fresh fish), saving you the walk into town and some cash. Owner Stelios will happily pick you up from the port or bus station.

Pension Dreams (☎ 22730 24350; Areos 9; d with/ without balcony €30/25; ☸) If you can swing the

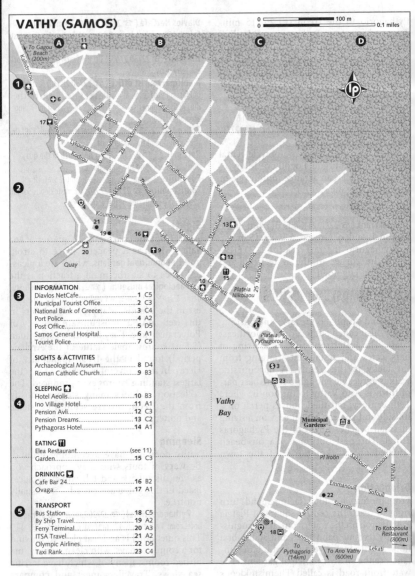

VATHY (SAMOS)

INFORMATION
Diavlos NetCafe	**1** C5
Municipal Tourist Office	**2** C3
National Bank of Greece	**3** C4
Port Police	**4** A2
Post Office	**5** D5
Samos General Hospital	**6** A1
Tourist Police	**7** C5

SIGHTS & ACTIVITIES
Archaeological Museum	**8** D4
Roman Catholic Church	**9** B3

SLEEPING
Hotel Aeolis	**10** B3
Ino Village Hotel	**11** A1
Pension Avli	**12** C3
Pension Dreams	**13** C2
Pythagoras Hotel	**14** A1

EATING
Elea Restaurant	(see 11)
Garden	**15** C3

DRINKING
Cafe Bar 24	**16** B2
Ovaga	**17** A1

TRANSPORT
Bus Station	**18** C5
By Ship Travel	**19** A2
Ferry Terminal	**20** A3
ITSA Travel	**21** A2
Olympic Airlines	**22** D5
Taxi Rank	**23** C4

*Vathy
Bay*

rooftop studio, this is what dreams are made of! Otherwise try for a balcony room, with garden views at this small, but central pension on a hill overlooking the harbour. The friendly owner speaks several languages.

Ino Village Hotel (☎ 22730 23241; www.inovillage .gr; Kalami; s/d/tr incl breakfast from €47/60/85; **P** ✦ 🖳 🏊) This is a well-manicured oasis

high above busy Vathy. Several ivy-covered buildings surround a central courtyard with pool. The quiet rooms are simple but stylish. The Elea Restaurant has a wonderful open terrace. In the high season it may be booked out by tour groups.

Hotel Aeolis (☎ 22730 28377; www.aeolis.gr; Themistokleous Sofouli 33; s/d incl breakfast €45/60; ✦ 🏊)

Stretch out and relax in this grand-looking establishment. Laze around in the rooftop garden which has a huge pool (one of two), Jacuzzi and taverna, or head downstairs to the popular bar which is generally the busiest on the strip. From your comfortable room you can stroll out onto the balcony, which just might have a view over the water.

Pension Avli (☎ 22730 22939; Areos 2; d €30) For something atmospheric, this traditional place is a former Roman Catholic convent built around a lovely courtyard. It was closed at time of writing, but you might have better luck.

Eating

When dining out on Samos don't forget to sample the Samian wine, extolled by Byron.

Kotopoula (☎ 22730 28415; Vlamaris; mezedes around €4, mains around €6) Hidden by a leafy plane tree in the backstreets, this vine-cloaked restaurant is a bit of a tourist enclave these days, but it still turns out delicious spit-roasted chicken (served only in the evenings) and tasty *revithokeftedes* (chickpea rissoles). Follow Ioannou Lekati inland for about 800m until you find it on your left.

Garden (☎ 22730 24033; Manolis Kalomiris; mains €4-9) This spot, just off Lykourgou Logotheti (entry is from the next street up to the north), has a garden setting with a vast and tree-filled outdoor terrace. The Greek standards are good, particularly the fish soup which makes a nice light meal.

Elea Restaurant (☎ 22730 23241; Kalami; mains from €6-8) This relaxed restaurant on the terrace of the Ino Village Hotel, serves up dishes as good as the views. The focus is on contemporary Greek specialities but there are often surprising specials, such as rooster in red-wine sauce with *parpadelle* pasta. There is also an extensive list of Samian wines.

Drinking

There are plenty of bars along the waterfront, all pretty much of a muchness. For something a bit more interesting, head to the bars by the water on Kefalopoulou, just past La Calma restaurant. These include Escape Music Bar, Cosy and **Ovaga** (☎ 22730 25476; Kefalopoulou 13), which has a stunning terrace by the water.

Café Bar 24 (off Themistokleous Sofouli) is an intimate little outdoor bar on a side street that plays excellent music and has an under-hyped candlelit ambience.

PYTHAGORIO ΠΥΘΑΓΟΡΕΙΟ
pop 1327

Pythagorio, on the southeast coast of the island, is reminiscent of a seaside retirement village. The place has a somewhat upmarket feel, perhaps because of the many over-priced cafés with multilingual menus which are squashed along the yacht-filled harbour. But dip into the pretty back streets, lined with red hibiscus and pink oleander, and you'll find a few family-run pensions and enough ancient sights to keep you happy for a day or two. There is also a rather attractive town beach just beyond the jetty.

Pythagorio stands on the site of the now World Heritage–listed ancient city of Samos. Although the settlement dates from the Neolithic era, most of the remains are from Polycrates' time (around 550 BC). All boats coming from Patmos, and other points south of Samos, dock at Pythagorio.

Orientation

From the ferry quay, turn right and follow the waterfront to the main thoroughfare of Lykourgou Logotheti, a turn-off to the left. Here there are supermarkets, travel agents and numerous car, motorcycle and bicycle rental outlets. The central square of Plateia Irinis is further along the waterfront. The bus stop is on the south side of Lykourgou Logotheti.

Information

Commercial Bank (Lykourgou Logotheti) Has ATM.
Digital World (☎ 22730 62722; Pythagora; per hr €4; ⊙ 11am-10.30pm) Has Internet access.
National Bank of Greece (Lykourgou Logotheti)
Post office (Lykourgou Logotheti)
Tourist office (☎ 22730 61389; deap5@otenet.gr; ⊙ 8am-9.30pm) On the south side of Lykourgou Logotheti. The English-speaking staff are particularly friendly and helpful and give out a town map, bus timetable and information about ferry schedules. It's also a currency exchange.
Tourist police (☎ 22730 61100; Lykourgou Logotheti) To the left of the tourist office.

Sights

Driving northeast from the town centre, a path on the left passes traces of an **ancient theatre**. The right fork past the theatre

PYTHAGORIO

INFORMATION		
Commercial Bank ATM	1	B1
Digital World	2	B2
National Bank of Greece	3	A1
Post Office	4	A1
Tourist Office	5	B2
Tourist Police	6	B2

SIGHTS & ACTIVITIES		
Castle of Lykourgos Logothetis	7	A2
Pythagorio Museum	8	C1
Ruins of Aphrodite	9	B2

SLEEPING		
Hotel Alexandra	10	B2
Hotel Evripili	11	B2
Pension Despina	12	C1
Polixeni Hotel	13	C2

EATING		
Anna's Garden	14	C1
Poseidonas	15	D2
Restaurant Remataki	16	D2
Taverna ta Platania	17	C2

TRANSPORT		
Bus Stop	18	A1
By Ship Travel	19	B2
Ferry Quay	20	D3
Olympic Airlines	21	A1
Taxi Rank	22	C2

leads up to **Moni Panagias Spilianis** (Monastery of the Virgin of the Grotto; ☎ 22730 61361; ◷ 9am-8pm). The **city walls** extend from here to the amazing Evpalinos Tunnel, which can also be reached along this path.

Back in town, the remains of the **Castle of Lykourgos Logothetis** are at the southern end of Metamorfosis Sotiros. The castle was built in 1824 and became a stronghold of Greek resistance during the War of Independence.

In the town hall at the back of Plateia Irinis, is the **Pythagorio Museum** (☎ 22730 61400; Plateia Irinis; admission free; ◷ 8.45am-2.30pm Tue-Sun), which has some finds from the Ireon.

Between Lykourgou Logotheti and the car park are the **ruins of Aphrodite**.

EVPALINOS TUNNEL

The 1034m-long **Evpalinos Tunnel** (☎ 22730 61400; adult/student €4/2; ◷ 8.45am-2.45pm Tue-Sun) is a remarkable feat of precision engineering. Constructed in 524 BC to channel mountain water to the city, the diggers laboriously chopped through a mountainside, beginning at each end and finally meeting in the middle.

In the Middle Ages the inhabitants of Pythagorio used the tunnel as a hide-out during pirate raids. The tunnel is, in effect, two tunnels: a service tunnel and a lower water tunnel that can be seen at various points along the narrow walkway.

The tunnel is fun to explore, though access to it is via a very constricted stairway. If you are tall, portly or suffer from claustrophobia, give it a miss!

The tunnel is most easily reached from the western end of Lykourgou Logotheti, from where it is signposted. If you arrive by road, a sign points you to the tunnel's southern mouth as you enter Pythagorio from Samos.

Sleeping

Much of Pythagorio's accommodation is block-booked by tour companies in the peak summer period.

Polixeni Hotel (☎ 22730 61590; fax 22730 61359; d €65; ✷) This homely place on the waterfront has nicely furnished, clean and comfortable rooms with balconies and very amiable staff. A good bet.

Pension Despina (☎ 22730 61677; despina@samos rooms.com; A Nikolaou; d €35) This quiet little pension is tucked away by the museum. There's a choice of tiled studios or uninspiring, but pleasant, rooms with balcony. Dig into the small book collection, and relax in the lovely plant-filled courtyard.

Hotel Evripili (☎ 22730 61096; fax 22730 61897; Konstantinou Kanari; s/d €45/60) Occupying a stone building not far from the waterfront this friendly place has cosy rooms which are nicely furnished with shutters to protect against the sun. Some rooms have balconies.

Hotel Alexandra (☎ 22730 61429; Metamorfosis Sotiros 22; d €25) A well-kept establishment offering eight small but fetching rooms, some with a sea view. The enclosed garden is a treat on hot summer days.

Eating

The waterfront is packed with restaurants, most offering the same expensive, unexciting fare.

Anna's Garden (☎ 22730 61635; Odyssea Orologa; mains €5-8; ☽ summer) Named for the owners' grandmother, Anna's bistro is set in a garden at the back of town. The menu is modest, but features home-made specialities which change daily. The atmosphere here is very different from the waterfront restaurants, and is definitely worth a stop.

Restaurant Remataki (☎ 22730 61104; mezedes €4-6; mains €7-10) This restaurant, at the beginning of the town beach, has an imaginative menu of carefully prepared food – but it is steadily getting pricier. Try a meal of various *mezedes* for a change: *revithokeftedes* (chickpea rissoles), *piperies Florinis* (Florina peppers) and *gigantes* (lima beans) make a good combination. The artichoke soup and dolmades (aromatic rice wrapped in vine leaves) are also excellent.

Poseidonas (☎ 22730 62530; mains €5-13) Next door to Remataki, this popular restaurant serves some interesting dishes, including Chinese-inspired seafood offerings as well as Greek food prepared with the freshest ingredients.

Taverna ta Platania (☎ 22730 61817; Plateia Irinis; mains €4-6) This taverna, opposite the museum, is away from the more expensive waterfront eateries. As a result, it tends to attract a relaxed, local crowd. It recently changed hands, so we are hoping the tasty Greek standards stay that way.

AROUND PYTHAGORIO

The Ireon Το Ηραίον

The Sacred Way, once flanked by thousands of statues, led from the city to the **Ireon** (☎ 22730 95277; adult/student €3/2; ☽ 8.30am-3pm Tue-Sun), the legendary birthplace of Hera. Every goddess needs a sanctuary and this one was built in the 6th century BC on swampy land where the River Imbrasos enters the sea. There had been a temple on the site since Mycenaean times, but the Ireon was enormous; four times the size of the Parthenon. As a result of plunderings and earthquakes only one column remains standing, although the extent of the temple can be gleaned from the foundations. Other remains on the site include a stoa, more temples and a 5th-century basilica.

The Ireon is now listed as a World Heritage site. It is situated on the coast 8km west of Pythagorio.

Mytilinii Μυτιληνιοί

The fascinating **palaeontology museum** (☎ 22730 52055; admission €2.50; ☽ 10am-2pm), on the main thoroughfare of the inland village of Mytilinii, between Pythagorio and Vathy (Samos), houses skeletons of prehistoric animals. Included in the collection are remains of animals that were the antecedents of the giraffe and elephant. From the museum it's a nice walk to **Agia Triada monastery**, where there's an ossuary.

Beaches

Sandy **Psili Ammos** (not to be confused with the beach near Votsalakia) is the finest beach near Pythagorio. This lovely cove is bordered by trees and looks across the water at Turkey. The gently sloping water makes it ideal for families and it's extremely popular, so get there early to grab your spot. There are a few reasonably priced tavernas off the beach that rent rooms. It can be reached by car or scooter from the Vathy–Pythagorio road (signposted), or by excursion boat (€15) from Pythagorio. There are also buses from Vathy (Samos). If you arrive by road, look out for the pond on your left that hosts a bevy of pink flamingos in the spring; it's about 1km before the beach.

Glykoriza Beach, nearer Pythagorio, is dominated by a few hotels, but is a clean, public beach of pebbles and sand.

SOUTHWEST SAMOS

The southwest coast of Samos remained unspoilt for longer than the north coast, but in recent years resorts have sprung up alongside the best beaches. The area east of Marathokampos was hit by fires in 2000, and the forests are only beginning to recover.

Ormos Marathokampou, 50km from Vathy (Samos), has a pebble beach. From here a road leads 6km inland to the village of **Marathokampos**, which is worth a visit for the stunning view down to the immense **Bay of Marathokampos**. **Votsalakia**, 4km west of Ormos Marathokampou and known officially as Kampos, and the much nicer **Psili Ammos**, 2km beyond, have long, sandy beaches. There are many *domatia* and tavernas on this stretch of coast, though it has a rather scrappy feel and lacks the intimacy of smaller coastal resorts.

With your own transport you may like to continue from Psili Ammos along a stunning route that skirts mighty **Mt Kerkis**, high above the totally undeveloped and isolated west coast. The road passes through the village of **Kallithea**, and continues to **Drakeí**, where it terminates.

NORTHERN SAMOS

The road that skirts the north coast passes many beaches and resorts. The fishing village of **Kokkari**, 10km from Vathy (Samos), is also a popular holiday resort with a long and narrow pebble beach. As it is exposed to the frequent summer winds it is a favourite with windsurfers. Rooms, studios and tavernas abound, all offering much the same quality.

Beaches extend from here to **Avlakia**, with **Lemonaki** and **Tsamadou Beaches** being the most accessible for walkers staying in Kokkari; clothing is optional at these two secluded beaches. Continuing west, beyond Avlakia, the road is flanked by trees, a foretaste of the scenery encountered on the roads leading inland from the coast.

A turn-off south along this stretch leads to the delightful mountain village of **Vourliotes**, from where you can walk another 3km to **Moni Panagias Vrondianis**. Built in the 1550s, this is the island's oldest extant monastery; a sign in the village points the way. Vourliotes is slightly larger than its alpine neighbour Manolates, and has multicoloured, shuttered houses surrounding a central square. It can be reached by a footpath from Kokkari.

Continue west, around the coast, until you reach a left hand turn-off. Here a 5km road winds its way up the lower slopes of Mt Ampelos (known as the Balcony of Samos) through thick, well-watered woodlands of pine and deciduous trees, to the gorgeous village of **Manolates**, which is

---

WALK ON BY

To see the island at its non-touristy best, take to the Kalderimia, the cobbled mule tracks which link the lush hills behind Kokkari. Samos has one of the most extensive networks of paths and walking routes of any Greek island, with plenty of shade for summer hiking.

For guidance, we recommend the *Landscapes of Samos* by Brian Anderson (Sunflower Publications), or see if you can get your hands on the discontinued booklet *Walks in the Kokkari Area of Samos* by Lance Chilton (Marengo Publications 2001). They both offer a wide variety of routes and accompanying notes.

Vourliotes–Manolates

Duration: 2½ hours. For spectacularly wild scenery start this walk from the Vourliotes carpark on the uphill road to Moni Vrondianis. Follow the sign to Manolates. Ignore the several disruptions to the track, and take the uphill fork which zigzags through woodland, vineyards and bare rock stream beds. It finally emerges above the Loukas taverna in Manolates.

Kokkari–Agios Pandeleimon/Mana Spring

Duration: One to two hours. From Kokkari take the Vourliotes footpath until you reach a wide dirt track, and turn left; this leads to the church of Agios Pandeleimon and a gorgeous picnic spot by the Mana Spring. From here the route is poorly marked but you can head uphill towards the entrance of the valley and then back down to Kokkari.

nearly encircled by mountains. The area is rich in bird life, with a proliferation of nightingales, warblers and thrushes whose chirpings echo through the steep old streets. The Samians say that if you have not visited either Vourliotes or Manolates, then you have not seen Samos. We would agree.

Back on the coast, the road continues to the pretty flower-filled village of **Agios Konstantinos**. Beyond here it winds through rugged coastal scenery to the town of **Karlovasi**, Samos' third port. The town consists of three contiguous settlements: Paleo (old), Meson (middle) and Neo (new). It once boasted a thriving tanning industry, but now it's a lacklustre place with little of interest for visitors. The nearest beach is the sand-and-pebble **Potami**, 2km west of town.

Sleeping

In the high season the **EOT** (Greek National Tourist Organisation; ☎ 22730 92217) in Kokkari will assist in finding accommodation. The bus stops on the main road at a large stone church, and the EOT is about 100m up the street next to the OTE (telephone office).

Kokkari Beach Hotel (☎ 22730 92238; fax 22730 92381; Kokkari; d incl breakfast €68-73; ❄ ⚓) For a touch of class try this place, about 1km west of the bus stop. The pretty yellow building is set back from the road, leaving the comfortably furnished rooms a quiet haven in this busy village. There is also a café right across the road which is great for chilling out.

Aidonokastro (☎ 22730 94686; fax 22730 94404; Valiondates; d/tr €60/75) Keen walkers, or anyone who wants to escape the busy coastline, should investigate these renovated apartments, set in five traditionally furnished houses with gorgeous mountain and forest views. The lovely English-speaking Yiannis has great tips on trekking the area. It's in Valiondates, a hamlet on the way up to Manolates.

Studio Angella (☎ 22730 94478, 21050 59708, in Athens ☎ 6972 975 722; Manolates; d €30) Try this studio built into the side of a hill at the edge of Manolates town. Rooms have balconies with spectacular views over the mountains.

Traditional Greek House (☎ 22730 94331, 22730 94174; Manolates; d €25) Phone to inquire about the studio in this nice little unnamed house in Manolates. The quiet and romantic room is large and tastefully furnished. It's in the centre of the village next to Giorgidas taverna.

Eating

There are many reasonably priced restaurants to be found in Kokkari, all offering the usual range of tourist fare, but the best eating is in the little mountain villages.

Grill Café (☎ 22730 93291; Vourliotes; mains from €5) This little taverna on the left of Vourliotes main square is run by two women who recommend their excellent plate of mixed vegetarian *mezedes*. But, for a mouthful of meat, the pita sandwiches with home-made sausage are unbelievable.

Loukas Taverna (☎ 22730 94541; mains €3-4.50) In Manolates, climb to the top of the hill to this taverna for the best and cheapest food around, as well as great views. Try the stuffed courgette flowers and the special home-made *moshato* (muscat) wines. Follow the prominent signs to the back end of the village.

CHIOS ΧΙΟΣ

area 859 sq km

Situated rather awkwardly on the ferry routes, and without a tangible international profile, Chios (*hee*-os) attracts curious travellers and expat Greeks rather than hordes of package tourists. Those who make the effort find the island subtly rewarding in its own distinct way. The mastic villages of the south are highly original, there are some decent beaches and a glorious profusion of tulips in the spring. The island is separated from Turkey's Karaburun Peninsula by the 8km-wide Chios Straits.

The one place you might be able to snag yourself a shipping magnate is Chios; a large number of highly successful ship owners come from the island and its dependencies, Inousses and Psara. This, and its mastic production, have meant that Chios has not needed to develop a large tourist industry. In recent years, however, package tourism has begun to make inroads, though it's limited to a fairly small coastal stretch south of Chios.

Getting There & Away

AIR

Chios has, on average, four flights daily to Athens (€69, 50 minutes), three weekly to Thessaloniki (€149, one hour 10 minutes) and two weekly to Lesvos (€43, 25 minutes). **Olympic Airlines** (☎ 22710 20359; www.olympic airlines.com; Leof Aigaiou) is in Chios Town. The airport is 4km from Chios Town. There is no Olympic Airlines bus, but a taxi to/from the airport should cost about €5.

FERRY

Domestic

In summer at least one ferry goes daily to Piraeus (€22.50, eight hours) and Lesvos (€12, three hours). There's one ferry per week to Thessaloniki (€34.20, 18 hours) via Limnos (€20, 11 hours), and Alexandrou-polis (€24.50, 12½ hours) via Limnos. There are three boats weekly to Samos (€11.70, four hours) and one each per week to Kos (€17.50, nine hours) and Rhodes (€30, 15 hours). Tickets for these routes can be bought from **NEL** (☎ 22710 23971; fax 22710 41319; Leof Aigaiou 16) in Chios Town.

Miniotis Lines (☎ 22710 24670; www.miniotis.gr; Neorion 23) in Chios Town runs small boats to Karlovasi (€10, four hours) and Vathy (€11, 4½ hours) on Samos twice a week. Three times a week these boats continue on to Fourni (€12.40, 7½ hours) and Ikaria (€13, 8½ hours). Miniotis also has three boats weekly to Psara (€9.90, 3½ hours). Mini-otis boats occasionally dock at the southern end of the harbour, at the corner of Leof Aigaiou and Kokali.

The *Oinoussai II*, another small local boat, runs to and from Inousses (€3 one-way, 1¼ hours, daily). Most days it leaves Chios in the afternoon and Inousses in the morning, so you must stay overnight. Purchase tickets on board. **Sunrise Tours** (☎ 22710 41390; Kanari 28) also runs day-trips to the island in the high season (€20) about twice a week. The price doesn't include lunch. There are also daily water taxis between Langada and Inousses (€35, shared between the passengers).

Aeolis Express sails three times weekly to Lesvos (€24.80, 1½ hours).

International

Boats to Turkey run all year from Chios. From May to October there are daily ferries to Çeşme, leaving Chios at 8.30am and returning at 6.30pm, except on Sunday when it returns at 5pm. The fare is €22 one way and €25 return. Further information and tickets can be obtained from **Miniotis Lines** (☎ 22710 24670; www.miniotis.gr; Neorion 23). The special daily excursion rates often work out cheaper. Check with local agencies offering such trips.

Turkish visas, where required, are issued upon arrival in Çeşme.

HYDROFOIL

From April to September there are about three hydrofoils a week departing for Les-vos (€25.50, two hours) and Piraeus (€38.50, four hours).

Getting Around

BUS

From the **long-distance bus station** (☎ 22710 27507; Leof Aigaiou) in Chios there are, in sum-mer, four buses from Monday to Saturday to Pyrgi (€2.20), three to Mesta (€2.70) and four to Kardamyla (€2.25) via Lan-gada. There are two buses a week to Volis-sos (€2.70). A few buses go to the main beaches of Kampia, Nagos and Lithi but the schedule may make it impractical to take day trips. Buses to Karfas Beach are serviced by the blue (city) bus company. Schedules are posted at both the **local bus station** (☎ 22710 22079), south of the park, and the long-distance bus station in Chios Town.

CAR & MOTORCYCLE

The numerous car-rental outlets in Chios Town include **Aegean Travel** (☎ 22710 41277; aegeantr@otenet.gr; Leof Aigaiou 114), underneath Chios Rooms. In summer it's a good idea to book in advance for weekends.

TAXI

There is a **taxi rank** (☎ 22710 41111; Plateia Vounakiou) in Chios Town.

CHIOS TOWN

pop 23,779

The town of Chios, on the east coast, is the island's port and capital, and home to almost half of the island's inhabitants. Its waterfront, flanked by concrete build-ings and happening bars, is pretty noisy, but the police appear to be cracking down on the inordinate number of extra-loud,

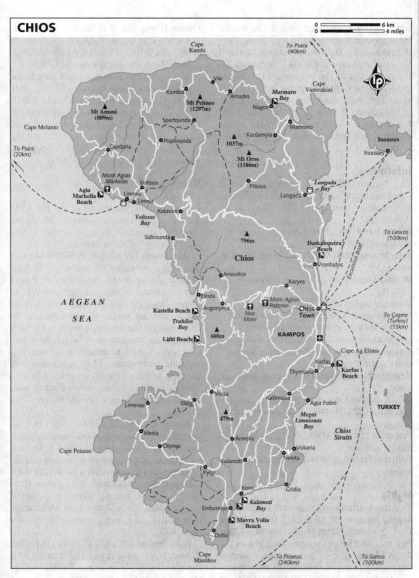

CHIOS

Cape Kambi
Viki
Kambia
Amades
Mt Amani (809m)
Mt Pelineo (1297m)
Spartounda
Marmaro Bay
Nagos
Cape Melanio
Dardaria
Pispilounda
Kardamyla
Marmaro
Cape Vamvakias
To Psara (20km)
1037m
Inousses
Inousses
Mt Oros (1186m)
Moni Agias Markelas
Volissos
Pitious
Langada Bay
Agia Markella Beach
Limnos
Limnia
Langada
Volissos Bay
Katavasi
Sidirounda
796m
To Lesvos (100km)
Daskalopetra Beach
Chios
Vrontados
A E G E A N
Anavatos
Karyes
S E A
Elinda
Moni Agion Pateron
Kastella Beach
Avgonyma
Nea Moni
Chios Town
To Çesme (Turkey) (15km)
Trahilos Bay
608m
Lithi Beach
KAMPOS
Cape Ag Elinas
Karfas
Karfas Beach
Thymiana
Vessa
Kallimasia
Agia Fotini
Limenas
Elata
479m
Megas Limnionas Bay
TURKEY
Mesta
Olympi
Armolia
Vokaria
Chios Straits
Cape Petasas
Kalamoti
Nenita
Pyrgi
Komi
Gridia
Emboreios
Kalamoti Bay
Mavra Volia Beach
Dotia
Cape Mastihos
To Piraeus (240km)
To Samos (100km)

To Psara (40km)

Excursion boat

0 ___ 6 km
0 ___ 4 miles

souped-up vehicles which career up and down. The atmospheric old quarter, with many traditional Turkish houses built around a Genoese castle, and the lively market area, are both worth taking the time to explore. Chios doesn't have its own beach; the nearest is the sand at Karfas, 6km south.

Orientation

Most ferries dock at the northern end of the waterfront at the western end of Neorion. Some ferries from Piraeus arrive at the very inconvenient time of 4am – worth remembering if you are planning to find a room. The old Turkish quarter (called Kastro) is to the north of the ferry quay. To reach the town centre from here, follow the waterfront around to the left and walk along Leof Aigaiou. Turn right onto Kanari to reach the central square of Plateia Vounakiou. To the northwest of the square are the public gardens, and to the southeast is the market area. The main shopping streets are south of the square. As you face inland, the local bus station is on the right side of the public gardens, and the long-distance bus station is on the left.

Information

The National Bank of Greece and most other banks are between Kanari and Plateia Vounakiou. There is an ATM halfway along Aplotarias.

Aegean Travel (☎ 22710 41277; aegeantr@otenet.gr; Leof Aigaiou 114)

Enter Internet Café (☎ 22710 41058; Leof Aigaiou 48; per hr €3.50)

Mr Quick Laundry (☎ 22710 26108; Prokymea 46; per kg €8)

Municipal Tourist office (☎ 22710 44389; infochio@otenet.gr; Kanari 18; 7am-10pm Apr-Oct, 7am-4pm Nov-Mar) Extremely helpful and friendly, it provides information on accommodation, car rental, bus and boat schedules, and more. The book *Hiking Routes of Chios* is available here for free.

Newsagent (cnr Leof Aigaiou & Rodokanaki) Sells foreign papers.

OTE (Dimokkratias Roidou) Public telephone.

Port police (☎ 22710 44432) At the eastern end of Neorion.

Post office (☎ 22710 44350; Omirou 2) One block back from the waterfront.

Tourist police (☎ 22710 44427) At the eastern end of Neorion.

Sights

The most interesting museum is the **Philip Argenti Museum** (☎ 22710 23463; Koraís; admission €1.50; museum & library 8am-2pm Mon-Fri, 5-7.30pm Fri, 8am-12.30pm Sat) in the same building as the **Koraís Library**, one of the country's largest libraries. The museum contains embroideries, traditional costumes and portraits of the wealthy Argenti family.

The town's other museums are not so compelling. The **archaeological museum** (☎ 22710 44239; Mihalon 10; admission €2; 8.30am-2.45pm Tue-Sun) contains sculptures, pottery and coins dating from the Neolithic period. The **Byzantine Museum** (☎ 22710 26866; Plateia Vounakiou) housed in a former mosque, the Medjitie Djami. It was closed at the time of writing, but when it re-opens there's a collection of sculptures that date from the 14th- to 15th-century Genoese occupation of Chios.

Just inside the Kastro's main gate is the tiny **Giustiniani Palace Museum** (☎ 22710 22819; admission €2 Mon-Sat, €1 Sun; 9am-3pm Tue-Sun). It holds a few restored wall paintings of prophets and other Byzantine bits and pieces. The most important works are the 12 Byzantine frescoes of the prophets, which date from the 13th century.

Sleeping

BUDGET

Call the municipal tourist office for a full listing of the town's *domatia*. Be aware though, accommodation in central Chios can be noisy – choose carefully.

Chios Rooms (☎ 22710 20198, 69728 33841; www.chiosrooms.gr; Leof Aigaiou 110; s/d/tr €25/30/40) This beautifully restored neoclassical house is a continual work in progress for Kiwi owner Don. He is passionate about finding interesting pieces of old furniture to complement the breezy rooms with high ceilings, the front ones of which have terrific water views. Rooms have private, but separate bathrooms. The 'penthouse' has its own terrace (doubles/triples €35/45). There's nothing better than relaxing with a cold beer on Don's sunny, flower-filled balcony.

Rooms Alex (☎ 22710 26054; Livanou 29; d incl breakfast €45) For another *domatia* option look for the roof garden of this place, festooned with flags. The rooms have an old-Greek-grandmother feel, and are a bit on the dark side, but the place does have personality. Alex will pick you up from your boat if you call him. He will also help with car or bike rentals and give general information on Chios.

Fedra Pension (☎ 22710 41129; fax 22710 41130; M Livanou 13; s/d €28/40) If you can actually find the unenthusiastic reception (try the downstairs bar) these seven attractive rooms succeed with a modern-meets-traditional décor in an old mansion house. Just beware of the noise from nearby bars.

MIDRANGE & TOP END

Hotel Kyma (☎ 22710 44500; kyma@chi.forthnet.gr; Evgenias Chandris 1; s/d/tr incl breakfast €61/78/97;) The Kyma occupies a charismatic century-old

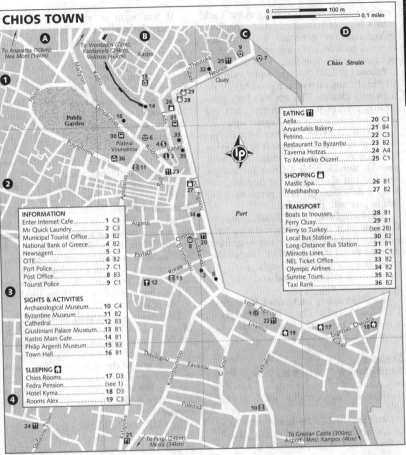

CHIOS TOWN

INFORMATION
Enter Internet Cafe	1 C3
Mr Quick Laundry	2 C3
Municipal Tourist Office	3 B2
National Bank of Greece	4 B2
Newsagent	5 C3
OTE	6 C3
Port Police	7 C1
Post Office	8 B3
Tourist Police	9 C1

SIGHTS & ACTIVITIES
Archaeological Museum	10 C4
Byzantine Museum	11 B2
Cathedral	12 B3
Giustiniani Palace Museum	13 B1
Kastro Main Gate	14 B1
Philip Argenti Museum	15 B3
Town Hall	16 B1

SLEEPING
Chios Rooms	17 D3
Fedra Pension	(see 1)
Hotel Kyma	18 D3
Rooms Alex	19 C3

EATING
Aella	20 C3
Arvanitakis Bakery	21 B4
Petrino	22 C3
Restaurant To Byzantio	23 B2
Taverna Hotzas	24 A4
To Meliotiko Ouzeri	25 C1

SHOPPING
Mastic Spa	26 B1
Mastihashop	27 B2

TRANSPORT
Boats to Inousses	28 B1
Ferry Quay	29 B1
Ferry to Turkey	(see 28)
Local Bus Station	30 B2
Long-Distance Bus Station	31 B2
Miniotis Lines	32 C1
NEL Ticket Office	33 B2
Olympic Airlines	34 B2
Sunrise Tours	35 B2
Taxi Rank	36 B2

mansion. If you can secure a room in the old part overlooking the sea you won't be disappointed, but the modern wing is a little too reminiscent of a hospital for our liking. The breakfast is magnificent. The helpful owners can organise driving itineraries that include accommodation in Mesta and Volissos.

Grecian Castle (☎ 22710 44740; www.greciancastle .gr; Enoseos; s/d/ste incl breakfast €100/125/200;) It's a pity that this boutique-style hotel is often overrun with tours, as it's not a bad place to stay. The pool overlooks the sea and there's an attractive garden filled with flowers and palms. Unfortunately the rooms, other than the suites, can't compete with the grounds and lack the atmosphere

of the communal areas. There are two restaurants, one of which offers the ubiquitous 'Greek Night'.

Eating

Taverna Hotzas (☎ 22710 42787; Kondyli 3; mains €5; dinner Mon-Sat, closed Jun) This taverna at the southern end of town is an institution, with lots of ugly cats and a lovely garden littered with lemon trees. Vegetarian-friendly dishes change regularly, but rice and mussels makes a tasty, filling meal. The *mastelo* (grilled cheese) and the grilled fish are also recommended, as is the house ouzo.

Restaurant To Byzantio (☎ 22710 41035; cnr Ralli & Roídou; mains from €4) This bright, unpretentious place serves good traditional steam-tray fare to a local crowd, at low prices. Tuck into a plate of stewed rabbit, or spaghetti bolognaise for generous portions and cheerful service. The cheese *pites* are great, but run out the door fast.

Petrino (☎ 22730 29797; Leof Aigaiou; mains from €7) This trendy eatery has a good handle on the Greek classics. Though it's a little pricier than average, it's well worth it, and there is a good choice of north Aegean wines.

Aella (☎ 22710 41465; Omiroi 4; meals from €2) Follow your nose, and the crowds to this *gyros* (Greek version of doner kebab) joint, with popular outside tables. Great for budget seekers, but also a treat for anyone who loves a delicious, perfectly prepared *souvlaki* in pita with fresh salad.

To Meliotiko Ouzeri (☎ 22710 40407; mains around €4-7) Line your stomach before a long ferry ride at this basic place on the waterfront near the police station. Pull up a street-side chair and dig into huge helpings of delicious Greek salads, seafood and vegetable appetisers. Be hungry.

Arvanitakis Bakery (cnr Katapola & Kountouriotou) The bread baked at Chios' largest bakery is some of the best you'll find in Greece. Try the wholewheat.

Shopping

Mastihashop (☎ 22710 81600; Leof Aigaiou 36) Products made out of local mastic – like lotions, toothpaste, soaps, condiments – are available here.

Mastic Spa (☎ 22710 28643; Leof Aigaiou 12) Mastic cosmetics can be found at this place.

See boxed text (opposite) for more.

CENTRAL CHIOS

North of Chios is an elongated beachside suburb leading to **Vrontados** where you can sit on the supposed stone chair of Homer, the **Daskalopetra**. It's a serene spot and it is not hard to imagine Homer nodding off here.

Immediately south of Chios is a warren of walled mansions, some restored, others crumbling, called the **Kampos**. Surrounded by lush, rambling gardens, and citrus groves, this was the preferred abode of wealthy Genoese and Greek merchant families from the 14th century onwards. It's ~~ea~~sy to get lost here so keep your wits about ~~you~~. It's best to tour the area by bicycle, ~~car~~d or car, since it is fairly extensive.

If you want to stay here, the 17th century **Perleas Mansion** (☎ 22710 32217; www .perleas.gr; Vitiadou; s/d/house for 4-5 people €75/110/16O) is an outstanding choice. More like a privat~~e~~ home than a guesthouse, it's set on a 4-acr~~e~~ organic farm where owner Claire teache~~s~~ traditional marmalade production.

Chios' main beach resort, **Karfas**, is also 7km south of Chios. The beach is sandy though comparatively small, with some moderate development and some A-class hotels; if you like your beaches quiet, look elsewhere. **Island Divers** (☎ 22710 32434; www .islanddivers.gr; Karfas) offers scuba diving and snorkelling day trips from €25 per person.

In the centre of the island is the **Nea Moni** (admission free; ⏱ 8am-1pm & 4-8pm). This large, 11th-century World Heritage–listed monastery stands in a beautiful mountain setting, 14km from Chios. At the time of writing, the monastery was under extensive renovations, with an unknown date of completion. You can still wander around the site, but most of the buildings are closed to the public.

Like many monasteries in Greece Nea Moni was built to house an icon of the Virgin Mary who appeared before the eyes of three shepherds. In its heyday the monastery was one of the richest in Greece with the most pre-eminent artists of Byzantium commissioned to create the mosaics in its *katholikon* (principal church of a monastic complex).

In 1822, the buildings were set on fire and all the resident monks were massacred by the Turks. There is a macabre display of their skulls in the ossuary at the monastery's little chapel. In the earthquake of 1881 the dome of the *katholikon* caved in, causing damage to the mosaics. Nonetheless, the mosaics still rank among the most outstanding examples of Byzantine art in Greece. Oddly, for a monastery, a few nuns now live there. The bus service is poor, but travel agents in Chios have excursions here and to Anavatos.

Ten kilometres from Nea Moni, at the end of a road that now takes no one home, stands the forlorn village of **Anavatos**. Its abandoned grey-stone houses stand as lonely sentinels to one of Chios' great tragedies. Nearly all the inhabitants of the village perished in 1822. It is a striking village, built on a precipitous cliff which

---

THE GUM MASTIC

'The Tear of a Shrub' is how the mastic industry describes its famous product. The resin drops that seep from the mastic tree, or lentisk bush, resemble tears, and the hard manual work required to harvest, dry and clean the product probably provokes them. Many ancient Greeks, including Hippocrates, proclaimed the pharmaceutical benefits of mastic, claiming that it cured stomach upsets, chronic coughs and diseases of the liver, intestines and bladder. It was also used as an antidote for snake bites. During Turkish rule Chios received preferential treatment from the sultans who, along with the ladies of the harem, were hooked on chewing gum made from mastic. It had the same value as gold, and those caught stealing mastic were hanged.

Conditions in southern Chios are ideal for the growth of the mastic tree. Until recently, mastic was widely used in the pharmaceutical industry, as well as in the manufacture of chewing gum and certain alcoholic drinks, particularly arak, a Middle Eastern liqueur. In most cases mastic has now been replaced by *raki,* a Greek firewater. But mastic production may yet have a future. Some adherents of alternative medicine claim that it stimulates the immune system and reduces blood pressure and cholesterol levels. Lotions, toothpaste, soaps, condiments and various other mastic products are available at **Mastihashop** (☎ 22710 81600; Leof Aigaiou 36), in Chios Town, and mastic cosmetics can be found at the **Mastic Spa** (☎ 22710 28643; Leof Aigaiou 12). Chewing gum made from mastic can be bought everywhere on Chios, under the brand name Elma.

---

the villagers chose to hurl themselves over, rather than be taken captive by the Turks. Narrow, stepped pathways wind between the houses to the summit but the general decrepitude makes the walk dangerous and the route is often closed. Nearby **Avgonyma** is an attractive hilltop village built in the 11th century which is undergoing a revival. **Spitakia** (☎ 22710 81200; www.spitakia.com; d from €90) offers unique studios in restored buildings.

The beaches on the mid-west coast are not spectacular, but they are quiet and generally undeveloped. **Lithi Beach**, the southernmost, is popular with weekenders and can get busy.

SOUTHERN CHIOS

Southern Chios is dominated by medieval villages that look as though they were transplanted from the Levant rather than built by Genoese colonisers in the 14th century. The rolling, scrubby hills are covered in low mastic trees that for many years were the main source of income for these scattered settlements.

There are some 20 Mastihohoria (mastic villages); the two best preserved ones are Pyrgi and Mesta. As mastic was a lucrative commodity in the Middle Ages, many an invader cast an acquisitive eye upon these villages, necessitating sturdy fortifications. The archways spanning the streets were to prevent the houses from collapsing during earthquakes. Because of the sultan's fondness for mastic chewing gum, the inhabitants of the Mastihohoria were spared in the 1822 massacre.

Pyrgi Πυργί
pop 1044

The fortified village of Pyrgi, 24km southwest of Chios, is the largest of the Mastihohoria and one of the most extraordinary villages in the whole of Greece. The vaulted streets of the fortified village are narrow and labyrinthine, but what makes Pyrgi unique are the building façades, decorated with intricate grey and white designs. Some of the patterns are geometric and others are based on flowers, leaves and animals. The technique used, called *xysta*, is achieved by coating the walls with a mixture of cement and black volcanic sand, painting over this with white lime, and then scraping off parts of the lime with the bent prong of a fork, to reveal the matt grey beneath.

From the main road, a fork heading to the right (coming from Chios) leads to the heart of the village and the central square. The little 12th-century **Church of Agios Apostolos** (☎ 10am-1pm Tue-Thu & Sat), just off the square, is profusely decorated with well-preserved 17th-century frescoes. It's usually open for Mass on Sunday and in the late afternoon. The façade of the larger church, on the opposite side of the square, has the most impressive *xysta* of all the buildings here.

Rooms are few and far between but there are three tavernas on the central square. Book ahead for the modern and renovated **Giannaki Rooms** (☎ 22710 25888, 69459 59889; fax 22710 22846; d €40; ⚇).

Emboreios Εμπορειός

Six kilometres south of Pyrgi, Emboreios was the *Mastihohoria's* port in the days when mastic production was big business. These days it is a quiet place, perfect for people who like to get away from it all. As you come from Chios, a sign points left to Emboreios, just before you arrive at Pyrgi.

Mavra Volia Beach, at the end of the road, has unusual black volcanic pebbles as its main attraction. The effect is striking but the wide beach is shadeless.

There is another more secluded beach, just over the headland along a paved track.

The comfortable **Studio Apartments Vasiliki** (☎ 22710 71422; d €45; ⚇) in Emboreios are often full, but the same people also have rooms in Mavra Volia.

On the main square the shady **Porto Emborios** (☎ 22710 70025; mains from €6, appetisers €3.50) is very pleasant, with an old stone façade decorated with fishing nets and hanging strings of chillies and garlic. It has good home-cooked food, including roast lamb and a number of vegetarian dishes.

Mesta Μεστά

Mesta has a very different atmosphere from that created by the striking visuals of Pyrgi, and should be on any visitor's itinerary. Nestled among low hills, the village is exquisite and completely enclosed within massive fortified walls. Entrance to the maze of streets is via one of four gates. This method of limiting entry to the settlement, and its disorienting maze of streets and tunnels, is a prime example of 14th-century defence architecture. The cobbled streets of bare stone houses and arches have a melancholy aura, and feel downright eerie at night. The sunny central square is a lovely place to sit over a coffee, with women chatting on their front steps as they shell almonds and fresh *revithia* (chickpeas) or tie bundles of sweet-smelling herbs.

ORIENTATION

Buses stop on Plateia Nikolaou Poumpaki, on the main road outside Mesta. To reach the central square of Plateia Taxiarhon, with your back to the bus shelter, turn right, and then immediately left, and you will see a sign pointing to the centre of the village.

SIGHTS

The village has two **churches of the Taxiarhes** (archangels). The older one dates from Byzantine times and has a magnificent 17th-century iconostasis. The second one, built in the 19th century, has very fine frescoes.

SLEEPING & EATING

There is a clearing house system for the comfortable, but generally dark, rooms in various houses around the village. Head to the Mesaonas restaurant on the square and ask for the proprietors of the following places.

Despina Floris Rooms (☎ 22710 76050; fax 22710 76529; d studio €45-50) Despina Floris speaks brilliant English and is a fount of information about the village.

Anna Floradis Rooms (☎ /fax 22710 76455; floradis@Internet.gr; s/d €40/50; ⚇) The French-speaking Anna Floradis has five studios with TV, next to the church.

Dhimitris Pipidhis Rooms (☎ 22710 76029; r €30-45) Dhimitris Pipidhis is charming.

Mesaonas (☎ 22710 76050; Plateia Taxiarhon; mains from €5) For excellent country cooking take an outside table at this restaurant on the square. It specialises in traditional recipes made with local ingredients. The wine, oil, cheese and, of course, the *souma* (an ouzo made from seasonal fruit, or a mastic firewater), are all from Mesta.

NORTHERN CHIOS

Northern Chios is characterised by its craggy peaks (Mt Pelineo, Mt Oros and Mt Amani), deserted villages and scrawny hillsides once blanketed in rich pine forests. The area is mainly for the adventurous and those not fazed by tortuous roads.

Volissos is the main focus for the villages of the northwestern quarter. Reputedly Homer's place of birth, it is today a quiet settlement, capped with an impressive Genoese fort. Volissos' port is **Limnia**, a workaday fishing harbour. It's not especially appealing, but has a welcoming taverna. You can continue to **Limnos**, 1km away, where caïques sometimes leave for Psara. The road onwards round the north end is very winding and passes some isolated villages.

On the eastern side a picturesque road leads out of Vrontados through a landscape that is somewhat more visitor-friendly than the western side. **Langada** is the first village, wedged at the end of a bay looking out towards Inousses. Next are **Kardamyla** and **Marmaro**, the two main settlements. If you fancy a dip, head a few kilometres further to the lush little fishing hamlet of **Nagos**, which has a nice beach with coloured pebbles.

Beyond Nagos, the road winds upwards, skirting craggy Mt Pelineo. The scenery is green enough, but settlements are ever fewer and more remote. **Amades** and **Viki** are two villages you will traverse before hitting the last village, **Kambia**, perched high up on a ridge overlooking bare hillsides and the sea far below. From here a mostly sealed road leads you round Mt Pelineo, past a futuristic phalanx of 10 huge wind-driven generators on the opposite side of the valley, and back to the trans-island route near Volissos.

Sleeping

Hotel Kardamyla (☎ 22720 23353; kyma@chi.forthnet .gr; Marmaro; s/d/tr €61/78/97.20; ❄) If you choose to stay in Marmaro, try this comfortable hotel run by the same management as Hotel Kyma in Chios. The sprawling establishment is right on a quiet cove just outside the village, making it an ideal spot for a beach holiday. If you call ahead, the owners will arrange for transport from Marmaro.

INOUSSES ΟΙΝΟΥΣΣΕΣ

pop 1050 / area 14 sq km
Off the northeastern coast of Chios lie nine tiny islets, collectively called Inousses. Only one of these, also called Inousses, is inhabited. Those who live here permanently make their living from fishing and sheep farming. The island has three fish farms and exports fish to Italy and France; it is hilly, covered in scrub and has good beaches.

Inousses is no ordinary Greek island. It may be small, but it is the ancestral home of around 30% of Greece's ship owners. Most of these wealthy maritime barons conduct their business from Athens, London and New York, but in summer, they return with their families to Inousses, where they own luxurious mansions.

There is a rumour that financial incentives are offered to discourage people from opening tavernas or *domatia* on the island, because they don't want to attract foreign tourists. It may not be possible to prove this but certainly no *domatia* owners come to meet the boat, there are no *domatia* signs and wandering around the streets fails to attract the usual offers of accommodation. There is one overpriced hotel and a couple of nearly deserted tavernas and the place has a curiously barren and sterile air since there are few tourist facilities and even fewer visitors.

On a more positive note – if these quirks have not discouraged you from going to Inousses – the island's town has some nice neoclassical mansions and abandoned houses, good beaches (Kastro Beach is the usual swimming stop for day-trippers) and no package tourists. In the town of Inousses there is a large naval boarding school and if you visit during term time you may well encounter the pupils parading around town to bellowed marching orders.

Getting There & Away

The best way to visit this island is on a day-long excursion (€15). These are run regularly between June and September. Try **Sunrise Tours** (☎ 22710 41390; Kanari 28) in Chios Town. The island is served only by the local ferry boat (€3, one hour) but the schedule is not always geared towards day trips. There are also daily **water taxis** (☎ 69441 68104) travelling to/from Langada. The one-way fare is €35, which is split between the passengers.

Getting Around

Inousses has no public transport and nowhere to rent wheels, but there is one taxi (ask at one of the tavernas).

PSARA ΨΑΡΑ

pop 422 / area 45 sq km
Psara (psah-*rah*) is a rocky island with little vegetation, which lies off the northwest coast of Chios. During Ottoman times Greeks settled on this remote island to escape Turkish oppression. By the 19th century, many of these inhabitants, like those of Chios and Inousses, had become successful ship owners. When the rallying cry for

self-determination reverberated through the country, the Psariots zealously took up arms and contributed a large number of ships to the Greek cause. In retaliation the Turks stormed the island and killed all but 3000 of the 20,000 inhabitants. The island never regained its former glory and today all of the inhabitants live in the island's one settlement, also called Psara.

Like Inousses, Psara sees few tourists but there are some *domatia* and a couple of tavernas.

Getting There & Away

Ferries leave Chios for Psara (€8.80, 3½ hours) at 7am or 8am three times weekly, but the schedule may mandate an overnight stay. Call **Miniotis Lines** (☎ 22710 24670) in Chios, or check with a local agent for current departure days, since these change from year to year. Local caïques also run from Limnos (€5, three hours) on the west coast of Chios about once a week, but departure times are unpredictable and often depend on the prevailing weather conditions.

LESVOS (MYTILINI)
ΛΕΣΒΟΣ (ΜΥΤΙΛΗΝΗ)

pop 93,428 / area 1637 sq km

Scenically, culturally, historically and gastronomically, the Lesvos (Mytilini) experience is hard to rival. The third-largest island in Greece, after Crete and Evia, Lesvos is predominantly mountainous, with wonderful opportunities for trekking and bird-watching, while the fertile south and east of the island are carpeted with olive groves producing the best olive oil in Greece. The terrain is ideal for grazing and the sheeps'-milk cheese of Lesvos (called *ladotyri*) is justifiably prized. The Gulf of Kalloni produces pungent sardines, eaten salted with local ouzo.

The artistic side of Lesvos is no less developed. Terpander, the musical composer, and Arion, the poet, were both born on the island in the 7th century BC. A few centuries later, Aristotle and Epicurus taught at an exceptional school of philosophy which flourished on Lesvos. Perhaps the island's most famous progeny was Sappho, one of the greatest poets of

ancient Greece, who was born on Lesvos around 630 BC. Unfortunately little of her poetry is extant, but what remains reveals a genius for combining passion with simplicity and detachment in verses of beauty and power. More recently, the primitive painter Theophilos (1866–1934) and the Nobel Prize-winning poet Odysseus Elytis (1911–96) were born on Lesvos. The island is to this day a spawning ground for innovative ideas in the arts and politics, and is the headquarters of the University of the Aegean.

Lesvos is becoming a popular package-holiday destination, but is large enough to absorb tourists without seeming to be overrun. Still, it's best to visit outside the peak tourist months of July and August. Early spring and late autumn are ideal for trekking. There's a lot to see here; you could easily spend two weeks taking in the sights and still feel you've run out of time to see everything.

Activities
TREKKING

Lesvos has some nice trekking trails in the north and south. Some of these were once marked with colour-coded signs, but these days only a few signs are left; nonetheless, the trails are easy to follow. These walks can be taken in sections, or over a few days, stopping off along the way where appropriate. They are a mixture of dirt vehicle tracks and pedestrian trails. The main trails are Vatera–Yera, Petra–Lapsarna, Kapi–Sykaminia and Sigri–Eresos. There are many other walking trails on the island, including those in the olive-growing region around Plomari (see boxed text, p382). Of these, the Skopelos–Karionas–Kastelos–Trigonas/Plagia day-trek is the most popular.

BIRD-WATCHING

Bird-watching is big business in Lesvos. The island is the transit point and home to over 279 species of birds ranging from raptors to waders. As a result, Lesvos is attracting an increasing number of visitors – human and feathered – particularly in spring. There are four main observation areas – Eresos, Petra, Skala Kallonis and Agiasos. The major aim of birders seems to be spotting the elusive Cinereous Bunting and Kruper's Nuthatch. *Birding on the Greek Island of Lesvos* (2002) by Richard Brooks, which can be bought in Kallonis, is the definitive guide.

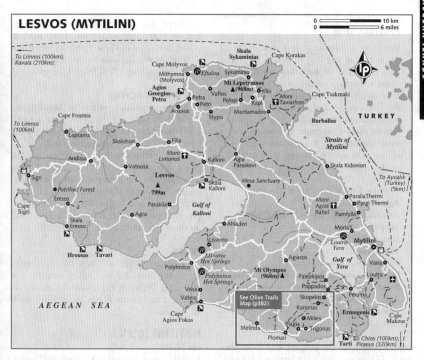

Festivals & Events

Throughout summer, villages hold festivals on the name day of their church. These two-day festas with very ancient origins usually involve the racing of beautifully decorated horses and the sacrifice of a bull. For a list of dates and villages, see the boxed text, p374.

If you're visiting Lesvos in February, don't miss carnival in the town of Agiasos – among other things, the locals perform hilariously vulgar comedies.

Getting There & Away

AIR

Olympic Airlines (☎ 22510 28659; www.olympicairlines .com; Kavetsou 44), in Mytilini, has at least four flights daily from Lesvos to Athens (€78) and one daily to Thessaloniki (€87), as well as two flights weekly to Chios (€28) and five weekly to Limnos (€46). **Aegean Airlines** (☎ 22510 61120; fax 22510 61801; www.aegeanair.com) flies between Lesvos and Athens (€68, one hour) three times a day and Thessaloniki (€84, one hour 10 minutes) once a day; they have an office at the airport. Note that Lesvos is referred to as Mytilene on air schedules. The airport

is 8km south of Mytilini. A taxi to/from the airport will cost about €7.

FERRY

Domestic

In summer there is at least one ferry daily to Piraeus (€27.90, 12 hours) via Chios (€12, three hours) and three weekly high-speed services (€50, six hours), also via Chios. There are two ferries weekly to Kavala (€24.70, 10 hours) via Limnos (€17.20, six hours), one weekly to Thessaloniki (€30.20, 13 hours), also via Limnos, and one weekly to Alexandroupolis (€21.60, nine hours). These ferries stop at Sigri not Mytilini. Ferry ticket offices line the eastern side of Pavlou Kountourioti in Mytilini. Get tickets from **Maritime Company of Lesvos** (NEL; ☎ 22510 28480; fax 22510 28601; Pavlou Kountourioti 67) or **Samiotis Tours** (☎ 22510 42574; fax 22510 41808; Pavlou Kountourioti 43).

Samiotis Tours also handles tickets for the high-speed *Aeolis Express,* which sails three times weekly to Chios (€24.80, 1½ hours) and Piraeus (€27.40, six hours).

Lesvos has a very strict anti-drug policy, and the port police sometimes conduct

NORHTEASTERN
AEGEAN ISLANDS

FESTIVAL TIME

One of the best times of year to be in Lesvos is during July and August when the days and nights are given over to wild bacchanals in honour of patron saints. At this time of year there's usually a lot of food, drink, live music and dancing, as well as horse races and the sacrifice of a bull, which is then cooked overnight with wheat and eaten the next day. This traditional dish is known as *keskek*. On 6 August Skala Kalloni holds a sardine festival, which is not to be missed.

Major festival dates are as follows:

Agia Paraskevi 1 July
Agiasos, Eresos, Plomari, Vrisa 20 July
Skopelos 22 July
Eresos 24 July
Skala Kalloni 25 July
Paleokipos, Plomari 26 July
Eresos, Gavathas, Perama, Plomari 27 July
Eresos, Andissa, Skala Kalloni 6 August
Agiasos, Kerami 15 August
Vafios 30 August

---

searches of ferry passengers who look 'suspect'. Heavy penalties are imposed for possession of any drugs.

International

Ferries to Ayvalık in Turkey run roughly four times a week in high season. One-way and return tickets cost €29 (including port taxes). The crossing takes 45 minutes. Tickets are available from **Aeolic Cruises** (☎ 22510 23266; aeolic@les.forthnet.gr; Pavlou Kountourioti 47).

Getting Around

BUS

Lesvos' transport hub is the capital, Mytilini. In summer, from the **long-distance bus station** (☎ 22510 28873; El Venizelou) there are three buses daily to Skala Eresou (€7.50, 2½ hours) via Eresos, five buses daily to Mithymna (€5, 1¾ hours) via Petra, and two buses daily to Sigri (€7.70, 2½ hours). There are five buses daily to the south coast resort of Plomari (€4, 1¼ hours).

Note, there are about half as many buses in the off season, with a schedule that may not allow day trips. A timetable is posted in the window at the long-distance bus station.

There are no direct buses between Eresos, Sigri and Mithymna. If you wish to travel from one of these villages to another, change buses in Kalloni, which is 48km from Eresos and 22km from Mithymna.

CAR & MOTORCYCLE

The many car-hire outlets in Mytilini include **Hertz** (☎ 22510 37355; Pavlou Kountourioti 87) and **Egeon Rent a Car** (☎ 22510 29820, 69776 53583; Chiou 2), but it's best to shop around.

Many motorcycle-rental firms are located along the same stretch of waterfront. You will, however, be better off hiring a motorcycle or scooter in Mithymna or Skala Eresou, since Lesvos is a large island and an underpowered two-wheeler is not really a practical mode of transport for getting around.

FERRY

In summer there are half-hourly ferries across the mouth of the Gulf of Yera (€1, five minutes), between Perama and Koundouroudia, near Loutra. Buses to Mytilini meet all ferries.

MYTILINI TOWN ΜΥΤΙΛΗΝΗ

pop 27,247

Mytilini, the capital and port of Lesvos, might not be Mykonos, but it does have its own attractions, including a lively harbour and nightlife, once-grand 19th-century mansions (that are gradually being renovated), and the Teriade Museum, with its astonishing collection of 20th-century modern art. Mytilini's jumbled streets, particularly the northern end of Ermou, are perfect for getting lost among the old-fashioned *zaharoplasteia*, bakers, grocers and ramshackle antique stores. There are also interesting ceramic and jewellery workshops run by local designers. With a large university campus and a year-round population, Mytilini – unlike most island towns – is also lively in winter.

Orientation

Mytilini is built around two harbours (north and south) that occupy both sides of a promontory and are linked by the main thoroughfare of Ermou. East of the harbours is a large fortress surrounded by a pine forest. All ferries dock at the southern harbour. The waterfront is called Pavlou Kountourioti. The northern harbour's waterfront is called Navmahias Ellis.

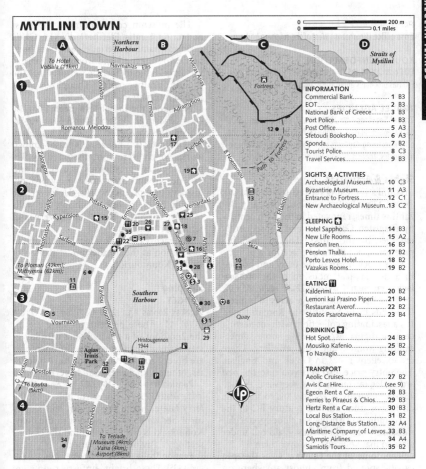

MYTILINI TOWN

0 _____ 200 m
0 _____ 0.1 miles

INFORMATION
Commercial Bank	1 B3
EOT	2 B3
National Bank of Greece	3 B3
Port Police	4 B3
Post Office	5 A3
Sfetoudi Bookshop	6 A3
Sponda	7 B3
Tourist Police	8 C3
Travel Services	9 B3

SIGHTS & ACTIVITIES
Archaeological Museum	10 C3
Byzantine Museum	11 A3
Entrance to Fortress	12 C1
New Archaeological Museum	13 C2

SLEEPING
Hotel Sappho	14 B3
New Life Rooms	15 A2
Pension Iren	16 B3
Pension Thalia	17 B2
Porto Lesvos Hotel	18 B2
Vazakas Rooms	19 B2

EATING
Kalderimi	20 B2
Lemoni kai Prasino Piperi	21 B4
Restaurant Averof	22 B4
Stratos Psarotaverna	23 B4

DRINKING
Hot Spot	24 B3
Mousiko Kafenio	25 B2
To Navagio	26 B2

TRANSPORT
Aeolic Cruises	27 B2
Avis Car Hire	(see 9)
Egeon Rent a Car	28 B3
Ferries to Piraeus & Chios	29 B3
Hertz Rent a Car	30 B3
Local Bus Station	31 B2
Long-Distance Bus Station	32 A4
Maritime Company of Lesvos	33 B3
Olympic Airlines	34 A4
Samiotis Tours	35 B2

Information

The Commercial Bank booth on Pavlou Kountourioti has an ATM, near the ferry terminal.

BOOKSHOPS

Sfetoudi Bookshop (☎ 22510 22287; Ermou 51) Sells good maps, postcards and books on Lesvos. Look for *39 Coffee Houses and a Barber's Shop*, a beautifully produced book of photos by Jelly Hadjidimitriou.

EMERGENCIES

Port police (☎ 22510 28827) Next to Picolo Travel on the east side of Pavlou Kountourioti.
Tourist police (☎ 22510 22776) At the entrance to the quay.

INTERNET ACCESS

Sponda (☎ 22510 41007; Komniaki; per hr €3) This pool hall has Internet access.

INTERNET RESOURCES

www.lesvos.com Information on Mytilini and Lesvos in general.

MEDICAL SERVICES

Bostaneio General Hospital (☎ 22510 43777; E Bostani 48)

MONEY

National Bank of Greece (Pavlou Kountourioti) Has an ATM. Other banks can also be found along Pavlou Kountourioti.

POST
Post office (Vournazon) West of the southern harbour.

TOURIST INFORMATION
EOT (☎ 22510 42511; Aristarhou 6; ☷ 9am-1pm Mon-Fri) Has brochures about the island.

TRAVEL AGENCIES
Travel Services (☎ 22530 71627; Pavlou Kountourioti 69; karablias@aias.gr) Helpful staff book ferry tickets, and offer interesting day tours with English and French speaking guides. There is also an Avis branch in the office.

Sights & Activities
Mytilini's imposing **fortress** (adult/student €2/1; ☷ 8am-2.30pm Tue-Sun) was built in early Byzantine times, renovated in the 14th century by Fragistco Gatelouzo, and subsequently enlarged by the Turks. The surrounding pine forest is a pleasant place for a picnic.

One block north of the quay and housed in a neoclassical mansion is the **archaeological museum** (☎ 22510 22087; adult/child €3/2; ☷ 8am-7.30pm). It has a large array of impressive finds from Neolithic to Roman times. It's a fascinating collection, with interesting ceramic figurines, including some somersaulting women, and gold jewellery. There are excellent notes in Greek and English. The entry price also gets you into the **new archaeological museum** (8 Noemvriou; ☷ 8am-7.30pm), 400m away, which aims to show life on Lesvos from the 2nd century BC to the 3rd century AD. Displays include spectacular mosaics – whole housefuls – laid out under glass so that you can walk over them.

The dome of the **Church of Agios Therapon** can be spotted from almost anywhere on the southern waterfront. The church has a highly ornate interior with a huge chandelier, an intricately carved iconostasis and priest's throne, and a frescoed dome. The **Byzantine Museum** (☎ 22510 28916; admission €2; ☷ 9am-1pm) in the church's courtyard houses some fine icons.

TERIADE & THEOPHILOS MUSEUMS
Four kilometres south of Mytilini is the village of **Varia**, the last place you would expect to find the **Teriade Museum** (☎ 22510 23372; adult/student €2/1; ☷ 9am-5pm Tue-Sun) which houses a jaw-dropping collection of works by 20th-century artists including such greats as Picasso, Chagall, Miro, Le Corbusier and Matisse.

The museum commemorates the artist and critic Stratis Eleftheriadis (he Gallicised his name to Teriade) who was born on Lesvos but lived and worked in Paris. It was largely due to Teriade's efforts that the prolific primitive painter Theophilos' work gained international renown.

Next door the **Theophilos Museum** (☎ 22510 41644; admission €2; ☷ 9am-2.30pm & 6-8pm Tue-Sun May-Sep, 9am-1pm & 4-6pm Tue-Sun Oct & Apr, 9am-2pm Tue-Sun Nov-Mar) houses his lesser-known works which were commissioned by Teriade. Several prestigious museums and galleries around the country now proudly display Theophilos' works. However, he lived in abject poverty, painting the walls of *kafeneia* (coffee house) and tavernas in return for sustenance.

To reach Varia, take a local bus from the bus station at the northernmost section of Pavlou Kountourioti.

Sleeping
BUDGET
Vazakas Rooms (☎ 22510 46571; Bizaniou 17; d/tr €30/40; ☒) These peaceful *domatia* are on the 2nd floor of a family home with lovely views over a citrus grove. The sunny rooms are breezy and inviting, some have balconies, others a kitchenette; all have TV.

Pension Iren (☎ 22510 22787; Komninaki 41; d incl breakfast €30/35) If you're stumbling off the ferry late at night, these clean and simply furnished *domatia* are nearest to the quay. Komninaki is one block behind the eastern section of Pavlou Kountourioti.

Pension Thalia (☎ 22510 24640; Kinikiou 1; d €30, studio €35) These bright, unfussy rooms are in a large family house with a small garden. The place is well-managed, but the friendly owners speak no English. The rooms are signposted from the corner of Ermou and Adramytiou.

MIDRANGE
Hotel Votsala (☎ 22510 71231; www.votsalahotel .com; Pyrgi Thermi; d incl breakfast €55-65) Only 11km north of Mytilini, this superb hotel near the fishing village of Pyrgi Thermi offers a simple but refined resort experience. The hotel, set in a garden of flowers and fruit trees, proudly forswears TVs and fabricated 'Greek Nights', promising classical music and the sound of gently lapping waves just outside your door. Simply furnished rooms

with a balcony have no air conditioning, 'the Aegean breeze does the trick.' Pedal boats and canoes are provided free.

Porto Lesvos Hotel (☎ 22510 22510; www.porto lesvos.gr; Komninaki 21; s/d €60/90; ✖) This intimate hotel has 12 rooms, of which two are attics. Those in the front have wraparound views of Mytilini. If slate and stone set into plaster is your idea of luxury then welcome. All rooms are well furnished and include a full selection of toiletries, bathrobe and slippers. The owners are helpful and pleased to show off the island.

New Life Rooms (☎ 22510 42650; Ermou 68) This brightly painted neoclassical mansion is a little on the kitsch side, but the nine rooms are simply furnished with wooden floors and interesting mouldings. As it's tucked into a cul-de-sac, it's likely to be quiet, despite the central location.

Hotel Sappho (☎ 22510 22888; sappho@microchip .gr; Pavlou Kountourioti 31; s/d €40/60; ✖) This business hotel on the waterfront is not a charmer but is fine for one night, especially if you get in late as there is a 24-hour reception. The pastel-painted rooms need some serious interior decorating advice, and it can get noisy first thing in the morning. Better rates can usually be negotiated.

Eating

Avoid the overpriced restaurants on the western section of the southern waterfront where the waiters tout for customers.

Kalderimi (☎ 22510 46577; Thasou 3; appetisers €2-4, mains around €6) For excellent *ouzeri* fare follow the locals to this pretty restaurant with tables that spill out into a vine-covered pedestrian street near the main harbour. The food is excellent (try the salty mackerel and the zucchini fritters) and the portions generous, but be prepared for slow service during the busy lunch period.

Restaurant Averof (☎ 22510 22180; Ermou 52; mains from €4) This place is a no-nonsense traditional restaurant that has been serving hearty Greek staples since 1925. It's pretty dark inside, so take a waterfront table and tuck into something from their wide menu, perhaps a beef grill or a steaming bowl of *patsas* (tripe soup).

Lemoni kai Prasino Piperi (☎ 22510 24014; cnr Pavlou Kountourioti & Hristougennon 1944; mains €7-12) For a bit of culinary excitement, check out this stylish restaurant, where the French-

trained chef turns out well-prepared Italian dishes. It's upstairs, above a *souvlaki* joint, and has tables on a large balcony that overlooks the port.

Stratos Psarotaverna (☎ 22510 21739; Hristougennon 1944; mains from €8) Head to this friendly place at the bottom of the main harbour for a tasty seafood meal of fried prawns and mussels *saganaki*. Tables from the surrounding restaurants take over the road in summer.

Locals recommend an ouzo at sunset at the *kafeneia* under the lighthouse.

Drinking

Mousiko Kafenio (cnr Mitropoleos & Vernardaki; ☽ 7.30am-2am) This is a hip place – arty without being pretentious. Drinks are mid-price range rather than cheap, but worth it for the terrific atmosphere.

Hot Spot (Pavlou Kountourioti; ☽ 10am-midnight) Borrow a board game from the bar, and kick back and enjoy the sunset from this relaxed spot on the east side of the harbour.

To Navagio (☎ 22510 21310; Arhipelagos 23) For great coffee or fresh juice take a patio seat at this sunny café-bar in the centre of the waterfront. The 2nd-floor wine bar and restaurant is a popular night spot. Check out the magazine style menu which has plenty of information on the island.

Getting There & Away

Mytilini has two bus stations: the long-distance bus station is just beyond the southwestern end of Pavlou Kountourioti; the local bus station is on the northernmost section of Pavlou Kountourioti. For motorists, there is a large free parking area just south of the main harbour.

NORTHERN LESVOS

Northern Lesvos is dominated economically and physically by the exquisitely preserved traditional town of Mithymna, which is of historical, and modern importance in Lesvos' commercial life. The neighbouring beach resort of Petra, 6km south, receives low-key package tourism and the villages surrounding Mt Lepetymnos are authentic and picturesque, well worth a day or two of exploration. Sykaminia, Mantamados and Agia Paraskevi in particular, are very pretty. Moni Taxiarhon, near Mantamados, is also worth a visit. Skala Sykaminias is a nice beach for a swim.

Mithymna Μήθυμνα

pop 1497

A one-time rival to Mytilini, picturesque Mithymna is nowadays the antithesis of the island capital. Its handsome stone houses, with their brightly coloured shutters, reach down to the fishing port and pebble beach from a castle-crowned hill. The winding, cobbled streets are shaded by vines and offer stunning views over the harbour. A surplus of tacky souvenir stores and package tourists has done little to detract from this incredibly charming and relaxing place.

Although the town has officially reverted to its ancient name of Mithymna (Methymna), most locals still refer to it as Molyvos.

ORIENTATION

From the bus stop, walk straight ahead towards the town. Where the road forks (at the Medical Centre sign), take the right fork into 17 Noemvriou. At the top of the hill, the road forks again; the right fork is Kastrou and the left fork is a continuation of 17 Noemvriou.

INFORMATION

The National Bank of Greece, with ATM, is next to the tourist office. The Commercial Bank booth directly opposite the National Bank of Greece also has an ATM.

Central Internet Café (per hr €4.40) On the road to the port.

Medical Centre (☎ 22530 71702)

Municipal tourist office (☎ 22530 71347) A small office on the left of Kastrou between the bus stop and the fork in the road.

Post office (Kastrou) Along the left of the street.

SIGHTS & ACTIVITIES

One of the most pleasant things to do in Mithymna is to stroll along its flower-shaded streets. If you have the energy, the ruined 14th-century **Byzantine-Genoese castle** (☎ 22530 71803; admission €2; ☉ 8.30am-7pm Tue-Sun) is worth clambering up to for fine views of the coastline and over the sea to Turkey. From this castle in the 15th century, Onetta d'Oria, wife of the Genoese governor, repulsed an onslaught by the Turks by putting on her husband's armour and leading the people of Mithymna into battle. In summer the castle is the venue for a **drama festival**; ask for details at the tourist office.

The beach at Mithymna is pebbled and crowded, but in summer **excursion boats** leave at 10.30am daily for the superior beaches of Eftalou, Skala Sykaminias and Petra. Trips cost around €20 and up, depending on the itinerary; sunset cruises and boat 'safaris' are also available. Contact **Faonas Travel** (☎ 22530 71630; tekes@otenet.gr), down at the port, for more information.

Eftalou's **hot spring** is an entrancing place on the beach – don't miss it (see Balm for the Soul boxed text, opposite).

SLEEPING

Budget

There are over 50 official *domatia* in Mithymna; most consist of only one or two rooms. All display *domatia* signs and most are of a high standard. The municipal tourist office will help you if you can't be bothered looking; otherwise, the best street to start at is 17 Noemvriou.

Camping Mithymna (☎ 22530 71169; sites per adult/tent €4/3.50; ☉ Jun-Oct) This excellent and refreshingly shady camping ground is 1.5km from town and signposted from near the tourist office. Although it opens in early June, you can usually camp if you arrive a bit earlier than that.

Nassos Guest House (☎ 22530 71432; www.nassosguesthouse.com; Arionos; d €20-35) This is the most fabulous place to stay in Mithymna; an old Turkish house oozing with character. The recently renovated rooms are brightly painted and have huge windows overlooking the harbour. Take a book from the large selection and relax on the sunny terrace. Tom, the manager, helps create an informal environment and an international feel – you may even want to rent the whole place (per night €200) out yourself, it sleeps 18.

Captain's View (☎ 22530 71241; meltheo@otenet.gr; up to 6 people €90-140; ☒) Groups of friends or family will love cooking up a storm in the well-equipped kitchen of this tastefully-restored home. Take a meal and some ouzo out on the balcony and enjoy the sunset, or chill in the cosy lounge. The house has two bedrooms, and a loft and sleeps up to six.

Midrange

Hotel Olive Press (☎ 22530 71205; www.olivepress-hotel.com; d with/without seaview €100/70; ☒ ☒) This converted olive-oil factory right on

BALM FOR THE SOUL

Lesvos has many mineral springs, most dating back to ancient times. The baths are usually housed in old whitewashed buildings that look like sunken church domes. Small holes in the roof let in rays of sunlight, creating a magical dappled effect on the water. The pools are usually made of marble.

In times past, before houses had their own bathrooms, these communal baths were the places people came to bathe and talk.

With the exception of the ramshackle abandoned hot springs at Thermi, which are still worth a visit (if you like faded grandeur), it's possible to take a dip at all of the baths. Most of the springs have separate bathing for men and women, unless they are empty. The properties of the waters are outlined in the following text.

Therma Yera

The largest **springs** (admission €2.50; 8am-6pm) on Lesvos are 5km west of Mytilini on the Gulf of Yera. It's thought that there was once a temple to Hera at this site, where ancient beauty pageants took place. The springs contain radium and are 39.7°C. They are recommended for infertility, rheumatism, arthritis, diabetes, bronchitis, gall stones, dropsy and more. The cool, white marble interior is steamy and dreamy.

Polyhnitos

Southeast of Polyhnitos, these **springs** (22520 41449; fax 22520 42678; admission €3; 7am-12pm & 3-8pm) are in a pretty, renovated Byzantine building. They are some of the hottest springs in all of Continental Europe, with a temperature of 87.6°C, and are recommended for rheumatism, arthritis, skin diseases and gynaecological problems.

Lisvorio

About 5km north of the Polyhnitos springs, these **springs** (22530 71245; admission €3; 8am-1pm & 3-8pm) are just outside the little village of Lisvorio. There are two quaint little baths here, situated on either side of a stream, with pretty vegetation all around. Ask in the village for directions as the baths are unmarked. The buildings are in disrepair but one of the baths is in reasonable condition and it's possible to have a soak. The temperature and the properties of the waters are similar to those at Polyhnitos.

Eftalou

These **baths** (admission old baths/new baths €3.50/5; old bathhouse 6am-8am & 6-10pm, new bathhouse 9am-6pm) on the beach not far from Mithymna are idyllic, with perfectly clear 46.5° water. You can choose between the old bathhouse, in a whitewashed vault with a pebbled floor, or a recently constructed new bathhouse that provides individual tubs for bathing. These springs are recommended for rheumatism, arthritis, neuralgia, hypertension, gall stones and gynaecological and skin problems.

the water has charming rooms and studios surrounding a lovely interior courtyard with ivy-covered walls. The sea-view rooms escape the noise of local motorbike hooligans, but are often full; call ahead and you might be in luck.

Amfitriti Hotel (22530 71741; fax 22530 71744; s/d/tr incl breakfast €54/77/95;) This very de luxe-looking place is just 50m from the beach. Built in the traditional stone style, the tiled rooms have all the mod cons, and

lovely views over the palm trees. The garden pool is particularly refreshing on a sweaty Lesvos day. The hotel is often booked up with package tourists, but staff are amiable to independent travellers.

Hotel Sea Horse (22530 71630; www.seahorse -hotel.com; d incl breakfast €75;) Down at the harbour, this renovated hotel has bright breezy rooms with balconies overlooking the cafés and fishing boats. It does a good breakfast, including real espresso for coffee

THE TENTH MUSE

Plato declared her the tenth muse, and Greek ruler Solon asked for someone to teach him her song 'because I want to learn it and die'. One of the greatest poets of the ancient world, Sappho is renowned as an artist of lyricism and love.

Born an aristocrat in Eresos around 630 BC she married a wealthy merchant whose fortune allowed her to live as a poet and teacher for a court of young women. Despite her fame, her reputation is based on only three complete poems, 63 complete single lines and up to 264 fragments.

Among Sappho's works were hymns, mythological poems and personal love songs. She uses sensuous images of nature to create her own special brand of erotic lyrical poetry, which has a simple yet melodious style. Most of her verses seem to have been addressed to a close, inner circle of female companions.

In 2004, a 2600-year-old Sappho poem written on papyrus was discovered in an Egyptian mummy, making it her fourth to survive. The subsequent commentary and translation has once again rekindled interest in what Martin West, a renowned translator of Greek lyric poetry calls 'a socio-historical enigma, a litterateurs' Lorelei, a feminist icon, a scholars' maypole'.

Lesvos, and Eresos in particular, is today visited by many lesbians paying homage to Sappho.

fiends, and has a small travel agency for arranging day tours and ferry tickets.

EATING

Betty's (☎ 22530 71421; 17 Noemvriou; mains from €5.50) Betty was born in a restaurant, and you can taste this in the delicious meals her sons serve up in this restored Turkish pasha's residence. All the food is cooked fresh every day and seafood is the speciality. For a vegetarian dish to gush over, try the zucchini flowers made by Betty's mother Maria. The home-made baklava is some of the best around. If you're looking for atmosphere, views and incredible home-style Greek food, Betty's is highly recommended. To get there, take the downhill fork after passing uphill through the tunnel.

Captain's Table (☎ 22530 71241; appetisers €3-6, mains €5-10; ☾ dinner) For more of a fishing-village feel, head down to the far end of the little harbour where there is a clutch of restaurants, the best of which is this Australian-Greek place. Chef Melinda turns out exquisite *mezedes* (try *adjuka* – a Ukrainian-inspired spicy aubergine dish) and high-quality seafood. The house white wine goes down well with smoked mackerel or the fabulous anchovies.

I Eftalou (☎ 22530 71049; mains from €5) For an idyllic setting, try this taverna just before the hot springs, 4km from Mithymna. The food is top notch – particularly the grilled sardines. Locals reckon the spinach and zucchini *pites* are the best on the island.

The beach opposite makes a nice spot for a pre-lunch swim.

Galley Restaurant (mains from €5.50) Regular visitors rave about this restaurant, the first place down by the harbour.

Petra Πέτρα

pop 1246

Petra, 5km south of Mithymna, is a popular package holiday resort, with a long sandy beach and seafront square shaded by tamarisk trees. While there are no concrete monstrosities, the few remaining traditional stone houses fight for space with ugly t-shirt shops, and bland cafés. Petra means 'rock', and looming over the village is an enormous, almost perpendicular rock that looks as if it has been lifted from Meteora in Thessaly. The rock is crowned by the 18th-century **Panagia Glykofilousa** (Church of the Sweet Kissing Virgin). You can reach it by climbing the 114 rock-hewn steps. The nearby village of **Petri**, to the east, has some nice old *kafeneia* and provides an excellent vantage point from which you can survey Petra and its surrounding landscape.

Petra has a post office, OTE, bank, medical facilities and bus connections. There's an interesting refurbished Turkish mansion, known as **Vareltzidaina's House** (admission free; ☾ 8am-7pm Tue-Sun), between the rock and the waterfront. It can be difficult to find, but the locals can point you in the right direction.

For accommodation, excursions, boat and air tickets, head to **Petra Tours** (☎ 22530 41390; petratours@otenet.gr) in the centre of town.

SLEEPING

Women's Agricultural Tourism Cooperative (☎ 22530 41238; womes@otenet.gr; s/d around €15/25) There are about 120 private rooms available in Petra, but your best bet for accommodation is to head straight for this women's collective, Greece's first (you don't have to be a woman to stay here). You may find yourself staying on a farm, or in a comfortable village studio. A large home-made breakfast is often included. The office is on the central square, upstairs in the restaurant above Cantina; enter from the street behind the waterfront.

Hotel Mediterraneo (☎ 22530 41778; fax 22530 41880; d €40; ✵) If you want to stay in the centre of things, try this simply furnished hotel, so close to the sea that you can practically dive in from the balcony of your room.

EATING

Syneterismos (☎ 22530 41238; fax 22530 41309; mains €4; ✵ summer) For mouth-watering *mousaka* (sliced eggplant and mincemeat, arranged in layers and baked) try this popular rooftop restaurant belonging to the Women's Agricultural Tourism Cooperative. Specials change daily as co-op members make their favourite dishes for the passing tourist trade. It's upstairs on the waterfront square, above Cantina; enter from the street running one block behind the waterfront.

0 Rigas (☎ 22530 41405; mains from €5; ✵ 7pm) For something very authentic, head up to the old village, to this wisteria-swathed taverna, which is the oldest in Petra. It has a very laid-back feel and the music is excellent. To get there walk uphill around the rock and keep going straight ahead for about 500m.

WESTERN LESVOS

Western Lesvos is different from the rest of the island, and this becomes apparent almost immediately as you wind westward out of Kalloni. The landscape becomes drier and barer, and there are fewer settlements, although they look very tidy and their red-tiled roofs add vital colour to an otherwise mottled green-brown landscape. The far western end is almost devoid of trees other than the petrified kind. Here you will find Lesvos' 'petrified forest' on a windswept and barren hillside. One resort,

a remote fishing village, and the birthplace of Sappho are what attract people to western Lesvos.

Skala Eresou Σκάλα Ερεσού
pop 1560

Surrounded by a riotously fertile agricultural plain, Skala Eresou, 90km from Mytilini, is a laid-back resort sitting on 2km of silvery-brown beach. The village has a certain female energy and bohemian vibe, as well as good restaurants, and slightly avant-garde nightlife. This may have to do with the considerable number of gay women who come on a kind of pilgrimage in honour of the ancient poet Sappho (c. 630–568 BC) who was born here. The village is very gay-friendly, with many businesses being lesbian-owned.

ORIENTATION & INFORMATION

From the bus turnaround at Skala Eresou, walk towards the sea to reach the central square of Plateia Anthis and Evristhenous, abutting the waterfront. The beach stretches to the left and right of this square. Turn right at the square onto Gyrinnis and just under 50m along you will come to a sign pointing left to the post office; the OTE is next door. Neither Skala Eresou nor Eresos has a bank but there is an ATM outside Sappho Travel in Skala Eresou.

Sappho Travel (☎ 22530 52140; www.sapphotravel .com) is incredibly helpful, whether you need accommodation in town or elsewhere in Lesvos. It can also help with car hire and has a range of tours.

FESTIVALS & EVENTS

The **Women Together** festival is held annually in September. For more information contact **Sappho Travel** (☎ 22530 52140; www.sappho travel.com).

SIGHTS

Eresos' **archaeological museum** (admission free; ✵ 8.30am-3pm Tue-Sun) houses archaic, classical Greek and Roman finds, including statues, coins and grave stelae. The museum, in the centre of Skala Eresou, stands near the remains of the early Christian Basilica of Agios Andreas.

The **petrified forest** (☎ 22530 54434; admission €1.50; ✵ 8am-4pm), as the EOT hyperbolically refers to this scattering of ancient tree stumps, is near the village of Sigri, on the west coast north of Skala Eresou. Experts reckon the petrified wood is at least 500,000 – but possibly 20 million – years old. If you're intrigued, the forest is easiest to reach on an excursion from Skala Eresou; enquire at Sappho Travel. If you're making your own way, the turn-off to the forest is signposted 7km before the village of Sigri.

The site is very exposed and hot, even in spring. A less sweaty suggestion is a visit to the very swish **Natural History Museum of the Lesvos Petrified Forest** (☎ 22530 54534; admission €3; 8.30am-4.30pm Tue-Sun) in Sigri, which has background information on the forest and, of course, a few tree stumps.

Sigri itself is a beautiful, peaceful fishing port where the road ends. 'Where The

---

OLIVE TRAILS

The most delightful way to experience the Plomari region is to walk. Old paths linking the hill villages have been restored and offer magical glimpses of the region's natural beauty. You'll pass through lush dells filled with old oaks, wild pears and pistachios, plane trees, pink hollyhocks, miscellaneous wild flowers and herbs, as well as higher, drier forests of pine and juniper. The wildlife is watered by a wealth of springs, fountains, rivers and streams that also served the olive mills and presses that dot the landscape. As you traverse the olive groves, you'll notice old *setia* (dry-walled terraces) and *damia* (small one-storey stone houses). To top it off, there are startling views down to the sea. In general, it's best to walk these paths in spring or autumn before or after the heat kicks in. The trails are clearly signposted and there are maps in villages and at the airport.

The major routes are as follows:

Melinda–Paleohori

Distance: 1.2km. Duration: 30 minutes. This trail starts at the fishing village of Melinda and follows the Selandas River for 200m. It ascends to the living village of Paleohori, passing a spring with potable water along the way. The trail ends at one of the village's two olive presses, where there is now a museum. You can continue southwest to Panagia Krifti and Drota Beach.

Paleohori–Rahidi

Distance: 1km. Duration: 30 minutes. The path here is 2m to 4m wide and paved with white stone. It ascends to Rahidi, which used to be the summer residence of the villagers from Paleohori. There are two springs along the way, and vineyards. There are about 40 nice old houses in

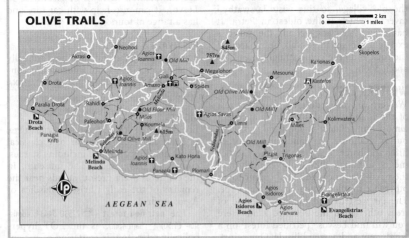

OLIVE TRAILS

AEGEAN SEA

Road Ends' is also the name of a guide to the area by author Roy Lawrence, which is worth picking up from travel agents for its interesting beach walks. The town has a real edge-of-the-world feeling to it, particularly if you're stumbling off a ferry at 2am. Call **Sigri Shipping Agency** (☎ 22530 54430; fax 22530 54273) before you arrive, to arrange a bed.

SLEEPING

Hotel Sappho (☎ 22530 53233; www.sapphohotel.com; s/d incl breakfast €32/52; April 1-Oct 15;) This was the first women-only hotel in Skala Eresou, and that superior attitude still pervades. It's perched right on the waterfront and the stark white rooms (some renovated, others showing their age) are a minimalist's dream, with the occasional piece of artwork,

---

Rahidi and a *kafeneio* (coffee house) that opens in summer. Rahidi, which now has a population of about five, first received electricity in 2001. There are stunning views from here. If you like, you can continue to Agios Ioannis along the same path.

Melinda–Kournela

Distance: 1.8km. Duration: 40 minutes. An old stone path climbs from the beach at Melinda to Kournela, a village of about 50 houses, with a population of three or four people. There are big shady plane trees, a triple-spouted fountain where people used to wash clothes, and an old steam-driven olive mill. There are good views across to Paleohori and Rahidi.

Kournela–Milos

Distance: 800m. Duration: 20 minutes. This trail descends to Milos, where there's an old flour mill. The village is at a crossroads, with paths leading to Paleohori, Melinda, Kournela and Megalohori.

Melinda–Milos

Distance: 2km. Duration: one hour. This level trail follows the Selandas River and passes a few houses, some ruined olive mills, one spring and two bridges. There is some unusual vegetation, including orange and mandarin trees. It's a shady trail, good for summer.

Milos–Amaxo

Distance: 1.75km. Duration: one hour. This very level trail follows the Melinda River, through vineyards and plane, poplar and pine forests. There are springs and fountains with good drinking water along the way. Nice wooden bridges made of chestnut cross the river. It's possible to start this walk from Amaxo, after driving from Plomari. If you're a good rider, you can mountain bike all the way from Amaxo down to Melinda.

Amaxo–Giali–Spides

Distance: 1.5km. Duration: 45 minutes. This trail follows a dirt road for about 500m to Giali, then ascends to Spides on a path. Halfway between Amaxo and Giali there's a little church with a picnic table that makes a nice spot for lunch.

Skopelos–Karionas–Kastelos–Trigonas/Plagia

Distance: 8km. Duration: three hours. This route follows a dirt road from Skopelos to Karionas, but there are cobbled paths the rest of the way. At the ruined castle known as Kastelos, there's now a small church. It's possible to take a detour to the village of Milies, where there is a fountain and some nice old houses. A path from Milies continues to Kolimvatera.

Plomari–Mesouna

Distance: 6km. Duration: three hours. The trail follows the Sedoundas River past many old houses. There's an olive-processing plant in the village of Limni, and about 4km upriver there's an old watermill that used to crush olives.

FASCINATING FOSSIL FIND

Lesvos is hardly the kind of place that you would associate with great excitement in the musty and dusty world of palaeontology. Nonetheless, the island has been thrust centre stage with the extraordinary discovery of animal, fish and plant fossils at Vatera, a sleepy beach resort on the south coast, hitherto more associated with grilled rather than fossilised fish.

Among the fossils found in the Vatera region are parts of a tortoise that was the size of a Volkswagen Beetle, and pieces of a gigantic horse. Dated up to 5.5 million years old, the fossils are displayed at the **Museum of Natural History** (☎ 22520 61890; admission €1; ☼ 9.30am-7.30pm) in the old school house in the village of Vrisa, just 2km from the excavation site.

---

or white cat lounging around. The popular restaurant downstairs, Sappho Restaurant, can get noisy, especially when the bar is used for their infamous summer parties.

Mascot Hotel (☎ 22530 52140; www.sapphotravel .com; s/d €35/60; ⬛) A few blocks back from the beach, this is a quieter, unpretentious alternative for women. The 10 cosy rooms are well-appointed with balconies that look out over citrus groves. The management is incredibly hospitable and has plenty of information on the area.

Hotel Galini (☎ 22530 53137/74; fax 22530 53155; s/d/tr €45/60/75) The straight option is a family-run hotel about 100m from the beach. This shady haven has small but airy rooms with private balcony, and there's a flower-filled garden. It is clearly signposted.

EATING & DRINKING

Along the shady promenade of Skala Eresou the many restaurants have sea views across to Chios, and drying octopuses hanging in the sun.

Sappho Restaurant (☎ 22530 53233; mains €7) Highly-regarded for its international menu, this lesbian-run restaurant is on the waterfront under the Hotel Sappho. Breakfast is served until 1pm, and after that daily specials can range from scrumptious spinach lasagne to beef mignon. The Eresou plate is packed with deliciously fresh *mezedes*. There is a chilled-out garden bar at the back.

Soulatso (☎ 22530 52078; mains €5) The place to come for a superb seafood pasta dish, this place, in the middle of the waterfront, also does wonderful sardines. Ask to try the speciality – spiced and salted mackerel which is then sun-dried and grilled – if it's available.

Eressos Palace (mains €5) Locals recommend this taverna for gutsy traditional cooking and efficient service. The menu offers a wide selection; try a meal of *mezedes* including the delightful marinated tuna in oil.

Margarita's (☎ 22530 53042) For a fortifying breakfast, and decent coffee, head straight for this waterfront café. Be sure to sample the scrumptious Austrian pastries, including a very delectable apple strudel (€6.50).

Popular watering holes for the lesbian set include Tenth Muse, on the square, an old favourite with a welcoming atmosphere and excellent fruit drinks; Parasol, on the waterfront with a funky tropical feel and exotic cocktails; and Notorious, at the far southeastern end of the promenade, in an isolated, romantic spot overlooking the water. During summer (June to September) most of these places are open from 10am to 1am.

SOUTHERN LESVOS

Southern Lesvos is dominated by Mt Olympus (968m). Pine forests and olive groves decorate its flanks.

The large village of **Agiasos** on the northern side of Mt Olympus features prominently in local tourist publications and is a popular day-trip destination. Agiasos is picturesque but not tacky, with artisan workshops making everything from handcrafted furniture to pottery. Its winding streets lead you to the church of the Panagia Vrefokratousa with its **Byzantine Museum** and **Popular Museum** in the courtyard.

Plomari on the south coast is a pleasant, crumbling resort town. A large, traditional village, it also has a laid-back beach settlement. Most people stay at **Agios Isidoros**, 3km to the east where there is a narrow, overcrowded beach. **Tarti**, east of Agios Isidoros, is a much nicer beach. West of Plomari, **Melinda** is a very pretty, serene fishing village with a beach. There are three tavernas in Melinda, all offering rooms and cheap hearty food.

About one hour's walk from Melinda, west along the coast, is the **Panagia Krifti**, a little church built in a cave near a hot spring.

The family resort of **Vatera**, over to the east, has an 8km stretch of beach that never seems to fill up. It is reached via the inland town of **Polyhnitos** where there are hot springs (see boxed text, Balm for the Soul, p379).

Sleeping & Eating

Hotel Vatera Beach (☎ 22520 61212; www.vatera beach.gr; s/d €55/90; 🅿 🖳) The secret to a successful beach hotel is not just sun, sand and a comprehensive bar, it is owners who remember your name, and your favourite dish. No wonder Barbara and George get so many return customers to their delightful resort. Relax in sea-view rooms, plonk yourself down with an English or German newspaper on the free sun-beds, or enjoy a wonderfully fresh Greek meal on the outside terrace. The hotel can help with car rental and sightseeing, and they offer excellent discounts for Internet bookings.

LIMNOS ΛΗΜΝΟΣ

pop 15,224 / area 482 sq km

For long, guilt-free days of dozing in the sun, you can't beat remote Limnos, an island seemingly ready to slip into eternal sleep. Its understated appeal rests on the lack of any cultural must-sees; there's just long sandy beaches, fine wine from the west coast, and gentle hills dusted with vibrant wildflowers in spring, and purple crocuses in autumn.

Flocks of flamingos wade through the placid lakes of eastern Limnos, the tranquillity only broken by the roar of fighter jets overhead. The garrison is due to Limnos' sensitive position near the Straits of the Dardanelles, midway between the Mt Athos Peninsula and Turkey. The far-from-ubiquitous military presence continues to subside as tourism makes inroads. But this is no package-holiday ghetto; tourist hubbub is minimal and mainly confined to northern Greeks holidaymakers in July and August, and expats on extended holidays.

Moudros Bay was the Allies' base for the disastrous Gallipoli campaign of WWI.

Getting There & Away

AIR

There is a daily flight to Limnos from Athens (€65, one hour), four weekly from Thessaloniki (€65, 45 minutes) and three flights weekly to Lesvos (€36, 35 minutes). **Olympic Airlines** (☎ 22540 22214; www.olympic airlines.com; Nikolaou Garoufallidou) is opposite Hotel Paris, in Myrina.

The airport is 22km east of Myrina; a taxi will cost about €14.

EXCURSION BOAT

Every Sunday in July and August, the *Aiolis* does a round trip to the small island of Agios Efstratios. The boat usually leaves at about 8am and returns at 5pm. Tickets cost €15 one-way/return and can be bought at **Myrina Tourist & Travel Agency** (☎ 22540 22460; root@mirina .lim.forthnet.gr) on the harbour front in Myrina.

FERRY

In summer four ferries weekly go from Limnos to Kavala (€15.30, five hours). In the high season there is usually one boat per week to Sigri in Lesvos (€20.50, six hours). There are also three to four boats weekly to Chios (€20.20, 11 hours) and Piraeus (€25.50, 13 hours) via Lesvos. There are two boats weekly to Thessaloniki (€22.10, eight hours) and one to two to Alexandroupolis (€17.90, five hours) via Samothraki (€11.50, three hours).

In addition, the *Aiolis*, a small local ferry, does the run to Agios Efstratios (one way/return €10/15, two hours) five times weekly. Tickets can be bought at **Myrina Tourist & Travel Agency** (☎ 22540 22460; root@mirina.lim .forthnet.gr), in Myrina.

Getting Around

BUS

Bus services on Limnos are poor. In summer there are two buses daily from Myrina to most of the villages but you may need to stay overnight in order to catch a bus back. Check the schedule (scribbled on a blackboard in Greek) at the **bus station** (☎ 22540 22464; Plateia Eleftheriou Venizelou).

CAR & MOTORCYCLE

In Myrina, cars and jeeps can be rented from **Myrina Rent a Car** (☎ 22540 24476; fax 22540 22484; Kyda-Karatza), near the waterfront. Prices range from €30 to €45 for a small car or jeep, depending on the season. There are several motorcycle-hire outlets on P Kyda-Karatza.

TAXI

There's a **taxi rank** (☎ 22540 23033) on the central square in Myrina.

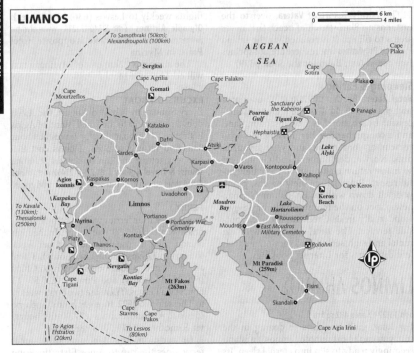

LIMNOS

To Samothraki (50km);
Alexandroupolis (100km)

AEGEAN SEA

Cape Plaka

Sergitsi

Cape Agrilia

Cape Falakro

Cape Sotira

Plaka

Cape Mourtzeflos

Gomati

Sanctuary of the Kabeiroi

Panagia

Katalako

Pournia Gulf

Tigani Bay

Dafni

Hephaistia

Sardes

Atsiki

Lake Alyki

Karpasi

Varos

Kontopouli

Kalliopi

Agios Ioannis

Kaspakas

Kornos

Cape Keros

Kaspakas Bay

Livadohon

Keros Beach

To Kavala (130km);
Thessaloniki (250km)

Limnos

Moudros Bay

Lake Hortarolimni

Portianos

Portianos War Cemetery

Roussopouli

Myrina

Kontias

Moudros

East Moudros Military Cemetery

Platy

Thanos

Poliohni

Nevgatis

Kontias Bay

Mt Fakos (263m)

Mt Paradisi (259m)

Cape Tigani

Fisini

Cape Stavros

Cape Fakos

Skandali

To Agios Efstratios (20km)

To Lesvos (80km)

Cape Agia Irini

0 — 6 km
0 — 4 miles

MYRINA ΜΥΡΙΝΑ
pop 5107

Surrounded by massive hunks of volcanic rock, and guarded by a looming Genoese castle, the capital of Limnos is not immediately perceived as a picturesque town. But as far as workaday fishing ports go, Myrina is animated and full of character. Colourful boats fill the harbour and the charming streets are sprinkled with little whitewashed stone dwellings, decaying neoclassical mansions and old-fashioned *kafeneia*.

The main thoroughfare of P Kyda-Karatza is where you will find traditional stores selling nuts and honey, and the local tipple, a Moschato Alexandrias muscat. There are also several barber shops – a testimony to the island's military presence. Down the side streets you'll see 19th-century wattle-and-daub houses, with wooden balconies, interspersed with the modern buildings.

With two wonderful, sandy beaches on either side of the town, and unfettered by establishments pandering to tourism, it's easy to spend a relaxing week here without stepping inside a car or bus.

Orientation
From the end of the quay turn right onto Plateia Ilia Iliou. Continue along the waterfront, passing Hotel Lemnos and the town hall. A little further along you will see the run-down Hotel Aktaion, set back from the waterfront. Turn left here, then immediately veer half-left onto the main thoroughfare P Kyda-Karatza. Proceeding up here you will reach Myrina's central square. Walk up P Kyda-Karatza and you will come to Plateia Eleftheriou Venizelou where you will see the town's bus station.

Information
The National Bank of Greece, on the central square, has an ATM. There's a small tourist information kiosk on the quay during the summer season.

Joy (☎ 22540 25453; per hr €4) Internet access is available here, two doors up from Olympic Airlines.

Laundrette (☎ 22540 24392; Nikolaou Garoufallidou) Opposite Olympic Airlines.

Myrina Rent a Car (☎ 22540 24476; fax 22540 24484; Kyda-Karatza) Near the waterfront.

Myrina Tourist & Travel Agency (☎ 22540 22460; root@mirina.lim.forthnet.gr) On the harbour front in Myrina, sells tickets for Aiolis' trips to Agios Efstratios.
Police station (☎ 22540 22201; Nikolaou Garoufallidou) At the far end of the street, on the right coming from P Kyda-Karatza.
Port police (☎ 22540 22225) On the waterfront near the quay.
Post office (Nikolaou Garoufallidou)
Theodoros Petrides Travel Agency (☎ 22540 22039; www.petridestravel.gr; Karatza 116)

Sights & Activities
As with any Greek-island **castle**, the one towering over Myrina is worth climbing up to. From its vantage point there are magnificent views over the sea to Mt Athos. As you walk from the harbour, take the first side street to the left by an old Turkish fountain. A sign here points you to the castle.

Myrina has two decent beaches right in town. The one closest is **Rea Maditos** which is wide and sandy. Another narrower but long swathe of sand begins on the other side of the castle as **Romeíkos Gialos**, which can be reached by walking along P Kyda-Karatza from the harbour, and taking any of the streets off to the left. It continues on to become **Riha Nera** (shallow water), so named because of its gently shelving beach that is ideal for children. Most of the nightlife is along this stretch.

In Myrina, and housed in a neoclassical mansion, is the **archaeological museum** (admission €2; ☽ 9am-3pm Tue-Sun). Worth a visit, it contains finds from all the three sites on Limnos – Poliohni, Sanctuary of the Kabeiroi and Hephaistia – exhibited in chronological order. The museum overlooks the beach, next to Hotel Kastro.

Tours
Theodoros Petrides Travel Agency (☎ 22540 22039; www.petridestravel.gr; ☽ Jun-Sep) organises round-the-island boat trips (€40) which include stops for swimming and lunch.

Sleeping
Romeíkos Gialos Pension (☎ 22540 23787; Sakhtouri 7; s/d/tr €45/57/67; ☒) Back in 1851, this beautiful stone-and-wood house was the islands' first hotel. Today it's had the typical boutique restoration, although the simple furnishings don't really live up to the splendour of the building. The charming owners

create a calm and relaxing atmosphere, and it's only 50m from the beach.
Hotel Lemnos (☎ 22540 22153; fax 22540 23329; s/d €35/45; ☒) This harbourside place has an ideal location. The rooms are relatively large and inviting, with balconies perfect for checking out the action at the port. It's run by the easy-going Stamboulis family, who will happily set you up with a taste of local ouzo while chatting about the island.
Hotel Filoktitis (☎ /fax 22540 23344; Ethnikis Antistaseos 14; s/d €50/60; ☒) If you can get past the gaudy reception you're in for excellent food, accommodating staff, and airy, spacious rooms with balcony, TV and fridge. There is also disabled access. The hotel is above the restaurant of the same name, a few blocks inland from Riha Nera; follow Maroulas (the continuation of P Kyda-Karatza) and take Ethnikis Antistaseos at the fork in the road.
Arion Beach Apartments (☎ 22540 22144; fax 22540 22147; d/tr €55/65; ☒) Families and self-caterers will love this homely place conveniently located a stone's throw from Riha Nera beach. There's enough room for an army in these studios, and if you need more, there are big shady balconies perfect for a summer-time siesta. To get there, take Seferi, the first street on your right as you walk over the hill to Riha Nera from Romeíkos Gialos. Look for the Arion's sign just a few doors up.
Apollo Pavillion (☎ /fax 22540 23712; www.apollo pavilion.gr; dm €11, d studios incl breakfast €50; ☒) Tucked away behind the port, this neoclassical wedding cake has friendly English-speaking owners, and enticing rooms with kitchenette and balconies. Breakfast served to you in your room. Book ahead in summer. Walk along Nikolaou Garoufallidou from P Kyda-Karatza and you will see the sign 150m along on the right.

Eating & Drinking
Several restaurants line the port, all offering seafood straight off the boat. May and September generally have the best offerings.
Glaros (☎ 22540 24061; mains from €5) The portside restaurants are much of a muchness but locals give the wonderfully fresh sardines here top marks. The mackerel and mouth-watering sea bream are also recommended in season.

O Platanos Taverna (☎ 22540 22070; mains from €5)
As soon as the locals close up their businesses for the afternoon, they head to this popular taverna halfway along P Kyda-Karatza. Tasty, but meat-heavy *mayirefta* (ready-cooked meals) is the order of the day. Vegetarians should select directly from the kitchen. Eating under the shady plane trees in the little square makes an attractive alternative to the waterfront establishments, but the menu is limited.

For a chilled-out sunset drink, follow the signs up to the castle where you will find Café Nefli halfway up. It has fine views of the coastline, but unfortunately the blaring radio does nothing for the serenity. Ask about their onsite studios.

WESTERN LIMNOS

North of Myrina, turn left just past the little village of **Kaspakas** and a narrow road leads down to the beach at **Agios Ioannis**. The beach is pleasant enough, but Agios Ioannis consists of a few desultory fishing shacks, scattered beach houses and a couple of tavernas, one of which has its tables set out in the embrace of a large volcanic rock.

Inland from Kaspakas, the barren hilly landscape dotted with sheep and rocks (particularly on the road to Katalako via Sardes and Dafni), looks more like the English Peak District than an Aegean island. The villages themselves have little to cause you to pause and you will certainly be an object of curiosity if you do. There is a remote and completely undeveloped beach at **Gomati** on the north coast and it can be reached by a good dirt road from Katalako.

Back on the beach road, if you continue south past Lemnos Village Resort Hotel, you will come to a sheltered sandy cove with an islet in the bay. The beach here is usually less crowded than Platy. **Thanos Beach** is the next bay around from Platy; it is also less crowded, and long and sandy. To get there, continue on the main road from Platy to the cute little village of Thanos, where a sign points to the beach. **Nevgatis**, the next bay along, is deserted but a trifle windy. Continuing along the coast road you'll come to the almost picturesque village of **Kontias**, marked by a row of old windmills.

CENTRAL LIMNOS

Central Limnos is the inspiration for the saying that no tree taller than parsley grows on the island. Impossibly flat, the agricultural area is dotted with wheat fields, small vineyards, and cattle and sheep farms. The island's huge air-force base is ominously surrounded by barbed-wire fences. The muddy and bleak Moudros Bay cuts deep into the interior, with **Moudros**, the second-largest town on the island, positioned on the eastern side of the bay. Moudros does not offer much for the tourist other than a couple of small hotels with tavernas on the waterfront. The harbour has none of Myrina's picturesque qualities.

One kilometre out of Moudros on the road to Roussopouli, you will come across the **East Moudros Military Cemetery**, where Commonwealth soldiers from the Gallipoli campaign are buried. Limnos, with its large protected anchorage, was occupied by a force of Royal Marines on 23 February 1915 and was the principal base for this ill-fated campaign. A metal plaque, inside the gates, gives a short history of the Gallipoli campaign. A second Commonwealth cemetery, **Portianos War Cemetery**, is at Portianos, about 6km south of Livadohori on the trans-island highway. The cemetery is not as obvious as the Australian-style blue-and-white street sign with the name 'Anzac St'. Follow Anzac St to the church and you will find the cemetery off a little lane behind it.

EASTERN LIMNOS

Eastern Limnos has three **archaeological sites** (admission free; ☉ 8am-7pm). The Italian School of Archaeologists has uncovered four ancient settlements at **Poliohni**, on the island's east coast. The most interesting was a sophisticated pre-Mycenaean city, which predated Troy VI (1800–1275 BC). The site is well laid out and there are good descriptions in Greek, Italian and English. However, there is nothing too exciting to be seen and the site is probably of greater interest to archaeological buffs than casual visitors.

The second site is that of the **Sanctuary of the Kabeiroi** (Ta Kaviria) in northeastern Limnos on the shores of remote Tigani Bay. This was originally a site for the worship of Kabeiroi gods which predates that of Samothraki (see p392). There is little of the splendour of Samothraki's sanctuary, but the layout of the site is obvious and excavations are still continuing.

The major site, which has 11 columns, is that of a **Hellenistic sanctuary**. The older site is further back and is still being excavated. Of additional interest is the **cave of Philoctetes**, the hero of the Trojan War, who was abandoned here while a gangrenous leg (the result of snakebite) healed. The sea cave can be reached by a path that leads down from the site. The cave can actually be entered by a hidden, narrow entrance (unmarked) to the left just past the main entrance.

You can reach the sanctuary easily, if you have your own transport, via a road that was built for the expensive tourist enclave, Kaviria Palace. The turn-off is 5km to the left, after the village of **Kontopouli**. From Kontopouli you can make a detour along a rough dirt track to the third site, **Hephaistia** (Ta Ifestia), once the most important city on the island. Hephaestus was the god of fire and metallurgy and, according to mythology, was thrown here from Mt Olympus by Zeus. The site is widely scattered over a scrub-covered, but otherwise desolate, small peninsula. There isn't much to see of the ancient city other than low walls and a partially excavated theatre.

The road to the northern tip of the island is worth exploring. There are some typical Limnian villages in the area and the often deserted beach at **Keros** is popular with windsurfers. Flocks of flamingos can sometimes be seen on shallow **Lake Alyki**. From the cape at the northeastern tip of Limnos you can see the islands of Samothraki, and Imvros (Gókçeada) in Turkey.

AGIOS EFSTRATIOS
ΑΓΙΟΣ ΕΥΣΤΡΑΤΙΟΣ

pop 371
The little-known island of Agios Efstratios, called Aí-Stratis locally, merits the title of perhaps the most isolated island in the Aegean. Stuck more or less plumb centre in the North Aegean some distance from its nearest neighbour Limnos, it has few cars and fewer roads, but sees a steady trickle of curious foreign island-hoppers seeking some peace and quiet.

Large numbers of political exiles were sent here for enforced peace and quiet before and after WWII. Among the exiled guests were such luminaries as composer Mikis Theodorakis and poets Kostas Varnalis and Giannis Ritsos.

The little village of Aí-Stratis was once picturesque, but in the early hours of the morning of 21 February 1968 a violent earthquake, with its epicentre in the seas between Limnos and Aí-Stratis, virtually destroyed the vibrant village in one fell swoop. Many people emigrated as a result and there are now large numbers of islanders living in Australia and elsewhere.

Ham-fisted intervention by the then ruling junta saw the demolition of most of the remaining traditional homes, and in their place cheaply built concrete boxes were erected to house the islanders.

Still, if you yearn for serenity and traffic-free bliss, and you enjoy walking, Agios Efstratios is a great place. It has a few fine beaches – though most are only accessible by caïque – some accommodation, and simple island food and nightlife.

There is a post office, one cardphone and one metered phone for the public.

Sights
BEACHES
Apart from the reasonable **village beach,** with its dark volcanic sand, the nearest beach worth making the effort to visit is **Alonitsi** on the northeast side of the island. It is a long, totally undeveloped, pristine strand and it can be all yours if you are prepared to walk the 90 minutes to reach it. To get there take the little track from the northeast side of the village, starting by a small bridge, and follow it up towards the power pylons. Halfway along, the track splits; take the right track for Alonitsi, or the left track for the **military lookout,** for great views. **Lidario,** a beach on the west side, can be reached – with difficulty – on foot, but is better approached by sea if you can get someone to take you there.

Sleeping & Eating
There are some 100 rooms available that can be booked through **Myrina Tourist & Travel Agency** (☎ 22540 22460; root@mirina.lim.forthnet.gr) or **Theodoros Petrides Travel Agency** (☎ 22540 22039; www.petridestravel.gr), both in Myrina on

Limnos, or fax the community fax machine at ☎ 22540 93210 to make a booking.

Places to eat are fairly inexpensive, though fish tends to be a bit on the steep side.

Xenonas Aí-Strati (☎ 22540 93329; Aí-Strati; d €40) Try this well-appointed, spotless and airy place run by the friendly Julia and Odysseas Galanakis. The rooms are in one of the few buildings that survived the earthquake on the northeastern side of the village.

Thanasis Taverna (☎ 22540 93269; mains around €5.50) The most obvious choice for food is this community-run taverna overlooking the harbour in Aí-Strati; it's open year-round.

Getting There & Away

Agios Efstratios is on the Kavala–Rafina ferry route, which includes Limnos. There are five services weekly to Limnos (€10, two hours) and one per week to Kavala (€15.50, 6¾ hours). In addition, the small local ferry *Aiolis* putters to and from Limnos every morning from Monday to Friday, and on Sundays in summer.

The harbour is exposed to the west winds, however, often causing ferry services to be cancelled or delayed. The island makes a good day-excursion; travel agencies in Limnos sell tickets for €18.

SAMOTHRAKI
ΣΑΜΟΘΡΑΚΗ

pop 2723 / area 176 sq km

Strange and beautiful Samothraki is full of secret treats. Cursed with awkward transportation links, few visitors make their way here but those who do are richly rewarded with sandy beaches that don't appear on any map, a hilltop capital hidden in a fold of mountains and the haunting Sanctuary of the Great Gods.

Samothraki's natural attributes are dramatic, big and untamed, culminating in the mighty peak of **Mt Fengari** (1611m), the highest mountain in the Aegean. Homer related that Poseidon watched the Trojan War from Mt Fengari's summit.

The jagged, boulder-strewn mountain looms over valleys of massive gnarled oak and plane trees, thick forests of olive and pine, dense shrubbery and damp, dark

glades where waterfalls plunge into deep, icy pools. On the gentler, western slopes of the island there are corn fields studded with poppies and other wild flowers in spring. Samothraki is also rich in fauna. Its springs are the habitat of a large number of frogs, toads and turtles; in its meadows you will see swarms of butterflies and may come across the occasional lumbering tortoise.

Samothraki's ancient site, the Sanctuary of the Great Gods, at Paleopolis evokes an epoch when Samothraki was a major religious centre. The mysterious cult of the Great Gods was brought to the island by the Thracians around 1000 BC, and by the 5th century BC luminaries from far and wide came to the site to be initiated. With the outlawing of paganism in the 4th century AD, the cult died out and the island dwindled into insignificance. Historians are unable to ascertain the nature of the rites performed here, but an aura of potent mysticism prevails over the whole island.

Getting There & Away
FERRY

Samothraki has daily ferry connections with Alexandroupolis (€8.30, two hours) and in summer there are at least two ferries per week to Kavala (€14, four hours) and two to Limnos (€12.20, three hours). There are also a couple of boats a week to Sigri (Lesvos) in peak season. Outside the high season, boats to/from Kavala are nonexistent. Ferry tickets can be bought at **Niki Tours** (☎ 25510 41465; fax 25510 41304), in Kamariotissa.

HYDROFOIL

In summer there are two or three hydrofoils daily between Samothraki and Alexandroupolis (€14.70, one hour). For departure details contact **Niki Tours** (☎ 25510 41465; fax 25510 41304).

Getting Around
BUS

In summer there are at least four buses daily from Kamariotissa to Hora (€0.75, 10 minutes) and Loutra (Therma; €1.15, 20 minutes), via Paleopolis (€0.75, 10 minutes). Some of the Loutra buses continue to the nearby camping grounds. There are four buses daily to Profitis Ilias (€1.15, 20 minutes), via Lakoma.

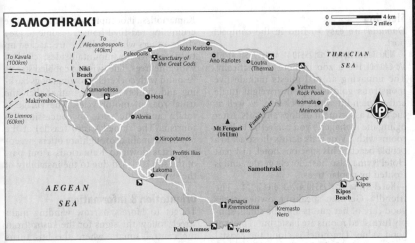

CAR & MOTORCYCLE

Cars and small jeeps can be rented from **X Rentals** (☎ 25510 42272) on the harbour and **Kyrkos Rent a Car** (☎ 25510 41620, 69728 39231). A small car is about €50. Motorcycles can be rented from **Rent A Motor Bike** (☎ 25510 41057), opposite the ferry quay.

EXCURSION BOAT

Depending on demand, caïques do trips from the Kamariotissa jetty to Pahia Ammos and Kipos Beaches, and the Samothraki excursion boat does trips around the island. For more information go to **Niki Tours** (☎ 25510 41465; fax 25510 41304).

TAXI

For a taxi, call ☎ 25510 41733, 25510 41341 or 25510 41077.

KAMARIOTISSA ΚΑΜΑΡΙΩΤΙΣΣΑ

pop 963

Kamariotissa may be Samothraki's largest town, but it is not much more than a one-boat port; so quiet you can hear the dice roll on a backgammon board. As the transport 'hub' of the island, you may wish to use it as a base for further explorations. It's not the most captivating of places but the leafy main drag is filled with flowers, and the exposed pebbly beach to the east is good for a contemplative stroll. Tourism is extremely low-key here. Speaking German is a big asset since the town has a great deal of people-traffic to and from Germany.

Orientation & Information

The bus stop is on the waterfront just east of the quay (turn left when you disembark). There is no EOT or tourist police, and the regular police are in Hora. There are two ATMs on the waterfront, but no post office or OTE – those also are in Hora.

Café Aktaion (☎ 25510 41056; per hr €4) Internet café at the end of the harbour.

Niki Tours (☎ 25510 41465; fax 25510 41304) Opposite the bus stop.

Port police (☎ 25510 41305) East along the waterfront.

www.samothraki.com Has general information about the island, including boat schedules.

X Rentals (☎ 25510 42272) On the harbour opposite the bus station, helpful to travellers; the English-speaking owner can provide a lot of information about the island.

Festivals & Events

Samothraki used to be home to Greece's largest electronic dance party. These days the **Samothraki World Music Festival** (www.samothrakifestival.com) has expanded, incorporating blues, roots, reggae, jazz and traditional music into the program. There is also a focus on art and ecology as the festival is heavily linked with Greenpeace, and other European environmental NGOs. The festival commandeers the Multilary Camping grounds and surrounding area for three days at the end of July. Tickets cost around €80 (the earlier you buy, the cheaper it is) and are on sale in outlets throughout Greece, and on the website.

Sleeping

Domatia are easy to find in the compact port.

Niki Beach Hotel (☎ 25510 41545; fax 25510 41461; s/d €40/60) It's a zoo in here – practically. The unpaying animal guests include five monstrous goldfish, an overweight turtle and a splendid white cockatoo, as well as the usual assortment of dogs and cats. After ogling the menagerie you can retire to large rooms with TV or walk across the street to a pebble beach. This spacious hotel, just past Hotel Kyma, also has a lovely garden and is fronted by poplar trees.

Hotel Kyma (☎ 25510 41263; d €45; ✸) The friendly German-speaking owner takes good care of her guests and the small, simply furnished rooms are basic, but represent good value. The hotel is along the coastal road towards Nikki Beach Hotel or Paleopolis, about 300m from the port.

Hotel Aeolos (☎ 25510 41595; fax 25510 41810; s/d incl breakfast €60/70; ✸ ✸) Behind Niki Beach Hotel, the Aeolos has a commanding position on a hill overlooking the sea. The rooms are comfortable enough, with TV and fridge, but nothing special. Those at the front overlook the large swimming pool and a mature garden, while rooms at the rear have views to Mt Fengari.

Eating

If you are just looking for a quick bite, try one of the *gyros* stands on the waterfront. A *souvlaki* or *gyros* costs about €4.50.

Klimitaria Restaurant (☎ 25510 41535; mains from €4.50) At the eastern end of the waterfront road, this is a pleasant place to relax under the shady trellis and dig into a large lunch. The restaurant serves an unusual specialty called *gianiotiko* (an oven-baked dish of diced pork, potatoes, egg and other goodies, €6). It also offers a good *pastitsio* (layers of buttery macaroni and seasoned lamb, €5) as well as a vegetarian option if you ask.

I Synantisi (☎ 25510 41308; fish from €5) For simple fresh fish and draught wine, try this *ouzeria* on the waterfront, between the ferry dock and the bus stop. The food is straightforward but excellent.

HORA ΧΩΡΑ

Hora is the island's capital, probably chosen more for its beauty than any practical reason. Concealed in the mountains above Kamariotissa it occupies a striking site. The crumbling red-tiled houses – some of grey stone, others whitewashed – are stacked up two steep rocky mountainsides, cloaked with pine trees. The twisting cobbled streets resound with cockerels crowing, dogs barking and donkeys braying, rather than the usual roar of motorcycles. The village is totally authentic with no concessions to tourism. The ruined *kastro* (castle) at the top of the main thoroughfare offers sweeping vistas down to Kamariotissa but part of the site is closed due to the instability of the structure.

Orientation & Information

To get to Hora's narrow winding main street, follow the signs for the *kastro* from the central square where the bus turns around. Here on the main street, which is nameless (as are all of Hora's streets; houses are distinguished by numbers), are the OTE, the Agricultural Bank and the post office. The **police station** (☎ 25510 41203) is in the ruined castle. Further up on the main street, on the right, a fountain gushes refreshing mountain water.

There are no hotels in Hora but if you ask in one of the *kafeneia* you will be put in touch with a room owner. Expect to pay €15 to €25 a double.

SANCTUARY OF THE GREAT GODS
ΤΟ ΙΕΡΟ ΤΩΝ ΜΕΓΑΛΩΝ ΘΕΩΝ

Next to the little village of Paleopolis, 6km northeast of Kamariotissa, is the **Sanctuary of the Great Gods** (admission €3/2, free Sun Nov 1-Mar 31 & public holidays; ❖ 8.30am-8.30pm Tue-Sun). The extensive site, lying in a valley of luxuriant vegetation between Mt Fengari and the sea, is one of the most magical in the whole of Greece. The Great Gods were of even greater antiquity than the Olympian gods worshipped in the official religion of ancient Greece. The principal deity, the Great Mother (Alceros Cybele), was worshipped as a fertility goddess.

When the original Thracian religion became integrated with the state religion, the Great Mother was merged with the Olympian female deities Demeter, Aphrodite and Hecate. The last of these was a mysterious goddess associated with darkness, the underworld and witchcraft. Other deities worshipped here were the Great Mother's consort, the virile young Kadmilos (god of the phallus), who was later integrated with the Olympian god Hermes; as well as the demonic Kabeiroi twins, Dardanos and Aeton, who were integrated with Castor and Pollux (the Dioscuri), the twin sons of Zeus and Leda. These twins were invoked by mariners to protect them against the perils of the sea. The formidable deities of Samothraki were venerated for their immense power. In comparison, the Olympian gods were a frivolous and fickle lot.

Initiates were sworn on punishment of death not to reveal what went on at the sanctuary; so there is only very flimsy knowledge of what the initiations involved. All archaeological evidence reveals is that there were two initiations, a lower and a higher. In the first initiation, gods were invoked to bring about a spiritual rebirth within the candidate. In the second initiation the candidate was absolved of transgressions. There was no prerequisite for initiation – it was available to anyone.

The site's most celebrated relic, the *Winged Victory of Samothrace* (now in the Louvre in Paris), was found by Champoiseau, the French consul, at Adrianople (present-day Edirne in Turkey) in 1863. Sporadic excavations followed in the late 19th and early 20th centuries, but did not begin in earnest until just before WWII when the Institute of Fine Arts, New York University, under the direction of Karl Lehmann and Phyllis Williams Lehmann, began digging.

Exploring the Site

The site is labelled in Greek and English. If you take the path that leads south from the entrance you will arrive at the rectangular **anaktoron**, on the left. At the southern end was a **sacristy**, an antechamber where candidates put on white gowns ready for their first (lower) initiation. The initiation ceremony took place in the main body of the anaktoron. Then, one by one, each initiate entered the holy of holies, a small inner temple at the northern end of the building, where a priest instructed them in the meanings of the symbols used in the ceremony. Afterwards the initiates returned to the sacristy to receive their initiation certificate.

The **arsinoein**, which was used for sacrifices, to the southwest of the anaktoron, was built in 289 BC and was at that time the largest cylindrical structure in Greece. It was a gift to the Great Gods from the Egyptian queen Arsinou. To the southeast of here you will see the **sacred rock**, the site's earliest altar, which was used by the Thracians.

The initiations were followed by a celebratory feast, which probably took place in the **temenos**, to the south of the arsinoein. This building was a gift from Philip II of Macedonia. The next building is the prominent Doric **hieron**, which is the most photographed ruin on the site; five of its columns have been reassembled. It was in this temple that candidates received the second initiation.

On the west side of the main path (opposite the hieron) are a few remnants of a **theatre**. Nearby, a path ascends to the **Nike monument** where the magnificent *Winged Victory of Samothrace* once stood. The statue was a gift from Demetrius Poliorketes (the 'besieger of cities') to the Kabeiroi for helping him defeat Ptolemy II in battle. To the northwest are the remains of a massive **stoa**, which was a two-aisled portico where pilgrims to the sanctuary sheltered. Names of initiates were recorded on its walls. North of the stoa are the ruins of the **ruinenviereck**, a medieval fortress.

Retrace your steps to the Nike monument and walk along the path leading east; on the left is a good plan of the site. The path continues to the southern **necropolis** which is the most important ancient cemetery so far found on the island. It was used from the Bronze Age to early Roman times. North of the cemetery was the **propylon**, an elaborate Ionic entrance to the sanctuary; it was a gift from Ptolemy II.

MUSEUM

The admission cost also includes the site's **museum** (☎ 25510 41474; 8.30am-3pm Tue-Sun) which is well laid out, with English labels. Exhibits include terracotta figurines, vases, jewellery and a plaster cast of the *Winged Victory of Samothrace*.

Sleeping & Eating

There are several *domatia* at Paleopolis, all of which are signposted from near the museum.

Kastro Hotel (☎ 25510 89400; www.kastrohotel.gr; s/d/tr incl breakfast €58/89/105;) Just west of Paleopolis, above the coast road, this hotel is simply humongous. Redolent with 70's charm, it offers dowdy rooms but spectacular sea views, which can be enjoyed while taking a dip in the pool or playing billiards. The restaurant is popular with groups in summer, who end up grooving to all hours thanks to the in-house musical entertainment.

I Asprovalta (☎ 25510 98250; Kato Kariotes; fish from around €5) Overlooking the sea, this serene little taverna in Kato Kariotes, about 4km east of Paleopolis, serves delicious fresh seafood.

AROUND SAMOTHRAKI
Loutra (Therma) Λουτρά (Θερμά)
Loutra, also called Therma, is 14km east of Kamariotissa and a short walk inland from the coast. It's in an attractive setting with a profusion of plane and horse chestnut trees, dense greenery and gurgling creeks. While not an authentic village, it is the nearest Samothraki comes to having a holiday resort. Many of its buildings are purpose-built *domatia*, and most visitors to the island seem to stay here. If you visit before mid-May, be prepared to find most places closed.

The village takes both its names from its therapeutic, sulphurous, mineral springs. Whether or not you are arthritic you may enjoy a **thermal bath** (☎ 25510 98229; admission €3; ◷ 6-11am & 5-7pm Jun-Sep), in the large white building by the bus stop. Alternatively, take the road to the right of the bathhouse and about 50m up on the right you'll see another small structure containing a thermal bath which is free. About 20m up the hill there are two more small baths, these outdoors.

SLEEPING & EATING
Samothraki's two official camping grounds are both near Loutra, on the beach to the east, and both are signposted 'Multilary Campings'; rest assured, this means municipal, not military, camping grounds.

It's a toss up between the shady, but basic **Multilary Camping** (Camping Plateia; ☎ 25510 41784; sites per adult/tent €3/3; ◷ Jun-Aug) to the left of the main road, 2km beyond the turn-off for Loutra coming from Kamariotissa, and the well-endowed **Multilary Camping** (☎ 25510 41491; sites per adult/tent €3/3; ◷ Jun-Aug) 2km further along the road. The latter has a minimarket, restaurant and hot showers, but is rather dry.

Mariva Bungalows (☎ 25510 98230; fax 25510 98374; d incl breakfast €80; ◲) These rambling

bungalows, set on a hillside in a secluded part of the island near a waterfall, are perhaps the loveliest place to stay on Samothraki. Rooms are airy and the bungalows are surrounded by lush foliage. To reach the hotel take the turning from the coast road which leads inland towards Loutra, and then the first left. Follow the signs to the hotel, which is 600m along this road.

Hotel Orpheas (☎ 25510 42213; fax 25510 98233; d/tr €55/65) On the road heading towards Mt Fengari, this pleasant family-run place is surrounded by greenery. The attractive terrace, with its colourful flowers, makes a great place to relax after a day spent stomping around ancient sites.

Paradisos Restaurant (☎ 25510 95267; mains from €4) Also at the back of the village this has a serene spot under the welcome shade of a huge plane tree; unfortunately the menu isn't as exciting. Take the road to the right from the bus stop to find it.

Fengari Restaurant (☎ 25510 98321; mains from €4) Has a better menu and is hidden away on a back street where food is cooked in traditional Samothraki ovens.

Kafeneio Ta Therma (☎ 25510 98325) After a soak in the baths, head to this place for coffee, and superb home-made sweets. Try the figs in syrup.

Fonias River
Visitors to the north coast should not miss the walk along the Fonias River to the **Vathres rock pools** (admission €1). The walk starts at the bridge over the river 4.7km east of Loutra, where there are a couple of ticket booths. The entry price is largely theoretical as the site is unfenced and the ticket booths are only open in the summer season. After an easy 40-minute walk along a fairly well-marked track you will come to a large rock-pool fed by a dramatic 12m-high waterfall. The water is pretty cold but very welcome on a hot day. Locals call the river the 'Murderer' and winter rains can transform the waters into a raging torrent. Although there are a total of six waterfalls, marked paths only run to the first two; after that, the walk becomes dangerously confusing.

Beaches
The gods did not over-endow Samothraki with good beaches. However, its one sandy beach, **Pahia Ammos**, on the south coast, is

superb. You can reach this 800m stretch of sand along an 8km winding road from Lakoma. In summer there are caïques from Kamariotissa to the beach. Around the headland is the equally superb **Vatos Beach**, used mainly by nudists.

Opposite Pahia Ammos, on a good day, you can see the mass of the former Greek island of Imvros (Gókçeada), ceded to the Turks under the Treaty of Lausanne in 1923.

Samothraki's other decent beach is the pebbled **Kipos Beach** on the southeast coast. It can be reached via the road skirting the north coast. There are no facilities here other than a shower and a freshwater fountain, however, and no shade; it pales in comparison to Pahia Ammos. Kipos Beach can also sometimes be reached by caïque from Kamariotissa. In summer there are boat excursions that take in both beaches for about €15.

Other Villages

The small villages of **Profitis Ilias**, **Lakoma** and **Xiropotamos** in the southwest, and **Alonia** near Hora, are all serene, unspoilt and charming. The hillside-perched Profitis Ilias, with many trees and springs, is particularly delightful and has several tavernas, of which **Vrahos** (☎ 25510 95264) is famous for its delicious roast kid (goat!). Asphalt roads lead to all of these villages.

THASOS ΘΑΣΟΣ

pop 13,530

Due to its proximity to the mainland – only 10km from Kavala – Thasos is a popular family-holiday spot for many northern Greeks. The tourist brochures tout it as the 'emerald isle' and, despite bad fires, Thasos is indeed a marvel of natural beauty. Mountain villages are shaded by huge oaks and plane trees, watered by streams and springs, while tiny inlets and coves are backed with rows of pines. The other main attraction of Thasos is its attractive white-sand beaches, and the archaeological remains in and around the capital, Thasos (Limenas). A good asphalt road runs around the island, so all the beaches are easily accessible.

Where there are beaches, tourists soon follow and they have come to Thasos in

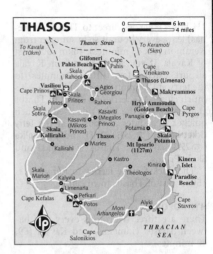

droves, mostly on package tours from Eastern Europe. Tourism is not all that Thasos relies upon, however. The island was once known for its gold. The Parians who founded the ancient city of Thasos (Limenas) in 700 BC struck gold at Mt Pangaion and it became the foundation for Thasos' lucrative export trade. With money came military power in the form of a navy as well as a number of notable painters and sculptors. Subsequent rulers, ranging from Athenians, Macedonians and Romans to the 18th-century Turks and 19th-century Egyptians, couldn't keep their hands away from Thasos' pot of money, taxing the island into penury.

In recent years Thasos has once again struck 'gold'. This time it is 'black gold', in the form of oil, and oil derricks can now be spotted at sea around the island. Thasos is also a major provider of very white marble – the quarries are fast creating huge holes in the island's mountainsides.

Outside of Limenas and Potos, there is little open in the way of hotels, tavernas and beach bars before the beginning of June. The months of July and August, along with summer weekends, are generally block-booked, but otherwise Thasos remains very quiet, almost eerily so.

Getting There & Away
FERRY

There are ferries every one or two hours, depending on the season, between Kavala, on the mainland, and Skala Prinos (€3.30,

1¼ hours). Ferries direct to Thasos (Limenas) leave every hour or so in summer from Keramoti (€2, 40 minutes), 46km southeast of Kavala. If you are coming from Kavala airport, catch a taxi (€10, 15 minutes) to the ferry at Keramoti instead of Kavala – it's much closer, the ferries go direct to Thasos (Limenas), and the ferry ride itself is much quicker. Schedules are posted at the **ferry ticket booths** (☎ 25930 22318) and **port police** (☎ 25930 22106) in Thasos (Limenas) and Skala Prinos.

The dock for the ferries to Keramoti is 150m west of Thasos town centre.

HYDROFOIL

There are three hydrofoils every day between Thasos (Limenas) and Kavala (€9, 40 minutes).

Getting Around

BICYCLE

Hire bicycles from **Babis Bikes** (☎ 25930 22129), on a side street between 18 Oktovriou and the central square in Limenas.

BUS

Thasos (Limenas) is the transport hub of the island; however, buses to various destinations meet all arriving ferries at Skala Prinos, so if you don't plan on staying in Thasos (Limenas) you can travel straight through. There are at least seven buses daily from Thasos (Limenas) to Limenaria via the west-coast villages (€3.30), and many to Skala Potamia at the southern end of Hrysi Ammoudia (Golden Beach) via Panagia and Potamia. There are five buses a day to Theologos and three to Alyki (€2.80). Five buses daily journey in a clockwise direction all the way around the island (€7.50, 3½ hours) and another five go anticlockwise. Timetables are available from the **bus station** (☎ 25930 22162) on the waterfront in Thasos town.

CAR & MOTORCYCLE

Cars can be hired from **Avis Rent a Car** Thasos (Limenas) (☎ 25930 22535; fax 25930 23124); Potamia (☎ 25930 61735); Skala Prinos (☎ 25930 72075). There are many other agencies, so you may want to shop around. In Thasos (Limenas) you can hire motorcycles and mopeds from **Billy's Bikes** (☎ 25930 22490), opposite the Newsagent, and **2 Wheels** (☎ 25930 23267), on the road to Prinos.

The coast road is around 100km all up, but due to winding mountain sections a full circuit with stops takes about a day.

EXCURSION BOAT

The **Eros 2 excursion boat** (☎ 25930 22285) makes full-day trips (€28) around the island three to four times a week, with stops for swimming and a barbecue. The boat leaves from the Old Harbour at 10am. There are also a couple of water taxis running regularly to Hrysi Ammoudia (Golden Beach) and Makryammos beach from the Old Harbour.

TAXIS

The taxi rank is in front of the bus stop in Thasos (Limenas).

THASOS (LIMENAS) ΘΑΣΟΣ (ΛΙΜΕΝΑΣ)

pop 2610 / area 375 sq km

Amid the uninspiring modern buildings and rows of tacky souvenir shops, the capital Thasos (also known as Limenas or Limin) offers a scattering of ancient ruins and a sandy beach just beyond the attractive old fishing harbour. As the island's transport hub, it makes a good base for exploring coastal resorts and villages.

Orientation & Information

The town's main thoroughfare is 18 Oktovriou, which is packed with tacky souvenir shops and tavernas.

The National Bank of Greece, on the waterfront, has an ATM.

Laundry Express (☎ 25930 22235)

Millennium Internet Café (☎ 25930 58089; ⏱ 8.30am-midnight; per hr €3) Has web access.

Newsagent (Theogenous) Sells English-language newspapers.

Port police (☎ 25930 22106)

Tourist police (☎ 25930 23111)

www.gothassos.com Has lots of useful information about the island.

Sights

Thasos' **archaeological museum** (☎ 25930 22180; ⏱ 9am-3pm Tue-Sun) next to the ancient agora (market) at the Old Harbour, has recently been renovated and opened for the first time in years. While occupying only two rooms, it's a well-designed, modern space with an interesting exhibition on Theagenes, a Thasos hero and strongman who won the Olympic Games (480–476 BC).

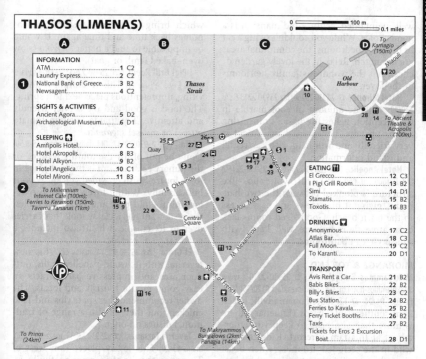

THASOS (LIMENAS)

INFORMATION
ATM.................................1 C2
Laundry Express.................2 C2
National Bank of Greece........3 B2
Newsagent........................4 C2

SIGHTS & ACTIVITIES
Ancient Agora....................5 D2
Archaeological Museum.........6 D1

SLEEPING
Amfipolis Hotel..................7 C2
Hotel Akropolis..................8 B3
Hotel Alkyon.....................9 B2
Hotel Angelica..................10 C1
Hotel Mironi....................11 B3

EATING
El Grecco........................12 C3
I Pigi Grill Room................13 B2
Simi.............................14 D1
Stamatis.........................15 B2
Toxotis..........................16 B3

DRINKING
Anonymous........................17 C2
Atlas Bar........................18 C3
Full Moon........................19 C2
To Karanti.......................20 D1

TRANSPORT
Avis Rent a Car..................21 B2
Babis Bikes......................22 B2
Billy's Bikes....................23 C2
Bus Station......................24 B2
Ferries to Kavala................25 B2
Ferry Ticket Booths..............26 B2
Taxis............................27 B2
Tickets for Eros 2 Excursion
Boat.............................28 D1

However, the museums' *pièce de résistance* is a colossal 6th-century BC *kouros* carrying a ram, that stands at 5m tall.

The **ancient agora** (admission free) next to the museum was the bustling marketplace of ancient and Roman Thasos – the centre of its civic, social and business life. It's a pleasant, verdant site with the foundations of stoas, shops and dwellings.

The **ancient theatre**, nearby, stages performances of ancient dramas and comedies as part of the Kavala Festival of Drama. The theatre is signposted from the small harbour.

From the theatre a path leads up to the **acropolis** of ancient Thasos, where there are substantial remains of a medieval fortress built on the foundations of the ancient walls that encompassed the entire city. From the topmost point of the acropolis there are magnificent views. From the far side of the acropolis, steps carved into the rock lead down to the foundations of the ancient wall. From here it's a short walk to the Limenas–Panagia road at the southern edge of town.

Festivals & Events
In July and August, performances of various ancient plays are held in the ancient theatre as part of the **Kavala Festival of Drama**. Not to be missed is the annual **Full Moon concert** that takes place each year in August. Admission is free and singers come from all over Greece to participate. Information and tickets can be easily obtained from the **EOT** (☎ 25102 22425) in Kavala or from the **tourist police** (☎ 25930 23111) on Thasos.

Sleeping
BUDGET
Hotel Alkyon (☎ 25930 22148; fax 25930 23662; 18 Oktovriou; s/d €25/35) A motherly welcome from owner Persephone is in store when you arrive at this harbour-front hotel. Certainly the best option in town for independent travellers, the hotel has spacious rooms with good size balconies, with sea or mountain views. Breakfast (€5) is served in the garden across the road.

Hotel Akropolis (☎ /fax 25930 22488; M Alexandrou; s/d incl breakfast €45/55; ❄) If you don't plan to spend too much time in your room, this well-maintained, century-old mansion is a good choice. While you couldn't swing a cat in the poky bedrooms, the communal areas are top notch. Relax in the lovely garden or check out the wondrous family heirlooms in the foyer.

Hotel Mironi (☎ 25930 23256; fax 25930 22132; s/d €30/40; ❄) The amount of cool marble in the reception belies the basic, uninspiring rooms upstairs. However, management is very friendly and will help with car rental and island information.

Hotel Angelica (☎ 25930 22387; fax 25930 22160; Old Harbour; d €60; ❄) This white box-like structure is plonked between the two harbours, giving it nice views and easy access to the town beach. Good-sized rooms lack decorative flair, but are well kept, with squeaky-clean bathrooms.

MIDRANGE & TOP END
Makryammos Bungalows (☎ 25930 22101; www.makryammos-hotel.gr; s/d/tr incl breakfast €120/150/188, f €285; P ❄ ⌘) Situated on an idyllic beach 2km southeast of Thasos (Limenas), there is more than sun beds to keep you entertained at this family resort. Kids can run wild in the secluded grounds, which boast a small zoo, mini-club, tennis and basketball courts, and a pool, while adults can indulge their inner self through yoga, tai chi and pottery classes. There are around 200 bungalows hidden in the forest behind the beach, all very private and furnished in an elegant, traditional style. There is a selection of restaurants and bars on site, a boat runs guests across to Thasos (Limenas) several times a day.

Amfipolis Hotel (☎ 25930 23101; fax 25930 22110; cnr 18 Oktovriou & Theogenous; s/d/ste incl breakfast €60/90/135; ❄ Jun-Oct; ❄ ⌘) Occupying a grand old tobacco factory, this lovely hotel has elegantly furnished rooms with interesting wood-panelled ceilings. The hotel has two bars and a well-regarded restaurant.

Eating
You can eat well in Thasos (Limenas), although too many restaurants are dumbing down their menus with poorly prepared versions of international standards.

Toxotis (☎ 25930 22720; mains from €4.50) No schnitzel and no multingual picture menus at this family-run joint. Instead, a warm atmosphere and well-prepared Greek food

which brings local and visiting gastronomes back time and time again. It would be impossible to find a better *klefyiko* (slow oven–baked lamb or goat).

I Pigi Grill Room (☎ 25930 22941; central square; mains €4-6; ☽ dinner) This restaurant is an inviting, unpretentious place next to a spring. The food is good and the service friendly and attentive. Try *stifado* (stew in tomato purée) or mussel *saganaki*.

Simi (☎ 25930 22517; Old Harbour; mains €5-8.50) Don't be put off by the touting waiters, or the hungry cats, as Simi is the best place in town for fresh fish provided you check your bill carefully. With a lovely position overlooking the old port and nicely set tables, the restaurant has a classy look that carries over to its cuisine, which also includes a good range of *mezedes*.

El Greco (☎ 25930 22874; mains €8) This new taverna, with its wood-panelled walls, outdoor area and impressive bar, attracts an easy-going mix of tourists and locals. The owner recommends her spare ribs and Thai chicken, but there is also a range of traditional dishes on offer.

Taverna Tarsanas (☎ 25930 23933; mezedes €2.50, mains €3-20) This lovely place, 1km west of Thasos on the site of a former boatbuilders, serves the most exquisite seafood on the island. There are lots of interesting seafood *mezedes* that you won't find anywhere else. Fresh lobster (per kilogram €44) – difficult to find on Thasos – is always available. Traditional meat dishes are also served.

Stamatis (☎ 25930 22131; 18 Oktovriou) The best place for an afternoon coffee and pastry is in the garden of this *zaharoplasteio* which has been going since 1958.

Drinking
There's no lager lout scene in Thasos, though on weekends and Greek holidays, the nightlife is young and active.

Atlas Bar (☎ 25930 22600; Street of French Archaeological School) Known for its reliably good music and casual atmosphere, the Atlas is run by an English-Dutch couple who are determined not to turn their welcoming bar into an English pub.

To Karanti (☎ 25930 24014; Miaouli) This outdoor *ouzeri*, next to the fishing boats on the Old Harbour, has one of the most beautiful settings in Thasos. Its relaxed atmosphere is enhanced by excellent Greek music. Aside from a full bar, breakfast and *mezedes* are available.

Karnagio (☎ 25930 23170) Beyond the Old Harbour, this is a lovely place to have a drink at sunset. Sited where wooden boats are still built, it has a dramatic locale at the end of the promontory.

Full Moon Bar (☎ 25930 23230; 18 Oktovriou) and **Anonymous** (☎ 25930 22847; 18 Oktovriou) are almost indistinguishable from each other. These two friendly cafés sit side by side, serving English-style pub grub and Guinness in a can, as well as a huge array of other beers.

EAST COAST

The hillside villages of **Panagia** and **Potamia** are a bit touristy but very picturesque. Both are 4km west of Hrysi Ammoudia (Golden Beach). The Greek-American artist Polygnotos Vagis was born in Potamia in 1894 and some of his work can be seen in the **Polygnotos Vagis Museum** (☎ 25930 61400; admission €3; ⏰ 8.30am-noon & 6-8pm Tue-Sat, 8.30am-noon Sun & holidays) in the village next to the main church. (The Municipal Museum of Kavala also has a collection of Vagis' work – see p111.) If you wish to walk to the highest point on the island, **Mt Ipsario** (1204m), you can follow the tractor trail west from Potamia to the end of the valley. Red waymarks on the trees and cairns point you in the right direction along a steep and unmaintained path up the mountain. Wear sturdy shoes, carry your own water, and give yourself a full day to get up and back.

It may get a trifle crowded, but the long and sandy **Hrysi Ammoudia** (Golden Beach) is one of the island's best beaches. Roads from both Panagia and Potamia lead to it, and the bus from Limenas calls at both villages before continuing to the southern end of the beach, which is known as Skala Potamia.

The next beach south is at the village of **Kinira**, and just south of here is the very pleasant **Paradise Beach**, preferred by nudists. The little islet just off the coast here is also called Kinira. **Alyki**, on the southeast coast, is a magical, spectacular place consisting of two quiet beaches back-to-back on a headland, and some quaint old houses. The southernmost beach is the better of the two. There is a small **archaeological site** near the beach and an ancient, submerged **marble**

quarry. Here marble was cut and loaded on to ships from the 6th century BC to the 6th century AD.

The road linking the east side of the island with the west side runs high across the cliffs, providing some great views of the bays to the south. Along here you will come to **Moni Arhangelou**, an old monastery built on top of cliffs directly opposite Mt Athos on the mainland. It's possible to visit, and the nuns sell some hand-painted icons, crosses and other paraphernalia.

Sleeping & Eating

As well as camping and hotel options, there are *domatia* at both Kinira and Alyki.

Golden Beach Camping (☎ 25930 61472; fax 25930 61473; sites per adult/tent €3.25/2.60) This place, smack in the middle of Hrysi Ammoudia, is the only camping ground on this side of the island; it's a stone's throw from the inviting water. Facilities are good and include a minimarket.

Thassos Inn (☎ 25930 61612; fax 25930 61027; d €45) This lovely hotel in Panagia is up the hill, in the cool of the forest. Built in traditional style, the balcony rooms have views over the slate rooftops of the village. From the bus stop, follow the small street leading from the fountain. Turn right at the sign to the hotel about 20m up the street, just past the honey shop, and follow the babbling brook.

Eric's Apartments/Studios (☎ 25930 61554; www.erics.gr; self-contained 2-/4-person studios €65/80; 🐾) If you've ever wanted to holiday with an ex-Manchester United footballer look no further than Stratos Papafilippou, the spitting image of Eric Catona, who owns these spacious, fully-equipped studios along the main road at Skala Potamia. There's a constant round of football matches on the satellite TV, full English breakfast and a popular bar.

Villa Zangas (☎ 25930 62031; www.villa-zangas .gmxhome.de; d €28.50) This villa, about 500m from Golden Beach, is an excellent budget option. There are only four rooms, so the whole house can be rented out by friends or family. A traditional stone oven in the garden is great for brushing up on your Greek cooking skills, and the vine covered deck has a leafy outlook.

Drosia/Platanos (☎ 25930 62172/1340; salads €2-4, mains €4-5) This popular taverna is on

Panagia's central square and serves pizza and spaghetti as well as traditional Greek dishes.

Fedra (☎ 25930 61474; mains €4-10) In the middle of Hrysi Ammoudia, this was one of the first restaurants on Thasos and is deservedly popular. The menu is huge, and the service friendly but not effusive.

Avalon (☎ 25930 62060; mains €4-10) In an imposing old monastery at the southern end of Hrysi Ammoudia in Skala Potamia, this establishment serves traditional fare as well as pizza and fish.

Restaurant Vigli (☎ 25930 61500; fish €5.50-10) At the north end of Hrysi Ammoudia, almost on the rocks, this is a great place for a drink or a fish dinner.

WEST COAST

The west coast consists of a series of beaches and seaside villages, most with *Skala* (literally 'step' or 'ladder', but also meaning 'little pier') before their names. Roads lead from each of these to inland villages with the same name (minus the 'skala'). Travelling from north to south the first beach is **Glifoneri**, closely followed by **Pahis Beach**.

The first village of any size is **Skala Rahoni**, a favourite of the package-tour companies, which has an excellent camping ground. A wide range of water-sports equipment can be hired from **Skala Rachonis Watersports** (☎ 25930 81056). The inland village of **Rahoni** remains unspoilt. **Pine Tree Paddock** (☎ 69451 18961; Rahoni; ☼ 10am-2pm & 5pm-sunset) has mountain ponies and a few horses for hire (per hour €20) or for guided trail rides (per hour €25). The owner needs 24 hours notice, so ring for an appointment.

Skala Prinos, the next coastal village and Thasos' second port, is nothing special. There is an ATM at the port and a few small hotels along the waterfront in case you get stuck. **Vasiliou**, about 1km south of the port, is a very nice beach backed by trees. The hillside villages of Mikros Prinos and Megalos Prinos, collectively known as **Kasaviti**, are gorgeous and lush, with excellent tavernas.

Skala Sotira and **Skala Kallirahis** are pleasant and both have small beaches. Kallirahi, 2km inland from Skala Kallirahis, is a peaceful village with steep narrow streets and old stone houses. It has a large population of skinny, anxious-looking cats and word has

it that the locals are scared of dogs. Judging by the graffiti and posters, there are also a lot of communists (though not as many as in Skala Potamia).

Skala Marion is a delightful fishing village and one of the least touristy places around the coast. It was from here, early in the 20th century, that the German Speidel Metal Company exported iron ore from Thasos to Europe. There are beaches at both sides of the village, and between here and Limenaria there are stretches of uncrowded beach. **Maries**, Skala Maries' inland sister village, is very pretty and has a lovely square.

Limenaria is Thasos' second-largest town. It's a crowded though pleasant resort, with a narrow sandy beach. The town was built in 1903 by the Speidel Metal Company. There are slightly less-crowded beaches around the coast at the old fishing villages of **Potos** and **Pefkari** which make very convenient bases for exploring the southern island.

From Potos a scenic 10km road leads inland to **Theologos**, which was the capital of the island in medieval and Turkish times. This is one of the island's most beautiful villages and the only mountain settlement served by public transport. The village houses are of whitewashed stone with slate roofs. It's a serene place, still unblemished by mass tourism.

Sleeping

Camping Daedalos (☎ /fax 25930 58251; sites per adult/tent around €5/2.50) This resort-style camping ground just north of Skala Sotira is a great option for would-be campers who didn't bring a tent – you can rent them here. Situated right on the beach, it also has a minimarket, and a restaurant with decent home-made food. Sailing, windsurfing and water-skiing lessons are also on offer.

Camping Pefkari (☎ 25930 51190; sites per adult/tent around €4.90/4.50; ☼ Jun-Sep) Campers have hit the jackpot with this attractive spot in a wooded area at Pefkari Beach, south of Limenaria. It has a family-atmosphere and very clean bathrooms, however it requires a minimum three-night stay.

All of the seaside villages have hotels and *domatia* and the inland villages have rooms in private houses. For information about these enquire in *kafeneia* or look for signs.

Aldebaran Pension (☎ 25930 52494; www.gothassos.com; Potos; d from €20; ☼) Just behind Potos beach, this lovely home away from home is run by the well travelled Yiannis and German-speaking Elke. The 10 rooms are simply decorated, but all have satellite TV and balconies big enough for a small party. Yiannis runs a Thasos website, so is a mine of information about island walking and birdwatching.

Esperia Hotel (☎ 25930 51342; info@hotel-esperia .gr; Pefkari; d/tr €45/50; 🍴) The ramshackle, leafy garden is the star of this otherwise standard hotel on Pefkari beach. Best enjoyed with a book underneath one of the many umbrellas, or from your balcony, it runs right down to the water. After a hard day on the beach, sink into an outdoor couch and order an ouzo from the well-stocked bar.

Alexandra Beach Hotel (☎ 25930 52391; www .alexandrabeach.gr; d incl full board from €150; P 🍴 🦽) Recognised as one of the island's best hotels, Alexandra Beach is now styling itself as a spa resort; guests can indulge in an 'anti-stress program' or a Swedish massage. For the more active, there's tennis, volleyball and even two mini-soccer fields. Unfortunately hardly any of the rooms have sea-views, a pity when the beach here is so attractive.

Eating

Taverna Glifoneri (mains from €4.50) At Glifoneri Beach, on the way from Thasos (Limenas) to Skala Rahoni, this place is on a small beach with a freshwater spring. Try the excellent home-made mussel *saganaki* with feta.

Pefkospilia (☎ 25930 81051; appetisers €2-3, mains €4-18) This cute, traditional, family-run taverna by the water at Pahis Beach, just off the road between Thasos (Limenas) and Skala Rahoni, is in a beautiful spot under a large pine tree. It serves delectable local specialities, including the sought-after fish known as *mourmoures* (per kilogram €25), *kravourosalata* (crab salad; €4) and *htapodokeftedes* (octopus rissoles; €3.50).

Taverna Drosia (☎ 25930 81270; mains €3-5) In a grove of plane and oak trees on the outskirts of Rahoni, this features live bouzouki on Friday, Saturday and Sunday evenings. Chargrilled meat is the speciality of the house, though it also has fresh seafood and precooked dishes.

Taverna O Andreas (☎ 25930 71760; mains from €3) This homespun taverna on Kasaviti's serene central square, shaded by ancient plane trees, serves excellent soup, vegetable dishes, meat and oven-cooked foods. The whole family participates in cooking and, judging by the food, they're passionate about it. Chirping birds, and cute cats chasing each other around the plane tree, will entertain you as you quietly savour your meal.

Vasilis (☎ 25930 72016; mains from €4) This beautiful, traditional wooden place on the road into Kasaviti has very good local food but is worth visiting for its stunning old-world architecture alone.

Zooom (☎ 25930 53059; mains €4-7.50) Regular Thasos visitors can't rave enough about the food and service at this *ouzeri* on the main road at Potos. Oven dishes are the speciality, but they also do a tasty grill. Daily specials are great for vegetarians, as are the freshly made salads.

Ciao Tropical Beach Bar (☎ 25930 81136) More Hawaiian than Hawaii, this beach bar in Pahis is quite a work of art. The owner has created everything by hand, from the umbrellas to the wood-carved lamps and furniture. You have to see it to believe it.

Evia & the Sporades
Εύβοια & Οι Σποράδες

Hugging the coastline of mainland Greece, the large island of Evia provides Athenians with a convenient destination for a weekend getaway. Much of the island, however, is relatively undeveloped and remains undiscovered by foreign tourists.

To the north, the villages of Loutra Edipsou and Limni draw Greeks in search of mineral spas and sandy beaches. In central Evia, trekkers head to the creek-side village of Steni at the foot of Mt Dirfys. To the island's south, the landscape changes from mountainsides carpeted in pine and poplar to arid hillsides dotted with olive trees and cut by rocky gorges. Above the coastal resort of Karystos you can visit the dragon houses, ancient Stonehenge-like landmarks set in seemingly impossible positions.

The Sporades (in Greek, 'scattered ones') lie northeast of Evia and southeast of the Pelion Peninsula, to which they were joined in prehistoric times. Indeed, with their dense vegetation and mountainous terrain, the islands seem like a continuation of this peninsula. There are 11 islands in the archipelago, four of which are inhabited. Skiathos claims the best beaches of the bunch and a throbbing tourist scene and nightlife, while Skopelos kicks back with an inviting postcard waterfront, sandy bays and lush forest trails. Alonnisos and Skyros, although by no means remote, are far less visited and retain more local character. The National Marine Park of Alonnisos encompasses seven islands, of which Alonnisos is the largest. The marine park is home to the endangered Mediterranean monk seal, and many island residents are dedicated to preserving the region's delicate ecology.

HIGHLIGHTS

- **Wining**
  Wine & Cultural Festival in Karystos (p408), Evia

- **Dining**
  The fish tavernas at Steni Vala (p423), Alonnisos

- **Sporting Event**
  The half-marathon (p426) across Skyros

- **Wildlife**
  Dolphin watching (p423) in the National Marine Park of Alonnisos

- **Adrenaline Rush**
  Scuba Diving (p413) off Tsougriaki Islet, Skiathos

- **Romantic Spot**
  The hide-away cove of Limnonari Beach (p418) on Skopelos

[Map showing: Alonnisos, Steni Vala, Tsougriaki, Limnonari Beach, Skyros, Karystos]

GETTING THERE & AWAY
Air
Skiathos airport receives charter flights from northern Europe and there are also domestic flights to Athens (see p409). Skyros airport has domestic flights to Athens (see p424), as well as occasional charter flights from the Netherlands.

Bus
From the Terminal B bus station in Athens (Liosion St) there are buses departing to Halkida (€5.10, 1¼ hours, every half-hour from 5.30am to 9pm), Paralia Kymis (€11.40, four hours, twice daily) and to Loutra Edipsou (€12.10, four hours, three daily). From the Mavromateon terminal in Athens (located opposite Aeros Park) there are buses to Rafina (for Karystos and Marmari; €1.90, one hour, every 45 minutes).

Ferry
There are daily ferries to the Sporades from both Agios Konstantinos and Volos, and weekly ferries from Thessaloniki to the Sporades, as well as five ferry routes connecting Evia to the mainland.

**FERRY CONNECTIONS TO EVIA
& THE SPORADES**

Origin	Destination	Dur	Fare	Freq
Agia Marina	Evia (Nea Styra)	1hr	€1.90	5 daily
Agios Konstantinos (jet ferry)	Alonnisos	4hr	€31.30	daily
	Skiathos	2½hr	€23.80	daily
	Skopelos	3½hr	€31.60	1-2 daily
Arkitsa	Evia (Loutra Edipsou)	45min	€2.10	12 daily
Evia (Paralia Kymis)	Skyros	1¾hr	€8.30	2 daily
Evia (Marmari)	Rafina	1hr	€5.10	5-6 daily
Glifa	Evia (Agiokambos)	30min	€1.50	6-7 daily
Skala Oropou	Evia (Eretria)	25min	€1.40	hourly
Thessaloniki	Skiathos	6hr	€17.70	weekly
Volos	Alonnisos	4½hr	€14.80	2 weekly
	Skiathos	2½hr	€13.10	2 daily
	Skopelos	3½hr	€16.90	1-2 daily

The table on this page lists ferries to this island group from mainland ports in high season. Further details and inter-island links can be found under each island entry in this chapter.

Summer ferry timetables are usually available in late April. The main companies include the following:

GA Ferries (☎ 210 451 1720; Akti Miaouli & 2 Kantharou, Piraeus)

Hellenic Seaways (☎ 210 419 9000; www.hellasferries .gr; Akti Kondyli & Etolikou 2, Piraeus)

Minoan Lines (☎ 281 033 0301; www.ferries.gr/minoan; Thermopylon 6-10, Piraeus)

Hydrofoil
There are frequent daily hydrofoil links from both Agios Konstantinos and Volos to the Northern Sporades (Skiathos, Skopelos and Alonnisos only). The table on this page lists hydrofoil connections during the high season. Further details and inter-island links can be found under each island entry in this chapter. The summer hydrofoil timetable is usually available in late April from **Hellenic Seaways** (☎ 210 419 9100; www .dolphins.gr; Akti Kondyli & Etolikou 2, Piraeus GR-185 45). The timetable is also available from local hydrofoil booking offices located in Volos and Agios Konstantinos.

**HYDROFOIL CONNECTIONS TO EVIA
& THE SPORADES**

Origin	Destination	Dur	Fare	Freq
Agios Konstantinos				
	Alonnisos	2¾hr	€31.30	2-3 daily
	Skiathos	1½hr	€23.20	2-3 daily
	Skopelos	2½hr	€27.40	2-3 daily
Volos	Alonnisos	2½hr	€27.80	3-4 daily
	Skiathos	1¼hr	€21.10	3-4 daily
	Skopelos	2¼hr	€26.30	3-4 daily
	Glossa	1¾hr	€24.10	3-4 daily

Train
There is an hourly train service from Athens' Larisis station to Halkida (€4.70, 1½ hours), and one intercity train to Volos, via Larisa (€19.50, five hours).

EVIA ΕΥΒΟΙΑ

The island of Evia (*eh-vih-ah*), a prime holiday destination for Greeks, remains less checked by foreign tourists. But Evia is well worthwhile for its scenic mountain roads (the best in Greece), good trekking destinations, unusual archaeological finds and uncrowded beaches. A mountainous spine runs north–south; the island's east coast consists of precipitous cliffs, whereas the gentler west coast has a string of beaches, resorts and spas. A number of ferry connections, as well as a short bridge over the Evripous Channel to the island's capital, Halkida, connect the island to the mainland.

At the mention of Evia, many Greeks will eagerly tell you that the current in this narrow channel changes direction around seven times daily, which it does, if you are prepared to hang around long enough to watch. The next bit of the story – that Aristotle became so perplexed at not finding an explanation for this mystifying occurrence that he threw himself into the channel and drowned – can almost certainly be taken with a grain of salt.

CENTRAL EVIA

After crossing the bridge to Halkida, the road veers south, following the coastline to Eretria, a bustling resort and major archaeological site. Further on, a string of hamlets and fishing villages dot the route until the junction at Lepoura, where the road forks north toward Kymi. Several branch roads to the sea are worth exploring, though the beach at Kalamos is exceptional. From the hillside town of Kymi, a rough mountain road leads west above the north coastline to Paralia Hiliadou (see p406).

Halkida Χαλκίδα

pop 54,558

Halkida (also Halkis) was an important city-state in ancient times, with several colonies dotted around the Mediterranean. The name derives from the bronze manufactured here in antiquity (*halkos* means 'bronze' in Greek). Today it's a lively industrial and agricultural town, but with nothing of sufficient note to warrant an overnight stay. However, if you have an hour or so to spare between buses, have a look at the **Archaeological Museum** (☎ 22210 60944; Leoforos Venizelou 13; admission €2; ☷ 8.30am-3pm Tue-Sun) with finds from Evia's three ancient cities of Halkida, Eretria and Karystos, including a chunk from the pediment of the Temple of Dafniforos Apollo at Eretria.

For emergencies, call the Halkida **tourist police** (☎ 22210 77777).

ACTIVITIES

The **Sport Apollon Scuba Diving Centre** (☎ 22210 86369; ☷ 9am-1:30pm & 5-9pm) in Halkida offers a range of diving activities for all levels of experience. The dives take place off the Alikes coast, north of Evia. A one-day dive costs about €45.

SLEEPING & EATING

Should your connections require you to stay overnight in this transport hub, head for **John's Hotel** (☎ /fax 22210 24996; s/d €45/65; P ☒), the best value among several waterfront options near the old bridge, and close to a string of tavernas.

GETTING THERE & AWAY

Halkida is the transport hub of Evia.

Bus

From **Halkida station** (☎ 22210 22640; cnr Papanastasiou & Venizelou) buses run to Athens (€5.10, 1¼ hours, hourly), Eretria (€1.50, 25 minutes, hourly), Kymi Town (€6.20, two hours, eight daily) via Eretria, two of which continue to Paralia Kymis to meet the ferry arrivals/departures. There are also buses to Steni (€3, one hour, twice daily), Limni (€5.80, two hours, two to three daily), Loutra Edipsou (€7.80, 2½ hours, two to three daily) and Karystos (€7.90, three hours, two to three daily) via Eretria. The port of Marmari (for ferry connections to/from Rafina) is 11km from Karystos, and can be reached by bus (€1.30) or taxi (€12).

Train

The **Halkida train station** (☎ 22210 22386) is on the mainland side of the bridge. Frequent trains make the run to Athens (€4.70, 1½ hours, hourly) and to Thessaloniki (via Oinoi: normal €14, 5½ hours, six daily; intercity €33, 4½ hours, three daily).

Eretria Ερέτρια

pop 3156

As you head east from Halkida, Eretria is the first major place of interest. Ancient Eretria was a major maritime power and also had an eminent school of philosophy. The city was destroyed in AD 87 during the Mithridatic War, fought between Mithridates (king of Pontos) and the Roman commander Sulla. The modern town was founded in the 1820s by islanders from

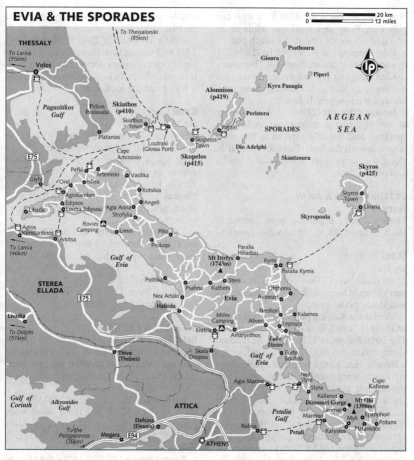

EVIA & THE SPORADES

Psara fleeing the Turkish. Despite its modern package-tourist patina, it remains one of Evia's major archaeological sites.

INFORMATION
There is no tourist information centre in Eritrea. For emergencies, call the Halkida **tourist police** (☎ 22210 77777). For Internet access, head to **Kristos Internet Cafe-Bar** (☎ 22290 61604; ☉ 9am-1am; per hr €3) on the waterfront.

SIGHTS
From the top of the **ancient acropolis**, at the northern end of town, there are splendid views over to the mainland. West of the acropolis are the remains of a palace, temple and theatre with a subterranean passage

once used by actors. Close by, the **Archaeological Museum of Eretria** (☎ 22290 62206; admission €2; ☉ 8am-3pm Tue-Sun) contains well-displayed finds from ancient Eretria. A walking path which begins at the museum focuses on the fascinating **House of Mosaics,** ending at the **Sanctuary of Apollo**.

SLEEPING & EATING
Sunrise Hotel Apartments (☎ 22290 60004; fax 22290 60648; Barbati St; d/f €40/60; P ⊠) This family-friendly self-catering apartment complex between the beach and central waterfront area features a tennis and basketball court.

Dreams Island Bungalows (☎ 22290 61224; fax 22290 61268; s/d/f incl breakfast €45/55/90; P ⊠) Tucked away on a nearby green islet, the bungalow setting is ideal for kids who can play Ping-Pong and mini-golf while mum and dad sip a cool one at the beach bar.

Milos Camping (☎ 22290 60460; fax 22110 60360; www.mxm.gr/milos; sites adult/tent €5/4) This clean, shaded camping ground on the coast 1km northwest of Eretria has a small restaurant, bar and narrow pebble beach.

Taverna Astra (☎ 22290 64111; Arheou Theatrou 48; mains €4-9) Just past the supermarket, this spacious and friendly taverna is the most reasonable on the waterfront for fresh fish, along with appetisers like *skordalia* (garlic and potato dip).

GETTING THERE & AWAY
Ferry
There's a ferry departing from Eretria to Skala Oropou (€1.40, 20 minutes, hourly).

Steni Στενή
pop 926

From Halkida, it's 31km to the lovely mountain village of Steni, with its gurgling springs and shady plane trees.

Steni is the starting point for the climb up **Mt Dirfys** (1743m), Evia's highest mountain. The **Dirfys Refuge**, at 1120m, can be reached along a 9km dirt road. From the refuge it's a steeper 7km to the summit. Allow about six hours from Steni to the summit. You should not attempt this walk unless you are an experienced trekker. For further information contact the **EOS** (Greek Alpine Club; ☎ 22210 25230; Angeli Gyviou 22, 341 33 Halkida GR). Serious trekkers should get the excellent topo/hiking map of Mt Dirfys published by Anavasi (No 25). A rough road continues from Steni to **Paralia Hiliadou**, on the north coast, where there is a fine pebble-and-sand beach, along with a few *domatia* and two tavernas. Campers can find shelter near the big rocks at the end of the beach.

SLEEPING & EATING
Hotel Dirfys (☎ 22280 51217; s/d €30/40) This is the best value of Steni's two hotels, and is 50m uphill from the bus terminal. It has comfortable, carpeted rooms with great views from the balconies.

Taverna Orea Steni (☎ 22280 51262; mains €3-8) The best and most attractive among ten brookside eateries, this taverna offers grills and traditional oven-ready dishes like the popular roast lamb with cheese, along with

salads prepared from locally gathered greens.

Mouria Taverna (☎ 22280 51234; mains €3-7) This welcoming taverna and *ouzeri* on the small central square serves mountain portions of grilled chicken and lamb chops and a very palatable local wine.

Kymi Κύμη
pop 3037

The untouristy, workaday town of Kymi is built on a cliff 250m above the sea. Things perk up at dusk when the town square comes to life. The port of Kymi (called Paralia Kymis), 4km downhill, is the only natural harbour on the precipitous east coast, and the departure point for ferries to Skyros.

The **Folklore Museum** (☎ 22220 22011; admission €1.50; ☑ 10am-1pm & 5-8pm), 30m downhill from main square, has an impressive collection of local costumes and historical photos, including a display commemorating Kymi-born Dr George Papanikolaou, inventor of the Pap smear test.

SLEEPING & EATING
Hotel Beis (☎ 22220 22604; fax 22220 29113; Paralia Kymis; s/d incl breakfast €35/45; ☒) This well-managed waterfront location features large and spotless rooms, and is just across from the ferry dock.

Hotel Carali (☎ 22220 22212; fax 22220 23353; Paralia Kymis; s/d €36/50; ℗ ☒) It's a 300m walk from the ferry dock to this quiet 21-room terraced hotel run by two sisters, Sofia and Evangelia.

Taverna Mouria (☎ 22220 22629; Galani 34; mains €3.50-7) Just north of the church on the square, this family-style eatery specialises in lamb grills and pasta (pastitsio).

In Paralia Kymis a string of tavernas and *ouzeria* lines the waterfront. Try **To Balkoni** (☎ 22220 24177) or **Taverna Aegeo** (☎ 22220 22641), both popular for fresh fish and oven-ready dishes and salads.

NORTHERN EVIA
From Halkida a road heads north to **Psahna**, the gateway to the highly scenic mountainous interior of northern Evia. The road climbs through pine forests to the beautiful agricultural village of **Prokopi**, 52km from Halkida. At Strofylia, 14km beyond Prokopi, a road heads southwest

to picturesque **Limni** then north to **Loutra Edipsou** and the ferry port at Agiokambos.

Loutra Edipsou Λουτρά Αιδηψού
pop 3600

The road continues to the sedate spa resort of **Loutra Edipsou,** whose therapeutic sulphur waters have been celebrated since antiquity. Many luminaries, including Aristotle, Plutarch and Sylla, sang the praises of these waters. The town's gradual expansion over the years has been tied to the improving technology required to carry the water further and further away from its thermal source. Today the town has two of Greece's most up-to-date hydrotherapy and physiotherapy centres. Even if you don't rank among the infirm you may enjoy a visit to this resort with its attractive port and beach tavernas.

INFORMATION
Dr Symeonides (☎ 22260 23220; Omirou 17) English-speaking doctor; recommended for emergencies.
Medical Centre (☎ 22260 53311; Istiea)
New Worlds Internet (☎ 22260 60682; Thermopotamou 17; per hr €3; ☺ 9am-12.30am) Next to the bus station.

ACTIVITIES
The more relaxing of the resort's two best-known spas is the **EOT Hydrotherapy-Physiotherapy Centre** (☎ 22260 23501; 25 March St 37; ☺ 7am-1pm & 5-7pm Jun 1-Oct 31), speckled with palm trees and a large outdoor pool and terrace overlooking the sea. Whirlpool bath treatments start at a modest €7.

The other is the posh **Thermae Sylla Hotel & Spa** (☎ 22260 60100; www.thermaesylla.gr; Posidonos 2; d €195-225; ☺ 24hr), with a somewhat late-Roman ambience befitting its name, and offering a wide range of health and beauty treatments, from mud baths to seaweed body wraps. Should you wish to stay in the hotel (d/ste €200/300), you'll find elegant designer rooms with high ceilings and clear views to the sea.

SLEEPING & EATING
Prices here reflect the higher summer season, 10 July to 10 October; off-season rates drop about 20%.
Hotel Aegli (☎ 22260 22215; fax 22260 22886; Paraliakis 18; s/d/tr €30/45/50) For charm and value, you can't beat this well-managed neoclassic

holdover from the 1930s. The lobby is decorated with framed autographs of luminaries who spent an evening here, including Greta Garbo, Aristotle Onassis and Winston Churchill. Like most hotels here, this one offers hydrotherapy baths for about €5.
Hotel Kentrikon (☎ /fax 22260 22502; 25 Martiou 14; s/d/tr €45/65/75; ☒ ☒) This efficient combination hotel and spa has an old-world charm about it, with large tiled rooms, many with wood ceilings and balcony views of the sea and hot springs.
Taverna Aegli (☎ 22260 22215; Paraliakis 18; mains €4-7.50) This leafy extension of the Hotel Aegli serves first-rate grills and salads. A few plates of sardines, fresh chips (not frozen), *horta* (wild greens) and wine runs about €10 per head.
Taverna Barous (☎ 22260 23111; mains €4-9) Opposite the ferry dock, Barous serves fine fish grills, pastas and *mezedes*. Pick a breezy outdoor table under the canopy to glimpse the harbour activity.

GETTING THERE & AWAY
Bus
From the **bus station** (☎ 22260 22250; Thermopotamou), 200m up from the port, buses run to Halkida (€7.80, 2½ hours, two to three daily), Athens (€12.10, four hours, three daily) and Thessaloniki (€20, five hours, once daily).

Ferry
The **ferry** (☎ 22260 31107) runs from mainland Glyfa to Agiokambos (€1.50, 25 minutes, every two hours from 7am to 8pm) and from mainland Arkitsa to Loutra Edipsou (€2.10, 30 minutes, hourly from 6am to 9pm).

Limni Λίμνη
pop 2072

One of Evia's most picturesque ports, little Limni faces seaward, its maze of white-washed houses and narrow lanes spilling onto a busy waterfront. The town's cultural **museum** (☎ 22270 32510; admission €2; ☺ 9am-1pm Mon-Sat, 10.30am-1pm Sun), just 40m south of the main square, features local archaeological finds along with antique looms, costumes and old coins.

With your own transport or a penchant for walking, you can visit the splendid 16th-century **Convent of Galataki,** 8km southeast of

Limni on a hillside above the road. The fine mosaics and frescoes in its *katholikon* merit a look, especially the *Entry of the Righteous into Paradise*. There are no official opening hours, but the convent is generally open from 9am to 6pm daily.

SLEEPING & EATING

Ostria Apartments (☎ /fax 22270 32248; www.holiday shop.gr/ostria; apt €100; P ⛱ ⛽) Olive trees and bougainvillea surround these 10 roomy self-catering apartments across the road from a pool and good pebble beach, 1km northwest of Limni.

Rovies Camping (☎ 22270 71120; sites adult/ tent €4.50/3; P) This well-tended camping ground is on the coast, 12km northwest of Limni, on a lovely stretch of sandy beach.

Zaniakos Domatia (☎ 22270 31667; Plateia; s/d €20/25; ⛱) At this humble *domatia*, not much English is in evidence, but the rooms are spotless and quiet.

Taverna Paradosiako (☎ 22270 31479; Plateia; mains €3.50-7.50) At the back of the shady plateia, this inviting family taverna serves traditional ready-to-eat dishes like stuffed tomatoes and peppers, and souvlaki.

SOUTHERN EVIA

Continuing east from Eretria, the road branches at Lepoura: the left fork leads north to Kymi, the right south to Karystos. A turn-off at Krieza, 3km from the junction, leads to Lake Distos, a shallow lake bed favoured by egrets and other wetland birds. Continuing south, you'll catch views of both coasts along this narrow bit of Evia as the landscape turns arid, until it reaches the sea at Karystos, near the base of Mt Ohi.

Karystos Κάρυστος
pop 4960

Set on the wide Karystian Bay below Mt Ohi (1398m), and flanked by two sandy beaches, Karystos is the most attractive of southern Evia's beach resorts. The town's central waterfront square, Plateia Amalias, faces onto the bay, overlooking the boat harbour. Further along, the remains of a 14th-century Venetian castle, the **Bourtzi**, contains bits of marble from a temple dedicated to Apollo. Karystos is the starting point for treks to Mt Ohi and the Dimosari Gorge.

INFORMATION

Polihoros Internet & Sports Cafe (☎ 22240 24421; Kriezotou 132; per hr €3; ⌚ 9am-1am) Next to the Galaxy Hotel.

South Evia Tours (☎ 22240 25700; fax 22240 29091; set@eviatravel.gr; Plateia Amalias 7) Help with local and island information, plus bookings and accommodations.

SIGHTS

Karystos is mentioned in Homer's *Iliad*, and was a powerful city-state during the Peloponnesian Wars. The **Karystos Museum** (☎ 22240 25661; admission €2; ⌚ 8.30am-3pm Tue-Sun), just opposite the Bourtzi, documents the town's archaeological heritage, including tiny Neolithic clay lamps, a stone plaque written in the Halkidian alphabet, 5th-century BC grave stelae depicting Zeus and Athena, and an exhibit of the 6th-century *drakospita* (dragon houses) of Mt Ohi and Styra.

TOURS

South Evia Tours (☎ 22240 25700; fax 22240 29091; set@eviatravel.gr) offers a range of services including car hire, accommodation and excursions. The latter include walks in the foothills of Mt Ohi, the 6th-century-BC Roman-built *drakospita* near Skyra, and a cruise around the Petali Islands.

FESTIVALS

Karystos hosts a summer **Wine & Cultural Festival** from early July until the last weekend in August. Most of the action happens on weekends, with plenty of traditional dancing to the tune of local musicians, and theatre performances, along with painting, photo and sculpture exhibits by local artists. The summer merrymaking concludes with the Wine Festival, featuring every local wine imaginable, free for the tasting. Festival schedules are available at the Karystos Museum (see above).

SLEEPING & EATING

Hotel Karystion (☎ 22240 22391; www.karystion.gr; Kriezotou 3; s/d incl breakfast €45/55; P ⛱) Well-managed and just 100m east of the Bourtzi, the bright and well-appointed rooms with seaview balconies are excellent value. A stairway off the courtyard leads to a sandy beach below.

Galaxy Hotel (☎ 22240 22600; fax 22240 22463; cnr Kriezotou & Odysseos; s/d incl breakfast €40/50; ⛱)

This low-key and welcoming waterfront hotel has simple and spacious rooms with music channels and balcony seaviews from the upper rooms.

Cavo d'Oro (☎ 22240 22326; mains €3-7) Join the locals in this cheery little alleyway restaurant one block west of the main square, where tasty oil-based dishes (*ladera*, or fasting food) cost from €3.20, perfect *spanakopita* (spinach pie) and *tiropita* (cheese pie) about €1.20, and a generous plate of fried *garida* (shrimp) fetches a modest €6.

Taverna Mesa-Exo (In-Out; ☎ 22240 23997; mains €3.50-8) This excellent boardwalk taverna is favoured by many locals for its grilled fish, *mezedes* and warm atmosphere. A plate of fried *gavros* (sardines), Greek salad and beer or house wine fetches about €10 per head.

DRINKING
For evening drinks and sounds from reggae to rock, walk west about 200m beyond the Galaxy Hotel to a string of late-night bars, such as **Club Archipelagos** (☎ 22240 25040), or head east to the hip **Club Kohili** (☎ 22240 24350), on the beach by the Apollon Suite Hotel.

Around Karystos
The ruins of **Castello Rossa** (Red Castle), a 13th-century Frankish fortress, are a two-hour walk from **Myli**, a delightful, well-watered village 4km inland from Karystos. A little beyond Myli there is an **ancient quarry** scattered with fragments of the once-prized Karystian marble.

With your own transport you can explore the nearby *drakospita* of Mt Ohi and Styra. The discovery of these Stonehenge-like dwellings hewn from rocks weighing up to several tons has spawned a number of theories regarding their origin, ranging from slave-built temples to UFO getaways.

Hikers can head north by car from Karystos to the summit of Mt Ohi where a footpath leads to the **Dimosari Gorge** and **Lenosei** village with views down to the coastal village of **Kallianos**. The 10km trail can usually be covered in about four hours, ending at the coastline near Kallianos village, where lunch is available. Inquire at South Evia Tours (opposite) in Karystos for trail conditions and maps.

For less strenuous walks, explore the villages and chestnut forests nestling in the foothills east of Mt Ohi. From **Epanohori**, a trail descends along an old school path and river bed before reaching the coastal village of **Potami** (about four hours).

GETTING THERE & AWAY
Bus
From the **Karystos bus station** (☎ 22240 26303), three blocks up from the plateia opposite Agios Nikolaos church, buses run to Halkida (€8.60, three hours, four daily) and to Athens (€6.80, two hours, twice daily).

Ferry
There is a regular ferry service between Marmari, 9km west of Karystos, and Rafina (€5.10, one hour, four to six daily). There is also a **ferry service** (☎ 22240 41533, 69449 82879) from Nea Styra (35km north of Karystos) to Agia Marina (€2.10, one hour, five daily).

SKIATHOS ΣΚΙΑΘΟΣ

pop 6160
The good news is that much of the pine-covered coast of Skiathos is blessed with exquisite beaches. The bad news is that in July and August the island is overrun with package tourists and prices soar. Despite the large presence of sun-starved northern Europeans, Skiathos is still a beautiful island and one of Greece's premier resorts.

The island's only major settlement, the port and capital of Skiathos Town, lies on the southeast coast. The rest of the south coast is a chain of holiday villas and hotels, plus a number of sandy beaches with pine trees for a backdrop. The north coast is precipitous and less accessible; in the 14th century the Kastro Peninsula served as a natural fortress against invaders. Today, most people come to Skiathos for the sun and nightlife, but the truly curious will discover inviting walks, picturesque monasteries, hilltop tavernas and even quiet beaches.

Getting There & Away
AIR
As well as the numerous charter flights from northern Europe to Skiathos, during summer there is one flight daily to Athens (€53). **Olympic Airlines** (☎ 24270 22200) has an office at the airport, not in town.

EVIA & THE SPORADES

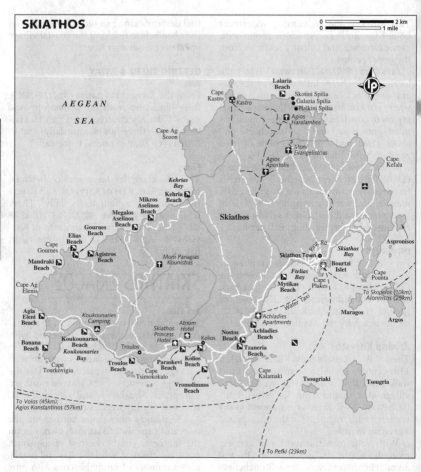

SKIATHOS

0 — 2 km
0 — 1 mile

AEGEAN SEA

Cape Kastro
Kastro

Lalaria Beach
Skotini Spilia
Galazia Spilia
Halkini Spilia

Cape Ag Sozon

Agios Haralambos

Moni Evangelistrias

Agios Apostolis

Cape Kefala

Kehrias Bay
Kehria Beach

Mikros Aselinos Beach

Megalos Aselinos Beach

Skiathos

Gournes Beach

Elias Beach

Cape Gournes

Agistros Beach

Mandraki Beach

Moni Panagias Kounistras

Ring Rd

Skiathos Bay

Aspronisos

Skiathos Town

Bourtzi Islet

Cape Ag Elenis

Ftelias Bay

Cape Plakes

Cape Pounta

To Skopelos (10km); Alonnisos (25km)

Agia Eleni Beach

Mytikas Beach

Water Taxi

Maragos

Argos

Koukounaries Camping

Achladies Apartments

Banana Beach

Koukounaries Beach

Koukounaries Bay

Skiathos Princess Hotel

Atrium Hotel

Nostos Beach

Achladies Beach

Troulos

Kolios

Cape Tourkovigia

Troulos Beach

Paraskevi Beach

Kolios Beach

Tzaneria Beach

Cape Tsimokokalo

Vromolimnos Beach

Cape Kalamaki

Tsougriaki

Tsougria

To Volos (45km); Agios Konstantinos (57km)

To Pefki (23km)

FERRY

In summer, there are ferries from Skiathos to Volos (€13.10, 2½ hours, twice daily), Agios Konstantinos (€23.20, 2½ hours by jet ferry, once daily) and Alonnisos (€10.70, two hours, twice daily) via Skopelos (€10.30, 1¼ hours).

From June through September, there is a weekly ferry service (Saturday) heading north to Thessaloniki (€17.70, six hours) on the mainland, and a weekly service travelling south to Tinos (€22.50, 7½ hours), Paros (€29.50, 10 hours), Santorini (€33.50, 13 hours) and Iraklio (€38, 17 hours). Heading to the east of Skiathos, there is a weekly service to Limnos (€15.50, seven hours).

Tickets can be purchased from **Skiathos Travel** (☎ 24270 22029; fax 24270 22750) at the bottom of Papadiamantis in Skiathos Town.

HYDROFOIL

In summer, there are hydrofoils from Skiathos to Volos (€21.10, 1¼ hours, three to four daily) and to Agios Konstantinos (€23.20, 1½ hours, two to three daily). A Flying Cat hydrofoil makes a daily run to Thessaloniki (€35.30, 3½ hours). And there is a regular service (four to six daily) from Skiathos to Alonnisos (€14.20, one hour) via Glossa on Skopelos (€6.10, 20 minutes) and Skopelos Town (€10, 35 minutes). Hydrofoil tickets can be purchased from Skiathos Travel (above).

Getting Around

BUS
Crowded buses leave Skiathos Town for Koukounaries Beach (€1.40, 30 minutes, every half-hour between 7.30am and 11pm). The buses stop at all the access points to the beaches along the south coast.

CAR & MOTORCYCLE
Reliable car-hire outlets in Skiathos Town include **Heliotropio Tourism & Travel** (☎ 24270 22430), next to Alpha Bank on the new port; **Mathinos Travel** (☎ 24270 23351; Papadiamantis 18) and **Euronet** (☎ 24270 24410), also near Alpha Bank. There are also heaps of motorcycle-hire outlets all along the town's waterfront.

TAXI
The **taxi stand** (☎ 24270 21460) is opposite the ferry dock.

WATER TAXI
Water taxis depart the terminal at the old port for Tzaneria Beach (€2, 20 minutes, hourly) and Achladies Beach.

SKIATHOS TOWN

Skiathos Town, with its red-roofed, white-washed houses, is built on two low hills. Opposite the waterfront lies inviting **Bourtzi Islet** (reached by a causeway) between the two small harbours. The town is a major tourist centre, with hotels, souvenir shops, travel agents, tavernas and bars dominating the waterfront and main thoroughfare.

Orientation
The quay (wharf) is in the middle of the waterfront, just north of Bourtzi Islet. To the right (as you face inland) is the straight, new harbour; to the left is the curving old harbour used by local fishing and excursion boats. The main thoroughfare of Papadiamanti strikes inland from opposite the quay. Plateia Trion Ierarhon is above the old harbour, next to a large church. The bus terminus is at the northern end of the new harbour.

Information

EMERGENCY
Port police (☎ 24270 22017)
Tourist police (☎ 24270 23172; 🕑 8am-9pm) Opposite the regular police station about halfway along Papadiamanti, next to the high school; open daily during the summer season.

INTERNET ACCESS
Enter Internet (☎ 24270 29330; per hr €4.50; 🕑 9am to 1am) From the port, walk up Papadiamanti and take the first left.
Internet Zone Café (☎ 24270 227671; Evangelistrias 28; per hr €4.50; 🕑 10am-1am) About 30m from the post office.

LAUNDRY
Snow White's Laundry (☎ 24270 24256; per load €10) Behind Alpha Bank.

MEDICAL SERVICES
Health Centre Hospital (☎ 24270 22222) At the beginning (west end) of ring road, above old port.

MONEY
The National Bank of Greece, Alpha Bank and numerous ATMs are on Papadiamanti and along the waterfront.

POST
Post office (☎ 24270 22011; cnr Papadiamantis & Evangelistra; 🕑 7:30am-2pm Mon-Fri)

Sights
Skiathos was the birthplace of popular Greek short-story writer and poet Alexandros Papadiamantis, as well as novelist Alexandros Moraïtidis. Papadiamantis' house is now a charming **museum** (☎ 24270 23843; Plateia Papadiamanti; admission €1; 🕑 9.30am-1pm & 5-8pm Tue-Sun) with a small collection documenting his life.

Tours
Excursion boats make full and half-day trips around the island (€12 to €17, approximately four to six hours), and usually include a visit to Kastro, Lalaria Beach and the three caves of Halkini Spilia, Skotini Spilia and Galazia Spilia, which are only accessible by boat. Contact **Mathinos Travel** (☎ 24270 23351; 18 Papadiamantis) or **Heliotropio Tourism & Travel** (☎ 24270 22430) at the new port, 20m from Papadiamantis.

Sleeping
Most accommodation is booked from July to the end of August, when prices quoted here are nearly double those of low season. There's a helpful quayside kiosk with information on hotel rooms and *domatia*.

Villa Orsa (☎ 24270 22430; s/d/f incl breakfast €70/80/110; ❄) Perched above the old harbour, this classic cliffside mansion features very comfortable, traditionally styled rooms, several with balcony views. Breakfast is served in a courtyard terrace overlooking the sea.

Pension Koula (☎ 24270 22025; koula@mathinos.gr; s/d incl breakfast €50/60) Above the old harbour and near the church, this well-managed traditional pension offers great sea views from a shaded patio where breakfast is served.

Hotel Akti (☎ 24270 22024; fax 24270 22430; s/d/ste €60/70/80; 🖭) You'll get a central waterfront location at the Akti, along with bright airy rooms. At the new port.

Also recommended:

Pothos Hotel (☎ 24270 21304; s/d €80/90; 🖭) A quiet sidestreet courtyard inn with spacious rooms and mini-fridges. Located on Evangelistrias, 30m west of post office.

Australia Hotel (☎ 24270 22488; Evangelistria; s/d €35/45; 🖭) A simple and spotless budget choice off the main drag.

Eating

Many eateries in Skiathos are geared to the tourist trade and are expensive. The following offer better value than most.

Maria's Pizza (☎ 24270 22292; Syngrou 6; mains €8-12) A popular hole-in-the-wall above the old port, Maria's offers superb handmade pizza, pasta and unique salads (salmon and arugula) in a flower-filled alleyway setting. A thinly-crusted pizza with salad for two, plus wine, runs about €25.

Psaradika Ouzeri (☎ 24270 23412; mains €3.50-10) This busy waterfront eatery at the far end of the old port specialises in fresh fish at decent prices; favourites include a hearty fish soup, *gavros* and grilled or fried calamari.

Taverna Alexandros (☎ 24270 22341; Mavrogiali; mains €4-9) Excellent lamb grills, traditional oven-roasted chicken and potatoes and live but low-key Greek music await at this friendly alleyway eatery under a canopy of mulberry trees.

Main Street (☎ 24270 21743; Papadiamantis; breakfasts €2-3) Next to the post office, this efficient and comfortable eatery serves the best-value breakfast in town, along with well-prepared wraps, burgers and fresh juices.

Taverna Ouzeri Kabourelia (☎ 24270 21112; mains €5-6) The only year-round eatery at the old port in Skiathos (just opposite the excursion boats), Kabourelia is favoured by locals for its grilled anchovies and *kalamaria* (calamari).

Also recommended:

Taverna Anemos (☎ 24270 21003; mains €4-10) Excellent seafood and Greek wine list. Take the steps at the end of the old harbour up 50m.

Taverna Meltemi (☎ 24240 65755; mains €4-8) The best of the waterfront eateries opposite the new harbour.

Amfiliki Cafe Restaurant (☎ 24270 22839; mains €7-12) Well regarded for its stuffed squid and superb ocean views. Opposite Medical Centre Hospital.

Porto Bello (☎ 24270 29051; Papadiamantis; mains €4-9) Good breakfast spot, with an all-you-can-eat English buffet, Internet access and 25 overhead fans.

Drinking

Kentavros Bar (☎ 24270 22980) The long-established and handsome Kentavros off Plateia Papadiamanti promises rock, soul, jazz and blues, and gets the thumbs up from locals and expats alike for its mellow ambience.

Bar Destiny (☎ 24270 24172) Look for the soft blue light coming from this hip sidestreet hole-in-the-wall parallel to Papadiamanti, with music videos, draught beer and a bit of dancing when the mood hits.

Rock & Roll Bar (☎ 24270 22944) Look for the huge pillows lining the steps outside this trendy bar by the old port. Huge beanbags have replaced a few of the pillows, resulting in fewer customers rolling off.

Kahlua Bar (☎ 24270 23205; Polytehniou) Like several clubs along the waterfront, this popular bar pulses with mainstream DJ sets and dancing drinkers.

Entertainment

Cinema Attikon (☎ 24270 22352; Papadiamanti; admission €7) You can catch recent English-language movies at this open-air cinema, sip a beer and practice speed-reading your Greek subtitles at the same time. (Greece is one of the few countries in Europe to show all films with original language intact, even on TV.)

Shopping

Loupos & his Dolphins (☎ 24270 23777; Plateia Papadiamanti; 🕙 10am-1.30pm & 6.30-11.30pm) This high-end gallery shop sells original icons, fine ceramics and jewellery. It's adjacent to the Papadiamantis Museum.

Archipelogos (☎ 24270 22163; Plateia Papadiamanti; 🕙 11am-1pm & 8-10pm) The work of contemporary Greek artists, along with elegant traditional weavings, stands out at this intimate shop.

Galerie Varsakis (☎ 24270 22255; Plateia Trion Ierarhon; ⏱ 10am-2pm & 6-11pm) This handsome shop features unusual antiques like 19th-century spinning sticks made by grooms for their intended brides.

AROUND SKIATHOS
Beaches

With some 65 beaches to choose from, beach-hopping on Skiathos can become a full-time occupation. Buses ply the south coast stopping at numbered beach access points. The ones nearest town are extremely crowded; the first one worth getting off the bus for is the pine-fringed, long and sandy **Vromolimnos Beach**. Further along, **Kolios Beach** and **Troulos** beaches are also good but both, alas, are very popular. The bus continues to **Koukounaries Beach**, backed by pine trees and a lagoon touted as the best beach in Greece. But nowadays it's best viewed at a distance, from where the 1200m long sweep of pale gold sand does indeed sparkle.

Banana Beach, known for its curving shape and soft white sand, lies at the other side of a narrow headland. It is nominally a nudist beach, though the skinny-dippers tend to abscond to **Little Banana Beach** (which also gets the big thumbs up from gay and lesbian sunbathers) around the rocky corner if things get too crowded.

Just west of Koukounaries, and 500m from bus stop No 23, **Agia Eleni Beach** is a favourite with windsurfers. The northwest coast's beaches are less crowded but are subject to the strong summer meltemi (northeasterly) winds. From Troulos (look for bus stop No 17), a road heads north to sandy **Moni Panagias Kounistras;** as you pass Moni Kounistra, the sealed road turns to a well-maintained dirt road. A right fork continues 300m to **Mikros Aselinos Beach** and 5km further on to secluded **Kehria Beach**.

Lalaria Beach, a tranquil strand of pale grey, egg-shaped pebbles on the northern coast, is easily the fairest of them all. It is much featured in tourist brochures, but only reached by excursion boat from Skiathos Town (see p411).

Kastro Κάστρο

Kastro, perched dramatically on a rocky headland above the north coast, was the fortified pirate-proof capital of the island from 1540 to 1829. It consisted of some 300 houses and 20 churches and the only access was by a drawbridge. Except for two churches, it is now in ruins. Access is by steps, and the views from it are tremendous. Excursion boats come to the beach below Kastro, from where it's an easy clamber up to the ruins.

Moni Evangelistrias Μονή Ευαγγελίστριας

The most appealing of the island's monasteries is the 18th-century **Moni Evangelistrias** (Annunciation; ☎ 24270 22012; ⏱ 8am-9pm), poised above a gorge 450m above sea level, and surrounded by pine and cypress trees. The monastery was a refuge for freedom fighters during the War of Independence. Once home to 70 monks, two monks now do the chores, which include wine-making. You can sample the tasty results of their efforts in the museum shop. An adjacent shed of old presses and vintage barrels recalls an earlier era, long before the satellite dish was installed above the courtyard.

Also worth a visit is **Moni Panagias Kounistras** (Holy Virgin), with fine frescoes adorning its *katholikon*. It's 4km inland from Troulos with your own transport.

Activities
DIVING

Dolphin Diving (☎ 24270 21599; www.ddiving.gr; Nostos Beach, bus stop No 12) This is the oldest diving school in the Sporades. Most single dives are in the €45 to €55 range (with equipment) including a beginners' dive off Tsougriaki Islet which explores locations to 30m deep.

Octopus Diving Centre (☎ 24270 24549; www.odc-skiathos.com; new harbour) Dive instructor team Theofanis and Eva conduct half-day dives around the islet of Tsougriaki for experts and beginners alike (from €40 to €50, equipment included).

TREKKING

A 6km-long trekking route begins at Moni Evangelistrias, eventually reaching **Cape Kastro,** before circling back through Agios Apostolis. Kastro is a spring mecca for bird-watchers who may catch glimpses of Mediterranean shags and singing thrushes.

Sleeping & Eating

Atrium Hotel (☎ 24270 49345; www.atriumhotel.gr; Paraskevi Beach; s/d/t €90/120/175; Ⓟ Ⓧ Ⓡ) This well-designed property (the winner in its

EVIA & THE SPORADES

top-end class) sits on a pine-covered hill-side overlooking Paraskevi Beach, with sparkling balconied rooms, satellite TV and gracious service. Facilities include a game lounge with billiards, and snack bar.

Achladies Apartments (☎ 24270 22486; Karvounis, PO Box 24, Achladies Bay, Skiathos Island, 37002 Greece; d/tr €50/65 2-night minimum; P) Look for the small yellow hand-painted sign to find this welcoming gem, 3km from Skiathos Town, with self-catering rooms, along with a tortoise sanctuary and a succulent garden winding down to a sandy beach, from where a water-taxi makes 20-minute runs to Skiathos Town.

Skiathos Princess Hotel (☎ 24270 49731; www .skiathos-princess.gr; Paraskevi Beach; s/d/ste incl breakfast €104/134/244; P 🖳 🗩) The best of the island's rambling resorts, the 131-room Princess sits just above Paraskevi Beach, 8km from town. Rooms feature marble baths and mini-fridges.

Koukounaries Camping (☎ /fax 24270 49250; sites per adult/tent €7/3.30; P) This excellent site at the eastern end of Koukounaries Beach is the only officially recognised camping ground in the Sporades. It has clean toilets and showers, a minimarket and a taverna.

Taverna Agnantio (☎ 24270 22016; mains €4-9) Family-run Agnantio attracts locals and tourists alike. Come early to catch house specialities like chicken in wine sauce. It's 400m off the ring road, with superb views down to Skiathos Town.

Panorama Pizza (☎ 69441 92066; 🕒 from 7pm) For excellent pizza with a Greek touch, follow the locals uphill to this place, where the views match the food. It's 2.4km from the ring road. A pizza for two averages €7.

SKOPELOS ΣΚΟΠΕΛΟΣ

pop 4700

Less commercialised than Skiathos, Skopelos is a beautiful island of pine forests, vineyards, olive groves and fruit orchards. It is noted for its plums and almonds, which are used in many local dishes.

Like Skiathos, the northwest coast is exposed, with high cliffs. The sheltered southeast coast harbours many beaches but, unlike Skiathos, most are pebbled. There are two large settlements: the capital and main port of Skopelos Town on the east

coast; and the lovely, unspoilt hill village of Glossa, the island's second port, 3km north of Loutraki on the west coast.

In 1936 Skopelos yielded an exciting archaeological find, a royal tomb dating to ancient times when the island was an important Minoan outpost ruled by Stafylos, the son of Ariadne and Dionysos in Greek mythology. Stafylos means grape in Greek and the Minoan ruler is said to have introduced wine-making here.

Getting There & Away
FERRY

In summer there are several daily ferries from Skopelos Town to Alonnisos (€7.70, 30 minutes, once or twice daily) and to Skiathos (€10.30, one hour, two to three times daily). There are also ferries to Volos (€16.90, 3½ hours, once or twice daily) and to Agios Konstantinos (€31.60, 3½ hours, one to two jet ferries daily). Tickets are available from **Skopelos Ferry Office** (☎ 24240 22767; fax 24240 23608) opposite the new quay, and **Lemonis Agency** (☎ 24240 22363) in Pension Lemonis toward the end of the new quay.

HYDROFOIL

Skopelos has two hydrofoil ports, one at Skopelos Town and the other to the northwest at Glossa's nearby (3km) port of Loutraki. During summer the main hydrofoil services from Skopelos Town are to Alonnisos (€7.70, 20 minutes, four daily) and Skiathos (€10.30, 45 minutes, four to five daily). From Glossa, there are services to Skopelos Town (€8.40, 30 minutes, four daily), to Skiathos (€6.30, 20 minutes, four daily) and to Alonnisos (€12.40, 55 minutes, four daily).

There are also hydrofoils that go to Volos (€26.30, 2¼ hours, three to four daily) and to Agios Konstantinos (€27.40, 2½ hours, two to three daily). You can purchase tickets from **Skopelos Ferry Office** (☎ 24240 22767; fax 24240 23060).

Getting Around
BUS

There are eight buses per day from Skopelos Town all the way to Glossa/Loutraki (€3.20, one hour), three that go only as far as Panormos (€1.70, 25 minutes) and Milia (€2.30, 35 minutes) and another two that go only as far as Agnontas (€1, 15 minutes) and Stafylos (€1, 15 minutes).

CAR & MOTORCYCLE

There are a fair number of car and motorcycle rental outlets in Skopelos Town, mostly located at the eastern end of the waterfront. Among your choices is the efficient **Motor Tours** (☎ 24240 22986; fax 24240 22602) next to Hotel Eleni.

TAXI

The taxi stand is next to the bus stop along the waterfront. A taxi to Stafylos is €5, to Glossa €22.

WATER TAXI

A regular water taxi departs at 11am for Glysteri Beach (€5 one way), and returns at about 5pm.

SKOPELOS TOWN

Skopelos Town is one of the most captivating towns in the Sporades. It skirts a semicircular bay and clambers in tiers up a hillside, culminating in a ruined fortress. Dozens of churches are interspersed among dazzling white houses with brightly shuttered windows and flower-adorned balconies.

Orientation

Skopelos Town's waterfront is flanked by two quays. The old quay is at the western end of the harbour and the new quay is at the eastern end, used by all ferries and hydrofoils. From the dock, turn right to reach the bustling waterfront lined with cafés, souvenir shops and travel agencies.

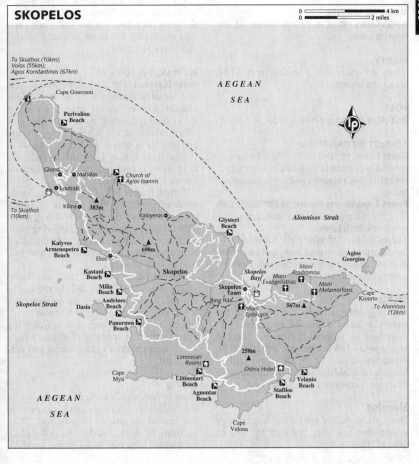

SKOPELOS

0 —— 4 km
0 —— 2 miles

To Skiathos (10km);
Volos (55km);
Agios Konstantinos (67km)

*AEGEAN
SEA*

Cape Gourouni

Perivoliou
Beach

Glossa   Mahalas
Loutraki   Church of
Agios Ioannis

To Skiathos
(10km)
Klima   383m

Kalyves
Armenopetra
Beach   Elios

Kaloyeros

Glysteri
Beach

Alonnisos Strait

690m

Kastani
Beach
Milia
Beach
Andrines
Beach

Skopelos

Skopelos
Bay   Moni
Evangelistrias

Moni
Pradromou

Agios
Georgios

Moni
Metamorfosis   Cape
Kiourto

Skopelos Strait   Dasia

Skopelos
Town

Ring Rd

Moni
Episkopis

567m

To Alonnisos
(12km)

Panormos
Beach

258m

Limnonari
Rooms

Cape
Myti   Limnonari
Beach

Agnontas
Beach

Ostria Hotel

Stafilos
Beach

Velanio
Beach

*AEGEAN
SEA*

Cape
Velona

The bus stop is just to the left of the new quay. The main square, Platanos Sq, is also known as Souvlaki Sq.

Information

EMERGENCY

Police (☎ 24240 22235) Above the National Bank.
Port police (☎ 24240 22180)

INTERNET ACCESS

Skopelos Internet Café (☎ 24240 23093; per hr €3.50) Next to the post office.

LAUNDRY

Blue Star Washing (☎ 24240 22844) On Hatzistamati between the Folk Art Museum and the OTE office, as you head up from the waterfront.

MEDICAL SERVICES

Health Centre (☎ 24240 22222) On the ring road, next to the fire station.

MONEY

There are three banks and several ATMs along the waterfront.

POST

Post office It's 100m past Platanos Square, on the right.

TOURIST INFORMATION

Madro Travel (☎ 24240 22300) At the end of the new port, Madro can provide help with booking accommodation and ticketing, and arrange walking trips and cooking lessons.
Rooms & Apartments Association (☎ 24240 24567; ◷ 8.30am-1.30pm) Can help with accommodation, sometimes in family homes.
Thalpos Holidays (☎ 24240 29036; thalpos@otenet.gr) The staff at this privately owned agency on the waterfront are helpful, offering a range of services including booking accommodation and tours around the island.

Sights

Strolling around town and sitting at the waterside cafés might be your chief occupations in Skopelos Town, but there is also a small **Folk Art Museum** (☎ 24240 23494; Hatzistamati; admission €2; ◷ 10am-10pm) with a Skopelean wedding room, complete with traditional costumes and bridal bed.

Sleeping

Hotel prices quoted are for the August high season, but are often reduced by 30% to 50% at other times.

BUDGET

Sotos Pension (☎ 24240 22549; fax 24240 23668; s/d €35/50; ▨) The delightful pine-floor rooms at this well-managed pension in the middle of the waterfront are each a bit different; an old brick oven serves as a handy shelf in one. There's a courtyard and well-equipped communal kitchen.

Hotel Regina (☎ 24240 22138; s/d incl breakfast €25/35; ▨) In a relatively quiet location less than 200m from the waterfront, this good budget choice has a shaded courtyard entrance and offers 11 spotless rooms with verandas. From the waterfront, turn right at Souvlaki Sq; the Regina is 40m along on your left.

Manos Apartments (☎ 24240 23973, 69452 98977; s/d €25/35; ℗ ▨) An excellent family budget option, the quiet Manos is 500m west of the ferry dock between the waterfront and ring road, with kitchenettes and a shaded children's play area.

MIDRANGE & TOP END

Hotel Dionyssos (☎ 24240 23210; www.dionyssos hotel.com; s/d incl breakfast €95/110; ℗ ▨ ▩) This elegant, low-key hotel occupies a quiet street below the ring road, near the post office. Many of the high-ceilinged pine-and-marble rooms offer balcony views of the harbour below. Even in summer, the large lobby is cool and inviting, and a pool bar awaits just outside.

Perivoli Studios (☎ 24240 58022; www.skopelos .net/perivoli; d/tr €60/70; ℗ ▨) These charming studios occupy a traditional building about 100m from the new quay, off the ring road. Each studio is simply but stylishly furnished with a well-equipped kitchen and a terrace overlooking an orchard.

Skopelos Village (☎ 24240 22517; www.skopelos village.gr; d/ste €70/110; ℗ ▨ ▩) On the southern side of the bay, overlooking the entire town, this upscale property features handsome one- and two-bedroom self-catering apartments. The landscaped grounds have a well-kept children's playground and tennis court.

Eating

Most of Skopelos' excellent eateries are in the budget to midrange category, even at the best of the pricier bistros. Just 100m up from the dock, Souvlaki Sq is the place for a quick bite, with good gyros, souvlaki, *tiropita* and *spanakopita*. Skopelos is known for a variety of plum- and prune-based recipes, and most tavernas will have one or two on the menu.

Taverna Ta Kymata O Angelos (☎ 24240 22381; mains €5-8) This modern but traditional-style taverna at the end of the old quay is the oldest on the island. The ready-to-eat *tou fournou* (oven) dishes include hearty staples like lamb *stifado* and stuffed zucchini.

Anna's Finikas Restaurant (☎ 24240 24734; Gifthorema; mains €7-15) Wind your way up the narrow streets of Skopelos Town, past the Folk Art Museum to find Anna's palm tree (in Greek, *finikas*) and swank courtyard bistro. The innovative menu makes use mostly of organic ingredients, including the table wine.

Taverna Peparithos (☎ 24240 23670; mains €4-8) On the ring road near the Health Centre, this low-key courtyard eatery makes a first-rate rabbit *stifado*, while a generous plate of *gavros* and *horta*, along with bread and beer will cost under €10.

Ouzeri Anatoli (☎ 24240 22851; mains €2.50-8; ☽ 7pm-2am, summer only) For *mezedes* and live music, head to this cosy *ouzeri*, high above the Kastro. From 11pm onwards you will hear *rembetika* music sung by Skopelos' own exponent of the Greek blues, Georgos Xindaris. Follow the path up the (steep) steps past Agio Apostolis church at the northern end of the quay.

Also recommended:

O Molos (☎ 24240 22551; mains €4-7) A reliable waterfront taverna with traditional ready-to-eat fare, including several vegie dishes.

Klimataria (☎ 24240 22273; mains €4-7) Practically sharing the tables next to O Molos, with similar offerings.

Nastas Ouzeri (☎ 24240 23441; mezedes €2.50-4, mains €6-10) Snappy ouzeri near the ring road with first-rate *mezedes*.

Le Bistro (☎ 24240 24741; mains €9-15) The town's newest upscale terrace bistro, just 10m north from Souvlaki Sq, strikes a good balance between local and Mediterranean flavours.

Drinking

Platanos Jazz Bar (☎ 24240 23661) You can hear jazz, blues and salsa at this leafy courtyard bar on the old quay. It's open all day and serves breakfast on its shady terrace – an ideal place to recover from a hangover, or to prepare for one.

Oionos Blue Bar (☎ 24240 23731) This cool little bar near the OTE in a traditional Skopelean house offers jazz, blues, soul and world beat music. It serves 17 types of beer, 25 malt whiskies and a wide range of cocktails.

Anemos Espresso Bar (☎ 24240 23564; coffees & snacks €2-4; 8am-1am) Start your day here, or get an afternoon caffeine jolt at this shaded and comfortable waterfront gathering spot.

Merkourios (☎ 24240 24593) Just 30m inland from overlooking the port, 25m from Souvlaki Sq, and next to the small Agios Merkourios church, this mellow bar plays jazz, samba and Greek tunes, all from the comfort of an old Skopelian house terrace overlooking the port.

Entertainment

For more entertainment there is a strip of clubs along Doulidi, toward the post office and the small church of Panagia Eleftherotria. Each attracts its own following; poke your nose in to see if you fit in. **Panselinos** (☎ 24240 24488; Doulidi; ☽ 10pm-3am) is the newest addition to the music block, Panselinos mixes Greek pop sounds with live performances on summer weekends. The popular **Metro Club** (☎ 24240 24478; Doulidi; ☽ 9pm-3am) plays mostly high-volume Greek pop.

GLOSSA ΓΛΩΣΣΑ

Glossa, Skopelos' other major settlement, is considerably quieter than the capital. Another whitewashed delight, it has miraculously managed to retain the feel of a pristine Greek village.

The bus stops in front of a large church at a T-junction. One road winds down 3km to the port of Loutraki and a few *domatia* and tavernas; the other leads nearby to a bank, pharmacy, bakery and a few small stores.

Sleeping & Eating

Pension Platanos (☎ 24240 33602; Glossa; s/d €20/30) This small pension, opposite the church, has clean and simple rooms and a welcoming owner.

Flisvos Taverna (☎ 24240 33856; Loutraki; mains €3-6.50) Perched at the end of the port at little Loutraki, this excellent end-of-the-road taverna offers fresh fish, homemade *mousaka*, and traditional dishes like *tara-masalata*. The owners pride themselves on serving nothing frozen.

Agnanti Taverna & Bar (☎ 24240 33076; Glossa; mains €4-9) It's worth a trip to Glossa just to enjoy the views over to Evia from the roof terrace while sampling a few of Agnanti's imaginative dishes like garlic feta with red peppers or simmered pork with plums.

AROUND SKOPELOS
Monasteries

Skopelos has several monasteries that can be visited on a scenic drive or day-long trek from Skopelos Town. Begin by following the road (Monastery Rd), which skirts the bay and then climbs inland. Continue beyond the signposted Hotel Aegeon until you reach a fork. Take the left fork for the 18th-century **Moni Evangelistrias,** now a convent. The monastery's prize, aside from the superb views, is a gilded iconostasis containing an 11th-century icon of the Virgin Mary.

The right fork leads to the uninhabited 16th-century **Moni Metamorfosis,** the island's oldest monastery. From here the track continues to the 18th-century **Moni Prodromou** (now a convent), 8km from Skopelos Town.

Moni Episkopis rests within the Venetian compound of a private Skopelian family. Ring **Apostolis** (☎ 69741 20450) for details. The small chapel within is a wonder of light and Byzantine icons.

Beaches

Skopelos' beaches are mostly pebbled, and almost all are on the sheltered southwest and west coasts. All buses stop at the beginning of paths that lead down to the beaches. The first beach you come to is the crowded sand-and-pebble **Stafylos Beach** (site of Stafylos' tomb), 4km southeast of Skopelos Town. From the eastern end of the beach a path leads over a small headland to the quieter **Velanio Beach,** the island's official nudist beach and a great snorkelling spot. **Agnontas,** 3km west of Stafylos, has a small pebble-and-sand beach and from here caïques sail to the superior and sandy **Limnonari Beach,** in a sheltered bay flanked by rocky outcrops. Limnonari is also a 1km walk from Agnontas.

From Agnontas the road cuts inland through pine forests before re-emerging at the sheltered **Panormos Beach**. One kilometre further, little **Andrines Beach** is sandy

and uncrowded. The next two beaches, **Milia** and **Kastani,** are considered two of the island's best for swimming.

Tours

If you can't tell a Cleopatra butterfly from a green bush cricket, join one of island resident Heather Parson's **guided walks** (☎ 24240 24022; www.skopelos-walks.com; €15-20). Her three-hour walk above Skopelos Town follows an old path into the hills, and offers views to Alonnisos and Evia. Her book, *Skopelos Trails,* contains graded trail descriptions, illustrated maps, and is available in waterfront stores (€16).

Day-long cruise boats depart from the new quay at 10am, and usually take in the Marine Park of Alonnisos (p423), pausing along the way for lunch and a swim. There's a good chance of spotting dolphins (striped, bottlenose and common). Nearby excursions start at €20, ranging to €45 for a tour of Kyra Panegia islet aboard the *Gorgona*. For bookings, contact **Thalpos Holidays** (☎ 24240 22947) on the waterfront, or **Madro Travel** (☎ 24240 22300), at the end of the waterfront, just past the Commercial Bank.

Sleeping & Eating

There are small hotels, *domatia* and tavernas at Stafylos, Limnonari, Panormos, Andrines and Milia.

Limnonari Rooms and Taverna (☎ 24240 23046; lemonisk@otenet.gr; Limnonari Beach; d/f/ste €40/60/100; P ⊠) This well-managed *domatia* at splendid Limnonari Beach features a dozen rooms and self-catering mini-studios, each airy and bright, along with a well-equipped communal kitchen and terrace.

Limnonari Taverna (☎ 24240 23046; mains €4-7) Locals think nothing of driving to Limnonari to sample traditionally prepared staples like stuffed calamari or several olive oil–based vegie dishes, as well as the owner's homemade olives and feta.

Taverna Pavlos (☎ 2424 022 409; Agnontas; mains €3-10) The most popular of the three waterside tavernas at Agnontas Beach, the Pavlos specialises in fresh fish, priced by the kilo.

Ostria Hotel (☎ 24240 22220; www.skopelos.net /ostria; Stafylos; s/d incl breakfast €55/70; P ⊠ ⊠) Less than 5km from Skopelos Town, next to the bus stop, the rooms at this well-managed midrange option are light and airy, and it's only a five minute walk to Stafylos Beach.

ALONNISOS ΑΛΟΝΝΗΣΟΣ

pop 2700

Alonnisos is an island of profuse greenery with thick stands of pine and oak, along with mastic and arbutus bushes, and fruit trees. The west coast is mostly precipitous cliffs but the east coast is speckled with pebble-and-sand beaches. The water around Alonnisos has been declared a national marine park, and is the cleanest in the Aegean. Every house has a cesspit, so no sewage enters the sea.

Starting in the 1950s, Alonnisos had its share of bad luck. A flourishing cottage wine industry came to a halt in 1952, when the vines were struck with the disease phylloxera. Robbed of their livelihood, many islanders moved away. Then, in 1965, an earthquake destroyed the hilltop capital of Alonnisos Town. The inhabitants were subsequently re-housed in hastily assembled concrete dwellings at Patitiri, a testament to the perseverance of these resourceful islanders.

Getting There & Away

FERRY

From Alonnisos, there are ferries to Skopelos Town (€4.60, 30 minutes, twice daily) and to Skiathos (€8.80, two hours, twice daily), to Volos (€14.80, 4½ hours, twice weekly), to Agios Konstantinos (€31.30,

ALONNISOS

0 —— 4 km
0 —— 2 miles

Cape Gerakas

Pelagonisos Strait

Gerakas Cove

Gerakas Marine Research Station

Cape Gregali

316m

Ydoneri

Merada

Diasello　Blue Cave　Cape Paliofanaro

AEGEAN SEA

Lehousa

Cape Kalami

Alonnisos　Mourtero

Agios Dimitrios Beach

180m

Cape Maistra

Kalamakia

Islet of Manolas

Glyfa Beach

Vasilikos Bay

348m

Steni Vala　Ikaros Camping

Agios Petros Beach

Peristera　260m

Megali Ammos Bay

Alonnisos Strait

Leftos Gialos Beach

Cape Kokkinokastro

Kokkinokastro Beach

Vrysitsa Beach

Old Alonnisos (Hora)　Votsi

Hrisi Milia Beach

Megalos Mourtias Beach

Patitiri

Cape Kokkinos

Vithisma Beach　Patitiri Bay

Excursion Boat

AEGEAN SEA

To Skopelos (12km);
Skiathos (25km);
Agios Konstantinos (79km)

Camping Rocks

Cape Marpounta

four hours by jet ferry, once daily, and to Thessaloniki (€35.30, three hours, once daily).

Tickets can be purchased from **Alonnisos Travel** (☎ 24240 65188) in Patitiri.

HYDROFOIL

In summer, hydrofoils connect Alonnisos to Skopelos Town (€7.70, 20 minutes, three to four daily), to Glossa (€12.20, one hour, three to four daily), to Skiathos (€14.70, 1½ hours, four to five daily), to Volos (€27.80, 2½ hours, three to four daily) and to Agios Konstantinos (€31.30, 2¾ hours, two to three daily). Tickets may be purchased from **Alkyon Travel** (☎ 24240 65220) in Patitiri.

Getting Around

BOAT

Alonnisos Travel rents out four-person 15 to 25 horsepower motorboats. The cost ranges from €48 to €70 per day in summer.

MOTORCYCLE

Several motorcycle-hire outlets can be found on Pelasgon, in Patitiri, including reliable **i'm Bike** (☎ 24240 65010). Be wary when riding down to the beaches since some of the sand-and-shale tracks are steep and slippery.

BUS

In summer, one bus plies the route between Patitiri (from opposite the quay) and Old Alonnisos (€1, hourly 9am to about 3pm). There is also a service to Steni Vala from Old Alonnisos via Patitiri (€1.10, twice daily).

TAXI

The four taxis on the island (Georgos, Periklis, Theodoros, Spyros) tend to congregate opposite the quay. It's €5 to Old Alonnisos, €8 to Megalos Mourtias and €12 to Steni Vala.

WATER TAXI

The easiest way during summer to get to and from the east coast beaches is by taking the **taxi boat** (☎ 24240 65461) that leaves from the quay at 11am and returns by about 5.30pm. The main stops are Kokkinokastro (€7), Steni Vala (€9) and Agios Dimitrios (€10).

PATITIRI ΠΑΤΗΤΗΡΙ

Patitiri sits between two sandstone cliffs at the southern end of the east coast. Not surprisingly, considering its hasty origins, it's not the most picturesque port town. Even so it makes a convenient base and has quite a relaxed atmosphere. Patitiri means 'wine press' and is where, in fact, grapes were processed prior to the demise of the wine industry in the 1950s.

Orientation

Finding your way around Patitiri is easy. The quay is in the centre of the waterfront and two roads lead inland. With your back to the sea, turn left for Pelasgon, or right for Ikion Dolopon. In truth, there are no road signs and most locals simply refer to them as the left-hand road (Pelasgon) and right-hand road (Ikion Dolopon).

Information

EMERGENCY

Police (☎ 24240 65205) At the northern end of Ikion Dolopon; there is no tourist police office.
Port police (☎ 24240 65595) On the quayside at Patitiri.

INTERNET ACCESS

Techno Plus (☎ 24240 29100; per hr €3; ☼ 9am-2pm & 5-9pm) Located 300m up the right-hand road, opposite the school.

LAUNDRY

Lena's Gardenia (☎ 24240 65831; Pelasgon; per load €8)

MONEY

National Bank of Greece At the southern end of Ikion Dolopon, it has an ATM.

POST & TELEPHONE

Post office (Ikion Dolopon) There is no OTE but there are cardphones in Patitiri, Old Alonnisos and Steni Vala.

TOURIST INFORMATION

Rooms to Let Service (☎ 24240 66188; fax 24240 65577; ☼ 9.30am-2pm & 6.30-10pm) In summer, opposite the quay, will help you find a room on Alonnisos.

Sights

Nothing is left to chance in detailing the heritage and customs of Alonnisos. The private collection at the **Historical & Folklore Museum of the Northern Sporades** (☎ 24240 66250; admission €3; ☼ 11am-7pm) is largely a labour of love by the Mavrikis family, and includes a pirates' exhibit, a horseshoe shop and antique nautical maps. A small café sits atop the museum with views of the harbour. Take the stone stairway at the far west end of the harbour to reach the museum.

Activities
WALKING
Walking opportunities abound on Alonnisos, and the best ones are waymarked. At the bus stop in Old Alonnisos a blue noticeboard details several walks. From Patitiri, a 2km donkey path begins at the blue walk signpost 400m up the left-hand road (Pelasgon), and winds up through shrubbery and orchards before bringing you to Old Alonnisos.

The informative *Alonnisos on Foot: A Walking & Swimming Guide* by Bente Keller & Elias Tsoukanas (€9) is available at waterfront shops.

CYCLING
The best mountain-bike riding is over on the southwest coast around the bay of Megali Ammos. There are several bicycle- and motorcycle-hire outlets on Ikion Dolopon. Be wary when riding to the beaches since some of the sand-and-shale tracks are steep and slippery.

Tours
For island excursions inquire at **Ikos Travel** (☎ 24240 65320; www.ikostravel.com). Ikos offers popular round-the-island excursions aboard the *Gorgona* that visit the **Blue Cave** on the northeast coast, and the islets of Kyra Panagia and Peristera. **Albedo Travel** (☎ 24240 65804; www.albedotravel.com) runs regular snorkelling and swimming excursions to **Skantzoura** and other islets, aboard the newest sailing vessel in the harbour, the *Odyssey*.

Consider a **walking tour** (☎ 69740 80039; www.alonnisoswalks.co.uk; €15-30) led by island resident Chris Browne. A half-day walk above Patitiri winds through pine forest trails, past churches and olive groves overlooking the sea.

Sleeping
Prices here are for the higher July to August season; expect discounts to 25% at other times.

BUDGET
Pension Pleiades (☎ 24240 65235; pleiades@Internet .gr; s/d €35/50; 🞩) This bright and cheerful budget option offers views of Patitiri Bay, along with nine immaculate, balconied rooms, plus two family-sized studios with kitchenette. Take the stairway behind Albedo Travel and the newsstand to reach the Pleiades.

Ilias Rent Rooms (☎ 24240 65451; fax 24240 65972; Pelasgon 27; d/2-/3-bed studios €30/45/50) These 12 simple and spotless rooms and studios share a communal kitchen (with kettle and sink).

MIDRANGE
Liadromia Hotel (☎ 24240 65521; fax 24240 65096; d/tr/ste incl breakfast €50/70/85; P   🞩) This welcoming and impeccably maintained hotel overlooking the harbour was Patitiri's first. All the rooms have a bit of character, from hand-embroidered curtains and old lamps to stone floors and traditional wood furnishings. Take the stairway directly opposite the National Bank of Greece.

Paradise Hotel (☎ 24240 65213; www.paradise -hotel.gr; s/d €62/77; P   🞩) Wood ceilings and stone-tiled floors give a rustic feel to the rooms here, most of which overlook the sea on one side or Patitiri harbour on the other. Room prices include a buffet breakfast served next to the pool. Follow the stairway opposite the National Bank to reach the Paradise.

Nina Studios (☎ 24240 65242; d/f €60/90; 🞩) Take the stairs opposite the bank to these handsome self-catering studios with stone floors and large bathrooms, along with vine-covered balcony views of the harbour below.

Follow the signposts in town for **Camping Rocks** (☎ 24240 65410; adult/tent €4/2), a rough but shaded coastal spot 2km off Pelasgon.

Eating
To Kamaki Ouzeri (☎ 24240 65245; Ikion Dolopon; mains €4-10) Start off with *mezedes* and ouzo at this traditional island eatery next to the bank, then move on to the stuffed *kalamaria* and peppers or blow the budget on fresh grilled lobster.

Café Flisvos (☎ 24240 65307; mains €5-8) Among the waterfront restaurants, this is the pick of the bunch. In the summer, sit under the canopy opposite the dock. It's not

---

THE AUTHOR'S CHOICE

Hayati (☎ 24240 66244; Old Alonnisos; snacks €2-4, mains €4-7; ☼ 9am-2am) Hayati is a Turkish word connoting comfort and relaxation, and that's what you'll find at this hill-top *glikopoliou* (sweets shop) and part-time taverna, where excellent food and song go hand in hand. This is one of those Greek gathering places that is suffused with the personality of its owners, in this case the gracious Meni and Angela, who cook, greet guests, circulate at tables and join in the music as the darkness gathers.

Hayati is both a snack shop at the upper entrance, and a taverna and piano bar below, offering sweeping views of the coastline from either level. Morning fare includes traditional *tiropita* and *spanakopita*, local yogurt and honey. Later, you'll find homemade pastas and rich sauces and souvlaki. Popular desserts include baklava, gelato, and *loukoumades* (a Greek doughnut dusted with cinnamon and drizzled with honey). Best of all, the terrace taverna sports a piano and most summer nights the music gets going by about 10pm, as the locals from nearby Patitiri arrive to seek the comforts of wine, food and song.

This versatile and inviting spot waits at the far end of Old Alonnisos and is accessible only on foot, a five-minute walk from the village square.

---

the quietest place, but the food and the homemade sweets are first rate.

Anais Restaurant & Pizzeria (☎ 24240 65243; mains €4-12; ☼ breakfast, lunch & dinner) Patitiri's first restaurant, located just opposite the hydrofoil dock, is still going strong. You'll find tasty versions of Greek basics like oven-baked chicken, along with swordfish souvlaki.

Drinking

En Plo (☎ 24240 66054) This is a local waterfront favourite, with a handsome bar and a good range of jazz, reggae and Greek pop on hand.

Harmony Bar (☎ 24240 66273) This lively favourite next to the Health Centre plays mostly rock and trance music, and serves an assortment of wines, beer and coffee.

Shopping

Ikos Traditional Products (☎ 24240 66270; Ikion Dolopon; ☼ 9am-2.30pm & 6-9.30pm) Walk 200m up the right-hand road from the dock to find this delightful cooperative run by the Women's Association of Alonnisos, selling handmade soaps and fresh herbs, along with local honey and tempting *glyka* (sweets).

OLD ALONNISOS ΠΑΛΙΑ ΑΛΟΝΝΙΣΟΣ

Old Alonnisos (also known as Hora or Palio Horio or Old Town) with its winding stepped alleys is a tranquil, picturesque place with lovely views. From the main road just outside the village an old donkey path leads down to pebbled Megalos Mourtias

Beach and other paths lead south to Vithisma and Marpounta Beaches.

Sleeping

Old Alonnisos has no hotels, but there are several well-managed *domatia*.

BUDGET

Pension Hiliadromia (☎ /fax 24240 65814; Plateia Hristou; d/2-bed studio €35/55; ☒) Several of the pine-and-stone-floor rooms at the Hiliadromia come with balcony views, and the studios have well-equipped kitchens.

Fantasia House (☎ 24240 65186; Plateia Hristou; s/d €30/40) Tucked away between the church and square, these simple rooms with exposed-beam ceilings are good value, and there is a snack bar in the courtyard.

MIDRANGE

Konstantina Studios (☎ 24240 66165; divlaiko@otenet .gr; s/d €50/60; ☒) Among the nicest accommodations on Alonnisos, these lovely and quiet self-catering studios with traditional styling come with balcony views of the southwest coast. Take the stairway about 20m down from Plateia Hristou.

Eating

Astrofengia (☎ 24240 65182; mains €5-12) This sophisticated place, signposted from the bus stop, offers exquisite *mezedes* like tzatziki (cucumber and garlic yogurt) and *saganaki* (fried cheese). Mains include cannelloni and grilled lamb. For dessert, try the homemade *galaktoboureko* (custard slice).

Megalos Mourtias Taverna (☎ 24240 65737; mains €3-7.50; ☺ breakfast, lunch & dinner) This welcoming beachside taverna 2km below Old Alonnisos serves fresh grilled fish and several tasty vegie dishes. Dutch co-owner Ria also gives Greek lessons to small groups on the side.

AROUND ALONNISOS

Alonnisos' main road reaches the northern tip of the island at Gerakas (19km), home to a marine research station. Six kilometres north of Patitiri, another sealed road branches off to the small fishing port and yacht harbour of Steni Vala, and follows the shore past Kalamakia for 5km. A third road takes you from Patitiri to Megalos Mourtias.

The first beach of note once you leave Patitiri is tiny **Rousoum** just before **Votsi,** and is very popular with local families. Next is the gently shelving **Hrisi Milia Beach**, another great beach for children. Next up is **Kokkinokastro,** a beach of red pebbles. This is the site of the ancient city of Ikos (once the capital); there are remains of city walls and a necropolis under the sea.

Steni Vala is a small fishing village with a permanent population of no more than 40 and has two good beaches, **Glyfa** just above

the village and **Agios Petros** just below. There are three tavernas opposite the small marina, of which **Ikion Taverna** (☎ 24240 65248) is the longest running. There are 30-odd rooms in *domatia*, as well as modest **Ikaros Camping** (☎ 24240 65772), next to the beach and decently shaded by olive trees. Try **Ikaros Café & Market** (☎ 24240 65390) for lodging information.

Kalamakia, 2km further north, is near a good beach and has a few *domatia* and tavernas. When the boats arrive at Steni Vala with the morning catch, they tie up directly in front of **Margarita's Taverna** (☎ 24240 65738), where the fresh fish seem to jump from boat to plate.

Beyond Kalamakia, the sealed road continues 3km to a wetland marsh and **Agios Dimitrios Beach,** a graceful stretch of white sand beyond which the road dwindles to a footpath heading inland.

ISLETS AROUND ALONNISOS

Alonnisos is surrounded by eight uninhabited islets, all of which are rich in flora and fauna. The largest remaining population of the monk seal, a Mediterranean sea mammal faced with extinction, lives in the waters around the Sporades. These factors were the incentive behind the formation of

EVIA & THE SPORADES

ALONNISOS MARINE PARK

The National Marine Park of Alonnisos – Northern Sporades is an ambitious project begun in 1992. Its prime aim was the protection of the endangered Mediterranean monk seal *(Monarchus monarchus),* and also the preservation of other rare plant and animal species.

The park is divided into two zones, A and B. Zone A, east of Alonnisos, is less accessible and comprises the islets of Kyra Panagia, Gioura, Psathoura, Skantzoura and Piperi. Restrictions on human activities apply on all islands in Zone A. In the case of Piperi, visitors are banned altogether, since the island is home to around 33 species of bird, including 350 to 400 pairs of Eleanora's falcon. Other threatened sea birds found on Piperi include the Mediterranean shag and Audouin's gull. Visitors may approach other islands with private vessels or on day trips organised from Alonnisos.

Zone B comprises Alonnisos itself and the nearer islands of Peristera, Lehousa, and Dio Adelphi (Two Brothers) off the southeast coast. Most nautical visitors to Alonnisos base themselves at the small yacht port of Steni Vala.

For the casual visitor, the Alonnisos Marine Park is somewhat inaccessible since tours to the various islands are limited and run during summer only. Bear in mind also that the park exists for the protection of marine animals and not for the entertainment of human visitors, so do not be surprised if you see very few animals at all. However, your chances of spotting any of the three dolphins (striped, bottlenose and common) in the area are especially good; and in June you stand a chance of catching sight of young dolphins swimming with their parents. In a country not noted in its recent history for long-sightedness in the protection of its fauna, the Alonnisos Marine Park is a welcome innovation.

the national marine park in 1992, which encompasses the sea and islets around Alonnisos (see p423). Its research station is on Alonnisos, near Gerakas Cove.

Piperi, the furthest island northeast of Alonnisos, is a refuge for the monk seal and is strictly off-limits. **Gioura** has many rare plants and a rare species of wild goat known for the crucifix-shaped marking on its spine. **Kyra Panagia** has good beaches and two abandoned monasteries. **Psathoura** boasts the submerged remains of an ancient city and the brightest lighthouse in the Aegean.

Peristera, just off Alonnisos' east coast, has several sandy beaches and the remains of a castle. Nearby **Lehousa** is known for its stalactite-filled sea caves. **Skantzoura,** to the southeast of Alonnisos, is the habitat of the Eleanora's falcon and the rare Audouin's seagull. The eighth island in the group, situated between Peristera and Skantzoura, is known as **Dio Adelphi** (Two Brothers); each 'brother' is actually a small island, both home to vipers, according to local fishermen who refuse to step foot on either.

SKYROS ΣΚΥΡΟΣ

pop 2602

Skyros is the largest of the Sporades islands, with rolling farmland and pine forests in the north, and barren hills and a rocky shoreline in the south. Solo women travellers are drawn to Skyros because of its reputation as a safe, hassle-free island, and a number of expats, particularly English and Dutch, have made Skyros their home.

In Byzantine times, rogues and criminals exiled here from the mainland entered into a mutually lucrative collaboration with invading pirates. The exiles became the elite of Skyrian society, decorating their houses with items brought by seafarers or looted by pirates from merchant ships: hand-carved furniture, plates and copper ornaments from Europe, the Middle East and East Asia. Today, almost every Skyrian house is decorated with similar items.

In Greek mythology, Skyros was the hiding place of young Achilles. See p426 for more information about the Skyros Lenten Carnival and its traditions, which allude to Achilles' heroic feats.

Skyros was also the last port of call for the English poet Rupert Brooke (1887–1915), who died of septicaemia at the age of 28 on a hospital ship off the coast of Skyros en route to Gallipoli.

Getting There & Away
AIR

In summer there are only two flights weekly (Wednesday and Saturday) between Athens and Skyros (€35, 35 minutes). Between Thessaloniki and Skyros, there are three flights weekly on Monday, Wednesday and Friday (€57, 40 minutes). For tickets go to the **Skyros Travel Agency** (☎ 22220 92123; www.skyrostravel.com; Agoras).

FERRY

A regular ferry service is provided by F/B *Achileas,* between the port of Kymi (Evia) and Skyros (€8.30, 1¾ hours). On weekdays, the ferry makes one crossing; on Saturday and Sunday, two crossings. You can buy tickets from **Lykomidis ticket office** (☎ 22220 91789; fax 22220 91791; Agoras), near the bank on Agoras in Skyros Town. There is also a ferry ticket kiosk at the dock in Linaria, and another at the dock in Kymi.

Skyros Travel Agency also sells tickets for the Kymi–Athens bus (€11.40, 3½ hours), which meets the ferry on arrival at Paralia Kymis (the port of Kymi). Services are twice daily June to September and once daily the rest of the year.

Getting Around
CAR & MOTORCYCLE

Cars and 4WD vehicles can be rented from **Theseus Rentals** (☎ 22220 91459) or **Pegasus Rentals** (☎ 22220 92123), both near the bus stop. A small car will cost about €35 to €40 per day, and a 4WD about €50 to €60. Scooters can be rented from nearby **Vayos Motorbikes** (☎ 22220 92957) for around €15 per day.

BUS & TAXI

In high season there are daily buses departing from Skyros Town to Linaria (€1) and to Molos (via Magazia). Buses for both Skyros Town and Molos meet the ferry at Linaria. However, outside of high season there are only one or two buses to Linaria (to coincide with the ferry arrivals) and none to Molos. A taxi from Skyros Town to Linaria is €10.

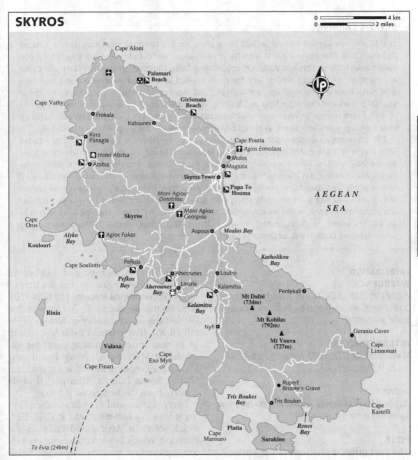

SKYROS

0 ——————— 4 km
0 ——————— 2 miles

Cape Aloni

Palamari Beach

Girismata Beach

Cape Vathy

Frokala

Katounes

Kyra Panagia

Cape Pouria

Agios Ermolaos

Hotel Atsitsa

Molos

Atsitsa

Magazia

Skyros Town

Papa To Houma

Moni Agiou Dimitriou

AEGEAN SEA

Moni Agiou Georgiou

Cape Oros

Skyros

Aspous

Mealos Bay

Alyko Bay

Agios Fokas

Katholikou Bay

Koulouri

Pefkos

Cape Souliotis

Aherounes

Loutro

Pentekali

Pefkos Bay

Linaria

Kalamitsa

Aherounes Bay

Mt Dafni (734m)

Rinia

Kalamitsa Bay

Nyfi

Mt Kohilas (792m)

Valaxa

Gerania Caves

Cape Exo Myti

Mt Vouva (727m)

Cape Limnonari

Cape Finari

Rupert Brooke's Grave

Tris Boukes Bay

Tris Boukes

Cape Kastelli

To Evia (24km)

Platia

Renes Bay

Cape Marmaro

Sarakino

EVIA & THE SPORADES

SKYROS TOWN

Skyros' capital is a striking, dazzlingly white town of flat-roofed Cycladic-style houses draped over a high rocky bluff and topped by a 13th-century fortress and the monastery of Agios Georgios. It is a gem of a place and a wander around its labyrinthine, whitewashed streets will often produce an invitation to admire a traditional Skyrian house by its proud owner.

Orientation

The bus stop is at the southern end of town on the main thoroughfare (Agoras) – an animated street lined with tavernas, snack bars and grocery shops and flanked by narrow winding alleyways. To reach the central square, known simply as the **Plateia,** walk straight ahead up the hill; the narrow road soon becomes even narrower, marking the beginning of the town's pedestrian zone. Motorbikes still squeeze through, but cars must park in the nearby car park.

About 100m beyond the Plateia, the main drag of Agoras forks. The right fork leads up to the **fortress** and **Moni Agiou Georgiou,** with its fine frescoes and sweeping views. The left fork zigzags to **Plateia Rupert Brooke,** where a simple bronze statue of a nude Rupert Brooke faces the sea. The frankness of the statue caused an outcry among the islanders when it was first installed in the 1930s. From this square the cobbled steps descend to Magazia Beach, 1km away.

SKYROS CARNIVAL

In this wild pre-Lenten festival, which takes place on the last four weekends before Kathara Deftera (Clean Monday – the first Monday in Lent, seven weeks before Easter), young men don goat masks, hairy jackets and dozens of copper goat bells. They then proceed to clank and dance around town, each with a partner (another man), dressed up as a Skyrian bride but also wearing a goat mask. During these revelries there is singing and dancing, performances of plays, recitations of satirical poems and much drinking and feasting. Women and children join in, wearing fancy dress as well. These strange goings-on are overtly pagan, with elements of Dionysian festivals, including goat worship. In ancient times, as today, Skyros was renowned for its goat's meat and milk.

The transvestism evident in the carnival seems to derive from the cult of Achilles associated with Skyros in Greek mythology. According to legend, the island was the childhood hiding place for the boy Achilles, whose mother, Thetis, feared a prophecy requiring her son's skills in the Trojan War. The boy was given to the care of King Lykomides of Skyros, who raised him disguised as one of his own daughters. Young Achilles was outwitted, however, by Odysseus who arrived with jewels and finery for the girls, along with a sword and shield. When the maiden Achilles alone showed interest in the weapons, Odysseus discovered his secret, then persuaded him to go to Troy where he distinguished himself in battle. This annual festival is the subject of Joy Koulentianou's book *The Goat Dance of Skyros*.

Information

EMERGENCY

Police (☎ 22220 91274) Take the first right after Skyros Travel Agency, and turn right at the T-junction; there is no tourist police office.

INTERNET ACCESS

Mano.com (☎ 22220 92473; Agoras; ☉ 9am-1.30pm & 6.30-11.30pm; per hr €3)

MONEY

National Bank of Greece (Agoras) With an ATM, it's on Agoras next to the central square.

POST

The post office is just west of the square.

TOURIST INFORMATION

Skyros Travel Agency (☎ 22220 91600; www.skyros travel.com; Agoras; ☉ 9am-2pm & 6.30-10pm, 9am-10pm in summer) They have island maps and can help with room bookings and travel reservations.

Sights & Activities

Skyros Town has two museums. The **Manos Faltaïts Museum** (☎ 22220 91232; Plateia Rupert Brooke; admission €2; ☉ 10am-2pm & 6-9pm) is a one-of-a-kind private museum housing the outstanding collection of a Skyrian ethnologist, Manos Faltaïts. The collection includes Skyrian costumes and furniture, antique ceramics, vintage books, photographs and more. You can join a morning tour with Niko Sikkes (€5 including museum admission)

detailing the mythology and folklore of Skyros; enquire at museum desk for times.

The **Archaeological Museum** (☎ 22220 91327; Plateia Rupert Brooke; admission €2; ☉ 8.30am-3pm Tue-Sun) features an impressive collection of locally discovered artefacts from Mycenaean to Roman times, including excellent examples of Mycenaean pottery found near Magazia. Interesting as well is a traditional Skyrian house interior, transported in its entirety from the benefactor's home.

Every year around early September, Skyros is host to a **half-marathon** (☎ 22220 92789), which starts in Atsitsa and ends on the Plateia in Skyros Town with drummers welcoming the first runners across the finish line. A mini-marathon for the children sets the tone, and the whole event is followed by music and dancing on the square.

Courses

At the **Reiki Centre** (☎ 22220 93510; Skyros Town; www.simplelifeskyros.com), longtime island resident and reiki Master Janet Smith offers small seven-day residential classes in reiki technique to visitors and locals alike. On the south edge of Skyros Town, 250m past Hotel Nefeli.

Skyros Centre (☎ 22220 93194; Atsitsa; www.skyros .com) is a holistic-based new-age centre which runs courses on a range of subjects, from Hatha yoga to windsurfing. Contact the centre, just north of Atsitsa, for detailed information on its fortnightly programmes.

Tours

Impromptu **walking tours** (☎ 22220 92158) are arranged by the versatile Nikos Sikkes (€10 to €15) around Skyros Town. A visit to his fine shop (Argos, p428), or the Faltaïts Museum, will get you a map and free advice as well.

A day-long boat excursion (€35) excursion to the Gerania sea caves on the southeast coast and nearby Sarakiniko Islet includes lunch and a swim. Contact **Skyros Travel** (☎ 22220 91600) for details.

Sleeping

Accommodation in Skyros Town varies from conventional small hotels and *domatia* to individual rooms in traditional Skyrian houses. If you arrive by bus, you'll usually be met with offers on nearby *domatia*; prices should range from €25 to €40 for a single/double. Failing that, head for Skyros Travel Agency (opposite). Prices quoted here are for the summer season.

BUDGET

Pension Nikolas (☎ 22220 91778; fax 22220 93400; r €40/60) This pension has attractive rooms on the quiet edge of Skyros Town. From the bus stop, walk south about 50m until the road splits. Take the road to the right, and continue another 150m.

Hotel Elena (☎ 22220 91738; s/d/tr €20/35/45; 🅷) The clean and simple Elena is a decent budget choice with 10 large rooms, each with a balcony and minibar. It's less than 100m north of the bus stop.

Atherinis Rooms (☎ 22220 93510; 69732 37797; d per person €30) Managed by reiki Master Janet Smith, Atherinis Rooms offers self-catering double rooms in a quiet bungalow with hand-tiled bath and wood balconies. Weekly rates of €280 include half board, featuring food from the organic garden and homemade wine.

MIDRANGE

Hotel Nefeli & Dimitrios Studios (☎ 22220 91964; www.skyros-nefeli.gr; s/d/studios €70/86/122; 🅿 🅷 🅽) This well-managed handsome hotel on the edge of town has modern well-appointed rooms with vintage photographs depicting traditional Skyrian life. The adjacent three- and four-bed studios are part of a large remodelled Skyrian house with traditional furnishings. Both properties share a saltwater swimming pool and bar.

Eating

Skyros welcomes a steady number of visiting Athenians, with the pleasant result that island cooks do not cater to touristy tongues. You can find a number of authentic Skyrian dishes in the smallest taverna, including several with goat's milk or meat.

O Pappous kai Ego (☎ 22220 93200; Agoras; mains €4-7.50) The name of this small taverna means 'my grandfather and me'. *Mezedes* are excellent, especially the Skyrian dolmades made with a touch of strained goat's milk. Tasty mains include nanny goat in lemon sauce and Skyrian squid with aniseed.

Maryetis Restaurant (☎ 22220 91311; Agoras; mains €4-8) Maryetis offers a menu featuring several local tastes, like octopus *stifado*, fava bean dip, as well as excellent grills and combination salads.

Liakos Café (☎ 22220 93509; mains €5-9) During the day, enjoy Liakos' serene interior where botanical prints grace the walls. In the evening, head to the roof terrace, where the fusion menu includes cold octopus salad and fava beans with sun-dried tomatoes.

Anemos Snack (☎ 22220 92155; snacks €2-4) Start the day with made-to-order eggs or just coffee and a roll at this snappy and reasonable eatery on Agoras.

Drinking

Nightlife in Skyros Town centres mostly around the bars on Agoras, all of which are tastefully decorated.

Nostos Cafe & Snack Bar (☎ 22220 91797; Agoras) On Agoras above the National Bank, this swank bar overlooking the plateia serves a range of mixed drinks, coffees and appetizers.

Artistiko Bar (☎ 22220 91864; Agoras) The music is all Greek all night under the beamed ceilings at little Artistiko, a hole-in-the-wall that buzzes till dawn.

Kalypso (☎ 22220 92696) The further north you go along Agoras the more mellow the sounds. Classy little Kalypso plays mostly jazz and blues.

Entertainment

Skyropoula Disco (☎ 22220 91180) On the ring road, Skyropoula draws a slightly older crowd, but still manages to belt out a danceable mix of pop European and Greek sounds.

MAGAZIA & MOLOS ΜΑΓΑΖΙΑ & ΜΩΛΟΣ

The resort of Magazia, a compact and attractive place of winding alleys, is at the southern end of a splendid, long sandy beach, situated a short distance north of Skyros Town; quieter and more arid Molos is at the northern end of the beach, with little more than a windmill and the adjacent rock-hewn Church of Agios Ermolaos to mark it.

Sleeping

Georgia Tsakami Rooms (☎ 22220 91357; Magazia; s/d/t €20/30/35; 🕲) You can't get much closer to the sand and sea than at these geranium-adorned and wood-panelled *domatia* 20m from the beach. Follow the Magazia Beach road about 150m in until you find a handy car park opposite. You can also ring the Athens office (☎ 210 282 0397) for reservations.

Didamia Hotel (☎ 22220 91270; s/d incl breakfast €35/45) An attractive budget option, just 30m in along the Magazia Beach road, on your left and well signed.

Angela Hotel (☎ 22220 91764; fax 22220 92030; Molos; s/d €60/75; ℗ 🕲 🕭) This oasis in arid Molos is only 100m from the beach; the welcoming Angela offers modern spacious rooms and a breakfast courtyard.

Eating & Drinking

Taverna Stefanos (☎ 22220 91272; mains €4-7.50) This traditional eatery, overlooking the southern end of Magazia Beach, offers a range of ready-to-eat oven dishes, along with good souvlaki and fresh fish.

Juicy Beach Bar (☎ 22220 933337; snacks €2-5; Magazia; 🕙 10am-1am) Escape the mid-day sun or chill out under the stars at this busy Magazia beach bar.

Shopping

Argos (☎ 22220 92158; Agoras) Argos specialises in high-quality copies of ceramics from the Faltaïts Museum, where owner Nikko Sekkes leads tours.

Andreou Woodcarving (☎ 22220 92926; Agoras) Get a close look at the intricate designs that distinguish traditional Skyrian furniture at this handsome shop on the main drag.

Several pottery workshops spin their wheels in Magazia without bothering to put a sign out front, but they are happy to see visitors, and some of their exceptional work is for sale. Most are on the small lane

between the Diadamia Hotel and Taverna Stephanos (left), including the workshops of **Efrossini Varsamou** (☎ 22220 91142), English-speaking **Amanda** (☎ 22220 92918), **Statius** (☎ 22220 92918) and **Nikolaou** (☎ 22220 91142).

AROUND SKYROS

Linaria Λιναριά

Linaria, the port of Skyros, is tucked into a small bay filled with bobbing fishing boats and lined with tavernas and *ouzeria*. Things perk up briefly whenever the Achileos ferry comes in, announcing its arrival with the impressive sound of Richard Strauss' *Also Sprach Zarathustra* blasting from the ship's huge speakers. The bus to Skyros Town coincides with the ferry's arrival and departure.

SLEEPING & EATING

King Lykomides Rooms (☎ 22220 93472; fax 22220 93412; s/d incl breakfast €35/40; ℗ 🕲) Just 50m to the right as you depart the ferry, you'll find these bright and spotless *domatia*, each with mini-fridge and balcony, managed by the hospitable Nikos Pappas.

Linaria Bay Hotel (☎ 22220 93274; fax 22220 93275; s/d €35/50) This attractive and quiet 11-room perch above the port at Linaria is just a few minutes' walk to the dock, and a good alternative to staying in Skyros Town.

Taverna Filipeous (☎ 22220 93276; mains €4-9) This busy fish taverna, located near the ferry dock, serves up lobster along with traditional ready-to-eat oven dishes like *briami* (mixed vegies) and pastitsio (baked macaroni and lamb).

Kavos Bar (☎ 22220 93213) This laid-back Linaria bar, perched on the hill overlooking the port, pulls in Skyrians from across the island for drinks and evening gossip.

Atsitsa Ατσίτσα

The quiet port village of Atsitsa on the island's west coast occupies a woodsy setting, shaded by pines surrounding a small, pebble beach.

For veranda seaviews, the seasonal **Hotel Atsitsa** (☎ /fax 22220 91917; s/d/tr incl breakfast €30/40/50; 🕙 Jun-Oct; ℗ 🕲) has clean and serviceable rooms. **Taverna Antonis** (☎ 22220 92990; mains €4-8) is about 20m from the small pier where the family's fishing boat ties up. Menu choices range from *gavros* to grilled fish by the kilo.

Beaches

At woodsy **Atsitsa,** on the west coast, there's a tranquil pebble beach shaded by pines, also good for freelance camping. Just to the north is the decent swimming beach of **Kyra Panagia,** named for the monastery on the hill above.

At **Pefkos Bay,** 10km southeast of Atsitsa, there is a beautiful horseshoe-shaped beach with a taverna and *domatia* at the south end. Nearby, the beach at **Aherounes** has a gentle sandy bottom, very nice for children. There are two tavernas opposite the road, next to a small hotel.

To the north and near the airport, **Pala-mari** is a graceful stretch of sandy beach that does not get crowded. Palamari is also the site of a well-marked **archaeological excavation** of a walled town dating from 2500 BC. Skinny-dippers can leave it all behind at the nudist beach of **Papa To Houma** at the southern end of Magazia.

Rupert Brooke's Grave

Rupert Brooke's well-tended grave is in a quiet olive grove just inland from Tris Boukes Bay in the south of the island. The actual grave is marked with a rough wooden sign in Greek on the roadside, but you can hardly miss it. The gravestone is inscribed with some of Brooke's verses, among which is the following apt epitaph:

> If I should die think only this of me:
> That there's some corner of a foreign field
> That is forever England.

From coastal Kalamitsa, a scenic road (built for the navy) passes the village of **Nyfi,** and brings you to Brookes' simple tomb. No buses come here, and travel is carefully restricted beyond this southernmost corner of the island dominated by the Greek Naval station on Tris Boukes Bay.

Ionian Islands
Τα Ιόνια Νησιά

It's not surprising that the Greeks invented the word *filoxenia* (hospitality). The word sums up the Ionian Islands, an archipelago that sweeps down the west coast of the mainland, and includes Corfu, Paxi, Lefkada, Ithaki, Kefallonia, Kythira and Zakynthos. The islands' natural beauty embraces a visitor; the vast olive groves, intriguing mountains, and iridescent waters of the Ionian Sea, offer something for adventure seekers, culture vultures and beach bums alike.

Each island boasts a distinct tradition, cuisine and architecture – the remaining influences of the former invading forces including the Venetians, French and British. These influences are obvious in Corfu Town where you can watch a cricket match on the Spianada, eat *stifado* (braised meat with onions) at a café under the Parisienne-style Liston arcade, and wander through the town's Venetian-style alleyways. Elsewhere in the Ionians – in the traditional fishing or mountain villages – stroll through central plazas shaded by bougainvillea and plane trees, or relax under a vine-covered canopy at a taverna with the soporific scent of jasmine.

Less appealing to the senses are the ultra-invasive package-tourist beach developments. But these can be avoided. Instead, explore in a boat to find your own isolated swimming coves. Cultural adventurers can wander through fortresses, Byzantine churches and Homeric sites. Adventure addicts can enjoy activities on tap including walking, cycling, bird watching, windsurfing, golf and scuba diving. And to top it all off: indulge in fresh, generous helpings of local dishes, served with a huge dollop of Ionian hospitality.

HIGHLIGHTS

- **Architecture**
  Wandering the narrow streets of Corfu's old town (p436) and admiring the fine Venetian buildings and nearby Mon Repos Villa (p438)

- **Getting Away From It All**
  Walking on the old donkey trails and through the ancient olive groves of Paxi (p445)

- **Scenic Splendours**
  Travelling along the lofty spine of Homeric Ithaki (p459)

- **Beauty Spot**
  Exploring the pretty village of Assos (p458) and then swimming in the iridescent blue waters of Myrtos Beach (p459) in Kefallonia

- **Live Music**
  Being entertained by the spirited performers at Arekia and Kostas' Brother restaurants in Zakynthos Town (p464)

Map labels: Corfu Town, Paxi, Assos, Ithaki, Myrtos Beach, Zakynthos Town

---

- POPULATION: 221,890
- AREA: 2432 SQ KM

GETTING THERE & AWAY
Air
Corfu, Kefallonia, Kythira and Zakynthos have airports; Lefkada has no airport, but Aktion airport, near Preveza on the mainland, is about 20km away. These airports have frequent flights to/from Athens. **Olympic Airlines** (www.olympicairlines.com) has introduced a useful service linking the Ionians: three times a week there are return flights from Corfu to Zakynthos, stopping en route at Aktion and Kefallonia.

From May to September, charter flights come from northern Europe and the UK to Corfu, Kefallonia, Zakynthos and Preveza. A new Air Sea Lines service flies between Corfu Town and Paxi, Corfu Town and Ioannina, and Paxi–Corfu–Ioannina (see p433).

Bus
KTEL (www.ktel.org) long-distance buses connect each major island with Athens and Thessaloniki, and usually also with Patra in the Peloponnese. Buses to Corfu, Lefkada, Kefallonia and Zakynthos depart from Athens' Terminal A bus station.

Ferry
DOMESTIC
The Peloponnese has two departure ports for the Ionian Islands: Patra for ferries to Corfu, Kefallonia and Ithaki; and Kyllini

---

WWW.PLANNING YOUR TRIP.COM

There's loads of websites devoted to the Ionians – here are some of the best we've found:

- **Ionian Islands** www.greeka.com/ionian
- **Corfu** www.kerkyra.gr, www.kerkyra .net, www.corfuhomepage.com
- **Paxi** www.paxos-greece.com, www .paxos.tk
- **Lefkada** www.lefkas.net, www.lefkada -greece.biz
- **Kefallonia** www.kefaloniathewaytogo .com, www.kefalonia.net.gr
- **Ithaki** www.ithacagreece.com
- **Zakynthos** www.zakynthos-net.gr, www.zanteweb.gr
- **Kythira** www.www.kythira.com

---

for ferries to Kefallonia and Zakynthos. On Epiros, Igoumenitsa serves Corfu and Paxi; and Astakos on Sterea Ellada serves Ithaki and Kefallonia (although only in the high season). The port of Neapoli on the southern tip of the Peleponnese serves Kythira. There are numerous websites offering information on ferry timetables; among the best is www.ferries.gr.

The following table details the scheduled domestic ferries to the Ionians from mainland ports in the high season.

DOMESTIC FERRY CONNECTIONS TO THE IONIAN ISLANDS

Origin	Destination	Dur	Fare	Freq
Astakos	Sami (Kefallonia)	3hr	€7.50	daily
	Piso Aetos (Ithaki)	2¾hr	€7	daily
Igoumenitsa	Corfu Town	1¼hr	€5.80	16 daily
	Lefkimmi (Corfu)	1hr	€3.90	6 daily
Igoumenitsa	Gaïos (Paxi)	1½hr	€6.70	daily
Kyllini	Zakynthos Town	1hr	€5.10	5 daily
	Argostoli (Kefallonia)	2½hr	€11.70	daily
	Poros (Kefallonia)	1½hr	€7.40	2-3 daily
Patra	Corfu Town	6½hr	€29.80	2 daily
	Sami (Kefallonia)	2¾hr	€15.40	2 daily
	Vathy/Piso Aetos (Ithaki)	3¾hr	€14	2 daily
Neapoli	Diakofti (Kythira)	1hr	€7	1-4 daily

It is not possible to island hop directly between the northern and southern islands. Corfu and Paxi are well connected by ferry and hydrofoil, but unfortunately there are no services from either Corfu or Paxi to Lefkada. Instead, travellers may be able to sail one way on hydrofoil day trips from Corfu to Kefallonia (offered twice weekly).

Within the southern Ionians, Lefkada, Kefallonia and Ithaki are well connected by ferry, and there's a twice-daily service between southern Kefallonia and northern Zakynthos (an alternative is to sail from Argostoli to Kyllini in the Peloponnese, and from there to Zakynthos Town). Further details can be found under each island entry.

INTERNATIONAL
Corfu has regular connections with three ports in Italy (Brindisi, Bari and Venice), operated by a handful of ferry companies sailing between Italy and Igoumenitsa and/or Patra. (Travellers can also sail between Ancona and Igoumenitsa, then transfer to a

IONIAN ISLANDS

IONIAN ISLANDS

local ferry.) Crossings are most frequent in July and August, but there are year-round services at least weekly between Corfu and Brindisi, Bari and Venice.

From Corfu it's also possible to cross to Albania, or to visit on a day trip.

Agoudimos Lines (www.agoudimos-lines.com) From Brindisi to Corfu and Igoumenitsa.

ANEK Lines (www.anek.gr) From Venice to Corfu.

Blue Star Ferries (www.bluestarferries.com) From Bari to Corfu, Igoumenitsa and Patra.

Fragline (www.fragline.gr) From Brindisi to Corfu and Igoumenitsa.

Minoan Lines (www.minoan.gr) From Venice to Igoumenitsa, Corfu and Patra.

SNAV (www.snav.it) High-season, high-speed catamaran services between Brindisi, Corfu and Paxi.

Superfast Ferries (www.superfast.com) From Bari to Corfu, Igoumenitsa and Patra.

Ventouris (www.ventouris.gr) From Bari to Corfu and Igoumenitsa.

HISTORY

The origin of the name Ionian is obscure but is thought to derive from the goddess Io. Yet another of Zeus' paramours, Io, while fleeing the wrath of a jealous Hera (in the shape of a heifer), happened to pass through the waters now known as the Ionian Sea.

If we are to believe Homer, the islands were important during Mycenaean times; however, no magnificent palaces or even modest villages from that period have been revealed, though Mycenaean tombs have been unearthed. Ancient history lies buried beneath tonnes of earthquake rubble – seismic activity has been constant on all Ionian islands.

By the 8th century BC, the Ionian Islands were in the clutches of the mighty city-state of Corinth, which regarded them as stepping stones on the route to Sicily and Italy. A century later, Corfu staged a successful revolt against Corinth, which was allied to Sparta, and became an ally of Sparta's archenemy, Athens. This alliance provoked Sparta into challenging Athens, thus precipitating the Peloponnesian Wars (431–404 BC). The wars left Corfu depleted, as they did all participants, and Corfu became little more than a staging post for whoever happened to be holding sway in Greece. By the end of the 3rd century BC, Corfu, along with the other Ionian Islands, fell under Roman rule. Following the decline of the

---

IONIAN KYTHIRA?

The island of Kythira (and its satellite, An-tikythira) dangles off the southern tip of the Peloponnese between the Ionian and Aegean Seas. Historically, Kythira is considered part of the Ionian Islands, but it mostly resembles the Cyclades in appearance and architecture, and today is administered from Piraeus. Due to its location and the lack of suitable ferry connections, visitors are unlikely to visit Kythira from its nearest Ionian neighbour, Zakynthos.

Roman Empire, the islands saw the usual waves of invaders that Greece suffered. After the fall of Constantinople, the islands became Venetian.

Corfu was never part of the Ottoman Empire. Paxi, Kefallonia, Zakynthos and Ithaki were variously occupied by the Turks, but the Venetians held them longest. The exception was Lefkada, which was Turkish for 200 years.

Venice fell to Napoleon in 1797. Two years later, under the Treaty of Campo Formio, the Ionian Islands were allotted to France. In 1799 Russian forces wrested the islands from Napoleon, but by 1807 they were his again. By then, the all-powerful British couldn't resist meddling. As a result, in 1815, after Napoleon's downfall, the islands became a British protectorate under the jurisdiction of a series of Lord High Commissioners.

British rule was oppressive but, on a more positive note, the British constructed roads, bridges, schools and hospitals, established trade links, and developed agriculture and industry. However, the nationalistic fervour throughout the rest of Greece soon reached the Ionian Islands, and a call for unity was realised in 1864 when Britain relinquished the islands to Greece.

In WWII the Italians invaded Corfu as part of Mussolini's plan to resurrect the mighty Roman Empire. Italy surrendered to the Allies in September 1943 and, in revenge, the Germans massacred thousands of Italians who had occupied the island. The Germans also sent some 5000 Corfiot Jews to Auschwitz.

The islands saw a great deal of emigration after WWII, and again following the earthquakes of 1948 and 1953 that devastated the region. But while Greeks left the islands, the foreign invasion has never really stopped, and these days takes the form of package tourism from northern Europe.

CORFU ΚΕΡΚΥΡΑ

pop 114,000

Corfu is the second-largest, the greenest Ionian island, and also the best known. In Greek, the island's name is Kerkyra (*ker-kih-rah*). It was Homer's 'beautiful and rich land', and Odysseus' last stop on his journey home to Ithaki. Shakespeare reputedly used it as a background for *The Tempest*. In the 20th century, the writers the Durrell brothers, among others, extolled its virtues.

With its beguiling landscape of wildflowers and cypress trees rising out of shimmering olive groves, Corfu is considered by many as Greece's most beautiful island. With the nation's highest rainfall, it's also a major vegetable garden and produces scores of herbs which gives the mountain air a pleasant scent.

Getting There & Away

AIR

Olympic Airlines (Map p437; ☎ 26610 22962; www .olympicairlines.com; Iakovou Polyla 11, Corfu Town) has a central office and a desk at the airport. The national airline has two flights to/from Athens daily (from €77), and four flights a week to/from Thessaloniki (€63). You can also fly three times weekly to Preveza (€35), Kefallonia (€35) and Zakynthos (€46).

Aegean Airlines (☎ 26610 27100; www.aegeanair .com) has two to three flights a day between Athens and Corfu (from €29). Its office is located at the airport and, if closed, calls will be diverted to their office in Athens.

AirSea Lines (Map p437; ☎ 26610 22900, 26610 99316; www.airsealines.com; Eleftheriou Venizilou 32, Corfu Town) is a new seaplane service which runs several flights a day between Corfu and Paxi (one-way/round trip €35/50), Corfu and Ioannina (€60 one-way, €100 round trip; twice daily), and Paxi–Corfu–Ioannina (€95 one-way, €160 round trip, twice daily). Children receive discounts. In Corfu, purchase tickets from the AirSea Lines office at the old port. A minibus will take/collect you from here to the departure point at Marina Gouvia, 8km away. Note the strict baggage

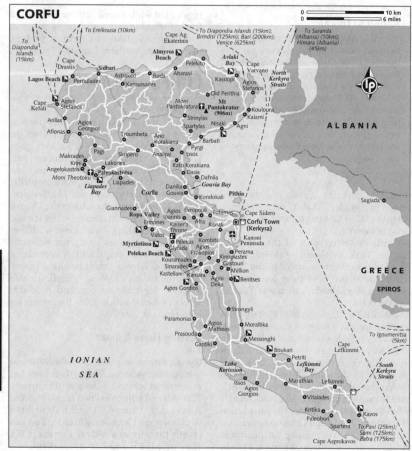

CORFU

0 — 10 km
0 — 6 miles

To Ereikousa (10km)
To Diapondia Islands (15km);
Brindisi (125km); Bari (200km);
Venice (625km)
To Saranda (Albania) (10km); Himara (Albania) (45km)
To Diapondia Islands (15km)
Cape Ag Ekaterinis
Cape Drastis
Almyros Beach
Pelekito
Avlaki Bay
Cape Varvano
North Kerkyra Straits
Lagos Beach
Sidhari
Astrakeri
Roda
Aharavi
Kassiopi
Agios Stefanos
Peroulades
Karoussades
Old Perithia
Arillas
Agios Stefanos
Cape Kefali
Moni Pantokratora
Mt Pantokrator (906m)
Kouloura
Kalami
ALBANIA
Afionas
Agios Georgios
Strinylas
Nisaki
Agni
Troumbeta
Ano Korakiana
Spartylas
Barbati
Makrades
Pagi
Skripero
Analipsi
Pyrgi
Ipsos
Krini
Lakones
Kato Korakiana
Angelokastro
Paleokastritsa
Dasia
Dafnila
Moni Theotoku
Liapades
Liapades Bay
Danilia
Gouvia
Gouvia Bay
Pithia
Corfu
Kondokali
Sagiada
Giannades
Ropa Valley
Agios Ioannis
Evropouli
Potamos
Cape Sidero
Ermones
Kaiser's Throne
Afra
Kanali
Corfu Town (Kerkyra)
Vatos
Pelekas
Kombitsi
Kanoni Peninsula
Myrtiotissa
Glyfada
Agios Prokopios
Perama
Kinopiastes
Pelekas Beach
Kouramades
Gastouri
Ahillion
GREECE
Sinarades
Kastellani
Kamara
Agioi Deka
Benitses
EPIROS
Agios Gordios
Strongyli
Paramonas
Agios Matheos
Moraitika
To Igoumenitsa (5km)
Prasouda
Messonghi
Gardiki
Boukari
Cape Lefkimmi
IONIAN SEA
Petriti
Lefkimmi Bay
South Kerkyra Straits
Lake Korission
Issos
Marathias
Lefkimmi
Agios Giorgios
Vitalades
Kritika
Kavos
Paleohon
Spartera
To Paxi (25km); Sami (125km); Patra (175km)
Cape Asprokavos

weight allowance (12kg, or an excess baggage fee of €2 per kilo per sector applies, plus 4kg of hand luggage).

BUS
KTEL (☎ 26610 39985) runs buses three times daily (via Lefkimmi in the island's south) between Corfu Town and Athens (€32.50, 8½ hours). There's also a twice-daily service to/from Thessaloniki (€30.80, eight hours); for both destinations budget an additional €3.90 for the ferry between Corfu and the mainland. Long-distance tickets should be purchased in advance from Corfu Town's bus station (opposite) on Avramiou, between Plateia San Rocco and the new port.

FERRY
Domestic
Hourly ferries travel daily between Corfu and Igoumenitsa (€5.80, 1¼ to two hours). Car ferries go to Paxi (€7.50, three hours) two or three times weekly (the hydrofoil is a better option as it's much more frequent). In high season you can travel to/from Patra on one of the international ferries that call at Corfu (€29, six hours) en route to/from Italy.

There are also six ferries daily between Lefkimmi in the island's south and Igoumenitsa (€3.90, one hour).

International
Corfu is on the Patra–Igoumenitsa ferry route to Italy (Brindisi, Bari, Ancona and Venice),

IONIAN ISLANDS

although ferries from Ancona don't stop at Corfu (passengers need to disembark at Igoumenitsa and cross to Corfu on a local ferry).

Ferries go a few times daily to Brindisi (€53, eight hours), and in summer usually once daily to Bari (€56, 10 to 12 hours) and Venice (€72, 24 to 26 hours depending if you go via Igoumenitsa). Fares listed here are for deck and airline-style seats (not cabin berths), one-way passage in the high season; there are sizable reductions in the low- and mid-seasons, and for return tickets. See also Igoumenitsa (p108) and Patra (p501) for more details.

SNAV (www.snav.it) operates daily high-speed catamaran services between Corfu and Brindisi from July to early September. The journey takes only 3¼ hours and fares range between €70 and €140, depending on the date of travel.

Shipping agencies selling tickets are found mostly in Corfu Town along Xenofondos Stratigou and Ethnikis Antistasis. **Agoudimos Lines** (Map p437; ☎ 26610 80030; www .agoudimos-lines.com; Ethnikis Antistasis 1), directly across from Corfu's new port, has extremely helpful staff who are happy to point you in the direction of the relevant international shipping lines if they can't help; the assortment of companies, routes and prices can be overwhelming.

For more information regarding Italian ferries to Corfu, see p431.

HYDROFOIL
Domestic
Petrakis Lines (p439) operates passenger-only hydrofoils between Corfu, Igoumenitsa and Paxi from May until mid-October. There are one to three services daily between Corfu and Paxi (€14.90, one hour), but only one service weekly between Corfu and Igoumenitsa (€11.50, 35 minutes) – on this route ferries are a much better option.

The same company also operates excursion day trips to Kefallonia (Sami and surrounds) twice weekly. The cost of the day trip is €60, but travellers can often use the hydrofoil for one-way passage for €43.10. This is the only direct sea link between the northern and southern Ionian Islands.

International
Hydrofoil services connecting Corfu and Albania are operated by Petrakis Lines

(p439). There are daily sailings to/from the town of Saranda (€15, 25 minutes), plus weekly Saturday services to/from Himara (€25, 1¼ hours). Travellers also pay €9 for a temporary visa for Albania. Alternatively, Petrakis Lines offers regular day excursions to historic areas around Saranda for €60, and no visa is required.

Petrakis Lines has daily ferries to the Albanian port of Saranda (€15, 25 minutes), plus twice-weekly services to Himara (€25, 1¼ hours) and Vlora (€38, 2½ hours).

Getting Around
TO/FROM THE AIRPORT
No bus service operates between Corfu Town and the airport. Bus Nos 6 and 10 from Plateia San Rocco in Corfu Town stop on the main road 800m from the airport (en route to Benitses and Ahillion). A taxi between the airport and Corfu Town costs around €10.

BUS
Long-distance KTEL buses (known as Green Buses) travel from Corfu Town's **long-distance bus station** (Map p437; ☎ 26610 30627; Avramiou).

LONG-DISTANCE (GREEN) BUSES FROM CORFU TOWN

Destination	Time	Frequency
Agios Gordios	45min	6 daily
Agios Stefanos	1½hr	4 daily
Aharavi (via Roda)	1¼hr	5 daily
Arillas (via Afionas)	1¼hr	2 daily
Barbati	45min	5 daily
Ermones	30min	4 daily
Glyfada	30min	7 daily
Kassiopi	45min	4 daily
Kavos	1½hr	10 daily
Messonghi	45min	6 daily
Paleokastritsa	45min	6 daily
Pyrgi	30min	9 daily
Sidhari	1¼hr	8 daily
Spartera	45min	2 daily

Fares cost €1.70 to €3.30. Organised Ioannis in the ticket kiosk will willingly give you a printed timetable. Sunday and holiday services are reduced considerably, or don't run.

Local buses (Blue Buses) depart from the **local bus station** (Map p439; ☎ 26610 31595; Plateia San Rocco) in Corfu Town.

IONIAN ISLANDS

LOCAL (BLUE) BUSES IN CORFU TOWN

Destination	Via	Bus	Frequency
Agios Ioannis	Afra	No 8	13 daily
Ahillion		No 10	7 daily
Analipsi		No 3	6 daily
Benitses		No 6	13 daily
Evropouli	Potamas	No 4	11 daily
Kanoni		No 2	half-hourly
Kombitsi	Kanali	No 14	4 daily
Kondokali & Dasia	Gouvia	No 7	half-hourly
Kouramades	Kinopiastes	No 5	13 daily
Pelekas		No 11	7 daily

Tickets are either €0.75 or €1 depending on the length of journey, and can be bought on board or from the booth on Plateia San Rocco. All trips are under 30 minutes.

CAR & MOTORCYCLE

Car- and motorbike-rental outlets are plentiful in Corfu Town and most of the resort towns on the island. Prices start at around €40 per day. Shop around to get a good deal. Most international car-rental companies are represented in Corfu Town and at the airport, and there are numerous local companies. Most have offices along the northern waterfront.

Budget (Map p437; ☎ 26610 28590; Iannou Theotoki 132)

Easy Rider (Map p437; ☎ 26610 43026) Opposite the new port, rents scooters and motorbikes.

Ocean (Map p439; ☎ 26610 44017; Eleftheriou Venizelou 22)

Sunrise (Map p437; ☎ 26610 26511; Ethnikis Anti-stasis 16)

Top Cars (Map p439; ☎ 26610 35237; Donzelot 25) A reliable choice along the waterfront near Hotel Konstantinopoulos.

CORFU TOWN

pop 28,200

Nicknamed 'Kastropolis' because of its position between two fortresses on a peninsula, Corfu Town can be summed up in three words: sophistication, beauty and charm. The town's architecture, culture and cuisine are a harmonious blend of Italian, French and British, with a contemporary Greek feel. Spot the foreign influences: the pink and ochre Venetian mansions in the old town's narrow alleys, the arcades of Paris' Rue de Rivoli in the Liston, a line of old buildings with an arched arcade and promenade, and an English-style cricket ground (come-village-green) on the Spianada. The town's cosmopolitan old and new sections merge seamlessly. Linger over a frappé and crowd watch from one of the many restaurants or bars in historic plazas and near Byzantine churches and museums.

Orientation

The town is separated into northern and southern sections. The old town is in the northern section between the Spianada and the Neo Frourio (New Fortress). To the east, the Palaio Frourio (Old Fortress) projects out to sea, cut off from the town by a moat. The southern section is the new town where you'll find most services including the post office, banks, clothes shops and some modern lively cafés.

The old port is north of the old town, and the new port is to the west. Between them is the hulking New Fortress. The long-distance bus station is off Avramiou between Plateia San Rocco and the new port. The local bus station is on Plateia San Rocco.

Information

EMERGENCY

Tourist police (Map p439; ☎ 26610 30265; 3rd fl, Samartzi 4) Off Plateia San Rocco.

INTERNET ACCESS

The going rate for Internet access is €3 to €5 per hour.

Netoikos (Map p439; Kaloheretou14) Between Church of Agios Spyridon and the Liston.

Eden (Map p439; Plateia San Rocco) Behind the tourist information booth.

MEDICAL SERVICES

Corfu General Hospital (Map p437; ☎ 26610 88200; Ioulias Andreadi)

MONEY

There are banks and ATMs around Plateia San Rocco, on Georgiou Theotoki and by both ports.

Alpha Bank (Map p439; Kapodistriou, behind the Liston)

National Bank of Greece (Map p439; Voulgareos)

POST

Post office (Map p437; Leof Alexandras)

TELEPHONE

Public telephones can be found on most major streets and squares. Prepaid telephone cards (€4) are available from kiosks.

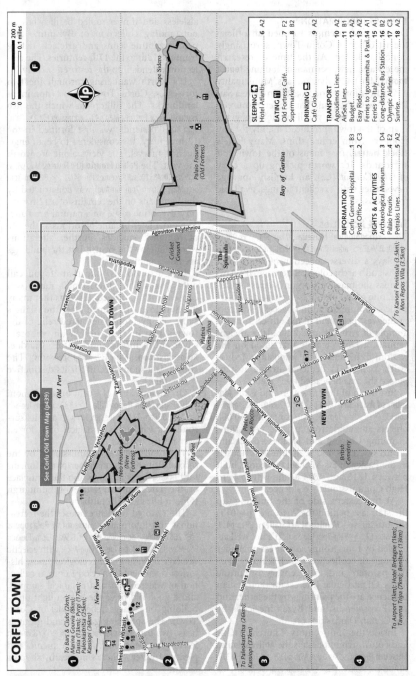

CORFU TOWN

IONIAN ISLANDS

TOURIST INFORMATION

Despite past attempts to open an official tourist office in Corfu Town, surprisingly none has lasted. At the time of research there was a new, permanent-looking **tourist booth** (Map p439; the sign says 'Municipality of Corfu Information Board') in Plateia San Rocco with helpful, but under-resourced staff. At the best you'll be able to get a map of the town, produced mainly for day troopers from cruise ships. Many hotels stock better, free maps of the town and surrounds. It's worth picking up a copy of *The Corfiot* (€2), an English-language newspaper with excellent listings, available from kiosks.

Sights & Activities

The **Archaeological Museum** (Map p437; ☎ 26610 30680; P Vraïla 5; admission €3; 8.30am-3pm Tue-Sun) displays a diverse collection of items from the island's archaeological heritage. It's hard to miss the massive Gorgon Medusa sculpture, one of the best-preserved pieces of Archaic sculpture found in Greece. It was part of the west pediment of the 6th-century BC Temple of Artemis at Corcyra (the ancient capital), a Doric temple that stood on the Kanoni Peninsula. The imposing Medusa (with snakes) is depicted in the instant before she was beheaded by Perseus.

Just north of the cricket ground is the **Museum of Asian Art** (Map p439; ☎ 26610 30443; admission €3; 8.30am-3pm Tue-Sun), containing 10,000 objects donated from private collections including Chinese and Japanese porcelain, bronzes, screens and sculptures. It's housed in the Palace of Sts Michael & George, built between 1818 and 1824 as the British Lord High Commissioner's residence.

At the eastern side of the building, up the staircase behind the Art Café (p440) is the oft-missed **Municipal Art Gallery** (Map p439; admission €2; 9am-7pm Tue-Sun). It's not well attended by tour groups so you can meander through the collection which features Corfiot painters and 15th-century Byzantine icons. Of particular interest for their Italian influence are the paintings by the father and son Prossalendis, and Byzantine icons by the Cretan Damaskinas.

Inside the 15th-century Church of Our Lady of Antivouniotissa is the **Antivouniotissa Museum** (Byzantine Museum; Map p439; ☎ 26610 38313; off Arseniou; admission €2; 8.30am-3pm Tue-Sun). This aisleless and timber-roofed basilica has an outstanding collection of Byzantine and post-Byzantine icons and artefacts dating from the 13th to the 17th centuries. The collection extends into the restored sacristy.

It's worth wandering through the two fortresses, Corfu Town's most dominant landmarks. The hilltop on which the **Neo Frourio** (New Fortress; Map p437; admission €2; 9am-9pm May-Oct) stands was first fortified in the 12th century. It's considered to be an engineering marvel. The views alone are worth the visit. The **Palaio Frourio** (Old Fortress; Map p439; ☎ 26610 48310; adult/concession €4/2; 8.30am-3pm Sep-May, 8.30am-7pm Jun-Aug) was constructed by the Venetians on the remains of a 12th-century Byzantine castle on a natural headland. The moat later became notorious as the site of romantic suicides. Further alterations were made by the British but the buildings are now mainly ruins.

In Corfu, locals joke that if you call out 'Spyros', half the island's males will come running. Indeed, it seems that many lucky fellows are named after the island's saint, St Spyridon. The sacred relic of the town's patron saint lies in an elaborate silver coffin in the 16th-century **Church of Agios Spyridon** (Map p439; Agiou Spyridonos). The church is also important for its distinctive campanile.

On the outskirts of Corfu on the Kanoni Peninsula, **Mon Repos Villa** (8.30am-3pm Tue-Sun Sep-May, 8.30am-7.30pm Tue-Sun Jun-Aug) and its surrounding gardens is a magical oasis for an over-heated traveller.

The residence was commissioned by the second British Commissioner of the Ionians for his Corfiot wife. It was also the birthplace of the UK's current Duke of Edinburgh (Queen Elizabeth II's husband).

The restored residence houses the recreational and informative **Museum of Palaeopolis** (☎ 26610 30680; admission €3; 8.30am-3pm Tue-Sun Sep-May, 8.30am-7.30pm Tue-Sun Jun-Aug), with eclectic displays including archaeological finds, historical documents, a Period Room, a collection of watercolours and botanical samples, and a good old press-the-button-light-up-a-building on a large relief model of Corfu Town. The sprawling gardens and grounds boast two **Doric temples** (admission free; 8am-5pm Sep-May, 8am-7pm Jun-Aug). Take a picnic and plenty of water – there's no nearby shop or kiosk.

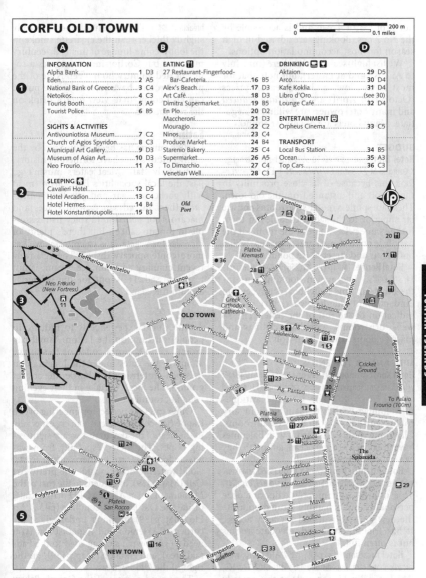

CORFU OLD TOWN

INFORMATION
Alpha Bank..............................1 D3
Eden..2 A5
National Bank of Greece........3 C4
Netoikos..................................4 C3
Tourist Booth..........................5 A5
Tourist Police..........................6 B5

SIGHTS & ACTIVITIES
Antivouniotissa Museum........7 C2
Church of Agios Spyridon........8 C3
Municipal Art Gallery..............9 D3
Museum of Asian Art.............10 D3
Neo Frourio...........................11 A3

SLEEPING
Cavalieri Hotel......................12 D5
Hotel Arcadion.....................13 C4
Hotel Hermes.......................14 B4
Hotel Konstantinoupolis.......15 B3

EATING
27 Restaurant-Fingerfood-
  Bar-Cafeteria....................16 B5
Alex's Beach.........................17 D3
Art Café................................18 D3
Dimitra Supermarket............19 B5
En Plo...................................20 D2
Maccheroni..........................21 D3
Mouragio..............................22 C2
Ninos....................................23 C4
Produce Market....................24 B4
Starenio Bakery....................25 C4
Supermarket.........................26 A5
To Dimarchio........................27 C4
Venetian Well.......................28 C3

DRINKING
Aktaion.................................29 D5
Arco......................................30 D4
Kafe Koklia...........................31 D4
Libro d'Oro........................(see 30)
Lounge Café.........................32 D4

ENTERTAINMENT
Orpheus Cinema...................33 C5

TRANSPORT
Local Bus Station..................34 B5
Ocean...................................35 A3
Top Cars...............................36 C3

Tours

Petrakis Lines (Map p437; 26610 31649; Ethnikis Antistasis 4) organises day trips from Corfu Town, including an excursion to ancient ruins in Albania; a boat trip taking in Paxi (and the Blue Caves) and Antipaxi; and a trip to Sami and surrounds in Kefallonia. Prices are from €35 to €75 depending on the trip.

Sleeping

Generally, cheaper accommodation choices in the old town are not great value and it's worth squeezing a little more from the purse for a huge leap in the quality. There are some good value options in the newer part of town. The nearest camping ground is Dionysus Camping Village (p443), 8km north of Corfu Town and is accessible by the No 7 bus. Bookings are advised in high season for most accommodation options.

We list high-season prices here (mid-July to August, and at Easter), but note that for most hotels, low- and mid-season prices (October to April) are *drastically reduced* and many hotel owners are willing to negotiate. Many hotels are open year round.

BUDGET

Hotel Bretagne (☎ 26610 30724; brhotel@otenet.gr; K Georgaki St 27; s/d/tr €47/70/90; 🔀) Don't overlook this because of its close proximity to the airport and distance from the old town. These are spotless motel-style rooms and are far superior to the jaded cheapies in town for the same price. Some of the rooms at the back face on to a small grassy garden, which buffets air and street noise pollution.

Hotel Hermes (Map p439; ☎ 26610 39268; G Markora 14; s/d €40/50) The ancient-looking plug-in-the-box telephone switchboard at reception (and pleasant elderly owner) give a good indication of the rest of the hotel. The 34 well-worn rooms, with high ceilings and massive doors, are clean, if noisy.

MIDRANGE & TOP END

Hotel Konstantinoupolis (Map p439; ☎ 26610 48716; www.konstantinoupolis.com.gr; K Zavitsianou 11; s/d incl breakfast €70/98; 🔀) The intimate antique-filled lounge extends to plain but light, airy rooms with aqua-coloured tiled bathrooms. Charming rooms at the front with balconies have great views of the ocean, although they can be a little noisy at night.

Hotel Atlantis (Map p437; ☎ 26610 35560; atlanker@ mail.otenet.gr; Xenofondos Stratigou 48; s/d €72/87; 🔀) This non-descript monolith doesn't ooze personality, but is handily located opposite the new port, so is useful for ferry access. It has friendly staff and adequate rooms but is often full.

Hotel Arcadion (Map p439; ☎ 26610 37670; www .arcadionhotel.com; Kapodistriou 44; s/d/tr €107/130/160; 🔀) Eat a Big Mac in style at this smartly refurbished boutique hotel incongruously situated above a McDonalds by the Liston. It's furnished with Corfiot furniture, and has double-glazed windows for tranquil views of the Spianada during the summer evening *voltas* (stroll).

Cavalieri Hotel (Map p439; ☎ 26610 39041; www .cavalieri-hotel.com; Kapodistriou 4; d €100-150 incl

breakfast; 🔀) The elegant drapes are only slightly thicker than the cigarette smoke in the lobby-come-lounge of this 17th-century mansion, but Corfiot furniture gives a sophisticated country home feel. Nine of the pleasant rooms have balconies. The public can also enjoy 'that' view over a drink on the rooftop bar.

Eating

Corfu's cuisine has been influenced by the many cultures that have formed its history, particularly Italy. Meat eaters mustn't go past the local specialities like *sofrito* (meat with garlic, vinegar and parsley), *pastitsada* (beef in red sauce, with spices and macaroni) or *bourdeto* (a spicy fish casserole in tomato sauce). But there's plenty of *mezedes* for vegetarians to enjoy, as well as more contemporary dishes. The relatively recent culinary addition, ice cream, is not to be missed. Look out for the gelaterias around the island.

CAFÉS

A true Corfu experience is to indulge in people-watching on the Liston. You'll pay around €3 to €5 for a coffee or fresh juice at any of the cafés under the loggia or in the open-air terraces that border the cricket ground. The locals partake in their evening *volta* at around eleven.

Other cafés are perfect for lingering over a frappé (ice-coffee drink) or snack, especially in the heat of the day to rest weary sightseeing bones. The views, especially from waterside locations, are further sensual feasts. Good watering holes include the pretty Art Café (Map p439), in gardens to the east of the Museum of Asian Art; the Old Fortress Café, inside the Old Fortress complex (p436); En Plo (Map p439), meaning 'under sail' at the corner of Arseniou and Kapodistriou (you need to go down a sloping road to the Faliraki area); and Aktaion (Map p439), on the right of the Old Fortress.

The proud owners of the **Starenio Bakery** (Map p439; ☎ 26610 47370; Guilford 59; snacks under €2) enjoy explaining their superb range of homemade gourmet pies, breads and gooey baklava.

RESTAURANTS

Stroll around pretty Plateia Dimarchiou (Town Hall Sq) and along Kapodistriou and its street off-shoots to peruse the menus of tavernas and more contemporary eateries.

Venetian Well (Map p439; ☎ 26610 44761; Plateia Kremasti; mains €14-20) A decorative well in a small square is not the only focus of this upmarket treat. The excellent choice of creative dishes includes stir-fried duck fillet with dried fruit, and wild boar. Turn left past the cathedral and follow the signs.

Mouragio (Map p439; ☎ 26610 33815; Arseniou 15; mains €5-10) The definite pick of this strip, despite the neighbouring (touristy) restaurants hogging the ocean view, this rustic and good-value place serves massive portions of *mezedes* and local dishes – *sofrito* and kebabs – and seafood delights. Popular with both local and foreign tourists.

Ninos (Chrisi; Map p439; ☎ 26610 46175; Sevastianou 44; mains €8-20) Started in 1920, this family concern is as authentic as Zorba. Line up with the locals to choose the generous portions of daily specials at the servery. Renowned for their *sofrito*.

27 Restaurant-Fingerfood-Bar-Cafeteria (Map p439; ☎ 26610 27270; Leof Alexandras; juices €4) The name implies that it delivers a lot – and it does. Come to view the eclectic mix of interiors, from the relaxing sofas and funky bar stools to the stylish, contemporary restaurant fittings. And while you're there enjoy a pricey – but nice – fresh juice.

Also recommended:

To Dimarchio (Map p439; ☎ 26610 39031; Plateia Dimarchiou; mains €8.50-21) Upmarket menu and a beautiful setting.

THE AUTHOR'S CHOICE

Tavern Tripa (☎ 26610 56333; www.tripas.gr; set banquet €30) If there's an entertainment and culinary experience never to be missed, it's this taverna, 7km southwest of Corfu Town in the tiny village of Kinopiastes. Since 1936, the owners have welcomed famous patrons including presidents, Jane Fonda and Anthony Quinn. One way or another you'll roll out the door, if not because of the bottomless jugs of homemade wine, then because of the banquet's delectable, and endless courses of freshly prepared Corfiot specialties. To top it off, there's a floor show of Greek dancing and singing. Try and fast beforehand, and book ahead.

Maccheroni (Map p439; ☎ 26610 44322; Kalocheretou 3) For pizza by the metre (€5 to €8) or by the slice (€1.50).

Alex's Beach (Faliraki) Unpretentious taverna by the sea serving good seafood starters, grills and kebabs.

SELF-CATERING

North of Plateia San Rocco is the bustling **produce market** (Map p439; ☒ closed Sun), open morning to early afternoon and selling fresh fruit, vegetables and fish. For groceries try **Dimitra supermarket** (Map p439; G Markora), next to Hotel Hermes, or other **supermarkets** (Map p437) by the long-distance bus station and on Avramiou Theotoki opposite the **main plaza** (Map p439).

Drinking

For unquestionably *the* best coffee in the Ionians, it's worth the effort to head to trendy **Café Gioia** (Map p437; 46 Xenofondos Stratigou) near the new port. Popular bars along the Liston and nearby include Kafe Koklia (Map p439), Arco (Map p439) and Libro d'Oro (Map p439) and Lounge Café (Map p439) and the classy rooftop bar at the Cavalieri Hotel (opposite).

Entertainment

To hang out with the cool crowds in the high-tech (and very late night) scene, head to Corfu's bar-come-disco strip, 2km northwest of the new port, along Ethnikis Antistasis (take a taxi). Recommended spots are the new, big and flashy Crystal, the hip and classy Privilege and more local Au Bar (Ω in Greek) caters to the locals. The €10 admission fee includes one freebie drink.

For visual entertainment, Corfu Town's **Orpheus cinema** (Map p439; ☎ 26610 39768; G Aspioti), screens English-language films with Greek subtitles. Look out about town for signs of music performances. An inaugural **Corfu Music Festival** (www.corfufestival.gr) was held in July 2005; high-profile musicians performed in the Ionian Academy, St George's Church and the Ahillion Palace.

NORTH OF CORFU TOWN

Much of the coast just north of Corfu Town is saturated by tourist mobs and tacky developments, though beyond **Pyrgi**, the winding, scenic road reveals some of Corfu's delights.

Just beyond Pyrgi take a detour to **Mt Pantokrator** (906m), the island's highest peak. On your way, wind your way around the many hairpin bends and through the picturesque villages of **Spartylas** and **Strinylas**. At Strinylas, stop for a drink or a snack under the greenery at **Taverna Oasis**. From here a road climbs through stark terrain to the mountain's summit, the **Moni Pantokrator** and stupendous views. Keep your eyes open for the wildflowers, including poppies, on the sides of the road. If you can ignore the presence of a massive telecommunications tower in the middle of its grounds, you can enjoy stupendous, if sometimes hazy, views.

Heading northeast from Pyrgi around the winding coastal road you will first hit **Barbati**, a developing resort with a long pebbled beach; pleasant family taverna **Akrogiali** on the edge of the cliff is a good drink stop. Further along, **Nisaki** is little more than a tiny cove with a pebble beach, a couple of tavernas and some rooms. **Agni** is renowned for its three tavernas – Taverna Toula, Taverna Nikolas, Taverna Agni – which serve excellent fare. The village of **Kalami** is famous for the White House, home to Lawrence Durrell and perched near water. The base of the building houses an inevitably touristy restaurant, while the house itself can be rented (see opposite). Just round the next headland is the pretty fishing harbour and beach of **Kouloura** which affords a good view of the neighbouring coast of Albania. **Agios Stefanos** is pretty in two respects – pretty upmarket (popular with the British villa vultures) and with a beautiful harbour and small shingle beach. The next bay **Avlaki** reveals a lovely long beach and a couple of tavernas and is a relaxing place surprisingly without the touristy hoards (yet).

Kassiopi is worth considering for a night's stop-over. Push your way through the blow-up beach paraphernalia dominating the modern part of town and head to the lower and attractive harbour. Opposite the church on the main street a small track leads to interesting, although neglected, castle ruins, and you can walk over the headland to the nearby Battaria and Kanoni Beaches. The main road continues inland to the touristy resorts of **Aharavi**, **Roda** and **Sidhari**.

Pleasant **Agios Stefanos**, further around the coast (not to be confused with the village of Agios Stefanos in the northeast), has a long sandy beach and high sand-cliffs. Regular boat excursions leave from the small harbour 1.5km from the village centre to the **Diapondia Islands**, a cluster of little-known and even less-visited satellite islands belonging administratively to Corfu. Of the five islands only three are inhabited. **San Stefanos Travel** (☎ 26630 51910; ☽ 9am-11pm May-Oct) can provide further information.

CORFU ACTIVITIES

Obviously the best activities in this part of the world are centred on, under or around water. If you're not fortunate enough to be sailing around the Ionians on your own private yacht, there are companies based at Marina Gouvia that offer yacht charter services, flotilla holidays or sailing lessons, including **Corfu Sea School** (☎ 26610 99470; www.corfuseaschool.com). For those who like smaller boats, there are many excellent opportunities to rent a **motorboat** and explore the coastal coves. Head to Marina Gouvia.

You can **dive** in the crystal-clear waters off Corfu, and there are diving operators in Kassiopi, Agios Gordios, Agios Giorgios, Ipsos, Gouvia and Paleokastritsa.

For land-lubbers, walking is a great way to experience the countryside and enjoy the unspoilt villages. Keen walkers should purchase *The Second Book of Corfu Walks* by Hilary Whitton Paipeti, available in bookshops around town. By the same author is *The Companion Guide to the Corfu Trail*; it's written to guide walkers tackling the **Corfu Trail** (www.travelling.gr/corfutrail), which traverses the island and takes between eight and 12 days to complete.

Given Corfu's hilly terrain, it's not surprising that mountain-biking is popular. **Corfu Mountainbike Shop** (☎ 26610 93344; www.mountainbikecorfu.gr) is based in Dasia and rents bikes for independent exploration, as well as organising day trips and cycling holidays.

Not far from Ermones on the island's west coast is the **Corfu Golf Club** (☎ 26610 94220; www.corfugolfclub.com), one of the few courses in Greece. Or you can go horse riding through olive groves with **Trailriders** (☎ 26630 23090), based in the small inland village of Ano Korakiana. Bird watchers should pigeon in the **Birdwatching Centre of Ropa Valley** (☎ 26610 94221).

Head inland to experience verdant landscapes plus hairpin bends that make the Monaco Grand Prix circuit seem like an airstrip. You'll pass through delightful hilltop villages including **Mesaria**, **Agios Athanasios** and **Agros**.

Sleeping & Eating

Dionysus Camping Village (☎ 26610 91417; www.dionysuscamping.gr; sites per adult/tent €5.20/3.60, huts per person €10; ⚡) The closest camping ground to Corfu Town, signposted between Tzavros and Dasia and well served by the No 7 bus. Olive terraces serve as the camping area and there's a pool, shop and restaurant. Alternatively, you can opt for simple pine-clad huts with straw roofs; tents can also be hired.

Manessis Apartments (☎ 26610 34990; diana@otenet.gr; Kassiopi; 4-person apt €100) These very homely bougainvillea- and vine-covered two-bedroom apartments are situated at the end of Kassiopi's picturesque harbour. The friendly Irish/Greek owners are enthusiastic walkers and know a lot about the island…not that you'll want to leave this beautiful spot.

White House (☎ 26630 91040; www.white-house-corfu.gr; €160) Durrell fans can stay in this writer's former residence which sleeps up to eight people. The basic interiors are nothing to write a book about – you are paying more for the novelty, the position and the wonderful outlook. For meals, head directly below to the **White House Taverna** (☎ 26610 91251; mains €7-12).

If you want to follow the lead of the British moneyed classes who visit Corfu's northeast, contact UK-based **CV Travel** (☎ 020-7591 2800; www.cvtravel.net), which rents out luxurious villas (many with pools) in the region on a weekly basis.

Ice Dream Gelateria (☎ 26630 98200) Five minutes drive north of Kassiopi, opposite an EPKO petrol station, is this obligatory stop. Authentic, creamy gelati made on the premises. Worth every lick.

SOUTH OF CORFU TOWN

The coast road continues south from Corfu Town with a turn-off to **Ahillion Palace** (☎ 26610 56245; admission €6; ◷ 9am-2.30pm Sep-May, 9am-7pm Jun-Aug), near the village of Gastouri and well signposted. In the 1890s it was the summer palace of Austria's Empress Elizabeth (King Otho of Greece was her uncle), and she dedicated the villa to Achilles. The

beautifully landscaped garden is guarded by kitsch statues of mythological heroes.

The narrow winding streets of the old village are the only thing that saves the suburban-feel resort town of **Benitses**. The towns of **Moraïtika** and **Messonghi** further south are in much the same league, although their beach scenes are much better. Off the beaten track along the winding coastal road south of Messonghi is **Boukari**. It ain't action-packed for the independent traveller and the beaches are pebbly, but it's tranquil and pretty. The non-intrusive tavernas on the edge of the water under oleander trees are a great place to unwind.

In Boukari you can stay at the **Golden Sunset Hotel** (☎ 26620 51853; www.corfusunset.gr; d/tr €45/60). Although 'motel modern' in character, the rooms are bright and spacious and have balconies with sea views, and a restaurant is attached.

A stopover in **Lefkimmi,** just over 10km from Boukari in the southern part of the island, is not the end of the world in any respect. The town – divided into a newer and older section – has some fascinating churches and a rather quaint, but sometimes odorous canal. If you do find yourself stuck here due to ferry connections, accommodation can be found at the pleasant **Maria Madalena Apartments** (☎ 26620 22386; d €25). To feel right at home, eat in the kitchen of Taverna Maria by the canal. For half a century the owners (now mother and daughter) have been cooking traditional dishes for a mainly local clientele. A basic meatballs and rice with bread costs around €5.

Don't bother heading further south to **Kavos** unless you want to join in with the lads (aka British louts) and liquor.

THE WEST COAST

Some of Corfu's prettiest countryside, villages and beaches are situated on or around the west coast. The beautiful and popular town of **Paleokastritsa**, 26km from Corfu Town, is set along a 3km stretch of road. Small coves are hidden between tall cliffs, and cypresses and olive trees appear through the lush green mountain backdrop. You can venture to nearby grottoes or one of the 15 nearby beaches by small excursion boat (per person €8, 30 minutes) or taxi boats can drop you off at a beach of your choice. Paddle boats cost €9 per hour and canoes €3 per person.

Perched on the rocky promontory at the end of Paleokastritsa is the interesting and icon-filled **Moni Theotokou** (admission free; ☺ 7am-1pm & 3-8pm Apr-Oct), a monastery founded in the 13th century (but the present building dates from the 18th century). Just off the monastery's garden – with ivy, vines, roses and pot plants – is a small **museum** (admission free; ☺ 7am-1pm & 3-8pm Apr-Oct) exhibiting everything from a giant clam to priestly vestments of the last century.

From Paleokastritsa a path ascends to the unspoilt village of **Lakones**, 5km inland by road. The 6km road west to **Krini** and **Makrades** meanders at elevated heights; many restaurant owners have capitalised on the vistas. Be sure to visit Krini's miniature town square. Alternatively, if you have time, wind your way up and down to **Pagi** and onto the resort of **Agios Georgios** for an eating experience at the Fisherman's Taverna (see opposite).

South of Paleokastritsa, and accessed by the inland road, the pebbly beach at **Ermones** is dominated by tasteless development, but is near the **Corfu Golf Club** (☎ /fax 26610 94220; Ropa Valley; 18 holes €50) if you're craving a round. Hilltop **Pelekas**, 4km away, is a good base for village and beach activities. This friendly village has a reasonable infrastructure yet attracts fewer package tourists and more independent travellers.

The nearby mountain village of **Sinarades** has maintained its traditional feel with old buildings, narrow streets, a beautiful clock tower and several excellent tavernas. Its fascinating **Folkloric Museum** (adult/concession €1.50/0.60; ☺ 9am-2pm Mon-Sat) is housed in a former farmhouse. The curator, Tasa, can tell you more about Greek history than Homer himself.

Near Pelekas village are two good sandy beaches, **Glyfada** and **Pelekas** (marked on some maps as Kontogialos and also a resort in its own right). These are quite developed, are backed by large hotels and accommodation options and have watersports and sunbeds galore. A free bus service runs from Pelekas village to these beaches. Further north is popular **Myrtiotissa** beach, although at the time of research travellers complained that it had severely reduced in size, so that the former unofficial nudist 'colony' had more or less merged with the happy families section. Warning: It's a long

---

A CUT ABOVE THE REST

Male travellers who may have 'let their hair down' during their vacation, should razor on down to the small village of Kouramades. This tiny place is home to a highly respected (and dare we say eccentric) barber, **Mr Yiangos Hytiris** (☎ 26610 54258). Since 1949 Mr Hytiris has been servicing hirsute clients, who come not only from around the island, but as far away as Athens. He is as well known for his quirky barber's shop which is housed in a distinctive rust-coloured building with green shutters. It's a legacy to the bygone era of the barber's art – cut-throat razors and other manual and technical gadgets are mounted on the walls, along with a collection of hundreds of ornaments and mirrors. If you decide to pay a visit, be respectful and dress appropriately – he's a proud and skilled artiste from the old-world – and would not appreciate clients rocking up in beach gear.

---

trek down a steep, unsealed road before you see a bottom of any kind (don't drive down – it's best to park in the olive grove at the top of the hill and walk).

Agios Gordios is a popular beach-bum hang out south of Glyfada. The long sandy beach can cope with the crowds. It's backdrop is a sparse and exposed flat landscape, but it appeals to travellers interested primarily in a serious sun scene.

Sleeping & Eating

Paleokastritsa has many hotels, studios and *domatia*. At the end of the main road, before the climb to the monastery, are some good options.

Hotel Zefiros (☎ 26630 41088; hotelzef@otenet .gr; Paleokastritsa; d €70) A family establishment since 1934, this good-value joint has simple décor, some larger family-sized rooms (with kitchenette), plus a café downstairs (which rather burns the savings from the good-value sleep-over). Its sea view rooms are partially marred by a large building on the beachfront.

Paleokastritsa Camping (☎ 26630 41204; Paleokastritsa; sites per adult/tent €4.60/3.20) On the right of the main approach road to town is this shady and well-organised campsite set on olive terraces and with minimarket close by. Beach bums might find it a bit of a trek to the water, however.

La Grotta (☎ 26630 41006; Paleokastritsa) The hippest of sun seekers will be content for the day at this cool café-bar set in a stunning rocky cove with café and diving board. To enter, descend the long flight of steps opposite the driveway up to Hotel Paleokastritsa on the main road. Sunbeds on the café platform cost €2.

Levant Hotel (☎ 26610 94230; www.levanthotel .com; s/d/f €55/90/160; ⊠ ⚹) Some might consider it a little over the top in every respect, but this elegant and luxurious neoclassical hotel near Kaiser's Throne lookout above Pelekas village has all the mod-cons, a swimming pool set in gardens and a restaurant (mains €6 to €9) and terrace with awesome views of the Adriatic and beyond.

Jimmy's Restaurant & Rooms (☎ 26610 94284; jimmyspelekas@hotmail.com; d €40; ⚹) Near the intersection of the roads to Pelekas Beach and Kaiser's Throne lookout is Jimmy's, with no-nonsense rooms and restaurant (mains €6 to €10). The eatery's menu features Corfiot dishes, and good vegetarian choices. The basic and clean rooms (with decent-sized bathrooms) have rooftop views of the village and church tower.

Rolling Stone (☎ 26610 94942; rollingstone@pelekas beach.com; Pelekas Beach; d €35-40) The psychedelic wind chime on this joint's massive terrace is possibly the most active thing in this atmospheric '70s kickback in Pelekas Beach. The laid-back hosts offer clean and spacious self-contained apartments and double rooms, decked out with shells and flowers. The porch – with its bar, funky bright stools, and outdoor sofa – provides the perfect chill pad. Ask locals for directions.

Pink Palace (☎ 26610 53103; www.thepinkpalace .com; Agios Gordios Beach, Sinarades; A-/B-class incl breakfast & dinner per person €18/25; ▢) This huge, garish complex is like a twenty-somethings' summer camp, and is considered the must-do hassle-free party palace for those on the European backpacker circuit. A massive dining area, a nightly disco, theme parties, booze cruises and water activities cater to its 900-capacity guests, and it's (in)famous for its debauchery (female travellers in particular might feel uneasy). Both hostel- and hotel-style rooms are available.

Fisherman's Taverna (☎ 69425 85550; Agios Georgios; mains for 2 people €25) Renowned for his occasional cantankerousness at impatient clientele, the owner serves up seafood dishes at turtle pace. Even a sign says, 'Dear Customer. We are sorry but we cannot serve you if you are in a hurry.' Since 1967 this small place has survived without electricity (generators are now used) in its hidden location by the sea. Head 1.1km up a dirt road from the southern end of Agios Georgos Beach (ignore the first taverna visible from the road whose sign also says 'Fish Taverna'). Go hungry and with money and time.

Recommended by younger travellers for the all-in hostel experience is **Sunrock** (☎ 26610 94637; www.geocities.com/sunrock_corfu; Pelekas Beach; r incl breakfast & dinner per person €18; ⚹ ▢).

PAXI ΠΑΞΟΙ

pop 2500
Don't let the 10km by 4km size fool you: the tiny alluring island package of Paxi offers big things.

The island is the smallest of the main islands and its three intimate harbour towns, Gaïos, Loggos and Lakka, feature pretty waterfronts with Venetian-style pink-and-cream storeyed buildings, set against hilly backdrops of lush greenery. Their nearby coves can be reached by motorboat, if not by car or on foot.

The smattering of inland villages sit by centuries-old olive groves, winding stone walls, ancient windmills and olive presses. On the less accessible west coast, sheer limestone cliffs plunge hundreds of metres and are punctuated by grottoes. Walkers can discover hidden delights along the old mule trails. Obligatory is the visually instructive *Bleasdale Walking Map* (€8) or book (€10.50), available from book shops on the island. Paxi has escaped the mass tourism of Corfu and caters to discriminating tour companies (mainly British) and Italians who arrive en masse in August. Its slow pace makes for a relaxing stay for like-minded visitors.

Accommodation in Paxi mostly consists of pre-booked apartments and villas; all the island's agencies can help with bookings. For independent travellers, there are a few 'Rooms for Rent' signs around.

Getting There & Away

AIR

AirSea Lines (www.airsealines.com), a new sea-plane service, runs several flights a day between Corfu and Paxi (one-way/return €35/50), Corfu and Ioannina (one-way/return €60/100), and Paxi–Corfu–Ioannina (one-way/return €95/160). Children receive discounts. On Paxi, purchase tickets at **Bouas Tours** (☎ 26620 32245). Note the strict baggage weight allowance (12kg, or excess baggage fee applies, plus 4kg of hand luggage).

BUS

There's a twice weekly direct bus service between Athens and Paxi (€39, plus €6.70 for ferry ticket between Paxi and Igoumenitsa, seven hours). On Paxi, tickets are available from Bouas Tours (above). The bus leaves from Terminal A in Athens.

FERRY

Domestic

Two (sometimes three) car ferries operate daily services between Paxi, Corfu and Igoumenitsa on the mainland. The Paxi–Igoumenitsa (€6.70) trip takes one to two hours; Paxi–Corfu (via Igoumenitsa; €7.50) can take four to five hours (depending on the stopover in Igoumenitsa). Tickets can be obtained from most travel agents on the island.

Ferries dock at Gaïos' new port 1km east of the central square. Excursion boats dock along the waterfront.

International

You can reach Corfu and Igoumenitsa from the major ports in Italy, then transfer to a local ferry to Paxi.

Hellenic Mediterranean Lines (www.hml.gr) has high-season (late June to August) connections a few times a week between Brindisi and Paxi (from €50, 10 hours). **SNAV** (www.snav.it) operates a high-speed catamaran between Brindisi and Paxi (€90 or €140 depending on date of travel, 4¾ hours), via Corfu, daily from July to early September. See Paxos Magic Holidays (opposite) in Gaïos for information.

HYDROFOIL

Popular passenger-only hydrofoils link Corfu and Paxi (and occasionally Igoumenitsa) from May until mid-October. There are one to two services daily (four on Mondays), between Corfu and Paxi (€14.90, one hour) and one service weekly from Igoumenitsa to Paxi (€13.40, 45 minutes).

For detailed information in Paxi contact Paxos Magic Holidays (opposite), Bouas Tours (left), or Petrakis Lines (p439) in Corfu.

Getting Around

The island's bus links Gaïos and Lakka via Loggos up to four times daily in either direction (€1.50). A taxi from Gaïos to Lakka or Loggos costs around €10; the taxi rank in Gaïos is on the waterfront by the main square.

Daily car hire costs vary between €45 and €90 in high season. Reliable **Alfa Hire** (☎ 26620 32505) in Gaïos offers car rental as does **Fougaros** (☎ 26620 32373). **Rent a Scooter Vassilis** (☎ 26620 32598), opposite the bus stop in Gaïos, has the biggest range of scooters and mopeds on the island, and are particular about driver experience. Many travel agencies offer the option of renting a small boat – this is a great way to access beach coves.

PAXI & ANTIPAXI

0 —————— 2 km
0 —————— 1 mile

To Corfu (10km)

To Igoumenitsa (25km)

South Kerkyra Straits

Lakka
Kastanitha Cave
Loggos
Paxi
Magazia
Fontana
Ortholithos Stack
Gaïos
Panagia Islet
Agios Nikolaos Islet
Bogdanatika
Agrilas Bay
Agrilas
Vellianitatika
Ozias
Trypitos

Mongonisi

Vrika Beach
Voutoumi Beach
Vigia
Agrapidia

IONIAN SEA

Antipaxi

GAÏOS ΓΑΪΟΣ

pop 560

Gaïos, on a sweeping, east-coast bay, is the island's small and well-equipped capital. Its pink, cream and whitewashed buildings line the bay, and the town's main Venetian square, swamped with the inevitable bars and cafés, abuts the waterfront.

The island is cosseted from the open sea by the nearby fortified islet of Agios Nikolaos. Panagia Islet, named after its monastery, lies at the northern entrance to the bay.

The main street (Panagioti Kanga) runs inland from the main square towards the back of town, where you'll find the bus stop. Banks and ATMs are near the square and a new **Internet café** (per hr €4; 11am-2pm & 6-11pm) is behind.

There's no tourist office, but the welcoming and helpful staff at **Paxos Magic Holidays** (26620 32269; www.paxosmagic.com) will happily direct you. They organise island excursions, including round-the-island boating trips and walks.

The **Cultural Museum** (admission €2; 10am-2.30pm & 6.30-11pm) in a former school on the southern waterfront, has an eclectic collection of local historical artefacts, including a 17th-century sex aid.

Sleeping

Thekli Studios (Clara Studios; 26620 32313; d €65;) It's hard to know what's more delightful, the cheery owner Thekli or her immaculate and well-equipped studios. Centrally located upstairs behind the creperie and overlooking the village and sea, this is a great base. Thekli is a fisher diver, so you might even score a trip in her boat. Call ahead and she'll meet you at the port.

Paxos Beach Hotel (26620 32211; www .paxosbeachhotel.gr; s/d/tr incl breakfast & dinner from €87/122/159;) The bungalows on this hillside complex, 1.5km south of Gaïos, are set a lobster claw apart, but they sprawl down to the sea in a pretty setting, and have tastefully furnished rooms and all the electronic trimmings. There's a private jetty, tennis court, beach, bar and restaurant.

San Giorgio Apartments (26620 32223; d €60-70) Pink, blue and white are the dated colours of these bright and airy rooms. But they're spotless, and boast all the necessary facilities. Located up signposted steps when heading towards town from the port by the lower (pedestrian) harbour road.

Eating

Taverna Vasilis (26620 32596; mains €6-14) Ignore the decorative plastic flowers and the international flag arrangement, this eatery has a seriously tasteful menu, ranging from soups to octopus. Go with the flow of the locals – try the lamb's intestines. To sweeten you up as you request the bill, the waiters may give you, on the house, delicious *loukoumades*, small donuts in a sticky syrup.

Capriccio Café Creperie (26620 32687; crepes €3-5; breakfast-late) A good place if you're 'moussaka'd out' or on a tight budget. For a filling experience head past the museum to this creperie. Tables are in a tranquil setting under large brollies near the seafront. It keeps long hours.

Taka Taka (26620 32329; mains €8-12) For a fishy experience of a positive kind, head to this upmarket place up behind the main square. The restaurant's name means 'immediately, immediately' and indeed, the fish (€20 to €50 per kg) are so fresh they might as well have swum their way there on demand.

Self-catering supplies can be found at the supermarket next door to Café Kalimera Espresso Bar (friendly owner Spyros serves excellent coffee), just west of the central square. A few doors from Café Italiano on the waterfront is an excellent bakery which serves Paxiot delights.

LOGGOS ΛΟΓΓΟΣ

Loggos is 5km north of Gaïos. The hub of this small fishing village is the intimate quay which is lined with chic bars and restaurants, and at one end, an old abandoned factory. It has a steep lush backdrop and some wonderful coves and pebble beaches nearby. **Café Bar Four Seasons** (per hr €5.50) has Internet facilities.

Sleeping & Eating

Arthur House (26620 31330; d €65, apt €95) While the name implies an English-style villa, these modest but spotless studios are above the owner's house, in the more local part of town, (a two-minute walk from the waterfront) and are the most reasonable deal around. Julia's boat and bike hire is part of the family deal.

Vasilis (☎ 26620 31587; mains €8-14) An in-house 'newspaper' is the menu cover at this classy terracotta-coloured family-run restaurant. It's been running since 1956 and current owner Kosta has the welcome mat out in a big way. Suckling pork is a speciality.

I Gonia (☎ 26620 31060; mains €5-12) Many locals recommend this no-frills joint for authentic, good-value grills.

Chill out over a juice (mega-cocktail) sundowner at the friendly and upbeat Roxy Bar, with a crowd and music to match. Move with your mood between the myriad of terraces. Next door, To Taxidi caters to a more bohemian crowd; the accordion-playing waiter gives impromptu performances.

LAKKA ΛΑΚΚΑ

The picturesque harbour of Lakka lies at the end of an almost circular bay on the north coast. It's a yachties' haven, with good bars and restaurants. There are a couple of decent beaches around either side of the bay's headland, including Harami Beach, and several pleasant walks.

Routsis Holidays (☎ 26620 31807; www.forthnet .gr/routsis-holidays) and **Planos Holidays** (☎ 02662 31744 okabis@itebet.gr) are helpful agencies responsible for well-appointed apartments and villas for all budgets.

Routsis will accommodate people for shorter-term stays at **Lefkothea** (d without bathroom €29) Don't do the white glove test on the communal kitchen and bathroom of this centrally located hotel-come-hostel, but the rooms themselves are clean and it's cheap and central.

Devour the lot at **La Bocca** (☎ 26620 31991; mains €7-15), an Italian restaurant serving tasty dishes in a tasteful setting, but with spicy prices. Savour your visit under the vine-covered patio or on the bar terrace sofas. Situated at the far end of the quay next to the renovated school house.

The best outlook for a drink is **Akis Bar** (☎ 26620 31665; snacks €4.50-10 & mains €9-17; 🖳). It has a pool table and Internet access (€7.50 per hour).

Tradition pervades the kafeneion on the small square near the car park, where the ancient owner still serves drinks. The old haunt's regular clients are as distinctive as its bare floors, faded prints and dusty bottles.

ANTIPAXI ΑΝΤΙΠΑΞΟΙ

pop 50

The diminutive satellite island of Antipaxi, 2km south of Paxi, is covered with grape vines, olives and small hamlets. Caïques and tourist boats run daily from Gaïos and Lakka, and pull in at two beach coves, the gently sandy **Vrika Beach** and the pretty, pebbly **Voutoumi Beach**. The water has dazzling clarity.

An inland path links the two beaches or energetic visitors can walk up to the scattered settlement of **Vigla**, or as far as the lighthouse at its southernmost tip (refer to the Bleasdale map and take plenty of water). Voutoumi Beach has one eatery; Vrika Beach has two:

Vrika Taverna (☎ 26620 31141; Vrika Beach; mains €5-10) Half-owner George declares you 'guests in his house' – you have free use of beach umbrellas and sunbeds and can drip on the shaded taverna terrace consuming tasty grilled and oven dishes.

Accommodation in a fully equipped villa for up to six people can be arranged through Spiros at nearby **Spiros Taverna** (☎ 26620 31172). Best done in advance.

Boats (€6 return) to Antipaxi leave Gaïos at 10am and return around 5.30pm.

LEFKADA ΛΕΥΚΑΔΑ

pop 22,500

Lefkada, also referred to as Lefkas, is the fourth-largest island in the Ionians. Joined to the mainland by a narrow isthmus until the occupying Corinthians dug a canal in the 8th century BC, its 25m strait is now spanned by a causeway.

Lefkada's mountainous peaks top 1000m and the island's fertile fields feature olive groves, vineyards, fir and pine forests. There are 10 satellite islets off the heavily developed east coast, and the less populated west coast boasts spectacular beaches.

Once a very poor island, Lefkada's beauty is also in its people, who display intense pride in their island. Many of the older women still wear traditional dress.

Getting There & Away

AIR

Lefkada has no airport, but the airport near Preveza (Aktion) on the mainland is about 20km away. There are daily flights between Athens and Preveza (€73.90), and flights three times a week to Corfu (€35) and Kefallonia (€30). Contact **Olympic Airlines** (☎ 26450 22881; Filippa Panagou 10, Lefkada Town) for bookings and information.

BUS
Departing Lefkada Town's **KTEL bus station** (☎ 26450 22364; Golemi), on the main waterfront road, are buses to Athens (€24.70, 5½ hours, four or five daily), Patra (€11.90, three hours, two weekly), Thessaloniki (€30.30, eight hours, one to two weekly) and Preveza (€2.30, 30 minutes, six daily).

FERRY
Four Islands Ferries runs a useful daily ferry service that sails to a complex and ever-changing schedule between Nydri (Lefkada), Frikes (Ithaki), Fiskardo (Kefallonia) and Vasiliki (Lefkada). Information and tickets can be obtained from **Borsalino Travel** (☎ 26450 92528) in Nydri and **Samba Tours** (☎ 26450 31520) in Vasiliki. Nydri to Frikes costs €5 and takes 1½ hours. Sailing from Nydri to Fiskardo (€6) takes 2½ hours as the ferry goes via Frikes; Vasiliki to Fiskardo (€6, one hour) is a direct route.

Getting Around
There's no reliable bus connection between Lefkada and Aktion airport, near Preveza. Taxis are costly (around €35); a cheaper option is to take a taxi to Preveza and then a bus to Lefkada.

From Lefkada Town, frequent buses ply the east coast, with up to 20 services daily to Nydri and Vlyho in high season, and five daily to Vasiliki. There are seven buses per day to Agios Nikitas, and two limited high-season services to Kalamitsi and Athani. There are seven daily services to the inland village of Karya. Other villages are served by one or two buses daily. Sunday services are reduced.

Car hire starts at €35 per day, depending on season and model. Cars can be hired from reliable **Europcar** (☎ 26450 22538; Panagou 16, Lefkada Town) or **Aris** (☎ 26450 22027; Iroon Politechniou 32). Rent a bike or moped from **Santas Motorcycle Rental** (☎ 26450 25250), next to the Ionian Star Hotel. There are countless car- and bike-rental companies in Nydri.

LEFKADA TOWN
pop 6900
The island's main town is built on a promontory at the southeastern corner of a salty lagoon. Earthquakes are a constant threat here and the town was devastated by one in 1948 (but unaffected in 1953), only to be rebuilt in a distinctively quake-proof and attractive style with upper floors in painted corrugated iron.

The town has a relaxed feel, with a vibrant main thoroughfare, a pleasant plaza and exquisite churches with separate bell towers to withstand seismic activity. The yachting crowd is serviced by a smart new marina.

Orientation & Information
The town's vibrant main pedestrian strip, Dorpfeld, starts south of the causeway at Hotel Nirikos. The street is named after 19th-century archaeologist Wilhelm Dorpfeld, who postulated that Lefkada, not Ithaki, was the home of Odysseus. Dorpfeld leads to Plateia Agiou Spyridonos, the main square, and continues with a different name, Ioannou Mela, which is lined with modern shops and cafés. Banks with ATMs and the post office are on Ioannou Mela. There's no tourist office. The bus station is on the southern waterfront.

Internet Cafezinho near the bus station offers OK Internet access (and great coffee), and **Internet Café** (Koutroubi), just off 8th Merarchias, offers high-tech access. It's a few minutes' walk southwest of the bus station.

Sights
Housed in the modern Cultural Centre at the western end of Agelou Sikelianou is the **Archaeological Museum** (☎ 26450 21635; admission €2; ☼ 8.30am-3pm Tue-Sun). It has a well-displayed and well-labelled collection of artefacts spanning the Palaeolithic Age to the Late Roman periods found on the island. The prize exhibit is a 6th-century-BC terracotta figurine of dancing nymphs.

Works by icon painters from the Ionian school and Russia dating back to 1500 are displayed in an impressive **collection of post-Byzantine icons** (☎ 26450 22502; Rontogianni; admission free; ☼ 8.30am-1.30pm Tue-Sat, 6-8.15pm Tue & Thu). It's in a classical building and also houses the public library off Ioannou Mela.

The 14th-century Venetian **Fortress of Agia Mavra** (☼ 9am-1.30pm Mon, 8.30am-1pm Tue-Sun) is

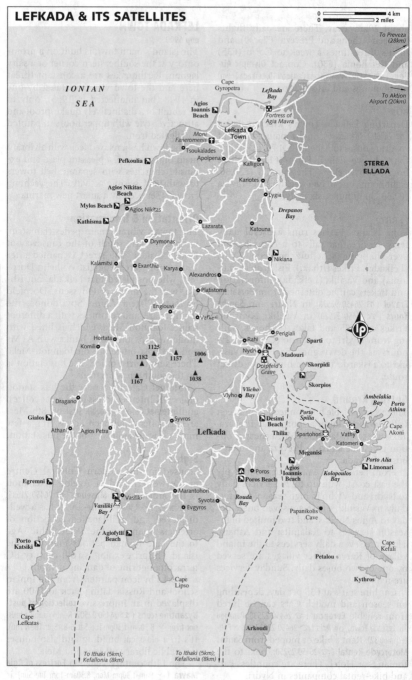

LEFKADA & ITS SATELLITES

0 — 4 km
0 — 2 miles

IONIAN SEA

To Preveza (28km)

Cape Gyropetra

Lefkada Bay

To Aktion Airport (20km)

Agios Ioannis Beach

Fortress of Agia Mavra

Moni Faneromenis

Lefkada Town

Tsoukalades
Apolpena

Kalligoni

STEREA ELLADA

Pefkoulia

Kariotes

Lygia

Agios Nikitas Beach

Drepanos Bay

Mylos Beach

Agios Nikitas

Kathisma

Lazarata

Katouna

Drymonas

Nikiana

Kalamitsi

Exanthia

Karya

Alexandros

Platistoma

Englouvi

Vafkeri

Rahi

Perigiali

Sparti

Hortata

Komili

1125

1157

1006

Nydri

Madouri

Skorpidi

1182

1167

1038

Dorpfeld's Grave

Skorpios

Vlyho

Vlicho Bay

Ambelakia Bay

Porto Athina

Dragano

Gialos

Syvros

Lefkada

Desimi Beach

Thilia

Porto Spilia

Spartohori

Vathy

Cape Akoni

Athani

Agios Petra

Katomeri

Meganisi

Porto Alia

Egremni

Poros
Poros Beach

Agios Ioannis Beach

Kolopoulos Bay

Limonari

Vasiliki

Marantohori

Syvota

Evgyros

Rouda Bay

Papanikolis Cave

Vasiliki Bay

Agiofylli Beach

Porto Katsiki

Cape Lipso

Cape Kefali

Petalou

Kythros

Cape Lefkatas

To Ithaki (5km); Kefallonia (8km)

To Ithaki (5km); Kefallonia (8km)

Arkoudi

IONIAN ISLANDS

immediately across the causeway. It was first established by the crusaders but the remains mainly date from the Venetian and Turkish occupations of the island. **Moni Faneromenis**, 3km west of town, was founded in 1634, destroyed by fire in 1886 and later rebuilt. The views of the lagoon and town are worth the ascent.

In the old town, look out for the attractive churches, with their separate iron **bell towers**.

Sleeping

Pension Pirofani (☎ 26450 25844; Dorpfeld; d/tr €67/80; ✷) Well-appointed, great-value rooms with all the trimmings, decent-sized super-hygienic bathrooms and a delightful owner. The balconies overlooking Dorpfeld are fun for crowd-watching, but rooms at the back will ensure a better night's kip.

Hotel Santa Maura (☎ 26450 21308; s/d/tr incl breakfast €50/72/86; ✷) Opposite Pension Pirofani is this bright and breezy place. The large immaculate rooms ooze character, but don't expect the single-glazed windows to muffle the street noise. Take your key with you at night – or it gets left on the front desk for your access on return. The entrance is on a side street just off Dorpfeld

Hotel Ianos (☎ 25450 22217; ianoshotel@altecnet.gr; Lefkada Marina; s/d/tr €80/100/120; ✷ ✹) Sail into this brand new, funky pad on the marina. With multi-shaped coloured sofas in the lobby, contemporary nautical-style corridors and Inca sun mirrors in each room, the modern and eclectic interiors provide a comfortable option, away from the town centre.

Eating

La Vinaria Taverna (☎ 26450 22910; S Vladi; mains €4-12) Don't get a shock when you see the owner/chef with a cigarette butt hanging from his bottom lip (it's unlit, he's trying to kick the smoking habit); his culinary skills – especially grills – are more savoury.

Mentioned because they'd be obvious by their absence are the pleasant, but over-hyped, **Regantos** (☎ 26450 22855; Vergioti 17; mains €5-12) and the **Lighthouse** (☎ 26450 25117; Filarmonikis 14; mains €5-12).

Stylish bars and cafés line the western side of the waterfront; **Il Posto** (Dorpfeld), at the start of Dorpfeld, is the place to see and be seen. Good people-watching spots are

also along Plateia Agiou Spyridonos. The marina offers alternative options for a more tranquil sundowner.

Self-caterers can pick up supplies from the **supermarket** (Golemi) next to the bus station or from the well-stocked **bakery** (Ioannou Mela 182).

NYDRI & SURROUNDS
ΝΥΔΡΙ & ΠΕΡΙΧΩΡΑ

Visitors either love or hate Nydri; it's a miniature Brighton with better weather. The main strip resembles neither a fishing village (which it was) nor summer town (which it's meant to be); it's a long strip of predominantly tourist and souvenir shops. The more pleasant quay is lined with eateries. Venture inland from the main drag, however, and you enter an oasis.

Nydri is the gateway to the islets of **Madouri**, **Sparti**, **Skorpidi** and **Skorpios**, plus **Meganisi**. Numerous excursions go to Meganisi and stop for a swim near Skorpios (€15 to €20) and some visit Ithaki and Kefallonia as well. To go it alone hire a motorboat from **Trident** (☎ 26450 92978) on the main drag. Helpful **Borsalino Travel** (☎ 26450 92528) on the main street can organise the travel gamut.

The privately owned islet of Madouri, where the Greek poet Aristotelis Valaoritis (1824–79) spent his last 10 years, is off limits. So too is Skorpios, where members of the Onassis family are buried in a cemetery, but cruise boats pause for a swim stop, off a sandy beach on the northern side of the island.

For immediate respite from the town's hustle and bustle, visit the **waterfalls**, 3km out of town (and another 400m past the tavern). The lovely walk follows a path through a ravine, but be careful of the slippery rocks as you reach the water.

Syvota, 15km south of Nydri, has been discovered by yachties, judging by the number of boats and 'showers here' signs; they've caught wind of the delights of this small harbour, a less hectic minor sibling of Vasiliki (p452).

Thankfully, that isn't to the detriment of the local fishermen, who anchor at harbour and fix their brightly coloured nets. It's a tranquil option for a base although you'd need transport to explore and there's no beach to speak of.

IONIAN ISLANDS

Sleeping & Eating

There are loads of rooms and studios in and around Nydri, though many are well and truly 'packaged up' by tour operators.

Gorgona Hotel (☎ 26450 92268; d €65, 4-person apt €75; 🖭) Friendly, family-run place with simple rooms and brand new bathrooms, and set in a lush garden. Push for the more spacious front rooms with a greener outlook than those of the dreary rear rooftops. It's down a side street diagonally opposite the Avis car-rental office.

Poros Beach Camping & Bungalows (☎ 26450 95452; www.porosbeach.com.gr; sites per adult/tent €6.50/4.50, studios €75-95; 🖭) Twelve kilometres south of Nydri is this unpretentious ultra-friendly complex overlooking pretty Poros Beach/Mikros Gialos. Its network of bungalows, studios and camping has a maze of prices to match, plus restaurant, minimarket, bar and swimming pool.

Barrell (☎ 26450 92906; mains €7-15) The owner declares that this is 'more than a Greek kitchen'. His prices are as well. But his long-standing European experience is reflected in high standards of imaginative international cuisine such as sausage with tomato and feta, served in a pan at the table.

In Syvota, ask for the helpful Dina, who can be found at one of the souvenir shops. Her three bright and modern **studios** (☎ 26450 31961, 26450 31567; d €55-60) have balconies perched over the quay with an unimpeded view of the water.

VASILIKI ΒΑΣΙΛΙΚΗ

Two types of people come to Vasiliki: the tanned and toned, and the sedate. Vasiliki is the centre of watersports and considered *the* windsurfing location in Europe, due to distinct thermal winds. But it's not all fast sailing; the winding waterfront, with the eucalyptus and canopy-covered eateries, provides a tranquil environment to relax in, unlike the stony beach strip. Caïques take visitors to the island's better beaches and coves including Agiofylli Beach, south of Vasiliki.

Along the beach numerous windsurfing and sailing (catamaran) companies have staked prominent claims with flags, equipment and their own hotels. They offer all-inclusive tuition and accommodation packages. If they've got spare gear, some will willingly rent it to the independent en-

thusiast for a day or two. Possible choices include **Club Vass** (UK ☎ 01920 484121; www.club vass.com), **Happy Surf** (Germany ☎ 030-3260 1733; www.happy-surf.de) and **Human Sports** (Germany ☎ 0241 69 988; www.human-sports.com). **Trekking Hellas** (☎ 26450 31130; www.trekking.gr) in the main street offers a great range of outdoor activities, from guided treks to sea kayaking, plus hire of ribs (zodiacs).

Sleeping & Eating

Pension Holidays (☎ 26450 31426; d €50; 🖭) Delightful Spiros offers Greek hospitality, breakfast on the balcony with harbour vista, and simply furnished but well-equipped rooms. In a quieter end of town towards the ferry dock.

Vasiliki Bay Hotel (☎ 26450 23567; s/d incl breakfast €50/80; 🖭) If you don't mind being away from the water, you can't go too wrong in this white, light and friendly place, up behind Alexander Restaurant. Prices reduced enormously outside August.

Alexander Restaurant (☎ 26450 31335; mains €5-12) The cats seem to flock to Alexander's more than other places – we like to think it's because of the higher quality seafood and grills – but it could be because of the many (generous) tourists who part with titbits. Good choice…if you're not allergic to feline (nor feline-loving) friends.

WEST COAST & AROUND

Serious beach bods should skip Lefkada's east coast and head straight for the west. The sea here actually lives up to the clichéd brochure spiel; it's an incredible turquoise blue and most beaches are sandy. The best beaches include the long stretches of **Pefkoulia** and **Kathisma** in the north (the latter beach is becoming more developed and there are a few studios for rent here), and remote **Egremni** and breathtaking **Porto Katsiki** in the south. These final two are a long drive south, signposted off the road leading to the island's southwestern promontory. You'll pass roadside stalls set up by locals selling olive oil, honey and wine.

Word is out about the picturesque town of **Agios Nikitas** and people flock to enjoy the holiday village's pleasant – if slightly claustrophic – atmosphere, plus the lovely **Mylos Beach** just around the headland (to walk, take the path by Taverna Poseidon. It's about 15 minutes up and over the peninsula, or for €2 you can take a taxi boat from the tiny Agios Nikitas beach, sea conditions permitting).

The town's accommodation options are plentiful, and include **Hotel Agios Nikitas** (☎ 26450 97460; www.agiosnikitas.com; Agios Nikitas; d incl breakfast €85, 4-person apt €90; ❄), a stylish hotel on the coastal road just north of the village. Tasteful rooms and apartments are in a secluded and tranquil complex of whitewashed buildings, set around a central courtyard, bordered by jasmine and bougainvillea. Both ocean and garden views are available.

Beach bums might like to base themselves at **Panorama** (☎ 26450 33291; d without bathroom €35) in one of the no-frills rooms on top of friendly Thomas' buzzing taverna of the same name. A beer with the views from the taverna terrace are the perfect sunburn cure. If this is full, try **Alex's** (☎ 26450 33484; d without bathroom €30) equally no-frills numbers diagonally opposite.

Further south near the turn-off to Porto Katsiki is **Taverna Oasis** (☎ 26450 33201; mains €6-9), a sprawling outdoor taverna set within an established pine grove. Its standard home-style favourites are said to be the best in the area. The taverna offers free **camping** for those with campervans and tents.

The spectacular central spine of Lefkada, with its traditional farming villages, lush green peaks, fragrant pine trees, olive groves and vines – plus occasional views of the islets – is well worth seeing if you have time and transport. The small village of **Karya** boasts a stunning square set on a massive terrace and surrounded by plane trees, tavernas and snack bars. Karya is famous for its special embroidery, introduced in the 19th century by one-handed local woman, Maria Koutsochero. Visit the **museum** for an interesting display of embroidery paraphernalia and local artifacts.

For food, **Taverna Karamboulias** (☎ 26450 41301; Karya; mains €5-9) is recommended for its meals, including Karsaniki salad, a salad in bread.

For accommodation options ask British Brenda Sherry at **Café Pierros** (☎ 26450 41760; Karya) who can arrange all (as well as a cup of tea and signature toasted sandwich). The island's highest village, **Englouvi**, is only a few kilometres south of Karya.

MEGANISI ΜΕΓΑΝΗΣΙ
pop 1090
Meganisi has the largest population of Lefkada's three inhabited satellite islets. The verdant landscape and deep bays of turquoise water, fringed by pebbled beaches, attract yachties and day visitors. A day trip (at minimum) is obligatory, either independently or on one of the excursion boats from Nydri (p451).

Meganisi has only three settlements: quiet and neat **Spartohori**, with narrow laneways and pretty, bougainvillea-bedecked houses and perched on a plateau above Porto Spilia (where the ferry docks; follow the steep road or steps behind). **Vathy** is the island's second attractive harbour and 800 metres behind it is the village of **Katomeri**. Those with more time up their sleeve can visit remote beaches, such as **Ambelakia**.

Sleeping & Eating
Hotel Meganisi (☎ 26450 51240; Katomeri; d incl breakfast €65; ❄ ❄) The welcoming aroma of Greek cuisine from the hotel kitchen is not the only pleasant aspect of this simple, but modern hotel in Katomeri. The sunny rooms with balconies have expansive outlooks to the country and sea, as does the generous-sized pool and terrace.

Camping is available behind Asteria Taverna near the ferry dock of Porto Spilia, run by **Taverna Salitzo** (☎ 26450 51646; Porto Spilia; sites per person €7). Regina and Christina at the **Twins Bar** (☎ 06450 51161) in Vathy will help travellers find accommodation with locals in the village.

Worthy dining options include **Asteria Taverna** (☎ 26450 51107; mains €4-10), near the ferry dock at Porto Spilia, whose helpful owner Panos Konidaris knows 'the lot' about the island; **Taverna Porto Vathy** (☎ 26450 51125; mains €6-14), a fish taverna perched out on a small quay in Vathy, and **Tropicana** (☎ 26450 51486), in Spartohori, which serves excellent pizzas.

Getting There & Away
The Meganisi ferry boat runs about six times daily between Nydri and Meganisi (€2, 25 to 40 minutes). It calls at Porto Spilia before Vathy (but the first ferry of the day stops at Vathy then Porto Spilia).

A local bus runs five to seven times per day between Spartohori and Vathy (via Katomeri) but it's worth considering bringing a bicycle or moped from Nydri (p451), as there's no rental places on the island.

KEFALLONIA
ΚΕΦΑΛΛΟΝΙΑ

pop 39,500

Kefallonia, the largest of the Ionian Islands, shouldn't be underestimated. It hides secrets below its rugged, towering mountain range: sprawling vineyards, stunning cliffs and beaches and unclassified Roman ruins. The highest point, Mt Enos (1627m), lays claim to the fir forest species, *Abies cephalonica*. Kefallonia was devastated in the 1953 earthquake so although much of the island's architectural aesthetics are modern, there's still plenty to occupy the traveller, including beautiful harbours, walking trails and the local cuisine.

Kefallonia's capital is Argostoli, the main port is Sami and ferry services also run from Fiskardo and Poros.

Getting There & Away

AIR

There are at least two daily flights between Kefallonia and Athens (€75), and connections to other Ionian Islands, including Zakynthos (€28) and Corfu (€35). **Olympic Airlines** (☎ 26710 28808; Rokou Vergoti 1, Argostoli) can help with information and bookings.

BUS

There are four daily buses connecting Athens and Kefallonia (via Patra) utilising the various ferry services (to/from Argostoli, Sami and Poros) to the mainland. All cost around €30 and take around seven hours (prices include ferry tickets). For information contact the **KTEL bus station** (☎ 26710 22276; Ioannou Metaxa) on the southern waterfront in Argostoli. The office also produces an excellent printed schedule.

FERRY
Domestic

There are frequent ferry services to Kyllini in the Peloponnese from both Poros (€7.40, 1½ hours, two to three daily) and Argostoli (€11.70, 2½ hours, one daily). One ferry goes from Sami to Astakos via Piso Aetos (€7.50, 3¾ hours) and Sami to Astakos direct (€7.50; 2½ hours) on alternate days.

Strintzis Lines (www.ferries.gr/strintzis) has two ferries daily connecting Sami with Patra

(€15.40, 2½ hours) and Vathy (€5.10) or Piso Aetos (€3.30, 45 minutes) on Ithaki.

Four Islands Ferries runs a daily ferry in the high season linking Sami with Piso Aetos (€2, 35 minutes). The same company operates a useful daily ferry service that sails to a complex, ever-changing schedule between Nydri (Lefkada), Frikes (Ithaki), Fiskardo (Kefallonia) and Vasiliki (Lefkada). Sailing from Fiskardo to Frikes (€3.20) takes just under an hour; Fiskardo–Vasiliki (€6) takes one hour; Fiskardo–Nydri (€6) takes 1½ hours direct, or 2½ hours via Frikes. Information and tickets for these routes can be obtained from **Blue Sea Travel** (☎ 26740 23007; www.samistar.com; Sami) and **Nautilus Travel** (☎ 26740 41440; Fiskardo).

From Pesada in the south there are two high-season services daily travelling to Agios Nikolaos (€4, 1¼ hours), on the northern tip of Zakynthos. There's two daily buses (in high season only and except Sundays) to the remote port of Pesada, and only two per week from Agios Nikolaos, making crossing without your own transport difficult (and costly if you rely on taxis). Another option is to travel from Argostoli or Poros to Kyllini, then catch a ferry from Kyllini to Zakynthos Town.

International

In the high season there are regular ferries plying the route between Sami, Patra, Igoumenitsa and Brindisi in Italy (Kefallonia–Brindisi costs €52 and takes around 14 hours). To get to other ports in Italy, you need to take the ferry first from Sami to Patra.

Tickets and information can be obtained from **Vassilatos Shipping** (☎ 26710 22618; Ioannou Metaxa 54, Argostoli), opposite the port authority, and from **Blue Sea Travel** (☎ 26740 23007; Sami), on the waterfront.

Getting Around

TO/FROM THE AIRPORT

The airport is 9km south of Argostoli. There's no airport bus service; a taxi costs around €14.

BUS

From Argostoli's **bus station** (☎ 26710 22276) on the southern waterfront there are nine buses daily heading to the Lassi Peninsula (€1), three buses departing for Sami

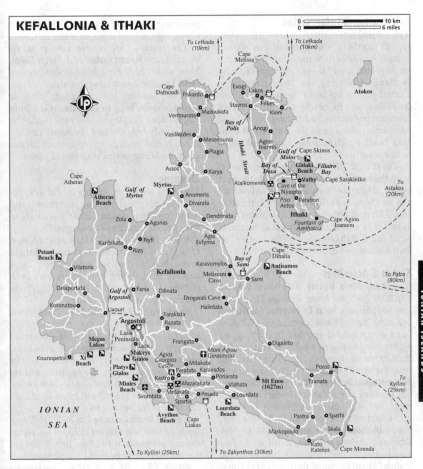

KEFALLONIA & ITHAKI

(map labels)

0 — 10 km
0 — 6 miles

To Lefkada (10km)
To Lefkada (10km)
Cape Melissa
Cape Dafnoudi
Fiskardo
Exogi
Lakos
Atokos
Ventourata
Mazoukata
Stavros
Frikes
Kioni
Vasilikades
Mesovounia
Bay of Polis
Anogi
Agios Ioannis
Gulf of Molos
Cape Skinos
Plagia
Ithaki Strait
Bay of Dexa
Gidaki Beach
Filiatro Bay
Assos
Karya
Alalkomenes
Vathy
Cape Sarakiniko
Cape Atheras
Myrtos
Cave of the Nymphs
To Astakos (20km)
Atheras Beach
Gulf of Myrtos
Anomeria
Piso Aetos
Perahori
Zola
Divarata
Ithaki
Agonas
Dendrinata
Fountain of Arethousa
Cape Agiou Ioannou
Kardakata
Nyfi
Agia Evfymia
Petani Beach
Riza
Kefallonia
Cape Dihalia
Vilatoria
Karavomylos
Bay of Sami
Antisamos Beach
Delaportata
Gulf of Argostoli
Farsa
Melissani Cave
Sami
To Patra (80km)
Koronatou
Dilinata
Lixouri
Drogarati Cave
Haliotata
Faraklata
Razata
Argostoli
Lassi Peninsula
Frangata
Digaleto
Megas Lakos
Lassi
Moni Agiou Gerasimou
Makrys Gialos
Agios Georgios Castle
Mitakata
Poros
Kounopetra
Xi Beach
Platys Gialos
Peratata
Karavados
Poriarata
Vlahata
Tzanata
To Kyllini (25km)
Minies Beach
Kastro
Mazarakata
Metaxata
Pesada
Lourdata
▲ Mt Enos (1627m)
Svorotata
Spartia
Lourdata Beach
Pastra
Spathi
IONIAN SEA
Avythos Beach
Cape Liakas
Markopoulo
Skala
To Kyllini (25km)
To Zakynthos (30km)
Kato Katelios
Cape Mounda

(€2.50), two to Poros (€3.50), two to Skala (€3) and two to Fiskardo (€4). There's a daily east-coast service linking Kato Katelios with Skala, Poros, Sami, Agia Evfymia and Fiskardo. No buses operate on Sunday.

CAR & MOTORCYCLE

The major resorts have loads of cars and bike rental joints. Lassi has the best choice around, and worth going if you can get there from Argostoli. In Argostoli, the best place for cars is **Reliable Rent a Car** (☎ 26710 23613; Rokou Vergoti 3). Prices start from €40 per day. Travellers have given the thumbs down to Sunbird for unreliability and broken promises.

FERRY

Car ferries run hourly (more frequently in high season) from 7.30am to 10.30pm between Argostoli and Lixouri, on the island's western peninsula. The journey takes 30 minutes, and tickets cost €1.30/3.60/1 per person/car/motorbike.

ARGOSTOLI ΑΡΓΟΣΤΟΛΙ
pop 8900

Argostoli was not rebuilt to its former Venetian splendour after the 1953 earthquake but it's a pleasant and lively place, and offers plentiful sleeping and eating options, plus shopping and nightlife. It has an authentic Greek feel and the whole town seems to gather in the evenings in the central plaza.

Orientation & Information

The main ferry quay is at the waterfront's northern end and the bus station is on the southern waterfront. The centre of Argostoli's social and culinary activity is Plateia Vallianou, the large palm-treed central square up from the waterfront off 21 Maïou, and its nearby surrounds. Other hubs are pedestrianised Lithostrotou, lined with smart shops, and the waterfront (Antoni Tristi, which becomes Ioannou Metaxa to the south).

The **EOT** (☎ 26710 22248; ⏰ 8am-2.30pm Mon-Fri) is on the northern waterfront beside the port police. There are banks with ATMs along the northern waterfront and on Lithostrotou. The post office is on Lithostrotou, and Internet is available at **Excelixis** (Minoos; per hr €2.50) and at **Web Café** (Plateia Vallianou; per hr €2.50) in the square's northeast corner.

Sights & Activities

The **Korgialenio History & Folklore Museum** (☎ 26710 28835; Ilia Zervou; admission €3; ⏰ 9am-2pm Mon-Sat) and **Focas-Kosmetatos Foundation** (☎ 26710 26595; Vallianou; admission €3; ⏰ 9.30am-1pm & 7-10pm Mon-Sat) provide interesting insights into Argostoli's cultural history, the former more general, the latter delving into the world of the nobility. The town's **Archaeological Museum** (☎ 26710 28300; Rokou Vergoti; admission €3; ⏰ 8.30am-3pm Tue-Sun) has a well displayed and labelled collection of island relics, including Mycenaean finds. The one-room **Divisione Acqui Museum** (☎ 69457 76294; Lithostratou; admission free), just south of Andrea Hoïda, details the disturbing history of the Italian 'Acqui Division' during their occupation of Kefallonia (and their slaughter by the Germans). Has irregular opening hours.

KTEL (☎ 26710 23364) runs excellent-value day tours (priced between €15 and €35) of Kefallonia, visiting several towns and villages around the island (including a Folkloric tour to monasteries), as well as tours to other islands (Ithaca and Zakynthos). Bookings can be made at the KTEL bus station building. Popular day-long **glass-bottom boat trips** (☎ 26710 23956) leave daily from just south of Argostoli's port (€50/35 adult/child, including beach barbecue lunch). Six kilometres from Argostoli in Davgata is the recently opened **Museum of Natural History** (☎ 26710 84400; admission €2.50; ⏰ 9am-3pm) with fascinating exhibits on the geological and natural

phenomenon of the island and an excellent topographical model of the island in relief.

The town's closest and largest sandy beaches are **Makrys Gialos** and **Platys Gialos**, 5km south in the package-resort area of **Lassi**. Regular buses serve the area.

Those wanting sun and sand, but little action, should head to **Lourdata**, 16km from Argostoli on the Argostoli–Poros road. The long, sandy beach offers the usual perks – sunbeds and brollies – plus a mountainous green backdrop dotted with pencil pines.

Sleeping

There's a string of shampoo-and-sewing-kit-style hotels along the waterfront and many options around Plateia Vallianou, with prices to suit most budgets.

Kyknos Studios (☎ 26710 23398; M Geroulanou 4; d €45) An historic well sits in front of these seven bright studios, surrounded by a creative garden with sunflowers and swan statues. The real charm is the delightfully relaxed and welcoming owner.

Hotel Ionian Plaza (☎ 26710 25581; Plateia Vallianou; s/d €54/78; ❄) It may be Argostoli's smartest hotel with a marble-decorated lobby, stylish public areas and well-appointed rooms with balconies, but it doesn't cater well to non-smokers. Those with a nose that knows, should first check their room, plus the double-glazed windows: keen ears can hear plaza noise, too.

Argostoli Beach Camping (☎ 26710 23487; www.argostolibeach.gr; sites adult/tent €6/3.50) This pleasant camping spot is near the lighthouse on the northernmost point of the peninsula.

Vivian Villa (☎ 26710 23396; www.kefalonia-vivianvilla.gr; Deladetsima 9; r/studio €60/65; ❄) Recommended for its bright rooms and owners. Prices are discounted for longer stays.

Thomatos Apartments (☎ 26710 31656; criti thomatos@yahoo.com; Lourdata; apt €90) The cleanliness of these brand spanking new, clean and white apartments rivals a hospital operating theatre…except they're far more appealing and have a better outlook; they face onto the beach. Based in Lourdata, 16km from Argostoli, these are a great place to feel anaesthetised.

Eating & Drinking

Givras Brothers (☎ 26710 24259; Vasili Vandorou 1; mains €4-8) A favourite old haunt of locals, this is one of Argostoli's most original and traditional

ARGOSTOLI

0 .... 200 m
0 .... 0.1 miles

INFORMATION
EOT...............................**1** B1
Excelixis.........................**2** B2
Port Police......................**3** B1
Post Office......................**4** B3
Web Café........................**5** B2

SIGHTS & ACTIVITIES
Archaeological Museum.........**6** B2
Divisione Acqui Museum.......**7** B3
Focas-Kosmetatos Foundation.....**8** B2
Glass-bottom Boat Trips.......**9** B2
Korgialenio History & Folklore
    Museum......................**10** B2

SLEEPING
Hotel Ionian Plaza.............**11** B2
Kyknos Studios.................**12** B1
Vivian Villa...................**13** A1

EATING
El Greco.........................**14** B2
Givras Brothers................**15** C3
Produce Market................**16** C3
Souvlatzidiko..................**17** B2

DRINKING
Polo Central Café..............**18** B2

ENTERTAINMENT
Cine Anny......................**19** A1

TRANSPORT
Ferries to Kyllini.............**20** B1
Ferries to Lixouri.............**21** B1
KTEL Bus Station..............**22** C4
Olympic Airlines...............**23** B2
Reliable Rent a Car...........**24** B2
Vassilatos Shipping............**25** B1

IONIAN ISLANDS

family run restaurants. Small, simple and it serves up a daily range of dishes, cooked by the owner himself. Basic rooms (double with bathroom €25) are available.

El Greco (☎ 26710 24449; Kalypsous Vergoti 3; mains €4.50-9) Despite the name, the restaurant's largely Italian menu features pizzas and seafood (not by the kilo – check how fresh it is) plus an excellent vegetarian and children's menu. There's a pretty garden out the back.

Hersona's Taverna (☎ 26710 69940; mains €3-9) A statue of two giant rams locked in battle signify that you've arrived at this carnivore's dream, 8km from Argostoli in the village of Troianata. The farmer-restaurateur's collection of cow bells and fresh carcasses hang on display in the kitchen from which

come superlative lamb *klefyiko* (baked meat in a tomato, onion, herb and garlic sauce) and chops. Wash it down with homemade wine on the outside balcony.

Among the pricey cafés on Plateia Vallianou is the popular **Souvlatzidiko** (gyros €1.50), next to Hotel Aeon, offering quick and tasty treats. You can pick up a range of self-catering supplies from the huge waterfront produce market and bakeries and supermarket opposite.

Entertainment
Plateia Vallianou is a barfly's delight with both crowds and music upbeat until late. The cool crowd people chill at Polo Central Café.

The outdoor cinema **Cine Anny** (☎ 26710 25880; Pan Harokopou 54) shows films between June and August (€7).

SAMI & SURROUNDS ΣΑΜΗ

pop 2290

Sami, 25km northeast of Argostoli and the main port of Kefallonia, was also flattened by the 1953 earthquake. Its exposed long concrete strip is made up of tourist-oriented cafés, but beyond this it's an attractive place, nestled in a bay and flanked by steep hills. The town is best known as the filming location of *Captain Corelli's Mandolin* (it was, in fact, a cleverly constructed set on the outskirts of town), but after the inevitable tourist rush, the fuss has now died down, save for the predictably named cafés. Sami is worthy of a stopover, if only as a base to visit the nearby caves, beaches or Ithaki on a day cruise. All facilities, including a post office and banks, are in town. Buses for Argostoli usually meet ferries.

Sights & Activities

Don't miss **Antisamos Beach**, 4km northeast of Sami. The long, stony beach is in a lovely green setting backed by hills. The drive here is also a highlight, offering dramatic views from cliff edges.

Most people rave about **Melissani Cave** (admission incl boat trip €5; ☼ 8am-8pm), a subterranean sea-water lake that turns an extraordinary blue when the sun is overhead; a visit at any other time is merely an expensive row in a boat in a dark and dank grotto. It is well-signposted and situated 2.5km from Sami. **Drogarati Cave** (☎ 26740 22950; admission €3.50; ☼ 8am-8pm) is the spot to view stalactites; concerts are held in its large (natural) chamber.

Sleeping & Eating

Akrogiali Rooms (☎ 26740 22494; Sami; d €55, 4-person apt €90) The pick of the bunch – new, clean and spacious apartments in the peaceful end of town, 400 metres past Hotel Kastro. Filalithis and his delightful elderly parents (little English spoken) warmly welcome guests and run the attached taverna, serving the Greek favourites (€5 to €12).

Karavomilos Beach Camping (☎ 26740 22480; www.camping-karavomilos.gr; sites per adult/tent €6.50/ 5.50; 🖳) A large, green and shady place in a glorious beach-front location, with all the facilities zipped up, too.

Hotel Melissani (☎ 26740 22464; d €60) Sixties-come-seventies, hip, hop and happenin'. Although built in the early '80s, a Maxwell Smart/Austin Powers morph would feel at home here, especially the bar – an eclectic décor of swivelling vinyl bar stools, retro lights, marble floors and groovy tiles. Smallish rooms with balconies have good views of mountains or sea.

Faros (☎ 26740 23041; mains €6.50-16) Claims to be the oldest post-earthquake restaurant. Pot plants provide welcome seclusion to re-energise over a Kefallonian meat pie (€7), stuffed chicken with green pepper and bacon or their signature dish, roasted lamb 'à la faros'.

AGIA EVFYMIA ΑΓΙΑ ΕΥΦΗΜΙΑ

The beautiful and understated fishing village of **Agia Evfymia** is set around a bay 10km north of Sami. En route there are coves ideal for swimming. This is a popular stop for those who love exploring the surrounding country, stumbling across Roman ruins (there's some in the town), and relaxing over a *robola* wine. There are hotels and studios here, as well as motorboat hire and a diving operator.

Friendly Gloria runs the '80s style **Moustakis Hotel** (☎ 26740 61060; www.moustakishotel.com; d incl breakfast €65; 🐾), a homely place whose communal lounge on the upper of a split-level floor gives it a summer ski-lodge feel. Side rooms are quieter with pleasant views.

The **Panorama Taverna** (☎ 26740 41225; mains €5.80-7) is as Greek as Zorba. The mainly local clientele sit on a large, vine-covered terrace, overlooking Ithaki, to consume homemade delights including roast lamb. Head to the north of town on the first promontory.

ASSOS ΑΣΟΣ

Tiny Assos is a gem of whitewashed and pastel houses, straddling the isthmus of a peninsula on which stands a Venetian fortress. Assos was more sensitively restored after the earthquake than other neighbouring towns.

For accommodation, check out the **Pension Gerania** (☎ 26740 51526; www.pensiongerania. gr; d €65; 🐾). The saucer-sized geraniums in this option's lush garden are as appealing as the spotless and well-equipped rooms. Follow the pension (and parking) sign as you enter town.

The sleek and sophisticated new kid in town, **Cosi's Inn** (☎ 26740 51420; www.cosisinn.gr; d €75; ✯), is not 'typically Greek' but a luxurious splurge. Iron beds and sofas, frosted lights and white décor are the marks of the young and hip interior designer owner.

Another favourite for quality and views is **Linardos Studios** (☎ 26740 51563; www.linardos apartments.gr; d €70, 4-person apt €85-95).

Assos's best value taverna, **Assos Restaurant** (☎ 6944 671804; mains €5-12), is set back from the waterfront under yet another vine-covered terrace. Try the veal with lemon sauce.

AROUND ASSOS

One of Greece's most breathtaking beaches can be found at **Myrtos**, 13km south of Assos along the hair-raising stretch of road going north to Fiskardo. Pull over at the designated viewing bay to admire and photograph the white sand and exquisite blue water set between tall limestone cliffs. There are minimal facilities at the beach itself (just a basic taverna and sunbed hire). Be aware that the beach drops off quickly and sharply.

FISKARDO ΦΙΣΚΑΡΔΟ
pop 225
Fiskardo, 50km north of Argostoli, was the only Kefallonian village not devastated by the 1953 earthquake. Framed by cypress-mantled hills and with fine Venetian buildings, it's a delightful, if slightly toy-townish, place. It's a favourite port-o'-call for yachties with attitude. Mr Bush Snr and his entourage are known to have anchored nearby.

The **Fiskardo Nautical and Environmental Club** (☎ 26740 41081; www.fnec.gr) is a not-for-profit organisation that runs a small local museum, environmental information centre and educational programme (up the stairs next to the church), as well as scuba-diving and dolphin-spotting activities. Volunteers are welcome.

Sleeping & Eating
Prices in Fiskardo are as high as a mainsail.
Pama Travel (☎ 26740 41033; www.pamatravel.com) on the harbour front can help with travel services including car and boat hire, plus it has Internet access.

Regina's Rooms (☎ 26740 41125; d €50-60) Friendly Regina runs a popular place with colourful rooms dotted with plastic flowers. Some rooms have kitchenettes and/or bal-

conies enjoying views over the water. The entrance faces onto a car park.

Stella Apartments (☎ 26740 41211; www.stella -apartments.gr; d €50-60, apt €160; ✯) Looking like a Greek, colourful version of Fawlty Towers from the outside, this yellow-and-green complex has immaculate, spacious studios with kitchen, TV, phone, air-con and balcony. It's situated about 800m from the main car park and a cove opposite provides great plunging possibilities.

For a fluffy bathrobe-type experience, spoil yourself at one of two luxury options.
Faros Suites (☎ 26740 41355; www.myrtoscorp .com; ste €100-140; ✯ ✯) Out of Africa comes to Greece. Possibly the most tastefully appointed rooms on the island, with more teak furniture and cream cotton-linen décor than a luxury safari lodge. Swimming pool and several indoor-outdoor relaxation areas.

Emelisse Hotel (☎ 26740 41200; ste from €150; ✯ ✯) Part of the Tsimaras Hotel chain. Simply stated: Greek chic. The design is minimalist with natural stone and wood décors. The hotel's accommodation range and price list are as long as its infinity pool.

Lagoudera (☎ 26740 41275; mains €4-10.50) The only place on the Ionians where you can sit in style with a €2 gyro. It's in a pretty setting just back from the harbour front and serves great grilled meats.

Also recommended for its atmosphere is **Café Tseleniti** (☎ 26740 41344; mains €6-15) housed in a 19th-century building that survived the 1953 earthquake. Be sure to view the fresco on the back wall, drawn by some wishful Greek patriots.

Getting There & Away
You can get to Fiskardo by ferry from Lefkada and Ithaki or by bus from Argostoli. The ferry is at one end of the waterfront; the bus will drop you at the car park behind town, and it's a ten minute walk to the ferry via the waterfront.

ITHAKI ΙΘΑΚΗ

pop 3700
Diminutive Ithaki is a tranquil and unaffected island. It is believed to be the mythical home of Homer's Odyssey, where his loyal wife Penelope patiently awaited his homecoming. It's two large peninsulas – joined by

a narrow isthmus – with sheer cliffs, precipitous mountainous passages and pockets of pine forest, cypresses and olive groves. Beautiful fishing hamlets (tastefully rebuilt after the 1953 earthquake) are nestled around this compact island, as are discreet pebbly coves. Monasteries and churches offer Byzantine delights and splendid views. The locals here are particularly welcoming.

Getting There & Away

Strintzis Lines (www.ferries.gr/strintzis-ferries) has two ferries daily connecting Vathy or Piso Aetos with Patra (€14, four hours), via Sami (€4, one hour) on Kefalonia.

Four Islands Ferries runs a daily ferry in the high season between Piso Aetos, Sami and Astakos on the mainland (€7, 2¾ hours direct from Piso Aetos to Astakos, four hours from Astakos to Piso Aetos via Sami). It also operates a useful daily ferry service that sails to a complex, ever-changing schedule between Nydri (Lefkada), Frikes (Ithaki), Fiskardo (Kefallonia) and Vasiliki (Lefkada). Sailing from Frikes to Fiskardo (€3.20) takes just under an hour; Frikes–Vasiliki (€6) goes via Fiskardo and takes two hours; Nydri–Frikes (one direction only) costs €5 and takes 1½ hours. Information and tickets for these routes can be obtained from Delas Tours (right) on the main square in Vathy.

Getting Around

Piso Aetos, on Ithaki's west coast, has no settlement; taxis often meet boats as does the municipal bus in high season only. The island's one bus runs twice daily (weekdays only) between Kioni and Vathy via Stavros and Frikes (€3.50). It's primarily a school bus so its limited schedule is not well suited to day trippers. Taxis are expensive (€25 for the Vathy–Frikes trip), so your best bet is to hire a moped or car (or a motorboat) to get around. In Vathy, **Rent a Scooter** (☎ 26740 32840) is down the laneway opposite the port authority, and Happy Cars lives up to its name – contact Polyctor Tours (right) on the plaza.

VATHY ΒΑΘΥ

pop 1820

Old mansions rise up from the elongated seafront of Vathy, Ithaki's main town. An attractive large square forms the social hub of the centre, otherwise made up of several twisting streets, cafés, restaurants and compact museums.

The ferry quay is on the western side of the bay. To reach the central square of Plateia Efstathiou Drakouli, turn left and follow the waterfront.

Ithaki has no tourist office, but the professional **Polyctor Tours** (☎ 26740 33120; www .ithakiholidays.com) and knowledgeable Stavros at **Delas Tours** (☎ 26740 32104; www.ithaca.com.gr), both on the main square, can help with tourist information. Banks with ATMs and the post office are also on the main square. Internet access is available at **Net** (per hr €4) on the main square.

Sights & Activities

Behind Hotel Mentor is an excellent **archaeological museum** (☎ 26740 32200; admission free; ⊙ 8.30am-3pm Tue-Sun). The informative **nautical & folklore museum** (admission €1; ⊙ 10am-2pm & 5-9pm Tue-Sat) is housed in an old generating station just back from the waterfront (signposted), and displays traditional clothing, household items and furniture, and shipping paraphernalia.

Boat excursions leave from Vathy harbour in the summer months and include day trips around Ithaki and to Fiskardo (€30); Lefkada (€30); and 'unknown islands' which include Atokos and Kalamos (€35). There's also a taxi boat to **Gidaki Beach**, inaccessible by road. **Walking** is a great way to explore Ithaki and Homeric sites, and keen walkers will not be disappointed – visit Stavros at Delas Tours (above); he is intending to publish a book of walking trails and willingly shares his routes and materials.

Sleeping

If you don't need a sea view, net a position in these nameless **apartments** (☎ 26740 32055; d €60-65; 🅿) run by Polly Servos that border onto the town's luminescent green soccer pitch. The clean and spacious living areas face onto distant hills and villages. Head east and turn right past Hotel Mentor and then left at the church. Continue for approximately 100m and look for the 'Apartments' sign on right.

Hotel Omirikon (☎ 26740 33596; www.omirikon hotel.com; d/tr €110/120; 🅿) The guests' Jacuzzi in the front is not the only sophisticated aspect of this small hotel on the eastern waterfront, about 10 minutes walk from

ODYSSEUS & ITHAKI

Ithaki has long been identified as the home of the mythical hero Odysseus (Ulysses); it was the island home he left to fight in the Trojan War. According to Homer's *The Iliad*, and more specifically *The Odyssey*, the hero Odysseus took 10 long years to return home to Ithaki from Troy on the Asia Minor coast.

Odysseus survived tempestuous seas, sea monsters and a cunning siren until finally, he was helped by friendly Phaeacians and Odysseus was returned to Ithaki. Here, disguised as a beggar he, along with his son Telemachus and his old swineherd Eumaeus, slayed the conniving suitors who'd been trying to woo Penelope, Odysseus' long-suffering wife who'd waited 20 years for him to return.

No mention of Ithaki appears in writings of the Middle Ages. As late as 1504 the island was almost uninhabited following repeated depredations by pirates so the Venetians induced settlers from neighbouring islands to repopulate it. Yet the island appears to be described in *The Odyssey*; it matches in many respects the physical nature of the island today. These sites include the 'Fountain of Arethousa' and the 'Cave of the Nymphs'. However, many Homerists have been hard-pressed to ascribe other locales described in *The Odyssey* – particularly Odysseus' castle – to actual places on the islands since scant archaeological remains assist the researcher.

the centre of town. The place is home to high-quality studio apartments, each with a distinct blue and green modern décor, plus a balcony overlooking the water.

Hotel Perantzada (☎ 26740 33496; perantzada@ arthotel.gr; Odissea Androutsou; d €118; ❄ ▯) A young Swiss banker-type crowd frequents this boutique number which must be given full marks for originality. Each room in this light-blue, neoclassical building (designed by 19th-century German architect Ernst Schiller) has been individually decorated with Italian-style flair and fabrics, including contemporary nautical and botanic themes. Highly tasteful or utterly pretentious, depending on your slant.

Eating

Eating at the restaurants along the western waterfront is a Ground Hog Day experience; identical menus in similar settings on the same patch. For a more distinct culinary sensation, head east 1km from town.

Gregory's Taverna/Paliocaravo (☎ 26740 32573; www.paliocaravo.sphosting.com; mains €6.50-10) For over 25 years this family concern has served gourmands, royalty and everyone in between, including (as they tell you), Mr Bean. Their specialty *savoro* (fried fish in a savory sauce) is worth the 1km stroll as is the ambience on the restaurant or waterfront terraces. Delightful Pagona can tell you heaps about the island.

Chez Manu (☎ 26740 33626; mains €6) New York meets Vathy in this new contemporary

bar-come-restaurant near the town hall. Black-and-white photos line the walls, funky Italian furniture fills the intimate space and a winding metal staircase leads to the most creative toilet in Greece. Oh, and the food? A delicious blend of Asian and Greek (owner Manu will explain...).

Café Karamela (☎ 26740 33580; snacks €2-6) A great breakfast spot is this new café on the western quay past the ferry dock. A massive window literally frames the bay view. Linger with the locals over the café's board games, books and TV.

For a sweet experience, try *rovani,* the local speciality made with rice, honey and cloves, at one of the patisseries on or near the main square.

AROUND ITHAKI

Ithaki proudly claims several sites associated with Homer's tale, *The Odyssey* (see above). There's a lot of hype about the locations and finding them can be an epic journey – signing is a bit scant. The most renowned is the **Fountain of Arethousa**, in the island's south, where Odysseus' swineherd, Eumaeus, brought his pigs to drink. The isolated trek – through unspoilt landscape with great sea views – takes 1½ to two hours (return) from the turnoff; this excludes the hilly 5km trek up the road to the sign itself. Take a hat and water.

A shorter trek is to the **Cave of the Nymphs** (closed at the time of research for excavations), near Dexa Beach, where Odysseus concealed the Phaeacians' gifts. Below the cave is the **Bay of Dexa**, thought to be ancient Phorkys where the Phaeacians safely delivered Odysseus home.

The location of Odysseus' palace has been much disputed and archaeologists have been unable to find conclusive evidence; some present-day archaeologists speculate it was on **Pelikata Hill** near Stavros, while German archaeologist Heinrich Schliemann believed it to be at **Alalkomenes**, near Piso Aetos. Useful for directionally challenged visitors, the main square of **Stavros** features a rather tired map which traces Odysseus' route from Troy to Ithaki. Also in Stavros visit the **archaeological museum** (☎ 26740 31305; free admission; ☾ 9am-2.30pm Tue-Sun) and speak to enthusiastic Fortini Couvaras who is aware of the current site theories.

Wandering away from Homeric myths, 14km north of Vathy is sleepy **Anogi**, the old capital. The restored church of **Agia Panagia** (claimed to be from the 12th century) has incredible Byzantine frescoes and a Venetian bell tower. Visit the neighbouring *kafeneio* (coffee house) and speak to the owner; he is the proud keeper of the keys.

The unsung fishing village of **Frikes** has a delightfully laid-back and uncontrived feel: it's set in among windswept cliffs and has good accommodation options, several waterfront restaurants, a popular bar and a relaxed ambience.

Sleeping & Eating
Fatouros Taverna (☎ 26740 31385; Stavros; mains €4.50-20) This place reinforces the saying about a book and its cover. Look past the outer to the homely interiors which have as much character as the hospitable owner. House specialties include lamb on the spit and eggplant rolls.

Mrs Vasilopoulos Rooms (☎ 26740 31027; Stavros; d/apt €45/70) In a lane diagonally off to the right hand side of Soris' Ways Café on the square are these sparkling and modern studios, set in a homely garden which overlooks olive and cypress groves. A great base from which to explore and visit the nearby Bay of Polis.

Kioni Κιόνι
Kioni is a small village draped around a verdant hillside and spilling down to a miniature harbour where yachties congregate. There are tavernas and a couple of bars and pretty flower-covered buildings – some of the houses survived the 1953 earthquake. Nearby swimming options are the bays between Kioni and Frikes.

Hamilton House (☎ 26740 31654) Owner Kostas Raftopoulos makes Homer look like an amateur: his story-telling antics are riveting. The idiosyncratic creaky interior of this imposing 19th-century, antique-filled mansion provides a quirky stay; the slightly tatty carpet just adds to the character. One night stays not permitted.

Captain's Apartments (☎ 26740 31481; www .captains-apartments.gr; d €65, 4-person apt €90) Put your anchor down at these berths – studios and apartments – owned by the (former) Captain Dellaporta. Each one is ship-shape with satellite TV and terrace or balcony. Follow the navigation signs as you enter Kioni.

Kalipso (☎ 26740 31066; mains €7-14) The pick of the bunch for panache, stylish traditional dishes, and position beside the small colourful boats. House specialty is onion pie.

ZAKYNTHOS ΖΑΚΥΝΘΟΣ

pop 38,600
Zakynthos (*zahk*-in-thos), also known as Zante, has inspired many superlatives. The Venetians called it Fior' di Levante (Flower of the Orient); the poet Dionysios Solomos wrote that 'Zakynthos could make one forget the Elysian Fields'. Indeed, on the whole, it is an island of exceptional natural beauty and outstanding beaches. The island has a split personality, reflected in its geography: a mountainous and rocky west and a fertile eastern plain. While most places in the west remain unspoiled, the coastal areas have been the victim of the worst manifestations of package tourism. Tourism is endangering the loggerhead turtle, or *Caretta caretta* (see the boxed text, p464). Still, if you're travelling outside of the high season and avoid resorts such as Laganas, you can enjoy a relaxing holiday here.

Getting There & Away
AIR
There's at least one daily flight between Zakynthos and Athens (€74), and connections to other Ionian Islands including Kefallonia (€28) and Corfu (€46). **Olympic Airlines** (☎ 26950 28322; Zakynthos Airport; ☎ 8am-4pm Mon-Fri) can help with information and bookings.

BUS

KTEL (☎ 26950 22255; Filita 42, Zakynthos Town) operates four buses daily between Zakynthos
Town and Patra (€5.20, 3½ hours), and four
daily connections to/from Athens (€18.90,
six hours). There's also a thrice-weekly
service to Thessaloniki (€36.20). Budget an
additional €5.40 for the ferry fare between
Zakynthos and Kyllini.

FERRY

Domestic

Depending on the season, between five
and eight ferries operate daily between
Zakynthos Town and Kyllini in the Peloponnese (€5.40, 1¼ hours). You can buy
tickets from the **Zakynthos Shipping Cooper-**
ative (☎ 26950 41500; Lombardou 40) in Zakynthos
Town.

From the northern port of Agios Nikolaos
a car ferry shuttles across to Pesada in
southern Kefallonia twice daily from May
to October and three times in August
(€4, 1¼ hours). In high season, there's
two daily buses from Pesada to Argostoli
(Kefallonia), and two per week to Agios
Nikolaos, making crossing without your
own transport difficult.

International

Hellenic Mediterranean Lines (www.hml.gr) has
high-season (July and August) services once
or twice a week between Brindisi and Zakynthos (€61 to €80 one way, about 18 hours).

ZAKYNTHOS

IONIAN ISLANDS

IONIAN ISLANDS

AT LOGGERHEADS

The Ionian Islands are home to the Mediterranean's loggerhead turtle *(Caretta caretta)*, one of Europe's most endangered marine species. The turtles prefer large tracts of clean, flat and un-inhabited sand, as do basking tourists, and this fateful convergence of interests has lead to the turtle being placed under the threat of extinction.

After laying around 120 eggs during the breeding season (nesting is from May to August, hatching from July to October), the female turtle returns to sea and after approximately 60 days the (surviving) hatchlings emerge. Zakynthos hosts the largest density of nests – between 800 and 1100 along the 5km Bay of Laganas. Many of the nests are destroyed by brollies and bikes, and the surviving young don't make it to the water – they are often disoriented by sunbeds, noise and lights.

The busy resort area has come under fire with conservation lobbyists clashing with local authorities and those in the tourist trade, as well as the government. Following pressure from the EU, in 1999 the Greek Government declared the Bay of Laganas area a national marine park and strict regulations were put in force regarding building, boating, mooring, fishing and watersports in designated zones. All designated nesting beaches are completely off-limits between dusk and dawn during the breeding season. Despite this, the regulations are ignored and enforcement is lax: dozens of illegal bars and tavernas operate in the area, illegal umbrellas and sunbeds are rented out to tourists and boats cruise through protected waters.

In 2001, Greece was condemned by the European Court of Justice for failing to implement EU nature protection legislation. Sadly, the situation had not improved. Several years later, at the time of research, the European Commission is about to refer the case of Zakynthos to the European Court of Justice.

Meanwhile WWF, Archelon (the Sea Turtle Protection Society of Greece) and Medasset continue their lobbying efforts. Volunteers from WWF (www.wwf.gr) and Archelon (www.archelon.gr) are providing informal wardens on the beaches. The two organisations also have excellent education and volunteer programmes. For further information, visit the information centre at Gerakas Beach.

While the Greek Government is accused of having its head in the sand over the issue and other interests are at loggerheads, visitors can do the following:

- Avoid using umbrellas on dry sand (use the wet part of the beach)
- Do not enter nesting beaches between dusk and dawn, and avoid visiting Daphni beach
- Be aware of boating trips – where they go and what's on offer
- Seek information regarding the protective regulation for the area, as well as sea turtle conservation efforts

Getting Around

There's no bus service between Zakynthos Town and the airport, 6km to the southwest. A taxi costs around €10. Frequent buses go from Zakynthos Town's **bus station** (☎ 26950 22255; Filita 42), one block back from the waterfront, to the developed resorts of Alikes, Tsilivi, Argasi, Laganas and Kalamaki (€1). Bus services to other villages are poor (one or two daily). There are several useful local buses that take the upper or lower main roads to Katastari and Volimes. These are not promoted to tourists – ask at the bus station.

Car- and moped-rental places are plentiful in the larger resorts. Zakynthos Town is also well-serviced. Options include **Europcar** (☎ 26950 41541; Plateia Agiou Louka), which

also has a branch at the airport, and **Hertz** (☎ 26950 45706; Lombardou 38). **HireAuto** (☎ 26950 24808; Lombardou 92), run through BesTours, offers competitive deals.

ZAKYNTHOS TOWN
pop 11,200

Zakynthos Town is the capital and port of the island. The town was devastated by the 1953 earthquake, but was reconstructed to its former layout with arcaded streets, imposing squares and gracious neoclassical public buildings. A Venetian fortress on a hill provides an attractive backdrop to the town. Despite its strung-out feel, there's at least a semblance of Greekness to Zakynthos Town in comparison to many of the overtouristed parts of the island. The northern area (around Plateia Agiou Markou) is of most interest to visitors, with hotels, restaurants and museums clustered around here.

Orientation & Information

Plateia Solomou is on the northern waterfront of Lombardou, opposite the ferry quay. Plateia Agiou Markou is behind it. The bus station is on Filita, one block back from the waterfront and south of the quay. The main thoroughfare is Alexandrou Roma, running parallel to the waterfront and several blocks inland.

Zakynthos Town has no tourist office but the **tourist police** (☎ 26950 27367; Lombardou 62) have one or two brochures for visitors. The

welcoming staff at **BesTours** (☎ 26950 24808; www.bestour.gr; Lomvardou Str & Logotheton 1) are particularly efficient when it comes to arranging accommodation and other travel services.

There are banks with ATMs along Lombardou and just west of Plateia Solomou. The **post office** (Tertseti 27) is one block west of Alexandrou Roma. **Connect Internet** (Agiou Dionysiou 18; per hr €4) offers cutting edge Internet access.

Sights & Activities

The **Byzantine museum** (☎ 26950 42714; Plateia Solomou; admission €3; ⏰ 8am-2.30pm Tue-Sun) houses an impressive collection of ecclesiastical art, rescued from churches razed in the earthquake. The nearby **Museum of Solomos** (☎ 26950 28982; Plateia Agiou Markou; admission

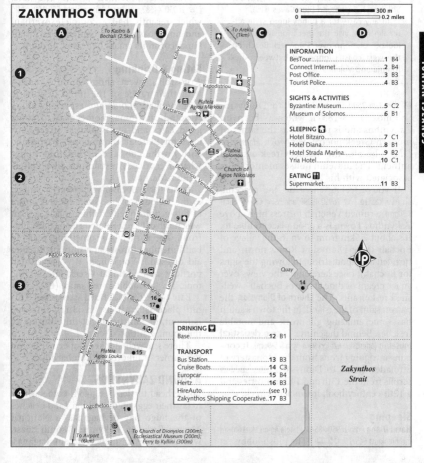

ZAKYNTHOS TOWN

0 — 300 m
0 — 0.2 miles

To Kastro & Bochali (2.5km)
To Arekia (1km)

INFORMATION	
BesTour.................................1	B4
Connect Internet.....................2	B4
Post Office.............................3	B3
Tourist Police.........................4	B3

SIGHTS & ACTIVITIES	
Byzantine Museum...................5	C2
Museum of Solomos.................6	B1

SLEEPING 🏠	
Hotel Bitzaro.........................7	C1
Hotel Diana...........................8	B1
Hotel Strada Marina.................9	B2
Yria Hotel............................10	C1

EATING 🍴	
Supermarket.........................11	B3

DRINKING 🍷	
Base...................................12	B1

TRANSPORT	
Bus Station..........................13	B3
Cruise Boats.........................14	C3
Europcar..............................15	B4
Hertz..................................16	B3
HireAuto.........................(see 1)	
Zakynthos Shipping Cooperative..17	B3

Zakynthos Strait

IONIAN ISLANDS

To Church of Dionysios (200m); Ecclesiastical Museum (200m); Ferry to Kyllini (300m)
To Airport (6km)

IONIAN ISLANDS

SHIPWRECK BEACH

The famous Shipwreck Beach (Navagio), whose photos grace virtually every tourist brochure about Zakynthos, is at the north-west tip of the island. It is a tad over-hyped, if splendid, beach and downright unap-pealing when the round-the-island (nine hours) excursion boats from Zakynthos Town disgorge trippers en masse. Your best bet is to take a small-boat trip to see Shipwreck Beach and/or the Blue Caves (in the island's northeast). The northeastern coastal road is lined with hawkers offering the 'same-trip-better-boat' deals. **Potamitis Trips** (☎ 26950 31132) offer good glass-bottom boat trips at Cape Skinari, 3km be-yond Agios Nikolaos. (Blue Caves only, €7.50; Shipwreck Beach and Blue Caves €15).

In any case, for a bungy-jump style ad-renalin rush, visit the precariously perched lookout platform over Shipwreck Beach on the west coast (signposted between Ana-fonitria and Volimes).

€3; ⏰ 9am-2pm) is dedicated to Dionysios Solomos (1798-1857), who was born on Zakynthos and is regarded as the father of modern Greek poetry. His work *Hymn to Liberty* became the stirring Greek national anthem. The museum houses memorabilia associated with his life.

If you're feeling energetic, the peaceful, shady **kastro** (☎ 26950 48099; admission €3; ⏰ 8am-7.30pm), a ruined Venetian fortress high above Zakynthos Town, is a good place to hike to. It's about 2.5km from town in the village of Bochali (take Dionysiou Roma north and turn left at Kapodistriou, following the signs for Bochali); once here enjoy the views over an ice cream or dine at one of Bochali's well-sited restaurants. The **Church of Dionysios**, the patron saint of the island, in the town's south has some amazing gilt work and notable frescoes. Behind the church is an **ecclesiastical museum** (admission €2; ⏰ 9am-1pm & 5-9pm). It con-tains intriguing icons from the Monastery of Strofades, home to Dionysios, plus speech scrolls from the 13th and 14th centuries and a 12th-century book in Ancient Greek.

Sleeping

Hotel Diana (☎ 26950 28547; Plateia Agiou Markou; s/d incl breakfast €45/75; ❌ 🖳) The plush lobby yet

stuffy corridors hint at the varying – but mainly high – standards of rooms here. The good-value (outer) rooms are well ap-pointed with fridge and TV, and the loca-tion is tops – close to all the action.

Hotel Strada Marina (☎ 26950 42761; strada marina@aias.gr; Lombardou 14; s/d €75/100; ❌ 🖳) This plush option in town offers no sur-prises – modern, well-equipped rooms with TV, phone and air-con – prices include buffet breakfast. Let's not forget the invit-ing rooftop pool and bar area.

Hotel Bitzaro (☎ 26950 23644; Dionysus Roma 46; s/d €40/50) The pleasant lobby is out of an '80s TV sit-com, complete with small patio dripping with plants. Its adequate rooms make it a good 'cheapo' choice.

Also recommended is the **Yria Hotel** (☎ 26950 44682; yriahotel@aias.gr; s/d €75/100; ❌) which recently had a complete overhaul and now boasts stylish contemporary Ital-ian décor in its small, but tasteful rooms.

Eating & Drinking

Argostoli's sweet shop windows entice with their range of the tooth-dissolving local nougat, *mandolato*, especially along Alexandrou Roma, home also to some good cafés and gyros places. Street ven-dors on Plateia Solomou sell barbecued corn on the cob, and decent (but some-what overpriced) restaurants line Plateia Agious Markou.

Arekia (☎ 26950 26346; mains under €10) Munch to the melodies of live *kantades* and *arekia* at this genuinely entertaining place, a 1km walk north of Plateia Solomou along the water-front. The spritely 80-something year-old band member throws in a ditty or three to aid digestion. You'll need it – gargantuan portions of traditional Greek fare set the tone. Try the rabbit in red sauce (€7).

Base (☎ 26950 42409; Plateia Agiou Markou) This hip place is great as an alfresco frappé hangout, or join the night-time throng of the young Zantiot 'it' crowd.

There's a well-stocked supermarket on the corner of Filioti and Lombardou.

AROUND ZAKYNTHOS

Loggerhead turtles (see p464) come ashore to lay their eggs on the golden-sand beaches of the huge Bay of Laganas, a National Marine Park, on Zakynthos' south coast, whereas party animals frequent Laganas, the highly developed, tacky resort. **Keri Beach** (turn off from Limni Keriou) is a prettier and more peaceful option, but the beach is narrow and stony. There's boat hire and a scuba diving centre here.

The **Vasilikos Peninsula**, southeast of Zakynthos Town beyond the busy resort of Argasi, is a pretty green area offering a number of ever-expanding beachfront settlements off the main road, with tavernas and accommodation options. The first decent place to stop is **Kaminia**, followed by the sandy cove of **Porto Zoro**. Virtually at the tip of the east coast, **Banana Beach** is a long (albeit narrow) strip of golden sand with plenty of watersports, umbrellas and sun lounges. **Agios Nikolaos** at the very end of the peninsula (not to be confused with Agios Nikolaos in the northeast) also has beach umbrellas and sunbeds for hire.

Beyond Mavratzis (dominated by the over-the-top Zante Palace Hotel) is the narrow and crowded **Porto Roma** beach – at the time of research, piles of pebbles were being dumped, presumably to stop erosion. On the other side of the peninsula, facing Laganas Bay, is Zakynthos' best beach, the long and sandy **Gerakas**. This is one of the main turtle-nesting beaches and access to the beach is forbidden between dusk and dawn during the breeding season (although sadly, this is not enforced – refer boxed text p464).

With your own transport, you can semi-escape from the tourist hype by visiting the accessible west coast coves, such as lovely **Limnionas** or **Kambi** (the latter has some rather tacky tavernas ideally positioned for the amazing sunsets), or head to the quieter northeast coast around **Agios Nikolaos**, where development is proceeding slowly. Known primarily as the ferry point, this tiny place has a few food and drink dwellings, a small stretch of beach with clear water, free sunbeds and a view of a tiny islet.

For a touch of rural tranquillity, head inland to the north and northwest of Zakynthos. Villages and settlements – some of which survived the 1953 earthquake – are scattered through the scrub and pines; here the welcoming locals have maintained their cultures and traditions and sell honey and other seasonal products. Churches and monasteries feature highly along this village route: **St Mavra** in **Maherado** is well-known for its peculiar belfry and sumptuous icons;

St Nikolaos in **Kiliomeno** features an unusual roofless campanile; the bell tower of **Agios Leon** (in the village of the same name) was formerly a windmill. Just off the main road in the small and charming hamlet of **Exo Hora** is a fascinating congregation of dried wells, and what is reputed to be the oldest olive tree on the island. **Volimes** is the unashamed sales centre for all traditional products.

Sleeping & Eating
Seaside Apartments (☎ 26950 22827; www.seaside .net.gr; d €65, 4-person apt €80; ✖ P ☐) Bright, breezy and well-equipped studios and apartments are above the beachfront Keri Tourist Center (really just a gift shop) at Keri Beach. The modern, creative décor is enhanced by artwork done by the friendly owner, and all have large balconies with wonderful sea views.

Tartaruga Camping (☎ 26950 51967; www.tar taruga-camping.com; sites per adult/tent €4.80/3.50, r per person €10) Happy campers should pitch up to this natural setting amid terraced olive groves, pines and plane trees that sprawl as far as the sea. Okay amenities, small store and café plus rooms for rent top off this well-signed spot on the road from Laganas to Keri.

Villa Contessa (☎ 26950 35161; www.villacontessa .gr; studio €50) This modern villa in Xirocastello is a great value studio alternative without the brash resort feel. The modern and spotless apartments are in one building set around a stone patio; there's no pool or facilities, but the beach is a steep 10-minute walk away. The owners speak little English. Take the turn-off to Kaminia Beach and look out for the pink building on the left.

If you fancy an impromptu stay in the area drop into the Earth Sea & Sky public information centre near Gerakas Beach. They will accommodate short term stays if available in villas and cottages.

At Cape Skinari, 3km north of Agios Nikolaos, blow in for a night and stay in one of two constructed **windmills** (☎ 26950 31132; d €75) which sleep two and four people. The cramped and tattier smaller one is less appealing than its neighbour, but the views are stupendous. A nearby snack bar–café and a lovely swimming area (down steep steps) serves visitors, plus it's the departure point for boat trips to the **Blue Caves** and shipwreck beach (see boxed text, opposite).

IONIAN ISLANDS

Behind Alykes in the lovely hillside village of Katstari is **Archontiko Village** (www
.archontikovillage.com; 2-person studio €90; ❄ ⚛). Go up the hill and back in time to these attractive studio-villas, part of a converted 19th-century olive oil factory; the tasteful rooms have most original features intact. The pool and bar area overlook pencil pines and olive groves. There is an extra charge for air-conditioning.

In Agios Nikolaos, in the north of the island near Cape Skinari, look no further than the modern, clean, bright-and-white **rooms** (☎ 26950 31160; s/d/tr €35/40/45) run by the friendly Theodosis/Fexoulis family (who don't speak English). Hike 600 metres up the hill from the ferry, turn left opposite Panorama Studios and the *domatia* are a further 200 metres at the road's end.

Kostas' Brother Tavern (☎ 26950 35347; mains €7-9.50) calls lovers of fine food and fun to a culinary and cultural experience on the Vasilikos Peninsula. For 26 years the owners have served their own farm's produce to large crowds on the restaurant's homely terrace and garden areas. Specialities include rabbit Vasilikos, and 'speciality of Alexandra', an eggplant and cheese goulash. The band sets the tone by taking requests. Situated on the sharp corner near the Banana Beach turnoff.

KYTHIRA & ANTIKYTHIRA

KYTHIRA ΚΥΘΗΡΑ
pop 3334

The island of Kythira (*kee*-thih-rah), 12km south of Neapoli, is the perfect destination for people who want to get away from it all and unwind for a few days.

Some 30km long and 18km wide, Kythira dangles off the tip of the Peloponnese's eastern Laconian Peninsula, between the Aegean and Ionian Seas.

The landscape is largely barren, dominated by a rocky plateau that covers most of the island. The population is spread among 40 villages scattered across the island, taking advantage of small pockets of agriculturally viable land. The villages are linked by narrow, winding lanes flanked by ancient dry-stone walls.

Despite its proximity to the mainland, Kythira is regarded by many Greeks as the

Holy Grail of island-hopping, a reputation that owes much to a well-known 1973 song by Dimitris Mitropanos called 'Road to Kythira', which portrayed the island as the never-reached end of a line.

Mythology suggests that Aphrodite was born in Kythira. She is supposed to have risen from the foam where Zeus had thrown Cronos' sex organ after castrating him. The goddess of love then re-emerged near Pafos in Cyprus, so both islands haggle over her birthplace.

Tourism remains low-key on Kythira for most of the year, but goes mad during July and August. Many of the visitors are members of the Kythiran diaspora returning from Australia to visit. Accommodation is virtually impossible to find, and restaurants are flat-out catering for the crowds. For the remaining 10 months of the year, Kythira is a peaceful island with fine, uncrowded beaches and clear water to be explored. The best times to plan a visit to Kythira are in late spring and around September/October. For information on the island, see www
.kythira.com.

GETTING THERE & AWAY
Air
There are daily flights between Kythira and Athens (€43, 40 minutes). The airport is 10km east of Potamos, and **Olympic Airlines** (☎ 27360 33362) is on the central square in Potamos. Book also at **Kythira Travel** (☎ 27360 31490) in Hora.

Ferry
The island's main ferry connection is between Diakofti and Neapoli (per person/car €7/31, one hour) in the Peloponnese. The frequency of the service ranges from four daily in July and August, down to one in winter. Tickets are sold at the quay.

ANEN Lines (www.anen.gr) calls at the southern port of Diakofti on its weekly schedule between Piraeus, Kythira, Antikythira, Kissamos-Kastelli (Crete) and Gythio (Peloponnese). From July to September there are five ferries weekly to Gythio (€9.90, 2½ hours) and five to Kissamos-Kastelli (€15.70, four hours), of which three call at Antikythira (€9, two hours). There are also two services weekly to Piraeus (€21.50, 6½ hours).

(Continued on page 477)

Caïque from Kalymnos (p326) to Telendos (p330)

Wine on tap (p66)

Beach near Cape Prasonisi (p291), Rhodes

Waterfalls, Petaloudes (p291), Rhodes

Makrygialos Bay (p297),
Karpathos

View from Asklipieion (p321), Rhodes

Castle of Lykourgos Logothetis (p360), Pythagorio, Samos

Cafés, Pyrgi (p369), Chios

Local birdlife (p53)

Potamia (p399), Lesvos

472

Kokkari (p362), Samos

DAVID TIPLING

Traditional Greek family lunch (p65)

ALAN BENSON

Facing Page:
Skyros Town (p425), Skyros

GEORGE TSAFOS

Cathedral, Karlovasi (p363), Samos

STELLA HELLA

VERONICA GA

Dining alfresco (p68)

STELLA HELLANDER

Traditional house, Kythira (p468)

Travelling by cart, Corfu Town (p436), Corfu

CHRIS CH

Corfu Town (p436), Corfu

Kouloura (p442), Corfu

Waterfront, Zakynthos Town (p464), Zakynthos

Ahillion Palace (p443),
Corfu

Moni Theotokou (p444), Corfu

Kathisma (p452), Lefkada

(Continued from page 468)

Information and tickets are available from **Porfyra Travel** (☎ /fax 27360 31888; porfyra@otenet .gr) in Livadi.

Hydrofoil

Hellenic Seaways (www.hellenicseaways.gr) services to Diakofti had been suspended at the time of research, and showed little prospect of resuming. Check www.hellenicseaways.gr for the latest news, or ask at **Kythira Travel** (☎ 27360 31490/390) on the main square in Hora.

GETTING AROUND

The only public transport on the island is provided by school buses, which are pressed into service during the July/August school holidays. Not surprisingly, there are taxis, but the best way to see the island is with your own transport. Panayotis at **Moto Rent** (☎ 27360 31600; fax 27360 31789) on Kapsali's waterfront rents cars and mopeds.

Hora Χώρα
pop 267

Hora (or Kythira), the island's capital, is a pretty village of Cycladic-style white, blue-shuttered houses, perched on a long, slender ridge stretching north from an impressive 13th-century Venetian *kastro*. The central square, planted with hibiscus, bougainvillea and palms, is Plateia Dimitriou Staï. The main street, Spiridonos Staï, runs south from the square to the *kastro*.

INFORMATION

Branches of the National Bank of Greece and Bank Agoritiki, both with ATMs, are on the central square.

Internet Service (☎ 27350 39016; Spiridonos Staï 38; per hr €5; 🕑 9am-2pm & 5.30-11pm Mon-Sat) Travellers can check email here.

Police station (☎ 27360 31206) Near the *kastro*.

Post office (🕑 7.30am-2pm Mon-Fri) On the central square.

SIGHTS

Hora's Venetian **kastro**, built in the 13th century, is at the southern end of town. If you walk to its southern extremity, passing the Church of Panagia, you will come to a sheer cliff – from here there's a stunning view of Kapsali and, on a clear day, of Antikythira.

The **archaeological museum** (☎ 27360 31789; admission free; 🕑 8.45am-3pm Tue-Sat, 9.30am-2.30pm Sun) is north of the central square, near the turn-off to Kapsali. It features gravestones of British soldiers who died on the island in the 19th century, and a large marble lion from around 550 BC.

Call in to **Stavros** (☎ 27360 31857), a store north of the square (opposite the turn-off to Kapsali) and pick up some of the local produce, including Greece's best honey.

SLEEPING

Hotel Margarita (☎ 27360 31711; www.hotel-margarita .com; off Spiridonos Staï; s/d €95/120; 🆇) This white-walled, blue-shuttered and generally charming hotel offers atmospheric rooms (all with TV and telephone) in a renovated 19th-century mansion. It features beautiful timber floors and a fine old spiral staircase. Breakfast is served on the whitewashed terrace which has fantastic port views.

Castello Rooms (☎ 27360 31069; jfatseas@otenet.gr; d/tr €40/45; 🆇) These comfortable rooms represent the best deal in town, set back from the main street and surrounded by a well-tended garden full of flowers, vegetables and fruit trees. The rooms have TV and most also have kitchen facilities. It is signposted at the southern end of Spiridonos Staï.

Myrtoon (☎ 27360 31705; mains €3-8) The standard taverna menu holds no surprises but the food's fine and it's reasonably priced.

Kapsali Καψάλι
pop 34

The picturesque village of Kapsali, just 2km south of Hora, served as Hora's port in Venetian times. It looks stunning viewed from Hora's castle, with its twin sandy bays and curving waterfront. Restaurants and cafés line the beach, and safe sheltered swimming is Kapsali's trademark. It can also get pretty crowded in high season.

Offshore you can see the stark rock island known as the **Avgo** (Egg) rearing above the water. It is here that Kytherians claim Aphrodite sprang from the sea.

Kapsali goes into hibernation in winter, coming to life between April and October. **Creperie Vanilia** (☎ 27360 31881) has a computer for Internet access (per hour €3). There's a small supermarket, and the **Kytherian Gallery** sells international newspapers as well as souvenirs.

IONIAN ISLANDS

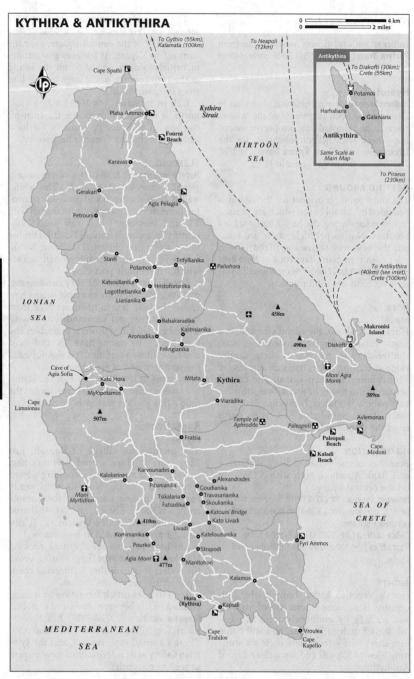

KYTHIRA & ANTIKYTHIRA

| 0 | 4 km |
| 0 | 2 miles |

To Gythio (55km);
Kalamata (100km)

To Neapoli
(12km)

Cape Spathi

Antikythira

To Diakofti (30km);
Crete (55km)

Potamos

Harhaliana

Galaniana

Antikythira

Same Scale as
Main Map

Platia Ammos

FOURNI
Beach

Kythira
Strait

M I R T O Ö N

S E A

Karavas

To Piraeus
(230km)

Gerakari

Agia Pelagia

Petrouni

To Antikythira
(40km) (see inset);
Crete (100km)

Stavli

Trifyllianika

Paliohora

Potamos

Katsoulianika

Hristoforianika

Logothetianika

Lianianika

I O N I A N

S E A

Babakaradika

458m

Kastrisianika

Aroniadika

490m

Frilingianika

Makronisi
Island

Diakofti

Cave of
Agia Sofia

Kato Hora

Mitata

Kythira

Mylopotamos

Moni Agia
Monis

Cape
Limnionas

507m

Viaradika

389m

Avlemonas

Temple of
Aphrodite

Paleopoli

Paleopoli
Beach

Fratsia

Cape
Modoni

Kaladi
Beach

Kalokerines

Karvounades

Pitsinianika

Alexandrades

S E A   O F

Tsikalaria

Goudianika

Travasarianika

C R E T E

Moni
Myrtidion

Fatsadika

Skoulianika

Katouni Bridge

Kato Livadi

410m

Kominianika

Livadi

Katelouzianika

Pourko

Fyri Ammos

Agia Moni

477m

Strapodi

Manitohori

Kalamos

M E D I T E R R A N E A N

S E A

Hora
(Kythira)

Kapsali

Cape
Trahilos

Vroulea

Cape
Kapello

ACTIVITIES

Panayotis at **Moto Rent** (☎ 27360 31600), on the waterfront, offers water-skiing lessons (€15) and hires canoes and pedal boats as well as cars, mopeds and bicycles.

SLEEPING & EATING

Spitia Vassilis (☎ 27360 31125; www.kythirabunga lowsvasili.gr; d €110, tr & q €120; **P**) This attractive green-and-white complex of studios has a wonderful setting overlooking Kapsali Beach. Olga, the friendly owner, offers spacious rooms with lovely timber floors and good bay views. It is on the right as you approach Kapsali from Hora.

Aphrodite Apartments (☎ 27360 31328; afro dite@aias.gr; s/d/tr studios €55/70/80; ❄) This place is ideally situated just 50m behind the main beach. The furnishings are pretty basic, but there are kitchen facilities and all the essentials.

Raikos Hotel (☎ 27360 31629; www.raikoshotel.gr; d/tr incl breakfast €120/144; **P** ❄ ❄) Signposted off the Hora–Kapsali road is this very smart, friendly hotel, offering spacious, pleasantly decorated rooms with terraces overlooking Kapsali and Hora's *kastro*. There's a lovely pool and bar area too, complete with billiards table.

Camping Kapsali (☎ 27360 31580; sites per person/tent €4.50/4; ☼ Jun-Sep 15) This small pine-shaded ground (well signposted on the road from Hora) is 400m from Kapsali's quay, behind the village. It's a quiet spot with minimum facilities and is better suited to small tents rather than large campervan set-ups.

Hydragogio (☎ 27360 31065; mains €6-12, lobster & fish priced per kg) Occupying a great spot overlooking the beach at the far end by the rocks, and specialising in fresh fish and mezedes, the Hydragogio is a good place to splurge on lobster (per kilogram €70) if your budget stretches that far. The wine list is comprehensive and excellent.

Estiatorio Magos (☎ 27360 31407; mains €2.80-6, fish priced per kg) The *magos* (magician) in question is owner Antonis, whose assortment of tricks includes pasta (€2.80) and a tasty fish soup (€3).

Potamos Ποταμός
pop 680

Potamos, 10km from Agia Pelagia, is the commercial hub. Its **Sunday morning market** seems to attract just about everyone on the island.

INFORMATION

The National Bank of Greece (with ATM) is on the central square.

Kafe Selena (☎ 27360 33997; per hr €3) Also on the square; has Internet access.

Post office (☼ 7.30am-2pm Mon-Fri) Just north of the square.

EATING

Ta Katsigouro (☎ 27360 33880; burgers & snacks €2-8) Ta Katsigouro has become something of a tourist attraction thanks to its sign featuring a wonderful New Age mythical beast with a kangaroo's body and a goat's head. Inside, former Sydneysider Maria turns out the best burger with the works (€3.50) west of Perth, as well as Greek fast food like *gyros* (Greek version of doner kebab) and *souvlaki* (cubes of meat on skewers).

Mylopotamos Μυλοπόταμος
pop 680

Mylopotamos is a charming village nestled in a small valley about 12km southwest of Potamos. Its square is flanked by a much-photographed church and the traditional **Kafeneio O Platanos** (☎ 27360 33397), which in summer becomes a restaurant, serving simple meals in a gorgeous setting. It's worth a stroll to the **Neraïda** (water nymph) waterfall, with luxuriant greenery and mature, shady trees. As you reach the church, take the right fork and follow the signs to an unpaved road leading down to the falls.

To reach the abandoned **kastro** of Mylopotamos, take the left fork after the *kafeneio* and follow the sign for **Kato Hora** (Lower Village). The road leads to the centre of Kato Hora, from where a portal leads into the spooky *kastro*, with derelict houses and well-preserved little churches (usually locked).

Further along the same road is the **Cave of Agia Sofia**, reached by a precipitous, unpaved 2km road. The staff at Kafeneio O Platanos can tell you if it's open.

Agia Pelagia Αγία Πελαγία
pop 280

Kythira's northern port of Agia Pelagia is a friendly waterfront village, ideal for relaxing and swimming. Mixed sand-and-pebble beaches are to either side of the quay. **Red**

Beach, south of the headland, is the best in the area, named for its red pebbles.

SLEEPING & EATING
Hotel Pelagia Aphrodite (☎ 27360 33926/7; pelagia@ otenet.gr; s/d/tr €65/80/96; Apr-Sep;) Has a great location on a small headland on the southern edge of the village. The hotel is modern and spotless with large, airy rooms, most with balconies overlooking the sea.

Moustakias (☎ 27360 33519; mains to €8.80) This *ouzeri*, next to the minimarket, is named after the moustache of cheerful owner Panayiotis. The menu includes all the Greek favourites and ranges from mezedes to grilled meats, including daily specials such as pork with ouzo, and seafood.

Around Kythira
If you have transport, a spin round the island is rewarding. The monasteries of **Agia Moni** and **Agia Elesis** are mountain refuges with superb views. **Moni Myrtidion** is a beautiful monastery surrounded by trees. From Hora, drive northeast to the picturesque village of **Avlemonas,** via **Paleopoli** with its wide, pebbled beach. Archaeologists spent years searching for evidence of a temple at Aphrodite's birthplace at Avlemonas. Be sure to also visit the spectacularly situated ruins of the Byzantine capital of **Paliohora,** in the island's northeast.

Just a bit north of the village of **Kato Livadi** make a detour to see the architecturally anomalous **Katouni Bridge,** a British-built legacy of Kythira's time as part of the British Protectorate in the 19th century. In the far north of the island the village of **Karavas** is verdant, very attractive and close to both Agia Pelagia and the reasonable beach at **Platia Ammos.** Beachcombers should seek out **Kaladi Beach,** near Paleopoli. **Fyri Ammos,** closer to Hora, is another good beach – but hard to access.

EATING
Estiatorion Pierros (☎ 27360 31014; Livadi; mains €3-7) Pierros, on the main road through Livadi, is a long-standing favourite where you'll find no-nonsense Greek staples. There's no menu – visit the kitchen to see what's being freshly cooked.

Rouga (☎ 27360 33766; Arionadika; mains €5-7; lunch & dinner) The place to sample some traditional Kythiran dishes like *kamares* (artichokes and leeks with lemon sauce, €4.50) and baked wild goat (€7). It also sells a range of home-made *gyka* (preserved fruit in syrup), which form a colourful counter display. Arionadika is about 4km south of Potamos.

Sotiris (☎ 27360 33722; Avlemonas; fish & lobster priced per kg; lunch & dinner) This popular fish taverna in pretty Avlemonas is famous for its lobster and its fish soup.

ANTIKYTHIRA ΑΝΤΙΚΥΘΗΡΑ
pop 70
The tiny island of Antikythira, 38km southeast of Kythira, is the most remote island in the Ionians. It has one settlement (Potamos), one doctor, one police officer, one teacher (with a few pupils), one telephone and a monastery. It has no post office or bank. The only accommodation is 10 basic rooms in two purpose-built blocks, open in summer only. Potamos has a *kafeneio* and a taverna.

Getting There & Away
ANEN Lines (www.anen.gr) calls at Antikythira on its route between Kythira and Kissamos-Kastelli on Crete, offering three services a week in each direction; single leg tickets are €9.10 and take two hours, while Kythira–Crete, costs €16.10. This is not an island for tourists on a tight schedule and will probably only appeal to those who really like isolation. For information and tickets, contact **Porfyra Travel** (☎ /fax 27360 31888; porfyra@otenet.gr) in Livadi on Kythira.

Directory

ACCOMMODATION

The Greek islands boast accommodation to suit every taste and budget. All places to stay are subject to strict price controls set by the tourist police. By law, a notice must be displayed in every room, which states the category of the room and the maximum price that can be charged. The price includes a 4.5% community tax and 8% VAT.

Accommodation owners may add a 10% surcharge for a stay of less than three nights, but this is not mandatory. A mandatory charge of 20% is levied if an extra bed is put into a room. During July and August, accommodation owners will charge the maximum price, but in spring and autumn, prices will drop by about 20%, and perhaps by even more in winter.

Rip-offs rarely occur, but if you do suspect that you have been exploited by an accommodation owner, make sure you report it to either the tourist police or regular police and they will act swiftly.

Throughout this book we have divided accommodation into budget (up to €80), midrange (€80 to €200) and top end categories (over €200), and within each section the options are listed in order of preference. This is a per-person rate in high season (July and August). Unless otherwise stated, all rooms have private bathroom facilities. It's difficult to generalise accommodation prices in Greece as rates depend entirely on the season and location. Don't expect to pay the same price for a double on one of the islands as you would in central Greece or even Athens.

Camping

Camping is a good option, especially in summer. There are almost 200 camping grounds dotted around the islands, some of them in

PRACTICALITIES

- Greece is two hours ahead of GMT/UTC and three hours ahead during daylight-saving time.
- Greece uses the metric system for weights and measures.
- Plug your electrical appliances into a two-pin adaptor before plugging into the electricity supply (220V AC, 50Hz).
- Keep up with Greek current affairs by reading the daily English-language edition of *Kathimerini* that comes with the *Herald Tribune*.
- Channel hop through a choice of nine free-to-air TV channels and an assortment of pay-TV channels.
- Be aware that Greece belongs to area 2 if you buy DVDs to watch back home, and uses the PAL TV system.

DIRECTORY

great locations. Standard facilities include hot showers, kitchens, restaurants and mini-markets – and often a swimming pool.

Most camping grounds are open only between April and October. The **Panhellenic Camping Association** (☎ /fax 2103 621 560; Solonos 102, Athens 106 80) publishes an annual booklet listing all camping grounds, their facilities and months of operation.

Camping fees are highest from 15 June to the end of August. Most camping grounds charge from €5 to €7 per adult and €3 to €4 for children aged four to 12. There's no charge for children aged under four. Tent sites cost from €4 per night for small tents, and from €5 per night for large tents. Caravan sites start at around €6.

Between May and mid-September the weather is warm enough to sleep out. Many camping grounds have covered areas where tourists who don't have tents can sleep in summer, so you can get by with a light-weight sleeping bag and foam bedroll. It's a good idea to have a foam pad to lie on and a waterproof cover for your sleeping bag. Pitching a tent in a nondesignated camping area is illegal, but the law is seldom enforced – to the irritation of camping-ground owners.

Domatia

Domatia are the Greek equivalent of the British bed and breakfast, minus the break-fast. Once upon a time *domatia* comprised little more than spare rooms in the family home that could be rented out to travellers in summer; nowadays, many are purpose-built appendages. Some come complete with fully-equipped kitchens. Standards of cleanliness are generally high.

The décor runs the gamut from cool marble floors, coordinated pine furniture and pretty lace curtains, to so much kitsch you're afraid to move in case you break an ornament.

Domatia remain a popular option for budget travellers. They are classified A, B or C. Expect to pay from €25 to €35 for a single, and €40 to €50 for a double, de-pending on the class, whether bathrooms are shared or private, the season and how long you plan to stay. *Domatia* are found on almost every island that has a permanent population. Many are open only between April and October.

From June to September *domatia* own-ers are out in force, touting for custom-ers. They meet buses and boats, shouting 'Room, room!' and often carrying photo-graphs of their rooms. In peak season, it can prove a mistake not to take up an offer – but be wary of owners who are vague about the location of their accommodation. 'Close to town' can turn out to be way out in the sticks. If you are at all dubious, insist they show you the location on a map.

Hostels

There is only one youth hostel in Greece affiliated to the International Youth Hos-tel Federation (IYHF), the **Athens Interna-tional Youth Hostel** (☎ 210 523 4170; fax 210 523 4015; www.interland.gr/athenshostel; Victor Hugo 16). You don't need a membership card to stay there; temporary membership costs €1.80 per day.

Most other youth hostels in Greece are run by the **Greek Youth Hostel Organisation** (☎ 210 751 9530; y-hostels@otenet.gr; Damareos 75, Athens 116 33). There are affiliated hostels in Athens, Olympia, Patra and Thessaloniki on the mainland, and on the islands of Crete and Santorini.

Hostel rates vary from €8 to €11 and you don't have to be a member to stay in any of them. Few have curfews.

Hotels

Hotels in Greece are divided into six cat-egories: deluxe, A, B, C, D and E. Hotels are categorised according to the size of the room, whether or not they have a bar, and the ratio of bathrooms to beds, rather than standards of cleanliness, comfort of the beds and friendliness of staff – all elements that may be of greater relevance to guests.

As one would expect, deluxe, A- and B-class hotels have many amenities, private bathrooms and constant hot water. C-class hotels have a snack bar, rooms have private bathrooms, but hot water may only be avail-able at certain times of the day. D-class ho-tels may or may not have snack bars, most rooms will share bathrooms, but there may be some with private bathrooms, and they may have solar-heated water, which means hot water is not guaranteed. E classes do not have a snack bar, bathrooms are shared and you may have to pay extra for hot water – if it exists at all.

Prices are controlled by the tourist police and the maximum rate that can be charged for a room must be displayed on a board behind the door of each room. The classification is not often much of a guide to price. Rates in D- and E-class hotels are generally comparable with *domatia*. You can pay from €35 to €60 for a single in high season in C class and €45 to €80 for a double. Prices in B class range from €50 to €80 for singles, and from €90 to €120 for doubles. A-class prices are not much higher.

Mountain Refuges

You are unlikely to need to stay at Greece's mountain refuges – unless of course you're going trekking in the mountains of Crete or Evia. The EOT (Ellinikos Organismos Tourismou; Greek National Tourist Organisation) publication *Greece: Mountain Refuges & Ski Centres* has details on all of the refuges in Greece; copies should be available at all EOT branches. See p494 for more information about EOT.

Pensions

Pensions in Greece are virtually indistinguishable from hotels. They are classed A, B or C. An A-class pension is equivalent in amenities and price to a B-class hotel, a B-class pension is equivalent to a C-class hotel and a C-class pension is equivalent to a D- or E-class hotel.

Rental Accommodation

There are plenty of places around the islands offering self-contained family apartments for rent, either long- or short-term. Prices vary considerably according to the season and the amenities offered.

If you're looking for long-term accommodation, it's worth checking out the classified section of the *Athens News* – although most of the places are in Athens. On the islands, the local *kafeneio* (coffee house) is a good place to start asking about your options.

Villas & Apartments

A really practical way to save on money and maximise comfort is to rent a furnished apartment or villa. Many are purpose built for tourists while others, especially villas, may be homes that are not being used by their owners. The main advantage is that you can accommodate a larger number of people under one roof and also save money by self-catering. This option is best for a stay of more than three days. In fact some owners may insist on a week's stay minimum. A good site to spot prospective villas is www.greekislands.com.

ACTIVITIES

For details on popular activities throughout the Greek islands, see the Greek Islands Outdoors chapter on p57.

BUSINESS HOURS

Banks are open 8am to 2pm Monday to Thursday, and 8am to 1.30pm Friday. Some banks in large towns and cities open between 3.30pm and 6.30pm in the afternoon and on Saturday morning.

Post offices are open from 7.30am to 2pm Monday to Friday. In the major cities they stay open until 8pm, and open 7.30am to 2pm Saturday.

In summer, the usual opening hours for shops are 8am to 1.30pm and 5.30pm to 8.30pm on Tuesday, Thursday and Friday, and 8am to 2.30pm on Monday, Wednesday and Saturday. Shops open 30 minutes later in winter.

These times are not always strictly adhered to. Many shops in tourist resorts are open seven days a week.

The opening hours of OTE offices (for long-distance and overseas telephone calls) vary according to the size of the town. In smaller towns they are usually open from 7.30am to 3pm daily, 6am to 11pm in larger towns, and 24 hours in major cities like Athens and Thessaloniki.

Department stores and supermarkets are open 8am to 8pm Monday to Friday, 8am to at least 3pm on Saturday and are closed Sunday.

Periptera (street kiosks) are open from early morning until late at night. They sell everything from bus tickets and cigarettes to hard-core pornography.

Restaurant opening hours vary enormously. They are normally open for lunch from 11am to 2pm, and for dinner between 7pm and 1am, while restaurants in tourist areas remain open all day. Cafés normally open at about 10am and stay open until midnight.

Bars open from 8pm until late, while nightclubs don't open until at least 10pm;

it's rare to find much of a crowd before midnight. They close at about 4am, later on Friday and Saturday.

CHILDREN

The Greek islands are a safe and relatively easy place to travel with children. Greeks are well known for making a fuss of children, who will always be made the centre of attention.

Despite this, it's usually quite rare for younger children to have much success making friends with local children their own age, partly because Greek children tend to play at home and partly because of the language barrier. The language barrier starts to recede by about the age of 12, by which time many local children are sufficiently advanced in their studies to communicate in English.

Matt Barrett's website (www.greektravel .com) has lots of useful tips for parents, while daughter Amarandi has put together some tips for kids (www.greece4kids.com).

Practicalities

Travelling is especially easy if you're staying at a resort hotel by the beach, where everything is set up for families with children. As well as facilities like paddling pools and playgrounds, they also have cots and highchairs.

Best of all, there's a strong possibility of making friends with other kids.

Elsewhere, it's rare to find cots and highchairs, although most hotels and restaurants will do their best to help.

Mobility is an issue for parents with very small children. Strollers (pushchairs) aren't much use. They are hopeless on rough stone paths and up steps, and a curse when getting on/off buses and ferries. Backpacks or front pouches are best.

Fresh milk is available in large towns and tourist areas, but not on the smaller islands. Supermarkets are the best place to look. Formula is available everywhere, as is condensed and heat-treated milk.

Disposable nappies are an environmental curse, but they can be a godsend on the road. They are also available everywhere.

Travel on ferries, buses and trains is free for children under four. They pay half fare up to the age of 10 (ferries) or 12 (buses and trains). Full fares apply otherwise. On domestic flights, you'll pay 10% of the fare to have a child under two sitting on your knee. Kids aged two to 12 pay half fare.

Sights & Activities

If you're travelling around, the shortage of decent playgrounds and other recreational facilities can be a problem, but it's impossible to be far from a beach anywhere on the islands.

Don't be afraid to take children to the ancient sites. Many parents are surprised by how much their children enjoy them. Young imaginations go into overdrive in a place like the 'labyrinth' at Knossos (p233).

CLIMATE

Greece has a mild Mediterranean climate but can be very hot during summer – in July and August the mercury can soar to 40°C (over 100°F) in the shade, just about anywhere in the country. Crete stays warm the longest of all the islands – you can swim off its southern coast from mid-April to November.

Summer is also the time of year when the *meltemi,* a strong northerly wind that sweeps the Aegean (particularly the Cyclades), is at its strongest. The *meltemi* starts off as a mild wind in May and June, and strengthens as the weather hots up – often blowing from a clear blue sky. In August and September it can blow at gale force for days on end. The wind is a mixed blessing: it reduces humidity, but plays havoc with ferry schedules.

The Ionian Islands escape the *meltemi,* but here the main summer wind is the *maïstros,* a light to moderate northwesterly that rises in the afternoon – it usually dies away at sunset.

In the winter, the Ionians are affected by the *gregali,* a northeasterly wind created by depressions moving east in the central Mediterranean.

The *gregali* can blow up to Force 8 on the 12-point Beaufort Scale used by Greek meteorologists.

November to February are the wettest months, and it can also get surprisingly cold. Snow is common on the mainland and in the mountains of Evia and Crete.

For tips on the best times to visit the Greek island see When to Go (p20). See also the climate charts (above).

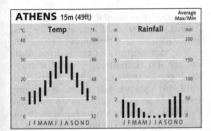

ATHENS 15m (49ft)

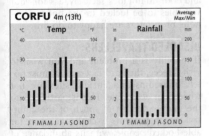

CORFU 4m (13ft)

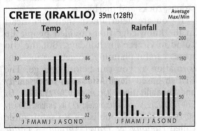

CRETE (IRAKLIO) 39m (128ft)

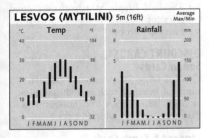

LESVOS (MYTILINI) 5m (16ft)

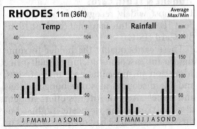

RHODES 11m (36ft)

COURSES

Cooking

Tasting Places (☎ 020-7460 0077; fax 020-7460 0029; www.tastingplaces.com) is a UK company that offers two-week courses on Santorini. Participants learn about the island's celebrated cuisine and its distinctive wines.

Dance

The **Dora Stratou Dance Company** (☎ 210 324 4395; fax 210 324 6921; www.grdance.org; Sholiou 8, Plaka, Athens 105 58) runs one-week courses for visitors at its headquarters in Plaka, Athens, during July and August.

Language

If you are serious about learning the language, an intensive course at the start of your stay is a good way to go about it. Most of the courses are in Athens, but there are also special courses on the islands in summer.

The **Hellenic Culture Centre** (☎ /fax 210 523 8149; www.hcc.gr; Halkokondyli 50, Athens 104 32) runs courses on the island of Lesvos from June to October. Two-week intensive courses for beginners cost €600 and involve 60 classroom hours or a 40 hour intermediate course costing €400. The centre can also arrange accommodation.

The **Athens Centre** (☎ 210 701 2268; fax 210 701 8603; www.athenscentre.gr; Arhimidous 48) in the suburb of Mets, runs courses on the island of Spetses in June and July. The three-week courses cost around €1100 and involve 60 hours of classwork.

Painting

Painting courses are becoming increasingly popular and British tour operators offer a range of possibilities.

Travelux (www.travelux.co.uk) offers a week in the wonderful Zagorohoria region of Epiros in northern Greece, followed by a week on the Ionian island of Lefkada.

Photography

Hania-based British photographer **Steve Outram** (☎ 2821 032 201; www.steveoutram.com) runs courses in Crete twice a year in May and October.

Photo-Tours Naxos (☎ 2285 022 367; www.naxos photoworkshop.com) runs one-day photo outings for small groups (€35 per person) with on-the-spot advice (from professional Stuart Thorpe) on taking better pictures.

DIRECTORY

CUSTOMS

There are no longer duty-free restrictions in the EU. This does not mean, however, that customs checks have been dispensed with; random searches for drugs are still made.

Upon entering the country from outside the EU, inspection is usually cursory for tourists. There may be spot checks, but you may not have to open your bags. A verbal declaration is usually all that is required.

You may bring the following duty-free: 200 cigarettes or 50 cigars; 1L of spirits or 2L of wine; 50g of perfume; 250mL of eau de cologne; one camera (still or video) and film; a pair of binoculars; a portable musical instrument; a portable radio or tape recorder; sports equipment; and dogs and cats (with a vet certificate).

Art and antiquities can be imported for free, but they must be declared, so that they can be re-exported. Import regulations for medicines are strict; if you are taking medication, make sure you get a statement from your doctor before you leave. It is illegal, for instance, to take codeine into Greece without an accompanying doctor's certificate.

An unlimited amount of foreign currency and travellers cheques may be brought into Greece. If you intend to leave the country with foreign banknotes in excess of US$1000, you must declare the sum upon entry.

Restrictions apply to the importation of sailboards into Greece. See the Greek Islands Outdoors chapter (p57) for more details.

It is strictly forbidden to export antiquities (anything over 100 years old) without an export permit. This crime is second only to drug smuggling in the penalties imposed. It is an offence to remove even the smallest article from an archaeological site.

The place to apply for an export permit is the Antique Dealers & Private Collections Section at the **Athens Archaeological Service** (Map p88; Polygnotou 13, Athens).

DANGERS & ANNOYANCES
Scams

Bar scams continue to be an unfortunate fact of life in Athens and are particularly prevalent in the Syntagma area. See p76 for the full run-down on this scam.

Theft

Crime, especially theft, is low in Greece, but unfortunately it's on the increase. The area worst affected is around Omonia in central Athens – keep track of your valuables here, on the metro and at the Sunday flea market.

The vast majority of thefts from tourists are still committed by other tourists; the biggest danger of theft is probably in dormitory rooms in hostels and at camping grounds – so make sure you do not leave valuables unattended in such places. If you are staying in a hotel room, and the windows and door do not lock securely, ask for your valuables to be locked in the hotel safe – hotel proprietors are happy to do this.

DISABLED TRAVELLERS

If mobility is a problem and you wish to visit Greece, the hard fact is that most hotels, museums and ancient sites are not wheelchair accessible. This is partly due to the uneven terrain of much of the country, which presents a challenge even for able-bodied people, with its abundance of stones, rocks and marble.

If you are determined, then take heart in the knowledge that disabled people do come to Greece for holidays. But the trip needs careful planning, so get as much information as you can before you go. The British-based **Royal Association for Disability and Rehabilitation** (Radar; ☎ 020-7250 3222; fax 020-7250 0212; www.radar.org.uk; 12 City Forum, 250 City Rd, London EC1V 8AF) publishes a useful guide called *Holidays & Travel Abroad: A Guide for Disabled People,* which gives a good overview of facilities available to disabled travellers in Europe.

DISCOUNT CARDS
Senior Cards

Card-carrying EU pensioners can claim a range of benefits, such as reduced admission at ancient sites and museums, and discounts on bus and train fares.

Student & Youth Cards

The most widely recognised form of student ID is the International Student Identity Card (ISIC).

These cards qualify the holder to some significant discounts including half-price admission to museums and ancient sites, and for discounts at some budget hotels and hostels. Aegean Airlines offers student discounts on some domestic flights, but there are none to be had on buses, ferries or trains. Students will find some good deals on international air fares.

Some travel agencies in Athens are licensed to issue cards. You must show documents proving you are a student, provide a passport photo and cough up €10.

Euro<26 (www.euro26.org) youth cards are not valid in Greece. Visit www.istc.org for more information.

EMBASSIES & CONSULATES
Greek Embassies
The following is a selection of Greek diplomatic missions abroad:

Albania (☎ 54-223 959; www.greekembassy.al; Ruga Frederik Shiroka, Tirana)

Australia (☎ 02-6273 3011; www.greekembassy.org .au; 9 Turrana St, Yarralumla, ACT 2600)

Bulgaria (☎ 2-946 1027; San Stefano 33, Sofia 1504)

Canada (☎ 613-238 6271; www.greekembassy.ca; 76-80 Maclaren St, Ottawa, Ontario K2P OK6)

Cyprus (☎ 02-680 670/671; Byron Blvd 8-10, Nicosia)

Denmark (☎ 33-114 533; Borgergade 16, 1300 Copenhagen K)

Egypt (☎ 02-795 0443; 18 Aisha el Taymouria, Garden City, Cairo)

France (☎ 01-47 23 72 28; www.amb-grece.fr; 17 Rue Auguste Vacquerie, Paris 75116)

Germany (☎ 30-213 7033/4; www.griechische-bot schaft.de; Jaegerstrasse 54-55, 10117 Berlin-Mitte)

Ireland (☎ 01-676 7254; 1 Upper Pembroke St, Dublin 2)

Israel (☎ 03-695 3060; Tower Bldg, Daniel Grise 3, Tel Aviv 64731)

Italy (☎ 06-853 7551; www.greekembassy.it; Via S Mercadante 36, Rome 00198)

Japan (☎ 03-3403 0871/0872; www.greekemb.jp; 3-16-30 Nishi Ajabu, Minato-ku, Tokyo 106-0031)

Netherlands (☎ 070-363 87 00; www.greekembassy .nl; Amaliastraat 1, 2514 JC, The Hague)

New Zealand (☎ 04-473 7775; 5-7 Willeston St, Wellington)

Norway (☎ 2244 2728; Nobels Gate 45, 0244 Oslo 2)

South Africa (☎ 12-430 7351;1003 Church St, Hatfield, Pretoria 0028)

Spain (☎ 01-564 4653; Avenida Doctor Arce 24, Madrid 28002)

Sweden (☎ 08-545 66 019; Riddargatan 60, 11457 Stockholm)

Switzerland (☎ 31-356 1414; Laubeggstrasse, 3006 Bern)

Turkey (☎ 312-436 8860; Ziya-ul-Rahman Caddesi 9-11, Gaziosmanpasa 06700, Ankara)

UK (☎ 020-7229 3850; www.greekembassy.org.uk;1A Holland Park, London W11 3TP)

USA (☎ 202-939 1300; www.greekembassy.org; 2221 Massachusetts Ave NW, Washington DC 20008)

Embassies in Greece
All foreign embassies in Greece are in Athens and its suburbs.

Albania (☎ 210 723 4412; Karahristou 1, 115 21)

Australia (☎ 210 645 0404; www.ausemb.gr; Dimitriou Soutsou 37, Ambelokipi, 115 21)

Bulgaria (☎ 210 674 8105; Stratigou Kalari 33a, Psyhiko, 154 52)

Canada (☎ 210 727 3400; www.dfait.maeci.gc.ca /canadaeuropa/greece; Gennadiou 4, 115 21)

Cyprus (Map p88; ☎ 210 723 7883; Irodotou 16, 106 75)

Egypt (☎ 210 361 8612; Leof Vasilissis Sofias 3)

France (Map p88; ☎ 210 361 1663; www.ambafrance -gr.org; Leof Vasilissis Sofias 7, 106 71)

Germany (Map p74; ☎ 210 728 5111; www.athen .diplo.de; Dimitriou 3 & Karaoli, Kolonaki, 106 75)

Hungary (☎ 210 672 5337; Kalvou 16, Psyhiko, 154 52)

Ireland (Map p74; ☎ 210 723 2771; Leof Vasilissis Sofias 60, 106 74)

Israel (☎ 210 671 9530; Marathonodromou 1, 154 52)

Italy (Map p74; ☎ 210 361 7260; Sekeri 2, 106 74)

Japan (☎ 210 775 8101; www.gr.emb-japan.go.jp; Athens Tower, Leof Mesogion 2-4, 115 27)

Netherlands (Map p88; ☎ 210 723 9701; www .dutchembassy.gr; Vasileos Konstantinou 5-7, 106 74)

New Zealand (Map p88; ☎ 210 687 4701; Kifisias 268, Halandri)

Serbia & Montenegro (☎ 210 777 4355; Leof Vasilissis Sofias 106, 115 21)

South Africa (☎ 210 680 6645; www.southafrica.gr; Kifisias 60, Marousi, 151 25)

Turkey (Map p88; ☎ 210 724 5915; Vasileos Georgiou 8, 106 74)

UK (Map p74; ☎ 210 723 6211; www.britishembassy .gr; Ploutarhou 1, 106 75)

USA (☎ 210 721 2951; http://athens.usembassy.gov; Leof Vasilissis Sofias 91, 115 21)

It's important to realise what your own embassy – the embassy of the country of which you are a citizen – can and can't do to help you if you get into trouble. Generally speaking, it won't be much help in emergencies if the trouble you're in is remotely your own fault. Remember that you are bound by the laws of the country you are in. Your embassy will not be sympathetic if you end up in jail after committing a crime locally, even if such actions are legal in your own country.

In genuine emergencies you might get some assistance, but only if other channels have been exhausted. For example, if you need to get home urgently, a free ticket home is exceedingly unlikely – the embassy would expect you to have insurance. If you have all your money and documents stolen, it might assist with getting a new passport, but a loan for onward travel is out of the question.

Some embassies used to keep letters for travellers or have a small reading room with home newspapers, but these days the mail-holding service has usually been stopped and even newspapers tend to be out of date.

FESTIVALS & EVENTS

The Greek year is a succession of festivals and events, some of which are religious, some cultural, others just an excuse for a good party, and some a combination of all three. The following is by no means an exhaustive list, but it covers the most important events, both national and regional. If you're in the right place at the right time, you'll certainly be invited to join the revelry.

More information about festivals and events can be found at www.cultureguide.gr.

January

Feast of Agios Vasilios (St Basil) The year kicks off with this festival on 1 January. A church ceremony is followed by the exchanging of gifts, singing, dancing and feasting; the New Year *vasilopitta* (pie) is cut and the person who gets the slice containing a coin will supposedly have a lucky year.

Epiphany (the Blessing of the Waters) The day of Christ's baptism by St John is celebrated throughout Greece on 6 January. Seas, lakes and rivers are blessed and crosses immersed in them. The largest ceremony occurs at Piraeus.

February

Carnival Season The three-week period before the beginning of Lent (the 40-day period before Easter, which is traditionally a period of fasting) is carnival season. The carnivals are ostensibly Christian pre-Lenten celebrations, but many derive from pagan festivals. There are many regional variations, but fancy dress, feasting, traditional dancing and general merry-making prevail. The Patra carnival (p107) is the largest and most exuberant, with elaborately decorated chariots parading through the streets. The most bizarre carnival takes place on the island of Skyros (p426), where the men transform themselves into grotesque 'half-man, half-beast' creatures by donning goat-skin masks and hairy jackets.

Shrove Monday (Clean Monday) On the Monday before Ash Wednesday (the first day of Lent), people take to the hills throughout Greece to have picnics and fly kites.

March

Independence Day The anniversary of the hoisting of the Greek flag by Bishop Germanos at Moni Agias Lavras is celebrated on 25 March with parades and dancing.

Germanos' act of revolt marked the start of the War of Independence. Independence Day coincides with the Feast of the Annunciation, so it is also a religious festival.

April

Easter This is the most important festival in the Greek Orthodox religion. Emphasis is placed on the Resurrection rather than on the Crucifixion, so it is a joyous occasion. The festival begins on the evening of Good Friday with the *perifora epitavios*, when a shrouded bier (representing Christ's funeral bier) is carried through the streets to the local church. This moving candle-lit procession can be seen in towns and villages throughout the country. From a spectator's viewpoint, the most impressive of these processions climbs Lykavittos Hill (p86) in Athens to the Chapel of Agios Georgios. The Resurrection Mass starts at 11pm on Saturday night. At midnight, packed churches are plunged into darkness to symbolise Christ's passing through the underworld. The ceremony of the lighting of candles, which follows, is the most significant moment in the Orthodox year, for it symbolises the Resurrection. Its poignancy and beauty are spellbinding. If you are in Greece at Easter you should endeavour to attend this ceremony, which ends with fireworks and candle-lit processions through the streets. The Lenten fast ends on Easter Sunday with the cracking of red-dyed Easter eggs and an outdoor feast of roast lamb followed by Greek dancing. The day's greeting is *Hristos anesti* (Christ is risen), to which the reply is *Alithos anesti* (Truly He is risen). On both Palm Sunday (the Sunday before Easter) and Easter Sunday, St Spyridon (the mummified patron saint of Corfu) is taken out for an airing and joyously paraded through Corfu Town. He is paraded again on 11 August.

Feast of Agios Georgos (St George) The feast day of St George, Greece's patron saint and patron saint of shepherds, takes place on 23 April or the Tuesday following Easter (whichever comes first).

May

May Day On the first day of May there is a mass exodus from towns to the country. During picnics, wildflowers are gathered and made into wreaths to decorate houses.

June

Navy Week The festival celebrates the long relationship between Greeks and the sea with events in fishing villages and ports throughout the country. Volos (p109) and Hydra (p124) each have unique versions of these celebrations. Volos re-enacts the departure of the Argo, for legend has it that Iolkos (from where Jason and the Argonauts set off in search of the Golden Fleece) was near the city. Hydra commemorates War of Independence-hero Admiral Andreas Miaoulis, who was born on the island, at its Miaoulia Festival, which includes a re-enactment of one of his naval victories, accompanied by feasting and fireworks.

Feast of St John the Baptist This feast day on 24 June is widely celebrated around Greece. Wreaths made on May Day are kept until this day, when they are burned on bonfires.
Hellenic Festival The Hellenic Festival is the most important of the many festivals staged throughout Greece during summer. It features performances of music, dance and drama at the Odeon of Herodes Atticus in Athens, and performances of ancient Greek drama at the world famous Theatre of Epidavros, near Nafplio in the Peloponnese.

July
Feast of Agia Marina (St Marina) This feast day is celebrated on 17 July in many parts of Greece and is a particularly important event on the Dodecanese island of Kasos (p300).
Feast of Profitis Ilias This feast day is celebrated on 20 July at the many hilltop churches and monasteries throughout Greece that are dedicated to the prophet Ilias.
Folegandros Festival The Folegandros Festival features a week-long programme of music and feasting at a range of locations around the island's beautiful old Hora (p205).

August
Assumption Greeks celebrate Assumption Day (15 August) with family reunions. The whole population seems to be on the move either side of the big day, so it's a good time to avoid public transport. The island of Tinos (p140) gets particularly busy because of its miracle-working icon of Panagia Evangelistria. It becomes a place of pilgrimage for thousands, who come to be blessed, healed or baptised.
Samothraki World Music Festival The Northeastern Aegean island of Samothraki (p391), plays host to a world music festival in late August incorporating blues, roots, reggae, jazz and traditional music.

September
Genesis Tis Panagias The birthday of the Virgin Mary is celebrated on 8 September throughout Greece with religious services and feasting.
Exaltation of the Cross This is celebrated on 14 September throughout Greece with processions and hymns.

October
Feast of Agios Dimitrios This feast day is celebrated in Thessaloniki (p100) on 26 October with wine drinking and revelry.
Ohi (No) Day Metaxas' refusal to allow Mussolini's troops free passage through Greece in WWII is commemorated on 28 October with remembrance services, military parades, folk dancing and feasting.

December
Christmas Day Although not as important as Easter, Christmas is still celebrated with religious services and feasting. Nowadays much 'Western' influence is apparent, including Christmas trees, decorations and presents.

FOOD
For large cities and towns, restaurant listings in this book are given in the following order: budget (under €15), midrange (€15 to €30) and top end (over €30), and within each section the restaurants are listed in order of preference. For information on the staples of Greek food, see the Food & Drink chapter (p62).

GAY & LESBIAN TRAVELLERS
In a country where the church still plays a prominent role in shaping society's views on issues such as sexuality, it should come as no surprise that homosexuality is generally frowned upon – especially outside the major cities. While there is no legislation against homosexual activity, it pays to be discreet and to avoid open displays of togetherness.

This has not prevented Greece from becoming an extremely popular destination for gay travellers. Athens has a busy gay scene – but most gay travellers head for the islands. Mykonos (p150) has long been famous for its bars, beaches and general hedonism, while Paros (and Antiparos), Rhodes, Santorini and Skiathos all have their share of gay hang-outs.

The town of Skala Eresou (p381) on the island of Lesvos (Mytilini), birthplace of the lesbian poet Sappho, has become something of a place of pilgrimage for lesbians.

Information
The *Spartacus International Gay Guide*, published by Bruno Gmünder (Berlin), is widely regarded as the leading authority on the gay travel scene. The Greek section contains a wealth of information on gay venues throughout the country.

There's also stacks of information on the Internet. For example, the website **Roz Mov** (www.geocities.com/WestHollywood/2225/index.html), is a good place to start. It has pages on travel information, gay health, the gay press, organisations, events and legal issues – and links to lots more sites.

Gayscape (www.gayscape.com/gayscape/menugreece.html) also has a useful website with lots of links.

HOLIDAYS
Public Holidays
All banks and shops and most museums and ancient sites close on public holidays.

The following are national public holidays in Greece:

New Year's Day 1 January
Epiphany 6 January
First Sunday in Lent February
Greek Independence Day 25 March
Good Friday March/April
(Orthodox) Easter Sunday March/April
Spring Festival/Labour Day 1 May
Feast of the Assumption 15 August
Ohi Day 28 October
Christmas Day 25 December
St Stephen's Day 26 December

School Holidays

The Greek school year is divided into three terms. The main school holidays are in July and August.

INSURANCE

A travel insurance policy to cover theft, loss and medical problems is a good idea. Some of these policies offer lower and higher medical-expense options; the higher ones are chiefly for countries such as the USA, which have extremely high medical costs. There is a wide variety of policies available, so check the small print.

Some policies specifically exclude 'dangerous activities', eg scuba diving, motorcycling, even trekking. A locally acquired motorcycle licence is not valid under some policies.

You may prefer a policy that pays doctors or hospitals directly rather than you having to pay on the spot and claim later. If you have to claim later make sure you retain all documentation related to the claim. Some policies ask you to call back (reverse charges) to a centre in your home country where an immediate assessment of your problem is made.

Check that the policy covers ambulances or an emergency flight home.

Buy travel insurance as early as possible. If you buy it just before you fly, you may find you're not covered for such problems as delays caused by industrial action. Make sure you have a separate record of all your ticket details – preferably a photocopy (for information on what else to copy see the boxed text, p495).

Paying for your ticket with a credit card sometimes provides limited travel insurance, and you may be able to reclaim the payment if the operator doesn't deliver. In the UK, for instance, credit-card providers are required by law to reimburse consumers if a company goes into liquidation and the amount in contention is more than UK£100.

INTERNET ACCESS

Internet cafés are to be found almost everywhere in Greece, and are listed under the Information section for cities and islands in this book. Some hotels also offer Internet access.

Some small islands may not have Internet access, though surprisingly you can find Internet in even the smallest of places. Charges range from €3 to a hefty €7 (when the owner has a monopoly and thinks they can get away with it). Connections can be slow or fast depending on whether they use dial-up or broadband. In short the islands are not any more lacking in resources and communication options than the mainland.

Check out www.netcafeguide.com for an up-to-date list of Internet cafés throughout Greece. You may also find public Net access in post offices, libraries, hostels, hotels, universities and so on.

Travelling with a portable computer is a great way to stay in touch with life back home, but unless you know what you're doing it's fraught with potential problems. If you plan to carry your notebook or palmtop computer with you, remember that the power-supply voltage in the countries you visit may vary from that at home, risking damage to your equipment. You'll also need a plug adaptor for each country you visit.

Also, your PC-card modem may not work away from your home country – and you won't know for sure until you try. The safest option is to buy a reputable 'global' modem before you leave home, or buy a local PC-card modem if you're spending an extended time in any one country. Keep in mind that the telephone socket in Greece will probably be different from the one at home, so ensure that you have at least a US RJ-11 telephone adaptor that works with your modem. You can almost always find an adaptor that will convert from RJ-11 to the local variety. For more information on travelling with a portable computer see www.teleadapt.com.

Email

Major Internet service providers such as **AOL** (www.aol.com) and **CompuServe** (www.compuserve.com)

have dial-in nodes throughout Europe; it's best to download a list of the dial-in numbers before you leave home. If you access your Internet email account at home through a smaller ISP or your office or school network, your best option is either to open an account with a global ISP, like those mentioned above, or to rely on Internet cafés and other public access points to collect your mail.

If you do intend to rely on Internet cafés, the best option to collect mail is to open a free Web-based email account online with, say, Yahoo! or Hotmail. You can then access your mail from anywhere in the world from any Net-connected machine running a standard Web browser.

LEGAL MATTERS
Arrests

It is a good idea to have your passport with you at all times in case you are stopped by the police and questioned. Greek citizens are presumed to always have identification on them; foreign visitors are similarly presumed to by the police. If you are arrested by police insist on an interpreter (*the*-lo dhi-ermi-*nea*) and/or a lawyer (*the*-lo dhi-ki-*go*-ro).

Drugs

Drug laws in Greece are the strictest in Europe. Greek courts make no distinction between the possession of drugs and dealing them. Possession of even a small amount of marijuana is likely to land you in jail.

MAPS

Unless you are going to trek or drive, the free maps given out by the EOT will probably suffice, although they are not 100% accurate. On islands where there is no EOT office there are usually tourist maps for sale for around €1.50 but, again, these are not very accurate.

The best maps are published by the Greek company Road Editions, whose maps are produced with the Hellenic Army Geographical Service. These maps are being updated using Global Positioning Satellite technology. There is a wide range of maps to suit various needs, starting with a 1:500,000 map of Greece. Crete is well covered by the company's maroon-covered 1:250,000 mainland series. Even the smallest roads and villages are clearly marked, and the distance indicators are spot-on – important when negotiating your way around the backblocks. Useful features include symbols to indicate the location of petrol stations and tyre shops.

The company's blue-cover Greek island series includes all the main islands. The scale ranges from 1:100,000 for larger islands like Corfu and Rhodes to 1:30,000 for Syros. It also publishes a 1:50,000 green-cover Greek mountain series, produced with trekkers in mind. The series includes *Mt Athos, Mt Olympia, Mt Parnitha, Mt Parnassos* and the *Pelion Peninsula (Pilio)*.

Freytag & Berndt's 15-map Greece series has good coverage of the islands and the Peloponnese.

MONEY

Greece dropped the drachma and adopted the euro at the beginning of 2002.

There are eight euro coins, in denominations of two and one euros; 50, 20, 10, five, two and one cents, and six notes: €5, €10, €20, €50, €100 and €200. Prices in many shops are still displayed in both drachma and euros.

See the inside front cover for currency exchange rates, and see p20 for information on costs in Greece.

ATMs

ATMs are to be found in every town large enough to support a bank – and certainly in all of the well-touristed areas. If you've got MasterCard or Visa/Access, there are plenty of places to withdraw money. Cirrus and Maestro users can make withdrawals in all major towns and tourist areas.

Automated foreign-exchange machines are common in major tourist areas. They take all the major European currencies, Australian and US dollars and Japanese yen, and can come in handy in an emergency. It's worth noting that you are charged a hefty commission though.

COMING OF AGE

For the record:

- You can drive when you're 18.
- The legal age for voting in Greece is 18.
- The age of consent for homosexual/ heterosexual sex for girls is 15/15 and boys 16/17.
- The legal drinking age is 16.

Cash

Nothing beats cash for convenience – or for risk. If you lose cash, it's gone for good and very few travel insurers will come to your rescue. It's best to carry no more cash than you need for the next few days, which means working out your potential costs whenever you change travellers cheques or withdraw cash from an ATM.

It's also a good idea to set aside a small amount of cash, say €100, as an emergency stash.

Credit Cards

The great advantage of credit cards is that they allow you to pay for major items without carrying around great wads of cash. Credit cards are now an accepted part of the commercial scene just about everywhere in Greece. They can be used to pay for a wide range of goods and services, such as meals (in better restaurants), accommodation, car hire and souvenirs.

Be sure to ask whether it's possible to have your card replaced in Greece if it is lost or stolen.

The main credit cards are MasterCard, Visa and Eurocard, all of which are widely accepted in Greece. They can also be used as cash cards to draw cash from the ATMs of affiliated Greek banks in the same way as at home. Daily withdrawal limits are set by the issuing bank. Cash advances are given in local currency only.

The main charge cards are American Express (Amex) and Diners Club, which are widely accepted in tourist areas but unheard of elsewhere.

Tipping

In restaurants a service charge is normally included in the bill and while a tip is not expected (as it is in North America), it is always appreciated and should be left if the service has been good. Taxi drivers expect you to round up the fare, while bellhops who help you with your luggage to your hotel room or stewards on ferries who take you to your cabin normally expect a small gratuity of up to €1.

Travellers Cheques

The main reason to carry travellers cheques rather than cash is the protection they offer against theft. Cheques are, however, losing popularity as more and more travellers opt to put their money in a bank at home and withdraw it from ATMs as they go along.

Amex, Visa and Thomas Cook cheques are all widely accepted and have efficient replacement policies. Maintaining a record of the cheque numbers and recording when you use them is vital when it comes to replacing lost cheques – keep this record separate from the cheques themselves.

PHOTOGRAPHY & VIDEO

Digital photography has taken over in a big way in Greece and a range of memory cards can now be bought from camera shops. Film is still widely available, although it can be expensive in smaller towns. You'll find all the gear you need in the photography shops of Athens and major cities.

It is possible to obtain video cartridges easily in large towns and cities, but make sure you buy the correct format. It is usually worth buying at least a few cartridges duty-free to start off your trip.

As elsewhere in the world, developing film is a competitive business. Most places charge around €8.80 to develop a roll of 36 colour prints.

Lonely Planet's *Travel Photography: A Guide to Taking Better Pictures* by well-known photographer Richard I'Anson offers a comprehensive guide to technical and creative travel photography.

Restrictions & Etiquette

Never photograph a military installation or anything else that has a sign forbidding photography. Flash photography is not allowed inside churches and it's considered taboo to photograph the main altar.

Greeks love having their photos taken but ask permission first. The same goes for video cameras, probably even more annoying and offensive for locals than a still camera.

POST

Tahydromia (post offices) are easily identifiable by the yellow signs outside. Regular post boxes are also yellow. The red boxes are for express mail only.

Postal Rates

The postal rate for postcards and airmail letters to destinations within the EU is €0.65 for up to 20g, €1 for up to 50g and €1.50 for up to

100g. To other destinations the rate is €0.65 for up to 20g and €1.15 for up to 150g. Post within Europe takes between five and eight days, and to the USA, Australia and New Zealand nine to 11 days. Some tourist shops also sell stamps, but with a 10% surcharge.

Express mail costs an extra €2 and should ensure delivery in three days within the EU – use the special red post boxes. Valuables should be sent registered post.

Sending Mail

Do not wrap a parcel until it has been inspected at a post office. In Athens, take your parcel to the **Parcel Post Office** (Map p74; ☎ 210 322 8940; Stadiou 4, Athens) in the arcade and elsewhere to the parcel counter of a regular post office.

Receiving Mail

You can receive mail poste restante (general delivery) at any main post office. The service is free, but you are required to show your passport. Ask senders to write your family name in capital letters and underline it, and also to mark the envelope 'poste restante'. It is a good idea to ask the post office clerk to check under your first name as well if letters you are expecting cannot be located. After one month, uncollected mail is returned to the sender. If you are about to leave a town and expected mail hasn't arrived, ask at the post office to have it forwarded to your next destination, c/o poste restante. Both Athens' **Central Post Office** (Map p74; Eolou 100, Omonia; 102 00; ⏲ 7.30am-8pm Mon-Fri, 7.30am-2pm Sat) and **Syntagma Post Office** (Map p88; cnr Mitropoleos & Plateia Syntagmatos 103 00; ⏲ 7.30am-8pm Mon-Fri, 7.30am-2pm Sat) hold poste-restante mail.

Parcels are not delivered in Greece; they must be collected from the parcel counter of a post office or, in Athens, from the Parcel Post Office.

SHOPPING

Shopping in Greece for Greeks and visitors alike is big business. At times a tourist town can look like one big shop with all kinds of goods and trinkets on display. The trouble is a lot of it is overpriced and of inferior quality so the moral of the story is don't shop in tourist areas. That said Athens' Flea Market (p93) has a bewildering array of items on sale and you can find some good bargains. Shoes and clothes are excellent buys,

especially in the post-seasonal sales; and if you have room in your suitcase or backpack there are some really excellent quality artisanal works to be picked up from small boutiques and galleries including pottery, jewellery and metalworked objets.

Bargaining

Getting a bit extra off the deal through bargaining is sadly a thing of the past in Greece nowadays. You might be offered a 'special deal' but the art and sport of bargaining has gone the way of the drachma: out the window. Instead know your goods and decide for yourself if the price you are being offered is worth it before accepting the deal.

SOLO TRAVELLERS

Greece is a great destination for solo travellers, especially in summer when the islands become an international meeting point. Hostels and other backpacker-friendly accommodation are good places to meet up with other solo travellers.

Many women travel alone in Greece. The crime rate remains relatively low and solo travel is probably safer than in most European countries. This does not mean that you should be lulled into complacency; bag snatching and rapes do occur, although violent offences are rare.

The biggest nuisance to foreign women travelling alone are the guys the Greeks have nicknamed *kamaki*. The word means 'fishing trident' and refers to the *kamaki*'s favourite pastime: 'fishing' for women. You will find them everywhere there are lots of tourists; young (for the most part), smooth-talking guys who aren't in the least bashful about sidling up to foreign women in the street. They can be very persistent, but they are a hassle rather than a threat.

The majority of Greek men treat foreign women with respect and are genuinely helpful.

TELEPHONE

The telephone service in Greece is maintained by the public corporation known as OTE (pronounced o-*teh*; Organismos Tilepikoinonion Ellados).

The system is modern and reasonably well maintained. There are public telephones just about everywhere, including some unbelievably isolated spots. The phones are easy to operate and can be used for local, long distance and international calls. The 'i' at the top left of the push-button dialling panel brings up the operating instructions in English.

Mobile Phones

Few countries in the world have embraced the mobile phone with such enthusiasm as Greece.

It has become the essential Greek accessory; everyone seems to have one.

If you have a compatible GSM mobile phone from a country with an overseas global roaming arrangement with Greece, you will be able to use your phone in Greece. You must inform your mobile phone service provider before you depart in order to have global roaming activated.

There are several mobile service providers in Greece – among which Panafon, CosmOTE and Telestet are the best known. Of these three, CosmOTE tends to have the best coverage in remote areas, so try re-tuning your phone to CosmOTE if you find mobile coverage is patchy.

All three companies offer pay-as-you-talk services by which you can buy a rechargeable SIM card and have your own Greek mobile number: a good idea if you plan to spend some time in Greece.

The Panafon system is called 'à la Carte', the Telestet system 'B-free' and CosmOTE's 'Cosmo Karta'.

USA and Canadian mobile phone users won't be able to use their mobile phones, unless their handset is quipped with a dual system.

Phonecards

All public phones use the OTE phonecards, known as *telekarta*, not coins. These cards (€3, €5 and €9) are widely available at *periptera*, corner shops and tourist shops. A local call costs €0.30 for three minutes.

It's also possible to use the public phones using a growing range of discount-card schemes, which involve dialling an access code and then punching in your card number. The OTE version of this card is known as 'Hronokarta'. The cards come with instructions in Greek and English. They are easy to use and buy double the time. The best of these cards is Smile, also widely available.

TIME

Greece maintains one time zone throughout the whole country and is two hours ahead of GMT/UTC and three hours ahead on daylight-saving time, which begins on the last Sunday in March, when clocks are put forward one hour.

Daylight saving ends on the last Sunday in September.

TOILETS

Most places in Greece have Western-style toilets. You'll occasionally come across Asian-style squat toilets in older houses, *kafeneia* and public toilets.

Public toilets are a rarity, except at airports and bus and train stations. Cafés are usually the best option if you happen to get caught short, but you'll most likely be expected to purchase something for the privilege.

One peculiarity of the Greek plumbing system is that it can't handle toilet paper; apparently the pipes are too narrow; flushing away tampons and sanitary napkins is guaranteed to block the system.

Whatever the reason, anything larger than a postage stamp seems to cause a serious problem. Toilet paper etc should be placed in the small bin that is provided near every toilet.

TOURIST INFORMATION

All of the tourist information is handled by the Greek National Tourist Organisation, known by the initials GNTO abroad and EOT (Ellinikos Organismos Tourismou) in Greece.

Local Tourist Offices

The EOT in Athens (p76) dispenses a variety of information, including a very useful timetable of the week's ferry departures from Piraeus. The office also provides details about public transport prices and schedules from Athens. Its free map of Athens is urgently in need of an update, although most places of interest are clearly marked. The office is about 500m from Ambelokipi metro station.

EOT offices can be found in most major tourist locations. Though these offices are increasingly being supplemented or sometimes even replaced by local municipality tourist offices.

Tourist Offices Abroad

GNTO offices abroad:

Australia (☎ 02-9241 1663/5; hto@tpg.com.au; 51-57 Pitt St, Sydney NSW 2000)

Austria (☎ 1-512 5317; grect@vienna.at; Opernring 8, Vienna A-10105)

Belgium (☎ 2-647 5770; fax 647 5142; 172 Ave Louise Louizalaan, B1050 Brussels)

Canada Montreal (☎ 514-871 1535; 1170 Place du Frère Andre, Montreal, Quebec H3B 3C6); Toronto (☎ 416-968 2220; gnto.tor@sympatico.ca; 91 Scollard St, Toronto, Ontario M5R 1G4)

Denmark (☎ 33-325 332; Vester Farimagsgade 1, 1606 Copenhagen)

France (☎ 01-42 60 65 75; eot@club-Internet.fr; 3 Ave de l'Opéra, Paris 75001)

Germany Berlin (☎ 30-217 6262; Wittenbergplatz 3A, 10789 Berlin 30); Frankfurt (☎ 69-236 561; info@gzf-eot.de; Neue Mainzerstrasse 22, 60311 Frankfurt); Hamburg (☎ 40-454 498; info-hamburg@gzf-eot.de; Neurer Wall 18, 20254 Hamburg); Munich (☎ 89-222 035/036; Pacellistrasse 5, 2W 80333 Munich)

Israel (☎ 3-517 0501; hellenic@netvision.net.il; 5 Shalom Aleichem St, Tel Aviv 61262)

Italy (www.enteturismoellenico.com); Milan (☎ 02-860 470; Piazza Diaz 1, 20123 Milano); Rome (☎ 06-474 4249; Via L Bissolati 78-80, 00187 Roma)

Japan (☎ 03-350 55 917; gnto-jpn@t3.rim.or.jp; Fukuda Bldg West, 5F 2-11-3 Akasaka, Minato-Ku, Tokyo 107)

Netherlands (☎ 20-625 4212; gnto@planet.nl; Kerkstraat 61, Amsterdam GC 1017)

Sweden (☎ 8-679 6480; grekiska.statens .turistbyra@swipnet.se; Birger Jarlsgatan 30, Box 5298 S, 10246 Stockholm)

Switzerland (☎ 01-221 0105; eot@bluewin.ch; Loewenstrasse 25, 8001 Zürich)

UK (☎ 020-7734 5997; 4 Conduit St, London W1R 0DJ)

USA (www.greektourism.com); Chicago (☎ 312-782 1084; Suite 600, 168 North Michigan Ave, Chicago, Illinois 60601); Los Angeles (☎ 213-626 6696; Suite 2198, 611 West 6th St, Los Angeles, California 92668); New York (☎ 212-421 5777; Olympic Tower, 645 5th Ave, New York, NY 10022)

Tourist Police

The tourist police work in cooperation with the regular Greek police and EOT. Each tourist-police office has at least one member of staff who speaks English. Hotels, restaurants, travel agencies, tourist shops, tourist guides, waiters, taxi drivers and bus drivers all come under the jurisdiction of the tourist police. If you think that you have been ripped off by any of these, report it to the tourist police and they will investigate.

If you need to report a theft or loss of passport, then go to the tourist police first, and they will act as interpreters between you and the regular police. The tourist police also fulfil the same functions as the EOT and municipal tourist offices, dispensing maps and brochures, and giving information on transport. They can often help to find accommodation.

VISAS

The list of countries whose nationals can stay in Greece for up to three months without a visa includes Australia, Canada, all EU countries, Iceland, Israel, Japan, New Zealand, Norway, Switzerland and the USA. Other countries included are the European principalities of Monaco and San Marino and most South American countries. The list changes – contact Greek embassies for the full list (up-to-date visa information is also available on www.lonelyplanet.com). Those not included can expect to pay about US$20 for a three-month visa.

Visa Extensions

If you wish to stay in Greece for longer than three months, apply at a consulate abroad or at least 20 days in advance to the **Aliens Bureau** (☎ 210 770 5711; Leof Alexandras 173; ⏰ 8am-1pm Mon-Fri) in the Athens Central Police Station. Take your passport and four passport photographs along. You may be asked for proof that you can support yourself financially, so keep all your bank exchange slips (or the equivalent from a post office). These slips are not always automatically given – you may have to ask for them. Elsewhere in Greece apply to the local police authority. You will be given a permit that will authorise you to stay in the country for a period of up to six months.

Most travellers manage to get around this by visiting Bulgaria or Turkey briefly and then re-entering Greece.

COPIES

All important documents (passport data page and visa page, credit cards, travel insurance policy, air/bus/train tickets, driving licence etc) should be photocopied before you leave home. Leave one copy with someone at home and keep another with you, separate from the originals.

DIRECTORY

WORK

EU nationals don't need a work permit, but they need a residency permit if they intend to stay longer than three months. Nationals of other countries are supposed to have a work permit.

Bar & Hostel Work

The bars of the Greek islands could not survive without foreign workers and there are thousands of summer jobs up for grabs every year. The pay is not fantastic, but you get to spend a summer in the islands. April and May is the time to go looking. Hostels and travellers hotels are other places that regularly employ foreign workers.

English Tutoring

If you're looking for a permanent job, the most widely available option is to teach English. A TEFL (Teaching English as a Foreign Language) certificate or a university degree is an advantage but not essential. In the UK, look through the *Times Educational Supplement* or Tuesday's edition of the *Guardian* newspaper for job opportunities – in other countries, contact the Greek embassy.

Another option is to find a job teaching English once in Greece. You will see language schools everywhere.

Strictly speaking, you need a licence to teach in these schools, but many will employ teachers without one. The best time to look is late summer.

Check out the notice board at the **Compendium** (p73) bookshop in Athens as it sometimes has advertisements looking for private English lessons.

Volunteer Work

The **Hellenic Society for the Study & Protection of the Monk Seal** (☎ 2105 222 888; fax 2105 222 450; Solomou 53, Athens 104 32) and **Archelon** (Sea Turtle Protection Society of Greece; ☎ /fax 2105 231 342; www .archelon.gr; Solomou 57, Athens 104 32) use volunteers for the monitoring programmes they run on the Ionian Islands.

The **Hellenic Wildlife Rehabilitation Centre** (Elliniko Kentro Perithalifis Agrion Zoon; ☎ 2297 028 367; www.ekpaz.gr in Greek; ☼ 11am-1pm) in Aegina welcomes volunteers, particularly during the winter months. The new centre has accommodation available for volunteer workers. For more information see p120.

Other Work

There are often jobs advertised in the classifieds section of English-language newspapers, or you can place an advertisement yourself. EU nationals can also make use of the OAED (Organismos Apasholiseos Ergatikou Dynamikou), the Greek National Employment Service. The OAED has offices throughout Greece.

Seasonal harvest work is mainly handled by migrant workers from Albania and other Balkan nations, and is no longer a viable option for travellers.

Transport

THINGS CHANGE...

The information in this chapter is particularly vulnerable to change. Check directly with the airline or a travel agent to make sure you understand how a fare (and ticket you may buy) works and be aware of the security requirements for international travel. Shop carefully. The details given in this chapter should be regarded as pointers and are not a substitute for your own careful, up-to-date research.

GETTING THERE & AWAY

ENTERING THE COUNTRY

Entry into Greece from the EU is nominally free of any formalities. Spot checks for contraband may be made of individuals or vehicles at the entry ports. Authorities may pay you more attention if entering from non-EU countries.

Passport

All visitors must have a passport – or ID card if a resident of the EU – and depending on your nationality, a visa.

For more detailed information on visas, see p495.

AIR

Most travellers arrive in Greece by air, which is often the cheapest and quickest way to get there.

Airports & Airlines

Greece has 16 international airports, but only those in Athens, Thessaloniki and Iraklio (Crete) take scheduled flights.

Athens (Eleftherios Venizelos International Airport; Code ATH; ☎ 2103 530 000; www.aia.gr)

Iraklio (Nikos Kazantzakis International Airport; Code HER; ☎ 2810 228 401)

Thessaloniki (Macedonia International Airport; Code SKG; ☎ 2310 473 700; users.otenet.gr/~cpnchris /skg.html)

Athens handles the vast majority of flights, including all intercontinental traffic. Thessaloniki has direct flights to Amsterdam, Belgrade, Berlin, Brussels, Cyprus, Düsseldorf, Frankfurt, İstanbul, London, Milan, Moscow, Munich, Paris, Stuttgart, Tirana, Vienna and Zürich. Most of these flights are with Greece's national airline, Olympic Airlines, or whichever flag carrier of the country concerned.

Iraklio has direct flights to Cyprus with Olympic, while Aegean Airlines flies direct to Paris, Germany and Italy.

Some airlines with offices in Athens include:

Aeroflot (airline code SU; ☎ 210 322 0986; www .aeroflot.org)

Air Berlin (AB; ☎ 210 353 5264; www.airberlin.com)

Air Canada (AC; ☎ 210 617 5321; www.aircanada.ca)

Air France (AF; ☎ 210 353 0380; www.airfrance.com)

Alitalia (AZ; ☎ 210 353 4284; www.alitalia.it)

American Airlines (AA; ☎ 210 331 1045; www .aa.com)

British Airways (BA; ☎ 210 890 6666; www.british airways.com)

Cyprus Airways (CY; ☎ 210 372 2722; www.cyprusair .com.cy)

Delta Airlines (DL; ☎ 210 331 1660; www.delta.com)

easyJet (U2; ☎ 210 967 0000; www.easyjet.com)

EgyptAir (MS; ☎ 210 353 1272; www.egyptair.com.eg)

El Al (LY; ☎ 210 353 1003; www.elal.co.il)

Emirates Airlines (EK; ☎ 210 933 3400; www .emirates.com)

Gulf Air (GF; ☎ 210 322 0851; www.gulfairco.com)

Iberia (IB; ☎ 210 323 4523; www.iberia.com)
Japan Airlines (JL; ☎ 210 324 8211; www.jal.co.jp)
KLM (KL; ☎ 210 353 1295; www.klm.com)
Lufthansa (LH; ☎ 210 617 5200; www.lufthansa.com)
SAS (SK; ☎ 210 361 3910; www.sas.se)
Singapore Airlines (SQ; ☎ 210 372 8000, 210 353 1259; www.singaporeair.com)
Thai Airways (TG; ☎ 210 353 1237; www.thaiairways.com)
Turkish Airlines (TK; ☎ 210 322 1035; www.turkishairlines.com)
Virgin Express (TV; ☎ 210 949 0777; www.virgin-express.com)

Other international airports that service the islands are found on Mykonos, Hania (Crete), Kos, Karpathos, Limnos, Chios, Kerkyra, Samos, Skiathos, Aktion (for Lefkada), Kefallonia, Santorini (Thira) and Zakynthos. These airports are used exclusively for charter flights, mostly from the UK, Germany and Scandinavia. Charter flights also fly to all of Greece's other international airports.

Olympic Airlines (OA; ☎ 2013 569 111; www.olympicairlines.com) is the country's national airline. Olympic is no longer Greece's only international airline. **Aegean Airlines** (A3; ☎ 8111 120 000; www.aegeanair.com) flies direct from Athens to Rome and Venice, and via Thessaloniki to Cologne, Düsseldorf, Frankfurt, Munich and Stuttgart.

Contact details for local Olympic and Aegean offices are listed in the appropriate sections throughout this book.

Asia

Most Asian countries offer fairly competitive deals, with Bangkok, Singapore and Hong Kong the best places to shop around for discount tickets.

Khao San Rd in Bangkok is the budget travellers' headquarters. Bangkok has a number of excellent travel agents, but there are also some suspect ones; ask the advice of other travellers before handing over your cash. **STA Travel** (☎ 02-236 0262; www.statravel.co.th) is a good place to start.

In Singapore, **STA Travel** (☎ 65-6737 7188; www.statravel.com.sg) offers competitive discount fares for most destinations. Singapore, like Bangkok, has hundreds of travel agents, so it is possible to compare prices on flights. Chinatown Point shopping centre on New Bridge Rd has a good selection of travel agents.

Hong Kong has a number of excellent, reliable travel agencies and some that are not so reliable. A good way to check on a travel agent is to look it up in the phone book: fly-by-night operators don't usually stay around long enough to get listed. In Hong Kong, **Four Seas Tours** (☎ 2200 7760; www.fourseastravel.com) is recommended, as is **Shoestring Travel** (☎ 2723 2306).

Australia

Two well-known agents for cheap fares are STA Travel and Flight Centre. **STA Travel** (☎ 1300 733 035; www.statravel.com.au) has its main office in Melbourne, but also has offices in all major cities and on many university campuses. Call for the location of your nearest branch. **Flight Centre** (☎ 133 133; www.flightcentre.com.au) has its central office in Sydney and dozens of offices throughout Australia.

Thai Airways International and Singapore Airlines both have convenient connections to Athens, as well as a reputation for good service. If you're planning on doing a bit of flying around Europe, it's worth checking around for special deals from the major European airlines. Alitalia, KLM and Lufthansa are three likely candidates with good European networks.

Canada

Canada's national student travel agency is **Travel CUTS** (☎ 1-866-246-9762; www.travelcuts.com), which has offices in all major cities. For online bookings try www.expedia.ca or www.travelocity.ca.

Olympic Airlines has two flights weekly from Toronto to Athens via Montreal. There are no direct flights from Vancouver, but there are connecting flights via Toronto, Amsterdam, Frankfurt and London on Canadian Airlines, KLM, Lufthansa and British Airways.

For courier flights originating in Canada, contact **FB On Board Courier Services** (☎ 514-631-7929) in Montreal.

Continental Europe

Athens is linked to every major city in Europe by either Olympic Airlines or the flag carrier of each country.

France has a large network of travel agencies that can supply discount tickets to travellers of all ages. They include **OTU**

Voyages (☎ 01 40 29 12 12; www.otu.fr), which has branches across the country and specialises in tickets for students and young people. Other recommendations include **Voyageurs du Monde** (☎ 01 42 86 16 00; www.vdm.com), **Voyages Wasteels** (☎ 08 03 88 70 04, Paris) and **Nouvelles Frontières** (nationwide ☎ 08 25 00 08 25, Paris ☎ 01 45 68 70 00; www.nouvelles-frontieres.fr).

In Germany, **STA Travel** (☎ 01805 456 422; www.statravel.de) has several offices around the country. For online fares try **Just Travel** (☎ 08 97 47 33 30; www.justtravel.de) and **Expedia** (☎ 018 05 00 60 25; www.expedia.de).

In the Netherlands, **Airfair** (☎ 020-620 5121; www.airfair.nl) and **My Travel** (☎ 0900 10 20 300; www.mytravel.nl) are recommended, while in Italy try **Passaggi** (☎ 06 47 409 23, Rome).

Cyprus

Both Olympic Airlines and Cyprus Airways share the Cyprus–Greece routes. Both airlines have three flights daily from Larnaka to Athens, and there are five flights weekly to Thessaloniki. Cyprus Airways also flies from Pafos to Athens once a week in winter, and twice a week in summer, while Olympic has two flights weekly between Larnaka and Iraklio.

Turkey

Olympic Airlines and Turkish Airlines share the İstanbul–Athens route, with at least one flight a day each. There are no direct flights from Ankara to Athens; all flights go via İstanbul.

UK & Ireland

Discount air travel is big business in London. Advertisements for several travel agencies appear in the travel pages of the weekend broadsheet newspapers, such as the *Independent* on Saturday and the *Sunday Times*. Look out for the free magazines, such as *TNT*, which are widely available in London – start by looking outside the main train and underground stations.

For students or travellers under 26, a popular travel agency in the UK is **STA Travel** (☎ 087-016 00 599; www.statravel.co.uk). It sells tickets to all travellers but caters especially to young people and students. Other recommended travel agents in London include **Trailfinders** (☎ 020-7938 3939; www.trailfinders.co.uk), **Bridge the World** (☎ 0870-443 2399; www.b-t-w.co.uk) and **Flightbookers** (☎ 087-0010 7000;

www.ebookers.com). Charter flights can work out as a cheaper alternative to scheduled flights, especially if you do not qualify for the under-26 and student discounts.

British Airways, Olympic Airlines and Virgin Atlantic operate daily flights between London and Athens. Pricing is very competitive, with all three offering return tickets for around UK£200+ in high season, plus tax. At other times, prices fall as low as UK£100, plus tax. British Airways has flights from Edinburgh, Glasgow and Manchester.

The cheapest scheduled flights are with **easyJet** (☎ 087-1750 0100; www.easyjet.com), the no-frills specialist, which has flights from Luton and Gatwick to Athens. There are numerous charter flights between the UK and Greece.

USA

STA Travel (☎ 800-781-4040; www.statravel.com) has offices in Boston, Chicago, Miami, New York, Philadelphia, San Francisco and other major cities. For online bookings try www.cheaptickets.com, www.expedia.com and www.orbitz.com.

New York has the widest range of options to Athens. The route to Europe is very competitive and there are new deals almost every day. Both Olympic Airlines and Delta Airlines have direct flights but there are numerous other connecting flights.

There are no direct flights to Athens from the west coast. There are, however, connecting flights to Athens from many US cities, either linking with Olympic Airlines in New York or flying with one of the European national airlines to their home country, and then on to Athens. Courier flights to Athens are occasionally advertised in the newspapers, or you could contact air-freight companies listed in the phone book. The **International Association of Air Travel Couriers** (☎ 561-582-8320; www.courier.org) sends members a bimonthly update of air-courier offerings.

LAND
Border Crossings
ALBANIA

There are four crossing points between Greece and Albania. The main one is at Kakavia, 60km northwest of Ioannina. The others are at Krystallopigi, 14km west of Kotas on the Florina–Kastoria road; at Mertziani, 17km west of Konitsa; and at Sagiada 28km north of Igoumenitsa.

BULGARIA

There are two Bulgarian border crossings; one at Promahonas, 109km northeast of Thessaloniki and 41km from Serres, and the other at Ormenio, in northeastern Thrace.

FORMER YUGOSLAV REPUBLIC OF MACEDONIA (FYROM)

There are three border crossings between Greece and FYROM. One is at Evzoni, 68km north of Thessaloniki. This is the main highway to Skopje, which continues to Belgrade. Another border crossing is at Niki, 16km north of Florina. This road leads to Bitola and continues to Ohrid, once a popular tourist resort on the shores of Lake Ohrid. The third one is at Doïrani, 31km north of Kilkis.

TURKEY

Crossing points are at Kipi, 43km northeast of Alexandroupolis, and at Kastanies, 139km northeast of Alexandroupolis. Kipi is probably more convenient if you're heading for İstanbul, but the route through Kastanies goes via the fascinating towns of Soufli and Didymotiho, in Greece, and Edirne (ancient Adrianople) in Turkey.

Albania
BUS

The Hellenic Railways Organization (OSE) operates a daily bus between Athens and Tirana (€35.20) via Ioannina and Gjirokastra. The bus departs Athens (500m west of the Larisis train station) daily, arriving in Tirana the following day. There are also buses from Thessaloniki to Korça (€20, six hours), travelling via Florina.

Bulgaria
BUS

OSE runs a bus from Athens to Sofia (€45.50, 15 hours) at 7am daily, except Monday. It also runs Thessaloniki–Sofia buses (€19, 7½ hours, four daily). There is a private service to Plovdiv (€29.50, six hours) and Sofia (€35.50, seven hours) from Alexandroupolis on Wednesday and Sunday at 8.30am.

TRAIN

There is a daily train to Sofia from Athens (€30.65, 18 hours) via Thessaloniki (€17.90, nine hours). From Sofia, there are connections to Budapest (€67.50) and Bucharest (€37.30).

Former Yugoslav Republic of Macedonia
TRAIN

There are two trains daily from Thessaloniki to Skopje (€14.50, three hours), crossing the border between Idomeni and Gevgelija. They continue from Skopje to the Serbian capital of Belgrade (€31.70, 12 hours).

There are no trains between Florina and FYROM, although there are trains to Skopje from Bitola on the FYROM side of the border.

Russia
TRAIN

There is one train service a week from Thessaloniki to Moscow. It departs Thessaloniki at 7.53am on Sunday and arrives in Moscow at 5.26am on Wednesday. It departs Moscow for the return trip at 11.32pm on the same day. The cost is €147.80 for a berth in a three-bed cabin.

Turkey
BUS

OSE operates a bus from Athens to İstanbul (22 hours) daily except Wednesday, leaving the Peloponnese train station in Athens at 7pm and travelling via Thessaloniki and Alexandroupolis.

One-way fares are €67.50 from Athens, €44 from Thessaloniki and €15 from Alexandroupolis. Students qualify for a 20% discount and children under 12 travel for half-fare. See the Getting There & Away sections for each city for information on where to buy tickets.

Buses from İstanbul to Athens leave the Anadolu Terminal (Anatolia Terminal) at the Topkapı *otogar* (bus station) at 10am daily except Sunday.

TRAIN

There are no direct trains between Athens and İstanbul. Travellers must take a train to Thessaloniki and connect with one of two daily services running to the Turkish city. The best option is the Filia-Tostluk Express service leaving Thessaloniki at 8pm (€48.25, 11½ hours) and arriving in İstanbul at 7.30am.

The other service is the indirect Intercity IC90 service to Orestiada leaving Thessaloniki at 7am; passengers for İstanbul change at Pythio on the Greece–Turkey border.

Western Europe

Overland travel between Western Europe and Greece is nowadays usually confined to heading to an Italian port and picking up the most geographically convenient ferry. While quite feasible, the route through Croatia, Serbia and the Former Yugoslav Republic of Macedonia is outweighed by the convenience of a 'mini-cruise' from an Italian port to one of Greece's two main entry ports, and the avoidance of fuel and hotel costs on the trip down through the Balkan peninsula.

BUS

There are no bus services to Greece from the UK, nor from anywhere else in northern Europe. Bus companies can no longer compete with cheap air fares.

CAR & MOTORCYCLE

Most intending drivers these days drive to an Italian port and take a ferry to Greece. The most convenient port is Venice with Ancona coming a close second. The route through Croatia, Serbia and the Former Yugoslav Republic of Macedonia takes on average 2½ days from Venice to Athens, whereas a high-speed ferry from Venice to Patra can be completed in around 26 hours. From Patra to Athens is a further 3½ hours driving.

TRAIN

Unless you have a Eurail pass or are aged under the age of 26 and eligible for a discounted fare, travelling to Greece by train is prohibitively expensive. Indeed, the chances of anyone wanting to travel from London to Athens by train are considered so remote, it's no longer possible to buy a single ticket for this journey. The trip involves travelling from London to Paris on the Eurostar, followed by Paris to Brindisi, then a ferry from Brindisi to Patra – and finally a train from Patra to Athens.

Greece is a part of the Eurail network. Eurail passes can only be bought by residents of non-European countries and are supposed to be purchased before arriving in Europe. They can, however, be bought in Europe as long as your passport proves that you've been there for less than six months. In London, head for the **Rail Europe Travel Centre** (☎ 087-0584 8848; 179 Piccadilly). Check the Eurail website (www.eurail.com) for full details of passes and prices.

If you are starting your European travels in Greece, you can buy your Eurail pass from the OSE office in Athens at Karolou 1, and at the stations in Patra and Thessaloniki.

Greece is also part of the **Inter-Rail** (www.interrailnet.com) pass system, available to residents in Europe for six months or more.

SEA

Albania

Corfu-based Petrakis Lines has daily ferries to the Albanian port of Saranda (€15, 25 minutes), plus twice-weekly services to Himara (€25, 1¼ hours) and Vlora (€38, 2½ hours).

Cyprus & Israel

Passenger services from Greece to Cyprus and Israel have been suspended indefinitely. **Salamis Lines** (www.viamare.com/Salamis) still operates the route, but carries only vehicles and freight.

Italy

There are ferries to Greece from the Italian ports of Ancona, Bari, Brindisi, Trieste and Venice. For more information about these services, see the Patra, Igoumenitsa, Corfu and Kefallonia sections.

The ferries can get very crowded in summer. If you want to take a vehicle across it's a good idea to make a reservation beforehand. In the UK, reservations can be made on almost all of these ferries through **Viamare Travel Ltd** (☎ 020-7431 4560; ferries@viamare.com).

You'll find all the latest information about ferry routes, schedules and services on the Internet. For an overview try www.greekferries.gr.

Most of the ferry companies have their own websites, including the following:
Agoudimos Lines (www.agoudimos-lines.com)
ANEK Lines (www.anek.gr)
Blue Star Ferries (www.bluestarferries.com)
Fragline (www.fragline.gr)
Hellenic Mediterranean Lines (www.hml.gr)
Minoan Lines (www.minoan.gr)
Superfast (www.superfast.com)
Ventouris Ferries (www.ventouris.gr)

The following ferry services are for high season (July and August), and prices are for one-way deck class. Deck class on these services means exactly that. If you want a reclining, aircraft-type seat, you'll be up for another

10% to 15% on top of the listed fares. All companies offer discounts for return travel. Prices are about 30% less in the low season.

ANCONA

The route to Igoumenitsa and Patra has become increasingly popular in recent years. There can be up to three boats daily in summer and at least one a day year round. All ferry operators in Ancona have booths at the *stazione marittima* (ferry terminal) off Piazza Candy, where you can pick up timetables and price lists and make bookings.

Blue Star Ferries and Superfast Ferries have two boats daily, taking 19 hours direct to Patra, or 21 hours via Igoumenitsa. Both charge €80 and sell tickets through **Morandi & Co** (☎ 071-20 20 33; Via XXIX Settembre 2/0). Superfast accepts Eurail passes. **ANEK Lines** (☎ 071-207 23 46; Via XXIX Settembre 2/0; €68) and **Minoan** (☎ 071-20 17 08; Via Astagno 3; €72) do the trip daily in 20½ hours via Igoumenitsa.

BARI

Superfast Ferries (☎ 080 52 11 416; Corso de Tullio 6) has daily sailings to Patra via Corfu and Igoumenitsa, and also accepts Eurail passes.

Ventouris Ferries (☎ 080-521 7609) has daily boats to Corfu (10 hours) and Igoumenitsa (11½ hours) for €53.

BRINDISI

The trip from Brindisi was once the most popular crossing, but it now operates only between April and early October. **Med Link** (Discovery Shipping; ☎ 0831-54 81 16/7; Costa Morena) and **Hellenic Mediterranean Lines** (☎ 0831 54 80 01; Costa Morena) offer at least one boat a day to Patra between them.

Hellenic Mediterranean calls at Igoumenitsa on the way, and also has services that call at Corfu, Kefallonia, Paxi and Zakynthos, while Med Link calls at Kefallonia during July and August. All these services cost €50. Hellenic Mediterranean accepts Eurail passes, and issues vouchers for travel with Med Link on days when there is no Hellenic Mediterranean service.

Agoudimos Lines (☎ 0831-55 01 80; Via Provinciale per Lecce 29) and **Fragline** (☎ 0831-54 85 40; Via Spalato 31) sail only to Igoumenitsa.

Italian Ferries (www.italianferries.it) operates highspeed catamaran services to Corfu (€57 to €85, 3¼ hours) and Paxi (€73 to €110, 4¾ hours) daily from July to mid-September.

TRIESTE

ANEK Lines (☎ 040-322 05 61; Via Rossini 2) has boats to Patra (€68, 32 hours) every day except Thursday, calling at Corfu and Igoumenitsa.

VENICE

Minoan Lines (☎ 041-240 71 77; Stazione Marittima 123) sails to Patra (€75, 29 hours) daily except Wednesday, calling at Corfu and Igoumenitsa. **Blue Star Ferries** (☎ 041-277 05 59; Stazione Marittima 123; €64) plies the route four times weekly.

Turkey

There are five regular ferry services between Turkey's Aegean coast and the Greek islands. Tickets for all ferries to Turkey must be bought a day in advance. You'll be asked to turn in your passport the night before the trip but don't worry, you'll get it back the next day before you board the boat. Port tax for departures to Turkey is €9.

See the relevant sections under individual island entries for more information.

RHODES

There are daily catamarans from Rhodes to Marmaris from June to September, dropping back to maybe only three or four services a week in winter. Tickets cost €30 one way plus €15 Turkish arrival tax. In addition there's a weekly passenger and car ferry service once a week on Friday at 4pm. The cost of ferrying one car to the Turkish mainland is €180 one way, while passengers pay €55 including taxes. Return rates usually work out cheaper.

KOS

There are daily ferries in summer from Kos to Bodrum (ancient Halicarnassus) in Turkey. Boats leave at 8.30am and return at 4.30pm. The one-hour journey costs €34. Port tax is extra.

CHIOS

There are daily Chios–Çeşme boats from July to September, dropping back to two boats a week in winter. Tickets cost €22/25 one way/return. Port tax is extra.

SAMOS

There are two boats daily to Kuşadası (for Ephesus) from Samos in summer, dropping to one or two boats weekly in winter. Tickets cost approximately €45 return, €37 one-way. Port tax is extra.

LESVOS

There are up to four boats weekly on this route in high season. Tickets cost €29 one-way or return, including port taxes.

GETTING AROUND

Greece is an easy place to travel around thanks to a comprehensive public transport system.

Buses are a mainstay of island transport, with a network that reaches out to the smallest villages. Trains are a good alternative, where available. To most visitors, though, travelling in the Greek islands means island-hopping on the multitude of ferries that crisscross the Adriatic and the Aegean. If you're in a hurry, Greece also has an extensive domestic air network.

The information in this chapter was for the 2005 high season. You'll find lots of travel information on the Internet. The website www.ellada.com has lots of useful links, including airline timetables.

AIR
Airlines in Greece

The vast majority of domestic flights are handled by the country's national carrier, **Olympic Airlines** (☎ 801 114 4444; www.olympicair lines.com), together with its offshoot, Olympic Aviation. Olympic has offices wherever there are flights, as well as in other major towns.

The prices listed in this book are for full-fare economy, and include domestic taxes and charges. Olympic also offers cheaper options between Athens and some of the more popular destinations such as Corfu, Iraklio, Lesvos, Rhodes and Thessaloniki. There are discounts for return tickets for travel between Monday and Thursday, and bigger discounts for trips that include a Saturday night away. You'll find full details on its website, as well as information on timetables.

The baggage allowance on all domestic flights is 15kg, or 20kg if the domestic flight is part of an international journey. Olympic offers a 25% student discount on domestic flights, but only if the flight is part of an international journey.

For more information on Olympic's domestic routes see p93.

Crete-based **Aegean Airlines** (☎ 801 112 0000, 210 626 1000; www.aegeanair.com) is the sole survivor of the clutch of new airlines that emerged to challenge Olympic following the 1993 decision by the government to end Olympic's monopoly on domestic flights.

It offers flights from Athens to Alexandroupolis, Corfu, Hania, Ioannina, Iraklio, Kavala, Lesvos, Mykonos, Rhodes, Santorini and Thessaloniki; from Thessaloniki to Iraklio, Lesvos, Mykonos, Rhodes and Santorini; and from Iraklio to Rhodes.

Full-fare economy costs much the same as Olympic, but Aegean often has special deals. It offers a 20% youth discount for travellers under 26, and a similar discount for the over-60s.

There is a comprehensive and useful website for Athens' Eleftherios Venizelos Airport at www.aia.gr.

AirSea Lines (☎ 26610 49800; www.airsealines.com) is a new seaplane service that runs flights between Corfu and Paxi, and Corfu and Ioannina. It has a strict baggage weight allowance of 12kg plus 4kg of hand luggage.

BICYCLE

Cycling is a cheap, healthy, environmentally sound and, above all, fun way of travelling around the Greek islands.

Crete is now a popular destination for cycling fans, but you'll find cyclists wherever the roads are good enough to get around. Most of them are foreigners; few locals show much enthusiasm for pedalling.

The time of year is an important consideration. It can get hot to cycle around in full summer and it can be very cold in winter, but for the rest of the year conditions are ideal. Frequent cooling winds on the Aegean Islands can bring some relief in summer.

If you want a decent touring bike, you should bring your own. Bicycles pose few problems for airlines.

You can take it to pieces and put it in a bike bag or box, but it's much easier simply to wheel your bike to the check-in desk, where it should be treated as a piece of baggage. You may have to remove the pedals and turn the handlebars sideways so that it takes up less space in the aircraft's hold; check all this with the airline well in advance. Bikes are carried free of charge on ferries.

One note of caution: before you leave home, go over your bike with a fine-toothed comb and fill your repair kit with every imaginable spare.

As with cars and motorbikes, you won't necessarily be able to buy spares for your machine if it breaks down in the middle of nowhere.

Hire

You can hire bicycles on only a few islands. Prices range from €5 to €12 per day, depending on the type and age of the bike. Only a few major islands sell bikes, eg Crete, Rhodes, Kos, Corfu, and prices are similar to the rest of EU Europe.

BOAT
Catamaran

High-speed catamarans have become an important part of the island travel scene. They are just as fast as hydrofoils – if not faster – and more comfortable. They are also less prone to cancellation in rough weather. Fares are the same as for hydrofoils.

Hellenic Seaways again is the major player. It operates giant, vehicle-carrying cats from Piraeus and Rafina to the Cyclades, and smaller Flying Cats from Rafina to the central and northern Cyclades and on many routes around the Saronic Gulf.

Blue Star Ferries operates its Seajet catamarans on the run from Rafina to Tinos, Mykonos and Paros.

Dodekanisos Naftiliaki runs two luxurious Norwegian-built passenger cats between Rhodes and Patmos in the Dodecanese.

Most services are very popular; book as far in advance as possible, especially if you want to travel on weekends.

Ferry

For most people, travel in Greece means island-hopping.

Every island will have a ferry service of some sort or other, although in winter services to some of the smaller islands are fairly skeletal. The services will start to pick up again from April onwards, and by July and August there are countless services crisscrossing the Aegean. Ferries come in all shapes and sizes, from the giant 'superferries' that work the major routes to the small, ageing, open ferries that chug around the backwaters.

The main ferry companies in Greece include the following:

ANEK Lines (☎ 210 419 7420; www.anek.gr) Serving Italy & Crete.

Blue Star Ferries (☎ 210 891 9800; www.bluestar ferries.com) Serving Italy, Crete and the Dodecanese.

GA Ferries (☎ 210 419 9100; www.gaferries.com) Mainly serving the Cyclades.

Hellenic Seaways (☎ 210 419 9000; www.hellenic seaways.gr) Serving the Sporades and Cyclades.

Italian Ferries (www.italianferries.it) Serving Italy.

LANE Lines (☎ 210 427 4011; www.lane.gr) Serving Rhodes via Milos, Crete, Kasos, Karpathos & Halki.

Minoan Lines (☎ 210 414 5700; www.minoan.gr) Serving Italy and Crete.

NEL Lines (☎ 22510 26299; www.nel.gr) Serving the Northeastern Aegean.

CLASSES

The large ferries usually have four classes: 1st class has air-con cabins and a posh lounge and restaurant; 2nd class has smaller cabins and sometimes a separate lounge; tourist class gives you a berth in a shared four-berth cabin; and 3rd (deck) class gives you access to a room with 'airline' seats, a restaurant, a lounge/bar and, of course, the deck.

Deck class remains an economical way to travel, while a 1st-class ticket can cost almost as much as flying on some routes. Children under four travel free, while children between four and 10 pay half fare. Full fares apply for children over 10. Unless you state otherwise, when purchasing a ticket you will automatically be given deck class. Prices quoted in this book are for deck class as this is the most popular with tourists.

Bear in mind that booking a half-decent cabin berth can often be almost as expensive as an airline ticket, particularly if it is with one of the superfast ferry operators such as Blue Star or Minoan.

COSTS

Prices are fixed by the government and are determined by the distance of the destination from the port of origin. The small differences in price you may find at ticket agencies are the results of some agents sacrificing part of their designated commission to qualify as a 'discount service'. The discount is seldom more than €0.50. Ticket prices include embarkation tax, a contribution to NAT (the seamen's union) and 10% VAT.

ROUTES

Ferries for the Ionian Islands leave from the Peloponnese ports of Patra (p107; for Kefallonia, Ithaki, Paxi and Corfu) and Kyllini (p108; for Kefallonia and Zakynthos); and from Igoumenitsa in Epiros (p108; for Corfu and Paxi).

Ferries heading for the Sporades leave from Volos, Thessaloniki, Agios Konstantinos, and Kymi on Evia (for Skyros only). The latter two ports are easily reached by bus from Athens.

Some of the Northeastern Aegean Islands have connections with Thessaloniki as well as Piraeus. The odd ones out are Thasos, which is reached from Kavala, and occasionally from Samothraki, which can be reached from Alexandroupolis year-round and also from Kavala in summer.

SCHEDULES

Ferry timetables change from year to year and season to season, and can be subject to delays and cancellations at short notice due to bad weather, strikes or the boats simply conking out. No timetable is infallible, but the comprehensive weekly list of departures from Piraeus put out by the EOT (Greek National Tourist Office) in Athens is as accurate as is humanly possible. The people to go to for the most up-to-date ferry information are the local *limenarheio* (port police), whose offices are usually on or near the quay.

There's lots of information about ferry services available on the Internet. Try www.greekferries.gr, which has a useful search programme and links, or www.gtp.gr. Many of the larger ferry companies have their own sites (see opposite).

Throughout the year there is at least one ferry a day from a mainland port to the major island in each group, and during the high season (from June to mid-September) there are considerably more. Ferries sailing from one island group to another are not so frequent, and if you're going to travel in this way you'll need to plan carefully, otherwise you may end up having to backtrack to Piraeus.

Travelling time can vary considerably from one ferry to another, depending on how many islands you decide to visit on the way to your destination. For example, the Piraeus–Rhodes trip can take between 15 and 18 hours depending on which route is taken. Before buying your ticket, check how many stops the boat is going to make, and its estimated arrival time. It can make a big difference.

TICKET PURCHASE

Given that ferries are prone to delays and cancellations, it's best not to purchase a ticket until it has been confirmed that the ferry is leaving. If you need to reserve a car space, however, you may need to pay in advance. If the service is then cancelled you can transfer your ticket to the next available service with that company.

Agencies selling tickets line the waterfront of most ports, but rarely is there one that sells tickets for every boat, and often an agency is reluctant to give you information about a boat they do not sell tickets for. This means you have to check the timetables displayed outside each agency to find out which ferry is next to depart – or ask the port police.

High-Speed Ferries

These are the latest addition to the ferry network, slashing travel times on some of the longer routes. **Nel Lines** (☎ 2251 026 299; www.ferries.gr/nel) leads the way with its futuristic-looking *F/B Aeolos Express* and *Aeolos Kenteris*, which operate from Piraeus to Syros, Tinos and Mykonos. These services cost about twice as much as standard ferries.

Blue Star Ferries (www.bluestarferries.com) is up there in almost the same league, and its fleet of modernistic boats serves many destinations in the Cycladic and Dodecanese islands, cutting travelling time considerably. Departure times tend to be in the late afternoon or evening, thus making an overnight sleep a necessity on the longer legs. It charges about 20% more than the regular ferries.

Hydrofoil

Hydrofoils offer a faster alternative to ferries on some routes, particularly to islands close to the mainland. They take half the time, but cost twice as much. They don't take cars or motorbikes. Most routes operate only during high season and according to demand, and all are prone to cancellations if the sea is rough.

Hellenic Seaways (☎ 210 419 9000; www.hellenicseaways.gr) runs the busy Argosaronic network linking Piraeus with the Saronic Gulf Islands and the ports of the eastern Peloponnese, as well as services to the Sporades from Agios Konstantinos and Volos.

Aegean Hydrofoils (☎ 2241 024 000), based in Rhodes, serves the Dodecanese and provides connections to the Northeastern Aegean islands of Ikaria and Samos. Other routes are between Kavala and Thasos in the Northeastern Aegean, and from Alexandroupolis to Samothraki and Limnos.

It's not possible to buy tickets on board hydrofoils – buy them in advance from an agent. You will be allocated a seat number.

Inter-island Boat

In addition to the large ferries that ply between the mainland ports and island groups, there are smaller boats that link islands within a group, and occasionally, an island in one group with an island in another.

In the past these boats were invariably caïques – sturdy old fishing boats – but gradually these are being replaced by new purpose-built boats, which are called express or excursion boats. Tickets tend to cost more than tickets for the large ferries, but the boats are useful if you're island-hopping.

Taxi Boat

Most islands have taxi boats – small speedboats that operate like taxis, transporting people to difficult-to-get-to places. Some owners charge a set price for each person, others charge a flat rate for the boat, and this cost is divided by the number of passengers. Either way, prices are usually quite reasonable.

BUS

All long-distance buses on the mainland and the islands are operated by regional collectives known as **KTEL** (Koino Tamio Eispraxeon Leoforion; www.ktel.org). Every prefecture on the mainland has a KTEL, which operates local services within the prefecture and services to the main towns of other prefectures. Fares are fixed by the government.

Island Buses

Island services are less simple to summarise! There's an enormous difference in the level of services. Crete (which is split into three prefectures) is organised in the same way as the mainland – each prefecture has its own KTEL providing local services and services to the main towns of other prefectures. Most

islands have just one bus company, some have just one bus.

On islands where the capital is inland, buses normally meet the boats. Some of the more remote islands have not yet acquired a bus, but most have some sort of motorised transport – even if it is only a bone-shaking, three-wheeled truck.

Mainland Buses

The network is comprehensive. All major ports on the mainland have daily connections to Athens. The islands of Corfu, Kefallonia and Zakynthos can also be reached directly from Athens by bus – the fares include the price of the ferry ticket. For details, see p94.

When you buy a ticket you will be allotted a seat number, which is noted on the ticket. The seat number is indicated on the back of each seat of the bus, not on the back of the seat in front; this can cause confusion among Greeks and tourists alike. You can board a bus without a ticket and pay on board, but this may mean that you have to stand. Keep your ticket for the duration of the journey; it will be checked several times en route.

Buses do not have toilets or refreshments on board, so make sure you are prepared on both counts. Buses stop about every three hours on long journeys. Smoking is prohibited on all buses in Greece; only the drivers dare to ignore the no-smoking signs.

Bus travel is very reasonably priced, with a journey costing approximately €5 per 100km. Following are fares and journey times on some of the major routes.

Route	Duration	Cost
Athens–Thessaloniki	7½hr	€31
Athens–Patra	3hr	€14
Athens–Volos	5hr	€20
Athens–Corfu*	5hr	€31
* including ferry		

CAR & MOTORCYCLE

Many of the islands are plenty big enough to warrant having your own vehicle. Roads have improved enormously in recent years, particularly on the larger, more visited islands, such as Crete.

Few people bother to bring their own vehicle from Europe; there are plenty of places to hire cars.

WARNING

The islands are not the best place to initiate yourself into the art of motorcycling. There are still a lot of gravel roads and dozens of tourists have accidents every year. If you are planning to use a motorcycle or moped, check that your travel insurance covers you for injury resulting from a motorbike accident. Many insurance companies don't offer this cover, so check the fine print!

Almost all islands are served by car ferries. Some sample prices for small vehicles include Piraeus–Mykonos (€76); Piraeus–Crete (Hania and Iraklio; €79); and Piraeus–Samos (€81). The charge for a large motorbike is about the same as the price of a 3rd-class passenger ticket.

Petrol in Greece is cheaper than in most other European countries, but by American or Australian standards it is expensive. Prices are generally set by the government but can vary from region to region. Leaded (super) and unleaded (amolyvdi) is always available, as is diesel (petreleo kinisis). Given the unprecedented rises in petrol costs of recent years it would be unwise to give a fixed figure, but by mid-2005 unleaded was around the €1 per litre mark. Diesel is usually cheaper.

Automobile Associations
Greece's domestic automobile association is **ELPA** (Elliniki Leschi Aftokinitou kai Periigiseon; www .elpa.gr).

Bring Your Own Vehicle
EU-registered vehicles are allowed free entry into Greece but may only stay six months without road taxes being due. Only a green card (international third-party insurance) is required. Your only proof of the date of entry – if requested by the police – is your ferry ticket (if coming from Italy), or your passport entry stamp if entering from elsewhere. Non-EU registered vehicles may be logged in your passport.

Driving Licence
Greece recognises all national driving licences, provided the licence has been held for at least one year. It also recognises an International Driving Permit, which should be obtained before you leave home.

Insurance
Insurance is always included in any vehicle hire agreements, but you are advised to check whether it is fully comprehensive or third party only. Otherwise you may be up for hefty costs in the event of any damage caused to your vehicle if you are at fault.

Rental
CAR
Rental cars are available almost everywhere, but it's best to hire from major cities where competition lowers the prices. All the multinational companies are represented in Athens, and most have branches in other major towns and tourist destinations. Smaller islands often have only one outlet.

High-season weekly rates with unlimited mileage start at about €280 for the smallest models, dropping to about €200 per week in winter. To these prices must be added VAT of 19%, or 14% on the islands of the Dodecanese, the Northeastern Aegean and the Sporades, and optional extras such as a collision damage waiver of €12 per day (more for larger models), without which you'll find yourself liable for the first €295 of the repairs (more for larger models). Other costs include a theft waiver (at least €6 per day) and personal accident insurance.

You can find better deals at local companies. Their advertised rates can be up to 50% cheaper, and they are normally more open to negotiation, especially if business is slow.

If you want to take a hire car to another country or onto a ferry, you will need advance written authorisation from the hire company. Unless you pay with a credit card, most hire companies will require a minimum deposit of €120 per day. See the Getting Around sections of cities and islands for details of places to rent cars.

The minimum driving age in Greece is 18 years, but most car-hire firms require you to be at least 21 – or 23 for larger vehicles.

Some of the major car-hire players in Greece are:
Avis (☎ 210 322 4951; www.avis.gr)
Budget (☎ 210 349 8800; www.budget.gr)
Europcar (☎ 210 960 2382; www.europcar.gr)
Hertz (☎ 210 626 4000; www.hertz.gr)

See their websites for their current rates and special offers.

MOTORCYCLE

Mopeds and motorcycles are available for hire wherever there are tourists to rent them. In many cases their maintenance has been minimal, so check the machine thoroughly before you hire it – especially the brakes: you'll need them!

Greece has introduced new regulations for hiring mopeds and motorcycles – to rent one you must produce a licence that shows proficiency in riding the category of bike you wish to rent; this applies to everything from 50cc up. Standard British driving licences are not sufficient – British citizens must obtain a Category A licence from the DVLA. In most other EU countries separate licences are automatically issued.

Motorbikes are a cheap way to travel around. Rates range from €10 to €15 per day for a moped or 50cc motorbike to €25 per day for a 250cc motorbike. Out of season these prices drop considerably, so use your bargaining skills. By October it is sometimes possible to hire a moped for as little as €5 per day. Most motorcycle hirers include third-party insurance in the price, but it's wise to check this. This insurance will not include medical expenses. Helmets are technically compulsory and rental agencies are obliged to offer one as part of the hire deal. Most riders ignore the regulation and go without.

Road Rules

In Greece, as in Continental Europe, you drive on the right and overtake on the left. Outside built-up areas, main road traffic has right of way at intersections. In towns, vehicles coming from the right have right of way. Seat belts must be worn in front seats, and in back seats if the car is fitted with them. Children under 12 years of age are not allowed in the front seat. It's compulsory to carry a first-aid kit, fire extinguisher and warning triangle, and it's forbidden to carry cans of petrol. Helmets are compulsory for motorcyclists if the motorbike is 50cc or more.

Outside residential areas the speed limit is 120km/h on highways, 90km/h on other roads and 50km/h in built-up areas. The speed limit for motorbikes up to 100cc is 70km/h and for larger motorbikes, 90km/h.

Drivers exceeding the speed limit by 20% are liable to receive a fine of €60; and by 40%, €150. In practice, most tourists escape with a warning.

The police have also cracked down on drink-driving laws – at last. A blood-alcohol content of 0.05% is liable to incur a fine of €150, and over 0.08% is a criminal offence.

If you are involved in an accident and no-one is hurt, the police will not be required to write a report, but it is advisable to go to a nearby police station and explain what happened. A police report may be required for insurance purposes. If an accident involves injury, a driver who does not stop and does not inform the police may face a prison sentence.

HITCHING

Hitching is never entirely safe in any country in the world, and we don't recommend it. Travellers who decide to hitch should understand that they are taking a small but potentially serious risk. People who do choose to hitch will be safer if they travel in pairs and should let someone know where they are planning to go.

Greece has a reputation for being a relatively safe place for women to hitch, but it is still unwise to do it alone. It's better for a woman to hitch with a companion, preferably a male one.

Hitching on the islands is not uncommon – even by locals – as local transport may be poor to non-existent. So be prepared to pick up as well as be picked up if you are using this method to get around. Local hitchers don't stick a thumb up, but rather they point a finger to the ground from an outstretched arm.

LOCAL TRANSPORT

Bus

Most Greek island towns are small enough to get around on foot. The only island towns where tourists are likely to use buses are Iraklio and Rhodes. The procedure for buying tickets for local buses is covered in the Getting Around section for each city.

Metro

Athens is the only city in Greece large enough to warrant the building of an underground system. For information see p96.

Taxi

Taxis are widely available except on the very smallest islands. They are reasonably priced by European standards, especially if three or four people share costs.

Cabs in mainland ports are metered. Flag fall is €0.75, followed by €0.28 per kilometre (€0.53 per kilometre outside town). These rates double between midnight and 5am. Costs additional to the per-kilometre rate are €3 from an airport, €0.80 from a bus, port or train station and €0.30 for each piece of luggage over 10kg.

Island taxis generally do not have meters, so you should always settle on a price before you start off.

TRAIN

None of the islands have trains. On the mainland trains are run by the **Greek Railways Organisation** (Organismos Sidirodromon Ellados; www.ose.gr), referred to as the OSE.

Trains are handy for getting to/from a number of mainland ports, ie Patra, Piraeus, Volos, Thessaloniki and Alexandroupolis. The network is of a good standard and is being constantly upgraded.

There are two types of service: regular (slow) trains that stop at all stations, and faster intercity trains that link major cities.

Slow trains are the country's cheapest public transport: 2nd-class fares are absurdly cheap, and even 1st class is cheaper than bus travel. Sample journey times and 1st- and 2nd-class fares include Athens–Thessaloniki (€21/14, 7½ hours) and Thessaloniki–Alexandroupolis (€15/10, seven hours).

Intercity trains linking the major ports are an excellent way to travel. Services aren't always express – Greece is too mountainous for that – but the trains are modern and comfortable.

Some sample Intercity train journey times and the 1st- and 2nd-class fares are Athens–Thessaloniki (€37.30/27.60, six hours) and Thessaloniki–Alexandroupolis (€21.90/16.20, 5½ hours).

Passes

Eurail and Inter-Rail passes are valid in Greece, but it's not worth buying one if Greece is the only place you plan to use it. The passes can be used for 2nd-class travel on Intercity services.

Health

BEFORE YOU GO

Prevention is the key to staying healthy while abroad. A little planning before departure, particularly for pre-existing illnesses, will save trouble later. Bring medications in their original, clearly labelled containers. A signed and dated letter from your physician describing your medical conditions and medications, including generic names, is also a good idea. If carrying syringes or needles, be sure to have a physician's letter documenting their medical necessity. If you are embarking on a long trip, make sure your teeth are OK and take your optical prescription with you.

INSURANCE

If you're an EU citizen, a European Health Insurance Card (EHIC; formerly the E111) covers you for most medical care but not emergency repatriation home or nonemergencies. It is available from health centres, and post offices in the UK. Citizens from other countries should find out if there is a reciprocal arrangement for free medical care between their country and Greece. If you do need health insurance, make sure you get a policy that covers you for the worst possible scenario, such as an accident requiring an emergency flight home. Find out in advance if your insurance plan will make payments directly to providers or reimburse you later for overseas health expenditures.

RECOMMENDED VACCINATIONS

No jabs are required to travel to Greece, but a yellow-fever vaccination certificate is required if you are coming from an infected area. The World Health Organization (WHO) recommends that all travellers should be covered for diphtheria, tetanus, measles, mumps, rubella and polio.

INTERNET RESOURCES

The WHO's publication *International Travel and Health* is revised annually and is available online at www.who.int/ith/. Other useful websites include www.mdtravel health.com (travel health recommendations for every country; updated daily), www.fit fortravel.scot.nhs.uk (general travel advice for the layperson), www.ageconcern.org .uk (advice on travel for the elderly) and www.mariestopes.org.uk (information on women's health and contraception).

IN TRANSIT

DEEP VEIN THROMBOSIS (DVT)

Blood clots may form in the legs during plane flights, chiefly because of prolonged immobility (the longer the flight, the greater the risk). The chief symptom of DVT is swelling or pain of the foot, ankle, or calf, usually but not always on just one side. When a blood clot travels to the lungs, it may cause chest pain and

---

WARNING

Codeine, which is commonly found in headache preparations, is banned in Greece; check labels carefully, or risk prosecution. There are strict regulations applying to the importation of medicines into Greece, so obtain a certificate from your doctor that outlines any medication you may have to carry into the country with you.

breathing difficulties. Travellers with any of these symptoms should immediately seek medical attention. To prevent the development of DVT on long flights you should walk about the cabin, contract the leg muscles while sitting, drink plenty of fluids and avoid alcohol and tobacco.

JET LAG
To avoid jet lag drink plenty of nonalcoholic fluids and eat light meals. Upon arrival, get exposure to natural sunlight and readjust your schedule (for meals, sleep etc) as soon as possible.

IN GREECE

AVAILABILITY & COST OF HEALTH CARE
If you need an ambulance in Greece call ☎ 166. There is at least one doctor on every island and larger islands have hospitals. Pharmacies can dispense medicines that are available only on prescription in most European countries, so you can consult a pharmacist for minor ailments.

All this sounds fine but, although medical training is of a high standard in Greece, the health service is badly underfunded. Hospitals can be overcrowded, hygiene is not always what it should be and relatives are expected to bring in food for the patient – which could be a problem for a tourist. Conditions and treatment are better in private hospitals, which are expensive. All this means that a good health-insurance policy is essential.

TRAVELLER'S DIARRHOEA
If you develop diarrhoea, be sure to drink plenty of fluids, preferably in the form of an oral rehydration solution such as dioralyte. If diarrhoea is bloody, persists for more than 72 hours or is accompanied by fever, shaking, chills or is severe abdominal pain you should seek medical attention.

ENVIRONMENTAL HAZARDS
Bites, Stings & Insect-Borne Diseases
Keep an eye out for sea urchins lurking around rocky beaches; if you get some of their needles embedded in your skin, olive oil should help to loosen them. If they are not removed they will become infected. You should also be wary of jellyfish, particularly during the months of September and October. Although jellyfish are not lethal in Greece, their stings can hurt. Dousing the affected area with vinegar will deactivate any stingers that have not 'fired'. Calamine lotion, antihistamines and analgesics may help reduce any reaction you experience and relieve the pain of any stings. Much more painful than either of these, but thankfully much rarer, is an encounter with the weever fish. The fish buries itself in the sand of the tidal zone with only its spines protruding, and injects a painful and powerful toxin if trodden on. Soaking your foot in very hot water (which breaks down the poison) should solve the problem. Weever fish stings can cause permanent local paralysis in the worst case.

Greece's only dangerous snake is the adder. To minimise the possibilities of being bitten, always wear boots, socks and long trousers when walking through undergrowth where snakes may be present. Don't put your hands into holes and crevices, and be careful when collecting firewood. Snake bites do not cause instantaneous death and an antivenin is widely available. Keep the victim calm and still, wrap the bitten limb tightly, as you would for a sprained ankle, and attach a splint to immobilise it. Seek medical help, if possible with the dead snake for identification. Don't attempt to catch the snake if there is a possibility of being bitten again. Tourniquets and sucking out the poison are now comprehensively discredited.

Always check all over your body if you have been walking through a potentially tick-infested area as ticks can cause skin infections and other more serious diseases. If a tick is found attached, press down around the tick's head with tweezers, grab the head and gently pull upwards. Avoid pulling the rear of the tick's body as this may squeeze the tick's gut contents through the attached mouth parts into the skin, increasing the risk of infection and disease.

Greece is now officially rabies-free, however even if the animal is not rabid, all animal bites should be treated seriously as they can become infected or can result in tetanus.

HEALTH

Heatstroke

Heatstroke occurs following excessive fluid loss with inadequate replacement of fluids and salt. Symptoms of heatstroke include headache, dizziness and tiredness. Dehydration is already happening by the time you feel thirsty – aim to drink sufficient water to produce pale, diluted urine. To treat heatstroke drink water and/or fruit juice, and cool the body with cold water and fans.

Hypothermia

Hypothermia occurs when the body loses heat faster than it can produce it. As ever, proper preparation will reduce the risks of getting it. Even on a hot day in the mountains, the weather can change rapidly so carry waterproof garments, warm layers and a hat, and inform others of your route. Hypothermia starts with shivering, loss of judgment and clumsiness. Unless rewarming occurs, the sufferer deteriorates into apathy, confusion and coma. Prevent further heat loss by seeking shelter, warm dry clothing, hot sweet drinks and shared bodily warmth.

TRAVELLING WITH CHILDREN

Make sure children are up to date with routine vaccinations and discuss possible travel vaccines well before departure as some vaccines are not suitable for children under a year old. Lonely Planet's *Travel with Children* includes travel health advice for younger children.

WOMEN'S HEALTH

Emotional stress, exhaustion and travelling through different time zones can all contribute to an upset in the menstrual pattern.

If using oral contraceptives, remember some antibiotics, diarrhoea and vomiting can stop the pill from working. Time zones, gastrointestinal upsets and antibiotics do not affect injectable contraception.

Travelling during pregnancy is usually possible but always consult your doctor before planning your trip. The most risky times for travel are during the first 12 weeks of pregnancy and after 30 weeks.

SEXUAL HEALTH

Condoms are readily available but emergency contraception may not be, so take the necessary precautions.

Language

CONTENTS

The Greek language is probably the oldest European language, with an oral tradition of 4000 years and a written tradition of approximately 3000 years. Its evolution over the four millennia was characterised by its strength during the golden age of Athens and the Democracy (mid-5th century BC); its use as a lingua franca throughout the Middle Eastern world, spread by Alexander the Great and his successors as far as India during the Hellenistic period (330 BC to AD 100); its adaptation as the language of the new religion, Christianity; its use as the official language of the Eastern Roman Empire; and its proclamation as the language of the Byzantine Empire (380–1453).

Greek maintained its status and prestige during the rise of the European Renaissance and was employed as the linguistic perspective for all contemporary sciences and terminologies during the period of Enlightenment. Today, Greek constitutes a large part of the vocabulary of any Indo-European language, and much of the lexicon of any scientific repertoire.

The modern Greek language is a southern Greek dialect which is now used by most Greek speakers both in Greece and abroad. It is the result of an intralinguistic influence and synthesis of the ancient vocabulary combined with words from Greek regional dialects, namely Cretan, Cypriot and Macedonian.

Greek is spoken throughout Greece by a population of around 10 million, and by some five million Greeks who live abroad.

PRONUNCIATION

All Greek words of two or more syllables have an acute accent which indicates where the stress falls. For instance, άγαλμα (statue) is pronounced *aghalma*, and αγάπη (love) is pronounced *aghapi*. In the following transliterations, italic lettering indicates where stress falls. Note also that **dh** is pronounced as 'th' in 'then' and **gh** is a softer, slightly guttural version of 'g'.

ACCOMMODATION

I'm looking for ...

psa·hno yi·a ...	Ψάχνω για ...
a room	
e·na dho·*ma*·ti·o	ένα δωμάτιο
a hotel	
e·na kse·no·dho·*chi*·o	ένα ξενοδοχείο
a youth hostel	
e·nan kse·*no*·na ne·o·ti·tas	έναν ξενώνα νεότητας

Where's a cheap hotel?
pou *i*·ne e·na fti·*no* xe·no·do·*hi*·o
Πού είναι ένα φτηνό ξενοδοχείο;
What's the address?
pya *i*·ne i dhi·*ef*·thin·si
Ποια είναι η διεύθυνση;
Could you write the address, please?
pa·ra·ka·*lo* bo·*ri*·te na *ghra*·pse·te ti· dhi·*ef*·thin·si
Παρακαλώ, μπορείτε να γράψετε τη διεύθυνση;
Are there any rooms available?
i·*par*·chun e·*lef*·the·ra dho·*ma*·ti·a
Υπάρχουν ελεύθερα δωμάτια;

I'd like to book ...

tha *i*·the·la na *kli*·so ...	Θα ήθελα να κλείσω ...
a bed	
e·na kre·*va*·ti	ένα κρεββάτι
a single room	
e·na mo·*no*·kli·o·no dho·*ma*·ti·o	ένα μονόκλινο δωμάτιο
a double room	
e·na *dhi*·kli·no dho·*ma*·ti·o	ένα δίκλινο δωμάτιο

THE GREEK ALPHABET & PRONUNCIATION

Greek	Pronunciation Guide		Example		
Α α	**a**	as in 'father'	αγάπη	a·gha·pi	love
Β β	**v**	as in 'vine'	βήμα	vi·ma	step
Γ γ	**gh**	like a rough 'g'	γάτα	gha·ta	cat
	y	as in 'yes'	για	ya	for
Δ δ	**dh**	as in 'there'	δέμα	dhe·ma	parcel
Ε ε	**e**	as in 'egg'	ένας	e·nas	one (m)
Ζ ζ	**z**	as in 'zoo'	ζώο	zo·o	animal
Η η	**i**	as in 'feet'	ήταν	i·tan	was
Θ θ	**th**	as in 'throw'	θέμα	the·ma	theme
Ι ι	**i**	as in 'feet'	ίδιος	i·dhyos	same
Κ κ	**k**	as in 'kite'	καλά	ka·la	well
Λ λ	**l**	as in 'leg'	λάθος	la·thos	mistake
Μ μ	**m**	as in 'man'	μαμά	ma·ma	mother
Ν ν	**n**	as in 'net'	νερό	ne·ro	water
Ξ ξ	**x**	as in 'ox'	ξύδι	ksi·dhi	vinegar
Ο ο	**o**	as in 'hot'	όλα	o·la	all
Π π	**p**	as in 'pup'	πάω	pa·o	I go
Ρ ρ	**r**	as in 'road'	ρέμα	re·ma	stream
		a slightly trilled 'r'	ρόδα	ro·dha	tyre
Σ σ, ς	**s**	as in 'sand'	σημάδι	si·ma·dhi	mark
Τ τ	**t**	as in 'tap'	τόπι	to·pi	ball
Υ υ	**i**	as in 'feet'	ύστερα	is·tera	after
Φ φ	**f**	as in 'find'	φύλλο	fi·lo	leaf
Χ χ	**h**	as the 'ch' in Scottish 'loch', or like a rough 'h'	χάνω	ha·no	I lose
			χέρι	he·ri	hand
Ψ ψ	**ps**	as in 'lapse'	ψωμί	pso·mi	bread
Ω ω	**o**	as in 'hot'	ώρα	o·ra	time

Combinations of Letters

The combinations of letters shown here are pronounced as follows:

Greek	Pronunciation Guide		Example		
ει	**i**	as in 'feet'	είδα	i·dha	I saw
οι	**i**	as in 'feet'	οικόπεδο	i·ko·pe·dho	land
αι	**e**	as in 'bet'	αίμα	e·ma	blood
ου	**u**	as in 'mood'	πού	pou	who/what
μπ	**b**	as in 'beer'	μπάλα	ba·la	ball
	mb	as in 'amber'	κάμπος	kam·bos	forest
ντ	**d**	as in 'dot'	ντουλάπα	dou·la·pa	wardrobe
	nd	as in 'bend'	πέντε	pen·de	five
γκ	**g**	as in 'God'	γκάζι	ga·zi	gas
γγ	**ng**	as in 'angle'	αγγελία	an·ge·lia	announcement
γξ	**ks**	as in 'minks'	σφιγξ	sfinks	sphynx
τζ	**dz**	as in 'hands'	τζάκι	dza·ki	fireplace

The pairs of vowels shown above are pronounced separately if the first has an acute accent, or the second a dieresis, as in the examples below:

γαϊδουράκι	gai·dhou·ra·ki	little donkey
Κάιρο	kai·ro	Cairo

Some Greek consonant sounds have no English equivalent. The υ of the groups αυ, ευ and ηυ is generally pronounced 'v'. The Greek question mark is represented with the English equivalent of a semicolon ';'.

a room with a double bed
e·na dho·ma·ti·o me	ένα δωμάτιο με
dhy·o kre·va·ti·a	δυό κρεββάτια

a room with a bathroom
e·na dho·ma·ti·o me	ένα δωμάτιο με
ba·ni·o	μπάνιο

I'd like to share a dorm.
tha i·the·la na mi·ra·so e·na ki·no dho·ma·ti·o
me al·la a·to·ma
θα ήθελα να μοιράσω ένα κοινό δωμάτιο
με άλλα άτομα

How much is it ...? po·so ka·ni ... Πόσο κάνει ...;
per night	ti ·vra·dhya	τη βραδυά
per person	to a·to·mo	το άτομο

May I see it?
bo·ro na to dho	Μπορώ να το δω;

Where's the bathroom?
pou i·ne to·ba·ni·o Πού είναι το μπάνιο;

I'm/We're leaving today.
fev·gho/fev·ghou·me	Φεύγω/φεύγουμε
si·me·ra	σήμερα

CONVERSATION & ESSENTIALS
Hello.
ya·sas (pol)	Γειά σας.
ya·su (inf)	Γειά σου.

Good morning.
ka·li me·ra   Καλή μέρα.
Good afternoon/evening.
ka·li spe·ra   Καλή σπέρα.
Good night.
ka·li nikh·ta   Καλή νύχτα.
Goodbye.
an·di·o   Αντίο.
Yes.
ne   Ναι.
No.
o·hi   Όχι.
Please.
pa·ra·ka·lo   Παρακαλώ.
Thank you.
ef·ha·ri·sto   Ευχαριστώ.
That's fine/You're welcome.
pa·ra·ka·lo   Παρακαλώ.
Sorry. (excuse me, forgive me)
sigh·no·mi   Συγγνώμη.
What's your name?
pos sas le·ne   Πώς σας λένε;
My name is ...
me le·ne ...   Με λένε ...
Where are you from?
a·po pou i·ste   Από πού είστε;

I'm from ...
i·me a·po ...   Είμαι από ...
I (don't) like ...
(dhen) ma·re·si ...   (Δεν) μ' αρέσει ...
Just a minute.
mi·so lep·to   Μισό λεπτό.

DIRECTIONS
Where is ...?
pou i·ne ...   Πού είναι...;
Straight ahead.
o·lo ef·thi·a   Ολο ευθεία.
Turn left.
strips·te a·ri·ste·ra   Στρίψτε αριστερά
Turn right.
strips·te dhe·ksi·a   Στρίψτε δεξιά
at the next corner
stin epo·me·ni gho·ni·a   στην επόμενη γωνία
at the traffic lights
sta fo·ta   στα φώτα

SIGNS
ΕΙΣΟΔΟΣ	Entry
ΕΞΟΔΟΣ	Exit
ΠΛΗΡΟΦΟΡΙΕΣ	Information
ΑΝΟΙΧΤΟ	Open
ΚΛΕΙΣΤΟ	Closed
ΑΠΑΓΟΡΕΥΕΤΑΙ	Prohibited
ΑΣΤΥΝΟΜΙΑ	Police
ΑΣΤΥΝΟΜΙΚΟΣ ΣΤΑΘΜΟΣ	Police Station
ΓΥΝΑΙΚΩΝ	Toilets (women)
ΑΝΔΡΩΝ	Toilets (men)

---

behind	pi·so	πίσω
in front of	bro·sta	μπροστά
far	ma·kri·a	μακριά
near (to)	kon·da	κοντά
opposite	a·pe·nan·di	απέναντι

acropolis	a·kro·po·li	ακρόπολη
beach	pa·ra·li·a	παραλία
bridge	yefira	γέφυρα
castle	ka·stro	κάστρο
island	ni·si	νησί
main square	ken·dri·ki· pla·ti·a	κεντρική πλατεία
market	a·gho·ra	αγορά
museum	mu·si·o	μουσείο
old quarter	pa·li·a po·li	παλιά πόλη
ruins	ar·he·a	αρχαία
sea	tha·las·sa	θάλασσα
square	pla·ti·a	πλατεία
temple	na·os	ναός

LANGUAGE

TRANSLITERATION & VARIANT SPELLINGS: AN EXPLANATION

The issue of correctly transliterating Greek into the Latin alphabet is a vexed one, fraught with inconsistencies and pitfalls. The Greeks themselves are not very consistent in this respect, though things are gradually improving. The word 'Piraeus', for example, has been variously represented by the following transliterations: *Pireas*, *Piraievs* and *Pireefs*; and when appearing as a street name (eg Piraeus St) you will also find *Pireos*!

This has been compounded by the linguistic minefield of diglossy, or the two forms of the Greek language. The purist form is called *Katharevousa* and the popular form is *Dimotiki* (Demotic). The Katharevousa form was never more than an artificiality and Dimotiki has always been spoken as the mainstream language, but this linguistic schizophrenia means there are often two Greek words for each English word. Thus, the word for 'baker' in everyday language is *fournos*, but the shop sign will more often than not say *artopoieion*. The baker's product will be known in the street as *psomi*, but in church as *artos*.

A further complication is the issue of anglicised vs hellenised forms of place names: Athina vs Athens, Patra vs Patras, Thiva vs Thebes, Evia vs Euboia – the list goes on and on! Toponymic diglossy (the existence of both an official and everyday name for a place) is responsible for Kerkyra/Corfu, Zante/Zakynthos, and Santorini/Thira. In this guide we usually provide modern Greek equivalents for town names, with one well known exception, Athens. For ancient sites, settlements or people from antiquity, we have tried to stick to the more familiar classical names; so we have Thucydides instead of Thoukididis, Mycenae instead of Mykines.

Problems in transliteration have particular implications for vowels, especially given that Greek has six ways of rendering the vowel sound 'ee', two ways of rendering the 'o' sound and two ways of rendering the 'e' sound. In most instances in this book, **y** has been used for the 'ee' sound when a Greek *upsilon* (υ, Υ) has been used, and **i** for Greek *ita* (η, Η) and *iota* (ι, Ι). In the case of the Greek vowel combinations that make the 'ee' sound, that is οι, ει and υι, an **i** has been used. For the two Greek 'e' sounds αι and ε, an **e** has been employed.

As far as consonants are concerned, the Greek letter *gamma* (γ, Γ) appears as **g** rather than **y** throughout this book. This means that *agios* (Greek for male saint) is used rather than *ayios*, and *agia* (female saint) rather than *ayia*. The letter *fi* (φ, Φ) can be transliterated as either **f** or **ph**. Here, a general rule of thumb is that classical names are spelt with a **ph** and modern names with an **f**. So Phaistos is used rather than Festos, and Folegandros is used rather than Pholegandros. The Greek *chi* (χ, Χ) has usually been represented as **h** in order to approximate the Greek pronunciation as closely as possible. Thus, we have Haralambos instead of Charalambos and Polytehniou instead of Polytechniou. Bear in mind that the **h** is to be pronounced as an aspirated 'h', much like the 'ch' in 'loch'. The letter *kapa* (κ, Κ) has been used to represent that sound, except where well known names from antiquity have adopted by convention the letter **c**, eg Polycrates, Acropolis.

Wherever reference to a street name is made, we have omitted the Greek word *odos*, but words for avenue (*leoforos*, abbreviated *leof*) and square (*plateia*) have been included.

HEALTH

| I'm ill. | *i*·me *a*·ro·stos | Είμαι άρρωστος. |
| It hurts here. | po·*nai*· e·*dho* | Πονάει εδώ. |

I have ...		
e·ho ...	Έχω ...	
asthma		
asth·ma	άσθμα	
diabetes		
za·ha·ro·dhi·a·*vi*·ti	ζαχαροδιαβήτη	
diarrhoea		
dhi·*a*·ri·a	διάρροια	
epilepsy		
e·pi·lip·*si*·a	επιληψία	

I'm allergic to ...		
i·me a·ler·yi·*kos*/	Είμαι αλλεργικός/	
a·ler·yi·*ki* ... (m/f)	αλλεργική ...	
antibiotics		
sta an·di·vi·o·ti·*ka*	στα αντιβιωτικά	
aspirin		
stin a·spi·*ri*·ni	στην ασπιρίνη	
penicillin		
stin pe·ni·ki·*li*·ni	στην πενικιλλίνη	
bees		
stis *me*·li·ses	στις μέλισσες	
nuts		
sta fi·*sti*·ki·a	στα φυστίκια	

condoms	pro·fi·la·kti·*ka* (ka·*po*·tez)	προφυλακτικά (καπότες)
contraceptive medicine	pro·fi·lak·ti·*ko* *farm*·a·ko	προφυλακτικό φάρμακο
sunblock cream	*kre*·ma i·*li*·u	κρέμα ηλίου
tampons	tam·*bon*	ταμπόν

LANGUAGE DIFFICULTIES

Do you speak English?
mi·*la*·te an·gli·*ka*   Μιλάτε Αγγλικά;
Does anyone speak English?
mi·*lai* ka·*nis* an·gli·*ka*   Μιλάει κανείς αγγλικά;
How do you say ... in Greek?
ps *le*·ghe·te ... sta   Πώς λέγεται ... στα
el·li·ni·*ka*   ελληνικά;
I understand.
ka·ta·la·*ve*·no   Καταλαβαίνω.
I don't understand.
dhen ka·ta·la·*ve*·no   Δεν καταλαβαίνω.
Please write it down.
ghrap·ste to pa·ra·ka·*lo*   Γράψτε το, παρακαλώ.
Can you show me on the map?
bo·*ri*·te na mo·u to   Μπορείτε να μου το
dhi·xe·te sto *har*·ti   δείξετε στο χάρτη;

NUMBERS

0	mi·*dhen*	μηδέν
1	e·nas	ένας (m)
	mi·a	μία (f)
	e·na	ένα (n)
2	*dhi*·o	δύο
3	tris	τρεις (m&f)
	tri·a	τρία (n)
4	te·se·ris	τέσσερεις (m&f)
	te·se·ra	τέσσερα (n)
5	*pen*·de	πέντε
6	e·xi	έξη
7	ep·*ta*	επτά
8	oh·*to*	οχτώ
9	e·*ne*·a	εννέα
10	dhe·ka	δέκα
20	ik·o·si	είκοσι
30	tri·*an*·da	τριάντα
40	sa·*ran*·da	σαράντα
50	pe·*nin*·da	πενήντα
60	exin·da	εξήντα
70	ev·dho·*min*·da	εβδομήντα
80	oh·*dhon*·da	ογδόντα
90	enen*in*da	ενενήντα
100	e·ka·*to*	εκατό
1000	hi·li·i	χίλιοι (m)
	hi·li·ez	χίλιες (f)
	hi·li·a	χίλια (n)
2000	dhi·*o* chi·*li*·a·dhez	δυό χιλιάδες

PAPERWORK

name
o·no·ma·te·*po*·ni·mo   ονοματεπώνυμο
nationality
i·pi·ko·o·*ti*·ta   υπηκοότητα
date of birth
i·me·ro·mi·*ni*·a   ημερομηνία
yen·*ni*·se·os   γεννήσεως

place of birth
to·pos yen·*ni*·se·os   τόπος γεννήσεως
sex (gender)
fil·lon   φύλον
passport
dhia·va·*ti*·ri·o   διαβατήριο
visa
vi·za   βίζα

QUESTION WORDS

Who/Which?
pi·*os*/pi·*a*/pi·*o* (sg m/f/n)   Ποιος/Ποια/Ποιο;
pi·*i*/pi·*es*/pi·*a* (pl m/f/n)   Ποιοι/Ποιες/Ποια;
Who's there?
pi·os *i*·ne e·*ki*   Ποιος είναι εκεί;
Which street is this?
pi·*a* o·*dhos i*·ne af·*ti*   Ποια οδός είναι αυτή;
What?
ti   Τι;
What's this?
ti *i*·ne af·*to*   Τι είναι αυτό;
Where?
pu   Πού;
When?
po·te   Πότε;
Why?
yi·a·*ti*   Γιατί;
How?
pos   Πώς;
How much?
po·so   Πόσο;
How much does it cost?
po·so ka·ni   Πόσο κάνει;

SHOPPING & SERVICES

I'd like to buy ...
the·lo n'a·gho·ra·so ...   Θέλω ν' αγοράσω ...
How much is it?
po·so ka·ni   Πόσο κάνει;
I don't like it
dhen mu a·re·si   Δεν μου αρέσει.
May I see it?
bo·ro na to dho   Μπορώ να το δω;
I'm just looking.
ap·los ki·ta·zo   Απλώς κοιτάζω.
It's cheap.
i·ne fti·no   Είναι φτηνό
It's too expensive.
i·ne po·li a·kri·vo   Είναι πολύ ακριβό.
I'll take it.
tha to pa·ro   Θα το πάρω

Do you accept ...?	dhe·che·ste ...	Δέχεστε ...;
credit cards	pi·sto·ti·ki kar·ta	πιστωτική κάρτα
travellers	tak·si·dhi·o·ti·kes	ταξιδιωτικές
cheques	e·pi·ta·ghes	επιταγές

more	pe·ri·so·te·ro	περισσότερο
less	li·gho·te·ro	λιγότερο
smaller	mi·kro·te·ro	μικρότερο
bigger	me·gha·li·te·ro	μεγαλύτερο

I'm looking for ...	psach·no ya ...	Ψάχνω για ...
a bank	mya tra·pe·za	μια τράπεζα
the church	tin ek·kli·si·a	την εκκλησία
the city centre	to ken·dro tis po·lis	το κέντρο της πόλης
the ... embassy	tin ... pres·vi·a	την ... πρεσβεία
the market	ti· lai·ki· a·gho·ra	τη λαϊκη αγορά
the museum	to mu·si·o	το μουσείο
the post office	to ta·chi·dhro·mi·o	το ταχυδρομείο
a public toilet	mya dhi·mo·sia tu·a·let·ta	μια δημόσια τουαλέττα
the telephone centre	to ti·le·fo·ni·ko ken·dro	το τηλεφωνικό κέντρο
the tourist office	to tu·ri·st·iko ghra·fi·o	το τουριστικό γραφείο

TIME & DATES

What time is it?	ti o·ra i·ne	Τι ώρα είναι;
It's (2 o'clock).	i·ne (dhi·o i· o·ra)	είναι (δύο η ώρα).
in the morning	to pro·i	το πρωί
in the afternoon	ta·po·yev·ma	το απόγευμα
in the evening	to vra·dhi	το βράδυ
When?	po·te	Πότε;
today	si·me·ra	σήμερα
tomorrow	av·ri·o	αύριο
yesterday	hthes	χθες

Monday	dhef·te·ra	Δευτέρα
Tuesday	tri·ti	Τρίτη
Wednesday	te·tar·ti	Τετάρτη
Thursday	pemp·ti	Πέμπτη
Friday	pa·ras·ke·vi	Παρασκευή
Saturday	sa·va·to	Σάββατο
Sunday	kyri·a·ki	Κυριακή

January	ia·nou·ar·i·os	Ιανουάριος
February	fev·rou·ar·i·os	Φεβρουάριος
March	mar·ti·os	Μάρτιος
April	a·pri·li·os	Απρίλιος
May	mai·os	Μάιος
June	i·ou·ni·os	Ιούνιος
July	i·ou·li·os	Ιούλιος
August	av·ghous·tos	Αύγουστος
September	sep·tem·vri·os	Σεπτέμβριος
October	ok·to·vri·os	Οκτώβριος
November	no·em·vri·os	Νοέμβριος
December	dhe·kem·vri·os	Δεκέμβριος

TRANSPORT
Public Transport

What time does the ... leave/ arrive?	ti o·ra fev·yi/ fta·ni to ...	Τι ώρα φεύγει/ φτάνει το ...;
boat	pli·o	πλοίο
(city) bus	a·sti·ko	αστικό
(intercity) bus	le·o·fo·ri·o	λεωφορείο
plane	ae·ro·pla·no	αεροπλάνο
train	tre·no	τραίνο

I'd like (a) ...	tha i·the·la (e·na) ...	Θα ήθελα (ένα) ...
one way ticket	a·plo isi·ti·ri·o	απλό εισιτήριο
return ticket	i·si·ti·ri·o me e·pi·stro·fi	εισιτήριο με επιστροφή
1st class	pro·ti· the·si	πρώτη θέση
2nd class	def·te·ri the·si	δεύτερη θέση

I want to go to ...
the·lo na pao sto/sti...
Θέλω να πάω στο/στη ...
The train has been cancelled/delayed.
to tre·no a·ki·rothi·ke/ka·thi·ste·ri·se
Το τραίνο ακυρώθηκε/καθυστέρησε

the first	to pro·to	το πρώτο
the last	to te·lef·te·o	το τελευταίο
platform number	a·rithmos a·po·va·thras	αριθμός αποβάθρας
ticket office	ek·dho·ti·ri·o i·si·ti·ri·on	εκδοτήριο εισιτηρίων

timetable
dhro·mo·*lo*·gio   δρομολόγιο
train station
si·dhi·ro·dhro·mi·*kos*   σιδηροδρομικός
stath·*mos*   σταθμός

Private Transport

I'd like to hire	tha *i*·the·la na	Θα ήθελα να
a ...	ni·ki·*a*·so ...	νοικιάσω ...
car	*e*·na af·ti·*ki*·ni·to	ένα αυτοκίνητο
4WD	*e*·na tes·se·ra	ένα τέσσερα
	e·*pi* tes·se·ra	επί τέσσερα
(a jeep)	(*e*·na tzip)	(ένα τζιπ)
motorbike	mya mo·to·si·	μια μοτοσυ·
	klet·ta	κλέττα
bicycle	*e*·na po·*dhi*·la·to	ένα ποδήλατο

Is this the road to ...?
af·*tos i*·ne o dhro·mos ya ...
Αυτός είναι ο δρόμος για ...
Where's the next service station?
pu *i*·ne to e·*po*·me·no ven·zi·na·dhi·ko
Πού είναι το επόμενο βενζινάδικο;
Please fill it up.
ye·*mi*·ste to pa·ra·ka·*lo*
Γεμίστε το, παρακαλώ.
I'd like (30) euros worth.
tha *i*·the·la (30) ev·ro
Θα ήθελα (30) ευρώ.

diesel	pet·*re*·le·o	πετρέλαιο
leaded petrol	*su*·per	σούπερ
unleaded petrol	a·*mo*·liv·dhi	αμόλυβδη

Can I park here?
bo·*ro* na par·*ka*·ro e·*dho*
Μπορώ να παρκάρω εδώ;
Where do I pay?
pu pli·*ro*·no
Πού πληρώνω;

Also available from Lonely Planet:
Greek Phrasebook

ΠΑΡΑΚΑΜΨΗ	Detour
ΑΠΑΓΟΡΕΥΕΤΑΙ Η ΕΙΣΟΔΟΣ	No Entry
ΑΠΑΓΟΡΕΥΕΤΑΙ Η ΠΡΟΣΠΕΡΑΣΗ	No Overtaking
ΑΠΑΓΟΡΕΥΕΤΑΙ Η ΣΤΑΘΜΕΥΣΗ	No Parking
ΕΙΣΟΔΟΣ	Entrance
ΜΗΝ ΠΑΡΚΑΡΕΤΕ ΕΔΩ	Keep Clear
ΔΙΟΔΙΑ	Toll
ΚΙΝΔΥΝΟΣ	Danger
ΑΡΓΑ	Slow Down
ΕΞΟΔΟΣ	Exit

The car/motorbike has broken down (at ...)
to af·to·*ki*·ni·to/mo·to·si·*klet*·ta cha·la·se sto ...
Το αυτοκίνητο/η μοτοσυκλέττα χάλασε στο ...
The car/motorbike won't start.
to af·to·*ki*·ni·to/mo·to·si·*klet*·ta dhen *per*·ni· bros
Το αυτοκίνητο/η μοτοσυκλέττα δεν παίρνει μπρος.
I have a flat tyre.
e·pa·tha *la*·sti·cho
Έπαθα λάστιχο.
I've run out of petrol.
e·*mi*·na a·*po* ven·*zi*·ni
Έμεινα από βενζίνη.
I've had an accident.
e·pa·tha a·*ti*·chi·ma
Έπαθα ατύχημα.

TRAVEL WITH CHILDREN

Is there a/an ...?	i·*par*·chi ...	Υπάρχει ...;
I need a/an ...	chri·*a*·zo·me ...	Χρειάζομαι ...
baby change room	*me*·ros nal·*lak*·so to mo·*ro*	μέρος ν' αλλάξω το μωρό
car baby seat	*ka*·this·ma ya mo·*ro*	κάθισμα για μωρό
child-minding service	ba·bi *sit*·ter	μπέιμπι σίττερ
children's menu	me·*nu* ya pe·*dhya*	μενού για παιδιά
(disposable) nappies/diapers	pan·nez Pam·pers	πάννες Pampers
(English-speaking) babysitter	ba·bi *sit*·ter pu mi·*la* an·*ghl*·ika	μπέιμπι σίττερ που μιλά αγγλικά
highchair	pe·dhi·*ki* ka·*rek*·la	παιδική καρέκλα
potty	yo·*yo*	γιογιό
stroller	ka·rot·*sa*·ki	καροτσάκι

Do you mind if I breastfeed here?
bo·*ro* na thi·*la*·so e·*dho*
Μπορώ να θηλάσω εδώ;
Are children allowed?
e·pi·*tre*·pon·de ta pe·*dhya*
Επιτρέπονται τα παιδιά;

Glossary

Achaean civilisation – see *Mycenaean civilisation*
acropolis – citadel; highest point of an ancient city
agia (f), agios (m) – saint
agora – commercial area of an ancient city; shopping precinct in modern Greece
Archaic period (800-480 BC) – also known as the Middle Age; period in which the city-states emerged from the 'dark age' and traded their way to wealth and power; the city-states were unified by a Greek alphabet and common cultural pursuits, engendering a sense of national identity
arhontika – 17th- and 18th-century AD mansions, which belonged to arhons, the leading citizens of a town
askitiria – mini-chapels; places of solitary worship

basilica – early Christian church
bouleuterion – council house
bouzouki – stringed lutelike instrument associated with *rembetika* music
bouzoukia – any nightclub where the *bouzouki* is played and low-grade blues songs are sung
Byzantine Empire (324 BC-AD 1453) – characterised by the merging of Hellenistic culture and Christianity and named after Byzantium, the city on the Bosphorus that became the capital of the Roman Empire; when the Roman Empire was formally divided in AD 395, Rome went into decline and the eastern capital, renamed Constantinople, flourished; the Byzantine Empire dissolved after the fall of Constantinople to the Turks in 1453

caïque – small, sturdy fishing boat often used to carry passengers
Classical period (480-323 BC) – era in which the city-states reached the height of their wealth and power after the defeat of the Persians in the 5th century BC; the period ended with the decline of the city-states as a result of the Peloponnesian Wars, and the expansionist aspirations of Philip II, King of Macedon (r 359-336 BC), and his son, Alexander the Great (r 336-323 BC)
Corinthian – order of Greek architecture recognisable by columns with bell-shaped capitals that have sculpted, elaborate ornaments based on acanthus leaves; see also *Doric* and *Ionic*
Cycladic civilisation (3000-1100 BC) – the civilisation that emerged following the settlement of Phoenician colonists on the Cycladic islands
cyclopes – mythical one-eyed giants

dark age (1200-800 BC) – period in which Greece was under *Dorian* rule

delfini – dolphin; common name for a hydrofoil
domatio (s), domatia (pl) – room, usually in a private home; cheap accommodation option
Dorians – Hellenic warriors who invaded Greece around 1200 BC, demolishing the city-states and destroying the *Mycenaean civilisation;* heralded Greece's 'dark age', when the artistic and cultural advancements of the Mycenaean's and Minoan's were abandoned; the Dorians later developed into land-holding aristocrats which encouraged the resurgence of independent city-states led by wealthy aristocrats
Doric – order of Greek architecture characterised by a column that has no base, a fluted shaft and a relatively plain capital, when compared with the flourishes evident on *Ionic* and *Corinthian* capitals; see also *Corinthian* and *Ionic*

Ellada or Ellas – see *Hellas*
ELTA – Ellinika Tahydromia; the Greek post office organisation
EOT – Ellinikos Organismos Tourismou; national tourism organisation that has offices in most major towns

Filiki Eteria – friendly society; a group of Greeks in exile; formed during Ottoman rule to organise an uprising against the Turks
flokati – shaggy woollen rug produced in Central and Northern Greece

Geometric period (1200-800 BC) – period characterised by pottery decorated with geometric designs; sometimes referred to as Greece's 'dark age'

Hellas – the Greek name for Greece; also known as *Ellada* or *Ellas*
Hellenistic period (323-146 BC) – prosperous, influential period of Greek civilisation ushered in by Alexander the Great's empire building and lasting until the Roman sacking of Corinth in 146 BC
hora – main town (usually on an island)
horio – village

Ionic – order of Greek architecture characterised by a column with truncated flutes and capitals with ornaments resembling scrolls; see also *Corinthian* and *Doric*

kafeneio (s), kafeneia (pl) – traditionally a male-only coffee house where cards and backgammon are played
kastro – walled-in town; also describes a fort and castle
katholikon – principal church of a monastic complex
kore – female statue of the Archaic period; see also *kouros*

kouros – male statue of the Archaic period, characterised by a stiff body posture and enigmatic smile; see also *kore*

KTEL – Kino Tamio Ispraxeon Leoforion; national bus cooperative; runs all long-distance bus services

leoforos – avenue; shortened to 'leof'

mayirefta – pre-cooked food in restaurants, as opposed to cooked to order

mayiria – cook houses

meltemi – northeasterly wind that blows throughout much of Greece during the summer

meze (s), mezedes (pl) – appetiser

Middle Age – see *Archaic period*

Minoan civilisation (3000-1100 BC) – Bronze Age culture of Crete named after the mythical king Minos, and characterised by pottery and metalwork of great beauty and artisanship

moni – monastery or convent

Mycenaean civilisation (1900-1100 BC) – the first great civilisation of the Greek mainland, characterised by powerful independent city-states ruled by kings; also known as the Achaean civilisation

odos – street

OSE – Organismos Sidirodromon Ellados; Greek railways organisation

OTE – Organismos Tilepikinonion Ellados; Greece's major telecommunications carrier

ouzeri (s), ouzeria (pl) – place that serves ouzo and light snacks

Panagia – Mother of God; name frequently used for churches

Pantokrator – painting or mosaic of Christ in the centre of the dome of a Byzantine church

periptero (s), periptera (pl) – street kiosk

plateia – square

rembetika – blues songs commonly associated with the underworld of the 1920s

Sarakatsani – Greek-speaking nomadic shepherd community from northern Greece

spilia – cave

stele (s), stelae (pl) – upright stone decorated with inscriptions or figures

stoa – long colonnaded building, usually in an *agora;* used as a meeting place and shelter in ancient Greece

taverna – traditional restaurant that serves food and wine

tholos – Mycenaean tomb shaped like a beehive

Vlach – traditional, seminomadic shepherds from Northern Greece who speak a Latin-based dialect

Behind the Scenes

THIS BOOK

This 3rd edition was updated by Paul Hellander, Kate Armstrong, Michael Clark, Des Hannigan, Victoria Kyriakopoulos, Miriam Raphael and Andrew Stone. The previous edition was coordinated by David Willett.

THANKS from the Authors

Paul Hellander To Mr Kim Sjögren and the indefatigable team at Triton Holidays in Rhodes a big *tak så mycket* for their assistance in putting together a very tight itinerary. It was a buzz, and it actually worked! To a scattering of very helpful individuals who also made my task a breeze may I say ευχαριστώ πολύ. Among these (in geographical order) are Emmanouil Manousos (Kasos), Takis Hrysovergis (Halki), Alexandra Arhondopoulou (Rhodes), Ilias Hrystofis (Tilos), Alex and Dionysia Zikas (Kos), Giakoumina Matheou (Patmos), Giannis and Elina Scoutaris (Patmos) and Angeliki Kanelli and Vana Kapsaski (Athens). Byron and Marcus – thanks for your good company and the good times.

Kate Armstrong Thanks to LP's Michala Green for giving me my break, Marina Kosmatos for her contacts and predecessor Carolyn Bain for paving a wonderful way. The rest was made possible by the hospitality of strangers in the Ionians. In Corfu, *efharisto poli* to Diana and Vincent, and Marilena Tombrou for helping to sort out the ferries, hydrofoils and everything in between; Debbie and Sandra in Lakka, and Carol and Kostas who really do perform magic in Paxos; John and Jane Fitzpatrick for their welcomed Irish humour; Dora and Eleni in

Lefkada; Alexander in Ithaki and Katarina Christoforou Bolidis in Zakynthos for her friendship and generosity. Finally, a huge thanks to Mark Tzilianos in Kefallonia whose huge heart, enthusiasm and gift of the gab is nothing but Greek.

Michael Clark My contribution to this book was made possible with the generous help of friends, relatives and acquaintances in Greece and at home, among them: my Athenian hosts Leonora Navari, and Tolis Choutzioumis and daughter Katerina; in Delphi, Yannis Christopoulos; in Kalambaka, Arthur, Thanassis and Toula; in the Pelion, Jill Sleeman and the Barber of Mouresi; in Skiathos, Keyrillos Sinioris and family; in Skopelos, Makis and Nana Kobro; in Alonnisos, Pakis of Ikos Travel; in Skyros, Janet and Dimitris; and in Evia, Alkis Triantafillou.

Closer to home, Kostas and Nana Vatsis, Angelo and Vangie Kallipolitis and Dessine Fricioni provided advice, opinions and humour. Special thanks to my ever-supportive commissioning editor Michala Green at LP, and fellow authors Paul Hellander for stellar road advice and Victoria Kyriakopoulos for the lunch trek in Athens. And to my splendiferous and patient family – Janet, Melina and Alexander – same time next year! Finally, I wish to dedicate this work to the memory of my mother, Mary Efimedia Raptis Kent, and my grandparents Stamatios Raptis and Despina Pavlos who started this voyage. Long may it continue.

Des Hannigan Warmest thanks to the many friends and passing acquaintances who helped and advised me, with good humour, wit and patience,

---

THE LONELY PLANET STORY

The story begins with a classic travel adventure: Tony and Maureen Wheeler's 1972 journey across Europe and Asia to Australia. There was no useful information about the overland trail then, so Tony and Maureen published the first Lonely Planet guidebook to meet a growing need.

From a kitchen table, Lonely Planet has grown to become the largest independent travel publisher in the world, with offices in Melbourne (Australia), Oakland (USA) and London (UK). Today Lonely Planet guidebooks cover the globe. There is an ever-growing list of books and information in a variety of media. Some things haven't changed. The main aim is still to make it possible for adventurous travellers to get out there – to explore and better understand the world.

At Lonely Planet we believe travellers can make a positive contribution to the countries they visit – if they respect their host communities and spend their money wisely. Every year 5% of company profit is donated to charities around the world.

during my work in Greece. Greatest thanks to those who know the business best of all; to Petros Koloventzos on Andros, Sharon Turner on Tinos, John van Lerberghe on Mykonos, Lisos Zilelides and Wiebke Godau on Santorini, Flavio Facciolo on Folegandros and Eleftheria Rafeletou on Sifnos. Special thanks yet again to, Kostas Karabetsos and Zelena Mihalopoyloy on Mykonos for great company and for the nightlife run; for insight, advice and good conversation, to Sophia Palermos on Salamina, Andrew Davies and Diane Thorstenson on Aegina, Yannis Karaoulanis on Andros, Giorgios Epitropakis on Paros, Maximos Fanariotis on Sifnos and Jouko Castrén for a Finnish perspective.

Thanks, as always, to my fellow authors for entertaining e-conferences and to Michala Green at Lonely Planet's London Office and coordinating author Paul Hellander, for holding it all together.

Victoria Kyriakopoulos My heartfelt thanks for the insight and support of friends and the kindness of many strangers during my travels and in researching this book.

In Athens, many thanks to Maria Zygourakis, Christina Pirovolakis, Eleni Bertes, Hector Cosmas, Vivienne Nilen, Antonis Bekiaris, Diane Shugart and Mary Retiniotis. Thanks to travelling companions Julie Psarologos, Vicky Valanos and Eric da Jong for sharing the journey in Crete. It was wonderful to be warmly welcomed back to Crete, where their famous hospitality is not a myth. Sincere thanks to Eleftherios Karatarakis (Lato Hotel), Dimitris Skoutelis and Sonia Panagiotidou in Iraklio, to Yiorgos Xylouris for the unforgettable wedding in Anogia, Dimitris Konstandinidis at Elounda, Manolis and Eftychis in Paleohora, Yiannis and Savas in Sougia, Tony Fennymore in Hania, Katerina Xekalou in Rethymno, Nikos Perakis in Kato Zakros, Foni and Stefi Patramani in Episkopi and Manolis, Kostas and Grigoris in Agios Nikolaos. Thanks also to Casa Del Fino and Hotel Amphora in Hania, Stella and Vangelis in Kissamos, Nikos Ailamakis in Sitia and Flora and Haris in Paleohora.

My gratitude to Michala Green in London and coordinating author Paul Hellander for their patience. In Australia, thanks to John and Suzie Rerakis, my family and Sam, Nikolas and Chris Anastassiades.

Miriam Raphael Firstly thanks to Paul and Byron Hellander for holding my hand during the first days of my northern Greece research. Byron you were a fantastic help in Ioannina and Zagoria, cheers! In Thessaloniki, thanks to Pat and Debs for showing me the best views in town and to ardent foodie Elena, at Capsis Bristol. I am grateful to Vasilli and Demetra,

Tom, Barbara and Don in the North Aegean islands for being warm, informative hosts. At Lonely Planet, thanks to Michala Green and the mapping crew. In Goreme, cheers to my friend Pat Yale, who lent me her home for the write-up, and to Ruth Lockwood, for her wonderful sense of humour and support.

Wherever I am in the world, my parents Ken and Deborah, are an ongoing source of love, encouragement and funny emails. Thanks to dad for his keen eye and helping me chop yet another chapter in half – I couldn't have done it without you this time, or last time. Finally, to my partner in crime Scott Brundell – you were wonderful company in the islands, even better in Goreme, where you dealt with my mess and moods with great charm, laughs and love. Thanks mate, your passion for travel never ceases to inspire me.

Andrew Stone My coauthors Paul Hellander and Victoria Kyriakopoulos deserve my sincere thanks for their generous help with my research trip and some good tips and recommendations. Thanks also to all those who assisted me with advice and recommendations on the way round including Nick in Monemvasia, Alkiviades and Ernestos in Ancient Olympia, the staff at the Patra Info Centre (the only switched-on tourist office on the Peloponnese), to fellow travellers Peter and Maureen Savic for many recommendations and an entertaining night in Nafplio and to Dimitris Koronis for his help with the wine information in this chapter. Finally my thanks go to Michala Green, my commissioning editor, for her help, humour and efficiency (and for offering me this gig in the first place).

CREDITS

This guidebook was commissioned in Lonely Planet's London office, and produced by the following:
Commissioning Editors Michala Green, Tasmin McNaughtan
Coordinating Editor Kate McLeod
Coordinating Cartographer Malisa Plesa
Coordinating Layout Designer Pablo Gastar
Managing Cartographer Mark Griffiths
Assisting Editor David Andrew
Assisting Proofreader Louisa Syme
Assisting Cartographers Chris Crook, Natasha Velleley
Cover Designer Nic Lehman
Colour Designer Pablo Gastar
Indexer Kate McLeod
Project Manager Eoin Dunlevy
Thanks to Melanie Dankel, Sally Darmody, Quentin Frayne, Imogen Hall, Rebecca Lalor, Adriana Mammarella, Suzannah Shwer, Gina Tsarouhas, Branislava Vladisavljevic and Celia Wood.

THANKS from Lonely Planet

Many thanks to the following travellers who used the last edition and wrote to us with helpful hints, useful advice and interesting anecdotes.

A Peter Acton, Jonathan Amies, Kostas Andreou, Aris Androutsos, Maria Anguita, Mary Ara, Nathalène Armand-Gouzi, Chris Ashdown, Tracey Atkinson **B** Hughie Baker, John Baker, Sarah Bangham, Shawn Banville, Raeder Barbara, Gabi Barkay, Alessandro Bavila, Adrian Beadles, Simon Best, Bob Blanchford, Joan Blanchford, Christine Blattert, Jason Bloomfield, Marcel Boer, Sanne Bogers, Caroline Borrie, Stacey Boulton, Euan Bowater, Luisa Braccesi, Terry Brace, Lynn Brazier, Ineke & Hans Breeman, Steve Burnhopr **C** Hilde Calberson, Lornie Caplan, Juan Casabonne, Fiona Charlton, Donna Childs, Edward & Connie Chung Ramos, Kalle Chydenius, Gillian Clark, Odile Ayral Claure, Beryl Coe, Marie Coffey, Belinda Cole, Nina Collins, Gael Connell, Daniel Cox **D** Hans Richard Damli, Michael Dansby, Michael Davis-Smith, German del Sol, Ern & Melva Della, Helen Dickinson, Evert Dijkema, Alexander Douglas, Chloe Druce, Richard Duggan, Louise Dulson **E** Jonathan Eaton, Peter Ellis, Jim Espie, John Ewing **F** Laura Fielding, Wendy Finch-Turner, Andrea Flachsmann, Katrin Flatscher, Nick Fountas, Laurent Francois **G** Cari Gardner, Heloise Gornall-Thode, John Grant, Fabio Graziosi, Frank Greenhill, Karen Grey **H** Kylie Hall, Cecilia Harris, Clive Harris, Paul Harris, Fiona Harrison, Jorgen Hastrup, David Haugh, Toril Havik, Marie Hazelwood, Sandi Heimlich, Dale Henderson, Peter Hendricks, Urska Hocevar, Andrew Hoshkiw, Wietske Hosper, Sandra Hribar **J** Robbie Jacobs, Linda Jensen, Laura Jones, Jude Jusayan **K** Line Kallstad, Olka Kolker, Stuart Krohn, Maja Kunzelmann **L** Don & Patricia Lawson, Bob Lee, Sandra Leffers, Riitta Liljander, Amanda Lindsay, John Lindsay, Nguyen Louie, Cassie Lovel, Charly Lynn **M** Rosemary Mahoney, Bjoern Mannsfeld, Bob Mark, Dubravaka Martinovic, Massimiliano Mattioli, Michael McKee, J P Michaels, Tiziana Milizia, Lucy Mitchell, Maria Mitropoulos, Stefaan Motte, Axel Mueller **N** Miriam Naccache, P A Nichols-Marzy, Karen Nielsen, Julia Niemann, Laura Nieri **O** F M Oddy, Joerg Oehlenschlaeger, Mike O'Flaherty, Grant James O'Neill **P** Giorgio Pagnotta, Tanya Pankhurst, Marina Papadopoulou, Tony Papalas, B E Payne, Kirk Penney, Richard Perry, Giovanni Pesce, Pigi Petratou, Bruce Probst, Bob Prosser, Thomas Psomas **R** Francesco Randisi, Bernt Rane, Jessica Raspe, Hernan Ratto, D A Reeve, Dan Robinson, David Rogers, Michaela Ronzoni, Jan Roscoe, Andrew Ross, Ewan Ross, Patrick & Deirdre Ruttledge **S** David Sack, Ashley Salisbury, Sally Salisbury, Lexie Scherer, Rebecca Schroeder, May Siao, Tanya Simmons, Tanya Skamene, Anne Smith, Muriel Smith, M E Sorley, Robyn Spurdle, Pamela Stokes, Lora Stylianou **T** Chris Tapp, Ryan Tracey **V** Francoise Van Den Bosch, D van Laan, Brons Veld **W** Richard Wade, Iris Wagner, Kerry Walker, Debbie Watson, David Wegman, Miriam Weinstein, Liz Westbrooke, Thelma White, Winston White, Alexandra Williams, Kate Wilson, Kyle Wilson, Thomas Winston, Ella Wise, Andy Wood, Alison Woodcock

ACKNOWLEDGMENTS

Many thanks to the following for the use of their content:

Globe on back cover © Mountain High Maps 1993 Digital Wisdom, Inc.

Portions of this document include intellectual property of EPSILON and are used herein by permission. Copyright ©2001 Epsilon International SA. All rights reserved.

SEND US YOUR FEEDBACK

We love to hear from travellers – your comments keep us on our toes and help make our books better. Our well-travelled team reads every word on what you loved or loathed about this book. Although we cannot reply individually to postal submissions, we always guarantee that your feedback goes straight to the appropriate authors, in time for the next edition. Each person who sends us information is thanked in the next edition – and the most useful submissions are rewarded with a free book.

To send us your updates – and find out about Lonely Planet events, newsletters and travel news – visit our award-winning website: **www.lonelyplanet.com/feedback**.

Note: We may edit, reproduce and incorporate your comments in Lonely Planet products such as guidebooks, websites and digital products, so let us know if you don't want your comments reproduced or your name acknowledged. For a copy of our privacy policy visit www.lonelyplanet .com/privacy.

Index

INDEX

INDEX

540

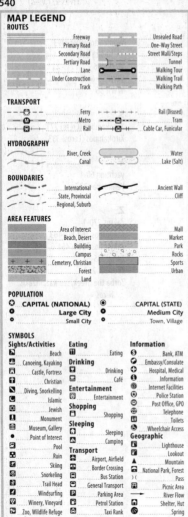

MAP LEGEND

ROUTES
Freeway	Unsealed Road
Primary Road	One-Way Street
Secondary Road	Street Mall/Steps
Tertiary Road	Tunnel
Lane	Walking Tour
Under Construction	Walking Trail
Track	Walking Path

TRANSPORT
Ferry	Rail (Disused)
Metro	Tram
Rail	Cable Car, Funicular

HYDROGRAPHY
River, Creek	Water
Canal	Lake (Salt)

BOUNDARIES
International	Ancient Wall
State, Provincial	Cliff
Regional, Suburb	

AREA FEATURES
Area of Interest	Mall
Beach, Desert	Market
Building	Park
Campus	Rocks
Cemetery, Christian	Sports
Forest	Urban
Land	

POPULATION
◉ CAPITAL (NATIONAL)	◉ CAPITAL (STATE)
● Large City	● Medium City
● Small City	○ Town, Village

SYMBOLS

Sights/Activities
- Beach
- Canoeing, Kayaking
- Castle, Fortress
- Christian
- Diving, Snorkelling
- Islamic
- Jewish
- Monument
- Museum, Gallery
- Point of Interest
- Pool
- Ruin
- Skiing
- Snorkeling
- Trail Head
- Windsurfing
- Winery, Vineyard
- Zoo, Wildlife Refuge

Eating
- Eating

Drinking
- Drinking
- Café

Entertainment
- Entertainment

Shopping
- Shopping

Sleeping
- Sleeping
- Camping

Transport
- Airport, Airfield
- Border Crossing
- Bus Station
- General Transport
- Parking Area
- Petrol Station
- Taxi Rank

Information
- Bank, ATM
- Embassy/Consulate
- Hospital, Medical
- Information
- Internet Facilities
- Police Station
- Post Office, GPO
- Telephone
- Toilets
- Wheelchair Access

Geographic
- Lighthouse
- Lookout
- Mountain
- National Park, Forest
-) (Pass
- Picnic Area
- River Flow
- Shelter, Hut
- Spring

LONELY PLANET OFFICES

Australia
Head Office
Locked Bag 1, Footscray, Victoria 3011
☎ 03 8379 8000, fax 03 8379 8111
talk2us@lonelyplanet.com.au

USA
150 Linden St, Oakland, CA 94607
☎ 510 893 8555, toll free 800 275 8555
fax 510 893 8572
info@lonelyplanet.com

UK
72–82 Rosebery Ave,
Clerkenwell, London EC1R 4RW
☎ 020 7841 9000, fax 020 7841 9001
go@lonelyplanet.co.uk

Published by Lonely Planet Publications Pty Ltd
ABN 36 005 607 983